CRITICAL THEORY SINCE 1965

CRITICAL THEORY SINCE 1965

edited by
HAZARD ADAMS
and
LEROY SEARLE

UNIVERSITY PRESSES OF FLORIDA
FLORIDA STATE UNIVERSITY PRESS
Tallahassee

Second printing, 1989

UNIVERSITY PRESSES OF FLORIDA is the central agency for scholarly publishing of the State of Florida's university system, producing books selected for publication by the faculty editorial committees of Florida's nine public universities: Florida A&M University (Tallahassee), Florida Atlantic University (Boca Raton), Florida International University (Miami), Florida State University (Tallahassee), University of Central Florida (Orlando), University of Florida (Gainesville), University of North Florida (Jacksonville), University of South Florida (Tampa), University of West Florida (Pensacola).

ORDERS for books published by all member presses should be addressed to University Presses of Florida, 15 NW 15th Street, Gainesville, FL 32603.

Library of Congress Cataloging-in-Publication Data

Critical theory since 1985.

Bibliography: p.
Includes index.
1. Criticism. 2. Aesthetics. 3. Semiotics.
4. Discourse analysis. I. Adams, Hazard, 1926–
II. Searle, Leroy.
PN94.C75 1986 801'.95 86–13216
ISBN 0–8130–0844–1

Printed in the U.S.A. on acid-free paper ∞
Typography by G&S Typesetters, Austin, Texas

Contents

APPENDIX

Preface

THIS ANTHOLOGY is a sequel to *Critical Theory Since Plato* (New York: Harcourt Brace Jovanovich, 1971) and attempts to bring the history of literary theory reasonably up to date. The year in the title marks approximately the ending date for selections in *Critical Theory Since Plato*, though a few of the essays that appear there were first published between 1966 and 1969. Except for two instances, here we have not published essays by authors who appeared in *Critical Theory Since Plato*, even though several of them continued to be active in the two decades that this book covers. As in the earlier volume, works of specifically critical practice—so-called practical criticism, structural analysis, hermeneutics, etc.—have been excluded, except in marginal cases like Heidegger's essay on Holderlin. (A historical collection of critical practice beginning with the earliest readers of Homer and Scripture is our next task.) This book follows roughly the plan of its predecessor, with one important addendum. A large appendix includes selections from sixteen writers not represented in *Critical Theory Since Plato*. Some of these writers could well have been there and are made available here to fill out the picture (Harcourt Brace Jovanovich has not wished to undertake a revision). Others are present here because, though not strictly literary theorists, they have been extremely influential or in their essay they address an issue of importance in an especially helpful way. The selections from Ferdinand de Saussure's *Course in General Linguistics* are an example of the former and Isaiah Berlin's "Verification" the latter.

The presence in the appendix, and even in the main body, of texts not addressed directly to literary matters reflects the fact that in recent years the world of literary theory has been greatly expanded. This change has made selection especially difficult. It has also made us look back at *Critical Theory Since Plato* and wish that certain texts of earlier ages had been included there. From the perspective of 1986, for example, Plato's *Cratylus* and parts of the *Phaedrus* take on an increased importance, as do certain texts of classical rhetoric. Our aim in the appendix has not been, however, to supplement the companion volume so much as to provide some of the necessary background for the main body of this text. The selections in *Critical Theory Since Plato* remain indispensable as background to this sequel. Any detachment of the study of modern and contemporary literary theory from the earlier history of criticism we regard as a serious mistake.

Selections in the text have been arranged chronologically by year of publication, writing, or first presentation as a lecture, rather than by some imposed rubric. Organization of the field by rubric has become increasingly difficult.

There are too many crossing and converging lines of force. In any case, we have not seen an anthology of the history of criticism arranged by rubric that has not been disconcerting to work with.

Our own views, of course, appear in the choice of selections, the headnotes, the introduction, and the afterword; we have attempted to be eclectic and to allow a wide hearing. In the present situation any other decision has presented itself as unthinkable. Our choices of texts have been sometimes for historical import and influence as well as for representation of certain kinds of theory. Limitations of space have prevented our including many works we would like to have seen here. We hope the bibliography helps to make up for these omissions.

We regret that we have been unable to obtain permission from Oxford University Press to reprint an essay by Tzevtan Todorov and have been refused permission to reprint an essay by Fredric Jameson.

We are in the debt of many scholars and critics who have generously responded to our requests for advice, and we wish to acknowledge their help here: M. H. Abrams, Carolyn Allen, Jonathan Arac, Douglas Collins, Northrop Frye, Sandra M. Gilbert, Geoffrey Hartman, E. D. Hirsch, Wolfgang Iser, Davor Kapetanic, Murray Krieger, Vincent B. Leitch, Wallace Martin, J. Hillis Miller, Walter J. Ong, S.J., Edward W. Said, Thomas H. Sebeok, Steven Shaviro, Barbara Herrnstein Smith, and Gayatri Chakravorty Spivak. The editors are particularly in the debt of Mary Gazlay, who has handled the securing of permissions and has proofread the text. Needless to say, the errors and omissions are our responsibility.

Acknowledgments of permission to reprint appear in bibliographical notes at the bottom of the first page of each selection. Footnotes are identified at the end of each by author [Au.], translator [Tr.], or editors [Eds.]. References citing *Critical Theory Since Plato* employ the acronym *CTSP.* Authors whose works are included in this text are indicated by the italicizing of their names, and readers who wish to consult their essays should go to the contents list.

HAZARD ADAMS
LEROY SEARLE

CRITICAL THEORY SINCE 1965

Introduction

by Hazard Adams

I

The year 1965 marks the midpoint in a decade of profound change and disquiet, particularly in its latter half, that did not leave the world of criticism and theory untouched. This change has been seen perhaps most dramatically in the United States, where it occurred more suddenly than elsewhere, principally because of the delay in the arrival of both European phenomenological and structuralist criticism in this country and the sudden demise or, some would say, transformation of the latter into poststructuralism or deconstruction. (American linguistics and anthropology had a structuralist phase, but it was exhausted before 1965.) As a result, North American criticism hardly had a structuralist phase at all—a phase that had developed over decades in Europe. As did its predecessor volume, this anthology naturally takes a North American point of view and thus, because of the phenomenon mentioned, somewhat skews the history of these matters, not only in this introduction but also in the selections made. It also limits itself to the history of criticism and theory in Western thought.

The other part of the title also reveals the North American perspective in its continued use of the term "critical theory." In North America the term has tended to mean the theory of *literary* criticism, whereas in Europe it has been associated with social thought and specifically identified with the so-called Frankfurt School of sociological analysis and critique of ideology. For our title we continue to use the term in the former sense, though we recognize the significance of the latter and its arrival long since in North America. Further, we recognize, and this anthology demonstrates, that much more than what had previously been thought of as relevant is involved today in questions about literature. Indeed, in some influential theories the term "literature," which does not have as long a history as one might suppose, has itself been put in question. The hidden, implied "literary" in our title we accept as problematical, even as we allow it to remain for quite practical reasons, one of which is that an anthology must establish boundaries, rough as they may be. The implied term means that this book holds works relevant to the theoretical concerns of criticism, imagined as the study of texts traditionally considered literary. We recognize at the same time the broader range of theory now thought important and even the view that there can be no firm boundaries established for such concerns or for literature itself. That we have felt compelled to make these remarks attests to the existence of a situation requiring a new anthology, which may do something toward clarifying the relations or differences among the many conflicting and independent positions being held or developed today. Never in the history of criticism has there been such a plethora of competing jargons and systems, to say nothing of antisystems.

II

In the effort to give some order to a large collection of separate pieces spanning over 2,000 years, the general introduction to *Critical Theory Since Plato* had recourse to the useful orientation of theories summarized by *M. H. Abrams* in his book *The Mirror and the Lamp* (1953). There he divided theories into four types called mimetic, pragmatic, expressive, and objective; and he noted that they predominated in the history of criticism, but not exclusively, roughly in the order in which they are given above—from the mimetic views held by Plato and Aristotle, through the pragmatic views of Horace and numerous medieval, Renaissance, and Enlightenment critics, to the expressive views of the romantic theorists, and finally the objectivism of the modernists.

In order to account for what is rather oddly called "postmodernism" and sometimes the "newer" criticism, successor in America to the New Criticism, one may profit by examining the history of criticism and theory from a somewhat different perspective, dividing it into three worlds that tend to overlap: those of ontology, epistemology, and linguistical thought. That would be to observe how criticism has moved along routes also taken by philosophy and other disciplines.[1] From this vantage, criticism and theory seem to be in the throes of sorting out the implications of a major shift to an interest in language that stirred late in the eighteenth century, flowered in the nineteenth, and threatened to sweep all before it in the twentieth. This shift was marked by the almost compulsive attention paid in almost all fields to language, symbols, and signs. The movement gathered momentum rapidly in this century—probably too rapidly for easy assimilation—on the tide of the previous epistemological movement, which it gradually replaced.

In the seventeenth century, epistemology had usurped the place of ontology, or the problem of being, which had dominated philosophy from its recorded beginning in ancient Greece. Mainly because of Plato, criticism received from the world of ontology two ideas that pervade it to this day, despite periodic campaigns to eradicate them: the ideas embodied by the terms "mimesis" and the "didactic." Under their domination, literature remained at best a handmaiden to philosophy and, in the Christian era, to theology. At worst it was regarded as an unruly child requiring surveillance and periodic correction, or even as an enemy to be destroyed or exiled from proper society.

The world of epistemology, usually marked in its beginnings by the science of Galileo, the empiricism of Francis Bacon and John Locke, and the rationalism of René Descartes, did not change abruptly the dominance of these two venerable terms. They persist to this day, sometimes in synonyms, and they have amply proved their staying power. But the famous bifurcation of nature, as A. N. Whitehead called it in his *Science and the Modern World* (1925), gave rise to a new emphasis. The bifurcation he refers to was the separation of human experi-

[1] *Abrams's* own analysis of the postobjective age of criticism, which he calls the "Age of Reading," can be found in this volume. Authors whose names are set in italics are included in this volume and can be found in the contents list beginning on p. v.

ence into objective and subjective or primary and secondary realms of knowledge. The problem of knowledge came to be regarded as prior to the problem of being. George Berkeley's criticism of Locke was that if the objective or primary qualities of experience were privileged—were accorded the status of the real—and the secondary qualities were merely subjective and a sort of illusion, how could we ever know the primary at all? After all, the primary qualities could be experienced only through the subjective, which had been declared relative and unreliable. Berkeley's form of subjective idealism was more successful as a criticism or *reductio ad absurdum* of Locke's distinction than as a route for philosophy, however; and the subject-object problem continued to dominate epistemology. It gave rise to David Hume's radical skepticism (*CTSP,* pp. 313–23), which in turn led to Immanuel Kant's critical philosophy (*CTSP,* pp. 377–99). It gave rise to ideas of the aesthetic, the imagination, and what Abrams called the "expressive" theoretical orientation in romantic criticism. The effort was to clear a space for human experiences the importance of which was not accounted for in a philosophy that accepted only scientific knowledge. Literary theory labored nevertheless under the domination of subjectivity and its inevitable but alien partner the objective. Aesthetics, which was systematically developed as the concept we know in the eighteenth century, involved the idea of experience and affect, particularly experience not reducible to objective measurement or to the Kantian categories of the understanding. "Imagination" in its many transmutations came to be regarded as a term denoting a creative mental power that overcame the implied and feared solipsism of the subjective by actually shaping experience into the real (see Coleridge, *CTSP,* pp. 468–70). "Expressive" is a term that describes the activity of the poet in bringing to externality the inner being or self. Theories of imagination and mental creativity sought to overcome the powerful bifurcation of subject and object and the isolation that threatened each individual in a world where subjectivity reduced to feeling apparently could not reach the object or beyond the enclosure of the self. Theories of pure subjectivity, in its extremity impressionism, accepted the bifurcation and in so doing acknowledged the inevitability of a radically solipsistic subjectivity for poet and critic alike. The classic text expressing this view is the conclusion to the *Renaissance* of Walter Pater (1893), for a while suppressed by its author as dangerous to youth. Its most famous sentences are "Experience, already reduced to a swarm of impressions, is ringed round for each one of us by that thick wall of personality through which no real voice has ever pierced on its way to us, or from us to that which we can only conjecture to be without. Every one of those impressions is the impression of the individual in his isolation, each mind keeping us a solitary prisoner in its own dream of a world." (The whole of the conclusion is in *CTSP,* pp. 643–45.) Anatole France's famous remark in his "Adventures of the Soul" (1888–93) expresses the same situation: "To be quite frank, the critic ought to say: 'Gentlemen, I am going to talk about myself on the subject of Shakespeare, or Racine, or Pascal, or Goethe—subjects that offer me a beautiful opportunity'" (*CTSP,* p. 671).

At about the same time the phenomenological movement, which was in part an attempt to reestablish the ontological world in the face of the epistemological world's new supremacy, attempted to heal the fissure between the subject and the world by rejecting the Kantian theory of the unknowability of things in themselves and promoting consciousness as knowing that is more than knowing in the epistemological sense of producing scientifically verifiable "truth." Consciousness is always the consciousness of something according to the putative founder of phenomenology, *Edmund Husserl*. Phenomenology in its many varieties in Europe, it was claimed, was an attack on epistemology, but the movement took only halfway measures, as shown by a term commonly used among phenomenological critics, "intersubjectivity." Intersubjectivity implies an objectivity somewhere; and, too, the shift from the term "knowledge" to "consciousness" was not a complete break. In any case, the phenomenological movement, the major aesthetician of which was *Roman Ingarden,* never dominated the scene in Europe. In America its related literary theory, the "criticism of consciousness," flourished briefly under the proprietorship of Georges Poulet (*CTSP,* pp. 1213–22) and his disciple at The Johns Hopkins University, *J. Hillis Miller.* Miller's career is a microcosm of one line of movement in American criticism in the period with which we are concerned. Trained at Harvard in the New Criticism, he passed through Poulet's influence and emerged in the seventies a Derridean deconstructionist, engaging in a polemic with M. H. Abrams on the question of whether textual meaning could be determinate or was inevitably indeterminate. Phenomenological theory with its emphasis on poetic consciousness mediated successfully by the literary work arrived comparatively late in North America, however. Indeed, even in Europe it was quickly enmeshed, as the work of *Martin Heidegger* on language shows, in the great web of language theory that transformed philosophical interest once again and brought to eminence the linguistic world.

We now recognize that the epistemological age carried the seeds of this transformation within itself. Giovanni Battista Vico (*CTSP,* pp. 293–301) anticipated the transformation with his theory of tropes as early as his *New Science* in 1725. It was latent in the first stirrings of a crude anthropology, etymology, and archeology in the eighteenth century and in the theories about mythology and the origin of language that continued to be offered into the nineteenth century. It was latent also in the thought of Kant, which seems to us today to cry out for transference of the notion of the constitutive from the mind to language. But on the whole philosophy remained concerned with problems of perception, knowing, and being with little attention paid to the mediation of language. There was, however, a strand of neo-Kantianism carried from Wilhelm von Humboldt to Ernst Cassirer, who published his three-volume *Philosophy of Symbolic Forms* in the 1920s, that did introduce language theory. Von Humboldt's brother Alexander had traveled widely in the Americas and gathered much information about languages, which Wilhelm put to use in his theories. In this neo-Kantian line, language became the medium of human creativity, the location of human imaginative power, an outgrowth or expression of human spirit. Cassirer, also in the debt of Vico, fled from the Nazis and arrived in the United States to write *An Essay on Man* (*CTSP,* pp. 993–1013), in which he regarded man as the *animal symbolicum.* This was a time during which the New Criticism succeeded in dominating critical fashion in America. Isolated from European developments, the New Criticism was in large part a reaction against the positivistic historical scholarship and pedagogy of the American academy. It came only belatedly to recognize that its practice had philosophical implications. This recognition came about gradually in the work of such peripheral figures as Monroe Beardsley (*CTSP*, pp. 1014–31), Eliseo Vivas (*CTSP*, pp. 1069–77), and Philip Wheelwright (*CTSP*, pp. 1102–12). It was supplemented and analyzed by Vivas's student *Murray Krieger* (*CTSP*, pp. 1223–49).

When Abrams wrote of the "objectivist" critical orientation, he had in mind this movement, which objectifies the Kantian product of aesthetic "purposiveness without purpose" or "internal purposiveness" in a linguistic artifact, apart from the historical author and separate from a subjective or empirically constituted reader. The New Criticism's considerable involvement with quite different positions—including the psychologism of I. A. Richards (*CTSP*, pp. 847–59) and self-styled classicisms of T. E. Hulme (*CTSP*, pp. 766–82) and T. S. Eliot (*CTSP*, pp. 783–90), its anti-Platonism, and its own curious positivism—cannot be charted here. Krieger's *The New Apologists for Poetry* (1956) remains an excellent analysis and one of the first rigorously theoretical works in American criticism. It is important to notice that the New Criticism in America did its work in ignorance of European phenomenology, which had preceded it chronologically but in America sought to succeed it. Neither had Europe been affected by the New Criticism, which took some time seeping into the academic bastions of England. The situation was the same with another European movement profoundly at odds with phenomenology but with some aspects of which phenomenology had directly to cope, specifically its direct concern with language.

This movement was, of course, structuralism, the origin of which is usually regarded as being the posthumously published *Course in General Linguistics* of *Ferdinand de Saussure*. Phenomenologists had been interested in language, of course. Heidegger is famous for remarking that language speaks man, that all man's thought is implicated in language. For Heidegger, however, language was mediatory, and the consciousness of the subject worked in and through it to the reader. For the structuralist, the "through" was eliminated, as was the phenomenological subject. De Saussure's aim was to establish a science of language on a firm foundation, and that meant to him that it would be necessary to isolate the object of study as a world or system of its own. The problem for such a study of language had always been, on the one hand, the supposedly originating human subject and, on the other, the troublesome referent. Both kept carrying into its study the baggage of externality. Actual speakers or real dogs and horses trotting through the world of language were certainly a nuisance to anyone attempting to establish a science dealing with it. Chemists do not want the "duckweed and a few fish" that the poet W. B. Yeats insisted on in water; they want that "poor naked creature H_2O." Physicists do not want dirt in their matter, which only clogs up the effort to constitute matter in and as number. Further, as Northrop Frye remarked in his *Anatomy of Criticism* (*CTSP*, pp. 1117–47), which begins as a plea for development of a true "science" of criticism, physicists study physics, not nature. Linguists, on this principle, would study linguistics, not language, and certainly not nature or human nature. Linguistics would have to be a science unconcerned with subjects or referents.

So language study and linguistically oriented philosophy which in their semantically oriented forms had always included acknowledgment of the referent and in their neo-Kantian forms had been supremely concerned with expression by a speaker, were reduced under the influence of de Saussure to the assumption that language was a binary system. Only the signifier (sound image, for de Saussure) and signified (concept) remained. This view has never fully won the day, however. Threefold systems which included the referent were influential before de Saussure, as the works of *Gottlob Frege* and *Charles Sanders Peirce* show, and after in their followers and others who insisted on language's capacity to bring the world into symbolic existence. The work of anthropological linguistics in many of its forms has emphasized the relation of human behavior to language (for example, *Benjamin Lee Whorf*). Indeed, as *Emile Benveniste,* himself inclined to a structuralist position, shows, de Saussure was equivocal or inconsistent about the status of the referent. Heidegger had been deliberately equivocal about the question of the subject, of whether if language speaks man, man does not also speak language. In Saussurean structuralism the banishment of the referent as a scientific irrelevance brought things down firmly on the side of the view that human beings are caught in the "prison house of language," as Fredric Jameson called it. Language had come to speak man—with a deterministic vengeance, even to the extent that the human subject, staple of the epistemological age, came into question. Indeed, language had seemed to replace the world and people, or rather the world had become linguistic rather in the same way that physicists had made the world mathematical.

This view happened to be congenial in some ways with a political position that had long identified the concept of the subject or "man" with an oppressive capitalism built on the notion of the laissez-faire economic individual. But this position was usually materialistic in Marxian fashion, and thus those who held it rebelled against the idea of the referentless "prison house," even as they were happy enough to dispatch the individual subject, regarded as a bourgeois invention. This whole situation perpetrated something of a crisis in Marxist literary theory, but crises in literary theory have almost always resulted in an influx of energy. Structuralism had leftist leanings on the whole, or rather leftist politics in France leaned toward some aspects of structuralism while at the same time remaining extremely wary of the formalist direction that structuralism, with both subject and referent gone, threatened to take. Those leaning toward leftist social theory have considered the structuralist and deconstructive movement that followed it in America a reactionary domestication.

Certainly deconstruction can be regarded as a carrying of structuralist principles to their logical conclusion, and some would call this movement a *reductio ad absurdum* like that of Berkeley.

The individual subject or "man" came under attack also in the work of the historian *Michel Foucault,* certainly associated with structuralist thought though he always angrily denied the appellation. Foucault's influential *The Order of Things* (1966) announced the disappearance of humanist man, which he regarded as a creation of the Renaissance *épistème.* With this disappearance, of course, went the idea of an author.

He viewed this demise as a liberation of sorts from a worldview responsible for various cultural institutions as we have known them—the madhouse, the hospital, the prison, and even the conventions of sexuality. This kind of "archeological" anthropology (or anti-anthropology) of Western culture had as its main characteristics the critique of institutions as such and could be looked on with interest by those who had studied the writings of the Frankfurt sociologists and philosophers *Theodor Adorno* and *Max Horkheimer,* though some in Europe regarded their work as not radical enough, especially Adorno's aestheticism.

Anthropology had been born in the individualistic entrepreneurial work of scholars in the "field" of so-called primitive societies. Though the researcher was likely to consider him- or herself an "observer" in good scientific fashion, anthropology tended to be interested in social or collective "man," not quite the "man" of whose existence Foucault called for the death knell. As "primitive" isolated societies (thus properly "laboratory" societies) disappeared, anthropology began to turn its methods back on Western "man." Closely in contact with structuralism, mainly through the broadly influential work of *Claude Lévi-Strauss,* anthropology, always difficult to define as a "human science," has become, for those outside it, a disseminator and meeting ground of ideas that have profoundly affected critical theory. Yet from the inside it appears chaotic; some of its major figures are dissenters (Lévi-Strauss can be regarded as a dissenter), and those who have invaded it from the outside, sometimes from literary criticism or for the purposes of literary criticism, remain interestingly marginal—*René Girard,* for example—perhaps more interesting than those inhabiting the main line. Part of the reason for this, as *Clifford Geertz* has indicated, is that there has been a change in modes of explanation in social sciences and a mixing of genres.

Lévi-Strauss's anthropological analysis of myths does not seem at first to be based on linguistics, but the method is in fact derived from de Saussure's treatment of language, and in that sense myths are treated as language. Linguistic method, specifically that of Hjelmslev, lay also at the base of Roland Barthes' treatment of everything from clothing fashions to literary texts as mythological. The term "text" came to include all cultural systems as if they were languages or made up of languages. The triumph of the linguistic world may be marked by the sudden ubiquity of "text" and the treatment of everything as if it were linguistic. Perhaps the phrase that most fully expresses this situation is *Jacques Derrida's* "Il n'y a pas de hors-texte," which is probably best translated as "There is no outside-the-text."

Fundamental principles of structuralist linguistics are, first, the arbitrary and, second, the diacritical nature of the sign. By the former is meant that there is no natural relation between the sound or appearance of a word and what it signifies. By the latter is meant that the sign is fundamentally expressive of a difference. Made up of a signifier (sound image) and a signified (concept) in arbitrary relationship, the sign is in itself differential. Furthermore, the sign is such by virtue of its difference from other signs in the system. A sign is therefore always defined by difference along a chain of such signs. Another fundamental principle is the difference between diachronic and synchronic approaches to linguistics. Diachrony emphasizes differences that relate successive terms in time and history.

Synchrony, more important in structuralism, is concerned with logical and psychological relations in an atemporal field. The concept of structure implies a differential system.

III

Despite the great importance of structuralism in European thought, as represented in this anthology and its predecessor by Barthes (see *CTSP*, pp. 1195–99), *Lévi-Strauss*, *Jacques Lacan* in psychoanalysis, Tzvetan Todorov in literary theory, and *Yurij Lotman* in aesthetics and cultural theory, its hegemony in North American criticism was short lived if it ever existed at all. This happened because even as it appeared on the scene it was subjected to powerful critique by a young French philosopher at a conference at The Johns Hopkins University in 1966. The conference, at which only European thinkers presented papers, was designed to introduce structuralist thought to the American literary academy. At this conference Jacques Derrida delivered the paper "Structure, Sign, and Play in the Discourse of the Human Sciences," a critique of the thought of structuralism's leading figure, Lévi-Strauss. Derrida's critique pointed to a fundamental contradiction in Lévi-Strauss's position and in structuralist thought generally. In positing a system of differences, structuralism did not recognize that such a system implies that there is no origin of meaning apart from itself to which it or its parts can be referred; or, if it does recognize this fact, it does not do so consistently and tends to smuggle in the idea of a "transcendental signified" to stabilize the system. The reason there can be no such transcendental signified, origin, or "center" is that every signified in the linguistic chain is but another signifier. Derrida claimed that a true structure or the "structure of structure" would have no boundaries and could only be bounded, or really unbounded, by a notion of infinite "play," which in turn could not be regarded as a concept in itself. This critique had enormous implications for the theory of meaning, and Derrida worked them out at once in a series of books in which the views of several major thinkers were "deconstructed" along similar lines. In *Of Grammatology* Derrida found the same sort of contradiction in de Saussure. Derrida accepted the notion that language was a differential network, but he rejected de Saussure's privileging of speech over writing and noted that this privileging leads back to the notion of an origin or "center" of meaning in the human speaking subject, the very thing in phenomenology that structuralism resisted. Derrida had made language an antisystem rather than a synchronic system. In *Speech and Phenomena* he analyzed Husserl's phenomenology on similar grounds in order to deconstruct the idea of a transcendental consciousness.

Fundamentally Derrida's attack was on the assumption lying behind the whole tradition of Western metaphysics as he saw it. Western metaphysics was the prisoner of the idea of "being as presence," that is, the notion of some anchor of being behind language, which was its ultimate truth or referent. He called this notion "logocentrism" and the tradition of privileging speech over writing "phonocentrism." The fundamental influence on Derrida, in addition to the structuralists and phenomenologists whom he deconstructs, is Friedrich Nietzsche, whom he regards as the first great deconstructor. Nietzsche's attack on Platonic dialectic and reason showed Plato to have employed the same rhetorical devices he attacks his opponents, the Sophists, for using. Nietzsche regarded Socratic reason as repression of the joyful play of language. Socrates would also suppress writing, where difference is clearly at play, there being in writing no present speaker to supply the illusion of meaning outside language. Derrida, of course, goes on to claim that it would make no difference if there were a speaker, since in the end speech can be shown to have the same differential character as writing anyway. In this sense, writing replaces speech as the model of language. It becomes Derrida's term for language's refusal of presence, of the concept as prior to it, and of the privileging of the signified over the signifier. Writing is the endless deferral and differing of meaning. For this condition Derrida coins a word in French that can only be written: *différance,* with an *a,* unknown to speech because it must be pronounced as if it were the same as *différence.* It combines, includes, and differs from the terms *différer* and *différence,* temporal and diachronic deferral and synchronic differing, respectively. Meaning is always subject to the "play" of *différance* along the linguistic chain. But because even *différance* threatens to become regarded as stabilized in meaning and thus subdued by the metaphysical tendency to assume a fixed meaning or center outside the antisystem, Derrida keeps inventing what he calls nonsynonymic relations to other terms. Some of these terms replacing *différance* for a time in his discourse are "supplement," "trace," "spacing," and "play" itself.

Another way of considering all this is to observe that if everything is always already in the web of language, then there is nowhere to stand outside of language in order to gain any leverage on it. All discussions of language employ the so-called object of discussion. Archimedes said that he could lift the universe if someone could point out where he should stand to do it. Derrida displaces this problem to the realm of the sign.

Derrida's move has the same elegance and, in the linguistic age, has created the same sort of interest that Berkeley's *reductio ad absurdum* of Locke's distinction between primary and secondary qualities had, and created, for the epistemological age. It is possible to think of it as the extension of structuralism to absurdity. Berkeley, having discovered solipsism, tried to evade it by involving the eternal mind of God in constant creation or perhaps retention. It was an attempt at a transcendental solution, which would return epistemology to metaphysics. But perhaps Derrida is not the linguistic Berkeley but the linguistic Kant, attacking metaphysics at the linguistic rather than the epistemological level. Like de Saussure, Derrida pays no attention to the referent. Referents cannot be known as other than belonging to the signified, which in itself is a signifier, which connects to (by means of difference from) yet another signifier. This chain is perhaps imaginable as a circle as large as language itself, potentially infinite, like the curved space of Einsteinian physics. An object on this track would return to its beginning in an infinite length of time. But the matter should perhaps be put the other way around: Einsteinian space is infinitely curved by its constitution in language. No word in the linguistic world is a beginning, for it is always already implicated in the infinite (yet closed and enclosed) system (antisystem), in which another word always precedes and follows it. There is no referent; neither is there an origin or center. Nor does Derrida bring in at the last moment a god from beyond the machine, as did Berkeley. There is only irony, inside and implicated. It is an irony of Nietzschean joyful play and performs the role in the linguistic world that romantic irony performed in the epistemological world. Because one can never escape entirely the rule of Western metaphysics and language's need to posit a center, origin, or transcendental signified even as its own differential behavior rejects it, one must write in language against language. One must write one's text against other texts, and even against one's own text. Derrida's books are confrontations with other texts, and in recent years they have actually been intermeshings with other texts so that it is uncertain quite what text is commenting on what and where one begins and another ends. Rather than endless Faustian striving for striving's ethical sake, or Byronic questing for questing's ethical sake, linguistic irony counsels joyous play along the linguistic chain. The identity of the romantic quester was not in doubt, or at least he was constantly in a state of becoming. In the linguistic world, no longer "man," the player disappears without identity into differential play, or (to reverse Yeats) there is no dancer, only the dance. (On this line in Yeats, see *Paul de Man*.) All that is left of "man" is a "trace" in the linguistic act. The old isolated epistemological subject is declared gone, or at least unknowable. The new subject, if that is what we can call it, is constituted by language, which is to say culture, and it is therefore always already alienated from any notion of a simple prelinguistic being or self simply located.

IV

Derrida's constant play across his own terms points to the notion that if one is to attempt interpretation it cannot come to an end, that there can never be anything but this play. Interpretation has been a problem through the history of criticism, and the issue has been, for the most part, the question of determinate or indeterminate meaning or even the meaning of the word "meaning" itself. The problem can be seen in the tradition of reading of both Homer and Scripture. Homer has been subjected to all kinds of readings, from strict decoding of a presumed allegory, as in the famous cave-of-the-nymphs scene from the *Odyssey*, which Porphyry read as a Neo-Platonic allegory of the descent of the soul into matter, to strict historical reading, which claimed the *Iliad* to depict real events and held the *Odyssey* to be the report of a sea voyage. Interpretation of Scripture traverses the same interpretive ground, made even more complicated by the tradition of rabbinical interpretation of the Old Testament, a method that tended to build an endless interpretation out of the text, and the contrasting Christian typological readings in which the New Testament was seen as historical fulfillment of Old Testament antitypes. Derrida's work could be seen as an extension of the rabbinical mode.

The problematical nature of interpretation is nothing new, however. In the secularization of hermeneutic practice from the nineteenth century onward there has been a quarrel over methods and ends. This centered first on Scripture, but soon it shifted to secular texts, including history. In *Validity in Interpretation* (*CTSP,* pp. 1177–94) E. D. Hirsch sought some years ago to locate a center of meaning in the reconstruction of authorial intention, a move that had been challenged long before Derrida in the arguments of the New Criticism against intention (see Wimsatt and Beardsley *CTSP,* pp. 1014–31). Hirsch, who may be identified with the tradition of nineteenth-century positivism, directly opposed the work of *Hans-Georg Gadamer,* identified with phenomenological hermeneutics, whose *Truth and Method* put forth the idea that to reconstruct the authorial outlook was always from a temporal "horizon" of our own and that what occurs in any interpretive act is a conversation of horizons between that of the text and that of the interpreter. In other words, every interpretation is the reading of a temporal relation of difference. Gadamer called the interpreter's horizon variously "prejudice" and "foreconcept." This foreconcept undergoes constant revision as time passes, and thus the past must constantly be reinterpreted. This view is connected to the Heideggerian notion of hermeneutic, which in his usual way Heidegger discloses via etymological search. "Hermeneutic" is "referable to the name of the god Hermes by a playful thinking that is more compelling than the rigor of science. Hermes is the divine messenger. He brings the message of destiny. *Hermeneuein* is that exposition which brings tidings because it can listen to a message." The phenomenological reading implicates a reader, an author, and a message, in contrast to deconstruction, but it recognizes an unresolvable problem or paradox of interpretation nevertheless, which it names the hermeneutic circle. This circle has two aspects. The first is the need for constant reinterpretation, because of the endless change of horizon in time. The second is the situation always present: In order to interpret, one must begin with either part or whole, but the part depends on the whole and the whole on the parts, so that what is required is an oscillation back and forth from a foreconcept of the whole to part to new foreconcept and so on. Heidegger is perhaps less cryptic than usual in the following remark about the hermeneutic act: "In interpreting we do not, so to speak, throw a 'signification' over some naked thing which is present at hand; but when something within the world is encountered as such, the thing in question already has an involvement which is disclosed in our understanding of the world, and this involvement is one that gets laid out by interpretation." Thus phenomenology, too, has its theory of difference, though it is a temporal and horizonal difference only.

V

This is not at all to say that the New Criticism, which the movements we have been considering replaced, was not conscious of these problems. The essay by *Stanley Cavell* that begins this anthology is deliberately chosen as a transition piece from one set of approaches to another. Cavell is concerned with two issues that he addresses in terms that would be familiar to anyone schooled in the tradition of aesthetics and in the New Criticism—the problem of paraphrase and the question of aesthetic judgment. With no connection to either structuralism or phenomenology, the New Criticism only came to recognize what relationship its problems had to those Kant had addressed. Kant's approach seems from one point of view old-fashioned and from another not so old-fashioned at all. The issues seem to recur in poststructuralist debate in other terms, somewhat displaced—the problem of meaning displacing the problem of aesthetic value, for example. As a general policy it might be well to look back on the Kantian and New Critical positions to see just how much change has actually taken place in North American theory. One may say fairly that the major result for critical practice has been the reaction against interpretation in the sense of the search for a fixed or "determinate" meaning of the text. The attitude is clearly stated in *Jonathan Culler*'s "Beyond Interpretation," where deconstruction and other recent developments in critical theory are regarded as freeing the text from the allegedly authoritarian notion of a center or origin of recoverable meaning. Cleanth Brooks, probably the model New Critic, could write "The Heresy of Paraphrase" (*CTSP*, pp. 1033–41), but his own practice tended to make from his idea of irony as a principle of structure what the poststructuralists called variously "closure" and "totalization." (For a radical dismissal of "totalization" see *Deleuze and Guattari,* even to the extent of proposing the idea of a "schizoid" work.) Derridean structure, of course, has no center. The structure of structure is centerlessness. New Critical irony becomes hypostatized, it is claimed, as an aesthetic center, objectifying the text and producing meaning, even as the idea of paraphrasable meaning is denied. This would allow for the possibility of "unity," ending the free play of signifiers in a *parole* of the text's own making. The poststructuralist position also rejects the New Critical notion that the language of poetry differs in any way from that of everyday language, or, if it does, it is only in degree and a very small degree at that. One thinks here of the work of John Crowe Ransom (*CTSP*, pp. 871–90). Ransom attempted to characterize the oddity of poetic language by dividing the poem into paraphrasable core and a texture of "irrelevant" detail. One thinks of Robert Penn Warren's notion of poetic "impurity" (*CTSP*, pp. 981–92) and of Philip Wheelwright's "depth language" (*CTSP*, pp. 1103–12). Poststructuralists insisted on seeing these attempts to define poetry as in some way special as a program to "privilege" poetic discourse, viewing this and the idea of the "autonomous" poetic object as closing off textual possibility and also as being suspect for political elitism. It is more accurate, however, to claim that the New Criticism tried to defend poetry against an already privileged positivistic view of language and science.

There is no doubt that Brooks in his discussion of poems in his book *The Well Wrought Urn* tended in the end to allegorize poems, his view being apparently that awareness of doing so was enough, if enough qualifications were made along the way. But this was not enough for the poststructuralists. Thus in Derrida one gets the following well-known remark: "From this language it is necessary to free ourselves. Not actually to try to free ourselves from it, for that is impossible without forgetting our historical condition. But to imagine it. Not actually to *free* ourselves from it, for that would be senseless and would deprive us of the light of sense. But to resist it as far as possible." This is a recognition that the language we employ in everything, including critical practice, tends toward the illusion of successful allegorization, "totalization," and closure and that there must be eternal vigilance even as one uses the language. From this point of view, Brooks was not disruptive enough of his own discourse.

VI

At this point it may be worthwhile to consider a little more how the idea of autonomy of the literary text, accused as it has been of elitism, privilege, and closure, developed in the first place, and what such autonomy did and did not imply, particularly an autonomy defined eventually in terms of language. The New Criticism, though it developed apart from structural linguistics, definitely belonged in its own way to the linguistic world. In any case, the idea of autonomy was by no means a New Critical invention.

At least since Aristotle, literature had been defined by differentiating it from history, it being tacitly agreed that to define something one had to find its difference from something else. Aristotle declared literature (or poetry) to be more universal than history, which he regarded as tied to particulars. In the Middle Ages, poetry was frequently compared to theology, either to its detriment or in order to defend it as offering moral fables supportive of theological teaching. But the rise of science generated need for a vigorous new defense and comparison. Aesthetics was to a great extent the outcome of this need, and of all aesthetic theories Kant's was the most rigorous and comprehensive. He attempted to carve out a place for a certain kind of judgment that did not move by means of the categories of understanding to subsume particulars under a general rule applicable to other particulars. Kant's aesthetic judgment was radically singular and in this sense autonomous, since it could not be brought under the laws of the understanding. This autonomy became transferred to the object when viewed as aesthetic. Kant was equivocal, however, about just exactly where this autonomy lay, because the object *as object* or "thing in itself" could not be known but only constituted in the pure forms of space and time and further submitted to a subjectively universal aesthetic judgment (see *CTSP*, pp. 379–99). Nor did Kant recognize adequately the linguistic nature of the literary aesthetic object.

It was nevertheless from Kant that the notion of the autonomous linguistic object, the poem, developed. Being made of language, the poem was apparently an employment of language in a different way from statements operating under the aegis of the externally purposive Kantian understanding, which always works toward generalization. Efforts to elaborate this difference abounded, often as parts of whole philosophical and aesthetic systems. Some of these theories imagined poetic behavior as a departure or deviation from a linguistic norm, the model of which was symbolic logic. This tendency was best exemplified in its extreme by the term invented for poetry (and later abandoned) by I. A. Richards, "pseudo-statement."

But though a number of these deviationist views were popular, a competing opposite view developed all through the modern period. It built in some versions on Vico's theory of the origin and growth of language and culture, which insisted on certain major tropes as actually central to or at least originally central to language. It was the language of science verging on mathematical symbolism that was the departure, or at least development, from this tropological source. The model of symbolic logic was the deviation. The true nature of language was Vico's "poetic logic." This view struggled for acceptance against a strongly scientific and positivistic intellectual tide which appears even in those who attempt to articulate it—Ernst Cassirer (*CTSP*, pp. 994–1013), Philip Wheelwright (*CTSP*, pp. 1103–12), Susanne Langer, and others. This tradition represents what might be called the positive side of a theory of tropes or, in the parlance of some of them, "myth" (see *Adams*). By contrast the deconstructive theory of tropes, in, for example, Paul de Man, emphasizes the duplicity, seductiveness, and unreliability of an inevitably tropological language.

Always opposed to the Derridean deconstruction and not associated with the Viconian line have been those theorists influenced by the analysis of language made by *Ludwig Wittgenstein* and those grouped around the speech-act theory of *J. L. Austin* and his disciple *John R. Searle.* As M. H. Abrams points out, there are similarities between Derrida and Wittgenstein in that both reject language as naively representational. But Wittgenstein did not concern himself so much with how language fails to transcend itself. Rather he inquired into how language pragmatically works, when it does. He was not interested in showing that language inevitably fails to accomplish what it seems to imply that it sets out to do—represent. In his *Philosophical Investigations,* Wittgenstein simply does not believe that it is to be judged as representation. This is a line with much influence in philosophy but less in critical theory at the present time, though a critic like *Charles Altieri* is strongly in the debt of Wittgenstein and speech-act theory, as is *Stanley Fish* with quite different results. Altieri subjects Derrida to scrutiny from that point of view. John Searle has criticized Derrida in print, as have linguists of other persuasions, critical of what they regard as a misunderstanding of de Saussure brought about by the recorders and editors of de Saussure's text. (De Saussure's text is based on notes taken down and edited by his students.) Derrida's answer to Searle shows that his position, thoroughly skeptical, is on its own terms impregnable, but its self-enclosure, even as it advises the joy of open play, may also be what eventually causes a draining away of interest in it.

VII

In the work of the major deconstructionist theorists the notion generated by Vico and the line emerging from it is rarely mentioned, perhaps because Vico's concerns were historical and the history he wrote sees with a certain ambivalence a later age of reason supplanting the age of tropological thinking. In Derrida and de Man there is a synchronic view of language, like de Saussure's, as not merely originally but always tropological. Philosophical, historical, scientific—all discourse is caught up in the infinite regress of the signifier as trope. Poetry swallows everything in sight. The need for a theory of aesthetic autonomy as a defense of poetry disappears because, everything being linguistic and all language being fundamentally poetic (for the trope is regarded in these systems as the essence of poetry), there remains nothing for poetry to be distinguished *from*.

It is no wonder that with this movement come declarations either of the death of literature or of the breakdown of distinctions between literature and other things including criticism itself. (On this point see *Geoffrey H. Hartman*.) Now suddenly the deviation is the norm, and there is nothing outside it. In Derrida's work everything disappears into the monolithic term *écriture*. So what began in the epistemological world as an attempt to defend poetry by defining it through difference proceeds in the linguistic world to subsume all linguistic behavior under literature, though the term is now effaced and *écriture* is written over it. With no difference from anything opposed to it, literature becomes everything and therefore nothing. It can be regarded as an irony of the history of criticism that a movement predicated on the idea of difference, beginning with the differential nature of the sign and invoking difference at every step, should end in the monolithic view that it does.

With the ubiquity of literature comes the displacement of the notion of autonomy. Now the whole system of language is autonomous, but because language is everywhere and everything the term "autonomy" actually disappears in the way that "literature" does. Poststructuralist thought rejects the notion of the autonomy of the literary text or any other kind of text, insisting on what is called intertextuality, refusing all ideas in any way suggesting "closure" or "totalization." This autonomous whole that is not a whole because it is endlessly open becomes the scene of Derridean play, parallel in the linguistic world to the ethical principle of disinterested play developed by Friedrich Schiller (*CTSP*, pp. 418–31) in the epistemological world. The poststructuralist move was hardly what Kant could have imagined when he posited a constitutive understanding and regulative reason, both seekers of unity, though the latter found itself embroiled in unresolvable contradictions.

Let us recall at this point that Dr. Johnson's response to Berkeley was to kick a stone. The parallel act in the linguistic age would be to kick a referent. Though Berkeley's answer to Locke was elegant, as is Derrida's to de Saussure, both positions cause the mind to boggle. But serious questions follow, as they did upon Berkeley. Is the whole movement really most important as a revision of the ground of ethics, despite its general attack on moralistic criticism? Is it driven by political considerations? Is it part of a general change in Foucauldian *épistème?* Jean-François Lyotard in *The Postmodern Condition* believes that it is and that it is marked by a tendency "not to supply reality but to invent allusions to the conceivable which cannot be presented."

With this turn comes the rise of studies that deliberately as a matter of principle disregard all traditional distinctions between kinds of writing. Studies employing contemporary critical styles occur, for example, of historical, philosophical, scientific, biographical, autobiographical, and fictive works. The term "narrative" supplants the venerable term "plot," identified with the old concept of unity, but "narrative" threatens to go the way of "literature," victim of its own ubiquity. A by-product of this development is the reappearance in literary criticism of the term "rhetoric," but it is turned inside out (see de Man). Classical rhetoric was the study of devices of speech that contributed to persuasion, delight, and transport. These devices were the classically defined tropes, regarded as useful decorations of linguistic utterances. They were deviations from a norm constituted by the structure of argument. In deconstruction, rhetoric reappears as the study of tropes, but now tropes are central to language, by no means merely devices of decoration or persuasion, though some of de Man's distrust of language may well come from this earlier though now rejected sense. The term now signifies the study of all utterance or, rather, writing. Argument and reasoning, once regarded as the center of writing, are now hopelessly enmeshed in a language the fabric of which is tropological in both warp and woof.

Now, since all tropes function in the endless play of signifiers, it appears that there can be no end to the possibilities for interpretation offered by any text. De Man's argument is that at any stage where a text seems to offer a fixed meaning, this meaning is dissipated or compromised by a play of tropes. Another meaning (and another) emerges to compromise any determined intention, whether constituted as internal or external. This is language speaking, not even language speaking man, but speaking its own undoing. (For Derrida it is language writing.) Further, the apparent intention of a text is blind to this undoing. Language is simply not to be trusted. Yet for de Man the unapproachable determinate remains truth, but a truth that cannot be achieved. Lamentation for this perpetual loss or unattainability is suppressed in favor of a tough welcoming of the knowledge of limitation. A de Manian deconstructive reading does not therefore emphasize openness and possibility so much as it deplores the delusion fostered by the idea of closure—a vain hope—and man's hopeless desire for it. Hope is to be scorned as weak. That Apollonian creative symbolic form of language emerging from locatable man (the view developed with certain important qualifications by Cassirer) is a delusion. The de Manian concept is more existential, though de Man would certainly claim to be less nostalgic than, say, Heidegger, denying any possibility of discovering truth in origins.

The Derridean concept is less concerned with loss or unattainability, though certainly it embraces absence, converting that embrace into a heroic gesture. This gesture has some affinity to that of Schiller, as has been suggested, but in style it is similar to that of Stéphane Mallarmé. Schiller's play was an outgrowth of the Kantian idea of internal purposiveness transferred to the realm of ethics, where paradoxically the ethical act becomes an expression of the irrelevance of self-interest. The romantic turns on this are many, from Faustian striving to the heroic thoughtless action of Yeats's Cuchulain. But Derrida's tradition is French, and the French exemplar is Mallarmé, whose elegant essays express a fastidious *sprezzatura*. The act requires a certain joyfulness, as Yeats remarked, transcending the dread that de Man would have us face full square.

The earlier work of Derrida does not exactly eschew interpretation so much as regard it as a continuing process, each act deconstructing the previous one in an endless movement. Even Culler does not unequivocally oppose interpretation in his attack on it. He opposes the fixed or fixing interpretation from which one is not supposed to see any reason to move on. The later Derrida, however, has developed techniques of evading even the momentary fixity of a reading. A text like *Glas* is so full of word play, so implicated in difference and juxtaposition with other texts, that it cannot be imagined as a reading of a text but only as an implication of itself with other texts that it takes into itself or opens itself to.

The idea of implication of one text with another (but in a far less radical sense) we have already noted in phenomenological hermeneutics as practiced by Gadamer. History is regarded here as always written from a temporal position so that all that can be recovered is really difference. In still another view, first developed by *Hayden White* under the initial influence of Northrop Frye, the writing of history is implicated in literature and tropes. A deconstructionist view makes it subject to the instabilities of language noted by de Man. Here, too, simple interpretation disappears, and the role of the critic is to demonstrate how texts resist interpretation even as they cry out for it.

VIII

Deconstruction is a strongly skeptical movement, calling all past theories into question. It has shaken faith in the possibility of discourse *about* a text. A refuge some critical practice has taken in response is to reconstitute the interpretive act radically and skeptically in the subjectivity of reading. In a sense, this is a parallel in the linguistic world to Anatole France's impressionism in the waning of the epistemological world. However, rather than assuming the isolation of the subject from the object, these orientations tend to declare the object *as object* nonexistent, or barely existent, and the text radically within the reader. The reader, however, is not France's critic talking about himself. The reader is a critical fiction, as in the work of *Wolfgang Iser*. Iser's version is, under the influence of Roman Ingarden's aesthetics, a phenomenological one. There is also the empirical study of reader-response, antithetical to the phenomenological dismissal of the empirical, which lodges meaning in a generalized reader, sometimes created in Freudian terms. There is the mode of literary history known as *rezeptionsasthetik*, represented here by *Hans Robert Jauss*, which under multiple influences, including Gadamer's, seeks to understand the work in terms of the history of its reception. Finally, there is the entirely skeptical disappearance of the text into the reader characterized by Stanley Fish's "Is There a Text in This Class?" The reader here is not the historical reconstruction but a version of "competence" based on a notion of cultural codes and communities. This literary competence is an analogy to the idea of linguistic competence found in the work of *Noam Chomsky*. In the case of Fish, however, the power to impose a reading replaces the idea of a possible objective reading to be achieved. Power and how it is exercised in communities of interpretation drive meaning. These views shift the center (usually a moving center) to the opposite side of the text from that of the poet's intention, favored by E. D. Hirsch. One theoretical position, that of *Harold Bloom,* turns the author into a reader, or rather inevitable misreader, of previous texts with which he is compelled to compete. Literary history becomes the history of poets misinterpreting (slaying?) their predecessors, the whole system being based on a Freudian Oedipal model. That sort of model is attacked by Gilles Deleuze and Felix Guattari in their *Anti-Oedipus* as a capitalistic fiction.

Fictive readers are called in question along with the author in poststructuralism to the extent that they represent a reappearance of the old epistemological subject. In the language-oriented version of Freudianism, or "French Freudianism" as it is sometimes called, especially that of Jacques Lacan, the subject is dissolved or, one might say, alienated from itself. In movement through the Lacanian imaginary into the symbolic stage, the stage characterized by the acquisition of language by the child, there comes establishment of a linguistically acculturated, imprisoned subject different from the old subject, which is left behind, unknowable outside of language. This new subject, alienated perpetually from itself, can know its existence only in and as language. It is a purely linguistic entity, subject to the world of difference and the law of the signifier. It has lost the self as we have thought of the self—some *thing* to which the word "self" refers, or one's own thinking being, as expressed in the Cartesian *cogito.* Language speaks man, but only the word "man." What began as a movement against Kantian aesthetics and autonomy ends by reasserting the unknowability of another thing in itself, the self in itself. Linguistic culture is now a gigantic solipsism, which is secure as long as it is also declared that there is nothing beyond. But in Lacan there is, or rather was, something beyond it, irrecoverably lost.

Generally speaking, recent theory has been involved, then, in the relation or disrelation of language to the subject, on the one hand, and to the reader, on the other, and to the question of language's cultural role—language as enclosure (or as all that there is), language as medium of cultural creation, or language as the controller of culture. To this extent, the *problems* of critical theory have not changed all that much since Plato, as a glance at the *Cratylus* and *Republic* will show. But there are new issues, or at least intensifications of them. Contemporary feminism, a politico-cultural movement of which literary theory is but a part, is concerned with the ways in which language codifies sexual oppression. It goes beyond this to question the established "canon" of great works as male-dominated (see *Robinson*). It finds something congenial in the Derridean notion of the possibility of a language working against the dominant language of the Western metaphysics of presence, transformed in feminist parlance to "patriarchy." (On this term see *Gilbert.*) But feminism in some of its appearances, especially in some of its American forms, is wary of the so-called formalism that some accuse Derrideanism of leading to, and in some cases it has taken a line that can be identified with the critique of ideology present in varieties of Marxism, while at the same time criticizing the patriarchal in Marx. Freud too comes under attack here. The idea of a feminine as against a masculine language is discussed, and it is identified in some views with Derridean play; but whether this is truly liberating, its own form of enclosure, or even any longer feminist is not agreed upon (see *Jardine*).

If there is a perceivable post-poststructuralist movement it is like a Wittgensteinian word-family with no common element. *Edward R. Said,* unhappy with the domestication of deconstruction especially in America, argues against the formalist isolation of domesticated critical theory and for a practice that is, as he calls it, "secular," "oppositional," and "ironic," that is suspicious of "guilds, special interests, imperialized fiefdoms, and orthodox habits of mind." In my own notion of the "secular symbolic" there is an appropriation of Vico and William Blake to arrive at a vision of culture privileging neither scientific nor poetic poles ("antimyth" and "myth") but insisting that the poetic play the Blakean "reprobate" role, providing a "contrary" to recognized opposites like subject and object. Murray Krieger's later work would hold for the special power of poetry to create the "illusion" of presence necessary to culture. *Northrop Frye*'s work after the influential *Anatomy of Criticism* (*CTSP,* pp. 1117–47) would connect his notion of literature to what he calls the "myth of concern." These are all, in quite different ways, efforts to return literature from isolation to culture and to build some sort of ethical vision.

In this confused scene, the fundamental questions may ultimately be ethical ones. It has been a convention since sometime in the nineteenth century for each new critical fashion coming on the scene to declare itself against moralism. This was part of the effort to free literature from the domination of philosophy and theology and the accompanying didactic. But every new critical fashion has made an ethical point. The call for a secular criticism, whether it is labeled "oppositional" or "reprobate," is also an insistence on attention to the ethical role of literature in the culture. The Derridean position, for example, invests play with an ethical significance. The ethical issue which seems to arise in poststructuralism is the question of freedom and justice. Contemporary critical debate may come to center on the question of whether we really want to dispense with the idea of the individual or the self, as the attack that has occurred in so many quarters on the subject seems to threaten. In varieties of poststructuralism the individual fades from view or is dissolved into the world of language. It is here that may be found the link between the linguistic side of poststructuralism and a political position that identifies the idea of the individual with bourgeois humanism, *laissez-faire* individualism, mastery, colonialism, authoritarianism, and male chauvinism or patriarchy. To submerge this dreadful individual in something greater, for the greater good is the end. Derrida has consistently claimed, against those on the left who declare his position formalist and reactionary, a radical stance. Yet many have held that at least the American form of deconstruction is but a further twist of the formalist reactionary screw.

This is the most recent form of a hoary argument in which each side prospers by deploring the supposed excesses of its opponent. One is reminded of situations in the sixties when any academic administrator who took anything resembling a position of reason was immediately vilified as a fascist. One remembers the academic communist-hunting of the late forties and early fifties, where confession of left-wing sinfulness and the turning of evidence gained absolution and often heroic status on the right. In the thirties some of the greatest writers of the century found themselves invited to choose sides, vilified no matter which of the apparently available choices they made, declared the real enemy if they chose neither side and tried to remain "oppositional" or "reprobate." Yeats, for example, whose concern was Irish politics at the time, which did not take a shape that gave particular sense to the choice elsewhere, found himself in a difficult position at the time of the Spanish Civil War and nearly did succumb (some declare that he did) to the fascistic view. He commented at the time: "When there is despair, public or private, when settled order seems lost, people look for strength within or without. Auden, Spender, all that seem the new movement *look* for strength in Marxian socialism, or in Major Douglas. They want marching feet. The lasting expression of our time is not this obvious choice but in a sense of something steel-like and cold within the will, something passionate and cold." This passage requires a reading. The question is whether it is a truly reprobate statement or simply an expression of a very ugly fascism. Or is this too obvious a choice, and should a reprobate reading reject it in favor of examining Yeats's struggle with the choices available to him in his concrete situation as an Anglo-Irishman? There is not space here to discuss this question, but it is possible to say that Yeats is *trying* to stake out a reprobate position, which were he successful would be contrary to the unproductive socialist/fascist opposition. A reprobate reading would try to recognize all of this and would probably recall in doing so that Yeats said of his reprobate work *A Vision* that its odd diagrams and gyres had helped him "to hold in a single thought reality and justice."

I have suggested that the establishment of a subject alienated from the original subject or self is identified in Lacan's work as the movement of the child through the imaginary order and into the symbolic or linguistic, where the subject becomes constituted in language, which is to say *as* language. Thus Lacan has posited an origin outside and prior to language. The Derridean must regard this as impossible to know. Further, it implies a psychoanalytical version of the theological myth of origin conflated with the myth of the fall. We are confronted with the notion of loss of our selves, as compared to a situation in which the self has and had no existence. Or nearly the loss, because Lacan holds on to the idea of something in the imaginary stage that endures into the symbolic. He holds onto a vestige of that outside-the-text, which remains in some unclear way apart from the alien figure of the constituted subject, locked in language, even as it *is* a part. There appears to be a crisis in Lacan over this matter, and it might be regarded as a repressed repetition of the stone-kicking of Dr. Johnson. It is a telling recalcitrance. The philosophy of a monolithic language that does more than speak man, that speaks the end of man, runs the risk of dissolving also freedom and perhaps justice and maybe even reality. Its collectivist implications could be unpleasant to contemplate.

Another question follows. What alternative is there to the negativing opposition between the old isolated subject alienated from the primary, valorized object (or the subject as master of the dispossessed) and the new linguistically constituted subject alienated from and negating the self? Perhaps we can consider again the idea of a mediating (symbolic), secular creativity in language, the idea of bringing things to symbolic existence even as we guard against the establishment of a fixed, stultified symbolic order. In "Subjectivity in Language" (1939), Emile Benveniste wrote: "The old antinomies of 'I' and 'the other,' of the individual and society, fall. It is a duality which is illegitimate and erroneous to reduce to a single primordial term, whether this unique term be the 'I,' which must be established in the individual's own consciousness in order to become accessible to that of the fellow human being, or whether it be, on the contrary, society, which as a totality would preexist the individual and from which the individual could only be disengaged gradually, in proportion to his acquisition of self-consciousness. It is in a dialectic reality that will incorporate the two terms and define them by mutual relationship that the linguistic basis of subjectivity is discovered." One can see the structuralist Benveniste struggling against a fall into the old subject/object relation and yet trying to hang on to the notion of a subject nevertheless. This is perhaps still the crisis of theory.

With the concept of the potentiality of linguistic creativity—requiring a subject in some sense but one that is reprobate to the prevailing opposition, definable in a relation of difference beyond the accepted opposition—there comes the possibility of a new reading ahead, a reading that our own reprobate reading ought to be prepared to embrace, not inevitably and not necessarily because it is better but because it might express adequately the renewal of life in that future moment. Some readings are better than others, and the test ought not to be submission to a prior jargon or political position. Rather, reading must be an act of mediation, of a closure not a closure because always prepared for the "yes but" of further discourse. It should be a reprobate act, "oppositional" in Said's sense, as its subject literature is at its most valuable—embodying something contrary to both fashionable alternatives.

We need criticism and interpretation, which, in order to do its cultural work, needs to be different from what it interprets. Inevitably that difference will have a sort of temporary fixity, in the throes of which we must employ a language of closures even as we strive to keep the poem open to the future. We know that there must be much tact about this activity. Our work must be mediational to allow some of the poem, at least, to flow out into the discourse of the culture. It should be celebratory of the reprobate in literature and it must condemn the unjust in it as well.

The poem always remains to be fully revealed, to be read again. All texts, we have learned, tell the story of their own evasiveness to our discourses about them. The theme of poststructuralism in its deconstructive phase is that poems resist interpretation. Demonstration of how this is so has been important (though not so new as some have thought), but repeated demonstration has already eventuated in its own form of reduction and thematization. Every text submitted to deconstruction considered as a critical method will yield the same theme, which may be true enough but remains only *that* story: the allegory of uninterpretability. It quickly becomes a repetition of the older formalist discovery that every text is about itself. It is no wonder that there has been a stirring—not so much a resistance against deconstruction (there has been that too, of course)—that expresses a desire to go beyond it. There has even been the idea of returning to Kant and trying again. But the dominant popular mood in critical theory as this is written is sociological and political, not surprising as a generation that came to adulthood in the sociologically and politically turbulent sixties gains positions of intellectual and academic power. Popular dominant moods do not often produce truly reprobate works except by oppositions that have to struggle for a hearing. Anthologists are always running the risk of dating their books even as they produce them, since the truly reprobate of the present may be obscured. It is clear enough that there is today renewal of a strong tendency throughout the history of criticism to bring the poem into the hurly-burly of culture and that criticism ought never to depart too far from this activity. But much of what is called critical theory today spends a minimum of time with literature as we have thought of the term and a maximum with sociological and political analysis. Thus this renewal may create in a few years a reaction. None of this is necessarily bad. In order for the truly reprobate to appear, criticism needs to be a continuous activity of many people. We know that much of it will pass away as it should, having done its work—as will some of the arguments anthologized here, when a new age replaces the linguistic. But not entirely, for problems of literary criticism have a way of returning in glamorous new disguises. We remind you that criticism has this sort of history and that what you have here is but the continuation of a story.

Stanley Cavell

b. 1926

In a 1964 essay, "Crisis in Criticism," Paul de Man suggested that perhaps "criticism" and "crisis" were redundant terms, arguing that genuine criticism seems to flow from crisis, even as critics remain unaware of the sources of their insights (*Blindness and Insight,* 1970). Stanley Cavell's essay, included here, may or may not be an example of this apparent paradox, but it contributes substantially to recording and partly explaining the "Spirit of the Age," ca. 1965. Cavell, as an ordinary language philosopher, approaches the subject of such a "spirit" cautiously, not altogether certain what "we would say." His argument that the powers of ordinary language philosophy closely resemble what Kant commended as aesthetic judgment comprises itself a recommendation for philosophers and critics, both uncertain what we should say or what we are going to say next.

Cavell records his sense "that philosophy is in one of its periodic crises of method, heightened by a worry . . . that method dictates to content." While this particular worry is that reliance on analytical techniques leads away from broader questions of human culture, Cavell proceeds in the hope that the analytical methods of ordinary language philosophy, especially as practiced by *Wittgenstein,* applied to aesthetic problems—and conversely, aesthetic analysis applied to philosophical problems—will yield a more satisfying engagement with issues that are not bare abstractions but concern our lives.

While many critics (including *Charles Altieri,* John Ellis, *Stanley Fish,* and others) have made significant use of the analytical techniques of ordinary language philosophy and the related philosophy of speech acts, Cavell's suggestion has not obviously borne fruit, in part because the tradition of the "aesthetic" was itself in a deeper crisis than Cavell may have appreciated, for similar reasons: that method, when it dictates content, may lead to an unwanted dissociation from vital concerns. This is evident in the two aesthetic problems to which Cavell turns: first, the problem of "paraphrase," or, as Cleanth Brooks expressed it, "the heresy of paraphrase"; second, the problem of the atonal avant-garde in music.

In the first case, Cavell responds altogether reasonably that Brooks's argument (rather, injunction) against paraphrase could not possibly be right, since Brooks himself cannot discuss any poem without paraphrase. Still, it is not altogether clear that Cavell has aimed at the right target, since the central problem for Brooks and the New Critics was the provenance and status of the poem as an "aesthetic" object (see *CTSP,* pp. 1032–48). In reviewing Yvor Winters's position, cited by Brooks, Cavell suggests that Winters, reasonable though he may be on the issue of paraphrase, comes close to being a reactionary crank in "defense of reason," since being "reasonable" in Winters's way would require forgoing "too much of modern art." There is no easy choice, however, no obviously "reasonable" choice, for the "aesthetic" object as such is itself liable to be a central case of "method dictat[ing] to content."

So it is, too, in the second case of avant-garde "atonal" music, with the difference that Cavell notes that such concepts as "tonality" or musical "cadence" belong to a "grammar" of music that admits a wide range of performance. When such a grammar is referred to one's own experience, it becomes, as Wittgenstein says, a "form of life"; and under such a condition of imagination, the problem is not solved, it is dissolved—in this case, by "naturalizing ourselves to a new form of life." Thus, while Cavell argues on behalf of the aesthetic, in the first case, the separateness of the "aesthetic" is itself the problem, which, in the second case, is not solved but dissolved by "naturalizing ourselves" to it. It then remains very much open to question whether the idea of the "aesthetic judgment" is itself necessary—particularly if such problems as "the heresy of paraphrase" and dilemmas of poetic interpretation are themselves a direct result of trying to separate the "aesthetic" from the nonaesthetic.

In any case, bringing analytic philosophy, aesthetics, and criticism into reflective relation to each other remains one of the most challenging problems of contemporary criticism.

Cavell's major works include *Must We Mean What We Say?* (1965); *The World Viewed: Reflections on the Ontology of Film* (1971); *The Senses of Walden* (1972; expanded edition, 1981); *The Claims of Reason: Wittgenstein, Skepticism, Morality, and Tragedy* (1979); and *Themes Out of School: Effects and Causes* (1984).

AESTHETIC PROBLEMS OF MODERN PHILOSOPHY

The Spirit of the Age is not easy to place, ontologically or empirically; and it is idle to suggest that creative effort must express its age, either because that cannot fail to happen, or because a new effort can create a new age. Still, one knows what it means when an art historian says, thinking of the succession of plastic styles, "not everything is possible in every period."[1] And that is equally true for every person and every philosophy. But then one is never sure what is possible until it happens; and when it happens it may produce a sense of revolution, of the past escaped and our problems solved—even when we also know that one man's solution is another man's problem.

Wittgenstein expressed his sense both of the revolutionary break his later methods descry in philosophy, and of their relation to methods in aesthetics and ethics.[2] I have tried, in what follows, to suggest

AESTHETIC PROBLEMS OF MODERN PHILOSOPHY originally appeared in *Philosophy in America*, ed. Max Black (Ithaca: Cornell University Press, 1965). It is reprinted here from Cavell, *Must We Mean What We Say?*, copyright 1976, by permission of Cambridge University Press.

[1] Heinrich Wolfflin, *Principles of Art History*, foreword to the 7th German edition. Quoted by E. H. Gombrich, *Art and Illusion* (New York: The Bollingen Series, Pantheon Press, 1960), p. 4. [Au.]

[2] Reported by G. E. Moore, "Wittgenstein's Lectures in 1930–33," reprinted in Moore's *Philosophical Papers* (London: George Allen and Unwin, 1959), p. 315. [Au.]

ways in which such feelings or claims can be understood, believing them to be essential in understanding Wittgenstein's later philosophy as a whole. The opening section outlines two problems in aesthetics each of which seems to yield to the possibilities of Wittgensteinian procedures, and in turn to illuminate them. The concluding section suggests resemblances between one kind of judgment recognizable as aesthetic and the characteristic claim of Wittgenstein—and of ordinary language philosophers generally—to voice "what we should ordinarily say."

What I have written, and I suppose the way I have written, grows from a sense that philosophy is in one of its periodic crises of method, heightened by a worry I am sure is not mine alone, that method dictates to content; that, for example, an intellectual commitment to analytical philosophy trains concern away from the wider, traditional problems of human culture which may have brought one to philosophy in the first place. Yet one can find oneself unable to relinquish either the method or the alien concern.

A free eclecticism of method is one obvious solution to such a problem. Another solution may be to discover further freedoms or possibilities within the method one finds closest to oneself. I lean here towards the latter of these alternatives, hoping to make philosophy yet another kind of problem for itself; in particular, to make the medium of philosophy—that is, of Wittgensteinian and, more generally, of ordinary language philosophy—a significant problem for aesthetics.

Two Problems of Aesthetics

Let us begin with a sheer matter of words—the controversy about whether a poem, or more modestly, a metaphor, can be paraphrased. Cleanth Brooks, in his *Well Wrought Urn,*[3] provided a convenient title for it in the expression "The Heresy of Paraphrase," the heresy, namely, of supposing that a "poem constitutes a 'statement' of some sort" (p. 179); a heresy in which "most of our difficulties in criticism are rooted" (p. 184).

> The truth of the matter is that all such formulations (of what a poem says) lead away from the center of the poem—not toward it; that the "prose sense" of the poem is not a rack on which the stuff of the poem is hung; that it does not represent the "inner" structure or the "essential" structure or the "real" structure of the poem (p. 182). We can very properly use paraphrases as pointers and as shorthand references provided that we know what we are doing. But it is highly important that we know what we are doing and that we see plainly that the paraphrase is not the real core of meaning which constitutes the essence of the poem (p. 180).

We may have some trouble in seeing plainly that the paraphrase is *not* the real core, or essence, or essential structure or inner or real structure of a poem; the same trouble we should have in understanding what *is* any or all of these things, since it takes so much philosophy just to state them. It is hard to imagine that someone has just flatly given it out that the essence, core, structure, and the rest, of a poem is its paraphrase. Probably somebody has been saying that poetry uses ornaments of style, or requires special poetic words; or has been saying what a poem means, or what it ought to mean—doing something that makes someone else, in a fit of philosophy, say that this is distorting a poem's essence. Now the person who is accused in Brooks' writ is probably going to deny guilt, feel that words are being put into his mouth, and answer that he knows perfectly well that a "paraphrase, of course, is not the equivalent of a poem; a poem is more than its paraphrasable content." Those are the words of Yvor Winters, whose work Professor Brooks uses as "[furnishing] perhaps the most respectable example of the paraphrastic heresy" (p. 183).[4] And so the argument goes, and goes. It has the gait of a false issue—by which I do not mean that it will be easy to straighten out.

One clear symptom of this is Brooks' recurrent concessions that, of course, a paraphrase is all right—if you know what you're doing. Which is

[3] *The Well Wrought Urn* (New York: Harcourt, Brace & Co., 1947). All page references to Brooks are to this edition. "The Heresy of Paraphrase" is the title of the concluding chapter. [Au.]

[4] For Winters' position, I have relied solely on his central essay, "The Experimental School in American Poetry," from *Primitivism and Decadence,* itself republished, together with earlier of his critical works, under the title *In Defense of Reason* (Denver: Alan Swallow, 1947). [Au.]

about like saying that of course criticism is all right, in its place; which is true enough. But how, in particular, are we to assess a critic's reading the opening stanza of Wordsworth's "Intimations" Ode and writing: ". . . the poet begins by saying that he has lost something" (Brooks, p. 116)? We can ransack that stanza and never find the expression "lost something" in it. Then the critic will be offended—rightly—and he may reply: Well, it does not actually say this, but it means it, it implies it; do you suggest that it does not mean that? And of course we do not. But then the critic has a *theory* about what he is doing when he says what a poem means, and so he will have to add some appendices to his readings of the poetry explaining that when he says what a poem means he does not say exactly quite just what the poem means; that is, he only points to its meaning, or rather "points to the area in which the meaning lies." But even this last does not seem to him humility enough, and he may be moved to a footnote in which he says that his own analyses are "at best crude approximations of the poem" (p. 189). By this time someone is likely to burst out with: But *of course* a paraphrase says what the poem says, and an *approximate* paraphrase is merely a bad paraphrase; with greater effort or sensibility you could have got it exactly right. To which one response would be: "Oh, I can tell you exactly what the Ode means," and then read the Ode aloud.

Is there no real way out of this air of self-defeat, no way to get *satisfying* answers? Can we discover what, in such an exchange, is causing that uneasy sense that the speakers are talking past one another? Surely each knows exactly what the other means; neither is pointing to the smallest fact that the other fails to see.

For one suggestion, look again at Brooks' temptation to say that his readings *approximate* to (the meaning of) the poem. He is not there confessing his personal ineptitude; he means that any paraphrase, the best, will be only an approximation. So he is not saying, what he was accused of saying, that his own paraphrase was, in some more or less definite way, inexact or faulty: he denies the ordinary contrast between "approximate" and "exact." And can he not do that if he wants to? Well, if I am right, he *did* do it. Although it is not clear that he *wanted* to. Perhaps he was *led* to it; and did he realize that, and would his realizing it make any difference? It may help to say: In speaking of the paraphrase as approximating to the poem (the meaning of the poem?) he himself furthers the suggestion that paraphrase and poem operate, as it were, at the same level, are the same kind of thing. (One shade of color approximates to another shade, it does not approximate, nor does it fail to approximate, to the object of which it is the color. An arrow pointing approximately north is exactly pointing somewhere. One paraphrase may be approximately the same, have approximately the same meaning, as another paraphrase.) And then he has to do everything at his philosophical disposal to keep paraphrase and poem from coinciding; in particular, speak of cores and essences and structures of the poem that are not reached by the paraphrase. It is as if someone got it into his head that really pointing to an object would require actually touching it, and then, realizing that this would make life very inconvenient, reconciled himself to common sense by saying: Of course we *can* point to objects, but we must realize what we are doing, and that most of the time this is only approximately pointing to them.

This is the sort of thing that happens with astonishing frequency in philosophy. We impose a demand for absoluteness (typically of some simple physical kind) upon a concept, and then, finding that our ordinary use of this concept does not meet our demand, we accommodate this discrepancy as nearly as possible. Take these familiar patterns: we do not really see material objects, but only see them indirectly; we cannot be certain of any empirical proposition, but only practically certain; we cannot really know what another person is feeling, but only infer it. One of Wittgenstein's greatest services, to my mind, is to show how constant a feature of philosophy this pattern is: this is something that his diagnoses are meant to explain ("We have a certain picture of how something must be"; "Language is idling; not doing work; being used apart from its ordinary language games"). Whether his diagnoses are themselves satisfying is another question. It is not very likely, because if the phenomenon is as common as he seems to have shown, its explanation will evidently have to be very much clearer and more complete than his sketches provide.

This much, however, is true: If you put such phrases as "giving the meaning," "giving a paraphrase," "saying exactly what something means (or what somebody said)," and so on, into the ordinary contexts (the "language games") in which they are used, you will not find that you are worried that you have not really *done* these things. We could say: *That* is what doing them really is. Only that serenity will last just so long as someone does not start philosophizing about it. Not that I want to stop him; only I want to know what it is he is then doing, and why he follows just those particular tracks.

We owe it to Winters to make it clear that he does not say any of the philosophical things Brooks attributes to him. His thesis, having expressed his total acquiescence in the fact that paraphrases are not poems, is that *some* poems cannot be paraphrased—in particular, poems of the chief poetic talent of the United States during the second and third decades of the twentieth century; that poems which are unparaphrasable are, in that specific way, defective; and that therefore this poetic talent was led in regrettable directions. The merit of this argument for us, whether we agree with its animus or not, and trying to keep special theories about poetic discourse at arm's length, is its recognition that paraphrasability is one definite characteristic of uses of language, a characteristic that some expressions have and some do not have. It suggests itself that uses of language can be distinguished according to whether or not they possess this characteristic, and further distinguished by the kind of paraphrase they demand. Let us pursue this suggestion with a few examples, following Wittgenstein's idea that we can find out what kind of object anything (grammatically) is (for example, a meaning) by investigating expressions which show the kind of thing said about it (for example, "explaining the meaning").

It is worth saying that the clearest case of a use of language having no paraphrase is its literal use. If I tell you, "Juliet [the girl next door] is not yet fourteen years old," and you ask me what I mean, I might do many things—ask you what *you* mean, or perhaps try to teach you the meaning of some expression you cannot yet use (which, as Wittgenstein goes to extraordinary lengths to show, is not the same thing as *telling* you what it means). Or again, if I say, "Sufficient unto the day is the evil thereof," which I take to be the literal truth, then if I need to explain my meaning to you I shall need to do other things: I shall perhaps not be surprised that you do not get my meaning and so I shall hardly ask you, in my former spirit, what you mean in asking me for it; nor shall I, unless my disappointment pricks me into offense, offer to teach you the meaning of an English expression. What I might do is to try to *put my thought another way,* and perhaps refer you, depending upon who you are, to a range of similar or identical thoughts expressed by others. What I cannot (logically) do in either the first or the second case is to *paraphrase* what I said.

Now suppose I am asked what someone means who says, "Juliet is the sun." Again my options are different, and specific. Again I am not, not in the same way, surprised that you ask; but I shall *not* try to put the thought another way—which seems to be the whole truth in the view that metaphors are unparaphrasable, that their meaning is bound up in the very words they employ. (The addition adds nothing: Where else is it imagined, in that context, that meanings are bound, or found?) I may say something like: Romeo means that Juliet is the warmth of his world; that his day begins with her; that only in her nourishment can he grow. And his declaration suggests that the moon, which other lovers use as emblems of their love, is merely her reflected light, and dead in comparison; and so on. In a word, I paraphrase it. Moreover, if I could not provide an explanation of this form, then that is a very good reason, a perfect reason, for supposing that I do not know what it means. Metaphors are paraphrasable. (And if that is true, it is tautologous.) When Croce denied the possibility of paraphrase, he at least had the grace to assert that there were no metaphors.

Two points now emerge: (1) The "and so on" which ends my example of paraphrase is significant. It registers what William Empson calls the "pregnancy" of metaphors, the burgeoning of meaning in them. Call it what you like; in this feature metaphors differ from some, but perhaps not all, literal discourse. And differ from the similar device of simile: the inclusion of "like" in an expression changes the rhetoric. If you say "Juliet is like the sun," two alterations at least seem obvious: the drive of it leads me to expect you to continue by saying in what definite respects they are like (similes are just a little bit pregnant); and, in complement, I *wait* for you to tell me what you mean, to deliver your meaning, so to speak. It is not up to me to find as much as I can in your words. The over-reading of metaphors so often complained of, no doubt justly, is a hazard they must run for their high interest.[5] (2) To give the paraphrase, to understand the metaphor, I must understand the ordinary or dictionary meaning of the words it contains, *and* understand that they are not there being used in their ordinary way, that the meanings they invite are not to be found opposite them in a dictionary. In this respect the words in metaphors function as they do in idioms. But idioms are, again, specifically different. "I fell flat on my face" seems an appropriate case. To explain its meaning is simply to *tell* it—one might say you don't *explain* it at all; either you know what it means or you don't; there is no richer and poorer among its explanations; you need imagine nothing special in the mind of the person using it. And you will find it in a dictionary, though in special locations; which suggests that, unlike metaphors, the number of idioms in a language is finite. In some, though not all, of these respects the procedure of "giving the meaning" of an idiom is like that in translating: one might think of it as translating from a given language into itself. Then how is it different from defining, or giving a synonym?

One final remark about the difference between idioms and metaphors. Any theory concerned to account for peculiarities of metaphor of the sort I have listed will wonder over the literal meaning its words, in that combination, have. This is a response, I take it, to the fact that a metaphorical expression (in the "*A* is *B*" form at least) sounds like an ordinary assertion, though perhaps not made by an ordinary mind. Theory aside, I want to look at the suggestion, often made, that what metaphors literally say is *false*. (This is a response to the well-marked characteristic of "psychic tension" set up in metaphors. The mark is used by Empson; I do not know the patent.) But to say that Juliet is the sun is not to say something false; it is, at best, wildly false, and that is not being just false. This is part of the fact that if we are to suggest that what the metaphor says is true, we shall have to say it is wildly true—mythically or magically or primitively true. (Romeo just may be young enough, or crazed or heretic enough, to have meant his words literally.) About some idioms, however, it is fair to say that their words literally say something that is quite false; something, that is, which could easily, though maybe comically, be imagined to be true. Someone might actually fall flat on his face, have a thorn in his side, a bee in his bonnet, a bug in his ear, or a fly in his ointment—even all at once. Then what are we to say about the literal meaning of a metaphor? That it has none? And that what it literally says is not false, *and* not true? And that it is not an assertion? But it sounds like one; and people do think it is true and people do think it is false. I am suggesting that it is such facts that will need investigating if we are to satisfy ourselves about metaphors; that we are going to keep getting philosophical theories about metaphor until such facts are investigated; and that this is not an occasion for adjudication, for the only thing we could offer now in that line would be: all the theories are right in what they say. And that seems to imply that all are wrong as well.

At this point we might be able to give more content to the idea that some modes of figurative language are such that in them what an expression means cannot be said at all, at least not in any of the more or less familiar, conventionalized ways so far noticed. Not because these modes are flatly literal—there is, as it were, room for an explanation, but we cannot enter it. About such an expression it may be right to say: I know what it means but I can't say what it means. And this would no longer suggest, as it would if said about a metaphor, that you really do not know what it means—or: it might suggest it, but you couldn't be sure.

Examples of such uses of language would, I think, characteristically occur in specific kinds of poetry, for example Symbolist, Surrealist or Imagist. Such a use seems to me present in a line like Hart Crane's "The mind is brushed by sparrow wings" (cited, among others, in the Winters essay), and in Wallace Stevens' "as a calm darkens among water-lights," from "Sunday Morning." Paraphrasing the lines, or

[5] [Added 1968. I should have made it more explicit that throughout this essay I am using "paraphrase" to name solely that specific form of account which suits metaphors (marked, for example, by its concluding sense of "and so on"). So when I say that stretches of literal prose "cannot be paraphrased," I mean to imply the specification ". . . in *that* way." Certainly an exercise useful in the teaching of reading can be given as "Paraphrase the following passage," where what is wanted is a resumé of the passage which shows a grasp of the difficult words and constructions in it and of its over-all sense. But in *that* context, paraphrase is explicitly not a candidate for anything likely to be taken as a *competitor* of the passage in question.] [Au.]

explaining their meaning, or telling it, or putting the thought another way—all these are out of the question. One may be able to say nothing except that a feeling has been voiced by a kindred spirit and that if someone does not get it he is not in one's world, or not of one's flesh. The lines may, that is, be left as touchstones of intimacy. Or one might try *describing* more or less elaborately a particular day or evening, a certain place and mood and gesture, in whose presence the line in question comes to seem a natural expression, the only expression.

This seems to be what Winters, who profitably distinguishes several varieties of such uses of language, distrusts and dislikes in his defense of reason, as he also seems prepared for the reply that this is not a *failing* of language but a feature of a specific approach of language. At least I think it is a reply of this sort, which I believe to be right, that he wishes to repudiate by appealing to "the fallacy of expressive (or imitative) form," instanced by him at one point as "Whitman trying to express a loose America by writing loose poetry," or "Mr. Joyce [endeavoring] to express disintegration by breaking down his form." It is useful to have a name for this fallacy, which no doubt some people commit. But his remarks seem a bit quick in their notation of what Whitman and Joyce were trying to express, and in their explanation of why they had to express themselves as they did; too sure that a break with the past of the order represented in modern art was not itself necessary in order to defend reason; too sure that convention can still be attacked in conventional ways. And they suggest scorn for the position that a high task of art has become, in our bombardment of sound, to create silence. (*Being* silent for that purpose might be a good example of the fallacy of imitative form. But that would depend on the context.) The fact is that I feel I would have to forgo too much of modern art were I to take his view of it.

Before we leave him, we owe it to Brooks to acknowledge a feature of Winters' position which may be causing his antipathy to it. Having wished to save Winters from a misconstruction of paraphrase, we gave back to that notion a specificity which, it now emerges, opens him to further objection. For his claim that poems that cannot be paraphrased—or, as he also puts it, do not "rest on a formulable logic"—are therefore defective now means or implies that all poems not made essentially of metaphorical language (and/or similes, idioms, literal statements) are defective. It is certainly to be hoped that all *criticism* be rational, to be demanded that it form coherent propositions about its art. But to suppose that this requires all poetry to be "formulable," in the sense that it must, whatever its form and pressure, yield to paraphrase, the way single metaphors specifically do, is not only unreasonable past defense but incurs what we might call the fallacy of expressive criticism.

In summary: Brooks is wrong to say that poems cannot in principle be fully paraphrased, but right to be worried about the relation between paraphrase and poem; Winters is right in his perception that some poetry is "formulable" and some not, but wrong in the assurance he draws from that fact; both respond to, but fail to follow, the relation between criticism and its object. And now, I think, we can be brought more unprotectedly to face the whole question that motivates such a conflict, namely what it is we are doing when we describe or explain a work of art; what function criticism serves; whether different arts, or forms of art, require different forms of criticism; what we may expect to learn from criticism, both about a particular piece of art and about the nature of art generally.

The second problem in aesthetics must be sketched even more swiftly and crudely.

Is such music as is called "atonal" (not distinguishing that, for our purposes now, from the term "twelve-tone") really without tonality? (The little I will say could be paralleled, I think, in discussing the nature of the painting or sculpture called abstract or non-objective.) The arguments are bitter and, to my knowledge, without issue; and many musicians have felt within themselves both an affirmative and a negative answer.[6] Against the idea that this music lacks tonality are (1) the theory that we are so trained to our perception of musical organization that we cannot help hearing it in a tonal frame of reference; and (2) the fact that one *can*, often, *say* what key a so-called "atonal" piece is in. In favor of the idea that it lacks tonality are (1) a theory of composition which says that it does, and whose point was just to escape that limitation, while yet maintaining coherence; and (2) the fact that it simply sounds so different. Without our now

[6] I am told, by Professor David Lewin, that this was true of Anton Webern, who was in doubt about his own music in this regard. [Au.]

even glancing at the theories, let us look at the fact we recorded as "being able to say, often, what key a piece is in." Does that have the weight it seems to have? An instance which once convinced me of its decisiveness was this: in listening to a song of Schoenberg's, I had a clear sense that I could, at three points, hear it cadence (I almost said, try to resolve) in F♯ minor. Then surely it is *in* F♯ minor? Well, the Chopin *Barcarolle* is in the key of F♯ major. How do I know that? Because I can hear it try to cadence in F♯ major? Three or more times? And after that I am convinced it is, feel slightly relieved and even triumphant that I have been able to hear some F♯ major? But that is absurd. I *know* the key; everyone knows it; everyone knows it from the opening measure—well, at least before the bass figure that begins on the pitch of F♯: it does not take a brick wall to fall on us. I would not even know how to go about doubting its key or *trying* to hear it in its key. And I know it because I know that now it has moved to the subdominant of the key, and now the dominant of the key is being extended, and now it is modulating, and now it is modulating to a more distant key. And to know all this is to know the grammar of the expression "musical key." Sometimes, to be sure, a solidly tonal composer will, especially in "development sections," obliterate the sense of placement in a key; but this is here a special effect, and depends upon an undoubted establishment of key. So if I insist upon saying that atonal music is really tonal (and to be said it has to be insisted upon) I have, so far as my ear goes, to forgo the grammar of the expression "tonality" or "musical key"—or almost all of it: I can retain "almost cadences in" and "sounds like the dominant of," but not "related key," "distant key," "modulation" etc. And then I am in danger of not knowing what I am saying. Wittgenstein says that ". . . the *speaking* of language is part of an activity, or of a form of life" (*Investigations,* §23), and also "To imagine a language means to imagine a form of life" (ibid., §19). The language of tonality is part of a particular form of life, one containing the music we are most familiar with; associated with, or consisting of, particular ways of being trained to perform it and to listen to it; involving particular ways of being corrected, particular ways of responding to mistakes, to nuance, above all to recurrence and to variation and modification. No wonder we want to preserve the idea of tonality: to give all *that* up seems like giving up the idea of music altogether. I think it *is*—*like* it.

I shall not try to say why it is not fully that. I shall only mention that it cannot be enough to point to the obvious fact that musical instruments, with their familiar or unfamiliar powers, are employed—because *that* fact does not prevent us from asking: But is it music? Nor enough to appeal to the fact that we can point to pitches, intervals, lines and rhythm—because we probably do not for the most part know what we are pointing to with these terms. I mean we do not know *which* lines are significant (try to play the "melody" or "bass" of a piece of Webern's) and which intervals to hear as organizing. More important, I think, is the fact that we may see an undoubted musician speak about such things and behave toward them in ways similar (not, I think, more than similar) to the ways he behaves toward, say, Beethoven, and then we may sense that, though similar, it is a new world and that to understand a new world it is imperative to concentrate upon its inhabitants. (Of course there will be the usual consequences of mimicry and pretension.) Moreover, but still perhaps even more rarely, we may find ourselves *within* the experience of such compositions, following them; and then the question whether this is music and the problem of its tonal sense, will be—not answered or solved, but rather they will disappear, seem irrelevant.

That is, of course, Wittgenstein's sense of the way philosophical problems end. It is true that for him, in the *Investigations* at any rate, this happens when we have gone through a process of bringing ourselves back into our natural forms of life, putting our souls back into our bodies; whereas I had to describe the accommodation of the new music as one of naturalizing ourselves to a new form of life, a new world. That a resolution of this sort is described as the solution of a philosophical problem, and as the goal of its particular mode of criticism, represents for me the most original contribution Wittgenstein offers philosophy. I can think of no closer title for it, in an established philosophical vocabulary, than Hegel's use of the term *Aufhebung*. We cannot translate the term: "cancelling," "negating," "fulfilling" etc. are all partial, and "sublate" transfers the problem. It seems to me to capture that sense of *satisfaction* in our representation of rival positions which I was asking for when I rehearsed the problems of Brooks and Winters. Of course we are no longer very apt to suppose, with Hegel, that History will make us a present of it: we are too aware of its brilliant ironies and its aborted revolutions for that. But as an ideal of (one kind of) philosophical criticism—a criticism in which it is pointless for one side to refute the other, because its cause and topic is the self getting in its own way—it seems about right.

In the *Tractatus* Wittgenstein says: "The solution of the problem of life is seen in the vanishing of the problem" (6.521); and in the *Investigations* he says: ". . . the clarity that we are aiming at is indeed *complete* clarity. But this simply means that the philosophical problems should *completely* disappear" (§133). Yet he calls these problems *solved* (*Investigations,* ibid.); and he says that ". . . when no questions remain . . . just that is the *answer*" (*Tractatus;* 6.52, my emphasis). In the central concept of his later work, this would seem to mean that the problems of life and the problems of philosophy have related grammars, because solutions to them both have the same form: their problems are solved only when they disappear, and answers are arrived at only when there are no longer questions—when, as it were, our accounts have cancelled them.

But in the *Investigations* this turns out to be more of an answer than, left this way, it seems to be; for it more explicitly dictates and displays the ways philosophy is to proceed in investigating problems, ways leading to what he calls "perspicuous representation" (*übersichtliche Darstellung*). It is my impression that many philosophers do not like Wittgenstein's comparing what he calls his "methods" to therapies (§133); but for me part of what he means by this comparison is brought out in thinking of the progress of psychoanalytic therapy. The more one learns, so to speak, the hang of oneself, and mounts one's problems, the less one is able to *say* what one has learned; not because you have *forgotten* what it was, but because nothing you said would seem like an answer or a solution: there is no longer any question or problem which your words would match. You have reached conviction, but not about a proposition; and consistency, but not in a theory. You are different, what you recognize as problems are different, your world is different. ("The world of the happy man is a different one from that of the unhappy man" (*Tractatus;* 6.43).) And this is the sense, the only sense, in which what a work of art means cannot be *said*. Believing it is seeing it.

When Wittgenstein says that "the concept of a perspicuous representation . . . earmarks the form of account we give" (§122), I take him to be making a grammatical remark about what he calls a "grammatical investigation," which is what his *Investigations* consist in (§90): no other form of resolution will count as philosophical. He says of his "form of account" that it is "the way we look at things"; and he then asks, parenthetically, "Is this a 'Weltanschauung'?" (§122). The answer to that question is, I take it, not No. Not, perhaps, Yes; because it is not a *special,* or competing, way of looking at things. But not No; because its mark of success is that the world seem—be—different. As usual, the claim to severe philosophical advance entails a reconception of the subject, a specific sense of revolution.

Aesthetic Judgment and a Philosophical Claim

Another good cause for stumbling over the procedures of ordinary language philosophy lies in its characteristic appeal to what "we" say and mean, or cannot or must say or mean. A good cause, since it is a very particular, not to say peculiar appeal, and one would expect philosophers dependent upon it themselves to be concerned for its investigation. I will suggest that the aesthetic judgment models the sort of claim entered by these philosophers, and that the familiar lack of conclusiveness in aesthetic argument, rather than showing up an irrationality, shows the kind of rationality it has, and needs.

Hume is always a respectable place to begin. Near the middle of his essay "Of the Standard of Taste,"[7] he has recourse to a story from *Don Quixote* which is to illustrate that "delicacy" of taste said to be essential to those critics who are to form our standard of it.

> It is with good reason, says Sancho to the squire with the great nose, that I pretend to have a judgment in wine: This is a quality hereditary in our family. Two of my kinsmen were once called in to give their opinion of a hogshead, which was supposed to be excellent, being old and of a good vintage. One of them tastes it; considers it; and after mature reflection pronounces the wine to be good, were it not for a small taste of leather, which he perceived in it. The other, after using the same precautions, gives also his verdict in

[7] *CTSP,* pp. 314–23. [Eds.]

> favour of the wine; but with the reserve of a taste of iron, which he could easily distinguish. You cannot imagine how much they were both ridiculed for their judgment. But who laughed in the end? On emptying the hogshead, there was found at the bottom, an old key with a leathern thong tied to it.

First of all, the fine drama of this gesture is greater than its factual decisiveness—a bit quixotic, so to say: for the taste may have been present and the object not, or the object present and the taste not. Second, and more important, the gesture misrepresents the efforts of the critic and the sort of vindication to which he aspires. It dissociates the exercise of taste from the discipline of accounting for it: but *all* that makes the critic's expression of taste worth more than another man's is his ability to produce for himself the thong and key of his response; and his vindication comes not from his pointing out that it is, or was, in the barrel, but in getting us to taste it there. Sancho's ancestors, he tells us, in each case after the precautions of reflection, both pronounced in favor of the wine; but he does not tell us what those reflections were, nor whether they were vindicated in their favorable verdict. Hume's essay, I take it, undertakes to explore just such questions, but in his understandable difficulty in directing us to the genuine critic and distinguishing him from the pretender, he says about him just what he, or anyone, says about art itself: that he is valuable, that we may disagree about his merits in a particular case, and that some, in the long run, "will be acknowledged by universal sentiment to have a preference above others." But this seems to put the critic's worth at the mercy of the history of taste; whereas his value to us is that he is able to make that history a part of his data, knowing that in itself, as it stands, it proves nothing—except popularity. His value to art and culture is not that he agrees with its taste—which would make him useful for guiding one's investments in the art market—but that he sets the terms in which our tastes, whatever they happen to be, may be protected or overcome. Sancho's descendants would, by the eighteenth century, have risen to gentlemen, exercising distinction in a world which knew what was right, and not needing to make their tastes their own. But it is Quixote who is the patron saint of the critic, desperate to preserve the best of his culture against itself, and surviving any failure but that of his honesty and his expression of it.

The idea of the agreement or "reconciliation" of taste controls Hume's argument; it is agreement that the standard of taste is to provide, so far as that is attainable. Hume's descendants, catching the assumption that agreement provides the vindication of judgment, but no longer able to hope for either, have found that aesthetic (and moral and political) judgments lack something: the arguments that support them are not conclusive the way arguments in logic are, nor rational the way arguments in science are. Indeed they are not, and if they were there would be no such subject as art (or morality) and no such art as criticism. It does not follow, however, that such judgments are not conclusive and rational.

Let us turn to Kant on the subject, who is, here as elsewhere, deeper and obscurer. Universal agreement, or as he also calls it, the "harmony of sentiment" or "a common sense of mankind," makes its appearance in the *Critique of Judgment* not as an empirical problem—which is scarcely surprising about Kant's procedure—but as an a priori requirement setting the (transcendental) conditions under which such judgments as we call aesthetic could be made *überhaupt*. Kant begins by saying that aesthetic judgment is not "theoretical," not "logical," not "objective," but one "whose determining ground can be *no other than subjective.*"[8] Today, or anyway the day before yesterday, and largely under his influence, we would have said it is not cognitive; which says so little that it *might* have been harmless enough. Kant goes on immediately to distinguish two kinds of "aesthetical judgments," or, as he also calls them, judgments of taste; and here, unfortunately, his influence trickled out. The first kind he calls the taste of sense, the second the taste of reflection; the former concerns merely what we find pleasant, the latter must—logically must, some of us would say—concern and claim more than that. And it is only the second whose topic is the beautiful, whose role, that is, would be aesthetic in its more familiar sense. The something more these judgments must do is to "demand" or "impute" or "claim" general validity, universal agreement with them; and when we make such judgments we go on claiming this agreement even though we know from experience that they will not receive it. (Are we, then, just willful or stupid in going on making them?) Kant also describes our feeling or belief

[8] All quotations from Kant are from sections 7 and 8 of the *Critique of Judgment*. [Au.] See *CTSP*, pp. 381–83. [Eds.]

when we make such judgments—judgments in which we demand "the assent of everyone," although we cannot "postulate" this assent as we could in making an ordinary empirical judgment—as one of "[speaking] with a universal voice." That is the sort of thing that we are likely nowadays to call a piece of psychology, which is no doubt right enough. But we would take that to mean that it marks an accidental accompaniment of such judgments; whereas Kant says about this claim to universal validity, this voice, that it "so essentially belongs to a judgment by which we describe anything as *beautiful* that, if this were not thought in it, it would never come into our thoughts to use the expression at all, but everything which pleases without a concept would be counted as pleasant."[9] The possibility of stupidity here is not one of continuing to demand agreement in the face of the fact that we won't attain it; but the stupidity of going on making aesthetic judgments at all (or moral or political ones) in the face of what they cost us, the difficulties of finding them for ourselves and the risk of explicit isolation.

Kant seems to be saying that apart from a certain spirit in which we make judgments we could have no concepts of the sort we think of as aesthetic.[10] What can the basis for such a claim be? Let us look at the examples he gives of his two kinds of aesthetic judgments.

> . . . [someone] is quite contented that if he says, "Canary wine is pleasant," another man may correct his expression and remind him that he ought to say, "It is pleasant *to me.*" And this is the case not only as regards the taste of the tongue, the palate, and the throat, but for whatever is pleasant to anyone's eyes and ears. . . . To strive here with the design of reproving as incorrect another man's judgment which is different from our own, as if the judgments were logically opposed, would be folly. . . .
>
> The case is quite different with the beautiful. It would (on the contrary) be laughable if a man who imagined anything to his own taste thought to justify himself by saying: "This object (the house we see, the coat that person wears, the concert we hear, the poem submitted to our judgment) is beautiful *for me.*" For he must not call it *beautiful* if it merely pleases him. . . .

What are these examples supposed to show? That using a form of expression in one context is all right, and using it in another is not all right. But what I wish to focus upon is the kind of rightness and wrongness invoked: it is not a matter of factual rectitude, nor of formal indiscretion but of saying something laughable, or which would be folly. It is such consequences that are taken to display a difference in the kind of judgment in question, in the nature of the concepts employed, and even in the nature of the reality the concepts capture. One hardly knows whether to call this a metaphysical or a logical difference. Kant called it a transcendental difference; Wittgenstein would call it a grammatical difference. And how can psychological differences like finding something laughable or foolish (which perhaps not *every* person would) be thought to betray such potent, or anyway different, differences?

Here we hit upon what is, to my mind, the most sensitive index of misunderstanding and bitterness between the positivist and the post-positivist components of analytical philosophy: the positivist grits his teeth when he hears an analysis given out as a logical one which is so painfully remote from formality, so obviously a question of how you happen to feel at the moment, so psychological; the philosopher who proceeds from everyday language stares back helplessly, asking, "Don't you feel the difference? Listen: you *must* see it." Surely, both know what the other knows, and each thinks the other is perverse, or irrelevant, or worse. (Here I must appeal to the experience of anyone who has

[9] One might compare with this Wittgenstein's question: "What gives us *so much as the idea* that living beings, things, can feel?" (*Investigations,* §283). [Au.]

[10] Another way of describing this assumption or demand, this thing of speaking with a universal voice, of judging "not merely for himself, but for all men," Kant also describes as "[speaking] of beauty as if it were a property of things." Only "as if" because it cannot be an ordinary property of things: its presence or absence cannot be established in the way ordinary properties are; that is, they cannot be established publicly, and we don't know (there aren't any) causal conditions, or usable rules, for producing, or altering, or erasing, or increasing this "property." Then why not just say it *isn't* a property of an object? I suppose there would be no reason not to say this, if we could find another way of recording our conviction that it is one, anyway that what we are pointing to is *there,* in the object; and our knowledge that men make objects that create this response in us, and make them exactly with the idea that they will create it; and the fact that, while we know not everyone will agree with us when we say it is present, we think they are *missing something* if they don't. [Au.]

been engaged in such encounters.) Any explanation of this is going to be hard to acquire. I offer the following guess, not because it can command much attention in itself, but as a way of suggesting the level I would expect a satisfying explanation to reach, a way of indicating why we lack as yet the concepts, even the facts, which must form a serious accommodation.

We know of the efforts of such philosophers as Frege and Husserl to undo the "psychologizing" of logic (like Kant's undoing Hume's psychologizing of knowledge): now, the shortest way I might describe such a book as the *Philosophical Investigations* is to say that it attempts to undo the psychologizing of psychology, to show the necessity controlling our application of psychological and behavioral categories; even, one could say, show the necessities in human action and passion themselves.[11] And at the same time it seems to turn all of philosophy into psychology—matters of what we call things, how we treat them, what their role is in our lives.

For one last glance, let us adapt Kant's examples to a form which is more fashionable, and think of the sort of reasons we offer for such judgments:

1. A: Canary wine is pleasant.
   B: How can you say that? It tastes like canary droppings.
   A: Well, I like it.
2. A: He plays beautifully doesn't he?
   B1: Yes; too beautifully. Beethoven is not Chopin.

Or he may answer:

B2: How can you say that? There was no line, no structure, no idea what the music was about. He's simply an impressive colorist.

[11] Consider, for example, the question: "Could someone have a feeling of ardent love or hope for the space of one second—*no matter what* preceded or followed this second?" (*Investigations,* §583). We shall not wish to say that this is logically impossible, or that it can in no way be imagined. But we might say: given our world this cannot happen; it is not, in our language, what "love" or "hope" mean; necessary in our world that this is not what love and hope are. I take it that our most common philosophical understanding of such notions as necessity, contingency, synthetic, and analytic statements, will not know what to make of our saying such things. [Au.]

Now, how will A reply? Can he now say: "Well, I liked it"? Of course he *can;* but don't we feel that here that would be a feeble rejoinder, a *retreat* to personal taste? Because B's reasons are obviously relevant to the evaluation of performance, and because they are *arguable,* in ways that anyone who knows about such things will know how to pursue. A *doesn't have* to pursue them; but if he doesn't, there is a price he will have to pay in our estimate of him. Is that enough to show it is a different kind of judgment? We are still in the realm of the psychological. But I wish to say that the price is necessary, and specific to the sorts of judgments we call aesthetic.

Go back to my saying, "he doesn't have to pursue" the discussion, and compare the following case:

A: There is a goldfinch in the garden.
B: How do you know?
A: From the color of its head.
B: But goldcrests also have heads that color.
A: Well, *I* think it's a goldfinch (it's a goldfinch to me).

This is no longer a feeble rejoinder, a retreat to personal opinion: and the price that would be paid here is not, as it would be in the former case, that he is not very articulate, or not discriminating, or has perverse tastes: the price here is that he is either mad, or doesn't know what the word "know" means, or is in some other way unintelligible to us. That is, *we rule him out* as a competent interlocutor in matters of knowledge (about birds?): whatever is going on, he *doesn't* know there is a goldfinch in the garden, whatever (else) he thinks he "knows." But we do not, at least not with the same flatness and good conscience, and not with the same consequences, rule out the person who liked the performance of the Beethoven: he still has a claim upon us, however attenuated; he *may* even have reasons for his judgment, or counters to your objections, which for some reason he can't give (perhaps because you've brow-beaten him into amnesia).

Leaving these descriptions so cruelly incomplete, I think one can now imagine the familiar response: "But you admit that arguments in the aesthetic case may go on, may perhaps never end, and that they needn't go on, perhaps can't go on in some cases, and that they may have different 'prices' (whatever that may mean), presumably depending on where they stop. How do you get logic out of that? What you cannot claim is that either party to the dispute, whether in the case Kant calls the taste of sense or the case he calls the taste of reflection, can *prove* his judgment. And would he want to, even if he could? Isn't that, indeed, what all your talk about criticism was about: The person accounts for his own feelings, and then, at best 'proves' them *to* another, shows them to whomever he wants to know them, the best way he can, the most effective way. That's scarcely logic; and how can you deny that it is psychology?"

It may help to reply to this: You call it psychology just because it so obviously is not logic, and it must be one or the other. (I do think that is the *entire* content of "psychology" in such objections. Such a person knows what he means by logic: how to do it, how to recognize it when he sees it done, what he can expect from it, etc. But who knows any of this about the "psychology" in question?) Contrariwise, I should admit that I call it "logic" mostly because it so obviously is not "psychology" in the way I think you mean it. I do not really think it is either of those activities, in the senses we attach to them now; but I cannot describe to anyone's satisfaction *what* it is. Wittgenstein called it "grammar"; others might call it "phenomenology."

Those of us who keep finding ourselves wanting to call such differences "logical" are, I think, responding to a sense of necessity we feel in them, together with a sense that necessity is, partly, a matter of the *ways* a judgment is supported, the ways in which conviction in it is produced: it is only by virtue of these recurrent patterns of support that a remark will count as—will be—aesthetic, or a mere matter of taste, or moral, propagandistic, religious, magical, scientific, philosophical. . . . It is essential to making an aesthetic judgment that at some point we be prepared to say in its support: don't you see, don't you hear, don't you dig? The best critic will know the best points. Because if you do not see *something,* without explanation, then there is nothing further to discuss. Which does not mean that the critic has no recourse: he can start training and instructing you and preaching at you—a direction in which criticism invariably will start to veer. (A critic like Ruskin can be a bit eager in seizing this direction, but it is a measure of his honesty, and his devotion to art, never to shrink from it; as it is part of the permanence of his writing to exemplify that moral passion which is a *natural* extension of the critical task.) At some point, the critic will have to say: This is what I see. Reasons—at definite points, for definite reasons, in different circumstances—come to an end. (Cf. *Investigations,* §217.)

Those who refuse the term "logic" are responding to a sense of arbitrariness in these differences, together with a sense that "logic" is a matter of arriving at conviction in such a way that anyone who can follow the argument must, unless he finds something definitely wrong with it, *accept the conclusion,* agree with it. I do not know what the gains or disadvantages would be of unfastening the term "logic" from that constant pattern of support or justification whose peculiarity is that it leads those competent at it to this kind of agreement, and extending it to patterns of justification having other purposes and peculiarities. All I am arguing for is that *pattern* and *agreement* are distinct features of the notion of logic.

If we say that the *hope* of agreement motivates our engaging in these various patterns of support, then we must also say, what I take Kant to have seen, that even were agreement in fact to emerge, our judgments, so far as aesthetic, would remain as essentially subjective, in his sense, as they ever were. Otherwise, art and the criticism of art would not have their special importance nor elicit their own forms of distrust and of gratitude. The problem of the critic, as of the artist, is not to discount his subjectivity, but to include it; not to overcome it in agreement, but to master it in exemplary ways. Then his work outlasts the fashions and arguments of a particular age. That is the beauty of it.

Kant's "universal voice" is, with perhaps a slight shift of accent, what we hear recorded in the philosopher's claims about "what we say": such claims are at least as close to what Kant calls aesthetical judgments as they are to ordinary empirical hypotheses. Though the philosopher seems to claim, or depend upon, severer agreement than is carried by the aesthetic analogue, I wish to suggest that it is a claim or dependence of the same kind.

We should immediately notice an obvious failure in the analogy between aesthetic judgments and the philosophical claim to voice what we say. The philosophical claim seems clearly open to refutation by an empirical collection of data about what people in fact say, whereas it makes no obvious sense to confirm or disconfirm such a judgment as "The *Hammerklavier* Sonata is a perverse work" by collecting data to find out whether the Sonata is in fact perverse. It is out of the question to enter into this difficult range of problems now. But I cannot forbear mentioning several points which I have tried elsewhere to suggest, with, to judge from results, evident unsuccess.[12]

1. I take it to be a phenomenological fact about philosophizing from everyday language that one feels empirical evidence about one's language to be irrelevant to one's claims. If such philosophizing is to be understood, then that fact about it must be understood. I am not saying that evidence about how (other) people speak can never make an ordinary language philosopher withdraw his typical claims; but I find it important that the most characteristic pressure against him is applied by producing or deepening an example which shows him that *he* would not say what he says "we" say.

2. The appeal to "what we should say if . . ." requires that we imagine an example or story, sometimes one more or less similar to events which may happen any day, sometimes one unlike anything we have known. Whatever the difficulties will be in trying to characterize this procedure fully and clearly, this much can be said at once: if we find we disagree about what we should say, it would make no obvious sense to attempt to confirm or disconfirm one or other of our responses by collecting data to show which of us is in fact right. What we should do is either (*a*) try to determine why we disagree (perhaps we are imagining the story differently)—just as, if we agree in response we will, when we start philosophizing about this fact, want to know why we agree, what it shows about our concepts; or (*b*) we will, if the disagreement cannot be explained, either find some explanation for *that,* or else discard the example. Disagreement is not disconfirming: it is as much a datum for philosophizing as agreement is. At this stage philosophizing has, hopefully, not yet begun.

3. Such facts perhaps only amount to saying that the philosophy of ordinary language is not about language, anyway not in any sense in which it is not also about the world. Ordinary language philosophy is about whatever ordinary language is about.

The philosopher appealing to everyday language turns to the reader not to convince him without proof but to get him to prove something, test something, against himself. He is saying: Look and find out whether you can see what I see, wish to say what I wish to say. Of course he often seems to answer or beg his own question by posing it in plural form: "We say . . . ; We want to say . . . ; We can imagine . . . ; We feel as if we had to penetrate phenomena, repair a spider's web; We are under the illusion . . . ; We are dazzled . . . ; The idea now absorbs us . . . ; We are dissatisfied . . . ." But this plural is still first person: it does not, to use Kant's word, "postulate" that "we," you and I and he, say and want and imagine and feel and suffer together. If we do not, then the philosopher's remarks are irrelevant to us. Of course he doesn't think they are irrelevant, but the implication is that philosophy, like art, is, and should be, powerless to *prove* its relevance; and that says something about the kind of relevance it wishes to have. All the philosopher, this kind of philosopher, can do is to express, as fully as he can, his world, and attract our undivided attention to our own.

Kant's attention to the "universal voice" expressed in aesthetic judgment seems to me, finally, to afford some explanation of that air of dogmatism which claims about what "we" say seem to carry for critics of ordinary language procedures, and which they find repugnant and intolerant. I think that air of dogmatism is indeed present in such claims; but if that is intolerant, that is because tolerance could only mean, as in liberals it often does, that the kind of claim in question is not taken seriously. It is, after all, a claim about *our lives;* it is differences, or oppositions, of these that tolerance, if it is to be achieved, must be directed toward. About what we should say when, we do not expect to have to tolerate much difference, believing that if we could articulate it fully we would have spoken for all men, found the necessities common to us all. Philosophy has always hoped for that; so, perhaps, has science. But philosophy concerns those necessities we cannot, being human, fail to know. Except that nothing is more human than to deny them.

[12] See J. Fodor and J. Katz, "The Availability of What We Say," in the *Philosophical Review,* Vol. LXXII (1963), an attack, primarily, on my paper "Must We Mean What We Say?" which appears as the first essay in this book. [Added 1968. A paper by Professor Richard Henson ("What We Say," *American Philosophical Quarterly,* Vol. 2/No. 1, January 1965, pp. 52–62) includes specific rejoinders to a number of the points raised by Fodor and Katz.] [Au.]

Noam Chomsky

b. 1928

NOAM CHOMSKY'S contributions to the development of modern linguistic theory have been massive and revolutionary. Indeed, one could argue that linguistic speculation prior to Chomsky was, in a sense, pretheoretical, inasmuch as there was no significant consensus as to what a "theory" of "linguistics" ought to explain—or even whether a "theory" ought to have an explanatory function. In this respect, Chomsky's importance is all the more remarkable, since he has not only formulated a descriptive theory of syntax of considerable elegance and power but has done exemplary philosophical work for linguistics on the role and limitations of "theory" itself.

Chomsky's first major work (*Syntactic Structures,* 1957) produced something of a sensation among American linguists particularly, since it showed by astute and logically scrupulous analytical methods that natural languages are based on recursive functions (e.g., "This is the house that Jack built; this is the malt that lay in the house that Jack built . . .") and logical transformations that affect every component of a language—phonemes, morphemes, and grammar. In the context of work by such linguists as Leonard Bloomfield, G. L. Trager, and Charles Fries, these fundamental insights were particularly unsettling, since they imply that the empirical search for linguistic "structure" in verbal behavior, whether sought in historical philology, anthropological fieldwork, or observations of psychological behavior, could never provide explanations for even the simplest linguistic phenomena.

Structural linguistics (of the so-called slot and substitution variety) simply foundered on such cases as "John is eager to please" and "John is easy to please," which appear to have the same manifest "structure" but are obviously (though not transparently) different. In the first case "John" is the subject of the sentence, but in the second "John" is the object of the verb. This elementary example, moreover, discloses that while a native speaker simply *never* makes a mistake in confusing the one with the other, there is no reason at all to suppose that the native speaker (even one who is verbally sophisticated) will be able to provide the slightest clue as to how one actually can tell the difference.

One might also note that such a case is even more destructive to the pretensions of a structuralist linguistics following *Saussure,* since Saussure's set of distinctions between "langue" and "parole," the "sign" and "signifier," and "paradigmatic" and "syntagmatic" structures do not permit the linguist even to state the problem as it affects the relation between syntactical and semantic domains. Indeed, following Saussure, there is no consistent way to sort out relations that are specifically "syntactical."

Chomsky's elaboration of linguistic theory has been based on three basic insights. First, there is a fundamental distinction between a speaker's "linguistic competence" and particular acts of speech, or "linguistic performance." While there is a superficial similarity between this distinction and Saussure's notion of "langue" as opposed to "parole," the two approaches are incommensurable, since Saussure's notion of "langue" as the totality of the language can only mystify the way in which that "language" is available to particular acts of cognition, and thereby creates a factitious problem about the "materiality" or "ideality" of language per se. For Chomsky, the idea of "linguistic competence" pertains fundamentally to a species-specific ability to acquire a language, more particularly to learn the basic grammatical relations on which the syntax of natural languages depend.

Chomsky's second major insight is that grammatical expressions in a language all present a bifurcated structure: the visible or "surface structure" of the language is correlatable with an implicit or "deep structure," connected in some fundamental way with the interpretability of the surface structure. That is, the actual expressions of a language are held to be derived from a "base component" transformed in particular ways to produce the actual expression. It is on this basis that a grammar can be described as "generative" and "transformational": the well-formed (grammatical) expressions of a language are generated from the base component by the application of transformational rules.

The third insight is that linguistic theory (or, for that matter, any theory whatever) can make no claim to some general "discovery procedure" or formulaic algorithm by which to find governing rules, laws, or explanatory principles. While this implies that specifically linguistic insight is not necessarily related to one's verbal proficiency—a good talker may have no significant insight into the structure of language—it also implies that a good theory developed from linguistic insights remains a theory about *linguistic* structure. That is to say, evidence of linguistic competence in the ability to recognize "grammatical" utterances does not depend on knowing the underlying grammatical principles explicitly; and the actual formulation of such principles, while it takes as its subject the linguistic competence (not the performance) of the native speaker, requires an explicit representational formalism suitable to linguistic evidence—which may or may not transfer to other subjects of study. Accordingly, theories of language should be held to two tests of adequacy: descriptive adequacy, in accounting for reproducible evidence, and explanatory adequacy, by positing underlying universals or laws that explain the regularities in described data.

In all of these areas, not surprisingly, Chomsky's work has been controversial. In the first case, Chomsky has taken obvious satisfaction in playing the role of nemesis for behaviorist psychology (see especially his review of B. F. Skinner's *Verbal Behavior*), since even the most trivial evidence concerning natural language syntax appears inconsistent with the foundational view of behaviorism—that the only relevant concern of the psychologist is empirical behavior. As Chomsky has developed his own view (which he has characterized as "Cartesian" linguistics), he has argued that the ability of human beings to acquire language is evidence in favor of "linguistic universals," similar to Descartes' notion of "innate ideas." Since this is a general philosophical issue not restricted to linguistics, Chomsky's views have provoked considerable debate.

In the second case, Chomsky's notion of the relation between the "base component" and "surface structure" poses difficult problems for the assignment of "meaning" to verbal structures. Chomsky's position on this issue, generally characterized as "interpretive semantics," is based on the view that the meaning of a grammatical sentence is determined by the deep structure of the base component and that, in general, transformations that generate surface structures are neutral with respect to meaning. The alternative view (as proposed by Charles Fillmore and others), "generative semantics," has held that transformations make decisive contributions to meaning, such that the meaning of the "surface structure" cannot be exclusively assigned to deep structure. (For its own part, generative semantics has not fared especially well, since it appears to involve a trade-off between a more elaborate account of meaning and a less elegant account of syntax.)

Finally, as a theorist and philosopher of language, Chomsky has provoked extensive debate concerning the implications of what Gustav Bergman has called the "linguistic turn" in philosophy, in both logical positivism and so-called ordinary language philosophy (see *Logic and Reality* [Madison: University of Wisconsin Press, 1964], p. 177). Jerrold Katz argues, for example, that both positivism and ordinary language philosophy presume that there is no "underlying reality" in natural language per se, so that one need attend only to surface features and observable uses of words (*The Underlying Reality of Language* [New York: Harper & Row, 1971], p. 179). A philosophy of language based on transformational-generative principles, on the other hand, would include as part of its structure and method the idea of linguistic universals as essential to the solution of philosophical problems.

While it would not be correct to say that there is any general consensus as to what would be acceptable intellectual doctrine on any of these issues, it is beyond doubt that Chomsky must be taken into account in any informed discussion of them.

Chomsky's major works include *Syntactic Structures* (1957); review of B. F. Skinner's *Verbal Behavior,* in *Language* 35 (1959): 26–58; *Current Issues in Linguistic Theory* (1965); *Aspects of the Theory of Syntax* (1965); *Cartesian Linguistics* (1966); *Topics in the Theory of Generative Grammar* (1966); *Language and Mind* (1968); *Reflections on Language* (1975); and *Rules and Representations* (1980). Chomsky has also written widely on social and political issues; see especially *American Power and the New Mandarins* (1969) and *Language and Responsibility* (1979). For an excellent introduction to Chomsky's contributions to linguistic theory, see John Lyons, *Noam Chomsky* (1970). See also Donald Davidson and Gilbert Harman, eds., *Semantics of Natural Langauge* (1972); Charles J. Fillmore, "The Case for Case," in *Universals in Linguistic Theory,* ed. E. Bach and R. Harms (1968); and Jay F. Rosenberg and Charles Travis, eds., *Readings in the Philosophy of Language* (1971).

FROM

ASPECTS OF THE THEORY OF SYNTAX

§ 1. Generative Grammars as Theories of Linguistic Competence

This study will touch on a variety of topics in syntactic theory and English syntax, a few in some detail, several quite superficially, and none exhaustively. It will be concerned with the syntactic component of a generative grammar, that is, with the rules that specify the well-formed strings of minimal syntactically functioning units (*formatives*) and assign structural information of various kinds both to these strings and to strings that deviate from well-formedness in certain respects.

The general framework within which this investigation will proceed has been presented in many places, and some familiarity with the theoretical and descriptive studies listed in the bibliography is presupposed. In this chapter, I shall survey briefly some of the main background assumptions, making no serious attempt here to justify them but only to sketch them clearly.

Linguistic theory is concerned primarily with an ideal speaker-listener, in a completely homogeneous speech-community, who knows its language perfectly and is unaffected by such grammatically irrelevant conditions as memory limitations, distractions, shifts of attention and interest, and errors (random or characteristic) in applying his knowledge of the language in actual performance. This seems to me to have been the position of the founders of modern general linguistics, and no cogent reason for modifying it has been offered. To study actual linguistic performance, we must consider the interaction of a variety of factors, of which the underlying competence of the speaker-hearer is only one. In this respect, study of language is no different from empirical investigation of other complex phenomena.

We thus make a fundamental distinction between *competence* (the speaker-hearer's knowledge of his language) and *performance* (the actual use of language in concrete situations). Only under the idealization set forth in the preceding paragraph is performance a direct reflection of competence. In actual fact, it obviously could not directly reflect competence. A record of natural speech will show numerous false starts, deviations from rules, changes of plan in mid-course, and so on. The problem for the linguist, as well as for the child learning the language, is to determine from the data of performance the underlying system of rules that has been mastered by the speaker-hearer and that he puts to use in actual performance. Hence, in the technical sense, linguistic theory is mentalistic, since it is concerned with discovering a mental reality underlying actual behavior.[1] Observed use of language or hypothesized

Selections from ASPECTS OF THE THEORY OF SYNTAX are from chapter 1, "Methodological Preliminaries," only part of which is included here. Bibliographic information cited in the notes appears at the end of the text. Reprinted by permission of the M.I.T. Press, copyright 1965.

[1] To accept traditional mentalism, in this way, is not to accept Bloomfield's dichotomy of "mentalism" versus "mechanism." Mentalistic linguistics is simply theoretical linguistics that uses performance as data (along with other data, for example, the data provided by introspection) for the determination of competence, the latter being taken as the primary object of its investigation. The mentalist, in this traditional sense, need make no assumptions about the possible phsyiological basis for the mental reality that he studies. In particular, he need not deny that there is such a basis. One would guess, rather, that it is the mentalistic studies that will ultimately be of greatest value for the investigation of neurophysiological mechanisms, since they alone are concerned with determining abstractly the properties that such mechanisms must exhibit and the functions they must perform.

In fact, the issue of mentalism versus antimentalism in linguistics apparently has to do only with goals and interests, and not with questions of truth or falsity, sense or nonsense. At least three issues are involved in this rather idle controversy: (*a*) dualism—are the rules that underlie performance represented in a nonmaterial medium?; (*b*) behaviorism—do the data of performance exhaust the domain of interest to the linguist, or is he also concerned with other facts, in particular those pertaining to the deeper systems that underlie behavior?; (*c*) introspectionism—should one make use of introspective data in the attempt to ascertain the properties of these underlying systems? It is the dualistic position against which Bloomfield irrelevantly inveighed. The behaviorist position is not an arguable matter. It is simply an expression of lack of interest in theory and explanation. This is clear, for example, in Twaddell's critique (1935) of Sapir's mentalistic phonology, which used informant responses and comments as evidence bearing on the psychological real-

dispositions to respond, habits, and so on, may provide evidence as to the nature of this mental reality, but surely cannot constitute the actual subject matter of linguistics, if this is to be a serious discipline. The distinction I am noting here is related to the *langue-parole* distinction of Saussure; but it is necessary to reject his concept of *langue* as merely a systematic inventory of items and to return rather to the Humboldtian conception of underlying competence as a system of generative processes. For discussion, see Chomsky (1964).

A grammar of a language purports to be a description of the ideal speaker-hearer's intrinsic competence. If the grammar is, furthermore, perfectly explicit—in other words, if it does not rely on the intelligence of the understanding reader but rather provides an explicit analysis of his contribution—we may (somewhat redundantly) call it a *generative grammar.*

A fully adequate grammar must assign to each of an infinite range of sentences a structural description indicating how this sentence is understood by the ideal speaker-hearer. This is the traditional problem of descriptive linguistics, and traditional grammars give a wealth of information concerning structural descriptions of sentences. However, valuable as they obviously are, traditional grammars are deficient in that they leave unexpressed many of the basic regularities of the language with which they are concerned. This fact is particularly clear on the level of syntax, where no traditional or structuralist grammar goes beyond classification of particular examples to the stage of formulation of generative rules on any significant scale. An analysis of the best existing grammars will quickly reveal that this is a defect of principle, not just a matter of empirical detail or logical preciseness. Nevertheless, it seems obvious that the attempt to explore this largely uncharted territory can most profitably begin with a study of the kind of structural information presented by traditional grammars and the kind of linguistic processes that have been exhibited, however informally, in these grammars.[2]

The limitations of traditional and structuralist grammars should be clearly appreciated. Although such grammars may contain full and explicit lists of exceptions and irregularities, they provide only examples and hints concerning the regular and productive syntactic processes. Traditional linguistic theory was not unaware of this fact. For example, James Beattie (1788) remarks that

> Languages, therefore, resemble men in this respect, that, though each has peculiarities, whereby it is distinguished from every other, yet all have certain qualities in common. The peculiarities of individual tongues are explained in their respective grammars and dictionaries. Those things, that all languages

ity of some abstract system of phonological elements. For Twaddell, the enterprise has no point because all that interests him is the behavior itself, "which is already available for the student of language, though in less concentrated form." Characteristically, this lack of interest in linguistic theory expresses itself in the proposal to limit the term "theory" to "summary of data" (as in Twaddell's paper, or, to take a more recent example, in Dixon, 1963, although the discussion of "theorics" in the latter is sufficiently vague as to allow other interpretations of what he may have in mind). Perhaps this loss of interest in theory, in the usual sense, was fostered by certain ideas (e.g., strict operationalism or strong verificationism) that were considered briefly in positivist philosophy of science, but rejected forthwith, in the early nineteen-thirties. In any event, question (*b*) poses no substantive issue. Question (*c*) arises only if one rejects the behaviorist limitations of (*b*). To maintain, on grounds of methodological purity, that introspective judgments of the informant (often, the linguist himself) should be disregarded is, for the present, to condemn the study of language to utter sterility. It is difficult to imagine what possible reason might be given for this. We return to this matter later. For further discussion, see Katz (1964*c*). [Au.]

[2] This has been denied recently by several European linguists (e.g., Dixon, 1963; Uhlenbeck, 1963, 1964). They offer no reasons for their skepticism concerning traditional grammar, however. Whatever evidence is available today seems to me to show that by and large the traditional views are basically correct, so far as they go, and that the suggested innovations are totally unjustifiable. For example, consider Uhlenbeck's proposal that the constituent analysis of "the man saw the boy" is [*the man saw*] [*the boy*], a proposal which presumably also implies that in the sentences [*the man put*] [*it into the box*], [*the man aimed*] [*it at John*], [*the man persuaded*] [*Bill that it was unlikely*], etc., the constituents are as indicated. There are many considerations relevant to the determination of constituent structure (cf. *Aspects*, p. 196); to my knowledge, they support the traditional analysis without exception against this proposal, for which the only argument offered is that it is the result of a "pure linguistic analysis." Cf. Uhlenbeck (1964), and the discussion there. As to Dixon's objections to traditional grammars, since he offers neither any alternative nor any argument (beyond the correct but irrelevant observation that they have been "long condemned by professional linguists"), there is nothing further to discuss, in this case. [Au.]

> have in common, or that are necessary to every language, are treated of in a science, which some have called *Universal or Philosophical* grammar.

Somewhat earlier, Du Marsais defines universal and particular grammar in the following way (1729; quoted in Sahlin, 1928, pp. 29–30):

> Il y a dans la grammaire des observations qui conviènnent à toutes les langues; ces observations forment ce qu'on appelle la grammaire générale: telles sont les remarques que l'on a faites sur les sons articulés, sur les lettres qui sont les signes de ces sons; sur la nature des mots, et sur les différentes manières dont ils doivent être ou arrangés ou terminés pour faire un sens. Outre ces observations générales, il y en a qui ne sont propres qu'à une langue particulière; et c'est ce qui forme les grammaires particulières de chaque langue.[3]

Within traditional linguistic theory, furthermore, it was clearly understood that one of the qualities that all languages have in common is their "creative" aspect. Thus an essential property of language is that it provides the means for expressing indefinitely many thoughts and for reacting appropriately in an indefinite range of new situations (for references, cf. Chomsky, 1964, forthcoming). The grammar of a particular language, then, is to be supplemented by a universal grammar that accommodates the creative aspect of language use and expresses the deep-seated regularities which, being universal, are omitted from the grammar itself. Therefore it is quite proper for a grammar to discuss only exceptions and irregularities in any detail. It is only when supplemented by a universal grammar that the grammar of a language provides a full account of the speaker-hearer's competence.

Modern linguistics, however, has not explicitly recognized the necessity for supplementing a "particular grammar" of a language by a universal grammar if it is to achieve descriptive adequacy. It has, in fact, characteristically rejected the study of universal grammar as misguided; and, as noted before, it has not attempted to deal with the creative aspect of language use. It thus suggests no way to overcome the fundamental descriptive inadequacy of structuralist grammars.

Another reason for the failure of traditional grammars, particular or universal, to attempt a precise statement of regular processes of sentence formation and sentence interpretation lay in the widely held belief that there is a "natural order of thoughts" that is mirrored by the order of words. Hence, the rules of sentence formation do not really belong to grammar but to some other subject in which the "order of thoughts" is studied. Thus in the *Grammaire générale et raisonnée* (Lancelot *et al.*, 1660) it is asserted that, aside from figurative speech, the sequence of words follows an "ordre naturel," which conforms "à l'expression naturelle de nos pensées." Consequently, few grammatical rules need be formulated beyond the rules of ellipsis, inversion, and so on, which determine the figurative use of language. The same view appears in many forms and variants. To mention just one additional example, in an interesting essay devoted largely to the question of how the simultaneous and sequential array of ideas is reflected in the order of words, Diderot concludes that French is unique among languages in the degree to which the order of words corresponds to the natural order of thoughts and ideas (Diderot, 1751). Thus "quel que soit l'ordre des termes dans une langue ancienne ou moderne, l'esprit de l'écrivain a suivi l'ordre didactique de la syntaxe française" (p. 390); "Nous disons les choses en français, comme l'esprit est forcé de les considérer en quelque langue qu'on écrive" (p. 371).[4] With admirable consistency he goes on to conclude that "notre langue *pédestre* a sur les autres l'avantage de l'utile sur l'agréable"[5] (p. 372); thus French is appropriate for the sciences, whereas Greek, Latin, Italian, and English "sont plus avantageuses pour les lettres." Moreover,

[3] There are in grammar some observations that apply to all languages; these observations form what one may call general grammar, such as remarks one makes on articulated sounds, on letters that are the signs of sounds, on the nature of words, and on the different ways in which they must be arranged or terminated in order to make sense. Further general observations that belong to particular languages make up the particular grammars of each language. [Eds.]

[4] Whatever the order of terms in a language, ancient or modern, the spirit of the writer has followed the didactic order of French syntax. . . . We say those things in French as the spirit is moved from considering the language in which it is written. [Eds.]

[5] Our pedestrian language has the advantage over the others of being useful as well as pleasing. [Eds.]

le bons sens choisirait la langue française; mais . . . l'imagination et les passions donneront la préférence aux langues anciennes et à celles de nos voisins . . . il faut parler français dans la société et dans les écoles de philosophie; et grec, latin, anglais, dans les chaires et sur les théâtres; . . . notre langue sera celle de la vérité, si jamais elle revient sur la terre; et . . . la grecque, la latine et les autres seront les langues de la fable et du mensonge. Le français est fait pour instruire, éclairer et convaincre; le grec, le latin, l'italien, l'anglais, pour persuader, émouvoir et tromper: parlez grec, latin, italien au peuple; mais parlez français au sage. (pp. 371–372)[6]

In any event, insofar as the order of words is determined by factors independent of language, it is not necessary to describe it in a particular or universal grammar, and we therefore have principled grounds for excluding an explicit formulation of syntactic processes from grammar. It is worth noting that this naïve view of language structure persists to modern times in various forms, for example, in Saussure's image of a sequence of expressions corresponding to an amorphous sequence of concepts or in the common characterization of language use as merely a matter of use of words and phrases (for example, Ryle, 1953).

But the fundamental reason for this inadequacy of traditional grammars is a more technical one. Although it was well understood that linguistic processes are in some sense "creative," the technical devices for expressing a system of recursive processes were simply not available until much more recently. In fact, a real understanding of how a language can (in Humboldt's words) "make infinite use of finite means" has developed only within the last thirty years, in the course of studies in the foundations of mathematics. Now that these insights are readily available it is possible to return to the problems that were raised, but not solved, in traditional linguistic theory, and to attempt an explicit formulation of the "creative" processes of language. There is, in short, no longer a technical barrier to the full-scale study of generative grammars.

Returning to the main theme, by a generative grammar I mean simply a system of rules that in some explicit and well-defined way assigns structural descriptions to sentences. Obviously, every speaker of a language has mastered and internalized a generative grammar that expresses his knowledge of his language. This is not to say that he is aware of the rules of the grammar or even that he can become aware of them, or that his statements about his intuitive knowledge of the language are necessarily accurate. Any interesting generative grammar will be dealing, for the most part, with mental processes that are far beyond the level of actual or even potential consciousness; furthermore, it is quite apparent that a speaker's reports and viewpoints about his behavior and his competence may be in error. Thus a generative grammar attempts to specify what the speaker actually knows, not what he may report about his knowledge. Similarly, a theory of visual perception would attempt to account for what a person actually sees and the mechanisms that determine this rather than his statements about what he sees and why, though these statements may provide useful, in fact, compelling evidence for such a theory.

To avoid what has been a continuing misunderstanding, it is perhaps worth while to reiterate that a generative grammar is not a model for a speaker or a hearer. It attempts to characterize in the most neutral possible terms the knowledge of the language that provides the basis for actual use of language by a speaker-hearer. When we speak of a grammar as generating a sentence with a certain structural description, we mean simply that the grammar assigns this structural description to the sentence. When we say that a sentence has a certain derivation with respect to a particular generative grammar, we say nothing about how the speaker or hearer might proceed, in some practical or efficient way, to construct such a derivation. These questions belong to the theory of language use—the theory of performance. No doubt, a reasonable model of language use will incorporate, as a basic component, the generative grammar that expresses the speaker-hearer's knowledge of the language; but this generative grammar does not, in itself, prescribe the

[6] Good sense will choose the French language; but . . . the imagination and passions will give preference to the ancient languages and their close relatives. . . . It is necessary to speak French in society and in the schools of philosophy; and Greek, Latin, English, in the pulpit and the theaters; . . . our language would be the language of truth, if ever it returned to the earth; . . . and Greek, Latin, and the others will be the language of fable and illusion. French is for teaching, illuminating, and convincing; Greek, Latin, Italian, English, for persuading, agitating, and beguiling: speak Greek, Latin, Italian to the people; but speak French to the wise man. [Eds.]

character or functioning of a perceptual model or a model of speech production. For various attempts to clarify this point, see Chomsky (1957), Gleason (1961), Miller and Chomsky (1963), and many other publications.

Confusion over this matter has been sufficiently persistent to suggest that a terminological change might be in order. Nevertheless, I think that the term "generative grammar" is completely appropriate, and have therefore continued to use it. The term "generate" is familiar in the sense intended here in logic, particularly in Post's theory of combinatorial systems.[7] Furthermore, "generate" seems to be the most appropriate translation for Humboldt's term *erzeugen,* which he frequently uses, it seems, in essentially the sense here intended. Since this use of the term "generate" is well established both in logic and in the tradition of linguistic theory, I can see no reason for a revision of terminology.

§ 2. Toward a Theory of Performance

There seems to be little reason to question the traditional view that investigation of performance will proceed only so far as understanding of underlying competence permits. Furthermore, recent work on performance seems to give new support to this assumption. To my knowledge, the only concrete results that have been achieved and the only clear suggestions that have been put forth concerning the theory of performance, outside of phonetics, have come from studies of performance models that incorporate generative grammars of specific kinds—that is, from studies that have been based on assumptions about underlying competence.[8] In particular, there are some suggestive observations concerning limitations on performance imposed by organization of memory and bounds on memory, and concerning the exploitation of grammatical devices to form deviant sentences of various types. . . . To clarify further the distinction between competence and performance, it may be useful to summarize briefly some of the suggestions and results that have appeared in the last few years in the study of performance models with limitations of memory, time, and access.

For the purposes of this discussion, let us use the term "acceptable" to refer to utterances that are perfectly natural and immediately comprehensible without paper-and-pencil analysis, and in no way bizarre or outlandish. Obviously, acceptability will be a matter of degree, along various dimensions. One could go on to propose various operational tests to specify the notion more precisely (for example, rapidity, correctness, and uniformity of recall and recognition, normalcy of intonation).[9] For present purposes, it is unnecessary to delimit it more carefully. To illustrate, the sentences of (1) are somewhat more acceptable, in the intended sense, than those of (2):

(1) (i) I called up the man who wrote the book that you told me about
(ii) quite a few of the students who you met who come from New York are friends of mine
(iii) John, Bill, Tom, and several of their friends visited us last night

(2) (i) I called the man who wrote the book that you told me about up
(ii) the man who the boy who the students recognized pointed out is a friend of mine

The more acceptable sentences are those that are more likely to be produced, more easily understood, less clumsy, and in some sense more natural.[10] The unacceptable sentences one would tend to

[7] Emil Post, American logician. [Eds.]

[8] Furthermore, it seems to me that speech perception is also best studied in this framework. See, for example, Halle and Stevens (1962). [Au.]

[9] Tests that seem to determine a useful notion of this sort have been described in various places—for example, Miller and Isard (1963). [Au.]

[10] These characterizations are equally vague, and the concepts involved are equally obscure. The notion "likely to be produced" or "probable" is sometimes thought to be more "objective" and antecedently better defined than the others, on the assumption that there is some clear meaning to the notion "probability of a sentence" or "probability of a sentence type." Actually, the latter notions are objective and antecedently clear only if probability is based on an estimate of relative frequency and if sentence type means something like "sequence of word or morpheme classes." (Furthermore, if the notion is to be at all significant, these classes must be extremely small and of mutually substitutable elements, or else unacceptable and ungrammatical sentences will be as "likely" and acceptable as grammatical ones.) But in this

avoid and replace by more acceptable variants, wherever possible, in actual discourse.

The notion "acceptable" is not to be confused with "grammatical." Acceptability is a concept that belongs to the study of performance, whereas grammaticalness belongs to the study of competence. The sentences of (2) are low on the scale of acceptability but high on the scale of grammaticalness, in the technical sense of this term. That is, the generative rules of the language assign an interpretation to them in exactly the way in which they assign an interpretation to the somewhat more acceptable sentences of (1). Like acceptability, grammaticalness is, no doubt, a matter of degree (cf. Chomsky, 1955, 1957, 1961), but the scales of grammaticalness and acceptability do not coincide. Grammaticalness is only one of many factors that interact to determine acceptability. Correspondingly, although one might propose various operational tests for acceptability, it is unlikely that a necessary and sufficient operational criterion might be invented for the much more abstract and far more important notion of grammaticalness. The unacceptable grammatical sentences often cannot be used, for reasons having to do, not with grammar, but rather with memory limitations, intonational and stylistic factors, "iconic" elements of discourse (for example, a tendency to place logical subject and object early rather than late; . . . and so on. Note that it would be quite impossible to characterize the unacceptable sentences in grammatical terms. For example, we cannot formulate particular rules of the grammar in such a way as to exclude them. Nor, obviously, can we exclude them by limiting the number of reapplications of grammatical rules in the generation of a sentence, since unacceptability can just as well arise from application of distinct rules, each being applied only once. In fact, it is clear that we can characterize unacceptable sentences only in terms of some "global" property of derivations and the structures they define—a property that is attributable, not to a particular rule, but rather to the way in which the rules interrelate in a derivation. . . .

case, though "probability of a sentence (type)" is clear and well defined, it is an utterly useless notion, since almost all highly acceptable sentences (in the intuitive sense) will have probabilities empirically indistinguishable from zero and will belong to sentence types with probabilities empirically indistinguishable from zero. Thus the acceptable or grammatical sentences (or sentence types) are no more likely, in any objective sense of this word, than the others. This remains true if we consider, not "likelihood," but "likelihood relative to a given situation," as long as "situations" are specified in terms of observable physical properties and are not mentalistic constructs. It is noteworthy that linguists who talk of hardheaded objective study of use of sentences in real situations, when they actually come to citing examples, invariably describe the "situations" in completely mentalistic terms. Cf., e.g., Dixon (1963, p. 101), where, in the only illustrative example in the book, a sentence is described as gaining its meaning from the situation "British Culture." To describe British culture as "a situation" is, in the first place, a category mistake; furthermore, to regard it as a pattern abstracted from observed behavior, and hence objectively describable in purely physical terms, betrays a complete misunderstanding of what might be expected from anthropological research. For further discussion, see Katz and Fodor (1964). [Au.]

§ 3. The Organization of a Generative Grammar

Returning now to the question of competence and the generative grammars that purport to describe it, we stress again that knowledge of a language involves the implicit ability to understand indefinitely many sentences.[11] Hence, a generative grammar must be a system of rules that can iterate to generate an indefinitely large number of structures. This system of rules can be analyzed into the three major components of a generative grammar: the syntactic, phonological, and semantic components.[12]

[11] It is astonishing to find that even this truism has recently been challenged. See Dixon (1963). However, it seems that when Dixon denies that a language has infinitely many sentences, he is using the term "infinite" in some special and rather obscure sense. Thus on the same page (p. 83) on which he objects to the assertion "that there are an infinite number of sentences in a language" he states that "we are clearly unable to say that there is any definite number, *N*, such that no sentence contains more than *N* clauses" (that is, he states that the language is infinite). Either this is a blatant self-contradiction, or else he has some new sense of the word "infinite" in mind. For further discussion of his remarks in this connection, see Chomsky (in press). [Au.]

[12] Aside from terminology, I follow here the exposition in Katz and Postal (1964). In particular, I shall assume throughout that the semantic component is essentially as they describe it and that the phonological component is essentially as described in Chomsky, Halle, and Lukoff (1956); Halle (1959*a*, 1959*b*, 1962*a*); Chomsky (1962*b*); Chomsky and Miller (1963); Halle and Chomsky (1960; forthcoming). [Au.]

The syntactic component specifies an infinite set of abstract formal objects, each of which incorporates all information relevant to a single interpretation of a particular sentence.[13] Since I shall be concerned here only with the syntactic component, I shall use the term "sentence" to refer to strings of formatives rather than to strings of phones. It will be recalled that a string of formatives specifies a string of phones uniquely (up to free variation), but not conversely.

The phonological component of a grammar determines the phonetic form of a sentence generated by the syntactic rules. That is, it relates a structure generated by the syntactic component to a phonetically represented signal. The semantic component determines the semantic interpretation of a sentence. That is, it relates a structure generated by the syntactic component to a certain semantic representation. Both the phonological and semantic components are therefore purely interpretive. Each utilizes information provided by the syntactic component concerning formatives, their inherent properties, and their interrelations in a given sentence. Consequently, the syntactic component of a grammar must specify, for each sentence, a *deep structure* that determines its semantic interpretation and a *surface structure* that determines its phonetic interpretation. The first of these is interpreted by the semantic component; the second, by the phonological component.[14]

[13] I assume throughout that the syntactic component contains a lexicon, and that each lexical item is specified in the lexicon in terms of its intrinsic semantic features, whatever these may be. [Au.]

[14] In place of the terms "deep structure" and "surface structure," one might use the corresponding Humboldtian notions "inner form" of a sentence and "outer form" of a sentence. However, though it seems to me that "deep structure" and "surface structure," in the sense in which these terms will be used here, do correspond quite closely to Humboldtian "inner form" and "outer form," respectively (as used of a sentence), I have adopted the more neutral terminology to avoid the question, here, of textual interpretation. The terms "depth grammar" and "surface grammar" are familiar in modern philosophy in something roughly like the sense here intended (cf. Wittgenstein's distinction of "*Tiefengrammatik*" and "*Oberflächengrammatik*," 1953, p. 168); Hockett uses similar terminology in his discussion of the inadequacy of taxonomic linguistics (Hockett, 1958, Chapter 29). Postal has used the terms "underlying structure" and "superficial structure" (Postal, 1964*b*) for the same notions.

It might be supposed that surface structure and deep structure will always be identical. In fact, one might briefly characterize the syntactic theories that have arisen in modern structural (taxonomic) linguistics as based on the assumption that deep and surface structures are actually the same (cf. Postal, 1964*a*, Chomsky, 1964). The central idea of transformational grammar is that they are, in general, distinct and that the surface structure is determined by repeated application of certain formal operations called "grammatical transformations" to objects of a more elementary sort. If this is true (as I assume, henceforth), then the syntactic component must generate deep and surface structures, for each sentence, and must interrelate them. This idea has been clarified substantially in recent work, in ways that will be described later. . . . For the moment, it

The distinction between deep and surface structure, in the sense in which these terms are used here, is drawn quite clearly in the Port-Royal *Grammar* (Lancelot *et al.*, 1660). See Chomsky (1964, pp. 15–16; forthcoming) for some discussion and references. In philosophical discussion, it is often introduced in an attempt to show how certain philosophical positions arise from false grammatical analogies, the surface structure of certain expressions being mistakenly considered to be semantically interpretable by means appropriate only to other, superficially similar sentences. Thus Thomas Reid (1785) holds a common source of philosophical error to lie in the fact that

> in all languages, there are phrases which have a distinct meaning; while at the same time, there may be something in the structure of them that disagrees with the analogy of grammar or with the principles of philosophy. . . . Thus, we speak of feeling pain as if pain was something distinct from the feeling of it. We speak of pain coming and going, and removing from one place to another. Such phrases are meant by those who use them in a sense that is neither obscure nor false. But the philosopher puts them into his alembic, reduces them to their first principles, draws out of them a sense that was never meant, and so imagines that he has discovered an error of the vulgar [pp. 167–168].

More generally, he criticizes the theory of ideas as based on a deviation from the "popular meaning," in which "to have an idea of anything signifies nothing more than to think of it" (p. 105). But philosophers take an idea to be "the object that the mind contemplates" (p. 105); to have an idea, then, is to possess in the mind such an image, picture, or representation as the immediate object of thought. It follows that there are two objects of thought: the idea, which is in the mind, and the thing represented by it. From this conclusion follow the ab-is sufficient to observe that although the Immediate Constituent analysis (labeled bracketing) of an actual string of formatives may be adequate as an account of surface structure, it is certainly not adequate as an account of deep structure. My concern in this book is primarily with deep structure and, in particular, with the elementary objects of which deep structure is constituted.

To clarify exposition, I shall use the following terminology, with occasional revisions as the discussion proceeds.

The *base* of the syntactic component is a system of rules that generate a highly restricted (perhaps finite) set of *basic strings,* each with an associated structural description called a *base Phrase-marker.* These base Phrase-markers are the elementary units of which deep structures are constituted. I shall assume that no ambiguity is introduced by rules of the base. This assumption seems to me correct, but has no important consequences for what follows here, though it simplifies exposition. Underlying each sentence of the language there is a sequence of base Phrase-markers, each generated by the use of the syntactic component. I shall refer to this sequence as the *basis* of the sentence that it underlies.

In addition to its base, the syntactic component of a generative grammar contains a *transformational* subcomponent. This is concerned with generating a sentence, with its surface structure, from its basis. Some familiarity with the operation and effects of transformational rules is henceforth presupposed.

Since the base generates only a restricted set of base Phrase-markers, most sentences will have a sequence of such objects as an underlying basis. Among the sentences with a single base Phrase-marker as basis, we can delimit a proper subset called "kernel sentences." These are sentences of a particularly simple sort that involve a minimum of transformational apparatus in their generation. The notion "kernel sentence" has, I think, an important intuitive significance, but since kernel sentences play no distinctive role in generation or interpretation of sentences, I shall say nothing more about them here. One must be careful not to confuse kernel sentences with the basic strings that underlie them. The basic strings and base Phrase-markers do, it seems, play a distinctive and crucial role in language use. . . .[15]

§ 8. Linguistic Theory and Language Learning

Certain problems of linguistic theory [can be] formulated as questions about the construction of a hypothetical language-acquisition device. This seems a useful and suggestive framework within

surdities, as Reid regards them, of the traditional theory of ideas. One of the sources of these absurdities is the failure of the philosopher to attend "to the distinction between the operations of the mind and the objects of these operations . . . although this distinction be familiar to the vulgar, and found in the structure of all languages . . ." (p. 110). Notice that these two senses of "having an idea" are distinguished by Descartes in the Preface to the *Meditations* (1641, p. 138). Reid's linguistic observation is made considerably earlier by Du Marsais, in a work published posthumously in 1769, in the following passage (pp. 179–180):

> Ainsi, comme nous avons dit *j'ai un livre, j'ai un diamant, j'ai une montre,* nous disons par imitation, *j'ai la fièvre, j'ai envie, j'ai peur, j'ai un doute, j'ai pitié, j'ai une idée,* etc. Mais *livre, diamant, montre* sont autant de noms d'objects réels qui existent indépendamment de notre manière de penser; au lieu que *santé, fièvre, peur, doute, envie,* ne sont que des termes métaphysiques qui ne désignent que des manières d'êtres considérés par des points de vue particuliers de l'esprit.
>
> Dans cet exemple, *j'ai une montre, j'ai* est une expression qui doit être prise dans le sens propre: mais dans *j'ai une idée, j'ai* n'est dit que par une imitation. C'est une expression empruntée. *J'ai une idée,* c'est-à-dire, *je pense, je conçois de telle ou telle manière. J'ai envie,* c'est-à-dire, *je désire; j'ai la volonté,* c'est-à-dire, *je veux,* etc.
>
> Ainsi, *idée, concept, imagination,* ne marquent point d'objets réels, et encore moins des êtres sensibles que l'on puisse unir l'un avec l'autre.

In more recent years, it has been widely held that the aims of philosophy should, in fact, be strictly limited to "the detection of the sources in linguistic idioms of recurrent misconstructions and absurd theories" (Ryle, 1931). [Au.]

[15] In the sections not reprinted here, Chomsky provides a detailed discussion of the justification of grammars, including his distinction between explanatory and descriptive adequacy (section 4); discussion of formal and substantive universals in language (section 5); a tentative model of language acquisition (or a "language-acquisition device") in terms of explanatory and descriptive theories (section 6); and a discussion of evaluation procedures (section 7). [Eds.]

which to pose and consider these problems. We may think of the theorist as given an empirical pairing of collections of primary linguistic data associated with grammars that are constructed by the device on the basis of such data. Much information can be obtained about both the primary data that constitute the input and the grammar that is the "output" of such a device, and the theorist has the problem of determining the intrinsic properties of a device capable of mediating this input-output relation.

It may be of some interest to set this discussion in a somewhat more general and traditional framework. Historically, we can distinguish two general lines of approach to the problem of acquisition of knowledge, of which the problem of acquisition of language is a special and particularly informative case. The empiricist approach has assumed that the structure of the acquisition device is limited to certain elementary "peripheral processing mechanisms"—for example, in recent versions, an innate "quality space" with an innate "distance" defined on it (Quine, 1960, pp. 83f),[16] a set of primitive unconditioned reflexes (Hull, 1943), or, in the case of language, the set of all "aurally distinguishable components" of the full "auditory impression" (Bloch, 1950). Beyond this, it assumes that the device has certain analytical data-processing mechanisms or inductive principles of a very elementary sort, for example, certain principles of association, weak principles of "generalization" involving gradients along the dimensions of the given quality space, or, in our case, taxonomic principles of segmentation and classification such as those that have been developed with some care in modern linguistics, in accordance with the Saussurian emphasis on the fundamental character of such principles. It is then assumed that a preliminary analysis of experience is provided by the peripheral processing mechanisms, and that one's concepts and knowledge, beyond this, are acquired by application of the available inductive principles to this initially analyzed experience.[17] Such views can be formulated clearly in one way or another as empirical hypotheses about the nature of mind.

A rather different approach to the problem of acquisition of knowledge has been characteristic of rationalist speculation about mental processes. The rationalist approach holds that beyond the periph-

[16] Actually, it is not clear that Quine's position should be taken as in any real sense an empiricist one. Thus he goes on to propose that in the innate quality space a red ball might be less distant from a green ball than from a red kerchief, so that we have not just a pre-experiential characterization of distance but also an innate analysis of this into distance in various respects. On the basis of these few comments, one might interpret him as proposing that such concepts as "ball" are innate ideas, hence as adopting an extreme form of nativism; at least, it is difficult to see wherein the cited proposal differs from this. In further support of such an antiempiricist interpretation, one may point to Quine's virtual renunciation of reinforcement theory (cf. my note 17).

Unfortunately, what are intended as empiricist views have generally been formulated in such an indefinite way that it is next to impossible to interpret them with any certainty, or to analyze or evaluate them. An extreme example, perhaps, is Skinner's account of how language is learned and used (Skinner, 1957). There seem to be only two coherent interpretations that one can give to this account. If we interpret the terms "stimulus," "reinforcement," "conditioning," etc., which appear in it, as having the meanings given to them in experimental psychology, then this account is so grossly and obviously counter to fact that discussion is quite beside the point. Alternatively, we may interpret these terms as metaphoric extensions of the (essentially homonymous) terms used in experimental psychology, in which case what is proposed is a mentalist account differing from traditional ones only in that many distinctions are necessarily obscured because of the poverty of the terminological apparatus available for paraphrase of the traditional mentalistic notions. What is particularly puzzling, then, is the insistent claim that this paraphrase is somehow "scientific" in a way in which traditional mentalism is not. [Au.]

[17] This application is perhaps mediated by "reinforcement," though many contemporary behaviorists use this term in such a loose way that reference to reinforcement adds nothing to the account of acquisition of knowledge that they propose. For example, Quine suggests (1960, pp. 82–83) that "some basic predilection for conformity" may take the place of "ulterior values," and that society's reinforcement of the response may consist "in no more than corroborative usage, whose resemblance to the child's effort is the sole reward." As Quine correctly notes, "this again is congenial enough to Skinner's scheme, for he does not enumerate the rewards" (this being one of the contributory factors to the near vacuity of Skinner's scheme). What this proposal comes to is that the only function of "reinforcement" may be to provide the child with information about correct usage; thus the empirical claim of "reinforcement theory" will be that learning of language cannot proceed in the absence of data. Actually, Skinner's concept of "reinforcement" is apparently still weaker than this, for he does not even require that the "reinforcing stimulus" impinge on the responding organism; it is sufficient that it be hoped for or imagined (for a collection of examples bearing on this matter, see Chomsky, 1959*b*). [Au.]

cral processing mechanisms,[18] there are innate ideas and principles of various kinds that determine the form of the acquired knowledge in what may be a rather restricted and highly organized way. A condition for innate mechanisms to become activated is that appropriate stimulation be presented. Thus for Descartes (1647), the innate ideas are those arising from the faculty of thinking rather than from external objects:

> . . . nothing reaches our mind from external objects through the organs of sense beyond certain corporeal movements . . . but even these movements, and the figures which arise from them, are not conceived by us in the shape they assume in the organs of sense. . . . Hence it follows that the ideas of the movements and figures are themselves innate in us. So much the more must the ideas of pain, colour, sound and the like be innate, that our mind may, on occasion of certain corporeal movements, envisage these ideas, for they have no likeness to the corporeal movements . . . [p. 443].

Similarly, such notions as that things equal to the same thing are equal to each other are innate, since they cannot arise as necessary principles from "particular movements." In general,

> sight . . . presents nothing beyond pictures, and hearing nothing beyond voices or sounds, so that all these things that we think of, beyond these voices or pictures, as being symbolized by them, are presented to us by means of ideas which come from no other source than our faculty of thinking, and are accordingly together with that faculty innate in us, that is, always existing in us potentially; for existence in any faculty is not actual but merely potential existence, since the very word "faculty" designates nothing more or less than a potentiality. . . . [Thus ideas are innate in the sense that] in some families generosity is innate, in others certain diseases like gout or gravel, not that on this account the babes of these families suffer from these diseases in their mother's womb, but because they are born with a certain disposition or propensity for contracting them . . . [p. 442].

Still earlier, Lord Herbert (1624) maintains that innate ideas and principles "remain latent when their corresponding objects are not present, and even disappear and give no sign of their existence"; they "must be deemed not so much the outcome of experience as principles without which we should have no experience at all . . . [p. 132]." Without these principles, "we could have no experience at all nor be capable of observations"; "we should never come to distinguish between things, or to grasp any general nature . . . [p. 105]." These notions are extensively developed throughout seventeenth-century rationalist philosophy. To mention just one example, Cudworth (1731) gives an extensive argument in support of his view that "there are many ideas of the mind, which though the cogitations of them be often occasionally invited from the motion or appulse of sensible objects without made upon our bodies; yet notwithstanding the ideas themselves could not possibly be stamped or impressed upon the soul from them, because sense takes no cognizance at all of any such things in those corporeal objects, and therefore they must needs arise from the innate vigour and activity of the mind itself . . . [Book IV]." Even in Locke one finds essentially the same conception, as was pointed out by Leibniz and many commentators since.

In the Port-Royal *Logic* (Arnauld, 1662), the same point of view is expressed in the following way:

> It is false, therefore, that all our ideas come through sense. On the contrary, it may be affirmed that no idea which we have in our minds has taken its rise from sense, except on occasion of those movements which are made in the brain through sense, the impulse from sense giving occasion to the mind to form different ideas which it would not have formed

[18] These mechanisms, as is now known, need not be at all elementary. Cf., for example, Lettvin *et al.* (1959), Hubel and Wiesel (1962), Frishkopf and Goldstein (1963). This work has demonstrated that peripheral processing in the receptor system or in lower cortical centers may provide a complex analysis of stimuli that, furthermore, seems to be rather specific to the animal's life-space and well correlated with behavior patterns. Thus it seems that not even peripheral processing can be described within the unstructured and atomistic framework that has been presupposed in empiricist thinking. [Au.]

> without it, though these ideas have very rarely any resemblance to what takes place in the sense and in the brain; and there are at least a very great number of ideas which, having no connection with any bodily image, cannot, without manifest absurdity, be referred to sense . . . [Chapter 1].

In the same vein, Leibniz refuses to accept a sharp distinction between innate and learned:

> I agree that we learn ideas and innate truths either in considering their source or in verifying them through experience. . . . And I cannot admit this proposition: *all that one learns is not innate.* The truths of numbers are in us, yet nonetheless one learns them,[19] either by drawing them from their source when we learn them through demonstrative proof (which shows that they are innate), or by testing them in examples, as do ordinary arithmeticians . . . [*New Essays,* p. 75]. [Thus] all arithmetic and all geometry are in us virtually, so that we can find them there if we consider attentively and set in order what we already have in the mind . . . [p. 78]. [In general,] we have an infinite amount of knowledge of which we are not always conscious, not even when we need it [p. 77]. The senses, although necessary for all our actual knowledge, are not sufficient to give it all to us, since the senses never give us anything but examples, i.e., particular or individual truths. Now all the examples which confirm a general truth, whatever their number, do not suffice to establish the universal necessity of that same truth . . . [pp. 42–43]. Necessary truths . . . must have principles whose proof does not depend on examples, nor consequently upon the testimony of the senses, although without the senses it would never have occurred to us to think of them. . . . It is true that we must not imagine that these eternal laws of the reason can be read in the soul as in an open book . . . but it is sufficient that they can be discovered in us by dint of attention, for which the senses furnish occasions, and successful experience serves to confirm reason . . . [p. 44]. [There are innate general principles that] enter into our thoughts, of which they form the soul and the connection. They are as necessary thereto as the muscles and sinews are for walking, although we do not at all think of them. The mind leans upon these principles every moment, but it does not come so easily to distinguish them and to represent them distinctly and separately, because that demands great attention to its acts. . . . Thus it is that one possesses many things without knowing it . . . [p. 74].

(as, for example, the Chinese possess articulate sounds, and therefore the basis for alphabetic writing, although they have not invented this).

Notice, incidentally, that throughout these classical discussions of the interplay between sense and mind in the formation of ideas, no sharp distinction is made between perception and acquisition, although there would be no inconsistency in the assumption that latent innate mental structures, once "activated," are then available for interpretation of the data of sense in a way in which they were not previously.

Applying this rationalist view to the special case of language learning, Humboldt (1836) concludes that one cannot really teach language but can only present the conditions under which it will develop spontaneously in the mind in its own way. Thus the *form of a language,* the schema for its grammar, is to a large extent given, though it will not be available for use without appropriate experience to set the language-forming processes into operation. Like Leibniz, he reiterates the Platonistic view that, for the individual, learning is largely a matter of *Wiedererzeugung,* that is, of drawing out what is innate in the mind.[20]

This view contrasts sharply with the empiricist

[19] I depart here from the Langley translation, which renders this passage inaccurately. The French original is as follows: ". . . je demeure d'accord que nous apprenons les idées et les véritées innées, soit en prenant garde à leur source, soit en les vérifiant par l'expérience. Ainsi je ne saurois admettre cette proposition, *tout ce qu'on apprend n'est pas inné.* Les vérités des nombres sont en nous, et on ne laisse pas de les apprendre, soit en les tirant de leur source lorsqu'on les apprend par raison démonstrative (ce qui fait voir qu'elles sont innées) soit en les éprouvant dans les exemples comme font les arithméticiens vulgaires. . . ." [Au.]

[20] Cf. Chomsky (1964) for additional discussion and quotations illustrating Humboldt's views on these questions. [Au.]

notion (the prevailing modern view) that language is essentially an adventitious construct, taught by "conditioning" (as would be maintained, for example, by Skinner or Quine) or by drill and explicit explanation (as was claimed by Wittgenstein), or built up by elementary "data-processing" procedures (as modern linguistics typically maintains), but, in any event, relatively independent in its structure of any innate mental faculties.

In short, empiricist speculation has characteristically assumed that only the procedures and mechanisms for the acquisition of knowledge constitute an innate property of the mind. Thus for Hume, the method of "experimental reasoning" is a basic instinct in animals and humans, on a par with the instinct "which teaches a bird, with such exactness, the art of incubation, and the whole economy and order of its nursery"—it is derived "from the original hand of nature" (Hume, 1748, § IX). The form of knowledge, however, is otherwise quite free. On the other hand, rationalist speculation has assumed that the general form of a system of knowledge is fixed in advance as a disposition of the mind, and the function of experience is to cause this general schematic structure to be realized and more fully differentiated. To follow Leibniz's enlightening analogy, we may make

> . . . the comparison of a block of marble which has veins, rather than a block of marble wholly even, or of blank tablets, i.e., of what is called among philosophers a *tabula rasa*. For if the soul resembled these blank tablets, truths would be in us as the figure of Hercules is in the marble, when the marble is wholly indifferent to the reception of this figure or some other. But if there were veins in the block which should indicate the figure of Hercules rather than other figures, this block would be more determined thereto, and Hercules would be in it as in some sense innate, although it would be needful to labor to discover these veins, to clear them by polishing, and by cutting away what prevents them from appearing. Thus it is that ideas and truths are for us innate, as inclinations, dispositions, habits, or natural potentialities, and not as actions; although these potentialities are always accompanied by some actions, often insensible, which correspond to them [Leibniz, *New Essays*, pp. 45–46].

It is not, of course, necessary to assume that empiricist and rationalist views can always be sharply distinguished and that these currents cannot cross. Nevertheless, it is historically accurate as well as heuristically valuable to distinguish these two very different approaches to the problem of acquisition of knowledge. Particular empiricist and rationalist views can be made quite precise and can then be presented as explicit hypotheses about acquisition of knowledge, in particular, about the innate structure of a language-acquisition device. In fact, it would not be inaccurate to describe the taxonomic, data-processing approach of modern linguistics as an empiricist view that contrasts with the essentially rationalist alternative proposed in recent theories of transformational grammar. Taxonomic linguistics is empiricist in its assumption that general linguistic theory consists only of a body of procedures for determining the grammar of a language from a corpus of data, the form of language being unspecified except insofar as restrictions on possible grammars are determined by this set of procedures. If we interpret taxonomic linguistics as making an empirical claim,[21] this claim must be that the grammars that result from application of the

[21] That this is a fair interpretation of taxonomic linguistics is not at all clear. For one thing, structural linguistics has rarely been concerned with the "creative" aspect of language use, which was a dominant theme in rationalistic linguistic theory. It has, in other words, given little attention to the production and interpretation of new, previously unheard sentences—that is, to the normal use of language. Thus the suggestion that the various theories of immediate constituent analysis might be interpreted as generative, phrase structure grammars (as in Chomsky, 1956, 1962*a*, or Postal, 1964*a*) certainly goes beyond what is explicitly stated by linguists who have developed these theories, and very likely beyond their intentions as well. Hence, the central problem of descriptive adequacy is not really raised within structural linguistics. Secondly, many "neo-Bloomfieldian" linguists, accepting Bloomfield's behaviorism under interpretation (*b*) of note 1 (as well as Firthians and "neo-Firthians" and many others), have thereby explicitly rejected any concern for descriptive adequacy, limiting the task of grammatical description, at least in theory, to organization of the primary linguistic data. Others have held that a grammar should at least describe the "habits" or "dispositions" of the speaker, though the sense in which language use might be regarded as a matter of habit or disposition has never been satisfactorily clarified. To be more precise, there is no clear sense of the term "habit" or "disposition" in accordance with which it would be correct to describe language as a "habit structure" or a "system of dispositions."

In general, it is not clear that most behaviorist tenden-

postulated procedures to a sufficiently rich selection of data will be descriptively adequate—in other words, that the set of procedures can be regarded as constituting a hypothesis about the innate language-acquisition system. In contrast, the discussion of language acquisition in preceding sections was rationalistic in its assumption that various formal and substantive universals are intrinsic properties of the language-acquisition system, these providing a schema that is applied to data and that determines in a highly restricted way the general form and, in part, even the substantive features of the grammar that may emerge upon presentation of appropriate data. A general linguistic theory of the sort roughly described earlier, and elaborated in more detail in the following chapters and in other studies of transformational grammar, must therefore be regarded as a specific hypothesis, of an essentially rationalist cast, as to the nature of mental structures and processes. See Chomsky (1959*b*, 1962*b*, 1964) and Katz (forthcoming) for some further discussion of this point.

When such contrasting views are clearly formulated, we may ask, as an empirical question, which (if either) is correct. There is no a priori way to settle this issue. Where empiricist and rationalist views have been presented with sufficient care so that the question of correctness can be seriously raised, it cannot, for example, be maintained that in any clear sense one is "simpler" than the other in terms of its potential physical realization,[22] and even if this could be shown, one way or the other, it would have no bearing on what is completely a factual issue. This factual question can be approached in several ways. In particular, restricting ourselves now to the question of language acquisition, we must bear in mind that any concrete empiricist proposal does impose certain conditions on the form of the grammars that can result from application of its inductive principles to primary data. We may therefore ask whether the grammars that these principles can provide, in principle, are at all close to those which we in fact discover when we investigate real languages. The same question can be asked about a concrete rationalist proposal. This has, in the past, proved to be a useful way to subject such hypotheses to one sort of empirical test.

If the answer to this question of adequacy-in-principle is positive, in either case, we can then turn to the question of feasibility: can the inductive procedures (in the empiricist case) or the mechanisms of elaboration and realization of innate schemata (in the rationalist case) succeed in producing grammars within the given constraints of time and access, and within the range of observed uniformity of output? In fact, the second question has rarely been raised in any serious way in connection with empiricist views (but cf. Miller, Galanter, and Pribram, 1960, pp. 145–148, and Miller and Chomsky, 1963, p. 430, for some comments), since study of the first question has been sufficient to rule out whatever explicit proposals of an essentially empiricist character have emerged in modern discussions of language acquisition. The only proposals that are explicit enough to support serious study are those that have been developed within taxonomic linguistics. It

cies should be regarded as varieties of empiricism at all, since, as distinct from classical empiricism, they renounce any interest in mental processes or faculties (that is, in the problems of descriptive or explanatory adequacy). [Au.]

[22] This is the only respect in which a comparison of such alternatives is relevant, apart from their relative success in accounting for the given facts of language acquisition. But this consideration apparently offers no information that has any bearing on the choice among alternative theories.

In general, it is important to bear in mind that an extremely specialized input-output relation does not necessarily presuppose a complex and highly structured device. Whether our assumption about the mind is that it contains the schema for transformational grammar or that it contains mechanisms for making arbitrary associations or for carrying out certain kinds of inductive or taxonomic operations, there is apparently little knowledge about the brain and little engineering insight into plausible physical systems that can be used to support these hypotheses. Similarly, there is no justification for the common assumption that there is an asymmetry between rationalist and empiricist views in that the former somehow beg the question, not showing how the postulated internal structure arises. Empiricist views leave open precisely the same question. For the moment, there is no better account of how the empiricist data-processing operations might have been developed, as innate structure, in a species, than there is of how the rationalist schema may arise through evolutionary processes or other determinants of the structure of organisms. Nor does comparison with species other than man help the empiricist argument. On the contrary, every known species has highly specialized cognitive capacities. It is important to observe that comparative psychology has not characteristically proceeded on empiricist assumptions about knowledge and behavior, and lends no support to these assumptions. [Au.]

seems to have been demonstrated beyond any reasonable doubt that, quite apart from any question of feasibility, methods of the sort that have been studied in taxonomic linguistics are intrinsically incapable of yielding the systems of grammatical knowledge that must be attributed to the speaker of a language (cf. Chomsky, 1956, 1957, 1964; Postal, 1962*b*, 1964*a*, 1964*c*; Katz and Postal, 1964, § 5.5, and many other publications for discussion of these questions that seems unanswerable and is, for the moment, not challenged). In general, then, it seems to me correct to say that empiricist theories about language acquisition are refutable wherever they are clear, and that further empiricist speculations have been quite empty and uninformative. On the other hand, the rationalist approach exemplified by recent work in the theory of transformational grammar seems to have proved fairly productive, to be fully in accord with what is known about language, and to offer at least some hope of providing a hypothesis about the intrinsic structure of a language-acquisition system that will meet the condition of adequacy-in-principle and do so in a sufficiently narrow and interesting way so that the question of feasibility can, for the first time, be seriously raised.

One might seek other ways of testing particular hypotheses about a language-acquisition device. A theory that attributes possession of certain linguistic universals to a language-acquisition system, as a property to be realized under appropriate external conditions, implies that only certain kinds of symbolic systems can be acquired and used as languages by this device. Others should be beyond its language-acquisition capacity. Systems can certainly be invented that fail the conditions, formal and substantive, that have been proposed as tentative linguistic universals in, for example, Jakobsonian distinctive-feature theory or the theory of transformational grammar. In principle, one might try to determine whether invented systems that fail these conditions do pose inordinately difficult problems for language learning, and do fall beyond the domain for which the language-acquisition system is designed. As a concrete example, consider the fact that, according to the theory of transformational grammar, only certain kinds of formal operations on strings can appear in grammars—operations that, furthermore, have no a priori justification. For example, the permitted operations cannot be shown in any sense to be the most "simple" or "elementary" ones that might be invented. In fact, what might in general be considered "elementary operations" on strings do not qualify as grammatical transformations at all, while many of the operations that do qualify are far from elementary, in any general sense. Specifically, grammatical transformations are necessarily "structure-dependent" in that they manipulate substrings only in terms of their assignment to categories. Thus it is possible to formulate a transformation that can insert all or part of the Auxiliary Verb to the left of a Noun Phrase that precedes it, independently of what the length or internal complexity of the strings belonging to these categories may be. It is impossible, however, to formulate as a transformation such a simple operation as reflection of an arbitrary string (that is, replacement of any string $a_1 \ldots a_n$, where each a_i is a single symbol, by $a_n \ldots a_1$), or interchange of the $(2n-1)^{th}$ word with the $2n^{th}$ word throughout a string of arbitrary length, or insertion of a symbol in the middle of a string of even length. Similarly, if the structural analyses that define transformations are restricted to Boolean conditions on *Analyzability*, as suggested later, it will be impossible to formulate many "structure-dependent" operations as transformations—for example, an operation that will iterate a symbol that is the leftmost member of a category (impossible, short of listing all categories of the grammar in the structural analysis), or an operation that will iterate a symbol that belongs to as many rightmost as leftmost categories). Hence, one who proposes this theory would have to predict that although a language might form interrogatives, for example, by interchanging the order of certain categories (as in English), it could not form interrogatives by reflection, or interchange of odd and even words, or insertion of a marker in the middle of the sentence. Many other such predictions, none of them at all obvious in any a priori sense, can be deduced from any sufficiently explicit theory of linguistic universals that is attributed to a language-acquisition device as an intrinsic property. For some initial approaches to the very difficult but tantalizing problem of investigating questions of this sort, see Miller and Stein (1963), Miller and Norman (1964).

Notice that when we maintain that a system is not learnable by a language-acquisition device that mirrors human capacities, we do not imply that this system cannot be mastered by a human in some other way, if treated as a puzzle or intellectual exercise of some sort. The language-acquisition device is only one component of the total system of intellectual structures that can be applied to problem solving and concept formation; in other words, the *faculté de langage* is only one of the faculties of the mind. What one would expect, however, is that there should be a qualitative difference in the way in which an organism with a functional language-acquisition system[23] will approach and deal with systems that are languagelike and others that are not.

The problem of mapping the intrinsic cognitive capacities of an organism and identifying the systems of belief and the organization of behavior that it can readily attain should be central to experimental psychology. However, the field has not developed in this way. Learning theory has, for the most part, concentrated on what seems a much more marginal topic, namely the question of species-independent regularities in acquisition of items of a "behavioral repertoire" under experimentally manipulable conditions. Consequently, it has necessarily directed its attention to tasks that are extrinsic to an organism's cognitive capacities—tasks that must be approached in a devious, indirect, and piecemeal fashion. In the course of this work, some incidental information has been obtained about the effect of intrinsic cognitive structure and intrinsic organization of behavior on what is learned, but this has rarely been the focus of serious attention (outside of ethology). The sporadic exceptions to this observation (see, for example, the discussion of "instinctual drift" in Breland and Breland, 1961) are quite suggestive, as are many ethological studies of lower organisms. The general question and its many ramifications, however, remain in a primitive state.

In brief, it seems clear that the present situation with regard to the study of language learning is essentially as follows. We have a certain amount of evidence about the character of the generative grammars that must be the "output" of an acquisition model for language. This evidence shows clearly that taxonomic views of linguistic structure are inadequate and that knowledge of grammatical structure cannot arise by application of step-by-step inductive operations (segmentation, classification, substitution procedures, filling of slots in frames, association, etc.) of any sort that have yet been developed within linguistics, psychology, or philosophy. Further empiricist speculations contribute nothing that even faintly suggests a way of overcoming the intrinsic limitations of the methods that have so far been proposed and elaborated. In particular, such speculations have not provided any way to account for or even to express the fundamental fact about the normal use of language, namely the speaker's ability to produce and understand instantly new sentences that are not similar to those previously heard in any physically defined sense or in terms of any notion of frames or classes of elements, nor associated with those previously heard by conditioning, nor obtainable from them by any sort of "generalization" known to psychology or philosophy. It seems plain that language acquisition is based on the child's discovery of what from a formal point of view is a deep and abstract theory—a generative grammar of his language—many of the concepts and principles of which are only remotely related to experience by long and intricate chains of unconscious quasi-inferential steps. A consideration of the character of the grammar that is acquired, the degenerate quality and narrowly limited extent of the available data, the striking uniformity of the resulting grammars, and their independence of intelligence, motivation, and emotional state, over wide ranges of variation, leave little hope that much of the structure of the language can be learned by an organism initially uninformed as to its general character.

It is, for the present, impossible to formulate an assumption about initial, innate structure rich enough to account for the fact that grammatical

[23] There is reason to believe that the language-acquisition system may be fully functional only during a "critical period" of mental development or, more specifically, that its various maturational stages (see *Aspects*, p. 206) have critical periods. See Lenneberg (forthcoming) for an important and informative review of data bearing on this question. Many other aspects of the problem of biologically given constraints on the nature of human language are discussed here and in Lenneberg (1960).

Notice that we do not, of course, imply that the functions of language acquisition are carried out by entirely separate components of the abstract mind or the physical brain, just as when one studies analyzing mechanisms in perception (cf. Sutherland, 1959, 1964), it is not implied that these are distinct and separate components of the full perceptual system. In fact, it is an important problem for psychology to determine to what extent other aspects of cognition share properties of language acquisition and language use, and to attempt, in this way, to develop a richer and more comprehensive theory of mind. [Au.]

knowledge is attained on the basis of the evidence available to the learner. Consequently, the empiricist effort to show how the assumptions about a language-acquisition device can be *reduced to a conceptual minimum*[24] is quite misplaced. The real problem is that of developing a hypothesis about initial structure that is sufficiently rich to account for acquisition of language, yet not so rich as to be inconsistent with the known diversity of language. It is a matter of no concern and of only historical interest that such a hypothesis will evidently not satisfy the preconceptions about learning that derive from centuries of empiricist doctrine. These preconceptions are not only quite implausible, to begin with, but are without factual support and are hardly consistent with what little is known about how animals or humans construct a "theory of the external world."

It is clear why the view that all knowledge derives solely from the senses by elementary operations of association and "generalization" should have had much appeal in the context of eighteenth-century struggles for scientific naturalism. However, there is surely no reason today for taking seriously a position that attributes a complex human achievement entirely to months (or at most years) of experience, rather than to millions of years of evolution or to principles of neural organization that may be even more deeply grounded in physical law—a position that would, furthermore, yield the conclusion that man is, apparently, unique among animals in the way in which he acquires knowledge. Such a position is particularly implausible with regard to language, an aspect of the child's world that is a human creation and would naturally be expected to reflect intrinsic human capacity in its internal organization.

In short, the structure of particular languages may very well be largely determined by factors over which the individual has no conscious control and concerning which society may have little choice or freedom. On the basis of the best information now available, it seems reasonable to suppose that a child cannot help constructing a particular sort of transformational grammar to account for the data presented to him, any more than he control his perception of solid objects or his attention to line and angle. Thus it may well be that the general features of language structure reflect, not so much the course of one's experience, but rather the general character of one's capacity to acquire knowledge—in the traditional sense, one's innate ideas and innate principles. It seems to me that the problem of clarifying this issue and sharpening our understanding of its many facets provides the most interesting and important reason for the study of descriptively adequate grammars and, beyond this, the formulation and justification of a general linguistic theory that meets the condition of explanatory adequacy. By pursuing this investigation, one may hope to give some real substance to the traditional belief that "the principles of grammar form an important, and very curious, part of the philosophy of the human mind" (Beattie, 1788).

[24] It is a curious fact that empiricism is commonly regarded as somehow a "scientific" philosophy. Actually, the empiricist approach to acquisition of knowledge has a certain dogmatic and aprioristic character that is largely lacking in its rationalist counterpart. In the particular case of language acquisition, the empiricist approach begins its investigation with the stipulation that certain arbitrarily selected data-processing mechanisms (e.g., principles of association, taxonomic procedures) are the only ones available to the language-acquisition device. It then investigates the application of these procedures to data, without, however, attempting to show that the result of this application corresponds to grammars that can be shown, independently, to be descriptively adequate. A nondogmatic alternative to empiricism would begin by observing that in studying language acquisition, what we are given is certain information about the primary data that are presented and the grammar that is the resulting product, and the problem we face is that of determining the structure of the device that mediates this input-output relation (the same is true of the more general problem of which language acquisition is a special case). There are no grounds for any specific assumptions, empiricist or otherwise, about the internal structure of this device. Continuing with no preconceptions, we would naturally turn to the study of uniformities in the output (formal and substantive universals), which we then must attribute to the structure of the device (or, if this can be shown, to uniformities in the input, this alternative rarely being a serious one in the cases that are of interest). This, in effect, has been the rationalist approach, and it is difficult to see what alternative there can be to it if dogmatic presuppositions as to the nature of mental processes are eliminated. [Au.]

Bibliography

Arnauld, A., and P. Nicole (1662). *La Logique, ou l'art de penser.*

Beattie, J. (1788). *Theory of Language.* London.

Bloch, B. (1950). "Studies in colloquial Japanese

IV: Phonemics." *Language, 26*, pp. 86–125. Reprinted in M. Joos (ed.), *Readings in Linguistics.* Washington, 1957.

Bloomfield, L. (1933). *Language.* New York: Holt.

Breland, K., and M. Breland (1961). "The misbehavior of organisms." *American Psychologist, 16*, pp. 681–684.

Chomsky, N. (1955). *The Logical Structure of Linguistic Theory.* Mimeographed, M.I.T. Library, Cambridge, Mass.

——— (1956). "Three models for the description of language." *I.R.E. Transactions on Information Theory,* Vol. IT-2, pp. 113–124. Reprinted, with corrections, in R. D. Luce, R. Bush, and E. Galanter (eds.), *Readings in Mathematical Psychology,* Vol. II. New York: Wiley, 1965.

——— (1957). *Syntactic Structures.* The Hague: Mouton & Co.

——— (1959*a*). "On certain formal properties of grammars." *Information and Control, 2*, pp. 137–167. Reprinted in R. D. Luce, R. Bush, and E. Galanter (eds.), *Readings in Mathematical Psychology,* Vol. II. New York: Wiley, 1965.

——— (1959*b*). Review of Skinner (1957). *Language, 35*, pp. 26–58. Reprinted in Fodor and Katz (1964).

——— (1961). "Some methodological remarks on generative grammar." *Word, 17*, pp. 219–239. Reprinted in part in Fodor and Katz (1964).

——— (1962*a*). "A transformational approach to syntax." In A. A. Hill (ed.), *Proceedings of the 1958 Conference on Problems of Linguistic Analysis in English,* pp. 124–148. Austin, Texas. Reprinted in Fodor and Katz (1964).

——— (1962*b*). "Explanatory models in linguistics." In E. Nagel, P. Suppes, and A. Tarski, *Logic, Methodology and Philosophy of Science.* Stanford, California: Stanford University Press.

——— (1963). "Formal properties of grammars." In R. D. Luce, R. Bush, and E. Galanter (eds.), *Handbook of Mathematical Psychology,* Vol. II, pp. 323–418. New York: Wiley.

——— (1964). *Current Issues in Linguistic Theory.* The Hague: Mouton & Co. A slightly earlier version appears in Fodor and Katz (1964). This is a revised and expanded version of a paper presented to the session "The logical basis of linguistic theory," at the Ninth International Congress of Linguists, Cambridge, Mass., 1962. It appears under the title of the session in H. Lunt (ed.), *Proceedings* of the Congress. The Hague: Mouton & Co., 1964.

——— (in press). "Topics in the theory of generative grammar." In T. A. Sebeok (ed.), *Current Trends in Linguistics.* Vol. III. *Linguistic Theory.* The Hague: Mouton & Co.

——— (forthcoming). "Cartesian Linguistics."

———, M. Halle, and F. Lukoff (1956). "On accent and juncture in English." In M. Halle, H. Lunt, and H. MacLean (eds.), *For Roman Jakobson,* pp. 65–80. The Hague: Mouton & Co.

———, and G. A. Miller (1963). "Introduction to the formal analysis of natural languages." In R. D. Luce, R. Bush, and E. Galanter (eds.), *Handbook of Mathematical Psychology,* Vol. II, pp. 269–322. New York: Wiley.

———, and M. P. Schützenberger (1963). "The algebraic theory of context-free languages." In P. Braffort and D. Hirschberg (eds.), *Computer Programming and Formal Systems,* pp. 119–161, *Studies in Logic Series.* Amsterdam: North-Holland.

Cudworth, R. (1731). *A Treatise Concerning Eternal and Immutable Morality.* Edited by E. Chandler.

Descartes, R. (1641). *Meditations.*

——— (1647). "Notes directed against a certain programme." Both works by Descartes translated by E. S. Haldane and G. T. Ross in *The Philosophical Works of Descartes,* Vol. I. New York: Dover, 1955.

Diderot, D. (1751). *Lettre sur les Sourds et Muets.* Page references are to J. Assézat (ed.), *Oeuvres Complètes de Diderot,* Vol. I (1875). Paris: Garnier Frères.

Dixon, R. W. (1963). *Linguistic Science and Logic.* The Hague: Mouton & Co.

Du Marsais, C. Ch. (1729). *Les véritables principes de la grammaire.* On the dating of this manuscript, see Sahlin (1928), p. ix.

Fodor, J. A., and J. J. Katz (eds.) (1964). *The Structure of Language: Readings in the Philosophy of Language.* Englewood, Cliffs, N.J.: Prentice-Hall.

Frishkopf, L. S., and M. H. Goldstein (1963). "Responses to acoustic stimuli from single units in the eighth nerve of the bullfrog." *Journal of the Acoustical Society of America, 35*, pp. 1219–1228.

Gleason, H. A. (1961). *Introduction to Descriptive Linguistics,* second edition. New York: Holt, Rinehart & Winston.

Halle, M. (1959*a*). "Questions of linguistics." *Nuovo Cimento, 13,* pp. 494–517.

——— (1959*b*). *The Sound Pattern of Russian.* The Hague: Mouton & Co.

——— (1962*a*). "Phonology in generative grammar." *Word, 18,* pp. 54–72. Reprinted in Fodor and Katz (1964).

———, and N. Chomsky (1960). "The Morphophonemics of English." *Quarterly Progress Report,* No. 58, Research Laboratory of Electronics, M.I.T., pp. 275–281.

——— (in preparation). *The Sound Pattern of English.* New York: Harper & Row.

———, and K. Stevens (1962). "Speech recognition: a model and a program for research." *I.R.E. Transactions in Information Theory,* Vol. IT-8, pp. 155–159. Reprinted in Fodor and Katz (1964).

Herbert of Cherbury (1624). *De Veritate.* Translated by M. H. Carré (1937). University of Bristol Studies, No. 6.

Hockett, C. F. (1958). *A Course in Modern Linguistics.* New York: Macmillan.

——— (1961). "Linguistic elements and their relations." *Language, 37,* pp. 29–53.

Hubel, D. H., and T. N. Wiesel (1962). "Receptive fields, binocular interaction and functional architecture in the cat's visual cortex." *Journal of Physiology, 160,* pp. 106–154.

Hull, C. L. (1943). *Principles of Behavior.* New York: Appleton-Century-Crofts.

Humboldt, W. von. (1836). *Über die Verschiedenheit des Menschlichen Sprachbaues.* Berlin.

Hume, D. (1748). *An Enquiry Concerning Human Understanding.*

Katz, J. J. (1964*a*). "Semi-sentences." In Fodor and Katz (1964).

——— (1964*b*). "Analyticity and contradiction in natural language." In Fodor and Katz (1964).

——— (1964*c*). "Mentalism in linguistics." *Language, 40,* pp. 124–137.

——— (1964*d*). "Semantic theory and the meaning of 'good.'" *Journal of Philosophy.*

——— (forthcoming). "Innate ideas."

———, and J. A. Fodor. "The structure of a semantic theory." *Language, 39,* pp. 170–210. Reprinted in Fodor & Katz (1964).

———, and J. A. Fodor (1964). "A reply to Dixon's 'A trend in semantics.'" *Linguistics, 3,* pp. 19–29.

———, and P. Postal (1964). *An Integrated Theory of Linguistic Descriptions.* Cambridge, Mass.: M.I.T. Press.

Lancelot, C., and A. Arnauld, *et al.* (1660). *Grammaire générale et raisonnée.*

Leibniz, G. W. *New Essays Concerning Human Understanding.* Translated by A. G. Langley. LaSalle, Ill.: Open Court, 1949.

Leitzmann, A. (1908). *Briefwechsel zwischen W. von Humboldt und A. W. Schlegel.* Halle: Niemeyer.

Lemmon, W. B., and G. H. Patterson (1964). "Depth perception in sheep." *Science, 145,* p. 835.

Lenneberg, E. (1960). "Language, evolution, and purposive behavior." In S. Diamond (ed.), *Culture in History: Essays in Honor of Paul Radin.* New York: Columbia University Press. Reprinted in a revised and extended version under the title "The capacity for language acquisition" in Fodor and Katz (1964).

——— (in preparation). *The Biological Bases of Language.*

Lettvin, J. Y., H. R. Maturana, W. S. McCulloch, and W. H. Pitts (1959). "What the frog's eye tells the frog's brain." *Proceedings of the I.R.E., 47,* pp. 1940–1951.

Miller, G. A., and N. Chomsky (1963). "Finitary models of language users." In R. D. Luce, R. Bush, and E. Galanter (eds.), *Handbook of Mathematical Psychology,* Vol. II, Ch. 13, pp. 419–492. New York: Wiley.

———, E. Galanter, and K. H. Pribram (1960). *Plans and the Structure of Behavior.* New York: Henry Holt.

———, and S. Isard (1963). "Some perceptual consequences of linguistic rules." *Journal of Verbal Learning and Verbal Behaviour,* 2, No. 3; pp. 217–220.

———, and S. Isard (1964). "Free recall of self-embedded English sentences." *Information and Control, 7,* pp. 292–303.

———, and D. A. Norman (1964). *Research on the Use of Formal Languages in the Behavioral Sciences.* Semi-annual Technical Report, Department of Defense, Advanced Research Projects Agency, January–June 1964, pp. 10–11. Cambridge: Harvard University, Center for Cognitive Studies.

——, and M. Stein (1963). *Grammarama.* Scientific Report No. CS-2, December. Cambridge: Harvard University, Center for Cognitive Studies.

Postal, P. M. (1962*a*). *Some Syntactic Rules in Mohawk.* Unpublished doctoral dissertation, New Haven, Yale University.

—— (1962*b*). "On the limitations of context-free phrase-structure description." *Quarterly Progress Report* No. 64, Research Laboratory of Electronics, M.I.T., pp. 231–238.

—— (1964*a*). *Constituent Structure: A Study of Contemporary Models of Syntactic Description.* The Hague: Mouton & Co.

—— (1964*b*). "Underlying and superficial linguistic structure." *Harvard Educational Review, 34*, pp. 246–266.

—— (1964*c*). "Limitations of phrase structure grammars." In Fodor and Katz (1964).

Quine, W. V. (1960). *Word and Object.* Cambridge, Mass.: M.I.T. Press, and New York: Wiley.

Reid, T. (1785). *Essays on the Intellectual Powers of Man.* Page references are to the abridged edition by A. D. Woozley, 1941. London: Macmillan and Co.

Ryle, G. (1931). "Systematically misleading expressions." *Proceedings of the Aristotelian Society.* Reprinted in A. G. N. Flew (ed.), *Logic and Language,* 1st. ser. Oxford: Blackwell, 1951.

—— (1953). "Ordinary language." *Philosophical Review,* 62, pp. 167–186.

Sahlin, G. (1928). *César Chesneau du Marsais et son rôle dans l'évolution de la grammaire générale.* Paris: Presses Universitaires.

Skinner, B. F. (1957). *Verbal Behavior.* New York: Appleton-Century-Crofts.

Sutherland, N. S. (1959). "Stimulus analyzing mechanisms." *Mechanization of Thought Processes,* Vol. II, National Physical Laboratory No. 10, London.

—— (1964). "Visual discrimination in animals." *British Medical Bulletin,* 20, pp. 54–59.

Twaddell, W. F. (1935). *On Defining the Phoneme. Language Monograph No. 16.* Reprinted in part in M. Joos (ed.), *Readings in Linguistics.* Washington: 1957.

Uhlenbeck, E. M. (1963). "An appraisal of transformation theory." *Lingua, 12*, pp. 1–18.

—— (1964). Discussion in the session "Logical basis of linguistic theory." In H. Lunt (ed.) *Proceedings of the Ninth Congress of Linguists,* pp. 981–983. The Hague: Mouton & Co.

Wittgenstein, L. (1953). *Philosophical Investigations.* Oxford: Blackwell's.

John R. Searle

b. 1932

WHILE MUCH of the interest in the idea of "speech acts" is diagnostic and taxonomic, in the effort to understand the purport and structure of ordinary language John R. Searle has developed the idea of speech acts with the intent of making it fit more precisely with other concerns of analytical philosophy, especially the relation of the speech act to propositions and descriptions, on the one hand, and general problems concerning the nature of human action, on the other.

In "What Is a Speech Act?" reprinted here, Searle develops a single case of an "illocutionary" act, as described by *J. L. Austin,* specifically the act of "promising." While the argument itself is meant as an example only (and, as such, is vulnerable to counterexamples), it illustrates how specific speech acts can be partially formalized according to necessary and sufficient conditions. Here, as in his book *Speech Acts: An Essay in the Philosophy of Language* (1969), Searle is particularly concerned to reconfigure philosophical problems, such that the methods of Austin and other ordinary language philosophers apply more felicitously without shifting attention away from the problem itself. Like *Stanley Cavell,* Searle is especially sensitive to the relation between philosophical method and content.

In *Speech Acts,* for example, Searle shows that such problems as "reference," "predication," and "description" are all directly tied to speech acts; and any philosophical analysis that presumes that a "reference" can be wholly dissociated from some referring expression and an act in which such an expression is produced and used invites its own confusion.

For literary critics, Searle's work has been of special interest on the distinction between regulative and constitutive rules (that is, rules such as speed limits or dress codes regulate behavior, while rules pertaining to such things as "touchdowns" in football or "checkmate" in chess constitute the thing they cover) and "brute" versus institutional facts in speech acts. According to Searle, brute facts are generally those that do not depend on specific kinds of human transactions, as, for example, in saying that "The large stone is to the left of the smaller stone"; institutional facts are the result of systems of constitutive rules, as, for example, when one says "These people are married" or "The Giants beat the Dodgers 3 to 1." Literary texts, for example, can be viewed as either "parasitic" on other acts of speech (but conforming to some of the rules relevant to speech acts in general) or as part of a set of institutional facts within which the production of a "poem" is itself a kind of speech act. While Searle has generally taken the former view (that literature is parasitic on normal speech acts, as, for example, when a pastor in a novel marries a couple, no one is actually married since the language of the marriage ceremony in the novel depends on there being such ceremonies outside the context of the fiction), his efforts to make the development of analytical procedures more exacting and precise are particularly important.

Searle's major works include *Speech Acts: An Essay in the Philosophy of Language* (1969); ed., *The Philosophy of Speech Acts* (1972). Of special interest are his two essays, "The Logical Status of Fictional Discourse," *New Literary History* 6 (1975), and his article on *Derrida,* "Reiterating the Differences," in *Glyph 1* (1977). For specifically literary applications of speech act philosophy, see Mary Louise Pratt, *Toward a Speech Act Theory of Literary Discourse* (1977).

WHAT IS A SPEECH ACT?

I. Introduction

In a typical speech situation involving a speaker, a hearer, and an utterance by the speaker, there are many kinds of acts associated with the speaker's utterance. The speaker will characteristically have moved his jaw and tongue and made noises. In addition, he will characteristically have performed some acts within the class which includes informing or irritating or boring his hearers; he will further characteristically have performed some acts within the class which includes referring to Kennedy or Khruschchev or the North Pole; and he will also have performed acts within the class which includes making statements, asking questions, issuing commands, giving reports, greeting, and warning. The members of this last class are what Austin[1] called illocutionary acts and it is with this class that I shall be concerned in this paper, so the paper might have been called 'What is an Illocutionary Act?' I do not attempt to define the expression 'illocutionary act', although if my analysis of a particular illocutionary act succeeds it may provide the basis for a definition. Some of the English verbs and verb phrases associated with illocutionary acts are: state, assert, describe, warn, remark, comment, command, order, request, criticize, apologize, censure, approve, welcome, promise, express approval, and express regret. Austin claimed that there were over a thousand such expressions in English.

By way of introduction, perhaps I can say why I think it is of interest and importance in the philosophy of language to study speech acts, or, as they are sometimes called, language acts or linguistic acts. I think it is essential to any specimen of linguistic communication that it involve a linguistic act. It is not, as has generally been supposed, the symbol or word or sentence, or even the token of the symbol or word or sentence, which is the unit of linguistic communication, but rather it is the *production* of the token in the performance of the speech act that constitutes the basic unit of linguistic communication. To put this point more precisely, the production of the sentence token under certain conditions is the illocutionary act, and the illocutionary act is the minimal unit of linguistic communication.

I do not know how to *prove* that linguistic communication essentially involves acts but I can think of arguments with which one might attempt to convince someone who was sceptical. One argument would be to call the sceptic's attention to the fact that when he takes a noise or a mark on paper to be an instance of linguistic communication, as a message, one of the things that is involved in his so taking that noise or mark is that he should regard it as having been produced by a being with certain intentions. He cannot just regard it as a natural phe-

WHAT IS A SPEECH ACT? first appeared in *Philosophy in America,* ed. Max Black, published by George Allen & Unwin, Ltd., copyright 1965. It is reprinted by permission of the publishers.

[1] J. L. Austin, *How To Do Things with Words* (Oxford, 1962). [Au.] (See *Austin*). [Eds.]

nomenon, like a stone, a waterfall, or a tree. In order to regard it as an instance of linguistic communication one must suppose that its production is what I am calling a speech act. It is a logical presupposition, for example, of current attempts to decipher the Mayan hieroglyphs that we at least hypothesize that the marks we see on the stones were produced by beings more or less like ourselves and produced with certain kinds of intentions. If we were certain the marks were a consequence of, say, water erosion, then the question of deciphering them or even calling them hieroglyphs could not arise. To construe them under the category of linguistic communication necessarily involves construing their production as speech acts.

To perform illocutionary acts is to engage in a rule-governed form of behaviour. I shall argue that such things as asking questions or making statements are rule-governed in ways quite similar to those in which getting a base hit in baseball or moving a knight in chess are rule-governed forms of acts. I intend therefore to explicate the notion of an illocutionary act by stating a set of necessary and sufficient conditions for the performance of a particular kind of illocutionary act, and extracting from it a set of semantical rules for the use of the expression (or syntactic device) which marks the utterance as an illocutionary act of that kind. If I am successful in stating the conditions and the corresponding rules for even one kind of illocutionary act, that will provide us with a pattern for analysing other kinds of acts and consequently for explicating the notion in general. But in order to set the stage for actually stating conditions and extracting rules for performing an illocutionary act I have to discuss three other preliminary notions: *rules, propositions,* and *meaning*. I shall confine my discussion of these notions to those aspects which are essential to my main purposes in this paper, but, even so, what I wish to say concerning each of these notions, if it were to be at all complete, would require a paper for each; however, sometimes it may be worth sacrificing thoroughness for the sake of scope and I shall therefore be very brief.

II. Rules

In recent years there has been in the philosophy of language considerable discussion involving the notion of rules for the use of expressions. Some philosophers have even said that knowing the meaning of the word is simply a matter of knowing the rules for its use or employment.[2] One disquieting feature of such discussions is that no philosopher, to my knowledge at least, has ever given anything like an adequate formulation of the rules for the use of even one expression. If meaning is a matter of rules of use, surely we ought to be able to state the rules for the use of expressions in a way which would explicate the meaning of those expressions. Certain other philosophers, dismayed perhaps by the failure of their colleagues to produce any rules, have denied the fashionable view that meaning is a matter of rules and have asserted that there are no semantical rules of the proposed kind at all. I am inclined to think that this scepticism is premature and stems from a failure to distinguish different sorts of rules, in a way which I shall now attempt to explain.

I distinguish between two sorts of rules: Some regulate antecedently existing forms of behaviour; for example, the rules of etiquette regulate interpersonal relationships, but these relationships exist independently of the rules of etiquette. Some rules on the other hand do not merely regulate but create or define new forms of behaviour. The rules of football, for example, do not merely regulate the game of football but as it were create the possibility of or define that activity. The activity of playing football is constituted by acting in accordance with these rules; football has no existence apart from these rules. I call the latter kind of rules constitutive rules and the former kind regulative rules. Regulative rules regulate a pre-existing activity, an activity whose existence is logically independent of the existence of the rules. Constitutive rules constitute (and also regulate) an activity the existence of which is logically dependent on the rules.[3]

Regulative rules characteristically take the form of or can be paraphrased as imperatives, e.g. 'When

[2] This view is generally derived from *Wittgenstein*. For an introduction to this controversial issue, see Donald Davidson, "Truth and Meaning," *Synthèse* 17 (1967): 304–23; reprinted in J. Rosenberg and C. Travis, eds., *Readings in the Philosophy of Language* (Englewood Cliffs, NJ: Prentice-Hall, 1971). In Rosenberg and Travis, see also Paul Ziff, "About What an Adequate Grammar Couldn't Do," pp. 548–56, and L. Jonathan Cohen, "Do Illocutionary Forces Exist?" pp. 580–99. [Eds.]

[3] This distinction occurs in J. Rawls, "Two Concepts of Rules", *Philosophical Review*, 1955, and J. R. Searle, "How to Derive 'Ought' from 'Is'", *Philosophical Review* 1964. [Au.]

cutting food hold the knife in the right hand,' or 'Officers are to wear ties to dinner'. Some constitutive rules take quite a different form, e.g. a checkmate is made if the king is attacked in such a way that no move will leave it unattacked; a touchdown is scored when a player crosses the opponents' goal line in possession of the ball while play is in progress. If our paradigms of rules are imperative regulative rules, such non-imperative constitutive rules are likely to strike us as extremely curious and hardly even as rules at all. Notice that they are almost tautological in character, for what the 'rule' seems to offer is a partial definition of 'checkmate' or 'touchdown'. But, of course, this quasi-tautological character is a necessary consequence of their being constitutive rules: the rules concerning touchdowns must define the notion of 'touchdown' in the same way that the rules concerning football define 'football'. That, for example, a touchdown can be scored in such and such ways and counts six points can appear sometimes as a rule, sometimes as an analytic truth; and that it can be construed as a tautology is a clue to the fact that the rule in question is a constitutive one. Regulative rules generally have the form 'Do *X*' or 'If *Y* do *X*'. Some members of the set of constitutive rules have this form but some also have the form '*X* counts as *Y*'.[4]

The failure to perceive this is of some importance in philosophy. Thus, e.g., some philosophers ask 'How can a promise create an obligation?' A similar question would be 'How can a touchdown create six points?' And as they stand both questions can only be answered by stating a rule of the form '*X* counts as *Y*'.

I am inclined to think that both the failure of some philosophers to state rules for the use of expressions and the scepticism of other philosophers concerning the existence of any such rules stem at least in part from a failure to recognize the distinctions between constitutive and regulative rules. The model or paradigm of a rule which most philosophers have is that of a regulative rule, and if one looks in semantics for purely regulative rules one is not likely to find anything interesting from the point of view of logical analysis. There are no doubt social rules of the form 'One ought not to utter obscenities at formal gatherings,' but that hardly seems a rule of the sort that is crucial in explicating the semantics of a language. The hypothesis that lies behind the present paper is that the semantics of a language can be regarded as a series of systems of constitutive rules and that illocutionary acts are acts performed in accordance with these sets of constitutive rules. One of the aims of this paper is to formulate a set of constitutive rules for a certain kind of speech act. And if what I have said concerning constitutive rules is correct, we should not be surprised if not all these rules take the form of imperative rules. Indeed we shall see that the rules fall into several different categories, none of which is quite like the rules of etiquette. The effort to state the rules for an illocutionary act can also be regarded as a kind of test of the hypothesis that there are constitutive rules underlying speech acts. If we are unable to give any satisfactory rule formulations, our failure could be construed as partially disconfirming evidence against the hypothesis.

[4]The formulation 'X counts as Y' was originally suggested to me by Max Black. [Au.]

III. PROPOSITIONS

Different illocutionary acts often have features in common with each other. Consider utterances of the following sentences:

(1) Will John leave the room?
(2) John will leave the room.
(3) John, leave the room!
(4) Would that John left the room.
(5) If John will leave the room, I will leave also.

Utterances of each of these on a given occasion would characteristically be performances of different illocutionary acts. The first would, characteristically, be a question, the second an assertion about the future, that is, a prediction, the third a request or order, the fourth an expression of a wish, and the fifth a hypothetical expression of intention. Yet in the performance of each the speaker would characteristically perform some subsidiary acts which are common to all five illocutionary acts. In the utterance of each the speaker *refers* to a particular person John and *predicates* the act of leaving the room of that person. In no case is that all he does, but in every case it is a part of what he does. I shall say, therefore, that in each of these cases, although the illocutionary acts are different, at least some of the non-illocutionary acts of reference and predication are the same.

The reference to some person John and predication of the same thing of him in each of these illocutionary acts inclines me to say that there is a common *content* in each of them. Something expressible by the clause 'that John will leave the room' seems to be a common feature of all. We could, with not too much distortion, write each of these sentences in a way which would isolate this common feature: 'I assert that John will leave the room', 'I ask whether John will leave the room', etc.

For lack of a better word I propose to call this common content a proposition, and I shall describe this feature of these illocutionary acts by saying that in the utterance of each of (1)–(5) the speaker expresses the proposition that John will leave the room. Notice that I do not say that the sentence expresses the proposition; I do not know how sentences could perform acts of that kind. But I shall say that in the utterance of the sentence the speaker expresses a proposition. Notice also that I am distinguishing between a proposition and an assertion or statement of that proposition. The proposition that John will leave the room is expressed in the utterance of all of (1)–(5) but only in (2) is that proposition asserted. An assertion is an illocutionary act, but a proposition is not an act at all, although the act of expressing a proposition is a part of performing certain illocutionary acts.

I might summarize this by saying that I am distinguishing between the illocutionary act and the propositional content of an illocutionary act. Of course, not all illocutionary acts have a propositional content, for example, an utterance of 'Hurrah!' or 'Ouch!' does not. In one version or another this distinction is an old one and has been marked in different ways by authors as diverse as Frege, Sheffer, Lewis, Reichenbach and Hare, to mention only a few.[5]

From a semantical point of view we can distinguish between the propositional indicator in the sentence and the indicator of illocutionary force. That is, for a large class of sentences used to perform illocutionary acts, we can say for the purpose of our analysis that the sentence has two (not necessarily separate) parts, the proposition-indicating element and the function-indicating device.[6] The function-indicating device shows how the proposition is to be taken, or, to put it in another way, what illocutionary force the utterance is to have, that is, what illocutionary act the speaker is performing in the utterance of the sentence. Function-indicating devices in English include word order, stress, intonation contour, punctuation, the mood of the verb, and finally a set of so-called performative verbs: I may indicate the kind of illocutionary act I am performing by beginning the sentence with 'I apologize,' 'I warn', 'I state', etc. Often in actual speech situations the context will make it clear what the illocutionary force of the utterance is, without its being necessary to invoke the appropriate function indicating device.

If this semantical distinction is of any real importance, it seems likely that it should have some syntactical analogue, and certain recent developments in transformational grammar tend to support the view that it does. In the underlying phrase marker of a sentence there is a distinction between those elements which correspond to the function-indicating device and those which correspond to the propositional content.

The distinction between the function-indicating device and the proposition-indicating device will prove very useful to us in giving an analysis of an illocutionary act. Since the same proposition can be common to all sorts of illocutionary acts, we can separate our analysis of the proposition from our analysis of kinds of illocutionary acts. I think there are rules for expressing propositions, rules for such things as reference and prediction, but those rules can be discussed independently of the rules for function indicating. In this paper I shall not attempt to discuss propositional rules but shall concentrate on rules for using certain kinds of function-indicating devices.

[5] See, for example, *Frege*, "On Sense and Meaning"; C. I. Lewis, *Modes of Knowledge and Valuation* (LaSalle, IL: Open Court Publishing Co., 1946), esp. chap. 3; Hans Reichenbach, *Elements of Symbolic Logic* (New York: Macmillan, 1947). See also Bertrand Russell's important discussion of "propositional functions" in *Introduction to Mathematical Philosophy* (London: Allen & Unwin, 1919) and Peter Geach, "Russell's Theory of Descriptions," *Analysis* 10 (1950): 84–88. [Eds.]

[6] In the sentence, 'I promise that I will come' the function-indicating device and the propositional element are separate. In the sentence 'I promise to come', which means the same as the first and is derived from it by certain transformations, the two elements are not separate. [Au.]

IV. MEANING

Speech acts are characteristically performed in the utterance of sounds or the making of marks. What is the difference between *just* uttering sounds or making marks and performing a speech act? One difference is that the sounds or marks one makes in the performance of a speech act are characteristically said to *have meaning*, and a second related difference is that one is characteristically said to *mean something* by those sounds or marks. Characteristically when one speaks one means something by what one says, and what one says, the string of morphemes that one emits, is characteristically said to have a meaning. Here, incidentally, is another point at which our analogy between performing speech acts and playing games breaks down. The pieces in a game like chess are not characteristically said to have a meaning, and furthermore when one makes a move one is not characteristically said to mean anything by that move.

But what is it for one to mean something by what one says, and what is it for something to have a meaning? To answer the first of these questions I propose to borrow and revise some ideas of Paul Grice. In an article entitled 'Meaning',[7] Grice gives the following analysis of one sense of the notion of 'meaning'. To say that *A* meant something by *x* is to say that '*A* intended the utterance of *x* to produce some effect in an audience by means of the recognition of this intention.' This seems to me a useful start on an analysis of meaning, first because it shows the close relationship between the notion of meaning and the notion of intention, and secondly because it captures something which is, I think, essential to speaking a language: In speaking a language I attempt to communicate things to my hearer by means of getting him to recognize my intention to communicate just those things. For example, characteristically, when I make an assertion, I attempt to communicate to and convince my hearer of the truth of a certain proposition; and the means I employ to do this are to utter certain sounds, which utterance I intend to produce in him the desired effect by means of his recognition of my intention to produce just that effect. I shall illustrate this with an example. I might on the one hand attempt to get you to believe that I am French by speaking French all the time, dressing in the French manner, showing wild enthusiasm for de Gaulle, and cultivating French acquaintances. But I might on the other hand attempt to get you to believe that I am French by simply telling you that I am French. Now, what is the difference between these two ways of my attempting to get you to believe that I am French? One crucial difference is that in the second case I attempt to get you to believe that I am French by getting you to recognize that it is my purported intention to get you to believe just that. That is one of the things involved in telling you that I am French. But of course if I try to get you to believe that I am French by putting on the act I described, then your recognition of my intention to produce in you the belief that I am French is not the means I am employing. Indeed in this case you would, I think, become rather suspicious if you recognized my intention.

However valuable this analysis of meaning is, it seems to me to be in certain respects defective. First of all, it fails to distinguish the different kinds of effects—perlocutionary versus illocutionary—that one may intend to produce in one's hearers, and it further fails to show the way in which these different kinds of effects are related to the notion of meaning. A second defect is that it fails to account for the extent to which meaning is a matter of rules or conventions. That is, this account of meaning does not show the connection between one's meaning something by what one says and what that which one says actually means in the language. In order to illustrate this point I now wish to present a counter-example to this analysis of meaning. The point of the counter-example will be to illustrate the connection between what a speaker means and what the words he utters mean.

Suppose that I am an American soldier in the Second World War and that I am captured by Italian troops. And suppose also that I wish to get these troops to believe that I am a German officer in order to get them to release me. What I would like to do is to tell them in German or Italian that I am a German officer. But let us suppose I don't know enough German or Italian to do that. So I, as it were, attempt to put on a show of telling them that I am a German officer by reciting those few bits of German that I know, trusting that they don't know enough German to see through my plan. Let us suppose I know only one line of German, which I remember

[7] *Philosophical Review*, 1957. [Au.]

from a poem I had to memorize in a high-school German course. Therefore I, a captured American, address my Italian captors with the following sentence: 'Kennst du das Land, wo die Zitronen blühen?' Now, let us describe the situation in Gricean terms. I intend to produce a certain effect in them, namely, the effect of believing that I am a German officer; and I intend to produce this effect by means of their recognition of my intention. I intend that they should think that what I am trying to tell them is that I am a German officer. But does it follow from this account that when I say 'Kennst du das Land . . .' etc., what I mean is, 'I am a German officer'? Not only does it not follow, but in this case it seems plainly false that when I utter the German sentence what I mean is 'I am a German officer', or even 'Ich bin ein deutscher Offizier', because what the words mean is, 'Knowest thou the land where the lemon trees bloom?' Of course, I want my captors to be deceived into thinking that what I mean is 'I am a German officer', but part of what is involved in the deception is getting them to think that that is what the words which I utter mean in German. At one point in the *Philosophical Investigations* Wittgenstein says 'Say "it's cold here" and mean "it's warm here"'.[8] The reason we are unable to do this is that what we can mean is a function of what we are saying. Meaning is more than a matter of intention, it is also a matter of convention.

Grice's account can be amended to deal with counter-examples of this kind. We have here a case where I am trying to produce a certain effect by means of the recognition of my intention to produce that effect, but the device I use to produce this effect is one which is conventionally, by the rules governing the use of that device, used as a means of producing quite different illocutionary effects. We must therefore reformulate the Gricean account of meaning in such a way as to make it clear that one's meaning something when one says something is more than just contingently related to what the sentence means in the language one is speaking. In our analysis of illocutionary acts, we must capture both the intentional and the conventional aspects and especially the relationship between them. In the performance of an illocutionary act the speaker intends to produce a certain effect by means of getting the hearer to recognize his intention to produce that effect, and furthermore, if he is using words literally, he intends this recognition to be achieved in virtue of the fact that the rules for using the expressions he utters associate the expressions with the production of that effect. It is this *combination* of elements which we shall need to express in our analysis of the illocutionary act.

V. How to Promise

I shall now attempt to give an analysis of the illocutionary act of promising. In order to do this I shall ask what conditions are necessary and sufficient for the act of promising to have been performed in the utterance of a given sentence. I shall attempt to answer this question by stating these conditions as a set of propositions such that the conjunction of the members of the set entails the proposition that a speaker made a promise, and the proposition that the speaker made a promise entails this conjunction. Thus each condition will be a necessary condition for the performance of the act of promising and taken collectively the set of conditions will be a sufficient condition for the act to have been performed.

If we get such a set of conditions we can extract from them a set of rules for the use of the function-indicating device. The method here is analogous to discovering the rules of chess by asking oneself what are the necessary and sufficient conditions under which one can be said to have correctly moved a knight or castled or checkmated a player, etc. We are in the position of someone who has learned to play chess without ever having the rules formulated and who wants such a formulation. We learned how to play the game of illocutionary acts, but in general it was done without an explicit formulation of the rules, and the first step in getting such a formulation is to set out the conditions for the performance of a particular illocutionary act. Our inquiry will therefore serve a double philosophical purpose. By stating a set of conditions for the performance of a particular illocutionary act we shall have offered a partial explication of that notion and shall also have paved the way for the second step, the formulation of the rules.

I find the statement of the conditions very difficult to do, and I am not entirely satisfied with the

[8] *Philosophical Investigations* (Oxford, 1953), para. 510. [Au.]

list I am about to present. One reason for the difficulty is that the notion of a promise, like most notions in ordinary language, does not have absolutely strict rules. There are all sorts of odd, deviant, and borderline promises; and counter-examples, more or less bizarre, can be produced against my analysis. I am inclined to think we shall not be able to get a set of knock-down necessary and sufficient conditions that will exactly mirror the ordinary use of the word 'promise.' I am confining my discussion, therefore, to the centre of the concept of promising and ignoring the fringe, borderline, and partially defective cases. I also confine my discussion to full-blown explicit promises and ignore promises made by elliptical turns of phrase, hints, metaphors, etc.

Another difficulty arises from my desire to state the conditions without certain forms of circularity. I want to give a list of conditions for the performance of a certain illocutionary act, which do not themselves mention the performance of any illocutionary acts. I need to satisfy this condition in order to offer an explication of the notion of an illocutionary act in general, otherwise I should simply be showing the relation between different illocutionary acts. However, although there will be no reference to illocutionary *acts,* certain illocutionary *concepts* will appear in the analysans as well as in the analysandum; and I think this form of circularity is unavoidable because of the nature of constitutive rules.

In the presentation of the conditions I shall first consider the case of a sincere promise and then show how to modify the conditions to allow for insincere promises. As our inquiry is semantical rather than syntactical, I shall simply assume the existence of grammatically well-formed sentences.

Given that a speaker *S* utters a sentence *T* in the presence of a hearer *H,* then, in the utterance of *T, S* sincerely (and non-defectively) promises that *p* to *H* if and only if:

(1) *Normal input and output conditions obtain.*

I use the terms 'input' and 'output' to cover the large and indefinite range of conditions under which any kind of serious linguistic communication is possible. 'Output' covers the conditions for intelligible speaking and 'input' covers the conditions for understanding. Together they include such things as that the speaker and hearer both know how to speak the language; both are conscious of what they are doing; the speaker is not acting under duress or threats; they have no physical impediments to communication, such as deafness, aphasia, or laryngitis; they are not acting in a play or telling jokes, etc.

(2) *S expresses that p in the utterance of T.*

This condition isolates the propositional content from the rest of the speech act and enables us to concentrate on the peculiarities of promising in the rest of the analysis.

(3) *In expressing that p, S predicates a future act A of S.*

In the case of promising the function-indicating device is an expression whose scope includes certain features of the proposition. In a promise an act must be predicated of the speaker and it cannot be a past act. I cannot promise to have done something, and I cannot promise that someone else will do something. (Although I can promise to see that he will do it.) The notion of an act, as I am construing it for present purposes, includes refraining from acts, performing series of acts, and may also include states and conditions: I may promise not to do something, I may promise to do something repeatedly, and I may promise to be or remain in a certain state or condition. I call conditions (2) and (3) the *propositional content conditions.*

(4) *H would prefer S's doing A to his not doing A, and S believes H would prefer his doing A to his not doing A.*

One crucial distinction between promises on the one hand and threats on the other is that a promise is a pledge to do something for you, not to you, but a threat is a pledge to do something to you, not for you. A promise is defective if the thing promised is something the promisee does not want done; and it is further defective if the promisor does not believe the promisee wants it done, since a non-defective promise must be intended as a promise and not as a threat or warning. I think both halves of this double condition are necessary in order to avoid fairly obvious counter-examples.

One can, however, think of apparent counter-examples to this condition as stated. Suppose I say to a lazy student 'If you don't hand in your paper on time I promise you I will give you a failing grade in the course'. Is this utterance a promise? I am inclined to think not; we would more naturally describe it as a warning or possibly even a threat. But why then is it possible to use the locution 'I promise' in such a case? I think we use it here because 'I promise' and 'I hereby promise' are among the strongest function-indicating devices for *commitment* provided by the English language. For that reason we often use these expressions in the performance of speech acts which are not strictly speaking promises but in which we wish to emphasize our commitment. To illustrate this, consider another apparent counter-example to the analysis along different lines. Sometimes, more commonly I think in the United States than in England, one hears people say 'I promise' when making an emphatic assertion. Suppose, for example, I accuse you of having stolen the money. I say, 'You stole that money, didn't you?' You reply 'No, I didn't, I promise you I didn't.' Did you make a promise in this case? I find it very unnatural to describe your utterance as a promise. This utterance would be more aptly described as an emphatic denial, and we can explain the occurrence of the function-indicating device 'I promise' as derivative from genuine promises and serving here as an expression adding emphasis to your denial.

In general the point stated in condition (4) is that if a purported promise is to be non-defective the thing promised must be something the hearer wants done, or considers to be in his interest, or would prefer being done to not being done, etc.; and the speaker must be aware of or believe or know, etc., that this is the case. I think a more elegant and exact formulation of this condition would require the introduction of technical terminology.

(5) *It is not obvious to both S and H that S will do A in the normal course of events.*

This condition is an instance of a general condition on many different kinds of illocutionary acts to the effect that the act must have a point. For example, if I make a request to someone to do something which it is obvious that he is already doing or is about to do, then my request is pointless and to that extent defective. In an actual speech situation, listeners, knowing the rules for performing illocutionary acts, will assume that this condition is satisfied. Suppose, for example, that in the course of a public speech I say to a member of my audience 'Look here, Smith, pay attention to what I am saying'. In order to make sense of this utterance the audience will have to assume that Smith has not been paying attention or at any rate that it is not obvious that he has been paying attention, that the question of his paying attention has arisen in some way; because a condition for making a request is that it is not obvious that the hearer is doing or about to do the thing requested.

Similarly with promises. It is out of order for me to promise to do something that it is obvious I am going to do anyhow. If I do seem to be making such a promise, the only way my audience can make sense of my utterance is to assume that I believe that it is not obvious that I am going to do the thing promised. A happily married man who promises his wife he will not desert her in the next week is likely to provide more anxiety than comfort.

Parenthetically I think this condition is an instance of the sort of phenomenon stated in Zipf's law.[9] I think there is operating in our language, as in most forms of human behaviour, a principle of least effort, in this case a principle of maximum illocutionary ends with minimum phonetic effort; and I think condition (5) is an instance of it.

I call conditions such as (4) and (5) *preparatory conditions*. They are *sine quibus non* of happy promising, but they do not yet state the essential feature.

(6) *S intends to do A.*

The most important distinction between sincere and insincere promises is that in the case of the sincere promise the speaker intends to do the act promised, in the case of the insincere promise he does not intend to do the act. Also in sincere promises the speaker believes it is possible for him to do the act (or refrain from doing it), but I think the proposition that he intends to do it entails that he thinks it is possible to do (or refrain from doing) it, so I am not stating that as an extra condition. I call this condition the *sincerity condition*.

(7) *S intends that the utterance of T will place him under an obligation to do A.*

The essential feature of a promise is that it is the undertaking of an obligation to perform a certain act. I think that this condition distinguishes promises

[9] Cf. George Kingsley Zipf [1902–50], *Human Behavior and the Principle of Least Effort: An Introduction to Human Ecology* (Cambridge, MA: Addison-Wesley Press, 1949). [Eds.]

(and other members of the same family such as vows) from other kinds of speech acts. Notice that in the statement of the condition we only specify the speaker's intention; further conditions will make clear how that intention is realized. It is clear, however, that having this intention is a necessary condition of making a promise; for if a speaker can demonstrate that he did not have this intention in a given utterance, he can prove that the utterance was not a promise. We know, for example, that Mr. Pickwick did not promise to marry the woman because we know he did not have the appropriate intention.

I call this the *essential condition.*

(8) *S intends that the utterance of T will produce in H a belief that conditions (6) and (7) obtain by means of the recognition of the intention to produce that belief, and he intends this recognition to be achieved by means of the recognition of the sentence as one conventionally used to produce such beliefs.*

This captures our amended Gricean analysis of what it is for the speaker to mean to make a promise. The speaker intends to produce a certain illocutionary effect by means of getting the hearer to recognize his intention to produce that effect, and he also intends this recognition to be achieved in virtue of the fact that the lexical and syntactical character of the item he utters conventionally associates it with producing that effect.

Strictly speaking this condition could be formulated as part of condition (1), but it is of enough philosophical interest to be worth stating separately. I find it troublesome for the following reason. If my original objection to Grice is really valid, then surely, one might say, all these iterated intentions are superfluous; all that is necessary is that the speaker should seriously utter a sentence. The production all these effects is simply a consequence of the hearer's knowledge of what the sentence means, which in turn is a consequence of his knowledge of the language, which is assumed by the speaker at the outset. I think the correct reply to this objection is that condition (8) explicates what it is for the speaker to 'seriously' utter the sentence, i.e. to utter it and mean it, but I am not completely confident about either the force of the objection or of the reply.

(9) *The semantical rules of the dialect spoken by S and H are such that T is correctly and sincerely uttered if and only if conditions (1)–(8) obtain.*

This condition is intended to make clear that the sentence uttered is one which by the semantical rules of the language is used to make a promise. Taken together with condition (8), it eliminates counter-examples like the captured soldier example considered earlier. Exactly what the formulation of the rules is, we shall soon see.

So far we have considered only the case of a sincere promise. But insincere promises are promises none the less, and we now need to show how to modify the conditions to allow for them. In making an insincere promise the speaker does not have all the intentions and beliefs he has when making a sincere promise. However, he purports to have them. Indeed it is because he purports to have intentions and beliefs which he does not have that we describe his act as insincere. So to allow for insincere promises we need only to revise our conditions to state that the speaker takes responsibility for having the beliefs and intentions rather than stating that he actually has them. A clue that the speaker does take such responsibility is the fact that he could not say without absurdity, e.g., 'I promise to do *A* but I do not intend to do *A*'. To say 'I promise to do *A*' is to take responsibility for intending to do *A*, and this condition holds whether the utterance was sincere or insincere. To allow for the possibility of an insincere promise then we have only to revise condition (6) so that it states not that the speaker intends to do *A*, but that he takes responsibility for intending to do *A*, and to avoid the charge of circularity I shall phrase this as follows:

(6*) *S intends that the utterance of T will make him responsible for intending to do A.*

Thus amended (and with 'sincerely' dropped from our analysandum and from condition (9)), our analysis is neutral on the question whether the promise was sincere or insincere.

VI. Rules for the Use of the Function-Indicating Device

Our next task is to extract from our set of conditions a set of rules for the use of the function-indicating device. Obviously not all of our conditions are equally relevant to this task. Condition (1) and conditions of the forms (8) and (9) apply generally to all kinds of normal illocutionary acts and are not peculiar to promising. Rules for the function-indicating device for promising are to be found corresponding to conditions (2)–(7).

The semantical rules for the use of any function-indicating device *P* for promising are:

> *Rule* 1. *P* is to be uttered only in the context of a sentence (or larger stretch of discourse) the utterance of which predicates some future act *A* of the speaker *S*.
>
> I call this the *propositional-content rule*. It is derived from the propositional-content conditions (2) and (3).
>
> *Rule* 2. *P* is to be uttered only if the hearer *H* would prefer *S*'s doing *A* to his not doing *A*, and *S* believes *H* would prefer *S*'s doing *A* to his not doing *A*.
>
> *Rule* 3. *P* is to be uttered only if it is not obvious to both *S* and *H* that *S* will do *A* in the normal course of events.
>
> I call rules (2) and (3) *preparatory rules*. They are derived from the preparatory conditions (4) and (5).
>
> *Rule* 4. *P* is to be uttered only if *S* intends to do *A*.
>
> I call this the *sincerity rule*. It is derived from the sincerity condition (6).
>
> *Rule* 5. The utterance of *P* counts as the undertaking of an obligation to do *A*.
>
> I call this the *essential rule*.

These rules are ordered: rules 2–5 apply only if rule 1 is satisfied, and rule 5 applies only if rules 2 and 3 are satisfied as well.

Notice that whereas rules 1–4 take the form of quasi-imperatives, i.e. they are of the form: utter *P* only if *x*, rule 5 is of the form: the utterance of *P* counts as *Y*. Thus rule 5 is of the kind peculiar to systems of constitutive rules which I discussed in section II.

Notice also that the rather tiresome analogy with games is holding up remarkably well. If we ask ourselves under what conditions a player could be said to move a knight correctly, we would find preparatory conditions, such as that it must be his turn to move, as well as the essential condition stating the actual positions the knight can move to. I think that there is even a sincerity rule for competitive games, the rule that each side tries to win. I suggest that the team which 'throws' the game is behaving in a way closely analogous to the speaker who lies or makes false promises. Of course, there usually are no propositional-content rules for games, because games do not, by and large, represent states of affairs.

If this analysis is of any general interest beyond the case of promising then it would seem that these distinctions should carry over into other types of speech act, and I think a little reflection will show that they do. Consider, e.g., giving an order. The preparatory conditions include that the speaker should be in a position of authority over the hearer, the sincerity condition is that the speaker wants the ordered act done, and the essential condition has to do with the fact that the utterance is an attempt to get the hearer to do it. For assertions, the preparatory conditions include the fact that the hearer must have some basis for supposing the asserted proposition is true, the sincerity condition is that he must believe it to be true, and the essential condition has to do with the fact that the utterance is an attempt to inform the hearer and convince him of its truth. Greetings are a much simpler kind of speech act, but even here some of the distinctions apply. In the utterance of 'Hello' there is no propositional content and no sincerity condition. The preparatory condition is that the speaker must have just encountered the hearer, and the essential rule is that the utterance indicates courteous recognition of the hearer.

A proposal for further research then is to carry out a similar analysis of other types of speech acts. Not only would this give us an analysis of concepts interesting in themselves, but the comparison of different analyses would deepen our understanding of the whole subject and incidentally provide a basis for a more serious taxonomy than any of the usual facile categories such as evaluative versus descriptive, or cognitive versus emotive.

Frank Kermode

b. 1919

FRANK KERMODE has written on a variety of subjects. In his first book he considered the idea of the image and the isolation of the artist as romantic notions fundamental to modern literature, and it remains an important study. More recently his concern has been narrative and the reading of fiction in general. His most influential work in this area is *The Sense of an Ending,* in which he studies the problem of fictions by considering the human need to establish beginnings and endings from the middle that we inhabit. In the chapter of this book that precedes the selection included here, which is part of chapter 2, Kermode begins to consider these basic requirements of fictions by studying the tradition of apocalyptic literature, or the fiction of an end. In making such fictions, human beings project themselves beyond the end to see history as a whole. That mistaken predictions of the end have seldom deterred people from predicting yet again or reinterpreting the prediction suggests that the concept of an end is more important than its truth or its achievement, being the imaginative investment in coherent pattern.

The tradition of apocalypse, therefore, has relevance to the existence and function of literary plots. The concept of *peripeteia,* for example, reflects reenactment of the readjustment of expectations when the end does not occur as we had expected. Yet it does occur in the fiction and thereby satisfies our yen for unity and wholeness, even though the end and the whole may be deliberately effected to violate our conventional sense even of *peripeteia,* as in the work of Robbe-Grillet, where the matter is transferred from plot to the manner of writing.

For his theory of fictions Kermode is particularly in the debt of two predecessors, Hans Vaihinger, author of the *Philosophy of "As If"*, and Wallace Stevens, on whom Kermode wrote a short book in 1960, six years before *The Sense of an Ending* appeared. Stevens is well known for his gnomic statements about fictions, one of which Kermode employs as one of the epigraphs for the chapter reproduced in part here: "the nicer knowledge of / Belief, that what it believes in is not true." Vaihinger's book, heavily influenced by Kant, reduces all symbolic structures to fictions and is faithful to Kant's stricture that things in themselves cannot be known, only our constitution of them. Kermode is particularly interested in valorizing fictions above myths, which he regards as fixed elicitors of dangerous belief—as for example the myths of Nazism. Literary fictions are, on the other hand—because untrue—useful to life, becoming mythical only when no longer dynamic, that is, no longer susceptible to new readings. Kermode's critical position is in the end pragmatic, and his attack is on the potential tyranny and deadness of mythic belief.

Among Kermode's books are *Romantic Image* (1957); *John Donne* (1957); *Wallace Stevens* (1960); *Puzzles and Epiphanies* (1962); *The Sense of an Ending* (1966); *The Classic* (1975); *The Genesis of Secrecy* (1979); *The Art of Telling* (1983); and *Forms of Attention* (1985).

FROM

FICTIONS

One of my tasks in this second talk is to answer some of the questions which I begged in the first. I wanted to concentrate on eschatological fictions, fictions of the End, in relation to apocalypse itself; and though I did say something about these as analogous to literary fictions, by means of which we impose other patterns on historical time, I did little to justify the analogy. And when I spoke of the degree to which fictions vary from the paradigmatic base, I again confined myself largely to straight apocalypse—the way the type figures were modified, made to refer not to a common End but to personal death or to crisis, or to epoch. I mentioned that literary fictions changed in the same way—perpetually recurring crises of the person, and the death of that person, took over from myths which purport to relate one's experience to grand beginnings and ends. And I suggested that there have been great changes, especially in recent times when our attitudes to fiction in general have grown so sophisticated; although it seems, at the same time, that in 'making sense' of the world we still feel a need, harder than ever to satisfy because of an accumulated scepticism, to experience that concordance of beginning, middle, and end which is the essence of our explanatory fictions, and especially when they belong to cultural traditions which treat historical time as primarily rectilinear rather than cyclic.

Obviously I now need to say more about the way I have been using such words as 'fiction' and 'concordance.' First, then, let us reflect that it is pretty surprising, given the range and minuteness of modern literary theory, that nobody, so far as I know, has ever tried to relate the theory of literary fictions to the theory of fictions in general, though I think something of the sort may have been in Ogden's mind when he assembled *Bentham's Theory of Fictions;* and there are relevant implications, not developed in this direction, in Richards on 'speculative instruments' and what he calls 'experimental submission.'[1] Richards is certainly concerned with the nature and quality of one's assent to fictions as a means to personal freedom or perhaps simply to personal comfort.

But that there *is* a simple relation between literary and other fictions seems, if one attends to it, more obvious than has appeared. If we think first of modern fictions, it can hardly be an accident that ever since Nietzsche generalized and developed the Kantian insights, literature has increasingly asserted its right to an arbitrary and private choice of fictional norms, just as historiography has become a discipline more devious and dubious because of our recognition that its methods depend to an unsuspected degree on myths and fictions. After Nietzsche it was possible to say, as Stevens did, that 'the final belief must be in a fiction.'[2] This poet, to whom the whole question was of perpetual interest, saw that to think in this way was to postpone the End—when the fiction might be said to coincide with reality—for ever; to make of it a fiction, an imaginary moment when 'at last' the world of fact and the *mundo* of fiction shall be one. Such a fiction—the last section of *Notes toward a Supreme Fiction* is, appropriately, the place where Stevens gives it his fullest attention—such a fiction of the end is like infinity plus one and imaginary numbers in mathematics, something we know does not exist, but which helps us to make sense of and to move in

FICTIONS, the last part of which does not appear here, is from *The Sense of an Ending: Studies in the Theory of Fiction,* copyright 1967, by the Oxford University Press, Inc. Reprinted by permission.

[1] C. K. Ogden, *Bentham's Theory of Fictions,* London, 1932; I. A. Richards, *The Philosophy of Rhetoric,* New York, 1936. [Au.] Jeremy Bentham (1748–1832), English philosopher. On Richards, see *CTSP,* pp. 847–59. [Eds.]

[2] Friedrich Wilhelm Nietzsche (1844–1900), German philosopher (see *CTSP,* pp. 635–41); Wallace Stevens (1879–1955), American poet (see *CTSP,* pp. 968–79). [Eds.]

the world. *Mundo* is itself such a fiction. I think Stevens, who certainly thought we have to make our sense out of whatever materials we find to hand, borrowed it from Ortega.[3] His general doctrine of fiction he took from Vaihinger, from Nietzsche, perhaps also from American pragmatism.

First, an ethical problem. If literary fictions *are* related to all others, then it must be said that they have some dangerous relations. 'The falseness of an opinion is not . . . any objection to it,' says Nietzsche, adding that the only relevant question is 'how far the opinion is life-furthering, life-preserving, species-preserving.' A man who thinks this is in some danger of resembling the Cretan Liar, for his opinion can be no less fictive than the opinions to which it alludes. He may be in worse danger; he may be encouraging people who hold the fictive view that death on a large scale is life-furthering and species-preserving. On the one hand you have a relatively innocent theory, a way of coming to terms with the modern way of recognizing the gulf between being and knowing, the sense that nature can always be made to answer our questions, comply with our fictions. This is what Wordsworth curiously and touchingly predicted when he asserted that 'Nature never did betray / The heart that loved her.' In its purely operational form this is the basis of the theoretical physicist's life, since he assumes that there will always be experimental confirmation for positions arrived at by pure mathematics. Naturally, the answers, like the questions, are purely human. 'Nature is patient of interpretation in terms of laws that happen to interest us,' as Whitehead remarked. But on the other hand you have the gas-chambers. Alfred Rosenberg used the innocent speculations of William James, John Dewey, and F. C. S. Schiller to argue that knowledge was at the service of 'organic' truth, which he identified with the furthering of the life of what he called the 'German race.'[4] If the value of an opinion is to be tested only by its success in the world, the propositions of dementia can become as valuable as any other fictions. The validity of one's opinion of the Jews can be proved by killing six million Jews.

[3] José Ortega y Gasset (1883–1955). See his *Man and Crisis,* translated by Mildred Adams, New York, 1958. [Au.]

[4] Alfred Rosenberg (1893–1946), German, Nazi political ideologist. William James (1842–1910), American philosopher and psychologist; John Dewey (1859–1952), American philosopher; Friedrich C. S. Schiller (1759–1805), German writer (see *CTSP,* pp. 417–31). [Eds.]

Hannah Arendt, who has written with clarity and passion on this issue, argues that the philosophical or anti-philosophical assumptions of the Nazis were not generically different from those of the scientist, or indeed of any of us in an age 'where man, wherever he goes, encounters only himself.'[5] How, in such a situation, can our paradigms of concord, our beginnings and ends, our humanly ordered picture of the world satisfy us, make sense? How can apocalypse or tragedy make sense, or more sense than any arbitrary nonsense can be made to make sense? If *King Lear* is an image of the promised end, so is Buchenwald; and both stand under the accusation of being horrible, rootless fantasies, the one no more true or more false than the other, so that the best you say is that *King Lear* does less harm.

I think we have to admit that the consciously false apocalypse of the Third Reich and the consciously false apocalypse of *King Lear* imply equally a recognition that it is ourselves we are encountering whenever we invent fictions. There may even be a real relation between certain kinds of effectiveness in literature and totalitarianism in politics. But although the fictions are alike ways of finding out about the human world, anti-Semitism is a fiction of escape which tells you nothing about death but projects it onto others; whereas *King Lear* is a fiction that inescapably involves an encounter with oneself, and the image of one's end. This is one difference; and there is another. We have to distinguish between myths and fictions. Fictions can degenerate into myths whenever they are not consciously held to be fictive. In this sense anti-Semitism is a degenerate fiction, a myth; and *Lear* is a fiction. Myth operates within the diagrams of ritual, which presupposes total and adequate explanations of things as they are and were; it is a sequence of radically unchangeable gestures. Fictions are for finding things out, and they change as the needs of sense-making change. Myths are the agents of stability, fictions the agents of change. Myths call for absolute, fictions for conditional assent. Myths make sense in terms of a lost order of time, *illud tempus* as Eliade calls it; fictions, if successful, make sense of the here and now, *hoc tempus.* It may be that treating literary fictions as myths sounds good just now, but as Marianne Moore so rightly said of poems, 'these things are important not because a /

[5] See her *Between Past and Future,* New York, 1963. [Au.]

high-sounding interpretation can be put upon them but because they are / useful.'

On Vaihinger's view, the fictional *as if* is distinguished also from hypothesis because it is not in question that at the end of the finding-out process it will be dropped. In some ways this is obviously true of the literary fictions. We are never in danger of thinking that the death of King Lear, which explains so much, is *true*. To the statement that he died thus and thus—speaking these words over Cordelia's body, calling for a looking-glass, fumbling with a button—we make an experimental assent. If we make it well, the gain is that we shall never quite resume the posture towards life and death that we formerly held. Of course it may be said that in changing ourselves we have, in the best possible indirect way, changed the world.

So my suggestion is that literary fictions belong to Vaihinger's category of 'the consciously false.' They are not subject, like hypotheses, to proof or disconfirmation, only, if they come to lose their operational effectiveness, to neglect. They are then thrown, in Stevens's figure, on to the 'dump'—'to sit among mattresses of the dead.' In this they resemble the fictions of science, mathematics, and law, and differ from those of theology only because religious fictions are harder to free from the mythical 'deposit.' I see no reason why we cannot apply to literary fictions what Vaihinger says of fictions in general, that they 'are mental structures. The psyche weaves this or that thought out of itself; for the mind is invention; under the compulsion of necessity, stimulated by the outer world, it discovers the store of contrivances hidden within itself. The organism finds itself in a world of contradictory sensations, it is exposed to the assaults of a hostile world, and in order to preserve itself is forced to seek every possible means of assistance.'[6] He distinguishes many different types of fiction: the paradigmatic, for example, which includes Utopias, and we may add apocalypses; the legal, where the fiction has a function in equity (as when a court may deem that a wife who died at the same instant as, or even some time later than her husband, pre-deceased him, so as to obviate an inequitable double payment of estate duties; or as when, after a certain lapse of time, after receipt, one is presumed to have accepted delivery of a postal packet); the fictive zero-cases of mathematics; the fictions of the thing-in-itself, or of causality; and what Vaihinger calls, in words remembered by Stevens, 'the last and greatest fiction,' 'the fiction of an Absolute.'[7] If we forget that fictions are fictive we regress to myth (as when the Neo-Platonists forgot the fictiveness of Plato's fictions and Professor Frye forgets the fictiveness of *all* fictions). This is as if we were to believe, because of the grace of the court, that by an immutable dispensation it always happens that when a husband and wife are involved in a car crash the wife dies first, though in ordinary life we may 'displace' or 'ironize' this basic truth. What Vaihinger calls 'reunion with reality' and I call 'making sense' or 'making human sense' is something that literature achieves only so long as we remember the status of fictions. They are not myths, and they are not hypotheses; you neither rearrange the world to suit them, nor test them by experiment, for instance in gas-chambers.

When Vaihinger had to deal with the situation that arises when men make fictions apparently too elaborate and ingenious to be explained simply in terms of survival in a hostile environment (more splendid than seems proper merely to the mitigation of 'poverty') he made up his Law of Preponderance of Means over End. We can do without this, but need to remember not only that we have what Bergson[8] called a *fonction fabulatrice,* but that we do set ourselves problems of the kind that would presumably not arise as a matter of simple biological necessity. When Nietzsche asked, 'why might not the world *which concerns us* be a fiction?' he was imagining a very large degree of human curiosity.

> Meanwhile the mind, from pleasure less,
> Withdraws into its happiness—

but having reached that point it does not cease to produce fictions beyond necessity:

> it creates, transcending these,
> Far other worlds and other seas.[9]

There are the green thoughts of fantasy, concerned not only with providing each kind with some convenient mental equivalent but projecting the desires

[6] See Hans Vaihinger, *The Philosophy of "As If"*, translated by C. K. Ogden, London, 1924. [Au.]

[7] Vaihinger, pp. 13–15. [Au.]

[8] Henri Bergson (1859–1941), French philosopher. [Eds.]

[9] Andrew Marvell (1621–78), "The Garden." [Eds.]

of the mind on to reality. When the fictions change, therefore, the world changes in step with them. This is what the poet[10] meant when he said that modern poetry was 'the act of finding / What will suffice.' He adds that this used to be easier than it is now, because 'the scene was set'—we had our paradigmatic fictions, which he calls 'Romantic tenements of rose and ice.' These no longer serve, and the fiction of the modern poet must 'speak words in the ear, / The delicatest ear of the mind, repeat, / Exactly, that which it wants to hear . . .' The satisfactions required are too subtle for the paradigms; but the poem needs to provide them. 'It must be the finding of a satisfaction, and may / Be of a man skating, a woman dancing, a woman / Combing.' It has moved, if you like, under the pressure of the Law of Preponderance of Means over End, away from the paradigm with its simpler biological function; it is a subtler matter now than utopia or apocalypse or tragedy. Those Noble Riders have come to look rigid, a bit absurd, as the same poet remarks.

Nor is it only in literary fictions that the satisfactions, especially the satisfactions of sceptical clerks, grow more devious and refined. The recognition, now commonplace, that the writing of history involves the use of regulative fictions, is part of the same process. World history, the imposition of a plot on time, is a substitute for myth, and the substitution of anti-historicist criticism for it is another step in the direction of harder satisfactions, in the clerkly rejection of romantic tenements. There is no history, says Karl Popper,[11] only histories; an insight in which he was anticipated by novelists, who wrote Histories (of, say, Tom Jones, or of the Life and Opinions of Tristram Shandy) in a period of paradigmatic historiography, as expounded by Carl Becker in his lectures called *The Heavenly City of the Eighteenth-Century Philosophers*.[12] The decline of paradigmatic history, and our growing consciousness of historiography's irreducible element of fiction, are, like the sophistication of literary plotting, contributions to what Wilde called 'the decay of lying.'[13] We fall into 'careless habits of accuracy.' We know that if we want to find out about ourselves, make sense, we must avoid the regress into myth which has deceived poet, historian, and critic. Our satisfactions will be hard to find.

And yet, it is clear, this is an exaggerated statement of the case. The paradigms do survive, somehow. If there was a time when, in Stevens's words, 'the scene was set,' it must be allowed that it has not yet been finally and totally struck. The survival of the paradigms is as much our business as their erosion. For that reason it is time to look more closely at them.

Now presumably it is true, in spite of all possible cultural and historical variations, that the paradigm will correspond, the more fully as one approaches a condition of absolute simplicity, to some basic human 'set,' biological or psychological. Right down at the root, they must correspond to a basic human need, they must make sense, give comfort. This root may be very primitive; the cultural differentiations must begin pretty far down. It may be that linguistic differentiae, which go very deep, reflect radically different styles of questions asked about the world. But on the other hand it has to be remembered that we know of no cultural group with whom communication is impossible, as a totally different attitude to time, or of course a totally different kind of time, would make it. At some very low level, we all share certain fictions about time, and they testify to the continuity of what is called human nature, however conscious some, as against others, may become of the fictive quality of these fictions.

It seems to follow that we shall learn more concerning the sense-making paradigms, relative to time, from experimental psychologists than from scientists or philosophers, and more from St. Augustine than from Kant or Einstein, because St. Augustine studies time as the soul's necessary self-extension before and after the critical moment upon which he reflects. We shall learn more from Piaget, from studies of such disorders as *déjà vu*, eidetic imagery, the Korsakoff syndrome, than from the learned investigators of time's arrow, or, on the other hand, from the mythic archetypes.[14]

Let us take a very simple example, the ticking of a clock. We ask what it *says:* and we agree that it says *tick-tock*. By this fiction we humanize it, make it talk our language. Of course, it is we who provide the fictional difference between the two sounds;

[10] Wallace Stevens. [Eds.]

[11] Karl Popper (b. 1902), Anglo-Austrian philosopher. [Eds.]

[12] See Carl Becker, *The Heavenly City of the Eighteenth-Century Philosophers*, New Haven, 1932. [Au.]

[13] See Wilde, *CTSP*, pp. 672–86. [Eds.]

[14] See G. J. Whitrow, *The Natural Philosophy of Time*, New York, 1959. [Au.]

tick is our word for a physical beginning, *tock* our word for an end. We say they differ. What enables them to be different is a special kind of middle. We can perceive a duration only when it is organized. It can be shown by experiment that subjects who listen to rhythmic structures such as *tick-tock,* repeated identically, 'can reproduce the intervals within the structure accurately, but they cannot grasp spontaneously the interval between the rhythmic groups,' that is, between *tock* and *tick,* even when this remains constant. The first interval is organized and limited, the second not. According to Paul Fraisse the *tock-tick* gap is analogous to the role of the 'ground' in spatial perception; each is characterized by a lack of form, against which the illusory organizations of shape and rhythm are perceived in the spatial or temporal object.[15] The fact that we call the second of the two related sounds *tock* is evidence that we use fictions to enable the end to confer organization and form on the temporal structure. The interval between the two sounds, between *tick* and *tock* is now charged with significant duration. The clock's *tick-tock* I take to be a model of what we call a plot, an organization that humanizes time by giving it form; and the interval between *tock* and *tick* represents purely successive, disorganized time of the sort that we need to humanize. Later I shall be asking whether, when *tick-tock* seems altogether too easily fictional, we do not produce plots containing a good deal of *tock-tick;* such a plot is that of *Ulysses.*

Tick is a humble genesis, *tock* a feeble apocalypse; and *tick-tock* is in any case not much of a plot. We need much larger ones and much more complicated ones if we persist in finding 'what will suffice.' And what happens if the organization is much more complex than *tick-tock?* Suppose, for instance, that it is a thousand-page novel. Then it obviously will not lie within what is called our 'temporal horizon'; to maintain the experience of organization we shall need many more fictional devices. And although they will essentially be of the same kind as calling the second of those two related sounds *tock,* they will obviously be more resourceful and elaborate. They have to defeat the tendency of the interval between *tick* and *tock* to empty itself; to maintain within that interval following *tick* a lively expectation of *tock,* and a sense that however remote *tock* may be, all that happens happens as if *tock* were certainly following. All such plotting presupposes and requires that an end will bestow upon the whole duration and meaning. To put it another way, the interval must be purged of simple chronicity, of the emptiness of *tock-tick,* humanly uninteresting successiveness. It is required to be a significant season, *kairos* poised between beginning and end. It has to be, on a scale much greater than that which concerns the psychologists, an instance of what they call 'temporal integration'—our way of bundling together perception of the present, memory of the past, and expectation of the future, in a common organization. Within this organization that which was conceived of as simply successive becomes charged with past and future: what was *chronos* becomes *kairos.* This is the time of the novelist, a transformation of mere successiveness which has been likened, by writers as different as Forster and Musil, to the experience of love, the erotic consciousness which makes divinely satisfactory sense out of the commonplace person.

As I intend to use this distinction again, I had better be plain about what I mean by the Greek words, *chronos* and *kairos.* Broadly speaking my usage is derived from the theologians who have developed this distinction in various ways, notably Oscar Cullmann in *Christ and Time,* and John Marsh in *The Fullness of Time.*[16] The distinction has been familiar in a general way for a good many years, having been given currency by Brabant's *Time and Eternity in Christian Thought,* of 1937. Tillich uses *kairos* idiosyncratically, but basically he means by it 'moment of crisis,' or, more obscurely, 'the fate of time'; in any case he has firmly associated it with a specifically modern sense of living in an epoch when 'the foundations of life quake beneath our feet.'[17] The notion recurs continually in modern thinking; one instance is Jaspers's 'boundary-situation,' which has to do with personal crisis—death, suffering, guilt—in relation to the data which constitute its historical determination.[18] But Cullmann and Marsh are seeking to use the words *kairos* and *chronos* in their historical, biblical senses: *chronos* is 'passing time' or 'waiting time'—

[15] See Paul Fraisse, *The Psychology of Time,* London, 1964. [Au.]

[16] See Oscar Cullmann, *Christ and Time,* London, 1951; John Marsh, *The Fullness of Time,* New York, 1952. [Au.]

[17] Paul Tillich (1866–1965), German-American theologian. [Eds.]

[18] Karl Jaspers (1883–1969), German philosopher. [Eds.]

that which, according to Revelation, 'shall be no more'—and *kairos* is the season, a point in time filled with significance, charged with a meaning derived from its relation to the end.

You can see that this is a very radical distinction. The Greeks, as Mr. Lampert observes, thought that even the gods could not change the past; but Christ did change it, rewrote it, and in a new way fulfilled it. In the same way the End changes all, and produces, in what in relation to it is the past, these seasons, *kairoi,* historical moments of intemporal significance. The divine plot is the pattern of *kairoi* in relation to the End. Not only the Greeks but the Hebrews lacked this antithesis; for Hebrew, according to Marsh, had no word for *chronos,* and so no contrast between time which is simply 'one damn thing after another' and time as concentrated in *kairoi.* It is the New Testament that lays the foundation for both the modern sense of epoch (it is very conscious of existing in an overlap of *aiones*) and the modern distinction between times: the coming of God's time (*kairos*), the fulfilling of the time (*kairos*—Mark i.15), the signs of the times (Matt. xvi.2,3) as against passing time, *chronos.* The notion of fulfilment is essential; the *kairos* transforms the past, validates Old Testament types and prophecies, establishes concord with origins as well as ends. The *chronos-kairos* distinction is therefore relevant to the typological interests of some modern theologians, and also some modern literary critics; Miss Helen Gardner has attacked both classes, justly in my view, for their typological obsessions, which, she thinks, diminish the force and actuality of the Gospels, as they do of secular literature.[19] The attractiveness of the types must in the end be explained in terms of the service they do to the man who senses his position in the middest, desiring these moments of significance which harmonize origin and end.

It would be wrong not to allude, at this point, to a critic of such distinctions, Professor James T. Barr.[20] He examines the work of Cullman, Marsh, J. A. T. Robinson, and others, calling it characteristic of modern biblical theology 'at its best' but arguing that all these scholars misinterpret the language of the Bible. The *chronos-kairos* distinction is simply not in the language of the New Testament. In Galatians 4.4. the words translated as 'the fulness of the time' are *pleroma tou chronou,* though Mark 1.15, already quoted, has *peplerotai ho kairos,* 'the time is fulfilled.' In Acts 1.7 and I. Thess. 5.1 the terms seem not to be differentiated: *hoi chronoi kai hoi kairoi,* which the Authorized Version translates 'the times and the seasons.' Also, says Barr, the Old Testament shows much more interest in passing-time, chronicity, than these scholars have suggested. In the New Testament, *kairos* and *chronos* can be opposed, but are sometimes interchangeable; perhaps *kairos* leans, as Augustine thought, towards 'critical time'; *chronos* is more quantitative. But we cannot, according to Barr, have a '*kairos* concept,' and to say, as G. A. F. Knight does, that "the story of the people of God is full of crises, *kairoi,* 'decisive moments,'" is not to use the word in a biblical sense at all.

Mr. Barr's authoritative book contains much more destructive criticism than this suggests. Among other things, it discourages too easy acceptance of sharp distinctions between Christian rectilinearity and Greek cyclism. But the main issue here is that Barr makes it impossible for anybody who is not willing to engage him on his own lexical terms to doubt that Marsh's distinction, which I have used, can have any very certain validity. It is overstated. The best one can hope for is that the words, in New Testament Greek, maintain a certain polarity, though they also shade off into one another—they cover the same ground as the word 'time' does in *Macbeth.* It makes one think of Wittgenstein's famous passage on games.[21] 'Back to the rough ground! Look and see!' Our notion of time includes, among much else, *kairos, chronos,* and *aion.* Even if their lexical methods are faulty, it is important that these modern theologians *want* these words to mean involved distinctions of the sort I have discussed. They play, as Wittgenstein might have said, and make up the rules as they go along. These rules are attractive; and they are so because we need, for our obscure cultural ends, to observe distinctions between mere chronicity and times which are concordant and full. Hence our use, for our own game, of *chronos, kairos,* and also *pleroma.*

We can use this kind of language to distinguish

[19] See Helen Gardner, *The Limits of Literary Criticism,* Oxford, 1956. [Au.]

[20] See James T. Barr, *Biblical Words for Time,* London, 1962. [Au.]

[21] See *Wittgenstein.* [Eds.]

between what we *feel* is happening in a fiction when mere successiveness, which we *feel* to be the chief characteristic in the ordinary going-on of time, is purged by the establishment of a significant relation between the moment and a remote origin and end, a concord of past, present, and future—three dreams which, as Augustine said, cross in our minds, as in the present of things past, the present of things present, and the present of things future. Normally we associate 'reality' with *chronos,* and a fiction which entirely ignored this association we might think unserious or silly or mad; only the unconscious is intemporal, and the illusion that the world can be made to satisfy the unconscious is an illusion without a future.

Yet in every plot there is an escape from chronicity, and so, in some measure, a deviation from this norm of 'reality.' When we read a novel we are, in a way, allowing ourselves to behave as young children do when they think of all the past as 'yesterday,' or like members of primitive cargo-cults when they speak of the arrival of Jesus a couple of generations back as a guarantee of another good cargo in the near future.[22] Our past is brief, organized by our desire for satisfaction, and simply related to our future. But there is a pattern of expectation improper to maturity. Having compared the novel-reader with an infant and a primitive, one can go further and compare him with a psychopath; and this I shall shortly be doing. But all I want to say at present is that any novel, however 'realistic,' involves some degree of alienation from 'reality.' You can see the difficulty Fielding, for example, felt about this, at the very beginning of the serious novel; he felt he had to reject the Richardsonian method of novels by epistolary correspondences, although this made sure that in the midst of voluminous detail intended to ensure realism, everything became *kairios* by virtue of the way in which letters coincided with critical moments. Fielding preferred to assume the right to convert one kind of time into another exactly as he pleased; if it is proper that a long period of time should elapse without producing anything notable, he will, he says, leave it 'totally unobserved.' In other words, Fielding allows the narrator to dispense with chronicity when he chooses, but feels it necessary to explain what he is doing. With some differences, he does what is done in the Greek romances. In fact Richardson is the more modern, and Fielding worries about it. His book, he says, is a 'history,' not a 'life'; and history isn't chronicle, ignores whatever is not concordant. *The History of Tom Jones* has nevertheless a critical 'middle,' the scene at Upton, in which the delayed arrivals, the split-second timing, as we now say, belong to the *kairos* of farce rather than to the *chronos* of reality; and he is especially proud of the concords he establishes with origins and ends in this passage. In short, he is, and would have been happy to hear it, of the family of Don Quixote, tilting with a hopeless chivalry against the dull windmills of a time-bound reality. All novelists must do so; but it is important that the great ones retreat from reality less perfunctorily than the authors of novelettes and detective stories.

Georges Poulet[23] argues that medieval men did not distinguish as we do between existence and duration; one can only say that they were very lucky, and less in need than we are of fictions relating to time—the kind that confer significance on the interval between *tick* and *tock*. For his medieval men, it seems, this significance was a simple property of the interval. We have to provide it. We still need the fullness of it, the *pleroma;* and it is our insatiable interest in the future (towards which we are biologically orientated) that makes it necessary for us to relate to the past, and to the moment in the middle, by plots: by which I mean not only concordant imaginary incidents, but all the other, perhaps subtler, concords that can be arranged in a narrative. Such concords can easily be called 'time-defeating,' but the objection to that word is that it leads directly to the questionable critical practice of calling literary structures *spatial.* This is a critical fiction which has regressed into a myth because it was not discarded at the right moment in the argument. 'Time-redeeming' is a better word, perhaps.

One implication of this argument is that the 'virtual' time of books—to use Mrs. Langer's word—is a kind of man-centred model of world-time. And books are indeed world-models.[24] St. Augustine found that the best model he could find for our ex-

[22] See P. M. Worsley, *The Trumpet Shall Sound,* London, 1957, and P. Lawrence, *Road Belong Cargo,* Manchester, 1964. [Au.]

[23] See Georges Poulet, *Studies in Human Time,* translated by Elliott Coleman, Baltimore, 1956. [Au.]

[24] See Susanne K. Langer, *Feeling and Form,* London, 1953. [Au.]

perience of past, present, and future was the recitation of a psalm. Thus he anticipated all the modern critics who wonder how it can be that a book can simultaneously be present like a picture (though in a way a picture has also to be recited) and yet extended in time. Curtius testifies to the durability of the book as a world-model in the Middle Ages.[25] Like the ziggurat, the Byzantine church, and most of all like the Gothic cathedral, it is a perpetual testimony to the set of our demands on the world. If the ziggurat is a topocosm, the book is a bibliocosm.[26] We can distribute our fictions in time as well as in space, which is why we must avoid an easy translation from the one to the other. E. H. Gombrich has recently been talking about the relevance of the great eleventh chapter of Augustine's *Confessions,* to which I have already referred, and finding in it the seeds of modern psychological speculation about the action of memory.[27] There is the matter of mere physiological persistence—which makes television possible. There is 'immediate memory,' or 'primary retention,' the registration of impressions we fail to 'take in,' but can recover a little later by introspection; and there is, finally, a kind of forward memory, familiar from spoonerisms and typing errors which are caused by anticipation, the mind working on an expected future. The second of these memories—registration of what we fail to 'take in'—is an essential tool of narrative fiction. It is familiar from the 'double-take' of the music-hall, and many literary kinds, from poems which catch up words and ideas into new significance, to complicated plots like that of *Tom Jones,* depend on it. Aristotle's notion of the best possible plot is a double-take. There is a sense in which *Macbeth* is an enormous dramatic extension of the double-take, for it is based on an initial deviation of attention which causes a temporal gap between the original apprehension of what the situation signifies and the final understanding that its significance was other. The third kind of memory is what enables writers to use the *peripeteia,* a falsification of expectation, so that the end comes as expected, but not in the manner expected.

Gombrich's argument is that we ignore these facts when we make a sharp *a priori* distinction between time and space; that in time our minds work in fashions that are not wholly and simply successive, while in spatial appreciations—as when one looks at a painting—there is a temporal element; one 'scans' the picture and could not do so without retinal persistence; one remembers what has passed, and has expectations about what is to come. These are matters on which he has previously spoken in *Art and Illusion.* I quote him in support of a revaluation of the element of temporal structure, memory, and expectation, as against the tendency to reduce our bibliocosms to merely spatial order. It seems obvious that in the experience of literature we use temporal expectation—a 'mental set,' as Gombrich puts it, which is 'a state of readiness to start projecting.' We remember that in Stevens the 'angel of reality' gives us the power 'to see the earth again / Cleared of its stiff and stubborn, man-locked set'; and that he aims at 'meanings said / By repetition of half-meanings'—by using the second kind of memory to play upon the expectations created by the third.

So we may call books fictive models of the temporal world. They will be humanly serviceable as models only if they pay adequate respect to what we think of as 'real' time, the chronicity of the waking moment. If we are normal we can guess the time—we can guess how long ago the lecture began, and also how long we shall have to wait for some desire to be gratified, for example, that the lecture should end.

[25] See E. Curtius, *European Literature in the Latin Middle Ages,* translated by Willard R. Trask, New York, 1953. [Au.]

[26] See Grace E. Cairns, *Philosophies of History,* New York, 1962; Mircea Eliade, *The Sacred and the Profane,* New York, 1959, p. 40. [Au.]

[27] See E. H. Gombrich, "Moment and Movement in Art," *Journal of the Warburg and Courtauld Institutes,* XXVI (1964), pp. 293ff. [Au.]

Jacques Derrida

b. 1930

THE FIRST of the three selections by Jacques Derrida included here was delivered at the Johns Hopkins University in 1966, at a conference presenting the varied work of French structuralism to an American audience. Significantly, the conference was titled "The Languages of Criticism and the Sciences of Man" (recalling R. S. Crane's arguments for critical pluralism in *The Languages of Criticism and the Structure of Poetry,* 1953; see *CTSP,* pp. 1079–1101); but the proceedings were published under the title *The Structuralist Controversy* (1970). Derrida's essay explains at least part of this change, since the conference, as an event, set out to offer a critical introduction to structuralism as what American critics might have viewed as another "approach" to literature, presumably to be welcomed as an alternative to weary native versions of formalism. Derrida's shrewd and penetrating commentary on the history, pretensions, and paradoxes of the idea of structure partakes of the character of commentaries on the emperor's new clothes. To pursue the metaphor, Derrida did not stop with the observation that the emperor was naked but memorialized the ultimate scandal: the "emperor" was not *there* at all.

As the principal exponent of what has since become generally known as deconstruction, Derrida has exerted a profound influence on contemporary criticism, both directly and indirectly. His densely self-reflexive prose has been the vehicle for philosophical analysis of exemplary penetration, just as it has been a frequent source of irritation, if not exasperation. To be sure, Derrida is very difficult to read but not because of any willful or perverse desire to antagonize the reader or to be deliberately obscure. It is, rather, that Derrida's philosophical position, like his method of analysis, systematically undermines the presumption of a stable interpretive context to which a reader may habitually appeal for the determination of meaning. For just this reason, Derrida's difficult prose cannot be dismissed as an incidental irritation, nor can it be deflected by the reactionary charge that it is in some way decadent or irrational. It is, rather, a radical challenge to prevailing notions of "meaning" or "rationality" that can be ignored only at the cost of demonstrating that the prevailing notions prevail by force of repression—a point Derrida frequently underscores.

Derrida's reception among English-speaking critics, especially in America, has been complicated by differences in historical background and training. While his work undermines conventional interpretive contexts, it arises from a very specific philosophical and historical context that one can rarely assume would be familiar to his American readers. While Derrida would no doubt find the problem of genesis in his own thought as vexed as he finds the problem of genesis in general, his view of "philosophy" could be traced to the skepticism of Montaigne and Descartes, the political and linguistic speculations of Rousseau, and the development of phenomenology since Hegel's *Phenomenology of Mind,* but especially the articulation of transcendental phenomenology by *Husserl.* Other major influences on Derrida's work include Nietzsche, *Heidegger,* Emmanuel Levinas, Sartre, and *de Saussure.*

It has been said, somewhat facetiously, that the range of modern philosophical styles falls between two extremes, defined by the posture of *Wittgenstein,* writing as if he were the First Philosopher who had read nothing, and the posture of Derrida, writing as if he were the Last Philosopher, who had read everything. But as Newton Garver suggests in his preface to the English translation of Derrida's *La Voix et le Phénomène,* extremes meet—or, in this case, given the presumptive evidence that early on, Derrida had not read Wittgenstein (or Whitehead or Russell or Carnap), they converge on similar preoccupations: problems of meaning, signification, and the radical critique of metaphysics. When Derrida refers to "Philosophy," however, the rhetoric of inclusion in fact represses what is most likely to be taught in Departments of Philosophy at most major American universities: logical analysis, conceptual elucidation, philosophy of science, all with a characteristic preference for empiricism or positivism. While it could be argued that the broad attack on metaphysics that has characterized logical empiricism or positivism at least from Comte and Mach to Russell and Carnap had so far succeeded as to divorce positivism from the main historical concerns of philosophy, it remains that Derrida's invocation of "Philosophy" is primarily rhetorical and is often as parochial as the response of his critics who might, for example, admit that Hegel and Nietzsche were philosophers without feeling compelled to take them very seriously as such.

Nevertheless, it remains that Derrida's work must be taken into account, no matter how one conceives of philosophical and critical traditions, simply on the strength of his most important insight. Derrida shows with exhaustive ingenuity that the fate of Western metaphysics is inextricably involved with the notion of the sign, and that the representation of the sign paradoxically requires a transcendental signified to be "present" to consciousness, even as that signified is always absent, always already displaced by another signifier.

In "Structure, Sign and Play," Derrida focuses his attention on the peculiarity of the idea of "structure," as it presumes to provide closure, coherence, and "totalization" for any system, that it cannot be directly reconciled with the element of play which, even as it generates the "structure," is repressed by the requirement of closure, if a structure is to be available *as* structured. Not coincidentally, Derrida associates the impulse to totalization with the notion of *totalitarian:* the very presumption that one could separate a "logical" relation from a political syndrome is itself an example of what Derrida means. The desire for closure, as guarantor of meaning and intelligibility, becomes the instrumentality of repression, particularly of the origin of processes of genesis by which a given structure is represented. While one may argue that Derrida, in asserting that such a relation is systemic, is himself presenting the problematic of structure as itself a structure, therefore subject to all of his strictures on the concept, this does not disarm his analysis but only adds to the layered self-reflexiveness of his style, inasmuch as he is obviously aware of the fact that his deconstructive analysis applies in principle to itself.

For literary critics, Derrida's work is all the more important because of the specific emphasis Derrida has placed on this problem. Bearing in mind that his immediate object for analysis is the problem of the transcendental signified, much of his work focuses more directly on the problem of writing. He argues that Western metaphysics has systematically privileged voice over writing, on the presumption that *logos,* as the a priori, transcendental power of knowledge and signifier of being, is immediately present in speech, whereas writing is displaced, one degree removed as the representation of speech. While this relation is essential to Plato's argument in Book X of *Republic* (see *CTSP,* pp. 33–41) that poetry, as an imitation of an imitation, is two removes from the truth, Derrida generalizes the issue to all signification and subverts the confidence of this Platonic gesture by showing that speech itself is subject to the same constraint and must itself be inscribed as the signifier of a still and always absent signified. Derrida's response is a project of "grammatology," described in the second selection here, from *Of Grammatology.* Working from within the tradition of "logocentric metaphysics" which the project of grammatology seeks to deconstruct, Derrida foregrounds "writing" (*écriture*), in contrast to the totalized "book," and proceeds, similarly, to differentiate grammatology from linguistics by proposing a model of writing that forgoes a positive ontology in preference for tracing the displacement of signifiers.

The excerpt from *Of Grammatology* illustrates Derrida's characteristic mode of analysis, always densely intertextual, tracing the "tension between gesture and statement" in other authors, in this case, de Saussure and Rousseau. In a complex gesture that recalls Hegel, Husserl, and Heidegger, Derrida begins by duplicating de Saussure's gesture in *Course in General Linguistics* of positing "semiology" as a science of the sign with a place staked out for it in advance—with the difference that Derrida posits "grammatology" and immediately proceeds to write as if it were already a science in existence. In one sense, it is: Derrida's "grammatology" occupies the body of its host, linguistics, insinuates its apparent genesis, and differentiates itself point by point. Where linguistics, for example, seeks its ground in phonology, Derrida notes that only in the inscription of writing is the idea of ideal objects possible, an idea essential to the statement of scientific "laws" or the description of general structures. Thus, when linguistics (following de Saussure, that is) permits to writing only a secondary and derivative status, Derrida's analysis, which may seem parasitic, may be more aptly likened to the return of the repressed. The relation between speech and writing, however, is not in Derrida's treatment a struggle for primacy or priority, in the fashion of Tweedledee and Tweedledum, for the crucial reason that the recovery of writing as the repressed does not put writing in the position of being the primary evidence of logos, from which speech derives. Rather, it empties the notion of presence and reinscribes the notion of difference: following de Saussure, Derrida assumes that the sign is "arbitrary" on the view that the system of language is entirely differential, and the meaning of a signifier does not lie in a relation of representation, as a word to a thing, but only in its difference from other signifiers.

The third essay reprinted here, "Différance," develops the complex character of difference, as differing and deferring. As Derrida uses the notion, the substitution of a letter which does not affect pronunciation makes of "différance" a term which is, according to Derrida, "neither a word nor a concept." The risk of falling into sophistical nonsense Derrida willingly accepts, since "différance" is not a concept (in the Kantian sense) because it is not categorially determinable, just as it is not a word (in the idiom of Saussurean linguistics) because it is not a signifier—or rather, as a signifier, it is null. Derrida's rhetorical ingenuity is put to a considerable test in this case, since what he wishes to mark is the intangible acknowledgment of difference and distinction, not simply between two items but as a process whereby the acknowledgment of difference also comprises an interval, a blank in time or space, that is the same in all cases of distinction.

It is noteworthy that Derrida, in taking on this problem as crucial for his notion of grammatology and the work of deconstruction, confronts virtually the same dilemma Plato addresses in the *Sophist,* where he finds it essential to include difference in a taxonomy of "kinds" among the Forms or Ideas—i.e., Motion and Rest, Sameness and Difference, and Existence. Plato's strategy resembles Derrida's, as he has the Eleatic Stranger demonstrate the paradoxical existence of "difference," in part to put an end to arguments contending that falsehood was impossible, since to lie is to "say what is not," and if "what is not" does not exist, how could it be uttered or represented in speech? That such arguments rest on a simple equivocation does not make them innocent; and in predicating existence of "difference" as something that paradoxically has and does not have positive existence of its own, Plato is protesting (as Derrida does implicitly) that to "exist" and to be a material body are not the same. Any metaphysic that denies that *this* difference exists is not only in error but irremediably obtuse.

Unlike Derrida, however, Plato's Stranger has slight patience even for his own demonstration of the paradoxicality of difference, as it may too easily lead to mere quibbling over a triviality. Instead, he urges a harder task, to follow such arguments that assert "that a different thing is the same or the same thing is different in a certain sense, [and] to take account of the precise sense and the precise respect in which they are said to be one or the other. Merely to show in some unspecified way that the same is different or the different is the same . . . and to take pleasure in perpetually parading such contradictions in argument—that is not genuine criticism, but may be recognized as the callow offspring of a too recent contact with reality" (*Sophist* 259d).

In this context, Derrida differs and defers with respect to both Plato and the Sophists; and his project of deconstruction, like the aims of the Sophists, cannot be peremptorily judged on logical grounds alone, since it is suffused with a practical and ethical resistance to oppression, even or especially in the name of "Truth" or "Being" or "Science." Perhaps Derrida's greatest contribution has been to confront what Joseph Conrad might have called the "flabby devil" of critical complacency and to insist with relentless energy that the problems of the linguistic sign are not local or limited but fundamental and deeply tied to the history of Western metaphysics.

Much of Derrida's work has appeared in English translation. Among the most important are *Speech and Phenomenon: Introduction to the Problem of Signs in Husserl's Phenomenology* (1967; trans. 1973); *Of Grammatology* (1967; trans. 1976); *Writing and Difference* (1967; trans. 1978); *Dissemination* (1972; trans. 1981); *Margins of Philosophy* (1972; trans. 1983); *Spurs: Nietzsche's Styles* (1976; trans. 1981); *Signeponge/Signsponge* (1985). *Positions* (1972; trans. 1981) contains several interviews with Derrida. See also especially Christopher Norris, *Deconstruction: Theory and Practice;* Jonathan Culler, "Jacques Derrida," in John Sturrock, ed., *Structuralism and Since: From Lévi-Strauss to Derrida;* Paul de Man, "The Rhetoric of Blindness," in his *Blindness and Insight;* Geoffrey H. Hartman, *Saving the Text: Literature/Derrida/Philosophy;* Gregory J. Ulmer, *Applied Grammatology;* and Robert Magliola, *Derrida on the Mend.*

STRUCTURE, SIGN AND PLAY IN THE DISCOURSE OF THE HUMAN SCIENCES

We need to interpret interpretations
more than to interpret things.

(Montaigne)

Perhaps something has occurred in the history of the concept of structure that could be called an "event," if this loaded word did not entail a meaning which it is precisely the function of structural—or structuralist—thought to reduce or to suspect. Let us speak of an "event," nevertheless, and let us use quotation marks to serve as a precaution. What would this event be then? Its exterior form would be that of a *rupture* and a redoubling.

STRUCTURE, SIGN AND PLAY IN THE DISCOURSE OF THE HUMAN SCIENCES was first presented in 1966 as a lecture at The Johns Hopkins University. It was published in *The Structuralist Controversy* (1970) and in *Writing and Difference* (1967; trans. 1978). This translation is by Alan Bass and is reprinted by permission of The University of Chicago Press.

It would be easy enough to show that the concept of structure and even the word "structure" itself are as old as the *epistēmē*[1]—that is to say, as old as Western science and Western philosophy—and that their roots thrust deep into the soil of ordinary language, into whose deepest recesses the *epistēmē* plunges in order to gather them up and to make them part of itself in a metaphorical displacement. Nevertheless, up to the event which I wish to mark out and define, structure—or rather the structurality of structure—although it has always been at work, has always been neutralized or reduced, and this by a process of giving it a center or of referring it to a point of presence, a fixed origin. The function of this center was not only to orient, balance, and organize the structure—one cannot in fact conceive of an unorganized structure—but above all to make sure that the organizing principle of the structure would limit what we might call the *play* of the structure. By orienting and organizing the coherence of the system, the center of a structure permits the play of its elements inside the total form. And even today the notion of a structure lacking any center represents the unthinkable itself.

Nevertheless, the center also closes off the play which it opens up and makes possible. As center, it is the point at which the substitution of contents,

[1] *epistēmē,* Greek, wisdom, scientific or philosophical knowledge. [Eds.]

elements, or terms is no longer possible. At the center, the permutation or the transformation of elements (which may of course be structures enclosed within a structure) is forbidden. At least this permutation has always remained *interdicted* (and I am using this word deliberately). Thus it has always been thought that the center, which is by definition unique, constituted that very thing within a structure which while governing the structure, escapes structurality. This is why classical thought concerning structure could say that the center is, paradoxically, *within* the structure and *outside it*. The center is at the center of the totality, and yet, since the center does not belong to the totality (is not part of the totality), the totality *has its center elsewhere*. The center is not the center. The concept of centered structure—although it represents coherence itself, the condition of the *epistēmē* as philosophy or science—is contradictorily coherent. And as always, coherence in contradiction expresses the force of a desire.[2] The concept of centered structure is in fact the concept of a play based on a fundamental ground, a play constituted on the basis of a fundamental immobility and a reassuring certitude, which itself is beyond the reach of play. And on the basis of this certitude anxiety can be mastered, for anxiety is invariably the result of a certain mode of being implicated in the game, of being caught by the game, of being as it were at stake in the game from the outset. And again on the basis of what we call the center (and which, because it can be either inside or outside, can also indifferently be called the origin or end, *archē* or *telos*), repetitions, substitutions, transformations, and permutations are always *taken* from a history of meaning [*sens*]—that is, in a word, a history—whose origin may always be reawakened or whose end may always be anticipated in the form of presence. This is why one perhaps could say that the movement of any archaeology, like that of any eschatology, is an accomplice of this reduction of the structurality of structure and always attempts to conceive of structure on the basis of a full presence which is beyond play.

If this is so, the entire history of the concept of structure, before the rupture of which we are speaking, must be thought of as a series of substitutions of center for center, as a linked chain of determinations of the center. Successively, and in a regulated fashion, the center receives different forms or names. The history of metaphysics, like the history of the West, is the history of these metaphors and metonymies. Its matrix—if you will pardon me for demonstrating so little and for being so elliptical in order to come more quickly to my principal theme—is the determination of Being as *presence* in all senses of this word. It could be shown that all the names related to fundamentals, to principles, or to the center have always designated an invariable presence—*eidos, archē, telos, energeia, ousia* (essence, existence, substance, subject) *alētheia*, transcendentality, consciousness, God, man, and so forth.

The event I called a rupture, the disruption I alluded to at the beginning of this paper, presumably would have come about when the structurality of structure had to begin to be thought, that is to say, repeated, and this is why I said that this disruption was repetition in every sense of the word. Henceforth, it became necessary to think both the law which somehow governed the desire for a center in the constitution of structure, and the process of signification which orders the displacements and substitutions for this law of central presence—but a central presence which has never been itself, has always already been exiled from itself into its own substitute. The substitute does not substitute itself for anything which has somehow existed before it. Henceforth, it was necessary to begin thinking that there was no center, that the center could not be thought in the form of a present-being, that the center had no natural site, that it was not a fixed locus but a function, a sort of nonlocus in which an infinite number of sign-substitutions came into play. This was the moment when language invaded the universal problematic, the moment when, in the absence of a center or origin, everything became discourse—provided we can agree on this word—that is to say, a system in which the central signified, the

[2]The reference, in a restricted sense, is to the Freudian theory of neurotic symptoms and of dream interpretation in which a given symbol is understood contradictorily as both the desire to fulfill an impulse and the desire to suppress the impulse. In a general sense the reference is to Derrida's thesis that logic and coherence themselves can only be understood contradictorily, since they presuppose the suppression of *différance*, "writing" in the sense of the general economy. Cf. "La pharmacie de Platon," in *La dissemination*, pp. 125–26, where Derrida uses the Freudian model of dream interpretation in order to clarify the contradictions embedded in philosophical coherence. [Tr.]

original or transcendental signified, is never absolutely present outside a system of differences. The absence of the transcendental signified extends the domain and the play of signification infinitely.

Where and how does this decentering, this thinking the structurality of structure, occur? It would be somewhat naïve to refer to an event, a doctrine, or an author in order to designate this occurrence. It is no doubt part of the totality of an era, our own, but still it has always already begun to proclaim itself and begun to *work*. Nevertheless, if we wished to choose several "names," as indications only, and to recall those authors in whose discourse this occurrence has kept most closely to its most radical formulation, we doubtless would have to cite the Nietzschean critique of metaphysics, the critique of the concepts of Being and truth, for which were substituted the concepts of play, interpretation, and sign (sign without present truth); the Freudian critique of self-presence, that is, the critique of consciousness, of the subject, of self-identity and of self-proximity or self-possession; and, more radically, the Heideggerean destruction of metaphysics, of onto-theology, of the determination of Being as presence. But all these destructive discourses and all their analogues are trapped in a kind of circle. This circle is unique. It describes the form of the relation between the history of metaphysics and the destruction of the history of metaphysics. There is no sense in doing without the concepts of metaphysics in order to shake metaphysics. We have no language—no syntax and no lexicon—which is foreign to this history; we can pronounce not a single destructive proposition which has not already had to slip into the form, the logic, and the implicit postulations of precisely what it seeks to contest. To take one example from many: the metaphysics of presence is shaken with the help of the concept of *sign*. But, as I suggested a moment ago, as soon as one seeks to demonstrate in this way that there is no transcendental or privileged signified and that the domain or play of signification henceforth has no limit, one must reject even the concept and word "sign" itself—which is precisely what cannot be done. For the signification "sign" has always been understood and determined, in its meaning, as sign-of, a signifier referring to a signified, a signifier different from its signified. If one erases the radical difference between signifier and signified, it is the word "signifier" itself which must be abandoned as a metaphysical concept. When Lévi-Strauss says in the preface to *The Raw and the Cooked* that he has "sought to transcend the opposition between the sensible and the intelligible by operating from the outset at the level of signs,"[3] the necessity, force, and legitimacy of his act cannot make us forget that the concept of the sign cannot in itself surpass this opposition between the sensible and the intelligible. The concept of the sign, in each of its aspects, has been determined by this opposition throughout the totality of its history. It has lived only on this opposition and its system. But we cannot do without the concept of the sign, for we cannot give up this metaphysical complicity without also giving up the critique we are directing against this complicity, or without the risk of erasing difference in the self-identity of a signified reducing its signifier into itself or, amounting to the same thing, simply expelling its signifier outside itself. For there are two heterogenous ways of erasing the difference between the signifier and the signified: one, the classic way, consists in reducing or deriving the signifier, that is to say, ultimately in *submitting* the sign to thought; the other, the one we are using here against the first one, consists in putting into question the system in which the preceding reduction functioned: first and foremost, the opposition between the sensible and the intelligible. For the *paradox* is that the metaphysical reduction of the sign needed the opposition it was reducing. The opposition is systematic with the reduction. And what we are saying here about the sign can be extended to all the concepts and all the sentences of metaphysics, in particular to the discourse on "structure." But there are several ways of being caught in this circle. They are all more or less naïve, more or less empirical, more or less systematic, more or less close to the formulation—that is, to the formalization—of this circle. It is these differences which explain the multiplicity of destructive discourses and the disagreement between those who elaborate them. Nietzsche, Freud, and Heidegger, for example, worked within the inherited concepts of metaphysics. Since these concepts are not elements or atoms, and since they are taken from a syntax and a system, every particular borrowing brings along with it the whole of meta-

[3] *The Raw and the Cooked*, trans. John and Doreen Wightman (New York: Harper and Row, 1969), p. 14. [Au.] (Translation somewhat modified.) [Tr.]

physics. This is what allows these destroyers to destroy each other reciprocally—for example, Heidegger regarding Nietzsche, with as much lucidity and rigor as bad faith and misconstruction, as the last metaphysician, the last "Platonist." One could do the same for Heidegger himself, for Freud, or for a number of others. And today no exercise is more widespread.

WHAT is the relevance of this formal schema when we turn to what are called the "human sciences"? One of them perhaps occupies a privileged place—ethnology. In fact one can assume that ethnology could have been born as a science only at the moment when a decentering had come about: at the moment when European culture—and, in consequence, the history of metaphysics and of its concepts—had been *dislocated,* driven from its locus, and forced to stop considering itself as the culture of reference. This moment is not first and foremost a moment of philosophical or scientific discourse. It is also a moment which is political, economic, technical, and so forth. One can say with total security that there is nothing fortuitous about the fact that the critique of ethnocentrism—the very condition for ethnology—should be systematically and historically contemporaneous with the destruction of the history of metaphysics. Both belong to one and the same era. Now, ethnology—like any science—comes about within the element of discourse. And it is primarily a European science employing traditional concepts, however much it may struggle against them. Consequently, whether he wants to or not—and this does not depend on a decision on his part—the ethnologist accepts into his discourse the premises of ethnocentrism at the very moment when he denounces them. This necessity is irreducible; it is not a historical contingency. We ought to consider all its implications very carefully. But if no one can escape this necessity, and if no one is therefore responsible for giving in to it, however little he may do so, this does not mean that all the ways of giving in to it are of equal pertinence. The quality and fecundity of a discourse are perhaps measured by the critical rigor with which this relation to the history of metaphysics and to inherited concepts is thought. Here it is a question both of a critical relation to the language of the social sciences and a critical responsibility of the discourse itself. It is a question of explicitly and systematically posing the problem of the status of a discourse which borrows from a heritage the resources necessary for the deconstruction of that heritage itself. A problem of *economy* and *strategy.*

If we consider, as an example, the texts of Claude Lévi-Strauss, it is not only because of the privilege accorded to ethnology among the social sciences, nor even because the thought of Lévi-Strauss weighs heavily on the contemporary theoretical situation. It is above all because a certain choice has been declared in the work of Lévi-Strauss and because a certain doctrine has been elaborated there, and precisely, in a *more or less explicit manner,* as concerns both this critique of language and this critical language in the social sciences.

In order to follow this movement in the text of Lévi-Strauss, let us choose as one guiding thread among others the opposition between nature and culture. Despite all its rejuvenations and disguises, this opposition is congenital to philosophy. It is even older than Plato. It is at least as old as the Sophists. Since the statement of the opposition *physis/nomos, physis/technē,*[4] it has been relayed to us by means of a whole historical chain which opposes "nature" to law, to education, to art, to technics—but also to liberty, to the arbitrary, to history, to society, to the mind, and so on. Now, from the outset of his researches, and from his first book (*The Elementary Structures of Kinship*) on, Lévi-Strauss simultaneously has experienced the necessity of utilizing this opposition and the impossibility of accepting it. In the *Elementary Structures,* he begins from this axiom or definition: that which is *universal* and spontaneous, and not dependent on any particular culture or on any determinate norm, belongs to nature. Inversely, that which depends upon a system of *norms* regulating society and therefore is capable of *varying* from one social structure to another, belongs to culture. These two definitions are of the traditional type. But in the very first pages of the *Elementary Structures* Lévi-Strauss, who has begun by giving credence to these concepts, encounters what he calls a *scandal,* that is to say, something which no longer tolerates the nature/culture opposition he has accepted, something which *simultaneously* seems to require the predicates of nature and of culture. This scandal is the *incest pro-*

[4] *physis, nomos, technē:* Greek, physical reality, custom, art. [Eds.]

hibition. The incest prohibition is universal; in this sense one could call it natural. But it is also a prohibition, a system of norms and interdicts; in this sense one could call it cultural:

> Let us suppose then that everything universal in man relates to the natural order, and is characterized by spontaneity, and that everything subject to a norm is cultural and is both relative and particular. We are then confronted with a fact, or rather, a group of facts, which, in the light of previous definitions, are not far removed from a scandal: we refer to that complex group of beliefs, customs, conditions and institutions described succinctly as the prohibition of incest, which presents, without the slightest ambiguity, and inseparably combines, the two characteristics in which we recognize the conflicting features of two mutually exclusive orders. It constitutes a rule, but a rule which, alone among all the social rules, possesses at the same time a universal character.[5]

Obviously there is no scandal except within a system of concepts which accredits the difference between nature and culture. By commencing his work with the *factum* of the incest prohibition, Lévi-Strauss thus places himself at the point at which this difference, which has always been assumed to be self-evident, finds itself erased or questioned. For from the moment when the incest prohibition can no longer be conceived within the nature/culture opposition, it can no longer be said to be a scandalous fact, a nucleus of opacity within a network of transparent significations. The incest prohibition is no longer a scandal one meets with or comes up against in the domain of traditional concepts; it is something which escapes these concepts and certainly precedes them—probably as the condition of their possibility. It could perhaps be said that the whole of philosophical conceptualization, which is systematic with the nature/culture opposition, is designed to leave in the domain of the unthinkable the very thing that makes this conceptualization possible: the origin of the prohibition of incest.

This example, too cursorily examined, is only one among many others, but nevertheless it already shows that language bears within itself the necessity of its own critique. Now this critique may be undertaken along two paths, in two "manners." Once the limit of the nature/culture opposition makes itself felt, one might want to question systematically and rigorously the history of these concepts. This is a first action. Such a systematic and historic questioning would be neither a philological nor a philosophical action in the classic sense of these words. To concern oneself with the founding concepts of the entire history of philosophy, to deconstitute them, is not to undertake the work of the philologist or of the classic historian of philosophy. Despite appearances, it is probably the most daring way of making the beginnings of a step outside of philosophy. The step "outside philosophy" is much more difficult to conceive than is generally imagined by those who think they made it long ago with cavalier ease, and who in general are swallowed up in metaphysics in the entire body of discourse which they claim to have disengaged from it.

The other choice (which I believe corresponds more closely to Lévi-Strauss's manner), in order to avoid the possibly sterilizing effects of the first one, consists in conserving all these old concepts within the domain of empirical discovery while here and there denouncing their limits, treating them as tools which can still be used. No longer is any truth value attributed to them; there is a readiness to abandon them, if necessary, should other instruments appear more useful. In the meantime, their relative efficacy is exploited, and they are employed to destroy the old machinery to which they belong and of which they themselves are pieces. This is how the language of the social sciences criticizes *itself*. Lévi-Strauss thinks that in this way he can separate *method* from *truth*, the instruments of the method and the objective significations envisaged by it. One could almost say that this is the primary affirmation of Lévi-Strauss; in any event, the first words of the *Elementary Structures* are: "Above all, it is beginning to emerge that this distinction between nature and society ('nature' and 'culture' seem preferable to us today), while of no acceptable historical significance, does contain a logic, fully justifying its use by modern sociology as a methodological tool."[6]

[5] *The Elementary Structures of Kinship*, trans. James Bell, John von Sturmer, and Rodney Needham (Boston: Beacon Press, 1969), p. 8. [Au./Tr.]

[6] Ibid., p. 3. [Au./Tr.]

Lévi-Strauss will always remain faithful to this double intention: to preserve as an instrument something whose truth value he criticizes.

On the one hand, he will continue, in effect, to contest the value of the nature/culture opposition. More than thirteen years after the *Elementary Structures, The Savage Mind* faithfully echoes the text I have just quoted: "The opposition between nature and culture to which I attached much importance at one time . . . now seems to be of primarily methodological importance." And this methodological value is not affected by its "ontological" nonvalue (as might be said, if this notion were not suspect here): "However, it would not be enough to reabsorb particular humanities into a general one. This first enterprise opens the way for others which . . . are incumbent on the exact natural sciences: the reintegration of culture in nature and finally of life within the whole of its physico-chemical conditions."[7]

On the other hand, still in *The Savage Mind,* he presents as what he calls *bricolage* what might be called the discourse of this method. The *bricoleur,* says Lévi-Strauss, is someone who uses "the means at hand," that is, the instruments he finds at his disposition around him, those which are already there, which had not been especially conceived with an eye to the operation for which they are to be used and to which one tries by trial and error to adapt them, not hesitating to change them whenever it appears necessary, or to try several of them at once, even if their form and their origin are heterogenous—and so forth. There is therefore a critique of language in the form of *bricolage,* and it has even been said that *bricolage* is critical language itself. I am thinking in particular of the article of G. Genette, "Structuralisme et critique littéraire," published in homage to Lévi-Strauss in a special issue of *L'Arc* (no. 26, 1965), where it is stated that the analysis of *bricolage* could "be applied almost word for word" to criticism, and especially to "literary criticism."

If one calls *bricolage* the necessity of borrowing one's concepts from the text of a heritage which is more or less coherent or ruined, it must be said that every discourse is *bricoleur.* The engineer, whom Lévi-Strauss opposes to the *bricoleur,* should be the one to construct the totality of his language, syntax, and lexicon. In this sense the engineer is a myth. A subject who supposedly would be the absolute origin of his own discourse and supposedly would construct it "out of nothing," "out of whole cloth," would be the creator of the verb, the verb itself. The notion of the engineer who supposedly breaks with all forms of *bricolage* is therefore a theological idea; and since Lévi-Strauss tells us elsewhere that *bricolage* is mythopoetic, the odds are that the engineer is a myth produced by the *bricoleur.* As soon as we cease to believe in such an engineer and in a discourse which breaks with the received historical discourse, and as soon as we admit that every finite discourse is bound by a certain *bricolage* and that the engineer and the scientist are also species of *bricoleurs,* then the very idea of *bricolage* is menaced and the difference in which it took on its meaning breaks down.

This brings us to the second thread which might guide us in what is being contrived here.

Lévi-Strauss describes *bricolage* not only as an intellectual activity but also as a mythopoetical activity. One reads in *The Savage Mind,* "Like *bricolage* on the technical plane, mythical reflection can reach brilliant unforeseen results on the intellectual plane. Conversely, attention has often been drawn to the mythopoetical nature of *bricolage.*"[8]

But Lévi-Strauss's remarkable endeavor does not simply consist in proposing, notably in his most recent investigations, a structural science of myths and of mythological activity. His endeavor also appears—I would say almost from the outset—to have the status which he accords to his own discourse on myths, to what he calls his "mythologicals." It is here that his discourse on the myth reflects on itself and criticizes itself. And this moment, this critical period, is evidently of concern to all the languages which share the field of the human sciences. What does Lévi-Strauss say of his "mythologicals"? It is here that we rediscover the mythopoetical virtue of *bricolage.* In effect, what appears most fascinating in this critical search for a new status of discourse is the stated abandonment of all reference to a *center,* to a *subject,* to a privileged *reference,* to an origin, or to an absolute *archia.* The theme of this decentering could be followed

[7] *The Savage Mind* (London: George Weidenfeld and Nicolson; Chicago: The University of Chicago Press, 1966), p. 247. [Au.]

[8] Ibid., p. 17. [Au.]

throughout the "Overture" to his last book, *The Raw and the Cooked.* I shall simply remark on a few key points.

1. From the very start, Lévi-Strauss recognizes that the Bororo myth which he employs in the book as the "reference myth" does not merit this name and this treatment. The name is specious and the use of the myth improper. This myth deserves no more than any other its referential privilege: "In fact, the Bororo myth, which I shall refer to from now on as the key myth, is, as I shall try to show, simply a transformation, to a greater or lesser extent, of other myths originating either in the same society or in neighboring or remote societies. I could, therefore, have legitimately taken as my starting point any one representative myth of the group. From this point of view, the key myth is interesting not because it is typical, but rather because of its irregular position within the group."[9]

2. There is no unity or absolute source of the myth. The focus and the source of the myth are always shadows and virtualities which are elusive, unactualizable, and nonexistent in the first place. Everything begins with structure, configuration, or relationship. The discourse on the acentric structure that myth itself is, cannot itself have an absolute subject or an absolute center. It must avoid the violence that consists in centering a language which describes an acentric structure if it is not to shortchange the form and movement of myth. Therefore it is necessary to forgo scientific or philosophical discourse, to renounce the *epistēmē* which absolutely requires, which is the absolute requirement that we go back to the source, to the center, to the founding basis, to the principle, and so on. In opposition to *epistemic* discourse, structural discourse on myths—*mythological* discourse—must itself be *mythomorphic*. It must have the form of that of which it speaks. This is what Lévi-Strauss says in *The Raw and the Cooked,* from which I would now like to quote a long and remarkable passage:

> The study of myths raises a methodological problem, in that it cannot be carried out according to the Cartesian principle of breaking down the difficulty into as many parts as may be necessary for finding the solution. There is no real end to methodological analysis, no hidden unity to be grasped once the breaking-down process has been completed. Themes can be split up *ad infinitum.* Just when you think you have disentangled and separated them, you realize that they are knitting together again in response to the operation of unexpected affinities. Consequently the unity of the myth is never more than tendential and projective and cannot reflect a state or a particular moment of the myth. It is a phenomenon of the imagination, resulting from the attempt at interpretation; and its function is to endow the myth with synthetic form and to prevent its disintegration into a confusion of opposites. The science of myths might therefore be termed "anaclastic," if we take this old term in the broader etymological sense which includes the study of both reflected rays and broken rays. But unlike philosophical reflection, which aims to go back to its own source, the reflections we are dealing with here concern rays whose only source is hypothetical. . . . And in seeking to imitate the spontaneous movement of mythological thought, this essay, which is also both too brief and too long, has had to conform to the requirements of that thought and to respect its rhythm. It follows that this book on myths is itself a kind of myth.[10]

This statement is repeated a little farther on: "As the myths themselves are based on secondary codes (the primary codes being those that provide the substance of language), the present work is put forward as a tentative draft of a tertiary code, which is intended to ensure the reciprocal translatability of several myths. This is why it would not be wrong to consider this book itself as a myth: it is, as it were, the myth of mythology."[11] The absence of a center is here the absence of a subject and the absence of an author: "Thus the myth and the musical work are like conductors of an orchestra, whose audience becomes the silent performers. If it is now asked where the real center of work is to be found, the answer is that this is impossible to determine. Music

[9] *The Raw and the Cooked,* p. 2. [Au.]

[10] Ibid., pp. 5–6. [Au.]

[11] Ibid., p. 12. [Au.]

and mythology bring man face to face with potential objects of which only the shadows are actualized. . . . Myths are anonymous."[12] The musical model chosen by Lévi-Strauss for the composition of his book is apparently justified by this absence of any real and fixed center of the mythical or mythological discourse.

Thus it is at this point that ethnographic *bricolage* deliberately assumes its mythopoetic function. But by the same token, this function makes the philosophical or epistemological requirement of a center appear as mythological, that is to say, as a historical illusion.

Nevertheless, even if one yields to the necessity of what Lévi-Strauss has done, one cannot ignore its risks. If the mythological is mythomorphic, are all discourses on myths equivalent? Shall we have to abandon any epistemological requirement which permits us to distinguish between several qualities of discourse on the myth? A classic, but inevitable question. It cannot be answered—and I believe that Lévi-Strauss does not answer it—for as long as the problem of the relations between the philosopheme or the theorem, on the one hand, and the mytheme or the mythopoem, on the other, has not been posed explicitly, which is no small problem. For lack of explicitly posing this problem, we condemn ourselves to transforming the alleged transgression of philosophy into an unnoticed fault within the philosophical realm. Empiricism would be the genus of which these faults would always be the species. Transphilosophical concepts would be transformed into philosophical naïvetés. Many examples could be given to demonstrate this risk: the concepts of sign, history, truth, and so forth. What I want to emphasize is simply that the passage beyond philosophy does not consist in turning the page of philosophy (which usually amounts to philosophizing badly), but in continuing to read philosphers *in a certain way.* The risk I am speaking of is always assumed by Lévi-Strauss, and it is the very price of this endeavor. I have said that empiricism is the matrix of all faults menacing a discourse which continues, as with Lévi-Strauss in particular, to consider itself scientific. If we wanted to pose the problem of empiricism and *bricolage* in depth, we would probably end up very quickly with a number of absolutely contradictory propositions concerning the status of discourse in structural ethnology. On the one hand, structuralism justifiably claims to be the critique of empiricism. But at the same time there is not a single book or study by Lévi-Strauss which is not proposed as an empirical essay which can always be completed or invalidated by new information. The structural schemata are always proposed as hypotheses resulting from a finite quantity of information and which are subjected to the proof of experience. Numerous texts could be used to demonstrate this double postulation. Let us turn once again to the "Overture" of *The Raw and the Cooked,* where it seems clear that if this postulation is double, it is because it is a question here of a language on language:

> If critics reproach me with not having carried out an exhaustive inventory of South American myths before analyzing them, they are making a grave mistake about the nature and function of these documents. The total body of myth belonging to a given community is comparable to its speech. Unless the population dies out physically or morally, this totality is never complete. You might as well criticize a linguist for compiling the grammar of a language without having complete records of the words pronounced since the language came into being, and without knowing what will be said in it during the future part of its existence. Experience proves that a linguist can work out the grammar of a given language from a remarkably small number of sentences. . . . And even a partial grammar or an outline grammar is a precious acquisition when we are dealing with unknown languages. Syntax does not become evident only after a (theoretically limitless) series of events has been recorded and examined, because it is itself the body of rules governing their production. What I have tried to give is an outline of the syntax of South American mythology. Should fresh data come to hand, they will be used to check or modify the formulation of certain grammatical laws, so that some are abandoned and replaced by new ones. But in no instance would I feel constrained to accept the aribitrary demand for a

[12] Ibid., pp. 17–18. [Au.]

> total mythological pattern, since, as has been shown, such a requirement has no meaning.[13]

Totalization, therefore, is sometimes defined as *useless,* and sometimes as *impossible.* This is no doubt due to the fact that there are two ways of conceiving the limit of totalization. And I assert once more that these two determinations coexist implicitly in Lévi-Strauss's discourse. Totalization can be judged impossible in the classical style: one then refers to the empirical endeavor of either a subject or a finite richness which it can never master. There is too much, more than one can say. But nontotalization can also be determined in another way: no longer from the standpoint of a concept of finitude as relegation to the empirical, but from the standpoint of the concept of *play.* If totalization no longer has any meaning, it is not because the infiniteness of a field cannot be covered by a finite glance or a finite discourse, but because the nature of the field—that is, language and a finite language—excludes totalization. This field is in effect that of *play,* that is to say, a field of infinite substitutions only because it is finite, that is to say, because instead of being an inexhaustible field, as in the classical hypothesis, instead of being too large, there is something missing from it: a center which arrests and grounds the play of substitutions. One could say—rigorously using that word whose scandalous signification is always obliterated in French—that this movement of play, permitted by the lack or absence of a center or origin, is the movement of *supplementarity.* One cannot determine the center and exhaust totalization because the sign which replaces the center, which supplements it, taking the center's place in its absence—this sign is added, occurs as a surplus, as a *supplement.*[14] The movement of signification adds something, which results in the fact that there is always more, but this addition is a floating one because it comes to perform a vicarious function, to supplement a lack on the part of the signified. Although Lévi-Strauss in his use of the word "supplementary" never emphasizes, as I do here, the two directions of meaning which are so strangely compounded within it, it is not by chance that he uses this word twice in his "Introduction to the Work of Marcel Mauss," at one point where he is speaking of the "overabundance of signifier, in relation to the signifieds to which this overabundance can refer":

> In his endeavor to understand the world, man therefore always has at his disposal a surplus of signification (which he shares out amongst things according to the laws of symbolic thought—which is the task of ethnologists and linguists to study). This distribution of a *supplementary* allowance [*ration supplémentaire*]—if it is permissible to put it that way—is absolutely necessary in order that on the whole the available signifier and the signified it aims at may remain in the relationship of complementarity which is the very condition of the use of symbolic thought."[15]

(It could no doubt be demonstrated that this *ration supplémentaire* of signification is the origin of the *ratio* itself.) The word reappears a little further on, after Lévi-Strauss has mentioned "this floating signifier, which is the servitude of all finite thought":

> In other words—and taking as our guide Mauss's precept that all social phenomena can be assimilated to language—we see in *mana, Wakau, oranda* and other notions of the same type, the conscious expression of a semantic function, whose role it is to permit symbolic thought to operate in spite of the contradiction which is proper to it. In this way are explained the apparently insoluble antinomies attached to this notion. . . . At one and the same time force and action, quality and state, noun and verb; abstract and concrete, omnipresent and localized—

[13] Ibid., pp. 7–8. [Au.]

[14] This double sense of supplement—to supply something which is missing, or to supply something additional—is at the center of Derrida's deconstruction of traditional linguistics in *De la grammatologie.* In a chapter entitled, "The Violence of the Letter: From Lévi-Strauss to Rousseau" (pp. 149ff.), Derrida expands the analysis of Lévi-Strauss begun in this essay in order to further clarify the ways in which the contradictions of traditional logic "program" the most modern conceptual apparatuses of linguistics and the social sciences. [Tr.]

[15] "Introduction à l'oeuvre de Marcel Mauss," in Marcel Mauss, *Sociologie et anthropologie* (Paris: P.U.F., 1950), p. xlix. [Au.]

> *mana* is in effect all these things. But is it not precisely because it is none of these things that *mana* is a simple form, or more exactly, a symbol in the pure state, and therefore capable of becoming charged with any sort of symbolic content whatever? In the system of symbols constituted by all cosmologies, *mana* would simply be a zero symbolic value, that is to say, a sign marking the necessity of a symbolic content *supplementary* [my italics] to that with which the signified is already loaded, but which can take on any value required, provided only that this value still remains part of the available reserve and is not, as phonologists put it, a "group-term."

Lévi-Strauss adds the note:

"Linguists have already been led to formulate hypotheses of this type. For example: 'A zero phoneme is opposed to all the other phonemes in French in that it entails no differential characters and no constant phonetic value. On the contrary, the proper function of the zero phoneme is to be opposed to phoneme absence.' (R. Jakobson and J. Lutz, "Notes on the French Phonemic Pattern," *Word* 5, no. 2 [August 1949]: 155). Similarly, if we schematize the conception I am proposing here, it could almost be said that the function of notions like *mana* is to be opposed to the absence of signification, without entailing by itself any particular signification."[16]

The *overabundance* of the signifier, its *supplementary* character, is thus the result of a finitude, that is to say, the result of a lack which must be *supplemented*.

It can now be understood why the concept of play is important in Lévi-Strauss. His references to all sorts of games, notably to roulette, are very frequent, especially in his *Conversations*,[17] in *Race and History*,[18] and in *The Savage Mind*. Further, the reference to play is always caught up in tension.

Tension with history, first of all. This is a classical problem, objections to which are now well worn. I shall simply indicate what seems to me the formality of the problem: by reducing history, Lévi-Strauss has treated as it deserves a concept which has always been in complicity with a teleological and eschatological metaphysics, in other words, paradoxically, in complicity with that philosophy of presence to which it was believed history could be opposed. The thematic of historicity, although it seems to be a somewhat late arrival in philosophy, has always been required by the determination of Being as presence. With or without etymology, and despite the classic antagonism which opposes these significations throughout all of classical thought, it could be shown that the concept of *epistēmē* has always called forth that of *historia,* if history is always the unity of becoming, as the tradition of truth or the development of science or knowledge oriented toward the appropriation of truth in presence and self-presence, toward knowledge in consciousness-of-self. History has always been conceived as the movement of a resumption of history, as a detour between two presences. But if it is legitimate to suspect this concept of history, there is a risk, if it is reduced without an explicit statement of the problem I am indicating here, of falling back into an ahistoricism of a classical type, that is to say, into a determined moment of the history of metaphysics. Such is the algebraic formality of the problem as I see it. More concretely, in the work of Lévi-Strauss it must be recognized that the respect for structurality, for the internal originality of the structure, compels a neutralization of time and history. For example, the appearance of a new structure, of an original system, always comes about—and this is the very condition of its structural specificity—by a rupture with its past, its origin, and its cause. Therefore one can describe what is peculiar to the structural organization only by not taking into account, in the very moment of this description, its past conditions; by omitting to posit the problem of the transition from one structure to another, by putting history between brackets. In this "structuralist" moment, the concepts of chance and discontinuity are indispensable. And Lévi-Strauss does in fact often appeal to them, for example, as concerns that structure of structures, language, of which he says in the "Introduction to the Work of Marcel Mauss" that it "could only have been born in one fell swoop":

> Whatever may have been the moment and the circumstances of its appearance on the scale

[16] Ibid., pp. xlix–l. [Au.]

[17] George Charbonnier, *Entretiens avec Claude Lévi-Strauss* (Paris: Plon, 1961). [Au.]

[18] *Race and History* (Paris: UNESCO Publications, 1958). [Au.]

> of animal life, language could only have been born in one fell swoop. Things could not have set about acquiring signification progressively. Following a transformation the study of which is not the concern of the social sciences, but rather of biology and psychology, a transition came about from a stage where nothing had a meaning to another where everything possessed it.[19]

This standpoint does not prevent Lévi-Strauss from recognizing the slowness, the process of maturing, the continuous toil of factual transformations, history (for example, *Race and History*). But, in accordance with a gesture which was also Rousseau's and Husserl's, he must "set aside all the facts" at the moment when he wishes to recapture the specificity of a structure. Like Rousseau, he must always conceive of the origin of a new structure on the model of catastrophe—an overturning of nature in nature, a natural interruption of the natural sequence, a setting aside *of* nature.

Besides the tension between play and history, there is also the tension between play and presence. Play is the disruption of presence. The presence of an element is always a signifying and substitutive reference inscribed in a system of differences and the movement of a chain. Play is always play of absence and presence, but if it is to be thought radically, play must be conceived of before the alternative of presence and absence. Being must be conceived as presence or absence on the basis of the possibility of play and not the other way around. If Lévi-Strauss, better than any other, has brought to light the play of repetition and the repetition of play, one no less perceives in his work a sort of ethic of presence, an ethic of nostalgia for origins, an ethic of archaic and natural innocence, of a purity of presence and self-presence in speech—an ethic, nostalgia, and even remorse, which he often presents as the motivation of the ethnological project when he moves toward the archaic societies which are exemplary societies in his eyes. These texts are well known.[20]

Turned towards the lost or impossible presence of the absent origin, this structuralist thematic of broken immediacy is therefore the saddened, *negative,* nostalgic, guilty, Rousseauistic side of the thinking of play whose other side would be the Nietzschean *affirmation,* that is the joyous affirmation of the play of the world and of the innocence of becoming, the affirmation of a world of signs without fault, without truth, and without origin which is offered to an active interpretation. *This affirmation then determines the noncenter otherwise than as loss of the center.* And it plays without security. For there is a *sure* play: that which is limited to the *substitution* of *given* and *existing, present,* pieces. In absolute chance, affirmation also surrenders itself to *genetic* indetermination, to the *seminal* adventure of the trace.

There are thus two interpretations of interpretation, of structure, of sign, of play. The one seeks to decipher, dreams of deciphering a truth or an origin which escapes play and the order of the sign, and which lives the necessity of interpretation as an exile. The other, which is no longer turned toward the origin, affirms play and tries to pass beyond man and humanism, the name of man being the name of that being who, throughout the history of metaphysics or of ontotheology—in other words, throughout his entire history—has dreamed of full presence, the reassuring foundation, the origin and the end of play. The second interpretation of interpretation, to which Nietzsche pointed the way, does not seek in ethnography, as Lévi-Strauss does, the "inspiration of a new humanism" (again citing the "Introduction to the Work of Marcel Mauss").

There are more than enough indications today to suggest we might perceive that these two interpretations of interpretation—which are absolutely irreconcilable even if we live them simultaneously and reconcile them in an obscure economy—together share the field which we call, in such a problematic fashion, the social sciences.

For my part, although these two interpretations must acknowledge and accentuate their difference and define their irreducibility, I do not believe that today there is any question of *choosing*—in the first place because here we are in a region (let us say, provisionally, a region of historicity) where the category of choice seems particularly trivial; and in the second, because we must first try to conceive of the common ground, and the *différance* of this irreducible difference. Here there is a kind of question, let us still call it historical, whose *conception, formation, gestation,* and *labor* we are only catching a

[19] "Introduction à l'oeuvre de Marcel Mauss," p. xlvi. [Au.]

[20] The reference is to *Tristes tropique,* trans. John Russell (London: Hutchinson and Co., 1961). [Tr.]

glimpse of today. I employ these words, I admit, with a glance toward the operations of childbearing—but also with a glance toward those who, in a society from which I do not exclude myself, turn their eyes away when faced by the as yet unnamable which is proclaiming itself and which can do so, as is necessary whenever a birth is in the offing, only under the species of the nonspecies, in the formless, mute, infant, and terrifying form of monstrosity.

FROM

OF GRAMMATOLOGY

LINGUISTICS AND GRAMMATOLOGY

The Outside and the Inside[1]

On the one hand, true to the Western tradition that controls not only in theory but in practice (*in the principle of its practice*) the relationships between speech and writing, Saussure does not recognize in the latter more than a *narrow* and *derivative* function. Narrow because it is nothing but one modality among others, a modality of the events which can befall a language whose essence, as the facts seem to show, can remain forever uncontaminated by writing. "Language does have an . . . oral tradition that is independent of writing" (*Cours de linguistique générale,* p. 46). Derivative because *representative:* signifier of the first signifier, representation of the self-present voice, of the immediate, natural, and direct signification of the meaning (of the signified, of the concept, of the ideal object or what have you). Saussure takes up the traditional definition of writing which, already in Plato and Aristotle, was restricted to the model of phonetic script and the language of words. Let us recall the Aristotelian definition: "Spoken words are the symbols of mental experience and written words are the symbols of spoken words." Saussure: "Language and writing are two distinct systems of signs; the second *exists for the sole purpose of representing* the first" (p. 45; italics added) [p. 23].[2] This representative determination, beside communicating without a doubt essentially with the idea of the sign, does not translate a choice or an evaluation, does not betray a psychological or metaphysical presupposition peculiar to Saussure; it describes or rather reflects the structure of a certain type of writing: phonetic writing, which we use and within whose element the *epistémè* in general (science and philosophy), and linguistics in particular, could be founded. One should, moreover, say *model* rather than *structure;* it is not a question of a system constructed and functioning perfectly, but of an ideal explicitly directing a functioning which *in fact* is never completely phonetic. In fact, but also for reasons of essence to which I shall frequently return.

To be sure this factum of phonetic writing is massive; it commands our entire culture and our entire science, and it is certainly not just one fact among others. Nevertheless it does not respond to any necessity of an absolute and universal essence. Using this as a point of departure, Saussure defines the project and object of general linguistics: "The linguistic object is not defined by the combination of the written word and the spoken word: *the spoken form alone constitutes the object*" (p. 45; italics added) [pp. 23–24].

The form of the question to which he responded thus entailed the response. It was a matter of knowing what sort of *word* is the object of linguistics and what the relationships are between the atomic uni-

OF GRAMMATOLOGY (*De la grammatologie*) was first published in 1967, translated by Gayatri C. Spivak in 1976. The selection below is from part I, chapter 2, only part of which is reproduced here. Reprinted by permission of The Johns Hopkins University Press, copyright 1977.

[1] The introductory section of this chapter provides a brief sketch of Derrida's notion of grammatology as "a science of writing," on the premise that "The concept of writing should define the field of a science" (p. 27). Derrida sets up the contrast between linguistics and grammatology by arguing that the instituting ground for claims of "scientific" status for linguistics is phonology, while the essential task has been taken to be demonstrating the "unity" of sound and meaning, which therefore appears to place writing "outside" the field of linguistics proper, as "the sign of a sign." [Eds.]

The title of the next section is "The Outside Is the Inside." In French, "is" (*est*) and "and" (*et*) "sound the same." For Derrida's discussion of the complicity between supplementation (and) and the copula (is), see, particularly, "Le supplément de copule: la philosophie devant la linguistique," in *Margins of Philosophy.* [Tr.]

[2] Hereafter, page numbers in parentheses refer to the original work and those in brackets to the English translation. [Tr.]

ties that are the written and the spoken word. Now the word (*vox*) is already a unity of sense and sound, of concept and voice, or, to speak a more rigorously Saussurian language, of the signified and the signifier. This last terminology was moreover first proposed in the domain of spoken language alone, of linguistics in the narrow sense and not in the domain of semiology ("I propose to retain the word *sign* [*signe*] to designate the whole and to replace *concept* and *sound-image* respectively by *signified* [*signifié*] and *signifier* [*signifiant*]" p. 99 [p. 67]). The *word* is thus already a constituted unity, an effect of "the somewhat mysterious fact . . . that 'thought-sound' implies divisions" (p. 156) [p. 112]. Even if the word is in its turn articulated, even if it implies other divisions, as long as one poses the question of the relationships between speech and writing in the light of the indivisible units of the "thought-sound," there will always be the ready response. Writing will be "phonetic," it will be the outside, the exterior representation of language and of this "thought-sound." It must necessarily operate from already constituted units of signification, in the formation of which it has played no part.

Perhaps the objection will be made that writing up to the present has not only not contradicted, but indeed confirmed the linguistics of the word. Hitherto I seem to have maintained that only the fascination of the unit called *word* has prevented giving to writing the attention that it merited. By that I seemed to suppose that, by ceasing to accord an absolute privilege to the word, modern linguistics would become that much more attentive to writing and would finally cease to regard it with suspicion. André Martinet comes to the opposite conclusion. In his study "The Word,"[3] he describes the necessity that contemporary linguistics obeys when it is led, if not to dispense everywhere with the concept of the word, at least to make its usage more flexible, to associate it with the concepts of smaller or greater units (monemes or syntagms). In accrediting and consolidating the division of language into words in certain areas of linguistics, writing would thus have encouraged classical linguistics in its prejudices. Writing would have constructed or at least condensed the "screen of the word."

> What a contemporary linguist can say of the word well illustrates the general revision of traditional concepts that the functionalist and structuralist research of the last thirty-five years had to undertake in order to give a scientific basis to the observation and description of languages. Certain applications of linguistics, like the researches relating to mechanical translation, by the emphasis they place on the written form of language, could make us believe in the fundamental importance of the divisions of the written text and make us forget that one must always start with the oral utterance in order to understand the real nature of human language. Also it is more than ever indispensable to insist on the necessity of pushing the examination beyond the immediate appearances and the structures most familiar to the researcher. It is behind the screen of the word that the truly fundamental characteristics of human language often appear.

One cannot but subscribe to this caution. Yet it must always be recognized that it throws suspicion only on a certain type of writing: phonetic writing conforming to the empirically determined and practiced divisions of ordinary oral language. The processes of mechanical translation to which it alludes conform similarly to that spontaneous practice. Be-

[3] *Diogène* 51, 1965, [p. 54]. [Parallel English, French, and Spanish editions of this journal are published simultaneously. My references are to the English *Diogenes*.] André Martinet alludes to the "courage" which would formerly have been "needed" to "foresee that the term 'word' itself might have to be put aside if . . . researches showed that this term could not be given a universally applicable definition" (p. 39) [p. 39]. "Semiology, as revealed by recent studies, has no need of the word" (p. 40) [p. 39]. . . . "Grammarians and linguists have long known that the analysis of utterances can be pursued beyond the word without going into phonetics, that is, ending with segments of speech, such as syllables or phonemes, which have nothing to do with meaning" (p. 41) [p. 40]. "We are touching here on what renders the notion of the word so suspect to all true linguists. They cannot accept traditional writing without verifying first whether it reproduces faithfully the true structure of the language which it is supposed to record" (p. 48) [p. 48]. In conclusion Martinet proposes the replacement "in linguistic practice" of the notion of word by that of "syntagm," any "group of several minimal signs" that will be called "monemes." [Au./Tr.]

yond that model and that concept of writing, this entire demonstration must, it seems, be reconsidered. For it remains trapped in the Saussurian limitation that we are attempting to explore.

In effect Saussure limits the number of systems of writing to two, both defined as systems of representation of the oral language, either representing *words* in a synthetic and global manner, or representing *phonetically* the elements of sounds constituting words:

> There are only two systems of writing: 1) In an ideographic system each word is represented by a single sign that is unrelated to the component sounds of the word itself. Each written sign stands for a whole word and, indirectly, for the idea expressed by the word. The classic example of an ideographic system of writing is Chinese. 2) The system commonly known as "phonetic" tries to reproduce the succession of sounds that make up a word. Phonetic systems are sometimes syllabic, sometimes alphabetic, i.e., based on the irreducible elements of speech. Moreover, ideographic systems freely become mixtures when certain ideograms lose their original value and become symbols of isolated sounds. (p. 47) [pp. 25–26].

This limitation is at bottom justified, in Saussure's eyes, by the notion of the arbitrariness of the sign. Writing being defined as "a system of signs," there is no "symbolic" writing (in the Saussurian sense), no figurative writing; there is no *writing* as long as graphism keeps a relationship of natural figuration and of some resemblance to what is then not *signified* but represented, drawn, etc. The concept of pictographic or natural writing would therefore be contradictory for Saussure. If one considers the now recognized fragility of the notions of pictogram, ideogram, etc., and the uncertainty of the frontiers between so-called pictographic, ideographic, and phonetic scripts, one realizes not only the unwiseness of the Saussurian limitation but the need for general linguistics to abandon an entire family of concepts inherited from metaphysics—often through the intermediary of a psychology—and clustering around the concept of arbitrariness. All this refers, beyond the nature/culture opposition, to a supervening opposition between *physis* and *nomos, physis* and *techné,* whose ultimate function is perhaps to *derive* historicity; and, paradoxically, not to recognize the rights of history, production, institutions etc., except in the form of the arbitrary and in the substance of naturalism. But let us keep that question provisionally open: perhaps this gesture, which in truth presides over metaphysics, is also inscribed in the concept of history and even in the concept of time.

In addition, Saussure introduces another massive limitation: "I shall limit discussion to the phonetic system and especially to the one used today, the system that stems from the Greek alphabet" (p. 48) [p. 26].

These two limitations are all the more reassuring because they are just what we need at a specific point to fulfill the most legitimate of exigencies; in fact, the condition for the scientificity of linguistics is that the field of linguistics have hard and fast frontiers, that it be a system regulated by an *internal* necessity, and that in a certain way its structure be closed. The representativist concept of writing facilitates things. If writing is nothing but the "figuration" (p. 44) [p. 23] of the language, one has the right to exclude it from the interiority of the system (for it must be believed that there is an *inside* of the language), as the image may be excluded without damage from the system of reality. Proposing as his theme "the representation of language by writing" Saussure thus begins by positing that writing is "unrelated to [the] . . . inner system" of language (p. 44) [p. 23]. External/internal, image/reality, representation/presence, such is the old grid to which is given the task of outlining the domain of a science. And of what science? Of a science that can no longer answer to the classical concept of the *epistémè* because the originality of its field—an originality that it inaugurates—is that the opening of the "image" within it appears as the condition of "reality"; a relationship that can no longer be thought within the simple difference and the uncompromising exteriority of "image" and "reality," of "outside" and "inside," of "appearance" and "essence," with the entire system of oppositions which necessarily follows from it. Plato, who said basically the same thing about the relationship between writing, speech, and being (or idea), had at least a more subtle, more critical, and less complacent theory of image, painting, and imitation than the one that presides over the birth of Saussurian linguistics.

It is not by chance that the exclusive consideration of phonetic writing permits a response to the exigencies of the "internal system." The basic functional principle of phonetic writing is precisely to respect and protect the integrity of the "internal system" of the language, even if in fact it does not succeed in doing so. *The Saussurian limitation does not respond, by a mere happy convenience, to the scientific exigency of the "internal system." That exigency is itself constituted, as the epistemological exigency in general, by the very possibility of phonetic writing and by the exteriority of the "notation" to internal logic.*

But let us not simplify: on that point Saussure too is not quite complacent. Why else would he give so much attention to that external phenomenon, that exiled figuration, that outside, that double? Why does he judge it impossible "to simply disregard" [literally "make abstraction of"] what is nevertheless designated as the abstract itself with respect to the inside of language? "Writing, though unrelated to its inner system, is used continually to represent language. We cannot simply disregard it. We must be acquainted with its usefulness, shortcomings, and dangers" (p. 44) [p. 23].

Writing would thus have the exteriority that one attributes to utensils; to what is even an imperfect tool and a dangerous, almost maleficent, technique. One understands better why, instead of treating this exterior figuration in an appendix or marginally, Saussure devotes so laborious a chapter to it almost at the beginning of the *Course*. It is less a question of outlining than of protecting, and even of restoring the internal system of the language in the purity of its concept against the gravest, most perfidious, most permanent contamination which has not ceased to menace, even to corrupt that system, in the course of what Saussure strongly wishes, in spite of all opposition, to consider as an external history, as a series of accidents affecting the language and befalling it *from without,* at the moment of "notation" (p. 45) [p. 24], as if writing began and ended with notation. Already in the *Phaedrus,* Plato says that the evil of writing comes from without (275a). The contamination by writing, the fact or the threat of it, are denounced in the accents of the moralist or preacher by the linguist from Geneva. The tone counts; it is as if, at the moment when the modern science of the logos would come into its autonomy and its scientificity, it became necessary again to attack a heresy. This tone began to make itself heard when, at the moment of already tying the *epistémè* and the *logos* within the same possibility, the *Phaedrus* denounced writing as the intrusion of an artful technique, a forced entry of a totally original sort, an archetypal violence: eruption of the *outside* within the *inside,* breaching into the interiority of the soul, the living self-presence of the soul within the true logos, the help that speech lends to itself. Thus incensed, Saussure's vehement argumentation aims at more than a theoretical error, more than a moral fault: at a sort of stain and primarily at a sin. Sin has been defined often—among others by Malebranche[4] and by Kant—as the inversion of the natural relationship between the soul and the body through passion. Saussure here points at the inversion of the natural relationship between speech and writing. It is not a simple analogy: writing, the letter, the sensible inscription, has always been considered by Western tradition as the body and matter external to the spirit, to breath, to speech, and to the logos. And the problem of soul and body is no doubt derived from the problem of writing from which it seems—conversely—to borrow its metaphors.

Writing, sensible matter and artificial exteriority: a "clothing." It has sometimes been contested that speech clothed thought. Husserl, Saussure, Lavelle have all questioned it. But has it ever been doubted that writing was the clothing of speech? For Saussure it is even a garment of perversion and debauchery, a dress of corruption and disguise, a festival mask that must be exorcised, that is to say warded off, by the good word: "Writing veils the appearance of language; it is not a guise for language but a disguise" (p. 51) [p. 30]. Strange "image." One already suspects that if writing is "image" and exterior "figuration," this "representation" is not innocent. The outside bears with the inside a relationship that is, as usual, anything but simple exteriority. The meaning of the outside was always present within the inside, imprisoned outside the outside, and vice versa.

Thus a science of language must recover the *natural*—that is, the simple and original—relationships between speech and writing, that is, between an inside and an outside. It must restore its absolute

[4] Nicolas Malebranche (1638–1715), French philosopher. [Eds.]

youth, and the purity of its origin, short of a history and a fall which would have perverted the relationships between outside and inside. Therefore there would be a *natural order* of relationships between linguistic and graphic signs, and it is the theoretician of the arbitrariness of the sign who reminds us of it. According to the historico-metaphysical presuppositions evoked above, there would be first a *natural* bond of sense to the senses and it is this that passes from sense to sound: "the natural bond," Saussure says, "the only true bond, the bond of sound" (p. 46) [p. 25]. This natural bond of the signified (concept or sense) to the phonic signifier would condition the natural relationship subordinating writing (visible image) to speech. It is this natural relationship that would have been inverted by the original sin of writing: "The graphic form [*image*] manages to force itself upon them at the expense of sound . . . and the natural sequence is reversed" (p. 47) [p. 25]. Malebranche explained original sin as inattention, the temptation of ease and idleness, by that *nothing* that was Adam's "distraction," alone culpable before the innocence of the divine word: the latter exerted no force, no efficacy, since *nothing* had taken place. Here too, one gave in to *ease*, which is curiously, but as usual, on the side of technical artifice and not within the bent of the natural movement thus thwarted or deviated:

> First, the graphic form [*image*] of words strikes us as being something permanent and stable, better suited than sound to constitute the unity of language throughout time. Though it creates a purely *fictitious* unity, the *superficial* bond of writing is much *easier* to grasp than the natural bond, the only true bond, the bond of sound (p. 46; italics added) [p. 25].

That "the graphic form of words strikes us as being something permanent and stable, better suited than sound to constitute the unity of language throughout time," is that not a natural phenomenon too? In fact a bad nature, "superficial" and "fictitious" and "easy," effaces a good nature by imposture; that which ties sense to sound, the "thought-sound." Saussure is faithful to the tradition that has always associated writing with the fatal violence of the political institution. It is clearly a matter, as with Rousseau for example, of a break with nature, of a usurpation that was coupled with the theoretical blindness to the natural essence of language, at any rate to the natural bond between the "instituted signs" of the voice and "the first language of man," the "cry of nature" (*Second Discourse*).[5] Saussure: "But the spoken word is so intimately bound to its written *image* that the latter manages to *usurp* the main role" (p. 45; italics added) [p. 24]. Rousseau: "Writing is nothing but the representation of speech; it is *bizarre* that one gives more care to the determining of the *image* than to the *object*." Saussure: "Whoever says that a certain letter must be pronounced a certain way is mistaking the written *image* of a sound for the sound itself. . . . [One] attribute[s] the oddity [*bizarrerie*] to an exceptional pronunciation" (p. 52) [p. 30].[6] What is intolerable and fascinating is indeed the intimacy intertwining image and thing, *graph, i.e.,* and phonè, to the point where by a mirroring, inverting, and perverting effect, speech seems in its turn the speculum of writing, which "manages to usurp the main role." Representation mingles with what it represents, to the point where one speaks as one writes, one thinks as if the represented were nothing more than the shadow or reflection of the representer. A dangerous promiscuity and a nefarious complicity between the reflection

[5] "Discours sur l'origine et les fondements de l'inégalité." Derrida's references are to the Pléiade edition, vol. 3, mine, placed within brackets, to "A Discourse on the Origin of Inequality," *The Social Contract and Discourses*, trans. G. D. H. Cole (London, 1913). [Tr.]

[6] Let us extend our quotation to bring out the tone and the affect of these theoretical propositions. Saussure *puts the blame on* writing: "Another result is that the less writing represents what it is supposed to represent, the stronger the tendency to use it as a basis becomes. Grammarians never fail to draw attention to the written form. Psychologically, the tendency is easily explained, but its consequences are annoying. Free use of the words 'pronounce' and 'pronunciation' sanctions the abuse and reverses the real, legitimate relationship between writing and language. Whoever says that a certain letter must be pronounced a certain way is mistaking the written image of a sound for the sound itself. For French *oi* to be pronounced *wa*, this spelling would have to exist independently; actually *wa* is written *oi*." Instead of meditating upon this strange proposition, the *possibility* of such a text ("actually *wa* is written *oi*"), Saussure argues: "To attribute the oddity to an exceptional pronunciation of *o* and *i* is also misleading, for this implies that language depends on its written form and that certain liberties may be taken in writing, as if the graphic symbols were the norm" (p. 52) [p. 30]. [Au.]

and the reflected which lets itself be seduced narcissistically. In this play of representation, the point of origin becomes ungraspable. There are things like reflecting pools, and images, an infinite reference from one to the other, but no longer a source, a spring. There is no longer a simple origin. For what is reflected is split *in itself* and not only as an addition to itself of its image. The reflection, the image, the double, splits what it doubles. The origin of the speculation becomes a difference. What can look at itself is not one; and the law of the addition of the origin to its representation, of the thing to its image, is that one plus one makes at least three. The historical usurpation and theoretical oddity that install the image within the rights of reality are determined as the *forgetting* of a simple origin. By Rousseau but also for Saussure. The displacement is hardly anagrammatic: "The result is that people forget that they learn to speak before they learn to write and the natural sequence is reversed" (p. 47) [p. 25]. The violence of forgetting. Writing, a mnemotechnic means, supplanting good memory, spontaneous memory, signifies forgetfulness. It is exactly what Plato said in the *Phaedrus,* comparing writing to speech as *hypomnesis* to *mnémè,* the auxilliary aide-mémoire to the living memory. Forgetfulness because it is a mediation and the departure of the logos from itself. Without writing, the latter would remain in itself. Writing is the dissimulation of the natural, primary, and immediate presence of sense to the soul within the logos. Its violence befalls the soul as unconsciousness. Deconstructing this tradition will therefore not consist of reversing it, of making writing innocent. Rather of showing why the violence of writing does not *befall* an innocent language. There is an originary violence of writing because language is first, in a sense I shall gradually reveal, writing. "Usurpation" has always already begun. The sense of the right side appears in a mythological effect of return.

"The sciences and the arts" have elected to live within this violence, their "progress" has consecrated forgetfulness and "corrupted manners [*moeurs*]." Saussure again anagrammatizes Rousseau: "The literary language adds to the undeserved importance of writing. . . . Thus writing assumes undeserved importance [*une importance à laquelle elle n'a pas droit*]" (p. 47) [p. 25]. When linguists become embroiled in a theoretical mistake in this subject, when they are taken in, they are *culpable,* their fault is above all *moral;* they have yielded to imagination, to sensibility, to passion, they have fallen into the "trap" (p. 46) [p. 25] of writing, have let themselves be fascinated by the "influence [*prestige*] of the written form" (ibid.), of that custom, that second nature. "The language does have a definite and stable oral tradition that is independent of writing, but the influence [*prestige*] of the written form prevents our seeing this." We are thus not blind to the visible, but blinded by the visible, dazzled by writing. "The first linguists confused language and writing, just as the humanists had done before them. Even Bopp.[7] . . . His immediate successors fell into the same trap." Rousseau had already addressed the same reproach to the Grammarians: "For the Grammarians, the art of speech seems to be very little more than the art of writing."[8] As usual, the "trap" is artifice dissimulated in nature. This explains why *The Course in General Linguistics* treats *first* this strange external system that is writing. As necessary preamble to restoring the natural to itself, one must first disassemble the trap. We read a little further on:

> To substitute immediately what is natural for what is artificial would be necessary; but this is impossible without first studying the sounds of what is language; detached from their graphic signs, sounds represent only vague notions, and the prop provided by writing, though deceptive, is still preferable. The first linguists, who knew nothing about the physiology of articulated sounds, were constantly falling into a trap; to let go of the letter was for them to lose their foothold; to me, it means a first step in the direction of truth (p. 55. Opening of the chapter on Phonology) [p. 32].

[7]Franz Bopp (1791–1867), German philologist, early analyst of connections among Indo-European languages. [Eds.]

[8]Manuscript included in the *Pléiade* edition under the title *Prononciation* (II, p. 1248). Its composition is placed circa 1761 (cf. editors' note in the *Pléiade*). The sentence that I have just cited is the last one of the fragment as published in the *Pléiade.* It does not appear in the comparable edition of the same group of notes by [M. G.] Streckeisen-Moultou, under the title of "Fragment d'un Essai sur les langues" and "Notes détachées sur le même sujet," in *Oeuvres et correspondances inédites de J. J. Rousseau* ([Paris], 1861), p. 295. [Au.]

For Saussure, to give in to the "prestige of the written form" is, as I have just said, to give in to *passion*. It is passion—and I weigh my word—that Saussure analyzes and criticizes here, as a moralist and a psychologist of a very old tradition. As one knows, passion is tyrannical and enslaving: "Philological criticism is still deficient on one point: it follows the written language slavishly and neglects the living language" (p. 14) [pp. 1–2]. "The tyranny of writing," Saussure says elsewhere (p. 53) [p. 31]. That tyranny is at bottom the mastery of the body over the soul, and passion is a passivity and sickness of the soul, the moral perversion is *pathological*. The reciprocal effect of writing on speech is "wrong [*vicieuse*]," Saussure says, "such mistakes are really pathological" (p. 53) [p. 31]. The inversion of the natural relationships would thus have engendered the perverse cult of the letter-image: sin of idolatry, "superstition of the letter" Saussure says in the *Anagrams*[9] where he has difficulty in proving the existence of a "phoneme anterior to all writing." The perversion of artifice engenders monsters. Writing, like all artificial languages one would wish to fix and remove from the living history of the natural language, participates in the monstrosity. It is a deviation from nature. The characteristic of the Leibnizian type and Esperanto would be here in the same position. Saussure's irritation with such possibilities drives him to pedestrian comparisons: "A man proposing a fixed language that posterity would have to accept for what it is would be like a hen hatching a duck's egg" (p. 111) [p. 76]. And Saussure wishes to save not only the *natural life* of language, but the natural habits of writing. Spontaneous life must be protected. Thus, the introduction of scientific exigencies and the taste for exactitude into ordinary phonetic writing must be avoided. In this case, rationality would bring death, desolation, and monstrousness. That is why common orthography must be kept away from the notations of the linguist and *the multiplying of diacritical signs must be avoided:*

> Are there grounds for substituting a phonologic alphabet for a system [*l'orthographe*] already in use? Here I can only broach this interesting subject. I think that phonological writing should be for the use of linguists only. First, how would it be possible to make the English, Germans, French, etc. adopt a uniform system! Next, an alphabet applicable to all languages would probably be weighed down by diacritical marks; and—to say nothing of the distressing appearance of a page of phonological writing—attempts to gain precision would obviously confuse the reader by obscuring what the writing was designed to express. The advantages would not be sufficient to compensate for the inconveniences. Phonological exactitude is not very desirable outside science (p. 57) [p. 34].

I hope my intention is clear. I think Saussure's reasons are good. I do not question, *on the level on which he says it,* the truth of *what Saussure says* in such a tone. And as long as an explicit problematics, a *critique* of the relationships between speech and writing, is not elaborated, what he denounces as the blind prejudice of classical linguists or of common experience indeed remains a blind prejudice, on the basis of a general presupposition which is no doubt common to the accused and the prosecutor.

I would rather announce the limits and the presuppositions of what seems here to be self-evident and what seems to me to retain the character and validity of evidence. The limits have already begun to appear: Why does a project of *general* linguistics, concerning the *internal system in general of language in general,* outline the limits of its field by excluding, as *exteriority in general, a particular* system of writing, however important it might be, even were it to be *in fact* universal?[10] A particular system which has precisely for its *principle* or at least for

[9] Text presented by Jean Starobinski in "Les anagrammes de Ferdinand de Saussure: textes inédits," *Mercure de France* (February 1964), [vol. 350; now published as *Les mots sous les mots: les anagrammes de Ferdinand de Saussure*, ed. Starobinski (Paris, 1971)]. [Au./Tr.]

[10] Rousseau is seemingly more cautious in the fragment on *Pronunciation:* "Thought is analyzed by speech, speech by writing; speech represents thought by conventional signs, and writing represents speech in the same way; thus the art of writing is nothing but a mediated representation of thought, *at least in the vocalic languages, the only ones that we use*" (p. 1249; italics added). Only seemingly, for even if, unlike Saussure, Rousseau here forbids himself to speak *in general* of the entire system, the notions of mediacy and of "vocalic languages" leave the enigma intact. I shall be obliged to return to this. [Au.]

its *declared* project to be exterior to the spoken language. Declaration of principle, pious wish and historical violence of a speech dreaming its full self-presence, living itself as its own resumption; self-proclaimed language, auto-production of a speech declared alive, capable, Socrates said, of helping itself, a logos which believes itself to be its own father, being lifted thus above written discourse, *infans* (speechless) and infirm at not being able to respond when one questions it and which, since its "parent['s help] is [always] needed" (toū patròs áeì deītai boīthoū—*Phaedrus* 275d) must therefore be born out of a primary gap and a primary *expatriation,* condemning it to wandering and blindness, to mourning. Self-proclaimed language but actually speech, deluded into believing itself completely alive, and violent, for it is not "capable of protect[ing] or defend[ing] [itself]" (dunatōs mēn amūnai éauto) except through expelling the other, and especially *its own* other, throwing it *outside* and *below,* under the name of writing. But however important it might be, and were it in fact universal or called upon to become so, that particular model which is phonetic writing *does not exist;* no practice is ever totally faithful to its principle. Even before speaking, as I shall do further on, of a radical and a priori necessary infidelity, one can already remark its massive phenomenon in mathematical script or in punctuation, in *spacing* in general, which it is difficult to consider as simple accessories of writing. That a speech supposedly alive can lend itself to spacing in its own writing is what relates it originarily to its own death.

Finally, the "usurpation" of which Saussure speaks, the violence by which writing would substitute itself for its own origin, for that which ought not only to have engendered it but to have been engendered from itself—such a reversal of power cannot be an accidental aberration. Usurpation necessarily refers us to a profound possibility of essence. This is without a doubt inscribed within speech itself and he should have questioned it, perhaps even started from it.

Saussure confronts the system of the spoken language with the system of phonetic (and even alphabetic) writing as though with the telos of writing. This teleology leads to the interpretation of all eruptions of the nonphonetic within writing as transitory crisis and accident of passage, and it is right to consider this teleology to be a Western ethnocentrism, a premathematical primitivism, and a preformalist intuitionism. Even if this teleology responds to some absolute necessity, it should be problematized as such. The scandal of "usurpation" invites us expressly and intrinsically to do that. How was the trap and the usurpation possible? Saussure never replies to this question beyond a psychology of the passions or of the imagination; a psychology reduced to its most conventional diagrams. This best explains why all linguistics, a determined sector inside semiology, is placed under the authority and superiority of psychology: "To determine the exact place of semiology is the task of the psychologist" (p. 33) [p. 16]. The affirmation of the essential and "natural" bond between the *phonè* and the sense, the privilege accorded to an order of signifier (which then becomes the major signified of all other signifiers) depend expressly, and in contradiction to the other levels of the Saussurian discourse, upon a psychology of consciousness and of intuitive consciousness. What Saussure does not question here is the essential possibility of nonintuition. Like Husserl, Saussure determines this nonintuition teleologically as *crisis.* The *empty* symbolism of the written notation—in mathematical technique for example—is also for Husserlian intuitionism that which exiles us far from the *clear* evidence of the sense, that is to say from the full presence of the signified in its truth, and thus opens the possibility of crisis. This is indeed a crisis of the logos. Nevertheless, for Husserl, this possibility remains linked with the very moment of truth and the production of ideal objectivity: it has in fact an essential need for writing.[11] By one entire aspect of his text, Husserl makes us think that the negativity of the crisis is not a mere accident. But it is then the concept of crisis that should be suspect, by virtue of what ties it to a dialectical and teleological determination of negativity.

On the other hand, to account for "usurpation" and the origin of "passion," the classical and very superficial argument of the solid permanence of the written thing, not to be simply false, calls forth descriptions which are precisely no longer within the province of psychology. Psychology will never be able to accommodate within its space that which constitutes the absence of the signatory, to say nothing of the absence of the referent. Writing is the

[11] Cf. *L'origine de la géométrie,* 1962. [Au.]

name of these two absences. Besides, is it not contradictory to what is elsewhere affirmed about language having "a definite and [far more] stable oral tradition that is independent of writing" (p. 46) [p. 24], to explain the usurpation by means of writing's power of *duration,* by means of the *durability* of the substance of writing? If these two "stabilities" were of the same nature, and if the stability of the spoken language were superior and independent, the origin of writing, its "prestige" and its supposed harmfulness, would remain an inexplicable mystery. It seems then as if Saussure wishes *at the same time* to demonstrate the corruption of speech by writing, to denounce the harm that the latter does to the former, *and* to underline the inalterable and natural independence of language. "Languages are independent of writing" (p. 45) [p. 24]. Such is the truth of nature. And yet nature is affected—from without—by an overturning which modifies it in its interior, denatures it and obliges it to be separated from itself. Nature denaturing itself, being separated *from itself,* naturally gathering its outside into its inside, is *catastrophe,* a natural event that overthrows nature, or *monstrosity,* a natural deviation within nature. The function assumed in Rousseau's discourse by the catastrophe (as we shall see), is here delegated to monstrousness. Let us cite the entire conclusion of Chapter VI of the *Course* ("Graphic Representation of Language"), which must be compared to Rousseau's text on *Pronunciation:*

> But the tyranny of writing goes even further. By imposing itself upon the masses, spelling influences and modifies language. This happens only in highly literary languages where written texts play an important role. Then visual images lead to wrong [*vicieuses*] pronunciations; such mistakes are really pathological. Spelling practices cause mistakes in the pronunciation of many French words. For instance, there were two spellings for the surname Lefèvre (from latin *faber*), one popular and simple, the other learned and etymological: *Lefèvre* and *Lefèbvre.* Because *v* and *u* were not kept apart in the old system of writing, *Lefèbvre* was read as *Lefébure,* with a *b* that has never really existed and a *u* that was the result of ambiguity. Now, the latter form is actually pronounced (pp. 53–54) [p. 31].

Where is the evil? one will perhaps ask. And what has been invested in the "living word," that makes such "aggressions" of writing intolerable? What investment begins by determining the constant action of writing as a deformation and an aggression? What prohibition has thus been transgressed? Where is the sacrilege? Why should the mother tongue be protected from the operation of writing? Why determine that operation as a violence, and why should the transformation be only a deformation? Why should the mother tongue not have a history, or, what comes to the same thing, produce its own history in a perfectly natural, autistic, and domestic way, without ever being affected by any outside? Why wish to punish writing for a monstrous crime, to the point of wanting to reserve for it, even within scientific treatments, a "special compartment" that holds it at a distance? For it is indeed within a sort of intralinguistic leper colony that Saussure wants to contain and concentrate the problem of deformations through writing. And, in order to be convinced that he would take in very bad part the innocent questions that I have just asked—for after all *Lefébure is not a bad name* and we can love this play—let us read the following. The passage below explains to us that the "play" is not "natural," and its accents are pessimistic: "Mispronunciations due to spelling will probably appear more frequently and as time goes on, the number of useless letters pronounced by speakers will probably increase." As in Rousseau in the same context, the Capital is accused: "Some Parisians already pronounce the *t* in *sept femmes* 'seven women.'" Strange example. The historical gap—for it is indeed history that one must stop in order to protect language from writing—will only widen:

> Darmsteter foresees the day when even the last two letters of *vingt* "twenty" will be pronounced—truly an orthographic *monstrosity.* Such phonic *deformations* belong to language but *do not stem from its natural functioning.* They are due to an *external* influence. Linguistics should put them into a *special compartment* for observation: they are *teratological* cases (p. 54; italics added) [pp. 31–32].

It is clear that the concepts of stability, permanence, and duration, which here assist thinking the relationships between speech and writing, are too lax and open to every uncritical investiture. They would require more attentive and minute analyses. The same is applicable to an explanation according to which "most people pay more attention to visual impressions simply because these are sharper and more lasting than aural impressions" (p. 46) [p. 25]. This explanation of "usurpation" is not only empirical in its form, it is problematic in its content, it refers to a metaphysics and to an old physiology of sensory faculties constantly disproved by science, as by the experience of language and by the body proper as language. It imprudently makes of visibility the tangible, simple, and essential element of writing. Above all, in considering the audible as the *natural* milieu within which language must *naturally* fragment and articulate its instituted signs, thus exercising its arbitrariness, this explanation excludes all possibility of some natural relationship between speech and writing at the very moment that it affirms it. Instead of deliberately dismissing the notions of nature and institution that it constantly uses, which ought to be done first, it thus confuses the two. It finally and most importantly contradicts the principal affirmation according to which "the thing that constitutes language [*l'essentiel de la langue*] is . . . unrelated to the phonic character of the linguistic sign" (p. 21) [p. 7]. This affirmation will soon occupy us; within it the other side of the Saussurian proposition denouncing the "illusions of script" comes to the fore.

What do these limits and presuppositions signify? First that a linguistics is not *general* as long as it defines its outside and inside in terms of *determined* linguistic models; as long as it does not rigorously distinguish essence from fact in their respective degrees of generality. The system of writing in general is not exterior to the system of language in general, unless it is granted that the division between exterior and interior passes through the interior of the interior or the exterior of the exterior, to the point where the immanence of language is essentially exposed to the intervention of forces that are apparently alien to its system. For the same reason, writing in general is not "image" or "figuration" of language in general, except if the nature, the logic, and the functioning of the image within the system from which one wishes to exclude it be reconsidered. Writing is not a sign of a sign, except if one says it of all signs, which would be more profoundly true. If every sign refers to a sign, and if "sign of a sign" signifies writing, certain conclusions—which I shall consider at the appropriate moment—will become inevitable. What Saussure saw without seeing, knew without being *able* to take into account, following in that the entire metaphysical tradition, is that a certain model of writing was necessarily but provisionally imposed (but for the inaccuracy in principle, insufficiency of fact, and the permanent usurpation) as instrument and technique of representation of a system of language. And that this movement, unique in style, was so profound that it permitted the thinking, *within language,* of concepts like those of the sign, technique, representation, language. The system of language associated with phonetic-alphabetic writing is that within which logocentric metaphysics, determining the sense of being as presence, has been produced. This logocentrism, this *epoch* of the full speech, has always placed in parenthesis, *suspended,* and suppressed for essential reasons, all free reflection on the origin and status of writing, all science of writing which was not *technology* and the *history of a technique,* itself leaning upon a mythology and a metaphor of a natural writing.[12] It is this logocentrism which, limiting the internal system of language in general by a bad abstraction, prevents Saussure and the majority of his successors[13] from determining fully and explicitly that which is called "the integral and concrete object of linguistics" (p. 23) [p. 7].

But conversely, as I announced above, it is when he is not expressly dealing with writing, when he feels he has closed the parentheses on that subject, that Saussure opens the field of a general gram-

[12] A play on "époque" (epoch) and "epoche," the Husserlian term for "bracketting" or "putting out of play" that constitutes phenomenological reduction. [Tr.] (See *Husserl.*) [Eds.]

[13] "The signifier aspect of the system of language can consist only of rules according to which the phonic aspect of the act of speech is ordered," [N. S.] Troubetzkoy, *Principes de phonologie,* tr. fr. [J. Cantineau (Paris, 1949); *Principles of Phonology,* tr. Christiane A. M. Baltaxe (Berkeley and Los Angeles, 1969)], p. 2. It is in the "Phonologie et phonétique" of Jakobson and Halle (the first part of *Fundamentals of Language,* collected and translated in *Essais de linguistique générale* [tr. Nicolas Ruwet (Paris, 1963)], p. 103) that the phonologistic strand of the Saussurian project seems to be most systematically and most rigorously defended, notably against Hjelmslev's "algebraic" point of view. [Au./Tr.]

matology. Which would not only no longer be excluded from general linguistics, but would dominate it and contain it within itself. Then one realizes that what was chased off limits, the wandering outcast of linguistics, has indeed never ceased to haunt language as its primary and most intimate possibility. Then something which was never spoken and which is nothing other than writing itself as the origin of language writes itself within Saussure's discourse. Then we glimpse the germ of a profound but indirect explanation of the usurpation and the traps condemned in Chapter VI. This explanation will overthrow even the form of the question to which it was a premature reply.

The Outside ~~is~~ the Inside

The thesis of the *arbitrariness* of the sign (so grossly misnamed, and not only for the reasons Saussure himself recognizes)[14] must forbid a radical distinction between the linguistic and the graphic sign. No doubt this thesis concerns only the necessity of relationships between specific signifiers and signifieds *within* an allegedly natural relationship between the voice and sense in general, between the order of phonic signifiers and the content of the signifieds ("the only natural bond, the only true bond, the bond of sound"). Only these relationships between specific signifiers and signifieds would be regulated by arbitrariness. Within the "natural" relationship between phonic signifiers and their signifieds *in general,* the relationship between each determined signifier and its determined signified would be "arbitrary."

Now from the moment that one considers the totality of determined signs, spoken, and a fortiori written, as unmotivated institutions, one must exclude any relationship of natural subordination, any natural hierarchy among signifiers or orders of signifiers. If "writing" signifies inscription and especially the durable institution of a sign (and that is the only irreducible kernel of the concept of writing), writing in general covers the entire field of linguistic signs. In that field a certain sort of instituted signifiers may then appear, "graphic" in the narrow and derivative sense of the word, ordered by a certain relationship with other instituted—hence "written," even if they are "phonic"—signifiers. The very idea of institution—hence of the arbitrariness of the sign—is unthinkable before the possibility of writing and outside of its horizon. Quite simply, that is, outside of the horizon itself, outside the world as space of inscription, as the opening to the emission and to the spatial *distribution* of signs, to the *regulated play* of their differences, even if they are "phonic."

Let us now persist in using this opposition of nature and institution, of *physis* and *nomos* (which also means, of course, a distribution and division regulated in fact by *law*) which a meditation on writing should disturb although it functions everywhere as self-evident, particularly in the discourse of linguistics. We must then conclude that only the signs called *natural,* those that Hegel and Saussure call "symbols," escape semiology as grammatology. But they fall a fortiori outside the field of linguistics as the region of general semiology. The thesis of the arbitrariness of the sign thus indirectly but irrevocably contests Saussure's declared proposition when he chases writing to the outer darkness of language. This thesis successfully accounts for a conventional relationship between the phoneme and the grapheme (in phonetic writing, between the phoneme, signifier-signified, and the grapheme, pure signifier), but by the same token it forbids that the latter be an "image" of the former. Now it was indispensable to the exclusion of writing as "external system," that it come to impose an "image," a "representation," or a "figuration," an exterior reflection of the reality of language.

It matters little, here at least, that there is in fact an ideographic filiation of the alphabet. This important question is much debated by historians of writing. What matters here is that in the synchronic structure and systematic principle of alphabetic writing—and phonetic writing in general—no relationship of "natural" representation, none of resemblance or participation, no "symbolic" relationship in the Hegelian–Saussurian sense, no "iconographic" relationship in the Peircian sense, be implied.

[14] Page 101. Beyond the scruples formulated by Saussure himself, an entire system of intralinguistic criticism can be opposed to the thesis of the "arbitrariness of the sign." Cf. Jakobson, "A la recherche de l'essence du langage," ["Quest for the Essence of Language,"] *Diogène,* 51, and Martinet, *La linguistique synchronique* [Paris 1965], p. 34. But these criticisms do not interfere—and, besides, do not pretend to interfere—with Saussure's profound intention directed at the discontinuity and immotivation proper to the structure if not the origin of the sign. [Au.]

One must therefore challenge, in the very name of the arbitrariness of the sign, the Saussurian definition of writing as "image"—hence as natural symbol—of language. Not to mention the fact that the phoneme is the *unimaginable* itself, and no visibility can *resemble* it, it suffices to take into account what Saussure says about the difference between the symbol and the sign (p. 101) [pp. 68–69] in order to be completely baffled as to how he can at the same time say of writing that it is an "image" or "figuration" of language and define language and writing elsewhere as "two distinct systems of signs" (p. 45) [p. 23]. For the property of the sign is not to be an image. By a process exposed by Freud in *The Interpretation of Dreams,* Saussure thus accumulates contradictory arguments to bring about a satisfactory decision: the exclusion of writing. In fact, even within so-called phonetic writing, the "graphic" signifier refers to the phoneme through a web of many dimensions which binds it, like all signifiers, to other written and oral signifiers, within a "total" system open, let us say, to all possible investments of sense. We must begin with the possibility of that total system.

Saussure was thus never able to think that writing was truly an "image," a "figuration," a "representation" of the spoken language, a symbol. If one considers that he nonetheless needed these inadequate notions to decide upon the exteriority of writing, one must conclude that an entire stratum of his discourse, the intention of Chapter VI ("Graphic Representation of Language"), was not at all scientific. When I say this, my quarry is not primarily Ferdinand de Saussure's intention or motivation, but rather the entire uncritical tradition which he inherits. To what zone of discourse does this strange functioning of argumentation belong, this coherence of desire producing itself in a near-oneiric way—although it clarifies the dream rather than allow itself to be clarified by it—through a contradictory logic? How is this functioning articulated with the entirety of theoretical discourse, throughout the history of science? Better yet, how does it work from within the concept of science itself? It is only when this question is elaborated—if it is some day—when the concepts required by this functioning are defined outside of all psychology (as of all sciences of man), outside metaphysics (which can now be "Marxist" or "structuralist"); when one is able to respect all its levels of generality and articulation—it is only then that one will be able to state rigorously the problem of the articulated appurtenance of a text (theoretical or otherwise) to an entire set: I obviously treat the Saussurian text at the moment only as a telling example within a given situation, without professing to use the concepts required by the functioning of which I have just spoken. My justification would be as follows: this and some other indices (in a general way the treatment of the concept of writing) already give us the assured means of broaching the deconstruction of *the greatest totality*—the concept of the *epistémè* and logocentric metaphysics—within which are produced, without ever posing the radical question of writing, all the Western methods of analysis, explication, reading, or interpretation.

Now we must think that writing is at the same time more exterior to speech, not being its "image" or its "symbol," and more interior to speech, which is already in itself a writing. Even before it is linked to incision, engraving, drawing, or the letter, to a signifier referring in general to a signifier signified by it, the concept of the *graphie* [unit of a possible graphic system] implies the framework of the *instituted trace,* as the possibility common to all systems of signification. My efforts will now be directed toward slowly detaching these two concepts from the classical discourse from which I necessarily borrow them. The effort will be laborious and we know a priori that its effectiveness will never be pure and absolute.

The instituted trace is "unmotivated" but not capricious. Like the word "arbitrary" according to Saussure, it "should not imply that the choice of the signifier is left entirely to the speaker" (p. 101) [pp. 68–69]. Simply, it has no "natural attachment" to the signified within reality. For us, the rupture of that "natural attachment" puts in question the idea of naturalness rather than that of attachment. That is why the word "institution" should not be too quickly interpreted within the classical system of oppositions.

The instituted trace cannot be thought without thinking the retention of difference within a structure of reference where difference appears *as such* and thus permits a certain liberty of variations among the full terms. The absence of *another* here-and-now, of another transcendental present, of *another* origin of the world appearing as such, presenting itself as irreducible absence within the presence of the trace, is not a metaphysical formula substituted for a scientific concept of writing. This formula, beside the fact that it is the questioning of metaphysics itself, describes the structure implied by the "arbitrariness of the sign," from the moment that one thinks of its possibility *short of* the derived opposition between nature and convention, symbol and sign, etc. These oppositions have meaning only after the possibility of the trace. The "unmotivatedness" of the sign requires a synthesis in which the completely other is announced as such—without any simplicity, any identity, any resemblance or continuity—within what is not it. *Is announced as such:* there we have all *history,* from what metaphysics has defined as "non-living" up to "consciousness," passing through all levels of animal organization. The trace, where the relationship with the other is marked, articulates its possibility in the entire field of the entity [*étant*], which metaphysics has defined as the being-present starting from the occulted movement of the trace. The trace must be thought before the entity. But the movement of the trace is necessarily occulted, it produces itself as self-occultation. When the other announces itself as such, it presents itself in the dissimulation of itself. This formulation is not theological, as one might believe somewhat hastily. The "theological" is a determined moment in the total movement of the trace. The field of the entity, before being determined as the field of presence, is structured according to the diverse possibilities—genetic and structural—of the trace. The presentation of the other as such, that is to say the dissimulation of its "as such," has always already begun and no structure of the entity escapes it.

That is why the movement of "unmotivatedness" passes from one structure to the other when the "sign" crosses the stage of the "symbol." It is in a certain sense and according to a certain determined structure of the "as such" that one is authorized to say that there is yet no immotivation in what Saussure calls "symbol" and which, according to him, does not—at least provisionally—interest semiology. The general structure of the unmotivated trace connects within the same possibility, and they cannot be separated except by abstraction, the structure of the relationship with the other, the movement of temporalization, and language as writing. Without referring back to a "nature," the immotivation of the trace has always *become.* In fact, there is no unmotivated trace: the trace is indefinitely its own becoming-unmotivated. In Saussurian language, what Saussure does not say would have to be said: there is neither symbol nor sign but a becoming-sign of the symbol.

Thus, as it goes without saying, the trace whereof I speak is not more *natural* (it is not the mark, the natural sign, or the index in the Husserlian sense) than *cultural,* not more physical than psychic, biological than spiritual. It is that starting from which a becoming-unmotivated of the sign, and with it all the ulterior oppositions between *physis* and its other, is possible.

In his project of semiotics, Peirce seems to have been more attentive than Saussure to the irreducibility of this becoming-unmotivated. In his terminology, one must speak of a becoming-unmotivated of the *symbol,* the notion of the symbol playing here a role analogous to that of the sign which Saussure opposes precisely to the symbol:

> Symbols grow. They come into being by development out of other signs, particularly from icons, or from mixed signs partaking of the nature of icons and symbols. We think only in signs. These mental signs are of mixed nature; the symbol parts of them are called concepts. If a man makes a new symbol, it is by thoughts involving concepts. So it is only out of symbols that a new symbol can grow. Omne symbolum de symbolo.[15]

Peirce complies with two apparently incompatible exigencies. The mistake here would be to sacrifice one for the other. It must be recognized that the symbolic (in Peirce's sense: of "the arbitrariness of the sign") is rooted in the nonsymbolic, in an anterior and related order of signification: "Symbols grow. They come into being by development out of other signs, particularly from icons, or from mixed signs." But these roots must not compromise the structural originality of the field of symbols, the autonomy of a domain, a production, and a play: "So it is only out of symbols that a new symbol can grow. Omne symbolum de symbolo."

But in both cases, the genetic root-system refers

[15] *Elements of Logic,* Bk. II, [*Collected Papers,* ed. Charles Hartshorne and Paul Weiss (Cambridge, Mass., 1931–58), vol. 2], p. 169, paragraph 302. [Au.] (See *Peirce.*) [Eds.]

from sign to sign. No ground of nonsignification—understood as insignificance or an intuition of a present truth—stretches out to give it foundation under the play and the coming into being of signs. Semiotics no longer depends on logic. Logic, according to Peirce, is only a semiotic: "Logic, in its general sense, is, as I believe I have shown, only another name for semiotics (*semeiotike*), the quasi-necessary, or formal, doctrine of signs." And logic in the classical sense, logic "properly speaking," nonformal logic commanded by the value of truth, occupies in that semiotics only a determined and not a fundamental level. As in Husserl (but the analogy, although it is most thought-provoking, would stop there and one must apply it carefully), the lowest level, the foundation of the possibility of logic (or semiotics) corresponds to the project of the *Grammatica speculativa* of Thomas d'Erfurt,[16] falsely attributed to Duns Scotus.[17] Like Husserl, Peirce expressly refers to it. It is a matter of elaborating, in both cases, a formal doctrine of conditions which a discourse must satisfy in order to have a sense, in order to "mean," even if it is false or contradictory. The general morphology of that meaning[18] (*Bedeutung, vouloir-dire*) is independent of all logic of truth.

> The science of semiotic has three branches. The first is called by Duns Scotus *grammatica speculativa*. We may term it *pure grammar*. It has for its task to ascertain what must be true of the representamen used by every scientific intelligence in order that they may embody any *meaning*. The second is logic proper. It is the science of what is quasi-necessarily true of the representamina of any scientific intelligence in order that they may hold good of any *object*, that is, may be true. Or say, logic proper is the formal science of the conditions of the truth of representations. The third, in imitation of Kant's fashion of preserving old associations of words in finding nomenclature for new conceptions, I call *pure rhetoric*. Its task is to ascertain the laws by which in every scientific intelligence one sign gives birth to another, and especially one thought brings forth another.[19]

Peirce goes very far in the direction that I have called the de-construction of the transcendental signified, which, at one time or another, would place a reassuring end to the reference from sign to sign. I have identified logocentrism and the metaphysics of presence as the exigent, powerful, systematic, and irrepressible desire for such a signified. Now Peirce considers the indefiniteness of reference as the criterion that allows us to recognize that we are indeed dealing with a system of signs. *What broaches the movement of signification is what makes its interruption impossible. The thing itself is a sign.* An unacceptable proposition for Husserl, whose phenomenology remains therefore—in its "principle of principles"—the most radical and most critical restoration of the metaphysics of presence. The difference between Husserl's and Peirce's phenomenologies is fundamental since it concerns the concept of the sign and of the manifestation of presence, the relationships between the re-presentation and the originary presentation of the thing itself (truth). On this point Peirce is undoubtedly closer to the inventor of the word *phenomenology:* Lambert proposed in fact to "reduce *the theory of things* to the *theory of signs*." According to the "phaneoroscopy" or "phenomenology" of Peirce, *manifestation* itself does not reveal a presence, it makes a sign. One may read in the *Principle of Phenomenology* that "the idea of *manifestation* is the idea of a sign."[20] There is thus no phenomenality reducing the sign or the representer so that the thing signified may be allowed to glow finally in the luminosity of its presence. The so-called "thing itself" is always already a *representamen* shielded from the simplicity of intuitive evidence. The *representamen* functions only by giving rise to an *interpretant* that itself becomes a sign and so on to infinity. The self-identity of the signified conceals itself unceasingly and is always on the move. The property of the *representamen* is to be itself and another, to be pro-

[16] Thomas d'Erfurt, thirteenth-century Scholastic philosopher. [Eds.]

[17] John Duns Scotus (ca. 1266–1308), Scholastic philosopher and theologian. [Eds.]

[18] I justify the translation of *bedeuten by vouloir-dire* [meaning, literally "wish-to-say"] in *La voix et le phénomène.* [Au.]

[19] *The Philosophy of Peirce: Selected Writings,* [ed. Justus Buchler (New York and London, 1940)], ch. 7, p. 99. [Au.]

[20] Page 93. Let us recall that Lambert opposes phenomenology to aletheiology. [Au.]

duced as a structure of reference, to be separated from itself. The property of the *representamen* is not to be *proper* [*propre*], that is to say absolutely *proximate* to itself (*prope, proprius*). The *represented* is always already a *representamen*. Definition of the sign:

> *Anything which determines something else (its interpretant) to refer to an object to which itself refers (its object) in the same way, this interpretant becoming in turn a sign, and so on ad infinitum.* . . . If the series of successive interpretants comes to an end, the sign is thereby rendered imperfect, at least.[21]

From the moment that there is meaning there are nothing but signs. We *think only in signs.* Which amounts to ruining the notion of the sign at the very moment when, as in Nietzsche, its exigency is recognized in the absoluteness of its right. One could call *play* the absence of the transcendental signified as limitlessness of play, that is to say as the destruction of ontotheology and the metaphysics of presence. It is not surprising that the shock, shaping and undermining metaphysics since its origin, lets itself *be named as such* in the period when, refusing to bind linguistics to semantics (which all European linguists, from Saussure to Hjemslev, still do), expelling the problem of *meaning* outside of their researches, certain American linguists constantly refer to the model of a game. Here one must think of writing as a game within language. (The *Phaedrus* (277e) condemned writing precisely as play—*paidia*—and opposed such childishness to the adult gravity [*spoudè*] of speech.) This *play,* thought as absence of the transcendental signified, is not a play *in the world,* as it has always been defined, for the purposes of *containing* it, by the philosophical tradition and as the theoreticians of play also consider it (or those who, following and going beyond Bloomfield, refer semantics to psychology or some other local discipline). To think play radically the ontological and transcendental problematics must first be seriously *exhausted;* the question of the meaning of being, the being of the entity and of the transcendental origin of the world—of the worldness of the world—must be patiently and rigorously worked through, thc critical movement of the Husserlian and Heideggerian questions must be effectively followed to the very end, and their effectiveness and legibility must be conserved. Even if it were crossed out, without it the concepts of play and writing to which I shall have recourse will remain caught within regional limits and an empiricist, positivist, or metaphysical discourse. The counter-move that the holders of such a discourse would oppose to the precritical tradition and to metaphysical speculation would be nothing but the worldly representation of their own operation. It is therefore *the game of the world* that must be first thought; before attempting to understand all the forms of play in the world.[22]

From the very opening of the game, then, we are within the becoming-unmotivated of the symbol. With regard to this becoming, the opposition of diachronic and synchronic is also derived. It would not be able to command a grammatology pertinently. The immotivation of the trace ought now to be understood as an operation and not as a state, as an active movement, a demotivation, and not as a given structure. Science of "the arbitrariness of the sign," science of the immotivation of the trace, science of writing before speech and in speech, grammatology would thus cover a vast field within which linguistics would, by abstraction, delineate its own area, with the limits that Saussure prescribes to its internal system and which must be carefully reexamined in each speech/writing system in the world and history.

By a substitution which would be anything but verbal, one may replace *semiology* by *grammatology* in the program of the *Course in General Linguistics:*

> I shall call it [grammatology]. . . . Since the science does not yet exist, no one can say what it would be; but it has a right to exis-

[21] *Elements of Logic,* Bk. I, 2, p. 302. [Au.]

[22] These Heideggerian themes obviously refer back to Nietzsche (cf. *La chose* [1950], tr. fr. in *Essais et conférences* [tr. André Préau (Paris, 1958)], p. 214 ["Das Ding," *Vorträge und Aufsätze* (Pfüllingen, 1954)], *Le principe de raison* (1955–56), tr. fr. [André Préau, Paris, 1962] pp. 240 f. [*Der Satz vom Grund* (Pfüllingen, 1957)]. Such themes are presented also in Eugen Fink (*Le jeu comme symbole du monde* [*Spiel als Weltsymbol*] (Stuttgart, 1960), and, in France, in Kostas Axelos, *Vers la pensée planétaire* ([Paris], 1964), and *Einführung in ein künftiges Denken: über Marx und Heidegger* (Tübingen, 1966). [Au./Tr.]

> tence, a place staked out in advance. Linguistics is only a part of [that] general science . . . ; the laws discovered by [grammatology] will be applicable to linguistics (p. 33) [p. 16].

The advantage of this substitution will not only be to give to the theory of writing the scope needed to counter logocentric repression and the subordination to linguistics. It will liberate the semiological project itself from what, in spite of its greater theoretical extension, remained *governed* by linguistics, organized as if linguistics were at once its center and its telos. *Even though semiology was in fact more general and more comprehensive than linguistics, it continued to be regulated as if it were one of the areas of linguistics. The linguistic sign remained exemplary for semiology,* it dominated it as the master-sign and as the generative model: the pattern [*patron*].

> One could therefore say that signs that are wholly arbitrary realize better than the others the ideal of the semiological process; that is why language, the most complex and universal of all systems of expression, is also the most characteristic; in this sense linguistics can become *the master-pattern for all branches* of *semiology* although language is only one particular semiological system (p. 101; italics added) [p. 68].

Consequently, reconsidering the order of dependence prescribed by Saussure, apparently inverting the relationship of the part to the whole, Barthes in fact carries out the profoundest intention of the *Course:*

> From now on we must admit the possibility of reversing Saussure's proposition some day: linguistics is not a part, even if privileged, of the general science of signs, it is semiology that is a part of linguistics.[23]

This coherent reversal, submitting semiology to a "translinguistics," leads to its full explication as linguistics historically dominated by logocentric metaphysics, for which in fact there is not and there should not be "any meaning except as named" (ibid.). Dominated by the so-called "civilization of writing" that we inhabit, a civilization of so-called phonetic writing, that is to say of the logos where the sense of being is, in its telos, determined as parousia. The Barthesian reversal is fecund and indispensable for the description of the *fact and the vocation of signification* within the closure of this epoch and this civilization that is in the process of disappearing in its very globalization.

Let us now try to go beyond these formal and architectonic considerations. Let us ask in a more intrinsic and concrete way, how language is not merely a sort of writing, "comparable to a system of writing" (p. 33) [p. 16]—Saussure writes curiously—but a species *of* writing. Or rather, since writing no longer relates to language as an extension or frontier, let us ask how language is a possibility founded on the general possibility of writing. Demonstrating this, one would give at the same time an account of that alleged "usurpation" which could not be an unhappy accident. It supposes on the contrary a common root and thus excludes the resemblance of the "image," derivation, or representative reflexion. And thus one would bring back to its true meaning, to its primary possibility, the apparently innocent and didactic analogy which makes Saussure say:

> Language is [comparable to] a system of signs that express ideas, and is therefore *comparable to writing,* the alphabet of deaf-mutes, symbolic rites, polite formulas, military signals, etc. But it is the most important of all these systems (p. 33; italics added) [p. 16].

Further, it is not by chance that, a hundred and thirty pages later, at the moment of explaining *phonic difference* as the condition of linguistic *value* ("from a material viewpoint"),[24] he must again borrow all his pedagogic resources from the example of writing:

[23] *Communications,* 4 (1964), p. 2. [Au.]

[24] "The conceptual side of value is made up solely of relations and differences with respect to the other terms of language, and the same can be said of its material side. The important thing in the word is not the sound alone but the phonic differences that make it possible to distinguish this word from all others, for differences carry signification. . . . A segment of language can never in the final analysis be based on anything except its noncoincidence with the rest" (p. 163) [pp. 117–18]. [Au.]

> Since an identical state of affairs is observable in writing, another system of signs, we shall use writing to draw some comparisons that will clarify the whole issue (p. 165) [p. 119].

Four demonstrative items, borrowing pattern and content from writing, follow.[25]

Once more, then, we definitely have to oppose Saussure to himself. Before being or not being "noted," "represented," "figured," in a "*graphie,*" the linguistic sign implies an originary writing. Henceforth, it is not to the thesis of the arbitrariness of the sign that I shall appeal directly, but to what Saussure associates with it as an indispensable correlative and which would seem to me rather to lay the foundations for it: the thesis of *difference* as the source of linguistic value.[26]

What are, from the grammatological point of view, the consequences of this theme that is now so well-known (and upon which Plato already reflected in the *Sophist*)?

By definition, difference is never in itself a sensible plenitude. Therefore, its necessity contradicts the allegation of a naturally phonic essence of language. It contests by the same token the professed natural dependence of the graphic signifier. That is a consequence Saussure himself draws against the premises defining the internal system of language. He must now exclude the very thing which had permitted him to exclude writing: sound and its "natural bond" [*lien naturel*] with meaning. For example: "The thing that constitutes language is, as I shall show later, unrelated to the phonic character of the linguistic sign" (p. 21) [p. 7]. And in a paragraph on difference:

> It is impossible for sound alone, a material element, to belong to language. It is only a secondary thing, substance to be put to use. All our conventional values have the characteristic of not being confused with the tangible element which supports them. . . . The linguistic signifier . . . is not [in essence] phonic but incorporeal—constituted not by its material substance but the differences that separate its sound-image from all others (p. 164) [pp. 118–19]. The idea or phonic substance that a sign contains is of less importance than the other signs that surround it (p. 166) [p. 120].

Without this reduction of phonic matter, the distinction between language and speech, decisive for Saussure, would have no rigor. It would be the same for the oppositions that happened to descend from it: between code and message, pattern and usage, etc. Conclusion: "Phonology—this bears repeating—is only an auxiliary discipline [of the science of language] and belongs exclusively to speaking" (p. 56) [p. 33]. Speech thus draws from this stock of writing, noted or not, that language is, and it is here that one must meditate upon the complicity between the two "stabilities." The reduction of the *phonè* reveals this complicity. What Saussure says, for example, about the sign in general and what he "confirms" through the example of writing, applies also to language: "Signs are governed by a principle of general semiology: continuity in time is coupled to change in time; this is confirmed by orthrographic systems, the speech of deaf-mutes, etc." (p. 111) [p. 16].

The reduction of phonic substance thus does not only permit the distinction between phonetics on the one hand (and a fortiori acoustics or the physiology of the phonating organs) and phonology on the other. It also makes of phonology itself an "auxiliary discipline." Here the direction indicated by

[25] "Since an identical state of affairs is observable in writing, another system of signs, we shall use writing to draw some comparisons that will clarify the whole issue. In fact:

"1) The signs used in writing are arbitrary; there is no connection, for example, between the letter *t* and the sound that it designates.

"2) The value of letters is purely negative and differential. The same person can write *t,* for instance, in different ways: *t* & t. The only requirement is that the sign for *t* not be confused in his script with the signs used for *l, d,* etc.

"3) Values in writing function only through reciprocal opposition within a fixed system that consists of a set number of letters. This third characteristic, though not identical to the second, is closely related to it, for both depend on the first. Since the graphic sign is arbitrary, its form matters little or rather matters only within the limitations imposed by the system.

"4) The means by which the sign is produced is completely unimportant, for it does not affect the system (this also follows from characteristic 1). Whether I make the letters in white or black, raised or engraved, with pen or chisel—all this is of no importance with respect to their signification" (pp. 165–66) [pp. 119–20]. [Au.]

[26] "*Arbitrary and differential* are two correlative qualities" (p. 163) [p. 118]. [Au.]

Saussure takes us beyond the phonologism of those who profess to follow him on this point: in fact, Jakobson believes indifference to the phonic substance of expression to be impossible and illegitimate. He thus criticizes the glossematics of Hjelmslev which requires and practices the neutralizing of sonorous substance. And in the text cited above, Jakobson and Halle maintain that the "theoretical requirement" of a research of invariables placing sonorous substance in parenthesis (as an empirical and contingent content) is:

1. *impracticable* since, as "Eli Fischer-Jorgensen exposes [it]," "the sonorous substance [is taken into account] at every step of the analysis."[27] But is that a "troubling discrepancy," as Jakobson and Halle would have it? Can one not account for it as a fact serving as an example, as do the phenomenologists who always need, keeping it always within sight, an exemplary empirical content in the reading of an essence which is independent of it by right?

2. *inadmissible in principle* since one cannot consider "that in language form is opposed to substance as a constant to a variable." It is in the course of this second demonstration that the literally Saussurian formulas reappear within the question of the relationships between speech and writing; the order of writing is the order of exteriority, of the "occasional," of the "accessory," of the "auxiliary," of the "*parasitic*" (pp. 116–17; italics added) [pp. 16–17]. The argument of Jakobson and Halle appeals to the factual genesis and invokes the secondariness of writing in the colloquial sense: "Only after having mastered speech does one graduate to reading and writing." Even if this commonsensical proposition were rigorously proved—something that I do not believe (since each of its concepts harbors an immense problem)—one would still have to receive assurance of its pertinence to the argument. Even if "after" were here a facile representation, if one knew perfectly well what one thought and stated while assuring that one learns to write *after* having learned to speak, would that suffice to conclude that what thus comes "after" is parasitic? And what is a parasite? And what if writing were precisely that which makes us reconsider our logic of the parasite?

[27] Jakobson and Halle, *Fundamentals of Language,* (1956), p. 16. [Tr.]

In another moment of the critique, Jakobson and Halle recall the imperfection of graphic representation; that imperfection is due to "the cardinally dissimilar patterning of letters and phonemes:"

> Letters never, or only partially, reproduce the different distinctive features on which the phonemic pattern is based and unfailingly disregard the structural relationship of these features (p. 116) [p. 17].

I have suggested it above: does not the radical dissimilarity of the two elements—graphic and phonic—exclude derivation? Does not the inadequacy of graphic representation concern only common alphabetic writing, to which glossematic formalism does not essentially refer? Finally, if one accepts all the phonologist arguments thus presented, it must still be recognized that they oppose a "scientific" concept of the spoken word to a vulgar concept of writing. What I would wish to show is that one cannot exclude writing from the general experience of "the structural relationship of these features." Which amounts, of course, to reforming the concept of writing.

In short, if the Jakobsonian analysis is faithful to Saussure in this matter, is it not especially so to the Saussure of Chapter VI? Up to what point would Saussure have maintained the inseparability of matter and form, which remains the most important argument of Jakobson and Halle (p. 117), [p. 17]? The question may be repeated in the case of the position of André Martinet who, in this debate, follows Chapter VI of the *Course* to the letter.[28] And

[28] This literal fidelity is expressed:

1. In the critical exposition of Hjelmslev's attempt ("Au sujet des fondements de la théorie linguistique de L. Hjelmslev," *Bulletin de la Société Linguistique de Paris,* vol. 42, p. 40): "Hjelmslev is perfectly consistent with himself when he declares that a written text has for the linguist exactly the same value as a spoken text, since the choice of the substance is not important. He refuses even to admit that the spoken substance is primitive and the written substance derived. It seems as if it would suffice to make him notice that, but for certain pathological exceptions, all human beings speak, but few know how to write, or that children know how to speak long before they learn how to write. *I shall therefore not press the point*" (italics added).

2. In the *Eléments de linguistique générale* [(Paris, 1961); *Elements of General Linguistics,* tr. Elisabeth Palmer (London, 1964)], where all the chapters on the

only Chapter VI, from which Martinet *expressly* dissociates the doctrine of what, in the *Course*, effaces the privilege of phonic substance. After having explained why "a dead language with a perfect ideography," that is to say a communication effective through the system of a generalized script, "could not have any real autonomy," and why *nevertheless*, "such a system would be something so particular that one can well understand why linguists *want to exclude it* from the domain of their science" (*La linguistique syncronique*, p. 18; italics added), Martinet criticizes those who, following a certain trend in Saussure, question the essentially phonic character of the linguistic sign: "Much will be attempted to prove that Saussure is right when he announces that 'the thing that constitutes language [*l'essentiel de la langue*] is . . . unrelated to the phonic character of the linguistic sign,' and, going beyond the teaching of the master, to declare that the linguistic sign does not necessarily have that phonic character" (p. 19).

On that precise point, it is not a question of "going beyond" the master's teaching but of following and extending it. Not to do it is to cling to what in Chapter VI greatly limits formal and structural research and contradicts the least contestable findings of Saussurian doctrine. To avoid "going beyond," one risks returning to a point that falls short.

I believe that generalized writing is not just the idea of a system to be invented, an hypothetical characteristic or a future possibility. I think on the contrary that oral language already belongs to this writing. But that presupposes a modification of the concept of writing that we for the moment merely anticipate. Even supposing that one is not given that modified concept, supposing that one is considering a system of pure writing as an hypothesis for the future or a working hypothesis, faced with that hypothesis, should a linguist refuse himself the means of thinking it and of integrating its formulation within his theoretical discourse? Does the fact that most linguists do so create a theoretical right? Martinet seems to be of that opinion. After having elaborated a purely "dactylological" hypothesis of language, he writes, in effect:

> It must be recognized that the parallelism between this "dactylology" and phonology is complete as much in synchronic as in diachronic material, and that the terminology associated with the latter may be used for the former, except of course when the terms refer to the phonic substance. Clearly, if we do not *desire* to exclude from the domain of linguistics the systems of the type we have just imagined, it is most important to modify traditional terminology relative to the articulation of signifiers so as to eliminate all reference to phonic substance; as does Louis Hjelmslev when he uses "ceneme" and "cenematics" instead of "phoneme" and "phonematics." *Yet it is understandable that the majority of linguists hesitate to modify completely the traditional terminological edifice for the only theoretical advantages of being able to include in the field of their science some purely hypothetical systems. To make them agree to envisage such a revolution,* they must be persuaded that, in attested linguistic systems, they have no advantage in considering the phonic substance of units of expression as to be of direct interest (pp. 20–21; italics added).

Once again, we do not doubt the value of these phonological arguments, the presuppositions behind which I have attempted to expose above. Once

vocal character of language pick up the words and arguments of Chapter VI of the *Course:* "[One learns to speak before learning to read:] reading comes as a reflection of spoken usage: *the reverse is never true*" (italics added. This proposition seems to me to be thoroughly debatable, even on the level of that common experience which has the force of law within this argument). Martinet concludes: "The study of writing is a discipline distinct from linguistics proper, although practically speaking it is one of its dependencies. Thus the linguist in principle operates without regard for written forms" (p. 11) [p. 17]. We see how the concepts of *dependency* and *abstraction* function: writing and its science are alien but not independent; which does not stop them from being, conversely, immanent but not essential. Just enough "outside" not to affect the integrity of the language *itself*, in its pure original self-identity, in its property; just enough "inside" not to have the right to any practical or epistemological independence. And vice versa.

3. In "The Word" (already cited): ". . . it is from speech that one should always start in order to understand the real nature of human language" (p. 53) [p. 54].

4. And finally and above all in "La double articulation du langage," *La linguistique synchronique*, pp. 8 f. and 18 f. [Au.]

one assumes these presuppositions, it would be absurd to reintroduce confusedly a derivative writing, in the area of oral language and within the system of this derivation. Not only would ethnocentrism not be avoided, but all the frontiers within the sphere of its legitimacy would then be confused. It is not a question of rehabilitating writing in the narrow sense, nor of reversing the order of dependence when it is evident. Phonologism does not brook any objections as long as one conserves the colloquial concepts of speech and writing which form the solid fabric of its argumentation. Colloquial and quotidian conceptions, inhabited besides—uncontradictorily enough—by an old history, limited by frontiers that are hardly visible yet all the more rigorous by that very fact.

I would wish rather to suggest that the alleged derivativeness of writing, however real and massive, was possible only on one condition: that the "original," "natural," etc. language had never existed, never been intact and untouched by writing, that it had itself always been a writing. An arche-writing whose necessity and new concept I wish to indicate and outline here; and which I continue to call writing only because it essentially communicates with the vulgar concept of writing. The latter could not have imposed itself historically except by the dissimulation of the arche-writing, by the desire for a speech displacing its other and its double and working to reduce its difference. If I persist in calling that difference writing, it is because, within the work of historical repression, writing was, by its situation, destined to signify the most formidable difference. It threatened the desire for the living speech from the closest proximity, it *breached* living speech from within and from the very beginning. And as we shall begin to see, difference cannot be thought without the *trace*.

This arche-writing, although its concept is *invoked* by the themes of "the arbitrariness of the sign" and of difference, cannot and can never be recognized as the *object of a science*. It is that very thing which cannot let itself be reduced to the form of *presence*. The latter orders all objectivity of the object and all relation of knowledge. That is why what I would be tempted to consider in the development of the *Course* as "progress," calling into question in return the uncritical positions of Chapter VI, never gives rise to a new "scientific" concept of writing.

Can one say as much of the algebraism of Hjelmslev, which undoubtedly drew the most rigorous conclusions from that progress?

The *Principes de grammaire générale* (1928) separated out within the doctrine of the *Course* the phonological principle and the principle of difference: It isolated a concept of *form* which permitted a distinction between formal difference and phonic difference, and this even within "spoken" language (p. 117). Grammar is independent of semantics and phonology (p. 118).

That independence is the very principle of glossematics as the formal science of language. Its formality supposes that "there is no necessary connexion between sounds and language."[29] That formality is itself the condition of a purely functional analysis. The idea of a linguistic function and of a purely linguistic unit—the glosseme—excludes then not only the consideration of the substance of expression (material substance) but also that of the substance of the content (immaterial substance). "Since language is a form and not a substance (Saussure), the glossemes are by definition independent of substance, immaterial (semantic, psychological and logical) and material (phonic, graphic, etc.)."[30] The study of the functioning of language, of its *play*, presupposes that the substance of *meaning* and, among other possible substances, that of *sound*, be placed in parenthesis. The unity of sound and of sense is indeed here, as I proposed above, the reassuring closing of play. Hjelmslev situates his concept of the *scheme* or *play* of language within Saussure's heritage—of Saussure's formalism and his theory of value. Although he prefers to compare linguistic value to the "value of exchange in the economic sciences" rather than to the "purely logicomathematical value," he assigns a limit to this analogy.

> An economic value is by definition a value with two faces: not only does it play the role of a constant vis-à-vis the concrete units of money, but it also itself plays the role of a variable vis-à-vis a fixed quantity of mer-

[29] "On the Principles of Phonematics" (1955), *Proceedings of the Second International Congress of Phonetic Sciences*, p. 51. [Au.]

[30] Louis Hjelmslev and H. J. Uldall, *Etudes de linguistique structurale organisées au sein du Cercle linguistique de Copenhauge* (Bulletin 11, 35, pp. 13 f.). [Au.]

> chandise which serves it as a standard. In linguistics on the other hand there is nothing that corresponds to a standard. That is why the game of chess and not economic fact remains for Saussure the most faithful image of a grammar. The scheme of language is in the last analysis *a game* and nothing more.[31]

In the *Prolegomena to a Theory of Language* (1943), setting forth the opposition *expression/content,* which he substitutes for the difference *signifier/signified,* and in which each term may be considered from the point of view of *form* or *substance,* Hjelmslev criticizes the idea of a language *naturally* bound to the substance of phonic expression. It is by mistake that it has hitherto been supposed "that the substance-expression of a spoken language should consist of 'sounds':"

> Thus, as has been pointed out by the Zwirners in particular, the fact has been overlooked that speech is accompanied by, and that certain components of speech can be replaced by, gesture, and that in reality, as the Zwirners say, not only the so-called organs of speech (throat, mouth, and nose), but very nearly all the striate musculature cooperate in the exercise of "natural" language. Further, it is possible to replace the usual sound-and-gesture substance with any other that offers itself as appropriate under changed external circumstances. Thus the same linguistic form may also be manifested in writing, as happens with a phonetic or phonemic notation and with the so-called phonetic orthographies, as for example the Finnish. Here is a "graphic" substance which is addressed exclusively to the eye and which need not be transposed into a phonetic "substance" in order to be grasped or understood. And this graphic "substance" can, precisely from the point of view of the substance, be of quite various sorts.[32]

Refusing to presuppose a "derivation" of substances following from the substance of phonic expression, Hjelmslev places this problem outside the area of structural analysis and of linguistics.

> Moreover it is not always certain what is derived and what not; we must not forget that the discovery of alphabetic writing is hidden in prehistory [n.: Bertrand Russell quite rightly calls attention to the fact that we have no means of deciding whether writing or speech is the older form of human expression (*An Outline of Philosophy* [London, 1927], p. 47)], so that the assertion that it rests on a phonetic analysis is only one of the possible diachronic hypotheses; it may also be rested on a formal analysis of linguistic structure. But in any case, as is recognized by modern linguistics, diachronic considerations are irrelevant for synchronic descriptions (pp. 104–05).

H. J. Uldall provides a remarkable formulation of the fact that glossematic criticism operates at the same time thanks to Saussure and against him; that, as I suggested above, the proper space of a grammatology is at the same time opened and closed by *The Course in General Linguistics.* To show that Saussure did not develop "all the theoretical consequences of his discovery," he writes:

> It is even more curious when we consider that the practical consequences have been widely drawn, indeed had been drawn thousands of years before Saussure, for it is only through the concept of a difference between form and substance that we can explain the possibility of speech and writing existing at the same time as expressions of one and the same language. If either of these two substances, the stream of air or the stream of ink, were an in-

[31] "Langue et parole" (1943), *Essais linguistiques* [Copenhagen, 1959], p. 77. [Au.]

[32] *Omkring sprogteoriens grundlaeggelse,* Copenhagen (1943), pp. 91–93 (translated as *Prolegomena to A Theory of Language,* [by Francis J. Whitfield (2nd edition, Baltimore, 1961)] pp. 103–04.

Cf. also "La stratification du langage" (1954), *Essais linguistiques* (*Travaux du Cercle linguistique de Copenhague,* XII [1959]). The project and the terminology of a *graphematics,* science of the substance of graphic expression, are there presented (p. 41). The complexity of the proposed algebra aims to remedy the fact that, from the point of view of the distinction between form and substance, "Saussure's terminology can lead to confusion" (p. 48). Hjelmslev demonstrates how "one and the same form of expression can be manifested by diverse substances: phonic, graphic, flag-signals, etc." (p. 49). [Au.]

> tegral part of the language itself, it would not be possible to go from one to the other without changing the language.[33]

Undoubtedly the Copenhagen School thus frees a field of research: it becomes possible to direct attention not only to the purity of a form freed from all "natural" bonds to a substance but also to everything that, in the stratification of language, depends on the substance of graphic expression. An original and rigorously delimited description of this may thus be promised. Hjelmslev recognizes that an "analysis of writing without regard to sound has not yet been undertaken" (p. 105). While regretting also that "the substance of ink has not received the same attention on the part of linguists that they have so lavishly bestowed on the substance of air," H. J. Uldall delimits these problems and emphasizes the mutual independence of the substances of expression. He illustrates it particularly by the fact that, in orthography, no grapheme corresponds to accents of pronunciation (for Rousseau this was the misery and the menace of writing) and that, reciprocally, in pronunciation, no phoneme corresponds to the spacing between written words (pp. 13–14).

Recognizing the specificity of *writing*, glossematics did not merely give itself the means of describing the *graphic* element. It showed how to reach the *literary* element, to what in literature passes through an irreducibly graphic text, tying the *play of form* to a determined substance of expression. If there is something in literature which does not allow itself to be reduced to the voice, to epos or to poetry, one cannot recapture it except by rigorously isolating the bond that links *the play of form* to the substance of graphic expression. (It will by the same token be seen that "pure literature," thus respected in its irreducibility, also risks limiting the play, restricting it. The desire to restrict play is, moreover, irresistible.) This interest in literature is effectively manifested in the Copenhagen School.[34] It thus removes the Rousseauist and Saussurian caution with regard to literary arts. It radicalizes the efforts of the Russian formalists, specifically of the O.PO.IAZ, who, in their attention to the being-literary of literature, perhaps favored the phonological instance and the literary models that it dominates. Notably poetry. That which, within the history of literature and in the structure of a literary text in general, escapes that framework, merits a type of description whose norms and conditions of possibility glossematics has perhaps better isolated. It has perhaps thus better prepared itself to study the purely graphic stratum within the structure of the literary text within the history of the becoming-literary of literality, notably in its "modernity."

Undoubtedly a new domain is thus opened to new and fecund researches. But I am not primarily interested in such a parallelism or such a recaptured parity of substances of expression. It is clear that if the phonic substance lost its privilege, it was not to the advantage of the graphic substance, which lends itself to the same substitutions. To the extent that it liberates and is irrefutable, glossematics still operates with a popular concept of writing. However original and irreducible it might be, the "form of expression" linked by correlation to the *graphic* "substance of expression" remains very determined. It is very dependent and very derivative with regard to the arche-writing of which I speak. This arche-writing would be at work not only in the form and substance of graphic expression but also in those of nongraphic expression. It would constitute not only the pattern uniting form to all substance, graphic or otherwise, but the movement of the *sign-function* linking a content to an expression, whether it be graphic or not. This theme could not have a place in Hjelmslev's system.

It is because arche-writing, movement of differance, irreducible arche-synthesis, opening in one and the same possibility, temporalization as well as relationship with the other and language, cannot,

[33] "Speech and Writing," 1938, *Acta Linguistica* 4 (1944): 11 f. Uldall refers also to a study by Dr. Joseph Vachek, "Zum Problem der geschriebenen Sprache" (*Travaux du Cercle linguistique de Prague* 8, 1939) in order to indicate "the difference between the phonologic and glossematic points of view."

Cf. also Eli Fischer-Jorgensen, "Remarques sur les principes de l'analyse phonémique," *Recherches structurales*, 1949 (*Travaux du Cercle linguistique de Prague*, vol. 5, pp. 231. f.); Bertha Siertsema, *A Study of Glossematics* ([The Hague] 1955), (especially ch. VI), and Hennings Spang-Hanssen, "Glossematics," *Trends in European and American Linguistics*, 1930–60 [ed. Christine Mohrmann (Utrecht,] 1961), pp. 147 f. [Au.]

[34] And already, in a very programmatic manner, in the *Prolegomena* (English translation, pp. 114–15). Cf. also Adolf Stender-Petersen, "Esquisse d'une théorie structurale de la littérature," and Stevan Johanson, "La notion de signe dans la glossématique et dans l'esthétique," *Travaux du Cercle linguistique de Copenhague* 5 (1949). [Au.]

as the condition of all linguistic systems, form a part of the linguistic system itself and be situated as an object in its field. (Which does not mean it has a real field *elsewhere, another* assignable *site.*) Its concept could in no way enrich the scientific, positive, and "immanent" (in the Hjelmslevian sense) description of the system itself. Therefore, the founder of glossematics would no doubt have questioned its necessity, as he rejects, en bloc and legitimately, all the extra-linguistic theories which do not arise from the irreducible immanence of the linguistic system.[35] He would have seen in that notion one of those appeals to experience which a theory should dispense with.[36] He would not have understood why the name writing continued to be used for that X which becomes so different from what has always been called "writing."

I have already begun to justify this word, and especially the necessity of the communication between the concept of arche-writing and the vulgar concept of writing submitted to deconstruction by it. I shall continue to do so below. As for the concept of experience, it is most unwieldy here. Like all the notions I am using here, it belongs to the history of metaphysics and we can only use it under erasure [*sous rature*]. "Experience" has always designated the relationship with a presence, whether that relationship had the form of consciousness or not. At any rate, we must, according to this sort of contortion and contention which the discourse is obliged to undergo, exhaust the resources of the concept of experience before attaining and in order to attain, by deconstruction, its ultimate foundation. It is the only way to escape "empiricism" and the "naive" critiques of experience at the same time. Thus, for example, the experience whose "theory," Hjelmslev says, "must be independent" is not the whole of experience. It always corresponds to a certain type of factual or regional experience (historical, psychological, physiological, sociological, etc.), giving rise to a science that is itself regional and, as such, rigorously outside linguistics. The parenthesizing of regions of experience or of the totality of natural experience must discover a field of transcendental experience. This experience is only accessible in so far as, after having, like Hjelmslev, isolated the specificity of the linguistic system and excluded all the extrinsic sciences and metaphysical speculations, one asks the question of the transcendental origin of the system itself, as a system of the objects of a science, and, correlatively, of the theoretical system which studies it: here of the objective and "deductive" system which glossematics wishes to be. Without that, the decisive progress accomplished by a formalism respectful of the originality of its object, of "the immanent system of its objects," is plagued by a scientificist objectivism, that is to say by another unperceived or unconfessed metaphysics. This is often noticeable in the work of the Copenhagen School. It is to escape falling back into this naive objectivism that I refer here to a transcendentality that I elsewhere put into question. It is because I believe that there is a short-of and a beyond of transcendental criticism. To see to it that the beyond does not return to the within is to recognize in the contortion the necessity of a pathway [*parcours*]. That pathway must leave a trace in the text. Without that trace, abandoned to the simple content of its conclusions, the ultra-transcendental text will so closely resemble the pre-critical text as to be indistinguishable from it. We must now form and meditate upon the law of this resemblance. What I call the erasure of concepts ought to mark the places of that future meditation. For example, the value of the transcendental arche [*archie*] must make its necessity felt before letting itself be erased. The concept of arche-trace must comply with both that necessity and that erasure. It is in fact contradictory and not acceptable within the logic of identity. The trace is not only the disappearance of origin—within the discourse that we sustain and according to the path that we follow it means that the origin did not even disappear, that it was never constituted except reciprocally by a non-origin, the trace, which thus becomes the origin of the origin. From then on, to wrench the concept of

[35] *Omkring,* p. 9 (*Prolegomena,* p. 8). [Au.]

[36] Page 14. Which does not prevent Hjelmslev from "venturing to call" his directing principle an "empirical principle" (p. 12, English translation, p. 11). "But," he adds, "we are willing to abandon the name if epistemological investigation shows it to be inappropriate. From our point of view this is merely a question of terminology, which does not affect the maintenance of the principle." This is only one example of the terminological conventionalism of a system, which, in borrowing all its concepts from the history of the metaphysics that it would hold at a distance (form/substance, context/expression, etc.), believes it can neutralize its entire historical burden by means of some declaration of intention, a preface or quotation marks. [Au.]

the trace from the classical scheme, which would derive it from a presence or from an originary non-trace and which would make of it an empirical mark, one must indeed speak of an originary trace or arche-trace. Yet we know that that concept destroys its name and that, if all begins with the trace, there is above all no originary trace.[37] We must then *situate,* as a simple *moment of the discourse,* the phenomenological reduction and the Husserlian reference to a transcendental experience. To the extent that the concept of experience in general—and of transcendental experience, in Husserl in particular—remains governed by the theme of presence, it participates in the movement of the reduction of the trace. The Living Present (*lebendige Gegenwart*) is the universal and absolute form of transcendental experience to which Husserl refers us. In the descriptions of the movements of temporalization, all that does not torment the simplicity and the domination of that form seems to indicate to us how much transcendental phenomenology belongs to metaphysics. But that must come to terms with the forces of rupture. In the originary temporalization and the movement of relationship with the outside, as Husserl actually describes them, nonpresentation or depresentation is as "originary" as presentation. *That is why a thought of the trace can no more break with a transcendental phenomenology than be reduced to it.* Here as elsewhere, to pose the problem in terms of choice, to oblige or to believe oneself obliged to answer it by a *yes* or *no,* to conceive of appurtenance as an allegiance or nonappurtenance as plain speaking, is to confuse very different levels, paths, and styles. In the deconstruction of the arche, one does not make a choice.

Therefore, I admit the necessity of going through the concept of the arche-trace. How does that necessity direct us from the interior of the linguistic system? How does the path that leads from Saussure to Hjelmslev forbid us to avoid the originary trace?

In that its passage through *form* is a passage through the *imprint.* And the meaning of differance in general would be more accessible to us if the unity of that double passage appeared more clearly.

In both cases, one must begin from the possibility of neutralizing the phonic substance.

On the one hand, the phonic element, the term, the plenitude that is called sensible, would not appear as such without the difference or opposition which gives them *form.* Such is the most evident significance of the appeal to difference as the reduction of phonic substance. Here the appearing and functioning of difference presupposes an originary synthesis not preceded by any absolute simplicity. Such would be the originary trace. Without a retention in the minimal unit of temporal experience, without a trace retaining the other as other in the same, no difference would do its work and no meaning would appear. It is not the question of a constituted difference here, but rather, before all determination of the content, of the *pure* movement which produces difference. *The (pure) trace is differance.* It does not depend on any sensible plenitude, audible or visible, phonic or graphic. It is, on the contrary, the condition of such a plenitude. Although it *does not exist,* although it is never a *being-present* outside of all plenitude, its possibility is by rights anterior to all that one calls sign (signified/signifier, content/expression, etc.), concept or operation, motor or sensory. This differance is therefore not more sensible than intelligible and it permits the articulation of signs among themselves within the same abstract order—a phonic or graphic text for example—or between two orders of expression. It permits the articulation of speech and writing—in the colloquial sense—as it founds the metaphysical opposition between the sensible and the intelligible, then between signifier and signified, expression and content, etc. If language were not already, in that sense, a writing, no derived "notation" would be possible; and the classical problem of relationships between speech and writing could not arise. Of course, the positive *sciences* of signification can only describe the *work* and the *fact* of differance, the determined differences and the determined presences that they make possible. There cannot be a science of differance itself in its operation, as it is impossible to have a science of the origin of presence itself, that is to say of a certain nonorigin.

Differance is therefore the formation of form. But it is *on the other hand* the being-imprinted of the imprint. It is well-known that Saussure distinguishes between the "sound-image" and the objec-

[37] As for this critique of the concept of origin in general (empirical and/or transcendental) we have elsewhere attempted to indicate the schema of an argument (Introduction to Husserl's *L'origine de la géométrie,* p. 60). [Au.]

tive sound (p. 98) [p. 66]. He thus gives himself the right to "reduce," in the phenomenological sense, the sciences of acoustics and physiology at the moment that he institutes the science of language. The sound-image is the structure of the appearing of the sound [*l'apparaître du son*] which is anything but the sound appearing [*le son apparaissant*]. It is the sound-image that he calls *signifier,* reserving the name *signified* not for the thing, to be sure (it is reduced by the act and the very ideality of language), but for the "concept," undoubtedly an unhappy notion here; let us say for the ideality of the sense. "I propose to retain the word *sign* [*signe*] to designate the whole and to replace *concept* and *sound-image* respectively by *signified* [*signifié*] and *signifier* [*significant*]." The sound-image is what is *heard;* not the *sound* heard but the being-heard of the sound. Being-heard is structurally phenomenal and belongs to an order radically dissimilar to that of the real sound in the world. One can only divide this subtle but absolutely decisive heterogeneity by a phenomenological reduction. The latter is therefore indispensable to all analyses of being-heard, whether they be inspired by linguistic, psychoanalytic, or other preoccupations.

Now the "sound-image," the structured appearing [*l'apparaître*] of the sound, the "sensory matter" *lived* and *informed* by differance, what Husserl would name the *hylè/morphé* structure, distinct from all mundane reality, is called the "psychic image" by Saussure: "The latter [the sound-image] is not the material sound, a purely physical thing, but the psychic imprint of the sound, the impression that it makes on our senses [*la représentation que nous en donne le témoignage de nos sens*]. The sound-image is sensory, and if I happen to call it 'material,' it is only in that sense, and by way of opposing it, to the other term of the association, the concept, which is generally more abstract" (p. 98) [p. 66]. Although the word "psychic" is not perhaps convenient, except for exercising in this matter a phenomenological caution, the originality of a certain place is well marked.

Before specifying it, let us note that this is not necessarily what Jakobson and other linguists could criticize as "the mentalist point of view":

> In the oldest of these approaches, going back to Baudouin de Courtenay and still surviving, the phoneme is a sound imagined or intended, opposed to the emitted sound as a "psychophonetic" phenomenon to the "physiophonetic" fact. It is the psychic equivalent of an exteriorized sound.[38]

Although the notion of the "psychic image" thus defined (that is to say according to a prephenomenological psychology of the imagination) is indeed of this mentalist inspiration, it could be defended against Jakobson's criticism by specifying: (1) that it could be conserved without necessarily affirming that "our internal speech . . . is confined to the distinctive features to the exclusion of the configurative, or redundant features;" (2) that the qualification *psychic* is not retained if it designates exclusively *another natural reality, internal and not external.* Here the Husserlian correction is indispensable and transforms even the premises of the debate. Real (*reell* and not *real*) component of lived experience, the *hylè/morphé* structure is not a reality (*Realität*). As to the intentional object, for example, the content of the image, it does not really (*reall*) belong either to the world or to lived experience: the nonreal component of lived experience. The psychic image of which Saussure speaks must not be an internal reality copying an external one. Husserl, who criticizes this concept of "portrait" in

[38] Op. cit., p. 111. Hjelmslev formulates the same reservations: "It is curious that linguistics, so long on guard against any suspicion of 'psychologism,' seems here, even if only to a certain extent and in very cautious proportions, to be on its way back to Saussure's 'accoustic image,' and equally to 'concept,' as long as that word is interpreted in strict conformity with the doctrine that I have just elaborated, in short to recognize, with however many necessary reservations, that, with the two aspects of the linguistic sign, one is in the presence of the 'purely psychological phenomenon' (*Course,* p. 28) [p. 11]. But it is rather a partial coincidence of nomenclatures than a real analogy. The terms introduced by Saussure, and the interpretations given in the *Course,* have been abandoned because they can be equivocal, and it is better not to make the same mistakes again. I too hesitate when I ask myself how much the researches advocated here may be considered as belonging to the psychological order: the reason being that psychology seems to be a discipline whose definition still leaves much to be desired" ("La stratification du langage" *Essais linguistiques* [1954], p. 56). Hjelmslev, posing the same problem, already evoked those "numerous nuances that the Genevan master could be fully aware of, but which he did not find it useful to insist upon; the motives behind this attitude naturally escape us" (p. 76). [Au.]

Ideen I[39] shows also in the *Krisis* (pp. 63 f.)[40] how phenomenology should overcome the naturalist opposition—whereby psychology and the other sciences of man survive—between "internal" and "external" experience. It is therefore indispensable to preserve the distinction between the appearing sound [*le son apparaissant*] and the appearing of the sound [*l'apparaître du son*] in order to escape the worst and the most prevalent of confusions; and it is in principle possible to do it without "attempt[ing] to overcome the antinomy between invariance and variability by assigning the former to the internal and the latter to the external experience" (Jakobson, op. cit., p. 112) [p. 12]. The difference between invariance and variability does not separate the two domains from each other, it divides each of them within itself. That gives enough indication that the essence of the *phonè* cannot be read directly and primarily in the text of a mundane science, of a psycho-physiophonetics.

These precautions taken, it should be recognized that it is in the specific zone of this imprint and this trace, in the temporalization of a *lived experience* which is neither *in* the world nor in "another world," which is not more sonorous than luminous, not more *in* time than *in* space, that differences appear among the elements or rather produce them, make them emerge as such and constitute the *texts,* the chains, and the systems of traces. These chains and systems cannot be outlined except in the fabric of this trace or imprint. The unheard difference between the appearing and the appearance [*l'apparaissant et l'apparaître*] (between the "world" and "lived experience") is the condition of all other differences, of all other traces, and *it is already a trace.* This last concept is thus absolutely and by rights "anterior" to all *physiological* problematics concerning the nature of the *engramme* [the unit of engraving], or *metaphysical* problematics concerning the meaning of absolute presence whose trace is thus opened to deciphering. *The trace is in fact the absolute origin of sense in general. Which amounts to saying once again that there is no absolute origin of sense in general. The trace is the differance* which opens appearance [*l'apparaître*] and signification. Articulating the living upon the nonliving in general, origin of all repetition, origin of ideality, the trace is not more ideal than real, not more intelligible than sensible, not more a transparent signification than an opaque energy and *no concept of metaphysics can describe it.* And as it is *a fortiori* anterior to the distinction between regions of sensibility, anterior to sound as much as to light, is there a sense in establishing a "natural" hierarchy between the sound-imprint, for example, and the visual (graphic) imprint? The graphic image is not seen; and the acoustic image is not heard. The difference between the full unities of the voice remains unheard. And, the difference in the body of the inscription is also invisible.

[39] *Ideen zu einer reinen Phänomenologie und phänomenologischen Philosophie.* I. Buch, *Gesammelte Werke* (The Hague, 1950), Band 3; *Ideas: General Introduction to Pure Phenomenology,* trans. W. R. Boyce (New York, 1931). [Tr.]

[40] *Husserliana. Gesammelte Werke,* ed. H. L. van Breda (The Hague, 1950–73), vol. 6. [Tr.]

DIFFÉRANCE

I will speak, therefore, of a letter.

Of the first letter, if the alphabet, and most of the speculations which have ventured into it, are to be believed.

I will speak, therefore, of the letter *a,* this initial letter which it apparently has been necessary to insinuate, here and there, into the writing of the word *difference;* and to do so in the course of a writing on writing, and also of a writing within writing whose different trajectories thereby find themselves, at certain very determined points, intersecting with a kind of gross spelling mistake, a lapse in the discipline and law which regulate writing and keep it seemly. One can always, de facto or de jure, erase or reduce this lapse in spelling, and find it (according to situations to be analyzed each time, although amounting to the same), grave or unseemly, that is, to follow the most ingenuous hypothesis, amusing. Thus, even if one seeks to pass over such an infraction in silence, the interest that one takes in it can be recognized and situated in advance as prescribed by the mute irony, the inaudible misplacement, of this literal permutation. One can always act as if it made no difference. And I must state here and now that today's discourse will be less a justification of, and even less an apology for, this silent lapse in spelling, than a kind of insistent intensification of its play.

On the other hand, I will have to be excused if I refer, at least implicitly, to some of the texts I have ventured to publish. This is precisely because I would like to attempt, to a certain extent, and even though in principle and in the last analysis this is impossible, and impossible for essential reasons, to reassemble in a *sheaf* the different directions in which I have been able to utilize what I would call provisionally the word or concept of *différance,* or rather to let it impose itself upon me in its neographism, although as we shall see, *différance* is literally neither a word nor a concept. And I insist upon the word *sheaf* for two reasons. On the one hand, I will not be concerned, as I might have been, with describing a history and narrating its stages, text by text, context by context, demonstrating the economy that each time imposed this graphic disorder; rather, I will be concerned with the *general system of this economy.* On the other hand, the word *sheaf* seems to mark more appropriately that the assemblage to be proposed has the complex structure of a weaving, an interlacing which permits the different threads and different lines of meaning—or of force—to go off again in different directions, just as it is always ready to tie itself up with others.

Therefore, preliminarily, let me recall that this discreet graphic intervention, which neither primarily nor simply aims to shock the reader or the grammarian, came to be formulated in the course of a written investigation of a question about writing. Now it happens, I would say in effect, that this graphic difference (*a* instead of *e*), this marked difference between two apparently vocal notations, between two vowels, remains purely graphic: it is read, or it is written, but it cannot be heard. It cannot be apprehended in speech, and we will see why it also bypasses the order of apprehension in general. It is offered by a mute mark, by a tacit monument, I would even say by a pyramid, thinking not only of the form of the letter when it is printed as a capital, but also of the text in Hegel's *Encyclopedia* in which the body of the sign is compared to the Egyptian Pyramid. The *a* of *différance,* thus, is not heard; it remains silent, secret and discreet as a tomb: *oikēsis.* And thereby let us anticipate the delineation of a site, the familial residence and tomb of the proper[1] in which is produced, by *différance,* the *economy of death.* This stone—provided that one knows how to decipher its inscription—is not far from announcing the death of the tyrant.[2]

DIFFÉRANCE was first presented as an address before the Société française de philosophie, January 27, 1968, published simultaneously in the *Bulletin de la société française de philosophie,* July–September 1968, and in *Théorie d'ensemble,* coll. Tel Quel (Paris, 1968). This translation by Alan Bass is reprinted from *Margins of Philosophy* (1972; trans. 1982), by permission of the University of Chicago Press.

[1] Throughout this book I will translate *le propre* as "the proper." Derrida most often intends all the senses of the word at once: that which is correct, as in *le sens propre* (proper, literal meaning), and that which is one's own, that which may be owned, that which is legally, correctly owned—all the links between proper, property, and propriety. [Tr.]

[2] The last three sentences refer elliptically and playfully to the following ideas. Derrida first plays on the "silence" of the *a* in *différance* as being like a silent tomb, like a pyramid, like the pyramid to which Hegel compares the body

And it is a tomb that cannot even be made to resonate. In effect, I cannot let you know through my discourse, through the speech being addressed at this moment to the French Society of Philosophy, what difference I am talking about when I talk about it. I can speak of this graphic difference only through a very indirect discourse on writing, and on the condition that I specify, each time, whether I am referring to difference with an *e* or *différance* with an *a*. Which will not simplify things today, and will give us all, you and me, a great deal of trouble, if, at least, we wish to understand each other. In any event, the oral specifications that I will provide—when I say "with an *e*" or "with an *a*"—will refer uncircumventably *to a written text* that keeps watch over my discourse, to a text that I am holding in front of me, that I will read, and toward which I necessarily will attempt to direct your hands and your eyes. We will be able neither to do without the passage through a written text, nor to avoid the order of the disorder produced within it—and this, first of all, is what counts for me.

The pyramidal silence of the graphic difference between the *e* and the *a* can function, of course, only within the system of phonetic writing, and within the language and grammar which is as historically linked to phonetic writing as it is to the entire culture inseparable from phonetic writing. But I would say that this in itself—the silence that functions within only a so-called phonetic writing—quite opportunely conveys or reminds us that, contrary to a very widespread prejudice, there is no phonetic writing. There is no purely and rigorously phonetic writing. So-called phonetic writing, by all rights and in principle, and not only due to an empirical or technical insufficiency, can function only by admitting into its system nonphonetic "signs" (punctuation, spacing, etc.). And an examination of the structure and necessity of these nonphonetic signs quickly reveals that they can barely tolerate the concept of the sign itself. Better, the play of difference, which, as Saussure reminded us, is the condition for the possibility and functioning of every sign, is in itself a silent play. Inaudible is the difference between two phonemes which alone permits them to be and to operate as such. The inaudible opens up the apprehension of two present phonemes such as they present themselves. If there is no purely phonetic writing, it is that there is no purely phonetic *phōnē*. The difference which establishes phonemes and lets them be heard remains in and of itself inaudible, in every sense of the word.

It will be objected, for the same reasons, that graphic difference itself vanishes into the night, can never be sensed as a full term, but rather extends an invisible relationship, the mark of an inapparent relationship between two spectacles. Doubtless. But, from this point of view, that the difference marked in the "differ( )nce" between the *e* and the *a* eludes both vision and hearing perhaps happily suggests that here we must be permitted to refer to an order which no longer belongs to sensibility. But neither can it belong to intelligibility, to the ideality which is not fortuitously affiliated with the objectivity of *theōrein* or understanding.[3] Here, therefore, we must let ourselves refer to an order that resists the opposition, one of the founding oppositions of philosophy, between the sensible and the intelligible. The order which resists this opposition, and resists it because it transports it, is announced in a movement of *différance* (with an *a*) between two differences or two letters, a *différance* which belongs nei-

of the sign. "Tomb" in Greek is *oikēsis*, which is akin to the Greek *oikos*—house—from which the word "economy" derives (*oikos*—house—and *nemein*—to manage). Thus Derrida speaks of the "economy of death" as the "familial residence and tomb of the proper." Further, and more elliptically still, Derrida speaks of the tomb, which always bears an inscription in stone, announcing the death of the tyrant. This seems to refer to Hegel's treatment of the Antigone story in the *Phenomenology*. It will be recalled that Antigone defies the tyrant Creon by burying her brother Polynices. Creon retaliates by having Antigone entombed. There she cheats the slow death that awaits her by hanging herself. The tyrant Creon has a change of heart too late, and—after the suicides of his son and wife, his *family*—kills himself. Thus family, death, inscription, tomb, law, economy. In a later work, *Glas*, Derrida analyzes Hegel's treatment of the *Antigone*. [Tr.]

[3] ". . . not fortuitously affiliated with the objectivity of *theōrein* or understanding." A play on words has been lost in translation here, a loss that makes this sentence difficult to understand. In the previous sentence Derrida says that the difference between the *e* and the *a* of *difference/différance* can neither be seen nor heard. It is not a sensible—that is, relating to the senses—difference. But, he goes on to explain, neither is this an intelligible difference, for the very names by which we conceive of objective intelligibility are already in complicity with sensibility. *Theōrein*—the Greek origin of "theory"—literally means "to look at," to *see;* and the word Derrida uses for "understanding" here is *entendement*, the noun form of *entendre*, to *hear*. [Tr.]

ther to the voice nor to writing in the usual sense, and which is located, as the strange space that will keep us together here for an hour, *between* speech and writing, and beyond the tranquil familiarity which links us to one and the other, occasionally reassuring us in our illusion that they are two.

What am I to do in order to speak of the *a* of *différance*? It goes without saying that it cannot be *exposed*. One can expose only that which at a certain moment can become *present*, manifest, that which can be shown, presented as something present, a being-present[4] in its truth, in the truth of a present or the presence of the present. Now if *différance* ~~is~~ (and I also cross out the "~~is~~") what makes possible the presentation of the being-present, it is never presented as such. It is never offered to the present. Or to anyone. Reserving itself, not exposing itself, in regular fashion it exceeds the order of truth at a certain precise point, but without dissimulating itself as something, as a mysterious being, in the occult of a nonknowledge or in a hole with indeterminable borders (for example, in a topology of castration).[5] In every exposition it would be exposed to disappearing as disappearance. It would risk appearing: disappearing.

So much so that the detours, locutions, and syntax in which I will often have to take recourse will resemble those of negative theology, occasionally even to the point of being indistinguishable from negative theology. Already we have had to delineate *that différance is not,* does not exist, is not a present-being (*on*) in any form; and we will be led to delineate also everything *that* it *is not,* that is, *everything;* and consequently that it has neither existence nor essence. It derives from no category of being, whether present or absent. And yet those aspects of *différance* which are thereby delineated are not theological, not even in the order of the most negative of negative theologies, which are always concerned with disengaging a superessentiality beyond the finite categories of essence and existence, that is, of presence, and always hastening to recall that God is refused the predicate of existence, only in order to acknowledge his superior, inconceivable, and ineffable mode of being. Such a development is not in question here, and this will be confirmed progressively. *Différance* is not only irreducible to any ontological or theological—ontotheological—reappropriation, but as the very opening of the space in which ontotheology—philosophy—produces its system and its history, it includes ontotheology, inscribing it and exceeding it without return.

For the same reason there is nowhere to *begin* to trace the sheaf or the graphics of *différance*. For what is put into question is precisely the quest for a rightful beginning, an absolute point of departure, a principal responsibility. The problematic of writing is opened by putting into question the value *arkhē*.[6] What I will propose here will not be elaborated simply as a philosophical discourse, operating according to principles, postulates, axioms or definitions, and proceeding along the discursive lines of a linear order of reasons. In the delineation of *différance* everything is strategic and adventurous. Strategic because no transcendent truth present outside the field of writing can govern theologically the totality of the field. Adventurous because this strategy is not a simple strategy in the sense that strategy orients tactics according to a final goal, a *telos* or theme of domination, a mastery and ultimate reappropriation of the development of the field. Finally, a strategy without finality, what might be called blind tactics, or empirical wandering if the value of empiricism did not itself acquire its entire meaning in its opposition to philosophical responsibility. If there is a certain wandering in the tracing of *différance*, it no more follows the lines of philosophical-logical discourse than that of its sym-

[4] As in the past, *être* (*Sein*) will be translated as Being. *Etant* (*Seiendes*) will be either beings or being, depending on the context. Thus, here *étant-present* is "being-present." For a justification of this translation see Derrida, *Writing and Difference,* trans. Alan Bass (Chicago: University of Chicago Press, 1978), Translator's Introduction, p. xvii. [Tr.]

[5] ". . . a hole with indeterminable borders (for example, in a topology of castration)." This phrase was added to "La Différance" for its publication in the French edition of this volume and refers to the polemic Derrida had already engaged (in *Positions;* elaborated further in *le Facteur de la verité*) with *Jacques Lacan*. For Derrida, Lacan's "topology of castration," which assigns the "hole" or lack to a place—"a hole with determinable borders"—repeats the metaphysical gesture (albeit a negative one) of making absence, the lack, the hole, a transcendental principle that can be pinned down as such, and can thereby *govern* a theoretical discourse. [Tr.]

[6] The Greek *arkhē* combines the values of a founding principle and of government by a controlling principle (e.g. *arche*ology, mon*archy*). [Tr.]

metrical and integral inverse, empirical logical discourse. The concept of *play* keeps itself beyond this opposition, announcing, on the eve of philosophy and beyond it, the unity of chance and necessity in calculations without end.

Also, by decision and as a rule of the game, if you will, turning these propositions back on themselves, we will be introduced to the thought of *différance* by the theme of strategy or the strategem. By means of this solely strategic justification, I wish to underline that the efficacity of the thematic of *différance* may very well, indeed must, one day be superseded, lending itself if not to its own replacement, at least to enmeshing itself in a chain that in truth it never will have governed. Whereby, once again, it is not theological.

I would say, first off, that *différance,* which is neither a word nor a concept, strategically seemed to me the most proper one to think, if not to master—thought, here, being that which is maintained in a certain necessary relationship with the structural limits of mastery—what is most irreducible about our "era." Therefore I am starting, strategically, from the place and the time in which "we" are, even though in the last analysis my opening is not justifiable, since it is only on the basis of *différance* and its "history" that we can allegedly know who and where "we" are, and what the limits of an "era" might be.

Even though *différance* is neither a word nor a concept, let us nevertheless attempt a simple and approximate semantic analysis that will take us to within sight of what is at stake.

We know that the verb *différer* (Latin verb *differre*) has two meanings which seem quite distinct;[7] for example in Littré they are the object of two separate articles. In this sense the Latin *differre* is not simply a translation of the Greek *diapherein,* and this will not be without consequences for us, linking our discourse to a particular language, and to a language that passes as less philosophical, less originally philosophical than the other. For the distribution of meaning in the Greek *diapherein* does not comport one of the two motifs of the Latin *differre,* to wit, the action of putting off until later, of taking into account, of taking account of time and of the forces of an operation that implies an economical calculation, a detour, a delay, a relay, a reserve, a representation—concepts that I would summarize here in a word I have never used but that could be inscribed in this chain: *temporization. Différer* in this sense is to temporize, to take recourse, consciously or unconsciously, in the temporal and temporizing mediation of a detour that suspends the accomplishment or fulfillment of "desire" or "will," and equally effects this suspension in a mode that annuls or tempers its own effect. And we will see, later, how this temporization is also temporalization and spacing, the becoming-time of space and the becoming-space of time, the "originary constitution" of time and space, as metaphysics or transcendental phenomenology would say, to use the language that here is criticized and displaced.

The other sense of *différer* is the more common and identifiable one: to be not identical, to be other, discernible, etc. When dealing with *differen(ts)(ds),* a word that can be written with a final *ts* or a final *ds,* as you will, whether it is a question of dissimilar otherness or of allergic and polemic otherness, an interval, a distance, *spacing,* must be produced between the elements other, and be produced with a certain perseverance in repetition.[8]

Now the word *différence* (with an *e*) can never refer either to *différer* as temporization or to *différends* as *polemos.*[9] Thus the word *différance* (with an *a*) is to compensate—economically—this loss of meaning, for *différance* can refer simultaneously to the entire configuration of its meanings. It is immediately and irreducibly polysemic, which will not be

[7] In English the two distinct meanings of the Latin *differre* have become two separate words: to defer and to differ. [Tr.]

[8] The next few sentences will require some annotation, to be found in this note and the next two. In this sentence Derrida is pointing out that two words that sound exactly alike in French (*différents, différends*) refer to the sense of *differre* that implies spacing, otherness—difference in its usual English sense. *Les différents* are different things; *les différends* are differences of opinion, grounds for dispute—whence the references to *all*ergy (from the Greek *allos,* other) and polemics. [Tr.]

[9] However, to continue the last note, *différence* (in French) does not convey the sense of active putting off, of deferring (*différance* in what would be its usual sense in French; if it were a word in common usage), or the sense of active polemical difference, actively differing with someone or something. ("Active" here, though, is not really correct, for reasons that Derrida will explain below.) The point is that there is no noun-verb, no gerund for either sense in French. [Tr.]

indifferent to the economy of my discourse here. In its polysemia this word, of course, like any meaning, must defer to the discourse in which it occurs, its interpretive context; but in a way it defers itself, or at least does so more readily than any other word, the *a* immediately deriving from the present participle (*différant*), thereby bringing us close to the very action of the verb *différer,* before it has even produced an effect constituted as something different or as *différence* (with an *e*).[10] In a conceptuality adhering to classical strictures "*différance*" would be said to designate a constitutive, productive, and originary causality, the process of scission and division which would produce or constitute different things or differences. But, because it brings us close to the infinitive and active kernel of *différer, différance* (with an *a*) neutralizes what the infinitive denotes as simply active, just as *mouvance* in our language does not simply mean the fact of moving, of moving oneself or of being moved. No more is resonance the act of resonating. We must consider that in the usage of our language the ending *-ance* remains undecided *between* the active and the passive. And we will see why that which lets itself be designated *différance* is neither simply active nor simply passive, announcing or rather recalling something like the middle voice, saying an operation that is not an operation, an operation that cannot be conceived either as passion or as the action of a subject on an object, or on the basis of the categories of agent or patient, neither on the basis of nor moving toward any of these *terms.* For the middle voice, a certain nontransitivity, may be what philosophy, at its outset, distributed into an active and a passive voice, thereby constituting itself by means of this repression.

Différance as temporization, *différance* as spacing. How are they to be joined?

Let us start, since we are already there, from the problematic of the sign and of writing. The sign is usually said to be put in the place of the thing itself, the present thing, "thing" here standing equally for meaning or referent. The sign represents the present in its absence. It takes the place of the present. When we cannot grasp or show the thing, state the present, the being-present, when the present cannot be presented, we signify, we go through the detour of the sign. We take or give signs. We signal. The sign, in this sense, is deferred presence. Whether we are concerned with the verbal or the written sign, with the monetary sign, or with electoral delegation and political representation, the circulation of signs defers the moment in which we can encounter the thing itself, make it ours, consume or expend it, touch it, see it, intuit its presence. What I am describing here in order to define it is the classically determined structure of the sign in all the banality of its characteristics—signification as the *différance* of temporization. And this structure presupposes that the sign, which defers presence, is conceivable only on the *basis* of the presence that it defers and *moving toward* the deferred presence that it aims to reappropriate. According to this classical semiology, the substitution of the sign for the thing itself is both *secondary* and *provisional:* secondary due to an original and lost presence from which the sign thus derives; provisional as concerns this final and missing presence toward which the sign in this sense is a movement of mediation.

In attempting to put into question these traits of the provisional secondariness of the substitute, one would come to see something like an originary *différance;* but one could no longer call it originary or final in the extent to which the values of origin, archi-, *telos, eskhaton,* etc. have always denoted presence—*ousa, parousia.*[11] To put into question the secondary and provisional characteristics of the sign, to oppose to them an "originary" *différance,* therefore would have two consequences.

1. One could no longer include *différance* in the concept of the sign, which always has meant the representation of a presence, and has been constituted in a system (thought or language) governed by and moving toward presence.

2. And thereby one puts into question the authority of presence, or of its simple symmetrical opposite, absence or lack. Thus one questions the limit which has always constrained us, which still constrains us—as inhabitants of a language and a system of thought—to formulate the meaning of

[10] Such a gerund would normally be constructed from the present participle of the verb: *différant.* Curiously then, the noun *différance* suspends itself between the two senses of *différant*—deferring, differing. We might say that it defers differing, and differs from deferring, in and of itself. [Tr.]

[11] *Ousia* and *parousia* imply presence as both origin and end, the founding principle (*arkhē-*) as that toward which one moves (*telos, eskhaton*). [Tr.]

Being in general as presence or absence, in the categories of being or beingness (*ousia*). Already it appears that the type of question to which we are redirected is, let us say, of the Heideggerian type, and that *différance seems* to lead back to the ontico-ontological difference. I will be permitted to hold off on this reference. I will note only that between difference as temporization-temporalization, which can no longer be conceived within the horizon of the present, and what Heidegger says in *Being and Time* about temporalization as the transcendental horizon of the question of Being, which must be liberated from its traditional, metaphysical domination by the present and the now, there is a strict communication, even though not an exhaustive and irreducibly necessary one.

But first let us remain within the semiological problematic in order to see *différance* as temporization and *différance* as spacing conjoined. Most of the semiological or linguistic researches that dominate the field of thought today, whether due to their own results or to the regulatory model that they find themselves acknowledging everywhere, refer genealogically to Saussure (correctly or incorrectly) as their common inaugurator. Now Saussure first of all is the thinker who put the *arbitrary character of the sign* and the *differential character* of the sign at the very foundation of general semiology, particularly linguistics. And, as we know, these two motifs—arbitrary and differential—are inseparable in his view. There can be arbitrariness only because the system of signs is constituted solely by the differences in terms, and not by their plenitude. The elements of signification function due not to the compact force of their nuclei but rather to the network of oppositions that distinguishes them, and then relates them one to another. "Arbitrary and differential," says Saussure, "are two correlative characteristics."

Now this principle of difference, as the condition for signification, affects the *totality* of the sign, that is the sign as both signified and signifier. The signified is the concept, the ideal meaning; and the signifier is what Saussure calls the "image," the "psychical imprint" of a material, physical—for example, acoustical—phenomenon. We do not have to go into all the problems posed by these definitions here. Let us cite Saussure only at the point which interests us: "The conceptual side of value is made up solely of relations and differences with respect to the other terms of language, and the same can be said of its material side . . . Everything that has been said up to this point boils down to this: in language there are only differences. Even more important: a difference generally implies positive terms between which the difference is set up; but in language there are only differences *without positive terms*. Whether we take the signified or the signifier, language has neither ideas nor sounds that existed before the linguistic system, but only conceptual and phonic differences that have issued from the system. The idea or phonic substance that a sign contains is of less importance than the other signs that surround it."[12]

The first consequence to be drawn from this is that the signified concept is never present in and of itself, in a sufficient presence that would refer only to itself. Essentially and lawfully, every concept is inscribed in a chain or in a system within which it refers to the other, to other concepts, by means of the systematic play of differences. Such a play, *différance,* is thus no longer simply a concept, but rather the possibility of conceptuality, of a conceptual process and system in general. For the same reason, *différance,* which is not a concept, is not simply a word, that is, what is generally represented as the calm, present, and self-referential unity of concept and phonic material. Later we will look into the word in general.

The difference of which Saussure speaks is itself, therefore, neither a concept nor a word among others. The same can be said, a fortiori, of *différance.* And we are thereby led to explicate the relation of one to the other.

In a language, in the *system* of language, there are only differences. Therefore a taxonomical operation can undertake the systematic, statistical, and classificatory inventory of a language. But, on the one hand, these differences *play:* in language, in speech too, and in the exchange between language and speech. On the other hand, these differences are themselves *effects.* They have not fallen from the sky fully formed, and are no more inscribed in a *topos noētos,* than they are prescribed in the gray matter of the brain. If the word "history" did not in and of itself convey the motif of a final repression of

[12] Ferdinand de Saussure, *Course in General Linguistics,* trans. Wade Baskin (New York: Philosophical Library, 1959), pp. 117–18, 120. [Tr.]

difference, one could say that only differences can be "historical" from the outset and in each of their aspects.

What is written as *différance,* then, will be the playing movement that "produces"—by means of something that is not simply an activity—these differences, these effects of difference. This does not mean that the *différance* that produces differences is somehow before them, in a simple and unmodified—in-different—present. *Différance* is the nonfull, non-simple, structured and differentiating origin of differences. Thus, the name "origin" no longer suits it.

Since language, which Saussure says is a classification, has not fallen from the sky, its differences have been produced, are produced effects, but they are effects which do not find their cause in a subject or a substance, in a thing in general, a being that is somewhere present, thereby eluding the play of *différance.* If such a presence were implied in the concept of cause in general, in the most classical fashion, we then would have to speak of an effect without a cause, which very quickly would lead to speaking of no effect at all. I have attempted to indicate a way out of the closure of this framework via the "trace," which is no more an effect than it has a cause, but which in and of itself, outside its text, is not sufficient to operate the necessary transgression.

Since there is no presence before and outside semiological difference, what Saussure has written about language can be extended to the sign in general: "Language is necessary in order for speech to be intelligible and to produce all of its effects; but the latter is necessary in order for language to be established; historically, the fact of speech always comes first."[13]

Retaining at least the framework, if not the content, of this requirement formulated by Saussure, we will designate as *différance* the movement according to which language, or any code, any system of referral in general, is constituted "historically" as a weave of differences. "Is constituted," "is produced," "is created," "movement," "historically," etc., necessarily being understood beyond the metaphysical language in which they are retained, along with all their implications. We ought to demonstrate why concepts like *production,* constitution, and history remain in complicity with what is at issue here. But this would take me too far today—toward the theory of the representation of the "circle" in which we appear to be enclosed—and I utilize such concepts, like many others, only for their strategic convenience and in order to undertake their deconstruction at the currently most decisive point. In any event, it will be understood, by means of the circle in which we appear to be engaged, that as it is written here, *différance* is no more static than it is genetic, no more structural than historical. Or is no less so; and to object to this on the basis of the oldest of metaphysical oppositions (for example, by setting some generative point of view against a structural-taxonomical point of view, or vice versa) would be, above all, not to read what here is missing from orthographical ethics. Such oppositions have not the least pertinence to *différance,* which makes the thinking of it uneasy and uncomfortable.

Now if we consider the chain in which *différance* lends itself to a certain number of nonsynonymous substitutions, according to the necessity of the context, why have recourse to the "reserve," to "archi-writing," to the "archi-trace," to "spacing," that is, to the "supplement," or to the *pharmakon,* and soon to the hymen, to the margin-mark-march, etc.[14]

Let us go on. It is because of *différance* that the movement of signification is possible only if each so-called "present" element, each element appearing on the scene of presence, is related to something other than itself, thereby keeping within itself the mark of the past element, and already letting itself be vitiated by the mark of its relation to the future element, this trace being related no less to what is

[13] Ibid., p. 18. [Tr.]

[14] All these terms refer to writing and inscribe *différance* within themselves, as Derrida says, according to the context. The supplement (*supplément*) is Rousseau's word to describe writing (analyzed in *Of Grammatology,* trans. Gayatri Spivak [Baltimore: Johns Hopkins University Press, 1976]). It means *both* the missing piece and the extra piece. The *pharmakon* is Plato's word for writing (analyzed in "Plato's Pharmacy" in *Dissemination,* trans. Barbara Johnson [Chicago: University of Chicago Press, 1981]), meaning *both* remedy and poison; the hymen (*l'hymen*) comes from Derrida's analysis of Mallarmé's writing and Mallarmé's reflections on writing ("The Double Session" in *Dissemination*) and refers *both* to virginity and to consummation; *marge-marque-marche* is the series *en différance* that Derrida applies to Sollers's *Nombres* ("Dissemination" in *Dissemination*). [Tr.]

called the future than to what is called the past, and constituting what is called the present by means of this very relation to what it is not: what it absolutely is not, not even a past or a future as a modified present. An interval must separate the present from what it is not in order for the present to be itself, but this interval that constitutes it as present must, by the same token, divide the present in and of itself, thereby also dividing, along with the present, everything that is thought on the basis of the present, that is, in our metaphysical language, every being, and singularly substance or the subject. In constituting itself, in dividing itself dynamically, this interval is what might be called *spacing*, the becoming-space of time or the becoming-time of space (*temporization*). And it is this constitution of the present, as an "originary" and irreducibly nonsimple (and therefore, *stricto sensu* nonoriginary) synthesis of marks, or traces of retentions and protentions (to reproduce analogically and provisionally a phenomenological and transcendental language that soon will reveal itself to be inadequate), that I propose to call archi-writing, archi-trace, or *différance*. Which (is) (simultaneously) spacing (and) temporization.

Could not this (active) movement of (the production of) *différance* without origin be called simply, and without neographism, *differentiation?* Such a word, among other confusions, would have left open the possibility of an organic, original, and homogeneous unity that eventually would come to be divided, to receive difference as an event. And above all, since it is formed from the verb "to differentiate," it would negate the economic signification of the detour, the temporizing delay, "deferral." Here, a remark in passing, which I owe to a recent reading of a text that Koyré (in 1934, in *Revue d'histoire et de philosophie réligieuse*, and reprinted in his *Etudes d'histoire de la pensée philosophique*) devoted to "Hegel in Jena." In this text Koyré gives long citations, in German, of the Jena *Logic*, and proposes their translation. On two occasions he encounters the expression *differente Beziehung* in Hegel's text. This word (*different*), with its Latin root, is rare in German and, I believe, in Hegel, who prefers *verschieden* or *ungleich*, calling difference *Unterschied* and qualitative variety *Verschiedenheit*. In the Jena *Logic* he uses the word *different* precisely where he treats of time and the present. Before getting to a valuable comment of Koyré's, let us look at some sentences from Hegel, such as Koyré translates them: "The infinite, in this simplicity, is, as a moment opposed to the equal-to-itself, the negative, and in its moments, although it is (itself) presented to and in itself the totality, (it is) what excludes in general, the point or limit; but in its own (action of) negating, it is related immediately to the other and negates itself by itself. The limit or moment of the present (*der Gegen-wart*), the absolute 'this' of time, or the now, is of an absolutely negative simplicity, which absolutely excludes from itself all multiplicity, and, by virtue of this, is absolutely determined; it is not whole or a *quantum* which would be extended in itself (and) which, in itself, also would have an undetermined moment, a diversity which, as indifferent (*gleichgultig*) or exterior in itself, would be related to an other (*auf ein anderes bezöge*), but in this is a relation absolutely different from the simple (*sondern es ist absolut differente Beziehung*)." And Koyré most remarkably specifies in a note: "different Relation: *differente Beziehung*. One might say: 'differentiating relation.'" And on the next page, another text of Hegel's in which one can read this: "*Diese Beziehung ist Gegenwart, als eine differente Beziehung* (This relationship is [the] present as a different relationship)." Another note of Koyré's: "The term *different* here is taken in an active sense."[15]

Writing "*différant*"[16] or "*différance*" (with an *a*) would have had the advantage of making it possible to translate Hegel at that particular point—which is also an absolutely decisive point in his discourse—

[15] Alexandre Koyré, "Hegel à Iena," in *Etudes d'histoire de la pensée philosophique* (Paris: Armand Colin, 1961), pp. 153–54. In his translation of "La différance" (in *Speech and Phenomena* [Evanston: Northwestern University Press, 1973]), David Allison notes (p. 144) that the citation from Hegel comes from "Jensener Logik, Metaphysik, und Naturphilosophie" in *Sämtliche Werke* (Leipzig: F. Meiner, 1925), XVIII, 202. Allison himself translated Hegel's text, and I have modified his translation. [Tr.]

[16] The point here, which cannot be conveyed in English, is that Koyré's realization that Hegel is describing a "differentiating relation," or "different" in an active sense, is precisely what the formation of *différance* from the participle *différant* describes, as explained in notes 9 and 10 above. And that it is the *present* that is described as differing from and deferring itself helps clarify Derrida's argument (at the end of the essay) that presence is to be rethought as the trace of the trace, as *différance* differed-and-deferred. [Tr.]

without further notes or specifications. And the translation would be, as it always must be, a transformation of one language by another. I contend, of course, that the word *différance* can also serve other purposes: first, because it marks not only the activity of "originary" difference, but also the temporizing detour of deferral; and above all because *différance* thus written, although maintaining relations of profound affinity with Hegelian discourse (such as it must be read), is also, up to a certain point, unable to break with that discourse (which has no kind of meaning or chance); but it can operate a kind of infinitesimal and radical displacement of it, whose space I attempt to delineate elsewhere but of which it would be difficult to speak briefly here.

Differences, thus, are "produced"—deferred—by *différance*. But *what* defers or *who* defers? In other words, *what is différance?* With this question we reach another level and another resource of our problematic.

What differs? Who differs? What is *différance?*

If we answered these questions before examining them as questions, before turning them back on themselves, and before suspecting their very form, including what seems most natural and necessary about them, we would immediately fall back into what we have just disengaged ourselves from. In effect, if we accepted the form of the question, in its meaning and its syntax ("what is?" "who is?" "who is it that?"), we would have to conclude that *différance* has been derived, has happened, is to be mastered and governed on the basis of the point of a present being, which itself could be some thing, a form, a state, a power in the world to which all kinds of names might be given, a *what*, or a present being as a *subject*, a *who*. And in this last case, notably, one would conclude implicitly that this present being, for example a being present to itself, as consciousness, eventually would come to defer or to differ: whether by delaying and turning away from the fulfillment of a "need" or a "desire," or by differing from itself. But in neither of these cases would such a present being be "constituted" by this *différance*.

Now if we refer, once again, to semiological difference, of what does Saussure, in particular, remind us? That "language [which only consists of differences] is not a function of the speaking subject." This implies that the subject (in its identity with itself, or eventually in its consciousness of its identity with itself, its self-consciousness) is inscribed in language, is a "function" of language, becomes a *speaking* subject only by making its speech conform—even in so-called "creation," or in so-called "transgression"—to the system of the rules of language as a system of differences, or at very least by conforming to the general law of *différance*, or by adhering to the principle of language which Saussure says is "spoken language minus speech." "Language is necessary for the spoken word to be intelligible and so that it can produce all of its effects."[17]

If, by hypothesis, we maintain that the opposition of speech to language is absolutely rigorous, then *différance* would be not only the play of differences within language but also the relation of speech to language, the detour through which I must pass in order to speak, the silent promise I must make; and this is equally valid for semiology in general, governing all the relations of usage to schemata, of message to code, etc. (Elsewhere I have attempted to suggest that this *différance* in language, and in the relation of speech and language, forbids the essential dissociation of speech and language that Saussure, at another level of his discourse, traditionally wished to delineate. The practice of a language or of a code supposing a play of forms without a determined and invariable substance, and also supposing in the practice of this play a retention and protention of differences, a spacing and a temporization, a play of traces—all this must be a kind of writing before the letter, an archi-writing without a present origin, without archi-. Whence the regular erasure of the archi-, and the transformation of general semiology into grammatology, this latter executing a critical labor on everything within semiology, including the central concept of the sign, that maintained metaphysical presuppositions incompatible with the motif of *différance*.)

One might be tempted by an objection: certainly the subject becomes a *speaking* subject only in its commerce with the system of linguistic differences; or yet, the subject becomes a *signifying* (signifying in general, by means of speech or any other sign) subject only by inscribing itself in the system of differences. Certainly in this sense the speaking or sig-

[17] Saussure, *Course in General Linguistics*, p. 37. [Tr.]

nifying subject could not be present to itself, as speaking or signifying, without the play of linguistic or semiological *différance*. But can one not conceive of a presence, and of a presence to itself of the subject before speech or signs, a presence to itself of the subject in a silent and intuitive consciousness?

Such a question therefore supposes that, prior to the sign and outside it, excluding any trace and any *différance,* something like consciousness is possible. And that consciousness, before distributing its signs in space and in the world, can gather itself into its presence. But what is consciousness? What does "consciousness" mean? Most often, in the very form of meaning, in all its modifications, consciousness offers itself to thought only as self-presence, as the perception of self in presence. And what holds for consciousness holds here for so-called subjective existence in general. Just as the category of the subject cannot be, and never has been, thought without the reference to presence as *hypokeimenon* or as *ousia,* etc., so the subject as consciousness has never manifested itself except as self-presence. The privilege granted to consciousness therefore signifies the privilege granted to the present; and even if one describes the transcendental temporality of consciousness, and at the depth at which Husserl does so, one grants to the "living present" the power of synthesizing traces, and of incessantly reassembling them.

This privilege is the ether of metaphysics, the element of our thought that is caught in the language of metaphysics. One can delimit such a closure today only by soliciting[18] the value of presence that Heidegger has shown to be the ontotheological determination of Being; and in thus soliciting the value of presence, by means of an interrogation whose status must be completely exceptional, we are also examining the absolute privilege of this form or epoch of presence in general that is consciousness as meaning[19] in self-presence.

Thus one comes to posit presence—and specifically consciousness, the being beside itself of consciousness—no longer as the absolutely central form of Being but as a "determination" and as an "effect." A determination or an effect within a system which is no longer that of presence but of *différance,* a system that no longer tolerates the opposition of activity and passivity, nor that of cause and effect, or of indetermination and determination, etc., such that in designating consciousness as an effect or a determination, one continues—for strategic reasons that can be more or less lucidly deliberated and systematically calculated—to operate according to the lexicon of that which one is delimiting.

Before being so radically and purposely the gesture of Heidegger, this gesture was also made by Nietzsche and Freud, both of whom, as is well known, and sometimes in very similar fashion, put consciousness into question in its assured certainty of itself. Now is it not remarkable that they both did so on the basis of the motif of *différance?*

Différance appears almost by name in their texts, and in those places where everything is at stake. I cannot expand upon this here; I will only recall that for Nietzsche "the great principal activity is unconscious," and that consciousness is the effect of forces whose essence, byways, and modalities are not proper to it. Force itself is never present; it is only a play of differences and quantities. There would be no force in general without the difference between forces; and here the difference of quantity counts more than the content of the quantity, more than absolute size itself. "Quantity itself, therefore, is not separable from the difference of quantity. The difference of quantity is the essence of force, the relation of force to force. The dream of two equal forces, even if they are granted an opposition of meaning, is an approximate and crude dream, a statistical dream, plunged into by the living but dispelled by chemistry."[20] Is not all of Nietzsche's thought a critique of philosophy as an active indifference to difference, as the system of adiaphoristic reduction or repression? Which according to the same logic, according to logic itself, does not exclude that philosophy lives *in* and *on différance,* thereby blinding itself to the *same,* which is not the

[18] The French *solliciter,* as the English *solicit,* derives from an Old Latin expression meaning to shake the whole, to make something tremble in its entirety. Derrida comments on this later, but is already using "to solicit" in this sense here. [Tr.]

[19] "Meaning" here is the weak translation of *vouloir-dire,* which has a strong sense of willing (*voluntas*) to say, putting the attempt to mean in conjunction with speech, a crucial conjunction for Derrida. [Tr.]

[20] Gilles Deleuze, *Nietzsche et la philosophie* (Paris: Presses Universitaires de France, 1970), p. 49. [Au.]

identical. The same, precisely, is *différance* (with an *a*) as the displaced and equivocal passage of one different thing to another, from one term of an opposition to the other. Thus one could reconsider all the pairs of opposites on which philosophy is constructed and on which our discourse lives, not in order to see opposition erase itself but to see what indicates that each of the terms must appear as the *différance* of the other, as the other different and deferred in the economy of the same (the intelligible as differing-deferring the sensible, as the sensible different and deferred; the concept as different and deferred, differing-deferring intuition; culture as nature different and deferred, differing-deferring; all the others of *physis—tekhnē, nomos, thesis,* society, freedom, history, mind, etc.—as *physis* different and deferred, or as *physis* differing and deferring. *Physis* in *différance.* And in this we may see the site of a reinterpretation of *mimēsis* in its alleged opposition to *physis*). And on the basis of this unfolding of the same as *différance,* we see announced the sameness of *différance* and repetition in the eternal return. Themes in Nietzsche's work that are linked to the symptomatology that always diagnoses the detour or ruse of an agency disguised in its *différance;* or further, to the entire thematic of active interpretation, which substitutes incessant deciphering for the unveiling of truth as the presentation of the thing itself in its presence, etc. Figures without truth, or at least a system of figures not dominated by the value of truth, which then becomes only an included, inscribed, circumscribed function.

Thus, *différance* is the name we might give to the "active," moving discord of different forces, and of differences of forces, that Nietzsche sets up against the entire system of metaphysical grammar, wherever this system governs culture, philosophy, and science.

It is historically significant that this diaphoristics, which, as an energetics or economics of forces, commits itself to putting into question the primacy of presence as consciousness, is also the major motif of Freud's thought: another diaphoristics, which in its entirety is both a theory of the figure (or of the trace) and an energetics. The putting into question of the authority of consciousness is first and always differential.

The two apparently different values of *différance* are tied together in Freudian theory: to differ as discernibility, distinction, separation, diastem, *spacing;* and to defer as detour, relay, reserve, *temporization.*

1. The concepts of trace (*Spur*), of breaching (*Bahnung*),[21] and of the forces of breaching, from the *Project* on, are inseparable from the concept of difference. The origin of memory, and of the psyche as (conscious or unconscious) memory in general, can be described only by taking into account the difference between breaches. Freud says so overtly. There is no breach without difference and no difference without trace.

2. All the differences in the production of unconscious traces and in the processes of inscription (*Niederschrift*) can also be interpreted as moments of *différance,* in the sense of putting into reserve. According to a schema that never ceased to guide Freud's thought, the movement of the trace is described as an effort of life to protect itself by *deferring* the dangerous investment, by constituting a reserve (*Vorrat*). And all the oppositions that furrow Freudian thought relate each of his concepts one to another as moments of a detour in the economy of *différance.* One is but the other different and deferred, one differing and deferring the other. One is the other in *différance,* one is the *différance* of the other. This is why every apparently rigorous and irreducible *opposition*(for example the opposition of the secondary to the primary) comes to be qualified, at one moment or another, as a "theoretical fiction." Again, it is thereby, for example (but such an example governs, and communicates with, everything), that the difference between the pleasure principle and the reality principle is only *différance* as detour. In *Beyond the Pleasure Principle* Freud writes: "Under the influence of the ego's instincts of self-preservation, the pleasure principle is replaced by the reality principle. This latter principle does not abandon the intention of ultimately obtaining pleasure, but it nevertheless demands and carries into effect the postponement of satisfaction, the abandonment of a number of possibilities of gaining

[21] Derrida is referring here to his essay "Freud and the Scene of Writing"in *Writing and Difference.* "Breaching" is the translation for *Bahnung* that I adopted there: it conveys more of the sense of breaking open (as in the German *Bahnung* and the French *frayage*) than the Standard Edition's "facilitation." The *Project* Derrida refers to here is the *Project for a Scientific Psychology* (1895), in which Freud attempted to cast his psychological thinking in a neurological framework. [Tr.]

satisfaction and the temporary toleration of unpleasure as a step on the long indirect road (*Aufschub*) to pleasure."[22]

Here we are touching upon the point of greatest obscurity, on the very enigma of *différance*, on precisely that which divides its very concept by means of a strange cleavage. We must not hasten to decide. How are we to think *simultaneously*, on the one hand, *différance* as the economic detour which, in the element of the same, always aims at coming back to the pleasure or the presence that have been deferred by (conscious or unconscious) calculation, and, on the other hand, *différance* as the relation to an impossible presence, as expenditure without reserve, as the irreparable loss of presence, the irreversible usage of energy, that is, as the death instinct, and as the entirely other relationship that apparently interrupts every economy? It is evident—and this is the evident itself—that the economical and the noneconomical, the same and the entirely other, etc., cannot be thought *together*. If *différance* is unthinkable in this way, perhaps we should not hasten to make it evident, in the philosophical element of evidentiality which would make short work of dissipating the mirage and illogicalness of *différance* and would do so with the infallibility of calculations that we are well acquainted with, having precisely recognized their place, necessity, and function in the structure of *différance*. Elsewhere, in a reading of Bataille, I have attempted to indicate what might come of a rigorous and, in a new sense, "scientific" *relating* of the "restricted economy" that takes no part in expenditure without reserve, death, opening itself to nonmeaning, etc., to a general economy that *takes into account* the nonreserve, that keeps in reserve the nonreserve, if it can be put thus. I am speaking of a relationship between a *différance* that can make a profit on its investment and a *différance* that misses its profit, the *investiture* of a presence that is pure and without loss here being confused with absolute loss, with death. Through such a relating of a restricted and a general economy the very project of philosophy, under the privileged heading of Hegelianism, is displaced and reinscribed. The *Aufhebung*—*la relève*—is constrained into writing itself otherwise. Or perhaps simply into writing itself. Or, better, into taking account of its consumption of writing.[23]

For the economic character of *différance* in no way implies that the deferred presence can always be found again, that we have here only an investment that provisionally and calculatedly delays the perception of its profit or the profit of its perception. Contrary to the metaphysical, dialectical, "Hegelian" interpretation of the economic movement of *différance*, we must conceive of a play in which

[22] *The Standard Edition of the Complete Psychological Works* (London: Hogarth Press, 1950 [hereafter cited as *SE*]), vol. 18, p. 10. [Tr.]

[23] Derrida is referring here to the reading of Hegel he proposed in "From Restricted to General Economy: A Hegelianism Without Reserve," in *Writing and Difference*. In that essay Derrida began his consideration of Hegel as the great philosophical *speculator;* thus all the economic metaphors of the previous sentences. For Derrida the deconstruction of metaphysics implies an endless confrontation with Hegelian concepts, and the move from a restricted, "speculative" philosophical economy—in which there is nothing that cannot be made to make sense, in which there is nothing *other* than meaning—to a "general" economy—which affirms that which exceeds meaning, the excess of meaning from which there can be no speculative profit—involves a reinterpretation of the central Hegelian concept: the *Aufhebung*. *Aufhebung* literally means "lifting up"; but it also contains the double meaning of conservation and negation. For Hegel, dialectics is a process of *Aufhebung:* every concept is to be negated and lifted up to a higher sphere in which it is thereby conserved. In this way, there is nothing from which the *Aufhebung* cannot profit. However, as Derrida points out, there is always an effect of *différance* when the same word has two contradictory meanings. Indeed it is this effect of *différance*—the excess of the trace *Aufhebung* itself—that is precisely what the *Aufhebung* can never *aufheben:* lift up, conserve, and negate. This is why Derrida wishes to constrain the *Aufhebung* to write itself otherwise, or simply to write itself, to take into account its consumption of writing. Without writing, the trace, there could be no words with double, contradictory meanings.

As with *différance*, the translation of a word with a double meaning is particularly difficult, and touches upon the entire problematics of writing and *différance*. The best translators of Hegel usually cite Hegel's own delight that the most speculative of languages, German, should have provided this most speculative of words as the vehicle for his supreme speculative effort. Thus *Aufhebung* is usually best annotated and left untranslated. (Jean Hyppolyte, in his French translations of Hegel, carefully annotates his rendering of *Aufheben* as both *supprimer* and *dépasser*. Baillies's rendering of *Aufhebung* as "sublation" is misleading.) Derrida, however, in his attempt to make *Aufhebung* write itself otherwise, has proposed a new translation of it that *does* take into account the effect of *différance* in its double meaning. Derrida's translation is *la relève*. The word comes from the verb *relever*, which means to lift up, as

whoever loses wins, and in which one loses and wins on every turn. If the displaced presentation remains definitively and implacably postponed, it is not that a certain present remains absent or hidden. Rather, *différance* maintains our relationship with that which we necessarily misconstrue, and which exceeds the alternative of presence and absence. A certain alterity—to which Freud gives the metaphysical name of the unconscious—is definitively exempt from every process of presentation by means of which we would call upon it to show itself in person. In this context, and beneath this guise, the unconscious is not, as we know, a hidden, virtual, or potential self-presence. It differs from, and defers, itself; which doubtless means that it is woven of differences, and also that it sends out delegates, representatives, proxies; but without any chance that the giver of proxies might "exist," might be present, be "itself" somewhere, and with even less chance that it might become conscious. In this sense, contrary to the terms of an old debate full of the metaphysical investments that it has always assumed, the "unconscious" is no more a "thing" than it is any other thing, is no more a thing than it is a virtual or masked consciousness. This radical alterity as concerns every possible mode of presence is marked by the irreducibility of the aftereffect, the delay. In order to describe traces, in order to read the traces of "unconscious" traces (there are no "conscious" traces), the language of presence and absence, the metaphysical discourse of phenomenology, is inadequate. (Although the phenomenologist is not the only one to speak this language.)

The structure of delay (*Nachträglichkeit*) in effect forbids that one make of temporalization (temporization) a simple dialectical complication of the living present as an originary and unceasing synthesis—a synthesis constantly directed back on itself, gathered in on itself and gathering—of retentional traces and protentional openings. The alterity of the "unconscious" makes us concerned not with horizons of modified—past or future—presents, but with a "past" that has never been present, and which never will be, whose future to come will never be a *production* or a reproduction in the form of presence. Therefore the concept of trace is incompatible with the concept of retention, of the becoming-past of what has been present. One cannot think the trace—and therefore, *différance*—on the basis of the present, or of the presence of the present.

A past that has never been present: this formula is the one that Emmanuel Levinas uses, although certainly in a nonpsychoanalytic way, to qualify the trace and enigma of absolute alterity: the Other.[24] Within these limits, and from this point of view at least, the thought of *différance* implies the entire critique of classical ontology undertaken by Levinas. And the concept of the trace, like that of *différance* thereby organizes, along the lines of these different traces and differences of traces, in Nietzsche's sense, in Freud's sense, in Levinas's sense—these "names of authors" here being only indices—the network which reassembles and traverses our "era" as the delimitation of the ontology of presence.

Which is to say the ontology of beings and beingness. It is the domination of beings that *différance* everywhere comes to solicit, in the sense that *sollicitare,* in old Latin, means to shake as a whole, to make tremble in entirety. Therefore, it is the determination of Being as presence or as beingness that is interrogated by the thought of *différance.* Such a question could not emerge and be understood unless the difference between Being and beings were somewhere to be broached. First consequence: *différance* is not. It is not a present being, however excellent, unique, principal, or transcendent. It governs nothing, reigns over nothing, and nowhere exercises any authority. It is not announced by any capital letter. Not only is there no kingdom of *différance,* but *différance* instigates the subversion of every kingdom. Which makes it obviously threatening and infallibly dreaded by everything within us

does *Aufheben.* But *relever* also means to relay, to relieve, as when one soldier on duty relieves another. Thus the conserving-and-negating lift has become *la relève,* a "lift" in which is inscribed an effect of substitution and difference, the effect of substitution and difference inscribed in the double meaning of *Aufhebung.* A. V. Miller's rendering of *Aufhebung* as "supersession" in his recent translation of the *Phenomenology* comes close to *relever* in combining the senses of raising up and replacement, although without the elegance of Derrida's maintenance of the verb meaning "to lift" (*heben, lever*) and change of prefix (*auf-, re-*). Thus we will leave *la relève* untranslated throughout, as with *différance.* For more on *la relève,* see below "*Ousia* and *Grammē,*" note 15; "The Pit and the Pyramid," note 16; and "The Ends of Man," note 14. [Tr.]

[24] On Levinas, and on the translation of his term *autrui* by "Other," see "Violence and Metaphysics," note 6, in *Writing and Difference.* [Tr.]

that desires a kingdom, the past or future presence of a kingdom. And it is always in the name of a kingdom that one may reproach *différance* with wishing to reign, believing that one sees it aggrandize itself with a capital letter.

Can *différance,* for these reasons, settle down into the division of the ontico-ontological difference, such as it is thought, such as its "epoch" in particular is thought, "through," if it may still be expressed such, Heidegger's uncircumventable meditation?

There is no simple answer to such a question.

In a certain aspect of itself, *différance* is certainly but the historical and epochal *unfolding* of Being or of the ontological difference. The *a* of *différance* marks the *movement* of this unfolding.

And yet, are not the thought of the *meaning* or *truth* of Being, the determination of *différance* as the ontico-ontological difference, difference thought within the horizon of the question *of Being,* still intrametaphysical effects of *différance?* The unfolding of *différance* is perhaps not solely the truth of Being, or of the epochality of Being. Perhaps we must attempt to think this unheard-of thought, this silent tracing: that the history of Being, whose thought engages the Greco-Western *logos* such as it is produced via the ontological difference, is but an epoch of the *diapherein.* Henceforth one could no longer even call this an "epoch," the concept of epochality belonging to what is within history as the history of Being. Since Being has never had a "meaning," has never been thought or said as such, except by dissimulating itself in beings, then *différance,* in a certain and very strange way, (is) "older" than the ontological difference or than the truth of Being. When it has this age it can be called the play of the trace. The play of a trace which no longer belongs to the horizon of Being, but whose play transports and encloses the meaning of Being: the play of the trace, or the *différance,* which has no meaning and is not. Which does not belong. There is no maintaining, and no depth to, this bottomless chessboard on which Being is put into play.

Perhaps this is why the Heraclitean play of the *hen diapheron heautōi,* of the one differing from itself, the one in difference with itself, already is lost like a trace in the determination of the *diapherein* as ontological difference.

To think the ontological difference doubtless remains a difficult task, and any statement of it has remained almost inaudible. Further, to prepare, beyond our *logos,* for a *différance* so violent that it can be interpellated neither as the epochality of Being nor as ontological difference, is not in any way to dispense with the passage through the truth of Being, or to "criticize," "contest," or misconstrue its incessant necessity. On the contrary, we must stay within the difficulty of this passage, and repeat it in the rigorous reading of metaphysics, wherever metaphysics normalizes Western discourse, and not only in the texts of the "history of philosophy." As rigorously as possible we must permit to appear/disappear the trace of what exceeds the truth of Being. The trace (of that) which can never be presented, the trace which itself can never be presented: that is, appear and manifest itself, as such, in its phenomenon. The trace beyond that which profoundly links fundamental ontology and phenomenology. Always differing and deferring, the trace is never as it is in the presentation of itself. It erases itself in presenting itself, muffles itself in resonating, like the *a* writing itself, inscribing its pyramid in *différance.*

The annunciating and reserved trace of this movement can always be disclosed in metaphysical discourse, and especially in the contemporary discourse which states, through the attempts to which we just referred (Nietzsche, Freud, Levinas), the closure of ontology. And especially through the Heideggerean text.

This text prompts us to examine the essence of the present, the presence of the present.

What is the present? What is it to think the present in its presence?

Let us consider, for example, the 1946 text entitled *Der Spruch des Anaximander* ("The Anaximander Fragment").[25] In this text Heidegger recalls that the forgetting of Being forgets the difference between Being and beings: ". . . to be the Being *of* beings is the matter of Being (*die Sache des Seins*). The grammatical form of this enigmatic, ambiguous genitive indicates a genesis (*Genesis*), the emergence (*Herkunft*) of what is present from presencing (*des Anwesenden aus dem Anwesen*). Yet the essence (*Wesen*) of this emergence remains concealed (*verbogen*) along with the essence of these two

[25] Martin Heidegger, *Holzwege* (Frankfurt: V. Klostermann, 1957). English translation ("The Anaximander Fragment") in *Early Greek Thinking,* trans. David Farrell Krell and Frank Capuzzi (New York: Harper and Row, 1975). All further references in the text. [Tr.]

words. Not only that, but even the very relation between presencing and what is present (*Anwesen und Anwesendem*)remains unthought. From early on it seems as though presencing and what is present were each something for itself. Presencing itself unnoticeably becomes something present . . . The essence of presencing (*Das Wesen des Anwesens*), and with it the distinction between presencing and what is present, remains forgotten. *The oblivion of Being is oblivion of the distinction between Being and beings*" (p. 50).

In recalling the difference between Being and beings (the ontological difference) as the difference between presence and the present, Heidegger advances a proposition, a body of propositions, that we are not going to use as a subject for criticism. This would be foolishly precipitate; rather, what we shall try to do is to return to this proposition its power to provoke.

Let us proceed slowly. What Heidegger wants to mark is this: the difference between Being and beings, the forgotten of metaphysics, has disappeared without leaving a trace. The very trace of difference has been submerged. If we maintain that *différance* (is) (itself) other than absence and presence, if it *traces,* then when it is a matter of the forgetting of the difference (between Being and beings), we would have to speak of a disappearance of the trace of the trace. Which is indeed what the following passage from "The Anaximander Fragment" seems to imply: "Oblivion of Being belongs to the self-veiling essence of Being. It belongs so essentially to the destiny of Being that the dawn of this destiny rises as the unveiling of what is present in its presencing. This means that the history of Being begins with the oblivion of Being, since Being—together with its essence, its distinction from beings—keeps to itself. The distinction collapses. It remains forgotten. Although the two parties to the distinction, what is present and presencing (*das Anwesende und das Anwesen*), reveal themselves, they do not do so as distinguished. Rather, even the early trace (*die frühe Spur*) of the distinction is obliterated when presencing appears as something present (*das Anwesen wie ein Anwesendes erscheint*) and finds itself in the position of being the highest being present (*in einem höchsten Anwesenden*)" (pp. 50–51).

Since the trace is not a presence but the simulacrum of a presence that dislocates itself, displaces itself, refers itself, it properly has no site—erasure belongs to its structure. And not only the erasure which must always be able to overtake it (without which it would not be a trace but an indestructible and monumental substance), but also the erasure which constitutes it from the outset as a trace, which situates it as the change of site, and makes it disappear in its appearance, makes it emerge from itself in its production. The erasure of the early trace (*die frühe Spur*) of difference is therefore the "same" as its tracing in the text of metaphysics. This latter must have maintained the mark of what it has lost, reserved, put aside. The paradox of such a structure, in the language of metaphysics, is an inversion of metaphysical concepts, which produces the following effect: the present becomes the sign of the sign, the trace of the trace. It is no longer what every reference refers to in the last analysis. It becomes a function in a structure of generalized reference. It is a trace, and a trace of the erasure of the trace.

Thereby the text of metaphysics is *comprehended.* Still legible; and to be read. It is not surrounded but rather traversed by its limit, marked in its interior by the multiple furrow of its margin. Proposing *all at once* the monument and the mirage of the trace, the trace simultaneously traced and erased, simultaneously living and dead, and, as always, living in its simulation of life's preserved inscription. A pyramid. Not a stone fence to be jumped over but itself stonelike, on a wall, to be deciphered otherwise, a text without voice.

Thus one can think without contradiction, or at least without granting any pertinence to such a contradiction, what is perceptible and imperceptible in the trace. The "early trace" of difference is lost in an invisibility without return, and yet its very loss is sheltered, retained, seen, delayed. In a text. In the form of presence. In the form of the proper. Which itself is only an effect of writing.

Having stated the erasure of the early trace, Heidegger can therefore, in a contradiction without contradiction, consign, countersign, the sealing of the trace. A bit further on: "However, the distinction between Being and beings, as something forgotten, can invade our experience only if it has already unveiled itself with the presencing of what is present (*mit dem Anwesen des Anwesenden*); only if it has left a trace (*eine Spur geprägt hat*) which remains preserved (*gewahrt bleibt*) in the language to which Being comes" (p. 51).

Still further on, while meditating on Anaximander's *to khreon,* which he translates as *Brauch* (usage), Heidegger writes this: "Enjoining order and reck (*Fug und Ruch verfügend*), usage delivers to each present being (*Anwesende*) the while into which it is released. But accompanying this process is the constant danger that lingering will petrify into mere persistence (*in das blosse Beharren verhärtet*). Thus usage essentially remains at the same time the distribution (*Aushändigung:* dismaintenance) of presencing (*des Anwesens*) into disorder (*in den Un-fug*). Usage conjoins the dis (*Der Brauch fügt das Un-*)" (p. 54).

And it is at the moment when Heidegger recognizes *usage* as *trace* that the question must be asked: can we, and to what extent, think this trace and the *dis* of *différance* as *Wesen des Seins?* Does not the *dis* of *différance* refer us beyond the history of Being, and also beyond our langauge, and everything that can be named in it? In the language of Being, does it not call for a necessarily violent transformation of this language by an entirely other language?

Let us make this question more specific. And to force the "trace" out of it (and has anyone thought that we have been tracking something down, something other than tracks themselves to be tracked down?), let us read this passage: "The translation of *to khreon* as 'usage' has not resulted from a preoccupation with etymologies and dictionary meanings. The choice of the word stems from a prior crossing *over* (*Über-setzen;* trans-lation) of a thinking which tries to think the distinction in the essence of Being (*im Wesen des Seins*) in the fateful beginning of Being's oblivion. The word 'usage' is dictated to thinking in the experience (*Erfahrung*) of Being's oblivion. What properly remains to be thought in the word 'usage' has presumably left a trace (*Spur*) in *to khreon*. This trace quickly vanishes (*alsbald verschwindet*) in the destiny of Being which unfolds in world history as Western metaphysics" (p. 54).

How to conceive what is outside a text? That which is more or less than a text's *own, proper* margin? For example, what is other than the text of Western metaphysics? It is certain that the trace which "quickly vanishes in the destiny of Being (and) which unfolds . . . as Western metaphysics" escapes every determination, every name it might receive in the metaphysical text. It is sheltered, and therefore, dissimulated, in these names. It does not appear in them as the trace "itself." But this is because it could never appear itself, *as such*. Heidegger also says that difference cannot appear as such: "Lichtung des Unterschiedes kann deshalb auch nicht bedeuten, dass der Unterschied als der Unterschied erscheint." There is no essence of *différance;* it (is) that which not only could never be appropriated in the *as such* of its name or its appearing, but also that which threatens the authority of the *as such* in general, of the presence of the thing itself in its essence. That there is not a proper essence[26] of *différance* at this point, implies that there is neither

[26] *Différance* is not a "species" of the genus *ontological difference.* If the "gift of presence is the property of Appropriating (*Die Gabe von Anwesen ist Eigentum des Ereignens*)" ["Time and Being," in *On Time and Being*, trans. Joan Stambaugh, New York: Harper and Row, 1972; p. 22], *différance* is not a process of propriation in any sense whatever. It is neither position (appropriation) nor negation (expropriation), but rather other. Hence it seems—but here, rather, we are marking the necessity of a future itinerary—that *différance* would be no more a species of the genus *Ereignis* than Being. Heidegger: ". . . then Being belongs into Appropriating (*Dann gehört das Sein in das Ereignen*). Giving and its gift receive their determination from Appropriating. In that case, Being would be a species of Appropriation (*Ereignis*), and not the other way around. To take refuge in such an inversion would be too cheap. Such thinking misses the matter at stake (*Sie denkt am Sachverhalt vorbei*). Appropriation (*Ereignis*) is not the encompassing general concept under which Being and time could be subsumed. Logical classifications mean nothing here. For as we think Being itself and follow what is its own (*seinem Eigenen folgen*), Being proves to be destiny's gift of presence (*gewahrte Gabe des Geschickes von Anwesenheit*), the gift granted by the giving (*Reichen*) of time. The gift of presence is the property of Appropriating (*Die Gabe von Anwesen ist Eigentum des Ereignens*)." (*On Time and Being*, pp. 21–22).

Without a displaced reinscription of this chain (Being, presence, -propriation, etc.) the relation between general or fundamental onto-logy and whatever ontology masters or makes subordinate under the rubric of a regional or particular science will never be transformed rigorously and irreversibly. Such regional sciences include not only political economy, psychoanalysis, semiolinguistics—in all of which, and perhaps more than elsewhere, the value of the *proper* plays an irreducible role—but equally all spiritualist or materialist metaphysics. The analyses articulated in this volume aim at such a preliminary articulation. It goes without saying that such a reinscription will never be contained in theoretical or philosophical discourse, or generally in any discourse or writing, but only on the scene of what I have called elsewhere the text in general (1972). [Au.]

a Being nor truth of the play of writing such as it engages *différance.*

For us, *différance* remains a metaphysical name, and all the names that it receives in our langauge are still, as names, metaphysical. And this is particularly the case when these names state the determination of *différance* as the difference between presence and the present (*Anwesen/Anwesend*), and above all, and is already the case when they state the determination of *différance* as the difference of Being and beings.

"Older" than Being itself, such a *différance* has no name in our language. But we "already know" that if it is unnameable, it is not provisionally so, not because our language has not yet found or received this *name,* or because we would have to seek it in another language, outside the finite system of our own. It is rather because there is no *name* for it at all, not even the name of essence or of Being, not even that of "*différance,*" which is not a name, which is not a pure nominal unity, and unceasingly dislocates itself in a chain of differing and deferring substitutions.

"There is no name for it": a proposition to be read in its *platitude.* This unnameable is not an ineffable Being which no name could approach: God, for example. This unnameable is the play which makes possible nominal effects, the relatively unitary and atomic structures that are called names, the chains of substitutions of names in which, for example, the nominal effect *différance* is itself *enmeshed,* carried off, reinscribed, just as a false entry or a false exit is still part of the game, a function of the system.

What we know, or what we would know if it were simply a question here of something to know, is that there has never been, never will be, a unique word, a master-name. This is why the thought of the letter *a* in *différance* is not the primary prescription or the prophetic annunciation of an imminent and as yet unheard-of nomination. There is nothing kerygmatic about this "word," provided that one perceives its decapita(liza)tion. And that one puts into question the name of the name.

There will be no unique name, even if it were the name of Being. And we must think this without *nostalgia,* that is, outside of the myth of a purely maternal or paternal language, a lost native country of thought. On the contrary, we must *affirm* this, in the sense in which Nietzsche puts affirmation into play, in a certain laughter and a certain step of the dance.

From the vantage of this laughter and this dance, from the vantage of this affirmation foreign to all dialectics, the other side of nostalgia, what I will call Heideggerian *hope,* comes into question. I am not unaware how shocking this word might seem here. Nevertheless I am venturing it, without excluding any of its implications, and I relate it to what still seems to me to be the metaphysical part of "The Anaximander Fragment": the quest for the proper word and the unique name. Speaking of the first word of Being (*das frühe Wort des Seins: to khreon*), Heidegger writes: "The relation to what is present that rules in the essence of presencing itself is a unique one (*ist eine einzige*), altogether incomparable to any other relation. It belongs to the uniqueness of Being itself (*Sie gehört zur Einzigkeit des Seins selbst*). Therefore, in order to name the essential nature of Being (*das wesende Seins*), language would have to find a single word, the unique word (*ein einziges, das einzige Wort*). From this we can gather how daring every thoughtful word (*denkende Wort*) addressed to Being is (*das dem Sein zugesprochen wird*). Nevertheless such daring is not impossible, since Being speaks always and everywhere throughout language" (p. 52).

Such is the question: the alliance of speech and Being in the unique word, in the finally proper name. And such is the question inscribed in the simulated affirmation of *différance.* It bears (on) each member of this sentence: "Being / speaks / always and everywhere / throughout / language."

Michel Foucault

1926–1984

THESE TWO TEXTS represent a juncture in Foucault's thought between his earlier "archeological" studies and his later "genealogical" ones. This is not to imply a definite break but rather a development in which the later work expands the range of concern established in the earlier. Foucault's earlier "archeological" studies—for example, his treatment of madness and the asylum—deal with historical systems of institutional and discursive practices. In those studies he unearths such systems as if they were autonomous wholes, avoiding questions of truth or meaning and rejecting wholesale the methods of hermeneutics and the idea of a meaning *behind* discursive practices. Archeology is "a task that consists of not—of no longer—treating discourses as groups of signs (signifying elements referring to contents or representations) but as practices that systematically form the objects of which they speak." Although this project clearly has a connection to structuralism, Foucault came to proclaim his difference from the structuralists. This difference became clearer as he adopted the concerns of what he called "genealogy," a term he adopted from Nietzsche. Genealogy asks the question of how such discourses function, and it led Foucault to questions of power. Structuralism, itself, he came to regard as a discursive practice interwoven with power. Foucault acknowledges that any analytical procedure is a product of the power relations that are immanent in it. This would have to apply to his own procedures. For Foucault, who argues that the day of the human subject (or as he calls it "man") as conceived in post-Kantian philosophy is over, power has no "origin" but is a diffusion through society, and knowledge at any given time is a projection of the prevailing relations of power, locatable only as an immanence everywhere. Genealogy thus goes beyond the concept of autonomous discourse to deal with historical situations (there are no other for Foucault) in which discursive practices are interwoven with social practices. Foucault is silent, however, on where discourse stops and social practices begin. The term "practices" emphasizes the radically historical view, marking him off from structuralism, that Foucault always holds. Practices are seen not as acts of individual subjects or as objective social structures but as the results of the diffusion of power.

Knowledge is governed by power relations. What is allowed (knowledge) and what is not allowed (the "unthought") are generated in relation to systems of authority, rules, hierarchy, and discipline, the last term including the interesting combination of a body of knowledge and practice and the results of training, suppression, and repression. Foucault's late work was principally concerned with the problem of the subject and power, the subject being taken in the sense of "subject to someone else by control and dependence, and tied to his own identity by a conscience or self-knowledge." Foucault regards his thought as not for or against the individual but against the effect of power that governs individualization, which for him is the legacy of the modern world and its invention "man."

Works of Foucault translated into English include *Madness and Civilization* (1961, trans. 1965); *The Birth of the Clinic* (1963, rev. 1972, trans. 1975); *The Order of Things* (1966, trans. 1970); *The Archeology of Knowledge* (1969, trans. 1972); *Discipline and Punish* (1975, trans. 1977); *The History of Sexuality I* (1976, trans. 1978); *Language, Counter-Memory, Practice: Selected Essays and Interviews* (1977); and *Power/Knowledge* (1980). See Charles C. Lemert and Garth Gillan, *Michel Foucault: Social Theory and Transgression,* which includes a bibliography of Foucault's writings; Herbert L. Dreyfuss and Paul Rabinow, *Michel Foucault: Beyond Structuralism and Hermeneutics,* which includes Foucault's "The Subject and Power"; John Rajchman, *Michel Foucault: The Freedom of Philosophy;* and Michael Clark, *Michel Foucault: A Bibliography.*

WHAT IS AN AUTHOR?

In proposing this slightly odd question, I am conscious of the need for an explanation. To this day, the "author" remains an open question both with respect to its general function within discourse and in my own writings; that is, this question permits me to return to certain aspects of my own work which now appear ill-advised and misleading. In this regard, I wish to propose a necessary criticism and reevaluation.

For instance, my objective in *The Order of Things* had been to analyse verbal clusters as discursive layers which fall outside the familiar categories of a book, a work, or an author. But while I considered "natural history," the "analysis of wealth," and "political economy" in general terms, I neglected a similar analysis of the author and his works; it is perhaps due to this omission that I employed the names of authors throughout this book in a naive and often crude fashion. I spoke of Buffon, Cuvier, Ricardo, and others as well, but failed to realize that I had allowed their names to function ambiguously.[1] This has proved an embarrassment to me in that my oversight has served to raise two pertinent objections.

It was argued that I had not properly described Buffon or his work and that my handling of Marx was pitifully inadequate in terms of the totality of his thought.[2] Although these objections were obviously justified, they ignored the task I had set myself: I had no intention of describing Buffon or Marx or of reproducing their statements or implicit meanings, but, simply stated, I wanted to locate the rules that formed a certain number of concepts and theoretical relationships in their works. In addition, it was argued that I had created monstrous families by bringing together names as disparate as Buffon and Linnaeus or in placing Cuvier next to Darwin in defiance of the most readily observable family resemblances and natural ties.[3] This objection also

WHAT IS AN AUTHOR? originally appeared in the *Bulletin de la Société française de Philosophie* in 1969. It is reprinted by permission of the society. It is from Foucault's *Language, Counter-Memory, Practice,* trans. (from the French) Donald F. Bouchard and Sherry Simon, ed. Donald F. Bouchard, copyright 1977, by Cornell University. Used by permission of the publisher, Cornell University Press.

[1] George Buffon (1707–88), French naturalist; Georges Cuvier (1769–1832), French naturalist; David Ricardo (1772–1823), British economist. [Eds.]

[2] See "Entretiens sur Michel Foucault" (directed by J. Proust), *La Pensée,* No. 137 (1968), pp. 6–7 and 11; and also Sylvie le Bon, "Un Positivisme désespérée," *Esprit,* No. 5 (1967), pp. 1317–1319. [Tr.]

[3] Linnaeus (Karl von Linne) (1707–78), Swedish botanist. [Eds.]

seems inappropriate since I had never tried to establish a genealogical table of exceptional individuals, nor was I concerned in forming an intellectual daguerreotype of the scholar or naturalist of the seventeenth and eighteenth century. In fact, I had no intention of forming any family, whether holy or perverse. On the contrary, I wanted to determine—a much more modest task—the functional conditions of specific discursive practices.

Then why did I use the names of authors in *The Order of Things?* Why not avoid their use altogether, or, short of that, why not define the manner in which they were used? These questions appear fully justified and I have tried to gauge their implications and consequences in a book that will appear shortly.[4] These questions have determined my effort to situate comprehensive discursive units, such as "natural history" or "political economy," and to establish the methods and instruments for delimiting, analyzing, and describing these unities. Nevertheless, as a privileged moment of individualization in the history of ideas, knowledge, and literature, or in the history of philosophy and science, the question of the author demands a more direct response. Even now, when we study the history of a concept, a literary genre, or a branch of philosophy, these concerns assume a relatively weak and secondary position in relation to the solid and fundamental role of an author and his works.

For the purposes of this paper, I will set aside a sociohistorical analysis of the author as an individual and the numerous questions that deserve attention in this context: how the author was individualized in a culture such as ours; the status we have given the author, for instance, when we began our research into authenticity and attribution; the systems of valorization in which he was included; or the moment when the stories of heroes gave way to an author's biography; the conditions that fostered the formulation of the fundamental critical category of "the man and his work." For the time being, I wish to restrict myself to the singular relationship that holds between an author and a text, the manner in which a text apparently points to this figure who is outside and precedes it.

Beckett supplies a direction: "What matter who's speaking, someone said, what matter who's speaking."[5] In an indifference such as this we must recognize one of the fundamental ethical principles of contemporary writing. It is not simply "ethical" because it characterizes our way of speaking and writing, but because it stands as an immanent rule, endlessly adopted and yet never fully applied. As a principle, it dominates writing as an ongoing practice and slights our customary attention to the finished product. For the sake of illustration, we need only consider two of its major themes. First, the writing of our day has freed itself from the necessity of "expression"; it only refers to itself, yet it is not restricted to the confines of interiority. On the contrary, we recognize it in its exterior deployment. This reversal transforms writing into an interplay of signs, regulated less by the content it signifies than by the very nature of the signifier. Moreover, it implies an action that is always testing the limits of its regularity, transgressing and reversing an order that it accepts and manipulates. Writing unfolds like a game that inevitably moves beyond its own rules and finally leaves them behind. Thus, the essential basis of this writing is not the exalted emotions related to the act of composition or the insertion of a subject into language. Rather, it is primarily concerned with creating an opening where the writing subject endlessly disappears.

The second theme is even more familiar: it is the kinship between writing and death. This relationship inverts the age-old conception of Greek narrative or epic, which was designed to guarantee the immortality of a hero. The hero accepted an early death because his life, consecrated and magnified by death, passed into immortality; and the narrative redeemed his acceptance of death. In a different sense, Arabic stories, and *The Arabian Nights* in particular, had as their motivation, their theme and pretext, this strategy for defeating death. Storytellers continued their narratives late into the night to forestall death and to delay the inevitable moment when everyone must fall silent. Scheherazade's story is a desperate inversion of murder; it is the effort, throughout all those nights, to exclude death from the circle of existence. This conception of a spoken or written narrative as a protection against death has been transformed by our culture. Writing

[4] *The Archeology of Knowledge* trans. A. M. Sheridan Smith (London: Tavistock, 1972) was published in France in 1969; for discussion of the author, see esp. pp. 92–96, 122. [Tr.]

[5] Samuel Beckett, *Texts for Nothing,* trans. Beckett (London: Calder and Boyars, 1974), p. 16. [Tr.]

is now linked to sacrifice and to the sacrifice of life itself; it is a voluntary obliteration of the self that does not require representation in books because it takes place in the everyday existence of the writer. Where a work had the duty of creating immortality, it now attains the right to kill, to become the murderer of its author. Flaubert, Proust, and Kafka are obvious examples of this reversal. In addition, we find the link between writing and death manifested in the total effacement of the individual characteristics of the writer; the quibbling and confrontations that a writer generates between himself and his text cancel out the signs of his particular individuality. If we wish to know the writer in our day, it will be through the singularity of his absence and in his link to death, which has transformed him into a victim of his own writing. While all of this is familiar in philosophy, as in literary criticism, I am not certain that the consequences derived from the disappearance or death of the author have been fully explored or that the importance of this event has been appreciated. To be specific, it seems to me that the themes destined to replace the privileged position accorded the author have merely served to arrest the possibility of genuine change. Of these, I will examine two that seem particularly important.

To begin with, the thesis concerning a work. It has been understood that the task of criticism is not to reestablish the ties between an author and his work or to reconstitute an author's thought and experience through his works and, further, that criticism should concern itself with the structures of a work, its architectonic forms, which are studied for their intrinsic and internal relationships. Yet, what of a context that questions the concept of a work? What, in short, is the strange unit designated by the term, work? What is necessary to its composition, if a work is not something written by a person called an "author?" Difficulties arise on all sides if we raise the question in this way. If an individual is not an author, what are we to make of those things he has written or said, left among his papers or communicated to others? Is this not properly a work? What, for instance, were Sade's papers before he was consecrated as an author? Little more, perhaps, than rolls of paper on which he endlessly unravelled his fantasies while in prison.

Assuming that we are dealing with an author, is everything he wrote and said, everything he left behind, to be included in his work? This problem is both theoretical and practical. If we wish to publish the complete works of Nietzsche, for example, where do we draw the line? Certainly, everything must be published, but can we agree on what "everything" means? We will, of course, include everything that Nietzsche himself published, along with the drafts of his work, his plans for aphorisms, his marginal notations and corrections. But what if, in a notebook filled with aphorisms, we find a reference, a reminder of an appointment, an address, or a laundry bill, should this be included in his works? Why not? These practical considerations are endless once we consider how a work can be extracted from the millions of traces left by an individual after his death. Plainly, we lack a theory to encompass the questions generated by a work and the empirical activity of those who naively undertake the publication of the complete works of an author often suffers from the absence of this framework. Yet more questions arise. Can we say that *The Arabian Nights,* and *Stromates* of Clement of Alexandria, or the *Lives* of Diogenes Laertes constitute works? Such questions only begin to suggest the range of our difficulties, and, if some have found it convenient to bypass the individuality of the writer or his status as an author to concentrate on a work, they have failed to appreciate the equally problematic nature of the word "work" and the unity it designates.

Another thesis has detained us from taking full measure of the author's disappearance. It avoids confronting the specific event that makes it possible and, in subtle ways, continues to preserve the existence of the author. This is the notion of *écriture.*[6] Strictly speaking, it should allow us not only to circumvent references to an author, but to situate his recent absence. The conception of *écriture,* as currently employed, is concerned with neither the act of writing nor the indications, as symptoms or signs within a text, of an author's meaning; rather, it stands for a remarkably profound attempt to elaborate the conditions of any text, both the conditions

[6] We have kept the French *écriture,* with its double reference to the act of writing and to the primordial (and metaphysical) nature of writing as an entity in itself, since it is the term that best identifies the program of Jacques Derrida. Like the theme of self-referential writing, it too builds on a theory of the sign and denotes writing as the interplay of presence and absence in that "signs represent the present in its absence." [Tr.] See *Derrida.* [Eds.]

of its spatial dispersion and its temporal deployment.

It appears, however, that this concept, as currently employed, has merely transposed the empirical characteristics of an author to a transcendental anonymity. The extremely visible signs of the author's empirical activity are effaced to allow the play, in parallel or opposition, of religious and critical modes of characterization. In granting a primordial status to writing, do we not, in effect, simply reinscribe in transcendental terms the theological affirmation of its sacred origin or a critical belief in its creative nature? To say that writing, in terms of the particular history it made possible, is subjected to forgetfulness and repression, is this not to reintroduce in transcendental terms the religious principle of hidden meanings (which require interpretation) and the critical assumption of implicit significations, silent purposes, and obscure contents (which give rise to commentary)? Finally, is not the conception of writing as absence a transposition into transcendental terms of the religious belief in a fixed and continuous tradition or the aesthetic principle that proclaims the survival of the work as a kind of enigmatic supplement of the author beyond his own death?[7]

This conception of *écriture* sustains the privileges of the author through the safeguard of the a priori; the play of representations that formed a particular image of the author is extended within a gray neutrality. The disappearance of the author—since Mallarmé, an event of our time—is held in check by the transcendental. Is it not necessary to draw a line between those who believe that we can continue to situate our present discontinuities within the historical and transcendental tradition of the nineteenth century and those who are making a great effort to liberate themselves, once and for all, from this conceptual framework?

It is obviously insufficient to repeat empty slogans: the author has disappeared; God and man died a common death.[8] Rather, we should reexamine the empty space left by the author's disappearance; we should attentively observe, along its gaps and fault lines, its new demarcations, and the reapportionment of this void; we should await the fluid functions released by this disappearance. In this context we can briefly consider the problems that arise in the use of an author's name. What is the name of an author? How does it function? Far from offering a solution, I will attempt to indicate some of the difficulties related to these questions.

The name of an author poses all the problems related to the category of the proper name. (Here, I am referring to the work of John Searle,[9] among others.) Obviously not a pure and simple reference, the proper name (and the author's name as well) has other than indicative functions. It is more than a gesture, a finger pointed at someone; it is, to a certain extent, the equivalent of a description. When we say "Aristotle," we are using a word that means one or a series of definite descriptions of the type: "the author of the *Analytics,*" or "the founder of ontology," and so forth.[10] Furthermore, a proper name has other functions than that of signification: when we discover that Rimbaud has not written *La Chasse spirituelle,* we cannot maintain that the meaning of the proper name or this author's name has been altered. The proper name and the name of an author oscillate between the poles of description and designation, and, granting that they are linked to what they name, they are not totally determined either by their descriptive or designative functions.[11] Yet—and it is here that the specific difficulties attending an author's name appear—the link between a proper name and the individual being named and the link between an author's name and that which it names are not isomorphous and do not function in the same way; and these differences require clarification.

To learn, for example, that Pierre Dupont does not have blue eyes, does not live in Paris, and is not a doctor does not invalidate the fact that the name, Pierre Dupont, continues to refer to the same person; there has been no modification of the designation that links the name to the person. With the name of an author, however, the problems are far more complex. The disclosure that Shakespeare was not born in the house that tourists now visit would not modify the functioning of the author's name, but, if it were proved that he had not written

[7] On "supplement" see Jacques Derrida, *Speech and Phenomena,* pp. 88–104. [Tr.]

[8] Nietzsche, *The Gay Science,* III, 108. [Au.]

[9] John Searle, *Speech Acts: An Essay in the Philosophy of Language* (Cambridge: Cambridge University Press, 1969), pp. 162–74. [Tr.]. See *Searle.* [Eds.]

[10] *Speech Acts,* p. 169. [Tr.]

[11] *Speech Acts,* p. 172. [Tr.]

the sonnets that we attribute to him, this would constitute a significant change and affect the manner in which the author's name functions. Moreover, if we establish that Shakespeare wrote Bacon's *Organon* and that the same author was responsible for both the works of Shakespeare and those of Bacon, we would have introduced a third type of alteration which completely modifies the functioning of the author's name. Consequently, the name of an author is not precisely a proper name among others.

Many other factors sustain this paradoxical singularity of the name of an author. It is altogether different to maintain that Pierre Dupont does not exist and that Homer or Hermes Trismegistus have never existed. While the first negation merely implies that there is no one by the name of Pierre Dupont, the second indicates that several individuals have been referred to by one name or that the real author possessed none of the traits traditionally associated with Homer or Hermes. Neither is it the same thing to say that Jacques Durand, not Pierre Dupont, is the real name of *X* and that Stendhal's name was Henri Beyle. We could also examine the function and meaning of such statements as "Bourbaki is this or that person," and "Victor Eremita, Climacus, Anticlimacus, Frater Taciturnus, Constantin Constantius, all of these are Kierkegaard."

These differences indicate that an author's name is not simply an element of speech (as a subject, a complement, or an element that could be replaced by a pronoun or other parts of speech). Its presence is functional in that it serves as a means of classification. A name can group together a number of texts and thus differentiate them from others. A name also establishes different forms of relationships among texts. Neither Hermes nor Hippocrates existed in the sense that we can say Balzac existed, but the fact that a number of texts were attached to a single name implies that relationships of homogeneity, filiation, reciprocal explanation, authentification, or of common utilization were established among them. Finally, the author's name characterizes a particular manner of existence of discourse. Discourse that possesses an author's name is not to be immediately consumed and forgotten; neither is it accorded the momentary attention given to ordinary, fleeting words. Rather, its status and its manner of reception are regulated by the culture in which it circulates.

We can conclude that, unlike a proper name, which moves from the interior of a discourse to the real person outside who produced it, the name of the author remains at the contours of texts—separating one from the other, defining their form, and characterizing their mode of existence. It points to the existence of certain groups of discourse and refers to the status of this discourse within a society and culture. The author's name is not a function of a man's civil status, nor is it fictional; it is situated in the breach, among the discontinuities, which gives rise to new groups of discourse and their singular mode of existence. Consequently, we can say that in our culture, the name of an author is a variable that accompanies only certain texts to the exclusion of others: a private letter may have a signatory, but it does not have an author; a contract can have an underwriter, but not an author; and, similarly, an anonymous poster attached to a wall may have a writer, but he cannot be an author. In this sense, the function of an author is to characterize the existence, circulation, and operation of certain discourses within a society.

IN dealing with the "author" as a function of discourse, we must consider the characteristics of a discourse that support this use and determine its difference from other discourses. If we limit our remarks to only those books or texts with authors, we can isolate four different features.

First, they are objects of appropriation; the form of property they have become is of a particular type whose legal codification was accomplished some years ago. It is important to notice, as well, that its status as property is historically secondary to the penal code controlling its appropriation. Speeches and books were assigned real authors, other than mythical or important religious figures, only when the author became subject to punishment and to the extent that his discourse was considered transgressive. In our culture—undoubtedly in others as well—discourse was not originally a thing, a product, or a possession, but an action situated in a bipolar field of sacred and profane, lawful and unlawful, religious and blasphemous. It was a gesture charged with risks long before it became a possession caught in a circuit of property values. But it was at the moment when a system of ownership and strict copyright rules were established (toward the end of the eighteenth and beginning of the nineteenth century) that the transgressive properties always intrinsic to the act of writing became the forceful imperative of literature. It is as if the author, at the moment he was accepted into the social order of property which governs our culture, was compensating for his new status by reviving the older bipolar field of discourse in a systematic practice of transgression and by restoring the danger of writing which, on another side, had been conferred the benefits of property.

Secondly, the "author-function" is not universal or constant in all discourse. Even within our civilization, the same types of texts have not always required authors; there was a time when those texts which we now call "literary" (stories, folk tales, epics, and tragedies) were accepted, circulated, and valorized without any question about the identity of their author. Their anonymity was ignored because their real or supposed age was a sufficient guarantee of their authenticity. Texts, however, that we now call "scientific" (dealing with cosmology and the heavens, medicine or illness, the natural sciences or geography) were only considered truthful during the Middle Ages if the name of the author was indicated. Statements on the order of "Hippocrates said . . ." or "Pliny tells us that . . ." were not merely formulas for an argument based on authority; they marked a proven discourse. In the seventeenth and eighteenth centuries, a totally new conception was developed when scientific texts were accepted on their own merits and positioned within an anonymous and coherent conceptual system of established truths and methods of verification. Authentification no longer required reference to the individual who had produced them; the role of the author disappeared as an index of truthfulness and, where it remained as an inventor's name, it was merely to denote a specific theorem or proposition, a strange effect, a property, a body, a group of elements, or pathological syndrome.

At the same time, however, "literary" discourse was acceptable only if it carried an author's name; every text of poetry or fiction was obliged to state its author and the date, place, and circumstance of its writing. The meaning and value attributed to the text depended on this information. If by accident or design a text was presented anonymously, every effort was made to locate its author. Literary anonymity was of interest only as a puzzle to be solved as, in our day, literary works are totally dominated by the sovereignty of the author. (Undoubtedly, these remarks are far too categorical. Criticism has been concerned for some time now with aspects of a text not fully dependent on the notion of an individual creator; studies of genre or the analysis of recurring textual motifs and their variations from a norm other than the author. Furthermore, where in mathematics the author has become little more than a handy reference for a particular theorem or group of propositions, the reference to an author in biology and medicine, or to the date of his research has a substantially different bearing. This latter reference, more than simply indicating the source of information, attests to the "reliability" of the evidence, since it entails an appreciation of the techniques and experimental materials available at a given time and in a particular laboratory.)

The third point concerning this "author-function" is that it is not formed spontaneously through the simple attribution of a discourse to an individual. It results from a complex operation whose purpose is to construct the rational entity we call an author. Undoubtedly, this construction is assigned a "realistic" dimension as we speak of an individual's "profundity" or "creative" power, his intentions or the original inspiration manifested in writing. Nevertheless, these aspects of an individual, which we designate as an author (or which comprise an individual as an author), are projections, in terms always more or less psychological, of our way of handling texts: in the comparisons we make, the traits we extract as pertinent, the continuities we assign, or the exclusions we practice. In addition, all these operations vary according to the period and the form of discourse concerned. A "philosopher" and a "poet" are not constructed in the same manner; and the author of an eighteenth-century novel was formed differently from the modern novelist. There are, nevertheless, transhistorical constants in the rules that govern the construction of an author.

In literary criticism, for example, the traditional methods for defining an author—or, rather, for determining the configuration of the author from existing texts—derive in large part from those used in the Christian tradition to authenticate (or to reject) the particular texts in its possession. Modern criticism, in its desire to "recover" the author from a work, employs devices strongly reminiscent of Christian exegesis when it wished to prove the value of a text by ascertaining the holiness of its author. In *De Viris Illustribus*, Saint Jerome maintains that homonymy is not proof of the common authorship of several works, since many individuals could have the same name or someone could have perversely appropriated another's name. The name, as an individual mark, is not sufficient as it relates to a textual tradition. How, then, can several texts be attributed to an individual author? What norms, related to the function of the author, will disclose the involvement of several authors? According to Saint Jerome, there are four criteria: the texts that must be eliminated from the list of works attributed to a single author are those inferior to the others (thus, the author is defined as a standard level of quality); those whose ideas conflict with the doctrine expressed in the others (here the author is defined as a certain field of conceptual or theoretical coherence); those written in a different style and containing words and phrases not ordinarily found in the other works (the author is seen as a stylistic uniformity); and those referring to events or historical figures subsequent to the death of the author (the author is thus a definite historical figure in which a series of events converge). Although modern criticism does not appear to have these same suspicions concerning authentication, its strategies for defining the author present striking similarities. The author explains the presence of certain events within a text, as well as their transformations, distortions, and their various modifications (and this through an author's biography or by reference to his particular point of view, in the analysis of his social preferences and his position within a class or by delineating his fundamental objectives). The author also constitutes a principle of unity in writing where any unevenness of production is ascribed to changes caused by evolution, maturation, or outside influence. In addition, the author serves to neutralize the contradictions that are found in a series of texts. Governing this function is the belief that there must be—at a particular level of an author's thought, of his conscious or unconscious desire—a point where contradictions are resolved, where the incompatible elements can be shown to relate to one another or to cohere around a fundamental and originating contradiction. Finally, the author is a particular source of expression who, in more or less finished forms, is manifested equally well, and with similar validity, in a text, in letters, fragments, drafts, and so forth. Thus, even while Saint Jerome's four principles of authenticity might seem largely inadequate to modern critics, they, nevertheless, define the critical modalities now used to display the function of the author.

However, it would be false to consider the function of the author as a pure and simple reconstruction after the fact of a text given as passive material, since a text always bears a number of signs that refer to the author. Well known to grammarians, these textual signs are personal pronouns, adverbs of time and place, and the conjugation of verbs. But it is important to note that these elements have a different bearing on texts with an author and on those without one. In the latter, these "shifters" refer to a real speaker and to an actual deictic situation, with certain exceptions such as the case of indirect speech in the first person. When discourse is linked to an author, however, the role of "shifters" is more complex and variable. It is well known that in a novel narrated in the first person, neither the first person pronoun, the present indicative tense, nor, for that matter, its signs of localization refer directly to the writer, either to the time when he wrote, or to the specific act of writing; rather, they stand for a "second self" whose similarity to the author is never fixed and undergoes considerable alteration within the course of a single book. It would be as false to seek the author in relation to the actual writer as to the fictional narrator; the "author-function" arises out of their scission—in the division and distance of the two. One might object that this phenomenon only applies to novels or poetry, to a context of "quasi-discourse," but, in fact, all discourse that supports this "author-function" is characterized by this plurality of egos. In a mathematical treatise, the ego who indicates the circumstances of composition in the preface is not identical, either in terms of his position or his function, to the "I" who concludes a demonstration within the body of the text. The former implies a unique individual who, at a given time and place, succeeded in completing a project, whereas the latter indicates an instance and plan of demonstration that anyone could perform provided the same set of axioms, preliminary operations, and an identical set of symbols were used. It is also possible to locate a third ego: one who speaks of the goals of his investigation, the obstacles encountered, its results, and the problems yet to be solved and this "I" would function in a field of existing or future mathematical discourses. We are not dealing with a system of dependencies where a first and essential use of the "I" is reduplicated, as a kind of fiction, by the other two. On the contrary, the "author-function" in such discourses operates so as to effect the simultaneous dispersion of the three egos.

Further elaboration would, of course, disclose other characteristics of the "author-function," but I have limited myself to the four that seemed the most obvious and important. They can be summarized in the following manner: the "author-function" is tied to the legal and institutional systems that circumscribe, determine, and articulate the realm of discourses; it does not operate in a uniform manner in all discourses, at all times, and in any given culture; it is not defined by the spontaneous attribution of a text to its creator, but through a series of precise and complex procedures; it does not refer, purely and simply, to an actual individual insofar as it simultaneously gives rise to a variety of egos and to a series of subjective positions that individuals of any class may come to occupy.

I AM aware that until now I have kept my subject within unjustifiable limits; I should also have spoken of the "author-function" in painting, music, technical fields, and so forth. Admitting that my analysis is restricted to the domain of discourse, it seems that I have given the term "author" an excessively narrow meaning. I have discussed the author only in the limited sense of a person to whom the production of a text, a book, or a work can be legitimately attributed. However, it is obvious that even within the realm of discourse a person can be the author of much more than a book—of a theory, for instance, of a tradition or a discipline within which new books and authors can proliferate. For convenience, we could say that such authors occupy a "transdiscursive" position.

Homer, Aristotle, and the Church Fathers played this role, as did the first mathematicians and the originators of the Hippocratic tradition. This type of author is surely as old as our civilization. But I believe that the nineteenth century in Europe produced a singular type of author who should not be confused with "great" literary authors, or the authors of canonical religious texts, and the founders of sciences. Somewhat arbitrarily, we might call them "initiators of discursive practices."

The distinctive contribution of these authors is that they produced not only their own work, but the possibility and the rules of formation of other texts. In this sense, their role differs entirely from that of a novelist, for example, who is basically never more than the author of his own text. Freud is not simply the author of *The Interpretation of Dreams* or of *Wit and its Relation to the Unconscious* and Marx is not simply the author of the *Communist Manifesto* or *Capital:* they both established the endless possibility of discourse. Obviously, an easy objection can be made. The author of a novel may be responsible for more than his own text; if he acquires some "importance" in the literary world, his influence can have significant ramifications. To take a very simple example, one could say that Ann Radcliffe did not simply write *The Mysteries of Udolpho* and a few other novels, but also made possible the appearance of Gothic Romances at the beginning of the nineteenth century. To this extent, her function as an author exceeds the limits of her work. However, this objection can be answered by the fact that the possibilities disclosed by the initiators of discursive practices (using the examples of Marx and Freud, whom I believe to be the first and the most important) are significantly different from those suggested by novelists. The novels of Ann Radcliffe put into circulation a certain number of resemblances and analogies patterned on her work—various characteristic signs, figures, relationships, and structures that could be integrated into other books. In short, to say that Ann Radcliffe created the Gothic Romance means that there are certain elements common to her works and to the nineteenth-century Gothic romance: the heroine ruined by her own innocence, the secret fortress that functions as a counter-city, the outlaw-hero who swears revenge on the world that has cursed him, etc. On the other hand, Marx and Freud, as "initiators of discursive practices," not only made possible a certain number of analogies that could be adopted by future texts, but, as importantly, they also made possible a certain number of differences. They cleared a space for the introduction of elements other than their own, which, nevertheless, remain within the field of discourse they initiated. In saying that Freud founded psychoanalysis, we do not simply mean that the concept of libido or the techniques of dream analysis reappear in the writings of Karl Abraham or Melanie Klein, but that he made possible a certain number of differences with respect to his books, concepts, and hypotheses, which all arise out of psychoanalytic discourse.

Is this not the case, however, with the founder of any new science or of any author who successfully transforms an existing science? After all, Galileo is indirectly responsible for the texts of those who mechanically applied the laws he formulated, in addition to having paved the way for the production of statements far different from his own. If Cuvier is the founder of biology and Saussure of linguistics, it is not because they were imitated or that an organic concept or a theory of the sign was uncritically integrated into new texts, but because Cuvier, to a certain extent, made possible a theory of evolution diametrically opposed to his own system and because Saussure made possible a generative grammar radically different from his own structural analysis. Superficially, then, the initiation of discursive practices appears similar to the founding of any scientific endeavor, but I believe there is a fundamental difference.

In a scientific program, the founding act is on an equal footing with its future transformations: it is merely one among the many modifications that it makes possible. This interdependence can take several forms. In the future development of a science, the founding act may appear as little more than a single instance of a more general phenomenon that has been discovered. It might be questioned, in retrospect, for being too intuitive or empirical and submitted to the rigors of new theoretical operations in order to situate it in a formal domain. Finally, it might be thought a hasty generalization whose validity should be restricted. In other words, the founding act of a science can always be rechanneled through the machinery of transformations it has instituted.

On the other hand, the initiation of a discursive practice is heterogeneous to its ulterior transformations. To extend psychoanalytic practice, as initiated by Freud, is not to presume a formal generality that was not claimed at the outset; it is to explore a number of possible applications. To limit it is to isolate in the original texts a small set of propositions or statements that are recognized as having an inaugurative value and that mark other Freudian concepts or theories as derivative. Finally, there are no "false" statements in the work of these initiators; those statements considered inessential or "prehistoric," in that they are associated with another discourse, are simply neglected in favor of the more pertinent aspects of the work. The initiation of a discursive practice, unlike the founding of a science, overshadows and is necessarily detached from its later developments and transformations. As a consequence, we define the theoretical validity of a statement with respect to the work of the initiator, whereas in the case of Galileo or Newton, it is based on the structural and intrinsic norms established in cosmology or physics. Stated schematically, the work of these initiators is not situated in relation to a science or in the space it defines; rather, it is science or discursive practice that relate to their works as the primary points of reference.

In keeping with this distinction, we can understand why it is inevitable that practitioners of such discourses must "return to the origin." Here, as well, it is necessary to distinguish a "return" from scientific "rediscoveries" or "reactivations." "Rediscoveries" are the effects of analogy or isomorphism with current forms of knowledge that allow the perception of forgotten or obscured figures. For instance, Chomsky in his book on Cartesian grammar[12] "rediscovered" a form of knowledge that had been in use from Cordemoy to Humboldt. It could only be understood from the perspective of generative grammar because this later manifestation held the key to its construction: in effect, a retrospective codification of an historical position. "Reactivation" refers to something quite different: the insertion of discourse into totally new domains of generalization, practice, and transformations. The history of mathematics abounds in examples of this phenomenon as the work of Michel Serres on mathematical anamnesis shows.[13]

The phrase, "return to," designates a movement with its proper specificity, which characterizes the initiation of discursive practices. If we return, it is because of a basic and constructive omission, an omission that is not the result of accident or incomprehension. In effect, the act of initiation is such, in its essence, that it is inevitably subjected to its own distortions; that which displays this act and derives from it is, at the same time, the root of its divergences and travesties. This nonaccidental omission must be regulated by precise operations

[12] Noam Chomsky, *Cartesian Linguistics* (New York: Harper & Row, 1966). [Tr.]

[13] *La Communication: Hermes I* (Paris: Editions de Minuit, 1968), pp. 78–112. [Tr.]

that can be situated, analysed, and reduced in a return to the act of initiation. The barrier imposed by omission was not added from the outside; it arises from the discursive practice in question, which gives it its law. Both the cause of the barrier and the means for its removal, this omission—also responsible for the obstacles that prevent returning to the act of initiation—can only be resolved by a return. In addition, it is always a return to a text in itself, specifically, to a primary and unadorned text with particular attention to those things registered in the interstices of the text, its gaps and absences. We return to those empty spaces that have been masked by omission or concealed in a false and misleading plenitude. In these rediscoveries of an essential lack, we find the oscillation of two characteristic responses: "This point was made—you can't help seeing it if you know how to read"; or, inversely, "No, that point is not made in any of the printed words in the text, but it is expressed through the words, in their relationships and in the distance that separates them." It follows naturally that this return, which is a part of the discursive mechanism, constantly introduces modifications and that the return to a text is not a historical supplement that would come to fix itself upon the primary discursivity and redouble it in the form of an ornament which, after all, is not essential. Rather, it is an effective and necessary means of transforming discursive practice. A study of Galileo's works could alter our knowledge of the history, but not the science, of mechanics; whereas, a reexamination of the books of Freud or Marx can transform our understanding of psychoanalysis or Marxism.

A last feature of these returns is that they tend to reinforce the enigmatic link between an author and his works. A text has an inaugurative value precisely because it is the work of a particular author, and our returns are conditioned by this knowledge. The rediscovery of an unknown text by Newton or Cantor will not modify classical cosmology or group theory; at most, it will change our appreciation of their historical genesis. Bringing to light, however, *An Outline of Psychoanalysis,* to the extent that we recognize it as a book by Freud, can transform not only our historical knowledge, but the field of psychoanalytic theory—if only through a shift of accent or of the center of gravity. These returns, an important component of discursive practices, form a relationship between "fundamental" and mediate authors, which is not identical to that which links an ordinary text to its immediate author.

These remarks concerning the initiation of discursive practices have been extremely schematic, especially with regard to the opposition I have tried to trace between this initiation and the founding of sciences. The distinction between the two is not readily discernible; moreover, there is no proof that the two procedures are mutually exclusive. My only purpose in setting up this opposition, however, was to show that the "author-function," sufficiently complex at the level of a book or a series of texts that bear a definite signature, has other determining factors when analysed in terms of larger entities—groups of works or entire disciplines.

Unfortunately, there is a decided absence of positive propositions in this essay, as it applies to analytic procedures or directions for future research, but I ought at least to give the reasons why I attach such importance to a continuation of this work. Developing a similar analysis could provide the basis for a typology of discourse. A typology of this sort cannot be adequately understood in relation to the grammatical features, formal structures, and objects of discourse, because there undoubtedly exist specific discursive properties or relationships that are irreducible to the rules of grammar and logic and to the laws that govern objects. These properties require investigation if we hope to distinguish the larger categories of discourse. The different forms of relationships (or nonrelationships) that an author can assume are evidently one of these discursive properties.

This form of investigation might also permit the introduction of an historical analysis of discourse. Perhaps the time has come to study not only the expressive value and formal transformations of discourse, but its mode of existence: the modifications and variations, within any culture, of modes of circulation, valorization, attribution, and appropriation. Partially at the expense of themes and concepts that an author places in his work, the "author-function" could also reveal the manner in which discourse is articulated on the basis of social relationships.

Is it not possible to reexamine, as a legitimate extension of this kind of analysis, the privileges of the subject? Clearly, in undertaking an internal and architectonic analysis of a work (whether it be a literary text, a philosophical system, or a scientific work) and in delimiting psychological and biographical references, suspicions arise concerning the absolute nature and creative role of the subject. But the subject should not be entirely abandoned. It should be reconsidered, not to restore the theme of an originating subject, but to seize its functions, its intervention in discourse, and its system of dependencies. We should suspend the typical questions: how does a free subject penetrate the density of things and endow them with meaning; how does it accomplish its design by animating the rules of discourse from within? Rather, we should ask: under what conditions and through what forms can an entity like the subject appear in the order of discourse; what position does it occupy; what functions does it exhibit; and what rules does it follow in each type of discourse? In short, the subject (and its substitutes) must be stripped of its creative role and analysed as a complex and variable function of discourse.

The author—or what I have called the "author-function"—is undoubtedly only one of the possible specifications of the subject and, considering past historical transformations, it appears that the form, the complexity, and even the existence of this function are far from immutable. We can easily imagine a culture where discourse would circulate without any need for an author. Discourses, whatever their status, form, or value, and regardless of our manner of handling them, would unfold in a pervasive anonymity. No longer the tiresome repetitions:

> "Who is the real author?"
> "Have we proof of his authenticity and originality?"
> "What has he revealed of his most profound self in his language?"

New questions will be heard:

> "What are the modes of existence of this discourse?"
> "Where does it come from; how is it circulated; who controls it?"
> "What placements are determined for possible subjects?"
> "Who can fulfill these diverse functions of the subject?"

Behind all these questions we would hear little more than the murmur of indifference:

> "What matter who's speaking?"

THE DISCOURSE ON LANGUAGE

I would really like to have slipped imperceptibly into this lecture, as into all the others I shall be delivering, perhaps over the years ahead. I would have preferred to be enveloped in words, borne way beyond all possible beginnings. At the moment of speaking, I would like to have perceived a nameless voice, long preceding me, leaving me merely to enmesh myself in it, taking up its cadence, and to lodge myself, when no one was looking, in its interstices as if it had paused an instant, in suspense, to beckon to me. There would have been no beginnings: instead, speech would proceed from me, while I stood in its path—a slender gap—the point of its possible disappearance.

Behind me, I should like to have heard (having been at it long enough already, repeating in advance what I am about to tell you) the voice of Molloy, beginning to speak thus: 'I must go on; I can't go on; I must go on; I must say words as long as there are words, I must say them until they find me, until they say me—heavy burden, heavy sin; I must go on; maybe it's been done already; maybe they've already said me; maybe they've already borne me to the threshold of my story, right to the door opening onto my story; I'd be surprised if it opened.'[1]

A good many people, I imagine, harbour a simi-

From THE DISCOURSE ON LANGUAGE by Michel Foucault, in *Social Science Information* (10), trans. Rupert Swyer, used by permission of Sage Publications, Ltd., London, The last few pages, in which Foucault pays homage to his teacher Jean Hippolyte, do not appear here.

[1] From Samuel Beckett's novel *Molloy*. [Eds.]

lar desire to be freed from the obligation to begin, a similar desire to find themselves, right from the outside, on the other side of discourse, without having to stand outside it, pondering its particular, fearsome, and even devilish features. To this all too common feeling, institutions have an ironic reply, for they solemnise beginnings, surrounding them with a circle of silent attention; in order that they can be distinguished from far off, they impose ritual forms upon them.

Inclination speaks out: 'I don't want to have to enter this risky world of discourse; I want nothing to do with it insofar as it is decisive and final; I would like to feel it all around me, calm and transparent, profound, infinitely open, with others responding to my expectations, and truth emerging, one by one. All I want is to allow myself to be borne along, within it, and by it, a happy wreck.' Institutions reply: 'But you have nothing to fear from launching out; we're here to show you discourse is within the established order of things, that we've waited a long time for its arrival, that a place has been set aside for it—a place which both honours and disarms it; and if it should happen to have a certain power, then it is we, and we alone, who give it that power'.

Yet, maybe this institution and this inclination are but two converse responses to the same anxiety: anxiety as to just what discourse is, when it is manifested materially, as a written or spoken object; but also, uncertainty faced with a transitory existence, destined for oblivion—at any rate, not belonging to us; uncertainty at the suggestion of barely imaginable powers and dangers behind this activity, however humdrum and grey it may seem; uncertainty when we suspect the conflicts, triumphs, injuries, dominations and enslavements that lie behind these words, even when long use has chipped away their rough edges.

What is so perilous, then, in the fact that people speak, and that their speech proliferates? Where is the danger in that?

Here then is the hypothesis I want to advance, tonight, in order to fix the terrain—or perhaps the very provisional theatre—within which I shall be working. I am supposing that in every society the production of discourse is at once controlled, selected, organised and redistributed according to a certain number of procedures, whose role is to avert its powers and its dangers, to cope with chance events, to evade its ponderous, awesome materiality.

In a society such as our own we all know the rules of *exclusion*. The most obvious and familiar of these concerns what is *prohibited*. We know perfectly well that we are not free to say just anything, that we cannot simply speak of anything, when we like or where we like; not just anyone, finally, may speak of just anything. We have three types of prohibition, covering objects, ritual with its surrounding circumstances, the privileged or exclusive right to speak of a particular subject; these prohibitions interrelate, reinforce and complement each other, forming a complex web, continually subject to modification. I will note simply that the areas where this web is most tightly woven today, where the danger spots are most numerous, are those dealing with politics and sexuality. It is as though discussion, far from being a transparent, neutral element, allowing us to disarm sexuality and to pacify politics, were one of those privileged areas in which they exercised some of their more awesome powers. In appearance, speech may well be of little account, but the prohibitions surrounding it soon reveal its links with desire and power. This should not be very surprising, for psychoanalysis has already shown us that speech is not merely the medium which manifests—or dissembles—desire; it is also the object of desire. Similarly, historians have constantly impressed upon us that speech is no mere verbalisation of conflicts and systems of domination, but that it is the very object of man's conflicts.

But our society possesses yet another principle of exclusion; not another prohibition, but a division and a rejection. I have in mind the opposition: reason and folly. From the depths of the Middle Ages, a man was mad if his speech could not be said to form part of the common discourse of men. His words were considered null and void, without truth or significance, worthless as evidence, inadmissible in the authentification of acts or contracts, incapable even of bringing about transubstantiation—the transformation of bread into flesh—at Mass. And yet, in contrast to all others, his words were credited with strange powers, of revealing some hidden truth, of predicting the future, of revealing, in all their naivete, what the wise were unable to perceive. It is curious to note that for centuries, in Europe, the words of a madman were either totally ignored or else were taken as words of truth. They either fell into a void—rejected the moment they were proffered—or else men deciphered in them a naive or cunning reason, rationality more rational than that of a rational man. At all events, whether excluded or secretly invested with reason, the madman's speech did not strictly exist. It was through his words that one recognised the madness of the madman; but they were certainly the medium within which this division became active; they were neither heard nor remembered. No doctor before the end of the eighteenth century had ever thought of listening to the content—how it was said and why—of these words; and yet it was these which signalled the difference between reason and madness. Whatever a madman said, it was taken for mere noise; he was credited with words only in a symbolic sense, in the theatre, in which he stepped forward, unarmed and reconciled, playing his role: that of masked truth.

Of course people are going to say all that is over and done with, or that it is in the process of being finished with, today; that the madman's words are no longer on the other side of this division; that they are no longer null and void, that, on the contrary, they alert us to the need to look for a sense behind them, for the attempt at, or the ruins of some '*œuvre*'; we have even come to notice these words of madmen in our own speech, in those tiny pauses when we forget what we are talking about. But all this is no proof that the old division is not just as active as before; we have only to think of the systems by which we decipher this speech; we have only to think of the network of institutions established to permit doctors and psychoanalysts to listen to the mad and, at the same time, enabling the mad to come and speak, or, in desperation, to withhold their meagre words; we have only to bear all this in mind to suspect that the old division is just as active as ever, even if it is proceeding along different lines and, via new institutions, producing rather different effects. Even when the role of the doctor consists of lending an ear to this finally liberated speech, this procedure still takes place in the context of a hiatus between listener and speaker. For he is listening to speech invested with desire, crediting itself—for its greater exultation or for its greater anguish—with terrible powers. If we truly require silence to cure monsters, then it must be an attentive silence, and it is in this that the division lingers.

It is perhaps a little risky to speak of the opposition between true and false as a third system of exclusion, along with those I have mentioned already. How could one reasonably compare the constraints of truth with those other divisions, arbitrary in origin if not developing out of historical contingency—not merely modifiable but in a state of continual flux, supported by a system of institutions imposing and manipulating them, acting not without constraint, not without an element, at least, of violence?

Certainly, as a proposition, the division between true and false is neither arbitrary, nor modifiable, nor institutional, nor violent. Putting the question in different terms, however—asking what has been, what still is, throughout our discourse, this will to truth which has survived throughout so many centuries of our history; or if we ask what is, in its very general form, the kind of division governing our will to knowledge—then we may well discern something like a system of exclusion (historical, modifiable, institutionally constraining) in the process of development.

It is, undoubtedly, a historically constituted division. For, even with the sixth century Greek poets, true discourse—in the meaningful sense—inspiring respect and terror, to which all were obliged to submit, because it held sway over all and was pronounced by men who spoke as of right, according to ritual, meted out justice and attributed to each his rightful share; it prophesied the future, not merely announcing what was going to occur, but contributing to its actual event, carrying men along with it and thus weaving itself into the fabric of fate. And yet, a century later, the highest truth no longer resided in what discourse *was,* nor in what it *did:* it lay in what was *said*. The day dawned when truth moved over from the ritualised act—potent and just—of enunciation to settle on what was enunciated itself: its meaning, its form, its object and its relation to what it referred to. A division emerged between Hesiod and Plato, separating true discourse from false; it was a new division for, henceforth, true discourse was no longer considered precious and desirable, since it had ceased to be discourse linked to the exercise of power. And so the Sophists were routed.[2]

This historical division has doubtless lent its general form to our will to knowledge. Yet it has never ceased shifting: the great mutations of science may well sometimes be seen to flow from some discov-

[2]See Plato, *CTSP*, pp. 11–46. [Eds.]

ery, but they may equally be viewed as the appearance of new forms of the will to truth. In the nineteenth century there was undoubtedly a will to truth having nothing to do, in terms of the forms examined, of the fields to which it addressed itself, nor the techniques upon which it was based, with the will to knowledge which characterised classical culture. Going back a little in time, to the turn of the sixteenth and seventeenth centuries—and particularly in England—a will to knowledge emerged which, anticipating its present content, sketched out a schema of possible, observable, measurable and classifiable objects; a will to knowledge which imposed upon the knowing subject—in some ways taking precedence over all experience—a certain position, a certain viewpoint, and a certain function (look rather than read, verify rather than comment), a will to knowledge which prescribed (and, more generally speaking, all instruments determined) the technological level at which knowledge could be employed in order to be verifiable and useful (navigation, mining, pharmacopoeia). Everything seems to have occurred as though, from the time of the great Platonic division onwards, the will to truth had its own history, which is not at all that of the constraining truths: the history of a range of subjects to be learned, the history of the functions of the knowing subject, the history of material, technical and instrumental investment in knowledge.

But this will to truth, like the other systems of exclusion, relies on institutional support: it is both reinforced and accompanied by whole strata of practices such as pedagogy—naturally—the book-system, publishing, libraries, such as the learned societies in the past, and laboratories today. But it is probably even more profoundly accompanied by the manner in which knowledge is employed in a society, the way in which it is exploited, divided and, in some ways, attributed. It is worth recalling at this point, if only symbolically, the old Greek adage, that arithmetic should be taught in democracies, for it teaches relations of equality, but that geometry alone should be reserved for oligarchies, as it demonstrates the proportions within inequality.

Finally, I believe that this will to knowledge, thus reliant upon institutional support and distribution, tends to exercise a sort of pressure, a power of constraint upon other forms of discourse—I am speaking of our own society. I am thinking of the way Western literature has, for centuries, sought to base itself in nature, in the plausible, upon sincerity and science—in short, upon true discourse. I am thinking, too, of the way economic practices, codified into precepts and recipes—as morality, too—have sought, since the eighteenth century, to found themselves, to rationalise and justify their currency, in a theory of wealth and production; I am thinking, again, of the manner in which such prescriptive ensembles as the Penal Code have sought their bases or justifications. For example, the Penal Code started out as a theory of Right; then, from the time of the nineteenth century, people looked for its validation in sociological, psychological, medical and psychiatric knowledge. It is as though the very words of the law had no authority in our society, except insofar as they are derived from true discourse. Of the three great systems of exclusion governing discourse—prohibited words, the division of madness and the will to truth—I have spoken at greatest length concerning the third. With good reason: for centuries, the former have continually tended toward the latter; because this last has, gradually, been attempting to assimilate the others in order both to modify them and to provide them with a firm foundation. Because, if the two former are continually growing more fragile and less certain to the extent that they are now invaded by the will to truth, the latter, in contrast, daily grows in strength, in depth and implacability.

And yet we speak of it least. As though the will to truth and its vicissitudes were masked by truth itself and its necessary unfolding. The reason is perhaps this: if, since the time of the Greeks, true discourse no longer responds to desire or to that which exercises power in the will to truth, in the will to speak out in true discourse, what, then, is at work, if not desire and power? True discourse, liberated by the nature of its form from desire and power, is incapable of recognising the will to truth which pervades it; and the will to truth, having imposed itself upon us for so long, is such that the truth it seeks to reveal cannot fail to mask it.

Thus, only one truth appears before our eyes: wealth, fertility and sweet strength in all its insidious universality. In contrast, we are unaware of the prodigious machinery of the will to truth, with its vocation of exclusion. All those who, at one moment or another in our history, have attempted to remould this will to truth and to turn it against truth at that very point where truth undertakes to justify the taboo, and to define madness; all those, from Nietzsche to Artaud and Bataille, must now stand as (probably haughty) signposts for all our future work.[3]

There are, of course, many other systems for the control and delimitation of discourse. Those I have spoken of up to now are, to some extent, active on the exterior; they function as systems of exclusion; they concern that part of discourse which deals with power and desire.

I believe we can isolate another group: internal rules, where discourse exercises its own control; rules concerned with the principles of classification, ordering and distribution. It is as though we were now involved in the mastery of another dimension of discourse: that of events and chance.

In the first place, commentary. I suppose, though I am not altogether sure, there is barely a society without its major narratives, told, retold and varied; formulae, texts, ritualised texts to be spoken in well-defined circumstances; things said once, and conserved because people suspect some hidden secret or wealth lies buried within. In short, I suspect one could find a kind of gradation between different types of discourse within most societies: discourse 'uttered' in the course of the day and in casual meetings, and which disappears with the very act which gave rise to it; and those forms of discourse that lie at the origins of a certain number of new verbal acts, which are reiterated, transformed or discussed; in short, discourse which *is spoken* and remains spoken, indefinitely, beyond its formulation, and which remains to be spoken. We know them in our own cultural system: religious or juridical texts, as well as some curious texts, from the point of view of their status, which we term '*literary*'; to a certain extent, scientific texts also.

What is clear is that this gap is neither stable, nor constant, nor absolute. There is no question of there being one category, fixed for all time, reserved for fundamental or creative discourse, and another for those which reiterate, expound and comment. Not a few major texts become blurred and disappear, and commentaries sometimes come to occupy the former position. But while the details of application may well change, the function remains the same, and the principle of hierarchy remains at work. The radical denial of this gradation can never be anything but play, utopia or anguish. Play, as Borges[4] uses the term, in the form of commentary that is nothing more than the reappearance, word for word (though this time it is solemn and anticipated) of the text commented on; or again, the play of a work of criticism talking endlessly about a work that does not exist. It is a lyrical dream of talk reborn, utterly afresh and innocent, at each point; continually reborn in all its vigour, stimulated by things, feelings or thoughts. Anguish, such as that of Janet when sick, for whom the least utterance sounded as the 'word of the Evangelist', concealing an inexhaustible wealth of meaning, worthy to be broadcast, rebegun, commented upon indefinitely: 'When I think,' he said on reading or listening; 'When I think of this phrase, continuing its journey through eternity, while I, perhaps, have only incompletely understood it . . .'

But who can fail to see that this would be to annul one of the terms of the relationship each time, and not to suppress the relationship itself? A relationship in continual process of modification; a relationship taking multiple and diverse forms in a given epoch: juridical exegesis is very different—and has been for a long time—from religious commentary; a single work of literature can give rise, simultaneously, to several distinct types of discourse. The *Odyssey*, as a primary text, is repeated in the same epoch, in Berand's translation, in infinite textual explanations and in Joyce's *Ulysses*.

For the time being, I would like to limit myself to pointing out that, in what we generally refer to as commentary, the difference between primary text and secondary text plays two interdependent roles. On the one hand, it permits us to create new discourses ad infinitum: the top-heaviness of the original text, its permanence, its status as discourse ever capable of being brought up to date, the multiple or hidden meanings with which it is credited, the reticence and wealth it is believed to contain, all this creates an open possibility for discussion. On the other hand, whatever the techniques employed, commentary's only role is to say *finally*, what has silently been articulated *deep down*. It must—and

[3] Friedrich Nietzsche (1844–1900), whose work most important to Foucault is *The Genealogy of Morals;* Antonin Artaud (1896–1948), French poet, actor and director; Georges Bataille (1897–1962), French writer. [Eds.]

[4] Jorge Luis Borges (b. 1899), Argentine writer. [Eds.]

the paradox is ever-changing yet inescapable—say, for the first time, what has already been said, and repeat tirelessly what was, nevertheless, never said. The infinite rippling of commentary is agitated from within by the dream of masked repetition: in the distance there is, perhaps, nothing other than what was there at the point of departure: simple recitation. Commentary averts the chance element of discourse by giving it its due: it gives us the opportunity to say something other than the text itself, but on condition that it is the text itself which is uttered and, in some ways, finalised. The open multiplicity, the fortuitousness, is transferred, by the principle of commentary, from what is liable to be said to the number, the form, the masks and the circumstances of repetition. The novelty lies no longer in what is said, but in its reappearance.

I believe there is another principle of rarefaction, complementary to the first: the author. Not, of course, the author in the sense of the individual who delivered the speech or wrote the text in question, but the author as the unifying principle in a particular group of writings or statements, lying at the origins of their significance, as the seat of their coherence. This principle is not constant at all times. All around us, there are sayings and texts whose meaning or effectiveness has nothing to do with any author to whom they might be attributed: mundane remarks, quickly forgotten; orders and contracts that are signed, but have no recognisable author; technical prescriptions anonymously transmitted. But even in those fields where it is normal to attribute a work to an author—literature, philosophy, science—the principle does not always play the same role; in the order of scientific discourse, it was, during the Middle Ages, indispensable that a scientific text be attributed to an author, for the author was the index of the work's truthfulness. A proposition was held to derive its scientific value from its author. But since the seventeenth century this function has been steadily declining; it barely survives now, save to give a name to a theorem, an effect, an example or a syndrome. In literature, however, and from about the same period, the author's function has become steadily more important. Now, we demand of all those narratives, poems, dramas and comedies which circulated relatively anonymously throughout the Middle Ages, whence they come, and we virtually insist they tell us who wrote them. We ask authors to answer for the unity of the works published in their names; we ask that they reveal, or at least display the hidden sense pervading their work; we ask them to reveal their personal lives, to account for their experiences and the real story that gave birth to their writings. The author is he who implants, into the troublesome language of fiction, its unities, its coherence, its links with reality.

I know what people are going to say: 'But there you are speaking of the author in the same way as the critic reinvents him after he is dead and buried, when we are left with no more than a tangled mass of scrawlings. Of course, then you have to put a little order into what is left, you have to imagine a structure, a cohesion, the sort of theme you might expect to arise out of an author's consciousness or his life, even if it is a little fictitious. But all that cannot get away from the fact the author existed, irrupting into the midst of all the words employed, infusing them with his genius, or his chaos'.

Of course, it would be ridiculous to deny the existence of individuals who write, and invent. But I think that, for some time, at least, the individual who sits down to write a text, at the edge of which lurks a possible *œuvre,* resumes the functions of the author. What he writes and does not write, what he sketches out, even preliminary sketches for the work, and what he drops as simple mundane remarks, all this interplay of differences is prescribed by the author-function. It is from his new position, as an author, that he will fashion—from all he might have said, from all he says daily, at any time—the still shaky profile of his *œuvre.*

Commentary limited the hazards of discourse through the action of an *identity* taking the form of *repetition* and *sameness.* The author principle limits this same chance element through the action of an *identity* whose form is that of *individuality* and the *I.*

But we have to recognise another principle of limitation in what we call, not sciences, but 'disciplines'. Here is yet another relative, mobile principle, one which enables us to construct, but within a narrow framework.

The organisation of disciplines is just as much opposed to the commentary-principle as it is to that of the author. Opposed to that of the author, because disciplines are defined by groups of objects, methods, their corpus of propositions considered to be true, the interplay of rules and definitions, of techniques and tools: all these constitute a sort of anonymous system, freely available to whoever wishes, or whoever is able to make use of them, without there being any question of their meaning or their validity being derived from whoever happened to invent them. But the principles involved in the formation of disciplines are equally opposed to that of commentary. In a discipline, unlike in commentary, what is supposed at the point of departure is not some meaning which must be rediscovered, nor an identity to be reiterated; it is that which is required for the construction of new statements. For a discipline to exist, there must be the possibility of formulating—and of doing so ad infinitum—fresh propositions.

But there is more, and there is more, probably, in order that there may be less. A discipline is not the sum total of all the truths that may be uttered concerning something; it is not even the total of all that may be accepted, by virtue of some principle of coherence and systematisation, concerning some given fact or proposition. Medicine does not consist of all that may be truly said about disease; botany cannot be defined by the sum total of the truths one could say about plants. There are two reasons for this, the first being that botany and medicine, like other disciplines, consist of errors as well as truths, errors that are in no way residuals, or foreign bodies, but having their own positive functions and their own valid history, such that their roles are often indissociable from that of the truths. The other reason is that, for a proposition to belong to botany or pathology, it must fulfil certain conditions, in a stricter and more complex sense than that of pure and simple truth: at any rate, other conditions. The proposition must refer to a specific range of objects; from the end of the seventeenth century, for example, a proposition, to be 'botanical', had to be concerned with the visible structure of plants, with its system of close and not so close resemblances, or with the behavior of its fluids; (but it could no longer retain, as had still been the case in the sixteenth century, references to its symbolic value or to the virtues and properties accorded it in antiquity). But without belonging to any discipline, a proposition is obliged to utilize conceptual instruments and techniques of a well-defined type; from the nineteenth century onwards, a proposition was no longer medical—it became 'non-medical', becoming more of an individual fantasy or item of popular imagery—if it employed metaphorical or qualitative terms or notions of essence (congestion, fermented liquids, desiccated solids); in return, it could—it had to—appeal to equally metaphorical notions, though constructed according to a different functional and physiological model (concerning irritation, inflammation or the decay of tissue). But there is more still, for in order to belong to a discipline, a proposition must fit into a certain type of theoretical field. Suffice it to recall that the quest for primitive language, a perfectly acceptable theme up to the eighteenth century, was enough, in the second half of the nineteenth century, to throw any discourse into, I hesitate to say error, but into a world of chimera and reverie—into pure and simple linguistic monstrosity.

Within its own limits, every discipline recognises true and false propositions, but it repulses a whole teratology of learning. The exterior of a science is both more, and less, populated than one might think: certainly, there is immediate experience, imaginary themes bearing on and continually accompanying immemorial beliefs; but perhaps there are no errors in the strict sense of the term, for error can only emerge and be identified within a well-defined process; there are monsters on the prowl, however, whose forms alter with the history of knowledge. In short, a proposition must fulfil some onerous and complex conditions before it can be admitted within a discipline; before it can be pronounced true or false it must be, as Monsieur Canguilhem might say, 'within the true'.[5]

People have often wondered how on earth nineteenth-century botanists and biologists managed not to see the truth of Mendel's statements.[6] But it was precisely because Mendel spoke of objects, employed methods and placed himself within a theoretical perspective totally alien to the biology of his time. But then, Naudin had suggested that hereditary traits constituted a separate element before him;[7] and yet, however novel or unfamiliar the principle may have been, it was nevertheless reconcilable, if only as an enigma, with biological discourse. Mendel, on the other hand, announced that

[5] Georges Canguilhem (b. 1904), French historian of science. [Eds.]

[6] Gregor Johann Mendel (1822–84), Austrian geneticist. [Eds.]

[7] Charles-Victor Naudin (1815–99), French botanist. [Eds.]

hereditary traits constituted an absolutely new biological object, thanks to a hitherto untried system of filtrage: he detached them from species, from the sex transmitting them, the field in which he observed being that infinitely open series of generations in which hereditary traits appear and disappear with statistical regularity. Here was a new object, calling for new conceptual tools, and for fresh theoretical foundations. Mendel spoke the truth, but he was not *dans le vrai* (within the true) of contemporary biological discourse: it simply was not along such lines that objects and biological concepts were formed. A whole change in scale, the deployment of a totally new range of objects in biology was required before Mendel could enter into the true and his propositions appear, for the most part, exact. Mendel was a true monster, so much so that science could not even properly speak of him. And yet Schleiden, for example, thirty years earlier, denying, at the height of the nineteenth century, vegetable sexuality, was committing no more than a disciplined error.[8]

It is always possible one could speak the truth in a void; one would only be in the true, however, if one obeyed the rules of some discursive 'policy' which would have to be reactivated every time one spoke.

Disciplines constitute a system of control in the production of discourse, fixing its limits through the action of an identity taking the form of a permanent reactivation of the rules.

We tend to see, in an author's fertility, in the multiplicity of commentaries and in the development of a discipline so many infinite resources available for the creation of discourse. Perhaps so, but they are nonetheless principles of constraint, and it is probably impossible to appreciate their positive, multiplicatory role without first taking into consideration their restrictive, constraining role.

There is, I believe, a third group of rules serving to control discourse. Here, we are no longer dealing with the mastery of the powers contained within discourse, nor with averting the hazards of its appearance; it is more a question of determining the conditions under which it may be employed, of imposing a certain number of rules upon those individuals who employ it, thus denying access to everyone else. This amounts to a rarefaction among speaking subjects: none may enter into discourse on a specific subject unless he has satisfied certain conditions or if he is not, from the outset, qualified to do so. More exactly, not all areas of discourse are equally open and penetrable; some are forbidden territory (differentiated and differentiating) while others are virtually open to the winds and stand, without any prior restrictions, open to all.

Here, I would like to recount a little story so beautiful I fear it may well be true. It encompasses all the constraints of discourse: those limiting its powers, those controlling its chance appearances and those which select from among speaking subjects. At the beginning of the seventeenth century, the Shogun heard tell of European superiority in navigation, commerce, politics and the military arts, and that this was due to their knowledge of mathematics. He wanted to obtain this precious knowledge. When someone told him of an English sailor possessed of this marvelous discourse, he summoned him to his palace and kept him there. The Shogun took lessons from the mariner in private and familiarised himself with mathematics, after which he retained power and lived to a very old age. It was not until the nineteenth century that there were *Japanese* mathematicians. But that is not the end of the anecdote, for it has its European aspect as well. The story has it that the English sailor, Will Adams, was a carpenter and an autodidact. Having worked in a shipyard he had learnt geometry. Can we see in this narrative the expression of one of the great myths of European culture? To the monopolistic, secret knowledge of oriental tyranny, Europe opposed the universal communication of knowledge and the infinitely free exchange of discourse.

This notion does not, in fact, stand up to close examination. Exchange and communication are positive forces at play within complex but restrictive systems; it is probable that they cannot operate independently of these. The most superficial and obvious of these restrictive systems is constituted by what we collectively refer to as ritual; ritual defines the qualifications required of the speaker (of who in dialogue, interrogation or recitation, should occupy which position and formulate which type of utterance); it lays down gestures to be made, behaviour, circumstances and the whole range of signs that must accompany discourse; finally, it lays down

[8] Matthias Jakob Schleiden (1804–81), German botanist. [Eds.]

the supposed, or imposed significance of the words used, their effect upon those to whom they are addressed, the limitations of their constraining validity. Religious discourse, juridical and therapeutic as well as, in some ways, political discourse are all barely dissociable from the functioning of a ritual that determines the individual properties and agreed roles of the speakers.

A rather different function is filled by 'fellowships of discourse', whose function is to preserve or to reproduce discourse, but in order that it should circulate within a closed community, according to strict regulations, without those in possession being dispossessed by this very distribution. An archaic model of this would be those groups of Rhapsodists, possessing knowledge of poems to recite or, even, upon which to work variations and transformations. But though the ultimate object of this knowledge was ritual recitation, it was protected and preserved within a determinate group, by the, often extremely complex, exercises of memory implied by such a process. Apprenticeship gained access both to a group and to a secret which recitation made manifest, but did not divulge. The roles of speaking and listening were not interchangeable.

Few such 'fellowships of discourse' remain, with their ambiguous interplay of secrecy and disclosure. But do not be deceived; even in true discourse, even in the order of published discourse, free from all ritual, we still find secret-appropriation and non-interchangeability at work. It could even be that the act of writing, as it is institutionalised today, with its books, its publishing system and the personality of the writer, occurs within a diffuse, yet constraining, 'fellowship of discourse.' The separateness of the writer, continually opposed to the activity of all other writing and speaking subjects, the intransitive character he lends to his discourse, the fundamental singularity he has long accorded to 'writing', the affirmed dissymmetry between 'creation' and any use of linguistic systems—all this manifests in its formulation (and tends moreover to accompany the interplay of these factors in practice) the existence of a certain 'fellowship of discourse.' But there are many others, functioning according to entirely different schemas of exclusivity and disclosure: one has only to think of technical and scientific secrets, of the forms of diffusion and circulation in medical discourse, of those who have appropriated economic or political discourse.

At first sight, 'doctrine' (religious, political, philosophical) would seem to constitute the very reverse of a 'fellowship of discourse'; for among the latter, the number of speakers were, if not fixed, at least limited, and it was among this number that discourse was allowed to circulate and be transmitted. Doctrine, on the other hand, tends to diffusion: in the holding in common of a single ensemble of discourse that individuals, as many as you wish, could define their reciprocal allegiance. In appearance, the sole requisite is the recognition of the same truths and the acceptance of a certain rule—more or less flexible—of conformity with validated discourse. If it were a question of just that, doctrines would barely be any different from scientific disciplines, and discursive control would bear merely on the form or content of what was uttered, and not on the speaker. Doctrinal adherence, however, involves both speaker and the spoken, the one through the other. The speaking subject is involved through, and as a result of, the spoken, as is demonstrated by the rules of exclusion and the rejection mechanism brought into play when a speaker formulates one, or many, inassimilable utterances; questions of heresy and unorthodoxy in no way arise out of fanatical exaggeration of doctrinal mechanisms; they are a fundamental part of them. But conversely, doctrine involves the utterances of speakers in the sense that doctrinc is, permanently, the sign, the manifestation and the instrument of a prior adherence—adherence to a class, to a social or racial status, to a nationality or an interest, to a struggle, a revolt, resistance or acceptance. Doctrine links individuals to certain types of utterance while consequently barring them from all others. Doctrine effects a dual subjection, that of speaking subjects to discourse, and that of discourse to the group, at least virtually, of speakers.

Finally, on a much broader scale, we have to recognise the great cleavages in what one might call the social appropriation of discourse. Education may well be, as of right, the instrument whereby every individual, in a society like our own, can gain access to any kind of discourse. But we well know that in its distribution, in what it permits and in what it prevents, it follows the well-trodden battle-lines of social conflict. Every educational system is a political means of maintaining or of modifying the appropriation of discourse, with the knowledge and the powers it carries with it.

I am well aware of the abstraction I am performing when I separate, as I have just done, verbal rituals, 'fellowships of discourse', doctrinal groups and social appropriation. Most of the time they are linked together, constituting great edifices that distribute speakers among the different types of discourse, and which appropriate those types of discourse to certain categories of subject. In a word, let us say that these are the main rules for the subjection of discourse. What is an educational system, after all, if not a ritualisation of the word; if not a qualification of some fixing of roles for speakers; if not the constitution of a (diffuse) doctrinal group; if not a distribution and an appropriation of discourse, with all its learning and its powers? What is 'writing' (that of 'writers') if not a similar form of subjection, perhaps taking rather different forms, but whose main stresses are nonetheless analogous? May we not also say that the judicial system, as well as institutionalised medicine, constitute similar systems for the subjection of discourse?

I wonder whether a certain number of philosophical themes have not come to conform to this activity of limitation and exclusion and perhaps even to reinforce it.

They conform, first of all, by proposing an ideal truth as a law of discourse, and an immanent rationality as the principle of their behaviour. They accompany, too, an ethic of knowledge, promising truth only to the desire for truth itself and the power to think it.

They then go on to reinforce this activity by denying the specific reality of discourse in general.

Ever since the exclusion of the activity and commerce of the sophists, ever since their paradoxes were muzzled, more or less securely, it would seem that Western thought has seen to it that discourse be permitted as little room as possible between thought and words. It would appear to have ensured that *to discourse* should appear merely as a certain interjection between speaking and thinking; that it should constitute thought, clad in its signs and rendered visible by words or, conversely, that the structures of language themselves should be brought into play, producing a certain effect of meaning.

This very ancient elision of the reality of discourse in philosophical thought has taken many forms in the course of history. We have seen it quite recently in the guise of many themes now familiar to us.

It seems to me that the theme of the founding subject permits us to elide the reality of discourse. The task of the founding subject is to animate the empty forms of language with his objectives; through the thickness and inertia of empty things, he grasps intuitively the meanings lying within them. Beyond time, he indicates the field of meanings—leaving history to make them explicit—in which propositions, sciences, and deductive ensembles ultimately find their foundation. In this relationship with meaning, the founding subject has signs, marks, tracks, letters at his disposal. But he does not need to demonstrate these passing through the singular instance of discourse.

The opposing theme, that of originating experience, plays an analogous role. This asserts, in the case of experience, that even before it could be grasped in the form of a *cogito,* prior significations, in some ways already spoken, were circulating in the world, scattering it all about us, and from the outset made possible a sort of primitive recognition. Thus, a primary complicity with the world founds, for us, a possibility of speaking of experience, in it, to designate and name it, to judge it and, finally, to know it in the form of truth. If there is discourse, what could it legitimately be if not a discrete reading? Things murmur meanings our language has merely to extract; from its most primitive beginnings, this language was already whispering to us of a being of which it forms the skeleton.

The theme of universal mediation is, I believe, yet another manner of eliding the reality of discourse. And this despite appearances. At first sight it would seem that, to discover the movement of a logos everywhere elevating singularities into concepts, finally enabling immediate consciousness to deploy all the rationality in the world, is certainly to place discourse at the centre of speculation. But, in truth, this logos is really only another discourse already in operation, or rather, it is things and events themselves which *insensibly* become discourse in the unfolding of the essential secrets. Discourse is no longer much more than the shimmering of a truth about to be born in its own eyes; and when all things come eventually to take the form of discourse, when everything may be said and when anything becomes an excuse for pronouncing a discourse, it will be because all things having manifested and exchanged meanings, they will then all be able to return to the silent interiority of self-consciousness.

Whether it is the philosophy of a founding subject, a philosophy of originating experience or a philosophy of universal mediation, discourse is really only an activity, of writing in the first case, of reading in the second and exchange in the third. This exchange, this writing, this reading never involve anything but signs. Discourse thus nullifies itself, in reality, in placing itself at the disposal of the signifier.

What civilization, in appearance, has shown more respect towards discourse than our own? Where has it been more and better honoured? Where have men depended more radically, apparently, upon its constraints and its universal character? But, it seems to me, a certain fear hides behind this apparent supremacy accorded, this apparent logophilia. It is as though these taboos, these barriers, thresholds and limits were deliberately disposed in order, at least partly, to master and control the great proliferation of discourse, in such a way as to relieve its richness of its most dangerous elements; to organise its disorder so as to skate round its most uncontrollable aspects. It is as though people had wanted to efface all trace of its irruption into the activity of our thought and language. There is undoubtedly in our society, and I would not be surprised to see it in others, though taking different forms and modes, a profound logophobia, a sort of dumb fear of these events, of this mass of spoken things, of everything that could possibly be violent, discontinuous, querulous, disordered even and perilous in it, of the incessant, disorderly buzzing of discourse.

If we wish—I will not say to efface this fear—but to analyse it in its conditions, its activity and its effects, I believe we must resolve ourselves to accept three decisions which our current thinking rather tends to resist, and which belong to the three groups of function I have just mentioned: to question our will to truth; to restore to discourse its character as an event; to abolish the sovereignty of the signifier.

These are the tasks, or rather, some of the themes which will govern my work in the years ahead. One can straight away distinguish some of the methodological demands they imply.

A principle of *reversal*, first of all. Where, according to tradition, we think we recognise the source of discourse, the principles behind its flourishing and continuity, in those factors which seem to play a positive role, such as the author, discipline, will to truth, we must rather recognise the negative activity of the cutting-out and rarefaction of discourse.

But, once we have distinguished these principles of rarefaction, once we have ceased considering them as a fundamental and creative action, what do we discover behind them? Should we affirm that a world of uninterrupted discourse would be virtually complete? This is where we have to bring other methodological principles into play.

Next, then, the principle of *discontinuity*. The existence of systems of rarefaction does not imply that, over and beyond them lie great vistas of limitless discourse, continuous and silent, repressed and driven back by them, making it our task to abolish them and at last to restore it to speech. Whether talking in terms of speaking or thinking, we must not imagine some unsaid thing, or an unthought, floating about the world, interlacing with all its forms and events. Discourse must be treated as a discontinuous activity, its different manifestations sometimes coming together, but just as easily unaware of, or excluding each other.

The principle of *specificity* declares that a particular discourse cannot be resolved by a prior system of significations; that we should not imagine that the world presents us with a legible face, leaving us merely to decipher it; it does not work hand in glove with what we already know; there is no pre–discursive fate disposing the word in our favour. We must conceive discourse as a violence that we do to things, or, at all events, as a practice we impose upon them; it is in this practice that the events of discourse find the principle of their regularity.

The fourth principle, that of *exteriority*, holds that we are not to burrow to the hidden core of discourse, to the heart of the thought or meaning manifested in it; instead, taking the discourse itself, its appearance and its regularity, that we should look for its external conditions of existence, for that which gives rise to the chance series of these events and fixes its limits.

As the regulatory principles of analysis, then, we have four notions: event series, regularity and the possible conditions of existence. Term for term we find the notion of event opposed to that of creation, the possible conditions of existence opposing signification. These four notions (signification, originality, unity, creation) have, in a fairly general way, dominated the traditional history of ideas; by general agreement one sought the point of creation, the unity of a work, of a period or a theme, one looked also for the mark of individual originality and the infinite wealth of hidden meanings.

I would like to add just two remarks, the first of which concerns history. We frequently credit contemporary history with having removed the individual event from its privileged position and with having revealed the more enduring structures of history. That is so. I am not sure, however, that historians have been working in this direction alone. Or, rather, I do not think one can oppose the identification of the individual event to the analysis of long term trends quite so neatly. On the contrary, it seems to me that it is in squeezing the individual event, in directing the resolving power of historical analysis onto official price-lists (*mercuriales*), title deeds, parish registers, to harbour archives analysed year by year and week by week, that we gradually perceive—beyond battles, decisions, dynasties and assemblies—the emergence of those massive phenomena of secular or multi-secular importance. History, as it is practised today, does not turn its back on events; on the contrary, it is continually enlarging the field of events, constantly discovering new layers—more superficial as well as more profound—incessantly isolating new ensembles—events, numerous, dense and interchangeable or rare and decisive: from daily price fluctuations to secular inflations. What is significant is that history does not consider an event without defining the series to which it belongs, without specifying the method of analysis used, without seeking out the regularity of phenomena and the probable limits of their occurrence, without enquiring about variations, inflexions and the slope of the curve, without desiring to know the conditions on which these depend. History has long since abandoned its attempts to understand events in terms of cause and effect in the formless unity of some great evolutionary process, whether vaguely homogeneous or rigidly hierarchised. It did not do this in order to seek out structures anterior to, alien or hostile to the event. It was rather in order to establish those diverse converging, and sometimes divergent, but never autonomous series that enable us to circumscribe the 'locus' of an event, the limits to its fluidity and the conditions of its emergence.

The fundamental notions now imposed upon us are no longer those of consciousness and continuity (with their correlative problems of liberty and causality), nor are they those of sign and structure. They are notions, rather, of events and of series, with the group of notions linked to these; it is around such an ensemble that this analysis of discourse I am thinking of is articulated, certainly not upon those traditional themes which the philosophers of the past took for 'living' history, but on the effective work of historians.

But it is also here that this analysis poses some, probably awesome philosophical or theoretical problems. If discourses are to be treated first as ensembles of discursive events, what status are we to accord this notion of event, so rarely taken into consideration by philosophers? Of course, an event is neither substance, nor accident, nor quality nor process; events are not corporeal. And yet, an event is certainly not immaterial; it takes effect, becomes effect, always on the level of materiality. Events have their place; they consist in relation to, coexistence with, dispersion of, the cross-checking accumulation and the selection of material elements; it occurs as an effect of, and in, material dispersion. Let us say that the philosophy of event should advance in the direction, at first sight paradoxical, of an incorporeal materialism. If, on the other hand, discursive events are to be dealt with as homogeneous, but discontinuous series, what status are we to accord this discontinuity? Here we are not dealing with a succession of instants in time, nor with the plurality of thinking subjects; what is concerned are those caesurae breaking the instant and dispersing the subject in a multiplicity of possible positions and functions. Such a discontinuity strikes and invalidates the smallest units, traditionally recognised and the least readily contested: the instant and the subject. Beyond them, independent of them, we must conceive—between these discontinuous series of relations which are not in any order of succession (or simultaneity) within any (or several) consciousnesses—and we must elaborate—outside of philosophies of time and subject—a theory of discontinuous systematisation. Finally, if it is true that these discursive, discontinuous series have their regularity, within certain limits, it is clearly no longer possible to establish mechanically causal links or an ideal necessity among their constitutive elements. We must accept the introduction of chance as a category in the production of events. There again, we feel the absence of a theory enabling us to conceive the links between chance and thought.

In the sense that this slender wedge I intend to slip into the history of ideas consists not in dealing with meanings possibly lying behind this or that discourse, but with discourse as regular series and distinct events, I fear I recognise in this wedge a tiny (odious, too, perhaps) device permitting the introduction, into the very roots of thought, of notions of *chance, discontinuity* and *materiality*. This represents a triple peril which one particular form of history attempts to avert by recounting the continuous unfolding of some ideal necessity. But they are three notions which ought to permit us to link the history of systems of thought to the practical work of historians; three directions to be followed in the work of theoretical elaboration.

Following these principles, and referring to this overall view, the analyses I intend to undertake fall into two groups. On the one hand, the 'critical' group which sets the reversal-principle to work. I shall attempt to distinguish the forms of exclusion, limitation and appropriation of which I was speaking earlier; I shall try to show how they are formed, in answer to which needs, how they are modified and displaced, which constraints they have effectively exercised, to what extent they have been worked on. On the other hand, the 'genealogical' group, which brings the three other principles into play: how series of discourse are formed, through, in spite of, or with the aid of these systems of constraint: what were the specific norms for each, and what were their conditions of appearance, growth and variation.

Taking the critical group first, a preliminary group of investigations could bear on what I have designated functions of exclusion. I have already examined one of these for a determinate period: the disjunction of reason and madness in the classical age. Later, we could attempt an investigation of a taboo system in language, that concerning sexuality from the sixteenth to the nineteenth century. In this, we would not be concerned with the manner in which this has progressively—and happily—disappeared, but with the way it has been altered and rearticulated, from the practice of confession, with its forbidden conduct, named, classified, hierarchised down to the smallest detail, to the belated, timid appearance of the treatment of sexuality in nineteenth-century psychiatry and medicine. Of course, these only amount to somewhat symbolic guidelines, but one can already be pretty sure that the stresses will not fall where we expect, and that taboos are not always to be found where we imagine them to be.

For the time being, I would like to address myself to the third system of exclusion. I will envisage it in two ways. Firstly, I would like to try to visualise the manner in which this truth within which we are caught, but which we constantly renew, was selected, but at the same time, was repeated, extended and displaced. I will take first of all the age of the Sophists and its beginning with Socrates, or at least with Platonic philosophy, and I shall try to see how effective, ritual discourse, charged with power and peril, gradually arranged itself into a disjunction between true and false discourse. I shall next take the turn of the sixteenth and seventeenth centuries and the age which, above all in England, saw the emergence of an observational, affirmative science, a certain natural philosophy inseparable, too, from religious ideology—for this certainly constituted a new form of the will to knowledge. In the third place, I shall turn to the beginning of the nineteenth century and the great founding acts of modern science, as well as the formation of industrial society and the accompanying positivist ideology. Three slices out of the morphology of our will to knowledge; three staging posts in our philistinism.

I would also like to consider the same question from quite another angle. I would like to measure the effect of a discourse claiming to be scientific—medical, psychiatric or sociological—on the ensemble of practices and prescriptive discourse of which the penal code consists. The study of psychiatric skills and their role in the penal system will serve as a point of departure and as basic material for this analysis.

It is within this critical perspective, but on a different level, that the analysis of the rules for the limitation of discourse should take place, of those among which I earlier designated the author principle, that of commentary and that of discipline. One can envisage a certain number of studies in this field. I am thinking, for example, of the history of medicine in the sixteenth to nineteenth centuries; not so much an account of discoveries made and concepts developed, but of grasping—from the construction of medical discourse, from all its supporting institutions, from its transmission and its reinforcement,—how the principles of author, commentary and discipline worked in practice; of seeking to know how the great author principle, whether Hippocrates, Galen, Paracelsus and Sydenham, or Boerhaave,[9] became a principle of limitation in medical discourse; how, even late into

[9]Galen (c. 130–c. 200), Greek physician; Paracelsus (Theophrastus von Hohenheim) (1493?–1541), Swiss physician and alchemist; Thomas Sydenham (1624–89), British physician; Hermann Boerhaave (1668–1738), Dutch physician. [Eds.]

the nineteenth century, the practice of aphorism and commentary retained its currency and how it was gradually replaced by the emphasis on case-histories and clinical training on actual cases; according to which model medicine sought to constitute itself as a discipline, basing itself at first on natural history and, later, on anatomy and biology.

One could also envisage the way in which eighteenth and nineteenth-century literary criticism and history have constituted the character of the author and the form of the work, utilising, modifying and altering the procedures of religious exegesis, biblical criticism, hagiography, the 'lives' of historical or legendary figures, of autobiography and memoirs. One day, too, we must take a look at Freud's role in psycho-analytical knowledge, so different from that of Newton in physics, or from that an author might play in the field of philosophy (Kant, for example, who originated a totally new way of philosophizing).

These, then, are some of the projects falling within the critical aspect of the task, for the analysis of instances of discursive control. The genealogical aspect concerns the effective formation of discourse, whether within the limits of control, or outside of them, or as is most frequent, on both sides of the delimitation. Criticism analyses the processes of rarefaction, consolidation and unification in discourse; genealogy studies their formation, at once scattered, discontinuous and regular. To tell the truth, these two tasks are not always exactly complementary. We do not find, on the one hand, forms of rejection, exclusion, consolidation or attribution, and, on a more profound level, the spontaneous pouring forth of discourse, which immediately before or after its manifestation, finds itself submitted to selection and control. The regular formation of discourse may, in certain conditions and up to a certain point, integrate control procedures (this is what happens, for example, when a discipline takes on the form and status of scientific discourse). Conversely, modes of control may take on life within a discursive formation (such as literary criticism as the author's constitutive discourse) even though any critical task calling instances of control into play must, at the same time, analyse the discursive regularities through which these instances are formed. Any genealogical description must take into account the limits at play within real formations. The difference between the critical and the genealogical enterprise is not one of object or field, but of point of attack, perspective and delimitation.

Earlier on I mentioned one possible study, that of the taboos in discourse on sexuality. It would be difficult, and in any case abstract, to try to carry out this study, without at the same time analysing literary, religious and ethical, biological and medical, as well as juridical discursive ensembles: wherever sexuality is discussed, wherever it is named or described, metaphorised, explained or judged. We are a very long way from having constituted a unitary, regular discourse concerning sexuality; it may be that we never will, and that we are not even travelling in that direction. No matter. Taboos are homogeneous neither in their forms nor their behaviour whether in literary or medical discourse, in that of psychiatry or of the direction of consciousness. Conversely, these different discursive regularities do not divert or alter taboos in the same manner. It will only be possible to undertake this study, therefore, if we take into account the plurality of series within which the taboos, each one to some extent different from all the others, are at work.

We could also consider those series of discourse which, in the sixteenth and seventeenth centuries, dealt with wealth and poverty, money, production and trade. Here, we would be dealing with some pretty heterogeneous ensembles of enunciations, formulated by rich and poor, the wise and the ignorant, protestants and catholics, royal officials, merchants or moralists. Each one has its forms of regularity and, equally, its systems of constraint. None of them precisely prefigures that other form of regularity that was to acquire the momentum of a discipline and which was later to be known, first as 'the study of wealth' and, subsequently, 'political economy'. And yet, it was from the foregoing that a new regularity was formed, retrieving or excluding, justifying or rejecting, this or that utterance from these old forms.

One could also conceive a study of discourse concerning heredity, such as it can be gleaned, dispersed as it was until the beginning of the twentieth century, among a variety of disciplines, observations, techniques and formulae; we would be concerned to show the process whereby these series eventually became subsumed under the single system, now recognised as epistemologically coherent, known as genetics. This is the work François Jacob has just completed, with unequalled brilliance and scholarship.[10]

[10]François Jacob (b. 1920), French biologist. [Eds.]

It is thus that critical and genealogical descriptions are to alternate, support and complete each other. The critical side of the analysis deals with the systems enveloping discourse; attempting to mark out and distinguish the principles of ordering, exclusion and rarity in discourse. We might, to play with our words, say it practises a kind of studied casualness. The genealogical side of discourse, by way of contrast, deals with series of effective formation of discourse: it attempts to grasp it in its power of affirmation, by which I do not mean a power opposed to that of negation, but the power of constituting domains of objects, in relation to which one can affirm or deny true or false propositions. Let us call these domains of objects positivist and, to play on words yet again, let us say that, if the critical style is one of studied casualness, then the genealogical mood is one of felicitous positivism.

At all events, one thing at least must be emphasised here: that the analysis of discourse thus understood, does not reveal the universality of a meaning, but brings to light the action of imposed rarity, with a fundamental power of affirmation. Rarity and affirmation; rarity, in the last resort of affirmation—certainly not any continuous outpouring of meaning, and certainly not any monarchy of the signifier.

And now, let those who are weak on vocabulary, let those with little comprehension of theory call all this—if its appeal is stronger than its meaning for them—structuralism.

Hans Robert Jauss

b. 1921

PARTICULARLY because of the importance of this essay, Jauss is regarded as the principal architect of the contemporary aesthetics of reception (*Rezeptionsästhetik*). Delivered as a lecture in 1967 at Constance, where Jauss teaches, the essay was originally titled "What is and for what purpose does one study literary history?" and was purposely identified with Friedrich Schiller's oration of 1798 entitled "What is and for what purpose does one study universal history?" Both have the character of manifestos, and both are concerned with the question of the relation of past to present in interpretation.

Jauss sees reception theory as an attempt to solve the problem of the impasse generated in European literary theory by the antithetical schools of Marxism and formalism. The Marxists give attention to history but only in terms of production and representation, while formalism, with all its analytical subtlety, neglects the historical. The common weakness of both, Jauss argues, is that they neglect one aspect of the fundamental triangle, author-work-public. It is the last, of course, that reception theory reintroduces to critical practice.

But there has always been a problem in locating a public. Is it to be identified with the present, the past, posterity, or tradition? Each of these presents problems of location in itself and, in addition, raises serious questions of adequacy, which Jauss discusses on the way to taking up a position advocating a study of reception as a historical process of the relation of production to reception. In this view, the literary work contains an ever unfolding potentiality of meaning, which can be seen as actualized in reception at various historical moments.

But these moments are always constituted as a relation of horizons of the historical moment and of the moment of constitution. This is not a historicism claiming a simple objectivity in its treatment of the past. However, it is also true that Jauss at times writes as if objectivity could be achieved in the constitution of a system of readerly expectations in any historical moment. Jauss is heavily influenced by the hermeneutic theory of *Hans-Georg Gadamer* in his theory of horizons, but he criticizes Gadamer's recourse to the idea of the classic and of tradition as a standard to which all horizons are ultimately referable. Jauss substitutes for this alleged recourse to a fixed standard a purely dialectical historical situation in which, it is declared, there is no external principle, no teleology, no sense that the interpreter stands at the *end* of things but at a vanishing point.

The essay here is printed without its first four sections, which are devoted to previous sorts of literary history, Marxism, criticism, and formalism. Jauss's most important essays are translated in two collections, *Toward an Aesthetic of Reception* (1982) with an introduction by *Paul de Man* and *Aesthetic Ex-*

perience and Literary Hermeneutics (1982), in which Jauss revises his earlier theory developed in the essay here. See Robert C. Holub, *Reception Theory: A Critical Introduction* (1984), and an interview with Jauss in *Diacritics* 5, 1 (1975):53–61.

FROM

LITERARY HISTORY AS A CHALLENGE TO LITERARY THEORY

V

In the question thus posed, I see the challenge to literary studies of taking up once again the problem of literary history, which was left unresolved in the dispute between Marxist and Formalist methods. My attempt to bridge the gap between literature and history, between historical and aesthetic approaches, begins at the point at which both schools stop. Their methods conceive the *literary fact* within the closed circle of an aesthetics of production and of representation. In doing so, they deprive literature of a dimension that inalienably belongs to its aesthetic character as well as to its social function: the dimension of its reception and influence. Reader, listener, and spectator—in short, the factor of the audience—play an extremely limited role in both literary theories. Orthodox Marxist aesthetics treats the reader—if at all—no differently from the author: it inquires about his social position or seeks to recognize him in the structure of a represented society. The Formalist school needs the reader only as a perceiving subject who follows the directions in the text in order to distinguish the [literary] form or discover the [literary] procedure. It assumes that the reader has the theoretical understanding of the philologist who can reflect on the artistic devices, already knowing them; conversely, the Marxist school candidly equates the spontaneous experience of the reader with the scholarly interest of historical materialism, which would discover relationships between superstructure and basis in the literary work. However, as Walther Bulst has stated, "no text was ever written to be read and interpreted philologically by philologists,"[1] nor, may I add, historically by historians. Both methods lack the reader in his genuine role, a role as unalterable for aesthetic as for historical knowledge: as the addressee for whom the literary work is primarily destined.

For even the critic who judges a new work, the writer who conceives of his work in light of positive or negative norms of an earlier work, and the literary historian who classifies a work in its tradition and explains it historically are first simply readers before their reflexive relationship to literature can become productive again. In the triangle of author, work, and public the last is no passive part, no chain of mere reactions, but rather itself an energy formative of history. The historical life of a literary work is unthinkable without the active participation of its addressees. For it is only through the process of its mediation that the work enters into the changing horizon-of-experience of a continuity in which the perpetual inversion occurs from simple reception to critical understanding, from passive to active reception, from recognized aesthetic norms to a new production that surpasses them. The historicity of literature as well as its communicative character presupposes a dialogical and at once processlike relationship between work, audience, and new work that can be conceived in the relations between message and receiver as well as between question and answer, problem and solution. The

LITERARY HISTORY AS A CHALLENGE TO LITERARY THEORY first appeared in Germany in 1967. It is reprinted in a translation by Timothy Bahti from *Toward an Aesthetic of Reception*, © 1982, by permission of the University of Minnesota Press.

[1] "Bedenken eines Philologen," *Studium generale* 7 (1954), 321–23. The new approach to literary tradition that R. Guiette has sought in a series of pioneering essays (partly in *Questions de littérature* [Ghent, 1960]), using his own method of combining aesthetic criticism with historical knowledge, corresponds almost literally to his (unpublished) axiom, "The greatest error of philologists is to believe that literature has been made for philologists." See also his "Eloge de la lecture," *Revue générale belge* (January 1966), pp. 3–14. [Au.]

closed circle of production and of representation within which the methodology of literary studies has mainly moved in the past must therefore be opened to an aesthetics of reception and influence if the problem of comprehending the historical sequence of literary works as the coherence of literary history is to find a new solution.

The perspective of the aesthetics of reception mediates between passive reception and active understanding, experience formative of norms, and new production. If the history of literature is viewed in this way within the horizon of a dialogue between work and audience that forms a continuity, the opposition between its aesthetic and its historical aspects is also continually mediated. Thus the thread from the past appearance to the present experience of literature, which historicism had cut, is tied back together.

The relationship of literature and reader has aesthetic as well as historical implications. The aesthetic implication lies in the fact that the first reception of a work by the reader includes a test of its aesthetic value in comparison with works already read.[2] The obvious historical implication of this is that the understanding of the first reader will be sustained and enriched in a chain of receptions from generation to generation; in this way the historical significance of a work will be decided and its aesthetic value made evident. In this process of the history of reception, which the literary historian can only escape at the price of leaving unquestioned the presuppositions that guide his understanding and judgment, the reappropriation of past works occurs simultaneously with the perpetual mediation of past and present art and of traditional evaluation and current literary attempts. The merit of a literary history based on an aesthetics of reception will depend upon the extent to which it can take an active part in the ongoing totalization of the past through aesthetic experience. This demands on the one hand—in opposition to the objectivism of positivist literary history—a conscious attempt at the formation of a canon, which, on the other hand—in opposition to the classicism of the study of traditions—presupposes a critical revision if not destruction of the received literary canon. The criterion for the formation of such a canon and the ever necessary retelling of literary history is clearly set out by the aesthetics of reception. The step from the history of the reception of the individual work to the history of literature has to lead to seeing and representing the historical sequence of works as they determine and clarify the coherence of literature, to the extent that it is meaningful for us, as the prehistory of its present experience.[3]

From this premise, the question as to how literary history can today be methodologically grounded and written anew will be addressed in the following seven theses.

VI

Thesis 1. A renewal of literary history demands the removal of the prejudices of historical objectivism and the grounding of the traditional aesthetics of production and representation in an aesthetics of reception and influence. The historicity of literature rests not on an organization of "literary facts" that is established *post festum,* but rather on the preceding experience of the literary work by its readers.

R. G. Collingwood's postulate, posed in his critique of the prevailing ideology of objectivity in history—"History is nothing but the re-enactment of past thought in the historian's mind"[4]—is even more valid for literary history. For the positivistic view of history as the "objective" description of a series of events in an isolated past neglects the artistic character as well as the specific historicity of literature. A literary work is not an object that stands by itself and that offers the same view to each reader in each period.[5] It is not a monument

[2] This thesis is one of the main points of the *Introduction à une esthétique de la littérature* by G. Picon (Paris, 1953); see esp. pp. 90 ff. [Au.]

[3] Correspondingly, Walter Benjamin (1931) formulated: "For it is not a question of representing the written works in relation to their time but of bringing to representation the time that knows them—that is our time—in the time when they originated. Thus literature becomes an organon of history and the task of literary history is to make it this—and not to make written works the material of history" (*Angelus Novus* [Frankfurt a.M., 1966], p. 456). [Au.] See *Benjamin.* [Eds.]

[4] *The Idea of History* (New York and Oxford, 1956), p. 228. [Au.]

[5] Here I am following A. Nisin in his criticism of the latent Platonism of philological methods, that is, of their belief in the timeless substance of a literary work and in a timeless point of view of the reader: "For the work of art, if it cannot incarnate the essence of art, is also not an object

that monologically reveals its timeless essence. It is much more like an orchestration that strikes ever new resonances among its readers and that frees the text from the material of the words and brings it to a contemporary existence: "words that must, at the same time that they speak to him, create an interlocutor capable of understanding them."[6] This dialogical character of the literary work also establishes why philological understanding can exist only in a perpetual confrontation with the text, and cannot be allowed to be reduced to a knowledge of facts.[7] Philological understanding always remains related to interpretation that must set as its goal, along with learning about the object, the reflection on and description of the completion of this knowledge as a moment of new understanding.

History of literature is a process of aesthetic reception and production that takes place in the realization of literary texts on the part of the receptive reader, the reflective critic, and the author in his continuing productivity. The endlessly growing sum of literary "facts" that winds up in the conventional literary histories is merely left over from this process; it is only the collected and classified past and therefore not history at all, but pseudo-history. Anyone who considers a series of such literary facts as a piece of the history of literature confuses the eventful character of a work of art with that of historical matter-of-factness. The *Perceval* of Chrétien de Troyes, as a literary event, is not "historical" in the same sense as, for example, the Third Crusade, which was occurring at about the same time.[8] It is not a "fact" that could be explained as caused by a series of situational preconditions and motives, by the intent of a historical action as it can be reconstructed, and by the necessary and secondary consequences of this deed. The historical context in which a literary work appears is not a factical, independent series of events that exists apart from an observer. *Perceval* becomes a literary event only for its reader, who reads this last work of Chrétien with a memory of his earlier works and who recognizes its individuality in comparison with these and other works that he already knows, so that he gains a new criterion for evaluating future works. In contrast to a political event, a literary event has no unavoidable consequences subsisting on their own that no succeeding generation can ever escape. A literary event can continue to have an effect only if those who come after it still or once again respond to it—if there are readers who again appropriate the past work or authors who want to imitate, outdo, or refute it. The coherence of literature as an event is primarily mediated in the horizon of expectations of the literary experience of contemporary and later readers, critics, and authors. Whether it is possible to comprehend and represent the history of literature in its unique historicity depends on whether this horizon of expectations can be objectified.

VII

Thesis 2. The analysis of the literary experience of the reader avoids the threatening pitfalls of psychology if it describes the reception and the influence of a work within the objectifiable system of expectations that arises for each work in the historical moment of its appearance, from a pre-understanding of the genre, from the form and themes of already familiar works, and from the opposition between poetic and practical language.

which we can regard according to the Cartesian rule 'without putting anything of ourselves into it but what can apply indiscriminately to all objects.'" *La Littérature et le lecteur* (Paris, 1959), p. 57 (see also my review in *Archiv für das Studium der neueren Sprachen* 197 [1960], 223–35). [Au.]

[6] Picon, *Introduction,* p. 34. This view of the dialogical mode of being of a literary work of art is found in Malraux (*Les voix du silence*) as well as in Picon, Nisin, and Guiette—a tradition of literary aesthetics which is still alive in France and to which I am especially indebted; it finally goes back to a famous sentence in Valéry's poetics, "It is the execution of the poem which is the poem." [Au.]

[7] Peter Szondi, "Über philologische Erkenntnis," *Hölderlin-Studien* (Frankfurt a.M., 1967), rightly sees in this the decisive difference between literary and historical studies, p. 11: "No commentary, no stylistic examination of a poem should aim to give a description of the poem that could be taken by itself. Even the least critical reader will want to confront it with the poem and will not understand it until he has traced the claim back to the acts of knowledge whence they originated." Guiette says something very similar in "Eloge de la lecture" (see note 1). [Au.]

[8] Note also J. Storost, "Das Problem der Literaturgeschichte," *Dante-Jahrbuch* 38 (1960), pp. 1–17, who simply equates the historical event with the literary event ("A work of art is first of all an artistic act and hence historical like the Battle of Isos"). [Au.]

My thesis opposes a widespread skepticism that doubts whether an analysis of aesthetic influence can approach the meaning of a work of art at all or can produce, at best, more than a simple sociology of taste. René Wellek in particular directs such doubts against the literary theory of I. A. Richards. Wellek argues that neither the individual state of consciousness, since it is momentary and only personal, nor a collective state of consciousness, as Jan Mukarovsky assumes the effect a work of art to be, can be determined by empirical means.[9] Roman Jakobson wanted to replace the "collective state of consciousness" by a "collective ideology" in the form of a system of norms that exists for each literary work as *langue* and that is actualized as *parole* by the receiver—although incompletely and never as a whole.[10] This theory, it is true, limits the subjectivity of the influence, but it still leaves open the question of which data can be used to comprehend the influence of a particular work on a certain public and to incorporate it into a system of norms. In the meantime there are empirical means that had never been thought of before—literary data that allow one to ascertain a specific disposition of the audience for each work (a disposition that precedes the psychological reaction as well as the subjective understanding of the individual reader). As in the case of every actual experience, the first literary experience of a previously unknown work also demands a "foreknowledge which is an element of the experience itself, and on the basis of which anything new that we come across is available to experience at all, i.e., as it were readable in a context of experience."[11]

A literary work, even when it appears to be new, does not present itself as something absolutely new in an informational vacuum, but predisposes its audience to a very specific kind of reception by announcements, overt and covert signals, familiar characteristics, or implicit allusions. It awakens memories of that which was already read, brings the reader to a specific emotional attitude, and with its beginning arouses expectations for the "middle and end," which can then be maintained intact or altered, reoriented, or even fulfilled ironically in the course of the reading according to specific rules of the genre or type of text. The psychic process in the reception of a text is, in the primary horizon of aesthetic experience, by no means only an arbitrary series of merely subjective impressions, but rather the carrying out of specific instructions in a process of directed perception, which can be comprehended according to its constitutive motivations and triggering signals, and which also can be described by a textual linguistics. If, along with W. D. Stempel, one defines the initial horizon of expectations of a text as paradigmatic isotopy, which is transposed into an immanent syntagmatic horizon of expectations to the extent that the utterance grows, then the process of reception becomes describable in the expansion of a semiotic system that accomplishes itself between the development and the correction of a system.[12] A corresponding process of the continuous establishing and altering of horizons also determines the relationship of the individual text to the succession of texts that forms the genre. The new text evokes for the reader (listener) the horizon of expectations and rules familiar from earlier texts, which are then varied, corrected, altered, or even just reproduced. Variation and correction determine the scope, whereas alteration and reproduction determine the borders of a genre-structure.[13] The interpretative reception of a text always presupposes the context of experience of aesthetic perception: the question of the subjectivity of the interpretation and of the taste of different readers or levels of readers can be asked meaningfully only when one has first clarified which transsubjective horizon of understanding conditions the influence of the text.

The ideal cases of the objective capability of such literary-historical frames of reference are works

[9] René Wellek, "The Theory of Literary History," *Études dediées au quatrième Congrès de linguistes–Travaux du Cercle Linguistique de Prague* (1936), p. 179. [Au.]

[10] In *Slovo a slovenost*, I, p. 192, cited by Wellek (1936), pp. 179 ff. [Au.]

[11] G. Buck, *Lernen und Erfahrung* (Stuttgart, 1967), p. 56, who refers here to Husserl (*Erfahrung und Urteil*, esp. § 8) but who more broadly goes beyond Husserl in a determination of the negativity in the process of experience that is of significance for the horizontal structure of aesthetic experience (cf. note 49 below). [Au.]

[12] Wolf Dieter Stempel, "Pour une description des genres littéraires," in *Actes du XIIe congrès international de linguistique Romane* (Bucharest, 1968), also in *Beiträge zur Textlinguistik*, ed. W. D. Stempel (Munich, 1970). [Au.]

[13] Here I can refer to my study, "Theory of Genres and Medieval Literature," Chapter 3, *Toward an Aesthetic of Reception*. [Au.]

that evoke the reader's horizon of expectations, formed by a convention of genre, style, or form, only in order to destroy it step by step—which by no means serves a critical purpose only, but can itself once again produce poetic effects. Thus Cervantes allows the horizon of expectations of the favorite old tales of knighthood to arise out of the reading of *Don Quixote,* which the adventure of his last knight then seriously parodies.[14] Thus Diderot, at the beginning of *Jacques le Fataliste,* evokes the horizon of expectations of the popular novelistic schema of the "journey" (with the fictive questions of the reader to the narrator) along with the (Aristotelian) convention of the romanesque fable and the providence unique to it, so that he can then provocatively oppose to the promised journey- and love-novel a completely unromanesque "vérité de l'histoire": the bizarre reality and moral casuistry of the enclosed stories in which the truth of life continually denies the mendacious character of poetic fiction.[15] Thus Nerval in the *Chimères* cites, combines, and mixes a quintessence of well-known romantic and occult motifs to produce the horizon of expectations of a mythical metamorphosis of the world only in order to signify his renunciation of romantic poetry. The identifications and relationships of the mythic state that are familiar or disclosable to the reader dissolve into an unknown to the same degree as the attempted private myth of the lyrical "I" fails, the law of sufficient information is broken, and the obscurity that has become expressive itself gains a poetic function.[16]

There is also the possibility of objectifying the horizon of expectations in works that are historically less sharply delineated. For the specific disposition toward a particular work that the author anticipates from the audience can also be arrived at, even if explicit signals are lacking, through three generally presupposed factors: first, through familiar norms or the immanent poetics of the genre; second, through the implicit relationships to familiar works of the literary-historical surroundings; and third, through the opposition between fiction and reality, between the poetic and the practical function of language, which is always available to the reflective reader during the reading as a possibility of comparison. The third factor includes the possibility that the reader of a new work can perceive it within the narrower horizon of literary expectations, as well as within the wider horizon of experience of life. I shall return to this horizonal structure, and its ability to be objectified by means of the hermeneutics of question and answer, in the discussion of the relationship between literature and lived praxis (see XII).

VIII

Thesis 3. Reconstructed in this way, the horizon of expectations of a work allows one to determine its artistic character by the kind and the degree of its influence on a presupposed audience. If one characterizes as aesthetic distance the disparity between the given horizon of expectations and the appearance of a new work, whose reception can result in a "change of horizons" through negation of familiar experiences or through raising newly articulated experiences to the level of consciousness, then this aesthetic distance can be objectified historically along the spectrum of the audience's reactions and criticism's judgment (spontaneous success, rejection or shock, scattered approval, gradual or belated understanding).

The way in which a literary work, at the historical moment of its appearance, satisfies, surpasses, disappoints, or refutes the expectations of its first audience obviously provides a criterion for the determination of its aesthetic value. The distance between the horizon of expectations and the work, between the familiarity of previous aesthetic experience and the "horizonal change"[17] demanded by the reception of the new work, determines the artistic character of a literary work, according to an aesthetics of reception: to the degree that this distance

[14] According to the interpretation of H. J. Neuschafer, *Der Sinn der Parodie im Don Quijote,* Studia Romanica 5 (Heidelberg, 1963). [Au.]

[15] According to the interpretation of Rainer Warning, *Illusion und Wirklichkeit in Tristam Shandy und Jacques le Fataliste,* Theorie und Geschichte der Literatur und der schönen Künste 4 (Munich, 1965), esp. pp. 80 ff. [Au.]

[16] According to the interpretation of Karl Heinz Stierle, *Dunkelheit und Form in Gérard de Nervals "Chimères",* Theorie und Geschichte der Literatur und der schönen Künste 5 (Munich, 1967), esp. pp. 55 and 91. [Au.]

[17] On this Husserlian concept, see Buck, *Lernen und Erfahrung,* pp. 64 ff. [Au.]

decreases, and no turn toward the horizon of yet-unknown experience is demanded of the receiving consciousness, the closer the work comes to the sphere of "culinary" or entertainment art [*Unterhaltungskunst*]. This latter work can be characterized by an aesthetics of reception as not demanding any horizonal change, but rather as precisely fulfilling the expectations prescribed by a ruling standard of taste, in that it satisfies the desire for the reproduction of the familiarly beautiful; confirms familiar sentiments; sanctions wishful notions; makes unusual experiences enjoyable as "sensations"; or even raises moral problems, but only to "solve' them in an edifying manner as predecided questions.[18] If, conversely, the artistic character of a work is to be measured by the aesthetic distance with which it opposes the expectations of its first audience, then it follows that this distance, at first experienced as a pleasing or alienating new perspective, can disappear for later readers, to the extent that the original negativity of the work has become self-evident and has itself entered into the horizon of future aesthetic experience, as a henceforth familiar expectation. The classical character of the so-called masterworks especially belongs to this second horizonal change;[19] their beautiful form that has become self-evident, and their seemingly unquestionable "eternal meaning" bring them, according to an aesthetics of reception, dangerously close to the irresistibly convincing and enjoyable "culinary" art, so that it requires a special effort to read them "against the grain" of the accustomed experience to catch sight of their artistic character once again (see section X).

The relationship between literature and audience includes more than the facts that every work has its own specific, historically and sociologically determinable audience, that every writer is dependent on the milieu, views, and ideology of his audience, and that literary success presupposes a book "which expresses what the group expects, a book which presents the group with its own image."[20] This objectivist determination of literary success according to the congruence of the work's intention with the expectations of a social group always leads literary sociology into a dilemma whenever later or ongoing influence is to be explained. Thus R. Escarpit wants to presuppose a "collective basis in space or time" for the "illusion of the lasting quality" of a writer, which in the case of Molière leads to an astonishing prognosis: "Molière is still young for the Frenchman of the twentieth century because his world still lives, and a sphere of culture, views, and language still binds us to him. . . . But the sphere becomes ever smaller, and Molière will age and die when the things which our culture still has in common with the France of Molière die" (p. 117). As if Molière had only mirrored the "mores of his time" and had only remained successful through this supposed intention! Where the congruence between work and social group does not exist, or no longer exists, as for example with the reception of a work in a foreign language, Escarpit is able to help himself by inserting a "myth" in between: "myths that are invented by a later world for which the reality that they substitute for has become alien" (p. 111). As if all reception beyond the first, socially determined audience for a work were only a "distorted echo," only a result of "subjective myths," and did not itself have its objective a priori once again in the received work as the limit and possibility of later understanding! The sociology of literature does not

[18] Here I am incorporating results of the discussion of "kitsch," as a borderline phenomenon of the aesthetic, which took place during the third colloquium of the research group "Poetik und Hermeneutik" (now in the volume *Die nicht mehr schönen Künste—Grenzphänomene des Ästhetischen,* ed. H. R. Jauss [Munich, 1968]). For the "culinary" approach, which presupposes mere entertainment art, the same thing holds as for kitsch, namely, that here the "demands of the consumers are *a priori* satisfied" (P. Beylin), that "the fulfilled expectation becomes the norm of the product" (Wolfgang Iser), or that "its work, without having or solving a problem, presents the appearance of a solution to a problem" (M. Imdahl), pp. 651–67. [Au.]

[19] As also the epigonal; on this, see Boris Tomashevsky, in *Théorie de la littérature. Textes des formalistes russes,* ed. T. Todorov (Paris, 1965), p. 306, n. 53: "The appearance of a genius always equals a literary revolution which dethrones the dominant canon and gives power to processes subordinated until then. . . . The epigones repeat a worn-out combination of processes, and as original and revolutionary as it was, this combination becomes stereotypical and traditional. Thus the epigones kill, sometimes for a long time, the aptitude of their contemporaries to sense the aesthetic force of the examples they imitate: they discredit their masters." [Au.]

[20] R. Escarpit, *Das Buch und der Leser: Entwurf einer Literatursoziologie* (Cologne and Opladen, 1961; first, expanded German edition of *Sociologie de la littérature* [Paris, 1958]), p. 116. [Au.]

view its object dialectically enough when it determines the circle of author, work, and audience so one-sidedly.[21] The determination is reversible: there are works that at the moment of their appearance are not yet directed at any specific audience, but that break through the familiar horizon of literary expectations so completely that an audience can only gradually develop for them.[22] When, then, the new horizon of expectations has achieved more general currency, the power of the altered aesthetic norm can be demonstrated in that the audience experiences formerly successful works as outmoded, and withdraws its appreciation. Only in view of such horizonal change does the analysis of literary influence achieve the dimension of a literary history of readers,[23] and do the statistical curves of the best-sellers provide historical knowledge.

A literary sensation from the year 1857 may serve as an example. Alongside Flaubert's *Madame Bovary,* which has since become world-famous, appeared his friend Feydeau's *Fanny,* today forgotten. Although Flaubert's novel brought with it a trial for offending public morals, *Madame Bovary* was at first overshadowed by Feydeau's novel: *Fanny* went through thirteen editions in one year, achieving a success the likes of which Paris had not experienced since Chateaubriand's *Atala.* Thematically considered, both novels met the expectations of a new audience that—in Baudelaire's analysis—had foresworn all romanticism, and despised great as well as naive passions equally:[24] they treated a trivial subject, infidelity in a bourgeois and provincial milieu. Both authors understood how to give to the conventional, ossified triangular relationship a sensational twist that went beyond the expected details of the erotic scenes. They put the worn-out theme of jealousy in a new light by reversing the expected relationship between the three classic roles: Feydeau has the youthful lover of the *femme de trente ans* become jealous of his lover's husband despite his having already fulfilled his desires, and perishing over this agonizing situation; Flaubert gives the adulteries of the doctor's wife in the provinces—interpreted by Baudelaire as a sublime form of *dandysme*—the surprise ending that precisely the laughable figure of the cuckolded Charles Bovary takes on dignified traits at the end. In the official criticism of the time, one finds voices that reject *Fanny* as well as *Madame Bovary* as a product of the new school of *réalisme,* which they reproach for denying everything ideal and attacking the ideas on which the social order of the Second Empire was founded.[25] The audience's horizon of expectations in 1857, here only vaguely sketched in, which did not expect anything great from the novel after Balzac's death,[26] explains the different success of the two novels only when the question of the effect of their narrative form is posed. Flaubert's formal innovation, his principle of "impersonal narration" (*impassibilité*)—attacked by Barbey d'Aurevilly with the comparison that if a story-telling machine could

[21] K. H. Bender, *König und Vasall: Untersuchungen zur Chanson de Geste des XII. Jahrhunderts,* Studia Romanica 13 (Heidelberg, 1967), shows what step is necessary to get beyond this one-sided determination. In this history of the early French epic, the apparent congruence of feudal society and epic ideality is represented as a process that is maintained through a continually changing discrepancy between "reality" and "ideology," that is, between the historical constellations of feudal conflicts and the poetic responses of the epics. [Au.]

[22] The incomparably more promising literary sociology of Erich Auerbach brought these aspects to light in the variety of epoch-making breaks in the relationship between author and reader; for this see the evaluation of Fritz Schalk in his edition of Auerbach's *Gesammeltc Aufsätze zur romanischen Philologie* (Bern and Munich, 1967), pp. 11 ff. [Au.]

[23] See Harald Weinrich, "Für eine Literaturgeschichte des Lesers," *Merkur* 21 (November, 1967), an attempt arising from the same intent as mine, which, analogously to the way that the linguistics of the speaker, customary earlier, has been replaced by the linguistics of the listener, argues for a methodological consideration of the perspective of the reader in literary history and thereby most happily supports my aims. Weinrich shows above all how the empirical methods of literary sociology can be supplemented by the linguistic and literary interpretation of the role of the reader implicit in the work. [Au.]

[24] In "*Madame Bovary* par Gustave Flaubert," Baudelaire, *Oeuvres complètes,* Pléiade ed. (Paris, 1951), p. 998: "The last years of Louis-Philippe witnessed the last explosions of a spirit still excitable by the play of the imagination; but the new novelist found himself faced with a completely worn-out society—worse than worn-out—stupified and gluttonous, with a horror only of fiction, and love only for possession." [Au.]

[25] Cf. *ibid.,* p. 999, as well as the accusation, speech for the defense, and verdict of the *Bovary* trial in Flaubert, *Oeuvres,* Pléiade ed. (Paris, 1951), I, pp. 649–717, esp. p. 717; also about *Fanny,* E. Montégut, "Le roman intime de la littérature réaliste," *Revue des deux mondes* 18 (1858), pp. 196–213, esp. pp. 201 and 209 ff. [Au.]

[26] As Baudelaire declares, *Oeuvres complètes,* p. 996: "for since the disappearance of Balzac . . . all curiosity relative to the novel has been pacified and put to rest." [Au.]

be cast of English steel it would function no differently than Monsieur Flaubert[27]—must have shocked the same audience that was offered the provocative contents of *Fanny* in the inviting tone of a confessional novel. It could also find incorporated in Feydeau's descriptions the modish ideals and surpressed desires of a stylish level of society,[28] and could delight without restraint in the lascivious central scene which Fanny (without suspecting that her lover is watching from the balcony) seduces her husband—for the moral indignation was already diminished for them through the reaction of the unhappy witness. As *Madame Bovary,* however, became a worldwide success, when at first it was understood and appreciated as a turning-point in the history of the novel by only a small circle of connoisseurs, the audience of novel-readers that was formed by it came to sanction the new canon of expectations; this canon made Feydeau's weaknesses—his flowery style, his modish effects, his lyrical-confessional cliches—unbearable, and allowed *Fanny* to fade into yesterday's bestseller.

IX

Thesis 4. The reconstruction of the horizon of expectations, in the face of which a work was created and received in the past, enables one on the other hand to pose questions that the text gave an answer to, and thereby to discover how the contemporary reader could have viewed and understood the work. This approach corrects the mostly unrecognized norms of a classicist or modernizing understanding of art, and avoids the circular recourse to a general "spirit of the age." It brings to view the hermeneutic difference between the former and the current understanding of a work; it raises to consciousness the history of its reception, which mediates both positions; and it thereby calls into question as a platonizing dogma of philological metaphysics the apparently self-evident claims that in the literary text, literature [Dichtung] is eternally present, and that its objective meaning, determined once and for all, is at all times immediately accessible to the interpreter.

THE METHOD of historical reception[29] is indispensable for the understanding of literature from the distant past. When the author of a work is unknown, his intent undeclared, and his relationship to sources and models only indirectly accessible, the philological question of how the text is "properly"—that is, "from its intention and time"—to be understood can best be answered if one foregrounds it against those works that the author explicitly or implicitly presupposed his contemporary audience to know. The creator of the oldest branches of the *Roman de Renart,* for example, assumes—as his prologue testifies—that his listeners know romances like the story of Troy and *Tristan,* heroic epics (*chansons de geste*), and verse fables (*fabliaux*), and that they are therefore curious about the "unprecedented war between the two barons, Renart and Ysengrin," which is to overshadow everything already known. The works and genres that are evoked are then all ironically touched on in the course of the narrative. From this horizonal change one can probably also explain the public success,

[27] For these and other contemporary verdicts see H. R. Jauss, "Die beiden Fassungen von Flauberts *Education sentimentale,*" *Heidelberger Jahrbücher* 2 (1958), pp. 96–116, esp. p. 97. [Au.]

[28] On this, see the excellent analysis by the contemporary critic E. Montégut (see note 25 above), who explains in detail why the dream-world and the figures in Feydeau's novel are typical for the audience in the neighborhoods "between the Bourse and the boulevard Montmartre" (p. 209) that needs an "alcool poétique," enjoys "seeing their vulgar adventures of yesterday and their vulgar projects of tomorrow poeticized" (p. 210), and subscribes to an "idolatry of the material," by which Montégut understands the ingredients of the "dream factory" of 1858—"a sort of sanctimonious admiration, almost devout, for furniture, wallpaper, dress, escapes like a perfume of patchouli from each of its pages" (p. 201). [Au.]

[29] Examples of this method, which not only follow the success, fame, and influence of a writer through history but also examine the historical conditions and changes in understanding him, are rare. The following should be mentioned: G. F. Ford, *Dickens and His Readers* (Princeton, 1955); A. Nisin, *Les Oeuvres et les siècles* (Paris, 1960), which discusses "Virgile, Dante et nous," Ronsard, Corneille, Racine; E. Lämmert, "Zur Wirkungsgeschichte Eichendorffs in Deutschland," *Festschrift für Richard Alewyn,* ed. H. Singer and B. von Wiese (Cologne and Graz, 1967). The methodological problem of the step from the influence to the reception of a work was indicated most sharply by F. Vodička already in 1941 in his study "Die Problematik der Rezeption von Nerudas Werk" (now in *Struktur vývoje* Prague, 1969) with the question of the changes in the work that are realized in its successive aesthetic perceptions. [Au.]

reaching far beyond France, of this rapidly famous work that for the first time took a position opposed to all the long-reigning heroic and courtly poetry.[30]

Philological research long misunderstood the originally satiric intention of the medieval *Reineke Fuchs* and, along with it, the ironic-didactic meaning of the analogy between animal and human natures, because ever since Jacob Grimm it had remained trapped within the romantic notion of pure nature poetry and naive animal tales. Thus, to give yet a second example of modernizing norms, one could also rightly reproach French research into the epic since Bédier for living—unconsciously—by the criteria of Boileau's poetics, and judging a nonclassical literature by the norms of simplicity, harmony of part and whole, probability, and still others.[31] The philological-critical method is obviously not protected by its historical objectivism from the interpreter who, supposedly bracketing himself, nonetheless raises his own aesthetic preconceptions to an unacknowledged norm and unreflectively modernizes the meaning of the past text. Whoever believes that the "timelessly true" meaning of a literary work must immediately, and simply through one's mere absorption in the text, disclose itself to the interpreter as if he had a standpoint outside of history and beyond all "errors" of his predecessors and of the historical reception—whoever believes this "conceals the involvement of the historical consciousness itself in the history of influence." He denies "those presuppositions—certainly not arbitrary but rather fundamental—that govern his own understanding," and can only feign an objectivity "that in truth depends upon the legitimacy of the questions asked."[32]

In *Truth and Method* Hans-Georg Gadamer, whose critique of historical objectivism I am assuming here, described the principle of the history of influence, which seeks to present the reality of history in understanding itself,[33] as an application of the logic of question and answer to the historical tradition. In a continuation of Collingwood's thesis that "one can understand a text only when one has understood the question to which it is an answer,"[34] Gadamer demonstrates that the reconstructed question can no longer stand within its original horizon because this historical horizon is always already enveloped within the horizon of the present: "Understanding is always the process of the fusion of these horizons that we suppose to exist by themselves."[35] The historical question cannot exist for itself; it must merge with the question "that the tradition is for us."[36] One thereby solves the question with which René Wellek described the aporia of literary judgment: should the philologist evaluate a literary work according to the perspective of the past, the standpoint of the present, or the "verdict of the ages"?[37] The actual standards of a past could be so narrow that their use would only make poorer a work that in the history of its influence had unfolded a rich semantic potential. The aesthetic judgment of the present would favor a canon of works that correspond to modern taste, but would unjustly evaluate all other works only because their function in their time is no longer evident. And the history of influence itself, as instructive as it might be, is as "authority open to the same objections as the authority of the author's contemporaries."[38] Wellek's conclusion—that there is no possibility of avoiding our own judgment; one must only make this judgment as objective as possible in that one does what every scholar does, namely, "isolate the object"[39]—is no solution to the aporia, but rather a relapse into objectivism. The "verdict of the ages" on a literary work is more than merely "the accumulated judgment of other readers, critics, viewers, and even professors";[40] it is the successive unfolding of the potential for meaning that is embedded in a work and actualized in the stages of its historical reception as it discloses itself to understanding judgment, so long as this faculty achieves in a controlled fashion the "fusion of horizons" in the encounter with the tradition.

[30] See H. R. Jauss, *Untersuchungen zur mittelalterlichen Tierdichtung* (Tübingen, 1959), esp. chap. IV A and D. [Au.]

[31] A. Vinaver, "A la recherche d'une poétique médiévale," *Cahiers de civilisation médiévale* 2 (1959), 1–16. [Au.]

[32] Gadamer, *Wahrheit und Methode*, pp. 284, 285; Eng., p. 268. [Au.]

[33] *Ibid.*, p. 283; Eng., p. 267. [Au.]. See Gadamer. [Eds.]

[34] *Ibid.*, p. 352; Eng., p. 333. [Au.]

[35] *Ibid.*, p. 289; Eng., p. 273. [Au.]

[36] *Ibid.*, p. 356; Eng., p. 337. [Au.]

[37] Wellek, 1936, p. 184; *ibid.*, "The Concept of Evolution in Literary History," *Concepts of Criticism* (New Haven, 1963), pp. 17–20. [Au.]

[38] *Ibid.*, p. 17. [Au.]

[39] *Ibid.*, [Au.]

[40] *Ibid.*, [Au.]

The agreement between my attempt to establish a possible literary history on the basis of an aesthetics of reception and H.-G. Gadamer's principle of the history of influence nonetheless reaches its limit where Gadamer would like to elevate the concept of the classical to the status of prototype for all historical mediation of past with present. His definition, that "what we call 'classical' does not first require the overcoming of historical distance—for in its own constant mediation it achieves this overcoming,"[41] falls out of the relationship of question and answer that is constitutive of all historical tradition. If classical is "what says something to the present as if it were actually said to it,"[42] then for the classical text one would not first seek the question to which it gives an answer. Doesn't the classical, which "signifies itself and interprets itself,"[43] merely describe the result of what I called the "second horizonal change": the unquestioned, self-evident character of the so-called "masterwork," which conceals its original negativity within the retrospective horizon of an exemplary tradition, and which necessitates our regaining the "right horizon of questioning" once again in the face of the confirmed classicism? Even with the classical work, the receiving consciousness is not relieved of the task of recognizing the "tensional relationship between the text and the present."[44] The concept of the classical that interprets itself, taken over from Hegel, must lead to a reversal of the historical relationship of question and answer,[45] and contradicts the principle of the history of influence that understanding is "not merely a reproductive, but always a productive attitude as well."[46]

This contradiction is evidently conditioned by Gadamer's holding fast to a concept of classical art that is not capable of serving as a general foundation for an aesthetics of reception beyond the period of its origination, namely, that of humanism. It is the concept of *mimesis,* understood as "recognition," as Gadamer demonstrates in his ontological explanation of the experience of art: "What one actually experiences in a work of art and what one is directed toward is rather how true it is, that is, to what extent one knows and recognizes something and oneself."[47] This concept of art can be validated for the humanist period of art, but not for its preceding medieval period and not at all for its succeeding period of our modernity, in which the aesthetics of mimesis has lost its obligatory character, along with the substantialist metaphysics ("knowledge of essence") that founded it. The epistemological significance of art does not, however, come to an end with this period-change, whence it becomes evident that art was in no way bound to the classical function of recognition.[48] The work of art can also mediate knowledge that does not fit into the Platonic schema if it anticipates paths of future experience, imagines as-yet-untested models of perception and behavior, or contains an answer to newly posed questions.[49] It is precisely concerning this virtual significance and productive function in the process of experience that the history of the influence of literature is abbreviated when one gathers the mediation of past art and the present under the concept of the *classical.* If, according to Gadamer, the classical *itself* is supposed to achieve the overcoming of historical distance through its constant mediation, it must, as a perspective of the hypostatized tradition, displace the insight that classical art at the time of its production did not yet appear "classical": rather, it could open up new ways of seeing things and preform new experiences that only in historical distance—in the recognition of what is now familiar—give rise to the appearance that a timeless truth expresses itself in the work of art.

The influence of even the great literary works of the past can be compared neither with a self-mediating event nor with an emanation: the tradi-

[41] *Wahrheit und Methode,* p. 274; Eng., p. 257. [Au.]

[42] *Ibid.,* [Au.]

[43] *Ibid.,* [Au.]

[44] *Ibid.,* p. 290; Eng., p. 273. [Au.]

[45] This reversal becomes obvious in the chapter "Die Logik von Frage und Antwort" (*ibid.,* pp. 351–60; Eng., pp. 333–41); see my "History of Art and Pragmatic History," Chapter 2 of *Toward an Aesthetics of Reception.* [Au.]

[46] *Ibid.,* p. 280; Eng., p. 264. [Au.]

[47] *Ibid.,* p. 109; Eng., p. 102. [Au.]

[48] See *ibid.,* p. 110; Eng., p. 103. [Au.]

[49] This also follows from Formalist aesthetics and especially from Viktor Shklovsky's theory of "deautomatization"; cf. Victor Erlich's summary, *Russian Formalism,* p. 76: "As the 'twisted, deliberately impeded form' interposes artificial obstacles between the perceiving subject and the object perceived, the chain of habitual association and of automatic responses is broken: thus, we become able to *see* things instead of merely *recognizing* them." [Au.]

tion of art also presupposes a dialogical relationship of the present to the past, according to which the past work can answer and "say something" to us only when the present observer has posed the question that draws it back out of its seclusion. When, in *Truth and Method,* understanding is conceived—analogous to Heidegger's "event of being" [*Seinsgeschehen*]—as "the placing of oneself within a process of tradition in which past and present are constantly mediated,"[50] the "productive moment which lies in understanding"[51] must be shortchanged. This productive function of progressive understanding, which necessarily also includes criticizing the tradition and forgetting it, shall in the following sections establish the basis for the project of a literary history according to an aesthetics of reception. This project must consider the historicity of literature in a threefold manner: diachronically in the interrelationships of the reception of literary works (see X), synchronically in the frame of reference of literature of the same moment, as well as in the sequence of such frames (see XI), and finally in the relationship of the immanent literary development to the general process of history (see XII).

X

Thesis 5. The theory of the aesthetics of reception not only allows one to conceive the meaning and form of a literary work in the historical unfolding of its understanding. It also demands that one insert the individual work into its "literary series" to recognize its historical position and significance in the context of the experience of literature. In the step from a history of the reception of works to an eventful history of literature, the latter manifests itself as a process in which the passive reception is on the part of authors. Put another way, the next work can solve formal and moral problems left behind by the last work, and present new problems in turn.

HOW CAN the individual work, which positivistic literary history determined in a chronological series and thereby reduced to the status of a "fact," be brought back into its historical-sequential relationship and thereby once again be understood as an "event"? The theory of the Formalist school, as already mentioned, would solve this problem with its principle of "literary evolution," according to which the new work arises against the background of preceding or competing works, reaches the "high point" of a literary period as a successful form, is quickly reproduced and thereby increasingly automatized, until finally, when the next form has broken through, the former vegetates on as a used-up genre in the quotidian sphere of literature. If one were to analyze and describe a literary period according to this program—which to date has hardly been put into use[52]—one could expect a representation that would in various respects be superior to that of the conventional literary history. Instead of the works standing in closed series, themselves standing one after another and unconnected, at best framed by a sketch of general history—for example, the series of the works of an author, a particular school, or one kind of style, as well as the series of various genres—the Formalist method would relate the series to one another and *discover the evolutionary alternating relationship of functions and forms.*[53] The works that thereby stand out from, correspond to, or replace one another would appear as moments of a process that no longer needs to be construed as tending toward some end point, since as the *dialectical self-production of new forms* it requires no teleology. Seen in this way, the autonomous dynamics of literary evolution would furthermore eliminate the dilemma of the criteria of selection: the criterion here is the work as a new form in the literary series, and not the self-reproduction of worn-out forms, artistic devices, and genres, which pass into the background until at a new moment in the evolution they are made "perceptible" once again. Finally, in the Formalist project of a literary history that understands itself as "evolution" and—contrary to the usual sense of this term—excludes any

[50] *Wahrheit und Methode,* p. 275; Eng., p. 258. [Au.]
[51] *Ibid.,* p. 280; Eng., p. 264. [Au.]

[52] In the 1927 article, "Uber literarische Evolution," by Jurij Tynjanov (in *Die literarischen Kunstmittel und die Evolution in der Literatur,* pp. 37–60), this program is most pregnantly presented. It was only partially fulfilled—as Jurij Striedter informed me—in the treatment of problems of structural change in the history of literary genres, as for example in the volume *Russkaja proza,* Voprosy poètiki 8 (Leningrad, 1926), or J. Tynjanov, "Die Ode als rhetorische Gattung" (1922), now in *Texte der russischen Formalisten,* II, ed. J. Striedter (Munich, 1970). [Au.]
[53] J. Tynjanov, "Über literarische Evolution," p. 59. [Au.]

directional course, the historical character of a work becomes synonymous with literature's historical character: the "evolutionary" significance and characteristics of a literary phenomenon presuppose innovation as the decisive feature, just as a work of art is perceived against the background of other works of art.[54]

The Formalist theory of "literary evolution" is certainly one of the most significant attempts at a renovation of literary history. The recognition that historical changes also occur within a system in the field of literature, the attempted functionalization of literary development, and, not least of all, the theory of automatization—these are achievements that are to be held onto, even if the one-sided canonization of change requires a correction. Criticism has already displayed the weaknesses of the Formalist theory of evolution: mere opposition or aesthetic variation does not suffice to explain the growth of literature; the question of the direction of change of literary forms remains unanswerable; innovation for itself does not alone make up artistic character; and the connection between literary evolution and social change does not vanish from the face of the earth through its mere negation.[55] My thesis XII responds to the last question; the problematic of the remaining questions demands that the descriptive literary theory of the Formalists be opened up, through an aesthetics of reception, to the dimension of historical experience that must also include the historical standpoint of the present observer, that is, the literary historian.

The description of literary evolution as a ceaseless struggle between the new and the old, or as the alternation of the canonization and automatization of forms reduces the historical character of literature to the one-dimensional actuality of its changes and limits historical understanding to their perception. The alterations in the literary series nonetheless only become a historical sequence when the opposition of the old and new form also allows one to recognize their specific mediation. This mediation, which includes the step from the old to the new form in the interaction of work and recipient (audience, critic, new producer) as well as that of past event and successive reception, can be methodologically grasped in the formal and substantial problem "that each work of art, as the horizon of the 'solutions' which are possible after it, poses and leaves behind."[56] The mere description of the altered structure and the new artistic devices of a work does not necessarily lead to this problem, nor, therefore, back to its function in the historical series. To determine this, that is, to recognize the problem left behind to which the new work in the historical series is the answer, the interpreter must bring his own experience into play, since the past horizon of old and new forms, problems and solutions, is only recognizable in its further mediation, within the present horizon of the received work. Literary history as "literary evolution" presupposes the historical process of aesthetic reception and production up to the observer's present as the condition for the mediation of all formal oppositions or "differential qualities" ["*Differenzqualitäten*"].[57]

Founding "literary evolution" on an aesthetics of reception thus not only returns its lost direction insofar as the standpoint of the literary historian becomes the vanishing point—but not the goal!—of the process. It also opens to view the temporal depths of literary experience, in that it allows one to recognize the variable distance between the actual and the virtual significance of a literary work. This means that the artistic character of a work, whose semantic potential Formalism reduces to innovation as the single criterion of value, must in no way always be immediately perceptible within the horizon of its first appearance, let alone that it could then also already be exhausted in the pure opposition between the old and the new form. The distance between the actual first perception of a work and its virtual significance, or, put another way, the resistance that the new work poses to the expectations

[54] "A work of art will appear as a positive value when it regroups the structure of the preceding period, it will appear as a negative value if it takes over the structure without changing it." (Jan Mukařovský, cited by R. Wellek, 1963, pp. 48, 49.) [Au.]

[55] See V. Erlich, *Russian Formalism,* pp. 254–57, R. Wellek, 1963, pp. 48 ff., and J. Striedter, *Texte der russischen Formalisten,* I, Introduction, § X. [Au.]

[56] Hans Blumenberg, in *Poetik und Hermeneutik 3* (see note 18), p. 692. [Au.]

[57] According to V. Erlich, *Russian Formalism,* p. 252, this concept meant three things to the Formalists: "on the level of the representation of reality, *Differenzqualität* stood for the 'divergence' from the actual, i.e., for creative deformation. On the level of language it meant a departure from current linguistic usage. Finally, on the place of literary dynamics, a . . . modification of the prevailing artistic norm." [Au.]

of its first audience, can be so great that it requires a long process of reception to gather in that which was unexpected and unusable within the first horizon. It can thereby happen that a virtual significance of the work remains long unrecognized until the "literary evolution," through the actualization of a newer form, reaches the horizon that now for the first time allows one to find access to the understanding of the misunderstood older form. Thus the obscure lyrics of Mallarmé and his school prepared the ground for the return to baroque poetry, long since unappreciated and therefore forgotten, and in particular for the philological reinterpretation and "rebirth" of Góngora. One can line up the examples of how a new literary form can reopen access to forgotten literature. These include the so-called "renaissances"—so-called, because the word's meaning gives rise to the appearance of an automatic return, and often prevents one from recognizing that literary tradition can not transmit itself alone. That is, a literary past can return only when a new reception draws it back into the present, whether an altered aesthetic attitude willfully reaches back to reappropriate the past, or an unexpected light falls back on forgotten literature from the new moment of literary evolution, allowing something to be found that one previously could not have sought in it.[58]

The new is thus not only an *aesthetic* category. It is not absorbed into the factors of innovation, surprise, surpassing, rearrangement, or alienation, to which the Formalist theory assigned exclusive importance. The new also becomes a *historical* category when the diachronic analysis of literature is pushed further to ask which historical moments are really the ones that first make new that which is new in a literary phenomenon; to what degree this new element is already perceptible in the historical instant of its emergence; which distance, path, or detour of understanding were required for its realization in content; and whether the moment of its full actualization was so influential that it could alter the perspective on the old, and thereby the canonization of the literary past.[59] How the relationship of poetic theory to aesthetically productive praxis is represented in this light has already been discussed in another context.[60] The possibilities of the interaction between production and reception in the historical change of aesthetic attitudes are admittedly far from exhausted by these remarks. Here they should above all illustrate the dimension into which a diachronic view of literature leads when it would no longer be satisfied to consider a chronological series of literary facts as already the historical appearance of literature.

XI

Thesis 6. The achievements made in linguistics through the distinction and methodological interrelation of diachronic and synchronic analysis are the occasion for overcoming the diachronic perspective—previously the only one practiced—in literary history as well. If the perspective of the history of reception always bumps up against the functional connections between the understanding of new works and the significance of older ones when changes in aesthetic attitudes are considered, it must also be possible to take a synchronic cross-section of a moment in the development, to arrange the heterogeneous multiplicity of contemporaneous works in equivalent, opposing, and hierarchical structures, and thereby to discover an overarching system of relationships in the literature of a historical moment. From this the principle of representation of a new literary history could be developed, if further cross-sections diachronically before and after were so arranged as to articulate historically the change in literary structures in its epoch-making moments.

SIEGFRIED Kracauer has most decisively questioned the primacy of the diachronic perspective in histo-

[58] For the first possibility the (antiromantic) reevaluation of Boileau and of the classical *contrainte* poetics by Gide and Valéry can be introduced; for the second, the belated discovery of Hölderlin's hymns or Novalis's concept of future poetry (on the latter see H. R. Jauss in *Romanische Forschungen* 77 [1965], pp. 174–83). [Au.]

[59] Thus, since the reception of the "minor romantic" Nerval, whose *Chimères* only attracted attention under the influence of Mallarmé, the canonized "major romantics" Lamartine, Vigny, Musset and a large part of the "rhetorical" lyrics of Victor Hugo have been increasingly forced into the background. [Au.]

[60] *Poetik und Hermeneutik 2 (Immanente Ästhetik—Ästhetische Reflexion)*, ed. W. Iser (Munich, 1966), esp. pp. 395–418. [Au.]

riography. His study "Time and History"[61] disputes the claim of "General History" to render comprehensible events from all spheres of life within a homogeneous medium of chronological time as a unified process, consistent in each historical moment. This understanding of history, still standing under the influence of Hegel's concept of the "objective spirit," presupposes that everything that happens contemporaneously is equally informed by the significance of this moment, and it thereby conceals the actual noncontemporaneity of the contemporaneous.[62] For the multiplicity of events of one historical moment, which the universal historian believes can be understood as exponents of a unified content, are de facto moments of entirely different time-curves, conditioned by the laws of their "special history,"[63] as becomes immediately evident in the discrepancies of the various "histories" of the arts, law, economics, politics, and so forth: "The shaped times of the diverse areas overshadow the uniform flow of time. Any historical period must therefore be imagined as a mixture of events which emerge at different moments of their own time."[64]

It is not in question here whether this state of affairs presupposes a primary inconsistency to history, so that the consistency of general history always only arises retrospectively from the unifying viewpoint and representation of the historian; or whether the radical doubt concerning "historical reason," which Kracauer extends from the pluralism of chronological and morphological courses of time to the fundamental antinomy of the general and the particular in history, in fact proves that universal history is philosophically illegitimate today. For the sphere of literature in any case, one can say that Kracauer's insights into the "coexistence of the contemporaneous and non-contemporaneous,"[65] far from leading historical knowledge into an aporia, rather make apparent the necessity and possibility of discovering the historical dimension of literary phenomena in synchronic cross-sections. For it follows from these insights that the chronological fiction of the moment that informs all contemporaneous phenomena corresponds as little to the historicity of literature as does the morphological fiction of a homogeneous literary series, in which all phenomena in their sequential order only follow immanent laws. The purely diachronic perspective, however conclusively it might explain changes in, for example, the histories of genres according to the immanent logic of innovation and automatization, problem and solution, nonetheless only arrives at the properly historical dimension when it breaks through the morphological canon, to confront the work that is important in historical influence with the historically worn-out, conventional works of the genre, and at the same time does not ignore its relationship to the literary milieu in which it had to make its way alongside works of other genres.

The historicity of literature comes to light at the intersections of diachrony and synchrony. Thus it must also be possible to make the literary horizon of a specific historical moment comprehensible as that synchronic system in relation to which literature that appears contemporaneously could be received diachronically in relations of noncontemporaneity, and the work could be received as current or not, as modish, outdated, or perennial, as premature or belated.[66] For if, from the point of view of

[61] In *Zeugnisse—Theodor W. Adorno zum 60. Geburtstag* (Frankfurt a.M., 1963), pp. 50–64, and also in "General History and the Aesthetic Approach," *Poetik und Hermeneutik* 3. See also *History: The Last Things Before the Last* (New York, 1969), esp. chap. 6: "Ahasuerus, or the Riddle of Time," pp. 139–63. [Au.]

[62] "First, in identifying history as a process in chronological time, we tacitly assume that our knowledge of the moment at which an event emerges from the flow of time will help us to account for its appearance. The date of the event is a value-laden fact. Accordingly, all events in the history of a people, a nation, or a civilization that take place at a given moment are supposed to occur then and there for reasons bound up, somehow, with that moment" (Kracauer, *History,* p. 141). [Au.]

[63] This concept goes back to H. Foccillon, *The Life of Forms in Art* (New York, 1948), and G. Kubler, *The Shape of Time: Remarks on the History of Things* (New Haven, 1962). [Au.]

[64] Kracauer, *History,* p. 53. [Au.]

[65] *Poetik und Hermeneutik* 3, p. 569. The formula of "the contemporaneity of the different," with which F. Sengle, "Aufgaben der heutigen Literaturgeschichtsschreibung," 1964, pp. 247 ff., refers to the same phenomenon, fails to grasp one dimension of the problem, which becomes evident in his belief that this difficulty of literary history can be solved by simply combining comparative methods and modern interpretation ("that is, carrying out comparative interpretation on a broader basis," p. 249). [Au.]

[66] In 1960 Roman Jakobson also made this claim in a lecture that now constitutes chap. 11, "Linguistique et poétique," of his book, *Essais de linguistique générale* (Paris, 1963). Cf. p. 212: "Synchronic description en-

an aesthetics of production, literature that appears contemporaneously breaks down into a heterogeneous multiplicity of the noncontemporaneous, that is, of works informed by the various moments of the "shaped time" of their genre (as the seemingly present heavenly constellations move apart astronomically into points of the most different temporal distance), this multiplicity of literary phenomena nonetheless, when seen from the point of view of an aesthetics of reception, coalesces again for the audience that perceives them and relates them to one another as works of *its* present, in the unity of a common horizon of literary expectations, memories, and anticipations that establishes their significance.

Since each synchronic system must contain its past and its future as inseparable structural elements,[67] the synchronic cross-section of the literary production of a historical point in time necessarily implies further cross-sections that are diachronically before and after. Analogous to the history of language, constant and variable factors are thereby brought to light that can be localized as functions of a system. For literature as well is a kind of grammar or syntax, with relatively fixed relations of its own: the arrangement of the traditional and the uncanonized genres; modes of expression, kinds of style, and rhetorical figures; contrasted with this arrangement is the much more variable realm of a semantics: the literary subjects, archetypes, symbols, and metaphors. One can therefore seek to erect for literary history an analogy to that which Hans Blumenberg has postulated for the history of philosophy, elucidating it through examples of the change in periods and, in particular, the successional relationship of Christian theology and philosophy, and grounding it in his historical logic of question and answer: a "formal system of the explanation of the world . . . , within which structure the reshufflings can be localized which make up the process-like character of history up to the radicality of period-changes."[68] Once the substantialist notion of a self-reproducing literary tradition has been overcome through a functional explanation of the processlike relationships of production and reception, it must also be possible to recognize behind the *transformation* of literary forms and contents those *reshufflings* in a literary system of world-understanding that make the horizonal change in the process of aesthetic experience comprehensible.

From these premises one could develop the principle of representation of a literary history that would neither have to follow the all too familiar high road of the traditional great books, nor have to lose itself in the lowlands of the sum-total of all texts that can no longer be historically articulated. The problem of selecting that which is important for a new history of literature can be solved with the help of the synchronic perspective in a manner that has not yet been attempted: a horizonal change in the historical process of "literary evolution" need not be pursued only throughout the web of all the diachronic facts and filiations, but can also be established in the altered remains of the synchronic literary system and read out of further cross-sectional analyses. In principle, a representation of literature in the historical succession of such systems would be possible through a series of arbitrary points of intersection between diachrony and synchrony. The historical dimension of literature, its eventful continuity that is lost in traditionalism as in positivism, can meanwhile be recovered only if the literary historian finds points of intersection and brings works to light that articulate the processlike character of "literary evolution" in its moments formative of history as well as its caesurae between periods. But neither statistics nor the subjective willfulness of the literary historian decides on this historical articulation, but rather the history of influence: that "which results from the event" and which from the perspective of the present constitutes the coherence of literature as the prehistory of its present manifestation.

visages not only the literary production of a given period, but also that part of the literary tradition which has remained alive or been resuscitated in the period in question. . . . Historical poetics, exactly like the history of language, if it wants to be truly comprehensive, ought to be conceived as a superstructure built upon a series of successive synchronic descriptions." [Au.]

[67] Jurij Tynjanov and Roman Jakobson, "Probleme der Literatur- und Sprachforschung" (1928), now in *Kursbuch* 5 (Frankfurt a.M., 1966), p. 75: "The history of the system itself represents another system. Pure synchrony now proves to be illusory: each synchronic system has its past and its future as inseparable structural elements of this system." [Au.]

[68] First in "Epochenschwelle und Rezeption," *Philosophische Rundschau* 6 (1958), pp. 101 ff., most recently in *Die Legitimatät der Neuzeit* (Frankfurt a.M., 1966); see esp. pp. 41 ff. [Au.]

XII

Thesis 7. The task of literary history is thus only completed when literary production is not only represented synchronically and diachronically in the succession of its systems, but also seen as "special history" in its own unique relationship to "general history." This relationship does not end with the fact that a typified, idealized, satiric, or utopian image of social existence can be found in the literature of all times. The social function of literature manifests itself in its genuine possibility only where the literary experience of the reader enters into the horizon of expectations of his lived praxis, preforms his understanding of the world, and thereby also has an effect on his social behavior.

THE functional connection between literature and society is for the most part demonstrated in traditional literary sociology within the narrow boundaries of a method that has only superficially replaced the classical principle of *imitatio naturae* with the determination that literature is the representation of a pregiven reality, which therefore must elevate a concept of style conditioned by a particular period—the "realism" of the nineteenth century—to the status of the literary category par excellence. But even the literary "structuralism" now fashionable,[69] which appeals, often with dubious justification, to the archetypal criticism of Northrop Frye or to the structural anthropology of Claude Lévi-Strauss, still remains quite dependent on this basically classicist aesthetics of representation with its schematizations of "reflection" [*Wiederspiegelung*] and "typification." By interpreting the findings of linguistic and literary structuralism as archaic anthropological constants disguised in literary myths—which it not infrequently manages only with the help of an obvious allegorization of the text[70]—it reduces on the one hand historical existence to the structures of an original social nature, on the other hand literature to this nature's mythic or symbolic expression. But with this viewpoint, it is precisely the eminently social, i.e., socially *formative* function of literature that is missed. Literary structuralism—as little as the Marxist and Formalist literary studies that came before it—does not inquire as to how literature "itself turns around to help inform . . . the idea of society which it presupposes" and has helped to inform the processlike character of history. With these words, Gerhard Hess formulated in his lecture on "The Image of Society in French Literature" (1954) the unsolved problem of a union of literary history and sociology, and then explained to what extent French literature, in the course of its modern development, could claim for itself to have first discovered certain law-governed characteristics of social existence.[71] To answer the question of the socially formative function of literature according to an aesthetics of reception exceeds the competence of the traditional aesthetics of representation. The attempt to close the gap between literary-historical and sociological research through the methods of an aesthetics of reception is made easier because the concept of the *horizon of expectations* that I introduced into literary-historical interpretation[72] also has played a role in the axiomatics of the social sciences since Karl Mannheim.[73] It likewise stands in the center of a methodological essay on "Natural Laws and Theoretical Systems" by Karl R. Popper, who would anchor the scientific formation of theory in the prescientific experience of lived praxis. Popper here develops the problem of observation from out of the presupposition of a "horizon of expectations," thereby offering a basis of comparison for my attempt to determine the specific achievement of literature in the general process of the formation of experience, and to delimit it vis-à-vis other forms of social behavior.[74]

[69] N.B. This was composed in 1967. (Tr.)

[70] Lévi-Strauss himself testifies to this involuntarily but extremely impressively in his attempt to "interpret" with the help of his structural method a linguistic description of Baudelaire's poem "Les chats" provided by Roman Jakobson. See *L'Homme* 2 (1962), pp. 5–21; Eng. in *Structuralism,* ed. Jacques Ehrmann (Garden City, N.Y., 1971), a reprint of *Yale French Studies* nos. 36–37 (1966). [Au.]

[71] Now in *Gesellschaft—Literatur—Wissenschaft: Gesammelte Schriften 1938–1966,* eds. H. R. Jauss and C. Müller-Daehn (Munich, 1967), pp. 1–13, esp. pp. 2 and 4. [Au.]

[72] First in *Untersuchungen zur mittelalterlichen Tierdichtung,* see pp. 153, 180, 225, 271; further in *Archiv für das Studium der neueren Sprachen* 197 (1961), pp. 223–25. [Au.]

[73] Karl Mannheim, *Mensch und Gesellschaft in Zeitalter des Umbaus* (Darmstadt, 1958), pp. 212 ff. [Au.]

[74] In *Theorie und Realität,* ed. H. Albert (Tübingen, 1964), pp. 87–102. [Au.]

According to Popper, progress in science has in common with prescientific experience the fact that each hypothesis, like each observation, always presupposes expectations, "namely those that constitute the horizon of expectations which first makes those observations significant and thereby grants them the status of observations."[75] For progress in science as for that in the experience of life, the most important moment is the "disappointment of expectations": "It resembles the experience of a blind person, who runs into an obstacle and thereby experiences its existence. Through the falsification of our assumptions we actually make contact with 'reality.' The refutation of our errors is the positive experience that we gain from reality."[76] This model certainly does not sufficiently explain the process of the scientific formation of theory,[77] and yet it can well illustrate the "productive meaning of negative experience" in lived praxis,[78] as well as shed a clearer light upon the specific function of literature in social existence. For the reader is privileged above the (hypothetical) nonreader because the reader—to stay with Popper's image—does not first have to bump into a new obstacle to gain a new experience of reality. The experience of reading can liberate one from adaptations, prejudices, and predicaments of a lived praxis in that it compels one to a new perception of things. The horizon of expectations of literature distinguishes itself before the horizon of expectations of historical lived praxis in that it not only preserves actual experiences, but also anticipates unrealized possibility, broadens the limited space of social behavior for new desires, claims, and goals, and thereby opens paths of future experience.

The pre-orientation of our experience through the creative capability of literature rests not only on its artistic character, which by virtue of a new form helps one to break through the automatism of everyday perception. The new form of art is not only "perceived against the background of other art works and through association with them." In this famous sentence, which belongs to the core of the Formalist credo, Viktor Shklovsky remains correct only insofar as he turns against the prejudice of classicist aesthetics that defines the beautiful as *harmony of form and content* and accordingly reduces the new form of the secondary function of giving shape to a pregiven content. The new form, however, does not appear just "in order to relieve the old form that already is no longer artistic." It also can make possible a new perception of things by preforming the content of a new experience first brought to light in the form of literature. The relationship between literature and reader can actualize itself in the sensorial realm as an incitement to aesthetic perception as well as in the ethical realm as a summons to moral reflection.[79] The new literary work is received and judged against the background of other works of art as well as against the background of the everyday experience of life. Its social function in the ethical realm is to be grasped according to an aesthetics of reception in the same modalities of question and answer, problem and so-

[75] *Ibid.*, p. 91. [Au.]

[76] *Ibid.*, p. 102. [Au.]

[77] Popper's example of the blind man does not distinguish between the two possibilities of a merely reactive behavior and an experimenting mode of action under specific hypotheses. If the second possibility characterizes reflected scientific behavior in distinction to the unreflected behavior in lived praxis, the researcher would be "creative" on his part, and thus to be placed above the "blind man" and more appropriately compared with the writer as a creator of new expectations. [Au.]

[78] G. Buck, *Lernen und Erfahrung*, pp. 70 ff. "[Negative experience] has its instructive effect not only by causing us to revise the context of our subsequent experience so that the new fits into the corrected unity of an objective meaning. . . . Not only is the object of the experience differently represented, but the experiencing consciousness itself reverses itself. The work of negative experience is one of becoming conscious of oneself. What one becomes conscious of are the motifs which have been guiding experience and which have remained unquestioned in this guiding function. Negative experience thus has primarily the character of self-experience, which frees one for a qualitatively new kind of experience." From these premises Buck developed the concept of a hermeneutics, which, as a "relationship of lived praxis that is guided by the highest interest of lived praxis—the agent's self-information," legitimizes the specific experience of the so-called humanities [*Geisteswissenschaften*] in contrast to the empiricism of the natural sciences. See his "Bildung durch Wissenschaft," in *Wissenschaft, Bildung und pädagogische Wirklichkeit* (Heidenheim, 1969), p. 24. [Au.]

[79] Jurij Striedter has pointed out that in the diaries and examples from the prose of Leo Tolstoy to which Shklovsky referred in his first explanation of the procedure of "alienation," the purely aesthetic aspect was still bound up with an epistemological and ethical aspect. "Shklovsky was interested—in contrast to Tolstoy—above all in the artistic 'procedure' and not in the question of its ethical presuppositions and effects." (*Poetik und Hermeneutik* 2 [see note 60], pp. 288 ff.) [Au.]

lution, under which it enters into the horizon of its historical influence.

How a new aesthetic form can have moral consequences at the same time, or, put another way, how it can have the greatest conceivable impact on a moral question, is demonstrated in an impressive manner by the case of *Madame Bovary,* as reflected in the trial that was instituted against the author Flaubert after the prepublication of the work in the *Révue de Paris* in 1857. The new literary form that compelled Flaubert's audience to an unfamiliar perception of the "well-thumbed fable" was the principle of impersonal (or uninvolved) narration, in conjunction with the artistic device of the so-called *style indirect libre,* handled by Flaubert like a virtuoso and in a perspectively consequential manner. What is meant by this can be made clear with a quotation from the book, a description that the prosecuting attorney Pinard accused in his indictment as being immoral in the highest degree. In the novel it follows upon Emma's first "false step" and relates how she catches sight of herself in the mirror after her adultery:

> Seeing herself in the mirror she wondered at her face. Never had her eyes been so large, so black, or so deep. Something subtle spread about her being transfigured her.
>
> She repeated: "I have a lover! a lover!", delighting at the idea as at that of a second puberty that had come to her. So at last she was going to possess those joys of love, that fever of happiness of which she had despaired. She was entering upon something marvelous where all would be passion, ecstasy, delirium.

The prosecuting attorney took the last sentences for an objective depiction that included the judgment of the narrator and was upset over the "glorification of adultery" which he held to be even much more dangerous and immoral than the false step itself.[80] Yet Flaubert's accuser thereby succumbed to an error, as the defense immediately demonstrated. For the incriminating sentences are not any objective statement of the narrator's to which the reader can attribute belief, but rather a subjective opinion of the character, who is thereby to be characterized in her feelings that are formed according to novels. The artistic device consists in bringing forth a mostly inward discourse of the represented character without the signals of direct discourse ("So I am at last going to possess") or indirect discourse ("She said to herself that she was therefore at last going to possess"), with the effect that the reader himself has to decide whether he should take the sentence for a true declaration or understand it as an opinion characteristic of this character. Indeed, Emma Bovary is "judged, simply through a plain description of her existence, out of her own feelings."[81] This result of a modern stylistic analysis agrees exactly with the counterargument of the defense attorney Sénard, who emphasized that the disillusion began for Emma already from the second day onward: "The dénouement for morality is found in each line of the book"[82] (only that Sénard himself could not yet name the artistic device that was not yet recorded at this time!). The consternating effect of the formal innovations of Flaubert's narrative style became evident in the trial: the impersonal form of narration not only compelled his readers to perceive things differently—"photographically exact," according to the judgment of the time—but at the same time thrust them into an alienating uncertainty of judgment. Since the new artistic device broke through an old novelistic convention—the moral judgment of the represented characters that is always unequivocal and confirmed in the description—the novel was able to radicalize or to raise new questions of lived praxis, which during the proceedings caused the original occasion for the accusation—alleged lasciviousness—to recede wholly into the background. The question with which the defense went on its counterattack turned the reproach, that the novel provides nothing other than the "story of a provincial woman's adulteries," against the society: whether, then, the subtitle to *Madame Bovary* must not more properly read, "story of the education too often provided in the

[80] Flaubert, *Oeuvres,* I, p. 657: "thus, as early as this first mistake, as early as this first fall, she glorified adultery, its poetry, its voluptuousness. Voilà, gentlemen, what for me is much more dangerous, much more immoral than the fall itself!" [Au.]

[81] Erich Auerbach, *Mimesis: Dargestellte Wirklichkeit in der abendländischen Literatur* (Bern, 1946), p. 430; Eng., *Mimesis: The Representation of Reality in Western Literature,* trans. Willard R. Trask (Princeton, 1953), p. 485. [Au.]

[82] Flaubert, *Oeuvres,* I. p. 673. [Au.]

provinces."[83] But the question with which the prosecuting attorney's *réquisitoire* reaches its peak is nonetheless not yet thereby answered: "Who can condemn that woman in the book? No one. Such is the conclusion. In the book there is not a character who can condemn her. If you find a wise character there, if you find a single principle there by virtue of which the adultery might be stigmatized, I am in error."[84]

If in the novel none of the represented characters could break the staff across Emma Bovary, and if no moral principle can be found valid in whose name she would be condemnable, then is not the ruling "public opinion" and its basis in "religious feeling" at once called into question along with the "principle of marital fidelity"? Before what court could the case of *Madame Bovary* be brought if the formerly valid social norms—public opinion, religious sentiment, public morals, good manners—are no longer sufficient to reach a verdict in this case?[85] These open and implicit questions by no means indicate an aesthetic lack of understanding and moral philistinism on the part of the prosecuting attorney. Rather, it is much more that in them the unsuspected influence of a new art form comes to be expressed, which through a new *manière de voir les choses* was able to jolt the reader of *Madame Bovary* out of the self-evident character of his moral judgment, and turned a predecided question of public morals back into an open problem. In the face of the vexation that Flaubert, thanks to the artistry of his impersonal style, did not offer any handhold with which to ban his novel on grounds of the author's immorality, the court to that extent acted consistently when it acquitted Flaubert as writer, but condemned the literary school that he was supposed to represent, but that in truth was the as yet unrecognized artistic device:

> Whereas it is not permitted, under the pretext of portraying character and local color, to reproduce in their errors the facts, utterances and gestures of the characters whom the author's mission it is to portray; that a like system, applied to works of the spirit as well as to productions of the fine arts, leads to a realism which would be the negation of the beautiful and the good, and which, giving birth to works equally offensive to the eye and to the spirit, would commit continual offences against public morals and good manners.[86]

Thus a literary work with an unfamiliar aesthetic form can break through the expectations of its readers and at the same time confront them with a question, the solution to which remains lacking for them in the religiously or officially sanctioned morals. Instead of further examples, let one only recall here that it was not first Bertolt Brecht, but rather already the Enlightenment that proclaimed the competitive relationship between literature and canonized morals, as Friedrich Schiller not least of all bears witness to when he expressly claims for the bourgeois drama: "The laws of the stage begin where the sphere of worldly laws end."[87] But the literary work can also—and in the history of literature this possibility characterizes the latest period of our modernity—reverse the relationship of question and answer and in the medium of art confront the reader with a new, "opaque" reality that no longer allows itself to be understood from a pregiven horizon of expectations. Thus, for example, the latest genre of novels, the much-discussed *nouveau roman,* presents itself as a form of modern art that according to Edgar Wind's formulation, represents the paradoxical case "that the solution is given, but the problem is given up, so that the solution might be understood as a problem."[88] Here the reader is excluded from the situation of the immediate audience and put in the position of an uninitiated third party who in the face of a reality still without significance must himself find the questions that will decode for him the perception of the world and the interpersonal problem toward which the answer of the literature is directed.

It follows from all of this that the specific achievement of literature in social existence is to be sought

[83] *Ibid.,* p. 670. [Au.]
[84] *Ibid.,* p. 666. [Au.]
[85] Cf. *ibid.,* pp. 666–67. [Au.]

[86] *Ibid.,* p. 717. [Au.]
[87] "Die Schaubühne als eine moralische Anstalt betrachtet," in *Schillers Sämtliche Werke,* Säkularausgabe, XI, p. 99. See also R. Koselleck, *Kritik und Krise* (Freiburg and Munich, 1959), pp. 82 ff. [Au.]
[88] "Zur Systematik der künstlerischen Probleme," *Jahrbuch für Ästhetik* (1925), p. 440; for the application of this principle to works of art of the present, see M. Imdahl, *Poetik und Hermeneutik* 3, pp. 493–505, 663–64. [Au.]

exactly where literature is not absorbed into the function of a *representational* art. If one looks at the moments in history when literary works toppled the taboos of the ruling morals or offered the reader new solutions for the moral casuistry of his lived praxis, which thereafter could be sanctioned by the consensus of all readers in the society, then a still-little-studied area of research opens itself up to the literary historian. The gap between literature and history, between aesthetic and historical knowledge, can be bridged if literary history does not simply describe the process of general history in the reflection of its works one more time, but rather when it discovers in the course of "literary evolution" that properly *socially formative* function that belongs to literature as it competes with other arts and social forces in the emancipation of mankind from its natural, religious, and social bonds.

If it is worthwhile for the literary scholar to jump over his ahistorical shadow for the sake of this task, then it might well also provide an answer to the question: toward what end and with what right can one today still—or again—study literary history?

Roman Ingarden

1893–1970

THIS posthumously published piece by perhaps the most distinguished of phenomenologically oriented aestheticians has a retrospective quality in its opening pages in that the author reviews briefly the history of aesthetics, particularly that line eventuating in phenomenological aesthetic theory. He then sets forth in a general way his position. Ingarden insists here on examining the whole aesthetic process, which he regards as a continuum from authorial activity to the activity of the viewer or reader. This process includes, at certain stages, the author's viewing of his own creation as it develops, as well as the viewer's process of aesthetic apprehension. In between is the *work* of art, being created on the one side and being experienced on the other. Unlike the phenomenological critic of consciousness Georges Poulet (*CTSP,* pp. 1212–22), Ingarden expresses relatively little interest in the conveyance and receipt of consciousness in art, though he does speak of a rapprochement or spiritual communion of sorts between artist and viewer. But this rapprochement appears to be achieved as a communion with the work itself. Nor does Ingarden address questions of time and history as complicating the interpretation of the artifact, as does the reception theorist *Hans Robert Jauss,* who was clearly influenced by his work. Rather, he remains in the tradition of aesthetics and considers the viewer's activity in terms of a word like "communion" rather than in the tradition of hermeneutics, where "meaning" might be a more appropriate term.

Certainly Ingarden's insistence on the viewer's having to bring the work to a "phenomenological immediate perception," to a "concretion and self-presentation of aesthetically significant qualities," emphasizes the viewer's act of reception, but the emphasis remains phenomenological. Ingarden did not depart from the view of his teacher, *Edmund Husserl,* that all consciousness is the consciousness of something.

In spite of the fact that his two major translated books have different emphases—one on the necessity of intrinsic analysis, the other on the cognition of the work—Ingarden was always concerned with a process that included the intentional acts of author and viewer. He was perfectly willing to assert that there are things a viewer ought *not* to do as viewer. Works of art were for him purely intentional objects beyond the purview of either idealism or reason. They were of a special mode of being requiring a certain treatment. This involved, in a sense, their completion—the filling of gaps in their structure. This notion, which requires the viewer to concretize the work, influenced *Wolfgang Iser* in his version of reception theory.

The major translated works of Ingarden are *The Literary Work of Art* (1931, trans. 1973); *The Cognition of the Literary Work of Art* (1937, trans. 1973); *Time and Modes of Being* (1964, trans. 1964); "On the Motives Which Led Husserl to Transcendental Idealism," *Phaenomenologica* 64 (1975). See Herbert Spiegelberg, *The Phenomenological Movement*, esp. pp. 223–32, which includes a bibliography of Ingarden's writings.

PHENOMENOLOGICAL AESTHETICS: AN ATTEMPT AT DEFINING ITS RANGE

Aesthetics, if one may apply the term to a period when it was not being used in the modern sense, has had a peculiar history. From its beginnings in ancient Greece aesthetic enquiry had oscillated between two extremes. On the one hand, it focused upon the "subjective," that is, creative experiences and activities which give birth to works of art, or it concentrated upon receptive experiences and behavior, upon the reception of sensations, the pleasure and delight in works of art (or other things for that matter) out of which, so it is commonly supposed, nothing further is born. At the other extreme it focused upon several distinct kinds of "objects" such as mountains, landscapes, and sunsets, or artificially produced objects usually called "works of art." From time to time these two lines of enquiry met, but this usually meant that emphasis was placed upon one of them, that their differences were underlined. Thus their separatedness was maintained. In the nineteenth century and in our own we have had frequent disputes as to whether aesthetics ought to be "subjectivist" or "objectivist."

We first detect this oscillation in Plato. In the *Ion* he concentrates upon the "subjective," namely the creativity or the creative experiences and activities of the artist, and particularly of the poet.[1] On the other hand in the *Phaedrus* he is concerned with literary works and considers the problems attaching to the Form of beauty. But he does not explain what in this field is the connection between the "subjective" and the "objective." In the *Poetics* Aristotle is concerned almost exclusively with the work of literary art, without any reference to the creative acts of the poet or the experiences of the reader or listener, save that in considering the nature of tragedy he tries to define it through the way it affects the consumer.[2] But this really is a sign of his failure to explain the nature of tragedy in any other way. This one-sided attitude toward a work of literature and its beauty had a long life both in antiquity, and later during the Renaissance (Scaliger) and in French neoclassicism (Boileau).[3] Lessing's *Laocöon* may also be considered an example of "objectively" directed aesthetics. The opposite position is taken up by Baumgarten[4] with his concept of "aesthetics" which he interprets as a specific mode of cognition, and in this he goes well beyond the modern concept of aesthetics. The situation is similar in Kant, both in the *Critique of Pure Reason* and in the *Critique of Judgment*.[5] In the first work, as we know, Kant is concerned with purely epistemological problems, and especially with the *a priori* form of intuition. But in the other work the concept of aesthetics is widened to include communion with beauty and with works of art, and thus Kant moves closer to what we understand to be aesthetic in character. Nevertheless, Kant is largely concerned with the

PHENOMENOLOGICAL AESTHETICS: AN ATTEMPT AT DEFINING ITS RANGE was delivered as a lecture in 1969 and was published in Polish in volume 3 of Ingarden's *Studia z estetyki* in 1970. This slightly abridged translation is by Adam Czerniawski and is reprinted with permission from the *Journal of Aesthetics and Art Criticism*.

[1] See *CTSP*, pp. 11–18. [Eds.]
[2] See *CTSP*, pp. 47–66. [Eds.]
[3] See *CTSP*, pp. 136–43. [Eds.]
[4] Alexander Gottlieb Baumgarten, author of *Aesthetica* (1750, 1758). [Eds.]
[5] See *CTSP*, pp. 377–99. [Eds.]

so-called "judgment of taste" (*Geschmacksurteil*), with its conditions and efficacy, confining his discussion of art to a few paragraphs in which there is very little that is new. The same applies to his discussion of the beautiful and the sublime. In Hegel the emphasis is upon what is beautiful in art (*Das Kunstschöne*) and upon works of art which, admittedly, are taken to be products of an artist and subordinated to "Mind" in a special way.[6] Nevertheless the internal connection between the objective and the subjective is not clarified.

The aesthetics of Frederick Theodor Vischer[7] and of his son Robert which is influenced by Hegel does, it is true, create a metaphysics of beauty and art, but from there it turns mainly towards the problem of the apprehension or cognition of works of art, and deals especially with the so-called "empathy" (*Einfühlung*), thereby opening up a perspective on related psychological problems which emerge. But the aesthetics which had turned against Hegel, for instance the work of Gustav Theodor Fechner (*Vorschule der Asthetik*) and of his many followers down to Theodor Lipps, and to a large extent that of Johann Volkelt, is decidedly subjectivist in orientation and has in the end turned into a branch of psychology.[8] If these people considered aesthetic objects (works of art), they psychologized them almost without exception, that is, treated them as something "mental." It is a remarkable fact that a number of works which had appeared much later and dealt with music, for instance the books by Kurth, G. Revesh, and others, had "psychology of music" in their titles.[9]

This particular development also influenced the first phenomenological works in this field. As far as I know, the first phenomenological work in aesthetics is called *Der ästhetische Gegenstand.* Its author is Waldemar Conrad who also published a book on drama.[10] He is concerned exclusively with a general analysis of works in different arts, that is, literature, music, painting, and so on. He had nothing to say about creative and receptive aesthetic experiences, and he regards works of art (aesthetic objects) as "ideal objects" in the sense Husserl gives them in *Logische Untersuchungen,* that is, as timeless and immutable objects.[11] Some years later Moritz Geiger began to publish his works in aesthetics. These still deal with the subjective, with conscious experiences, and this happens even where certain problems which concern the nature of art begin to emerge. This leads Geiger to certain inconsistencies in his conception of aesthetic problems. The titles of his works are: *Prolegomena to the Phenomenology of Aesthetic Delight* (*Beigräge zur Phänomenologie des äesthetischen Genusses*), *The Nature and Role of Empathy, The Problem of the Empathy of Mood* (*Zum Problem der Stimmungseinfühlung*), *Dilettantism in Artistic Experience, The Superficial and the Deep Workings of Art* and *The Mental Significance of Art.*

What is noteworthy is what Geiger writes in the introduction to his book *Zugänge zur Ästhetik (Approaches to Art)* which is a collection of some of the papers I have mentioned: "Our approach to aesthetics lies ultimately in our own aesthetic experiences," which at times however develop inappropriately: "Only by purifying experiences will we again open up an approach to aesthetics." Only in his paper entitled "Psychische Bedeutung der Kunst" ("The Mental Meaning of Art") and in the article entitled "Phenomenological Aesthetics" does Geiger clearly refer to works of art and specifically discuss questions regarding the nature of a work of art and of aesthetic value as subjects for aesthetic investigation. He here takes aesthetic value, that is, something inhering in the work itself, as that which defines the unity of the realm of aesthetic investigation. But in these papers too the emphasis is upon experiences, and psychological aesthetics is frequently referred to as a discipline which does not stand in need of justification. In other papers, for instance, in his paper on aesthetic delight, Geiger emphasizes that this aesthetic "delight" of "savoring" is always directed at something (some object). He here postulates an "object aesthetics" ("Gegenstandsästhetik"). In this paper, then, we have the clearest example of the oscillation between the two

[6] See *CTSP,* pp. 517–31. [Eds.]

[7] Friedrich Theodor Vischer, author of *Ästhetik* (1846–47) and *Die Kunst* (1851–57) and his son Robert, author of *Das Optische Formgefuhl* (1873). [Eds.]

[8] Gustav Fechner, author of *Vorschule der Ästhetik* (1876); Theodor Lipps, author of *Ästhetik* (1903–6); Johannes Volkelt (1848–1930), German philosopher. [Eds.]

[9] Ernst Kurth (1886–1946), German musicologist; Geza Revesh (1878–1955), Hungarian musicologist. [Eds.]

[10] Waldemar Conrad (1878–1915), German aesthetician. [Eds.]

[11] See *Edmund Husserl.* [Eds.]

lines of aesthetic enquiry, while the absence of an explanation of the connection between the two is felt quite acutely. It is also surprising that this should happen in the case of the most distinguished phenomenological investigator in the realm of aesthetics who, as can be seen from his paper on "Dilettantism in Artistic Experience," was fully aware of the boundaries which demarcate aesthetics.

Of the later phenomenological works in aesthetics included in the 1929 Husserl *Festschrift* there is a subjectivist bias in L. F. Clauss's "Das Verstehen des sprachlichen Kunstwerks" ("Understanding a Linguistic Work of Art") and in F. Kaufmann's "Die Bedeutung der künstlerischen Stimmung" ("The Meaning of Artistic Mood"), while O. Becker's "Von der Hinfälligkeit des Schönen und die Abenteuererlichkeit des Künstlers" ("The Fragility of Beauty and the Artist's Search for Adventure") has an objectivist thrust, the author arguing that Phenomenology is an "ontological enquiry in the realm of aesthetic problems."

Thus in this respect phenomenological aesthetics is no different from earlier enquiries. Because Conrad's work did not prove influential it looked as though phenomenology too was inclined towards subjectivist oriented aesthetics. This, together with the then steadily growing psychologically motivated aesthetics, led to a reaction by some philosophers and historians of art. These included Max Dessoir (in 1907) and Emil Utitz who was close to phenomenology and who in 1914 raised the cry of "a general science of art," setting this science up as a study parallel to aesthetics, as is clear from the title of the quarterly which Dessoir published over several years: "Zeitschrift für Ästhetik und allgemeine Kunstwissenschaft." This dual title showed that there are two different lines of investigation, the one applying to art, to its works, whose general structure and properties have to be elucidated, while the other was to concern itself with aesthetic experience, but in fact turned out to be a focal point for remarkably diverse enquiries. The connection between those two lines of investigation was somehow lost. The title "A General Science of Art" was also a source of misunderstandings in that it seemed to emphasize its opposition to aesthetics as a philosophical discipline. But from the very beginning it was unclear what precisely this "general science" of art was to be: whether it was truly a science or a branch of philosophy. In practice one got the impression of a philosophical enquiry, with the only difference that in contrast to other philosophical enquiries in this field, there was some reference to actual works of art. But the slogan appeared to emphasize the term "Wissenschaft" ("science"). A science, however, interested not in the history of the subject, but in systematizations in general fields like, say, the theory of art. This impression is reinforced by the works of eminent art historians published at almost the same time. Wölfflin's *Principles of Art History* and Worringer's *Abstraction and Empathy* attempted through an investigation of actual works of art to discover general characteristics of works in specific artistic movements in the visual arts.[12] A similar tendency also manifested itself in the analysis of literature exemplified by Walzel's *Gehalt und Gestalt*.[13] We now began to hear about "a general science of literature" ("allgemeine Literaturwissenschaft") and in Poland about "theory of literature." In Germany, as far as I know, only Ermatinger used the expression "philosophy of literature" in a collection of essays entitled *Philosophie der Literatur* (1930).

It is not clear how one is to interpret these three concepts. Nor is the meaning of that generality clear, especially of the way in which "general" predication was to be arrived at. Was it to be by empirical generalizations based on the experience of specific works, and what sort of "experience" was it to be? Was it, for instance, to be achieved in the way that it is done in comparative literature studies, or in some other manner: for instance, through a consideration of specific works, through an analysis of the general content of a work of art, as the phenomenologists themselves wished to do?

When in 1927 I began writing my first book on this subject it was quite clear to me that one cannot employ the method of empirical generalization in aesthetics, but that one must carry through an eidetic analysis of the idea of a literary work of art or a work of art in general. So I thought it a mistake to set against each other the two lines of enquiry: (a) the general enquiry into a work of art, and (b) the aesthetic experience, whether in the sense of the author's creative experience or as a receptive experi-

[12] Heinrich Wölfflin (1864–1945), Swiss art historian; Wilhelm Worringer (1881–1965), German philosopher. [Eds.]

[13] Oskar Walzel (1864–1944), German literary historian. [Eds.]

ence of the reader or observer. I had therefore suitably shaped the thesis of my book, even though its title was *Das literarische Kunstwerk,*[14] and even though the German edition of my *Untersuchungen zur Ontologie der Kunst* (*Ontological Investigations in Art*) published thirty years later also has a title suggesting a purely object-directed aesthetic enquiry, with not a word about aesthetics. But this happened because the book was intended as a prolegomena to the discussion of several fundamental philosophical problems, specifically the problem of idealism and realism, with the aesthetic problems playing then a secondary role. But in fact my method of investigation and the way I had presented the problem put the case quite differently. From the start the work of art was assumed to be a purely intentional product of an artist's creative acts. At the same time, as a schematic entity having certain potential elements, it was contrasted with its "concretions." A work which for its inception required an author, but also the recreative receptive experiences of a reader or observer, so that right from the beginning, on account of its very nature and the mode of its existence, it pointed towards essentially different experiential histories, different mental subjects, as the necessary conditions of its existence and its mode of appearing (*Erscheinungsweise*), while in the annals of its existence (in its "life," as I used to say) it pointed to a whole community of such readers, observers, or listeners. And conversely, these experiences can come about only in such a way that by their very nature they refer to a certain object: the work of art. Moreover, it transpired at the same time that it requires for its existence not only these various experiences but additionally a certain physical object like a book, a piece of marble, a painted canvas, which must be suitably shaped by the artist and suitably perceived and apprehended by the consumer, in order that against this background the given work of art might appear and that, while remaining for a period of time unchanged, it should assist its many consumers in identifying the work. In this manner, in addition to the bodily and conscious behavior of various people and to the works of art themselves we have also drawn into the discussion certain real material objects as the physical ontological basis of a work of art. What is more, the creative behavior of an artist covers not only his productive experiences, but also certain physical actions which suitably shape a particular thing or process, so that it can perform the function of an ontological basis of a painting, a sculpture, a poem, or a sonata. On the other hand, the already produced work of art, the schematic entity, must be completed (concretized) by the consumer in many ways and must be actualized in its potential elements before it can acquire the shape of an aesthetic object valuable in a specific way. For this the work requires an observer who must achieve a certain particular experience, namely the aesthetic experience. In this way the internal connection of the work of art with its creator and its observer who is fulfilling the aesthetic experience became manifest. The material world enters as a background and displays itself in the shape of the ontological foundation of the work of art. All these elements form a single true whole of a higher order which gives a unity to the field which includes the work and the human being in communion with it. We can therefore assign it to a uniform philosophical discipline, namely aesthetics.

When in the course of my enquiry the problem of aesthetic value began to press itself with growing force which I could not ignore, the internal unity of the whole range of problems began to appear to me with increasing clarity, and at the same time I became aware that it is necessary to discover such a concept of aesthetics as would guarantee such unity.

So, at the Third International Congress of Aesthetics in Venice in 1956, I therefore proposed that we should take as a starting point of our enquiry into the definition of aesthetics the fundamental fact of the encounter or communion between the artist or the observer and a certain object, in particular, a work of art: a quite specific encounter, which leads in certain cases to the emergence of, on the one hand, the work of art or the aesthetic object, and on the other, to the birth of the creative artist or of the aesthetically experiencing observer or critic. As expected, the leading figures at that Congress—the Chairman of that session was Thomas Munro, and the Chairman of the Congress was Etienne Souriau—ignored this suggestion with a certain degree of contempt, especially since in my address I remarked that we should treat this encounter as crucial, while Munro clearly favored empirical psychology as a means of tackling aesthetic problems. At that time only my *Das literarische*

[14] Published in 1931. [Eds.]

Kunstwerk was known in the West, so that for the time being my attempt at a different orientation or definition of aesthetics proved abortive. I hope that conditions are now more favorable to my approach which I shall try to sketch in the following paragraphs.

First of all, it has to be stressed that it is inappropriate to regard all the experiences and behavior out of which a work of art flows as being active, while regarding those experiences and actions which terminate in aesthetic apprehension or cognition of a work of art as passive and purely receptive. In both situations there are phases of passivity and receptivity—of apprehension and acceptance—and phases of activity, of movement beyond what is already given, and to the production of something new which has not existed before and which is an honest product of the artist or of the observer. In the first instance the process does not exhaust itself in the productive experiencing by the artist: it discharges itself in a certain active bodily behavior during which the physical ontological foundation of the work of art is shaped. This shaping is directed by the creative experience and by the work of art which begins to outline itself and to shine through that experience, which is to be seemingly embodied in the work. This leads to results which are controlled by the artist and which must be subjected to such control if the artist is successfully to realize his intentions. From this several consequences follow.

Firstly, there are the specific phases in the shaping of the physical foundation, and this occurs on each occasion. Secondly, there is the developing structure of the work of art which dawns upon the artist in the course of this structuring of the foundation, the work being initially swathed in a protoplasmic state. And finally, the effectiveness coming into being during the shaping of the physical foundation, an effectiveness in performing the function of embodying and presenting the intended work of art in its immediacy. The artist controls and checks these results, this control taking place during the receptive experience which apprehends the properties of the object (the work of art). The painter, for instance, must see the products of the particular phases of his activity, of what is already painted on the canvas, and what artistic effectiveness it possesses. The composer in putting his work together, possibly noting it down in a score, has to hear how the particular parts sound, and for this purpose he often uses an instrument in order to be able to hear the particular fragments. It is this seeing or hearing that enables the artist to continue the work and shaping its physical foundation, leading the artist to make revisions or even to a complete recasting of the work. Only occasionally, in the case of poetry, do we get the poet composing "at one go" without having to read through his draft, and without any revisions or alterations. This is closely interwoven with the creative process and yet is itself an act of receptivity, of aesthetic apprehension. We may say that in this case the artist becomes an observer of his own emerging work, but even then it is not completely passive apprehension but an active, receptive behavior. On the other side, the observer too does not behave in a completely passive or receptive way, but being temporarily disposed to the reception and recreation of the work itself, is also not only activity, but in a certain sense at least creative. From the initially receptive phases of his experience there emerge creative phases at the moment when the already apprehended and reconstructed work of art stimulates the consumer to pass from looking to that phase of aesthetic experience in which the apprehending subject moves beyond the schematic work of art itself and in a creative way completes it. He swathes the work in aesthetically significant qualities suggested by the work and then brings about the constitution of the work's aesthetic value. (This need not always be the case. Sometimes these qualities are imposed by the observer without any suggestion, or without sufficient suggestion from the work itself. Then the value of the constituted aesthetic object also does not have a sufficient basis in the work of art itself. It is in these various different situations that we find a basis for resolving the problem of the objectivity of value in each particular case.) This is creative behavior, which is not only stimulated and guided by what has already been apprehended in a work of art, but also demands the observer's creative initiative, in order for him not only to guess with what aesthetically significant qualities a certain area of indeterminatedness in the work of art is to be filled, but also to imagine in immediate perception how the aesthetically significant congruence which has arisen in the work concretized by that completion by those new elements as yet unembodied in the work itself will sound. Frequently this achievement of bringing the concretized work into immediate perception, saturated with aesthetically significant qualities, comes about with the aid of considerable activity on the observer's part, without which everything would be savorless and lifeless. This phase of aesthetic shaping and live manifestation of the aesthetic value leads in turn to the phase of the apprehension of the essence of the constituted valuable aesthetic object, while the shape of the object blossoming in this apprehension stimulates the observer into an active response towards the already apprehended value, and to an assessment of this value.

This process, be it (a) active-passive or receptive, or (b) active-creative, is not the product of man's purely conscious behavior. It is the whole man endowed with defined mental and bodily powers, which during the process undergo certain characteristic changes which will differ, depending upon how the encounter is taking place and upon the shape of the work of art, or the relevant aesthetic object, that is being created. If this process leads to the creation of a true and honest work of art, then both this process and the manifest face of the work leaves a permanent mark in the artist's soul. To some extent, the same happens when the observer encounters a great work of art, an encounter which produces the constitution of a highly valuable aesthetic object. He, too, then undergoes a permanent and significant change.

The various processes and changes in the artist or the observer are paralleled by appropriate changes taking place in the object. In the case of the work of art in the process of being created this is obvious: the work of art comes into being gradually. And during this period, which may be prolonged, the changes occur in the shape and the properties of the emerging work corresponding to the particular phases of its coming into being. Similarly, just as the way in which a work of art is being created may vary, so may the changes it undergoes. On the whole it would be very difficult to say whether and within what boundaries there exist certain norms governing the coming into being of a work of art. In specific cases it is very difficult to discover these changes and prove their existence, especially when we see the work in its finished state and it shows no signs of the history of its coming into being. There can however, be no doubt that these changes which a work of art undergoes as it comes into being do exist, and that they correspond to the process of its coming into being.

It is not so easy to demonstrate that when the observer is apprehending a finished work of art there are similar changes to the ones just described. This process appears possible and understandable in the case where the observer's apprehension of the work goes astray and he comprehends it faultily, but generally we do demand and expect that during the process of apprehending a work of art there should be no deficiency, that it should be apprehended adequately and that it should stand before the observer's eyes in a faithful reconstruction. In such a case we could ascribe to the particular phases of the work's apprehension only the process of discovery of particular parts and characteristics of the work and of their emergence in immediate perception. We would then again be having two interwoven parallel processes: on the one hand, the apprehension, and on the other, the revelation and the appearance in immediate perception of the work of art, which together would produce the phenomenon of the encounter (communion?) between the observer and the work. It is, however, rare for the encounter to take such a course as to produce exclusively a pure reconstruction of the work of art, and were it to happen always in the case of a particular work of art, it would mean that as a work of art it is really dead, aesthetically inert, and therefore does not really perform its function. The process of apprehending the work which is better suited to its character does not appear until the time when, apart from its pure reconstruction, an aesthetic concretion is achieved which bestows upon the naked scheme of the work of art a plenitude of aesthetic qualities and aesthetic values. This process shrouds the aesthetic object until the observer has achieved a certain type of final completion (*Vollendung*) and constitution resulting in a quiescence in his behavior.

He himself now feels that the completion of the aesthetic object has been achieved and that he has accomplished the task of constituting the object. Now he only has to respond properly to the already constituted value of the aesthetic object in order to do justice to it. The task of performing an evaluation of the aesthetically concretized work of art, consonant with a response to value, may possibly arise and must be solved in such a way that nothing is altered or disturbed in the already concretized object, so that the process of evaluation should not produce any further change in the object. For it to be just and to preserve the untouchability of the evaluated object this evaluation must not be active. One may of course speculate whether this is always possible, but it is the essential meaning and function of evaluation.

And once again I must stress that the process of the concretion and the constitution of a valuable aesthetic object may run very differently in the case of one and the same work of art because the very constitutive experience and the circumstances in which it takes place may be different. This diversity is increased further due to the fact that works of art are quite different in their individuality and in the essentials of their kind. So they may influence the observer variously with their artistic activity and may arouse him occasionally to quite disparate aesthetic experience when he apprehends the work. There are thus considerable difficulties in describing these changes. For the time being we are only concerned to state that there is a "correlativity" and a mutual dependence between two parallel processes: in the experiencing subject and in the object which reveals itself to the observer and at the same time comes into being through this manifestation. These processes cannot be separated and neither can be studied in complete isolation from the other. This is the basic postulate of an aesthetics which has realized that the fundamental fact, with the elucidation of which it ought to start its investigation, is the encounter between man and an external object different from him and for the time being independent of him.

This object, thing, process, or event may be something purely physical, or a certain fact in the life and experience of the observer, or a musical motif, a snatch of a melody, or a harmony of sounds, a color contrast, or a particular metaphysical quality. All this comes from the outside and puts a particular pressure on the artist in the unfolding of an extremely rare intuition, even though it is only an intuition of the imagination. The role of this "object" is to move the artist in a particular way: it forces him out of a natural quotidian attitude and puts him into a completely new disposition.

This "object" may be a particularly eye-catching quality of some thing, as for instance, of a pigment both saturated and "shining," or a specific shape. It must however be a quality which draws our attention to itself because it excites in us an emotionally colored experience and an atmosphere of a certain surprise at its particularity and its wonderfully penetrating character. The German word *reizend* describes this quality. It may be of such a kind that one's drawing towards it may change into a "savoring" of its specificity and it may satisfy through its very presence the spectator's or listener's awakening desire to be in communion with it. Should the quality fully succeed in this, it then creates a certain primitive, simple aesthetic object. The experiencing observer's encounter with this quality gives rise to a certain kind of surprise, interest, delight, and later even happiness in the immediate communion with that specific quality.

This quality may, however, be seemingly qualitatively incomplete, heteronymous. It may consequently demand completion and through its embryonic manifestation it makes the observer aware of a certain lack which may at times become very unpleasant. This lack persuades the observer to seek other qualities that would complement that first quality and would bring the whole phenomenon to a saturation or final completion (*Vollendung*), thereby removing that unpleasant lack. Thus, the observer may find himself undergoing a lengthy process lasting until he is able to find that complementing quality, which would not only forge a connection with that first quality, but would also possess a synthetic overtone acting as a "shape" which envelops the whole phenomenon. This search constitutes the beginning of the creative process which depends not only on discovering this overtone, but which also creates the qualitative entity in which that shape finds its ontological base and upon which it concretely manifests itself.

This entity, say a certain combination of sounds, a three-dimensional structure, or a certain linguistic whole consisting of sentences, must be suitably shaped in order that upon it (or in it) that synthetic shape may manifest itself in immediate perception. We call this shape the work of art. It is seemingly created by the artist on top of that aesthetically significant synthetic overtone which as yet is not fully manifest. Naturally, the work of art is in itself qualitatively determined. If that aesthetically active shape is to manifest itself, this can only come about through a "harmony," a congruence between the shape and the work's qualitative definition, so that the whole which comes about in this way is self-sufficient and brings about a complete self-presentation of that aesthetically active synthetic shape. It may also happen that the already composed whole leads to an immediately perceived presence of one or more completely new aesthetically active qualities not initially envisaged by the artist, although he is far from indifferent to them. The process of shaping the work of art then moves further. If however the newly created whole can fulfill the artist's longing and desire to achieve a direct communion and a delight in the self-present whole ultimately emerging from the process, this brings him satisfaction and peace. The restless search and creation turns into a wholly peaceful observation and contemplation. That which brings fulfillment and peace has the character of something valuable, but not because it is something which we try to reach but, on the contrary, because it is in itself complete and perfect.

This new intentionally produced object may for the time be only "painted" in the imagination. It therefore does not achieve complete self-presence and does not bring about either an honest fulfillment of desires or peace. On the contrary, it rouses one's desire to "see" it in reality. What is more, the purely intentional object conceived in imagination quickly passes together with the image itself, and one should perhaps perform a new act of imagination before one can commune with the same work again, even in imagination. One does not often succeed in repeating this kind of creative vision without the object undergoing significant changes. Hence arises the thought that the created work must somehow be "fixed" in a comparatively durable material. The artist is therefore concerned with bringing about changes in the surrounding material world, be that in some thing, or be that in order to start the unfolding of a certain process so as to make possible an almost perceptible presence of the work and a certain kind of embodiment on the basis of, for example, a suitably carved stone, as well as the self-presentation of the aesthetically significant qualities manifesting themselves upon it. The artist therefore tries to shape his creative experience in a way enabling it to discharge itself in a certain mental and bodily behavior or activity which brings about the formation of a thing or a process due to serve as the physical basis of the existence of the work of art.

If he is a painter he covers a canvas with paints, if he is an architect he builds a house, and if he is a poet he writes a poem. In this he is motivated by the structure of the properties of a work of art which at first appear only in imagination or, more likely, by means of a certain fragment of leaven. Then the painting or poem in the process of being created helps him to finish the details of a work which originally appeared to him rather sketchily and had only the capacity to suggest a vision of an aesthetically valuable shape. Although the pigmented canvas or the carved stone never, as we frequently say, fully "realize" the work of art, embody it in themselves or constitute the sufficient condition for the visible manifestation on their basis of the work of art, nevertheless they do provide a certain kind of support for the intentional feigning or recreation of, for instance, a painting or a musical work. And given a suitable behavior by the artist or observer, they impose upon the concretion of the work a liveliness and fullness of an almost perceptible manifestation, thereby making possible the self-presence of aesthetically valuable qualities. If for example in the case of an already shaped literary text, our reading a certain poem silently—assuming of course that the poem is already "written"—is not enough to call forth that self-presentation of the aesthetically valuable qualities, we then resort to reading aloud, recitation, or in the case of a dramatic work, to a presentation on the stage which possesses a higher level of liveliness and effectiveness in affecting the spectator. We then frequently talk of the "realization" of the drama on stage or on film. But we must not forget that there are works, lyrics for instance, in the case of which recitation, especially an unduly "realistic" or "vivid" recitation, interferes with the self-presentation of emotionally colored subtle aesthetically valuable qualities. In their case it is enough for them to appear in the imaginative intuition in order to manifest themselves in their delicate subtlety and thus move us most profoundly. But this is probably true only of literature, for could it also be true of unpainted paintings or effectively unplayed symphonies?

It may happen that when an artist is creating the physical ontological foundation of his work of art, and has not finished composing his work in his imagination but only has a certain outline which, however, moves him aesthetically, he has a particularly vivid idea of some of its features. He is then also sometimes aware that some of them tend, if anything, to interfere with the presentation of aesthetically significant qualities or that through a different shaping of the physical foundation of the work, and thereby of the work itself, he would succeed in getting better artistic effects. The artist then changes the composition of his work, perfects it, and sometimes, discouraged, abandons it altogether. But not in every case does he then have to reject the, as we say, intrinsic "idea," that is, be persuaded that the aesthetically valuable shape which originally germinated in the imagination is valueless. On the contrary, despite everything, he affirms its value and continues to expect that, should he be able to present it against a background of a differently composed object (a work of art), it would then be properly "realized" and embodied, and would manifest itself in the fullness of its value. So once more he constructs an object: a painting, a cathedral, a symphony, or a literary work, or completely changes the material of the ontological foundation of the work. For instance, instead of bronze he now employs Carrara marble, instead of one range of pigments a different range with the same aesthetically valuable overtones. In the course of these various changes and operations it transpires that neither during the shaping of the physical foundation of the work nor during the development of the initial conception and the working out of the various details of the work does the artist behave in a purely creative way. Rather, during many phases of his activity he assumes the position of an observer of already educed details of the physical foundation and of the various parts and traits of the work itself appearing against this background.

The variety of the basic structures of works in the different arts, which I had once demonstrated, leads to the conclusion that the process of the creative composition of works of art, which in their properties are to constitute the basis for the aesthetically valuable qualities and the formation of the physical foundation of the work, runs very differently. Each of these two factors introduces different difficulties to be overcome.

On the one hand, it can be the resistance of the physical materials or the aesthetic ineffectiveness of the artistic entity itself which demands from the author various skills and activities to control a variety of techniques or to find completely new techniques, the latter the more difficult to perfect. On the other hand, in this technical battle with the material the artist needs the ability not to lose the basic intuition of the aesthetically active synthetic shape which directs him in his "realization" of his work. The genius of the original intuition and the toil of hard labor have to go hand in hand, and when their harmonization fails to occur, we get a technically abortive entity, which nevertheless allows us to guess at what it was meant to manifest. Or the fundamental intuition gets lost and, for all the excellent techniques, there is now nothing in the complete work of the aesthetically valuable quality inspired by that intuition: the entity may be perfect in its "workmanship" and yet inert, having nothing to tell us. But despite all these varieties of creative behavior on the artist's part the work nevertheless has in each case the same basic structure which belongs to the work's essence.

I trust that some details of this structure are becoming obvious from what I am here trying to say, but I must refrain from a more detailed analysis, which perhaps is not in any case required. For I am here concerned only with the thesis that it is a process which often undergoes several phases, in which there is a constant contact and encounter between the acting experiencing artist and a certain object, or rather two objects: the work of art in course of creation and the physical foundation undergoing change through his influence. Moreover, both these elements undergo correlative mutually dependent changes. It is not a collision of dead matter but a living encounter full of activity.

In order to make my central thesis clearer it may be worthwhile characterizing briefly the behavior of an observer of a work of art, both in his perceptual (receptive) experiences and in certain of his bodily actions. It is customary to talk of the "aesthetic experience" and to mean by it a momentary and homogeneous experience: there are many such theories in twentieth-century aesthetics. I had once attempted to show that it consists of many various rationally connected elements and occupies many phases. Here I would only add that this could occur in two different ways. The experience starts either with a sense-perception of a certain physical foundation of a work of art (a painted surface, a lump of stone, and so on) whose certain details enable the observer to "read" the shape of the work. Whereupon the work comes to be constituted in his receptive experience or, alternatively, the observer instantaneously perceives the work of art itself, that is, he sees a picture or a sculpture representing someone. While in subsequent phases of the process the perceived painting now begins to work aesthetically upon the observer who, passing on into an aesthetic attitude actualizes the aesthetically valuable qualities which the work of art has suggested to him and he brings about the constitution of the aesthetic value of the whole. In order to highlight this difference in the manner of the observer's behavior when he apprehends the work of art I shall consider his behavior through the example of his communion with an Impressionist painting.

In the first instance the observer sees for the time being an area of canvas or paper covered with colored patches. Some of these flow into each other, others stand out in sharper contrast. In stopping to consider these patches more closely the observer behaves in the way that we do today when we observe a purely abstract painting where the collection of these patches of paint appears to us self-sufficient. Soon however some of these patches, either in their disposition or through their color, begin to work upon the observer, rousing him to adopt an aesthetic attitude: he now begins to sense rather than see certain aesthetically significant qualities suggested by the disposition, color, and shape of the patches. At a certain moment he focuses his attention upon them, apprehends them in full focus and delights in them. Finally, he reacts towards them with either a positive or a negative emotion which represents his response to their aesthetically valuable disposition of contrasting colors. But it may also happen that perceiving a certain variety of colored patches which appear to him completely devoid of any interconnection produces in him a shock arising from his incomprehension. This leads him to ask: "What is this supposed to be?" or "What does this represent?" This state of disquietude, of incomprehension, may pass into an attempt at understanding what precisely the painting is all about. And then suddenly the observer realizes that he is looking at the painting faultily, regarding the colored patches as objective determinations, as the properties of the canvas or wood which has been painted over for no apparent reason, whereas he should make use of the colored patches to receive a certain quantity of experiential data which, seemingly of their own accord, arrange themselves into a certain aspect of an object seen from a certain point of view under certain lighting conditions.

The observer allows himself to be drawn and then suddenly everything becomes "comprehensible." From the multiplicity of colored patches a human face emerges: for instance the face of a girl reading a book, as in Renoir's *La liseuse,* or a collection of many colored objects illuminated by a lively light, as in Sisley's *Le brouillard* or Pissarro's *Femme dans un clos* and his *Arbres en fleur.* Now, on the one hand, the look of the painting changes.[15] Only now does it begin to appear as a painting which "represents" something, in which objects and people appear illuminated by a certain light in very vibrating, glistening, unstable aspects, while the variety of colored patches which lie at the basis of this painting do not quite disappear from the field of vision, although they are not that which we see and upon which our interest rests.

But, on the other hand, the observer's behavior also undergoes change. He now accomplishes an act of "seeing" which is almost like that of normal visual perception, of things presented "in the picture." In Claude Monet's *Regattes à Argenteuil* he sees sailing boats at the seaside and reflections of their sails in the waves. At the same time, upon the basis of that "seeing," he performs an act of comprehension of what is to be presented in the painting, what is to manifest itself as though present when he sees the painting in a proper way. And it is inappropriate to say that we look "upon" the picture or that we "see" it. For although we in fact do look "at the picture," we perceive in the picture just the objects we have already mentioned, which are manifested to us through our apprehension of multicolored patches of whose disposition on the canvas we are not at that moment aware. For had we been aware of these dispositions we would be seeing a smeared or blotched canvas, or an abstract painting, and we would not be seeing either the sailing boats or the wavy reflections of their white sails on the rippling blue waters of the sea.

But something else occurs which is peculiar, and of whose peculiarity we are not normally aware, precisely because we have experienced it so frequently as something completely "natural" and far from surprising, namely that looking upon a human face emerging from a play of patches and light we

[15] I am not here saying that the painting itself changes, only that its "look" or perhaps "aspect" does. I am expressing myself very carefully because I do not wish at this stage to decide upon the difficult issue of the identity of a painting persisting through the various ways it is perceived. [Au.]

perceive something more: a friendly smile, satisfaction, joyfulness, or deep sorrow. We say, and this goes for spectators as well as for painters themselves or the so-called critics, that a certain "expression" of the person presented in the painting imposes itself upon us. This occurs chiefly in good portraits like those by Rembrandt or Van Gogh. Here the term "expression" may mean two different, although related things: a certain actual mood, commotion or mental state, or a certain defined trait of the character of the presented person, of psychological maturity or kindheartedness such as we can see in certain self-portraits by the older Rembrandt, in, for instance, his portrait in the New York Frick Gallery. These two elements do not appear in all portraits with equal clarity. The observer's apprehension of this type of features in a painting brings about a change in the painting's aspects or looks. The element of the mental and of the mental states brought in by the perceptual content livens up the whole painting in a specific way, often giving it a character of depth and subtlety because it reveals that part of the human soul which is normally hidden or difficult to reach. But this leads to a change in the observer's behavior. He now understands the sense of the "facial expression" of the person presented or, conversely, in other instances, he stumbles upon something incomprehensible or puzzling in that expression (and this too is a certain positive phenomenon) and is unable to formulate an opinion as to what, as we sometimes say, lies hidden behind this incomprehensible smile or look. But while in the first instance this leads to a positive reaction, in the second instance he may find himself more or less hurt or put in a weird mood. When the observer comes to understand the psychological element of the painting, this frequently produces an emotional reaction in him: kindliness calls forth a state of kindliness, while hostility or a trait of malice apparent in someone's face produces a rather negative attitude in the spectator.

But these are seemingly extra-aesthetic elements in the observer's experience. Of greater importance is what in this experience has consequences for aesthetics. If for instance an expression of a mental state or a trait of character is manifested in the painting in a sharp, imposing, and unambiguous manner, so that the presented person appears to the spectator as though "alive," the spectator undergoes a different experience. This is a feeling of admiration for the mastery of the painter who succeeded through purely painterly means, through a certain disposition and shape, through differently colored patches, to bring about the manifestation of something as different from the pigments as the joy or the maturity of the presented person. The spectator asks how was it possible that, for instance, a character trait of the presented person should become visible by these means; what is more, that something should impose itself upon him with considerable force, so that he is unable to free himself from, as we sometimes say, this "sensation."[16] What dispositions of colors and lines are required to manifest a look full of love or kindliness with which a person views another person? The spectator who puts this question to himself and who looks for an answer in a further examination of the picture, changes—and here his behavior alters radically—from a "naive" spectator who simply communes emotionally with people presented in the painting and reacts to their behavior with his own behavior in the way that his occurs in ordinary life in interpersonal relationships, into a person who treats the given painting *as a work of art,* as a peculiar entity which fulfills special functions. He now investigates its specific strata: what is represented and the means of representation. He critically examines their functions and evaluates their artistic effectiveness or ineffectiveness. Finally he arrives either at a high valuation of the work or rejects it and condemns it as kitsch.

In this new attitude he begins to understand the given work quite differently. This understanding now concerns not what is being expressed of the mental life of the presented person, but rather considers what the individual strata of the painting contribute to its whole, what they effect, what is the "calculation" behind the whole painting, what is most important in it artistically and aesthetically, and what is merely the means to achieve this goal, what is a mannerism acquired from others (an intolerable mannerism, we sometimes say), and what is a new technical achievement or a new discovery, either in the realm of the presented world or in the field of aesthetically significant qualities and the ul-

[16] This is not the discovery of the Expressionists. They merely place a greater *emphasis* upon manifesting by painterly means of momentary mental actions, with a stress upon strange, shocking, and gloomy appearances which can be found in older painters like Breughel. [Au.]

timate overtones of aesthetic value. By behaving in this way the spectator becomes a "connoisseur" of painterly art, of its various effects and artistic and aesthetic achievements. This behavior on the part of the spectator endows the observed picture with a new character: it now stands before him as, for instance, a masterpiece, and also as a work of a master, testifying to his ability and his spirit, to his mode of evaluation and the world of his values with which he is in communion; values which he tries to make manifest to his spectators and through his work to enable the spectators to share these values. All this brings it about that on the one hand justice is rendered to the given work of art as a work of art, that it is grasped and understood in its proper function and in the values realized in it, while on the other hand, that between the observer and the artist, the master, there arises a specific *reapproachment,* even a certain kind of spiritual communion, although the master is absent and may well be long since dead.

This sketchy account of the observer's communion with a painting must of course be checked against many other examples, enriched with new details and deepened.[17] Its primary purpose is to justify and to give a firmer foundation to my main thesis regarding the encounter of the artist or observer with a work of art. If this thesis is true and adequately substantiated, then it may serve as a principle of demarcation of aesthetic enquiry, endowing it with a certain unity which is not provided by either the so-called "subjectivist" or the "objectivist" aesthetics. This thesis points to a certain fundamental fact from the analysis of which in its collective totality it is possible to move further in two directions.

(1) Towards an analysis of the emerging or the already finished work of art and (2) towards the investigation of the activity of the artist-creator and the behavior of the spectator, the recreator, and the critic. So, in an analytical structural enquiry into the work of art we shall not forget that works of art arise out of defined creative acts by an artist, and that they are therefore shaped in a certain purposeful manner, namely in the intention of realizing a certain artistic or aesthetic project and achievement; that they are also the products of a behavior in which the basic and essential role is played by conscious intentional experiences and that in their capacity as such products, these experiences may acquire only a certain particular mode of existence and, derivatively, of acting in various human communities. Because of their mode of existence they must, when they are being contemplated by the spectator, be brought by him to a phenomenal immediate perception, to a concretion and a self-presentation of aesthetically significant qualities, and of the aesthetic value resting upon them. In our investigation of the creative acts by the artist we shall never forget what their aim is and what they can achieve. In investigating the behavior of the spectator or of the observer in general, we shall remember what it is that he as an observer of a work of art must emphasize, in what way he can do justice to the work of art, how the work's value or lack of it may be revealed and made manifest to other people, how he can and ought to carry out their evaluation, and lastly, what he does not do and ought not to do as a consumer and observer of a work of art, rather than as an idealogue or as a public-spirited citizen.

In pointing to a close connection between the two sides—the works of art and the people who are in communion with them or produce them—I am not altering my existing conviction which I have tried to develop and justify in many of my works. It is that works of art, although they are only purely intentional objects—admittedly resting on physical ontological foundations—after all form a special sphere of being whose peculiarity and specific endowment ought to be preserved in any investigation. It must not be violated by postulates which are foreign to it. Works of art have a right to expect to be properly apprehended by observers who are in communion with them and to have their special value justly treated.

[17] The descriptions given here are of course idealizations. Their function is to sketch a *possible* and *typical* course of the encounter and of the processes which occur in it. These descriptions systematize, or perhaps rationally order their course. In reality we get certain considerable departures from this order because these processes are usually influenced by variable incidental conditions which disturb this course. But these are matters of interest to psychology rather than aesthetics, which in fact attempts to reconstruct the phases of the course of the process of the encounter. Aesthetics investigates their function in order to obtain, on the one hand, the constitution of the aesthetic object in communion with the appropriate work of art and, on the other, to acquire a cognition both of that object and of the work of art lying at its basis. [Au.]

It would take me too far if I were now to attempt to develop the problem of philosophical aesthetics as I have defined it and understood it above. But I wish to add that what may be self-explanatory within phenomenological aesthetics must here be touched upon to show that I am not in any way abandoning the conviction that works of art, aesthetic objects, as well as their creators and consumers, and the connections between the two, may and ought to be investigated phenomenologically. This method aims above all at bringing its objects of enquiry to an immediate givenness in a suitably shaped experience and to a faithful description of the data of that experience. I also continue to be convinced that it is both possible and justified to achieve in these enquiries a disposition towards the essence of facts and the search for the contents of general ideas entering into the object under enquiry. It seems to me that this method may produce results which it may be difficult to achieve in differently organized enquiries. I can support my conviction with the results of my enquiries over several decades, although I do not deny that they should always be submitted to checks and amplifications, that they should be deepened by fresh investigations. In declaring my position I am very far from wishing to state that only the phenomenological method is effective in aesthetic enquiry and that every other method is doomed to failure. Neither do I have any desire to impose this method upon others. Every enquirer must assimilate the method which suits his talents and his scientific convictions and enables him to achieve results which are honest and at least probable. That goes for me, too.

Paul de Man

1919–1983

PAUL DE MAN'S "The Rhetoric of Temporality" (1969) is one of the most influential essays written in the period represented by this anthology. Today, after he published two highly influential books, it can be seen also as presaging his movement toward his own version of deconstruction. In 1969, the word was still "demystification," borrowed from existential theology. De Man's reading of *Jacques Derrida* and his continuing interest in Nietzsche propelled him beyond the 1969 essay to a more thoroughly deconstructive position, which is to say, in his case, a deeper attention to the inevitable contradiction or *aporia* which he believed to be discoverable in any text.

In "The Rhetoric of Temporality," de Man reverses what he regards as the romantic valorization of symbol over allegory (see, for example, Coleridge, *CTSP*, pp. 467–68), arguing that symbolism is a mystification in which "the substance and the representation do not differ in their being" and allegory is recognition of difference. In a well-known statement, de Man says, "Whereas the symbol postulates the possibility of an identity or identification, allegory designates primarily a distance in relation to its own origin, and, renouncing the nostalgia and the desire to coincide, it establishes its language in the void of this temporal difference." Clearly this view is in agreement with the structuralist notion of the differential nature of the sign and the notion of temporal deferral—two ideas that Derrida combines in his coinage *différance.* De Man's argument is that romantic literature is in fact an allegorical art.

But then, of course, so is all art and, in the end, all writing. The question remains only to what extent writing knows this. On the whole most writing does not, or only half knows it, and must be told. This is the task of deconstructive criticism as de Man sees it, and he performs it relentlessly in the books that follow. In *Blindness and Insight* it is proposed that the critic's insight is identical with his blind spot, that it exists inevitably entwined with his error to form a crisis that further criticism comes to unravel. Except, of course, that the unraveling must become subject to yet another unraveling.

In the later *Allegories of Reading* the error is named metaphor, its synonym "symbol" having been previously demystified. However, by this time the term "deconstruction" has replaced "demystification." For de Man, resemblances always disguise differences, and the void present in language is revealed when the seductive (a term de Man likes) disguise is swept away in a close reading that reveals not an organic whole but an unresolvable contradiction. Reading is therefore never the choice of one interpretation over another but the recognition of both assertion and denial and ultimately the understanding that language itself is the abyss, that rhetoric or the trope undoes intention. Though de Man rejects all dogma as mystification, it appears that traces of an existential theology remain, though always on the move and never content with a formulation that would allow even for a negative certainty.

De Man's books are *Blindness and Insight: Essays in the Rhetoric of Contemporary Criticism* (1971, rev. 1983); *Allegories of Reading: Figural Language in Rousseau, Nietzsche, Rilke, and Proust* (1979); and *The Rhetoric of Romanticism* (1985). Both works take the form of collections of essays written at different times. See Stanley Corngold, "Error in Paul de Man," in *The Yale Critics,* ed. J. Arac, W. Godzich, and W. Martin, which includes a bibliography of de Man's writings; Frank Lentricchia, *After the New Criticism;* Christopher Norris, *Deconstruction: Theory and Practice,* and *The Lesson of Paul De Man,* Yale French Studies 69.

THE RHETORIC OF TEMPORALITY

I. Allegory and Symbol

Since the advent, in the course of the nineteenth century, of a subjectivistic critical vocabulary, the traditional forms of rhetoric have fallen into disrepute. It is becoming increasingly clear, however, that this was only a temporary eclipse: recent developments in criticism[1] reveal the possibility of a rhetoric that would no longer be normative or descriptive but that would more or less openly raise the question of the intentionality of rhetorical figures. Such concerns are implicitly present in many works in which the terms "mimesis," "metaphor," "allegory," or "irony" play a prominent part. One of the main difficulties that still hamper these investigations stems from the association of rhetorical terms with value judgments that blur distinctions and hide the real structures. In most cases, their use is governed by assumptions that go back at least as far as the romantic period; hence the need for historical clarification as a preliminary to a more systematic treatment of an intentional rhetoric. One has to return, in the history of European literature, to the moment when the rhetorical key-terms undergo significant changes and are at the center of important tensions. A first and obvious example would be the change that takes place in the latter half of the eighteenth century, when the word "symbol" tends to supplant other denominations for figural language, including that of "allegory."

Although the problem is perhaps most in evidence in the history of German literature, we do not intend to retrace the itinerary that led the German writers of the age of Goethe to consider symbol and

THE RHETORIC OF TEMPORALITY originally appeared in *Interpretation,* ed. Charles Singleton (Johns Hopkins University Press, 1969), and is reprinted from *Blindness and Insight* (2d ed. rev.) by permission of the University of Minnesota Press, Minneapolis. Copyright 1983 by the University of Minnesota. We are grateful to Jeffrey Peck and Azade Seyhan for translating passages quoted in German. [Eds.]

[1] The trend is apparent in various critical movements that develop independently of one another in several countries. Thus, for example, in the attempt of some French critics to fuse the conceptual terminology of structural linguistics with traditional terms of rhetoric (see, among others, Roland Barthes, "Elements de semiologie," in *Communications* 4 [1964], trans. Annette Lavers, and Colin Smith, *Elements of Semiology* [New York; Hill and Wang, 1967]; Gérard Genette, *Figures* [Paris: Seuil, 1966]; Michel Foucault, *Les Mots et les choses* [Paris: Gallimard, 1966], trans. *The Order of Things* [New York: Random House, Inc., 1970]). In Germany a similar trend often takes the form of a rediscovery and reinterpretation of the allegorical and emblematic style of the baroque (see, among others, Walter Benjamin, *Ursprung des deutschen Trauerspiels* [Berlin: 1982, reissued in Frankfurt: Suhrkamp, 1963], trans. John Osborne, *The Origin of German Tragic Drama* [London: NLB, 1977]; Albrecht Schöne, *Emblematik und Drama im Zeitalter des Barock* [Munich: Beck, 1964]). The evolution from the New Criticism to the criticism of Northrop Frye in North America tends in the same direction. [Au.]

allegory as antithetical, when they were still synonymous for Winckelmann. The itinerary is too complex for cursory treatment. In *Wahrheit und Methode,* Hans-Georg Gadamer makes the valorization of symbol at the expense of allegory coincide with the growth of an aesthetics that refuses to distinguish between experience and the representation of this experience. The poetic language of genius is capable of transcending this distinction and can thus transform all individual experience directly into general truth. The subjectivity of experience is preserved when it is translated into language; the world is then no longer seen as a configuration of entities that designate a plurality of distinct and isolated meanings, but as a configuration of symbols ultimately leading to a total, single, and universal meaning. This appeal to the infinity of a totality constitutes the main attraction of the symbol as opposed to allegory, a sign that refers to one specific meaning and thus exhausts its suggestive potentialities once it has been deciphered. "Symbol and allegory," writes Gadamer, "are opposed as art is opposed to non-art, in that the former seems endlessly suggestive in the indefiniteness of its meaning, whereas the latter, as soon as its meaning is reached, has run its full course."[2] Allegory appears as dryly rational and dogmatic in its reference to a meaning that it does not itself constitute, whereas the symbol is founded on an intimate unity between the image that rises up before the senses and the supersensory totality that the image suggests. In this historical perspective, the names of Goethe, Schiller, and Schelling stand out from the background of the classical idea of a unity between incarnate and ideal beauty.

Even within the area of German thought other currents complicate this historical scheme. In the perspective of traditional German classicism, allegory appears as the product of the age of Enlightenment and is vulnerable to the reproach of excessive rationality. Other trends, however, consider allegory as the very place where the contact with a superhuman origin of language has been preserved. Thus the polemical utterances of Hamann against Herder on the problem of the origin of language are closely related to Hamann's considerations on the allegorical nature of all language,[3] as well as with his literary praxis that mingles allegory with irony. It is certainly not in the name of an enlightened rationalism that the idea of a transcendental distance between the incarnate world of man and the divine origin of the word is here being defended. Herder's humanism encounters in Hamann a resistance that reveals the complexity of the intellectual climate in which the debate between symbol and allegory will take place.

These questions have been treated at length in the historiography of the period. We do not have to return to them here, except to indicate how contradictory the origins of the debate appear to be. It is therefore not at all surprising that, even in the case of Goethe, the choice in favor of the symbol is accompanied by all kinds of reservations and qualification. But, as one progresses into the nineteenth century, these qualifications tend to disappear. The supremacy of the symbol, conceived as an expression of unity between the representative and the semantic function of language, becomes a commonplace that underlies literary taste, literary criticism, and literary history. The supremacy of the symbol still functions as the basis of recent French and English studies of the romantic and post-romantic eras, to such an extent that allegory is frequently considered an anachronism and dismissed as nonpoetic.

Yet certain questions remain unsolved. At the very moment when properly symbolic modes, in the full strength of their development, are supplanting allegory, we can witness the growth of metaphorical styles in no way related to the decorative allegorism of the rococo, but that cannot be called "symbolic" in the Goethian sense. Thus it would be difficult to assert that in the poems of Hölderlin, the island Patmos, the river Rhine, or, more generally, the landscapes and places that are often described at the beginning of the poems would be symbolic landscapes or entities that represent, as by analogy, the spiritual truths that appear in the more abstract parts of the text. To state this would be to misjudge the literality of these passages, to ignore that they derive their considerable poetic authority from the fact that they are not synecdoches designating a to-

[2] Hans-Georg Gadamer, *Wahrheit und Methode* (Tubingen: J. C. B. Mohr, 1960; 4th ed., 1975), p. 70; trans. G. Barden and J. Cumming, *Truth and Method* (New York: Seabury Press, 1975), p. 67. [Au.]

[3] Johann Georg Hamann, "Die Rezension der Herderschen Preisschrift," in *J. G. Hamann's Hauptschriften erklärt, vol 4 (Uber den Ursprung der Sprache),* Elfriede Buchsel (Gutersloh: Gerd Mohn, 1963). [Au.]

tality of which they are a part, but are themselves already this totality. They are not the sensorial equivalence of a more general, ideal meaning; they are themselves this idea, just as much as the abstract expression that will appear in philosophical or historical form in the later parts of the poem. A metaphorical style such as Hölderlin's can at any rate not be described in terms of the antimony between allegory and symbol—and the same could be said, albeit in a very different way, of Goethe's late style. Also, when the term "allegory" continues to appear in the writers of the period, such as Friedrich Schlegel, or later in Solger or E. T. A. Hoffmann, one should not assume that its use is merely a matter of habit, devoid of deeper meaning. Between 1800 and 1832, under the influence of Creuzer and Schelling, Friedrich Schlegel substitutes the word "symbolic" for "allegorical" in the oft-quoted passage of the "Gespräch über die Poesie": " . . . alle Schönheit ist Allegorie. Das Höchste kann man eben weil es unaussprechlich ist, nur allegorisch sagen."[4] But can we deduce from this, with Schlegel's editor Hans Eichner, that Schlegel "simply uses allegory where we would nowadays say symbol"?[5] It could be shown that, precisely because it suggests a disjunction between the way in which the world appears in reality and the way it appears in language, the word "allegory" fits the general problematic of the "Gespräch," whereas the word "symbol" becomes an alien presence in the later version.

We must go even further than this. Ever since the study of *topoi* has made us more aware of the importance of tradition in the choice of images, the symbol, in the post-romantic sense of the term, appears more and more as a special case of figural language in general, a special case that can lay no claim to historical or philosophical priority over other figures. After such otherwise divergent studies as those of E. R. Curtius, of Erich Auerbach, of Walter Benjamin,[6] and of H.-G. Gadamer, we can no longer consider the supremacy of the symbol as a "solution" to the problem of metaphorical diction. "The basis of aesthetics during the nineteenth century," writes Gadamer, "was the freedom of the symbolizing power of the mind. But is this still a firm basis? Is the symbolizing activity not actually still bound today by the survival of a mythological and allegorical tradition?"[7]

To make some headway in this difficult question, it may be useful to leave the field of German literature and see how the same problem appears in English and French writers of the same period. Some help may be gained from a broader perspective.

The English contemporary of Goethe who has expressed himself most explicitly in the relationship between allegory and symbol is, of course, Coleridge. We find in Coleridge what appears to be, at first sight, an unqualified assertion of the superiority of the symbol over allegory. The symbol is the product of the organic growth of form; in the world of the symbol, life and form are identical: "such as the life is, such is the form."[8] Its structure is that of the synecdoche, for the symbol is always a part of the totality that it represents. Consequently, in the symbolic imagination, no disjunction of the constitutive faculties takes place, since the material perception and the symbolical imagination are continuous, as the part is continuous with the whole. In contrast, the allegorical form appears purely mechanical, an abstraction whose original meaning is even more devoid of substance than its "phantom proxy," the allegorical representative; it is an immaterial shape that represents a sheer phantom devoid of shape and substance.[9]

But even in the passage from *The Statesman's Manual,* from which this quotation is taken, a certain degree of ambiguity is manifest. After associating the essential thinness of allegory with a lack of substantiality, Coleridge wants to stress, by contrast, the worth of the symbol. One would expect the latter to be valued for its organic or material richness, but instead the notion of "translucence" is

[4] Friedrich Schlegel, "Gespräch über die Poesie," in *Kritische Ausgabe,* Band 2, *Charakteristiken und Kritiken I, (1796–1801),* Hans Eichner, ed. (Paderborn: Ferdinand Schöningh, 1967), pp. 324ff. [Au.] "All beauty is allegory. One can express the loftiest allegorically since it is unspeakable." . . . [Hier, versiegt . . .] "Here, the source from which the editor of these pages has created dries up suddenly." [Eds.]

[5] *Ibid,* p. xci, n. 2. [Au.]

[6] See note 1 above. [Au.]

[7] Gadamer, p. 76, Eng., p. 72. [Au.]

[8] S. T. Coleridge, *Essays on Shakespeare and Some Other Old Poets and Dramatists* (London: Everyman, 1907), p. 46. [Au.]

[9] S. T. Coleridge, *The Statesman's Manual,* W. G. T. Shedd, ed. (New York: Harper and Brothers, 1875), pp. 437–38, quoted in Angus Fletcher, *Allegory: The Theory of a Symbolic Mode* (Ithaca, N.Y.: Cornell University Press, 1964), p. 16, n. 29. [Au.] See *CTSP,* pp. 467–68. [Eds.]

suddenly put in evidence: "The symbol is characterized by the translucence of the special in the individual, or of the general in the special, or of the universal in the general; above all by the translucence of the eternal through and in the temporal."[10]

The material substantiality dissolves and becomes a mere reflection of a more original unity that does not exist in the material world. It is all the more surprising to see Coleridge, in the final part of the passage, characterize allegory negatively as being *merely* a reflection. In truth, the spiritualization of the symbol has been carried so far that the moment of material existence by which it was originally defined has now become altogether unimportant; symbol and allegory alike now have a common origin beyond the world of matter. The reference, in both cases, to a transcendental source, is now more important than the kind of relationship that exists between the reflection and its source. It becomes of secondary importance whether this relationship is based, as in the case of the symbol, on the organic coherence of the synecdoche, or whether, as in the case of allegory, it is a pure decision of the mind. Both figures designate, in fact, the transcendental source, albeit in an oblique and ambiguous way. Coleridge stresses the ambiguity in a definition of allegory in which it is said that allegory ". . . convey[s], while in disguise, either moral qualities or conceptions of the mind that are not in themselves objects of the senses . . . ," but then goes on to state that, on the level of language, allegory can "combine the parts to form a consistent whole."[11] Starting out from the assumed superiority of the symbol in terms of organic substantiality, we end up with a description of figural language as translucence, a description in which the distinction between allegory and symbol has become of secondary importance.

It is not, however, in this direction that Coleridge's considerable influence on later English and American criticism has been most manifest. The very prominent place given in this criticism to the study of metaphor and imagery, often considered as more important than problems of metrics or thematic considerations, is well enough known. But the conception of metaphor that is being assumed, often with explicit reference to Coleridge, is that of a dialectic between object and subject, in which the experience of the object takes on the form of a perception or a sensation. The ultimate intent of the image is not, however, as in Coleridge, translucence, but synthesis, and the mode of this synthesis is defined as "symbolic" by the priority conferred on the initial moment of sensory perception.

The main interpretative effort of English and American historians of romanticism has focused on the transition that leads from eighteenth-century to romantic nature poetry. Among American interpreters of romanticism, there is general agreement about the importance of eighteenth-century antecedents for Wordsworth and Coleridge, but when it comes to describing just in what way romantic nature poetry differs from the earlier forms, certain difficulties arise. They center on the tendency shared by all commentators to define the romantic image as a relationship between mind and nature, between subject and object. The fluent transition in romantic diction, from descriptive to inward, meditative passages, bears out the notion that this relationship is indeed of fundamental importance. The same applies to a large extent to eighteenth-century landscape poets who constantly mix descriptions of nature with abstract moralizings; commentators tend to agree, however, that the relationship between mind and nature becomes much more intimate toward the end of the century. Wimsatt was the first to show convincingly, by the juxtaposition of a sonnet of Coleridge and a sonnet of Bowles that, for all external similitudes, a fundamental change in substance and in tone separated the two texts.[12] He points to a greater specificity in Coleridge's details, thus revealing a closer, more faithful observation of the outside object. But this finer attention given to the natural surfaces is accompanied, paradoxically enough, by a greater inwardness, by experiences of memory and of reverie that stem from deeper regions of subjectivity than in the earlier writer. How this closer attention to surfaces engenders greater depth remains problematic. Wimsatt writes: "The common feat of the romantic nature poets was to read meanings into the landscape. The meaning

[10] *Ibid.* [Au.]

[11] S. T. Coleridge, *Miscellaneous Criticism,* T. M. Raysor, ed. (London: Constable and Co., Ltd., 1936), p. 30; also quoted by Fletcher, p. 19. [Au.]

[12] William Wimsatt, "The Structure of Romantic Nature Imagery," *The Verbal Icon* (Lexington, Ky.: University of Kentucky Press, 1954), pp. 106–110. [Au.]

might be such as we have seen in Coleridge's sonnet, but it might more characteristically be more profound, concerning the spirit or soul of things—'the one life within us and abroad.' And that meaning especially was summoned out of the very surface of nature itself."[13] The synthesis of surface and depth would then be the manifestation, in language, of a fundamental unity that encompasses both mind and object, "the one life within us and abroad." It appears, however, that this unity can be hidden from a subject, who then has to look outside, in nature, for the confirmation of its existence. For Wimsatt, the unifying principle seems to reside primarily within nature, hence the necessity for the poets to start out from natural landscapes, the sources of the unifying "symbolic" power.

The point receives more development and ampler documentation in recent articles by Meyer Abrams and Earl Wasserman that make use of very similar, at times even identical material.[14] The two interpreters agree on many issues, to the point of overlapping. Both name, for instance, the principle of analogy between mind and nature as the basis for the eighteenth-century habit of treating a moral issue in terms of a descriptive landscape. Abrams refers to Renaissance concepts of theology and philosophy as a main source for the later *paysage moralisé:* ". . . the divine Architect has designed the universe analogically, relating the physical, moral, and spiritual realms by an elaborate system of correspondences. . . . The metaphysics of a symbolic and analogical universe underlay the figurative tactics of the seventeenth-century metaphysical poets."[15] A "tamed and ordered" version of this cosmology, "smoothed to a neo-classic decency" and decorum, then becomes the origin of the eighteenth-century loco-descriptive poem, in which "sensuous phenomena are coupled with moral statements." And Wasserman points to eighteenth-century theoreticians of the imagination, such as Akenside, who "can find [the most intimate relation] between subject and object is that of associative analogy, so that man beholds 'in lifeless things / The Inexpressive semblance of himself, / Of thought and passion.'"[16]

The key concept here is, in Wasserman's correct phrasing, that of an *associative* analogy, as contrasted with a more vital form of analogy in the romantics. Abrams makes it seem, at times, as if the romantic theory of imagination did away with analogy altogether and that Coleridge in particular replaced it by a genuine and working monism. "Nature is made thought and thought nature," he writes, "both by their sustained interaction and by their seamless metaphoric continuity."[17] But he does not really claim that this degree of fusion is achieved and sustained—at most that it corresponds to Coleridge's desire for a unity toward which his thought and poetic strategy strive. Analogy as such is certainly never abandoned as an epistemological pattern for natural images; even within the esoteric vocabulary of as late a version of a monistic universe as Baudelaire's correspondences, the expression "*analogie universelle*" is still being used.[18] Nevertheless, the relationship between mind and nature becomes indeed a lot less formal, less purely associative and external than it is in the eighteenth century. As a result, the critical—and even, at times, the poetic—vocabulary attempts to find terms better suited to express this relationship than is the somewhat formal concept of analogy. Words such as "affinity," or "sympathy," appear instead of the more abstract "analogy." This does not change the fundamental pattern of the structure, which remains that of a formal resemblance between entities that, in other respects, can be antithetical. But the new terminology indicates a gliding away from the formal problem of a congruence between the two poles to that of the ontological priority of the one over the other. For terms such as "affinity" or "sympathy" apply to the relationships between subjects rather than to relationships between a subject and an object. The relationship with nature has been superseded by an intersubjective, interpersonal

[13] *Ibid.* p. 110. [Au.]

[14] Meyer Abrams, "Structure and Style in the Greater Romantic Lyric," in *From Sensibility to Romanticism: Essays Presented to F. A. Pottle,* F. W. Hillis and H. Bloom, eds. (New York: Oxford University Press, 1965). Earl Wasserman, "The English Romantics, The Grounds of Knowledge," *Essays in Romanticism,* 4 (Autumn, 1964). [Au.]

[15] Abrams, p. 536. [Au.]

[16] Wasserman, p. 19. [Au.]

[17] Abrams, p. 551. [Au.]

[18] Charles Baudelaire, "Réflexions sur quelques-uns de mes contemporains, Victor Hugo." in *Curiosités esthétiques: L'Art romantique et autre Oeuvres critiques,* H. Lemaître, ed. (Paris: Garnier, 1962), p. 735. [Au.]

relationship that, in the last analysis, is a relationship of the subject toward itself. Thus the priority has passed from the outside world entirely within the subject, and we end up with something that resembles a radical idealism. Both Abrams and Wasserman offer quotations from Wordsworth and Coleridge, as well as summarizing comments of their own, that seem to suggest that romanticism is, in fact, such an idealism. Both quote Wordsworth: "I was often unable to think of external things as having external existence, and I communed with all that I saw as something not apart from, but inherent in, my own immaterial nature"—and Wasserman comments that "Wordsworth's poetic experience seeks to recapture that condition."[19]

Since the assertion of a radical priority of the subject over objective nature is not easily compatible with the poetic praxis of the romantic poets, who all gave a great deal of importance to the presence of nature, a certain degree of confusion ensues. One can find numerous quotations and examples that plead for the predominance, in romantic poetry, of an analogical imagination that is founded on the priority of natural substances over the consciousness of the self. Coleridge can speak, in nearly Fichtean terms, of the infinite self in opposition to the "necessarily finite" character of natural objects, and insist on the need for the self to give life to the dead forms of nature.[20] But the finite nature of the objective world is seen, at that moment, in spatial terms, and the substitution of vital (i.e., in Coleridge, intersubjective) relationships that are dynamic, for the physical relationships that exist between entities in the natural world is not necessarily convincing. It could very well be argued that Coleridge's own concept of organic unity as a dynamic principle is derived from the movements of nature, not from those of the self. Wordsworth is more clearly conscious of what is involved here when he sees the same dialectic between the self and nature in temporal terms. The movements of nature are for him instances of what Goethe calls *Dauer im Wechsel,* endurance within a pattern of change, the assertion of a metatemporal, stationary state beyond the apparent decay of a mutability that attacks certain outward aspects of nature but leaves the core intact. Hence we have famous passages such as the description of the mountain scenes in *The Prelude* in which a striking temporal paradox is evoked:

> . . . these majestic floods—these shining
> cliffs
> The untransmuted shapes of many worlds,
> Cerulian ether's pure inhabitants,
> These forests unapproachable by death,
> That shall endure as long as man en-
> dures . . . ;

or

> The immeasurable height
> Of woods decaying, never to be decayed
> The stationary blast of waterfalls. . . .

Such paradoxical assertions of eternity in motion can be applied to nature but not to a self caught up entirely within mutability. The temptation exists, then, for the self to borrow, so to speak, the temporal stability that it lacks from nature, and to devise strategies by means of which nature is brought down to a human level while still escaping from "the unimaginable touch of time." This strategy is certainly present in Coleridge. And it is present, though perhaps not consciously, in critics such as Abrams and Wasserman, who see Coleridge as the great synthesizer and who take his dialectic of subject and object to be the authentic pattern of romantic imagery. But this forces them, in fact, into a persistent contradiction. They are obliged, on the one hand, to assert the priority of object over subject that is implicit in an organic conception of language. So Abrams states: "The best Romantic meditations on a landscape, following Coleridge's example, all manifest a transaction between subject and object in which the thought incorporates and makes explicit what was already implicit in the outer scene."[21] This puts the priority unquestionably in the natural world, limiting the task of the mind to interpreting what is given in nature. Yet this statement is taken from the same paragraph in which Abrams quotes the passages from Wordsworth and Coleridge that confer an equally absolute priority to the self over nature. The contradiction reaches a genuine impasse. For what are we to believe? Is romanticism a

[19] Wasserman, p. 26. [Au.]
[20] *Ibid.*, p. 29. [Au.]

[21] Abrams, p. 551. [Au.]

subjective idealism, open to all the attacks of solipsism that, from Hazlitt to the French structuralists, a succession of de-mystifiers of the self have directed against it? Or is it instead a return to a certain form of naturalism after the forced abstraction of the Enlightenment, but a return which our urban and alienated world can conceive of only as a nostalgic and unreachable past? Wasserman is caught in the same impasse: for him, Wordsworth represents the extreme form of subjectivism whereas Keats, as a quasi-Shakespearean poet of negative capability, exemplifies a sympathetic and objective form of material imagination. Coleridge acts as the synthesis of this antithetical polarity. But Wasserman's claim for Coleridge as the reconciler of what he calls "the phenomenal world of understanding with the noumenal world of reason"[22] is based on a quotation in which Coleridge simply substitutes another self for the category of the object and thus removes the problem from nature altogether, reducing it to a purely intersubjective pattern. "To make the object one with us, we must become one with the object—ergo, an object. Ergo, the object must be itself a subject—partially a favorite dog, principally a friend, wholly God, *the* Friend."[23] Wordsworth was never guilty of thus reducing a theocentric to an interpersonal relationship.

Does the confusion originate with the critics, or does it reside in the romantic poets themselves? Were they really unable to move beyond the analogism that they inherited from the eighteenth century and were they trapped in the contradiction of a pseudo dialectic between subject and object? Certain commentators believe this to be the case;[24] before following them, we should make certain that we have indeed been dealing with the main romantic problem when we interpret the romantic image in terms of a subject-object tension. For this dialectic originates, it must be remembered, in the assumed predominance of the symbol as the outstanding characteristic of romantic diction, and this predominance must, in its turn, be put into question.

It might be helpful, at this point, to shift attention from English to French literary history. Because French pre-romanticism occurs, with Rousseau, so early in the eighteenth century, and because the Lockian heritage in France never reached, not even with Condillac, the degree of automaticism against which Coleridge and Wordsworth had to rebel in Hartley, the entire problem of analogy, as connected with the use of nature imagery, is somewhat clearer there than in England. Some of the writers of the period were at least as aware as their later commentators of what was involved in a development of the general taste that felt attracted toward a new kind of landscape. To take one example: in his *De la composition des paysages sur le terrain,* which dates from 1777, the Marquis de Girardin describes a landscape explicitly as "romantic," made up of dark woods, snow-capped mountains, and a crystalline lake with an island on which an idyllic "*ménage rustique*" enjoys a happy combination of sociability and solitude among cascades and rushing brooks. And he comments on the scene as follows: "It is in situations like this that one feels all the strength of this analogy between natural beauty and moral sentiment."[25] One could establish a long list of similar quotations dating from the same general period, all expressing the intimate proximity between nature and its beholder in a language that evokes the material shape of the landscape as well as the mood of its inhabitants.

Later historians and critics have stressed this close unity between mind and nature as a fundamental characteristic of romantic diction. "Often the outer and the inner world are so deeply intermingled," writes Daniel Mornet, "that nothing distinguishes the images perceived by the senses from the chimera of the imagination."[26] The same emphasis, still present in the more recent writings on the period,[27] closely resembles the opinion expressed in Anglo-American criticism. There is the same stress on the analogical unity of nature and consciousness, the same priority given to the symbol as the unit of language in which the subject-object synthesis can take place, the same tendency

[22] Wasserman, p. 30. [Au.]

[23] *Ibid.*, pp. 29–30. [Au.]

[24] As one instance among others see E. E. Bostetter, *The Romantic Ventriloquists* (Seattle: University of Washington Press, 1963). [Au.]

[25] Quoted in Daniel Mornet, *Le Sentiment de la Nature en France au XVIIIe siècle de Jean-Jacques Rousseau à Bernardin de Saint-Pierre* (Paris, 1932), p. 248. [Au.]

[26] *Ibid*, p. 187. [Au.]

[27] See, for example, Herbert Dieckmann, "Zur Theorie der Lyrik im 18. Jahrhundert in Frankreich, mit gelegentlicher Berucksichtigung der Englischen Kritik," in *Poetik und Hermeneutik,* vol. 2, W. Iser, ed. (Munich: Wilhelm Fink, 1966), p. 108. [Au.]

to transfer into nature attributes of consciousness and to unify it organically with respect to a center that acts, for natural objects, as the identity of the self functions for a consciousness. In French literary history dealing with the period of Rousseau to the present, ambivalences closely akin to those found in the American historians of romanticism could be pointed out, ambivalences derived from an illusionary priority of a subject that had, in fact, to borrow from the outside world a temporal stability which it lacked within itself.

In the case of French romanticism, it is perhaps easier than it is in English literature to designate the historical origin of this tendency. One can point to a certain number of specific texts in which a symbolic language, based on the close interpenetration between observation and passion, begins to acquire a priority that it will never relinquish during the nineteenth and twentieth centuries. Among these texts none is more often singled out than Rousseau's novel *La Nouvelle Héloïse*. It forms the basis of Daniel Mornet's study on the sentiment of nature in the eighteenth century.[28] In more recent works, such as Robert Mauzi's *Idée du bonheur dans la littérature française du 18ème siècle,*[29] the same predominant importance is given to Rousseau's novel. "When one knows *Cleveland* and *La Nouvelle Héloïse,* there is little left to discover about the 18th century," Mauzi asserts in his preface.[30] There is certainly no better reference to be found than *La Nouvelle Héloïse* for putting to the test the nearly unanimous conviction that the origins of romanticism coincide with the beginnings of a predominantly symbolical diction.

Interpreters of Rousseau's epistolary novel have had no difficulty in pointing out the close correspondence between inner states of the soul and the outward aspect of nature, especially in passages such as the Meillerie episode in the fourth part of the novel.[31] In this letter, St. Preux revisits, in the company of the now-married Julie, the deserted region on the northern bank of the lake from which he had, in earlier days, written the letter that sealed their destiny. Rousseau stresses that the *lieu solitaire* he describes is like a wild desert "*sauvage et désert; mais plein de ces sortes de beautés qui ne plaisent qu'aux âmes sensibles et paraissent horribles aux autres.*"[32] A polemical reference to current taste is certainly present here, and such passages can be cited to illustrate the transition from the eighteenth-century, idyllic landscape that we still find in Girardin to the somber, tormented scenes that are soon to predominate in Macpherson. But this polemic of taste is superficial, for Rousseau's concerns are clearly entirely different. It is true that the intimate analogy between scenery and emotion serves as a basis for some of the dramatic and poetic effects of the passage: the sensuous passion, reawakened by memory and threatening to disturb a precarious tranquility, is conveyed by the contrasting effects of light and setting which give the passage its dramatic power. The analogism of the style and the sensuous intensity of the passion are closely related. But this should not blind us to the explicit thematic function of the letter, which is one of temptation and near-fatal relapse into former error, openly and explicitly condemned, without any trace of ambiguity, in the larger context of Rousseau's novel.

In this respect, the reference to the Meillerie landscape as a wilderness is particularly revealing, especially when contrasted with other landscapes in the novel that are not emblematic of error, but of the virtue associated with the figure of Julie. This is the case for the central emblem of the novel, the garden that Julie has created on the Wolmar estate as a place of refuge. On the allegorical level the garden functions as the landscape representative of the "beautiful soul." Our question is whether this garden, the Elysium described at length in the eleventh letter of the fourth part of the novel, is based on the same kind of subject/object relationship that was thematically and stylistically present in the Meillerie episode.

A brief consideration of Rousseau's sources for the passage is enlightening. The main non-literary source has been all too strongly emphasized by Mornet in his critical edition of the novel:[33] Rous-

[28] See note 25 above.[Au.]

[29] Robert Mauzi, *L'Idée du bonheur dans la littérature et la pensée française du XVIIIe siècle* (Paris: A. Colin, 1960). [Au.]

[30] *Ibid.*, p. 10 [Au.]

[31] J. J. Rousseau, *Julie ou la Nouvelle Héloïse,* pt. 4, letter 17, in *Oeuvres complètes,* B. Gagnebin and Marcel Raymond, eds. (Paris: Gallimard [Bibliotheque de la Pleiade, 1961), 2:514ff. [Au.]

[32] *Ibid.* p. 518. [Au.] "savage and deserted, but full of beauties of a kind that please only sensitive souls, and appear horrible to others." [Eds.]

[33] *La Nouvelle Héloïse,* Daniel Mornet, ed. (Paris: 1925), Introduction, 1:67–74, and notes, 3:223–47. [Au.]

seau derives several of the exterior aspects of his garden from the so-called *jardins anglais,* which, well before him, were being preferred to the geometrical abstraction of the classical French gardens. The excessive symmetry of Le Nôtre, writes Rousseau, echoing a commonplace of sophisticated taste at the time, is *"ennemie de la nature et de la variété."*[34] But this "natural" look of the garden is by no means the main theme of the passage. From the beginning we are told that the natural aspect of the site is in fact the result of extreme artifice, that in his bower of bliss, contrary to the tradition of the *topos,* we are entirely in the realm of art and not that of nature. "Il est vrai," Rousseau has Julie say, "que la nature a tout fait [dans ce jardin] mais sous ma direction, et il n'y a rien là que je n'aie ordonné."[35] The statement should at least alert us to the literary sources of the gardens of the passage that Mornet, preoccupied as he was with the outward history of taste, was led to neglect.

Confining ourselves to the explicit literary allusions that can be found in the text, the reference to "*une Ile déserte . . (où) je n'aperçois aucuns pas d'hommes*"[36] points directly toward Rousseau's favorite contemporary novel, the only one considered suitable for Emile's education, Defoe's *Robinson Crusoe,* whereas the allusion to the *Roman de la rose* in the pages immediately preceding the letter on Julie's Elysium[37] is equally revealing. The combination of *Robinson Crusoe* with the *Roman de la rose* may not look very promising at first sight, but it has, in fact, considerable hidden possibilities. The fact that the medieval romance, re-issued in 1735 and widely read in Rousseau's time,[38] had given the novel its subtitle of *"La Nouvelle Héloïse"* is well known, but its influence is manifest in many other ways as well. The close similarity between Julie's garden and the love garden of Deduit, which appears in the first part of Guillaume de Lorris' poem, is obvious. There is hardly a detail of Rousseau's description that does not find its counterpart in the medieval text: the self-enclosed, isolated space of the "*asile*"; the special privilege reserved to the happy few who possess a key that unlocks the gate; the traditional enumeration of natural attributes—a catalogue of the various flowers, trees, fruits, perfumes, and, above all, of the birds, culminating in the description of their song.[39] Most revealing of all is the emphasis on water, on fountains and pools that, in *Julie* as in the *Roman de la rose,* are controlled not by nature but by the ingenuity of the inhabitants.[40] Far from being an observed scene or the expression of a personal *état d'âme,* it is clear that Rousseau has deliberately taken all the details of his setting from the medieval literary source, one of the best-known versions of the traditional *topos* of the erotic garden.

In linguistic terms, we have something very different, then, from the descriptive and metaphorical language that, from Chateaubriand on, will predominate in French romantic diction. Rousseau does not even pretend to be observing. The language is purely figural, not based on perception, less still on an experienced dialectic between nature and consciousness. Julie's claim of domination and control over nature ("*il n'y a rien là que je n'aie ordonné*") may well be considered as the fitting emblem for a language that submits the outside world entirely to its own purposes, contrary to what happens in the Meillerie episode, where the language fuses together the parallel movements of nature and of passion.

In the first part of the *Roman de la rose,* however, the use of figural language in no way conflicts with the exalted treatment of erotic themes; quite to the contrary, the erotic aspects of the allegory hardly need to be stressed. But in *La Nouvelle Héloïse* the emphasis on an ethic of renunciation conveys a moral climate that differs entirely from the moralizing sections of the medieval romance. Rousseau's theme of renunciation is far from being one-sided and is certainly not to be equated with a puritanical denial of the world of the senses. Nevertheless, it is in the use of allegorical diction rather than of the language of correspondences that the medieval and

[34] Rousseau, p. 483. [Au.]

[35] *Ibid.,* p. 472. [Au.] "It is true that nature has made everything [in the garden] but under my direction, and there is nothing which I have not ordered." [Eds.]

[36] *Ibid.,* p. 479. [Au.] "a desert isle . . . [where] I discern no other people." [Eds.]

[37] "Richesse ne fait pas riche, dit le Roman de la Rose," quoted in letter 10 of pt. 4, *ibid.,* p. 466 and n. [Au.]

[38] *Ibid.,* p. 1606, n. 2. I have consulted a copy of the Lenglet du Fresnoy edition which, at first sight, offers no variants that are immediately relevant to our question. [Au.]

[39] Guillaume de Lorris and Jean de Meun, *Le Roman de la rose,* Félix Lecoy, ed. (Paris: Champion, 1965) vol. 1, esp. 11. 499ff., 629ff., 1345ff. [Au.]

[40] *Ibid.,* 11. 1385ff. [Au.]

eighteenth-century sources converge. Recent studies of Defoe, such as G. A. Starr's *Defoe and Spiritual Autobiography*[41] and Paul Hunter's *The Reluctant Pilgrim,*[42] have reversed the trend to see in Defoe one of the inventors of a modern "realistic" idiom and have rediscovered the importance of the puritanical, religious element to which Rousseau responded. Paul Hunter has strongly emphasized the stylistic importance of this element, which led Defoe to make an allegorical rather than a metaphorical and descriptive use of nature. Thus Defoe's gardens, far from being realistic natural settings, are stylized emblems, quite similar in structure and detail to the gardens of the *Roman de la rose*. But they serve primarily a redemptive, ethical function. Defoe's garden, writes Paul Hunter, "is not . . . a prelapsarian paradise but rather an earthly paradise *in posse,* for Crusoe is postlapsarian man who has to toil to cultivate his land into full abundance."[43] The same stress on hardship, toil, and virtue is present in Julie's garden, relating the scene closely to the Protestant allegorical tradition of which the English version, culminating in Bunyan, reached Rousseau through a variety of sources, including Defoe. The stylistic likeness of the sources supersedes all further differences between them; the tension arises not between the two distant literary sources, the one erotic, the other puritanical, but between the allegorical language of a scene such as Julie's Elysium and the symbolic language of passages such as the Meillerie episode. The moral contrast between these two worlds epitomizes the dramatic conflict of the novel. This conflict is ultimately resolved in the triumph of a controlled and lucid renunciation of the values associated with a cult of the moment, and this renunciation establishes the priority of an allegorical over a symbolic diction. The novel could not exist without the simultaneous presence of both metaphorical modes, nor could it reach its conclusion without the implied choice in favor of allegory over symbol.

Subsequent interpreters of *La Nouvelle Héloïse* have, in general, ignored the presence of allegorical elements in shaping the diction of the novel, and it is only recently that one begins to realize how false the image of Rousseau as a primitivist or as a naturalist actually is. These false interpretations, very revealing in their own right, resist correction with a remarkable tenacity, thereby indicating how deeply this correction conflicts with the widespread "*idées reçues*" on the nature and the origins of European romanticism.

For, if the dialectic between subject and object does not designate the main romantic experience, but only one passing moment in a dialectic, and a negative moment at that, since it represents a temptation that has to be overcome, then the entire historical and philosophical pattern changes a great deal. Similar allegorizing tendencies, though often in a very different form, are present not only in Rousseau but in all European literature between 1760 and 1800. Far from being a mannerism inherited from the exterior aspects of the baroque and the rococo, they appear at the most original and profound moments in the works, when an authentic voice becomes audible. The historians of English romanticism have been forced, by the nature of things, to mention allegory, although it is often a problem of secondary importance. Wimsatt has to encounter it in dealing with Blake; he quotes two brief poems by Blake, entitled "To Spring" and "To Summer," and comments: "Blake's starting point . . . is the opposite of Wordsworth's and Byron's, not the landscape but a spirit personified or allegorized. Nevertheless, this spirit as it approaches the 'western isle' takes on certain distinctly terrestrial hues. . . . These early romantic poets are examples of the Biblical, classical, and Renaissance tradition of allegory as it approaches the romantic condition of landscape naturalism—as Spring and Summer descend into the landscape and are fused with it."[44] Rather than such a continuous development from allegory to romantic naturalism, the example of Rousseau shows that we are dealing instead with the rediscovery of an allegorical tradition beyond the sensualistic analogism of the eighteenth century. This rediscovery, far from being spontaneous and easy, implies instead the discontinuity of a renunciation, even of a sacrifice. Taking for his starting point the descriptive poem of

[41] G. A. Starr, *Defoe and Spiritual Autobiography* (Princeton, N.J.: Princeton University Press, 1965). [Au.]

[42] J. Paul Hunter, *The Reluctant Pilgrim: Defoe's Emblematic Method and Quest in Robinson Crusoe* (Baltimore: Johns Hopkins University Press, 1966). [Au.]

[43] *Ibid.*, p. 172. [Au.]

[44] Wimsatt, p. 113. [Au.]

the eighteenth century, Abrams can speak with more historical precision. After having stressed the thematic resemblance between the romantic lyric and the metaphysical poem of the seventeenth century, he writes: "There is a very conspicuous and significant difference between the Romantic lyric and the seventeenth-century meditation on created nature. . . . [In the seventeenth century] the 'composition of place' was not a specific locality, nor did it need to be present to the eyes of the speaker, but was a typical scene or object, usually called up . . . before 'the eyes of the imagination' in order to set off and guide the thought by means of correspondences whose interpretation was firmly controlled by an inherited typology."[45] The distinction between seventeenth- and late eighteenth-century poetry is made in terms of the determining role played by the geographical *place* as establishing the link between the language of the poem and the empirical experience of the reader. However, in observing the development of even as geographically concrete a poet as Wordsworth, the significance of the locale can extend so far as to include a meaning that is no longer circumscribed by the literal horizon of a given place. The meaning of the site is often made problematic by a sequence of spatial ambiguities, to such an extent that one ends up no longer at a specific place but with a mere name whose geographical significance has become almost meaningless. Raising the question of the geographical locale of a given metaphorical object (in this case, a river), Wordsworth writes: "The spirit of the answer [as to the whereabouts of the river] through the word might be a certain stream, accompanied perhaps with an image gathered from a Map, or from a real object in nature—these might have been the latter, but the spirit of the answer must have been, as inevitably—a receptacle without bounds or dimensions;—nothing less than infinity."[46] Passages in Wordsworth such as the crossing of the Alps or the ascent of Mount Snowden, or texts less sublime in character, such as the sequence of poems on the river Duddon, can no longer be classified with the locodescriptive poem of the eighteenth century. In the terminology proposed by Abrams, passages of this kind no longer depend on the choice of a specific locale, but are controlled by "a traditional and inherited typology," exactly as in the case of the poems from the sixteenth and seventeenth centuries—with this distinction, however, that the typology is no longer the same and that the poet, sometimes after long and difficult inner struggle, had to renounce the seductiveness and the poetic resources of a symbolical diction.

Whether it occurs in the form of an ethical conflict, as in *La Nouvelle Héloïse,* or as an allegorization of the geographical site, as in Wordsworth, the prevalence of allegory always corresponds to the unveiling of an authentically temporal destiny. This unveiling takes place in a subject that has sought refuge against the impact of time in a natural world to which, in truth, it bears no resemblance. The secularized thought of the pre-romantic period no longer allows a transcendence of the antinomies between the created world and the act of creation by means of a positive recourse to the notion of divine will; the failure of the attempt to conceive of a language that would be symbolical as well as allegorical, the suppression, in the allegory, of the analogical and anagogical levels, is one of the ways in which this impossibility becomes manifest. In the world of the symbol it would be possible for the image to coincide with the substance, since the substance and its representation do not differ in their being but only in their extension: they are part and whole of the same set of categories. Their relationship is one of simultaneity, which, in truth, is spatial in kind, and in which the intervention of time is merely a matter of contingency, whereas, in the world of allegory, time is the originary constitutive category. The relationship between the allegorical sign and its meaning (*signifié*) is not decreed by dogma; in the instances we have seen in Rousseau and in Wordsworth, this is not at all the case. We have, instead, a relationship between signs in which the reference to their respective meanings has become of secondary importance. But this relationship between signs necessarily contains a constitutive temporal element; it remains necessary, if there is to be allegory, that the allegorical sign refer to another sign that precedes it. The meaning constituted by the allegorical sign can then consist only in the *repetition* (in the Kierkegaardian sense of the term) of a previous sign with which it can never coincide, since it is

[45] Abrams, p. 556. [Au.]

[46] W. Wordsworth, "Essay upon Epitaphs," in *The Poetical Works* (Oxford, 1949) 4:446. [Au.]

of the essence of this previous sign to be pure anteriority. The secularized allegory of the early romantics thus necessarily contains the negative moment which in Rousseau is that of renunciation, in Wordsworth that of the loss of self in death or in error.

Whereas the symbol postulates the possibility of an identity or identification, allegory designates primarily a distance in relation to its own origin, and, renouncing the nostalgia and the desire to coincide, it establishes its language in the void of this temporal difference. In so doing, it prevents the self from an illusory identification with the non-self, which is now fully, though painfully, recognized as a non-self. It is this painful knowledge that we perceive at the moments when early romantic literature finds its true voice. It is ironically revealing that this voice is so rarely recognized for what it really is and that the literary movement in which it appears has repeatedly been called a primitive naturalism or a mystified solipsism. The authors with whom we are dealing had often gone out of their way to designate their theological and philosophical sources: too little attention has been paid to the complex and controlled set of literary allusions which, in *La Nouvelle Héloïse,* established the link between Rousseau and his Augustinian sources, mostly by way of Petrarch.

We are led, in conclusion, to a historical scheme that differs entirely from the customary picture. The dialectical relationship between subject and object is no longer the central statement of romantic thought, but this dialectic is now located entirely in the temporal relationships that exist within a system of allegorical signs. It becomes a conflict between a conception of the self seen in its authentically temporal predicament and a defensive strategy that tries to hide from this negative self-knowledge. On the level of language the asserted superiority of the symbol over allegory, so frequent during the nineteenth century, is one of the forms taken by this tenacious self-mystification. Wide areas of European literature of the nineteenth and twentieth centuries appear as regressive with regards to the truths that come to light in the last quarter of the eighteenth century. For the lucidity of the pre-romantic writers does not persist. It does not take long for a symbolic conception of metaphorical language to establish itself everywhere, despite the ambiguities that persist in aesthetic theory and poetic practice. But this symbolical style will never be allowed to exist in serenity; since it is a veil thrown over a light one no longer wishes to perceive, it will never be able to gain an entirely good poetic conscience.

II. Irony

Around the same time that the tension between symbol and allegory finds expression in the works and the theoretical speculations of the early romantics, the problem of irony also receives more and more self-conscious attention. At times, a concern with the figural aspects of language and, more specifically, an awareness of the persistence of allegorical modes go hand in hand with a theoretical concern for the trope "irony" as such. This is by no means always the case. We cited Rousseau and Wordsworth, and alluded to Hölderlin, as possible instances of romantic allegorism; the use of irony is conspicuously absent from all these poets. In others, however, the implicit and rather enigmatic link between allegory and irony which runs through the history of rhetoric seems to prevail. We mentioned Hamann;[47] in Germany alone, the names of Friedrich Schlegel, Friedrich Solger, E. T. A. Hoffmann, and Kierkegaard would be obvious additions to the list. In all these instances a more-or-less systematic theory of figural language, with explicit stress on allegory, runs parallel with an equally prevalent stress on irony. Friedrich Schlegel, of course, is well known as the main theoretician of romantic irony. That he was also affected, as well as somewhat puzzled, by the problem of metaphorical diction is clear from many of the *Fragmenten,* as well as from the revisions he made between the 1800 and 1823 editions of his works.[48] A similar parallelism between the problem of allegory and that of irony is certainly present in Solger, who elevates irony to the constitutive mode of all literature and suggestively distinguishes between symbol and allegory in terms of a dialectic of identity and difference.[49]

Nevertheless, the connection and the distinction between allegory and irony never become, at that time, independent subjects for reflection. The terms

[47] See note 3 above. [Au.]

[48] Schlegel, Band 2, p. xci. [Au.]

[49] Friedrich Solger, *Erwin: Vier Gespräche über das Schöne und die Kunst* (Leipzig, 1829). [Au.]

are rarely used as a means to reach a sharper definition, which, especially in the case of irony, is greatly needed. It obviously does not suffice to refer back to the descriptive rhetorical tradition which, from Aristotle to the eighteenth century, defines irony as "saying one thing and meaning another" or, in an even more restrictive context, as "blame-by-praise and praise-by-blame"[50] This definition points to a structure shared by irony and allegory in that, in both cases, the relationship between sign and meaning is discontinuous, involving an extraneous principle that determines the point and the manner at and in which the relationship is articulated. In both cases, the sign points to something that differs from its literal meaning and has for its function the thematization of this difference. But this important structural aspect may well be a description of figural language in general; it clearly lacks discriminatory precision. The relationship between allegory and irony appears in history as a casual and apparently contingent fact, in the form of a common concern of some writers with both modes. It is this empirical event that has to receive a more general and theoretical interpretation.

The question is made more complex, but also somewhat more concrete, by an additional connection between a concern with irony and the development of the modern novel. The link is made in many critical texts: in Goethe, in Friedrich Schlegel, more recently in Lukács and in structuralist studies of narrative form. The tie between irony and the novel seems to be so strong that one feels tempted to follow Lukács in making the novel into the equivalent, in the history of literary genres, of irony itself. From the very beginning, the possibility of extending the trope to make it encompass lengthy narratives existed; in the *Institutio,* Quintilian described irony as capable of coloring an entire discourse pronounced in a tone of voice that did not correspond to the true situation, or even, with reference to Socrates, as pervading an entire life.[51] The passage from the localized trope to the extended novel is tempting, although the correlation between irony and the novel is far from simple. Even the superficial and empirical observation of literary history reveals this complexity. The growth of theoretical insight into irony around 1800 bears a by no means obvious relationship to the growth of the nineteenth-century novel. In Germany, for instance, the advent of a full-fledged ironic consciousness, which will persist from Friedrich Schlegel to Kierkegaard and to Nietzsche, certainly does not coincide with a parallel blossoming of the novel. Friedrich Schlegel, writing on the novel, has to take his recent examples from Sterne and Diderot and has to strain to find a comparable level of ironic insight in *Wilhelm Meisters Lehrjahre* and in Jean Paul Richter.[52] The opposite is true in France and England, where the spectacular development of the novel is not necessarily accompanied by a parallel interest in the theory of irony; one has to wait until Baudelaire to find a French equivalent of Schlegel's penetration. It could be argued that the greatest ironists of the nineteenth century generally are not novelists: they often tend toward novelistic forms and devices—one thinks of Kierkegaard, Hoffmann, Baudelaire, Mallarmé, or Nietzsche—but they show a prevalent tendency toward aphoristic, rapid, and brief texts (which are incompatible with the duration that is the basis of the novel), as if there were something in the nature of irony that did not allow for sustained movements. The great and all-important exception is, of course, Stendhal. But it should be clear by now that, aside from having to give insight into the relationship between irony and allegory, an intentional theory of irony should also deal with the relationship between irony and the novel.

In the case of irony one cannot so easily take refuge in the need for a historical de-mystification of the term, as when we tried to show that the term "symbol" had in fact been substituted for that of "allegory" in an act of ontological bad faith. The tension between allegory and symbol justified this procedure: the mystification is a fact of history and must therefore be dealt with in a historical manner before actual theorization can start. But in the case of irony one has to start out from the structure of the trope itself, taking one's cue from texts that are de-mystified and, to a large extent, themselves ironical. For that manner, the target of their irony is very often the claim to speak about human matters as if they were facts of history. It is a historical fact that irony

[50] Norman Knox, *The Word Irony and Its Context, 1500–1755* (Durham, N.C.: Duke University Press, 1961). [Au.]

[51] Quintilian, *Institutio* 9.2. 44–53, quoted in Knox. [Au.]

[52] Schlegel, 'Brief uber den Roman,' in "Gesprache uber die Poesie," pp. 331ff. [Au.]

becomes increasingly conscious of itself in the course of demonstrating the impossibility of our being historical. In speaking of irony we are dealing not with the history of an error but with a problem that exists within the self. We cannot escape, therefore, the need for a definition toward which this essay is oriented. On the other hand, a great deal of assistance can be gained from existing texts on irony. Curiously enough, it seems to be only in describing a mode of language which does not mean what it says that one can actually say what one means.

Thus freed from the necessity of respecting historical chronology, we can take Baudelaire's text, "De l'essence du rire," as a starting point. Among the various examples of ridicule cited and analyzed, it is the simplest situation of all that best reveals the predominant traits of an ironic consciousness: the spectacle of a man tripping and falling into the street. "Le comique," writes Baudelaire, "la puissance du rire est dans le rieur et nullement dans l'objet du rire. Ce n'est point l'homme qui tombe qui rit de sa propre chute, à moins qu'il ne soit un philosophe, un homme qui ait acquis, par habitude, la force de se dédoubler rapidement et d'assister comme spectateur désintéressé aux phénomènes de son *moi*."[53] In this simple observation several key concepts are already present. In the first place, the accent falls on the notion of *dédoublement* as the characteristic that sets apart a reflective activity, such as that of the philosopher, from the activity of the ordinary self caught in everyday concerns. Hidden away at first in side-remarks such as this one, or masked behind a vocabulary of superiority and inferiority, of master and slave, the notion of self-duplication or self-multiplication emerges at the end of the essay as the key concept of the article, the concept for the sake of which the essay has in fact been written.

> . . . pour qu'il y ait comique, c'est-à-dire émanation, explosion, dégagement de comique, il faut qu'il y ait deux êtres en présence;—que c'est spécialement dans le rieur, dans le spectateur, que gît le comique;—que cependant, relativement à cette loi d'ignorance, il faut faire une exception pour les hommes qui ont fait métier de développer en eux le sentiment du comique et de le tirer d'eux-mêmes pour le divertissement de leurs semblables, lequel phénomène rentre dans la classe de tous les phénomènes artistiques qui dénotent dans l'être humain l'existence d'une dualité permanente, la puissance d'être à la fois soi et un autre.[54]

The nature of this duplication is essential for an understanding of irony. It is a relationship, within consciousness, between two selves, yet it is not an intersubjective relationship. Baudelaire spends several pages of his essay distinguishing between a simple sense of comedy that is oriented toward others, and thus exists on the necessarily empirical level of interpersonal relationships, and what he calls "*le comique absolu*" (by which he designates that which, at other moments in his work, he calls irony), where the relationship is not between man and man, two entities that are in essence similar, but between man and what he calls nature, that is, two entities that are in essence different. Within the realm of intersubjectivity one would indeed speak of difference in terms of the superiority of one subject over another, with all the implications of will to power, of violence, and possession which come into play when a person is laughing at someone else—including the will to educate and to improve. But, when the concept of "superiority" is still being used when the self is engaged in a relationship not to other subjects, but to what is precisely not a self, then the so-called superiority merely designates the *distance* constitutive of all acts of reflection. Superi-

[53] Charles Baudelaire, "De l'essence du rire," in *Curiosités esthétiques: L'Art romantique et autres Oeuvres critiques*, H. Lemaître, ed. (Paris: Garnier, 1962), pp. 215ff. [Au.] "The comic and the capacity for laughter are in the one who laughs, not at all in the object of laughter. It is not the man who stumbles who laughs at his own fall, unless he be a philosopher, a man who has formed by habit the power of rapid self-doubling, and thus assisting as a disinterested spectator at the phenomenon of his own self." [Eds.]

[54] *Ibid.*, p. 262. [Au.] "For there to be the comic, that is to say, emanation, explosion, the discharge of the comic, it is necessary that there be two beings present—that it is especially in the laugher, the spectator, that the comic resides; yet still, relative to that law of ignorance, it is necessary to make an exception for those who have made it their business to develop in themselves the comic sensibility and to draw it forth for their fellows, which phenomenon enters into the class of all artistic phenomena which point to the existence of a permanent duality in human nature, the capacity to be at the same time both oneself and an other." [Eds.]

ority and inferiority then become merely spatial metaphors to indicate a discontinuity and a plurality of levels within a subject that comes to know itself by an increasing differentiation from what is not. Baudelaire insists that irony, as "*comique absolu,*" is an infinitely higher form of comedy than is the intersubjective kind of humor he finds so frequently among the French; hence his preference for Italian *commedia dell'arte,* English pantomime, or the tales of E. T. A. Hoffmann over Molière, the typical example of a certain French comic spirit that is unable to rise above the level of intersubjectivity. Daumier is dismissed in the same terms in favor of Hogarth and Goya in the essays on caricature.[55]

The *dédoublement* thus designates the activity of a consciousness by which a man differentiates himself from the non-human world. The capacity for such duplication is rare, says Baudelaire, but belongs specifically to those who, like artists or philosophers, deal in language. His emphasis on a professional vocabulary, on "*se faire un métier,*" stresses the technicality of their action, the fact that language is their material, just as leather is the material of the cobbler or wood is that of the carpenter. In everyday, common existence, this is not how language usually operates; there it functions much more as does the cobbler's or the carpenter's hammer, not as the material itself, but as a tool by means of which the heterogeneous material of experience is more-or-less adequately made to fit. The reflective disjunction not only occurs *by means of* language as a privileged category, but it transfers the self out of the empirical world into a world constituted out of, and in, language—a language that it finds in the world like one entity among others, but that remains unique in being the only entity by means of which it can differentiate itself from the world. Language thus conceived divides the subject into an empirical self, immersed in the world, and a self that becomes like a sign in its attempt at differentiation and self-definition.

More important still, in Baudelaire's description the division of the subject into a multiple consciousness takes place in immediate connection with a fall. The element of falling introduces the specifically comical and ultimately ironical ingredient. At the moment that the artistic or philosophical, that is, the language-determined, man laughs at himself falling, he is laughing at a mistaken, mystified assumption he was making about himself. In a false feeling of pride the self has substituted, in its relationship to nature, an intersubjective feeling (of superiority) for the knowledge of a difference. As a being that stands upright (as in the passage at the beginning of Ovid's *Metamorphoses* to which Baudelaire alludes elsewhere[56]), man comes to believe that he dominates nature, just as he can, at times, dominate others or watch others dominate him. This is, of course, a major mystification. The Fall, in the literal as well as the theological sense, reminds him of the purely instrumental, reified character of his relationship to nature. Nature can at all times treat him as if he were a thing and remind him of his factitiousness, whereas he is quite powerless to convert even the smallest particle of nature into something human. In the idea of fall thus conceived, a progression in self-knowledge is certainly implicit: the man who has fallen is somewhat wiser than the fool who walks around oblivious of the crack in the pavement about to trip him up. And the fallen philosopher reflecting on the discrepancy between the two successive stages is wiser still, but this does not in the least prevent him from stumbling in his turn. It seems instead that his wisdom can be gained only at the cost of such a fall. The mere falling of others does not suffice; he has to go down himself. The ironic, twofold self that the writer or philosopher constitutes by his language seems able to come into being only at the expense of his empirical self, falling (or rising) from a stage of mystified adjustment into the knowledge of his mystification. The ironic language splits the subject into an empirical self that exists in a state of inauthenticity and a self that exists only in the form of a language that asserts the knowledge of this inauthenticity. This does not, however, make it into an authentic language, for to know inauthenticity is not the same as to be authentic.

It becomes evident that the disjunction is by no means a reassuring and serene process, despite the fact that it involves laughter. When the contemporary French philosopher V. Jankélévitch entitled a book on irony *L'Ironie ou la bonne conscience,* he

[55] Baudelaire, "Quelques caricaturistes français," *ibid.*, p. 281. [Au.]

[56] For example in the poem "Le Cygne":

> Je vois malhereux, mythe étrange et fatal,
> Vers le ciel quelquefois, comme l'homme
> d'Ovide. . . .

The allusion is to *Metamorphoses* 1. 84–86. [Au.]

certainly was far removed from Baudelaire's conception of irony—unless, of course, the choice of the title itself was ironic. For Baudelaire, at any rate, the movement of the ironic consciousness is anything but reassuring. The moment the innocence or authenticity of our sense of being in the world is put into question, a far from harmless process gets underway. It may start as a casual bit of play with a stray loose end of the fabric, but before long the entire texture of the self is unraveled and comes apart. The whole process happens at an unsettling speed. Irony possesses an inherent tendency to gain momentum and not to stop until it has run its full course; from the small and apparently innocuous exposure of a small self-deception it soon reaches the dimensions of the absolute. Often starting as litotes or understatement, it contains within itself the power to become hyperbole. Baudelaire refers to this unsettling power as "*vertige de l'hyperbole*" and conveys the feeling of its effect in his description of the English pantomime he saw at the Théâtre des Variétés:

> Une des choses les plus remarquables comme comique absolu, et, pour ainsi dire, comme métaphysique du comique absolu, était certainement le début de cette belle pièce, un prologue plein d'une haute esthétique. Les principaux personnages de la pièce, Pierrot, Cassandre, Harlequin, Colombine . . . sont [d'abord] à peu près raisonnables et ne diffèrent pas beaucoup des braves gens qui sont dans la salle. Le souffle merveilleux qui va les faire se mouvoir extraordinairement n'a pas encore soufflé sur leurs cervelles. . . . Une fée s'intéresse à Harlequin . . . elle lui promet sa protection et, pour lui en donner une preuve immédiate, elle promène avec un geste mystérieux et plein d'autorité sa baguette dans les airs. Aussitôt le vertige est entré, le vertige circule dans l'air; on respire le vertige; c'est le vertige qui remplit les poumons et renouvelle le sang dans le ventricule. Qu'est-ce que ce vertige? C'est le comique absolu; il s'est emparé de chaque être. Ils font des gestes extraordinaires, qui démontrent clairement qu'ils se sentent introduits de force dans une existence nouvelle. . . . Et ils s'élancent à travers l'oeuvre fantastique qui, à proprement parler, ne commence que là, c'est-à-dire sur la frontière du merveilleux.[57]

Irony is unrelieved *vertige*, dizziness to the point of madness. Sanity can exist only because we are willing to function within the conventions of duplicity and dissimulation, just as social language dissimulates the inherent violence of the actual relationships between human beings. Once this mask is shown to be a mask, the authentic being underneath appears necessarily as on the verge of madness. "Le rire est généralement l'apanage des fous," writes Baudelaire, and the term "*folie*" remains associated throughout with that of "*comique absolu.*" "Il est notoire que tous les fous des hôpitaux ont l'idée de leur supériorité développée outre mesure. Je ne connais guère de fous d'humilité. Remarquez que le rire est une des expressions les plus fréquentes et les plus nombreuses de la folie. . . . [Le rire] sorti des conditions fondamentales de la vie . . . est un rire qui ne dort jamais, comme une maladie qui va toujours son chemin et exécute un ordre providentiel."[58] And, most clearly of all, in the

[57] Baudelaire, "De l'essence du rire," pp. 259–60. [Au.] "One of the most remarkable things in the way of absolute comedy and, so to speak, the metaphysics of absolute comedy, was certainly the beginning of this beautiful piece, a prologue filled with a high aesthetic. The main characters of the piece, Pierrot, Cassandre, Harlequin, Colombine . . . are at first sight reasonable creatures, not much different from the fine people in the hall. The wondrous breath which is about to move them to their extraordinary antics has not yet touched their brains . . . A fairy intercedes for Harlequin . . . she promises her protection and, for immediate proof, she waves her wand mysteriously but with authority in the air. At once, vertigo is abroad; madness swirls in the air—and we breathe it in. It is the intoxication which fills the lungs and renews the blood in the heart. What is this dizziness? It is the comic absolute; it has taken over each of them. They make their extraordinary gestures, which demonstrate clearly that they feel themselves forced into a new existence. . . . And they leap through this fantastic work, which, properly speaking, only starts at that point—which is to say, on the frontiers of the marvelous." [Eds.]

[58] *Ibid.*, pp. 248–50. [Au.] "Laughter is generally the lot of madmen. . . . It is notorious that all the madmen in the asylum have an exaggerated idea of their own superiority. I know of hardly any with the madness of humility. Note that laughter is one of the most frequent and numerous expressions of madness. . . . [Laughter] which departs from the fundamental conditions of life . . . is a laughter which never sleeps, like a disease which con-

essay on caricature he states, in reference to Brueghel: "Je défie qu'on explique le capharnaüm diabolique et drôlatique de Breughel le Drôle autrement que par une espèce de grâce spéciale et satanique. Au mot grâce spéciale substituez, si vous voulez, le mot folie, ou hallucination; mais le mystère restera presque aussi noir."[59]

When we speak, then, of irony originating at the cost of the empirical self, the statement has to be taken seriously enough to be carried to the extreme: absolute irony is a consciousness of madness, itself the end of all consciousness; it is a consciousness of a non-consciousness, a reflection on madness from the inside of madness itself. But this reflection is made possible only by the double structure of ironic language: the ironist invents a form of himself that is "mad" but that does not know its own madness; he then proceeds to reflect on his madness thus objectified.

This might be construed to mean that irony, as a "*folie lucide*" which allows language to prevail even in extreme stages of self-alienation, could be a kind of therapy, a cure of madness by means of the spoken or written word. Baudelaire himself speaks of Hoffmann, whom he rightly considers to be an instance of absolute irony, as "*un physiologiste ou un médecin de fous des plus profonds, et qui s'amuserait à revêtir cette profonde science de formes poétiques.*" Jean Starobinski, who has written very well on the subject, allows that irony can be considered a cure for a self lost in the alienation of its melancholy. He writes:

> Nothing prevents the ironist from conferring an expansive value to the freedom he has conquered for himself: he is then led to dream of a reconciliation of the spirit and the world, all things being reunited in the realm of the spirit. Then the great, eternal Return can take place, the universal reparation of what evil had temporarily disrupted. This general recovery is accomplished through the mediation of art. More than any other romantic, Hoffmann longed for such a return to the world. The symbol of this return could be the "bourgeois" happiness that the young comedian couple finds at the end of the *Prinzessin Brambilla*—the Hoffmann text to which Baudelaire had alluded in the essay on laughter as a "*haut bréviaire d'esthétique*" and which is also cited by Kierkegaard in his journals.[60]

Yet the effect of irony seems to be the opposite of what Starobinski here proposes. Almost simultaneously with the first duplication of the self, by means of which a purely "linguistic" subject replaces the original self, a new disjunction has to take place. The temptation at once arises for the ironic subject to construe its function as one of assistance to the original self and to act as if it existed for the sake of this world-bound person. This results in an immediate degradation to an intersubjective level, away from the "*comique absolu*" into what Baudelaire calls "*comique significatif,*" into a betrayal of the ironic mode. Instead, the ironic subject at once has to ironize its own predicament and observe in turn, with the detachment and disinterestedness that Baudelaire demands of this kind of spectator, the temptation to which it is about to succumb. It does so precisely by avoiding the return to the world mentioned by Starobinski, by reasserting the purely fictional nature of its own universe and by carefully maintaining the radical difference that separates fiction from the world of empirical reality.

Hoffmann's *Prinzessin Brambilla* is a good case in point. It tells the story of a young comedian couple thoroughly mystified into believing that the fine and moving parts they are made to play on the stage give them an equally exalted station in life. They are finally "cured" of this delusion by the discovery of irony, manifest in their shift from a tragic to a comical repertory, from the tearful tragedies of the Abbato Chiari to a Gozzi-like type of *commedia dell'arte*. Near the end of the story, they exist indeed

tinues on and completes its destined course." Note that in the original, Baudelaire is referring specifically to C. R. Maturin's *Melmouth the Wanderer* (1820).] [Eds.]

[59] Baudelaire, "Quelques caricaturistes étrangers," *ibid.*, p. 303. [Au.] "I defy anyone to explain the diabolical and amusing Capharnaum (cf. *John* 6:10, Eds.) of Breughel the Droll otherwise than as a kind of special, satanic grace. For the words, 'special grace' substitute, if you will, the words 'madness' or 'hallucination'; but the mystery will persist almost as black." [Eds.]

[60] Jean Starobinski, "Ironie et mélancolie: Gozzi, Hoffman, Kierkegaard," in *Estratto da Sensibilitá e Razionalitá nel Settecento* (Florence, 1967), p. 459. [Au.]

in a state of domestic bliss that might give credence to Starobinski's belief that art and the world have been reconciled by the right kind of art. But it takes no particular viciousness of character to notice that the bourgeois idyl of the end is treated by Hoffmann as pure parody, that the hero and the heroine, far from having returned to their natural selves, are more than ever playing the artificial parts of the happy couple. Their diction is more stilted, their minds more mystified, than ever before. Never have art and life been farther apart than at the moment they seem to be reconciled. Hoffmann has made the point clear enough throughout: at the very moment that irony is thought of as a knowledge able to order and to cure the world, the source of its invention immediately runs dry. The instant it construes the fall of the self as an event that could somehow benefit the self, it discovers that it has in fact substituted death for madness. "Der Moment, in dem der Mensch umfällt, ist der erste, in dem sein wahrhaftes Ich sich aufrichtet,"[61] Hoffmann has his mythical king, initiated into the mysteries of irony, proclaim—and, lest we imagine that this is the assertion of a positive, hopeful future for prince and country, he immediately drops dead on the spot. Similarly, in the last paragraph of the text, when the prince pompously proclaims that the magical source of irony has given humanity eternal happiness in its ascent to self-knowledge, Hoffmann pursues: "Hier, versiegt plötzlich die Quelle, aus der . . . der Herausgeber dieser Blätter geschöpft hat"—and the story breaks off with the evocation of the painter Callot, whose drawings have indeed been the "source" of the story. These drawings represent figures from the *commedia dell'arte* floating against a background that is precisely *not* the world, adrift in an empty sky.

Far from being a return to the world, the irony to the second power of "irony of irony" that all true irony at once has to engender asserts and maintains its fictional character by stating the continued impossibility of reconciling the world of fiction with the actual world. Well before Baudelaire and Hoffmann, Friedrich Schlegel knew this very well when he defined *irony*, in a note from 1797, as "*eine permanente Parekbase.*"[62] Parabasis is understood here as what is called in English criticism the "self-conscious narrator," the author's intrusion that disrupts the fictional illusion. Schlegel makes clear, however, that the effect of this intrusion is not a heightened realism, an affirmation of the priority of a historical over a fictional act, but that it has the very opposite aim and effect: it serves to prevent the all too readily mystified reader from confusing fact and fiction and from forgetting the essential negativity of the fiction. The problem is familiar to students of point of view in a fictional narrative, in the distinction they have learned to make between the persona of the author and the persona of the fictional narrator. The moment when this difference is asserted is precisely the moment when the author does not return to the world. He asserts instead the ironic necessity of not becoming the dupe of his own irony and discovers that there is no way back from his fictional self to his actual self.

It is also at this point that the link between irony and the novel becomes apparent. For it is at this same point that the temporal structure of irony begins to emerge. Starobinski's error in seeing irony as a preliminary movement toward a recovered unity, as a reconciliation of the self with the world by means of art, is a common (and morally admirable) mistake. In temporal terms it makes irony into the prefiguration of a future recovery, fiction into the promise of a future happiness that, for the time being, exists only ideally. Commentators of Friedrich Schlegel have read him in the same way. To quote one of the best among them, this is how Peter Szondi describes the function of the ironic consciousness in Schlegel:

> The subject of romantic irony is the isolated, alienated man who has become the object of his own reflection and whose consciousness has deprived him of his ability to act. He nostalgically aspires toward unity and infinity; the world appears to him divided and finite. What he calls irony is his attempt to bear up under his critical predicament, to change his situation by achieving distance toward it. In an ever-expanding act of reflec-

[61] E. T. A. Hoffmann, *Prinzessin Brambilla*, chap. 5. [Au.] "The moment in which the human being (man) falls is the first moment in which his real self rights itself." [Eds.]

[62] Schlegel, "Fragment 668," in *Kritische Ausgabe*, Band 18, *Philosophische Lehrjahre (1796–1806)*, Ernst Behler, ed. (Paderborn: Ferdinand Schöningh, 1962), p. 85. [Au.]

tion[63] he tries to establish a point of view beyond himself and to resolve the tension between himself and the world on the level of fiction [*des Scheins*]. He cannot overcome the negativity of his situation by means of an act in which the reconciliation of finite achievement with infinite longing could take place; through prefiguration of a future unity, *in which he believes,* the negative is described as temporary [*vorläufig*] and, by the same token, it is kept in check and reversed. This reversal makes it appear tolerable and allows the subject to dwell in the subjective region of fiction. Because irony designates and checks the power of negativity, it becomes itself, although originally conceived as the overcoming of negativity, the power of the negative. Irony allows for fulfillment only in the past and in the future; it measures whatever it encounters in the present by the yardstick of infinity and thus destroys it. The knowledge of his own impotence prevents the ironist from respecting his achievements: therein resides his danger. Making this assumption about himself, he closes off the way to his fulfillment. Each achievement becomes in turn inadequate and finally leads into a void: therein resides his tragedy.[64]

Every word in this admirable quotation is right from the point of view of the mystified self, but wrong from the point of view of the ironist. Szondi has to posit the belief in a reconciliation between the ideal and the real as the result of an action or the activity of the mind. But it is precisely this assumption that the ironist denies. Friedrich Schlegel is altogether clear on this. The dialectic of the self-destruction and self-invention which for him, as for Baudelaire, characterizes the ironic mind is an endless process that leads to no synthesis. The positive name he gives to the infinity of this process is freedom, the unwillingness of the mind to accept any stage in its progression as definitive, since this would stop what he calls its "infinite agility." In temporal terms it designates the fact that irony engenders a temporal sequence of acts of consciousness which is endless. Contrary to Szondi's assertion, irony is not temporary (*vorläufig*) but repetitive, the recurrence of a self-escalating act of consciousness. Schlegel at times speaks of this endless process in exhilarating terms, understandably enough, since he is describing the freedom of a self-engendering invention. "(Die romantische Poesie)," he writes—and by this term he specifically designates a poetry of irony—

> kann . . . am meisten zwischen dem Dargestellten und dem Darstellenden, frei von allem realen und idealen Interesse, auf den Flügeln der poetischen Reflexion in der Mitte schweben, diese Reflexion immer wieder potenzieren und wie in einer endlosen Reihe von Spiegeln vervielfachen. . . . Die romantische Dichtart ist noch im Werden; ja das ist ihr eigentliches Wesen, daß sie ewig nur werden, nie vollendet sein kann. . . . Nur eine divinatorische Kritik dürfte es wagen, ihr Ideal charakterisieren zu wollen. Sie allein ist unendlich, wie sie allein frei ist, und das als ihr erstes Gesetz anerkennt, daß die Willkür des Dichters kein Gesetz über sich leide.[65]

But this same endless process, here stated from the positive viewpoint of the poetic self engaged in its own development, appears as something very close to Baudelaire's lucid madness when a slightly older Friedrich Schlegel describes it from a more personal point of view. The passage is from the curious essay in which he took leave from the readers of the *Athenäum;* written in 1798 and revised for the 1800 publication, it is entitled, ironically enough,

[63] "In immer wieder potenzierter Reflexion . . ." is a quotation from Schlegel, "Athenäum Fragment 116," Band 2, p. 182. [Au.]

[64] Peter Szondi, "Friedrich Schlegel und die Romantische Ironie," *Satz und Gegensatz* (Frankfurt: Insel-Verlag, 1964), pp. 17–18; the italics are ours. [Au.]

[65] Schlegel, "Athenaum Fragment 116," pp. 182–83. [Au.] "[Romantic poetry] can be raised again and again to a higher power, most often between that which is represented and the representer, free from all real and ideal interests on the wings of poetic reflection and multiply itself as if in an endless series of mirrors. . . . The romantic art of creation is still in the process of becoming; that is, in fact, its very essence, that it is eternally only becoming, can never be completed. . . . [The following sentence omitted in the quotation: "It cannot be exhausted by any theory."] Only a divinatory criticism might dare to characterize its ideal. This poetry alone is infinite, as it alone is free and recognizes as its first law, that the free will of the poet cannot allow a law above it." [Eds.]

"Über die Unverständlichkeit." It evokes, in the language of criticism, the same experience of "*vertige de l'hyperbole*" that the spectacle of the pantomime awakened in Baudelaire. Schlegel has described various kinds of irony and finally comes to what he calls "the irony of irony."

> . . . Im allgemeinen ist das wohl die gründlichste Ironie der Ironie, daß man sie doch eben auch überdrüssig wird, wenn sie uns überall und immer wieder geboten wird. Was wir aber hier zunächst unter Ironie der Ironie verstanden wissen wollen, das entsteht auf mehr als einem Wege. Wenn man ohne Ironie von der Ironie redet, wie es soeben der Fall war; wenn man mit Ironie von einer Ironie redet, ohne zu merken, daß man sich zu eben der Zeit in einer andren viel auffallenderen Ironie befindet; wenn man nicht wieder aus der Ironie herauskommen kann, wie es in diesem Versuch über die Unverständlichkeit zu sein scheint; wenn die Ironie Manier wird, und so den Dichter gleichsam wieder ironiert; wenn man Ironie zu einem überflüssigen Taschenbuche versprochen hat, ohne seinen Vorrat vorher zu überschlagen und nun wider Willen Ironie machen muß, wie ein Schauspielkünstler, der Leibschmerzen hat; wenn die Ironie wild wird, und sich gar nicht mehr regieren läßt.
>
> Welche Götter werden uns von allen diesen Ironien erretten können? Das einzige wäre, wenn sich eine Ironie fände, welche die Eigenschaft hätte, alle jene großen und kleinen Ironien zu verschlucken und zu verschlingen, daß nichts mehr davon zu sehen wäre, und ich muß gestehen, daß ich eben dazu in der meinigen eine merkliche Disposition fühle. Aber auch das würde nur auf kurze Zeit helfen können. Ich fürchte . . . es würde bald eine neue Generation von kleinen Ironien entstehn: denn wahrlich die Gestirne deuten auf phantastisch. Und gesetzt es blieb auch während eines langen Zeitraums alles ruhig, so wäre doch nicht zu trauen. Mit der Ironie ist durchaus nicht zu scherzen. Sie kann unglaublich lange nachwirken. . . .[66]

Our description seems to have reached a provisional conclusion. The act of irony, as we now understand it, reveals the existence of a temporality that is definitely not organic, in that it relates to its source only in terms of distance and difference and allows for no end, for no totality. Irony divides the flow of temporal experience into a past that is pure mystification and a future that remains harassed forever by a relapse within the inauthentic. It can know this inauthenticity but can never overcome it. It can only restate and repeat it on an increasingly conscious level, but it remains endlessly caught in the impossibility of making this knowledge applicable to the empirical world. It dissolves in the narrowing spiral of a linguistic sign that becomes more and more remote from its meaning, and it can find no escape from this spiral. The temporal void that it reveals is the same void we encountered when we found allegory always implying an unreachable anteriority. Allegory and irony are thus linked in their common discovery of a truly temporal predicament. They are also linked in their common demystification of an organic world postulated in a symbolic mode of analogical correspondences or in a mimetic mode of representation in which fiction and reality could coincide. It is especially against the latter mystification that irony is directed: the regression in critical insight found in the transition from an allegorical to a symbolic theory of poetry

[66] Schlegel, "Über die Unverständlichkeit," Band 2, p. 369. [Au.] "In general, possibly the most basic irony of irony is that it indeed becomes superfluous when we are confronted with it everywhere, again and again. But firstly what we want to be understood under irony of irony, is that it originates in more than one way. If one speaks of irony without irony, as was just the case; if one speaks of irony without noticing, that one finds oneself precisely at that moment in a much more noticeable irony; if one can no longer disengage oneself from irony any more, as it appears to be the case in this essay on incommensurability; if irony becomes habit and therefore ironizes the poet so to speak; if one has promised irony for a trivial book without first checking one's reserves and now against one's will must produce irony, like a thespian in pain; if irony gets out of hand and cannot be controlled.

"Which gods will save us from all of these ironies? The only one would be when an irony would be discovered which had the characteristic of absorbing and swallowing up all large and small ironies so that nothing more of these were to be seen, and I must admit that I am markedly disposed in this direction. But that would only be able to help for a short time. I fear that a new generation of small ironies would arise: for truthfully the stars point to the fantastic. And even if it also remained thoroughly quiet for a long time, it is not to be trusted. One can't take irony lightly at all. It can have an unbelievably long after-effect." [Eds.]

would find its historical equivalent in the regression from the eighteenth-century ironic novel, based on what Friedrich Schlegel called *"Parekbase,"* to nineteenth-century realism.

This conclusion is dangerously satisfying and highly vulnerable to irony in that it rescues a coherent historical picture at the expense of stated human incoherence. Things cannot be left to rest at the point we have reached. More clearly even than allegory, the rhetorical mode of irony takes us back to the predicament of the conscious subject; this consciousness is clearly an unhappy one that strives to move beyond and outside itself. Schlegel's rhetorical question "What gods will be able to rescue us from all these ironies?" can also be taken quite literally. For the later Friedrich Schlegel, as for Kierkegaard, the solution could only be a leap out of language into faith. Yet a question remains: certain poets, who were Schlegel's actual, and Baudelaire's spiritual, contemporaries, remained housed within language, refused to escape out of time into apocalyptic conceptions of human temporality, but nevertheless were not ironic. In his essay on laughter Baudelaire speaks, without apparent irony, of a semimythical poetic figure that would exist beyond the realm of irony: "si dans ces mêmes nations ultra-civilisées, une intelligence, poussée par une ambition supérieure, veut franchir les limites de l'orgueil mondain et s'élancer hardiment vers la poésie pure, dans cette poésie, limpide et profonde comme la nature, le rire fera défaut comme dans l'âme du Sage."[67] Could we think of certain texts of that period—and it is better to speak here of texts than of individual names—as being truly meta-ironical, as having transcended irony without falling into the myth of an organic totality or bypassing the temporality of all language? And, if we call these texts "allegorical," would the language of allegory then be the overcoming of irony? Would some of the definitely non-ironic, but, in our sense of the term, allegorical, texts of the late Hölderlin, of Wordsworth, or of Baudelaire himself be this "pure poetry from which laughter is absent as from the soul of the Sage"? It would be very tempting to think so, but, since the implications are far-reaching, it might be better to approach the question in a less exalted mood, by making a brief comparison of the temporal structure of allegory and irony.

The text we can use for our demonstration has the advantage of being exceedingly brief and very well known. It would take some time to show that it falls under the definition of what is here being referred to as "allegorical" poetry; suffice it to say that it has the fundamentally profigurative pattern that is one of the characteristics of allegory. The text clearly is not ironic, either in its tonality or in its meaning. We are using one of Wordsworth's Lucy Gray poems:

> A slumber did my spirit seal;
> I had no human fears:
> She seemed a thing that could not feel
> The touch of earthly years.
>
> No motion has she now, no force;
> She neither hears nor sees;
> Rolled round in earth's diurnal course,
> With rocks, and stones, and trees.

Examining the temporal structure of this text, we can point to the successive description of two stages of consciousness, one belonging to the past and mystified, the other to the *now* of the poem, the stage that has recovered from the mystification of a past now presented as being in error; the "slumber" is a condition of non-awareness. The event that separates the two states is the radical discontinuity of a death that remains quite impersonal; the identity of the unnamed "she" is not divulged. Lines 3 and 4 are particularly important for our purpose;

> She seemed a thing that could not feel
> The touch of earthly years.

These lines are curiously ambiguous, with the full weight of the ambiguity concentrated in the word "thing." Within the mystified world of the past, when the temporal reality of death was repressed or forgotten, the word "thing" could be used quite innocently, perhaps even in a playfully amorous way (since the deceased entity is a "she"). The line could almost be a gallant compliment to the well-preserved youth of the lady, in spite of the somewhat ominous "seemed." The curious shock of the poem, the very Wordsworthian "shock of mild surprise," is that this innocuous statement becomes literally true in the retrospective perspective of the eternal "now" of the second part. She now has become a *thing* in the full sense of the word, not unlike Baudelaire's falling man who became a thing in the grip of gravity, and, indeed, she exists beyond

[67] Baudelaire, "De l'essence du rire," p. 251. [Au.]

the touch of earthly years. But the light-hearted compliment has turned into a grim awareness of the de-mystifying power of death, which makes all the past appear as a flight into the inauthenticity of a forgetting. It could be said that, read within the perspective of the entire poem, these two lines are ironic, though they are not ironic in themselves or within the context of the first stanza. Nor is the poem, as a whole, ironic. The stance of the speaker, who exists in the "now," is that of a subject whose insight is no longer in doubt and who is no longer vulnerable to irony. It could be called, if one so wished, a stance of wisdom. There is no real disjunction of the subject; the poem is written from the point of view of a unified self that fully recognizes a past condition as one of error and stands in a present that, however painful, sees things as they actually are. This stance has been made possible by two things: first, the death alluded to is not the death of the speaker but apparently that of someone else; second, the poem is in the third person and uses the feminine gender throughout. If this were truly relevant, the question would remain whether Wordsworth could have written in the same manner about his own death. For the informed reader of Wordsworth the answer to this question is affirmative; Wordsworth is one of the few poets who can write proleptically about their own death and speak, as it were, from beyond their own graves. The "she" in the poem is in fact large enough to encompass Wordsworth as well. More important than the otherness of the dead person is the seemingly obvious fact that the poem describes the demystification as a temporal sequence: first there was error, then the death occurred, and now an eternal insight into the rocky barrenness of the human predicament prevails. The *difference* does not exist within the subject, which remains unique throughout and therefore can resolve the tragic irony of lines 3 and 4 in the wisdom of the concluding lines. The difference has been spread out over a temporality which is exclusively that of the poem and in which the conditions of error and of wisdom have become successive. This is possible within the ideal, self-created temporality engendered by the language of the poem, but it is not possible within the actual temporality of experience. The "now" of the poem is not an actual now, which is that of the moment of death, lies hidden in the blank space between the two stanzas. The fundamental structure of allegory reappears here in the tendency of the language toward narrative, the spreading out along the axis of an imaginary time in order to give duration to what is, in fact, simultaneous within the subject.

The structure of irony, however, is the reversed mirror-image of this form. In practically all the quotations from Baudelaire and Schlegel, irony appears as an instantaneous process that takes place rapidly, suddenly, in one single moment: Baudelaire speaks of "*la force de se dédoubler* rapidement," "*la puissance d'être* à la fois *soi-même et un autre*"; irony is instantaneous like an "explosion" and the fall is sudden. In describing the pantomime, he complains that his pen cannot possibly convey the simultaneity of the visual spectacle: "*avec une plume tout cela est pâle et glacé.*"[68] His later, most ironic works, the prose poems of the *Tableaux parisiens,* grow shorter and shorter and always climax in the single brief moment of a final *pointe.* This is the instant at which the two selves, the empirical as well as the ironic, are simultaneously present, juxtaposed within the same moment but as two irreconcilable and disjointed beings. The structure is precisely the opposite from that of the Wordsworth poem: the difference now resides in the subject, whereas time is reduced to one single moment. In this respect, irony comes closer to the pattern of factual experience and recaptures some of the factitiousness of human existence as a succession of isolated moments lived by a divided self. Essentially the mode of the present, it knows neither memory nor prefigurative duration, whereas allegory exists entirely within an ideal time that is never here and now but always a past or an endless future. Irony is a synchronic structure, while allegory appears as a successive mode capable of engendering duration as the illusion of a continuity that it knows to be illusionary. Yet the two modes, for all their profound distinctions in mood and structure, are the two faces of the same fundamental experience of time. One is tempted to play them off against each other and to attach value judgments to each, as if one were intrinsically superior to the other. We mentioned the temptation to confer on allegorical writers a wisdom superior to that of ironic writers; an

[68] *Ibid.*, p. 259. [Au.]

equivalent temptation exists to consider ironists as more enlightened than their assumedly naïve counterparts, the allegorists. Both attitudes are in error. The knowledge derived from both modes is essentially the same; Hölderlin's or Wordsworth's wisdom could be stated ironically, and the rapidity of Schlegel or Baudelaire could be preserved in terms of general wisdom. Both modes are fully demystified when they remain within the realm of their respective languages but are totally vulnerable to renewed blindness as soon as they leave it for the empirical world. Both are determined by an authentic experience of temporality which, seen from the point of view of the self engaged in the world, is a negative one. The dialectical play between the two modes, as well as their common interplay with mystified forms of language (such as symbolic or mimetic representation), which it is not in their power to eradicate, make up what is called literary history.

We can conclude with a brief remark on the novel, which is caught with the truly perverse assignment of using both the narrative duration of the diachronic allegory and the instantaneity of the narrative present; to try for less than a combination of the two is to betray the inherent *gageure* of the genre. Things seem very simple for the novel when author and narrator are considered to be one and the same subject and when the time of the narrative is also assumed to be the natural time of days and years. They get somewhat more complex when, as in the scheme proposed by René Girard, the novel begins in error but works itself almost unwittingly into the knowledge of this error; this allows for a mystified structure that falls apart at the hand and makes the novel into a pre-ironic mode. The real difficulty starts when we allow for the existence of a novelist who has all these preliminary stages behind him, who is a full-fledged ironist as well as an allegorist and has to seal, so to speak, the ironic moments within the allegorical duration.

Stendhal, in the *Chartreuse de Parme,* is a good example. We readily grant him irony, as in the famous Stendhalian speed that allows him to dispose of a seduction or a murder in the span of two brief sentences. All perceptive critics have noticed the emphasis on the moment with the resulting discontinuity. Georges Poulet, among others, describes it very well:

> In none of [Stendhal's truly happy moments] is the moment connected with other moments to form a continuous totality of fulfilled existence, as we almost always find it, for instance, in the characters of Flaubert, of Tolstoi, of Thomas Hardy, of Roger Martin du Gard. They all seem, at all times, to carry the full weight of their past (and even in their future destiny) on their shoulders. But the opposite is true of Stendhal's characters. Always living exclusively in their moments, they are entirely free of what does not belong to these moments. Would this mean that they lack an essential dimension, a certain consistency which is the consistency of duration? It could be. . . .[69]

This is true of Stendhal the ironist, whose reflective patterns are very thoroughly described in the rest of the article, although Poulet never uses the term "irony." But, especially in the *Chartreuse de Parme,* there clearly occur slow, meditative movements full of reverie, anticipation, and recollection: one thinks of Fabrice's return to his native town and the night he spends there in the church tower,[70] as well as of the famous courtship episodes in the high tower of the prison. Stephen Gilman[71] has very convincingly shown how these episodes, with their numerous antecedents in previous works of literature, are allegorical and emblematic, just as Julie's garden in *La Nouvelle Héloïse* was found to be. And he has also shown very well how these allegorical episodes act prefiguratively and give the novel a duration that the *staccato* of irony would never be able, by definition, to achieve. It remains to be said that this successful combination of allegory and irony also determines the thematic substance of the novel as a whole, the underlying *mythos* of the allegory. The novel tells the story of two lovers who, like Eros and Psyche, are never allowed to come into full contact with each other. When they can see each other they are separated by an unbreachable distance; when they can touch, it has to be in a darkness imposed

[69] Georges Poulet, *Mesure de l'instant* (Paris: Plon, 1968), p. 250. [Au.]

[70] Stendhal, *La Chartreuse de Parme* (1839), chap. 8. [Au.]

[71] Stephen Gilman, *The Tower as Emblem,* Analecta Romanica, vol. 22 (Frankfurt: Vittorio Klostermann, 1967). [Au.]

by a totally arbitrary and irrational decision, an act of the gods. The myth is that of the unovercomable distance which must always prevail between the selves, and it thematizes the ironic distance that Stendhal the writer always believed prevailed between his pseudonymous and nominal identities. As such, it reaffirms Schlegel's definition of irony as a "permanent parabasis" and singles out this novel as one of the few novels of novels, as the allegory of irony.

SEMIOLOGY AND RHETORIC

To judge from various recent publications, the spirit of the times is not blowing in the direction of formalist and intrinsic criticism. We may no longer be hearing too much about relevance but we keep hearing a great deal about reference, about the nonverbal "outside" to which language refers, by which it is conditioned and upon which it acts. The stress falls not so much on the fictional status of literature—a property now perhaps somewhat too easily taken for granted—but on the interplay between these fictions and categories that are said to partake of reality, such as the self, man, society, "the artist, his culture and the human community," as one critic puts it. Hence the emphasis on hybrid texts considered to be partly literary and partly referential, on popular fictions deliberately aimed towards social and psychological gratification, on literary autobiography as a key to the understanding of the self, and so on. We speak as if, with the problems of literary form resolved once and forever, and with the techniques of structural analysis refined to near-perfection, we could now move "beyond formalism" towards the questions that really interest us and reap, at last, the fruits of the ascetic concentration on techniques that prepared us for this decisive step. With the internal law and order of literature well policed, we can now confidently devote ourselves to the foreign affairs, the external politics of literature. Not only do we feel able to do so, but we owe it to ourselves to take this step: our moral conscience would not allow us to do otherwise. Behind the assurance that valid interpretation is possible, behind the recent interest in writing and reading as potentially effective public speech acts, stands a highly respectable moral imperative that strives to reconcile the internal, formal, private structures of literary language with their external, referential, and public effects.

I want, for the moment, to consider briefly this tendency in itself, as an undeniable and recurrent historical fact, without regard for its truth or falseness or for its value as desirable or pernicious. It is a fact that this sort of thing happens, again and again, in literary studies. On the one hand, literature cannot merely be received as a definite unit of referential meaning that can be decoded without leaving a residue. The code is unusually conspicuous, complex, and enigmatic; it attracts an inordinate amount of attention to itself, and this attention has to acquire the rigor of a method. The structural moment of concentration on the code for its own sake cannot be avoided, and literature necessarily breeds its own formalism. Technical innovations in the methodical study of literature only occur when this kind of attention predominates. It can legitimately be said, for example, that, from a technical point of view, very little has happened in American criticism since the innovative works of New Criticism. There certainly have been numerous excellent books of criticism since, but in none of them have the techniques of description and interpretation evolved beyond the techniques of close reading established in the thirties and forties. Formalism, it seems, is an all-absorbing and tyrannical muse; the hope that one can be at the same time technically original and discursively eloquent is not borne out by the history of literary criticism.

On the other hand—and this is the real mystery—no literary formalism, no matter how accurate and enriching in its analytic powers, is ever allowed to come into being without seeming reductive. When form is considered to be the external trappings of literary meaning or content, it seems superficial and expendable. The development of intrinsic, formalist criticism in the twentieth century

SEMIOLOGY AND RHETORIC is reprinted from *Allegories of Reading: Figural Language in Rousseau, Nietzsche, Rilke, and Proust* (1979) published by Yale University Press, by permission of the editor of *Diacritics,* where it first appeared in 1975.

has changed this mode: form is now a solipsistic category of self-reflection, and the referential meaning is said to be extrinsic. The polarities of inside and outside have been reversed, but they are still the same polarities that are at play: internal meaning has become outside reference, and the outer form has become the intrinsic structure. A new version of reductiveness at once follows this reversal: formalism nowadays is mostly described in an imagery of imprisonment and claustrophobia: the "prison house of language," "the impasse of formalist criticism," etc. Like the grandmother in Proust's novel ceaselessly driving the young Marcel out into the garden, away from the unhealthy inwardness of his closeted reading, critics cry out for the fresh air of referential meaning. Thus, with the structure of the code so opaque, but the meaning so anxious to blot out the obstacle of form, no wonder that the reconciliation of form and meaning would be so attractive. The attraction of reconciliation is the elective breeding-ground of false models and metaphors; it accounts for the metaphorical model of literature as a kind of box that separates an inside from an outside, and the reader or critic as the person who opens the lid in order to release in the open what was secreted but inaccessible inside. It matters little whether we call the inside of the box the content or the form, the outside the meaning or the appearance. The recurrent debate opposing intrinsic to extrinsic criticism stands under the aegis of an inside/outside metaphor that is never being seriously questioned.

Metaphors are much more tenacious than facts, and I certainly don't expect to dislodge this age-old model in one short try. I merely wish to speculate on a different set of terms, perhaps less simple in their differential relationships than the strictly polar, binary opposition between inside and outside and therefore less likely to enter into the easy play of chiasmic reversals. I derive these terms (which are as old as the hills) pragmatically from the observation of developments and debates in recent critical methodology.

One of the most controversial among these developments coincides with a new approach to poetics or, as it is called in Germany, poetology, as a branch of general semiotics. In France, a semiology of literature comes about as the outcome of the long-deferred but all the more explosive encounter of the nimble French literary mind with the category of form. Semiology, as opposed to semantics, is the science or study of signs as signifiers; it does not ask what words mean but how they mean. Unlike American New Criticism, which derived the internalization of form from the practice of highly self-conscious modern writers, French semiology turned to linguistics for its model and adopted Saussure and Jakobson rather than Valéry or Proust for its masters. By an awareness of the arbitrariness of the sign (Saussure)[1] and of literature as an autotelic statement "focused on the way it is expressed" (Jakobson)[2] the entire question of meaning can be bracketed, thus freeing the critical discourse from the debilitating burden of paraphrase. The demystifying power of semiology, within the context of French historical and thematic criticism, has been considerable. It demonstrated that the perception of the literary dimensions of language is largely obscured if one submits uncritically to the authority of reference. It also revealed how tenaciously this authority continues to assert itself in a variety of disguises, ranging from the crudest ideology to the most refined forms of aesthetic and ethical judgment. It especially explodes the myth of semantic correspondence between sign and referent, the wishful hope of having it both ways, of being, to paraphrase Marx in the German Ideology, a formalist critic in the morning and a communal moralist in the afternoon, of serving both the technique of form and the substance of meaning. The results, in the practice of French criticism, have been as fruitful as they are irreversible. Perhaps for the first time since the late eighteenth century, French critics can come at least somewhat closer to the kind of linguistic awareness that never ceased to be operative in its poets and novelists and that forced all of them, including Sainte Beuve, to write their main works "contre Sainte Beuve."[3] The distance was never so considerable in England and the United States, which does not mean, however, that we may be able, in this country, to dispense altogether with some preventative semiological hygiene.

One of the most striking characteristics of literary semiology as it is practiced today, in France and elsewhere, is the use of grammatical (especially syntactical) structures conjointly with rhetorical structures, without apparent awareness of a possible discrepancy between them. In their literary analyses,

[1] See *de Saussure*. [Eds.]

[2] For a note on Jakobson and an example of his work see *CTSP*, pp. 1113–16. [Eds.]

[3] See Sainte Beuve, *CTSP*, pp. 555–62. [Eds.]

Barthes, Genette, Todorov, Greimas, and their disciples all simplify and regress from Jakobson in letting grammar and rhetoric function in perfect continuity, and in passing from grammatical to rhetorical structures without difficulty or interruption. Indeed, as the study of grammatical structures is refined in contemporary theories of generative, transformational, and distributive grammar, the study of tropes and of figures (which is how the term *rhetoric* is used here, and not in the derived sense of comment or of eloquence or persuasion) becomes a mere extension of grammatical models, a particular subset of syntactical relations. In the recent *Dictionnaire encyclopédique des sciences du langage,* Ducrot and Todorov write that rhetoric has always been satisfied with a paradigmatic view over words (words substituting for each other), without questioning their syntagmatic relationship (the contiguity of words to each other). There ought to be another perspective, complementary to the first, in which metaphor, for example, would not be defined as a substitution but as a particular type of combination. Research inspired by linguistics or, more narrowly, by syntactical studies, has begun to reveal this possibility—but it remains to be explored. Todorov, who calls one of his books a *Grammar of the Decameron,* rightly thinks of his own work and that of his associates as first explorations in the elaboration of a systematic grammar of literary modes, genres, and also of literary figures. Perhaps the most perceptive work to come out of this school, Genette's studies of figural modes, can be shown to be assimilations of rhetorical transformations or combinations to syntactical, grammatical patterns. Thus a recent study, now printed in *Figures III* and entitled *Metaphor and Metonymy in Proust,* shows the combined presence, in a wide and astute selection of passages, of paradigmatic, metaphorical figures with syntagmatic, metonymic structures. The combination of both is treated descriptively and nondialectically without considering the possibility of logical tensions.

One can ask whether this reduction of figure to grammar is legitimate. The existence of grammatical structures, within and beyond the unit of the sentence, in literary texts is undeniable, and their description and classification are indispensable. The question remains if and how figures of rhetoric can be included in such a taxonomy. This question is at the core of the debate going on, in a wide variety of apparently unrelated forms, in contemporary poetics. But the historical picture of contemporary criticism is too confused to make the mapping out of such a topography a useful exercise. Not only are these questions mixed in and mixed up within particular groups or local trends, but they are often copresent, without apparent contradiction, within the work of a single author.

Neither is the theory of the question suitable for quick expository treatment. To distinguish the epistemology of grammar from the epistemology of rhetoric is a redoubtable task. On an entirely naïve level, we tend to conceive of grammatical systems as tending towards universality and as simply generative, i.e., as capable of deriving an infinity of versions from a single model (that may govern transformations as well as derivations) without the intervention of another model that would upset the first. We therefore think of the relationship between grammar and logic, the passage from grammar to propositions, as being relatively unproblematic; no true propositions are conceivable in the absence of grammatical consistency or of controlled deviation from a system of consistency no matter how complex. Grammar and logic stand to each other in a dyadic relationship of unsubverted support. In a logic of acts rather than of statements, as in Austin's theory of speech acts,[4] that has had such a strong influence on recent American work in literary semiology, it is also possible to move between speech acts and grammar without difficulty. The performance of what is called illocutionary acts such as ordering, questioning, denying, assuming, etc., within the language is congruent with the grammatical structures of syntax in the corresponding imperative, interrogative, negative, optative sentences. "The rules for illocutionary acts," writes Richard Ohmann in a recent paper, "determine whether performance of a given act is well-executed, in just the same way as *grammatical* rules determine whether the product of a locutionary act—a sentence—is well formed. . . . But whereas the rules of grammar concern the relationships among sound, syntax, and meaning, the rules of illocutionary acts concern relationships among people."[5] And since rhetoric is then conceived exclusively as persuasion, as actual action upon others (and not as an intralinguistic figure or trope), the continuity between

[4] See *Austin* and *Searle.* [Eds.]

[5] "Speech, Literature, and the Space in Between," *New Literary History* 4 (Autumn 1972): 50. [Au.]

the illocutionary realm of grammar and the perlocutionary realm of rhetoric is self-evident. It becomes the basis for a new rhetoric that, exactly as is the case for Todorov and Genette, would also be a new grammar.

Without engaging the substance of the question, it can be pointed out, without having to go beyond recent and American examples, and without calling upon the strength of an age-old tradition, that the continuity here assumed between grammar and rhetoric is not borne out by theoretical and philosophical speculation. Kenneth Burke mentions *deflection* (which he compares structurally to Freudian displacement), defined as "any slight bias or even unintended error," as the rhetorical basis of language, and deflection is then conceived as a dialectical subversion of the consistent link between sign and meaning that operates within grammatical patterns; hence Burke's well-known insistence on the distinction between grammar and rhetoric.[6] Charles Sanders Peirce, who, with Nietzsche and Saussure, laid the philosophical foundation for modern semiology, stressed the distinction between grammar and rhetoric in his celebrated and so suggestively unfathomable definition of the sign.[7] He insists, as is well known, on the necessary presence of a third element, called the interpretant, within any relationship that the sign entertains with its object. The sign is to be interpreted if we are to understand the idea it is to convey, and this is so because the sign is not the thing but a meaning derived from the thing by a process here called representation that is not simply generative, i.e., dependent on a univocal origin. The interpretation of the sign is not, for Peirce, a meaning but another sign; it is a reading, not a decodage, and this reading has, in its turn, to be interpreted into another sign, and so on *ad infinitum*. Peirce calls this process by means of which one sign gives birth to another pure rhetoric, as distinguished from pure grammar, which postulates the possibility of unproblematic, dyadic meaning, and pure logic, which postulates the possibility of the universal truth of meanings. Only if the sign engendered meaning in the same way that the object engenders the sign, that is, by representation, would there be no need to distinguish between grammar and rhetoric.

These remarks should indicate at least the existence and the difficulty of the question, a difficulty which puts its concise theoretical exposition beyond my powers. I must retreat therefore into a pragmatic discourse and try to illustrate the tension between grammar and rhetoric in a few specific textual examples. Let me begin by considering what is perhaps the most commonly known instance of an apparent symbiosis between a grammatical and a rhetorical structure, the so-called rhetorical question, in which the figure is conveyed directly by means of a syntactical device. I take the first example from the sub-literature of the mass media; asked by his wife whether he wants to have his bowling shoes laced over or laced under, Archie Bunker answers with a question: "What's the difference?" Being a reader of sublime simplicity, his wife replies by patiently explaining the difference between lacing over and lacing under, whatever this may be, but provokes only ire. "What's the difference" did not ask for difference but means instead "I don't give a damn what the difference is." The same grammatical pattern engenders two meanings that are mutually exclusive: the literal meaning asks for the concept (difference) whose existence is denied by the figurative meaning. As long as we are talking about bowling shoes, the consequences are relatively trivial; Archie Bunker, who is a great believer in the authority of origins (as long, of course, as they are the right origins) muddles along in a world where literal and figurative meanings get in each other's way, though not without discomforts. But suppose that it is a *de*-bunker rather than a "Bunker," and a de-bunker of the arche (or origin), an archie Debunker such as Nietzsche or Jacques Derrida[8] for instance, who asks the question "What is the Difference"—and we cannot even tell from his grammar whether he "really" wants to know "what" difference is or is just telling us that we shouldn't even try to find out. Confronted with the question of the difference between grammar and rhetoric, grammar allows us to ask the question, but the sentence by means of which we ask it may deny the very possibility of asking. For what is the use of asking, I ask, when we cannot even authoritatively decide whether a question asks or doesn't ask?

The point is as follows. A perfectly clear syntactical paradigm (the question) engenders a sentence that has at least two meanings, of which the one as-

[6] Kenneth Burke, *A Grammar of Motives* (1945) and *A Rhetoric of Motives* (1950). [Eds.]
[7] See *Peirce*. [Eds.]

[8] See *Derrida*. [Eds.]

serts and the other denies its own illocutionary mode. It is not so that there are simply two meanings, one literal and the other figural, and that we have to decide which one of these meanings is the right one in this particular situation. The confusion can only be cleared up by the intervention of an extra-textual intention, such as Archie Bunker putting his wife straight; but the very anger he displays is indicative of more than impatience; it reveals his despair when confronted with a structure of linguistic meaning that he cannot control and that holds the discouraging prospect of an infinity of similar future confusions, all of them potentially catastrophic in their consequences. Nor is this intervention really a part of the mini-text constituted by the figure which holds our attention only as long as it remains suspended and unresolved. I follow the usage of common speech in calling this semiological enigma "rhetorical." The grammatical model of the question becomes rhetorical not when we have, on the one hand, a literal meaning and on the other hand a figural meaning, but when it is impossible to decide by grammatical or other linguistic devices which of the two meanings (that can be entirely incompatible) prevails. Rhetoric radically suspends logic and opens up vertiginous possibilities of referential aberration. And although it would perhaps be somewhat more remote from common usage, I would not hesitate to equate the rhetorical, figural potentiality of language with literature itself. I could point to a great number of antecedents to this equation of literature with figure; the most recent reference would be to Monroe Beardsley's insistence in his contribution to the *Essays* to honor William Wimsatt, that literary language is characterized by being "distinctly above the norm in ratio of implicit [or, I would say rhetorical] to explicit meaning."[9]

Let me pursue the matter of the rhetorical question through one more example. Yeats's poem "Among School Children" ends with the famous line: "How can we know the dancer from the dance?" Although there are some revealing inconsistencies within the commentaries, the line is usually interpreted as stating, with the increased emphasis of a rhetorical device, the potential unity between form and experience, between creator and creation. It could be said that it denies the discrepancy between the sign and the referent from which we started out. Many elements in the imagery and the dramatic development of the poem strengthen this traditional reading; without having to look any further than the immediately preceding lines, one finds powerful and consecrated images of the continuity from part to whole that makes synecdoche into the most seductive of metaphors: the organic beauty of the tree, stated in the parallel syntax of a similar rhetorical question, or the convergence, in the dance, of erotic desire with musical form:

> O chestnut-tree, great-rooted blossomer,
> Are you the leaf, the blossom or the bole?
> O body swayed to music, O brightening
> glance,
> How can we know the dancer from the
> dance?

A more extended reading, always assuming that the final line is to be read as a rhetorical question, reveals that the thematic and rhetorical grammar of the poem yields a consistent reading that extends from the first line to the last and that can account for all the details in the text. It is equally possible, however, to read the last line literally rather than figuratively, as asking with some urgency the question we asked earlier within the context of contemporary criticism; *not* that sign and referent are so exquisitely fitted to each other that all difference between them is at times blotted out but, rather, since the two essentially different elements, sign and meaning, are so intricately intertwined in the imagined "presence" that the poem addresses, how can we possibly make the distinctions that would shelter us from the error of identifying what cannot be identified? The clumsiness of the paraphrase reveals that it is not necessarily the literal reading which is simpler than the figurative one, as was the case in our first example; here, the figural reading, which assumes the question to be rhetorical, is perhaps naïve, whereas the literal reading leads to greater complication of theme and statement. For it turns out that the entire scheme set up by the first reading can be undermined, or deconstructed, in the terms of the second, in which the final line is read literally as meaning that, since the dancer and the dance are not the same, it might be useful, perhaps even des-

[9]"The Concept of Literature," in *Literary Theory and Structure: Essays in Honor of W. K. Wimsatt*, ed. Frank Brady, John Palmer, and Martin Price (New Haven, 1973), p. 37. [Au.]

perately necessary—for the question can be given a ring of urgency, "Please tell me, how *can* I know the dancer from the dance"—to tell them apart. But this will replace the reading of each symbolic detail by a divergent interpretation. The oneness of trunk, leaf, and blossom, for example, that would have appealed to Goethe, would find itself replaced by the much less reassuring Tree of Life from the Mabinogion that appears in the poem "Vacillation," in which the fiery blossom and the earthly leaf are held together, as well as apart, by the crucified and castrated God Attis, of whose body it can hardly be said that it is "not bruised to pleasure the soul." This hint should suffice to suggest that two entirely coherent but entirely incompatible readings can be made to hinge on one line, whose grammatical structure is devoid of ambiguity, but whose rhetorical mode turns the mood as well as the mode of the entire poem upside down. Neither can we say, as was already the case in the first example, that the poem simply has two meanings that exist side by side. The two readings have to engage each other in direct confrontation, for the one reading is precisely the error denounced by the other and has to be undone by it. Nor can we in any way make a valid decision as to which of the readings can be given priority over the other; none can exist in the other's absence. There can be no defiance without a dancer, no sign without a referent. On the other hand, the authority of the meaning engendered by the grammatical structure is fully obscured by the duplicity of a figure that cries out for the differentiation that it conceals.

Yeats's poem is not explicitly "about" rhetorical questions but about images or metaphors, and about the possibility of convergence between experiences of consciousness such as memory or emotions—what the poem calls passion, piety, and affection—and entities accessible to the senses such as bodies, persons, or icons. We return to the inside/outside model from which we started out and which the poem puts into question by means of a syntactical device (the question) made to operate on a grammatical as well as on a rhetorical level. The couple grammar/rhetoric, certainly not a binary opposition since they in no way exclude each other, disrupts and confuses the neat antithesis of the inside/outside pattern. We can transfer this scheme to the act of reading and interpretation. By reading we get, as we say, *inside* a text that was first something alien to us and which we now make our own by an act of understanding. But this understanding becomes at once the representation of an extra-textual meaning; in Austin's terms, the illocutionary speech act becomes a perlocutionary actual act—in Frege's terms, *Bedeutung* becomes *Sinn.*[10] Our recurrent question is whether this transformation is semantically controlled along grammatical or along rhetorical lines. Does the metaphor of reading really unite outer meaning with inner understanding, action with reflection, into one single totality? The assertion is powerfully and suggestively made in a passage from Proust that describes the experience of reading as such a union. It describes the young Marcel, near the beginning of Combray, hiding in the closed space of his room in order to read. The example differs from the earlier ones in that we are not dealing with a grammatical structure that also functions rhetorically but have instead the representation, the dramatization, in terms of the experience of a subject, of a rhetorical structure—just as, in many other passages, Proust dramatizes tropes by means of landscapes or descriptions of objects. The figure here dramatized is that of metaphor, an inside/outside correspondence as represented by the act of reading. The reading scene is the culmination of a series of actions taking place in enclosed spaces and leading up to the "dark coolness" of Marcel's room.

> I had stretched out on my bed, with a book, in my room which sheltered, tremblingly, its transparent and fragile coolness from the afternoon sun, behind the almost closed blinds through which a glimmer of daylight had nevertheless managed to push its yellow wings, remaining motionless between the wood and the glass, in a corner, posed like a butterfly. It was hardly light enough to read, and the sensation of the light's splendor was given me only by the noise of Camus . . . hammering dusty crates; resounding in the sonorous atmosphere that is peculiar to hot weather, they seemed to spark off scarlet stars; and also by the flies executing their little concert, the chamber music of summer: evocative not in the manner of a human tune that, heard perchance during the summer, af-

[10] See *Frege.* [Eds.]

> terwards reminds you of it but connected to summer by a more necessary link: born from beautiful days, resurrecting only when they return, containing some of their essence, it does not only awaken their image in our memory; it guarantees their return, their actual, persistent, unmediated presence.
>
> The dark coolness of my room related to the full sunlight of the street as the shadow relates to the ray of light, that is to say it was just as luminous and it gave my imagination the total spectacle of the summer, whereas my senses, if I had been on a walk, could only have enjoyed it by fragments; it matched my repose which (thanks to the adventures told by my book and stirring my tranquility) supported, like the quiet of a motionless hand in the middle of a running brook the shock and the motion of a torrent of activity.[11]

For our present purpose, the most striking aspect of this passage is the juxtaposition of figural and metafigural language. It contains seductive metaphors that bring into play a variety of irresistible objects: chamber music, butterflies, stars, books, running brooks, etc., and it inscribes these objects within dazzling fire- and water-works of figuration. But the passage also comments normatively on the best way to achieve such effects; in this sense, it is metafigural: it writes figuratively about figures. It contrasts two ways of evoking the natural experience of summer and unambiguously states its preference for one of these ways over the other: the "necessary link" that unites the buzzing of the flies to the summer makes it a much more effective symbol than the tune heard "perchance" during the summer. The preference is expressed by means of a distinction that corresponds to the difference between metaphor and metonymy, necessity and chance being a legitimate way to distinguish between analogy and contiguity. The inference of identity and totality that is constitutive of metaphor is lacking in the purely relational metonymic contact: an element of truth is involved in taking Achilles for a lion but none in taking Mr. Ford for a motor car. The passage is *about* the aesthetic superiority of metaphor over metonymy, but this aesthetic claim is made by means of categories that are the ontological ground of the metaphysical system that allows for the aesthetic to come into being as a category. The metaphor for summer (in this case, the synesthesia set off by the "chamber music" of the flies) guarantees a presence which, far from being contingent, is said to be essential, permanently recurrent and unmediated by linguistic representations or figurations. Finally, in the second part of the passage, the metaphor of presence not only appears as the ground of cognition but as the performance of an action, thus promising the reconciliation of the most disruptive of contradictions. By then, the investment in the power of metaphor is such that it may seem sacrilegious to put it in question.

Yet, it takes little perspicacity to show that the text does not practice what it preaches. A rhetorical reading of the passage reveals that the figural praxis and the metafigural theory do not converge and that the assertion of the mastery of metaphor over metonymy owes its persuasive power to the use of metonymic structures. I have carried out such an analysis in a somewhat more extended context;[12] at this point, we are more concerned with the results than with the procedure. For the metaphysical categories of presence, essence, action, truth, and beauty do not remain unaffected by such a reading. This would become clear from an inclusive reading of Proust's novel or would become even more explicit in a language-conscious philosopher such as Nietzsche who, as a philosopher, has to be concerned with the epistemological consequences of the kind of rhetorical seductions exemplified by the Proust passage. It can be shown that the systematic critique of the main categories of metaphysics undertaken by Nietzsche in his late work, the critique of the concepts of causality, of the subject, of identity, of referential and revealed truth, etc., occurs along the same pattern of deconstruction that was operative in Proust's text; and it can also be shown that this pattern exactly corresponds to Nietzsche's description, in texts that precede *The Will to Power* by more than fifteen years, of the structure of the main rhetorical tropes. The key to this critique of metaphysics, which is itself a recurrent gesture throughout the history of thought, is the rhetorical model of the trope or, if one prefers to call it that, literature. It turns out that in these innocent-

[11] *Swann's Way* (Paris: Pléiade, 1954), p. 83. [Au.]

[12] On pp. 59–67 of *Allegories of Reading* (New Haven: Yale University Press, 1979). [Eds.]

looking didactic exercises we are in fact playing for very sizeable stakes.

It is therefore all the more necessary to know what is linguistically involved in a rhetorically conscious reading of the type here undertaken on a brief fragment from a novel and extended by Nietzsche to the entire text of post-Hellenic thought. Our first examples dealing with the rhetorical questions were rhetorizations of grammar, figures generated by syntactical paradigms, whereas the Proust example could be better described as a grammatization of rhetoric. By passing from a paradigmatic structure based on substitution, such as metaphor, to a syntagmatic structure based on contingent association such as metonymy, the mechanical, repetitive aspect of grammatical forms is shown to be operative in a passage that seemed at first sight to celebrate the self-willed and autonomous inventiveness of a subject. Figures are assumed to be inventions, the products of a highly particularized individual talent, whereas no one can claim credit for the programmed pattern of grammar. Yet, our reading of the Proust passage shows that precisely when the highest claims are being made of the unifying power of metaphor, these very images rely in fact on the deceptive use of semi-automatic grammatical patterns. The deconstruction of metaphor and of all rhetorical patterns such as mimesis, paronomasia, or personification that use resemblance as a way to disguise differences, takes us back to the impersonal precision of grammar and of a semiology derived from grammatical patterns. Such a reading puts into question a whole series of concepts that underlie the value judgments of our critical discourse: the metaphors of primacy, of genetic history, and, most notably, of the autonomous power to will of the self.

There seems to be a difference, then, between what I called the rhetorization of grammar (as in the rhetorical question and the grammatization of rhetoric, as in the readings of the type sketched out in the passage from Proust. The former end up in indetermination, in a suspended uncertainty that was unable to choose between two modes of reading, whereas the latter seems to reach a truth, albeit by the negative road of exposing an error, a false pretense. After the rhetorical reading of the Proust passage, we can no longer believe the assertion made in this passage about the intrinsic, metaphysical superiority of metaphor over metonymy. We seem to end up in a mood of negative assurance that is highly productive of critical discourse. The further text of Proust's novel, for example, responds perfectly to an extended application of this pattern: not only can similar gestures be repeated throughout the novel, at all the crucial articulations or all passages where large aesthetic and metaphysical claims are being made—the scenes of involuntary memory, the workshop of Elstir, the septette of Vinteuil, the convergence of author and narrator at the end of the novel—but a vast thematic and semiotic network is revealed that structures the entire narrative and that remained invisible to a reader caught in naïve metaphorical mystification. The whole of literature would respond in similar fashion, although the techniques and the patterns would have to vary considerably, of course, from author to author. But there is absolutely no reason why analyses of the kind here suggested for Proust would not be applicable, with proper modifications of technique, to Milton or to Dante or to Hölderlin. This will in fact be the task of literary criticism in the coming years.

It would seem that we are saying that criticism is the deconstruction of literature, the reduction to the rigors of grammar of rhetorical mystifications. And if we hold up Nietzsche as the philosopher of such a critical deconstruction, then the literary critic would become the philosopher's ally in his struggle with the poets. Criticism and literature would separate around the epistemological axis that distinguishes grammar from rhetoric. It is easy enough to see that this apparent glorification of the critic-philosopher in the name of truth is in fact a glorification of the poet as the primary source of this truth; if truth is the recognition of the systematic character of a certain kind of error, then it would be fully dependent on the prior existence of this error. Philosophers of science like Bachelard or Wittgenstein are notoriously dependent on the aberrations of the poets.[13] We are back at our unanswered question: does the grammatization of rhetoric end up in negative certainty or does it, like the rhetorization of grammar, remain suspended in the ignorance of its own truth or falsehood?

Two concluding remarks should suffice to answer the question. First of all, it is not true that Proust's text can simply be reduced to the mystified asser-

[13] See *Wittgenstein*. [Eds.]

tion (the superiority of metaphor over metonymy) that our reading deconstructs. The reading is not "our" reading, since it uses only the linguistic elements provided by the text itself: the distinction between author and reader is one of the false distinctions that the reading makes evident. The deconstruction is not something we have added to the text but it constituted the text in the first place. A literary text simultaneously asserts and denies the authority of its own rhetorical mode, and by reading the text as we did we were only trying to come closer to being as rigorous a reader as the author had to be in order to write the sentence in the first place. Poetic writing is the most advanced and refined mode of deconstruction; it may differ from critical or discursive writing in the economy of its articulation, but not in kind.

But if we recognize the existence of such a moment as constitutive of all literary language, we have surreptitiously reintroduced the categories that this deconstruction was supposed to eliminate and that have merely been displaced. We have, for example, displaced the question of the self from the referent into the figure of the narrator, who then becomes the *signifié* of the passage. It becomes again possible to ask such naïve questions as what Proust's, or Marcel's, motives may have been in thus manipulating language: was he fooling himself, or was he represented as fooling himself and fooling us into believing that fiction and action are as easy to unite, by reading, as the passage asserts? The pathos of the entire section, which would have been more noticeable if the quotation had been a little more extended, the constant vacillation of the narrator between guilt and well-being, invites such questions. They are absurd questions, of course, since the reconciliation of fact and fiction occurs itself as a mere assertion made in a text, and is thus productive of more text at the moment when it asserts its decision to escape from textual confinement. But even if we free ourselves of all false questions of intent and rightfully reduce the narrator to the status of a mere grammatical pronoun, without which the narrative could not come into being, this subject remains endowed with a function that is not grammatical but rhetorical, in that it gives voice, so to speak, to a grammatical syntagm. The term *voice*, even when used in a grammatical terminology as when we speak of the passive or interrogative voice, is, of course, a metaphor inferring by analogy the intent of the subject from the structure of the predicate. In the case of the deconstructive discourse that we call literary, or rhetorical, or poetic, this creates a distinctive complication illustrated by the Proust passage. The reading revealed a first paradox: the passage valorizes metaphor as being the "right" literary figure, but then proceeds to constitute itself by means of the epistemologically incompatible figure of metonymy. The critical discourse reveals the presence of this delusion and affirms it as the irreversible mode of its truth. It cannot pause there however. For if we then ask the obvious and simple next question, whether the rhetorical mode of the text in question is that of metaphor or metonymy, it is impossible to give an answer. Individual metaphors, such as the chiaroscuro effect or the butterfly, are shown to be subordinate figures in a general clause whose syntax is metonymic; from this point of view, it seems that the rhetoric is superseded by a grammar that deconstructs it. But this metonymic clause has as its subject a voice whose relationship to this clause is again metaphorical. The narrator who tells us about the impossibility of metaphor is himself, or itself, a metaphor, the metaphor of a grammatical syntagm whose meaning is the denial of metaphor stated, by antiphrasis, as its priority. And this subject-metaphor is, in its turn, open to the kind of deconstruction to the second degree, the rhetorical deconstruction of psycholinguistics, in which the more advanced investigations of literature are presently engaged, against considerable resistance.

We end up therefore, in the case of the rhetorical grammatization of semiology, just as in the grammatical rhetorization of illocutionary phrases, in the same state of suspended ignorance. Any question about the rhetorical mode of a literary text is always a rhetorical question which does not even know whether it is really questioning. The resulting pathos is an anxiety (or bliss, depending on one's momentary mood or individual temperament) of ignorance, not an anxiety of reference—as becomes thematically clear in Proust's novel when reading is dramatized, in the relationship between Marcel and Albertine, not as an emotive reaction to what language does, but as an emotive reaction to the impossibility of knowing what it might be up to. Literature as well as criticism—the difference between them being delusive—is condemned (or privileged) to be forever the most rigorous and, consequently, the most unreliable language in terms of which man names and transforms himself.

Theodor Adorno

1903–1969

"THE GREATNESS of works of art lies solely in their power to let those things be heard which ideology conceals," remarked Adorno in a posthumously published essay. Well known for his connection with the so-called Frankfurt School of social theorists, Adorno was its principal aesthetician, and it is this interest and the direction it took that most easily differentiate him from the other theorists of the group. Adorno had studied music both as a musician and as a composer in Vienna in the twenties and had become a strong advocate of the music of Schoenberg. His own thought remained always in the debt of Schoenberg's techniques of composition—to the extent that his thought has frequently been called atonal. This is a metaphor, of course, but it is a powerful one that emphasizes Adorno's profound distrust of all rational resolutions. It is no surprise that Adorno's best-known work is entitled *Negative Dialectics* and that commentators on the poststructuralist critical scene have noticed connections between his thought and deconstruction. Adorno's work bristles with terms clearly designed to oppose what is frequently called "totalization." In his powerful *Minima Moralia* he remarks, "The whole is the false," and he characteristically attacks the imperialistic tendencies of both sides of our usual oppositions, particularly subject/object. He attacks the passive subject of positivism but also the active constitutive subject of various idealisms. The Enlightenment, he argues in his collaboration with *Max Horkheimer,* has resulted in instrumentalism and human domination of nature. The subject is neither a passive recipient of the object nor a solipsist. Yet Adorno always holds out for individuality, though an individuality that is a creation of a complex cultural reality.

There is, then, no philosophy of identity in Adorno but rather a resistance or opposition to all closures or totalities except the artifice, which whole is not organic or rational but "autonomous" because it is known to be illusory and is therefore not to be employed as either escape from or consolation for reality. For Adorno, the Kantian notion of uselessness is, in fact, a resistance to the culture of instrumentalism and is thus always in its apartness and refusal of closure revolutionary. But he recognizes the danger in a theory of uselessness and so keeps his negative dialectic moving.

Adorno is deeply pessimistic, the exponent of a "melancholy science" against the "gay science" of Nietzsche, from whom he borrowed much. He is also optimistic in that he never abandons a utopian vision, though he is certain that it will not come about and would be its own totalizing corruption if it did. Still, for him, it is a necessary vision.

As a Marxist, Adorno had no attachment to any socialist government and remained always a political outsider, no less so for his strong aesthetic interests—

though he would de-aestheticize art—and his profound distaste for mass culture and bureaucracy. His *Aesthetic Theory,* left unfinished at his death, seeks to find in art what William Blake would have called a "reprobate" role, opposing culture's attempts at closure, identity, and thus repression.

The principal translated works of Adorno in addition to *Aesthetic Theory* are *Dialectic of Enlightenment* (1947, trans. 1972) with Max Horkheimer; *Minima Moralia* (1951, trans. 1974); *The Jargon of Authenticity* (1964, trans. 1973); *Negative Dialectics* (1966, trans. 1973); and *Prisms: Cultural Criticism and Society* (1955, trans. 1967). See Martin Jay, *The Dialectical Imagination: A History of the Frankfurt School of Social Research;* Susan Buck-Morss, *The Origin of Negative Dialectics;* Gillian Rose, *The Melancholy Science;* A. Orato and E. Gebhart, *The Essential Frankfurt School Reader;* and Martin Jay, *Adorno.*

FROM

AESTHETIC THEORY

On the Relation Between Art and Society

Aesthetic refraction is as incomplete without the refracted object as imagination is without the imagined object. This has special significance for the problem of the inherent functionality of art. Tied to the real world, art adopts the principle of self-preservation of that world, turning it into the ideal of self-identical art, the essence of which Schönberg once summed up in the statement that the painter paints a picture rather than what it represents. Implied here is the idea that every work of art spontaneously aims at being identical with itself, just as in the world outside a fake identity is everywhere forcibly imposed on objects by the insatiable subject. Aesthetic identity is different, however, in one important respect: it is meant to assist the non-identical in its struggle against the repressive identification compulsion that rules the outside world. It is by virtue of its separation from empirical reality that the work of art can become a being of a higher order, fashioning the relation between the whole and its parts in accordance with its own needs. Works of art are after-images or replicas of empirical life, inasmuch as they proffer to the latter what in the outside world is being denied them. In the process they slough off a repressive, external-empirical mode of experiencing the world. Whereas the line separating art from real life should not be fudged, least of all by glorifying the artist, it must be kept in mind that works of art are alive, have a life *sui generis.* Their life is more than just an outward fate. Over time, great works reveal new facets of themselves, they age, they become rigid, and they die. Being human artefacts, they do not 'live' in the same sense as human beings. Of course not. To put the accent on the artefactual aspect in works of art seems to imply that the way in which they came to be is important. It is not. The emphasis must be on their inner constitution. They have life because they speak in ways nature and man cannot. They talk because there is communication between their individual constituents, which cannot be said of things that exist in a state of mere diffusion.

As artefacts, works of art communicate not only internally but also with the external reality which they try to get away from and which none the less is the substratum of their content. Art negates the conceptualization foisted on the real world and yet harbours in its own substance elements of the empirically existent. Assuming that one has to differentiate form and content before grasping their mediation, we can say that art's opposition to the real world is in the realm of form; but this occurs, generally speaking, in a mediated way such that aesthetic form is a sedimentation of content. What seem like pure forms in art, namely those of traditional music, do in all respects, and all the way down to details of musical idiom, derive from exter-

AESTHETIC THEORY was originally published in Germany in 1970. The selection reprinted here is translated by C. Lenhardt from *Aesthetic Theory,* © 1984, by permission of Routledge and Kegan Paul.

nal content such as dance. Similarly, ornaments in the visual arts originally tended to be cult symbols. Members of the Warburg Institute were following this lead, studying the derivability of aesthetic forms from contents in the context of classical antiquity and its influence on later periods. This kind of work needs to be undertaken on a larger scale.

The manner in which art communicates with the outside world is in fact also a lack of communication, because art seeks, blissfully or unhappily, to seclude itself from the world. This non-communication points to the fractured nature of art. It is natural to think that art's autonomous domain has no more in common with the outside world than a few borrowed elements undergoing radical change in the context of art. But there is more to it than that. There is some truth to the historical cliché which states that the developments of artistic methods, usually lumped together under the term 'style', correspond to social development. Even the most sublime work of art takes up a definite position *vis-à-vis* reality by stepping outside of reality's spell, not abstractly once and for all, but occasionally and in concrete ways, when it unconsciously and tacitly polemicizes against the condition of society at a particular point in time.

How can works of art be like windowless monads, representing something which is other than they? There is only one way to explain this, which is to view them as being subject to a dynamic or immanent historicity and a dialectical tension between nature and domination of nature, a dialectic that seems to be of the same kind as the dialectic of society. or to put it more cautiously, the dialectic of art resembles the social dialectic without consciously imitating it. The productive force of useful labour and that of art are the same. They both have the same teleology. And what might be termed aesthetic relations of production—defined as everything that provides an outlet for the productive forces of art or everything in which these forces become embedded—are sedimentations of social relations of production bearing the imprint of the latter. Thus in all dimensions of its productive process art has a twofold essence, being both an autonomous entity and a social fact in the Durkheimian sense of the term.

It is through this relationship to the empirical that works of art salvage, albeit in neutralized fashion, something that once upon a time was literally a shared experience of all mankind and which enlightenment has since expelled. Art, too, partakes of enlightenment, but in a different way: works of art do not lie; what they say is literally true. Their reality however lies in the fact that they are answers to questions brought before them from outside. The tension in art therefore has meaning only in relation to the tension outside. The fundamental layers of artistic experience are akin to the objective world from which art recoils.

The unresolved antagonisms of reality reappear in art in the guise of immanent problems of artistic form. This, and not the deliberate injection of objective moments or social content, defines art's relation to society. The aesthetic tensions manifesting themselves in works of art express the essence of reality in and through their emancipation from the factual façade of exteriority. Art's simultaneous dissociation from and secret connection with empirical being confirms the strength of Hegel's analysis of the nature of a conceptual barrier (*Schranke*): the intellect, argues Hegel against Kant, no sooner posits a barrier than it has to go beyond it, absorbing into itself that against which the barrier was set up.[1] We have here, among other things, a basis for a non-moralistic critique of the idea of *l'art pour l'art* with its abstract negation of the empirical and with its monomaniac separatism in aesthetic theory.

Freedom, the presupposition of art and the self-glorifying conception art has of itself, is the cunning of art's reason. Blissfully soaring above the real world, art is still chained by each of its elements to the empirical other, into which it may even sink back altogether at every instant. In their relation to empirical reality works of art recall the theologumenon that in a state of redemption everything will be just as it is and yet wholly different. There is an unmistakable similarity in all this with the development of the profane. The profane secularizes the sacred realm to the point where the latter is the only secular thing left. The sacred realm is thus objectified, staked out as it were, because its moment of untruth awaits secularization as much as it tries to avert it through incantation.

It follows that art is not defined once and for all by the scope of an immutable concept. Rather, the concept of art is a fragile balance attained now and

[1] Cf. G. W. F. Hegel, *Science of Logic*, 1, Section 1, ch. 2. [Tr.]

then, quite similar to the psychological equilibrium between id and ego. Disturbances continually upset the balance, keeping the process in motion. Every work of art is an instant; every great work of art is a stoppage of the process, a momentary standing still, whereas a persistent eye sees only the process. While it is true that works of art provide answers to their own questions, it is equally true that in so doing they become questions for themselves. Take a look at the widespread inclination (which to this day has not been mitigated by education) to perceive art in terms of extra-aesthetic or pre-aesthetic criteria. This tendency is, on the one hand, a mark of atrocious backwardness or of the regressive consciousness of many people. On the other hand, there is no denying that that tendency is promoted by something in art itself. If art is perceived strictly in aesthetic terms, then it cannot be properly perceived in aesthetic terms. The artist must feel the presence of the empirical other in the foreground of his own experience in order to be able to sublimate that experience, thus freeing himself from his confinement to content while at the same time saving the being-for-itself of art from slipping into outright indifference toward the world.

Art is and is not being-for-itself. Without a heterogeneous moment, art cannot achieve autonomy. Great epics that survive their own oblivion were originally shot through with historical and geographical reporting. Valéry, for one, was aware of the degree to which the Homeric, pagan-germanic and Christian epics contained raw materials that had never been melted down and recast by the laws of form, noting that this did not diminish their rank in comparison with 'pure' works of art. Similarly, tragedy, the likely origin of the abstract idea of aesthetic autonomy, was also an after-image of pragmatically oriented cult acts. At no point in its history of progressive emancipation was art able to stamp out that moment. And the reason is not that the bonds were simply too strong. Long before socialist realism rationally planned its debasement, the realistic novel, which was at its height as a literary form in the nineteenth century, bears the marks of reportage, anticipating what was later to become the task of social science surveys. Conversely, the fanatic thoroughness of linguistic integration that characterizes *Madame Bovary,* for instance, is probably the result of the contrary moment. The continued relevance of this work is due to the unity of both.

In art, the criterion of success is twofold: first, works of art must be able to integrate materials and details into their immanent law of form; and, second, they must not try to erase the fractures left by the process of integration, preserving instead in the aesthetic whole the traces of those elements which resisted integration. Integration as such does not guarantee quality. There is no privileged single category, not even the aesthetically central one of form, that defines the essence of art and suffices to judge its product. In short, art has defining characteristics that go against the grain of what philosophy of art ordinarily conceives as art. Hegel is the exception. His aesthetics of content recognized the moment of otherness inherent in art, thus superseding the old aesthetic of form. The latter seems to be operating with too pure a concept of art, even though it has at least one advantage, which is that it does not, unlike Hegel's (and Kierkegaard's) substantive aesthetics, place obstacles in the way of certain historical developments such as abstract painting. This is one weakness of Hegel's aesthetic. The other is that, by conceiving form in terms of content, Hegel's theory of art regresses to a position that can only be called 'pre-aesthetic' and crude. Hegel mistakes the replicatory *(abbildende)* or discursive treatment of content for the kind of otherness that is constitutive of art. He sins, as it were, against his own dialectical concept of aesthetics, with results that he could not foresee. He in effect helped prepare the way of the banausic tendency to transform art into an ideology of repression.

The moment of unreality and non-existence in art is not independent of the existent, as though it were posited or invented by some arbitrary will. Rather, that moment of unreality is a structure resulting from quantitative relations between elements of being, relations which are in turn a response to, and an echo of, the imperfections of real conditions, their constraints, their contradictions, and their potentialities. Art is related to its other like a magnet to a field of iron filings. The elements of art as well as their constellation, or what is commonly thought to be the spiritual essence of art, point back to the real other. The identity of the works of art with existent reality also accounts for the centripetal force that enables them to gather unto themselves the traces and *membra disiecta*[2] of real life. Their affinity with the world lies in a principle that is con-

[2] Scattered parts. [Tr.]

ceived to be a contrast to that world but is in fact no different from the principle whereby spirit has dominated the world. Synthesis is not some process of imposing order on the elements of a work of art. It is important, rather, that the elements interact with each other; hence there is a sense in which synthesis is a mere repetition of the pre-established interdependence among elements, which interdependence is a product of otherness, of non-art. Synthesis, therefore, is firmly grounded in the material aspects of works of art.

There is a link between the aesthetic moment of form and non-violence. In its difference from the existent, art of necessity constitutes itself in terms of that which is not a work of art yet is indispensable for its being. The emphasis on non-intentionality in art, noticeable first in the sympathy for popular art in Apollinaire, early Cubism and Wedekind (who derided what he called 'art-artists'), indicates that art became aware, however dimly, that it interacted with its opposite. This new self-conception of art gave rise to a critical turn signalling an end to the illusory equation of art with pure spirituality.

Kant and Freud on Art

Freud's theory of art as wish-fulfilment has its antithesis in the theory of Kant. Kant states at the start of the 'Analytic of the Beautiful' that the first moment of a judgment of taste is disinterested satisfaction,[3] where interest is defined as 'the satisfaction which we combine with the representation of the existence of an object.'[4] Right away there is an ambiguity. It is impossible to tell whether Kant means, by representation of the existence of an object, the empirical object dealt with in a work of art, in other words its subject matter or content, or whether he means the work of art itself. Is he referring to the pretty nude model or to the sweetly pleasing sound of a piece of music (which, incidentally, can be pure artistic trash or an integral part of artistic quality)? Kant's stress on representation flows directly from his subjectivist approach, which locates the aesthetic quality in the effect a work of art has upon the viewer. This is in accord with the rationalist tradition, notably Moses Mendelssohn.[5] While staying in the old tradition of an aesthetic that emphasizes effect *(Wirkungsaesthetik)*, the *Critique of Judgment* is none the less a radical immanent critique of then contemporary rationalist aesthetics. Let us remember that the significance of Kantian subjectivism as a whole lies in its objective intention, its attempt to salvage objectivity by means of an analysis of subjective moments.

It is through the concept of disinterestedness that Kant breaks up the supremacy of pleasure in aesthetics. Satisfaction is meant to preserve effect but disinterestedness draws away from it. Bereft of what Kant calls interest, satisfaction and pleasure become wholly indeterminate, losing the capacity to define the beautiful. All the same, the doctrine of disinterested satisfaction is impoverished in view of the richness of aesthetic phenomena. It reduces them either to the formally beautiful—a questionable entity when viewed in isolation—or in the case of natural objects to the sublime. The reduction of art to absolute form misses the point about the why and wherefore of art. Kant's murky footnote,[6] which says that a judgment about an object of satisfaction is disinterested, i.e. not based on interest, even though it may be 'interesting', i.e. capable of evoking an interest, testifies honestly, if indirectly, to the fact that he was aware of a difficulty. Kant separates aesthetic feeling—and therefore, according to his own understanding, virtually the whole of art—from the faculty of desire at which the 'representation of the existence of an object' is aimed. Or, as he puts it, satisfaction in such a prepresentation 'always has reference to the faculty of desire.'[7] Kant was the first to have gained an insight that was never to be forgotten since: namely, that aesthetic conduct is free of immediate desire. Thus he rescued art from the greedy clutches of a kind of insensitivity that forever wants to touch and savour it.

Comparing Kant and Freud, it is interesting to note that the Kantian motif is not entirely foreign to the Freudian theory. Even for Freud, works of art, far from being direct wish-fulfilment, transform repressed libido into socially productive accomplishments. What is, of course, uncritically presupposed in this theory is the social value of art, whose quality as art simply rests on public reputation. By putting the difference between art, on the one hand, and the faculty of desire and empirical re-

[3] Kant, *Critique of Judgment*, tr. J. H. Bernard (New York, 1951), p. 39. [Tr.] See *CTSP*, pp. 377–99. [Eds.]

[4] Ibid., p. 38. [Tr.]

[5] Moses Mendelssohn (1729–86), German philosopher. [Eds.]

[6] Op. cit., p. 39. [Tr.]

[7] Ibid., p. 38. [Tr.]

ality, on the other, into much sharper relief than Freud, Kant does more than simply idealize art. Isolating the aesthetic from the empirical sphere, he constitutes art. He then, however, proceeds to arrest this process of constitution in the framework of his transcendental philosophy, simplistically equating constitution with the essence of art and ignoring the fact that the subjective instinctual components of art crop up, in different form, even in the most mature manifestations of art.

In his theory of sublimation, on the other hand, Freud was more clearly aware of the dynamic nature of art. The price he paid was no smaller than Kant's. For Freud, the spiritual essence of art remains hidden. For Kant, it does emerge from the distinctions between aesthetic, practical and appetitive behaviour, Kant's preference for sensuous intuition notwithstanding. In the Freudian view works of art, although products of sublimation, are little more than plenipotentiaries of sensuous impulses made unrecognizable to some degree by a kind of dream-work.

A comparison between two thinkers as different as Kant and Freud—Kant, for example, not only rejected philosophical psychologism but with age also became hostile to psychology as such—is justified by the presence of a common denominator that outweighs the differences between the Kantian construction of the transcendental subject and the Freudian focus on the empirical subject. Where they differ is in their positive and negative approaches, respectively, to the faculty of desire. What they have in common, however, is the underlying subjective orientation. For both, the work of art exists only in relation to the individual who contemplates or produces it. There is a mechanism in Kant's thought that forces him, both in moral and in aesthetic philosophy, to consider the ontic, empirical individual to a larger extent than seems warranted by the notion of the transcendental subject. In aesthetics this implies that there can be no pleasure without a living being to whom an object is pleasing. Without explicit recognition, Kant devotes the entire *Critique of Judgment* to an analysis of *constituta*. Therefore, despite the programmatic idea of building a bridge between theoretical and practical pure reason, the faculty of judgment turns out to be *sui generis* in relation to both forms of reason.

Perhaps the most important taboo in art is the one that prohibits an animal-like atittude toward the object, say, a desire to devour it or otherwise to subjugate it to one's body. Now, the strength of such a taboo is matched by the strength of the repressed urge. Hence, all art contains in itself a negative moment from which it tries to get away. If Kant's disinterestedness is to be more than a synonym for indifference, it has to have a trace of untamed interest somewhere. Indeed, there is much to be said for the thesis that the dignity of works of art depends on the magnitude of the interest from which they were wrested. Kant denies this in order to protect his concept of freedom from spurious heteronomies that he saw lurking everywhere. In this regard, his theory of art is tainted by an insufficiency of his theory of practical reason. In the context of Kant's philosophy, the idea of a beautiful object possessing a kind of independence from the sovereign ego must seem like a digression into intelligible worlds. The source from which art antithetically originates, as well as the content of art, are of no concern to Kant, who instead posits something as formal as aesthetic satisfaction as the defining characteristic of art. His aesthetics presents the paradox of a castrated hedonism, of a theory of pleasure without pleasure. This position fails to do justice either to artistic experience wherein satisfaction is a subordinate moment in a larger whole, or to the material-corporeal interest, i.e. repressed and unsatisfied needs that resonate in their aesthetic negations—the works of art—turning them into something more than empty patterns.

Aesthetic disinterestedness has moved interest beyond particularity. Objectively, the interest in constituting an aesthetic totality entailed an interest in the proper arrangement of the social whole. In the last analysis aesthetic interest aimed not at some particular fulfilment, but at the fulfilment of infinite possibilities, which in turn cannot be thought without fulfilment of the particular.

A corresponding weakness can be noticed in Freud's theory of art, which is a good deal more idealistic than Freud had thought it was. By placing works of art squarely into a realm of psychic immanence, Freud's theory loses sight of their antithetical relation to the non-subjective, which thus remains unmolested, as it were, by the thorns pointed toward it by works of art. As a result, psychic processes like instinctual denial and adaptation are left as the only relevant aspects of art. Psychologistic interpretations of art are in league with the philistine view that art is a conciliatory force capable of smoothing over differences, or that it is the dream of a better life, never mind the fact that such dreams should recall the negativity from which they were forcibly extracted. Psychoanalysis in conformist fashion simply takes over the prevalent view of art as some sort of beneficent culture heritage. To this corresponds the aesthetic hedonism which has psychoanalysis banish all negativity from art *qua* result, pushing the analysis of that negativity back to the level of instinctual conflict. Once successful sublimation and integration become the be-all and end-all of a work of art, it loses the power to transcend mere existence. However, as soon as we conceive of the work of art in terms of its ability to keep a hold on the negativity of the real and to enter into a definite relation to it, we have to change the concept of disinterestedness as well. In contrast to the Kantian and Freudian views on the matter, works of art necessarily evolve in a dialectic of interests and disinterestedness.

There is a grain of validity even in a contemplative attitude towards art, inasmuch as it underscores the important posture of art's turning away from immediate praxis and refusing to play the worldly game. This has long been a component of artistic behaviour. We see here, incidentally, that works of art are tied up with specific modes of behavior; indeed, that they *are* modes of behaviour. Now it is only those works of art that manifest themselves as modes of behaviour which have a reason for being. Art is like a plenipotentiary of a type of praxis that is better than the prevailing praxis of society, dominated as it is by brutal self-interest. This is what art criticizes. It gives the lie to the notion that production for production's sake is necessary, by opting for a mode of praxis beyond labour. Art's *promesse du bonheur,*[8] then, has an even more emphatically critical meaning: it not only expresses the idea that current praxis denies happiness, but also carries the connotation that happiness is something beyond praxis. The chasm between praxis and happiness is surveyed and measured by the power of negativity of the work of art.

Surely a writer like Kafka does anything but appeal to our faculty of desire. Prose writings such as *Metamorphosis* and *Penal Colony,* on the contrary, seem to call forth in us responses like real anxiety, a violent drawing back, an almost physical revulsion. They seem to be the opposite of desire. yet these phenomena of psychic defence and rejection have more in common with desire than with the old Kantian disinterestedness. Kafka and the literature that followed his example have swept away the notion of disinterestedness. In relation to Kafka's works, disinterestedness is a completely inadequate concept of interpretation. In the last analysis the postulate of disinterestedness debases all art, turning it into a pleasant or useful plaything, in accord with Horace's *ars poetica.*[9] Idealist aesthetics and its contemporaneous art products have emancipated themselves from this misconception. The precondition for the autonomy of artistic experience is the abandonment of the attitude of tasting and savouring. The trajectory leading to aesthetic autonomy passes through the stage of disinterestedness; and well it should, for it was during this stage that art emancipated itself from cuisine and pornography, an emancipation that has become irrevocable. However, art does not come to rest in disinterestedness. It moves on. And in so doing it reproduces, in different form, the interest inherent in disinterestedness. In a false world all *hedone* is false. This goes for artistic pleasure, too. Art renounces happiness for the sake of happiness, thus enabling desire to survive in art.

[8] Promise of happiness. [Eds.]

[9] See *CTSP,* pp. 67–75. [Eds.]

Louis Althusser

b. 1918

Louis Althusser became prominent as a structural Marxist in the early sixties with his attack on humanism and those who would return to the early so-called humanist Marx rather than the later antihumanistic precursor of structuralist social thought. For Althusser, the earliest Marx, who was first an ethical idealist influenced by Kant and Fichte and then a naturalistic humanist following Feuerbach, was superseded by a Marx whose thought posits a historical process without a humanist subject, the real subject being the social relations of production. Althusser advocates a reading of the late Marx's text, not Marx, denying that the significance of the text lies in Marx's recoverable intention. It is here that one of Althusser's major terms appears: "problematic," which has been much used by literary theorists. The problematic of a text is the unconscious infrastructure, the forms that determine how the text will behave and can be allowed to be thought. The problematic lies beneath the text, as the base to the superstructure, but it is unspoken. Further, the problematic is not thought by the individual subject (there is no such subject); instead it thinks through what in the past we have habitually called the subject: "We must go further than the unmentioned presence of the thoughts of a living author to the presence of his *potential thoughts,* to his *problematic,* that is, to the constitutive unity of the effective thoughts that make up the domain of the existing *ideological field* with which a particular author must settle accounts in his own thought." There is here no "constitutive subject" but instead a structure of ideas and relations among them.

This notion has something in common with the idea of "paradigm" set forth by *Thomas Kuhn* in *The Structure of Scientific Revolutions.* Althusser's notion of the "epistemological break" (*coupure*) or rupture also has some relation to Kuhn's notion of "paradigm shift." For Althusser, there are radical discontinuities in history, and one of these is apparent in miniature, so to speak, between the thought of the early and that of the late Marx—from ideology to science. Althusser claims that although certain key terms like "alienation" and "fetishism" appear in both the early and late works of Marx, they inhabit different problematics and thus perform different functions. Still, that residue of language and the struggle with it, which so often characterize revolutionary texts, suggest that no "coupure" is absolutely clean.

Althusser's antihumanism has been attacked by, for example, E. P. Thompson in *The Poverty of Theory* as having affinities with Stalinism. Althusser did not publicly disown Stalin, but his views are perhaps better understood as related to Spinozaism, and his work in general is an effort to create a structuralist Marxism that would be opposed to the subject as conceived by phenomenology and the bourgeois tradition reaching back into the empiricism of Locke.

The selection here is part of one of Althusser's most influential essays. One of its principal contributions to criticism is its analysis of education as part of ideological state apparatus.

Works by Althusser translated into English include *Politics and History* (1959 ff., trans. 1972); *For Marx* (1965, trans. 1969); *Reading Capital* (1965–68, trans. 1970); *Lenin and Philosophy* (1969, trans. 1970); and *Essays in Self-Criticism* (1974, trans. 1976). See Alex Callinicos, *Althusser's Marxism,* and Steven B. Smith, *Reading Althusser,* which includes a useful bibliography.

FROM

IDEOLOGY AND IDEOLOGICAL STATE APPARATUSES

On Ideology

When I put forward the concept of an Ideological State Apparatus, when I said that the ISAs 'function by ideology', I invoked a reality which needs a little discussion: ideology.

It is well known that the expression 'ideology' was invented by Cabanis, Destutt de Tracy and their friends, who assigned to it as an object the (genetic) theory of ideas. When Marx took up the term fifty years later, he gave it a quite different meaning, even in his Early Works. Here, ideology is the system of the ideas and representations which dominate the mind of a man or a social group. The ideologico-political struggle conducted by Marx as early as his articles in the *Rheinische Zeitung* inevitably and quickly brought him face to face with this reality and forced him to take his earliest intuitions further.

However, here we come upon a rather astonishing paradox. Everything seems to lead Marx to formulate a theory of ideology. In fact, *The German Ideology* does offer us, after the *1844 Manuscripts,* an explicit theory of ideology, but . . . it is not Marxist (we shall see why in a moment). As for *Capital,* although it does contain many hints towards a theory of ideologies (most visibly, the ideology of the vulgar economists), it does not contain the theory itself, which depends for the most part on a theory of ideology in general.

I should like to venture a first and very schematic outline of such a theory. The theses I am about to put forward are certainly not off the cuff, but they cannot be sustained and tested, i.e. confirmed or rejected, except by much thorough study and analysis.

Ideology has no History

One word first of all to expound the reason in principle which seems to me to found, or at least to justify, the project of a theory of ideology *in general,* and not a theory of particular ideolog*ies,* which, whatever their form (religious, ethical, legal, political), always express *class positions.*

It is quite obvious that it is necessary to proceed towards a theory of ideolog*ies* in the two respects I have just suggested.[1] It will then be clear that a theory of ideolog*ies* depends in the last resort on the history of social formations, and thus of the modes of production combined in social formations, and of the class struggles which develop in them. In this sense it is clear that there can be no question of a theory of ideolog*ies in general,* since ideolog*ies* (defined in the double respect suggested above: re-

IDEOLOGY AND IDEOLOGICAL STATE APPARATUSES (NOTES TOWARDS AN INVESTIGATION), of which only part is printed here, first appeared in French in *La Pensée* in 1970. It is reprinted from *Lenin and Philosophy and Other Essays,* trans. Ben Brewster, © 1971 by New Left Books. Reprinted, by permission of Monthly Review Foundation.

[1] Earlier in the essay Althusser has distinguished between state power and state apparatus, on the one hand, and the more subtle expressions of power and repression, ideological state apparatuses, on the other: the different churches, educational institutions, the family, the legal ideology, the political, trade unions, the arts, sports, etc. [Eds.]

gional and class) have a history, whose determination in the last instance is clearly situated outside ideologies alone, although it involves them.

On the contrary, if I am able to put forward the project of a theory of ideology *in general*, and if this theory really is one of the elements on which theories of ideolog*ies* depend, that entails an apparently paradoxical proposition which I shall express in the following terms: *ideology has no history.*

As we know, this formulation appears in so many words in a passage from *The German Ideology*. Marx utters it with respect to metaphysics, which, he says, has no more history than ethics (meaning also the other forms of ideology).

In *The German Ideology*, this formulation appears in a plainly positivist context. Ideology is conceived as a pure illusion, a pure dream, i.e. as nothingness. All its reality is external to it. Ideology is thus thought as an imaginary construction whose status is exactly like the theoretical status of the dream among writers before Freud. For these writers, the dream was the purely imaginary, i.e. null, result of 'day's residues', presented in an arbitrary arrangement and order, sometimes even 'inverted', in other words, in 'disorder'. For them, the dream was the imaginary, it was empty, null and arbitrarily 'stuck together' (*bricolé*), once the eyes had closed, from the residues of the only full and positive reality, the reality of the day. This is exactly the status of philosophy and ideology (since in the book philosophy is ideology *par excellence*) in *The German Ideology*.

Ideology, then, is for Marx an imaginary assemblage (*bricolage*), a pure dream, empty and vain, constituted by the 'day's residues' from the only full and positive reality, that of the concrete history of concrete material individuals materially producing their existence. It is on this basis that ideology has no history in *The German Ideology*, since its history is outside it, where the only existing history is, the history of concrete individuals, etc. In *The German Ideology*, the thesis that ideology has no history is therefore a purely negative thesis, since it means both:

1. ideology is nothing insofar as it is a pure dream (manufactured by who knows what power: if not by the alienation of the division of labour, but that, too, is a *negative* determination);

2. ideology has no history, which emphatically does not mean that there is no history in it (on the contrary, for it is merely the pale, empty and inverted reflection of real history) but that it has no history *of its own*.

Now, while the thesis I wish to defend formally speaking adopts the terms of *The German Ideology* ('ideology has no history'), it is radically different from the positivist and historicist thesis of *The German Ideology*.

For on the one hand, I think it is possible to hold that ideolog*ies have a history of their own* (although it is determined in the last instance by the class struggle); and on the other, I think it is possible to hold that ideology *in general has no history*, not in a negative sense (its history is external to it), but in an absolutely positive sense.

This sense is a positive one if it is true that the peculiarity of ideology is that it is endowed with a structure and a functioning such as to make it a non-historical reality, i.e. an *omni-historical* reality, in the sense in which that structure and functioning are immutable, present in the same form throughout what we can call history, in the sense in which the *Communist Manifesto* defines history as the history of class struggles, i.e. the history of class societies.

To give a theoretical reference-point here, I might say that, to return to our example of the dream, in its Freudian conception this time, our proposition: ideology has no history, can and must (and in a way which has absolutely nothing arbitrary about it, but, quite the reverse, is theoretically necessary, for there is an organic link between the two propositions) be related directly to Freud's proposition that the *unconscious is eternal*, i.e. that it has no history.

If eternal means, not transcendent to all (temporal) history, but omnipresent, trans-historical and therefore immutable in form throughout the extent of history, I shall adopt Freud's expression word for word, and write *ideology is eternal*, exactly like the unconscious. And I add that I find this comparison theoretically justified by the fact that the eternity of the unconscious is not unrelated to the eternity of ideology in general.

That is why I believe I am justified, hypothetically at least, in proposing a theory of ideology *in general*, in the sense that Freud presented a theory of the unconscious *in general*.

To simplify the phrase, it is convenient, taking into account what has been said about ideologies, to use the plain term ideology to designate ideology in general, which I have just said has no history, or, what comes to the same thing, is eternal, i.e. omnipresent in its immutable form throughout history (the history of social formations containing social classes). For the moment I shall restrict myself to 'class societies' and their history.

Ideology is a 'Representation' of the Imaginary Relationship of Individuals to their Real Conditions of Existence

In order to approach my central thesis on the structure and functioning of ideology, I shall first present two theses, one negative, the other positive. The first concerns the object which is 'represented' in the imaginary form of ideology, the second concerns the materiality of ideology.

THESIS I: Ideology represents the imaginary relationship of individuals to their real conditions of existence.

We commonly call religious ideology, ethical ideology, legal ideology, political ideology, etc., so many 'world outlooks'. Of course, assuming that we do not live one of these ideologies as the truth (e.g. 'believe' in God, Duty, Justice, etc. . . .), we admit that the ideology we are discussing from a critical point of view, examining it as the ethnologist examines the myths of a 'primitive society', that these 'world outlooks' are largely imaginary, i.e. do not 'correspond to reality'.

However, while admitting that they do not correspond to reality, i.e. that they constitute an illusion, we admit that they do make allusion to reality, and that they need only be 'interpreted' to discover the reality of the world behind their imaginary representation of that world (ideology = *illusion/allusion*).

There are different types of interpretation, the most famous of which are the *mechanistic* type, current in the eighteenth century (God is the imaginary representation of the real King), and the *'hermeneutic'* interpretation, inaugurated by the earliest Church Fathers, and revived by Feuerbach[2] and the theologico-philosophical school which descends from him, e.g. the theologian Barth (to Feuerbach, for example, God is the essence of real Man). The essential point is that on condition that we interpret the imaginary transposition (and inversion) of ideology we arrive at the conclusion that in ideology 'men represent their real conditions of existence to themselves in an imaginary form'.

Unfortunately, this interpretation leaves one small problem unsettled: why do men 'need' this imaginary transposition of their real conditions of existence in order to 'represent to themselves' their real conditions of existence?

The first answer (that of the eighteenth century) proposes a simple solution: Priests or Despots are responsible. They 'forged' the Beautiful Lies so that, in the belief that they were obeying God, men would in fact obey the Priests and Despots, who are usually in alliance in their imposture, the Priests acting in the interests of the Despots or *vice versa,* according to the political positions of the 'theoreticians' concerned. There is therefore a cause for the imaginary transposition of the real conditions of existence: that cause is the existence of a small number of cynical men who base their domination and exploitation of the 'people' on a falsified representation of the world which they have imagined in order to enslave other minds by dominating their imaginations.

The second answer (that of Feuerbach, taken over word for word by Marx in his Early Works) is more 'profound', i.e. just as false. It, too, seeks and finds a cause for the imaginary transposition and distortion of men's real conditions of existence, in short, for the alienation in the imaginary of the representation of men's conditions of existence. This cause is no longer Priests or Despots, nor their active imagination and the passive imagination of their victims. This cause is the material alienation which reigns in the conditions of existence of men themselves. This is how, in *The Jewish Question* and elsewhere, Marx defends the Feuerbachian idea that men make themselves an alienated (= imaginary) representation of their conditions of existence because these conditions of existence are themselves alienating (in the *1844 Manuscripts:* because these conditions are dominated by the essence of alienated society—*'alienated labour'*).

All these interpretations thus take literally the thesis which they presuppose, and on which they depend, i.e. that what is reflected in the imaginary representation of the world found in an ideology is the conditions of existence of men, i.e. their real world.

Now I can return to a thesis which I have already

[2]Ludwig Andreas Feuerbach (1804–72), German philosopher, first a Hegelian, later a natural materialist. [Eds.]

advanced: it is not their real conditions of existence, their real world, that 'men' 'represent to themselves' in ideology, but above all it is their relation to those conditions of existence which is represented to them there. It is this relation which is at the centre of every ideological, i.e. imaginary, representation of the real world. It is this relation that contains the 'cause' which has to explain the imaginary distortion of the ideological representation of the real world. Or rather, to leave aside the language of causality it is necessary to advance the thesis that it is the *imaginary nature of this relation* which underlies all the imaginary distortion that we can observe (if we do not live in its truth) in all ideology.

To speak in a Marxist language, if it is true that the representation of the real conditions of existence of the individuals occupying the posts of agents of production, exploitation, repression, ideologization and scientific practice, does in the last analysis arise from the relations of production, and from relations deriving from the relations of production, we can say the following: all ideology represents in its necessarily imaginary distortion not the existing relations of production (and the other relations that derive from them), but above all the (imaginary) relationship of individuals to the relations of production and the relations that derive from them. What is represented in ideology is therefore not the system of the real relations which govern the existence of individuals, but the imaginary relation of those individuals to the real relations in which they live.

If this is the case, the question of the 'cause' of the imaginary distortion of the real relations in ideology disappears and must be replaced by a different question: why is the representation given to individuals of their (individual) relation to the social relations which govern their conditions of existence and their collective and individual life necessarily an imaginary relation? And what is the nature of this imaginariness? Posed in this way, the question explodes the solution by a 'clique'[3] by a group of individuals (Priests or Despots) who are the authors of the great ideological mystification, just as it explodes the solution by the alienated character of the real world. We shall see why later in my exposition. For the moment I shall go no further.

[3] I use this very modern term deliberately. For even in Communist circles, unfortunately, it is a commonplace to 'explain' some political deviation (left or right opportunism) by the action of a 'clique'. [Au.]

THESIS II: Ideology has a material existence.

I have already touched on this thesis by saying that the 'ideas' or 'representations', etc., which seem to make up ideology do not have an ideal (*idéale* or *idéelle*) or spiritual existence, but a material existence. I even suggested that the ideal (*idéale, idéelle*) and spiritual existence of 'ideas' arises exclusively in an ideology of the 'idea' and of ideology, and let me add, in an ideology of what seems to have 'founded' this conception since the emergence of the sciences, i.e. what the practicians of the sciences represent to themselves in their spontaneous ideology as 'ideas', true or false. Of course, presented in affirmative form, this thesis is unproven. I simply ask that the reader be favourably disposed towards it, say, in the name of materialism. A long series of arguments would be necessary to prove it.

This hypothetical thesis of the not spiritual but material existence of 'ideas' or other 'representations' is indeed necessary if we are to advance in our analysis of the nature of ideology. Or rather, it is merely useful to us in order the better to reveal what every at all serious analysis of any ideology will immediately and empirically show to every observer, however critical.

While discussing the ideological State apparatuses and their practices, I said that each of them was the realization of an ideology (the unity of these different regional ideologies—religious, ethical, legal, political, aesthetic, etc.—being assured by their subjection to the ruling ideology). I now return to this thesis: an ideology always exists in an apparatus, and its practice, or practices. This existence is material.

Of course, the material existence of the ideology in an apparatus and its practices does not have the same modality as the material existence of a paving-stone or a rifle. But, at the risk of being taken for a Neo-Aristotelian (NB Marx had a very high regard for Aristotle), I shall say that 'matter is discussed in many senses', or rather that it exists in different modalities, all rooted in the last instance in 'physical' matter.

Having said this, let me move straight on and see what happens to the 'individuals' who live in ideology, i.e. in a determinate (religious, ethical, etc.) representation of the world whose imaginary distortion depends on their imaginary relation to their conditions of existence, in other words, in the last instance, to the relations of production and to class relations (ideology = an imaginary relation to real relations). I shall say that this imaginary relation is itself endowed with a material existence.

Now I observe the following.

An individual believes in God, or Duty, or Justice, etc. This belief derives (for everyone, i.e. for all those who live in an ideological representation of ideology, which reduces ideology to ideas endowed by definition with a spiritual existence) from the ideas of the individual concerned, i.e. from him as a subject with a consciousness which contains the ideas of his belief. In this way, i.e. by means of the absolutely ideological 'conceptual' device (*dispositif*) thus set up (a subject endowed with a consciousness in which he freely forms or freely recognizes ideas in which he believes), the (material) attitude of the subject concerned naturally follows.

The individual in question behaves in such and such a way, adopts such and such a practical attitude, and, what is more, participates in certain regular practices which are those of the ideological apparatus on which 'depend' the ideas which he has in all consciousness freely chosen as a subject. If he believes in God, he goes to Church to attend Mass, kneels, prays, confesses, does penance (once it was material in the ordinary sense of the term) and naturally repents and so on. If he believes in Duty, he will have the corresponding attitudes, inscribed in ritual practices 'according to the correct principles'. If he believes in Justice, he will submit unconditionally to the rules of the Law, and may even protest when they are violated, sign petitions, take part in a demonstration, etc.

Throughout this schema we observe that the ideological representation of ideology is itself forced to recognize that every 'subject' endowed with a 'consciousness' and believing in the 'ideas' that his 'consciousness' inspires in him and freely accepts, must '*act* according to his ideas', must therefore inscribe his own ideas as a free subject in the actions of his material practice. If he does not do so, 'that is wicked'.

Indeed, if he does not do what he ought to do as a function of what he believes, it is because he does something else, which, still as a function of the same idealist scheme, implies that he has other ideas in his head as well as those he proclaims, and that he acts according to these other ideas, as a man who is either 'inconsistent' ('no one is willingly evil') or cynical, or perverse.

In every case, the ideology of ideology thus recognizes, despite its imaginary distortion, that the 'ideas' of a human subject exist in his actions, or ought to exist in his actions, and if that is not the case, it lends him other ideas corresponding to the actions (however perverse) that he does perform. This ideology talks of actions: I shall talk of actions inserted into *practices. And* I shall point out that these practices are governed by the *rituals* in which these practices are inscribed, within the *material existence of an ideological apparatus,* be it only a small part of that apparatus: a small mass in a small church, a funeral, a minor match at a sports' club, a school day, a political party meeting, etc.

Besides, we are indebted to Pascal's[4] defensive 'dialectic' for the wonderful formula which will enable us to invert the order of the notional schema of ideology. Pascal says more or less: 'Kneel down, move your lips in prayer, and you will believe.' He thus scandalously inverts the order of things, bringing, like Christ, not peace but strife, and in addition something hardly Christian (for woe to him who brings scandal into the world!)—scandal itself. A fortunate scandal which makes him stick with Jansenist defiance to a language that directly names the reality.

I will be allowed to leave Pascal to the arguments of his ideological struggle with the religious ideological State apparatus of his day. And I shall be expected to use a more directly Marxist vocabulary, if that is possible, for we are advancing in still poorly explored domains.

I shall therefore say that, where only a single subject (such and such an individual) is concerned, the existence of the ideas of his belief is material in that *his ideas are his material actions inserted into material practices governed by material rituals which are themselves defined by the material ideological apparatus from which derive the ideas of that subject.* Naturally, the four inscriptions of the adjective 'material' in my proposition must be affected by different modalities: the materialities of a displacement for going to mass, of kneeling down, of the gesture of the sign of the cross, or of the *mea culpa,* of a sentence, of a prayer, of an act of contrition, of a penitence, of a gaze, of a hand-shake, of an external verbal discourse or an 'internal' verbal discourse (consciousness), are not one and the same materiality. I shall leave on one side the problem of a the-

[4]Blaise Pascal (1623–62), French philosopher and scientist. [Eds.]

ory of the differences between the modalities of materiality.

It remains that in this inverted presentation of things, we are not dealing with an 'inversion' at all, since it is clear that certain notions have purely and simply disappeared from our presentation, whereas others on the contrary survive, and new terms appear.

> Disappeared: the term *ideas*.
> Survive: the terms *subject, consciousness, belief, actions*.
> Appear: the terms *practices, rituals, ideological apparatus*.

It is therefore not an inversion or overturning (except in the sense in which one might say a government or a glass is overturned), but a reshuffle (of a non-ministerial type), a rather strange reshuffle, since we obtain the following result.

Ideas have disappeared as such (insofar as they are endowed with an ideal or spiritual existence), to the precise extent that it has emerged that their existence is inscribed in the actions of practices governed by rituals defined in the last instance by an ideological apparatus. It therefore appears that the subject acts insofar as he is acted by the following system (set out in the order of its real determination): ideology existing in a material ideological apparatus, prescribing material practices governed by a material ritual, which practices exist in the material actions of a subject acting in all consciousness according to his belief.

But this very presentation reveals that we have retained the following notions: subject, consciousness, belief, actions. From this series I shall immediately extract the decisive central term on which everything else depends: the notion of the *subject*.

And I shall immediately set down these two conjoint theses:

1. there is no practice except by and in an ideology;
2. there is no ideology except by the subject and for subjects.

I can now come to my central thesis.

Ideology Interpellates Individuals as Subjects

This thesis is simply a matter of making my last proposition explicit: there is no ideology except by the subject and for subjects. Meaning, there is no ideology except for concrete subjects, and this destination for ideology is only made possible by the subject: meaning, *by the category of the subject* and its functioning.

By this I mean that, even if it only appears under this name (the subject) with the rise of bourgeois ideology, above all with the rise of legal ideology,[5] the category of the subject (which may function under other names: e.g., as the soul in Plato, as God, etc.) is the constitutive category of all ideology, whatever its determination (regional or class) and whatever its historical date—since ideology has no history.

I say: the category of the subject is constitutive of all ideology, but at the same time and immediately I add that *the category of the subject is only constitutive of all ideology insofar as all ideology has the function* (*which defines it*) of 'constituting' concrete individuals as subjects. In the interaction of this double constitution exists the functioning of all ideology, ideology being nothing but its functioning in the material forms of existence of that functioning.

In order to grasp what follows, it is essential to realize that both he who is writing these lines and the reader who reads them are themselves subjects, and therefore ideological subjects (a tautological proposition), i.e. that the author and the reader of these lines both live 'spontaneously' or 'naturally' in ideology in the sense in which I have said that 'man is an ideological animal by nature'.

That the author, insofar as he writes the lines of a discourse which claims to be scientific, is completely absent as a 'subject' from 'his' scientfic discourse (for all scientific discourse is by definition a subject-less discourse, there is no 'Subject of science' except in an ideology of science) is a different question which I shall leave on one side for the moment.

As St Paul admirably put it, it is in the 'Logos', meaning in ideology, that we 'live, move and have our being'. It follows that, for you and for me, the category of the subject is a primary 'obviousness' (obviousnesses are always primary): it is clear that you and I are subjects (free, ethical, etc. . . .). Like all obviousnesses, including those that make a word 'name a thing' or 'have a meaning' (therefore in-

[5] Which borrowed the legal category of 'subject in law' to make an ideological notion: man is by nature a subject. [Au.]

cluding the obviousness of the 'transparency' of language), the 'obviousness' that you and I are subjects—and that that does not cause any problems—is an ideological effect, the elementary ideological effect.[6] It is indeed a peculiarity of ideology that it imposes (without appearing to do so, since these are 'obviousnesses') obviousnesses as obviousnesses, which we cannot *fail to recognize* and before which we have the inevitable and natural reaction of crying out (aloud or in the 'still, small voice of conscience'): 'That's obvious! That's right! That's true!'

At work in this reaction is the ideological *recognition* function which is one of the two functions of ideology as such (its inverse being the function of *misrecognition—méconnaissance*).

To take a highly 'concrete' example, we all have friends who, when they knock on our door and we ask, through the door, the question 'Who's there?', answer (since 'it's obvious') 'It's me'. And we recognize that 'it is him', or 'her'. We open the door, and 'it's true, it really was she who was there'. To take another example, when we recognize somebody of our (previous) acquaintance ((*re*)-*connaissance*) in the street, we show him that we have recognized him (and have recognized that he has recognized us) by saying to him 'Hello, my friend', and shaking his hand (a material ritual practice of ideological recognition in everyday life—in France, at least; elsewhere, there are other rituals).

In this preliminary remark and these concrete illustrations, I only wish to point out that you and I are *always already* subjects, and as such constantly practice the rituals of ideological recognition, which guarantee for us that we are indeed concrete, individual, distinguishable and (naturally) irreplaceable subjects. The writing I am currently executing and the reading you are currently[7] performing are also in this respect rituals of ideological recognition, including the 'obviousness' with which the 'truth' or 'error' of my reflections may impose itself on you.

But to recognize that we are subjects and that we function in the practical rituals of the most elementary everyday life (the hand-shake, the fact of calling you by your name, the fact of knowing, even if I do not know what it is, that you 'have' a name of your own, which means that you are recognized as a unique subject, etc.)—this recognition only gives us the 'consciousness' of our incessant (eternal) practice of ideological recognition—its consciousness, i.e. its *recognition*—but in no sense does it give us the (scientific) *knowledge* of the mechanism of this recognition. Now it is this knowledge that we have to reach, if you will, while speaking in ideology, and from within ideology we have to outline a discourse which tries to break with ideology, in order to dare to be the beginning of a scientific (i.e. subject-less) discourse on ideology.

Thus in order to represent why the category of the 'subject' is constitutive of ideology, which only exists by constituting concrete subjects as subjects, I shall employ a special mode of exposition: 'concrete' enough to be recognized, but abstract enough to be thinkable and thought, giving rise to knowledge.

As a first formulation I shall say: *all ideology hails or interpellates concrete individuals as concrete subjects,* by the functioning of the category of the subject.

This is a proposition which entails that we distinguish for the moment between concrete individuals on the one hand and concrete subjects on the other, although at this level concrete subjects only exist insofar as they are supported by a concrete individual.

I shall then suggest that ideology 'acts' or 'functions' in such a way that it 'recruits' subjects among the individuals (it recruits them all), or 'transforms' the individuals into subjects (it transforms them all) by that very precise operation which I have called *interpellation* or hailing, and which can be imagined along the lines of the most commonplace everyday police (or other) hailing: 'Hey, you there!'[8]

Assuming that the theoretical scene I have imagined takes place in the street, the hailed individual will turn round. By this mere one-hundred-and-eighty-degree physical conversion, he becomes a *subject.* Why? Because he has recognized that the

[6] Linguists and those who appeal to linguistics for various purposes often run up against difficulties which arise because they ignore the action of the ideological effects in all discourses—including even scientific discourses. [Au.]

[7] NB: this double 'currently' is one more proof of the fact that ideology is 'eternal', since these two 'currentlys' are separated by an indefinite interval; I am writing these lines on 6 April 1969, you may read them at any subsequent time. [Au.]

[8] Hailing as an everyday practice subject to a precise ritual takes quite 'special' form in the policeman's practice of 'hailing' which concerns the hailing of 'suspects'.[Au.]

hail was 'really' addressed to him, and that 'it was *really him* who was hailed' (and not someone else). Experience shows that the practical telecommunication of hailings is such that they hardly ever miss their man: verbal call or whistle, the one hailed always recognizes that it is really him who is being hailed. And yet it is a strange phenomenon, and one which cannot be explained solely by 'guilt feelings', despite the large numbers who 'have something on their consciences'.

Naturally for the convenience and clarity of my little theoretical theatre I have had to present things in the form of a sequence, with a before and an after, and thus in the form of a temporal succession. There are individuals walking along. Somewhere (usually behind them) the hail rings out: 'Hey, you there!' One individual (nine times out of ten it is the right one) turns round, believing/suspecting/knowing that it is for him, i.e. recognizing that 'it really is he' who is meant by the hailing. But in reality these things happen without any succession. The existence of ideology and the hailing or interpellation of individuals as subjects are one and the same thing.

I might add: what thus seems to take place outside ideology (to be precise, in the street), in reality takes place in ideology. What really takes place in ideology seems therefore to take place outside it. That is why those who are in ideology believe themselves by definition outside ideology: one of the effects of ideology is the practical *denegation* of ideological character of ideology by ideology: ideology never says, 'I am ideological'. It is necessary to be outside ideology, i.e. in scientific knowledge, to be able to say: I am in ideology (a quite exceptional case) or (the general case): I was in ideology. As is well known, the accusation of being in ideology only applies to others, never to oneself (unless one is really a Spinozist or a Marxist, which, in this matter, is to be exactly the same thing). Which amounts to saying that ideology *has no outside* (for itself), but at the same time *that it is nothing but outside* (for science and reality).

Spinoza[9] explained this completely two centuries before Marx, who practised it but without explaining it in detail. But let us leave this point, although it is heavy with consequences, consequences which are not just theoretical, but also directly political, since, for example, the whole theory of criticism and self-criticism, the golden rule of the Marxist-Leninist practice of the class struggle, depends on it.

Thus ideology hails or interpellates individuals as subjects. As ideology is eternal, I must now suppress the temporal form in which I have presented the functioning of ideology, and say: ideology has always-already interpellated individuals as subjects, which amounts to making it clear that individuals are always-already interpellated by ideology as subjects, which necessarily leads us to one last proposition: *individuals are always-already subjects*. Hence individuals are 'abstract' with respect to the subjects which they always-already are. This proposition might seem paradoxical.

That an individual is always-already a subject, even before he is born, is nevertheless the plain reality, accessible to everyone and not a paradox at all. Freud shows that individuals are always 'abstract' with respect to the subjects they always-already are, simply by noting the ideological ritual that surrounds the expectation of a 'birth', that 'happy event'. Everyone knows how much and in what way an unborn child is expected. Which amounts to saying, very prosaically, if we agree to drop the 'sentiments', i.e. the forms of family ideology (paternal/maternal/conjugal/fraternal) in which the unborn child is expected: it is certain in advance that it will bear its Father's Name, and will therefore have an identity and be irreplaceable. Before its birth, the child is therefore always-already a subject, appointed as a subject in and by the specific familial ideological configuration in which it is 'expected' once it has been conceived. I hardly need add that this familial ideological configuration is, in its uniqueness, highly structured, and that it is in this implacable and more or less 'pathological' (presupposing that any meaning can be assigned to that term) structure that the former subject-to-be will have to 'find' 'its' place, i.e. 'become' the sexual subject (boy or girl) which it already is in advance. It is clear that this ideological constraint and pre-appointment, and all the rituals of rearing and then education in the family, have some relationship with what Freud studied in the forms of the pre-genital and genital 'stages' of sexuality, i.e. in the 'grip' of what Freud registered by its effects as being the unconscious. But let us leave this point, too, on one side.

Let me go one step further. What I shall now turn

[9]Baruch Spinoza (1632–77), Jewish-Dutch philosopher, a monist and pantheist. [Eds.]

my attention to is the way the 'actors' in this *mise en scene* of interpellation, and their respective roles, are reflected in the very structure of all ideology.

An Example: The Christian Religious Ideology

As the formal structure of all ideology is always the same, I shall restrict my analysis to a single example, one accessible to everyone, that of religious ideology, with the proviso that the same demonstration can be produced for ethical, legal, political, aesthetic ideology, etc.

Let us therefore consider the Christian religious ideology. I shall use a rhetorical figure and 'make it speak', i.e. collect into a fictional discourse what it 'says' not only in its two Testaments, its Theologians, Sermons, but also in its practices, its rituals, its ceremonies and its sacraments. The Christian religious ideology says something like this:

It says: I address myself to you, a human individual called Peter (every individual is called by his name, in the passive sense, it is never he who provides his own name), in order to tell you that God exists and that you are answerable to Him. It adds: God addresses himself to you through my voice (Scripture having collected the Word of God, Tradition having transmitted it, Papal Infallibility fixing it for ever on 'nice' points). It says: this is who you are: you are Peter! This is your origin, you were created by God for all eternity, although you were born in the 1920th year of Our Lord! This is your place in the world! This is what you must do! By these means, if you observe the 'law of love' you will be saved, you, Peter, and will become part of the Glorious Body of Christ! Etc. . . .

Now this is quite a familiar and banal discourse, but at the same time quite a surprising one.

Surprising because if we consider that religious ideology is indeed addressed to individuals,[10] in order to 'transform them into subjects', by interpellating the individual, Peter, in order to make him a subject, free to obey or disobey the appeal, i.e. God's commandments; if it calls these individuals by their names, thus recognizing that they are always-already interpellated as subjects with a personal identity (to the extent that Pascal's Christ says: 'It is for you that I have shed this drop of my blood!'); if it interpellates them in such a way that the subject responds: *'Yes, it really is me!'* if it obtains from them the *recognition* that they really do occupy the place it designates for them as theirs in the world, a fixed residence: 'It really is me, I am here, a worker, a boss or a soldier!' in this vale of tears; if it obtains from them the recognition of a destination (eternal life or damnation) according to the respect or contempt they show to 'God's Commandments', Law become Love;—if everything does happen in this way (in the practices of the well-known rituals of baptism, confirmation, communion, confession and extreme unction, etc. . . .), we should note that all this 'procedure' to set up Christian religious subjects is dominated by a strange phenomenon: the fact that there can only be such a multitude of possible religious subjects on the absolute condition that there is a Unique, Absolute, *Other Subject,* i.e. God.

It is convenient to designate this new and remarkable Subject by writing Subject with a capital S to distinguish it from ordinary subjects, with a small s.

It then emerges that the interpellation of individuals as subjects presupposes the 'existence' of a Unique and central Other Subject, in whose Name the religious ideology interpellates all individuals as subjects. All this is clearly[11] written in what is rightly called the Scriptures. 'And it came to pass at that time that God the Lord (Yahweh) spoke to Moses in the cloud. And the Lord cried to Moses, "Moses!" And Moses replied "It is (really) I! I am Moses thy servant, speak and I shall listen!" And the Lord spoke to Moses and said to him, *"I am that I am"*'.

God thus defines himself as the Subject *par excellence,* he who is through himself and for himself ('I am that I am'), and he who interpellates his subject, the individual subjected to him by his very interpellation, i.e. the individual named Moses. And Moses, interpellated-called by his Name, having recognized that it 'really' was he who was called by God, recognizes that he is a subject, a subject *of* God, a subject subjected to God, *a subject through the Subject and subjected to the Subject.* The proof: he obeys him, and makes his people obey God's Commandments.

God is the Subject, and Moses and the innu-

[10] Although we know that the individual is always already a subject, we go on using this term, convenient because of the contrasting effect it produces. [Au.]

[11] I am quoting in a combined way, not to the letter but 'in spirit and truth'. [Au.]

merable subjects of God's people, the Subject's interlocutors-interpellates: his *mirrors,* his *reflections.* Were not men made *in the image* of God? As all theological reflection proves, whereas He 'could' perfectly well have done without men, God needs them, the Subject needs the subjects, just as men need God, the subjects need the Subject. Better: God needs men, the great Subject needs subjects, even in the terrible inversion of his image in them (when the subjects wallow in debauchery, i.e. sin).

Better: God duplicates himself and sends his Son to the Earth, as a mere subject 'forsaken' by him (the long complaint of the Garden of Olives which ends in the Crucifixion), subject but Subject, man but God, to do what prepares the way for the final Redemption, the Resurrection of Christ. God thus needs to 'make himself' a man, the Subject needs to become a subject, as if to show empirically, visibly to the eye, tangibly to the hands (see St Thomas)[12] of the subjects, that, if they are subjects, subjected to the Subject, that is solely in order that finally, on Judgement Day, they will re-enter the Lord's Bosom, like Christ, i.e. re-enter the Subject.[13]

Let us decipher into theoretical language this wonderful necessity for the duplication of *the Subject into subjects* and of *the Subject itself into a subject-Subject.*

We observe that the structure of all ideology, interpellating individuals as subjects in the name of a Unique and Absolute Subject is *speculary,* i.e. a mirror-structure, and *doubly* speculary: this mirror duplication is constitutive of ideology and ensures its functioning. Which means that all ideology is *centred,* that the Absolute Subject occupies the unique place of the Centre, and interpellates around it the infinity of individuals into subjects in a double mirror-connexion such that it *subjects* the subjects to the Subject, while giving them in the Subject in which each subject can contemplate its own image (present and future) the *guarantee* that this really concerns them and Him, and that since everything takes place in the Family (the Holy Family: the Family is in essence Holy), 'God will *recognize* his own in it', i.e. those who have recognized God, and have recognized themselves in Him, will be saved.

[12] St. Thomas Aquinas (1225–74), Italian philosopher and churchman. [Eds.]

[13] The dogma of the Trinity is precisely the theory of the duplication of the Subject (the Father) into a subject (the Son) and of their mirror connexion (the Holy Spirit). [Au.]

Let me summarize what we have discovered about ideology in general.

The duplicate mirror-structure of ideology ensures simultaneously:

1. the interpellation of 'individuals' as subjects;
2. their subjection to the Subject;
3. the mutual recognition of subjects and Subject, the subjects' recognition of each other, and finally the subject's recognition of himself;[14]
4. the absolute guarantee that everything really is so, and that on condition that the subjects recognize what they are and behave accordingly, everything will be all right; Amen—'*So be it*'.

Result: caught in this quadruple system of interpellation as subjects, of subjection to the Subject, of universal recognition and of absolute guarantee, the subjects 'work', they 'work by themselves' in the vast majority of cases, with the exception of the 'bad subjects' who on occasion provoke the intervention of one of the detachments of the (repressive) State apparatus. But the vast majority of (good) subjects work all right 'all by themselves', i.e. by ideology (whose concrete forms are realized in the Ideological State Apparatuses). They are inserted into practices governed by the rituals of the ISAs. They 'recognize' the existing state of affairs *(das Bestehende),* that 'it really is true that it is so and not otherwise', and that they must be obedient to God, to their conscience, to the priest, to de Gaulle, to the boss, to the engineer, that thou shalt 'love thy neighbour as thyself', etc. Their concrete, material behaviour is simply the inscription in life of the admirable words of the prayer: '*Amen—So be it*'.

Yes, the subjects 'work by themselves'. The whole mystery of this effect lies in the first two moments of the quadruple system I have just discussed, or, if you prefer, in the ambiguity of the term *subject.* In the ordinary use of the term, subject in fact means: (1) a free subjectivity, a centre of initiatives, author of and responsible for its actions; (2) a subjected being, who submits to a higher authority, and is therefore stripped of all freedom except that of freely accepting his submission. This last note gives

[14] Hegel is (unknowingly) an admirable 'theoretician' of ideology insofar as he is a 'theoretician' of Universal Recognition who unfortunately ends up in the ideology of Absolute Knowledge. Feuerbach is an astonishing 'theoretician' of the mirror connexion, who unfortunately ends up in the ideology of the Human Essence. To find the material with which to construct a theory of the guarantee, we must turn to Spinoza. [Au.]

us the meaning of this ambiguity, which is merely a reflection of the effect which produces it: the individual *is interpellated as a (free) subject in order that he shall submit freely to the commandments of the Subject, i.e. in order that he shall (freely) accept his subjection,* i.e. in order that he shall make the gestures and actions of his subjection 'all by himself'. *There are no subjects except by and for their subjection.* That is why they 'work all by themselves'.

'So be it! . . .' This phrase which registers the effect to be obtained proves that it is not 'naturally' so ('naturally': outside the prayer, i.e. outside the ideological intervention). This phrase proves that it *has* to be so if things are to be what they must be, and let us let the words slip: if the reproduction of the relations of production is to be assured, even in the processes of production and circulation, every day, in the 'consciousness', i.e. in the attitudes of the individual-subjects occupying the posts which the socio-technical division of labour assigns to them in production, exploitation, repression, ideologization, scientific practice, etc. Indeed, what is really in question in this mechanism of the mirror recognition of the Subject and of the individuals interpellated as subjects, and of the guarantee given by the Subject to the subjects if they freely accept their subjection to the Subject's 'commandments'? The reality in question in this mechanism, the reality which is necessarily *ignored* (*méconnue*) in the very forms of recognition (ideology = misrecognition/ignorance) is indeed, in the last resort, the reproduction of the relations of production and of the relations deriving from them.

January-April 1969

P.S. If these few schematic theses allow me to illuminate certain aspects of the functioning of the Superstructure and its mode of intervention in the Infrastructure, they are obviously *abstract* and necessarily leave several important problems unanswered, which should be mentioned:

1. The problem of the *total process* of the realization of the reproduction of the relations of production.

As an element of this process, the ISAs *contribute* to this reproduction. But the point of view of their contribution alone is still an abstract one.

It is only within the processes of production and circulation that this reproduction is *realized.* It is realized by the mechanisms of those processes, in which the training of the workers is 'completed', their posts assigned them, etc. It is in the internal mechanisms of these processes that the effect of the different ideologies is felt (above all the effect of legal-ethical ideology).

But this point of view is still an abstract one. For in a class society the relations of production are relations of exploitation, and therefore relations between antagonistic classes. The reproduction of the relations of production, the ultimate aim of the ruling class, cannot therefore be a merely technical operation training and distributing individuals for the different posts in the 'technical division' of labour except in the ideology of the ruling class: every 'technical' division, every 'technical' organization of labour is the form and mask of a *social* (= class) division and organization of labour. The reproduction of the relations of production can therefore only be a class undertaking. It is realized through a class struggle which counterposes the ruling class and the exploited class.

The *total process* of the realization of the reproduction of the relations of production is therefore still abstract, insofar as it has not adopted the point of view of this class struggle. To adopt the point of view of reproduction is therefore, in the last instance, to adopt the point of view of the class struggle.

2. The problem of the class nature of the ideologies existing in a social formation.

The 'mechanism' of ideology *in general* is one thing. We have seen that it can be reduced to a few principles expressed in a few words (as 'poor' as those which, according to Marx, define production *in general,* or in Freud, define *the* unconscious *in general*). If there is any truth in it, this mechanism must be *abstract* with respect to every real ideological formation.

I have suggested that the ideologies were *realized* in institutions, in their rituals and their practices, in the ISAs. We have seen that on this basis they contribute to that form of class struggle, vital for the ruling class, the reproduction of the relations of production. But the point of view itself, however real, is still an abstract one.

In fact, the State and its Apparatuses only have meaning from the point of view of the class struggle, as an apparatus of class struggle ensuring class oppression and guaranteeing the conditions of exploitation and its reproduction. But there is no class struggle without antagonistic classes. Whoever says class struggle of the ruling class says resistance, revolt and class struggle of the ruled class.

That is why the ISAs are not the realization of ideology *in general,* nor even of the conflict-free realization of the ideology of the ruling class. The ideology of the ruling class does not become the ruling ideology by the grace of God, nor even by virtue of the seizure of State power alone. It is by the installation of the ISAs in which this ideology is realized and realizes itself that it becomes the ruling ideology. But this installation is not achieved all by itself; on the contrary, it is the stake in a very bitter and continuous class struggle: first against the former ruling classes and their positions in the old and new ISAs, then against the exploited class.

But this point of view of the class struggle in the ISAs is still an abstract one. In fact, the class struggle in the ISAs is indeed an aspect of the class struggle, sometimes an important and symptomatic one: e.g. the anti-religious struggle in the eighteenth century, or the 'crisis' of the educational ISA in every capitalist country today. But the class struggles in the ISAs is only one aspect of a class struggle which goes beyond the ISAs. The ideology that a class in power makes the ruling ideology in its ISAs is indeed 'realized' in those ISAs, but it goes beyond them, for it comes from elsewhere. Similarly, the ideology that a ruled class manages to defend in and against such ISAs goes beyond them, for it comes from elsewhere.

It is only from the point of view of the classes, i.e. of the class struggle, that it is possible to explain the ideolog*ies* existing in a social formation. Not only is it from this starting-point that it is possible to explain the realization of the ruling ideology in the ISAs and of the forms of class struggle for which the ISAs are the seat and the stake. But it is also and above all from this starting-point that it is possible to understand the provenance of the ideologies which are realized in the ISAs and confront one another there. For if it is true that the ISAs represent the *form* in which the ideology of the ruling class must *necessarily* be realized, and the form in which the ideology of the ruled class must *necessarily* be measured and confronted, ideologies are not 'born' in the ISAs but from the social classes at grips in the class struggle: from their conditions of existence, their practices, their experience of the struggle, etc.

April 1970

Northrop Frye

b. 1912

NORTHROP FRYE'S earliest work, *Fearful Symmetry: A Study of William Blake* (1947), exerted a strong influence not only on Blake study but also on the criticism of the romantic period. His subsequent *Anatomy of Criticism* (1957), strongly Blakean in inspiration, had a like influence on the direction of critical theory (it is excerpted in *CTSP,* pp. 1117–47), providing both an alternative to and, in certain respects, an encompassment of New Critical principles. It was perhaps the appropriation of certain remarks of T. S. Eliot in Frye's theory that led in some quarters to criticism of his work for lack of social concern. To some, if the New Criticism had isolated the individual literary work in its own structure of irony, Frye had simply expanded the solipsism to that of the structure of literature itself. Frye's work after the *Anatomy* was designed in part to answer such critics as well as to proceed with the unfolding of a theory of the relation of literature to society and culture that, in his view, had always been his direction. *The Critical Path* is not the only document in this unfolding, though in some ways it may be the most important and the most revealing. A book known mainly in Canada, *The Modern Century* (1967), proposes the dialectic of open and closed mythologies, which in *The Critical Path* is given more complexity by showing such so-called myths to belong to the larger idea of the myth of concern, which is in turn opposed by the myth of freedom. These two Frye sees as necessarily opposed, the myth of freedom, with its recourse to the authority of reason and evidence, acting as a check and balance against myths of concern taken as authority in the sense of rigid literal belief (though Frye does not use "literal" in this sense) and fixed and final interpretation. The main and often terrifying problem of a myth of concern, which Frye identifies with religious stories and literature in general, is that it can become an article of absolutely closed belief, whereas the appropriate movement ought to be toward openness and toleration. Myths of concern must be kept open to interpretation rather than closed into fixed doctrine, and this means in all cases the renunciation of the "finality of one's understanding of the truth."

Frye's book on Blake was in large measure the result of his knowledge of the Bible, gained in theological training that eventuated in his ordination as a young man in the United Church of Canada. Though he became a professor of literature at the University of Toronto, his interest in the Bible continued to help form his theory of interpretation, and in recent years he has turned to treating it directly as a literary text in *The Great Code* and works still promised. It is no surprise that the title of his book on the Bible is taken from Blake, whose remark is quoted in the selection below in support of Frye's view of the Bible as a text that in the end calls us to proceed beyond belief to what can be imagined.

Frye's work since *The Critical Path* includes a collection of essays, *Spiritus Mundi* (1976); *The Secular Scripture* (1976); *Northrop Frye on Culture and Literature* (1978); and *The Great Code* (1981). On Frye's work, see Hazard Adams, *Philosophy of the Literary Symbolic* (1983), chapter 10.

FROM

THE CRITICAL PATH

We may perhaps arrive at some tentative conclusions from our quasi-historical survey before we turn to the contemporary scene. In the first place, the great dream of the deductive synthesis, in which faith and knowledge are indissolubly linked, seems to be fading. The confidence in the completeness and adequacy of the Thomist synthesis, expressed so eloquently by Maritain[1] in the last generation, is clearly not what it was in this more fragmented age. In Marxism it is obvious that the deductive synthesis, whenever it has become socially established, comes to depend more and more for its support on third-rate bureaucrats rather than on first-rate writers or thinkers. Evidently we must come to terms with the fact that mythical and logical languages are distinct. The vision of things as they could or should be certainly has to depend on the vision of things as they are. But what is between them is not so much a point of contact as an existential gap, a revolutionary and transforming act of choice. The beliefs we hold and the kind of society we try to construct are chosen from infinite possibilities, and the notion that our choices are inevitably connected with things as they are, whether through the mind of God or the constitution of nature, always turns out to be an illusion of habit. The mythical and the factual or logical attitudes are really connected by analogy. If, for example, such a philosopher as Bergson or Lloyd Morgan bases a metaphysical or religious structure on the conception of evolution, what he is working with is not really the same principle as the biological hypothesis of evolution, but is rather a mythical analogy of that hypothesis.[2]

It seems equally futile to expect any one myth of concern to establish itself all over the world. The more widely any such myth spreads, the deeper the rifts that develop within it. One reason for this is that concern, if unchecked by any internal or intellectual opposition, must have an enemy.[3] Marxist countries must have imperialistic aggressors; bourgeois societies must have Communist subversives, just as medieval Christendom had to have a pretext for starting the Crusades. We said earlier that a myth of concern draws a *temenos* or spellbinding line around a society. This bounding line has two aspects. A society enriches itself by what it includes; it defines itself by what it excludes. Whether or not good fences make good neighbours, the fence creates the neighbour. In *A Passage to India* E. M. Forster shows us how three great cultural complexes, Hinduism, Islam and Christianity, each accept ideals of universal brotherhood; their better and more sensitive members believe in these ideals and struggle to achieve them. And yet in the long run they all define themselves by exclusion, and those who do not wish to exclude anything run the risk of losing their identity and having their total inclusiveness turn into its terrible opposite, the sense of a totally meaningless universe, the ironic vision of the absurd, which comes to Mrs. Moore in the cave.

The only practicable solution seems to be the one hit on by democracy when it was trying to pare the

THE CRITICAL PATH, chapter 5, was published in 1971 and is reprinted here by permission of the Indiana University Press, copyright 1971.

[1]Jacques Maritain (1882–1973), Thomist philosopher. [Eds.]

[2]Henri Bergson (1859–1941), French philosopher; Conwy Lloyd Morgan (1852–1936), English psychologist and zoologist. [Eds.]

[3]Here Frye invokes the Blakean notion of contraries as opposed to negations. [Eds.]

claws of Christian temporal power. This is to accept, as part of a permanent tension between concern and freedom, a plurality of myths of concern, in which the state assumes the responsibility for keeping the peace among them. I return here to a distinction I have made elsewhere between closed and open mythologies.[4] A society with a closed myth of concern makes it compulsory for all its citizens to say that they support it, or at least will not overtly oppose it. Only a society with an open mythology is capable of a genuine and functional toleration. There are limits to toleration, of course, but the distinction between a society that imposes a belief and a society that imposes a kind of rules-of-the-game order within which dissent and opposition can operate is a practical distinction, however difficult to formulate in theory.

We saw earlier that every myth of concern is religious, in the sense of establishing a *religio* or common body of acts and beliefs for the community. Such a religion may be theistic and deny the finality of death, like Christianity, or atheistic and assert it, like Marxism. Marxism, and Christianity as long as it had temporal power, have tended to assume that a definite position on such points was obligatory on society as a whole, and hence, even if they could tolerate a group with a different position, they could not recognize such a difference as inevitable, certainly not as desirable. The tendency of a closed myth is to move from such broad general principles to more specific ones, prescribing more and more of a citizen's beliefs, and obliterating the varieties of social attitude. Jews, for instance, are a minority group with a myth of concern peculiar to themselves: consequently any society with a closed myth which contains Jews is bound sooner or later to turn anti-Semitic. Occasionally we find it suggested that breaking up closed myths of concern may be part of the historical function of Judaism. The King of Persia complains, in (the Greek additions to) The Book of Esther: "in all nations throughout the world there is scattered a certain malicious people, that have laws contrary to all nations . . . so as the uniting of our kingdoms, honorably intended by us, cannot go forward."

A society with an open mythology may still have its own predominant myth of concern. Nobody would say that "the American way of life" was less concerned than any other community's way of life. The principle of openness, however, is, so far as I can see, the only possible basis for a world community, assuming that no myth of concern can ever become world-wide. What is potentially world-wide is an assumption, too broad in itself to constitute a myth of concern, that life is better than death, freedom better than slavery, happiness better than misery, health better than sickness, for all men everywhere without exception. A society with an open myth can accommodate itself to such an assumption; a society with a closed one cannot. The latter can only pursue its own ends, deciding at each step how much misery and slavery may be necessary (of course only temporarily, it is always added) to advance those ends.

An open mythology establishes the relativity of each myth of concern within it, and so emphasizes the element of construct or imaginative vision in the myth. This would not affect the reality of, say, the Christian myth for anyone who holds it, but it puts it on the kind of basis on which communication, or what is now often called "dialogue," becomes possible with Jews or Moslems or Marxists, or even other Christians. When a myth of concern claims truth of correspondence as well as truth of vision, and assumes that its postulates are or can be established as facts, it can hardly produce any "dialogue" except the single exasperated formula: "But can't you *see* how wrong you are?" When it renounces this claim, it acquires the kind of humility which makes it possible to see intellectual honesty on the other side too. As for one's own side, one is not renouncing its truth: what one renounces is the finality of one's own understanding of that truth.

In all societies the pressure in the direction of a closed myth is also the tendency within society to become a mob, that is, a social body without individuals or critical attitudes, united by slogans or clichés against some focus of hatred. A myth of concern, by itself, cannot prevent this kind of social degeneration. Faith, or participation in a myth of concern, is not in itself verifiable, but to some extent it can be verified in experience. Some myths of concern obviously make a fuller life possible than others do. Charity, in the sense of respect for human life, is doubtless the primary criterion, but there is an important secondary one: the ability of a

[4] In *The Modern Century* (1967). [Eds.]

myth of concern to come to terms with the myth of freedom. A faith which permits intellectual honesty is clearly better in practice than one which tries to deny elementary facts of history or science. And perhaps the two standards, of charity and of intellectual honesty, are ultimately the same standard. Certainly such a myth of concern as Nazism, which ranks so low on the scale of charity, could not avoid the falsifying of history and science, and I suspect that the two vices always go together.

The basis of all tolerance in society, the condition in which a plurality of concerns can co-exist, is the recognition of the tension between concern and freedom. This issue becomes crucial as soon as it is obvious that the study of man's environment cannot be confined to the non-human environment. Human society, in the present as in the past, is an objective fact too. Sooner or later, therefore, the scientific spirit and the search for truth of correspondence will invade the structures of concern themselves, studying human mythology in the same spirit that they study nature. This collision between concern and freedom may well be the most important kind of what is now called "culture shock" that we have. In weak or insecure minds such a collision produces immediate panic, followed by elaborate defensive reactions. Efforts to bring the spirit of inquiry into the Christian religion met with such responses as (to give a relatively mild example): "If you destroy our faith with your rational and analytical questions, what will you put in its place?" Many Marxist theologians similarly must insist that, as everybody exists in a specific social context, there is no such thing as complete detachment from a social attitude, and consequently all inquiry is rooted in a social attitude which must be either revolutionary, and so in agreement with them, or counter-revolutionary. One still often hears the argument among student militants and others that because complete objectivity is impossible, differences in degree of objectivity are not significant.

It would be a grave error to associate this kind of resistance only with the immature or the easily frightened. We all have such fears, and can look at them in perspective only from a later historical age, when battles previously fought have since been won, or at least stopped. Meanwhile, it is clearly one of the unavoidable responsibilities of educated people to show by example that beliefs may be held and examined at the same time. We noted the encyclopaedic drive of concern: there is nothing that is not the concern of concern, and similarly there is nothing that can be excluded from free inquiry and the truth of correspondence. Concern and freedom both occupy the whole of the same universe: they interpenetrate, and it is no good trying to set up boundary stones. Some, of course, meet the collision of concern and freedom from the opposite side, with a naive rationalism which expects that before long all myths of concern will be outgrown and only the appeal to reason and evidence and experiment will be taken seriously. I hope it is clear from the general argument of this essay why I consider such a view entirely impossible. The growth of nonmythical knowledge tends to eliminate the incredible from belief, and helps to shape the myth of concern according to the outlines of what experience finds possible and vision desirable. But the growth of knowledge cannot in itself provide us with the social vision which will suggest what we should do with our knowledge.

This is where the central question of the present essay, the social function of criticism, comes in. Let us follow up this problem of the examining of a myth of concern by the standards of a myth of freedom, and see what happens as a result. The obvious example to choose is Christianity and the myth centered in the Bible. Within the last century there has been a crisis in the response to the Biblical Christian myth which is often called a crisis of belief, but is really a crisis in understanding the language of belief. The crisis begins in Victorian times, and immediately provokes the kind of resistance that one expects at the beginning of such a movement. In Newman's lectures on education, particularly in connection with science, we see how calmly reasonable the tone is as long as mathematics and the physical sciences are being discussed, and how edgy and nervous it becomes as soon liberal theology begins to appear, however distantly, on the horizon.[5] Then we are sharply warned that science ought not to go beyond its province and invade the field of religion. Matthew Arnold, though holding an entirely different view of religion, reacted quite as strongly to the iconoclastic attacks of Bishop

[5] John Henry Newman (1801–90), English theologian. See Frye's essay "The Problem of Spiritual Authority in the Nineteenth Century," in *The Stubborn Structure* (1970). [Eds.]

Colenso on the historicity of the Pentateuch.[6] It was wrong to confuse science and religion; it was wrong to take such matters to the general public, because only a few are capable, etc.; above all it was wrong to write crudely and bluntly about these subjects, as Colenso did. However, of course, the movement proceeded in spite of such resistance.

When I am asked if I "believe in" ghosts, I usually reply that ghosts, from all accounts, appear to be matters of experience rather than of belief, and that so far I have had no experience of them. But the fact that the question takes such a form indicates that belief is usually connected in the mind with a vision of possibilities, of what might or could be true. On the other hand, we often use the term "believe" to mean a suspended sense experience. "I believe you will find a telephone on the next floor" means that if I were on the next floor I should see a telephone. In reference to past time this suspended sense experience becomes the acceptance of a historical fact. "I believe Julius Caesar existed" implies that I think that if I had lived when and where he is said to have lived I should have seen him. "I believe in God" can hardly refer to a belief of this kind, but under the influence of the mental habits of a writing culture, concerned belief also has come to be associated with historical fact.

This leads to such curious aberrations as "believing the Bible," i.e., of ascribing special virtue to asserting that in another culture, a few years ago and a few miles away, Jonah was swallowed by a great fish and Elijah carried up to heaven in a fiery chariot, and that if we had been present at those events we should have seen precisely what is described in the sacred text. Such belief is really a voluntarily induced schizophrenia, and is probably a fruitful source of the infantilism and the hysterical anxieties about belief which are so frequently found in the neighborhood of religion, at least in its more uncritical areas. One thinks of Don Quixote's remark to Sancho Panza, that the Golden Age would soon return if people would only see things as they are, and not allow themselves to be deluded by enchanters who make hundred-armed giants look like windmills.

In the seventeenth century Sir Thomas Browne, reflecting on such matters as the fact that conditions in Noah's ark, after thirty-eight days or so, might become a trifle slummy, remarked "methinks there be not enough impossibilities in religion for an active faith."[7] But of course when a faith beyond reason is looked at in this sort of playful or ironic light, it tends to become unconcerned. The more genuinely concerned faith is, the more quickly a hierarchy is established in it, in which "essential" beliefs are retained and less essential ones regarded as expendable. But this conception of "essential" belief is, in spite of the word, introducing an existential element into belief. What we really believe is not what we say or think we believe but what our actions show that we believe, and no belief which is not an axiom of behavior is a genuinely concerned belief. Marxism has a similar conception of unessential belief, the "ideology" which is to be talked about but not acted upon, and which has the function of decorating the facade of a conservative attitude. Many of my readers would call what I am calling a myth of concern an ideology, and though, as I have indicated, I have specific reasons for using the term myth, those who prefer ideology may substitute it in most contexts.

For Milton writing *Paradise Lost* Adam and Eve were historical characters, his own literal ancestors, and Milton is fond of contrasting the plain and sober Scriptural accounts with the extravagances of the heathen. Simplicity however is not an infallible sign of historical credibility, and we today are struck rather by the similarity of the Biblical stories of the fall and the flood to other myths in other cultures. As the Old Testament narrative proceeds, myth gives place to legend and what German critics call *Sage,* legend to historical reminiscence, historical reminiscence to didactic and manipulated history, and so on. But there are no clear boundary lines: all that seems clear is that whatever in the Old Testament may be historically accurate is not there because it is historically accurate, but for quite different reasons. Further, historical accuracy has no relation to spiritual significance. The Book of Job, which is avowedly an imaginative drama, is clearly more significant in the development of religion than the begats in Chronicles, which may well contain authentic records.

With the Gospels, however, surely things must be

[6]See *CTSP,* p. 591. [Eds.]

[7]Sir Thomas Browne (1605–82), English physician and author. Frye refers to remarks in Browne's *Religio Medici.* [Eds.]

different, for Christianity has always insisted on the historical nature of its central event. We soon begin to wonder, however, whether the verbal presentation of that event is as historical as the event itself. We notice that the life of Christ in the Gospels is not presented biographically, as a piece of continuous prose writing founded on historical evidence, but as a discontinuous sequence of appearances (pericopes), which have a strongly mythical quality about them. If the approach were biographical we should want only one definitive Gospel, and of course the historical belief in them has always rested on some "harmony" of their narratives rather than on the four as they stand.

Naturally many efforts have been made to extract a credible continuous narrative from what seems a mass of mythical accretions. Thus a century ago Ernest Renan, in his *Vie de Jésus,* began confidently with the statement that Jesus was born in Nazareth, the story that he was born in Bethlehem having been inserted later to harmonize with Micah's prophecy that the Messiah was to be born in Bethlehem.[8] But, arguing on those terms, if the only reason for associating Jesus with Bethlehem is the passage in Micah, the only reason for associating him with Galilee is a similar passage in Isaiah (ix), and the only reason for associating him with Nazareth is to enable Matthew to make a dubious pun on "Nazirite." Renan's historical and credible statement, on his own basis of argument, dissolves into two more myths.

As we go through the Gospels, with their miracles of healing and miraculous feeding and raising the dead and the like, we begin to wonder how much there is that must be historical, that is unambiguous evidence for a historical Jesus. The authors of the Gospels seem to care nothing for the kind of evidence that would interest a biographer; the only evidence they concern themselves with is coincidence with Old Testament prophecies of the Messiah. The result is that our historical evidence for the life of Jesus, besides being hermetically sealed within the New Testament, seems to melt away, as we try to grasp it, into echoes from the Old Testament or from contemporary Jewish ritual. As some factual basis for Jesus's life was obviously available to the authors, why did they make so oblique and limited a use of it?

For any uncommitted reader of the Gospels, the question "could it really have happened just like that?" is bound to occur with great frequency. But at a certain point the question begins to turn into the form: "if I had been there, is that what I should have seen and experienced?" At this point the doubts become overwhelming, because most of these doubts are of one's own capacity for spiritual experience. Sir Thomas Browne's "I thank God that I never saw Christ or his disciples" begins to sound like a very shrewd remark. If I had been out on the hills of Bethlehem on the night of the birth of Christ, with the angels singing to the shepherds, I think that I should not have heard any angels singing. The reason why I think so is that I do not hear them now, and there is no reason to suppose that they have stopped.

If, under the influence of the mental habits of a writing culture, we insist on regarding a myth as a disguised way of presenting a real situation, we should have to regard the accounts of Jesus in the Gospels as highly suspect, if not actually fraudulent. But the impression of authority they convey is too strong to take the possibility of fraud seriously. It is much more probable that it is our conception of myth that is wrong, and it seems better to think of the authors as too concerned about the importance of their message to entrust what they had to say to merely historical or biographical idioms of language. The historian tries to put his reader where the event is, in the past. If he is writing about the assassination of Julius Caesar, he tries to make us see what we should have seen if we had been there, while keeping the additional understanding afforded by the distance in time. The apostle feels that if we had been "there," we should have seen nothing, or seen something utterly commonplace, or missed the whole significance of what we did see. So he comes to us, with his ritual drama of a Messiah, presenting a speaking picture which has to be, as Paul says, spiritually discerned.

Myth is the language of the present tense, even of what is expressed by the vogue-word "confrontation." There is a moral aspect of literature, stressed by Sidney among others, which literature possesses through its power of idealized example.[9] When poetry is the "companion of camps," a heroic achievement in the past is linked to another in the future of

[8] Ernest Renan (1823–92), French historian. [Eds.]

[9] See Sidney, *CTSP,* pp. 154–77. [Eds.]

which the reader is the potential hero. The best way to connect the two, for Sidney, is to present the former in its universal shape, combining the historical example with the abstract precept or model. If we wish to be inspired by Achilles we must read Homer, and may well thank God that we never saw Achilles or his myrmidons. Of course the historical criticism of the Bible plays the same liberalizing role here that it does elsewhere: it helps to ensure that a book set in an ancient Near Eastern culture, remote from ours in language and social assumptions, can never be completely kidnapped by provincial bigotry in our day. But the direct connection of religion with concern, where "go thou and do likewise" is always a part of the presentation, decreases the importance of this.

The Bible, it may be said, is not a story-book or an epic poem; but it is much closer to being a work of literature than it is to being a work of history or doctrine, and the kind of mental response that we bring to poetry has to be in the forefront of our understanding of it. This is, I think, what Matthew Arnold meant when he suggested that poetry would increasingly take on a religious importance in modern culture.[10] It is not that poetry will become a substitute or replacement for religion, a situation that could only produce phony literature as well as a phony religion. It is rather that religion will come to be understood increasingly as having a poetic rather than a rational language, and that it can be more effectively taught and learned through the imagination than through doctrine or history. Imagination is not in itself concern, but for a culture with a highly developed sense of fact and of the limits of experience, the road to concern runs through the language of imagination.

What applies to the Bible applies also, in some degree, to every scripture of concern, from the Vedic hymns to the Communist Manifesto. One question that arises is evidently the relation of myth to the ordinary standards of truth of correspondence. The connection between the growth of a myth of concern and the falsifying of history is so frequent as to be the rule, and it is not merely a vulgarizing of language that has given the word "mythical" the overtones of "false." When we see a myth of concern in process of formation, as with the contemporary black myth, we can see that rigid adherence to historical or sociological fact may not be the only moral principle involved.

There is also the conflict of loyalties between the demands of objective truth and the demands of concerned tactics, especially, in our day, the tactics of publicity. I remember a friend who was deeply committed to what he felt was a genuine social issue, and found himself watching a carefully rigged scene in which a member of his side produced an impression, for the benefit of the television cameras, of being brutally beaten by members of the other side. He was told that this kind of thing was tactically necessary, with the implication that if he so much as remembered that he saw what he did see he was working for the other side. A properly disciplined faith, perhaps, would forget, rationalize, or make no account of the total unreality of the incident. One would surely have a much higher opinion, however, of a person who felt, as my friend felt, some sense of violated integrity. It seems curious that hardly anybody rejects the values of contemporary civilization to the point of disbelieving in the necessity or effectiveness of public relations. Yet the invariable tendency of public relations, whatever they are working for, is to destroy the critical intelligence and its sense of the gap between appearance and reality. Bertrand Russell remarked in an interview just before his death that the skeptical element in him was stronger than the positive one, but "when you're in propaganda you have to make positive statements." He was clearly implying that the skeptical side of him would have considered many of his positive statements false if he had allowed it to do so. A more disturbing question is whether there can ever be truth of concern that is not in some degree falsehood of correspondence; whether myth must lie, and whether there can be any piety, to whatever church or state, without some kind of pious fraud.

Certainly in a world as complicated as ours there is bound to be the kind of oversimplifying tactic that may be called concerned tokenism. One of the commonest features of concern is the anxiety, usually conservative, that finds a symbolic focus in some change of fashion or custom. A history of preaching would include a long record of thunderous denunciations of new fashions in clothes or entertainment, where there has clearly been an unconscious choice of something relatively trivial to represent the devil's master plan to destroy man-

[10] See Arnold, *CTSP*, esp. p. 596. [Eds.]

kind. Even yet, the few square inches of the body still covered on bathing beaches can serve as an intense focus of anxiety for the anxious. But even serious concern has to pick one issue out of many, and sometimes the disproportion between the concern and the chosen issue indicates the ascendancy of rhetoric over reality that is an element in all lying. Thus Bryan's "you shall not crucify mankind upon a cross of gold" sounds a trifle over-apocalyptic for the fact that his party had decided to fight an election on the issue of bimetallism.[11] And while one may not warmly sympathize with Arnold's attitude to the deceased wife's sister bill in *Culture and Anarchy,* one does have to recognize the existence of deceased-wife's-sister liberalism (or radicalism or conservatism): the choosing of an issue more or less at random, not only to satisfy the need for action but to serve as a symbolic anxiety-substitute for a more demanding concern. All scapegoat figures, from Shelley's king and priest to Ezra Pound's usurers, are symbolic substitutes of this kind.

We have recurrently found throughout this discussion that there is an element in concern that resists final or ultimate formulation. Every myth of concern, as we pursue it, eventually retreats from what can be believed to what can be imagined. It seems clear that the standards of a myth of freedom, the standards of logic and evidence and a sense of objective reality, are also approximations. They too are analogies of a model world that may not exist, yet they must be there as ideals of procedure, however impossible it may be to realize them completely. In times of stress the inadequacy or impossibility of objective truth, and the consequent necessity of noble lies, is much insisted on, though as a rule with a kind of bravado that indicates some self-hypnotism. The original noble lie, in Plato's *Republic,* was to the effect that some men are golden, others silver, others of base metal. I suspect that every tactically necessary lie is a variant of the Platonic one, and has for its ultimate end the setting up of a hierarchy in which some people are assumed to be of more human worth than others. As Orwell's *1984* in particular has so trenchantly shown, lying weakens the will power, and therefore the will to resist being taken over by a police state.

There is also a philosophical issue involved which concerns the degree to which anything in words can tell the truth at all, in terms of the truth as correspondence. In truth of correspondence a verbal structure is aligned with the phenomena it describes, but every verbal structure contains mythical and fictional features simply because it is a verbal structure. Even the subject-predicate-object relationship is a verbal fiction, and arises from the conditions of grammar, not from those of the subject being studied. Then again, anything presented in words has a narrative shape (*mythos*) and is partly conditioned by the demands of narrative. These demands are those of a verbal causality which is *sui generis,* and has no direct connexion with any other kind of causality or sequence of events. To go further with this subject would take another book, and one that I am not in the least competent to write, although it would deal with a central issue of literary criticism. Some less ambitious considerations may be dealt with here.

We have seen that the integrity of the Bible as a myth has a good deal to do with its unreliability as history. Its relation to doctrine and concept is very similar. The conceptual aspect of the Bible is presented mainly in the discontinuous or concerned prose that we have already discussed, in such forms as commandment, oracle, proverb, parable, pericope, dialogue, and fable. Once again we see that the Biblical tradition adheres closely to its oral origin. A body of teachings presented in this way, assuming an overall coherence, can readily be systematized, that is, translated into the sequential and continuous prose of doctrine. But, like the "underthought" of poetry, it resists the *definitive* synthesis, because the discontinuity indicates other contexts than that of logical or sequential connexion. So the question arises, to what other contexts do such statements of concern belong?

In theistic religions, God speaks and man listens. Neither conception is simple, for all the efforts to make them so. God speaks, by hypothesis, in *accommodated* language, putting his thoughts and commandments into a humanly comprehensible form. Once the primary revelation is received, in prophecy or gospel or sura or oracle, man's listening takes the form of interpretation, which means critical reconstruction. There is no "literal" way of receiving a message from an infinite mind in finite language. So every myth of concern, even if it is assumed to start with the voice of God himself, is in-

[11] William Jennings Bryan (1860–1925), thrice Democratic presidential nominee. [Eds.]

volved by its own nature in a complex operation of critical commentary.

Statements of belief or concern are existential, and therefore one very obvious context for them, apart from doctrinal synthesis, is the life of the person who makes or inspires them, and who is usually a leader or culture-hero of some kind. In religious leaders particularly we notice the link with the oral tradition. Jesus, Buddha, even Mohammed, do not write, but make their utterances usually in connexion with specific occasions, some of their disciples acting as secretaries, like the author of the collection of sayings of Jesus (Q) which is preserved in Matthew and Luke. Once a myth of concern is socially established, the personal focus falls on the leader or interpreter who is centrally responsible for sustaining the myth in history.

This line of succession may derive from such figures as Paul, whose letters, like the pamphlets of Lenin later, deal with specific tactical decisions in a way that leads to far-reaching theoretical principles. Or it may take the form of a succession of leaders who are regarded as definitive interpreters of the myth of concern, like the Pope with his *ex cathedra* infallibility in Catholic Christianity or the Marxist leaders. Such leaders are regarded as incarnations of a dialectic, like Plato's philosopher-king. In other contexts the incarnation may be a purely symbolic figure like Elizabeth II, in her role of "defender of the faith." The most primitive form of such a conception is the kind represented by the *Führerprinzip* of Nazism. A much more open and sophisticated one is that of the Constitution of the United States, which was theoretically dictated by an inspired people to a prophetic group of founding fathers. When two myths of concern collide, this personal focus is usually prominent in the collision. It was the repudiation of the largely symbolic cult of the deified Caesar that marked Christians and Jews off from the Roman world; and when Julian the Apostate tried to set up a more philosophical and "open" alternative to Christianity he could hardly avoid putting his own cult at the centre of it.

The earlier stages of a myth of concern usually include a development of an oracular and mainly oral philosophy, associated with wise men, prophets or gurus whose sayings may also be recorded, often very haphazardly, by disciples or scribes. A strong esoteric tendency to distinguish between an inner and an outer court of hearers, or between deep and shallow comprehension of the same doctrines, is notable here. The practice of reserving special teachings for a smaller group of initiates has run through philosophy from Pythagoras to Wittgenstein. Similar esoteric movements make their way, sometimes in the form of philosophical heresies, into the great religions, producing various Gnostic developments in Christianity, Sufism in Islam, and what eventually became the Mahayana form of Buddhism. A secret tradition, believed to be authentically derived from the same source as the exoteric one, but possessing qualities that the latter would fear and distrust, may serve as a kind of back door or fire escape for a myth of freedom in persecuting times.

Any personality at the centre of a myth of concern whose life is the context of a body of teaching must be regarded as having reached a definitive level of truth. But as truth of concern is not truth of correspondence, and cannot be verified and expanded like the established principles of a science, it follows that such a central personality is bound to create a hierarchy of response. This hierarchy of response is often represented, as above, by an inner group of specially enlightened followers. But in a socially ascendant myth it tends to become formalized in an institution, which becomes the acknowledged interpreter of the myth of concern, again on a hierarchical basis.

The more open the myth, the more the task of interpreting it begins to show analogies to literary criticism. The myth of concern usually exists as a body of words drawn up in the past, sometimes a remote past, and this body of words is, like the critic's text, unalterable. The variable factor is the new social situation provided by the interpreter's age; and, as there is an indefinite series of such new situations, it follows that the original structure, again like the critic's text, is not only unalterable but must be inexhaustible in reference. Thus the Supreme Court in America may not alter the Constitution, but must say what an eighteenth-century principle means in a twentieth-century world. The assumption is that the principles are comprehensible enough to be applicable to any current situation.

We notice that in this interpreting process what may have been originally sequential or systematic arguments tend to break down into a discontinuous series of general principles, each of which acquires a different context in the commentary attached to it. In other words it acquires the detached oracular structure of the prose of concern. Such commentary is of course very similar to criticism in literature, and it is clear that the different forms of critical interpretation cannot be sharply separated, whether they are applied to the plays of Shakespeare, the manuscripts of the Bible, the American Constitution, or the oral traditions of an aboriginal tribe. In the area of general concern they converge, however widely the technical contexts in law, theology, literature or anthropology may differ.

The analogy of literary criticism to the interpreting of a myth of concern suggests that statements of belief or concern can have a literary context as well as the existential one of a leader's life. In literature such statements have the context of a story, from which they emerge as comments or applications. From a literary point of view every statement of belief or concern can be seen as the moral of a fable. We referred earlier to the importance of the sententious element in literature: for centuries epigrams on the human situation, embedded in a Classical author, were regarded as the pearls of literature, worth opening the oyster to get. We also noted a social and intellectual contrast in the forms of concerned prose between oracular statements, the dark sayings of the wise, which tend to be esoteric in reference, and proverbs, which tend to be the expression of popular wisdom and to circulate in gregarious swarms, there being something about the proverb, in all ages, that seems to stir the collector's instinct. It is not surprising that in later literature we find oracular aphorisms more frequently attached to tragedies and proverbial ones to comedy and satire. The fable traditionally has a moral at the end: the convention of *beginning* a story with a sententious comment, already well established in Boccaccio, appears in *Rasselas* and is expanded into a major feature of *Tom Jones*. It is still going strong in the opening sentences of *Anna Karenina* and (in the key of delicate parody) *Pride and Prejudice*.

On a larger scale, statements of Christian belief are inseparable from the story of the Bible, which in its literary aspect is a comic romance. Similarly the Greek belief in fate, or whatever was meant by such words as ananke, moira, and heimarmene, is essentially chorus comment on the narrative form of tragedy which the Greeks invented. In our day we tend to go from the three R's in our education to a belief in, or at least an assent to, the three A's: anxiety, alienation, and absurdity. But these concepts again are noble sentiments derived from a prevailingly ironic age of fable.

When Raphael in *Paradise Lost* was sent down to talk to Adam, the reason for sending him was to impress Adam with the importance of not touching the forbidden tree. Raphael, however, refers only obliquely to the tree: what he mainly does is to tell Adam the story of the fall of Satan. The implication is that teaching through parable, the typical method of Jesus, is the appropriate way of educating a free man, like Adam before his fall. After his fall, Adam gets from Michael a similar emblematic and illustrative instruction, though within his new and fallen category of linear time, where the events are prophecies of an inevitable future to him, records of an inescapable past to the reader. Yet education is still by story or "speaking picture," with morals attached, and the total containing structure of the teaching is the Christian romantic comedy of salvation. Angels, evidently, teach by fable; teaching by morals is merely human, and only the officially and institutionally human at that.

Educating through the fable rather than through the moral involves all the responsibilities of a greater freedom, including the responsibility of rejecting censorship. Of all the things that Milton says about censorship in the *Areopagitica*, the most far-reaching in its implications seems to me to be his remark that a wise man will make a better use of an idle pamphlet than a fool would of Holy Scripture. That is, the reader himself is responsible for the moral quality of what he reads, and it is the desire to dodge this responsibility, either on one's own behalf or that of others, that produces censorship. Statements of concern are either right or wrong, which means, as the truth involved is not directly verifiable, that they are accepted as right or wrong. For the deeply concerned, all arguments are personal, in a bad sense, because all arguments are either for them or against them, and hence their proponent, to be acclaimed or refuted, needs simply to be identified as one of us or one of the enemy. In a tense situation within an open myth of concern, when pressure groups are starting up to try to close it, the formula "you only say that because you're a (whatever is appropriate)" is often regarded as penetrating the reality behind a hypocritical facade. The preservation of the open myth depends on giving the foreground of impersonal argument its own validity; the other direction leads inevitably to censorship and an *index expurgatorius*. One sees the hierarchical institution beginning to take shape here, with the censors forming an elite.

The most unattractive quality of the censor is his contempt for other people. The censor says: "I want this play banned, because, while it can't possibly do me any harm, there are all those people over there who will be irreparably damaged in their morals if they see it." Similarly, the person who attaches a smear label to whatever he disagrees with is really saying: "It may be all very well to appeal to me with logical arguments, because I can see through them; but there are all those people over there who are not so astute." The same habit of mind is common among those who are anxious to save themselves trouble in thinking or reading. I note in several Freudian books a tendency to describe Freudian revisionists or heretics as "reactionary." I mention Freud because he was in so many respects a conservative, pessimistic, even "reactionary" thinker who has been made into the founder of a myth of revolutionary optimism. The implication is that calling anyone a reactionary, or any similar epithet, if it relates to qualities assumed to be inherent in his work, is intellectually dishonest. Nobody's *work* is inherently revolutionary or reactionary, whatever the writer's own views in his lifetime: it is the use made of the work which determines what it is, and any writer may be potentially useful to anybody, in any way.

A more difficult assumption of responsibility relates to the writer's beliefs, and the particular concerns that he participates in. We have already met the principle that in reading poetry the "overthought," or explicit statement, is expendable to some degree, and that the "underthought" or progression of image and metaphor is the decisive meaning. When a myth of concern is derived from the teachings of a single man, or series of accredited teachers, those teachers must be regarded as in a very special sense wise or inspired men. No such respect need be accorded the poet so far as he represents a belief or attitude, however important and essential the belief may be to the poet himself. Hopkins and Claudel would probably never have bothered to keep on writing poetry without the drive of a powerful Catholic belief; but what makes them poets is their skill in using the language of concern, and hence they can be studied with the greatest devotion by readers who share none of their commitments. Still, most reasonable readers would respect a Catholic belief, whatever their own: a much more crucial example would be, say, Céline, who is a significant and important writer to many readers who could not possibly regard his views with anything but contempt.

The principles involved here are, first, that while the teacher of a myth of concern must be a wise or great or inspired man to his followers, the poet, or speaker of the language of concern, may be an important poet, and yet, in certain other respects, almost any kind of a damned fool. Second, the subordination of reader to poet is tactical only: he studies his author with full attention, but the end at which he aims is a transfer of the poet's vision to himself. Poetry is not, then, to be merely enjoyed and appreciated, but to be possessed as well. Third, there are no negative visions: all poets are potentially positive contributors to man's body of vision, and no *index expurgatorius* or literary hell (to use Milton's figure in *Areopagitica*) exists on any basis acceptable to a student of literature. Therefore, fourth, criticism does not aim at evaluation, which always means that the critic wants to get into the concern game himself, choosing a canon out of literature and so making literature a single gigantic allegory of his own anxieties.

We spoke earlier, however, of a canonical group of myths at the centre of an oral verbal culture. As writing, secular literature, and a myth of concern develop, the language of concern shifts to the conceptual, the statement of belief. Doctrine and creed replace such formulas as "in the eternal dream time." Meanwhile, literature goes its own way, continuing to produce stories, images and metaphors. When the critic arrives at the stage indicated by Shelley's *Defence*,[12] of being able to conceive of literature as a totality, an imaginative body and not simply an aggregate, the centrifugal movements of concern and literature begin to come together again. The critic begins to see literature as presenting the range of imaginative possibilities of belief, its stories the encyclopaedia of visions of human life and destiny which form the context of belief.

"The Old and New Testaments are the Great Code of Art," said Blake, indicating the context of

[12] See Shelley, *CTSP*, pp. 498–513. [Eds.]

his own work, and similarly literature is the "great code" of concern. Many mythical stories, like those of the fall or the flood, seem increasingly puerile when one tries to rationalize or historicize them, but approached in the universalized terms of the imagination, they become conceivable as visionary sources of belief. Other myths of concern, democratic, Marxist, or what not, are also founded on visions of human life with a generic literary shape, usually comic. Literature as a whole is also, like religious and political movements, to be related to a central life, but its central life is the life of humanity, and its inspired teacher the verbal imagination of man. Once again, literature in its totality is not a super-myth of concern, truer because more comprehensive than all existing ones combined. Literature is not to be believed in: there is no "religion of poetry": the whole point about literature is that it has no direct connection with belief. That is why it has such a vast importance in indicating the horizons beyond all formulations of belief, in pointing to an infinite total concern that can never be expressed, but only indicated in the variety of the arts themselves.

In modern times the classical statement of the relation of concern and freedom is Kierkegaard's *Either/Or,* from which the existentialist traditions of our day mainly descend. For Kierkegaard the detached, liberal, and impersonal attitude fostered by the study of an objective environment, and which flowers into comprehensive intellectual systems like that of Hegel, is an "aesthetic" attitude. It is fundamentally immature because with this attitude man tries to fit himself into a larger container, the general outlines of which he can see with his reason, but forgetting that his reason built the container. The crisis of life comes when we pass over into the commitment represented by "or," take up our primary concern, and thus enter the sphere of genuine personality and ethical freedom.

The postulates of Kierkegaard's ethical freedom are Christian postulates, and his commitment is an acceptance of faith. The acceptance is fundamentally uncritical, because, so the argument runs, man is not a spectator of his own life. But, we saw, the context of Christian faith is a context of vision and fable and myth, and Kierkegaard does not really come to terms with the implications of this fact. Milton's portrayal of Adam looking at the sequence of Adamic life presented in the Bible, where the Christian faith becomes a total informing vision which Adam contemplates as a spectator, shows a far profounder grasp, not only of Christianity, but of the whole problem of concern. If we stop with the voluntary self-blinkering of commitment, we are no better off than the "aesthetic": on the other side of "or" is another step to be taken, a step from the committed to the creative, from iconoclastic concern to what the literary critic above all ought to be able to see, that in literature man *is* a spectator of his own life, or at least of the larger vision in which his life is contained. This vision is nothing external to himself and is not born out of nature or any objective environment. Yet it is not subjective either, because it is produced by the power of imaginative communication, the power that enables men, in Aristotle's phrase, not merely to come together to form a social life, but to remain together to form the good life.

What applies to a Christian commitment in Kierkegaard applies also to commitments to other myths of concern, where Kierkegaard's "aesthetic" would be replaced by "escapist" or "idealistic" or what not. Kierkegaard is saying, in our terms, that concern is primary and freedom a derivation from it, as the present discussion has also maintained. The individual who does not understand the primacy of concern, the fact that we belong to something before we are anything, is, it is quite true, in a falsely individualized position, and his "aesthetic" attitude may well be parasitic. But Kierkegaard, like so many deeply concerned people, is also saying that passing over to concern gives us the genuine form of freedom, that concern and freedom are ultimately the same thing. This is the bait attached to all "either-or" arguments, but it does not make the hook any more digestible.

It is worth pausing a moment on this point, because Kierkegaard is not really satisfied with his own argument. He clearly understood the fact that freedom can only be realized in the individual, and sought for a Christianity that would escape from what he calls "Christendom," the merely social conformity or *religio* of Christianity. He speaks of the personal as in itself a subversive and revolutionary force, and sees the threat of what we should now call the totalitarian mob in the "impersonal." For him the highest form of truth is personally possessed truth, and he is not afraid to face the implications of what I think of as the "paranoia principle." This is the principle, lurking in all conceptions of a personal truth transcending the truth of concern, that it is only what is true only for me that is really true. This principle brings us back to the conception of a definitive experience, which we met at the end of the first section, as an unattained reality of which literature appears to be an analogy.

Concern raises the question of belief, and belief raises the question of authority, the question "Who says so?" I have tried to show that the authority of concern, in itself, is always the authority of a social establishment. Even if its answer is "God says so," its effective answer is always "it doesn't matter who originally said so: we say so now, and you will accept it or else." It is different with the authority of reason and evidence and repeatable experiment: granted that there is no absolute objectivity, etc., it is still true that this kind of authority is the only genuine form of spiritual authority. That is, it is the only kind of authority that enhances, instead of encroaching on, the dignity and the freedom of the individual who accepts it. Unless the autonomy of this kind of authority is fully recognized and respected, there can be no escape from "Christendom" or whatever other conforming mob may be thrown up by concern. What I have been calling an open mythology is really the recognition of this autonomy, a readiness on the part of society to accept a "both-and" rather than an "either-or" situation.

The context of the myth of freedom is the environment of physical nature, and this environment is one of alienation, a sub-moral and sub-human world. Concern is an essential part of the attempt to escape from this alienation by forming a human community. The myth of freedom is born from concern, and can never replace concern or exist without it; nevertheless it creates a tension against it. One necessary development of this tension is the collision between the two kinds of authority when a myth of concern is approached from the standards of a myth of freedom. What emerges from the conflict is the sense of an imaginative world as forming the wider context of belief, a total potential of myth from which every specific myth of concern has been crystallized. The imaginative world opens up for us a new dimension of freedom, in which the individual finds himself again, detached but not separated from his community. Hence, though we cannot simply accept the view of Shelley that the poetic imagination speaks the language of freedom as well as concern, still one essential aspect of freedom is the release of the language of concern, or allowing freedom to the poetic imagination.

Again, this new dimension of freedom, which includes the released imagination, cannot take the place of concern: we can neither live continuously in the imaginative world nor bring it into existence. The tension has to continue. But maintaining the tension is difficult, like standing on a pinnacle, and there are constant temptations to throw ourselves off. The temptation listened to by Kierkegaard, and by so many existentialists and others since, is the temptation to identify freedom with the power of choice. As we can really choose only what commits us, this means that, like Adam in Eden, we can express our freedom only by annihilating it. This is an irony of the human situation. But irony, as students of literature realize, is not the centre of human reality but only one of several modes of imaginative expression, and it is a function of the critic to provide some perspective for irony.

Irony in literature has a great deal to do with a conception of freedom which identifies freedom with freedom of the will. Such freedom is usually thought of as opposed to necessity, and the irony consists in the fact that such freedom eventually collapses into the fatality it tries to fight against. If we associate a free will of this kind with God, we embark on that dismal theological chess game that ends with predestination in time, with the God of Burns's Holy Willie who

> Sends ane to heaven and ten to hell
> A' for thy glory

and whom anyone less obsessed with concern would find great difficulty in distinguishing from the devil. If we associate it with an individual, he soon becomes a tyrant who acts by whim and caprice, and so is not free but a slave of his own compulsions. If we associate it with a society, we get the kind of "will of the people" which is mob rule, where the leaders play the same enslaving role that compulsions do in the tyrant. The only genuine freedom is a freedom of the will which is informed by a vision, and this vision can only come to us through the intellect and the imagination, and through the arts and sciences which embody them, the analogies of whatever truth and beauty we can reach. In this kind of freedom the opposition to necessity disappears: for scientists and artists and scholars, as such, what they want to do and what they have to do become the same thing. This is the core of the freedom that no concern can ever include or replace, and everything else that we associate with freedom proceeds from it.

René Girard

b. 1923

René Girard's work is less influenced by anthropological thought than by a continuing dialogue with it. Beginning as a literary critic, he has more and more moved into the arena of the philosophy of culture and history. His recent turn to the study of Shakespeare has been to show how the theories resulting from the anthropological dialogue are endorsed by Shakespeare's treatment of desire and tragedy.

Perhaps the two key concepts in Girard's work have to do with mimesis and sacrifice. In his *Deceit, Desire, and the Novel* (1961), he attempted a radical redefinition of human desire as not a relation of lack to an object but rather the result of the imitation of a preexistent desire discovered in some esteemed other person. This sets up, presumably, an infinite chain of desire with no origin, and it also sees imitation as conflictual because an act of appropriation. "When a gesture of appropriation is imitated," Girard remarks in an interview, "it simply means that two hands will reach for the same object simultaneously." Plato's theory of imitation Girard rejects; it is persistent, perhaps, because people esteem and copy Plato. The object of desire, always displaced, can only be in the end transcendental. But mimetic desire, as Girard calls it, being itself unlimited, must be controlled in some way or it will produce intolerable and unlimited violence. In *Violence and the Sacred* (1972), of which the selection below is the second chapter, Girard proposes that the mechanism of sacrifice was devised by men to escape the prospect of uncontrolled violence and chaos. Sacrifice becomes the origin of culture. It is also the acknowledgment and, indeed, the insistence upon difference, the memory of violence, and the repression and channeling of it. It is difference for Girard that leads away from the equilibrium that inevitably, for him, breeds violence, as has, he believes, the disappearance of sacrificial rituals, which reassert difference in the fate of the victim and bind together society by defining it as apart from that Other.

Girard's view has been regarded, and frequently attacked, as reactionary. Clearly it is conservative and religious. Ultimately it valorizes Christianity but in a way foreign to most Christian apologists because of its insistence on sacrifice and the Other as a social need. It is based on a metaphysical principle, the result of which is an explanation for the phenomenon of the scapegoat unnerving to conventional religious thought, particularly since Girard argues that the only good scapegoats are the ones we are unable to acknowledge as such.

Mimetic desire, for Girard, precedes everything. Girard's untranslated *Des Choses cachés depuis la fondation du monde* (1978), perhaps his most important book, appearing in the form of a conversation with two psychiatrists, Jean-

Michel Oughourlian and Guy Lefort, contains audacious applications of this principle to various texts, including the Bible.

Girard's books translated into English are *Deceit, Desire, and the Novel* (1965), published originally in France as *Mensonge romantique et verité romanesque* (1961); *Violence and the Sacred* (1972, trans. 1977); and *To Double Business Bound: Essays on Literature, Mimesis, and Anthropology* (1978). Books available in French only are *Critique dans un souterrain,* principally on Dostoyevsky (1976); *Des Choses cachés depuis la fondation du monde* (1978); *Le Bouc émissaire,* further essays on scapegoating in the Bible (1982); and *La Route antique des hommes parvers* (1985). Girard's work on Shakespeare is represented by "Myth and Ritual in Shakespeare: A Midsummer Night's Dream," in *Textual Strategies,* ed. J. V. Harari (1979). See *Diacritics* 8, 1 (Spring 1978), devoted to Girard's work and containing an interview with him.

THE SACRIFICIAL CRISIS

As we have seen, the proper functioning of the sacrificial process requires not only the complete separation of the sacrificed victim from those beings for whom the victim is a substitute but also a similarity between both parties. This dual requirement can be fulfilled only through a delicately balanced mechanism of associations.

Any change, however slight, in the hierarchical classification of living creatures risks undermining the whole sacrificial structure. The sheer repetition of the sacrificial act—the repeated slaughter of the same type of victim—inevitably brings about such change. But the inability to adapt to new conditions is a trait characteristic of religion in general. If, as is often the case, we encounter the institution of sacrifice either in an advanced state of decay or reduced to relative insignificance, it is because it has already undergone a good deal of wear and tear.

Whether the slippage in the mechanism is due to "too little" or "too much" contact between the victim and those whom the victim represents, the results are the same. The elimination of violence is no longer effected; on the contrary, conflicts within the community multiply, and the menace of chain reactions looms ever larger.

If the gap between the victim and the community is allowed to grow too wide, all similarity will be destroyed. The victim will no longer be capable of attracting the violent impulses to itself; the sacrifice will cease to serve as a "good conductor," in the sense that metal is a good conductor of electricity. On the other hand, if there is *too much* continuity the violence will overflow its channels. "Impure" violence will mingle with the "sacred" violence of the rites, turning the latter into a scandalous accomplice in the process of pollution, even a kind of catalyst in the propagation of further impurity.

These are postulates that seem to take form a priori from our earlier conclusions. They can also be discerned in literature—in the adaptations of certain myths in classical Greek tragedy, in particular in Euripides' version of the legend of Heracles.

Euripides' *Heracles* contains no tragic conflict, no debate between declared adversaries. The real subject of the play is the failure of a sacrifice, the act of sacrificial violence that suddenly *goes wrong.* Heracles, returning home after the completion of his labors, finds his wife and children in the power of a usurper named Lycus, who is preparing to offer them as sacrificial victims. Heracles kills Lycus. After this most recent act of violence, committed in the heart of the city, the hero's need to purify himself is greater than ever, and he sets about preparing a sacrifice of his own. His wife and children are with him when Heracles, suddenly seized by mad-

THE SACRIFICIAL CRISIS first appeared in France in 1972. It is reprinted from *Violence and the Sacred,* trans. Patrick Gregory, by permission of its publisher, The Johns Hopkins University Press, copyright 1977.

ness, mistakes them for his enemies and *sacrifices* them.

Heracles' misidentification of his family is attributed to Lyssa, goddess of madness, who is operating as an emissary of two other goddesses, Iris and Hera, who bear Heracles ill will. The preparations for the sacrifice provide an imposing setting for the homicidal outburst; it is unlikely that their dramatic significance passed unnoticed by the author. In fact, it is Euripides himself who directs our attention to the ritualistic origins of the onslaught. After the massacre, Heracles' father, Amphitryon, asks his son: "My child, what happened to you? How could this horror have taken place? Was it perhaps the spilt blood that turned your head?" Heracles, who is just returning to consciousness and remembers nothing, inquires in turn: "Where did the madness overtake me? Where did it strike me down?" Amphitryon replies: "Near the altar, where you were purifying your hands over the sacred flames."

The sacrifice contemplated by the hero succeeded only too well in polarizing the forces of violence. Indeed, it produced a superabundance of violence of a particularly virulent kind. As Amphitryon suggested, the blood shed in the course of the terrible labors and in the city itself finally turned the hero's head. Instead of drawing off the violence and allowing it to ebb away, the rites brought a veritable flood of violence down on the victim. The sacrificial rites were no longer able to accomplish their task; they swelled the surging tide of impure violence instead of channeling it. The mechanism of substitutions had gone astray, and those whom the sacrifice was designed to protect became its victims.

The difference between sacrificial and nonsacrificial violence is anything but exact; it is even arbitrary. At times the difference threatens to disappear entirely. There is no such thing as truly "pure" violence. Nevertheless, sacrificial violence can, in the proper circumstances, serve as an agent of purification. That is why those who perform the rites are obliged to purify themselves at the conclusion of the sacrifice. The procedure followed is reminiscent of atomic power plants; when the expert has finished decontaminating the installation, he must himself be decontaminated. And accidents can always happen.

The catastrophic inversion of the sacrificial act would appear to be an essential element in the Heracles myth. The motif reappears, thinly con cealed behind secondary themes, in another episode of his story, in Sophocles' *The Women of Trachis*.

Heracles had mortally wounded the centaur Nessus, who had assaulted Heracles' wife, Deianira. Before dying, the centaur gave the young woman a shirt smeared with his sperm—or, in Sophocles' version, smeared with his blood mixed with the blood of a Hydra. (Once again, as in the *Ion,* we encounter the theme of the two kinds of blood mingling to form one.)

The subject of the tragedy, as in Euripides' *Heracles,* is the return of the hero. In this instance Heracles is bringing with him a pretty young captive, of whom Deianira is jealous. Deianira sends a servant to her husband with a welcoming gift, the shirt of Nessus. With his dying breath the centaur had told her that the shirt would assure the wearer's eternal fidelity to her; but he cautioned her to keep it well out of the way of any flame or source of heat.

Heracles puts on the shirt, and soon afterward lights a fire for the rites of sacrificial purification. The flames activate the poison in the shirt; it is the rite itself that unlooses the evil. Heracles, contorted with pain, presently ends his life on the pyre he has begged his son to prepare. Before dying, Heracles kills the servant who delivered the shirt to him; this death, along with his own and the subsequent suicide of his wife, contributes to the cycle of violence heralded by Heracles' return and the failure of the sacrifice. Once again, violence has struck the beings who sought the protection of sacrificial rites.

A number of sacrifice motifs intermingle in these two plays. A special sort of impurity clings to the warrior returning to his homeland, still tainted with the slaughter of war. In the case of Heracles, his sanguinary labors render him particularly impure.

The returning warrior risks carrying the seed of violence into the very heart of his city. The myth of Horatius, as explicated by Georges Dumézil, illustrates this theme: Horatius kills his sister before any ritual purification has been performed. In the case of Heracles the impurity triumphs over the rite itself.

If we examine the mechanism of violence in these two tragedies, we notice that when the sacrifice goes wrong it sets off a chain reaction of the sort

[1]The first chapter of *Violence and the Sacred* is entitled "Sacrifice." [Eds.]

defined in the first chapter.[1] The murder of Lycus is presented in the Euripides play as a last "labor" of the hero, a still-rational prelude to the insane outburst that follows. Seen from the perspective of the ritualist, it might well constitute a first link of impure violence. With this incident, as we have noted, violence invades the heart of the city. This initial murder corresponds to the death of the old servant in *The Women of Trachis*.

Supernatural intervention plays no part in these episodes, except perhaps to cast a thin veil over the true subject: the sacrificial celebration that has gone wrong. The goddess Lyssa, Nessus' shirt—these add nothing to the meaning of the two stories; rather, they act as a veil, and as soon as the veil is drawn aside we encounter the same theme of "good" violence turning into "bad." The mythological accompaniments to the stories can be seen as redundant. Lyssa, the goddess of madness, sounds more like a refugee from an allegorical tale than a real goddess, and Nessus' shirt joins company with all the acts of violence that Heracles carries on his back.

The theme of the Warrior's Return is not, strictly speaking, mythological, and readily lends itself to sociological or psychological interpretations. The conquering hero who threatens to destroy the liberty of his homeland belongs to history, not myth. Certainly that is the way Corneille seems to approach the subject in *Horace,* although in his version of the tale the ideology is somewhat reversed—the returning warrior is rightly shocked by his sister's lack of patriotism. We could easily translate the "case histories" of Heracles and Horatius into psychological or psychoanalytical terms and come up with numerous working theories, each at variance with the other. But we should avoid this temptation, for in debating the relative merits of each theory we would lose sight of the role played by ritual—a subject that has nothing to do with such debates, even though it may, as we shall see, open the way to them. Being more *primitive,* ritualistic action is hospitable to all ideological interpretations and dependent on none. It has only one axiom: the contagious nature of the violence encountered by the warrior in battle—and only one prescription: the proper performance of ritual purification. Its sole purpose is to prevent the resurgence of violence and its spread throughout the community.

The two tragedies we have been discussing present in anecdotal form, as if dealing exclusively with exceptional individuals, events that are significant because they affect the community as a whole. Sacrifice is a social act, and when it goes amiss the consequences are not limited to some "exceptional" individual singled out by Destiny.

Historians seem to agree that Greek tragedy belonged to a period of transition between the dominance of an archaic theocracy and the emergence of a new, "modern" order based on statism and laws. Before its decline the archaic order must have enjoyed a certain stability; and this stability must have reposed on its religious element—that is, on the sacrificial rites.

Although they predate the tragedians, the pre-Socratics are often regarded as the philosophers of classical tragedy. In their writings we can find echoes of the religious crisis we are attempting to define. The fifth fragment of Heraclitus quite clearly deals with the decay of sacrificial rites, with their inability to purify what is impure. Religious beliefs are compromised by the decadent state of the ritual: "In vain do they strive for purification by besmirching themselves with blood, as the man who has bathed in the mire seeks to cleanse himself with mud. Such antics can only strike the beholder as utter folly! In addressing their prayers to images of the gods, they might just as well be speaking to the walls, without seeking to know the true nature of gods or heroes."

The difference between blood spilt for ritual and for criminal purposes no longer holds. The Heraclitus fragment appears in even sharper relief when compared to analogous passages in the Old Testament. The preexilian prophets Amos, Isaiah, and Micah denounce in vehement terms the impotence of the sacrificial process and ritual in general. In the most explicit manner they link the decay of religious practices to the deterioration of contemporary behavior. Inevitably, the eroding of the sacrificial system seems to result in the emergence of reciprocal violence. Neighbors who had previously discharged their mutual aggressions on a third party, joining together in the sacrifice of an "outside" victim, now turn to sacrificing one another. Empedocles' *Purifications* brings us even closer to the problem:

> 136. When will the sinister noise of this carnage cease? Can you not see that you are devouring one another with your callous hearts?
>
> 137. The father seizes hold of the son, who

> has changed form; in his mad delusion he kills him, murmuring prayers. The son cries out, imploring his insane executioner to spare him. But the father hears him not, and cuts his throat, and spreads a great feast in his palace. In the same way the son takes hold of the father, the children their mother, one slaughtering the other and devouring their own flesh and blood.

The concept of a "sacrificial crisis" may be useful in clarifying certain aspects of Greek tragedy. To a real extent it is sacrificial religion that provides the language for these dramas; the criminal in the plays sees himself not so much as a righter-of-wrongs as a performer-of-sacrifices. We always view the "tragic flaw" from the perspective of the new, emergent order; never from that of the old order in the final stages of decay. The reason for this approach is clear: modern thought has never been able to attribute any real function to the practice of sacrifice, and because the nature of the practice eludes us, we naturally find it difficult to determine when and if this practice is in the process of disintegration. In the case of Greek tragedy it is not enough merely to believe in the existence of the old order; we must look deeper if we hope to discover the religious problems of the era. Unlike the Jewish prophets, whose viewpoint was historical, the Greek tragedians evoked their own sacrificial crisis in terms of legendary figures whose forms were fixed by tradition.

All the bloody events that serve as background to the plays—the plagues and pestilences, civil and foreign wars—undoubtedly reflect the contemporary scene, but the images are unclear, as if viewed through a glass darkly. Each time, for example, a play of Euripides deals with the collapse of a royal house (as in *Heracles, Iphigenia in Aulis,* or *The Bacchae*), we are convinced that the poet is suggesting that the scene before our eyes is only the tip of the iceberg, that the real issue is the fate of the entire community. At the moment when Heracles is slaughtering his family offstage, the chorus cries out: "Look, look! The tempest is shaking the house; the roof is falling in."

If the tragic crisis is indeed to be described in terms of the sacrificial crisis, its relationship to sacrifice should be apparent in all aspects of tragedy—either conveyed directly through explicit reference or perceived indirectly, in broad outline, underlying the texture of the drama.

If the art of tragedy is to be defined in a single phrase, we might do worse than call attention to one of its most characteristic traits: the opposition of symmetrical elements. There is no aspect of the plot, form, or language of a tragedy in which this symmetrical pattern does not recur. The third actor, for instance, hardly constitutes the innovation that critics have claimed. Third actor or no third actor, the core of the drama remains the tragic dialogue; that is, the fateful confrontation during which the two protagonists exchange insults and accusations with increasing earnestness and rapidity. The Greek public brought to these verbal contests the same educated sense of appreciation that French audiences many centuries later evinced for their own classic drama—for Théramène's famous speech from the last act of *Phèdre,* for example, or for almost any passage from *Le Cid.*

The symmetry of the tragic dialogue is perfectly mirrored by the stichomythia, in which the two protagonists address one another in alternating lines. In tragic dialogue hot words are substituted for cold steel. But whether the violence is physical or verbal, the suspense remains the same. The adversaries match blow for blow, and they seem so evenly matched that it is impossible to predict the outcome of the battle. The structural similarity between the two forms of violence is illustrated by the description of the duel between the brothers Eteocles and Polyneices in Euripides' *Phoenician Women.* There is nothing in this account that does not apply equally to both brothers: their parries, thrusts, and feints, their gestures and postures, are identical: "If either saw the other's eye peer over the rim of his shield, He raised his spear."

Polyneices loses his spear in the fight, and so does Eteocles. Both are wounded. Each blow upsets the equilibrium, threatening to decide the outcome then and there. It is immediately followed by a new blow that not only redresses the balance but creates a symmetrical disequilibrium that is itself, naturally enough, of short duration. The tragic suspense follows the rhythm of these rapid exchanges, each one of which promises to bring matters to a head—but never quite does so. "They struggle now on even terms, each having spent his spear. Swords are unsheathed, and the two brothers are locked in close combat. Shield clashes with shield, and a great clamor engulfs them both." Even death fails to tip the balance. "They hit the dust and lay together side by side; and their heritage was still unclaimed."

The death of the brothers resolves nothing; it simply perpetuates the symmetry of the battle. Each had been his army's champion, and the two armies now resume the struggle, reestablish the symmetry. Oddly enough, however, the conflict is now transferred to a purely verbal plane, transforming itself into a true tragic dialogue. Tragedy now assumes its proper function as a verbal extension of physical combat, an interminable debate set off by the chronically indecisive character of an act of violence committed previously:

> The soldiers then leapt to their feet, and the argument began. We claimed that our king had won; they claimed the victory for Polyneices. The captains quarreled, too. Some said that Polyneices had struck the first blow; others replied that death had snatched the palm of victory from both claimants.

The indecisiveness of the first combat spreads quite naturally to the second, which then sows it abroad. The tragic dialogue is a debate without resolution. Each side resolutely continues to deploy the same arguments, emphases, goals; *Gleichgewicht* is Hölderlin's word for it. Tragedy is the balancing of the scale, not of justice but of violence. No sooner is something added to one side of the scale than its equivalent is contributed to the other. The same insults and accusations fly from one combatant to the other, as a ball flies from one player to another in tennis. The conflict stretches on interminably because between the two adversaries there is no difference whatsoever.

The equilibrium in the struggle has often been attributed to a so-called tragic impartiality; Hölderlin's word is *Impartialität*. I do not find this interpretation quite satisfactory. Impartiality implies a deliberate refusal to take sides, a firm commitment to treat both contestants equally. The impartial party is not eager to resolve the issue, does not want to know if there is a resolution; nor does he maintain that resolution is impossible. His impartiality-at-any-price is not unfrequently simply an unsubstantiated assertion of superiority. One of the adversaries is right, the other wrong, and the onlooker is obliged to take sides; either that, or the rights and wrongs are so evenly distributed between the two factions that taking sides is impossible. The self-proclaimed advocate of impartiality does not want to commit himself to either course of action. If pushed toward one camp, he seeks refuge in the other. Men always find it distasteful to admit that the "reasons" on both sides of a dispute are equally valid—which is to say that *violence operates without reason.*

Tragedy begins at that point where the illusion of impartiality, as well as the illusions of the adversaries, collapses. For example, in *Oedipus the King,* Oedipus, Creon, and Tiresias are each in turn drawn into a conflict that each had thought to resolve in the role of impartial mediator.

It is not clear to what extent the tragedians themselves managed to remain impartial. For example, Euripides in *The Phoenician Women* barely conceals his preference for Eteocles—or perhaps we should say his preference for the Athenian public's approval. In any case, his partiality is superficial. The preferences registered for one side or another never prevent the authors from constantly underlining the symmetrical relationship between the adversaries.

At the very moment when they appear to be abandoning impartiality, the tragedians do their utmost to deprive the audience of any means of taking sides. Aeschylus, Sophocles, and Euripides all utilize the same procedures and almost identical phraseology to convey symmetry, identity, reciprocity. We encounter here an aspect of tragic art that has been largely overlooked by contemporary criticism. Nowadays critics tend to assess a work of art on the basis of its *originality.* To the extent that an author cannot claim exclusive rights to his themes, his style, and his esthetic effects, his work is deemed deficient. In the domain of esthetics, singularity reigns supreme.

Such criteria cannot apply, of course, to Greek tragedy, whose authors were not committed to the doctrine of originality at any price. Nevertheless, our frustrated individualism still exerts a deleterious effect on modern interpretations of Greek tragedy.

It is readily apparent that Aeschylus, Sophocles, and Euripides shared certain literary traits and that the characters in their plays have certain characteristics in common. Yet there is no reason to label these resemblances mere stereotypes. It is my belief that these "stereotypes" contain the very essence of Greek tragedy. And if the tragic element in these plays still eludes us, it is because we have obstinately averted our attention from these similarities.

The tragedians portray men and women caught up in a form of violence too impersonal in its workings, too brutal in its results, to allow any sort of value judgment, any sort of distinction, subtle or simplistic, to be drawn between "good" and "wicked" characters. That is why most modern interpretations go astray; we have still not extricated ourselves entirely from the "Manichean" frame of reference that gained sway in the Romantic era and still exerts its influence today.

In Greek tragedy violence invariably effaces the differences between antagonists. The sheer impossibility of asserting their differences fuels the rage of Eteocles and Polyneices. In Euripides' *Heracles* the hero kills Lycus to keep him from sacrificing his family, and next he does what he wanted to prevent his enemy from doing, thereby falling victim to the ironic humor of a Destiny that seems to work hand in glove with violence. In the end it is Heracles who carries out the crime meditated by his counterpart. The more a tragic conflict is prolonged, the more likely it is to culminate in a violent mimesis; the resemblance between the combatants grows ever stronger until each presents a mirror image of the other. There is a scientific corollary: modern research suggests that individuals of quite different make-up and background respond to violence in essentially the same way.

It is the act of reprisal, the repetition of imitative acts of violence, that characterizes tragic plotting. The destruction of differences is particularly spectacular when the hierarchical distance between the characters, the amount of respect due from one to the other, is great—between father and son, for instance. This scandalous effacement of distinctions is apparent in Euripides' *Alcestis*. Father and son are engaged in a tragic dialogue; each accuses the other of fleeing from death and leaving the heroine to die. The symmetry is perfect, emphasized by the symmetrical interventions of the members of the Chorus, who first castigate the son ("Young man, remember to whom you are speaking; do not insult your father"), and then rebuke the father ("Enough has been said on this subject; cease, we pray you, to abuse your own son.").

In *Oedipus the King* Sophocles frequently puts in Oedipus's mouth words that emphasize his resemblance to his father: resemblance in desires, suspicions, and course of action. If the hero throws himself impetuously into the investigation that causes his downfall, it is because he is reacting just as Laius did in seeking out the potential assassin who, according to the oracles, would replace him on the throne of Thebes and in the bed of the queen.

Oedipus finally kills Laius, but it is Laius who, at the crossroads, first raised his hand against his son. The patricide thus takes part in a reciprocal exchange of murderous gestures. It is an act of reprisal in a universe based on reprisals.

At the core of the Oedipus myth, as Sophocles presents it, is the proposition that all masculine relationships are based on reciprocal acts of violence. Laius, taking his cue from the oracle, violently rejects Oedipus out of fear that his son will seize the throne and invade his conjugal bed. Oedipus, taking his cue from the oracle, does away with Laius, violently rebuffs the sphinx, then takes their places—as king and "scourge of the city," respectively. Again, Oedipus, taking his cue from the oracle, plots the death of that unknown figure who may be seeking to usurp his own position. Oedipus, Creon, and Tiresias, each taking his cue from the oracle, seek one another's downfall.

All these acts of violence gradually wear away the differences that exist not only in the same family but throughout the community. The tragic combat between Oedipus and Tiresias pits the community's chief spiritual leaders against one another. The enraged Oedipus seeks to strip the aura of "mystery" from his rival, to prove that he is a false prophet, nothing more:

> Come tell us: have you truly shown yourself a prophet? When the terrible sphinx held sway over our countrymen, did you ever whisper the words that would have delivered them? That riddle was not to be answered by anyone; the gift of prophecy was called for. Yet that gift was clearly not yours to give; nor was it ever granted to you, either by the birds or by the gods.

Confronted by the king's frustration and rage at being unable to uncover the truth, Tiresias launches his own challenge. The terms are much the same: "If you are so clever at solving enigmas, why are you powerless to solve this one?" Both parties in this tragic dialogue have recourse to the same tactics, use the same weapons, and strive for the same goal: destruction of the adversary. Tiresias poses as the champion of tradition, taking up the cudgels on behalf of the oracles flouted by Oedipus. However, in so doing he shows himself insolent to royal authority. Although the targets are individuals, it is the institutions that receive the blows. Legitimate authority trembles on its pedestal, and the combatants finally assist in the downfall of the very order they strove to maintain. The impiety referred to by the chorus—the neglect of the oracles, the general decadence that pervades the religion of the community—is surely part of the same phenomenon that works away at the undermining of family relationships, as well as of religious and social hierarchies.

The *sacrificial crisis,* that is, the disappearance of the sacrificial rites, coincides with the disappearance of the difference between impure violence and purifying violence. When this difference has been effaced, purification is no longer possible and impure, contagious, reciprocal violence spreads throughout the community.

The sacrificial distinction, the distinction between the pure and the impure, cannot be obliterated without obliterating all other differences as well. One and the same process of violent reciprocity engulfs the whole. The sacrificial crisis can be defined, therefore, as a crisis of distinctions—that is, a crisis affecting the cultural order. This cultural order is nothing more than a regulated system of distinctions in which the differences among individuals are used to establish their "identity" and their mutual relationships.

In the first chapter the danger threatening the community with the decay of sacrificial practices was portrayed in terms of physical violence, of cyclical vengeance set off by a chain reaction. We now discover more insidious forms of the same evil. When the religious framework of a society starts to totter, it is not exclusively or immediately the physical security of the society that is threatened; rather, the whole cultural foundation of the society is put in jeopardy. The institutions lose their vitality; the protective façade of the society gives way; social values are rapidly eroded, and the whole cultural structure seems on the verge of collapse.

The hidden violence of the sacrificial crisis eventually succeeds in destroying distinctions, and this destruction in turn fuels the renewed violence. In short, it seems that anything that adversely affects the institution of sacrifice will ultimately pose a threat to the very basis of the community, to the principles on which its social harmony and equilibrium depend.

A SINGLE principle is at work in primitive religion and classical tragedy alike, a principle implicit but fundamental. Order, peace, and fecundity depend on cultural distinctions; it is not these distinctions but the loss of them that gives birth to fierce rivalries and sets members of the same family or social group at one another's throats.

Modern society aspires to equality among men and tends instinctively to regard all differences, even those unrelated to the economic or social status of men, as obstacles in the path of human happiness. This modern ideal exerts an obvious influence on ethnological approaches, although more often on the level of technical procedure than that of explicit principle. The permutations of this ideal are complex, rich in potential contradictions, and difficult to characterize briefly. Suffice it to say that an "antidifferential" prejudice often falsifies the ethnological outlook not only on the origins of discord and conflict but also on all religious modes. Although usually implicit, its principles are explicitly set forth in Victor Turner's *The Ritual Process:* "Structural differentiation, both vertical and horizontal, is the foundation of strife and factionalism, and of struggles in dyadic relations between incumbents of positions or rivals for positions."[2] When differences come unhinged they are generally identified as the cause of those rivalries for which they also furnish the stakes. This has not always been their role. As in the case of sacrificial rites, when they no longer serve as a dam against violence, they serve to swell the flood.

In order to rid ourselves of some fashionable intellectual attitudes—useful enough in their place, but not always relevant in dealing with the past—we might turn to Shakespeare, who in the course of the famous speech of Ulysses in *Troilus and Cressida* makes some interesting observations on the interaction of violence and "differences." The point of view of primitive religion and Greek tragedy could not be better summarized than by this speech.

The Greek army has been besieging Troy for a long time and is growing demoralized through want of action. In commenting on their position, Ulysses strays from the particular to a general reflection on the role of "Degree," or distinctions, in human endeavors. "Degree," or *gradus,* is the underlying

[2]Victor Turner, *The Ritual Process* (Chicago, 1969), p. 179. [Au.]

principle of all order, natural and cultural. It permits individuals to find a place for themselves in society; it lends a meaning to things, arranging them in proper sequence within a hierarchy; it defines the objects and moral standards that men alter, manipulate, and transform. The musical metaphor describes that order as a "structure," in the modern sense of the word, a system of chords thrown into disharmony by the sudden intervention of reciprocal violence:

> . . . O when Degree is shaked
> Which is the ladder to all high designs,
> The enterprise is sick! How could communities,
> Degrees in schools, and brotherhoods in cities,
> Peaceful commerce from dividable shores,
> The primogenitive and due of birth,
> Prerogative of age, crowns, sceptres, laurels,
> But by degree, stand in authentic place?
> Take but degree away, untune that string,
> And, hark, what discord follows! Each thing meets
> In mere oppugnancy: the bounded waters
> Should lift their bosoms higher than the shores,
> And make a sop of all this solid globe:
> Strength should be lord of imbecility,
> And the rude son should strike his father dead:
> Force should be right; or rather, right and wrong
> Between whose endless jar justice resides,
> Should lose their names, and so should justice too.

As in Greek tragedy and primitive religion, it is not the differences but the loss of them that gives rise to violence and chaos, that inspires Ulysses' plaint. This loss forces men into a perpetual confrontation, one that strips them of all their distinctive characteristics—in short, of their "identities." Language itself is put in jeopardy. "Each thing meets / In mere oppugnancy:" the adversaries are reduced to indefinite objects, "things" that wantonly collide with each other like loose cargo on the decks of a storm-tossed ship. The metaphor of the floodtide that transforms the earth's surface to a muddy mass is frequently employed by Shakespeare to designate the undifferentiated state of the world that is also portrayed in Genesis and that we have attributed to the sacrificial crisis.

In this situation no one and nothing is spared; coherent thinking collapses and rational activities are abandoned. All associative forms are dissolved or become antagonistic; all values, spiritual or material, perish. Of course, formal education, as represented by academic "degrees," is rendered useless, because its value derives from the now inoperative principle of universal differentiation. To say that this speech merely reflects a Renaissance commonplace, the great chain of being, is unsatisfactory. Who has ever seen a great chain of being collapse?

Ulysses is a career soldier, authoritarian in temper and conservative in inclination. Nevertheless, the order he is committed to defend is secretly acknowledged as arbitrary. The end of distinctions means the triumph of the strong over the weak, the pitting of father against son—the end of all human justice, which is here unexpectedly defined in terms of "differences" among individuals. If perfect equilibrium invariably leads to violence, as in Greek tragedy, it follows that the relative nonviolence guaranteed by human justice must be defined as a sort of imbalance, a difference between "good" and "evil" parallel to the sacrificial difference between "pure" and "impure." The idea of justice as a balanced scale, an exercise in exquisite impartiality, is utterly foreign to this theory, which sees the roots of justice in differences among men and the demise of justice in the elimination of these differences. Whenever the terrible equilibrium of tragedy prevails, all talk of right and wrong is futile. At that point in the conflict one can only say to the combatants: Make friends or pursue your own ruin.

If the two-in-one crisis that we have described is indeed a fundamental reality—if the collapse of the cultural structure of a society leads to reciprocal violence and if this collapse encourages the spread of violence everywhere—then we ought to see signs of this reality outside the restricted realms of Greek tragedy or Shakespearean drama. The closer our contact with primitive societies, the more rapidly these societies tend to lose their distinctive qualities; but this loss is in some cases effected through a *sacrificial crisis*. And in some cases these crises have been directly observed by ethnologists. Scholarly literature on the subject is rather extensive; rarely, however, does a coherent picture emerge. More often than not the accounts are fragmentary, mingled with commentary relating to purely structural matters. A remarkable exception, well worth our attention here, is Jules Henry's *Jungle People,* which deals with the Kaingang Indians of Santa Katarina in Brazil.[3] The author came to live with the Indians shortly after they had been transferred to a reservation, when the consequences of that last and radical change had not yet completely taken hold. He was thus able to observe at first hand, or through the testimony of witnesses, the process I call the sacrificial crisis.

The extreme poverty of the Kaingang culture on a religious as well as a technological level made a strong impression on Henry, who attributed it to the blood feuds (that is, the cyclical vengeance) carried on among close relatives. To describe the effects of this reciprocal violence he instinctively turned to the hyperbolic imagery of the great myths, in particular to the image of plague: "Feuds spread, cleaving the society asunder like a deadly axe, blighting its life like the plague."[4]

These are the very symptoms that we have made bold to identify with the sacrificial crisis, or crisis of distinctions. The Kaingang seem to have abandoned all their old mythology in favor of stories of actual acts of revenge. When discussing internecine murders, "they seem to be fitting together the parts of a machine, the intricate workings of which they know precisely. Their absorbed interest in the history of their own destruction has impressed on their minds with flawless clarity the multitudinous cross-workings of feuds."[5]

Although the Kaingang blood feuds represent the decadence of a system that once enjoyed relative stability, the feuds still retain some remnant of their original "sacrificial" nature. They constitute, in fact, a more forceful, more violent—and therefore less effective—effort to keep a grip on the "good" violence, with all its protective and constraining powers. Indeed, the "bad" violence does not yet penetrate the defenses of those Indians who are said to "travel together"; that is, go out together on hunting expeditions. However, this group is always small in number, and the relative peace that reigns within it is in sharp contrast to the violence that rages triumphantly outside—*between* the different groups.

Within the group there is a spirit of conciliation. The most inflammatory challenges pass unacknowledged; adultery, which provokes an instant and bloody reprisal among members of rival groups, is openly tolerated. As long as violence does not cross a certain threshold of intensity, it remains sacrificial and defines an inner circle of nonviolence essential to the accomplishment of basic social functions—that is, to the survival of the society. Nonetheless, the moment arrives when the inner group is contaminated. As soon as they are installed on a reservation, members of a group tend to turn against one another. They can no longer polarize their aggressions against outside enemies, the "others," the "different men."[6]

The chain of killings finally reaches the heart of the individual group. At this point, the very basis of the social life of the group is challenged. In the case of the Kaingang, outside factors—primarily the Brazilian authorities—intervened assuring the physical survival of the last remnants of the Kaingang while guaranteeing the extinction of their culture.

In acknowledging the existence of an internal process of self-destruction among the Kaingang, we are not attempting to diminish or dismiss the part played by the white man in this tragedy. The problem of Brazilian responsibility would not be resolved even if the new settlers had refrained from using hired assassins to speed up the process of destruction. Indeed, it is worth asking whether the impetus behind the Kaingang's dismemberment of their culture and the inexorable character of their self-destruction were not ultimately due to the pressure of a foreign culture. Even if this were the case, cyclical violence still presents a threat to any society, whether or not it is under pressure from a foreign culture or from any other external interference. The process is basically internal.

Such is Henry's conclusion after contemplating the terrible plight of the Kaingang. He uses the phrase "social suicide," and we must admit that the

[3] Jules Henry, *Jungle People* (New York, 1964). [Au.]

[4] Ibid., p. 50. [Au.]

[5] Ibid., p. 51. [Au.]

[6] The Kaingang use one and the same term to refer to (1) differences of all kinds; (2) men of rival groups, who are always close relatives; (3) Brazilians, the traditional enemy; and (4) the dead and all mythological figures, demonic and divine, generally spoken of as "different things." [Au.]

potentiality for such self-destruction always exists. In the course of history a number of communities doubtless succumbed to their own violent impulses and disappeared without a trace. Even if we have certain reservations about his interpretation of the case under discussion, Henry's conclusions have direct pertinence to numberless groups of human beings whose histories remain unknown. "This group, excellently suited in their physical and psychological endowments to cope with the rigors of their natural environment, were yet unable to withstand the internal forces that were disrupting their society, and having no culturally standardized devices to deal with them, were committing social suicide."[7]

The fear generated by the kill-or-be-killed syndrome, the tendency to "anticipate" violence by lashing out first (akin to our contemporary concept of "preventive war") cannot be explained in purely psychological terms. The notion of a *sacrificial crisis* is designed to dissipate the psychological illusion; even in those instances when Henry borrows the language of psychology, it is clear that he does not share the illusion. In a universe both deprived of any transcendental code of justice and exposed to violence, everybody has reason to fear the worst. The difference between a projection of one's own paranoia and an objective evaluation of circumstances has been worn away.[8]

Once that crucial distinction has vanished, both psychology and sociology falter. The professional observer who distributes good or bad marks to individuals and cultures on the basis of their "normality" and "abnormality" is obliged to make his observations from the particular perspective of someone *who does not run the risk of being killed.* Psychologists and other social scientists ordinarily suppose a peaceable substructure for their subjects; indeed, they tend to take this pacific quality for granted. Yet nothing in their mode of reasoning, which they like to regard as radically "enlightened," solidly based, and free of idealistic nonsense, justifies such an assumption—as Henry's study makes clear: "With a single murder the murderer enters a locked system. He must kill and kill again, he must plan whole massacres lest a single survivor remain to avenge his kin."[9]

Henry encountered some particularly bloodthirsty specimens among the Kaingang, but he also fell in with individual members of the tribe who were peaceable and perspicacious and who sought in vain to free themselves from the machinery of destruction. *"Kaingang murderers are like characters of a Greek tragedy in the grip of a natural law whose processes once started can never be stayed."*[10]

ALTHOUGH they approached the subject more obliquely, the Greek tragedians were concerned, like Jules Henry, with the destruction of a cultural order. The violent reciprocity that engulfs their characters is a manifestation of this destructive process. Our own concern with sacrificial matters shows the vital role the ritualistic crisis—the abolition of all distinctions—plays in the formation of tragedy. In turn, a study of tragedy can clarify the nature of this crisis and those aspects of primitive religion that are inseparably linked to it. For in the final analysis, the sole purpose of religion is to prevent the recurrence of reciprocal violence.

I am inclined, then, to assert that tragedy opens a royal way to the great dilemmas of religious ethnology. Such a stand will no doubt elicit the scorn of "scientific" researchers as well as fervent Hellenophiles, from the defenders of traditional humanism to the disciples of Nietzsche and Heidegger. The scientifically inclined have a tendency to regard literary folk as dubious company, whose society grows increasingly dangerous as their own efforts remain obstinately theoretical. As for the Hellenophiles, they are quick to see blasphemy in any parallel drawn between classical Greece and primitive societies.

It is essential to make it clear, once and for all, that to draw on tragic literature does not mean to relinquish scholarly standards of research; nor does it constitute a purely "esthetic" approach to the

[7] Henry, *Jungle People,* p. 7. [Au.]

[8] "When Yakwa says to me, 'My cousin wants to kill me,' I know he wants to kill his cousin, who slaughtered his pigs for rooting up his corn; and when he says 'Eduardo (the Agent) is angry with me,' I realize that he is angry with the Agent for not having given him a shirt. Yakwa's state of mind is a pale reflection of the Kaingang habit of projecting their own hate and fear into the minds of those whom they hate and fear. Yet one cannot always be sure that it is just a projection, for in these feuds currents of danger may radiate from any number of points of conflict, and there is often good and sufficient cause for any fear" (ibid., p. 54). [Au.]

[9] Ibid., p. 53. [Au.]

[10] Ibid. [Au.]

subject. At the same time we must manage to appease the men of letters who tremble at the thought of applying scientific methods of any kind to literature, convinced as they are that such methods can only lead to facile "reductionism" of the works of art, to sterile analyses that disregard the spirit of the literature. The conflict between the "two cultures," science and literature, rests on a common failure, a negative complicity shared by literary critics and religious specialists. Neither group perceives the underlying principle on which their objects are based. The tragedians seem to have labored in vain to make this principle manifest. They never achieve more than partial success, and their efforts are perpetually undone by the differentiations imposed on their work by literary critics and social scientists.

Ethnologists are not unaware that ritual impurity is linked to the dissolution of distinctions between individuals and institutions.[11] However, they fail to recognize the dangers inherent in this dissolution. As we have noted, the modern mind has difficulty conceiving of violence in terms of a loss of distinctions, or of a loss of distinctions in terms of violence. Tragedy can help to resolve this difficulty if we agree to view the plays from a radical perspective. Tragic drama addresses itself to a burning issue—in fact, to *the* burning issue. The issue is never directly alluded to in the plays, and for good reason, since it has to do with the dissolution by reciprocal violence of those very values and distinctions around which the conflict of the plays supposedly revolves. Because this subject is taboo—and even more than taboo, almost unspeakable in the language devoted to distinctions—literary critics proceed to obscure with their own meticulously differentiated categories the relative lack of difference between antagonists that characterizes a tragic confrontation in classical drama.

The primitive mind, in contrast, has no difficulty imagining an affiliation between violence and nondifferentiation and, indeed, is often obsessed by the possible consequences of such a union. Natural differences are conceived in terms of cultural differences, and vice versa. Where we would view the loss of a distinctive quality as a wholly natural phenomenon having no bearing on human relationships, the primitive man might well view this occurrence with deep dread. Because there is no real difference between the various modes of differentiation, there is in consequence no difference between the manner in which things fail to differ; the disappearance of natural differences can thus bring to mind the dissolution of regulations pertaining to the individual's proper place in society—that is, can instigate a sacrificial crisis.

Once we have grasped this fact, certain religious phenomena never explained by traditional approaches suddenly become intelligible. A brief glance at one of the more spectacular of these phenomena will, I think, serve to demonstrate the usefulness of applying the tragic tradition to religious ethnology.

In some primitive societies twins inspire a particular terror. It is not unusual for one of the twins, and often both, to be put to death. The origin of this terror has long puzzled ethnologists.

Today the enigma is presented as a problem of classification. Two individuals suddenly appear, where only one had been expected; in those societies that permit them to survive, twins often display a single social personality. The problem of classification as defined by structuralism does not justify the death of the twins. The reasons that prompt men to do away with certain of their children are undoubtedly bad reasons, but they are not frivolous ones. Culture is not merely a jigsaw puzzle where the extra pieces are discarded once the picture has been completed. If the problem of classification becomes crucial, that is because its implications are crucial.

Twins invariably share a cultural identity, and they often have a striking physical resemblance to each other. Wherever differences are lacking, violence threatens. Between the biological twins and the sociological twins there arises a confusion that grows more troubled as the question of differences reaches a crisis. It is only natural that twins should awaken fear, for they are harbingers of indiscriminate violence, the greatest menace to primitive societies. As soon as the twins of violence appear they multiply prodigiously, by scissiparity, as it were, and produce a sacrificial crisis. It is essential to prevent the spread of this highly contagious disease. When faced with biological twins the normal reaction of the culture is simply to avoid contagion. The way primitive societies attempt to accomplish this offers a graphic demonstration of the kind of danger they

[11] Cf. Mary Douglas, *Purity and Danger* (London 1966). [Au.]

associate with twins. In societies where their very existence is considered dangerous, the infants are "exposed"; that is, abandoned outside the community under conditions that make their death inevitable. Any act of *direct* physical violence against the anathema is scrupulously avoided. Any such act would only serve to entrap the perpetrators in a vicious circle of violence—the trap "bad" violence sets for the community and baits with the birth of twins.

An inventory of the customs, prescriptions, and interdictions relating to twins in those societies where they are regarded with dread reveals one common concern: the fear of pollution. The divergences from one culture to the next are easily explained in terms of the religious attitudes defined above, which pertain to the strictly empirical—that is, terror-stricken—character of the precautions taken against "bad" violence. In the case of twins, the precautions are misdirected; nevertheless, they become quite intelligible once we recognize the terror that inspires them. Although the menace is somewhat differently perceived from society to society, it is fundamentally the same everywhere, and a challenge with which all religious institutions are obliged to cope.

The Nyakyusa maintain that the parents of twins are contaminated by "bad" violence, and there is a certain logic about that notion, since the parents are, after all, responsible for engendering the twins. In reference to the twins the parents are designated by a term that is applied to all threatening individuals, all monstrous or terrifying creatures. In order to prevent the spread of pollution the parents are required to isolate themselves and submit to rites of purification; only then are they allowed to rejoin the community.[12]

It is not unreasonable to believe that the relatives and close friends of the twins' parents, as well as other immediate neighbors, are those most directly exposed to the infection. "Bad" violence is by definition a force that works on various levels—physical, familial, social—and spreads from one to the other.

Twins are impure in the same way that a warrior steeped in carnage is impure, or an incestuous couple, or a menstruating woman. All forms of violence lead back to violence. We overlook this fact because the primitive concept of a link between the loss of distinctions and violence is strange to us; but we need only consider the calamities primitive people associate with twins to perceive the logic of this concept. Deadly epidemics can result from contact with twins, as can mysterious illnesses that cause sterility in women and animals. Even more significant to us is the role of twins in provoking discord among neighbors, a fatal collapse of ritual, the transgression of interdictions—in short, their part in instigating a sacrificial crisis.

As we have seen, the sacred embraces all those forces that threaten to harm man or trouble his peace. Natural forces and sickness are not distinguished from the threat of a violent disintegration of the community. Although man-made violence plays a dominant role in the dialectics of the sacred and is never completely omitted from the warnings issued by religion, it tends to be relegated to the background and treated as if it emanated from outside man. One might say that it has been deliberately hidden away almost out of sight behind forces that are genuinely exterior to man.

Behind the image of twins lurks the baleful aspect of the sacred, perceived as a disparate but formidably unified force. The sacrificial crisis can be viewed as a general offensive of violence directed against the community, and there is reason to fear that the birth of twins might herald this crisis.

In the primitive societies where twins are not killed they often enjoy a privileged position. This reversal corresponds to the attitudes we have noted in regard to menstrual blood. Any phenomenon linked to impure violence is capable of being inverted and rendered beneficent; but this can take place only within the immutable and rigorous framework of ritual practice. The purifying and pacifying aspects of violence take precedence over its destructive aspects. The apparition of twins, then, if properly handled, may in certain societies be seen to presage good events, not bad ones.

If the statements above are valid, two brothers need not be twins for their resemblance to arouse anxiety. We can assume almost a priori that in some societies the mere fact of familial similarity is cause for alarm. The verification of such a hypothesis would, I believe, confirm the inadequacy of previous theories regarding twins. If the twin phobia can

[12] Monica Wilson, *Rituals of Kinship among the Nyakyusa* (Oxford, 1957). [Au.]

be extended to other members of the family it can no longer be explained solely in terms of "a problem of classification." Twins could no longer be said to cause alarm because two individuals had turned up where only one was expected; their *physical resemblance* would now be perceived as the disruptive factor.

At this point we may well wonder how something so commonplace as the resemblance between siblings can be officially proscribed without causing enormous inconvenience, not to say total chaos. After all, a community cannot categorize a majority of its inhabitants as probationary criminals without creating an intolerable situation. Nevertheless, the phobia of resemblance is a fact. Malinowski's *The Father in Primitive Psychology* offers formal proof. The study demonstrates how the phobia can perpetuate itself without disastrous consequences. The ingenuity of man, or rather of his cultural systems, copes with the problem by categorically denying the existence of the dreaded phenomenon, or even its possibility:

> In a matrilineal society, as in the Trobriands, where all maternal relatives are considered to be of the "same body," and the father to be a "stranger," we would naturally expect and have no doubt that the facial and bodily similarity would be traced to the mother's family alone. The contrary is the case, and this is affirmed with an extremely strong social emphasis. Not only is it a household dogma, so to speak, that a child never resembles its mother, any of its brothers or sisters, or any of its maternal kinsmen, but it is extremely bad form and a great offence to hint at any such similarity. . . .
>
> I was introduced to this rule of *savoir vivre* in the usual way by making a *faux pas*. One of my bodyguards in Omarakana, named Moradeda, was endowed with a peculiar cast of features which had struck me at first sight. . . . One day I was struck by the appearance of an exact counterpart to Moradeda and asked his name and whereabouts. When I was told that he was my friend's elder brother, living in a distant village, I exclaimed: "Ah, truly! I asked about you because your face is alike—alike to that of Moradeda." There came such a hush over all the assembly that I noticed it at once. The man turned round and left us, while part of the company present, after looking away in a manner half-embarrassed, half-offended, soon dispersed. I was then told by my confidential informants that I had committed a breach of custom, that I had perpetrated what is called *"taputaki migila,"* a technical expression referring only to this act, which might be translated, "to-defile-by-comparing-to-a-kinsman-his-face." What astonished me in this discussion was, that in spite of the striking resemblance between the two brothers, my informants refused to admit it. In fact, they treated the question as if no one could possibly ever resemble his brother, or, for the matter of that, any maternal kinsman. I made my informants quite angry and displeased with me by arguing the point.
>
> This incident taught me never to hint at such a resemblance in the presence of the people concerned. But I thrashed the matter out well with many natives in subsequent general conversations. I found that every one in the Trobriands will, in the teeth of all the evidence, deny stoutly that similarity can exist between matrilineal kinsmen. You simply irritate and insult a Trobriander if you point to striking instances, exactly as you irritate your next-door neighbor in our own society if you bring before him a glaring truth which contradicts some of his cherished opinions, political, religious, or moral, or which is still worse, runs counter to his personal interests.[13]

Negation here serves as affirmation. There would be nothing untoward in mentioning resemblances if they were not a matter of great importance. To accuse two close relatives of resembling one another is to assert that they are a menace to the community, the carriers of an infectious disease. Malinowski tells us further that the accusation is a traditional form of insult among the Trobriands, the most wounding at their disposal. His account inspires confidence precisely because he presents the phenomenon as a complete enigma, proposing no interpretation of his own.

On the other hand, the Trobriands not only tolerate references to the resemblance between fathers

[13] Bronislaw Malinowski, *The Father in Primitive Psychology* (New York, 1966), pp. 88–91. [Au.]

and children but virtually demand its acknowledgment. This society formally denies the father's role in the reproductive process; between father and children, then, no parental link is said to exist.

Malinowski's description demonstrates that a paternal resemblance is perceived by the Trobriands, paradoxically enough, *in terms of differences.* It is the father who serves to differentiate the children from one another. He is literally the bearer of a difference, among whose characteristics we recognize the phallic element so dear to psychoanalysts. Because the father sleeps with the mother, because he is so often near her, he is said to "mold the face of the child." Malinowski informs us that the word *kuli*—"coagulate," "mold," "leave an impression"—recurred constantly in the discussions of resemblances. The father evidently represents form, the mother matter. In this capacity the father makes the children different from their mother and from one another. That explains why the children resemble him, and why *a resemblance to the father, common to all children, does not imply a resemblance of one child to another:* "It was often pointed out to me how strongly one or the other of the sons of To'uluwa, chief of Omarakana, resembled his father. . . . Whenever I pointed out that this similarity to the father implied similarity among each other, such a heresy was indignantly repudiated."[14]

At this point it seems appropriate to juxtapose the basic mythical theme of *enemy brothers* with the phobia concerning twins and other fraternal resemblances. Clyde Kluckhohn asserts that the most common of all mythical conflicts is the struggle between brothers, which generally ends in fratricide. In some regions of black Africa the mythical protagonists are brothers "born in immediate sequence."[15] If I understand this phrase correctly, it includes twins but is not strictly limited to them. The continuity between the theme of twins and the fraternal motif in general is not peculiar to the Trobriand Islands.

Even when the brothers are not twins, the difference between them is less than that between all other degrees of relations. They share the same mother, father, gender; in most instances they occupy the same position in respect to other relatives, both close and distant. Brothers seem to have more rights, duties, and functions in common than other family members. Twins are in a sense reinforced brothers whose final objective difference, that of age, has been removed; it is virtually impossible to distinguish between them.

We instinctively tend to regard the fraternal relationship as an affectionate one; yet the mythological, historical, and literary examples that spring to mind tell a different story: Cain and Abel, Jacob and Esau, Eteocles and Polyneices, Romulus and Remus, Richard the Lion-Hearted and John Lackland. The proliferation of enemy brothers in Greek myth and in dramatic adaptations of myth implies the continual presence of a sacrificial crisis, repeatedly alluded to in the same symbolic terms. The fraternal theme is no less "contagious" qua theme for being buried deep in the text than is the malevolent violence that accompanies it. In fact, the theme itself is a form of violence.

When Polyneices departs from Thebes, leaving his brother to take his turn on the throne, he carries the fraternal conflict with him as an integral part of his being. Everywhere he goes he literally draws from the earth the brother who seems expressly designed to thwart him, just as Cadmus sowed the dragon's teeth and brought forth a harvest of fully armed warriors ready to do battle with one another.

An oracle had announced to Adrastus that his two daughters would marry a lion and a wild boar respectively—animals very different in appearance, but of equally violent temper. In Euripides' *Supplices* Adastrus recounts how he came upon his future sons-in-law Polyneices and Tydeus, both poverty-stricken exiles who were fighting for shelter outside his door:

> ADRASTUS: The two exiles came to my door one night.
> THESEUS: Which two? What were their names?
> ADRASTUS: Tydeus and Polyneices. And each fell on the other's throat.
> THESEUS: And you recognized them as the beasts for whom your daughters were destined?
> ADRASTUS: They looked exactly like two wild beasts.
> THESEUS: How had they wandered so far from their homeland?
> ADRASTUS: Tydeus was banished for having killed a kinsman.

[14] Ibid., p. 92. [Au.]

[15] Clyde Kluckhohn, "Recurrent Themes in Myths and Mythmaking," in *Myth and Mythmaking,* ed. Henry A. Murray (Boston, 1968), p. 52. [Au.]

Theseus: And Oedipus's son, why had he left Thebes?
Adrastus: A father's curse: that he should kill his brother.

The ferocity of the two young men, the symmetry of their family situations, and their forthcoming marriages to two sisters—reconstituting, as it were, a properly "fraternal" relationship—all conspire to recreate the Polyneices / Eteocles relationship and, indeed, all other instances of fraternal rivalry.

Once our attention has been drawn to the "distinctive" traits of fraternal strife we seem to rediscover them, recurring singly or in clusters, throughout classical myth and tragedy. In addition to true brothers, such as Eteocles and Polyneices, we find brothers-in-law (that is, quasi-brothers), like Polyneices and Tydeus, Oedipus and Creon; or other close relatives of the same generation, like the first cousins Pentheus and Dionysus. Ultimately, the insufficient difference in the family relationships serves to symbolize the dissolution of family distinctions; in other words, it *desymbolizes.* Such relationships thus finally contribute to the symmetry of conflicts that is concealed in myth, but vigorously proclaimed in tragedy, which betrays this hidden process simply by *representing* the mythological material on stage.

Nothing can be further from the truth than the statement that tragedy lacks universality because it is totally preoccupied with family distinctions. It is the elimination of these distinctions that leads directly to fraternal strife and to the religious phobia regarding twins. The two themes are essentially the same; however, there is a shade of difference between them that deserves our attention.

Twins offer a symbolic representation, sometimes remarkably eloquent, of the symmetrical conflict and identity crisis that characterize the sacrificial crisis. But the resemblance is entirely accidental. There is no real connection between biological and sociological twins; twins are no more predisposed to violence than any other men—or, at least, any other brothers. There is something decidedly arbitrary about the relationship between sacrificial crises and the essential quality of twinship, which is not of the same order of arbitrariness as that of the linguistic sign, since the representative element is always present. Ultimately, the classic definition of the symbol seems to apply to the correspondence between twins and the sacrificial crisis.

In the case of fraternal strife the representative element becomes blurred. Fraternal relationships normally take form within the framework of the family, where differences, no matter how small, are readily recognized and acknowledged. In passing from twins to the general category of brothers, we lose something on the level of symbolic representation, but gain something on that of social reality; in fact, the shift puts our feet securely on the ground. Because in most societies the fraternal relationship implies only a minimum of differences, it obviously constitutes a vulnerable point in a system structured on differences, a point dangerously exposed to the onset of a sacrificial crisis. The fear of twins, qua twins, is clearly mythic and has little basis in reality, but one can hardly say the same for the thematic concern with fraternal rivalry. It is not only in myths that brothers are simultaneously drawn together and driven apart by something they both ardently desire and which they will not or cannot share—a throne, a woman or, in more general terms, a paternal heritage.

Rival brothers, unlike twins, straddle both forms of "desymbolization," the purely symbolic and the concrete variety—the variety that constitutes the true sacrificial crisis. In some African monarchies the death of the king precipitates a struggle for the succession and transforms the king's sons into *fraternal enemies.* It is difficult if not impossible to determine to what extent this struggle is symbolic, a matter of ritual, and to what extent it is a real historical event, pregnant with unforeseen consequences. In other words, it is hard to know whether one is dealing with a real-life struggle or with ritual mimicry whose cathartic effects are believed to ward off the impending crisis it imitates so faithfully.

If we have difficulty grasping what twins, or even rival brothers, represent, it is because we do not consider their presence a genuine threat. We cannot imagine how the mere appearance of a pair of twins or rival brothers can convey the entire course of sacrificial crisis; how the pair can *epitomize the entire crisis,* in terms not of formal rhetoric but of real violence. Any violent effacement of differences, even if initially restricted to a single pair of twins, reaches out to destroy a whole society.

We cannot be held entirely responsible for our lack of comprehension. None of the mythological themes can, by itself, point to the truth concerning the sacrificial crisis. In the case of twins, symmetry and identity are represented in extraordinarily explicit terms, nondifference is present in concrete, literal form, but this form is itself so exceptional as to constitute a new difference. Thus the *representation* of nondifference ultimately becomes the very exemplar of difference, a classic monstrosity that plays a vital role in sacred ritual.

In the case of enemy brothers the domestic context in which they operate brings us back into contact with reality: we are no longer dealing with outlandish phenomena that provoke either amusement or dread. But the very concreteness of the conflict tends to efface its symbolic significance; to lend it the character of a real historical event. With enemy brothers, as with twins, the sign cannot fail to betray the thing signified because that "thing" is the destruction of all signification. It is violent reciprocity, on the rampage everywhere, that truly destroys differences; yet this process can never be fully signified. Either a degree of difference survives and we remain within the framework of a cultural order, surrounded by meanings that ought to have been wiped out. Or perhaps all differences have indeed been effaced, but the nondifference immediately appears as a new and outlandish difference, a monstrosity such as twins, for example.

Being made up of differences, language finds it almost impossible to express undifferentiation directly. Whatever it may say on the subject, language invariably says at once too much and too little, even in such concise statements as "Each thing meets / In mere oppugnancy" or "sound and fury, / Signifying nothing."

No matter how diligently language attempts to catch hold of it, the reality of the sacrificial crisis invariably slips through its grasp. It invites anecdotal history on the one hand, and on the other, a visitation of monsters and grotesques. Mythology succumbs to the latter; tragedy is constantly threatened by the former.

Monstrosities recur throughout mythology. From this we can only conclude that myths make constant reference to the sacrificial crisis, but do so only in order to disguise the issue. Myths are the retrospective transfiguration of sacrificial crises, the reinterpretation of these crises in the light of the cultural order that has arisen from them.

The traces of sacrificial crisis are less distinct in myth than in tragedy. Or rather, tragedy is by its very nature a partial deciphering of mythological motifs. The poet brings the sacrificial crisis back to life; he pieces together the scattered fragments of reciprocity and balances elements thrown out of kilter in the process of being "mythologized." He whistles up a storm of violent reciprocity, and differences are swept away in this storm just as they were previously dissolved in the real crisis that must have generated the mythological transfiguration.

Tragedy envelops all human relationships in a single tragic antagonism. It does not differentiate between the fraternal conflict of Eteocles and Polyneices, the father-son conflict of *Alcestis* or *Oedipus the King,* the conflict between men who share no ancestral ties, such as Oedipus and Tiresias. The rivalry of the two prophets is indistinguishable from the rivalry between brothers. Tragedy tends to restore violence to mythological themes. It in part fulfills the dire forebodings primitive men experience at the sight of twins. It spreads the pollution abroad and multiplies the mirror images of violence.

Tragedy has a particular affinity for myth, but that does not mean it takes the same course. The term *desymbolism* is more appropriate to tragedy than is *symbolism.* It is because most of the symbols of the sacrificial crisis—in particular the symbol of the enemy brother—lend themselves so readily to *both* the tragic and the ritual situations that tragedy has been able to operate, at least to some extent, within and also contrary to mythological patterns. I have already noted this dual aspect of symbolic reference in connection with the monarchic succession in certain African states; it is virtually impossible to determine whether the fraternal rivalry that occurs in that connection is ritualistic or part of the "tragedy of history."

Symbolized reality becomes, paradoxically, the loss of all symbolism; the loss of differences is necessarily betrayed by the differentiated expression of language. The process is a peculiar one, utterly foreign to our usual notions of symbolism. Only a close reading of tragedy, a radically "symmetrical" reading, will help us to understand the phenomenon, to penetrate to the source of tragic inspiration. If the tragic poet touches upon the violent reciprocity underlying all myths, it is because he perceives these myths in a context of weakening distinctions and growing violence. His work is inseparable, then, from a new sacrificial crisis, the one referred to at the opening of this chapter.

To know violence is to experience it. Tragedy is therefore directly linked to violence; it is a child of the sacrificial crisis. The relationship between tragedy and myth as it is now taking shape can perhaps be understood more easily if we consider an analogous relationship, that of the Old Testament prophets to the Pentateuchal texts they cite as exemplars. For example, we find in Jeremiah (9:3–5):

> Beware a brother,
> for every brother plays the role of Jacob,
> and every friend spreads scandal.
> One deceives the other. . . .
> Fraud upon fraud, deceit upon deceit.

The concept of enemy brothers previously mentioned in connection with Jacob is precisely the same as the concept governing Euripides' version of the Eteocles/Polyneices story. It is the symmetry of the conflict that defines the fraternal relationship, and this symmetry, originally limited to a few tragic heroes, now reaches out to include the entire community. It loses its particularized quality and acquires a predominantly social meaning. The allusion to Jacob is subordinated to the main design, which is the description of the sacrificial crisis; violence engulfs the whole society, all its members confronting one another as enemy brothers. Specific stylistic effects underline the symmetry and mirror the violent reciprocity: "One deceives the other. . . . Fraud upon fraud, deceit upon deceit."

The books of the Old Testament are rooted in sacrificial crises, each distinct from the other and separated by long intervals of time, but analogous in at least some respects. The earlier crises are reinterpreted in the light of the later ones. And the experience of previous crises is of great value in coping with subsequent ones. Jeremiah's treatment of the historical figure of Jacob seems to bear this out. Contact has been established between the time of Genesis and the crisis of the sixth century; as a result, light is shed on both eras. Like tragedy, the prophetic act constitutes a return to violent reciprocity; so it, too, levels all mythological distinctions and does so even more effectively than tragedy. However, this leads us to a subject that deserves separate consideration, a subject I will turn to in another work.

Although the source of inspiration emerges more dimly and indirectly in tragedy than in biblical examples, the pattern is the same. The passage quoted above might well be taken for a fragment of a tragic drama drawn from the Book of Genesis—a tragedy of enemy brothers, perhaps Jacob and Esau.

Tragic and prophetic inspiration do not draw strength from historical or philological sources but from a direct intuitive grasp of the role played by violence in the cultural order and in disorder as well, in mythology and in the sacrificial crisis. England, in the throes of religious upheaval, provided Shakespeare with such an inspiration for his *Troilus and Cressida*. There is no reason to believe that advances in scholarship will, by the process of continuous enrichment so dear to the positivist cause, increase our understanding of the great tragedies; for however real and valuable this process may be, it fails to touch on the true tragic spirit. This spirit, never widespread even in periods of crisis, vanishes without a trace during periods of cultural stability.

At a given moment the violent effacement of distinctions ceases and the process begins to reverse itself, giving way to mythical elaboration. Mythical elaboration gives way in turn to the inverse operation of tragic inspiration. What sets off these metamorphoses? What mechanism governs the shift from cultural order to disorder? This is the question that concerns us; and this question elicits yet another, which touches on the final stages of the sacrificial crisis. Once violence has penetrated a community it engages in an orgy of self-propagation. There appears to be no way of bringing the reprisals to a halt before the community has been annihilated.

If there are really such events as sacrificial crises, some sort of braking mechanism, an automatic control that goes into effect before everything is destroyed, must be built into them. In the final stages of a sacrificial crisis the very viability of human society is put in question. Our task is to discover what these final stages involve and what makes them possible. It is likely that they must serve as a point of departure for both ritual and myth. Everything we can learn about this phase of the crisis, then, will enhance our knowledge of the nature of ritual and myth.

To find an answer to these questions let us address ourselves to one myth in particular, the story of Oedipus. Our previous investigations gave us reason to believe that the most useful approach lay by way of tragedy. We will turn our attention, therefore, to Sophocles' *Oedipus the King*.

Gilles Deleuze

b. 1925

and

Felix Guattari

b. 1936

THE collaboration of Gilles Deleuze and Felix Guattari, a philosopher and a psychoanalyst, both immediately and pervasively concerned with political praxis, conveys the affect of inevitability, as if it were the mutual fate of philosophy and psychoanalysis to meet on the field of social and political action. Their *Anti-Oedipus* is, however, unmistakably marked as a work of the late 1960s and early 1970s, of the period of Vietnam, wars of national liberation, indeed, of an ethic of liberation tried and still being tested in all the registers of social and political action: racial, sexual, economic, political.

Part of the difficulty of choosing representative excerpts from this work lies in the exuberance—and exorbitance—of its argument. In Freudian terms, one might say the argument is "polymorphously perverse," at least in its rejection of repression as a presumably civilizing force and its seemingly infinite appetite for examples and illustrations drawn from every arena of experience. Like R. D. Laing (in *The Politics of Experience*), Deleuze and Guattari are trying not just to work out a theory but to identify a syndrome and describe a possible praxis that always bears in mind that healing should be a response to suffering, not merely an occasion for discourse. From this point of view, when Deleuze and Guattari are outrageous, it is because they are outraged at our seemingly infinite capacity to do violence in the name of noble principles. Unlike Laing, however, their concern is not clinical, and they do have a theory to work out, a theory that challenges deeply rooted presuppositions about society and politics, the psyche and the "self," knowledge and representation. For Deleuze and Guattari, "Oedipus" represents the central dogma of psychoanalysis, a self determined by the triangle of the nuclear family ("daddy-mommy-me") and, by extension, reflecting the nuclear (and molecular) structure of capitalism.

The "wars of liberation" that one might associate with Third World nations, institutional racism, and sexual discrimination have theoretical correlates, which Deleuze and Guattari attempt to educe. The period of Vietnam, for example, coincided with the height of critical revision in political theory, as in *Althusser*'s analysis of ideology or the dissemination of critical theory from the Frankfurt School (see, for example, *Horkheimer, Adorno,* and *Benjamin*), just as it was a period of intense revision in psychoanalysis, principally in the work of *Jacques Lacan,* and a period of radical criticism in history, language theory, and philosophy, particularly in the work of *Michel Foucault, Noam Chomsky,* and *Jacques Derrida.* It is not surprising that *Anti-Oedipus* is an argument that resembles an "event," since it happens, as it were, where three roads meet: political theory, psychoanalytic theory, and the theory of the sign. To pursue the metaphor, they do not find, at that triple crossroad, a violent Laius with a goad but blind Oedipus, a figure for an idea of the "self" that is guilty of incest only in the sense that it turns against its own flesh, a self-generated tyrant, at once the object and the agent of revulsion and desire.

These are not, however, the terms in which the analysis proceeds. Deleuze and Guattari start from a model of desire that appropriates from Marx the idea of production, to undo the traditional model of desire since Plato (but particularly as one finds it in Freud), which treats desire as privation or "lack." The central idea in *Anti-Oedipus* is that desire is a process, always involved in production, and we err fundamentally when we make desire self-reflexive, as if it belonged to the psychic economy of the individual alone. The "self" is already the product of repression and denial, not a good to be attained; and desire, according to Deleuze and Guattari, is reciprocal or dialectical and always binary. Instead of a Freudian ego or a Cartesian self, they posit "desiring-machines," not metaphorically intended: "An organ-machine is plugged into an energy-source machine: the one produces a flow that the other interrupts. The breast is a machine that produces milk, and the mouth a machine coupled to it."

Like Blake's notion of the "prolific" and the "devourer," the "desiring-machines" of Deleuze and Guattari are involved in all human processes. But in a gesture that recalls Nietzsche, they energize their own arguments by reversing the semantic field of normative terms. Most notably, the schizophrenic is not taken as the apogee of the abnormal but as "the universal producer" who is *not* neurotic precisely as he has ceased to believe in the "ego," presumed to be the site of the disease. While such a strategy runs the risk of ignoring pain to make a point, the critical point is that neurosis, as a symptom of the Freudian, "Oedipal" self, mobilizes repression in the ontology of representation, as it appears from a view of desire as lack.

As Deleuze and Guattari put it, "If desire is the lack of the real object, its very nature as a real entity depends on an 'essence of lack' that produces the fantasized object." From this view, the idea of production is perverted into representations always taken to be fantasy or illusion, so that what is represented is always what is absent. Like the dog chasing his own tail, the "self" can never be satisfied, since representation has usurped the place of a directly material, bodily process of the "desiring-machine." In this respect, their analysis of desire, or rather their diagnosis of alienated desire, mirrors Marx's analysis of alienated labor in *Capital.*

The two selections reprinted below are the conclusion to the first chapter, "The Desiring Machines," and the middle section of the last chapter, "Introduction to Schizoanalysis." The concluding sections of *Anti-Oedipus* present the "positive tasks" of "schizoanalysis," to facilitate the identification of the "desiring-machines" that may actually operate first for individuals, second in the social field, and finally in historical and political action.

Michel Foucault, writing in praise of Deleuze's earlier work, ventured the opinion that "perhaps one day, this century will be known as Deleuzian." Foucault's enthusiasm for that earlier work (like his praise of *Anti-Oedipus* in his preface to the English translation) seems, even at the distance of a decade, a gesture of enthusiasm and a recognition of critical problems for which no one has adequate solutions. Deleuze and Guattari themselves characterize their method as resembling delirium, an observation that loses some of its ironic bite with passing time. Be that as it may, there can be little question that the problems engaged in *Anti-Oedipus,* at that intersection of psychoanalysis, politics, and representation, comprise an important evocation of underlying critical problems central to the period represented by this anthology.

In addition to *Anti-Oedipus: Capitalism and Psychoanalysis* (1972, trans. 1977), Deleuze has collaborated with Guattari on two other studies, *Kafka: Pour une littéraire mineure* (1975) and *Rhizôme* (1976). Other works by Deleuze available in English translation include *Proust and Signs* (1964; revised edition, 1970, trans. 1972) and "The Schizophrenic and Language: Surface and Depth in Lewis Carroll and Antonin Artaud," in *Textual Strategies: Perspectives in Post-Structuralist Criticism,* ed. Josué Harari. See also Michel Foucault's essay "Theatrum Philosophicum" in *Language, Counter-Memory, Practice* (1977), and an interview with Guattari in *Diacritics: A Review of Contemporary Criticism* (Fall 1974).

FROM

ANTI-OEDIPUS: CAPITALISM AND PSYCHOANALYSIS

The Whole and Its Parts [1]

In desiring-machines everything functions at the same time, but amid hiatuses and ruptures, breakdowns and failures, stalling and short circuits, distances and fragmentations, within a sum that never succeeds in bringing its various parts together so as to form a whole. That is because the breaks in the process are productive, and are reassemblies in and of themselves. Disjunctions, by the very fact that they are disjunctions, are inclusive. Even consumptions are transitions, processes of becoming, and returns. Maurice Blanchot[2] has found a way to pose the problem in the most rigorous terms, at the level of the literary machine: how to produce, how to think about fragments whose sole relationship is sheer difference—fragments that are related to one another only in that each of them is different—without having recourse either to any sort of original totality (not even one that has been lost), or to a subsequent totality that may not yet have come about?[3] It is only the category of multiplicity, used as a substantive and going beyond both the One

The selections reprinted here are from Deleuze and Guattari, ANTI-OEDIPUS: CAPITALISM AND PSYCHOANALYSIS, trans. Helen R. Lane, Robert Hurley, and Mark Seem, chaps. 1 and 4, only parts of which are included.

[1] This is sec. 6 from chap. 1. In earlier sections, the authors have defined "desiring-machines" as binary processes, in which "desire" is not associated with the absence or lack of an object, but with a process of production. See headnote. [Eds.]

[2] See *Blanchot.* [Eds.]

[3] Maurice Blanchot, *L'entretien infini* (Paris: Gallimard, 1969), pp. 451–52. [Au.]

and the many, beyond the predicative relation of the One and the many, that can account for desiring-production: desiring-production is pure multiplicity, that is to say, an affirmation that is irreducible to any sort of unity.

We live today in the age of partial objects, bricks that have been shattered to bits, and leftovers. We no longer believe in the myth of the existence of fragments that, like pieces of an antique statue, are merely waiting for the last one to be turned up, so that they may all be glued back together to create a unity that is precisely the same as the original unity. We no longer believe in a primordial totality that once existed, or in a final totality that awaits us at some future date. We no longer believe in the dull gray outlines of a dreary, colorless dialectic of evolution, aimed at forming a harmonious whole out of heterogeneous bits by rounding off their rough edges. We believe only in totalities that are peripheral. And if we discover such a totality alongside various separate parts, it is a whole *of* these particular parts but does not totalize them; it is a unity *of* all of these particular parts but does not unify them; rather, it is added to them as a new part fabricated separately.

"It comes into being, but applying this time to the whole as some inspired fragment composed separately. . . ." So Proust writes of the unity of Balzac's creation, though his remark is also an apt description of his own *oeuvre*.[4] In the literary machine that Proust's *In Search of Lost Time* constitutes, we are struck by the fact that all the parts are produced as asymmetrical sections, paths that suddenly come to an end, hermetically sealed boxes, noncommunicating vessels, watertight compartments, in which there are gaps even between things that are contiguous, gaps that are affirmations, pieces of a puzzle belonging not to any one puzzle but to many, pieces assembled by forcing them into a certain place where they may or may not belong, their unmatched edges violently bent out of shape, forcibly made to fit together, to interlock, with a number of pieces always left over. It is a schizoid work par excellence: it is almost as though the author's guilt, his confessions of guilt are merely a sort of joke. (In Kleinian terms, it might be said that the depressive position is only a cover-up for a more deeply rooted schizoid attitude.) For the rigors of the law are only an apparent expression of the protest of the One, whereas their real object is the absolution of fragmented universes, in which the law never unites anything in a single Whole, but on the contrary measures and maps out the divergences, the dispersions, the exploding into fragments of something that is innocent precisely because its source is madness. This is why in Proust's work the apparent theme of guilt is tightly interwoven with a completely different theme totally contradicting it; the plantlike innocence that results from the total compartmentalization of the sexes, both in Charlus's encounters and in Albertine's slumber, where flowers blossom in profusion and the utter innocence of madness is revealed, whether it be the patent madness of Charlus or the supposed madness of Albertine.

Hence Proust maintained that the Whole itself is a product, produced as nothing more than a part alongside other parts, which it neither unifies nor totalizes, though it has an effect on these other parts simply because it establishes aberrant paths of communication between noncommunicating vessels, transverse unities between elements that retain all their differences within their own particular boundaries. Thus in the trip on the train in *In Search of Lost Time*, there is never a totality of what is seen nor a unity of the points of view, except along the transversal that the frantic passenger traces from one window to the other, "in order to draw together, in order to reweave intermittent and opposite fragments." This drawing together, this reweaving is what Joyce called re-embodying. The body without organs is produced as a whole, but in its own particular place within the process of production, alongside the parts that it neither unifies nor totalizes. And when it operates on them, when it turns back upon them (*se rabat sur elles*), it brings about transverse communications, transfinite summarizations, polyvocal and transcursive inscriptions on its own surface, on which the functional breaks of partial objects are continually intersected by breaks in the signifying chains, and by breaks effected by a subject that uses them as reference points in order to locate itself. The whole not only coexists with all the parts; it is contiguous to them, it exists as a product that is produced

[4] All quotes from Proust are translated by Richard Howard. We also retain the title *In Search of Lost Time*, used by Richard Howard in his translation of Gilles Deleuze, *Proust and Signs* (New York: Braziller, 1972), p. 1. This title stresses the notion of search and voyage. [Tr.]

apart from them and yet at the same time is related to them. Geneticists have noted the same phenomenon in the particular language of their science: ". . . amino acids are assimilated individually into the cell, and then are arranged in the proper sequence by a mechanism analogous to a template onto which the distinctive side chain of each acid keys into its proper position."[5] As a general rule, the problem of the relationships between parts and the whole continues to be rather awkwardly formulated by classic mechanism and vitalism, so long as the whole is considered as a totality derived from the parts, or as an original totality from which the parts emanate, or as a dialectical totalization. Neither mechanism nor vitalism has really understood the nature of desiring-machines, nor the twofold need to consider the role of production in desire and the role of desire in mechanics.

There is no sort of evolution of drives that would cause these drives and their objects to progress in the direction of an integrated whole, any more than there is an original totality from which they can be derived. Melanie Klein was responsible for the marvelous discovery of partial objects, that world of explosions, rotations, vibrations. But how can we explain the fact that she has nonetheless failed to grasp the logic of these objects? It is doubtless because, first of all, she conceives of them as fantasies and judges them from the point of view of consumption, rather than regarding them as genuine production. She explains them in terms of causal mechanisms (introjection and projection, for instance), of mechanisms that produce certain effects (gratification and frustration), and of mechanisms of expression (good or bad)—an approach that forces her to adopt an idealist conception of the partial object. She does not relate these partial objects to a real process of production—of the sort carried out by desiring-machines, for instance. In the second place, she cannot rid herself of the notion that schizoparanoid partial objects are related to a whole, either to an original whole that has existed earlier in a primary phase, or to a whole that will eventually appear in a final depressive stage (the complete Object). Partial objects hence appear to her to be derived from (*prélevés sur*) global persons; not only are they destined to play a role in totalities aimed at integrating the ego, the object, and drives later in life, but they also constitute the original type of object relation between the ego, the mother, and the father. And in the final analysis that is where the crux of the matter lies. Partial objects unquestionably have a sufficient charge in and of themselves to blow up all of Oedipus and totally demolish its ridiculous claim to represent the unconscious, to triangulate the unconscious, to encompass the entire production of desire. The question that thus arises here is not at all that of the relative importance of what might be called the *pre-oedipal* in relation to Oedipus itself, since "pre-oedipal" still has a developmental or structural relationship to Oedipus. The question, rather, is that of the absolutely *anoedipal* nature of the production of desire. But because Melanie Klein insists on considering desire from the point of view of the whole, of global persons, and of complete objects—and also, perhaps, because she is eager to avoid any sort of contretemps with the International Psycho-Analytic Association that bears above its door the inscription "Let no one enter here who does not believe in Oedipus"—she does not make use of partial objects to shatter the iron collar of Oedipus; on the contrary, she uses them—or makes a pretense of using them—to water Oedipus down, to miniaturize it, to find it everywhere, to extend it to the very earliest years of life.

If we here choose the example of the analyst least prone to see everything in terms of Oedipus, we do so only in order to demonstrate what a forcing was necessary for her to make Oedipus the sole measure of desiring-production. And naturally this is all the more true in the case of run-of-the-mill practitioners who no longer have the slightest notion of what the psychoanalytic "movement" is all about. It is no longer a question of suggestion, but of sheer terrorism. Melanie Klein herself writes: "The first time Dick came to me . . . he manifested no sort of affect when his nurse handed him over to me. When I showed him the toys I had put ready, he looked at them without the faintest interest. I took a big train and put it beside a smaller one *and called them* 'Daddy-train' and 'Dick-train.' Thereupon he picked up the train I called 'Dick' and made it roll to the window and said 'Station.' *I explained:* 'The station is mummy; Dick is going into mummy.' He left the train, ran into the space between the outer and inner doors of the room, shutting himself in, say-

[5] J. H. Rush, *The Dawn of Life* (Garden City, N.Y.: Hanover House, 1957), p. 148. [Au.]

ing 'dark,' and ran out again directly. He went through this performance several times. *I explained to him:* 'It is dark inside mummy. Dick is inside dark mummy.' Meantime he picked up the train again, but soon ran back into the space between the doors. While I was saying that he was going into dark mummy, he said twice in a questioning way: 'Nurse?' . . . *As his analysis progressed . . . Dick had also discovered* the wash-basin as symbolizing the mother's body, and he displayed an extraordinary dread of being wetted with water."[6] Say that it's Oedipus, or you'll get a slap in the face. The psychoanalyst no longer says to the patient: "Tell me a little bit about your desiring-machines, won't you?" Instead he screams: "Answer daddy-and-mommy when I speak to you!" Even Melanie Klein. So the entire process of desiring-production is trampled underfoot and reduced to (*rabuttu sur*) parental images, laid out step by step in accordance with supposed pre-oedipal stages, totalized in Oedipus, and the logic of partial objects is thereby reduced to nothing. Oedipus thus becomes at this point the crucial premise in the logic of psychoanalysis. For as we suspected at the very beginning, partial objects are only apparently derived from (*prélevés sur*) global persons; they are really produced by being drawn from (*prélevés sur*) a flow or a nonpersonal *hylè*, with which they re-establish contact by connecting themselves to other partial objects. The unconscious is totally unaware of persons as such. Partial objects are not representations of parental figures or of the basic patterns of family relations; they are parts of desiring-machines, having to do with a process and with relations of production that are both irreducible and prior to anything that may be made to conform to the Oedipal figure.

When the break between Freud and Jung is discussed, the modest and practical point of disagreement that marked the beginning of their differences is too often forgotten: Jung remarked that in the process of transference the psychoanalyst frequently appeared in the guise of a devil, a god, or a sorcerer, and that the roles he assumed in the patient's eyes went far beyond any sort of parental images. They eventually came to a total parting of the ways, yet Jung's initial reservation was a telling one. The same remark holds true of children's games. A child never confines himself to playing house, to playing only at being daddy-and-mommy. He also plays at being a magician, a cowboy, a cop or a robber, a train, a little car. The train is not necessarily daddy, nor is the train station necessarily mommy. The problem has to do not with the sexual nature of desiring-machines, but with the family nature of this sexuality. Admittedly, once the child has grown up, he finds himself deeply involved in social relations that are no longer familial relations. But since these relations supposedly come into being at a later stage in life, there are only two possible ways in which this can be explained: it must be granted either that sexuality is sublimated or neutralized in and through social (*and* metaphysical) relations, in the form of an analytic "afterward"; or else that these relations bring into play a nonsexual energy, for which sexuality has merely served as the symbol of an anagogical "beyond."

It was their disagreement on this particular point that eventually made the break between Freud and Jung irreconcilable. Yet at the same time the two of them continued to share the belief that the libido cannot invest a social or metaphysical field without some sort of mediation. This is not the case, however. Let us consider a child at play, or a child crawling about exploring the various rooms of the house he lives in. He looks intently at an electrical outlet, he moves his body about like a machine, he uses one of his legs as though it were an oar, he goes into the kitchen, into the study, he runs toy cars back and forth. It is obvious that his parents are present all this time, and that the child would have nothing were it not for them. But that is not the real matter at issue. The matter at issue is to find out whether everything he touches is experienced as a representative of his parents. Ever since birth his crib, his mother's breast, her nipple, his bowel movements are desiring-machines connected to parts of his body. It seems to us self-contradictory to maintain, on the one hand, that the child lives among partial objects, and that on the other hand he conceives of these partial objects as being his parents, or even different parts of his parents' bodies. Strictly speaking, it is not true that a baby experiences his mother's breast as a separate part of her body. It exists, rather, as a part of a desiring-machine connected to the baby's mouth, and is experienced as an object providing a nonpersonal flow of milk, be it copious

[6] Melanie Klein, *Contributions to Psycho-Analysis, with an Introduction by Ernest Jones* (London: Hogarth Press, 1930), pp. 242–43 (emphasis added). [Au.]

or scanty. A desiring-machine and a partial object do not represent anything. A partial object is not representative, even though it admittedly serves as a basis of relations and as a means of assigning agents a place and a function; but these agents are not persons, any more than these relations are intersubjective. They are relations of production as such, and agents of production and antiproduction. Ray Bradbury demonstrates this very well when he describes the nursery as a place where desiring-production and group fantasy occur, as a place where the only connection is that between partial objects and agents.[7] The small child lives with his family around the clock; but within the bosom of this family, and from the very first days of his life, he immediately begins having an amazing nonfamilial experience that psychoanalysis has completely failed to take into account. Lindner's painting[8] attracts our attention once again.

It is not a question of denying the vital importance of parents or the love attachment of children to their mothers and fathers. It is a question of knowing what the place and the function of parents are within desiring-production, rather than doing the opposite and forcing the entire interplay of desiring-machines to fit within (*rabattre tout le jeu des machines désirantes dans*) the restricted code of Oedipus. How does the child first come to define the places and the functions that the parents are going to occupy as special agents, closely related to other agents? From the very beginning Oedipus exists in one form and one form only: open in all directions to a social field, to a field of production directly invested by libido. It would seem obvious that parents indeed make their appearance on the recording surface of desiring-production. But this is in fact the crux of the entire Oedipal problem: What are the precise forces that cause the Oedipal triangulation to close up? Under what conditions does this triangulation divert desire so that it flows across a surface within a narrow channel that is not a natural conformation of this surface? How does it form a type of inscription for experiences and the workings of mechanisms that extend far beyond it in every direction? It is in this sense and this sense only that the child *relates* the breast as a partial object to the person of his mother, and constantly watches the expression on his mother's face. The word "relate" in this case does not designate a natural productive relationship, but rather a *relation* in the sense of a report or an account, an inscription within the over-all process of inscription, within the Numen. From his very earliest infancy, the child has a wide-ranging life of desire—a whole set of nonfamilial relations with the objects and the machines of desire—that is not related to the parents from the point of view of immediate production, but that is ascribed to them (with either love or hatred) from the point of view of the recording of the process, and in accordance with the very special conditions of this recording, including the effect of these conditions upon the process itself (feedback).

It is amid partial objects and within the nonfamilial relations of desiring-production that the child lives his life and ponders what it means to live, even though the question must be "related" to his parents and the only possible tentative answer must be sought in family relations. "I remember that ever since I was eight years old, and even before that, I always wondered who I was, what I was, and why I was alive; I remember that at the age of six, in a house on the Boulevard de la Blancarde in Marseilles (number 29, to be precise), just as I was eating my afternoon snack—a chocolate bar that a certain woman known as my mother gave me—I asked myself what it meant to exist, to be alive, what it meant to be conscious of oneself breathing, and I remember that I wanted to inhale myself in order to prove that I was alive and to see if I liked being alive, and if so why."[9] That is the crucial point: a question occurs to the child that will perhaps be "related" to the woman known as mommy, but that is not formulated in terms of her, but rather produced within the interplay of desiring-machines—at the level, for example, of the mouth-air machine or the tasting-machine: What does it mean to be alive? What does it mean to breathe? What am I? What sort of thing is this breathing-machine on my body without organs?

The child is a metaphysical being. As in the case

[7] Ray Bradbury, *The Illustrated Man* (Garden City, N.Y.: Doubleday, 1951). [Au.]

[8] The painting referred to is Richard Linder's *Boy with Machine*, 1954, reprinted in the original French edition by permission of Mr. and Mrs. C. L. Harrison. In the painting, the boy is so integrated with the machine as to be virtually a part of it. [Eds.]

[9] Antonin Artaud, "Je n'ai jamais rien étudié . . . ," *84*, December, 1950. [Au.]

of the Cartesian *cogito*, parents have nothing to do with these questions. And we are guilty of an error when we confuse the fact that this question is "related" to the parents, in the sense of being recounted or communicated to them, with the notion that it is "related" to them in the sense of a fundamental connection with them. By boxing the life of the child up within the Oedipus complex, by making familial relations the universal mediation of childhood, we cannot help but fail to understand the production of the unconscious itself, and the collective mechanisms that have an immediate bearing on the unconscious: in particular, the entire interplay between primal psychic repression, the desiring-machines, and the body without organs. For *the unconscious is an orphan*, and produces itself within the identity of nature and man. The autoproduction of the unconscious suddenly became evident when the subject of the Cartesian *cogito* realized that it had no parents, when the socialist thinker discovered the unity of man and nature within the process of production, and when the cycle discovers its independence from an indefinite parental regression. To quote Artaud once again: "I got no/papamummy."

We have seen how a confusion arose between the two meanings of "process": process as the metaphysical production of the demoniacal within nature, and process as social production of desiring-machines within history. Neither social relations nor metaphysical relations constitute an "afterward" or a "beyond." The role of such relations must be recognized in all psychopathological processes, and their importance will be all the greater when we are dealing with psychotic syndromes that would appear to be the most animal-like and the most desocialized. It is in the child's very first days of life, in the most elementary behavior patterns of the suckling babe, that these relations with partial objects, with the agents of production, with the factors of antiproduction are woven, in accordance with the laws of desiring-production as a whole. By failing from the beginning to see what the precise nature of this desiring-production is, and how, under what conditions, and in response to what pressures, the Oedipal triangulation plays a role in the recording of the process, we find ourselves trapped in the net of a diffuse, generalized oedipalism that radically distorts the life of the child and his later development, the neurotic and psychotic problems of the adult, and sexuality as a whole. Let us keep D. H. Lawrence's reaction to psychoanalysis in mind, and never forget it. In Lawrence's case, at least, his reservations with regard to psychoanalysis did not stem from terror at having discovered what real sexuality was. But he had the impression—the purely instinctive impression—that psychoanalysis was shutting sexuality up in a bizarre sort of box painted with bourgeois motifs, in a kind of rather repugnant artificial triangle, thereby stifling the whole of sexuality as production of desire so as to recast it along entirely different lines, making of it a "dirty little secret," the dirty little family secret, a private theater rather than the fantastic factory of Nature and Production. Lawrence had the impression that sexuality possessed more power or more potentiality than that. And though psychoanalysis may perhaps have managed to "disinfect the dirty little secret," the dreary, dirty little secret of Oedipus-the-modern-tyrant benefited very little from having been thus disinfected.

Is it possible that, by taking the path that it has, psychoanalysis is reviving an age-old tendency to humble us, to demean us, and to make us feel guilty? Foucault has noted that the relationship between madness and the family can be traced back in large part to a development that affected the whole of bourgeois society in the nineteenth century: the family was entrusted with functions that became the measuring rod of the responsibility of its members and their possible guilt. Insofar as psychoanalysis cloaks insanity in the mantle of a "parental complex," and regards the patterns of self-punishment resulting from Oedipus as a confession of guilt, its theories are not at all radical or innovative. On the contrary: *it is completing the task begun by nineteenth-century psychology*, namely, to develop a moralized, familial discourse of mental pathology, linking madness to the "half-real, half-imaginary dialectic of the Family," deciphering within it "the unending attempt to murder the father," "the dull thud of instincts hammering at the solidity of the family as an institution and at its most archaic symbols."[10] Hence, instead of participating in an undertaking that will bring about genuine liberation, psy-

[10] Michel Foucault, *Madness and Civilization: A History of Insanity in the Age of Reason*, trans. Richard Howard (New York: Random House, 1971). The English version is an edition, abridged by the author himself, of his French text: Michel Foucault, *Histoire de la folie à l'âge classique* (Paris: Plon, 1961). [Au./Tr.]

choanalysis is taking part in the work of bourgeois repression at its most far-reaching level, that is to say, keeping European humanity harnessed to the yoke of daddy-mommy and *making no effort to do away with this problem once and for all.*

Psychoanalysis and Capitalism[11]

The schizoanalytic argument is simple: desire is a machine, a synthesis of machines, a machinic arrangement—desiring-machines. The order of desire is the order of *production;* all production is at once desiring-production and social production. We therefore reproach psychoanalysis for having stifled this order of production, for having shunted it into *representation.* Far from showing the boldness of psychoanalysis, this idea of unconscious representation marks from the outset its bankruptcy or its abnegation: an unconscious that no longer produces, but is content to *believe.* The unconscious believes in Oedipus, it believes in castration, in the law. It is doubtless true that the psychoanalyst would be the first to say that, everything considered, belief is not an act of the unconscious; it is always the preconscious that believes. Shouldn't it even be said that it is the psychoanalyst who believes—the psychoanalyst in each of us? Would belief then be an effect on the conscious material that the unconscious representation exerts from a distance? But inversely, who or what reduced the unconscious to this state of representation, if not first of all a system of beliefs put in the place of productions? In reality, social production becomes alienated in allegedly autonomous beliefs at the same time that desiring-production becomes enticed into allegedly unconscious representations. And as we have seen, it is the same agency—the family—that performs this double operation, distorting and disfiguring social desiring-production, leading it into an impasse.

Thus the link between *representation-belief* and the family is not accidental; it is of the essence of representation to be a familial representation. But production is not thereby suppressed, it continues to rumble, to throb beneath the representative agency (*instance représentative*) that suffocates it, and that it in return can make resonate to the breaking point. Thus in order to keep an effective grip on the zones of production, representation must inflate itself with all the power of myth and tragedy, it must give a *mythic and tragic presentation* of the family—and a familial presentation of myth and tragedy. Yet aren't myth and tragedy, too, productions—forms of production? Certainly not; they are production only when brought into connection with real social production, real desiring-production. Otherwise they are ideological forms, which have taken the place of the units of production. *Who believes in all this*—Oedipus, castration, etc.? The Greeks? Then the Greeks did not produce in the same way they believed? The Hellenists? Do the Hellenists believe that the Greeks produced according to their beliefs? This is true at least of the nineteenth-century Hellenists, about whom Engels said: you'd think they really believed in all that—in myth, in tragedy. Is it the unconscious that represents itself through Oedipus and castration? Or is it the psychoanalyst—the psychoanalyst in us all, who represents the unconscious in this way? For never has Engels's remark regained so much meaning: you'd think the psychoanalysts really believed in all this—in myth, in tragedy. (They go on believing, whereas the Hellenists have long since stopped.)

The Schreber case again applies: Schreber's father invented and fabricated astonishing little machines, sadistico-paranoiac machines—for example head straps with a metallic shank and leather bands, for restrictive use on children, for making them straighten up and behave.[12] These machines play no role whatever in the Freudian analysis. Perhaps it would have been more difficult to crush the entire

[11]This is sec. 3 from chap. 4, "Introduction to Schizoanalysis." [Eds.]

[12]Daniel Paul Schreber was a German judge who began psychiatric treatment in 1884 at the age of forty-two, and spent the remaining twenty-seven years of his life in and out of mental institutions. In 1903, at the age of sixty-one, he published his *Denkwürdigkeiten eines Nervenkranken* (*Memoirs of a Nervous Illness*), which Freud used as the basis of his influential 1911 study on paranoia, "Psycho-Analytic Notes. . . ," *Collected Papers* (New York: Basic Books, 1959), pp. 390–472. [Translator's note, from chapter 1, p. 2.]

W. G. Niederland discovered and reproduced Schreber's father's machines: see especially, "Schreber, Father and Son," *Psychoanalytic Quarterly,* Vol. 28 (1959), pp. 151–69. Quite similar instruments of pedagogical torture are to be found in the Contesse de Ségur: thus "the good behavior belt," "with an iron plate for the back and an iron rod to hold the chin in place" (*Comédies et proverbes, On ne prend pas les mouches*). [Au.]

sociopolitical content of Schreber's delirium if these desiring-machines of the father had been taken into account, as well as their obvious participation in a pedagogical social machine in general. For the real question is this: of course the father acts on the child's unconscious—but does he act as a head of a family in an expressive familial transmission, or rather as the agent of a machine, in a machinic information or communication? Schreber's desiring-machines communicate with those of his father; but it is in this very way that they are from early childhood the libidinal investment of a social field. *In this field the father has a role only as an agent of production and antiproduction.* Freud, on the contrary, chooses the first path: it is not the father who indicates the action of machines, but just the opposite; thereafter there is no longer even any reason for considering machines, whether as desiring-machines or as social machines. In return, the father will be inflated with all the "forces of myth and religion" and with phylogenesis, so as to ensure that the little familial representation has the appearance of being coextensive with the field of delirium. The production couple—the desiring-machines and the social field—gives way to a representative couple of an entirely different nature: family-myth. Once again, have you ever seen a child at play: how he already populates the technical social machines with his own desiring-machines, O sexuality—while the father or mother remains in the background, from whom the child borrows parts and gears according to his need, and who are there as agents of transmission, reception, and interception: kindly agents of production or suspicious agents of antiproduction.

Why was mythic and tragic representation accorded such a senseless privilege? Why were expressive forms and a whole *theater* installed there where there were fields, workshops, factories, units of production? The psychoanalyst parks his circus in the dumbfounded unconscious, a real P. T. Barnum in the fields and in the factory. That is what Miller, and already Lawrence, have to say against psychoanalysis (the living are not believers, the seers do not believe in myth and tragedy): "By retracing the paths to the earlier heroic life . . . you defeat the very element and quality of the heroic, for the hero never looks backward, nor does he ever doubt his powers. Hamlet was undoubtedly a hero to himself, and for every Hamlet born the only true course to pursue is the very course which Shakespeare describes. But the question, it seems to me, is this: are we *born* Hamlets? Were *you* born Hamlet? *Or did you not rather create the type in yourself?* Whether this be so or not, what seems infinitely more important is—*why revert to myth?* . . . This ideational rubbish out of which our world has erected its cultural edifice is now, by a critical irony, being given its poetic immolation, its mythos, *through a kind of writing which,* because it is *of* the disease and therefore *beyond,* clears the ground for fresh superstructures. (In my own mind the thought of 'fresh superstructures' is abhorrent, but this is merely the awareness of a process and not the process itself.) Actually, in process, I believe with each line I write that I am scouring the womb, giving it the *curette,* as it were. Behind this process lies the idea not of 'edifice' and 'superstructure,' which is culture and hence false, but of continuous birth, renewal, *life, life.* . . . In the myth there is no life for us. Only the myth lives in the myth. . . . *This ability to produce the myth is born out of awareness, out of ever-increasing consciousness.* That is why, speaking of the *schizophrenic nature* of our age, I said—'until the process is completed the belly of the world shall be the Third Eye." Now, Brother Ambrose, just what did I mean by that? What could I mean except that from this intellectual world in which we are swimming there must body forth a new world; but this new world can only be bodied forth in so far as it is *conceived.* And to conceive there must first be desire, . . . Desire is instinctual and holy: it is only through desire that we bring about the immaculate conception."[13]

Everything is said in these pages from Miller: Oedipus (or Hamlet) led to the point of autocritique; the expressive forms—myth and tragedy—denounced as conscious beliefs or illusions, nothing more than ideas; the necessity of a scouring of the unconscious, schizoanalysis as a curettage of the unconscious; the matrical fissure in opposition to the line of castration; the splendid affirmation of the orphan- and producer-unconscious; the exaltation of the process as a schizophrenic process of deterritorialization that must produce a new earth;

[13] Henry Miller, *Hamlet* (Puerto Rico: Carrefour, 1939), Vol. 1, pp. 124–29. [Au.]

and even the functioning of the desiring-machines against tragedy, against "the fatal drama of the personality," against "the inevitable confusion between mask and actor." It is obvious that Miller's correspondent, Michael Fraenkel, does not understand. He talks like a psychoanalyst, or like a nineteenth-century Hellenist: yes, myth, tragedy, Oedipus, and Hamlet are good expressions, pregnant forms; they express the true permanent drama of desire and knowledge. Fraenkel calls to his aid all the commonplaces, Schopenhauer, and the Nietzsche of *The Birth of Tragedy*. He thinks Miller is unaware of these things, and never wonders for a second why Nietzsche himself broke with *The Birth of Tragedy*, why he stopped believing in tragic representation.

Michel Foucault has convincingly shown what break (*coupure*) introduced the irruption of production into the world of representation. Production can be that of labor or that of desire, it can be social or desiring, it calls forth forces that no longer permit themselves to be contained in representation, traversing it through and through: "an immense expanse of shade" extended beneath the level of representation.[14] And this collapse or sinking of the classical world of representation is assigned a date by Foucault; the end of the eighteenth and the beginning of the nineteenth century. So it seems that the situation is far more complex than we made it out to be, since psychoanalysis participates to the highest degree in this discovery of the units of production, which subjugate all possible representations rather than being subordinated to them. Just as Ricardo founds political or social economy by discovering quantitative labor as the principle of every representable value, Freud founds desiring-economy by discovering the quantitative libido as the principle of every representation of the objects and aims of desire. Freud discovers the subjective nature or abstract essence of desire, just as Ricardo discovers the subjective nature or abstract essence of labor, beyond all representations that would bind it to objects, to aims, or even to particular sources. Freud is thus the first to disengage desire itself (*le désir tout court*), as Ricardo disengages labor itself (*le travail tout court*), and thereby the sphere of production that effectively eclipses representation. And subjective abstract desire, like subjective abstract labor, is inseparable from a movement of deterritorialization that discovers the interplay of machines and their agents underneath all the specific determinations that still linked desire or labor to a given person, to a given object in the framework of representation.

Desiring-production and machines, psychic apparatuses and machines of desire, desiring-machines and the assembling of an analytic machine suited to decode them: the domain of free syntheses where everything is possible; partial connections, included disjunctions, nomadic conjunctions, polyvocal flows and chains, transductive[15] breaks; the relation of desiring-machines as formations of the unconscious with the molar formations that they constitute statistically in organized crowds; and the apparatus of social and psychic repression resulting from these formations—such is the composition of the analytic field. And this subrepresentative field will continue to survive and work, even through Oedipus, even through myth and tragedy, which nevertheless mark the reconciliation of psychoanalysis with representation. The fact remains that a conflict cuts across the whole of psychoanalysis, the conflict between mythic and tragic familial representation and social and desiring-production. For myth and tragedy are systems of symbolic representations that still refer desire to determinate exterior conditions as well as to particular objective codes—the body of the Earth, the despotic body—and that in this way confound the discovery of the abstract or subjective essence. It has been remarked in this context that each time Freud brings to the fore the study of the psychic apparatuses, the social and desiring-machines, the mechanisms of the drives, and the institutional mechanisms, his interest in myth and tragedy tends to diminish, while at the

[14] Michel Foucault, *The Order of Things* (New York: Random House, 1970), pp. 208–11 (on the opposition between desire or desiring-production and representation); pp. 253–56 (on the opposition between social production and representation, in Adam Smith and especially Ricardo). [Au.]

[15] For a definition of transduction with respect to production and representation, see "Interview/Felix Guattari" in *Diacritics: A Review of Contemporary Criticism,* Fall 1974, p. 39: "Signs work as much as matter. Matter expresses as much as signs. . . . Transduction is the idea that, in essence, something is conducted, something happens between chains of semiotic expression, and material chains." [Tr.]

same time he denounces in Jung, then in Rank, the re-establishment of an exterior representation of the essence of desire as an objective desire, alienated in myth or tragedy.[16]

How can this very complex ambivalence of psychoanalysis be explained? Several different things must be distinguished. In the first place, symbolic representation indeed grasps the essence of desire, but by referring it to large "objectities" (*objectités*)[17] as to the specific elements that determine its objects, aims, and sources. It is in this way that myth ascribes desire to the element of the earth as a full body, and to the territorial code that distributes prescriptions and prohibitions. Likewise tragedy ascribes desire to the full body of the despot and to the corresponding imperial code. Consequently, the understanding of symbolic representations may consist in a systematic phenomenology of these elements and objectities (as in the old Hellenists or even Jung); or else these representations may be understood by historical study that assigns them to their real and objective social conditions (as with recent Hellenists). Viewed in the latter fashion, representation implies a certain lag, and expresses less a stable element than the conditioned passage from one element to another: mythic representation does not express the element of the earth, but rather the conditions under which this element fades before the despotic element; and tragic representation does not express the despotic element properly speaking, but the conditions under which—in fifth-century Greece, for example—this element diminishes in favor of the new order of the city-state.[18] It is obvious that neither one of these ways of treating myth or tragedy is suited to the psychoanalytic approach. The psychoanalytic method is quite different: rather than referring symbolic representation to determinate objectities and to objective social conditions, psychoanalysis refers them to the subjective and universal essence of desire as libido. Thus the operation of *decoding* in psychoanalysis can no longer signify what it signifies in the sciences of man; the discovery of the secret of such and such a code. Psychoanalysis must undo the codes so as to attain the quantitative and qualitative flows of libido that traverse dreams, fantasies, and pathological formations as well as myth, tragedy, and the social formations. Psychoanalytic interpretation does not consist in competing with codes, adding a code to the codes already recognized, but in decoding in an absolute way, in eliciting something that is uncodable by virtue of its polymorphism and its polyvocity.[19] It appears then that the interest psychoanalysis has in myth (or in tragedy) is an essentially critical interest, since the specificity of myth, understood objectively, must melt under the rays of the subjective libido: it is indeed the world of representation that crumbles, or tends to crumble.

It follows that, in the second place, the link between psychoanalysis and capitalism is no less profound than that between political economy and capitalism. This discovery of the decoded and deterritorialized flows is the same as that which takes place for political economy and in social production, in the form of subjective abstract labor, and for psychoanalysis and in desiring-production, in the form of subjective abstract libido. As Marx

[16] Didier Anzieu distinguishes between two periods in particular: 1906–1920, which "constitutes the great period of mythological works in the history of psychoanalysis"; then a period of relative discredit, as Freud turns toward the problems of the second topography [Tr.: the id, ego, and superego], and the relationships between desire and institutions, and takes less of an interest in a systematic exploration of myths ("Freud et la mythologie," in *Incidences de la psychanalyse,* no. 1 [1970], pp. 126–29). [Au.]

[17] *objectités:* This term corresponds to the German *objektität.* The following definition appears in *Vocabulaire technique et critique de la philosphie* (Paris: Presses Universitaires de France, 1968): "the form in which the thing-in-itself, the real, appears as an object." [Tr.]

[18] On myth as the expression of the organization of a despotic power that represses the Earth, see Jean-Pierre Vernant, *Les origines de la pensée grecque* (Paris: Presses Universitaires de France, 1962), pp. 109–16; and on tragedy as the expression of an organization of the city-state that represses in its turn the fallen despot, Vernant, "Oedipe sans complexe," *Raison présente,* August 1967. [Au.]

[19] It cannot be said, therefore, that psychoanalysis adds a code—a psychological one—to the social codes through which histories and mythologists explain myth. Freud pointed this out apropos dreams: it is not a question of a deciphering process according to a code. In this regard see Jacques Derrida's comments in *L'Écriture et la différance* (Paris: Editions du Seuil, 1967), pp. 310ff.: "It is doubtless true that [dream writing] works with a mass of elements codified in the course of an individual or collective history. But in its operations, its lexicon, and its syntax, a purely idiomatic residue remains irreducible, that must carry the whole weight of the interpretation, in the communication among unconsciouses. The dreamer invents his own grammar." [Au.]

says, in capitalism the essence becomes subjective—*the activity of production in general*—and abstract labor becomes something real from which all the preceding social formations can be reinterpreted from the point of view of a generalized decoding or a generalized process of deterritorialization: "The simplest abstraction, then, which modern economics places at the head of its discussions, and which expresses an immeasurably ancient relation valid in all forms of society, nevertheless achieves practical truth as an abstraction only as a category of the most modern society." This is also the case for desire as abstract libido and as subjective essence. Not that a simple parallelism should be drawn between capitalist social production and desiring-production, or between the flows of money-capital and the shit-flows of desire. The relationship is much closer: desiring-machines are in social machines and nowhere else, so that the conjunction of the decoded flows in the capitalist machine tends to liberate the free figures of a universal subjective libido. In short, the discovery of an activity of production *in general and without distinction*, as it appears in capitalism, is the identical discovery of *both* political economy *and* psychoanalysis, beyond the determinate systems of representation.

Obviously this does not mean that the capitalist being, or the being in capitalism, desires to work or that he works according to his desire. But the identity of desire and labor is not a myth, it is rather the active utopia par excellence that designates the capitalist limit to be overcome through desiring-production. But why, precisely, is desiring-production situated at the always counteracted limit of capitalism? Why, at the same time as it discovers the subjective essence of desire and labor—a common essence, inasmuch as it is the activity of production in general—is capitalism continually realienating this essence, and without interruption, in a repressive machine that divides the essence in two, and maintains it divided—abstract labor on the one hand, abstract desire on the other: political economy *and* psychoanalysis, political economy *and* libidinal economy? Here we are able to appreciate the full extent to which psychoanalysis belongs to capitalism. For as we have seen, capitalism indeed has as its limit the decoded flows of desiring-production, but it never stops repelling them by binding them in an axiomatic that takes the place of the codes. Capitalism is inseparable from the movement of deterritorialization, but this movement is exorcised through factitious and artificial reterritorializations. Capitalism is constructed on the ruins of the territorial and the despotic, the mythic and the tragic representations, but it re-establishes them in its own service and in another form, as images of capital.

Marx summarizes the entire matter by saying that the subjective abstract essence is discovered by capitalism only to be put in chains all over again, to be subjugated and alienated—no longer, it is true, in an exterior and independent element as objectity, but in the element, itself subjective, of private property: "What was previously being external to oneself—man's externalization in the thing—has merely become the act of externalizing—the process of alienating." It is, in fact, the form of private property that conditions the conjunction of the decoded flows, which is to say their axiomatization in a system where the flows of the means of production, as the property of the capitalists, is directly related to the flow of so-called free labor, as the "property" of the workers (so that the State restrictions on the substance or the content of private property do not at all affect this form). It is also the form of private property that constitutes the center of the factitious reterritorializations of capitalism. And finally, it is this form that produces the images filling the capitalist field of immanence, "the" capitalist, "the" worker, etc. In other terms, capitalism indeed implies the collapse of the great objective determinate representations, for the benefit of production as the universal interior essence, but it does not thereby escape the world of representation. It merely performs a vast conversion of this world, by attributing to it the new form of an infinite subjective representation.[20]

We seem to be straying from the main concern of psychoanalysis, yet never have we been so close. For here again, as we have seen previously, it is in the interiority of its movement that capitalism requires and institutes not only a social axiomatic, but an application of this axiomatic to the privatized family. Representation would never be able to ensure its

[20] Michel Foucault shows that "the human sciences" found their principle in production and were constituted on the collapse of representation, but that they immediately re-establish a new type of representation, as unconscious representation (*The Order of Things*, pp. 352–67). [Au.]

own conversion without this application that furrows deep into it, cleaves it, and forces it back upon itself. Thus subjective abstract Labor as represented in private property has, as its correlate, subjective abstract Desire as represented in the privatized family. Psychoanalysis undertakes the analysis of this second term, as political economy analyzes the first. Psychoanalysis is the technique of application, for which political economy is the axiomatic. In a word, psychoanalysis disengages the second pole in the very movement of capitalism, which substitutes the infinite subjective representation for the large determinate objective representations. It is in fact essential that the limit of the decoded flows of desiring-production be doubly exorcised, doubly displaced, once by the position of immanent limits that capitalism does not cease to reproduce on an ever expanding scale, and again by the marking out of an interior limit that reduces this social reproduction to restricted familial reproduction.

Consequently, the ambiguity of psychoanalysis in relation to myth or tragedy has the following explanation: psychoanalysis undoes them as objective representations, and discovers in them the figures of a subjective universal libido; but it reanimates them, and promotes them as subjective representations that extend the mythic and tragic contents to infinity. Psychoanalysis does treat myth and tragedy, but it treats them *as* the dreams and the fantasies of private man, *Homo familia*—and in fact dream and fantasy are to myth and tragedy as private property is to public property. What acts in myth and tragedy at the level of objective elements is therefore reappropriated and raised to a higher level by psychoanalysis, but as an unconscious dimension of subjective representation (myth as humanity's *dream*). What acts as an objective and public element—the Earth, the Despot—is now taken up again, but as the expression of a subjective and private reterritorialization: Oedipus is the fallen despot—banished, deterritorialized—but a reterritorialization is engineered, using the Oedipus complex conceived of as the daddy-mommy-me of today's everyman. Psychoanalysis and the Oedipus complex gather up all beliefs, all that has ever been believed by humanity, but only in order to raise it to the condition of a *denial* that preserves belief without believing in it (it's only a dream: the strictest piety today asks for nothing more). Whence this double impression, that psychoanalysis is opposed to mythology no less than to mythologists, but at the same time extends myth and tragedy to the dimensions of the subjective universal: if Oedipus himself "has no complex," the Oedipus complex has no Oedipus, just as narcissism has no Narcissus.[21] Such is the ambivalence that traverses psychoanalysis, and that extends beyond the specific problem of myth and tragedy: with one hand psychoanalysis undoes the system of objective representations (myth, tragedy) for the benefit of the subjective essence conceived as desiring-production, while with the other hand it reverses this production in a system of subjective representations (dream and fantasy, with myth and tragedy posited as their developments or projections). Images, nothing but images. What is left in the end is an intimate familial theater, the theater of private man, which is no longer either desiring-production or objective representation. The unconscious as a stage. A whole theater put in the place of production, a theater that disfigures this production even more than could tragedy and myth when reduced to their meager ancient resources.

Myth, tragedy, dream, and fantasy—and myth and tragedy reinterpreted in terms of dream and fantasy—are the representative series that psychoanalysis substitutes for the line of production: social and desiring-production. A theater series, instead of a production series. But why in fact does representation, having become subjective representation, assume this theatrical form ("There is a mysterious tie between psychoanalysis and the theater")? We are familiar with the eminently modern reply of certain recent authors: the theater elicits the finite structure of the infinite subjective representation. What is meant by "elicit" is very complex, since the structure can never present more than its own absence, or represent something not represented in the representation: but it is claimed that the theater's privilege is that of staging this metaphoric and metonymic causality that marks

[21] Didier Anzieu, "Freud et la mythologie," pp. 124, 128: "Freud grants myth no specificity. This is one of the points that have most seriously encumbered the subsequent relations between psychoanalysts and anthropologists. . . . Freud undertakes a veritable leveling. . . . The article 'On Narcissism: An Introduction,' which constitutes an important step toward the revision of the theory of the drives, contains no allusion to the myth of Narcissus." [Au.]

both the presence and the absence of the structures in its effects. While André Green expresses reservations about the adequacy of the structure, he does so only in the name of a theater necessary for the actualization of this structure, playing the role of revealer, a place by which the structure becomes visible.[22] In her fine analysis of the phenomenon of belief, Octave Mannoni likewise uses the theater model to show how the denial of belief in fact implies a transformation of belief, under the effect of a structure that the theater embodies or places on stage.[23] We should understand that representation, when it ceases to be objective, when it becomes subjective infinite—that is to say, imaginary—effectively loses all consistency, unless it is supported by a structure that determines the place and the functions of the subject of representation, as well as the objects represented as images, and the formal relations between them all. "Symbolic" thus no longer designates the relation of representation to an objectity as an element; it designates the ultimate elements of subjective representation, pure signifiers, pure nonrepresented representatives whence the subjects, the objects, and their relationships all derive. In this way the structure designates the unconscious of subjective representation. The series of this representation now presents itself: (imaginary) infinite subjective representation-theatrical representation-structural representation. And precisely because the theater is thought to stage the latent structure, as well as to embody its elements and relations, it is in a position to reveal the universality of this structure, even in the objective representations that it salvages and reinterprets in terms of hidden representatives, their migrations and variable relations. All former beliefs are gathered up and revived in the name of a structure of the unconscious: we are still pious. Everywhere, the great game of the symbolic signifier that is embodied in the signifieds of the Imaginary—Oedipus as a universal metaphor.

Why the theater? How bizarre, this theatrical and pasteboard unconscious: the theater taken as the model of production. Even in Louis Althusser we are witness to the following operation: the discovery of social production as "machine" or "machinery," irreducible to the world of objective representation (*Vorstellung*); but immediately the reduction of the machine to structure, the identification of production with a structural and theatrical representation (*Darstellung*).[24] Now the same is true of both desiring-production and social production: every time that production, rather than being apprehended in its originality, in its reality, becomes *reduced (rabattue)* in this manner to a representational space, it can no longer have value except by its own absence, and it appears as a lack within this space. In search of the structure in psychoanalysis, Moustafa Safouan is able to present it as a "contribution to a theory of lack." It is in the structure that the fusion of desire with the impossible is performed, with lack defined as castration. From the structure there arises the most austere song in honor of castration—yes, yes, we enter the order of desire through the gates of castration—once desiring-production has spread out in the space of a representation that allows it to go on living only as an absence and a lack unto itself. For a *structural unity* is imposed on the desiring-machines that joins them together in a molar aggregate; the partial objects are referred to a totality that can appear only as that which the partial objects lack, and as that which is lacking unto itself while being lacking in them (the Great Signifier "symbolizable by the inherency of a -1 in the ensemble of signifiers"). Just how far will one go in the development of a lack of lack traversing the structure? Such is the structural operation: it distributes lack in the molar aggregate. The limit of desiring-production—the border line separating the molar aggregates and their molecular elements, the objective representations and the machines of desire—is now completely displaced. The limit now passes only within the molar aggregate itself, inasmuch as the latter is furrowed by the line of castration. The formal operations of the structure are those of extrapolation, application, and biuni-

[22] André Green goes very far in the analysis of the representation-theater-unconscious relations: *Un oeil en trop* (Paris: Editions de Minuit, 1969), Prologue (especially p. 43, concerning "the representation of the nonrepresented in representation"). However, the criticism that Green makes of the structure is not conducted in the name of production, but in the name of representation, and invokes the necessity for extrastructural factors that must do nothing more than reveal the structure, and reveal it as Oedipal. [Au.]

[23] Octave Mannoni, *Clefs pour l'imaginaire ou l'autre scène* (Paris: Editions du Seuil, 1969), Ch. 1 and 7. [Au.]

[24] Louis Althusser and Etienne Balibar, *Reading Capital*, trans. Ben Brewster (New York: Pantheon, 1970). [Au.]

vocalization, which reduce the social aggregate of departure to a familial aggregate of destination, with the familial relation becoming "metaphorical for all the others" and hindering the molecular productive elements from following their own line of escape.

When André Green looks for the reasons that establish the affinity of psychoanalysis with the theatrical and structural representation it makes visible, he offers two that are especially striking: the theater raises the familial relation to the condition of a universal metaphoric structural relation, whence the imaginary place and interplay of persons derives; and inversely, the theater forces the play and the working of machines into the wings, behind a limit that has become impassible (exactly as in fantasy the machines are there, but *behind the wall*). In short, the displaced limit no longer passes between objective representation and desiring-production, but between the two poles of subjective representation, as infinite imaginary representation, and as finite structural representation. Thereafter it is possible to oppose these two aspects to each other, the imaginary variations that tend toward the night of the indeterminate or the nondifferentiated, and the symbolic invariant that traces the path of the differentiations: the same thing is found all over, following a rule of inverse relation, or double bind. All of production is conducted into the double impasse of subjective representation. Oedipus can always be consigned to the Imaginary, but no matter, it will be encountered again, stronger and more whole, more lacking and triumphant by the very fact that it is lacking, it will be encountered again in its entirety in symbolic castration. And it's a sure thing that structure affords us no means for escaping familialism; on the contrary, it adds another turn, it attributes a universal metaphoric value to the family at the very moment it has lost its objective literal values. Psychoanalysis makes its ambition clear: to relieve the waning family, to replace the broken-down familial bed with the psychoanalyst's couch, to make it so that the "analytic situation" is *incestuous in its essence*, so that it is its own proof or voucher, on a par with Reality.[25]

In the final analysis that is indeed what is at issue, as Octave Mannoni shows: how can belief continue after repudiation, how can we continue to be pious? We have repudiated and lost all our beliefs that proceeded by way of objective representations. The earth is dead, the desert is growing: the old father is dead, the territorial father, and the son too, the despot Oedipus. We are alone with our bad conscience and our boredom, our life where nothing happens; nothing left but images that revolve within the infinite subjective representation. We will muster all our strength so as to believe in these images, from the depths of a structure that governs our relationships with them and our identifications as so many effects of a symbolic signifier. The "good identification." We are all Archie Bunker at the theater, shouting out before Oedipus: there's my kind of guy, there's my kind of guy! Everything, the myth of the earth, the tragedy of the despot, is taken up again as shadows projected on a stage. The great territorialities have fallen into ruin, but the structure proceeds with all the subjective and private reterritorializations. What a perverse operation psychoanalysis is, where this neoidealism, this rehabilitated cult of castration, this ideology of lack culminates: *the anthropomorphic representation of sex!* In truth, they don't know what they are doing, nor what mechanism of repression they are fostering, for their intentions are often progressive. But no one today can enter an analyst's consulting room without at least being aware that everything has been *played out* in advance: Oedipus and castration, the Imaginary and the Symbolic, the great lesson of the inadequacy of being or of dispossession. Psychoanalysis as a gadget, Oedipus as a reterritorialization, a retimbering of modern man on the "rock" of castration.

The path marked out by Lacan[26] led in a completely different direction. He is not content to turn, like the analytic squirrel, inside the wheel of the Imaginary and the Symbolic; he refuses to be caught up in the Oedipal Imaginary and the oedipalizing structure, the imaginary identity of persons and the structural unity of machines, everywhere knocking against the impasses of a molar representation that the family closes round itself. What is the use of going from the imaginary dual order to the symbolic third (or fourth), if the latter is biunivocalizing whereas the first is biunivocalized? As partial objects the desiring-machines undergo two totalizations, one when the socius confers on them a struc-

[25] Serge Leclaire, *Démasquer le réel* (Paris: Editions du Seuil, 1971), pp. 28–31. [Au.]

[26] See *Lacan*. [Eds.]

tural unity under a symbolic signifier acting as absence and lack in an aggregate of departure, the other when the family imposes on them a personal unity with imaginary signifieds that distribute, that "vacuolize" lack in an aggregate of destination: a double abduction of the orphan machines, inasmuch as the structure applies its articulation to them, inasmuch as the parents lay their fingers on them. To trace back from images to the structure would have little significance and would not rescue us from representation, *if the structure did not have a reverse side* that is like the real production of desire.

This reverse side is the "real inorganization" of the molecular elements: partial objects that enter into indirect syntheses or interactions, since they are not partial (*partiels*) in the sense of extensive parts, but rather partial (*"partiaux"*)[27] like the intensities under which a unit of matter always fills space in varying degrees (the eye, the mouth, the anus as degrees of matter); pure positive multiplicities where everything is possible, without exclusiveness or negation, syntheses operating without a plan, where the connections are transverse, the disjunctions included, the conjunctions polyvocal, indifferent to their underlying support, since this matter that serves them precisely as a support receives no specificity from any structural or personal unity, but appears as the body without organs that fills the space each time an intensity fills it; signs of desire that compose a signifying chain but that are not themselves signifying, and do not answer to the rules of a linguistic game of chess, but instead to the lottery drawings that sometimes cause a word to be chosen, sometimes a design, sometimes a thing or a piece of a thing, depending on one another only by the order of the random drawings, and holding together only by the absence of a link (nonlocalizable connections), having no other statutory condition than that of being dispersed elements of desiring-machines that are themselves dispersed.[28] It is this entire reverse side of the structure that Lacan discovers, with the "o" as machine, and the "O" as nonhuman sex: schizophrenizing the analytic field, instead of oedipalizing the psychotic field.

Everything hinges on the way in which the structure is elicited from the machines, according to planes of consistency or of structuration, and lines of selection that correspond to the large statistical aggregates or molar formations, and that determine the links and reduce production to representation—*that* is where the disjunctions become exclusive (and the connections global, and the conjunctions, biunivocal), at the same time that the support gains a specificity under a structural unity, and the signs themselves become signifying under the action of a despotic symbol that totalizes them in the name of its own absence or withdrawal. Yes, in fact, there the production of desire can be *represented* only in terms of an extrapolated sign that joins together all the elements of production in a constellation of which it is not itself a part. There the absence of a tie necessarily appears as an absence, and no longer as a positive force. There desire is necessarily referred to a missing term, whose very essence is to be lacking. The signs of desire, being nonsignifying, become signifying in representation only in terms of a signifier of absence or lack.

[27] *partiel:* partial, incomplete; (*pl. partiaux*): partial, biased, as a biased judge. We have chosen to translate *objets partiels* throughout as "partial objects" rather than as "part-objects" (as in Melanie Klein), in anticipation of this point in the book where Deleuze and Guattari shift from Klein's concept of the partial objects as "part of," hence as an incomplete part of a lost unity or totality (molar), toward a concept of the partial objects as biased, evaluating intensities that know no lack and are capable of selecting organs (molecular). [Tr.]

[28] Lacan, *Écrits*, pp. 657–59. Serge Leclaire has made a profound attempt to define within this perspective the reverse side of the structure as the "pure being of desire" ("La réalité du désir" pp. 242–49). In desire he sees a multiplicity of prepersonal singularities, or indifferent elements that are defined precisely by the absence of a link. But this absence of a link—and of a meaning—is positive, "it constitutes the specific force of coherence of this constellation." Of course, meaning and link can always be re-established, if only by inserting fragments assumed to be forgotten: this is even the very function of Oedipus. But *"if the analysis again discovers the link between the two elements, this is a sign that they are not the ultimate, irreducible terms of the unconscious."* It will be noticed here that Leclaire uses the exact criterion of real distinction in Spinoza and Leibniz: the ultimate elements (the infinitive attributes) are attributable to God, because they do not depend on one another and do not tolerate any relation of opposition or contradiction among themselves. The absence of direct links guarantees their common participation in the divine substance. Likewise for the partial objects and the body without organs: the body without organs is substance itself, and the partial objects, the ultimate attributes or elements of substance. [Au.]

The structure is formed and appears only in terms of the symbolic term defined as a lack. The great Other as the nonhuman sex gives way, in representation, to a signifier of the great Other as an always missing term, the all-too-human sex, the phallus of molar castration.[29]

Here too Lacan's approach appears in all its complexity; for it is certain that he does not enclose the unconscious in an Oedipal structure. He shows on the contrary that Oedipus is imaginary, nothing but an image, a myth; that this or these images are produced by an oedipalizing structure; that this structure acts only insofar as it reproduces the element of castration, which itself is not imaginary but symbolic. There we have the three major planes of structuration, which correspond to the molar aggregates: Oedipus as the imaginary reterritorialization of private man, produced under the structural conditions of capitalism, inasmuch as capitalism reproduces and revives the archaism of the imperial symbol or the vanished despot. All three are necessary—precisely in order to lead Oedipus to the point of its self-critique. The task undertaken by Lacan is to lead Oedipus to such a point. (Likewise, Elisabeth Roudinesco has clearly seen that, in Lacan, the hypothesis of an unconscious-as-language does not closet the unconscious in a linguistic structure, but leads linguistics to the point of its autocritique, by showing how the structural organization of signifiers still depends on a despotic Great Signifier acting as an archaism.)[30]

What is this point of self-criticism? It is the point where the structure, beyond the images that fill it and the Symbolic that conditions it within representation, reveals its reverse side as a positive principle of nonconsistency that dissolves it: where desire is shifted into the order of production, related to its molecular elements, and where it lacks nothing, because it is defined as *the natural and sensuous objective being,* at the same time as the Real is defined as *the objective being of desire.* For the unconscious of schizoanalysis is unaware of persons, aggregates, and laws, and of images, structures, and symbols. It is an orphan, just as it is an anarchist and an atheist. It is not an orphan in the sense that the father's name would designate an absence, but in the sense that the unconscious reproduces itself wherever the names of history designate present intensities ("the sea of proper names"). The unconscious is not figurative, since its *figural* is abstract, the figure-schiz. It is not structural, nor is it symbolic, for its reality is that of the Real in its very production, in its very inorganization. It is not representative, but solely machinic, and productive.

Destroy, destroy. The task of schizoanalysis goes by way of destruction—a whole scouring of the unconscious, a complete curettage. Destroy Oedipus, the illusion of the ego, the puppet of the superego, guilt, the law, castration. It is not a matter of pious destructions, such as those performed by psychoanalysis under the benevolent neutral eye of the analyst. For these are Hegel-style destructions, ways of conserving. How is it that the celebrated neutrality, and what psychoanalysis calls—dares to call—the disappearance or the dissolution of the Oedipus complex, do not make us burst into laughter? We are told that Oedipus is indispensable, that it is the source of every possible differentiation, and that it saves us from the terrible nondifferentiated mother. But this terrible mother, the sphinx, is herself part of Oedipus; her nondifferentiation is merely the reverse of the exclusive differentiations created by Oedipus, she is herself created by Oedipus: Oedipus necessarily operates in the form of this double impasse. We are told that Oedipus in its turn must be overcome, and that this is achieved through castration, latency, desexualization, and sublimation. But what is castration if not still Oedipus, to the *n*th power, now symbolic, and therefore all the more virulent? And what is latency, this pure fable, if not the silence imposed on desiring-machines so that Oedipus can develop, be fortified in us, so that

[29] Lacan, *Écrits,* p. 819: "For want of this signifier, all the others would represent nothing." Serge Leclaire shows how this structure is organized around a missing term, or rather a signifier of lack: "It is the elective signifier of the absence of a link, the phallus, that we find again in the unique privilege of its relation to the essence of lack—an emblem of difference par excellence—the irreducible difference, the difference between the sexes. . . . If man can talk, this is because at one point in the language system there is a guarantor of the irreducibility of lack: the phallic signifier" ("La réalité du désir," p. 251). How strange all this is! [Au.]

[30] Elisabeth Roudinesco, "L'action d'une métaphore," *La Pensée,* February 1972. See in Jacques Lacan, *Écrits* (Paris: Editions du Seuil), p. 821, the way in which Lacan raises the idea of a "signifier of the lack of this symbol" above the "zero symbol" taken in its linguistic sense. [Au.]

it can accumulate its poisonous sperm and gain the time necessary for propagating itself, and for passing on to our future children? And what is the elimination of castration anxiety in its turn—desexualization and sublimation—if not divine acceptance of, and infinite resignation to, bad conscience, which consists for the woman of "the appeased wish for a penis . . . destined to be converted into a wish for a baby and for a husband," and for the man in assuming his passive attitude and in "[subjecting] himself to a father substitute"?[31]

We are all the more "extricated" from Oedipus as we become a living example, an advertisement, a theorem in action, so as to attract our children to Oedipus: we have evolved in Oedipus, we have been structured in Oedipus, and under the neutral and benevolent eye of the substitute, we have learned the song of castration, the lack-of-being-that-is-life; "yes it is through castration / that we gain access / to Deeeeesire." What one calls the disappearance of Oedipus is Oedipus become an idea. Only the idea can inject the venom. Oedipus has to become an idea so that it sprouts each time a new set of arms and legs, lips and mustache: "In tracing back the 'memory deaths' your ego becomes a sort of mineral theorem which constantly proves the futility of living."[32] We have been triangulated in Oedipus, and will triangulate it in turn. From the family to the couple, from the couple to the family. In actuality, the benevolent neutrality of the analyst is very limited: it ceases the instant one stops responding daddy-mommy. It ceases the instant one introduces a little desiring-machine—the tape-recorder—into the analyst's office; it ceases as soon as a flow is made to circulate that does not let itself be stopped by Oedipus, the mark of the triangle (they tell you you have a libido that is too viscous, or too liquid, contraindications for analysis).

When Fromm[33] denounces the existence of a psychoanalytic bureaucracy, he still doesn't go far enough, because he doesn't see what the stamp of this bureaucracy is, and that an appeal to the pre-oedipal is not enough to escape this stamp: the pre-oedipal, like the post-oedipal, is still a way of bringing all of desiring-production—the anoedipal—back to Oedipus. When Reich[34] denounces the way in which psychoanalysis joins forces with social repression, he still doesn't go far enough, because he doesn't see that the tie linking psychoanalysis with capitalism is not merely ideological, that it is infinitely closer, infinitely tighter; and that psychoanalysis depends directly on an economic mechanism (whence its relations with money) through which the decoded flows of desire, as taken up in the axiomatic of capitalism, must necessarily be reduced to a familial field where the application of this axiomatic is carried out: Oedipus as the last word of capitalist consumption—sucking away at daddy-mommy, being blocked and triangulated on the couch; "So it's . . ." Psychoanalysis, no less than the bureaucratic or military apparatus, is a mechanism for the absorption of surplus value, nor is this true from the outside, extrinsically; rather, its very form and its finality are marked by this social function. It is not the pervert, nor even the autistic person, who escapes psychoanalysis; the whole of psychoanalysis is an immense perversion, a drug, a radical break with reality, starting with the reality of desire; it is a narcissism, a monstrous autism: the characteristic autism and the intrinsic perversion of the machine of capital. At its most autistic, psychoanalysis is no longer measured against any reality, it no longer opens to any outside, but becomes itself the test of reality and the guarantor of its own test: reality as the lack to which the inside and the outside, departure and arrival, are reduced. Psychoanalysis *index sui,* with no other *reference* than itself or "the analytic situation."

Psychoanalysis states clearly that unconscious representation can never be apprehended independently of the deformations, disguises, or displacements it undergoes. Unconscious representation therefore comprises essentially, by virtue of its own *law,* a represented that is displaced in relation to an agency in a constant state of displacement. But from this, two unwarranted conclusions are drawn: that this agency can be discovered by way of the displaced represented; and this, precisely because this

[31] Sigmund Freud, "Analysis Terminable and Interminable," *Standard Edition,* Vol. 23, pp. 251–52. [Au.]

[32] Miller, *Hamlet,* pp. 124–25. [Au.]

[33] Erich Fromm (1900–), German psychoanalyst and author, member of the International Institute for Social Research (Frankfurt School). [Eds.]

[34] Wilhelm Reich (1897–1957), Austrian psychiatrist and associate of Freud, who later broke with Freud and the psychoanalytic movement. [Eds.]

agency itself belongs to representation, as a non-represented representative, or as a lack "that juts out into the overfull (*trop-plein*) of a representation." This results from the fact that displacement refers to very different movements: at times, the movement through which desiring-production is continually overcoming the limit, becoming deterritorialized, causing its flows to escape, going beyond the threshold of representation; at times, on the contrary, the movement through which the limit itself is displaced, and now passes to the interior of the representation that performs the artificial reterritorializations of desire. If the displacing agency can be concluded from the displaced, this is only true in the second sense, where molar representation is organized around a representative that displaces the represented. But this is certainly not true in the first sense, where the molecular elements are continually passing through the links in the chain. We have seen in this perspective how the law of representation perverted the productive forces of the unconscious, and induced in its very structure a false image that caught desire in its trap (the impossibility of concluding from the prohibition as to what is actually prohibited). Yes, Oedipus is indeed the displaced represented; yes, castration is indeed the representative, the displacing agency (*le déplaçant*), the signifier—but none of that constitutes an unconscious material, nor does any of it concern the productions of the unconscious. Oedipus, castration, the signifier, etc., exist at the crossroads of two operations of capture: one where repressive social production becomes replaced by beliefs, the other where repressed desiring-production finds itself replaced by representations. To be sure, it is not psychoanalysis that makes us believe: Oedipus and castration are demanded, then demanded again, and these demands come from elsewhere and from deeper down. But psychoanalysis did find the following means, and fills the following function: causing beliefs to survive even after repudiation; causing those who no longer believe in anything to continue believing; reconstituting a private territory for them, a private Urstaat, a private capital (dreams as capital, said Freud).

That is why, inversely, schizoanalysis must devote itself with all its strength to the necessary destructions. Destroying beliefs and representations, theatrical scenes. And when engaged in this task no activity will be too malevolent. Causing Oedipus and castration to explode, brutally intervening each time the subject strikes up the song of myth or intones tragic lines, carrying him back *to the factory*. As Charlus says, "A lot we care about your grandmother, you little shit!" Oedipus and castration are no more than reactional formations, resistances, blockages, and armorings whose destruction can't come fast enough. Reich intuits a fundamental principle of schizoanalysis when he says that the destruction of resistances must not wait upon the discovery of the material.[35] But the reason for this is even more radical than he thought: there is no unconscious material, so that schizoanalysis has nothing to interpret. There are only resistances, and then machines desiring-machines. Oedipus is a resistance; if we have been able to speak of the intrinsically perverted nature of psychoanalysis, this is due to the fact that perversion in general is the artificial reterritorialization of the flows of desire, whose machines on the contrary are indices of deterritorialized production. The psychoanalyst reterritorializes on the couch, in the representation of Oedipus and castration. Schizoanalysis on the contrary must disengage the deterritorialized flows of desire, in the molecular elements of desiring-production. We should again call to mind the practical rule laid down by Leclaire, following Lacan, the rule of the right to non-sense as well as to the absence of a link: you will not have reached the ultimate and irreducible terms of the unconscious so long as you find or restore a link between two elements. (But how then can one see in this extreme dispersion—machines dispersed in every machine—nothing more than a pure "fiction" that must give way to Reality defined as a lack, with Oedipus and castration back at a gallop, at the same time that one reduces the absence of a link to a "signifier" of absence charged with representing the absence, with linking this absence itself, and with moving us back and forth from one pole of displacement to the other? One falls back into the molar hole while claiming to unmask the real.)

What complicates everything is that there is indeed a necessity for desiring-production to be induced from representation, to be discovered through its lines of escape. But this is true in a way al-

[35] Wilhelm Reich, *The Function of the Orgasm*, trans. Vincent R. Carfagno (New York: Simon & Schuster, 1973), pp. 167–68. See also Wilhelm Reich, *Character Analysis* (New York: Simon & Schuster, 1974). [Au.]

together different from what psychoanalysis believes it to be. The decoded flows of desire form the free energy (libido) of the desiring-machines. The desiring-machines take form and train their sights along a tangent of deterritorialization that traverses the representative spheres, and that runs along the body without organs. Leaving, escaping, but while causing more escapes. The desiring-machines themselves are the flows-schizzes or the breaks-flows that break and flow at the same time on the body without organs: not the gaping wound represented in castration, but the myriad little connections, disjunctions, and conjunctions by which every machine produces a flow in relation to another that breaks it, and breaks a flow that another produces. But how would these decoded and deterritorialized flows of desiring-production keep from being reduced to some representative territoriality, how would they keep from forming for themselves yet another such territory, even if on the body without organs as the indifferent support for a last representation? Even those who are best at "leaving," those who make leaving into something as natural as being born or dying, those who set out in search of nonhuman sex—Lawrence, Miller—stake out a far-off territoriality that still forms an anthropomorphic and phallic representation: the Orient, Mexico, or Peru. Even the schizo's stroll or voyage does not effect great deterritorializations without borrowing from territorial circuits: the tottering walk of Molloy and his bicycle preserves the mother's room as the vestige of a goal; the vacillating spirals of *The Unnamable* keep the familial tower as an uncertain center where it continues to turn while treading its own underfoot; the infinite series of juxtaposed and unlocalized parks in *Watt* still contains a reference to Mr. Knott's house, the only one capable of "pushing the soul out-of-doors," but also of summoning it back to its place. We are all little dogs, we need circuits, and we need to be taken for walks. Even those best able to disconnect, to unplug themselves, enter into connections of desiring-machines that re-form little earths. Even Gisela Pankow's great deterritorialized subjects are led to discover the image of a family castle under the roots of the uprooted tree that crosses through their body without organs.[36]

Previously we distinguished two poles of delirium, one as the molecular schizophrenic line of escape, and the other as the paranoiac molar investment. But the perverted pole is equally opposed to the schizophrenic pole, just as the reconstitution of territorialities is opposed to the movement of deterritorialization. And if perversion in the narrowest sense of the word performs a certain very specific type of reterritorialization within the artifice, perversion in the broad sense comprises all the types of reterritorializations, not merely artificial, but also exotic, archaic, residual, private, etc.: thus Oedipus and psychoanalysis as perversion. Even Raymond Roussel's schizophrenic machines turn into perverse machines in a theater representing Africa. In short, there is no deterritorialization of the flows of schizophrenic desire that is not accompanied by global or local reterritorializations, reterritorializations that always reconstitute shores of representation. What is more, the force and the obstinacy of a deterritorialization can only be evaluated through the types of reterritorialization that represent it; the one is the reverse side of the other. Our loves are complexes of deterritorialization and reterritorialization. What we love is always a certain mulatto—male or female. The movement of deterritorialization can never be grasped in itself, one can only grasp its indices in relation to the territorial representations. Take the example of dreams: yes, dreams are Oedipal, and this comes as no surprise, since dreams are a perverse reterritorialization in relation to the deterritorialization of sleep and nightmares. But *why return to dreams,* why turn them into the royal road of desire and the unconscious, when they are in fact the manifestation of a superego, a superpowerful and superarchaized ego (the Urszene of the Urstaat)? Yet at the heart of dreams themselves—as with fantasy and delirium—machines function as indices of deterritorialization. In dreams there are always machines endowed with the strange property of passing from hand to hand, of escaping and causing circulations, of carrying and being carried away. The airplane of parental coitus, the father's car, the grandmother's sewing machine, the little brother's bicycle, all objects of flight and theft, stealing and stealing away—the machine is always infernal in the family dream. The machine intro-

[36] Gisela Pankow, *L'homme et sa psychose* (Paris: Aubier, 1969), pp. 68–72. And on the role of the house: "La dynamique de l'espace et le temps vécu," *Critique,* February 1972. [Au.]

duces breaks and flows that prevent the dream from being reconfined in its scene and systematized within its representation. It makes the most of an irreducible factor of non-sense, which will develop elsewhere and from without, in the conjunctions of the real as such. Psychoanalysis, with its Oedipal stubbornness, has only a dim understanding of this; for one reterritorializes on persons and surroundings, but one deterritorializes on machines. Is it Schreber's father who acts through machines, or on the contrary is it the machines themselves that function through the father? *Psychoanalysis settles on the imaginary and structural representatives of reterritorialization, while schizoanalysis follows the machinic indices of deterritorialization.* The opposition still holds between the neurotic on the couch—as an ultimate and sterile land, the last exhausted colony—and the schizo out for a walk in a deterritorialized circuit.

The following excerpt from an article by Michel Cournot on Chaplin helps us understand what schizophrenic laughter is, as well as the schizophrenic line of escape or breakthrough, and the process as deterritorialization, with its machinic indices: "The moment Charlie Chaplin makes the board fall a second time on his head—a psychotic gesture—he provokes the spectator's laughter. Yes, but what laughter is this? And what spectator? For example, the question no longer applies at all, at this point in the film, of knowing whether the spectator must see the accident coming or be surprised by it. It is as though the spectator, at that very moment, were no longer in his seat, were no longer in a position to observe things. A kind of perceptive gymnastics has led him, progressively, not to identify with the character of *Modern Times,* but to experience so directly the resistance of the events that he accompanies this character, has the same surprises, the same premonitions, the same habits as he. Thus it is that the famous *eating machine,* which in a sense, by its excess, is foreign to the film (Chaplin had invented it twenty-two years before the film), is merely the formal, absolute exercise that prepares for the conduct—also psychotic—of the worker trapped in the machine, with only his upside-down head sticking out, and who has Chaplin feed him his lunch, since it is lunch time. If laughter is a reaction that takes certain circuits, it can be said that Charlie Chaplin, as the film's sequences unfold, progressively *displaces* the reactions, causes them to recede, level by level, until the moment when the spectator is no longer master of his own circuits, and tends to spontaneously take either a shorter path, which is not passable, which is barred, or else a path that is very explicitly posted as leading nowhere. After having suppressed the spectator as such, Chaplin perverts the laughter, which comes to be like so many *short-circuits of a disconnected piece of machinery.* Critics have occasionally spoken of the pessimism of *Modern Times* and of the optimism of the final image. Neither term suits the film. Charles Chaplin in *Modern Times* sketches rather, *on a very small scale,* with a precise stroke, the finished design of several oppressive and fundamental manifestations. The leading character, played by Chaplin, has to be neither active nor passive, neither consenting nor insubordinate, since he is the pencil point that traces the design, he is the stroke itself. . . . That is why the final image is without optimism. One does not see what optimism would be doing at the conclusion of this statement. This man and this woman seen from the back, all black, whose shadows are not projected by any sun, advance toward nothing. The wireless telegraph poles that run along the left side of the road, the barren trees that dot the right side, do not meet at the horizon. There is no horizon. The bald hills facing the spectator only form a line that merges with the void hanging over them. Anyone can see that this man and this woman are no longer alive. There is no pessimism here either. What had to happen happened. They did not kill each other. They were not brought down by the police. And it will not be necessary to go looking for the alibi of an accident. Charles Chaplin did not dwell on this. He went quickly, as usual. He traced the finished design."[37]

In its destructive task, schizoanalysis must proceed as quickly as possible, but it can also proceed only with great patience, great care, by successively undoing the representative territorialities and reterritorializations through which a subject passes in his individual history. For there are several layers, several planes of resistance that come from within or are imposed from without. Schizophrenia as a process, deterritorialization as a process, is inseparable from the stases that interrupt it, or aggravate

[37] Michel Cournot, *Le Nouvel Observateur,* Nov. 1, 1971. [Au.]

it, or make it turn in circles, and reterritorialize it into neurosis, perversion, and psychosis. To a point where the process cannot extricate itself, continue on, and reach fulfillment, except insofar as it is capable of creating—what exactly?—a new land. In each case we must go back by way of old lands, study their nature, their density; we must seek to discover how the machinic indices are grouped on each of these lands that permit going beyond them. How can we reconquer the process each time, constantly resuming the journey on these lands—Oedipal familial lands of neurosis, artificial lands of perversion, clinical lands of psychosis? *In Search of Lost Time* as a great enterprise of schizoanalysis: all the planes are traversed until their molecular line of escape is reached, their schizophrenic breakthrough; thus in the kiss where Albertine's face jumps from one plane of consistency to another, in order to finally come undone in a nebula of molecules. The reader always risks stopping at a given plane and saying yes, *that* is where Proust is explaining himself. But the narrator-spider never ceases undoing webs and planes, resuming the journey, watching for the signs or the indices that operate like machines and that will cause him to go on further. This very movement is humor, black humor. Oh, the narrator does not homestead in the familial and neurotic lands of Oedipus, there where the global and personal connections are established; he does not remain there, he crosses these lands, he desecrates them, he penetrates them, he liquidates even his grandmother with a machine for tying shoes. The perverse lands of homosexuality, where the exclusive disjunctions of women with women, and men with men, are established, likewise break apart in terms of the machinic indices that undermine them. The psychotic earths, with their conjunctions in place (Charlus is therefore surely mad, and Albertine too, perhaps!), are traversed in their turn to a point where the problem is no longer posed, no longer posed in this way. The narrator continues his own affair, until he reaches the *unknown country,* his own, the *unknown land,* which alone is created by his own work in progress, the *Search of Lost Time "in progress,"* functioning as a desiring-machine capable of collecting and dealing with all the indices. He goes toward these new regions where the connections are always partial and nonpersonal, the conjunctions nomadic and polyvocal, the disjunctions included, where homosexuality and heterosexuality cannot be distinguished any longer: the world of transverse communications, where the finally conquered nonhuman sex mingles with the flowers, a new earth where desire functions according to its molecular elements and flows. Such a voyage does not necessarily imply great movements in extension; it becomes immobile, in a room and on a body without organs—an intensive voyage that undoes all the lands for the benefit of the one it is creating.

The patient resumption of the process, or on the contrary its interruption—the two are so closely interrelated that they can only be evaluated each within the other. How would the schizo's voyage be possible independent of certain circuits, how could it exist without a land? But inversely, how can we be certain that these circuits don't reconstitute the lands—only too well known—of the asylum, the artifice, or the family? We always return to the same question: from what does the schizo suffer, he whose sufferings are unspeakable? Does he suffer from the process itself, or rather from its interruptions, when he is neuroticized in the family, in the land of Oedipus; when the one who does not allow himself to be Oedipalized is psychoticized in the land of the asylum; when the one who escapes the family and the asylum is perverted in the artificial locales? Perhaps there is only one illness, neurosis, the Oedipal decay against which all the pathogenic interruptions of the process should be measured. Most of the modern endeavors—outpatient centers, inpatient hospitals, social clubs for the sick, family care, institutions, and even antipsychiatry—remain threatened by a common danger, a danger which Jean Oury has been able to analyze in depth: how does one avoid the institution's re-forming an asylum structure, or constituting perverse and reformist artificial societies, or residual paternalistic or mothering pseudo families? We do not have in mind the so-called community psychiatry endeavors, whose admitted purpose is to triangulate, to Oedipalize everyone—people, animals, and things—to a point where we will witness a new race of sick people implore by reaction that they can be given back an asylum, or a little Beckettian land, a garbage can, so they can become catatonic in a corner. But in a less openly repressive manner, who says that the family is a good place, a good circuit for the deterritorialized schizo? Such a thing would be very surprising, to say the least: "the therapeutic potentialities of the familial surroundings." The whole town, then, the whole neighborhood? What molar unit will constitute a sufficiently nomadic circuit? How does one prevent the unit chosen, even if a specific institution, from constituting a perverted society of tolerance, a mutual-aid society that hides the real problems? Will the structure of the institution save it? But how will the structure break its relationship with neuroticizing, perverting, psychoticizing castration? How will this structure produce anything but a subjugated group? How will it give free play to the process, when its entire molar organization has the function of binding the molecular process? Even antipsychiatry—especially sensitive to the schizophrenic breakthrough and the intense voyage—tires out and proposes the image of a subject-group that would become immediately reperverted, with former schizos guiding the most recent ones, and, as relays, little chapels, or better yet, a convent in Ceylon.

The only thing that can save us from these impasses is an effective politicization of psychiatry. And doubtless, with R. D. Laing and David Cooper antipsychiatry went very far in this direction. But it seems to us that they still conceive of this politicization in terms of the structure and the event, rather than the process itself. Furthermore, they localize social and mental alienation on a single line, and tend to consider them as identical by showing how the familial agent extends the one into the other.[38] Between the two, however, the relationship is rather that of an *included disjunction*. This is because the decoding and the deterritorialization of flows define the very process of capitalism—that is, its essence, its tendency, and its external limit. But we know that the process is continually interrupted, or the tendency counteracted, or the limit displaced, by subjective reterritorializations and representations that operate as much at the level of capital as a subject (the axiomatic), as at the level of the persons serving as capital's agents (application of the axiomatic). But we seek in vain to assign social alienation and mental alienation to one side or the other, as long as we establish a relation of exclusion between the two. The deterritorialization of flows in general effectively merges with mental alienation, inasmuch as it *includes* the reterritorializations that permit it to subsist only as the state of a particular flow, a flow of madness that is defined thus because it is charged with representing whatever escapes the axiomatics and the applications of reterritorialization in other flows. Inversely, one can find the form of social alienation in action in all the reterritorializations of capitalism, inasmuch as they keep the flows from escaping the system, and maintain labor in the axiomatic framework of property, and desire in the applied framework of the family; but this social alienation includes in its turn mental alienation, which finds itself represented or reterritorialized in neurosis, perversion, and psychosis (the mental illnesses).

A true politics of psychiatry, or antipsychiatry, would consist therefore in the following praxis: (1) undoing all the reterritorializations that transform madness into mental illness; (2) liberating the schizoid movement of deterritorialization in all the flows, in such a way that this characteristic can no longer qualify a particular residue as a flow of madness, but affects just as well the flows of labor and desire, of production, knowledge and creation in their most profound tendency. Here, madness would no longer exist as madness, not because it would have been transformed into "mental illness," but on the contrary because it would receive the support of all the other flows, including science and art—once it is said that madness is called madness and appears as such only because it is deprived of this support, and finds itself reduced to testifying all alone for deterritorialization as a universal process. It is merely its unwarranted privilege, a privilege beyond its capacities, that renders it mad. In this perspective Foucault announced an age when madness would disappear, not because it would be lodged within the controlled space of mental illness ("great tepid aquariums"), but on the contrary because the exterior limit designated by madness would be over-

[38] David Cooper, "Aliénation mentale et aliénation sociale," *Recherches*, December 1968, pp. 48–49: "Social alienation comes for the most part to overlap the diverse forms of mental alienation. . . . Those admitted into a psychiatric hospital are admitted not so much because they are sick, as because they are protesting in a more or less adequate way against the social order. The social system in which they are caught thereby comes to reinforce the damages wrought by the familial system in which they grew up. This autonomy that they seek to affirm with regard to a microsociety acts as an indicator of a massive alienation performed by society as a whole." [Au.]

come by means of other flows escaping control on all sides, and carrying us along.[39]

It should therefore be said that one can never go far enough in the direction of deterritorialization: you haven't seen anything yet—an irreversible process. And when we consider what there is of a profoundly artificial nature in the perverted reterritorializations, but also in the psychotic reterritorializations of the hospital, or even the familial neurotic reterritorializations, we cry out, "More perversion! More artifice!"—to a point where the earth becomes so artificial that the movement of deterritorialization creates of necessity and by itself a new earth. Psychoanalysis is especially satisfying in this regard: its entire perverted practice of the cure consists in transforming familial neurosis into artificial neurosis (of transference), and in exalting the couch, a little island with its commander, the psychoanalyst, as an autonomous territoriality of the ultimate artifice. A little additional effort is enough to overturn everything, and to lead us finally toward other far-off places. The schizoanalytic flick of the finger, which restarts the movement, links up again with the tendency, and pushes the simulacra to a point where they cease being artificial images to become indices of the new world. That is what the completion of the process is: not a promised and a pre-existing land, but a world created in the process of its tendency, its coming undone, its deterritorialization. The movement of the theater of cruelty; for it is the only theater of production, there where the flows cross the threshold of deterritorialization and produce the new land—not at all a hope, but a simple "finding," a "finished design," where the person who escapes causes other escapes, and marks out the land while deterritorializing himself. An active point of escape where the revolutionary machine, the artistic machine, the scientific machine, and the (schizo) analytic machine become parts and pieces of one another.

[39] Michel Foucault, "La folie, l'absence d'oeuvre," *La Table ronde,* May 1964: "Everything that we experience today in the mode of the *limit,* or of strangeness, or of the unbearable, will have joined again with the serenity of the positive." [Au.]

Hélène Cixous

b. 1937

HÉLÈNE CIXOUS'S feminist work is strongly in the mode of French poststructuralism. One sees in her language the words of *Derrida, Lacan,* and Barthes (the last two perhaps through the first), whose notion of dissemination Cixous appropriates to her idea of "libidinal feminist" writing. The history of writing, the history of reason, the phallocentric tradition, the dominating syntax and grammar—all these form a chain of relationships that suppress the feminine. The feminine is therefore impossible to define, for definition captures the feminine in the masculine phallocentric order. Cixous acknowledges the impossibility of complete escape: "A little bit of phallus" must remain. But her work deliberately seeks to overthrow the prevailing mode of writing, whether the writing is literary criticism (as in her later essay on Joyce) or a feminist "tract," as in the immensely influential "Laugh of the Medusa," presented here, in which she urges woman to "write herself." This writing is a political act, a writing *through the body* that would sweep away syntax.

But the "libidinal feminine" is not to be regarded as belonging to women, nor is the libidinal masculine the sole property of men. Cixous finds Heinrich Kleist, the eighteenth-century German poet, and Clarice Lispector, the modern Brazilian writer, both of whom she has studied in her seminar at the University of Paris VIII, feminine in this sense. A feminine libidinal economy is flexible toward the concept of property, tolerates separation, the otherness of the other, and difference; that is to say, it is conducive to freedom. For Cixous, this is not a matter of taking a position *between* the masculine and the feminine. Rather, it is to be always "on the side *with*" and on the side of movement. The literary text of the libidinal feminine must tolerate freedom from self-limitation and from neat borders, from beginnings, middles, and ends, from chapters. Such texts will be disquieting. Clearly Joyce's texts interest Cixous by belonging to this class or, as she would surely insist, anticlass.

Cixous strives to go beyond the initial feminist questions of equal rights to radical questions involving deep cultural change. In a recent interview she asks: "Are we going to be the equal of men, are we going to be as phallic as they are? Or do we want to save something else, something more positive, more archaic, much more on the side of *jouissance,* of pleasure, less socializable? If so, how and at what price?" Of her own writing, she asserts, it is useful only if there is a women's movement.

Several of Cixous's works have been translated into English, including *The Exile of James Joyce or the Art of Replacement* (1968, trans. 1972) and *La Jeune Née* (1975, trans. 1985). See also *Boundary 2* 12 (Summer 1984) and Verena Andermatt Conley, *Hélène Cixous: Writing the Feminine* (1984).

THE LAUGH OF THE MEDUSA

I shall speak about women's writing: about *what it will do.* Woman must write her self: must write about women and bring women to writing, from which they have been driven away as violently as from their bodies—for the same reasons, by the same law, with the same fatal goal. Woman must put herself into the text—as into the world and into history—by her own movement.

The future must no longer be determined by the past. I do not deny that the effects of the past are still with us. But I refuse to strengthen them by repeating them, to confer upon them an irremovability the equivalent of destiny, to confuse the biological and the cultural. Anticipation is imperative.

Since these reflections are taking shape in an area just on the point of being discovered, they necessarily bear the mark of our time—a time during which the new breaks away from the old, and, more precisely, the (feminine) new from the old (*la nouvelle de l'ancien*). Thus, as there are no grounds for establishing a discourse, but rather an arid millennial ground to break, what I say has at least two sides and two aims: to break up, to destroy; and to foresee the unforeseeable, to project.

I write this as a woman, toward women. When I say "woman," I'm speaking of woman in her inevitable struggle against conventional man; and of a universal woman subject who must bring women to their senses and to their meaning in history. But first it must be said that in spite of the enormity of the repression that has kept them in the "dark"—that dark which people have been trying to make them accept as their attribute—there is, at this time, no general woman, no one typical woman. What they have *in common* I will say. But what strikes me is the infinite richness of their individual constitutions: you can't talk about *a* female sexuality, uniform, homogeneous, classifiable into codes—any more than you can talk about one unconscious resembling another. Women's imaginary is inexhaustible, like music, painting, writing: their stream of phantasms is incredible.

I have been amazed more than once by a description a woman gave me of a world all her own which she had been secretly haunting since early childhood. A world of searching, the elaboration of a knowledge, on the basis of a systematic experimentation with the bodily functions, a passionate and precise interrogation of her erotogeneity. This practice, extraordinarily rich and inventive, in particular as concerns masturbation, is prolonged or accompanied by a production of forms, a veritable aesthetic activity, each stage of rapture inscribing a resonant vision, a composition, something beautiful. Beauty will no longer be forbidden.

I wished that that woman would write and proclaim this unique empire so that other women, other unacknowledged sovereigns, might exclaim: I, too, overflow; my desires have invented new desires, my body knows unheard-of songs. Time and again I, too, have felt so full of luminous torrents that I could burst—burst with forms much more beautiful than those which are put up in frames and sold for a stinking fortune. And I, too, said nothing, showed nothing; I didn't open my mouth, I didn't repaint my half of the world. I was ashamed. I was afraid, and I swallowed my shame and my fear. I said to myself: You are mad! What's the meaning of these waves, these floods, these outbursts? Where is the ebullient, infinite woman who, immersed as she was in her naiveté, kept in the dark about herself, led into self-disdain by the great arm of parental-conjugal phallocentrism,[1] hasn't been ashamed of her strength? Who, surprised and horrified by the fantastic tumult of her drives (for she was made to believe that a well-adjusted normal woman has a . . . divine composure), hasn't accused herself of being a monster? Who, feeling a funny desire stirring inside her (to sing, to write, to dare to speak, in short, to bring out something new), hasn't thought she was sick? Well, her shameful sickness is that she resists death, that she makes trouble.

And why don't you write? Write! Writing is for you, you are for you; your body is yours, take it. I know why you haven't written. (And why I didn't write before the age of twenty-seven.) Because writ-

THE LAUGH OF THE MEDUSA originally appeared in French in 1975. It is reprinted here from *Signs* 1 (Summer 1976) by permission of the University of Chicago Press. The translation is by Keith Cohen and Paula Cohen.

[1]Phallocentrism is identified in the work of Derrida and deconstruction generally with the logocentric "origin" or, as in the work of Lacan, the "law of the father." See *Derrida* and *Lacan*. [Eds.]

ing is at once too high, too great for you, it's reserved for the great—that is for "great men"; and it's "silly." Besides, you've written a little, but in secret. And it wasn't good, because it was in secret, and because you punished yourself for writing, because you didn't go all the way, or because you wrote, irresistibly, as when we would masturbate in secret, not to go further, but to attenuate the tension a bit, just enough to take the edge off. And then as soon as we come, we go and make ourselves feel guilty—so as to be forgiven; or to forget, to bury it until the next time.

Write, let no one hold you back, let nothing stop you: not man; not the imbecilic capitalist machinery, in which publishing houses are the crafty, obsequious relayers of imperatives handed down by an economy that works against us and off our backs; and not *yourself*. Smug-faced readers, managing editors, and big bosses don't like the true texts of women—female-sexed tests. That kind scares them.

I write woman: woman must write woman. And man, man. So only an oblique consideration will be found here of man; it's up to him to say where his masculinity and femininity are at: this will concern us once men have opened their eyes and seen themselves clearly.[2]

Now women return from afar, from always: from "without," from the heath where witches are kept alive; from below, from beyond "culture"; from their childhood which men have been trying desperately to make them forget, condemning it to "eternal rest." The little girls and their "ill-mannered" bodies immured, well-preserved, intact unto themselves, in the mirror. Frigidified. But are they ever seething underneath! What an effort it takes—there's no end to it—for the sex cops to bar their threatening return. Such a display of forces on both sides that the struggle has for centuries been immobilized in the trembling equilibrium of a deadlock.

HERE they are, returning, arriving over and again, because the unconscious is impregnable. They have wandered around in circles, confined to the narrow room in which they've been given a deadly brainwashing. You can incarcerate them, slow them down, get away with the old Apartheid routine, but for a time only. As soon as they begin to speak, at the same time as they're taught their name, they can be taught that their territory is black: because you are Africa, you are black. Your continent is dark. Dark is dangerous. You can't see anything in the dark, you're afraid. Don't move, you might fall. Most of all, don't go into the forest. And so we have internalized this horror of the dark.

Men have committed the greatest crime against women. Insidiously, violently, they have led them to hate women, to be their own enemies, to mobilize their immense strength against themselves, to be the executants of their virile needs. They have made for women an antinarcissism! A narcissism which loves itself only to be loved for what women haven't got! They have constructed the infamous logic of antilove.

We the precocious, we the repressed of culture, our lovely mouths gagged with pollen, our wind knocked out of us, we the labyrinths, the ladders, the trampled spaces, the bevies—we are black and we are beautiful.

We're stormy, and that which is ours breaks loose from us without our fearing any debilitation. Our glances, our smiles, are spent; laughs exude from all our mouths; our blood flows and we extend ourselves without ever reaching an end; we never hold back our thoughts, our signs, our writing; and we're not afraid of lacking.

What happiness for us who are omitted, brushed aside at the scene of inheritances; we inspire ourselves and we expire without running out of breath, we are everywhere!

From now on, who, if we say so, can say no to us? We've come back from always.

It is time to liberate the New Woman from the Old by coming to know her—by loving her for getting by, for getting beyond the Old without delay,

[2] Men still have everything to say about their sexuality, and everything to write. For what they have said so far, for the most part, stems from the opposition activity/passivity from the power relation between a fantasized obligatory virility meant to invade, to colonize, and the consequential phantasm of woman as a "dark continent" to penetrate and to "pacify." (We know what "pacify" means in terms of scotomizing the other and misrecognizing the self.) Conquering her, they've made haste to depart from her borders, to get out of sight, out of body. The way man has of getting out of himself and into her whom he takes not for the other but for his own, deprives him, he knows, of his own bodily territory. One can understand how man, confusing himself with his penis and rushing in for the attack, might feel resentment and fear of being "taken" by the woman, of being lost in her, absorbed or alone. [Au.]

by going out ahead of what the New Woman will be, as an arrow quits the bow with a movement that gathers and separates the vibrations musically, in order to be more than her self.

I say that we must, for, with a few rare exceptions, there has not yet been any writing that inscribes femininity; exceptions so rare, in fact, that, after plowing through literature across languages, cultures, and ages,[3] one can only be startled at this vain scouting mission. It is well known that the number of women writers (while having increased very slightly from the nineteenth century on) has always been ridiculously small. This is a useless and deceptive fact unless from their species of female writers we do not first deduct the immense majority whose workmanship is in no way different from male writing, and which either obscures women or reproduces the classic representations of women (as sensitive—intuitive—dreamy, etc.)[4]

Let me insert here a parenthetical remark. I mean it when I speak of male writing. I maintain unequivocally that there is such a thing as *marked* writing; that, until now, far more extensively and repressively than is ever suspected or admitted, writing has been run by a libidinal and cultural—hence political, typically masculine—economy; that this is a locus where the repression of women has been perpetuated, over and over, more or less consciously, and in a manner that's frightening since it's often hidden or adorned with the mystifying charms of fiction; that this locus has grossly exaggerated all the signs of sexual opposition (and not sexual difference), where woman has never *her* turn to speak—this being all the more serious and unpardonable in that writing is precisely *the very possibility of change,* the space that can serve as a springboard for subversive thought, the precursory movement of a transformation of social and cultural structures.

[3]I am speaking here only of the place "reserved" for women by the Western World. [Au.]

[4]Which works, then, might be called feminine? I'll just point out some examples: one would have to give them full readings to bring out what is pervasively feminine in their significance. Which I shall do elsewhere. In France (have you noted our infinite poverty in this field?—the Anglo-Saxon countries have shown resources of distinctly greater consequence), leafing through what's come out of the twentieth century—and it's not much—the only inscriptions of femininity that I have seen were by Colette, Marguerite Duras, . . . and Jean Genet. [Au.]

Nearly the entire history of writing is confounded with the history of reason, of which it is at once the effect, the support, and one of the privileged alibis. It has been one with the phallocentric tradition. It is indeed that same self-admiring, self-stimulating, self-congratulatory phallocentrism.

With some exceptions, for there have been failures—and if it weren't for them, I wouldn't be writing (I-woman, escapee)—in that enormous machine that has been operating and turning out its "truth" for centuries. There have been poets who would go to any lengths to slip something by at odds with tradition—men capable of loving love and hence capable of loving others and of wanting them, of imagining the woman who would hold out against oppression and constitute herself as a superb, equal, hence "impossible" subject, untenable in a real social framework. Such a woman the poet could desire only by breaking the codes that negate her. Her appearance would necessarily bring on, if not revolution—for the bastion was supposed to be immutable—at least harrowing explosions. At times it is in the fissure caused by an earthquake, through that radical mutation of things brought on by a material upheaval when every structure is for a moment thrown off balance and an ephemeral wildness sweeps order away, that the poet slips something by, for a brief span, of woman. Thus did Kleist[5] expend himself in his yearning for the existence of sister-lovers, maternal daughters, mother-sisters, who never hung their heads in shame. Once the palace of magistrates is restored, it's time to pay: immediate bloody death to the uncontrollable elements.

But only the poets—not the novelists, allies of representationalism. Because poetry involves gaining strength through the unconscious and because the unconscious, that other limitless country, is the place where the repressed manage to survive: women, or as Hoffmann would say, fairies.[6]

She must write her self, because this is the invention of a *new insurgent* writing which, when the moment of her liberation has come, will allow her to carry out the indispensable ruptures and transformations in her history, first at two levels that cannot be separated.

a) Individually. By writing her self, woman will

[5]Heinrich von Kleist (1777–1811), German dramatic poet. [Eds.]

[6]E.T. A. Hoffmann (1776–1822), German writer. [Eds.]

return to the body which has been more than confiscated from her, which has been turned into the uncanny stranger on display—the ailing or dead figure, which so often turns out to be the nasty companion, the cause and location of inhibitions. Censor the body and you censor breath and speech at the same time.

Write your self. Your body must be heard. Only then will the immense resources of the unconscious spring forth. Our naphtha will spread, throughout the world, without dollars—black or gold—nonassessed values that will change the rules of the old game.

To write. An act which will not only "realize" the decensored relation of woman to her sexuality, to her womanly being, giving her access to her native strength; it will give her back her goods, her pleasures, her organs, her immense bodily territories which have been kept under seal; it will tear her away from the superegoized structure in which she has always occupied the place reserved for the guilty (guilty of everything, guilty at every turn: for having desires, for not having any; for being frigid, for being "too hot"; for not being both at once; for being too motherly and not enough; for having children and for not having any; for nursing and for not nursing. . .)—tear her away by means of this research, this job of analysis and illumination, this emancipation of the marvelous text of her self that she must urgently learn to speak. A woman without a body, dumb, blind, can't possibly be a good fighter. She is reduced to being the servant of the militant male, his shadow. We must kill the false woman who is preventing the live one from breathing. Inscribe the breath of the whole woman.

b) An act that will also be marked by woman's *seizing* the occasion to *speak,* hence her shattering entry into history, which has always been based *on her suppression*. To write and thus to forge for herself the antilogos weapon. To become *at will* the taker and initiator, for her own right, in every symbolic system, in every political process.

It is time for women to start scoring their feats in written and oral language.

Every woman has known the torment of getting up to speak. Her heart racing, at times entirely lost for words, ground and language slipping away—that's how daring a feat, how great a transgression it is for a woman to speak—even just open her mouth—in public. A double distress, for even if she transgresses, her words fall almost always upon the deaf male ear, which hears in language only that which speaks in the masculine.

It is by writing, from and toward women, and by taking up the challenge of speech which has been governed by the phallus, that women will confirm women in a place other than that which is reserved in and by the symbolic, that is, in a place other than silence. Women should break out of the snare of silence. They shouldn't be conned into accepting a domain which is the margin or the harem.

Listen to a woman speak at a public gathering (if she hasn't painfully lost her wind). She doesn't "speak," she throws her trembling body forward; she lets go of herself, she flies; all of her passes into her voice, and it's with her body that she vitally supports the "logic" of her speech. Her flesh speaks true. She lays herself bare. In fact, she physically materializes what she's thinking; she signifies it with her body. In a certain way she *inscribes* what she's saying, because she doesn't deny her drives the intractable and impassioned part they have in speaking. Her speech, even when "theoretical" or political, is never simple or linear or "objectified," generalized: she draws her story into history.

There is not that scission, that division made by the common man between the logic of oral speech and the logic of the text, bound as he is by his antiquated relation—servile, calculating—to mastery. From which proceeds the niggardly lip service which engages only the tiniest part of the body, plus the mask.

In women's speech, as in their writing, that element which never stops resonating, which, once we've been permeated by it, profoundly and imperceptibly touched by it, retains the power of moving us—that element is the song: first music from the first voice of love which is alive in every woman. Why this privileged relationship with the voice? Because no woman stockpiles as many defenses for countering the drives as does a man. You don't build walls around yourself, you don't forego pleasure as "wisely" as he. Even if phallic mystification has generally contaminated good relationships, a woman is never far from "mother" (I mean outside her role functions: the "mother" as nonname and as source of goods). There is always within her at least a little of that good mother's milk. She writes in white ink.

Woman for women.—There always remains in woman that force which produces/is produced by the other—in particular, the other woman. *In* her, matrix, cradler; herself giver as her mother and child; she is her own sister-daughter. You might object, "What about she who is the hysterical offspring of a bad mother?" Everything will be changed once woman gives woman to the other woman. There is hidden and always ready in woman the source; the locus for the other. The mother, too, is a metaphor. It is necessary and sufficient that the best of herself be given to woman by another woman for her to be able to love herself and return in love the body that was "born" to her. Touch me, caress me, you the living no-name, give me my self as myself. The relation to the "mother," in terms of intense pleasure and violence, is curtailed no more than the relation to childhood (the child that she was, that she is, that she makes, remakes, undoes, there at the point where, the same, she mothers herself). Text: my body—shot through with streams of song; I don't mean the overbearing, clutchy "mother" but, rather, what touches you, the equivoice that affects you, fills your breast with an urge to come to language and launches your force; the rhythm that laughs you; the intimate recipient who makes all metaphors possible and desirable; body (body? bodies?), no more describable than god, the soul, or the Other; that part of you that leaves a space between yourself and urges you to inscribe in language your woman's style. In women there is always more or less of the mother who makes everything all right, who nourishes, and who stands up against separation; a force that will not be cut off but will knock the wind out of the codes. We will rethink womankind beginning with every form and every period of her body. The Americans remind us, "We are all Lesbians"; that is, don't denigrate woman, don't make of her what men have made of you.

Because the "economy" of her drives is prodigious, she cannot fail, in seizing the occasion to speak, to transform directly and indirectly *all* systems of exchange based on masculine thrift. Her libido will produce far more radical effects of political and social change than some might like to think.

Because she arrives, vibrant, over and again, we are at the beginning of a new history, or rather of a process of becoming in which several histories intersect with one another. As subject for history, woman always occurs simultaneously in several places. Woman un-thinks[7] the unifying, regulating history that homogenizes and channels forces, herding contradictions into a single battlefield. In woman, personal history blends together with the history of all women, as well as national and world history. As a militant, she is an integral part of all liberations. She must be farsighted, not limited to a blow-by-blow interaction. She foresees that her liberation will do more than modify power relations or toss the ball over to the other camp; she will bring about a mutation in human relations, in thought, in all praxis: hers is not simply a class struggle, which she carries forward into a much vaster movement. Not that in order to be a woman-in-struggle(s) you have to leave the class struggle or repudiate it; but you have to split it open, spread it out, push it forward, fill it with the fundamental struggle so as to prevent the class struggle, or any other struggle for the liberation of a class or people, from operating as a form of repression, pretext for postponing the inevitable, the staggering alteration in power relations and in the production of individualities. This alteration is already upon us—in the United States, for example, where millions of night crawlers are in the process of undermining the family and disintegrating the whole of American sociality.

The new history is coming; it's not a dream, though it does extend beyond men's imagination, and for good reason. It's going to deprive them of their conceptual orthopedics, beginning with the destruction of their enticement machine.

It is impossible to *define* a feminine practice of writing, and this is an impossibility that will remain, for this practice can never be theorized, enclosed, coded—which doesn't mean that it doesn't exist. But it will always surpass the discourse that regulates the phallocentric system; it does and will take place in areas other than those subordinated to philosophico-theoretical domination. It will be conceived of only by subjects who are breakers of automatisms, by peripheral figures that no authority can ever subjugate.

HENCE the necessity to affirm the flourishes of this writing, to give form to its movement, its near and distant byways. Bear in mind to begin with (1) that sexual opposition, which has always worked for man's profit to the point of reducing writing, too, to his laws, is only a historico-cultural limit. There is, there will be more and more rapidly pervasive now, a fiction that produces irreducible effects of femi-

[7] *Dé-pense,* a neologism formed on the verb *penser,* hence "unthinks," but also "spends" (from *dépenser*). [Tr.]

ninity. (2) That it is through ignorance that most readers, critics, and writers of both sexes hesitate to admit or deny outright the possibility or the pertinence of a distinction between feminine and masculine writing. It will usually be said, thus disposing of sexual difference: either that all writing, to the extent that it materializes, is feminine; or, inversely—but it comes to the same thing—that the act of writing is equivalent to masculine masturbation (and so the woman who writes cuts herself out a paper penis); or that writing is bisexual, hence neuter, which again does away with differentiation. To admit that writing is precisely working (in) the in-between, inspecting the process of the same and of the other without which nothing can live, undoing the work of death—to admit this is first to want the two, as well as both, the ensemble of the one and the other, not fixed in sequences of struggle and expulsion or some other form of death but infinitely dynamized by an incessant process of exchange from one subject to another. A process of different subjects knowing one another and beginning one another anew only from the living boundaries of the other: a multiple and inexhaustible course with millions of encounters and transformations of the same into the other and into the in-between, from which woman takes her forms (and man, in his turn; but that's his other history).

In saying "bisexual, hence neuter," I am referring to the classic conception of bisexuality, which, squashed under the emblem of castration fear and along with the fantasy of a "total" being (though composed of two halves), would do away with the difference experienced as an operation incurring loss, as the mark of dreaded sectility.

To this self-effacing, merger-type bisexuality, which would conjure away castration (the writer who puts up his sign: "bisexual written here, come and see," when the odds are good that it's neither one nor the other), I oppose the *other bisexuality* on which every subject not enclosed in the false theater of phallocentric representationalism has founded his/her erotic universe. Bisexuality: that is, each one's location in self (*répérage en soi*) of the presence—variously manifest and insistent according to each person, male or female—of both sexes, nonexclusion either of the difference or of one sex, and, from this "self-permission," multiplication of the effects of the inscription of desire, over all parts of my body and the other body.

Now it happens that at present, for historico-cultural reasons, it is women who are opening up to and benefiting from this vatic bisexuality which doesn't annul differences but stirs them up, pursues them, increases their number. In a certain way, "woman is bisexual"; man—it's a secret to no one—being poised to keep glorious phallic monosexuality in view. By virtue of affirming the primacy of the phallus and of bringing it into play, phallocratic ideology has claimed more than one victim. As a woman, I've been clouded over by the great shadow of the scepter and been told: idolize it, that which you cannot brandish. But at the same time, man has been handed that grotesque and scarcely enviable destiny (just imagine) of being reduced to a single idol with clay balls. And consumed, as Freud and his followers note, by a fear of being a woman! For, if psychoanalysis was constituted from woman, to repress femininity (and not so successful a repression at that—men have made it clear), its account of masculine sexuality is now hardly refutable; as with all the "human" sciences, it reproduces the masculine view, of which it is one of the effects.

Here we encounter the inevitable man-with-rock, standing erect in his old Freudian realm, in the way that, to take the figure back to the point where linguistics is conceptualizing it "anew," Lacan[8] preserves it in the sanctuary of the phallos (ɸ) "sheltered" from *castration's lack!* Their "symbolic" exists, it holds power—we, the sowers of disorder, know it only too well. But we are in no way obliged to deposit our lives in their banks of lack, to consider the constitution of the subject in terms of a drama manglingly restaged, to reinstate again and again the religion of the father. Because we don't want that. We don't fawn around the supreme hole. We have no womanly reason to pledge allegiance to the negative. The feminine (as the poets suspected) affirms: ". . . And yes," says Molly, carrying *Ulysses* off beyond any book and toward the new writing; "I said yes, I will Yes."[9]

The Dark Continent is neither dark nor unexplorable.—It is still unexplored only because we've been made to believe that it was too dark to be explorable. And because they want to make us believe that what interests us is the white continent, with

[8] See *Jacques Lacan*. [Eds.]

[9] The last words of James Joyce's *Ulysses*. [Eds.]

its monuments to Lack. And we believed. They riveted us between two horrifying myths: between the Medusa and the abyss. That would be enough to set half the world laughing, except that it's still going on. For the phallologocentric sublation[10] is with us, and it's militant, regenerating the old patterns, anchored in the dogma of castration. They haven't changed a thing: they've theorized their desire for reality! Let the priests tremble, we're going to show them our sexts!

Too bad for them if they fall apart upon discovering that women aren't men, or that the mother doesn't have one. But isn't this fear convenient for them? Wouldn't the worst be, isn't the worst, in truth, that women aren't castrated, that they have only to stop listening to the Sirens (for the Sirens were men) for history to change its meaning? You only have to look at the Medusa straight on to see her. And she's not deadly. She's beautiful and she's laughing.

Men say that there are two unrepresentable things: death and the feminine sex. That's because they need femininity to be associated with death; it's the jitters that gives them a hard-on! for themselves! They need to be afraid of us. Look at the trembling Perseuses moving backward toward us, clad in apotropes. What lovely backs! Not another minute to lose. Let's get out of here.

Let's hurry: the continent is not impenetrably dark. I've been there often. I was overjoyed one day to run into Jean Genet. It was in *Pompes funèbres*.[11] He had come there led by his Jean. There are some men (all too few) who aren't afraid of femininity.

Almost everything is yet to be written by women about femininity: about their sexuality, that is, its infinite and mobile complexity, about their eroticization, sudden turn-ons of a certain miniscule-immense area of their bodies; not about destiny, but about the adventure of such and such a drive, about trips, crossings, trudges, abrupt and gradual awakenings, discoveries of a zone at one time timorous and soon to be forthright. A woman's body, with its thousand and one thresholds of ardor—once, by smashing yokes and censors, she lets it articulate the profusion of meanings that run through it in every direction—will make the old single-grooved mother tongue reverberate with more than one language.

We've been turned away from our bodies, shamefully taught to ignore them, to strike them with that stupid sexual modesty; we've been made victims of the old fool's game: each one will love the other sex. I'll give you your body and you'll give me mine. But who are the men who give women the body that women blindly yield to them? Why so few texts? Because so few women have as yet won back their body. Women must write through their bodies, they must invent the impregnable language that will wreck partitions, classes, and rhetorics, regulations and codes, they must submerge, cut through, get beyond the ultimate reserve-discourse, including the one that laughs at the very idea of pronouncing the word "silence," the one that, aiming for the impossible, stops short before the word "impossible" and writes it as "the end."

Such is the strength of women that, sweeping away syntax, breaking that famous thread (just a tiny little thread, they say) which acts for men as a surrogate umbilical cord, assuring them—otherwise they couldn't come—that the old lady is always right behind them, watching them make phallus, women will go right up to the impossible.

When the "repressed" of their culture and their society returns, it's an explosive, *utterly* destructive, staggering return, with a force never yet unleashed and equal to the most forbidding of suppressions. For when the Phallic period comes to an end, women will have been either annihilated or borne up to the highest and most violent incandescence. Muffled throughout their history, they have lived in dreams, in bodies (though muted), in silences, in aphonic revolts.

And with such force in their fragility; a fragility, a vulnerability, equal to their incomparable intensity. Fortunately, they haven't sublimated; they've saved their skin, their energy. They haven't worked at liquidating the impasse of lives without futures. They have furiously inhabited these sumptuous bodies: admirable hysterics who made Freud succumb to many voluptuous moments impossible to confess, bombarding his Mosaic statue with their carnal and passionate body words, haunting him with their inaudible and thundering denunciations, dazzling, more than naked underneath the seven

[10] Standard English term for the Hegelian *Aufhebung*, the French *la relève*. [Tr.]

[11] Jean Genet, *Pompes funèbres* (Paris 1948), p. 185 (privately published). [Au.]

veils of modesty. Those who, with a single word of the body, have inscribed the vertiginous immensity of a history which is sprung like an arrow from the whole history of men and from biblico-capitalist society, are the women, the supplicants of yesterday, who come as forebears of the new women, after whom no intersubjective relation will ever be the same. You, Dora,[12] you the indomitable, the poetic body, you are the true "mistress" of the Signifier. Before long your efficacity will be seen at work when your speech is no longer suppressed, its point turned in against your breast, but written out over against the other.

In body.—More so than men who are coaxed toward social success, toward sublimation, women are body. More body, hence more writing. For a long time it has been in body that women have responded to persecution, to the familial-conjugal enterprise of domestication, to the repeated attempts at castrating them. Those who have turned their tongues 10,000 times seven times before not speaking are either dead from it or more familiar with their tongues and their mouths than anyone else. Now, I-woman am going to blow up the Law: an explosion henceforth possible and ineluctable; let it be done, right now, *in* language.

Let us not be trapped by an analysis still encumbered with the old automatisms. It's not to be feared that language conceals an invincible adversary, because it's the language of men and their grammar. We mustn't leave them a single place that's any more theirs alone than we are.

If woman has always functioned "within" the discourse of man, a signifier that has always referred back to the opposite signifier which annihilates its specific energy and diminishes or stifles its very different sounds, it is time for her to dislocate this "within," to explode it, turn it around, and seize it; to make it hers, containing it, taking it in her own mouth, biting that tongue with her very own teeth to invent for herself a language to get inside of. And you'll see with what ease she will spring forth from that "within"—the "within" where once she so drowsily crouched—to overflow at the lips she will cover the foam.

Nor is the point to appropriate their instruments, their concepts, their places, or to begrudge them their position of mastery. Just because there's a risk of identification doesn't mean that we'll succumb. Let's leave it to the worriers, to masculine anxiety and its obsession with how to dominate the way things work—knowing "how it works" in order to "make it work." For us the point is not to take possession in order to internalize or manipulate, but rather to dash through and to "fly."[13]

Flying is woman's gesture—flying in language and making it fly. We have all learned the art of flying and its numerous techniques; for centuries we've been able to possess anything only by flying; we've lived in flight, stealing away, finding, when desired, narrow passageways, hidden crossovers. It's no accident that *voler* has a double meaning, that it plays on each of them and thus throws off the agents of sense. It's no accident: women take after birds and robbers just as robbers take after women and birds. They (*illes*)[14] go by, fly the coop, take pleasure in jumbling the order of space, in disorienting it, in changing around the furniture, dislocating things and values, breaking them all up, emptying structures, and turning propriety upside down.

What woman hasn't flown/stolen? Who hasn't felt, dreamt, performed the gesture that jams sociality? Who hasn't crumbled, held up to ridicule, the bar of separation? Who hasn't inscribed with her body the differential, punctured the system of couples and opposition? Who, by some act of transgression, hasn't overthrown successiveness, connection, the wall of circumfusion?

A feminine text cannot fail to be more than subversive. It is volcanic; as it is written it brings about an upheaval of the old property crust, carrier of masculine investments; there's no other way. There's no room for her if she's not a he. If she's a her-she, it's in order to smash everything, to shatter the framework of institutions, to blow up the law, to break up the "truth" with laughter.

For once she blazes *her* trail in the symbolic, she cannot fail to make of it the chaosmos of the "personal"—in her pronouns, her nouns, and her clique of referents. And for good reason. There will have been the long history of gynocide. This is known by the colonized peoples of yesterday, the workers, the nations, the species off whose backs the history of

[12] Dora. See Freud's *Fragment of an Analysis of a Case of Hysteria* (1905). [Eds.]

[13] Also, "to steal." Both meanings of the verb *voler* are played on, as the text itself explains in the following paragraph. [Tr.]

[14] *Illes* is a fusion of the masculine pronoun *ils*, which refers back to birds and robbers, with the feminine *elles*, which refers to women. [Tr.]

men has made its gold; those who have known the ignominy of persecution derive from it an obstinate future desire for grandeur; those who are locked up know better than their jailers the taste of free air. Thanks to their history, women today know (how to do and want) what men will be able to conceive of only much later. I say woman overturns the "personal," for if, by means of laws, lies, blackmail, and marriage, her right to herself has been extorted at the same time as her name, she has been able, through the very movement of moral alienation, to see more closely the inanity of "propriety," the reductive stinginess of the masculine-conjugal subjective economy, which she doubly resists. On the one hand she has constituted herself necessarily as that "person" capable of losing a part of herself without losing her integrity. But secretly, silently, deep down inside, she grows and multiplies, for, on the other hand, she knows far more about living and about the relation between the economy of the drives and the management of the ego than any man. Unlike man, who holds so dearly to his title and his titles, his pouches of value, his cap, crown, and everything connected with his head, woman couldn't care less about the fear of decapitation (or castration), adventuring, without the masculine temerity, into anonymity, which she can merge with, without annihilating herself: because she's a giver.

I shall have a great deal to say about the whole deceptive problematic of the gift. Woman is obviously not that woman Nietzsche dreamed of who gives only in order to.[15] Who could ever think of the gift as a gift-that-takes? Who else but man, precisely the one who would like to take everything?

If there is a "propriety of woman," it is paradoxically her capacity to depropriate unselfishly, body without end, without appendage, without principal "parts." If she is a whole, it's a whole composed of parts that are wholes, not simple partial objects but a moving, limitlessly changing ensemble, a cosmos tirelessly traversed by Eros, an immense astral space not organized around any one sun that's any more of a star than the others.

This doesn't mean that she's an undifferentiated magma, but that she doesn't lord it over her body or her desire. Though masculine sexuality gravitates around the penis, engendering that centralized body (in political anatomy) under the dictatorship of its parts, woman does not bring about the same regionalization which serves the couple head/genitals and which is inscribed only within boundaries. Her libido is cosmic, just as her unconscious is worldwide. Her writing can only keep going, without ever inscribing or discerning contours, daring to make these vertiginous crossings of the other(s) ephemeral and passionate sojourns in him, her, them, whom she inhabits long enough to look at from the point closest to their unconscious from the moment they awaken, to love them at the point closest to their drives; and then further, impregnated through and through with these brief, identificatory embraces, she goes and passes into infinity. She alone dares and wishes to know from within, where she, the outcast, has never ceased to hear the resonance of fore-language. She lets the other language speak—the language of 1,000 tongues which knows neither enclosure nor death. To life she refuses nothing. Her language does not contain, it carries; it does not hold back, it makes possible. When id is ambiguously uttered—the wonder of being several—she doesn't defend herself against these unknown women whom she's surprised at becoming, but derives pleasure from this gift of alterability. I am spacious, singing flesh, on which is grafted no one knows which I, more or less human, but alive because of transformation.

Write! and your self-seeking text will know itself better than flesh and blood, rising, insurrectionary dough kneading itself, with sonorous, perfumed ingredients, a lively combination of flying colors, leaves, and rivers plunging into the sea we feed. "Ah, there's her sea," he will say as he holds out to me a basin full of water from the little phallic mother from whom he's inseparable. But look, our seas are what we make of them, full of fish or not, opaque or transparent, red or black, high or smooth, narrow or bankless; and we are ourselves sea, sand, coral, seaweed, beaches, tides, swimmers, children, waves . . . More or less wavily sea, earth, sky—what matter would rebuff us? We know how to speak them all.

Heterogeneous, yes. For her joyous benefits she is erogenous; she is the erotogeneity of the heterogeneous: airborne swimmer, in flight, she does not

[15] Reread Derrida's text, "Le style de la femme," in *Nietzsche aujourd'hui* (Union Générale d'Editions, Coll. 10/18), where the philosopher can be seen operating an *Aufhebung* of all philosophy in its systematic reducing of woman to the place of seduction: she appears as the one who is taken for; the bait in person, all veils unfurled, the one who doesn't give but who gives only in order to (take). [Au.]

cling to herself; she is dispersible, prodigious, stunning, desirous and capable of others, of the other woman that she will be, of the other woman she isn't, of him, of you.

Woman be unafraid of any other place, of any same, or any other. My eyes, my tongue, my ears, my nose, my skin, my mouth, my body-for-(the)-other—not that I long for it in order to fill up a hole, to provide against some defect of mine, or because, as fate would have it, I'm spurred on by feminine "jealousy"; not because I've been dragged into the whole chain of substitutions that brings that which is substituted back to its ultimate object. That sort of thing you would expect to come straight out of "Tom Thumb," out of the *Penisneid* whispered to us by old grandmother ogresses, servants to their father-sons. If they believe, in order to muster up some self-importance, if they really need to believe that we're dying of desire, that we are this hole fringed with desire for their penis—that's their immemorial business. Undeniably (we verify it at our own expense—but also to our amusement), it's their business to let us know they're getting a hard-on, so that we'll assure them (we the maternal mistresses of their little pocket signifier) that they still can, that it's still there—that men structure themselves only by being fitted with a feather. In the child it's not the penis that the woman desires, it's not that famous bit of skin around which every man gravitates. Pregnancy cannot be traced back, except within the historical limits of the ancients, to some form of fate, to those mechanical substitutions brought about by the unconscious of some eternal "jealous woman"; not to penis envies; and not to narcissism or to some sort of homosexuality linked to the ever-present mother! Begetting a child doesn't mean that the woman or the man must fall ineluctably into patterns or must recharge the circuit of reproduction. If there's a risk there's not an inevitable trap: may women be spared the pressure, under the guise of consciousness-raising, of a supplement of interdictions. Either you want a kid or you don't—*that's your business*. Let nobody threaten you; in satisfying your desire, let not the fear of becoming the accomplice to a sociality succeed the old-time fear of being "taken." And man, are you still going to bank on everyone's blindness and passivity, afraid lest the child make a father and, consequently, that in having a kid the woman land herself more than one bad deal by engendering all at once child—mother—father—family? No; it's up to you to break the old circuits. It will be up to man and woman to render obsolete the former relationship and all its consequences, to consider the launching of a brand-new subject, alive, with defamilialization. Let us demater-paternalize rather than deny woman, in an effort to avoid the cooptation of procreation, a thrilling era of the body. Let us defetishize. Let's get away from the dialectic which has it that the only good father is a dead one, or that the child is the death of his parents. The child is the other, but the other without violence, bypassing loss, struggle. We're fed up with the reuniting of bonds forever to be severed, with the litany of castration that's handed down and genealogized. We won't advance backward anymore; we're not going to repress something so simple as the desire for life. Oral drive, anal drive, vocal drive—all these drives are our strengths, and among them is the gestation drive—just like the desire to write: a desire to live self from within, a desire for the swollen belly, for language, for blood. We are not going to refuse, if it should happen to strike our fancy, the unsurpassed pleasures of pregnancy which have actually been always exaggerated or conjured away—or cursed—in the classic texts. For if there's one thing that's been repressed, here's just the place to find it: in the taboo of the pregnant woman. This says a lot about the power she seems invested with at the time, because it has always been suspected, that, when pregnant, the woman not only doubles her market value, but—what's more important—takes on intrinsic value as a woman in her own eyes and, undeniably, acquires body and sex.

There are thousands of ways of living one's pregnancy; to have or not to have with that still invisible other a relationship of another intensity. And if you don't have that particular yearning, it doesn't mean that you're in any way lacking. Each body distributes in its own special way, without model or norm, the nonfinite and changing totality of its desires. Decide for yourself on your position in the arena of contradictions, where pleasure and reality embrace. Bring the other to life. Women know how to live detachment; giving birth is neither losing nor increasing. It's adding to life an other. Am I dreaming? Am I misrecognizing? You, the defenders of "theory," the sacrosanct yes-men of Concept, enthroners of the phallus (but not of the penis):

Once more you'll say that all this smacks of "idealism," or what's worse, you'll splutter that I'm a "mystic."

And what about the libido? Haven't I read the "Signification of the Phallus"? And what about separation, what about that bit of self for which, to be born, you undergo an ablation—an ablation, so they say, to be forever commemorated by your desire?

Besides, isn't it evident that the penis gets around in my texts, that I give it a place and appeal? Of course I do. I want all. I want all of me with all of him. Why should I deprive myself of a part of us? I want all of us. Woman of course has a desire for a "loving desire" and not a jealous one. But not because she is gelded; not because she's deprived and needs to be filled out, like some wounded person who wants to console herself or seek vengeance. I don't want a penis to decorate my body with. But I do desire the other for the other, whole and entire, male or female; because living means wanting everything that is, everything that lives, and wanting it alive. Castration? Let others toy with it. What's a desire originating from a lack? A pretty meager desire.

The woman who still allows herself to be threatened by the big dick, who's still impressed by the commotion of the phallic stance, who still leads a loyal master to the beat of the drum: that's the woman of yesterday. They still exist, easy and numerous victims of the oldest of farces: either they're cast in the original silent versions in which, as titanesses lying under the mountains they make with their quivering, they never see erected that theoretic monument to the golden phallus looming, in the old manner, over their bodies. Or, coming today out of their *infans* period and into the second, "enlightened" version of their virtuous debasement, they see themselves suddenly assaulted by the builders of the analytic empire and, as soon as they've begun to formulate the new desire, naked, nameless, so happy at making an appendage, they're taken in their bath by the new old men, and then, whoops! Luring them with flashy signifiers, the demon of interpretation—oblique, decked out in modernity—sells them the same old handcuffs, baubles, and chains. Which castration do you prefer? Whose degrading do you like better, the father's or the mother's? Oh, what pwetty eyes, you pwetty little girl. Here, buy my glasses and you'll see the Truth-Me-Myself tell you everything you should know. Put them on your nose and take a fetishist's look (you are me, the other analyst—that's what I'm telling you) at your body and the body of the other. You see? No? Wait, you'll have everything explained to you, and you'll know at last which sort of neurosis you're related to. Hold still, we're going to do your portrait, so that you can begin looking like it right away.

Yes, the naives to the first and second degree are still legion. If the New Women, arriving now, dare to create outside the theoretical, they're called in by the cops of the signifier, fingerprinted, remonstrated, and brought into the line of order that they are supposed to know; assigned by force of trickery to a precise place in the chain that's always formed for the benefit of a privileged signifier. We are pieced back to the string which leads back, if not to the Name-of-the-Father, then, for a new twist, to the place of the phallic-mother.

Beware, my friend, of the signifier that would take you back to the authority of a signified! Beware of diagnoses that would reduce your generative powers. "Common" nouns are also proper nouns that disparage your singularity by classifying it into species. Break out of the circles; don't remain within the psychoanalytic closure. Take a look around, then cut through!

And if we are legion, it's because the war of liberation has only made as yet a tiny breakthrough. But women are thronging to it. I've seen them, those who will be neither dupe nor domestic, those who will not fear the risk of being a woman; who will not fear any risk, any desire, any space still unexplored in themselves, among themselves and others or anywhere else. They do not fetishize, they do not deny, they do not hate. They observe, they approach, they try to see the other woman, the child, the lover—not to strengthen their own narcissism or verify the solidity or weakness of the master, but to make love better, to invent.

Other love.—In the beginning are our differences. The new love dares for the other, wants the other, makes dizzying, precipitous flights between knowledge and invention. The woman arriving over and over again does not stand still; she's everywhere, she exchanges, she is the desire-that-gives. (Not enclosed in the paradox of the gift that takes nor under the illusion of unitary fusion. We're past that.) She comes in, comes-in-between herself me and you, between the other me where one is always infinitely more than one and more than me, without the fear of ever reaching a limit; she thrills in our becoming. And we'll keep on becoming! She cuts through defensive loves, motherages, and devourations: beyond selfish narcissism, in the moving, open, transitional space, she runs her risks. Beyond the struggle-to-the-death that's been removed to the bed, beyond the love-battle that claims to represent exchange, she scorns at an Eros dynamic that would be fed by hatred. Hatred: a heritage, again, a reminder, a duping subservience to the phallus. To love, to watch-think-seek the other in the other, to despecularize, to unhoard. Does this seem difficult? It's not impossible, and this is what nourishes life—a love that has no commerce with the apprehensive desire that provides against the lack and stultifies the strange; a love that rejoices in the exchange that multiplies. Wherever history still unfolds as the history of death, she does not tread. Opposition, hierarchizing exchange, the struggle for mastery which can end only in at least one death (one master—one slave, or two nonmasters ≠ two dead)—all that comes from a period in time governed by phallocentric values. The fact that this period extends into the present doesn't prevent woman from starting the history of life somewhere else. Elsewhere, she gives. She doesn't "know" what she's giving, she doesn't measure it; she gives, though, neither a counterfeit impression nor something she hasn't got. She gives more, with no assurance that she'll get back even some unexpected profit from what she puts out. She gives that there may be life, thought, transformation. This is an "economy" that can no longer be put in economic terms. Wherever she loves, all the old concepts of management are left behind. At the end of a more or less conscious computation, she finds not her sum but her differences. I am for you what you want me to be at the moment you look at me in a way you've never seen me before: at every instant. When I write, it's everything that we don't know we can be that is written out of me, without exclusions, without stipulation, and everything we will be calls us to the unflagging, intoxicating, unappeasable search for love. In one another we will never be lacking.

Jonathan Culler

b. 1944

JONATHAN CULLER'S *Structuralist Poetics* (1975) provides a significant measure of the impact of Continental structuralism on a new generation of American critics who had been trained by the so-called New Critics—just as it provides essential background for his vigorous argument concerning the role of interpretation reprinted here. In *Structuralist Poetics,* Culler at once embraced and transformed structuralism, by interpreting it through a more local Anglo-American history—with the ironic peculiarity that the local history inculcates a predisposition to universalizing technique as "science." Thus, Culler argued for a more rigorous approach to the study of literary structure by borrowing from structuralist and transformational linguistics, substituting the idea of "literary competence" for Chomsky's notion of "linguistic competence" and turning from the anthropological focus of such theorists as *Lévi-Strauss* to the specific "poetic" deployment of the diverse conventions and codes in poems and novels.

The case is especially interesting since it illustrates the subtle problem of commensurability when a term such as "structure" assumes a privileged role in different cultural and intellectual traditions. New Critics (and their collegial antagonists, the neo-Aristotelians) had appealed to an idea of literary structure as distinctive, differentiating poetry from both ordinary speech and the language of science. (See *CTSP,* pp. 927–47, 1032–48, 1078–1101 for selections by Allen Tate, Cleanth Brooks, and R. S. Crane.) From this point of view, the appeal of criticism, especially theoretical criticism, lies partly in the fact that the presumed autonomy of the text and the "objectivity" of its structure would appear to offer criticism a clear rationale for its own existence as a profession, and make literature and its values accessible without respect to one's social status or even one's learning. The inability of the New Critics (or the neo-Aristotelians) to resolve controversies concerning "form" and "structure" and, more specifically, rival interpretations of texts was therefore not merely a technical difficulty but an ideological defeat. Appeals to critical pluralism, as if theoretical differences could be tolerated, failed for both theoretical and political reasons—in the first case because the claim that "form" or "structure" was intrinsic and "objective" presupposes that agreement could be insulated from ideological commitments, and in the second because the theoretical vulnerability indicated by disagreement implies that literary form or structure, though it may be intrinsic and objective, surely cannot be insulated from ideology.

In the concluding chapters of *Structuralist Poetics,* Culler notes this irony in his discussion of the *Tel Quel* group, notably *Derrida* and *Kristeva* while defending the structuralist program he outlines as conducive to a "criticism which focuses on the adventures of meaning." Part of what he means by "the adventures of meaning" is explicated by the essay reprinted here, "Beyond Interpretation." Culler does not address the New Critics' dilemma over interpretation directly, except to suggest that its characteristic focus on developing a "reading" of the single, isolated text is radically insufficient—just as he had earlier suggested in *Structuralist Poetics* that the insistence on "organic unity" for the individual text makes a fetish of the idea of the end or telos presumed to be realized in the text itself. Even so, Culler's pursuit of semiotics is (as he indicates in the title of another essay in *The Pursuit of Signs*) the elaboration of "Semiotics as a Theory of Reading." As such, Culler's work remains within the tradition he seeks to go beyond, expanding the scope and scale of the New Criticism to include what he calls in the essay here an "analysis of the conditions of meaning." This is not at all to diminish the importance of Culler's objection to interpretation, as if it were the defining task of criticism, but only to place that objection within a history. Indeed, just as Culler suggests that "one source of energy for criticism in the coming years may be the reinvention of literary history," so too a source of energy for theory may be the reinvention of the history of criticism.

Culler's works include *Flaubert: The Uses of Uncertainty* (1974); *Structuralist Poetics* (1975); *The Pursuit of Signs* (1981); and *On Deconstruction* (1982).

BEYOND INTERPRETATION

In the years since World War II, the New Criticism has been challenged, even vilified, but it has seldom been effectively ignored. The inability if not reluctance of its opponents simply to evade its legacy testifies to the dominant position it has come to occupy in American and British universities. Despite the many attacks on it, despite the lack of an organized and systematic defense, it seems not unfair to speak of the hegemony of New Criticism in this period and of the determining influence it has exercised on our ways of writing about and teaching literature. Whatever critical affiliations we may proclaim, we are all New Critics, in that it requires a strenuous effort to escape notions of the autonomy of the literary work, the importance of demonstrating its unity, and the requirement of 'close reading.'

In many ways the influence of the New Criticism has been beneficent, especially on the teaching of literature. Those old enough to have experienced the transition, its emergence from an earlier mode of literary study, speak of the sense of release, the new excitement breathed into literary education by the assumption that even the meanest student who lacked the scholarly information of his betters could make valid comments on the language and structure of the text. No longer was discussion and evaluation of a work something which had to wait upon acquisition of a respectable store of literary, historical, and biographical information. No longer was the right to comment something earned by months in a library. Even the beginning student of literature was now confronted with poems, asked to read them closely, and required to discuss and evaluate their use of language and thematic organization. To make the experience of the text itself central to literary education and to relegate the accumulation of information about the text to an ancillary status was a move which gave the study of literature a new focus and justification, as well as promoting a more precise and relevant understanding of literary works.

BEYOND INTERPRETATION appears as chapter 1 of Culler, *The Pursuit of Signs: Semiotics, Literature, Deconstruction,* © 1981 Jonathan Culler. It is reprinted with the permission of the publisher, Cornell University Press. An earlier version of the essay was published in *Comparative Literature* 28 (1976).

But what is good for literary education is not necessarily good for the study of literature in general, and those very aspects of the New Criticism which ensured its success in schools and universities determined its eventual limitations as a program for literary criticism. Commitment to the autonomy of the literary text, a fundamental article of faith with positive consequences for the teaching of literature, led to a commitment to interpretation as the proper activity of criticism. If the work is an autonomous whole, then it can and should be studied in and for itself, without reference to possible external contexts, whether biographical, historical, psychoanalytic, or sociological. Distinguishing what was external from what was internal, rejecting historical and causal explanation in favor of internal analysis, the New Criticism left readers and critics with only one recourse. They must interpret the poem; they must show how its various parts contribute to a thematic unity, for this thematic unity justifies the work's status as autonomous artifact. When a poem is read in and for itself critics must fall back upon the one constant of their situation: there is a poem being read by a human being. Whatever is external to the poem, the fact that it addresses a human being means that what it says about human life is internal to it. The critic's task is to show how the interaction of the poem's parts produces a complex and ontologically privileged statement about human experience.

Though they may occasionally attempt to disguise the fact, the basic concepts of the New Critics and their followers derive from this thematic and interpretive orientation. The poem is not simply a series of sentences; it is spoken by a *persona,* who expresses an *attitude* to be defined, speaking in a particular *tone* which puts the attitude in one of various possible modes or degrees of commitment. Since the poem is an autonomous whole its value must lie within it, in richness of attitude, in complexity of judgment, in delicate balance of values.

Hence one finds in poems *ambivalence, ambiguity, tension, irony, paradox.* These are all thematic operators which permit one to translate formal features of the language into meanings so that the poem may be unified as a complex thematic structure expressing an attitude toward the world. And in place of a theory of reading which would specify how order was to be achieved, the New Criticism deployed a common humanism or, as R. S. Crane calls it, a 'set of reduction terms' toward which analysis of ambivalence, tension, irony, and paradox was to move: 'life and death, good and evil, love and hate, harmony and strife, order and disorder, eternity and time, reality and appearance, truth and falsity . . . emotion and reason, simplicity and complexity, nature and art."[1] A repertoire of contrasting attitudes and values relevant to the human situation served as a target language in the process of thematic translation. To analyze a poem was to show how all its parts contributed to a complex statement about human problems.

In short, it would be possible to demonstrate that, given its premises, the New Criticism was necessarily an interpretive criticism. But in fact this is scarcely necessary since the most important and insidious legacy of the New Criticism is the widespread and unquestioning acceptance of the notion that the critic's job is to interpret literary works. Fulfillment of the interpretive task has come to be the touchstone by which other kinds of critical writing are judged, and reviewers inevitably ask of any work of literary theory, linguistic analysis, or historical scholarship, whether it actually assists us in our understanding of particular works. In this critical climate it is therefore important, if only as a means of loosening the grip which interpretation has on critical consciousness, to take up a tendentious position and to maintain that, while the experience of literature may be an experience of interpreting works, in fact the interpretation of individual works is only tangentially related to the understanding of literature. To engage in the study of literature is not to produce yet another interpretation of *King Lear* but to advance one's understanding of the conventions and operations of an institution, a mode of discourse.

There are many tasks that confront criticism, many things we need to advance our understanding of literature, but one thing we do not need is more interpretations of literary works. It is not at all difficult to list in a general way critical projects which would be of compelling interest if carried through to some measure of completion; and such a list is in itself the best illustration of the potential fecundity of other ways of writing about literature. We have

[1] R. S. Crane, *The Languages of Criticism and the Structure of Poetry,* University of Toronto Press, 1953, pp. 123–4. [Au.]

no convincing account of the role or function of literature in society or social consciousness. We have only fragmentary or anecdotal histories of literature as an institution: we need a fuller exploration of its historical relation to the other forms of discourse through which the world is organized and human activities are given meaning. We need a more sophisticated and apposite account of the role of literature in the psychological economies of both writers and readers; and in particular we ought to understand much more than we do about the effects of *fictional* discourse. As Frank Kermode emphasized in his seminal work, *The Sense of an Ending,* criticism has made almost no progress toward a comprehensive theory of fictions, and we still operate with rudimentary notions of 'dramatic illusion' and 'identification' whose crudity proclaims their unacceptability. What is the status and what is the role of fictions, or, to pose the same kind of problem in another way, what are the relations (the historical, the psychic, the social relationships) between the real and the fictive? What are the ways of moving between life and art? What operations or figures articulate this movement? Have we in fact progressed beyond Freud's simple distinction between the figures of condensation and displacement? Finally, or perhaps in sum, we need a typology of discourse and a theory of the relations (both mimetic and nonmimetic) between literature and the other modes of discourse which make up the text of intersubjective experience.

The fact that we are so far from possessing these things in what is, after all, an age of criticism—an age where unparalleled industry and intelligence have been invested in writing about literature—is in part due to the preeminent role accorded to interpretation. Indeed, one of the best ways of talking about the failures of contemporary criticism is to look at the fate which has befallen three very intelligent and promising attempts to break away from the legacy of the New Criticism. In each case the failure to combat the notion of interpretation itself, or rather the conscious or unconscious persistence of the notion that a critical approach must justify itself by its interpretive results, has emasculated a highly promising mode of investigation.

My first case, in many ways the most significant, is that of Northrop Frye's *Anatomy of Criticism.* Frye's polemical introduction is, of course, a powerful indictment of contemporary criticism and an argument for a systematic poetics: criticism is in a state of 'naïve induction,' trying to study individual works of literature without a proper conceptual framework. It must recognize that literature is not a simple aggregate of discrete works but a conceptual space which can be coherently organized; and it must, if it is to become a discipline, make a 'leap to a new ground from which it can discover what the organizing or containing forms of its conceptual framework are.'[2] Working on this new ground involves assuming the possibility of 'a coherent and comprehensive theory of literature, logically and scientifically organized, some of which the student unconsciously learns as he goes on, but the main principles of which are as yet unknown to us.'[3]

This is certainly a direct attack on the atomism of the New Criticism and the assumption that one should approach each individual work with as few preconceptions as possible in order to experience directly the words on the page, but Frye does not realize the importance of attacking interpretation itself. He hovers on the edge of the problem, characterizing as 'one of the many slovenly illiteracies that the absence of systematic criticism has allowed to grow up' the notion that 'the critic should confine himself to "getting out" of a poem exactly what the poet may vaguely be assumed to have been aware of "putting in"'; but the function of this argument in his overall enterprise is anything but clear. It is wrongly assumed, he continues, that the critic needs no conceptual framework and that his job is simply 'to take a poem into which a poet has diligently stuffed a specific number of beauties or effects, and complacently to extract them one by one, like his prototype Little Jack Horner.'[4]

One might take this sentence as a general attack on interpretation, especially interpretation of a complacent and fundamentally tautological kind, but in fact, as the earlier sentence makes clear, Frye's real target is interpretation of an intentionalist kind. Joining the New Critics in rejecting criticism which is guilty of the intentional fallacy, Frye has picked the wrong enemy and opened the door to a trivialization of his enterprise. The systematic poetics for which he calls and to which he makes a sub-

[2] Northrop Frye, *Anatomy of Criticism,* New York, Atheneum, 1965, p. 16. [Au.]
[3] Ibid., p. 11. [Au.]
[4] Ibid., pp. 17–18. [Au.]

stantial contribution can thus be seen as a prelude to interpretation. Approaching the text with a conceptual framework—the theories of Modes, Symbols, Myths, and Genres as outlined in the *Anatomy*—the critic can interpret the work not by pulling out what the poet was aware of putting in but by extracting the elements of the various modes, genres, symbols, and myths which may have been put in without the author's explicit knowledge. In this case, interpretation would still be the test of a critical method, and the value of Frye's approach would be that it enabled one to perceive meanings which hitherto had been obscure.

Certainly this is not the justification Frye would wish to give his project. His repeated assertions that criticism must seek a comprehensive view of what it is doing, that it must try to attain an understanding of the fundamental principles which make it a discipline and mode of knowledge, show that he has other goals in mind. But his failure to question interpretation as a goal creates a fundamental ambiguity about the status of his categories and schemas. In identifying Spring, Summer, Autumn, and Winter as the four mythic categories, what exactly is Frye claiming? He might be suggesting that these categories form a general conceptual map which we have assimilated through our experience of literature and which lead us to interpret literature as we do. In other words, he might be claiming that in order to account for the meanings and effects of literary works one must bring to light these fundamental distinctions which are constantly at work in our reading of literature. Alternatively, he might be claiming that he has discovered categories of experience basic to the human psyche and that in order to discover the true or deepest meaning of literary works we must apply to them these categories, as hermeneutic devices.

Though the difference between these alternatives may seem slight, it is in fact crucial to the project of a poetics. In the second case one is claiming to have discovered distinctions which serve as a method of interpretation: which enable one to produce new and better readings of literary works. In the first case one is not offering a method of interpretation but is claiming to explain why we interpret literary works as we do. In the context of the polemical introduction and the suggestion that we should try to make explicit the implicit theory of literature which students unconsciously acquire in their literary education, the first interpretation would certainly be preferable; but in terms of the traditional tasks and preoccupations of criticism, which Frye has not thought to reject, the second interpretation is more likely to prevail.

In fact, this is exactly what has happened. Though it began as a plea for a systematic poetics, Frye's work has done less to promote work in poetics than to stimulate a mode of interpretation which has come to be known as "myth-criticism" or archetypal criticism. The assumption that the critic's task is to interpret individual works remains unchanged, only now, on the theory that the deepest meanings of a work are to be sought in the archetypal symbols or patterns which it deploys, Frye's categories are used as a set of labeling devices. Frye failed to recognize that the enemy of poetics is not just atomism but the interpretive project to which atomism ministers, and this led not only to deflection of systematic energy but to the promotion of a rather anodyne mode of interpretation.

The second example of a potentially powerful theoretical mode that had adopted the project of interpreting works is psychoanalytic criticism. In the 1960s the best works of psychoanalytic criticism avoided the questions concerning the status and effects of fiction which might have been elucidated by a psychoanalytic approach and concentrated on interpretation, as if they could only prove themselves by demonstrating their interpretive prowess. In *The Sins of the Fathers: Hawthorne's Psychological Themes* Frederick Crews demonstrates the appropriateness of a psychoanalytic method for making sense of many powerful and puzzling elements in Hawthorne's work. Oddities of plot, character, and fantasy become more interesting and their force more intelligible when they are analyzed as representations of the consequences of unresolved Oedipal conflicts: the works 'rest on fantasy, but on the shared fantasy of mankind, and this makes for a more interesting fiction than would any illusionistic slice of life.'[5]

The Sins of the Fathers is admirable, except in its implication that the goal of the psychoanalytic critic is to identify and interpret what the subtitle calls 'psychological themes.' If critics devote themselves to identifying in literary works the forces and

[5] Frederick Crews, *The Sins of the Fathers*, New York, Oxford University Press, p. 263. [Au.]

elements described by psychoanalytic theory, if they make psychoanalysis a source of themes, they restrict the impact of potentially valuable theoretical developments, such as the insights that have emerged from recent French rereadings of Freud. This body of work provides, among other things, an account of processes of textual transference by which critics find themselves uncannily repeating a displaced version of the narrative they are supposed to be comprehending—just as the psychoanalyst, through the process of transference and countertransference, finds himself caught up in the reenactment of the analysand's drama.[6] Contemporary psychoanalytic theory might have much to teach us about the logic of our interaction with texts but it is impoverished when it is treated as a repository of themes—themes to be identified when interpreting literary works. Leo Bersani's perceptive and original *Baudelaire and Freud* slides into this perspective in treating *Les Fleurs du Mal* as a drama of the struggle between what Lacan calls the Symbolic and the Imaginary.[7] In Lacan these are two modes of representation. Interpretive criticism makes them two psychic conditions, one good and the other bad, and translates events of the narrative into a struggle between them, thus producing something like an updated version of the hunt for Oedipus complexes and phallic symbols.

My third case is the 'Affective Stylistics' of Stanley Fish, which begins with a determined attempt to break away from the assumptions and procedures of the New Criticism but which, again, fails to identify interpretation as the real enemy and so compromises the theoretical insights on which it is based. Wimsatt and Beardsley had argued that one must not confuse the poem and its effects ('what it *is* and what it *does*') lest 'the poem itself, as an object of specifically critical judgment . . . disappear.'[8] This is precisely what should happen, replies Fish, for meaning lies not in the object but in the event or experience of reading. To ask about the meaning of a word or sentence is to ask what it *does* in the work, and to specify what it does one must analyze 'the developing responses of the reader in relation to the words as they succeed one another in time.'[9]

This is a fruitful reorientation, for reasons to be discussed later. Above all, it makes clear the need for a poetics, for if the meaning of works lies in the successive effects of their elements on readers, then one needs a powerful theory that will account for these effects by analyzing the norms, conventions, and mental operations on which they depend. A theory focussed on the reader and reading ought to undertake to make explicit the implicit knowledge that readers deploy in responding as they do.

But Fish fails to take this step because he assumes that the task of criticism is to interpret individual works, and he proposes to do this—for *Paradise Lost* and then for a series of 'self-consuming' seventeenth-century artifacts—by describing the reader's experience of hazarding judgments and then finding them proved wrong. In fact, this interpretive orientation has placed him in a rather tight corner: to claim simultaneously that one is describing the experience of the reader and that one is producing valuable new interpretations is a difficult act to sustain, and despite Fish's skill and energy he will not sustain it for long.[10] The future lies, rather, in the theoretical project that he flees.

These three cases, though very different in the content of their proposals and results, suggest a gloomy prognosis: the principle of interpretation is so strong an unexamined postulate of American criticism that it subsumes and neutralizes the most forceful and intelligent acts of revolt. However, the increasing influence of European criticism is making available a greater variety of ways of writing about literature, and if we can refrain from redirecting them to the restricted task of interpretation, American criticism will be much the richer.

At its most basic the lesson of contemporary European criticism is this: the New Criticism's dream of a self-contained encounter between innocent

[6] See Shoshana Felman, 'Turning the Screw of Interpretation,' *Yale French Studies*, 55/56 (1977) pp. 94–207, and Cynthia Chase, 'Oedipal Textuality: Reading Freud's Reading of *Oedipus*,' *Diacritics*, 9:1 (Spring 1979) pp. 54–71, for excellent discussions and applications. [Au.]

[7] Leo Bersani, *Baudelaire and Freud*, Berkeley, University of California Press, 1977. [Au.]

[8] W. K. Wimsatt, *The Verbal Icon*, Lexington, Kentucky, University of Kentucky Press, 1954, p. 21. [Au.] See *CTSP*, pp. 1022–31. [Eds.]

[9] Stanley Fish, *Self-Consuming Artifacts*, Berkeley, University of California Press, 1972, pp. 387–8. [Au.]

[10] Fish's later book, *The Living Temple: George Herbert and Catechizing*, Berkeley, University of California Press, 1978, combines a description of readers' responses to Herbert's poems with a historical thesis about Herbert's model of organization. The redescription of response alone would not suffice to produce a new and valuable interpretation. [Au.] See *Fish*. [Eds.]

reader and autonomous text is a bizarre fiction. To read is always to read in relation to other texts, in relation to the codes that are the products of these texts and go to make up a culture. And thus, while the New Criticism could conceive of no other possibility than interpreting the text, there are other projects of greater importance which involve analysis of the conditions of meaning. If works were indeed autonomous artifacts, there might be nothing to do but to interpret each of them, but since they participate in a variety of systems—the conventions of literary genres, the logic of story and the teleologies of emplotment, the condensations and displacements of desire, the various discourses of knowledge that are found in a culture—critics can move through texts towards an understanding of the systems and semiotic processes which make them possible.

Criticism informed by these principles may take many guises. A semiotics of literature would attempt to describe in systematic fashion the modes of significance of literary discourse and the interpretive operations embodied in the institution of literature. Alternatively, Fredric Jameson proposes to work towards a dialectical criticism which would not attempt to resolve difficulties but would take as its object of enquiry a work's resistance to interpretation. In defining the nature of a work's opacity one would attempt to discover its historical grounds: 'Thus our thought no longer takes official problems at face value but walks behind the screen to assess the very origin of the subject-object relationship in the first place.'[11] The product or result of dialectical criticism is not an interpretation of the work but a broader historical account of why interpretation should be necessary and what is signified by the need for particular types of interpretation.

Jameson's enterprise would lead, he says, 'to a dialectical rhetoric in which the various mental operations are understood not absolutely, but as moments and figures, tropes, syntactical paradigms of our relationship to the real itself, as, altering irrevocably in time, it nonetheless obeys a logic that like the logic of a language can never be fully distinguished from its object.'[12] A Marxist criticism conceived in this spirit would demonstrate that the relationship between a literary work and a social and historical reality is one not of reflected content but of a play of forms. Social reality includes paradigms of organization, figures of intelligibility; and the interplay between a literary work and its historical ground lies in the way its formal devices exploit, transform, and supplement a culture's ways of producing meaning.

Another version of this historical project is the *Rezeptionsästhetik* proposed by Hans Robert Jauss. Emphasizing that the meaning of a work depends upon the horizon of expectations against which it is received and which poses the questions to which the work comes to function as an answer, Jauss has inaugurated the vast and complex enterprise of describing these horizons, which are of course the product of the discourses of a culture. *Rezeptionsästhetik* is not a way of interpreting works but an attempt to understand their changing intelligibility by identifying the codes and interpretive assumptions that give them meaning for different audiences at different periods.[13]

These two examples suggest that one source of energy for criticism in the coming years may be the reinvention of literary history. The historical perspective enables one to recognize the transience of any interpretation, which will always be succeeded by other interpretations, and to take as object of reflection the series of interpretive acts by which traditions are constituted and meaning produced. This new historical orientation seems the common factor in the work of three otherwise very different critics, Geoffrey Hartman, Harold Bloom, and Paul de Man. Drawing sustenance from a historically conceived romantic poetry rather than from an ahistorical Metaphysical or Modernist verse, invoking as the stimulus of repeated quest and failure the impossible calling of high Romanticism, they treat literature and reading as a repeated historical error or deformation. 'History,' writes Hartman, 'is the wake of a mobile mind falling in and out of love with the things it detaches by its attachment.'[14] This becomes the temporal scheme of Harold Bloom's *The Anxiety of Influence:* each poet must slay his poetic

[11] Fredric Jameson, *Marxism and Form,* Princeton University Press, 1971, p. 341. [Au.]

[12] Ibid., p. 374. [Au.]

[13] See Hans Robert Jauss, *Literaturgeschichte als Provokation,* Frankfurt, Suhrkamp, 1970, and in English, 'Literary History as a Challenge to Literary Theory,' *New Directions in Literary History,* ed. Ralph Cohen, Baltimore, Johns Hopkins University Press, 1974, pp. 11–41. [Au.] See *Jauss.* [Eds.]

[14] Geoffrey Hartman, 'History-writing as Answerable Style,' in ibid., p. 100. [Au.]

father; he must displace his precursors by a revisionary misreading which creates the historical space in which his own poetry takes place. The hidden order of literary history is based on a negative and dialectical principle, which also orders the relationship between reader and text: the reader, like the new poet, is a latecomer bound to misconstrue the text so as to serve the meanings required by his own moment in literary history. That the greatest insights are produced in the process of necessary and determinate misreadings is the claim of another theorist of deformation, Paul de Man, for whom interpretation is always in fact covert literary history and inevitable error, since it takes for granted historical categorizations and obscures its own historical status.[15]

These critics certainly do not oppose interpretation; indeed, they publicly indulge in it, but by defining it as necessary error they lead us to enquire about its nature and status and thus to consider central questions about the nature of literary language. The effect of their writings has been to broaden the possibilities of literary investigation, but since they do not question the assumption that interpretation is the purpose of criticism they are immediately assimilated to the project of interpretation, at the cost of some confusion.

Consider the case of Harold Bloom. He proposes a theory of how poems come into being. Few critics would claim that an account of a poem's genesis is an account of its meaning, but since we assume that the task of critics is to interpret poems, we leap to the conclusion that when Bloom writes about a poem he is telling us its meaning. Even when he warns us that poems do not have meanings at all or that 'the meaning of a poem can only be a poem, but *another poem,* a *poem not itself,*'[16] we ignore his statement and take what he says about a poem and its intertextual, tropological genesis as an interpretation, even though it is not another poem—after which we are affronted that his 'interpretation' should be so extravagant, so different from what the poem appears to say. The assumption that critics *must* interpret is so powerful that we will not allow Bloom's writing to be anything else, and one suspects that Bloom himself is influenced by this assumption, against the explicit claims of his own theory.

Or consider *deconstruction.* Although Derrida's writings all involve close engagement with various texts, they seldom involve interpretations as traditionally conceived. There is no deference to the integrity of the text, no search for a unifying purpose that would assign each part its appropriate role. Derrida characteristically concentrates on elements which others find marginal, seeking not to elucidate what a text says but to reveal an uncanny logic that operates in and across texts, whatever they say. His treatment of Rousseau in *Of Grammatology* is part of an investigation of the place of writing in Western discussions of language, a disclosure of the process which has preserved an idealized model of speech by attributing certain problematical features of language to writing and then setting writing aside as secondary and derivative. Derrida notes that terms Rousseau uses to describe writing, the noun *supplément* and the verb *suppléer,* appear in discussions of other phenomena such as education and masturbation, and in following up these references in fictional, autobiographical, and expository texts, he describes what he calls the 'logic of supplementarity,' a general operation which we can now see at work as a source of energy in a wide variety of texts.[17] Is this an interpretation of Rousseau? It omits most of the contents of every text it mentions and fails to identify a thematic unity or a distinctive meaning for any of Rousseau's writings. Derrida is working, rather, to describe a general process through which texts undo the philosophical system to which they adhere by revealing its rhetorical nature.

But when deconstruction comes to America a shift takes place, subtly inaugurated in Paul de Man's critique of Derrida in *Blindness and Insight.* De Man argues that Rousseau's text already carries out the deconstructive operations which Derrida claims to perform on it, so that Derrida is in fact elucidating Rousseau, though he pretends to be doing something else because it makes, as de Man

[15] Paul de Man, *Blindness and Insight,* New York, Oxford University Press, 1971, p. 165. [Au.]

[16] Harold Bloom, *The Anxiety of Influence,* New York, Oxford University Press, 1973, p. 70. [Au.]

[17] Jacques Derrida, *Of Grammatology,* Baltimore, Johns Hopkins University Press, 1976, part II, ch. 2. For further discussion, see Jonathan Culler, *On Deconstruction: Literary Theory in the 1970s,* Ithaca, Cornell University Press/London, Routledge & Kegan Paul, forthcoming. [Au.]

puts it, a better story.[18] This displacement has since been transformed into a central methodological principle by J. Hillis Miller, who argues not just that a text already contains the operation of self-deconstruction, in which two contradictory principles or lines of argument confront one another, but that this undecidability 'is always thematized in the text itself in the form of metalinguistic statements.'[19] In other words, the text does not just contain or perform a self-deconstruction but is *about* self-deconstruction, so that a deconstructive reading is an interpretation of the text, an analysis of what it says or means. 'Great works of literature,' Miller insists, 'have anticipated explicitly any deconstruction the critic can achieve,' so that energetic deference and interpretive elucidation are the appropriate critical stances. Thus is deconstruction tamed by the critical assumption and made into a version of interpretation.

In the hands of its best practitioners, such as Paul de Man and Barbara Johnson, deconstruction is an interpretive mode of unusual power and subtlety.[20] In other hands there is always the danger that it will become a process of interpretation which seeks to identify particular themes, making undecidability, or the problem of writing, or the relationship between performative and constative, privileged themes of literary works. It seems to me that just because it easily becomes a method of interpretation, deconstruction has succeeded in America in a way that Marxism and structuralism have not. Marxism is committed to the immense and difficult project of working out the complicated processes of mediation between base and superstructure. When enlisted to interpret a particular work it is bound to seem, as we say, 'vulgar.' Structuralism is also committed to large-scale projects, such as elaborating a grammar of plot structure or the possible relations between story and discourse, and has thus seemed irrelevant except in so far as its concepts and categories can be 'applied' in the activity of interpretation. The possibility of pursuing these larger projects depends on our ability to resist the assumption that interpretation is the task of criticism.

Of course, in one sense all projects involve interpretation: selecting facts that require explanation is already an act of interpretation, as is positing descriptive categories and organizing them into theories. But this is no reason to take as the only valid form of critical writing the highly specialized exercise of developing for one work after another an interpretation sufficiently grounded in tradition to seem valid and sufficiently new to be worth proposing. This exercise has a strategic place in the production of literary tradition, but that does not mean that it should dominate literary studies. Readers will continue to read and interpret literary works, and interpretation will continue in the classroom, since it is through interpretation that teachers attempt to transmit cultural values, but critics should explore ways of moving beyond interpretation. E. D. Hirsch, for many years a leading champion of interpretation, has reached the conclusion that criticism should no longer devote itself to the goal of producing ever more interpretations: 'A far better solution to the problem of academic publishing would be to abandon the idea that has dominated scholarly writing for the past forty years: that interpretation is the only truly legitimate activity for a professor of literature. There are other things to do, to think about, to write about.'[21]

[18] Paul de Man, *Blindness and Insight,* ch. 7, pp. 102–41. [Au.]

[19] J. Hillis Miller, 'Deconstructing the Deconstructors,' *Diacritics,* 5:2 (Summer 1975) pp. 30–1. [Au.]

[20] See Paul de Man, *Allegories of Reading,* New Haven, Yale University Press, 1979; and Barbara Johnson, *Défigurations du langage poétique,* Paris, Flammarion, 1979. [Au.]

[21] E. D. Hirsch, 'Carnal Knowledge,' *New York Review of Books,* 26:10 (14 June 1979) p. 20. [Au.]

Harold Bloom

b. 1930

HAROLD BLOOM'S early work, mainly on the romantic poets, belongs to that phase of American criticism that revived interest in the romantics in response to the New Critics' tendency to denigrate them. This countermovement came in part in the wake of Northrop Frye's work on Blake. Bloom's early writing shows Frye's influence but breaks more thoroughly with the New Criticism by emphasizing the visionary qualities of Shelley and Blake. His first book enters the corpus of Shelley's poetry by way of Martin Buber's distinction between I-it and I-Thou relationships and attributes to Shelley a visionary energy disregarded by a previous generation of critics under the influence of the taste of T. S. Eliot.

Bloom's later work continues to valorize energy, but it expresses a much darker view of energy and employs a new and different critical language gathered up principally from psychoanalysis and the history of rhetoric. This criticism marks itself off from most poststructuralism by its insistence on an interest in authors, thus maintaining a typically romantic concern. But the author that Bloom rescues is hardly the author of traditional humanism. Rather, he is a creature of savage will to power, who comes on the scene always too late, always embattled by the fact that a strong precursor was there first. He must do battle with this precursor by creatively misreading him. For Bloom all poetry is interpretation of a previous writing. Indeed, it is inevitably *mis*interpretation, as is all criticism as well. The question is only whether it is "strong" or "weak," the "strong" misreading being one in which the poet, or the critic, triumphs through his "anxiety of influence" over that influence by a creative misprision. Lesser or "weak" writers do not assimilate their predecessors to their own creativity but merely follow along. From the beginning one notices in Bloom's work the frequent appearance of the word "stance," which valorizes the role of ego in a world of psychic warfare with the father-poet. This is a war the poet wages by means of what Bloom calls "revisionary ratios" or rhetorical maneuvers (Bloom provides a whole vocabulary of these) employed as defensive-aggressive acts in order to misread the predecessor: "Poems are not psyches, nor things, nor are they renewable archetypes in a verbal universe [here Bloom subjects his predecessor Frye to misprision], nor are they architectonic units of balanced stresses. They are defensive procedures in constant change, which is to say that poems themselves are *acts of reading*."

One senses strongly that Bloom would make the act of critical reading strong, that the distinction between poem and critical essay is inclined to disappear (see *Hartman*) beneath the hand of a strong critic. Bloom's own criticism recalls the famous line of Blake's character Los: "I must create a system or be enslav'd by another man's."

Bloom's development of his theory of the "anxiety of influence" occurs in a series of four books: *The Anxiety of Influence* (1973); *A Map of Misreading* (1975); *Kabbalah and Criticism* (1975); and *Poetry and Repression* (1976). These were followed by *Agon: Towards a Theory of Revisionism* (1981) and *The Breaking of the Vessels* (1982). Earlier works include *Shelley's Mythmaking* (1959); *The Visionary Company* (1961); *Blake's Apocalypse* (1963); *Yeats* (1970); *The Ringers in the Tower* (1971); and *Wallace Stevens: The Poems of Our Climate* (1976). See Jean-Pierre Mileur, *Literary Revisionism and the Burden of Modernity*, and David File, *Harold Bloom: The Rhetoric of Romantic Fiction.*

POETRY, REVISIONISM, REPRESSION

Jacques Derrida asks a central question in his essay on Freud and the Scene of Writing: "What is a text, and what must the psyche be if it can be represented by a text?"[1] My narrower concern with poetry prompts the contrary question: "What is a psyche, and what must a text be if it can be represented by a psyche?" Both Derrida's question and my own require exploration of three terms: "psyche," "text," "represented."

"Psyche" is ultimately from the Indo-European root *bhes,* meaning "to breathe," and possibly was imitative in its origins. "Text" goes back to the root *teks,* meaning "to weave," and also "to fabricate." "Represent" has as its root *es:* "to be." My question thus can be rephrased: "What is a breath, and what must a weaving or a fabrication be so as to come into being again as a breath?"

In the context of post-Enlightenment poetry, a breath is at once a *word,* and a *stance* for uttering that word, a word and a stance *of one's own.* In this context, a weaving or a fabrication is what we call a poem, and its function is to represent, to bring back into being again, an individual stance and word. The poem, as text, is represented or seconded by what psychoanalysis calls the psyche. But the text *is* rhetoric, and as a persuasive system of tropes can be carried into being again only by another system of tropes. Rhetoric can be seconded only by rhetoric, for all that rhetoric can *intend* is more rhetoric. If a text and a psyche can be represented by one another, this can be done only because each is a departure from proper meaning. Figuration turns out to be our only link between breathing and making.

The strong word and stance issue only from a strict will, a will that dares the error of reading all of reality as a text, and all prior texts as openings for its own totalizing and unique interpretations. Strong poets present themselves as looking for truth *in the world,* searching in reality and in tradition, but such a stance, as Nietzsche said, remains under the mastery of desire, of instinctual drives. So, in effect, the strong poet wants pleasure and not truth; he wants what Nietzsche named as "the belief in truth and the pleasurable effects of this belief." No strong poet can admit that Nietzsche was accurate in this insight, and no critic need fear that any strong poet will accept and so be hurt by demystification. The concern of this book, as of my earlier studies in poetic misprision, is only with strong poets, which in this series of chapters is exemplified by the major sequence of High Romantic British and American poets: Blake, Wordsworth, Shelley, Keats, Tennyson, Browning, Yeats, Emerson, Whitman, and Stevens, but also throughout by two of the strongest poets in the European Romantic tradition: Nietzsche and Freud. By "poet" I therefore do not mean only verse-writer, as the instance of Emerson also should make clear.

POETRY, REVISIONISM, REPRESSION is reprinted here from *Poetry and Repression: Revisionism from Blake to Stevens,* by permission of the Yale University Press, copyright 1976.

[1] *Writing and Difference,* trans. Alan Bass (Chicago: University of Chicago Press, 1978), p. 199. [Eds.]

A poetic "text," as I interpret it, is not a gathering of signs on a page, but is a psychic battlefield upon which authentic forces struggle for the only victory worth winning, the divinating triumph over oblivion, or as Milton sang it:

> Attir'd with Stars, we shall for ever sit,
> Triumphing over Death, and Chance, and
> thee O Time.[2]

Few notions are more difficult to dispel than the "commonsensical" one that a poetic text is self-contained, that it has an ascertainable meaning or meanings without reference to other poetic texts. Something in nearly every reader wants to say: "*Here* is a poem and *there* is a meaning, and I am reasonably certain that the two can be brought together." Unfortunately, poems are not things but only words that refer to other words, and *those* words refer to still other words, and so on, into the densely overpopulated world of literary language. Any poem is an inter-poem, and any reading of a poem is an inter-reading. A poem is not writing, but *rewriting,* and though a strong poem is a fresh start, such a start is a starting-again.

In some sense, literary criticism has known always this reliance of texts upon texts, but the knowing changed (or should have changed) after Vico, who uncovered the genuine scandal of poetic origins, in the complex defensive trope or troping defense he called "divination." Poetry began, according to Vico, out of the ignorance and mortal fear of the gentile giants, who sought to ward off danger and death through interpreting the auguries, through divination: "Their poetic wisdom began with this poetic metaphysics . . . and they were called theological poets . . . and were properly called divine in the sense of diviners, from *divinari,* to divine or predict."[3] These were the giants or poets before the Flood, for Vico a crucial image of two modes of encroachment always threatening the human mind, a divine deluge and a natural engulfment. Edward Said eloquently interprets Vico's own influence-anxieties:

> These threatening encroachments are described by Vico as the result of a divinely willed flood, which I take to be an image for the inner crisis of self-knowledge that each man must face at the very beginning of any conscious undertaking. The analogy, in Vico's *Autobiography,* of the universal flood is the prolonged personal crisis of self-alienation from full philosophic knowledge and self-knowledge that Vico faces until the publication of his major work, the *New Science.* His minor successes with his orations, his poems, his treatises, reveal bits of the truth to him, but he is always striving with great effort to come literally into his own.[4]

Said's commentary illuminates the remarkable passage in Vico's early *On the Study Methods of Our Time,* where Vico suddenly appears to be the precursor of Artaud, arguing that the great masterpieces of anterior art must be destroyed, if any great works are still to be performed. Or, if great art is to be retained, let it be for "the benefit of lesser minds," while men of "surpassing genius, should put the masterpieces of their art out of their sight, and strive with the greatest minds to appropriate the secret of nature's grandest creation." Vico's primary precursor was Descartes, whom he repudiated in favor of Bacon as a more distant and antithetical precursor, but it could be argued that Vico's *New Science* as a "severe poem" is a strong misprision of Descartes.

Language for Vico, particularly poetic language, is always and necessarily a revision of previous language. Vico, so far as I know, inaugurated a crucial insight that most critics still refuse to assimilate, which is that every poet is belated, that every poem is an instance of what Freud called *Nachträglichkeit* or "retroactive meaningfulness." Any poet (meaning even Homer, if we could know enough about his precursors) is in the position of being "after the Event," in terms of literary language. His art is necessarily an *aftering,* and so at best he strives for a selection, through repression, out of the traces of the language of poetry; that is, he represses some of the traces, and remembers others. This remembering is a misprision, or creative misreading, but no matter how strong a misprision, it cannot achieve an autonomy of meaning, or a meaning *fully* present, that is, free from all literary context. Even the strongest poet must take up his stance *within* liter-

[2] Milton, "On Time." [Eds.]

[3] *The New Science, CTSP,* p. 298. [Eds.]

[4] *Beginnings: Intention and Method* (New York: Basic Books, 1975), p. 365. [Eds.]

ary language. If he stands *outside* it, then he cannot begin to write poetry. For poetry lives always under the shadow of poetry. The caveman who traced the outline of an animal upon the rock always retraced a precursor's outline.

The curse of an increased belatedness, a dangerously self-conscious belatedness, is that creative envy becomes the ecstasy, the Sublime, of the sign-system of poetic language. But this is, from an altered perspective, a loss that can become a shadowed gain, the blessing achieved by the latecomer poet as a wrestling Jacob, who cannot let the great depart finally, without receiving a new name all his own. Nothing is won for the reader we all need to become if this wrestling with the dead is idealized by criticism. The enormous distinction of Vico, among all critical theorists, is that he idealized least. Vico understood, as almost no one has since, that the link between poetry and Hebrew-Christian theology was perpetual. In Vico's absolute distinction between gentile and Jew, the gentile is linked both to poetry and history, through the revisionary medium of language, while the Jew (and subsequently the Christian) is linked to a sacred origin transcending language, and so has no relation to human history or to the arts. We only know what we ourselves have made, according to Vico, and so his science excludes all knowledge of the true God, who can be left to the Church and its theologians. The happy consequence, for Vico, is that the world of the indefinite, the world of ambivalent and uncertain images, which is the universe of poetry, becomes identical with our fallen state of being in the body. To be in the body, according to Vico, is to suffer a condition in which we are ignorant of causation and of origins, yet still we are very much in quest of origins. Vico's insight is that poetry is born of our ignorance of causes, and we can extend Vico by observing that if any poet knows too well what causes his poem, then he cannot write it, or at least will write it badly. He must repress the causes, including the precursor-poems, but such forgetting, as this book will show, itself is a condition of a particular exaggeration of style or hyperbolical figuration that tradition has called the Sublime.

2

How does one read a strong poem? How does one write a strong poem? What makes a poem strong? There is a precarious identity between the Over-reader and the Over-poet, both of them perhaps forms of the Over-man, as prophesied by Nietzsche's Zarathustra. Strong poetry is a paradox, resembling nothing so much as Durkheim on Marxism, or Karl Kraus on Freudianism.[5] Durkheim said that socialism was not a sociology or miniature science, but rather a cry of grief; not so much a scientific formulation of social facts, as itself a social fact. Following the aphorism of Kraus, that psychoanalysis itself was the disease for which it purported to be the cure, we can say that psychoanalysis is more a psychic fact than a formulation of psychic facts. Similarly, the reading of strong poetry is just as much a poetic fact as is the writing of such poetry. Strong poetry is strong only by virtue of a kind of textual usurpation that is analogous to what Marxism encompasses as its social usurpation or Freudianism as its psychic usurpation. A strong poem does not *formulate* poetic facts any more than strong reading or criticism formulates them, for a strong reading *is* the only poetic fact, the only revenge against time that endures, that is successful in canonizing one text as opposed to a rival text.

There is no textual authority without an act of imposition, a declaration of property that is made figuratively rather than properly or literally. For the ultimate question a strong reading asks of a poem is: Why? Why should it have been written? Why must we read it, out of all the too many other poems available? Who does the poet think he is, anyway? Why is his poem?

By defining poetic strength as usurpation or imposition, I am offending against civility, against the social conventions of literary scholarship and criticism. But poetry, when it aspires to strength, is necessarily a competitive mode, indeed an obsessive mode, because poetic strength involves a self-representation that is reached only through trespass, through crossing a daemonic threshold. Again, resorting to Vico gives the best insight available for the nature and necessity of the strong poet's self-proclamation.

Vico says that "the true God" founded the Jewish religion "on the prohibition of the divination on which all the gentile nations arose." A strong poet, for Vico or for us, is precisely like a gentile nation; he must divine or invent himself, and so attempt the

[5] Emile Durkheim (1858–1917), French sociologist; Karl Kraus (1874–1936), Austrian writer. [Eds.]

impossibility of *originating himself*. Poetry has an origin in the body's ideas of itself, a Vichian notion that is authentically difficult, at least for me. Since poetry, unlike the Jewish religion, does not go back to a truly divine origin, poetry is always at work *imagining its own origin,* or telling a persuasive lie about itself, to itself. Poetic strength ensues when such lying persuades the reader that his own origin has been reimagined by the poem. Persuasion, in a poem, is the work of rhetoric, and again Vico is the best of guides, for he convincingly relates the origins of rhetoric to the origins of what he calls poetic logic, or what I would call poetic misprision.

Angus Fletcher, writing on *The Magic Flute,* observes that: "To begin is always uncertain, nextdoor to chaos. To begin requires that, uncertainly, we bid farewell to some thing, some one, some where, some time. Beginning is still ending." Fletcher, by emphasizing the uncertainty of a beginning, follows Vico's idea of the indefiniteness of all secular origins. But this indefiniteness, because it is made by man, can be interpreted by man. Vico says that "ignorance, the mother of wonder, made everything wonderful to men who were ignorant of everything." From this followed a poetic logic or language "not . . . in accord with the nature of the things it dealt with . . . but . . . a fantastic speech making use of physical substances endowed with life and most of them imagined to be divine."

For Vico, then, the trope comes from ignorance. Vico's profundity as a philosopher of rhetoric, beyond all others ancient and modern except for his true son, Kenneth Burke, is that he views tropes as defenses. Against what? Initially, against their own origins in ignorance, and so against the powerlessness of man in relation to the world:

> . . . man in his ignorance makes himself the rule of the universe, for in the examples cited he has made of himself an entire world. So that, as rational metaphysics teaches that man becomes all things by understanding them, this imaginative metaphysics shows that man becomes all things by *not* understanding them; and perhaps the latter proposition is truer than the former, for when man understands he extends his mind and takes in the things, but when he does not understand he makes the things out of himself and becomes them by transforming himself into them.[6]

Vico is asking a crucial question, which could be interpreted reductively as, What is a poetic image, or what is a rhetorical trope, or what is a psychic defense? Vico's answer can be read as a formula: poetic image, trope, defense are all forms of a ratio between human ignorance making things out of itself, and human self-identification moving to transform us into the things we have made. When the human ignorance is the trespass of a poetic repression of anteriority, and the transforming movement is a new poem, then the ratio measures a rewriting or an act of revision. As poetic image, the ratio is a phenomenal masking of the mind taking in the world of things, which is Vico's misprision of the Cartesian relationship between mind and the *res extensa.* An image is necessarily an imitation, and its coverings or maskings in poetic language necessarily center in certain fixed areas: presence and absence, partness and wholeness, fullness and emptiness, height and depth, insideness and outsideness, earliness and lateness. Why these? Because they are the inevitable categories of our makings and our becomings, or as inevitable as such categories can be, within the fixities and limits of space and time.

As trope, the ratio between ignorance and identification takes us back to the realization, by Vico, that the first language of the gentiles was not a "giving of names to things according to the nature of each," unlike the sacred Hebrew of Adam, but rather was fantastic and figurative. In the beginning was the trope, is in effect Vico's formula for pagan poetry. Kenneth Burke, the Vico of our century, gives us a formula for why rhetoric rises:

> In pure identification there would be no strife. Likewise, there would be no strife in absolute separateness, since opponents can join battle only through a mediatory ground that makes their communication possible, thus providing the first condition necessary for their interchange of blows. But put identification and division ambiguously together, so that you cannot know for certain just

[6] Vico, *CTSP,* p. 300. [Eds.]

> where one ends and the other begins, and you have the characteristic invitation to rhetoric. Here is a major reason why rhetoric, according to Aristotle, "proves opposites."[7]

Vico saw rhetoric as being defensive; Burke tends to emphasize what he calls the realistic function of rhetoric: "the use of language as a symbolic means of inducing cooperation in beings that by nature respond to symbols." But Vico, compared to Burke, is more of a magical formalist, like his own primitives, his "theological poets." Vico's giants divinate so as to defend against death, and they divinate through the turns of figurative language. As a ratio between ignorance and identification, a psychic defense in Vichian terms is not significantly different from the Freudian notion of defense. Freud's "mechanisms" of defense are directed toward Vico's "ignorance," which in Freud is "instinct" or "drive." For Freud and Vico alike the "source" of all our drives is the body, and defense is finally against drive itself. For though defense takes instinct as its object, defense becomes contaminated by instinct, and so becomes compulsive and at least partly repressed, which rhetorically means hyperbolical or Sublime.

A specific defense is for Freud an operation, but for Vico a trope. It is worth noting that the root-meaning of our word "defense" is "to strike or hurt," and that "gun" and "defense" are from the same root, just as it is interesting to remember that *tropos* meaning originally "turn, way, manner" appears also in the name *Atropos* and in the word "entropy." The trope-as-defense or ratio between ignorance and identification might be called at once a warding-off by turning and yet also a way of striking or manner of hurting. Combining Vico and Freud teaches us that the origin of any defense is its stance towards death, just as the origin of any trope is its stance towards proper meaning. Where the psychic defense and the rhetorical trope take the same particular phenomenal maskings in poetic images, there we might speak of the ultimate ratio between ignorance and identification as expressing itself in a somber formula: death is the most proper or literal of meanings, and literal meaning partakes of death.

Talbot Donaldson, commenting upon Chaucer's *Nun's Priest's Tale,* speaks of rhetoric as "a powerful weapon of survival in a vast and alien universe," a mode of satisfying our need for security.[8] For a strong poet in particular, rhetoric is also what Nietzsche saw it as being, a mode of interpretation that is the will's revulsion against time, the will's revenge, its vindication against the necessity of passing away. Pragmatically, a trope's revenge is against an earlier trope, just as defenses tend to become operations against one another. We can define a strong poet as one who will not tolerate words that intervene between him and the Word, or precursors standing between him and the Muse. But that means the strong poet in effect takes up the stance of the Gnostic, ancestor of all major Western revisionists.

3

What does the Gnostic *know*? These are the injunctions of the Gnostic adept Monoimus, who sounds rather like Emerson:

> Abandon the search for God and the creation. . . . Look for him by taking *yourself* as the starting point. Learn who it is who *within you* makes everything his own and says, "*My* god, *my* mind, *my* thought, *my* soul, *my* body." Learn the sources of sorrow, joy, love, hate. Learn how it happens that one watches without willing, rests without willing, becomes angry without willing, loves without willing. If you search these matters you will find him *in yourself*.[9]

What the Gnostic knows is his own subjectivity, and in that self-consciousness he seeks his own freedom, which he calls "salvation" but which pragmatically seems to be freedom from the anxiety of being influenced by the Jewish God, or Biblical Law, or nature. The Gnostics, by temperament, were akin both to Vico's magic primitives and to post-

[7] *A Rhetoric of Motives* (New York: Prentice-Hall, 1950), p. 25. [Eds.]

[8] Talbot Donaldson, *Chaucer's Poetry* (New York: Ronald Press, 1975), pp. 940–44. [Eds.]

[9] In Hippolytus, *Refutatio* Viii. 15. 1–2. Bloom is quoting the passage from R. M. Grant, *Gnosticism and Early Christianity* (New York: Columbia University Press, 1959), p. 9. [Eds.]

Enlightenment poets; their quarrel with the words dividing them from their own Word was essentially the quarrel of any belated creator with his precursor. Their rebellion against religious tradition as a process of supposedly benign transmission became the prophecy of all subsequent quarrels with poetic tradition. R. M. Grant, in his *Gnosticism and Early Christianity,* remarks of the proto-Gnostic yet still Jewish *Prayer of Joseph* that it "represents an attempt to supplant an archangel of the older apocalyptic by a new archangel who makes himself known by a new revelation." But Gnostics, as Grant indicates, go beyond apocalyptic thought, and abandon Judaism (and Christianity) by denying the goodness and true divinity of the Creator god, as well as the law of Moses and the vision of the Resurrection.

Part of the deep relevance of Gnosticism to any theory of poetic misprision is due to the attempt of Simon Magus to revise Homer as well as the Bible, as in this Simonian misreading of the *Iliad,* where Virgil's stationing of Helen is ascribed to Homer, an error wholly typical of all strong misinterpretation:

> She who at that time was with the Greeks and Trojans was the same who dwelt above before creation. . . . She is the one who now is with me; for her sake I descended. She waited for my coming; for she is the Thought called Helen in Homer. So Homer has to describe her as having stood on the tower and signaling with a torch to the Greeks the plot against the Phrygians. Through its shining he signified the light's display from above. . . . As the Phrygians by dragging in the wooden horse ignorantly brought on their own destruction, so the gentiles, the men apart from my gnosis, produce perdition for themselves.[10]

Simon is writing his own poem, and calling it Homer, and his peculiar mixture in this passage of Homer, Virgil, the Bible, and his own Gnosis amounts to a revisionary freedom of interpretation, one so free that it transgresses all limits and becomes its own creation. Christianity has given Simon a bad name, but in a later time he might have achieved distinction as a truly audacious strong poet, akin to Yeats.

Valentinus, who came after Simon, has been compared to Heidegger by Hans Jonas,[11] and I myself have found the Valentinian speculation to be rather more useful for poetic theory than the Heideggerian. Something of that usefulness I attempt to demonstrate in the chapter on Yeats in this book; here I want to cite only a single Valentinian passage, for its view of the Demiurge is precisely the view taken of a strong precursor poet by a strong ephebe or latecomer poet:

> When the Demiurge further wanted to imitate also the boundless, eternal, infinite and timeless nature of [the original eight Aeons in the Pleroma], but could not express their immutable eternity, being as he was a fruit of defect, he embodied their eternity in times, epochs, and great numbers of years, under the delusion that by the quantity of times he could represent their infinity. Thus truth escaped him and he followed the lie. Therefore he shall pass away when the times are fulfilled.[12]

This is a misprision-by-parody of Plato, as Plotinus eloquently charged in his *Second Ennead IX,* "Against the Gnostics; or, Against Those that Affirm the Creator of the Cosmos and the Cosmos Itself to be Evil." Hans Jonas observes the specific parody of the *Timaeus* 37C ff:

> When the father and creator saw the creature which he had made moving and living, the created image of the eternal gods, he rejoiced, and in his joy determined to make the copy still more like the original, and as this was an eternal living being, he sought to make the universe eternal, so far as might be. Now the nature of the ideal being was everlasting, but to bestow this attribute in its fullness upon a creature was impossible. Wherefore he resolved to have a moving image of eternity, and when he set in order the heaven, he made this image eternal but moving according to number, while eternity itself rests in unity, and this image we call time.[13]

[10] In Epiphanus, *Panorium* XXI. 3. 1–3. Again Bloom quotes from Grant (see n. 9), p. 78. [Eds.]

[11] *The Gnostic Religion* (Boston: Beacon Press, 1963), p. 64. [Eds.]

[12] Quoted in Jonas, pp. 194–95. [Eds.]

[13] Ibid., p. 194. [Eds.]

The Demiurge of Valentinus lies against eternity, and so, against the Demiurge, Valentinus lies against time. Where the Platonic model suggests a benign transmission (though with loss) through imitation, the Gnostic model insists upon a doubly malign misinterpretation, and a transmission through catastrophe. Either way, the belated creator achieves the uniqueness of his own consciousness through a kind of fall, but these kinds are very different, the Platonic model positing time as a necessity, the Valentinian misprision condemning time as a lie. While the major traditions of poetic interpretation have followed Platonic and/or Aristotelian models, I think that the major traditions of post-Enlightenment poetry have tended more to the Gnostic stance of misprision. The Valentinian doctrine of creation could serve my own revisionist purpose, which is to adopt an interpretative model closer to the stance and language of "modern" or post-Enlightenment poetry than the philosophically oriented models have proved to be. But, again like the poets, so many of whom have been implicitly Gnostic while explicitly even more occult, I turn to the medieval system of Old Testament interpretation known as Kabbalah, particularly the doctrines of Isaac Luria.[14] Kabbalah, demystified, is a unique blend of Gnostic and Neoplatonic elements, of a self-conscious subjectivity founded upon a revisionist view of creation, combined with a rational but rhetorically extreme dialectic of creativity. My turn to a Kabbalistic model, particularly to a Lurianic and "regressive" scheme of creation, may seem rather eccentric, but the readings offered in this book should demonstrate the usefulness of the Lurianic dialectics for poetic interpretation.

The quest for interpretative models is a necessary obsession for the reader who would be strong, since to refuse models explicitly is only to accept other models, however unknowingly. All reading is translation, and all attempts to communicate a reading seem to court reduction, perhaps inevitably. The proper use of any critical paradigm ought to lessen the dangers of reduction, yet clearly most paradigms are, in themselves, dangerously reductive. Negative theology, even where it verges upon theosophy, rather than the reasoning through negation of Continental philosophy, or structuralist linguistics, seems to me the likeliest "discipline" for revisionary literary critics to raid in their incessant quest after further metaphors for the act of reading. But so extreme is the situation of strong poetry in the post-Enlightenment, so nearly identical is it with the anxiety of influence,[15] that it requires as interpretative model the most dialectical and negative of theologies that can be found. Kabbalah provides not only a dialectic of creation astonishingly close to revisionist poetics, but also a conceptual rhetoric ingeniously oriented towards defense.

Kabbalah, though the very word means "tradition" (in the particular sense of "reception") goes well beyond orthodox tradition in its attempt to *restore* primal meanings to the Bible. Kabbalah is necessarily a massive misprision of both Bible and Talmud, and the initial sense in which it accurately was "tradition" is the unintentionally ironic one that means Neoplatonic and Gnostic traditions, rather than Jewish ones. The cosmology of Kabbalah, as Gershom Scholem definitively observes, is Neoplatonic.[16] Scholem locates the originality in a "new religious impulse," yet understandably has difficulty in defining such an impulse. He distinguishes Kabbalistic theories of the emanation of the *sefirot,* from Neoplatonic systems, by noting that, in the latter, the stages of emanation "are not conceived as processes within the Godhead." Yet he grants that certain Gnosticisms also concentrated on the life within the Godhead, and we can notice the same emphasis in the analysis of the Valentinian Speculation by Hans Jonas: "The distinguishing principle . . . is the attempt to place the origin of darkness, and thereby of the dualistic rift of being, *within* the godhead itself."[17] Jonas adds that the Valentinian vision relies on "terms of divine error" and this *is* the distinction between Gnosticism and Kabbalah, for Kabbalah declines to impute error to the Godhead.

Earlier Kabbalah from its origins until Luria's older contemporary Cordovero,[18] saw creation as an outgoing or egressive process. Luria's startling originality was to revise the *Zohar's* dialectics of creation into an ingoing or regressive process, a creation by contraction, destruction, and subsequent restitution. This Lurianic story of creation-

[14] Isaac Luria (1534–72), Jewish Kabbalist. [Eds.]

[15] Title of Bloom's earlier book. [Eds.]

[16] Gershom Scholem, *Kabbalah* (1974). [Eds.]

[17] Jonas, p. 174. [Eds.]

[18] Moses Cordovero (1522–1570), rabbi and Kabbalist. [Eds.]

by-catastrophe is a genuine dialectic or dialectical process by the ordeal of the toughest-minded account of dialectic I know, the one set forth by the philosopher Karl Popper in his powerful collection, *Conjectures and Refutations: The Growth of Scientific Knowledge,* which has a decisive essay, "What Is Dialectic?" in which neither Hegel nor Marx passes the Popperian test.

The Lurianic story of creation begins with an act of self-limitation on God's part that finds its aesthetic equivalent in any new poet's initial rhetoric of limitation, that is, in his acts of re-seeing what his precursors had seen before him. These re-seeings are translations of desires into verbal acts, instances of substantive thinking, and tend to be expressed by a nominal style, and by an imagery that stresses states of absence, of emptiness, and of estrangement or "outsideness." In the language of psychoanalysis, these modes of aesthetic limitation can be called different degrees of sublimation, as I will explain in this chapter's last section. Lurianic *zimzum* or divine contraction, the first step in the dialectic of creation, can be called God's sublimation of Himself, or at least of His own Presence. God begins creation by taking a step inside Himself, by voiding His own Presence. This *zimzum,* considered rhetorically, is a composite trope, commencing as an irony for the creative act, since it says "withdrawal" yet means the opposite, which is absolute "concentration." Making begins with a regression, a holding-in of the Divine breath, which is also, curiously, a kind of digression.

Even so, the strong poems of the post-Enlightenment, from Blake through Stevens, begin with the parabasis of rhetorical irony. But the psychic defense concealed in the irony is the initial defense that Freud called reaction-formation, the overt attitude that opposes itself directly to a repressed wish, by a rigidity that expresses the opposite of the instinct it battles. The Kabbalistic contraction/withdrawal is both trope and defense, and in seeking an initial term for it I have settled upon the Epicurean-Lucretian *clinamen,* naturalized as a critical term long before me, by Coleridge in his *Aids to Reflection.* The *clinamen* or "swerve" is the trope-as-misreading, irony as a dialectical alternation of images of presence and absence, or the beginnings of the defensive process. Writing on *The Magic Flute,* Angus Fletcher ventures some very useful observations upon irony as an aesthetic limitation:

> Irony is merely a darkened awareness of that possibility of change, of transformation, which in its fixed philosophic definition is the "crossing over" of dialectic process. But we can never say too often that irony implies the potential defeat of action, defeat at the hands of introspection, self-consciousness, etc., modes of thought which sap the body and even the mind itself of its apparent motivation.

Kenneth Burke notes that dialectic irony provides us with a kind of technical equivalent for the doctrine of original sin, which for a strong new poem is simply a sin of transgression *against origins.* The Lurianic dialectic follows its initial irony of Divine contraction, or image of limitation, with a process it calls the breaking-of-the-vessels, which in poetic terms is the principle of rhetorical substitution, or in psychic terms is the metamorphic element in all defenses, their tendency to turn into one another, even as tropes tend to mix into one another. What follows in the later or regressive Kabbalah is called *tikkun* or "restitution" and is symbolic representation. Here again, Coleridge can be our guide, as he identified Symbol with the trope of synecdoche, just as Freud located the defense of turning-against-the-self, or masochistic reversal, within a thinking-by-synecdoche. Here, seeking for a broader term to hold together synecdoche and reversal within the part/whole image, I have followed Mallarmé and Lucan by using the word *tessera,* not in its modern meaning as a mosaic-building unit, but in its ancient, mystery-cult meaning of an antithetical completion, the device of recognition that fits together the broken parts of a vessel, to make a whole again.

There is an opening movement of *clinamen* to *tessera,* in most significant poems of our era, that is, of the last three centuries. I am aware that such a statement, between its home-made terminology and its apparent arbitrariness, is rather outrageous, but I offer it as merely descriptive and as a useful mapping of how the reading of poems begins. By "reading" I intend to mean the work both of poet and of critic, who themselves move from dialectic irony to synecdochal representation as they confront the text before them. The movement is from a troubled awareness of dearth, of signification having wandered away and gotten lost, to an even more troubled awareness that the self represents only part of a mutilated or broken whole, whether in relation to what it believes itself once to have been, or still somehow hopes to become.

Clinamen is a swerve or step inside, and so is a movement of internalization, just as *tessera* is necessarily an antithetical completion that necessarily fails to complete, and so is less than a full externalization. That is reason enough for strong modern poems passing into a middle movement, where as terms-for-mapping I have employed *kenosis*, St. Paul's word for Christ's "humbling" or emptying-out of his own divinity, and *daemonization*, founded upon the ancient notion of the daemonic as the intervening stage between the human and the divine. *Kenosis* subsumes the trope of metonymy, the imagistic reduction from a prior fullness to a later emptiness, and the three parallel Freudian defenses of regression, undoing, and isolating, all of them repetitive and compulsive movements of the psyche.

Daemonization, which usually marks the climax or Sublime crisis point of the strong poem, subsumes the principal Freudian defense, repression, the very active defense that produces or accumulates much of what Freud calls the Unconscious. As trope, poetic repression tends to appear as an exaggerated representation, the overthrow called hyperbole, with characteristic imagery of great heights and abysmal depths. Metonymy, as a reification by contiguity, can be called an extension of irony, just as hyperbole extends synecdoche. But both extremes lack finality, as their psychic equivalents hint, since the reductiveness of metonymy is only the linguistic version of the hopelessly entropic backward movements of the regressing, undoing, and isolating psyche. The metonymizer is a compulsive cataloger, and the contents of the poetic self never can be wholly emptied out. Similarly, there is no end to repression in strong poetry, as again I will indicate in the last section of this chapter. The dialectics of revisionism compel the strong poem into a final movement of ratios, one that sets space against time, space as a metaphor of limitation and time as a restituting metalepsis or transumption, a trope that murders all previous tropes.

I take the name, *askesis*, for the revisionary ratio that subsumes metaphor, the defense of sublimation, and the dualistic imagery of inside consciousness against outside nature, from Walter Pater, who himself took it from pre-Socratic usage. Pater said of *askesis* (which he spelled *ascesis*) that in a stylistic context it equalled "self-restraint, a skillful economy of means,"[19] and in his usually subtle play on etymological meaning, he hinted at the athlete's self-discipline. Even more subtly, Pater was attempting to refine the Romantic legacy of Coleridge, with its preference for mind/nature metaphors over all other figurations. To Pater belongs the distinction of noting that the secularized epiphany, the "privileged" or good moment of Romantic tradition, was the ultimate and precarious form of this inside/outside metaphor. The third and final dialectical movement of modern strong poems tends to begin with such a sublimating metaphor, but again this is another limitation of meaning, another achieved dearth or realization of wandering signification. In the final breaking-of-the-vessels of Romantic figuration, an extraordinary substitution takes place, for which I have proposed the name *apophrades*, the unlucky days, dismal, when the Athenian dead return to reinhabit their former houses, and ritualistically and momentarily drive the living out of doors.

Defensively, this poetic final movement is frequently a balance between introjection (or identification) and projection (or casting-out the forbidden). Imagistically, the balance is between earliness and belatedness, and there are very few strong poems that do not attempt, somehow, to conclude by introjecting an earliness and projecting the affliction of belatedness. The trope involved is the unsettling one anciently called metalepsis or transumption, the only trope-reversing trope, since it substitutes one word for another in earlier figurations. Angus Fletcher follows Quintilian in describing transumption as a process "in which commonly the poet goes from one word to another that sounds like it, to yet another, thus developing a chain of auditory associations getting the poem from one image to another more remote image." Kenneth Burke, commenting upon my *A Map of Misreading*, sees daemonic hyperbole and transumption as heightened versions of synecdoche, representations related to Plato's transcendentalized eros:

> The *Phaedrus* takes us from seed in the sense of sheer sperm to the heights of the Socratic erotic, as transcendentally embodied in the idea of doctrinal insemination. And similarly, via hyperbole and metalepsis, we'd ad-

[19] "Style," *Appreciations* (1889) (London: Macmillan, 1920), p. 17. [Eds.]

> vance from an ephebe's sheer *physical* release
> to a poetically ejaculatory analogue.

Metalepsis or transumption thus becomes a total, final act of taking up a poetic stance in relation to anteriority, particularly to the anteriority of poetic language, which means primarily the loved-and-feared poems of the precursors. Properly accomplished, this stance figuratively produces the illusion of having fathered one's own fathers, which is the greatest illusion, the one that Vico called "divination," or that we could call poetic immortality.

What is the critic's defense for so systematic a mapping of the poet's defenses? Burke, in the preface to his first book, *Counter-Statement,* said that his set-piece, his "Lexicon Rhetoricae," was "frankly intended as a machine—machine for criticism, however, not for poetry,"[20] since poetry "is always beyond the last formula." I too offer a "machine for criticism," though I sometimes fear that poetry itself increasingly has become the last formula. Modern poetry, as Richard Rorty sums it up, lives under a triple curse: (1) Hegel's prophecy that any future will be transcended automatically by a future future, (2) Marx's prophecy of the end of all individual enterprise, (3) Freud's prophetic analysis of the entropic drive beyond the Pleasure Principle, an analysis uneasily akin to Nietzsche's vision of the death of Man, a vision elaborated by Foucault, Deleuze, and other recent speculators. As Rorty says: "Who can see himself as caught in a dialectical moment, enmeshed in a family romance, parasitic upon the last stages of capitalism, yet still in competition with the mighty dead?" The only answer I know is that the strongest artists, but only the strongest, can prevail even in this entrapment of dialectics. They prevail by reattaining the Sublime, though a greatly altered Sublime, and so I will conclude this chapter by a brief speculation upon that fresh Sublime, and its dependence upon poetic equivalents of repression.

4

The grandfathers of the Sublime are Homer and the Bible, but in English, Milton is the severe father of the Sublime mode. Erich Auerbach said that "the *Divine Comedy* is the first and in certain respects the only European poem comparable in rank and quality to the sublime poetry of antiquity," a judgment that seems to exclude *Paradise Lost* from Europe. I suppose that Dante's superiority over Milton, insofar as it exists, best might be justified by Auerbach's beautiful observations upon Dante's personal involvement in his own Sublime:

> Dante . . . is not only the narrator; he is at the same time the suffering hero. As the protagonist of his poem which, far greater in scope than the Homeric epics, encompasses all the sufferings and passions, all the joys and blessings of human existence, he himself is involved in all the movements of his immense action. . . . it is he himself who, held fast in the depths of hell, awaits the savior in a moment of extreme peril. What he relates accordingly, is not a mere happening, but something that happens to him. He is not outside, contemplating, admiring, and describing the sublime. He is in it, at a definite point in the scene of action, threatened and hard pressed; he can only feel and describe what is present to him at this particular place, and what presents itself is the divine aid he has been awaiting.

Elsewhere in the same book *(Literary Language and Its Public in Late Latin Antiquity and in the Middle Ages),* Auerbach sets Petrarch above even Dante in one respect, which I believe is also the one in which the English line that goes from Spenser through Milton on to Wordsworth surpassed even Petrarch:

> The Italians learned to control the devices of rhetoric and gradually to rid them of their coldness and obtrusive pedantry. In this respect Petrarch's Italian is markedly superior even to Dante's, for a feeling for the limits of expressibility had become second nature to Petrarch and accounts in good part for his formal clarity, while Dante had to struggle for these acquisitions and had far greater difficulty in maintaining them in the face of his far greater and more profound undertaking. With Petrarch lyrical subjectivism achieved perfection for the first time since antiquity,

[20] *Counter-Statement* (1931) (Berkeley and Los Angeles: University of California Press, 1968), p. ix. [Eds.]

> not impaired but, quite on the contrary, enriched by the motif of Christian anguish that always accompanies it. For it was this motif that gave lyrical subjectivism its dialectical character and the poignancy of its emotional appeal.

The dialectical character of lyrical subjectivism is indeed my subject, and is what I attempt to map through my interplay of revisionary ratios. Auerbach, in the same book, says of Vico that "In the rhetorical figures of the schools he saw vestiges of the original, concrete, and sensuous thinking of men who believed that in employing words and concepts they were seizing hold of things themselves." Auerbach is thus in Vico's tradition when he praises Dante for being *in* his own Sublime, as though the Sublime were not so much a word or concept but somehow was the thing itself, or Dante was one with his own severe poem. The lyrical subjectivism of Petrarch knows more clearly its distance from the thing itself, its reliance upon words apart from things. Perhaps this is why John Freccero so persuasively can nominate Petrarch as the first strong instance in Western poetry of the anxiety of influence, an anxiety induced by the greatness of Dante. Petrarch, like Spenser and Milton after him, suffers several dialectical anguishes, besides the anguish of attempting to reconcile poetry and religion.

Milton does stand outside his own Sublime; his astonishing invention was to place Satan inside the Sublime, as even a momentary comparison of the Satans of Dante and Milton will show. I am an unreconstructed Romantic when I read *Paradise Lost;* I continue to be less surprised by sin than I am surprised by Satan. If I can recognize the Sublime in poetry, then I find it in Satan, in what he is, says, does; and more powerfully even in what he is not, does not say, and cannot do. Milton's Satan is his own worst enemy, but that is his strength, not his weakness, in a dualizing era when the self can become strong only by battling itself in others, and others in itself. Satan is a great rhetorician, and nearly as strong a poet as Milton himself, but more important he is Milton's central way through to the Sublime. As such, Satan prophesies the post-Enlightenment crisis-poem, which has become our modern Sublime.

I find that my map of misprision with its dialectic of limitation/substitution/representation, and its three pairs of ratios, alternating with one another, works well enough for the pattern of Satan's major soliloquies, possibly because these are among the ancestors of the crisis-of-poetic-vision poem, by way of the eighteenth-century Sublime ode. Satan's hyperbolic rhetoric is wonderfully described by a theoretician of the Sublime, Martin Price, in a passage which tries only to explicate Longinus, but which nevertheless conveys the force of Satan's characteristic imagery:

> One finds, then, a conception of passion that transcends material objects, that moves through the sensible universe in search of its grandest forms and yet can never find outward grandeur adequate to its inherent vision and its capacities of devotion. The intensity of the soul's passions is measured by the immensity of its objects. The immensity is, at its extreme, quite literally a boundlessness, a surpassing of measurable extension.

The hyperbole or intensified exaggeration that such boundlessness demands exacts a psychic price. To "exaggerate" etymologically means "to pile up, to heap," and the function of the Sublime is to heap us, as Moby Dick makes Ahab cry out "He heaps me!" Precisely here I locate the difference between the strong poets and Freud, since what Freud calls "repression" is, in the greater poets, the imagination of a Counter-Sublime. By attempting to show the poetic ascendancy of "repression" over "sublimation" I intend no revision of the Freudian trope of "the Unconscious," but rather I deny the usefulness of the Unconscious, as opposed to repression, as a literary term. Freud, in the context of poetic interpretation, is only another strong poet, though the strongest of modern poets, stronger even than Schopenhauer, Emerson, Nietzsche, Marx, and Browning; far stronger than Valéry, Rilke, Yeats, Stevens. A critic, "using" Freud, does nothing different in kind from "using" Milton or Valéry. If the critic chooses to employ Freud reductively, as a supposed scientist, whatever that is, then the critic forgets that tropes or defenses are primarily figures of willed falsification rather than figures of unwilled knowledge. There is willed knowing, but that process does not produce poems.

Whatever the criticism of poetry that I urge is,

and whether it proves to be, as I hope, a necessary error, or just another useless mistake, it has nothing in common with anything now miscalled "Freudian literary criticism." To say that a poem's true subject is its repression of the precursor poem is not to say that the later poem reduces to the process of that repression. On a strict Freudian view, a good poem is a sublimation, and not a repression. Like any work of substitution that replaces the gratification of prohibited instincts, the poem, as viewed by the Freudians, may contain antithetical effects but not unintended or counterintended effects. In the Freudian valorization of sublimation, the survival of those effects would be flaws in the poem. But poems are actually stronger when their counterintended effects battle most incessantly against their overt intentions.

Imagination, as Vico understood and Freud did not, is the faculty of self-preservation, and so the proper use of Freud, for the literary critic, is not so to apply Freud (or even revise Freud) as to arrive at an Oedipal interpretation of poetic history. I find such to be the usual misunderstanding that my own work provokes. In studying poetry we are not studying the mind, nor the Unconscious, even if there is an unconscious. We are studying a kind of labor that has its own latent principles, principles that can be uncovered and then taught systematically. Freud's lifework is a severe poem, and its own latent principles are more useful to us, as critics, than its manifest principles, which frequently call for interpretation as the misprisions of Schopenhauer and Nietzsche that they are, despite their own intentions.

Poems are not psyches, nor things, nor are they renewable archetypes in a verbal universe, nor are they architectonic units of balanced stresses. They are defensive processes in constant change, which is to say that poems themselves are *acts of reading.* A poem is, as Thomas Frosch says, a fierce, proleptic debate *with itself,* as well as with precursor poems. Or, a poem is a dance of substitutions, a constant breaking-of-the-vessels, as one limitation undoes a representation, only to be restituted in its turn by a fresh representation. Every strong poem, at least since Petrarch, has known implicitly what Nietzsche taught us to know explicitly: that there is only interpretation, and that every interpretation answers an earlier interpretation, and then must yield to a later one.

I conclude by returning to the poetic equivalent of repression, to the Sublime or the Counter-Sublime of a belated *daemonization,* because the enigma of poetic authority can be resolved only in the context of repression. Geoffrey Hartman, in *The Fate of Reading,* calls the poetic will "sublimated compulsion." I myself would call it "repressed freedom." Freud, expounding repression, was compelled to posit a "primal repression," a purely hypothetical first phase of repression, in which the very idea representing a repressed instinct itself was denied any entrance into consciousness. Though the French Freudians courageously have tried to expound this splendidly outrageous notion, their efforts have left it in utter darkness. To explain repression at all, Freud overtly had to create a myth of an archaic fixation, as though he were saying: "In the beginning was repression, even before there was any drive to be repressed or any consciousness to be defended by repression." If this is science, then so is the Valentinian Speculation, and so is Lurianic Kabbalah, and so is Ferenczi's *Thalassa,* and perhaps all of them are. But clearly they are also something else, poems that commence by defensive processes, and that keep going through an elaboration of those processes.

A primal fixation or repression, as I have tried to show in *A Map of Misreading,* takes us back not to the Freudian Primal Scene of the Oedipus Complex, nor to the Freudian Primal History Scene of *Totem and Taboo,* nor to Derrida's Scene of Writing, but to the most poetically primal of scenes, the Scene of Instruction, a six-phased scene that strong poems must will to overcome, by repressing their own freedom into the patterns of a revisionary misinterpretation. Thomas Frosch's lucid summary is more admirably concise than I have been able to be, and so I borrow it here:

> . . . a Primal Scene of Instruction [is] a model for the unavoidable imposition of influence. The Scene—really a complete play, or process—has six stages, through which the ephebe emerges: election (seizure by the precursor's power); covenant (a basic agreement of poetic vision between precursor and ephebe); the choice of a rival inspiration (e.g., Wordsworth's Nature vs. Milton's Muse); the self-presentation of the ephebe as a new incarnation of the "Poetical Character"; the

> ephebe's interpretation of the precursor; and the ephebe's revision of the precursor. Each of these stages then becomes a level of interpretation in the reading of the ephebe's poem.

To this, I would add now only the formula that a poem both takes its origin in a Scene of Instruction and finds its necessary aim or purpose there as well. It is only by repressing creative "freedom," through the initial fixation of influence, that a person can be reborn as a poet. And only by revising that repression can a poet become and remain strong. Poetry, revisionism, and repression verge upon a melancholy identity, an identity that is broken afresh by every new strong poem, and mended afresh by the same poem.

Geoffrey H. Hartman

b. 1929

AMONG THOSE American critics associated with Yale University, the most difficult to characterize or identify with some well-known phrase is Geoffrey H. Hartman. His career is marked by certain stopping places, but it would be hard to identify him with any one of them. Though a theorist, he is in some ways evasive of theory, or has become so, as if a theory will limit the possibilities inherent in the critical essay, the form which his later work has taken.

From his earliest work Hartman showed himself capable of the most subtle close reading but without the commitments of the New Critics. In *The Unmediated Vision* he addressed the problem of "mediation" bequeathed to him by a European tradition of criticism not well understood by American critics at the time. In his long study of Wordsworth's poetry, the same concerns were brought to bear on problems of consciousness and self-consciousness in that poet. With Harold Bloom and others he helped reestablish the reputations of the romantic poets after their denigration by the New Criticism. The titles of his three subsequent books—all collections of separate essays—describe his path: *Beyond Formalism, The Fate of Reading,* and *Criticism in the Wilderness.* In these books Hartman further emancipates his work from notions that the interpretive critic is writing on a level secondary to the texts he discusses. He expresses a certain independence from system. His treatment of specific works has taken on more and more the character of a performance, abetted by his adoption, in practice at least, of an interest in Derridean undecidability and openness. Indeed, it is the undecidability principle that supports Hartman's practice of reading, which deliberately maintains at crucial points openness to possibility. It is also, perhaps, that principle that brings the critical essay into literature, which is viewed as a network of interpretations. For Hartman, the hope of an unmediated view of nature for the poet—at least in language—was early abandoned. His later writing acknowledges that an unmediated view of the poem is equally impossible. Hartman's study of Derrida's *Glas* is the nearest thing he has done recently that might seem at first glance secondary to the work it addresses. But here, nevertheless, the text of Derrida is a pretext for a meditation. The book's full title is *Saving the Text: Literature/Derrida/Philosophy.* The first phrase suggests an interesting ambiguity. Hartman is enough of a traditionalist to wish to save the text from those—perhaps Derrida himself or at least some of his followers—who would dissolve the text into the great sea of *écriture.* At the same time the phrase can be read as "except the text," suggesting the critic's freedom from it. The rest of the title places the name of Derrida, the ostensible subject, between literature and philosophy, where it seems to mediate. Hartman thus cunningly indicates a special role for the critic, just as he has noted Derrida's unusually mediative role.

It is probably best to describe Hartman not as a deconstructionist at all (though there is no denying Derrida's influence) but rather as the writer of meditative essays on the phenomenon of criticism itself, where the division between criticism and literary creation is always at least in dispute and perhaps obliterated. Certainly he is wary of theory because of a fear that it can be transformed into fixed law and then applied ruthlessly. His remark about aesthetics at the conclusion of the essay here shows him evasive of any principle of exclusion. This elusiveness penetrates his style and gives his work a quality of perpetual provocation.

Hartman's books are *The Unmediated Vision* (1954); *Wordsworth's Poetry* (1964); *Beyond Formalism* (1970); *The Fate of Reading* (1975); *Criticism in the Wilderness* (1980); *Saving the Text: Literature/Derrida/Philosophy* (1981); and *Easy Pieces* (1985). See Christopher Norris, *Deconstruction: Theory and Practice.*

LITERARY COMMENTARY AS LITERATURE

The school of Derrida confronts us with a substantial problem. What are the proper relations between the "critical" and "creative" activities, or between "primary" and "secondary" texts? In 1923, writing his own essay on "The Function of Criticism," T. S. Eliot accused Matthew Arnold of distinguishing too bluntly between critical and creative. "He overlooks the capital importance of criticism in the work of creation itself."[1] Eliot's perception was, of course, partially based on the literary work of French writers since Flaubert and Baudelaire, including Mallarmé, Laforgue, and Valéry. But Eliot is wary lest his charge against Arnold, and in favor of the critical element in creative writing, be misapplied. "If so large a part of creation is really criticism, is not a large part of what is called 'critical writing' really creative? If so, is there not creative criticism in the ordinary sense?" Thus, having let the cat out of the bag, Eliot at once tries to contain the damage and deny, like Arnold, that criticism can find its own justification, and be creative or independent.

> The answer seems to be, that there is no equation. I have assumed as axiomatic that a creation, a work of art, is autotelic; and that criticism, by definition, is *about* something other than itself. Hence you cannot fuse creation with criticism as you can fuse criticism with creation. The critical activity finds its highest, its true fulfilment in a kind of union with creation in the labor of the artist.[2]

In 1956, talking at the University of Minnesota on "The Frontiers of Criticism," Eliot is still uneasy about the "creative" potential in criticism. Characterizing his earlier essay as a reaction to the "impressionistic" type of criticism prevailing in his day, and fearing that now the "explanatory" type has become predominant, Eliot concludes: "These last thirty years have been, I think, a brilliant period in literary criticism in both Britain and America. It may even come to seem, in retrospect, too brilliant. Who knows?"[3]

How can anything be too brilliant? Such defensiveness is neoclassical, and used to be directed against the plague of wit or glitter or enthusiasm in art. Having helped to establish, after Coleridge, that art not only has a logic of its own but that this logic is not discontinuous with the critical faculty—and that Matthew Arnold, who thought the Romantic poets did not "know" enough, should have recognized even more explicitly that art was a kind of avant-garde criticism—Eliot draws back

LITERARY COMMENTARY AS LITERATURE originally appeared in *Comparative Literature*. It is reprinted from *Criticism in the Wilderness* by permission of the Yale University Press, copyright 1981.

[1] *Selected Essays, 1917–1932* (New York: Harcourt, Brace and Co., 1932), p. 18. [Eds.]

[2] Ibid., p. 19. [Eds.]

[3] "The Frontiers of Criticism," in *On Poetry and Poets* (New York: 1961), p. 131. [Eds.]

from what seems to him an ultimate and dangerous sophistication. Criticism cannot be a creative activity. "You cannot fuse creation with criticism as you can fuse criticism with creation."

But this fusion of creation with criticism is occurring in the writings of contemporary critics. We are in the presence of something that, if not entirely new, is now methodically pursued, and without the backing of any specifically literary authority. I mean that we accept more easily the idea of a creative element in the critical essay if its author is a poet or novelist: then his authority in the creative realm carries over into the critical. So no one will deny the difficult and curiously "creative" investment of Mallarmé's prose, or the claim that "La musique et les lettres" is as interesting a piece of writing as a poem—even perhaps a poem by Mallarmé.[4] But Derrida is no poet or even man of letters in the tradition of Mallarmé, Valéry, Malraux, Arnold, and Eliot. He is a professional philosopher as intense and focused as Heidegger. He does not tend to write critiques of the latest works of art or review segments of literary history. Other practitioners of the new philosophic criticism, such as Theodor Adorno and Walter Benjamin,[5] are also not "creative writers" in the accepted sense of that phrase, though their criticism has often a practical cast and engages directly the notion of technology, culture, and the "culture industry."

The basic question is that of creative criticism: what to make of the "brilliance" of this phenomenon, which liberates the critical activity from its positive or reviewing function, from its subordination to the thing commented on, whether artifact or general theme. The new philosophic criticism had a scope that, though not autotelic, seems to stand in a complex and even crossover relation to both art and philosophy. To elucidate this problem I turn back to a writer who anticipates it in an essay on the essay contemporary with an early story of that most intellectual of novelists, Thomas Mann. I refer to Georg Lukács's "The Nature and Form of the Essay" (1910),[6] published at almost the same time as Mann's *Death in Venice*.

LUKÁCS does not accept subordination as a defining characteristic of the essay. For him the great essayists, among whom he places Plato and Montaigne, use events or books merely as occasions to express their own "criticism of life"—a phrase he cites from Matthew Arnold, who had applied it to poetry. Does the essay, then, we might ask with Lukács, and the literary essay in particular, have a form of its own, a shape or perspective that removes it from the domain of positive knowledge *(Wissenschaft)* to give it a place beside art, yet without confusing the boundaries of scholarship and art? Is it at least *possible* for the essay to muster enough vigor to institute a renewal of ideas ("die Kraft zu einem begrifflichen Neuordnen des Leben") while remaining essayistic, distinct from a scientific philosophy's striving for absolute truths (the "eisig-endgültige Vollkommenheit der Philosophie")? The central question, thus, is criticism, the essay, as work of art, as art genre. "Also: die Kritik, der Essay—oder nenne es vorläufig was Du willst—als Kunstwerk, als Kunstgattung."

Lukács is aware that his position is timely, that it comes out of a movement of impressionist criticism whose great practitioners, after Romantic beginnings, were Pater and Wilde. "The Critic as Artist" is a phrase we associate with Wilde.[7] It is against this movement that, a decade later, I. A. Richards and others launched their search for a stricter, more principled, even "scientific" or theoretically founded study of art. This occurred at the very time that Russian formalism was beginning its own quest for a rigorous definition of "literariness." In England, what Richards started at Cambridge soon became embroiled in the question of "scientism"; and while the striving for a theory of literature, or minimally for principles of criticism, maintained itself, the antitheoretical bias of F. R. Leavis[8] and practical pressures, which make the profession of English studies short on bishops and long on country clergy, complicated though by no means killed the issue as Lukács stated it. In Germany itself, the influence of Dilthey,[9] who had fanned the hope

[4]For examples of Mallarmé's essays see *CTSP*, pp. 687–94. [Eds.]

[5]See *Adorno; Benjamin.* [Eds.]

[6]See Lukács, *Soul and Form* (Cambridge, MA: MIT Press, 1974), pp. 1–18. [Eds.]. "Über Wesen und Form des Essays: Ein Brief an Leo Popper." In *Die Seele und die Formen,* translated as *Soul and Form.* [Au.]

[7]See "The Critic as Artist" in Wilde's *Intentions* (1891), and Richard Ellmann's fine essay "The Critic as Artist as Wilde" introducing his selection from Wilde, *The Artist as Critic: Critical Writings of Oscar Wilde.* [Au.]

[8]F. R. Leavis, English critic (1895–1978), author of *The Great Tradition, New Bearings in English Poetry,* and other works. [Eds.]

[9]Wilhelm Dilthey (1833–1911), German philosopher. [Eds.]

for a humanistic type of science standing on its own theoretical base *(Geisteswissenschaft)*, diverted Lukács's question; and in the 1930s Lukács himself was to join the search for a science of literature from the Marxist side.

Let us return, now, to the diverted question: the status of the essay in Lukács's discussion of 1910. Lukács, one feels, isn't talking about the essay alone but about the inner tendency of all reflective, self-critical discourse. The chances are, in fact, that his understanding of the relation of the essay to "dialectic"—and so of a literary form to philosophy—was mediated by Walter Pater's *Plato and Platonism* (1893). By a peculiar twist of intellectual history, Lukács seems to view the German Romantics, and especially Hegel, through Pater's conception of Socratic conversation—which, looking back at Pater now, seems suspiciously like an idealized version of Oxford tutorials.[10] "The Platonic dialogue," Pater claims, "in its conception, its peculiar opportunities, is essentially an essay—an essay, now and then passing into the earlier form of philosophic poetry, the prose poem of Heraclitus." He distinguishes treatise from essay by saying that the former is an instrument of dogmatic philosophy that starts with axiom or definition, while "the essay or dialogue . . . as the instrument of dialectic, does not necessarily so much as conclude in one; like that long dialogue with oneself, that dialectic process, which may be coextensive with life. It does in truth little more than clear the ground, or the atmosphere, or the mental tablet." Socratic irony also belongs to this "tentative character of dialectic, of question and answer as the method of discovery, of teaching and learning, to the position, in a word, of the philosophic *essayist*."

These intuitions are developed by Lukács in his own way. He asserts that while the tragic mode of existence is crowned by its ending, in an essayistic mode everything, including the ending, is always arbitrary or ironic: the one question dissolves into the many, and even the external as distinguished from the internal interruptions serve to keep things open. The consciously occasional nature of the essay prevents closure. Lukács then interprets this open or occasional character in a way similar to, yet quite different from, contemporary semiotic or language-inspired explanations. Lukács says that it is ideally (and we are in the presence of a viewpoint shaped by German idealism) a counterpart, perhaps counterpoint, to mysticism's desire for ultimate issues. That the critic should talk about ultimate issues only in the guise of reviewing pictures or books is considered a deep-irony. "Ironisch fügt er sich in diese Kleinheit ein, in die ewige Kleinheit der tiefsten Gedankenarbeit dem Leben gegenüber" ("The critic accommodates himself ironically to this minuteness, to the eternal minuteness of the deepest labor of thought vis-à-vis life").

How are we to understand such a strange assertion? Lukács, of course, inherited this enlarged concept of irony from the German Romantics. In *Soul and Form* there is a dialogue on Laurence Sterne that reminds us in many respects of Friedrich Schlegel. Irony, in any case, in Lukács as in German Romanticism, and perhaps in Sterne, is a kind of familiar demon, a domesticated compulsion, the will to truth or even the demon of absolute knowledge transformed by the magic of art into something close to a human and socializing grace. The essay form is a secret relative of the Romantic "fragment": it acknowledges occasionalism, stays within it, yet removes from accident and contingency that taint of gratuitousness which the mind is always tempted to deny or else to mystify. All occasions inform the essayist as they do the typological preacher, but in a purely secular way. This nontragic, nonreligious idealism could make the essayist take as his emblem a famous formula slightly altered: "Der liebe Gott steckt—ironisch—im Detail."[11]

It is still our situation today. Perhaps all the more so, with the influx of books, artifacts, and pseudo-events. Keeping up means becoming the victim of flux unless sustained by an ironic idealism of this sort. Lukács gives no hint, however, as to whether this kind of irony can be realized. He asserts, on the

[10] While Pater's discussion of dialectic in chapter 7 contains strong remarks on method as a journey or an endless dialogue that always takes you a step further toward the ideal of a single imaginative act that would intuit "all the transitions of a long conversation . . . all the seemingly opposite contentions of all the various speakers at once" (cf. the evocation of a "gallery of spirits" at the end of Hegel's *Phenomenology* as well as Bakhtin's "concept of polyphony"), it also etiolates the anagogic thrust of Hegel or Plato by statements that suggest a pedagogy of the (with)drawing room: "If one, if Socrates, seemed to become the teacher of another it was but by thinking that other as he went along that difficult way which each one must really prosecute for himself, however full such comradeship might be of happy occasions for the awakening of the latent knowledge," etc. [Au.]

[11] "Almighty God stuck—ironically—to detail." [Eds.]

one hand, that the modern essayist has lost ground compared to Plato and others, since each writer must now draw his critical standards out of himself, and, on the other, that the essay hasn't evolved enough to attain its destined form: genuine independence from naïvely representational—didactic, moralistic, review-subordinated—aims. The very "frivolity" of style that often enters the essay in the modern period is said to point to this exacerbated situation which obliges the critic to "represent" or "review" an artifact while being interested, really, in a transcendent *idea.* This is, primarily, the idea of fiction *(Dichtung)* as prior and greater than all possible fictions; and the critic, in his ironic or casual way, is exclusively in the service of that idea. He is therefore unlikely to engage in polemics or minute judgments: the fact that he carries with him the "atmosphere of the idea" should be enough to pass judgment on the individual work of art—to free it of all false, obsolete, or partial wisdom.

Just as we are about to give him up for the idealism he later exorcised, Lukács proposes a seminal and very practical definition. The essayist-critic, he adds, cannot himself embody the idea. He heralds it, wakes our sense for it, but remains its precursor. "Er ist der reine Typus des Vorläufers."[12] Vorläufer, literally "pre-courser," "forerunner," has a resonance in German easily lost in translation. This resonance can be restored if we translate it as "provisional," the one who foresees but is a threshold figure, like Moses or John the Baptist. He can bring us no further than the penultimate stage. In a strong paragraph Lukács delimits strictly the dignity of the essay: "Ruhig und stolz darf der Essay sein Fragmentarisches den kleinen Vollendungen wissenschaftlicher Exaktheit und impressionistischer Frische entgegenstellen, kraftlos aber wird seine reinste Erfüllung, sein starkestes Erreichen, wenn die grosse Ästhetik gekommen ist" ("The essay can insist quietly and proudly on its fragmentary character against the minor perfections of scientific precision or impressionistic vividness, but its strongest achievement will prove impotent when the great aesthetics has arrived").

I confess I am drawn strongly to Lukács's essay on the essay. So much of contemporary intellectual life consists in reading these all-purpose forms, these baggy miniature monsters which like certain demons are only too serviceable. Lukács, moreover, is as plastic as Kant or Schiller in his elaboration of distinctions, each of which is given its dignity. He is never trapped by categories. Even when he has defined the essay as something intrinsically devoted to obsolescence, as a prelude or propadeutic for "die grosse Ästhetik"[13] (he will complete his own in the 1960s), he assigns it also an independent existential value.

Though the essay as *parergon* will surely be subsumed, as in the case of Schopenhauer, by the system, yet such *parerga,* or *Beispiele,*[14] show the system as a living, evolving entity ("seine Verwachsenheit mit dem lebendigen Leben").[15] So that, in a sense, they stand forever there, *beside* the system. Pater rescued "dialectic" from the philosophers and vested it in a form whose method or path was circuitous, but Lukács, more explicitly than Pater, attributes the essay form to both irony and desire *(Sehnsucht),* to a double, complementary or contrary, infinitizing. The essay lives off a desire that has an in-itself, that is more than something merely waiting to be completed, and removed, by absolute knowledge. On finishing Lukács, we have the uncanny impression that his exemplum has enacted the entire problem. This "real" letter to a friend, Leo Popper, dated formally "Florence, October 1910," is much more than the letter-preface to a book of essays, more than an essay even: it is an "intellectual poem," as A. W. Schlegel[16] called Hemsterhuis' essays.[17] It delimits its own position in the life of the intellect but meanwhile incorporates so much living thought that its narrower function of *Gericht* expands into the form of a *Gedicht.*[18]

IF THE essay is indeed an intellectual poem, it is unflattering to observe that very few such poems exist in the sphere of literary or cultural criticism. The uneasy coexistence, in essays, of their referential function as commentary with their ambition to *be*

[12] "He is the clear type of forerunner." [Eds.]

[13] "The great aesthetic." [Eds.]

[14] *Parergon:* supplement, frame, appendage. *Beispiele:* illustration, example. [Eds.]

[15] Hartman has interpreted the phrase, which is difficult to translate literally. An approximation is "Its having grown together with a vital life." [Eds.]

[16] A. W. Schlegel (1767–1845), German poet and critic. [Eds.]

[17] Frans Hemsterhuis (1721–90), Dutch philosopher. [Eds.]

[18] *Gericht:* judgment. *Gedicht:* poem. [Eds.]

literature and not only be about it makes for a medley of insight and idiosyncratic self-assertion. There is a charm, of course, to many nineteenth-century essays, which preserves them from this fate. Arnold or Pater or Wordsworth can be read as interesting *prose,* sustained by valid if occasionally dated remarks. We are not threatened, not imposed on, by the force of their observation, or not any longer. Pater and Arnold are now part of the heaven of English literature, like Wordsworth himself. The ideal proposed by Lukács is, however, a harder one, and as unlikely of realization as a poem that must carry along, and not shirk, a strong weight of ratiocination or of opinion with the force of fact.

How scarce this commodity is, this essay which is an intellectual poem, can be gauged by a guess that, with the early exception of Friedrich Schlegel, only Valéry habitually attained it: one thinks of his masterful construction of the figure of Leonardo da Vinci or of "Poetry and Abstract Thought,"[19] both of which, it happens, raise the issue of the relation between artistic and scientific thinking. One might add such essays as Ortega's "In Search of Goethe from Within."[20] Certain of Freud's or Heidegger's essays are also constructions of this kind, severe intellectual poems.

Yet neither Valéry nor Ortega nor Freud nor Heidegger engages very often in the close reading of literature or the close viewing of art. Their notion of detail, when it comes to art, is less exigent, and their exposition less grainy than ours. The critical essay today, to qualify as such, must contain some close-ups: it tends to proceed, in fact, by shifts of perspective (as in some kinds of sequential art or concrete poetry) that expose the non-homogeneity of the fact at hand, the arbitrariness of the knots that bind the work into a semblance of unity. The close-ups are not there merely to illustrate or reinforce a suppositious unity but to show what simplifications, or institutional processes, are necessary for achieving any kind of unitary, consensual view of the artifact.

The process of institutionalization or the normalization called "objective reality" is what is focused on: though not, always, to subvert it. Subversion can be one aim, as in much avant-garde criticism; yet today, on the whole, such criticism, whether in the form of radical art or advanced commentary, seeks to remove the naiveté of formalization rather than to challenge its necessity. There is, of course, no avoiding the disillusion that comes to all, when what is taken to be nature is unmasked as rhetoric or ideology or second nature—when we see leading strings maintained into maturity and becoming bonds or even chains we at best shake a little. The critical essay is critical: we are allowed to survive but not to substantialize our illusions.

A curious reversal may therefore occur in the world of letters. Often poems seem to be less demanding than essays. To be precise, poems, especially today, are there as identity marks, written because to write is part of the contemporary heraldry of identity. Many writers read merely in order to write, not in order to discover whether it is needful for them to add their testimony. The same may be true of the essayists. Yet it seems to me that the essays of the more intellectual practitioners of the art of literary or philosophical criticism make greater demands on the reader: that they ask him to read so as not to write, that they even make the text a little harder to understand and the visible a little harder to see. They increase rather than lighten the burden of tradition, in an anti-evangelical and depressing manner.

Though less distinguished in their decorum, many essays are now more exacting than the "familiar" prose which aimed, in the previous century, to expand the family of readers. Hazlitt makes you feel equal to, or different only in degree from, Wordsworth. And while this democratic ethos (which Wordsworth shared) remains valid, the virulence of nationalistic and separatist movements has taught us how dangerous it is to assume intimacy or common standards. The labor involved in understanding something foreign or dissident without either colonizing it or becoming oneself a cultural transvestite meets us fully as the reality, the otherness, to be faced.[21]

[19] The essay appears in *CTSP,* pp. 914–26. [Eds.]

[20] José Ortega y Gasset (1883–1955), Spanish man of letters. [Eds.]

[21] Hazlitt himself, a prime political dissident, insists fiercely enough on the difference between a writer's greatness as a writer and his politics (see, for example, the ending of the essay on Sir Walter Scott in *The Spirit of the Age,* 1825). His own political philosophy assumes, however, not only a wide audience, as in modern journalism, but also one whose politics and culture could be harmonized. [Au.]

It may well be that some of the difficult critics of whom I speak (whether Adorno or Blackmur or Derrida) are frustrated poets, and this can be held against them; but they are frustrated because they realize the discipline and learning involved, and do not want merely to exploit the past. Though not paralyzed by the heavy task of emulating past-masters or alien traditions, they know that culture has often progressed by *contamination;* and this produces an anguish and a self-scrutiny leading to a vacillating or deeply equivocal recuperation of what Northrop Frye has prematurely named "the secular scripture."[22] Frye suggests that art becomes secular by being recuperated; yet woe to him (I must add) by whom this recuperation comes! He may profane the tradition, just as the New Testament runs the risk of profaning the Old, by giving it a universality that at once redeems and cheapens the barbarous, that is, ethnocentric, element.

Like Lukács in his pre-Marxist phase, Frye places the critical essay closer to *Gedicht* than *Gericht.* With him too the "atmosphere of the idea," not any imperious or ideological truth, changes our consciousness of fact or artifact. There is some anxiety about the past in Frye, but mainly a refusal to be anxious about, and so to overdefine, the future. "To recreate the past and bring it into the present," he writes, "is only half the operation. The other half consists of bringing something into the present which is potential or possible, and in that sense belongs to the future." It is, however, hard to know what Frye means by the "potential" or the "possible" unless it is precisely that sacred and untamed element, the "wish-fulfillment element in romance," which so often has an ethnocentric basis, and which art opposes to itself as to any institutionalization.

Here, certainly, is one "bind" that makes the critical essay both severe and essential, and more than a time-serving device. It is always at once timely and untimely: it stands at the very intersection of what is perceived to be a past to be carried forward, and a future that must be kept open. In Lukács's idealism, as in Frye's, the futuristic element is "desire," or whatever fuels wishing, and cannot achieve fulfillment. When institutionalized, this desire produces superstition; kept free it produces a frivolous or disinterested irony.

It is mere common sense, then, to put the critical essay on the side of irony, but this may turn out to be more defensive than correct. What lies beyond wish fulfillment or the pleasure principle is not irony but something daemonic to which Freud ventured to give the name of reality-mastery. Lukács's career as critic veers dialectically, and perhaps daemonically, toward a reality-mastery in which desire, wish fulfillment, and formal irony play only a subordinate role. The process of incorporating what continues to violate one's identity—I mean on the level of cultural conflict or exchange—may lie beyond the range of values associated with such words as *pleasure, taste, civility, irony, accommodation.* This beyond may also become the domain of the literary essay, the more urgent and severe its aim.

"I AM always amused," Wilde says characteristically, "by the silly vanity of those writers and artists of our day who seem to imagine that the primary function of the critic is to chatter about their second-rate work."[23] The problem is what to do about first-rate work, or that which is great enough to reduce all critical comment to chatter.

The English tradition in criticism is sublimated chatter; but it is also animated by its fierce ability to draw reputation into question. Even Shakespeare had once to be made safe; and Milton is restored, after Leavis, to his bad eminence. This power to alter reputations is formidable, and it shows that criticism has an unacknowledged penchant for reversal in it, which is near-daemonic and which brings it close to the primacy of art. This penchant, of course, can be dismissed as the sin of envy: as a drive for primacy like Satan's or Iago's. Yet, Lukács remarked, there *is* something ironic about the critic's subordination of himself to the work reviewed. At best he keeps testing that work, that apparent greatness, and by force of doubt or enthusiasm puts it more patently before us. He plays the role now of accuser and now of God. A judicious rather than judicial criticism will, needless to say, not try for a single verdict: like Dr. Johnson's, it will expose virtues and weaknesses, strong points and failings together. But it can also frighten us by opening a breach—or the possibility of transvalua-

[22] *The Secular Scripture* (1976). My later quotation comes from this work. [Au.]

[23] "The Critic as Artist," in *Literary Criticism of Oscar Wilde* (Lincoln: University of Nebraska Press, 1968), p. 222. [Eds.]

tion—in almost every received value. Even Romantic irony, therefore, seems unable to digest Wilde's insouciance. "The fact of a man being a poisoner is nothing against his prose."

Wilde means, of course, a poisoner in life, like Thomas Wainewright.[24] But can we help thinking, at the same time, of the poison or immorality that may lodge in art and that made Plato compare a certain kind of rhetor to a dangerous cook? A breach is opened by Wilde between morality and art paralleling that between morality and religion in certain pronouncements of Christ or, for that matter, Blake and Kierkegaard. This parallel may put too great a strain on art, as Eliot feared; and it may also put too great a strain on the critic, who knows that poisons can be remedies.[25] Still, since Wilde (with anticipations in Poe and Baudelaire), the theory of art has been striving to understand the daemonic artist, even the artist-criminal. Not as an empirical or social phenomenon so much but as a theory-enabling fiction that could reveal the problematic depths of *persona* and *intention*.[26] Wilde tears apart face and mask, while the modern persona theory tries to repair the breach. Yet the issue of an intention too faceless to be envisaged still defeats us; and for that reason Derrida suggests that we should substitute the word *sfeinctor* for *author*.

Nor is it an accident, then, that Derrida interests himself in Genet and the "precious bane" of his style. Derrida's *Glas*,[27] a work in which commentary becomes literature, by interweaving philosophical discourse, figurative elaboration, and literary criticism, begins one column with Genet's evocation of a "Rembrandt déchiré."[28] But the theme of the torn picture (viz. manuscript) does not express an iconoclasm nourished by the simple opposition of art-appearance and reality *(Dorian Gray)*, or art and religion, or art and a claimant absolute. It expresses, rather, the insufferable coexistence, even crossover, of holiness and profaneness in art. This crossover tears us apart; and we imaginatively take our revenge by tearing at it, or prudently and hygienically—by means of a *genre tranché*[29] critical theory—denying the crossover, and separating the daemonry of art from the civility of criticism, or discursive from literary discourse, or persona from person, and so forth. Yet everyone has known the feeling that in Henry James or Sartre, let alone Borges, criticism is not independent of the fictional drive. The more insidious question is whether any critic has value who is only a critic: who does not put us in the presence of "critical fictions"[30] or make us aware of them in the writings of others.

WHAT I am saying, then—pedantically enough, and reducing a significant matter to its formal effect—is that literary commentary may cross the line and become as demanding as literature: it is an unpredictable or unstable genre that cannot be subordinated, a priori, to its referential or commentating function. Commentary certainly remains one of the defining features, for it is hardly useful to describe as "criticism" an essay that does not review in some way an existing book or other work. But the perspectival power of criticism, its strength of recontextualization, must be such that the critical essay should not be considered a supplement to something else. Though the irony described by Lukács may formally subdue the essay to a given work, a reversal must be possible whereby this "secondary" piece of writing turns out to be "primary."

We have viewed the critical essay too reductively, just as, in the history of literature itself, we often find types of fiction defined by arbitrary rules from which they break loose. Let us remember, too, that instrumental music, before a certain time, was strictly subordinated to text or programmatic function. Later the instruments become speculative. The same holds true of criticism: its speculative instruments are now exercising their own textual powers rather than performing, explaining, or reifying existing texts. What is happening is neither an inflation of criticism at the expense of creative writing nor a promiscuous intermingling of both. It is, rather, a creative testing and illumination of *limits:*

[24] See "Pen, Pencil, and Poison," in *Intentions*. [Au.]

[25] Cf. Jacques Derrida's "La pharmacie de Platon," in *La Dissémination*. [Au.]

[26] There is a convergence, at this point, of the problem of intention in a secular context with the same problem in a sacred context. The depth interpretations of sacred hermeneutics, whether rabbinical or patristic or kabbalistic, are based on divine revelations that are close to being faceless, i.e., "dark with excessive bright." [Au.]

[27] See Hartman's *Saving the Text* for a discussion of *Glas*. [Eds.]

[28] "Rembrandt torn." [Eds.]

[29] "A determined grace." [Eds.]

[30] *Critical Fictions* is the title of Joseph Halpern's book on Sartre's criticism (1976). [Au.]

the limits of what Hegel called "absolute knowledge" and Dewey the "quest for certainty."[31]

I have argued previously that the more pressure we put on a text, in order to interpret or decode it, the more indeterminacy appears. As in science, the instruments of research begin to be part of the object viewed. All knowledge, then, remains knowledge of a text, or rather of a textuality so complex and interwoven that it seems abysmal. There is an "echappé de vue ins Unendliche,"[32] as Friedrich Schlegel quaintly says. Or, as Derrida puts it, the act of reading to which we are "abandoned" by the critic forbids a single theme or resolution to emerge. "Laissez flotter le filet, le jeu infiniment retors des noeuds."[33] We see, then, that English and French waves have an inspiration in common: whatever the difference—and it is considerable—Derrida's radical attention to the skein of language is still part of the "repudiation of the metaphysics" also aimed at by Ogden and Richards in *The Meaning of Meaning* (1923). But now the starting point, in France, is the pataphysical heritage[34] as well as a linguistic critique of metaphysics, or Hegel's concept of "absolute knowledge."

There is no absolute knowledge but rather a textual infinite, an interminable web of texts or interpretations; and the fact that we discern periods or sentences or genres or individual outlines or unities of various kinds is somewhat like computing time. We can insist that time has a beginning and an end; or, more modestly, that Romanticism, for example, began circa 1770 and ended circa 1830; but this is a silly if provoking mimicry of providential or historical determinism. Such linearity is precisely what stimulates Derrida and others to cross the line: to accept, that is, the need for lineation and delineation, but in the form of a textuality as disconcerting as a new geometry might be.

BEFORE turning again to Derrida for an example of how literary commentary is literature, two cautionary remarks. The first is that, in criticism, we deal not with language as such, nor with the philosophy of language, but with how books or habits of reading *penetrate* our lives. Arnold's "The Function of Criticism at the Present Time,"[35] still a classic essay for our discipline in terms of its quality of self-reflection, takes its power from the courage of adjudicating between English and French literature—*literature* in the broadest sense, as the character displayed by our laws, our magazines, our political writings, as well as poetry and criticism.

My second caution (still thinking of Arnold) is that a hundred years is not long in the eyes of God, if endless in the eyes of each generation. One can exaggerate the newness of the present moment in criticism. There has certainly been some speed-up in the rhythm of events even if we discount such extreme statements as Péguy's, on the eve of the Great War: "The world has changed less since Jesus Christ than in the last thirty years." Arnold himself was struck by the speed-up, and his very focus on the function of criticism acknowledges it. He sees the critic aiding the creative mind to find its proper "atmosphere," which lies "amidst the order of ideas" and beyond the provincialism of its era. And he welcomed the "epoch of expansion" that was opening in England. Yet he also feared the example of France, where the Revolution had produced a commitment to "the force, truth and universality of the ideas it took for its laws." For these ideas were not really free, but imprisoned by particular ideologies, by the French "mania for giving [them] an immediate political and practical application." My caution is that things have not changed all that much since Arnold's essay of 1864; that despite the increased tempo and complexity of modern life, what was true in his contrast of France and England may still be so.

In fact, even Lukács's notion of the essayist as a precursor type may have a direct relation to Arnold. Lukács substantializes the idea of a critic and puzzles over the paradox of a type whose essence is transience. For Arnold too the critic is a precursor, but Arnold does not claim an interest in the critic as such. His view is determined by concrete historical considerations, in particular by the stirring up of ideas in the era of the French Revolution. That stirring up is part of a great stream of tendency and must be for the good, but criticism itself is not that

[31] Title of one of the books of John Dewey (1859–1952), American philosopher. [Eds.]

[32] "Unending vista." [Eds.]

[33] "Let the string waver, the infinitely cunning play of intricacy." [Eds.]

[34] For a fine account of this heritage see Roger Shattuck, *The Banquet Years*. [Au.] "Pataphysics" is a coinage describing an utterly whimsical science in Alfred Jarry's *Ubu Roi* (1896). [Eds.]

[35] See *CTSP*, pp. 583–95. [Eds.]

good. Arnold therefore makes a sharper distinction than the young Lukács between precursor-critic and creative genius, insisting that criticism merely prepares the ground for the latter by stimulating a living current of ideas. It was because that current had not been sufficiently present in England when the Romantics wrote that they failed to match the glory of the writers of the Renaissance; and Arnold ends "The Function of Criticism" by foreseeing a new epoch of creativity that the movement of modern criticism will usher in. "There is the promised land, toward which criticism can only beckon. That promised land will not be ours to enter, and we shall die in the wilderness: but to have desired to enter it, to have saluted it from afar, is already perhaps the best distinction among contemporaries." To which one can only reply: Ah, Wilderness. It is precisely that purely functional notion of criticism, or that great divide between criticism and creation, which is now in dispute.

AGAINST Derrida's *Glas,* from which I will take my example of literary commentary as literature, it can be urged that bad cases make bad law. Exceptional this work certainly is, but can it represent criticism in any save an extreme contemporary form? It is not for me to decide that question. What seems extreme today may not be so a decade or a century hence. Books have their own fate; and I am sufficiently convinced that *Glas,* like *Finnegans Wake,*[36] introduces our consciousness to a dimension it will not forget, and perhaps not forgive. It is not only hard to say whether *Glas* is "criticism" or "philosophy" or "literature," it is hard to affirm it is a book. *Glas* raises the specter of texts so tangled, contaminated, displaced, deceptive that the idea of a single or original author fades, like virginity itself, into the charged Joycean phrase: "Jungfraud's messonge book."[37]

In *Glas,* as elsewhere, Derrida exerts a remarkable pressure on privileged theoretical constructs, in particular those of origin, self, author, and book. It seems difficult to let go of the concept of authorial identity: of a unified person or message characterized by a name that authenticates it within a clearly circumscribed text. Yet *Glas* not only interanimates many sources (Hegel, Nietzsche, Genet) by inner quotation and surrealist wit; it not only incorporates, in particular, passages from Genet's *Journal du voleur* (1948), but does so to become a thievish book in essence.

Genet's self-identification as a thief is developed, by Derrida, to embrace all writers. We are led beyond a psychoanalytic perspective to the haunting notion of a "vol anthique" (sometimes "question anthologique," viz. "ontologique"). This ancient theft recalls Prometheus and Hermes; but since *vol* also means flight, allusion is made to Icarus or the eaglelike aspiration of religion, science, and (Hegel's) philosophy to absolute knowledge. Most literally, though, "vol anthique" is *Blütenstaub*—"dissemination"—and expresses Derrida's counter-encyclopedic notion of the propagation of the word (with roots, possibly, in Novalis and the German Romantics) and the curious floweriness of Genet's style: a pastoral purification of an immoral subject matter equal yet opposite to Promethean fire. The *Journal du voleur* is made to betray a vol-ition as high as that of other myths, and which by contagion or camaraderie also informs *Glas.*

Glas, then, is Derrida's own *Journal du voleur,* and reveals the vol-onto-theology of writing. Writing is always theft or bricolage of the logos. The theft redistributes the logos by a new principle of equity, as unreferable to laws of property, boundary, etc. (Roman, capitalistic, paternal, national) as the volatile seed of flowers. Property, even in the form of the *nom propre,* is *non-propre,* and writing is an act of crossing the line of the text, of making it indeterminate, or revealing the *midi* as the *mi-dit.* "La force rare du texte, c'est que vous ne puissiez pas le surprendre (et donc limiter) à dire: *ceci est cela*" (*Glas,* p. 222).[38]

Does it amount to more, though, than a dignifying of bricolage?[39] Genet, Derrida, might turn out to be mere pastiche, a resynthesizing of older notions or myths. The objection Marx lodged against costume-drama revolution (resurrecting the idea of Rome in 1789 leads to the Napoleonic eagle) could be relevant. There seems to be no way of killing off,

[36] Hartman makes some comparisons to *Finnegans Wake* in *Saving the Text.* [Eds.]

[37] *Finnegans Wake* 460:20 [Eds.]

[38] "The rare force of the text is that you are not able to catch (and thus to confine) oneself to say this is that." [Eds.]

[39] "Bricolage" is a term brought into theory via Claude Lévi-Strauss, characterizing the work of a handyman who uses the tools at hand. Lévi-Strauss applies it to the logic of myth. [Eds.]

by bricolage, the exemplary Grand Story. Consider Doctorow's *Ragtime,* which rags (among other things) Kleist's *Michael Kohlhaas.* Surely it is only a matter of time before that story is recovered, not as some ultimate or privileged source but as a pre-text exploding its new frame and revealing not merely its priority but the stronger understanding in it of revolutionary fantasy.

It should be stated explicitly that the intertextual bricolage characteristic of *Glas* does not recuperate either Genet or "sacred" source texts. Derrida is not directly interested in the origin, psychic or literary, of Genet's work. To be exact, the very notion of origin is understood as a (Heideggerian) *Ursprung,*[40] a hyperbolic leaping like that of Icarus, which sustains itself by bricolage: by the technical exploitation or reframing of correlative structures that hold it up, fuel it falsely or failingly, but still, somehow, let it spin out the line—the tightrope even—of the "glue" of "aleatory" writing. Derrida repeats as a refrain: "La glu de l'aléa fait sens."[41]

There is, obviously, some exhibitionism in this: art no longer hides art. But only because there is nothing to hide. We know what is to be known, that every act of presence, every "ici" or "midi" is infinitely mediated, and yet as vulnerable—*coupable*—as an unmediated venture, a flight beyond what is, out of nothing, into nothing.

The line of exegesis will therefore tend to be as precariously extensible as the line of the text. The subject matter of exegesis is, in fact, this "line." Yet criticism as commentary *de linea* always crosses the line and changes to one *trans lineam.*[42] The commentator's discourse, that is, cannot be neatly or methodically separated from that of the author: the relation is contaminating and chiastic; source text and secondary text, though separable, enter into a mutually supportive, mutually dominating relation. It is hard to find the right analogy, the right figure, for this relation; better to describe what happens in the exemplary case.

So in *Glas* the presence of Genet is not (even on the first page) restricted to one column: it crosses the line into the commentary on Hegel. Yet to follow this crossing needs an understanding of the link between, for example, Genet's Rembrandt essay and a passage from the *Journal du voleur.*[43] Also an understanding of that *Journal* passage in its own right, as it deals with the very theme or "antheme" of *crossing the line.* Also perhaps an understanding of the volatility of the syllable "éc . . ." as it *echo*es not only through the right-hand column of the first page of *Glas* but establishes a continuing series by drawing in "IC" and "aig/le" ("Je m'éc . . ." "Je m'aig/le")—and even "glas," if we remember that the cry ascribed to eagles is "glatir." (See illustration on pages 140–41 for the opening paragraphs of *Glas.*) By such "contagion" or "circulation infinie de l'*é*quivalence générale," we approach, even before we reach Derrida's discussion of the "zero signification" of Genet's flowery style, what he terms "les glas de la signification" or "le texte anthrographique, marginal et parafant: qui ne signifie plus" (*Glas,* p. 37). "La force rare du texte" is "à la limite, nulle" (*Glas,* p. 222).[44]

Here, of course, the notion of transgression (of limits) and indeterminacy (of endlessly approaching the limit we call a meaning) seem to merge. It is as if two very different types of discourse—that of Blanchot, say, and that of Georges Bataille—were being melded into one.[45] The attempt to join such disparates is itself a transgression, and one cannot—as yet—determine whether Derrida is demystifying dialectic thinking (or other types of logic) or erecting literary wit into a new logic, at once corrosive and creative.

The Genet text that quietly pervades the Hegel

[40] My reference is to Heidegger's "Der Ursprung des Kunstwerks" (1936), first published in *Holzwege* (1950). [Au.]

[41] "The glue of the aleatory [chance] makes sense." [Eds.]

[42] The cultural and historical implications of "nonlinear" thinking are very differently expounded in such writings as Ernst Jünger's *Über die Linie* and Heidegger's réplique; in Marshall McLuhan's *The Gutenberg Galaxy*; in Derrida's translation (Paris, 1962) of Husserl's *Ursprung der Geometrie,* and in his *De la grammatologie,* pp. 127–131. Also in relation to the concept of time (including the historian's) in Derrida's "Ousia et grammè," *Marges de la philosophie.* Cf. J. Hillis Miller, "Ariadne's Web: Repetition and the Narrative Line," in *Critical Inquiry* (1976). [Au.]

[43] For Genet's essay on Rembrandt, see his *Oeuvres completes,* 4: 19–31. The passage from the *Journal du voleur* is analyzed below. Since the "crossing" of all these texts is complex enough, I omit the additional knot provided by a section of Nietzsche's *Also sprach Zarathustra* which deals with the theme of purity via the opposition of "Adler" and "Ekel." [Au.]

[44] *Glas:* knell; "the knell of signification"; "the anthropographical text, marginal and signed, which no longer signifies"; "the rare force of the text"; "at the limit, the null." [Eds.]

[45] See *Blanchot.* Georges Bataille (1897–1962), French writer. [Eds.]

column is later quoted and analyzed by Derrida himself (*Glas,* pp. 211–19). While Genet denies that he decided to be a thief at a precisely definable epoch in his life, he does recall detaching himself forcibly from the companionship of army life by an act of treachery that involved stealing from a buddy. This theft, he claims, strengthened him toward the "moral solitude" he desired, and which eventually made him break all ties of affection and love. He then continues without transition:

> Le tapisserie intitulée "La Dame à la Licorne" m'a bouleversé pour des raisons que je n'entreprendrai pas ici d'énumérer. Mais, quand je passai, de Tchécoslovaquie en Pologne, la frontière, c'était un midi, l'été. La ligne idéale traversait un champ de seigle mûr, dont la blondeur était celle de la chevelure des jeunes Polonais; il avait la douceur un peu beurrée de la Pologne dont je savais qu'au cours de l'historie elle fut toujours blessée et plainte. J'étais avec un autre garçon expulsé comme moi par la police tchèque, mais je le perdis de vue très vite, peut-être s'égara-t-il derrière un bosquet ou voulut-il m'abandonner: il disparut. Ce champ de seigle était bordé du côté polonais par un bois dont l'orée n'était que de bouleaux immobiles. Du côté tchèque d'un autre bois, mais de sapins. Longtemps je restai accroupi au bord, attentif à me demander ce que recélait ce champ, si je le traversais quels douaniers les seigles dissimulaient. Des lièvres invisibles devaient le parcourir. J'étais inquiet. A midi, sous un ciel pur, la nature entière me proposait une ènigme, et me la proposait avec suavité.
>
> —S'il se produit quelque chose, me disais-je, c'est l'apparition d'une licorne. Un tel instant et en tel endroit ne peuvent accoucher que d'une licorne.
>
> La peur, et la sorte d'émotion que j'éprouve toujours quand je passe une frontière, suscitaient à midi, sous un soleil de plomb la première féerie. Je me hasardai dans cette mer dorée comme on entre dans l'eau. Debout je traversai les seigles. Je m'avançai lentement, sûrement, avec la certitude d'être le personnage héraldique pour qui s'est formé un blason naturel: azur, champ d'or, soleil, forêts. Cette imagerie où je tenais ma place se compliquait de l'imagerie polonaise.
>
> —"Dans ce ciel de midi doit planer, invisible, l'aigle blanc!"
>
> En arrivant aux bouleaux, j'étais en Pologne. Un enchantement d'un autre ordre m'allait être proposé. La "Dame à la Licorne" m'est l'expression hautaine de ce passage de la ligne à midi. Je venais de connaître, grâce à la peur, un trouble en face du mystère de la nature diurne, quand la campagne française où j'errai surtout la nuit était toute peuplée du fantôme de Vacher, le tueur de bergers. En la parcourant j'écoutais en moi-même les airs d'accordéon qu'il devait y jourer et mentalement j'invitais les enfants à venir s'offrir aux mains de l'égorgeur. Cependant, je viens d'en parler pour essayer de vous dire vers quelle époque la nature m'inquiéta, provoquant en moi la création spontanée d'une faune fabuleuse, ou de situations, d'accidents dont j'étais le prisonnier craintif et charmé.[46]

[46] "The tapestry entitled 'The Lady and the Unicorn' overwhelmed me for reasons that I will attempt to enumerate here. One summer day, at noon, I crossed the border from Czechoslovakia to Poland. My line of sight traversed a field of ripe rye, the blondness of which was that of the hair of the young Poles; it had the buttery sweetness of the Poland that I knew over the course of its history to be always moaning and wounded. I was with another boy who had been expelled like me by the Czech police, but I soon lost contact with him—perhaps he got lost in a thicket, or wanted to leave me. He disappeared. This field of rye was bordered on the Polish side by a forest, the edge of which was made up of immobile birch trees. On the Czech side there was another forest, but pine. For a long time I remained crouched at the edge, wondering what might be obscured by these woods and whether there might be border police hidden in the rye. Invisible rabbits were probably crossing the field. I was anxious. At noon, under a clear sky, all of nature presented me with an enigma, and presented it to me with sweetness.

"—If something appears, I told myself, it will be the apparition of the unicorn. Such a moment and such a place can only give birth to a unicorn.

"The fear, and the sort of emotion that I always feel when I cross a border, called forth, at noon, beneath a leaden sky, the most exceptional magic spectacle. I ventured into this golden sea as one enters into water. Upright, I crossed the field of rye. I advanced slowly, surely, with the certainty of a heraldic figure, for whom the azure, the field of gold, the sun, and the forests furnished a natural coat of arms. This imagery within which I had my place was complicated by the Polish imagery.

"—'In this midday sky there must be flying, invisible, the white eagle!'

"Upon reaching the birch trees, I had arrived in Po-

What theory of allusion can account for the presence/absence of this passage on the opening page of *Glas?* If "Rembrandt déchiré" inaugurates the right-hand column of the book, embedded in the left with its marginal introduction of the Immaculate Conception ("IC") is another work of art ("la tapisserie intitulée 'La Dame à la Licorne'"). *That* seems untorn, virginal; yet does not an eagle hover invisibly in the sky, and is not crossing over (the "frontière" or "ligne") accompanied by a fear mingled with the kind of emotion that, at noon, incites "la première féerie"? What is that? May we translate it "the primal fantasy"? But what is *that?*

"Je me hasardai," Genet's next sentence reads, "dans cette mer dorée comme on entre dans l'eau. Debout je traversai les seigles." Since Genet has previously told us that "par elle dont je porte le nom le monde végétal m'est familier,"[47] he is entering as "le roi—peut-être la fée" (p. 46), a *mére dorée.* He is himself the Unicorn of this heraldic moment ("je pénétrais moins dans un pays qu'à l'intérieur d'une image,"[48] admits the paragraph following the passage on pp. 50–51). Or he is the royal prisoner, if not victim, of a Mother Nature associated twice with killers of children (here with Vacher, a page or so earlier with Gilles de Rais). "La première féerie" would seem to be the "family romance" of the absent mother, torn yet most whole, criminal and virginal, unstained like Nature herself by all the blood and suffering that should cry from that ground.

No wonder, then, that the first verse Genet wrote, as a note added to page 51 informs us, was "moissonneur des souffles coupés."[49] It is indeed a question of breath, of maintaining the line, not genetically but as a writer. Genet as "vainqueur du vent"[50] takes one's breath away with his imitation of Nature's impassibility, troubled rhythmically here and there yet remaining sublimely flowery. The wind is conquered or harvested; the text sustained. "Moissonneur des souffles coupés": who is the harvester alluded to? Is it Death, or Nature, or Vacher ("tueur de bergers"), or Genet himself?[51]

The scene with its "soleil de plomb," almost its noonday demon, is like a still out of Coleridge's *Ancient Mariner,* "All in a hot and copper sky / The bloody sun at noon. . . ." But the horror is now merely a "trouble," something "unquiet" in this quiet, and the blondness of the rye is compared to the "douceur un peu beurrée de la Pologne dont je savais qu'au cours de l'histoire elle fut toujours blessée et plainte."[52] How far, yet how near, are we from a strangled cry like *"Je m'éc . . ."?*

Is that cry not a "souffle coupé," as of butchered children? A muted, self-inflicted violence, as if Genet, that child of nature, had become a "bourreau berceur" (Derrida's phrase) like his mother? The cry's reflexiveness suggests that the "souffle coupé" may also be a "souffle coupable." *Je m'aigle:* I am my own vulture. Or as Derrida puts it: "Je seigle ou m'aigle" (*Glas,* p. 211). But that is some two hundred pages after the "aigle de plomb ou d'or, blanc ou noir" has appeared on the Hegel side of the balanced page.

Something is "mal enchaîné." The eagle referred to, via the pun on Hegel's name, is a national emblem shared, or competed for, by several nation-states, but also the Promethean torment of striving for absolute knowledge, "savoir absolu." With all boundaries in dispute (between nation and nation, outside and inside, text and commentary, Hegel and

land. An enchantment of another kind awaited me here. The 'Lady with the Unicorn' is to me the lofty expression for this movement of my line of vision to the south. I came to know, because of my fear, a commotion before the mystery of diurnal nature, when the French countryside where I wandered, especially at night, was thick with the presence of the ghost of Vacher, the killer of shepherds. While wandering through it I listened to the accordion tunes that must have been playing within me, and mentally I invited the children to come and offer themselves to the hands of the murderer. Nevertheless, I have just described this in order to try to tell you of that period in my life when I was frightened by nature, when it provoked in me the spontaneous creation of a fabulous fauna, of situations and events of which I was the frightened and charmed prisoner." [Eds.]

[47] "Par elle," i.e., his mother, whose name "Genet" ("genet," the broom flower) he retains. [Au.] "By her whose name I carry, the vegetal world is familiar to me." [Eds.]

[48] "I penetrate less into a place than into the interior of an image." [Eds.]

[49] "Harvester of cut breaths." [Eds.]

[50] "Vanquisher of the wind." [Eds.]

[51] When we extend the notion of "ligne" to include sounds (or the "glue" that builds phonemes into words and meanings) "moissonneur" could come apart as "moi sonneur," and lead Derrida to the theme of *Glas* once again. [Au.]

[52] The verisimilar yet oneiric truth of Genet's landscape is heightened by our knowledge that Jarry had set *Ubi Roi* (1896) in a Poland that continued to be ravaged by border disputes. "The action, which is about to begin, takes place in Poland, that is to say: 'Nowhere'." [Au.]

Genet, German and French, literature and philosophy, left and right margins) Genet's vaunted detachment dissolves into a self-penetration, a "s'avoir absolu" erected into a specular, heraldic image of self-presence. "Hieroglyphics of hysteria, blazons of phobia," these are what we interpret, says Jacques Lacan.

Derrida understands Genet's "pénêtre" (*Glas*, p. 215) so well that he sounds or extends that "souffle coupé" by following a "ligne idéale" through the "mer dorée" of the "seigle" until we come to the "mère dorée" of the "sigle": the IC (close to "ici") denoting the Immaculate Conception, or "Un tel instant et un tel endroit [qui] ne peuvent accoucher que d'une licorne." This IC/ici, therefore, is as much a personal fantasy as a final knowledge: it evokes the ecstatic desire for a here and now (an "ici, maintenant") or a pure self-presence which defines the inaugural as well as ultimate state of the odyssey of the spirit toward consciousness of itself in Hegel's system.

THERE are those who maintain that "the corruption of the poet is the generation of the critic." Or that, as the same authority alleges, there is a danger lest the auxiliary forces of criticism become the enemy of the creative writer. "Are they from our seconds become principals against us?"[53] Yet Dryden, of course, was blasting the nit-picking, censorious or "minute" critics of his time, the overzealous schoolmasters and arbiters of taste. Today our problem is more with the critics of critics: with those that bite or bark at their own kind, not only in their "rage to get things right" but also in order to idealize creative genius or to separate out, bureaucratically, the functions of critic and artist.

The example of Derrida, therefore, is an unsettling one, even more for litterateurs than for philosophers. In philosophy there is not quite so much formal difference made between "primary" philosophizing and "secondary" criticism. There is good and bad philosophy.

Still, I want to emphasize the problem rather than pretend to solve it. It has been with us for some time; perhaps most acutely since the German Romantics, who tried to achieve a synthesis of *poetry* and *philosophy*. "Nicht auf der Grenze schwebst du, sondern in deinem Geiste haben sich Poesie und Philosophie innig durchdrungen," runs Friedrich Schlegel's tribute to Novalis.[54] Yet the tribute is an epilogue to Schlegel's series of fragments entitled "Ideas": as in Novalis, the synthesis could only take a fragmentary form. Hegel then turned this ferment of fragments into a living system of ideas: mobile, interpenetrating, yet consequent and systematic. Hegel, Derrida remarks in *Of Grammatology*, was the last philosopher of the book and the first of "writing." His image of the consummate philosopher or absolute spirit (see the close of the *Phenomenology*) stands to Schlegel's portrait of Novalis as fulfillment to figure.

Derrida also does not wish to sit on the fence, or hover as an eternal precursor on the border of some elusive synthesis of poetry and philosophy. He therefore produces a text: not a book, exactly, perhaps even an antibook; not an encyclopedic system, perhaps even a counterencyclopedia. But the word *text*, so current now, and suspect, means something quite specific: historically viewed, it is a development of the Romantic fragment, a sustained fragment as it were, or—seen from the Hegelian system of absolute knowledge—an essayistic totality.

To identify that which must be synthesized as "poetry" and "philosophy" may seem very general or old-fashioned. Changing the terms does not, however, change the problem. "Il n'existe d'ouvert à la recherche mentale que deux voies, en tout, oú bifurque notre besoin, à savoir, l'esthétique d'une part et aussi l'économie politique."[55] So Mallarmé. The quote is aptly chosen by Fredric Jameson as one epigraph for his *Marxism and Form*. As we read *Glas*, we are made to think more often of aesthetics and political economy than of poetry and philosophy. And Lukács's "grosse Ästhetik," foretold by him in 1910, turned out to be, in 1950–60, precisely that attempt to marry the experience of art and the lessons of political economy.

Meanwhile one can doubt that *Glas*, or Lukács's magnum opus, transcends its condition of text, of sustained fragment or essayistic totality. Any

[53] Dryden, "Dedication" of *Examen Poeticum* (1693). [Au.]

[54] "You do not hover at the border, but in your spirit Poetry and Philosophy have thoroughly interpenetrated." Though Hegel subsumes this ideal, he engages in a devious polemic against Schlegel and Romantic irony that is well summarized in Ernst Behler's *Klassische Ironie, Romantische Ironie, Tragische Ironie*, pp. 112ff. [Au.]

[55] "There exist only a total of two paths, where our need bifurcates, that make possible entrance into the life of the mind, namely aesthetics and political economy." [Eds.]

grand Aesthetics, I suspect, will turn out to be an Xthetics, where *X* signifies something excluded, something X-ed from a previous system and now redeemed: the "ugly," for instance, or "low" or "mad" or economic factors. *X* also, therefore, signifies the chiasmus, a more powerful sign today than Aquarius or the Circle. What has been excluded is allowed to cross the line, or to be present even when absent, like a horizon. Literary criticism is now crossing over into literature. For in the period that may be said to begin with Arnold—a period characterized by increasing fears that the critical would jeopardize the creative spirit, and self-consciousness the energies of art—literary criticism is acknowledged at the price of being denied literary status and assigned a clearly subordinate, service function. There is no mysticism, only irony, in the fact that literary commentary today is creating texts—a literature—of its own.

Wolfgang Iser

b. 1926

THE TITLES of Iser's two books, *The Implied Reader* and *The Act of Reading,* indicate the emphasis of his work to be that of reception theory. As such it invites comparison with the theories of *Hans Robert Jauss,* his colleague at the University of Constance. There are significant differences between them. While Jauss has recourse to literary history, Iser, for all his emphasis on readers, tends in the end to place more emphasis on textual structures. The "implied reader" of his earlier work seems sometimes to be a fiction projected by the text; and even the act of reading does not, for Iser, involve a "real" reader, subject of a psychological analysis, which Iser goes to great lengths to avoid. While Jauss seems most influenced by the tradition of phenomenological hermeneutics, Iser's roots are in the phenomenological aesthetics of *Roman Ingarden.* Iser attempts to avoid the objectivization of the text along lines characteristic of the New Criticism; he substitutes not quite an object but a constitutive process in which potentialities inherent in the text as a structure are revealed in the act of reading. But this act is in the end ideal, involving a situation in which the work can exercise its effect. "Effect" seems a more adequate word, in Iser's view, then "meaning," because it implies that the important question is what a literary work *does.* It is here that speech act theory invades Iser's phenomenologically oriented position, and the selection here demonstrates how Iser employs it.

Iser's term "repertoire" is important in describing the situation necessary for any act of reading to occur. It is the "conditions necessary for the establishment of a situation." It is this which supplies something determinate, a ground for communication. It is the familiar or what is there to be known. Yet his theory holds that a literary situation brings something new into play and always works as a complement to the prevailing thought system. Indeed, it appears to fill a void in the repertoire by providing what is absent, as if no prevailing repertoire ever adequately contains reality, conceived of as a whole of some sort.

In the act of reading, Iser's unempirical and ideal reader must operate by inferences, particularly with respect to what he calls "blanks" in a text, which a reader must fill up. Such blanks are characteristic of narrative shifts, where the reader must perform a transition and complete the structure of the text. At times Iser treats the text as determining what the reader does with these blanks or at least limiting that act. To this extent, Iser continues to objectify the text as a structure of meaning.

Iser's major works are *The Implied Reader* (1972, trans. 1974) and *The Act of Reading* (1976, trans. 1978). Also available in English are "Indeterminacy and the Reader's Response," in *Aspects of Narrative,* ed. J. H. Miller (1971), and "The Current Situation of Literary Theory," *New Literary History* 11 (1979). See Robert C. Holub, *Reception Theory: A Critical Introduction* (1984), and Stanley Fish, "Why No One's Afraid of Wolfgang Iser," *Diacritics* 11 (1981) and Iser's reply in *Diacritics* 11 (1981).

THE REPERTOIRE

STARTING POINT

Every textual model involves certain heuristic decisions; the model cannot be equated with the literary text itself, but simply opens up a means of access to it. Whenever we analyze a text, we never deal with a text pure and simple, but inevitably apply a frame of reference specifically chosen for our analysis. Literature is generally regarded as fictitious writing, and, indeed, the very term *fiction* implies that the words on the printed page are not meant to denote any given reality in the empirical world, but are to represent something which is not given. For this reason 'fiction' and 'reality' have always been classified as pure opposites, and so a good deal of confusion arises when one seeks to define the 'reality' of literature. At one moment it is viewed as autonomous, the next as heteronomous,[1] in accordance with whatever frame of reference is being applied. Whatever the frame, the basic and misleading assumption is that fiction is an antonym of reality. In view of the tangled web of definitions resulting from this juxtaposition, the time has surely come to cut the thread altogether and replace ontological arguments with functional arguments, for what is important to readers, critics, and authors alike is what literature *does* and not what it *means.* If fiction and reality are to be linked, it must be in terms not of opposition but of communication, for the one is not the mere opposite of the other—fiction is a means of telling us something about reality. Thus we need no longer search for a frame of reference embracing both ends of a reality scale, or for the different attributes of truth and fiction. Once we are released from this obligation, the question inevitably arises as to what actually constitutes fiction. If it is not reality, this is not because it lacks the attributes of reality, but because it tells us something about reality, and the conveyer cannot be identical to what is conveyed. Furthermore, once the time-honored opposition has been replaced by the concept of communication, attention must be paid to the hitherto neglected recipient of the message. Now if the reader and the literary text are partners in a process of communication, and if what is communicated is to be of any value, our prime concern will no longer be the *meaning* of that text (the hobbyhorse ridden by the critics of yore) but its *effect.* Herein lies the function of literature, and herein lies the justification for approaching literature from a functionalist standpoint.

This approach must focus on two basic, interdependent areas: one, the intersection between text and reality, the other, that between text and reader, and it is necessary to find some way of pinpointing these intersections if one is to gauge the effectiveness of fiction as a means of communication. Our interest, then, is directed toward the pragmatics of literature—"pragmatic" in Morris's sense of relating the signs of the text to the "interpretant." The pragmatic use of signs always involves some kind of manipulation, as a response is to be elicited from the recipient of the signs. "Such terms as 'interpreter,' 'interpretant,' 'convention' (when applied to signs), 'taking-account-of' (when a function of signs) . . . are terms of pragmatics, while many strictly semiotical terms such as 'sign', 'language', 'truth', and

THE REPERTOIRE is chapter 3 of *The Act of Reading,* which appeared originally in Germany in 1976. The translation is reprinted by permission of The Johns Hopkins University Press, copyright 1979.

[1] See, for instance, Roman Ingarden, *The Literary Work of Art,* transl. by George G. Grabowicz (Evanston, 1973), pp. 245ff. [See *Ingarden.* (Eds.)] After completing this chapter (1972), I came across a similar view of literature in Johannes Anderegg's book, *Fiktion und Kommunikation* (Göttingen, 1973), pp. 97, 154f. He relates his study of the communicative processes of the "Fiktivtext" mainly to the intrinsic structure of the text, so that he develops the idea in a different direction from my own. [Au.]

'knowledge' have important pragmatical components."[2] Clearly, then, pragmatics, as usage of signs, cannot be abstracted from syntax—the interrelation of signs, or semantics—the relation of signs to objects. Indeed, pragmatics generally presuppose syntax and semantics, for these are implicit in the relation between the signs and the interpretant.

Speech-Act Theory

The pragmatic nature of language has been most clearly brought into focus by ordinary language philosophy. This has developed concepts which, although they are not meant to be applied to fiction, can nevertheless serve as a starting point for our study of the pragmatic nature of literary texts. The speech-act theory derived from ordinary language philosophy is an attempt to describe those factors that condition the success or failure of linguistic communication. These factors also pertain to the reading of fiction, which is a linguistic action in the sense that it involves an understanding of the text, or of what the text seeks to convey, by establishing a relationship between text and reader. Our task is to examine these factors as well as to describe the process by which a reality can be produced by means of language.

The speech act as outlined by J. L. Austin and systematized by John Searle represents a basic unit of communication. Searle writes:

> The reason for concentrating on the study of speech acts is simply this: all linguistic communication involves linguistic acts. The unit of linguistic communication is not, as has generally been supposed, the symbol, word or sentence, or even the token of the symbol, word or sentence, but rather the production or issuance of the symbol or word or sentence in the performance of the speech act. To take the token as a message is to take it as a produced or issued token. More precisely, the production or issuance of a sentence token under certain conditions is a speech act, and speech acts . . . are the basic or minimal units of linguistic communication.[3]

[2] Charles Morris, *Writings on the General Theory of Signs* (The Hague, 1971), p. 46. [Au.]

[3] John R. Searle, *Speech Acts* (Cambridge, 1969), p. 16. [Au.] See *Searle.* [Eds.]

The speech act, as a unit of communication, must not only organize the signs but also condition the way in which these signs are to be received. Speech acts are not just sentences. They are linguistic utterances in a given situation or context, and it is through this context that they take on their meaning. In brief, then, speech acts are units of linguistic communication through which sentences are situated and take on meaning in accordance with their usage.

The fact that the utterances of speech acts are situated within a context is of extra significance in view of the lingering conviction in some circles of literary criticism that "it's all on the printed page." The pragmatic nature of a text can only come to full fruition by way of the complete range of contexts which the text absorbs, collects, and stores. This in itself is a straightforward idea, but less straightforward is the question why the many references to realities outside the text should take on a different significance from that to be found in their original, nontextual setting. This problem will be discussed in detail later on. For the moment, it is sufficient for us to take the speech act as our heuristic guideline in considering the fact that the written utterance continually transcends the margins of the printed page, in order to bring the addressee into contact with nontextual realities.

At the beginning of his posthumously published series of lectures, *How to Do Things with Words,* J. L. Austin differentiates between two basic forms of linguistic utterance, which he calls "constative" and "performative."[4] The first makes statements about facts and must be measured against the criteria of truth or falsehood, and the second produces an action which can be measured against the standards of success or failure.[5] According to Austin's original distinction, the constative utterance is true or false in itself, is thus independent of any situation, and so is free from all pragmatic contexts. "With the constative utterance . . . we use an over-simplified notion of correspondence with facts. . . . We aim at the ideal of what would be right to say in all circumstances, for any purpose, to any audience."[6] Even if we do occasionally meet with such

[4] J. L. Austin, *How to Do Things with Words,* J. O. Urmson, ed. (Cambridge, Mass., 1962), pp. 2–8. [Au.] See *Austin.* [Eds.]

[5] See ibid., pp. 12f., 16, 25, 54. [Au.]

[6] Ibid., pp. 144f. [Au.]

ideal cases, Austin does not regard the constative utterance as the paradigm of the speech act. This is rather to be found in the performative utterance, which produces something that only begins to exist at the moment when the utterance is made. In Austin's terms it entails "*doing* something . . . rather than *reporting* something."[7] It brings about a change within its situational context, and, indeed, it is only through their situational usage that performative utterances actually take on their meaning. They are called performative precisely because they produce an action: "The name is derived, of course, from 'perform', the usual verb with the noun 'action': it indicates that the issuing of the utterance is the performing of an action—it is not normally thought of as just saying something."[8]

If a linguistic action is to be successful, there are certain conditions that must be fulfilled, and these conditions are basic to the speech act itself. The utterance must invoke a *convention* that is as valid for the recipient as for the speaker. The application of the convention must tie in with the situation—in other words, it must be governed by *accepted procedures*. And, finally, the willingness of the participants to engage in a linguistic action must be proportionate to the degree in which the *situation* or context of the action is defined.[9] If these conditions are not fulfilled, or if definitions are too vague or inaccurate, the utterance will run the risk of remaining empty and so failing to achieve its ultimate goal, which is "to effect the transaction."[10]

In addition to these possible flaws on the part of the speaker, there may be others on the part of the recipient, as has been noted by von Savigny. The attempt at communication may fail if the utterance is not properly received—i.e., if the intention is missed—or if certain factors undermine its determinacy, either because they are missing or because they are not overt.[11] This does not mean, however, that such "transactions" rarely succeed. Misunderstandings, indeterminacy, or obscurity can usually be cleared up by questions from the recipient, who can then latch onto the speaker's intention and so enable the utterance to give rise to the action intended.

[7] Ibid., p. 13. [Au.]
[8] Ibid., pp. 6f. [Au.]
[9] See ibid., pp. 14f., 23f., 26, 34. [Au.]
[10] Ibid., p. 7. [Au.]
[11] Eike von Savigny, *Die Philosophie der normalen Sprache* (Frankfort, 1969), p. 144. [Au.]

In gauging the success or failure of a linguistic action, it is not enough merely to establish a difference between constative and performative utterances. What is of prime importance is the link between the utterance and the action. Furthermore, the inherent limitations of the *accepted procedures*—which are essential to the success of the action—make it necessary to distinguish between those forms of the performative utterance that exercise total or only relative control over the intended effect.[12] Thus the distinctions suggested by Austin now require further differentiation. He postulates three speech acts, each of which leads to different types of performance:

> We first distinguished a group of things we do in saying something, which together we summed up by saying we perform a *locutionary act,* which is roughly equivalent to uttering a certain sentence with a certain sense and reference, which again is roughly equivalent to 'meaning' in the traditional sense. Second, we said that we also perform *illocutionary acts* such as informing, ordering, warning, undertaking, &c., i.e., utterances which have a certain (conventional) force. Thirdly, we may also perform *perlocutionary acts:* what we bring about or achieve *by* saying something, such as convincing, persuading, deterring, and even, say, surprising or misleading. Here we have three, if not more, different senses or dimensions of the 'use of a sentence' or of 'the use of langauge.' . . . All these three kinds of 'actions' are, simply of course as actions, subject to the usual troubles and reservations about attempt as distinct from achievement, being intentional as distinct from being unintentional, and the like.[13]

For our study of the pragmatic nature of literary texts, it is the illocutionary and perlocutionary speech acts that are of particular interest. When an utterance has the desired effect on the recipient and so produces the right consequence, it has the quality of the perlocutionary act: what is meant arises out of what is said. This presupposes the fulfillment of all those conditions which Austin described as *conventions* and *procedures*. The illocutionary act, on the other hand, has only a potential effect *(force)*,

[12] See Austin, *How to Do Things,* p. 101. [Au.]
[13] Ibid., pp. 108f. [Au.]

and its signals can only produce a particular type of access *(securing uptake)*, attentiveness *(taking effect)*, and an appropriate reaction on the part of the recipient *(inviting responses.)*.[14] The precise nature of the *illocutionary force* in the speech act is something the recipient can generally derive only from the situational context. Only through this can he recognize the speaker's intention, though again this presupposes that speaker and recipient share the same *conventions* and *procedures*, and that neither would sanction persistent deviation from such modes or any unconventional application of them. Only when the recipient shows by his *responses* that he has correctly received the speaker's intention are the conditions fulfilled for the success of the linguistic action. Von Savigny was therefore surely right to translate Austin's term *illocutionary force* as *illocutionary role*,[15] for the speech acts denoted by this term are successful to the degree in which the recipient is aware of and assumes the role intended for him by the speaker.

The distinction between speech acts is so fundamental for Austin that his original division of linguistic utterances into constative and performative recedes into the background. The reason for this lies in the control necessary if the speech act is to lead to a felicitous action. Generally such an action will only come about if it is rooted in a true statement. Thus the locutionary and perlocutionary acts have to be based on a constative utterance. This revision of his original distinctions brings Austin to the following conclusion:

> What then finally is left of the distinction of the performative and constative utterance? Really we may say that what we had in mind here was this:
>
> *(a)* With the constative utterance, we abstract from the illocutionary . . . aspects of the speech act, and we concentrate on the locutionary . . . we use an over-simplified notion of correspondence with the facts. . . . We aim at the ideal of what would be right to say in all circumstances, for any purpose, to any audience, &c. Perhaps this is sometimes realized.
>
> *(b)* With the performative utterance, we attend as much as possible to the illocutionary force of the utterance, and abstract from the dimension of correspondence with facts.[16]

According to this restricted definition, the performative utterance merely denotes one central aspect of the linguistic action, namely, its quality of productiveness. This quality cannot be identified with "correspondence with facts," but is actually abstracted from it.

Austin himself must have realized the similarity between this form of the speech act and the language of literature, for when he is discussing the effects of speech acts, he finds himself obliged to distinguish between the two: "a performative utterance will, for example, be *in a peculiar way* hollow or void if said by an actor on the stage, or if introduced in a poem, or spoken in soliloquy. . . . Language in such circumstances is in special ways—intelligibly—used not seriously, but in ways *parasitic* upon its normal use. . . . All this we are *excluding* from consideration. Our performative utterances, felicitous or not, are to be understood as issued in ordinary circumstances."[17] Austin regards the poetic utterance as void because it does not produce a linguistic action. To call it "parasitic," however, means that it has the inherent qualities of a performative utterance, but simply applies them inadequately. In other words, literature imitates the illocutionary speech act, but what is said does not produce what is meant. This raises the question of whether nothing at all is produced, or whether what is produced can only be regarded as a failure.

When Hamlet abuses Ophelia, Austin would call the utterance parasitic. The actor playing Hamlet is merely imitating a speech act which will remain void in any case because Hamlet does not actually want to abuse Ophelia at all, but means something different from what he says. But no one in the audience will have the impression that this is a parasitic, that is, a void speech act. On the contrary, Hamlet's speech 'quotes' the whole context of the drama, which in turn may evoke all that the spectator knows about human relations, motives, and situations. A speech act that can evoke such weighty matters is surely not "void," even if it does not bring about a real action in a real context. Indeed, the fictional context of the speech may well be transcended, and the spectator may find himself con-

[14] Ibid., p. 120. [Au.]
[15] See von Savigny, *Die Philosophie*, pp. 144, 158ff. [Au.]
[16] Austin, *How to Do Things*, pp. 144f. [Au.]
[17] Ibid., p. 22. [Au.]

templating the real world, or experiencing real emotions and real insights, in which case again the terms "void" and "parasitic" become highly suspect, even if the "performance" may be somewhat different from what Austin had in mind.

In his analysis of the basic premises of ordinary language philosophy, Stanley Cavell has shown that comprehension does not take place only through what is said, but also through what is implied: "Intimate understanding is understanding which is implicit. . . . Since saying something is never *merely* saying something, but is saying something with a certain tone and at a proper cue while executing the appropriate business, the sounded utterance is only a salience of what is going on when we talk."[18] If this were not so, i.e., if all linguistic actions were explicit, then the only threat to communication would be acoustic. As what is meant can never be totally translated into what is said, the utterance is bound to contain implications, which in turn necessitate interpretation. Indeed, there would never be any dyadic interaction if the speech act did not give rise to indeterminacies that needed to be resolved. According to the theory of speech acts, these indeterminate elements must be kept in check by means of conventions, procedures, and rules, but even these cannot disguise the fact that indeterminacy is a prerequisite for dyadic interaction, and hence a basic constituent of communication. Austin recognizes this fact at least indirectly by laying emphasis on sincerity[19] as the main condition for a successful linguistic action: *"our word is our bond."*[20] This condition makes two things clear: (1) The implications of an utterance are the productive prerequisite for its comprehension, and so comprehension itself is a productive process. (2) The very fact that a speech act automatically carries implications with it means that the fulfillment of the underlying intention of that speech act cannot be guaranteed by language alone, and sincerity of intention imposes clear moral obligations on the utterance.

The language of literature resembles the mode of the illocutionary act, but has a different function. As we have seen, the success of a linguistic action depends on the resolution of indeterminacies by means of conventions, procedures, and guarantees of sincerity. These form the frame of reference within which the speech act can be resolved into a context of action. Literary texts also require a resolution of indeterminacies but, by definition, for fiction there can be no such given frames of reference. On the contrary, the reader must first discover for himself the code underlying the text, and this is tantamount to bringing out the meaning. The process of discovery is itself a linguistic action in so far as it constitutes the means by which the reader may communicate with the text.

Austin and Searle excluded literary language from their analysis on the grounds that from a pragmatic standpoint it is void;[21] for them, language gains its function, and therefore its meaning, through its controlled usage. It therefore seems not unreasonable to differentiate between literary and pragmatic language in terms of its functional application. As has already been observed, fictional language does not lead to real actions in a real context, but this does not mean that it is without any real effect. Its success is less assured than that of an explicit, performative utterance, and its effect cannot be precisely defined as an "action," but even if these circumstances justified the epithet "void," they would still not suffice to deny this language its own pragmatic dimension.

For Austin, literary speech is void because it cannot invoke conventions and accepted procedures, and because it does not link up with a situational context which can stabilize the meaning of its utterances. In other words, it lacks the basic preconditions for a successful linguistic action. But this is not altogether true. It has already been pointed out that if literary langauge is "parasitic," it must have some qualities of the speech acts it imitates and, indeed, only differs from them in its mode of application. Now fictional language is not in fact without conventions at all—it merely deals with conventions in a different way from ordinary performative utterances. The latter will fail if conventions are not strictly adhered to—Austin illustrates this with the following question: "When the saint baptized the penguins, was this void because the procedure of baptizing is inappropriate to be applied to penguins, or because there is no accepted procedure of

[18] Stanley Cavell, *Must We Mean What We Say* (New York, 1969), pp. 12, 32f. [Au.]

[19] On the function of the *sincerity rule,* see also Searle, *Speech Acts,* pp. 63, 66f. [Au.]

[20] Austin, *How to Do Things,* p. 10. [Au.]

[21] See Austin, *How to Do Things,* pp. 22, and Searle, *Speech Acts,* pp. 78f. [Au.]

baptizing anything except humans?"[22] It is obvious from this what Austin, and through him the theory of speech acts as a whole, understands by convention and accepted procedure, namely, a normative stability. We might call this a vertical structure, in the sense that values of the past also apply to the present. This means, however, that the speech act does not evoke convention so much as conventional validity, and it is this validity that literary language calls into question—not because it is without conventions (for then it could not call their validity into question)—but because it disrupts this vertical structure and begins to reorganize conventions horizontally. The fictional text makes a selection from a variety of conventions to be found in the real world, and it puts them together as if they were interrelated. This is why we recognize in a novel, for instance, so many of the conventions that regulate our society and culture. But by reorganizing them horizontally, the fictional text brings them before us in unexpected combinations, so that they begin to be stripped of their validity. As a result, these conventions are taken out of their social contexts, deprived of their regulating function, and so become subjects of scrutiny in themselves. And this is where fictional language begins to take effect: it depragmatizes the conventions it has selected, and herein lies its pragmatic function. We call upon a vertical convention when we want to act; but a horizontal combination of different conventions enables us to see precisely what it is that guides us when we do act.

As far as the reader is concerned, he finds himself obliged to work out why certain conventions should have been selected for his attention. This process of discovery is in the nature of a performative action, for it brings out the motivation governing the selection. In this process the reader is guided by a variety of narrative techniques, which might be called the strategies of the text. These strategies correspond to the *accepted procedures* of speech acts, in so far as they provide an orientation in the search for intentions underlying the selection of conventions. But they differ from the *accepted procedures* in that they combine to thwart stabilized expectations or expectations which they themselves have initially stabilized.

Let us sum up our findings so far: fictional language has the basic properties of the illocutionary act. It relates to conventions which it carries with it, and it also entails procedures which, in the form of strategies, help to guide the reader to an understanding of the selective processes underlying the text. It has the quality of "performance," in that it makes the reader produce the code governing this selection as the actual meaning of the text. With its horizontal organization of different conventions, and its frustration of established expectations, it takes on an *illocutionary force,* and the potential effectiveness of this not only arouses attention but also guides the reader's approach to the text and elicits responses to it.

Situation-Building

We have seen that fictional language possesses many of the properties of the illocutionary act, but we have not yet dealt in any detail with one of the main component parts of all linguistic utterances, namely, their situational context. All utterances have their place in a situation, arising from it and conditioned by it. Speech devoid of situation is practically inconceivable, except perhaps as a symptom of some sort of mental disturbance—though even this is in itself a situation. Furthermore, speech is almost always directed at an addressee—usually in an attempt to stabilize the variable factors left open by the actual situation. This attempt to reach an addressee by means of illocutionary or perlocutionary acts is shaped by the choice of words, syntax, intonation, and other linguistic signs, as well as by the frame of reference, the proposition, and the predication of the utterance. This is how the situation, with all its attendant circumstances, takes on a definite form, and this, in turn, conditions subsequent utterances which can only be properly understood in relation to that situation. The theory of speech acts shows clearly the degree to which the context illuminates and stabilizes the meaning of the utterance.

The verbal structure of literary speech—especially that of prose fiction—is so similar to that of ordinary speech that it is often difficult to distinguish between the two. This is why Austin and Searle called it "parasitic." Ingarden, too, found that the similarity posed an intriguing problem, which emerged at a central point of his argument, when he was attempting to define the sentence cor-

[22] Austin, *How to Do Things,* p. 24. [Au.]

relates of literary works. For Ingarden, the sentences are the basic prerequisite for the production of the literary object. But the sentences in the work of art seem just like those used to describe real objects, although the two types have completely different functions to perform. According to Ingarden, the literary object is prefigured in the sequence of sentences, and takes on the character of an object by being offered to the conscious mind of the reader, who may thus imagine and comprehend it. But how can one and the same mode of sentence both describe an existing object and also prefigure an otherwise nonexistent literary one? In order to indicate the different functions of the sentences, Ingarden calls those of literary texts *"quasi-judgments."*[23] It is not surprising that this term should have caused a good many brows to furrow.[24] What Ingarden intended to show was that literary sentences have the same verbal structure as judgment sentences, without actually *being* judgment sentences, for they lack "the anchoring of the intentions of the meaning contents in the proper reality,"[25] i.e., they have no real context. The following statement shows the extent to which Ingarden regarded this as the basic problem in defining the literary work of art: "This great and mysterious achievement of the literary work of art has its source primarily in the peculiar, and certainly far from thoroughly investigated quasi-judgmental character of assertive propositions."[26]

As these assertions lack a real situational context with attendant circumstances, it seems as if they have freed themselves from those factors which have caused and conditioned them. Indeed, it is almost as if this lack of a context threatens to do away with the very meaning that the assertions are supposed to convey. And what is therefore especially mysterious is the impression that this form of speech, which has lost everything that endows normal speech with meaning, is nevertheless meaningful.

In their reflections on the nature of literary language, Ingarden, Austin, and Searle have one thing in common: they all regard this mode of language as an imitation of and not a deviation from ordinary speech. Thus they successfully avoid the problem of having to explain the langauge of literature in terms of norms and the violation of norms. However, they make it virtually impossible to grasp the nature of this application of language, when at one moment they call it "parasitic," and the next "mysterious." An imitation of the normal use of language ought to produce similar consequences to those of normal use. And yet in fiction it is claimed at one moment that the imitation is inferior to what it imitates (parasitic) and at another that it transcends it (mysterious). If this is so—which we will not dispute, at least for the time being—then "imitation" and "quasi-judgment" would both seem to be equally inadequate descriptions of literary language, since each fails totally to cover the other.

The parting of the ways between literary and ordinary speech is to be observed in the matter of situational context. The fictional utterance seems to be made without reference to any real situation, whereas the speech act presupposes a situation whose precise definition is essential to the success of that act. This lack of context does not, of course, mean that the fictional utterance must therefore fail; it is just a symptom of the fact that literature involves a different application of language, and it is in this application that we can pinpoint the uniqueness of literary speech.

Ernst Cassirer wrote, in his *Philosophy of Symbolic Forms,* "that the concept, in accordance with its characteristic attitude must, unlike direct perception, move its object off into a kind of ideal distance, in order to bring it within its horizon. The concept must annul 'presence' in order to arrive at 'representation'."[27] The concept, as a paradigm of symbol usage, makes an existing object knowable by translating it into something it is not. Perception without aids is as impossible as cognition without aids. There must always be an element of the nongiven in the given, if the latter is to be grasped at all, from whatever angle. Symbols are what constitute this nongiven element, without which we could have no access to empirical reality. "Before the aggregate of the visible could be constituted as a

[23] See Ingarden, *Literary Work of Art,* pp. 160ff. [Au.]

[24] See, among others, Käte Hamburger, *Die Logik der Dichtung* (Stuttgart, 1968), pp. 25ff. [Au.]

[25] Ingarden, *Literary Work of Art,* p. 171. [Au.]

[26] Ibid., p. 172. [Au.]

[27] Ernst Cassirer, *The Philosophy of Symbolic Forms,* transl. by Ralph Manheim (New Haven, 1953), III, 307. See also the interesting essay by Barbara Herrnstein Smith, "Poetry as Fiction," *New Directions in Literary History,* Ralph Cohen, ed. (London, 1974), pp. 165–87. [Au.] On Cassirer, see *CTSP,* pp. 993–1013. [Eds.]

whole, as the totality of an intuitive cosmos, it required certain basic forms of vision which, though they may be disclosed through visible objects, cannot be confounded with them, and cannot themselves be taken as visible objects. Without the relations of unity and otherness, of similarity and dissimilarity, of identity and difference, the world of intuition can acquire no fixed form; but these relations themselves belong to the makeup of this world only to the extent that they are *conditions* for it, and not parts of it."[28] Symbols enable us to perceive the given world because they do not embody any of the qualities or properties of the existing reality; in Cassirer's terms, it is their very *difference* that makes the empirical world accessible. Perception and comprehension are not qualities inherent in the objects themselves, and so the world must be translated into something it is not, if it is to be perceived and understood. But if symbols enable us to perceive the existing world and yet are independent of the visible, they must also in principle enable us to see a nonexistent world.

Fictional language represents such an arrangement of symbols, for in Ingarden's terms it is not anchored in reality, and in Austin's terms it has no situational context. The symbols of literary language do not 'represent' any empirical reality, but they do have a representative function. As this does not relate to an existing object, what is represented must be language itself. This means that literary speech represents ordinary speech, for it uses the same symbolic mode, but as it is without any of the empirical references, it must increase the density of instructions to be imparted by the symbolic arrangement. As a representation of speech, it can only represent that which speech is or accomplishes. In simple terms, we may say that fictional language provides instructions for the building of a situation and so for the production of an imaginary object.

This observation may be supported by arguments drawn from semiotics. Charles Morris describes signs in literature and art as icons or iconic signs. In this way he stresses the self-reference of these signs. But self-reference is not the same as self-sufficiency, for the latter would mean that there was no possible means of access to art or literature. Morris himself therefore suggests that the icon he regarded as a total representation of the designated object—in other words, he says that iconic signs no longer denote something, but themselves constitute what is denoted.[29] This definition may sound convincing for the pictorial arts, but it requires considerable modification if it is to be applied to literature. Eco has developed the argument as follows:

> The iconic sign therefore constructs a model of relationship . . . basically the same as the model of perception-relationships which we construct recognizing or remembering objects. If the iconic sign does have qualities in common with something else, it is not with the object but with the ways in which the object is perceived. This perception model can be constructed and recognized by means of the same mental operations we perform in constructing the thing we perceive, independently of the material object through which the relationships are brought into being.[30]

This observation sheds further light on the representational function of fictional language. If iconic signs do denote anything at all, it is certainly not the qualities of a given object, for there *is* no given object except for the sign itself. What is designated is the condition of *con*ception and *per*ception which enable the observer to construct the object intended by the signs. And here we have a definition that can certainly be applied to literature as much as to the pictorial arts. The iconic signs of literature constitute an organization of signifiers which do not serve to designate a signified object, but instead designate *instructions* for the *production* of the signified.

As an illustration, we may take the character of Allworthy in Fielding's *Tom Jones*. Allworthy is introduced to us as the perfect man, but he is at once brought face to face with a hypocrite, Captain Blifil, and is completely taken in by the latter's feigned piety. Clearly, then, the signifiers are not meant solely to designate perfection. On the con-

[28] Cassirer, *Symbolic Forms*, p. 300. [Au.]

[29] See Charles Morris, "Esthetics and the Theory of Signs," *Journal of Unified Science*, 8 (1939): 131–50; and the relevant corrections in Charles Morris, *Signification and Significance* (Cambridge, Mass., 1964), pp. 68ff. See also Charles Morris, *Signs, Language and Behavior* (New York, 1955), pp. 190ff. [Au.]

[30] Umberto Eco, *Einführung in die Semiotik* (Munich, 1972), p. 213. [Au.]

trary, they denote instructions to the reader to build up the signified, which represents not a quality of perfection, but in fact a vital defect, namely, Allworthy's lack of judgment. The signifiers therefore do not add up to the perfection they seem to denote, but rather designate the conditions whereby perfection is to be conceived—a characteristic mode of iconic sign usage. The iconic signs fulfill their function to the degree in which their relatedness to identifiable objects begins to fade or is even blotted out. For now something has to be imagined which the signs have not denoted—though it will be preconditioned by that which they do denote. Thus the reader is compelled to transform a denotation into a connotation. In our present example, the consequence is that the 'perfect man's' lack of judgment causes the reader to redefine what he means by perfection, for the signified which he has built up in turn becomes a signifier: it invokes his own concepts of perfection by means of this significant qualification (the 'perfect man's' lack of judgment), not only bringing them into the conscious mind but also demanding some form of correction. Through such transformations, guided by the signs of the text, the reader is induced to construct the imaginary object. It follows that the involvement of the reader is essential to the fulfillment of the text, for materially speaking this exists only as a potential reality—it requires a 'subject' (i.e., a reader) for the potential to be actualized. The literary text, then, exists primarily as a means of communication, while the process of reading is basically a kind of dyadic interaction.

All forms of dialogue and communication run the continual risk of failure, for reasons already listed. Although the literary text incorporates conventions that may provide a degree of common ground between itself and the reader, these conventions tend to be organized in such a way that their validity is, at best, called into question. The new arrangement of old norms constitutes one of the risks, as it is not related to the reader's own disposition, and another risk lies in the fact that, in contrast to ordinary speech acts, the literary text has no concrete situation to refer to. Indeed, it is this very lack of an existing situation that brings about two ranges of indeterminacy: (1) between text and reader, (2) between text and reality. The reader is compelled to reduce the indeterminacies, and so to build a situational frame to encompass himself and the text. Unlike the situational frame presupposed by the speech-act theory, the fictional situation does not exist until it is linguistically produced, which means that it is bound to be different in character and consequences from one that is already given and defined. (The danger here is that the very openness of the text may prevent the establishment of common ground; the advantage, however, is that there must then be more than just one form of interaction.) Here we might follow up an observation of J. M. Lotman's: "Apart from its ability to concentrate an enormous amount of information within the 'space' of a short text . . . the literary text has another special quality: it delivers different information to different readers—each in accordance with the capacity of his comprehension; furthermore, it also gives the reader the language to help him appropriate the next portion of data as he reads on. The literary text acts like a sort of living organism, which is linked to the reader, and also instructs him, by means of a feedback system."[31] If we view the relation between text and reader as a kind of self-regulating system, we can define the text itself as an array of sign impulses (signifiers) which are received by the reader. As he reads, there is a constant 'feedback' of 'information' already received, so that he himself is bound to insert his own ideas into the process of communication. This can again be illustrated by the Fielding example. Scarcely has Allworthy made the acquaintance of Captain Blifil, when he is deceived by him. The very fact that he lets himself be duped then has to be fed back into the text as follows: the linguistically denoted perfection lacks certain essential attributes that prevent it from being 'really' perfect. Thus events which were originally unpredictable, in the light of information denoted by the language signs (the name Allworthy, his virtues, his residence in Paradise Hall), now become acceptable, but this process involves two important factors: (1) the reader has constructed a signified which was not denoted by the signifiers, and (2) by doing so, he creates a basic condition of comprehension that enables him to grasp the peculiar nature of the 'perfection' intended by the text. But these signifieds, which the reader himself produces, are constantly changing in the course of his reading. If we stay

[31] J. M. Lotman, *Die Struktur literarischer Texte* (Munich, 1972), pp. 42f. [Au.] See *Lotman and Uspensky.* [Eds.]

with the Fielding example, we will find that after the reader has corrected his initial signified, as regards Allworthy's perfection, the latter has to pass judgment on an ambivalent action of Tom's. Instead of judging by appearances—as we would now expect him to do—Allworthy recognizes the hidden motive. This information again has to be fed back into the reader's signified, which must be corrected to the extent that evidently Allworthy is not lacking in judgment when good motives are being thwarted by bad circumstances. Once more, then, an unpredictable event has to be fitted into the overall picture, and in this case the adjustment is all the finer because the reader has had to modify the signified, which he himself had produced. Thus the reader's communication with the text is a dynamic process of self-correction, as he formulates signifieds which he must then continually modify. It is cybernetic in nature as it involves a feedback of effects and information throughout a sequence of changing situational frames; smaller units progressively merge into bigger ones, so that meaning gathers meaning in a kind of snowballing process.

The dynamic interaction between text and reader has the character of an event, which helps to create the impression that we are involved in something real. This impression is paradoxical in so far as the fictional text neither denotes a given reality, nor caters overtly to the possible range of its reader's dispositions. It does not even have to relate to any cultural code common to itself and its readers, for its 'reality' arises out of something even more basic: the nature of reality itself. A. N. Whitehead writes:

> One all-pervasive fact, inherent in the very character of what is real is the transition of things, the passage one to another. This passage is not a mere linear procession of discrete entities. However we fix a determinate entity, there is always a narrower determination of something which is presupposed in our first choice. Also there is always a wider determination into which our first choice fades by transition beyond itself. . . . These unities, which I call events, are the emergence into actuality of something. How are we to characterise the something which thus emerges? The name *'event'* given to such a unity, draws attention to the inherent transitoriness, combined with the actual unity. But this abstract word cannot be sufficient to characterise what the fact of the reality of an event is in itself. A moment's thought shows us that no one idea can in itself be sufficient. For every idea which finds its significance in each event must represent something which contributes to what realisation is in itself. . . . Aesthetic attainment is interwoven in the texture of realisation.[32]

Events are a paradigm of reality in that they designate a process, and are not merely a "discrete" entity. Each event represents the intersecting point of a variety of circumstances, but circumstances also change the event as soon as it has taken on a shape. As a shape, it marks off certain borderlines, so that these may then be transcended in the continuous process of realization that constitutes reality. In literature, where the reader is constantly feeding back reactions as he obtains new information, there is just such a continual process of realization, and so reading itself 'happens' like an event, in the sense that what we read takes on the character of an open-ended situation, at one and the same time concrete and yet fluid. The concreteness arises out of each new attitude we are forced to adopt toward the text, and the fluidity out of the fact that each new attitude bears the seeds of its own modification. Reading, then, is experienced as something which is happening—and happening is the hallmark of reality. For Whitehead the process of realization entails aesthetic attainment, because reality can only be conceived in a sequence of transitory shapes. These shapes are the signifieds which are in reading constantly being shifted into different situational frames, thus effecting a constant shift of position. The text can never be grasped as a whole—only as a series of changing viewpoints, each one restricted in itself and so necessitating further perspectives. This is the process by which the reader 'realizes' an overall situation.

The Referential System of the Repertoire

Text and reader converge by way of a situation which depends on both for its 'realization.' If the

[32] A. N. Whitehead, *Science and the Modern World* (Cambridge, 1953), pp. 116f. [Au.]

literary communication is to be successful, it must bring with it all the components necessary for the construction of the situation, since this has no existence outside the literary work. We may recall that Austin listed three main conditions for the success of the performative utterance: conventions common to speaker and recipient, procedures accepted by both, and the willingness of both to participate in the speech action. We may assume that, generally, text and reader will fulfill the condition of willingness, but as far as conventions and procedures are concerned, these must first be established by the text. We must now take a closer look at these basic components, and we should perhaps begin by naming them a little more precisely. The *conventions* necessary for the establishment of a situation might more fittingly be called the repertoire of the text. The *accepted procedures* we shall call the strategies, and the reader's participation will henceforth be referred to as the realization.

The repertoire consists of all the familiar territory within the text. This may be in the form of references to earlier works, or to social and historical norms, or to the whole culture from which the text has emerged—in brief, to what the Prague structuralists have called the "extratextual" reality.[33] The fact that this reality is referred to has a two-fold implication: (1) that the reality evoked is not confined to the printed page, (2) that those elements selected for reference are not intended to be a mere replica. On the contrary, their presence in the text usually means that they undergo some kind of transformation, and, indeed, this is an integral feature of the whole process of communication. The manner in which conventions, norms, and traditions take their place in the literary repertoire varies considerably, but they are always in some way reduced or modified, as they have been removed from their original context and function. In the literary text they thus become capable of new connections, but at the same time the old connections are still present, at least to a certain degree (and may themselves appear in a new light); indeed, their original context must remain sufficiently implicit to act as a background to offset their new significance. Thus the repertoire incorporates both the origin and the transformation of its elements, and the individuality of the text will largely depend on the extent to which their identity is changed.

The determinacy of the repertoire supplies a meeting point between text and reader, but as communication always entails conveying something new, obviously this meeting point cannot consist entirely of familiar territory. "The newness essential to art cannot be clearly marked off from the 'old.' I feel that more important than such considerations is the task of explaining the relationship of the new to the 'repetition.' This relationship does not consist in a linear course of regressions and progressions; the newness and the repetition approach one another . . . without ever merging into a single harmonic identity."[34] The absence of any such identity is an indication that the familiar territory is interesting not because it *is* familiar, but because it is to lead in an unfamiliar direction. The new significance of old norms cannot be defined by the text, because any definition would have to be in terms of existing norms, and so at best we can say that the repertoire presents existing norms in a state of suspended validity—thus turning the literary text into a kind of halfway house between past and future. The text itself becomes present to the reader as an open event because the importance of the familiar components cannot lie in their familiarity, and yet the intention underlying the selection of these components has not been formulated. It is this indeterminate position that endows the text with its dynamic, aesthetic value—"aesthetic" in the sense described by Robert Kalivoda: "In our eyes, the paramount discovery of scientific aesthetics is the recognition of the fact that the aesthetic vaue is an *empty* principle which organizes extraaesthetic qualities."[35] As such, aesthetic value is something that cannot be grasped. If it organizes nonaesthetic realities (which in themselves are not organized, or at least not organized in precisely that way), clearly, it is manifesting itself in the alteration of what is familiar. Aesthetic value, then, is like the wind—we know of its existence only through its effects.

The repertoire consists of a selection of norms and allusions, and the question arises as to what

[33] See Jan Mukařovský, *Kapitel aus der Ästhetik* (Frankfort, 1970), pp. 11ff. [Au.] on Mukařovský, see *CTSP*, pp. 1049–57. [Eds.]

[34] Herbert Malecki, *Spielräume: Aufsätze zur ästhetischen Aktion* (Frankfort, 1969), pp. 80f. [Au.]

[35] Robert Kalivoda, *Der Marxismus und die moderne geistige Wirklichkeit* (Frankfort, 1970), p. 29. [Au.]

principles govern this selection, which after all cannot be purely arbitrary. However, before we answer this question, we ought first to have a closer look at what is meant by the 'reality' out of which the selections are made. The term *reality* is already suspect in this connection, for no literary text relates to contingent reality as such, but to models or concepts of reality,[36] in which contingencies and complexities are reduced to a meaningful structure.[37] We call these structures world-pictures or systems. Every epoch has had its own thought system and social system, and each dominant system, in turn, has other systems as its historical environment, relegating them to subsystems, and so imposing a hierarchical order on what is considered to be the reality of the respective epoch. We tend to differentiate between epochs in history by the changes to which this pattern of hierarchically graded systems is subjected—in consequence of which the order imposed on contingent reality is reshuffled. According to General Systems Theory, each system has a definite structure of regulators which marshal contingent reality into a definitive order.[38] These regulators have several interrelated functions: they provide a framework for social action; they serve as a protection against insecurities arising out of the contingent world; they supply an operational set of norms that claim universal validity and so offer a reliable basis for our expectations; they must also be flexible enough to adapt to changes in their respective environments. In order to fulfill these functions, each system must effect a meaningful reduction of complexity by accentuating some possibilities and neutralizing or negating others. (Reduction, of course, should not be equated with simplification, for the latter would make the system too vulnerable to changing circumstances.) The selective process that brings about this reduction gives stability to the dominant possibilities by offsetting them against the background of those that have been excluded. "All systems are linked to the world around them by means of selective references, for they are less complex than that world, and so can never incorporate it in its totality. . . . The world around the system can, to a certain extent, be . . . immobilised through the *institutionalisation* of *particular forms* of *experience-processing* (habits of perception, interpretations of reality, values). A variety of systems are linked to the same, or similar concepts, so that the infinity of . . . possible modes of conduct is reduced and the complementarity of expectations is secured."[39] Every system thus brings about the stabilization of certain expectations, which take on normative and continual validity and so are enabled to regulate the "experience-processing" of the world.

Every system therefore represents a model of reality based on a structure inherent to all systems. Each meaningful reduction of contingency results in a division of the world into possibilities that fade from the dominant to the neutralized and negated, the latter being retained in the background, and thus offsetting and stabilizing the chosen possibilities of the system. This structure is emphasized by General Systems Theory, because reduction of contingency should not result in eliminating possibilities but only in deactivating some of them, so that the system can adapt to a changing world. The literary text, however, interferes with this structure, for generally it takes the prevalent thought system or social system as its context, but does not reproduce the frame of reference which stabilizes these systems. Consequently, it cannot produce those "expected expectations"[40] which are provided by the system. What it can and does do is set up a parallel frame within which meaningful patterns are to form. In this respect, the literary text is also a system, which shares the basic structure of overall systems as it brings out dominant meanings against a background of neutralized and negated possibilities. However, this structure becomes operative not in relation to a contingent world, but in relation to the ordered pattern of systems with which the text interferes or is meant to interfere. Although in structure basically identical to the overall system,

[36] See Siegfried J. Schmidt, *Texttheorie* (Munich, 1973), p. 45; and in particular, H. Blumenberg, "Wirklichkeitsbegriff und Möglichkeiten des Romans," *Nachahmung und Illusion* (*Poetik und Hermeneutik* I), H. R. Jauss, ed. (Munich, 1969), pp. 9-27. [Au.]

[37] See Jürgen Habermas and Niklas Luhmann, *Theorie der Gesellschaft oder Sozialtechnologie* (Frankfort, 1971), pp. 32f. On the function of the concept of meaning as a reduction of complexity, see Niklas Luhmann, *Soziologische Aufklärung* (Opladen, 1971), p. 73. [Au.]

[38] Niklas Luhmann, *Zweckbegriff und Systemrationalität* (Frankfort, 1973), pp. 182ff. [Au.]

[39] Ibid., pp. 182f. [Au.]

[40] See Habermas and Luhmann, *Sozialtechnologie*, pp. 63f. [Au.]

the literary text differs from it in its intention. Instead of reproducing the system to which it refers, it almost invariably tends to take as its dominant 'meaning' those possibilities that have been neutralized or negated by that system. If the basic reference of the text is to the penumbra of excluded possibilities, one might say that the borderlines of existing systems are the starting point for the literary text. It begins to activate that which the system has left inactive.

Herein lies the unique relationship between the literary text and 'reality,' in the form of thought systems or models of reality. The text does not copy these, and it does not deviate from them either—though the mirror-reflection theory and the stylistics of deviation would have us believe otherwise. Instead, it represents a reaction to the thought systems which it has chosen and incorporated in its own repertoire. This reaction is triggered by the system's limited ability to cope with the multifariousness of reality, thus drawing attention to its deficiencies. The result of this operation is the rearranging and, indeed, reranking of existing patterns of meaning. The above observations can perhaps best be understood through a concrete example. The Lockean philosophy of empiricism was the predominant thought system in eighteenth-century England. This philosophy is based on a number of selective decisions pertaining to the acquisition of human knowledge—a process that was of increasing concern at the time, in view of the general preoccupation with self-preservation. The dominance of this system may be gauged from the fact that existing systems endeavored to adapt themselves and so were relegated to subsystems. This was especially so in regard to theology, which accepted empirical premises concerning the acquisition of knowledge through experience, and so continually searched for natural explanations of supernatural phenomena. By this subjugation of theological systems, empiricism extended the validity of its own assumptions. However, a system can only become stable by excluding other possibilities. In this case, the possibility of a priori knowledge was negated, and this meant that knowledge could only be acquired subjectively. The advantage of such a doctrine was that knowledge could be gained from man's own experience; the disadvantage was that all traditional postulates governing human conduct and relations had to be called in question. "Hence it comes to pass that men's names of very compound *ideas,* such as for the most part are moral words, have seldom in two different men the same precise signification, since one man's complex *idea* seldom agrees with another's, and often differs from his own, from that which he had yesterday or will have tomorrow."[41] Here lies the boundary of the empirical system, and like all such boundaries it can only stabilize itself by means of neutralizations or negations. Locke solves the problem of how man is to acquire his knowledge (i.e., from experience), but in so doing he throws up a new problem of possible bases for human conduct and relations.

All thought systems are bound to exclude certain possibilities, thus automatically giving rise to deficiencies, and it is to these deficiencies that literature applies itself. Thus in the eighteenth-century novel and drama, there was an intense preoccupation with questions of morality. Eighteenth-century literature balanced out the deficiencies of the dominant thought system of the time. Since the whole sphere of human relations was absent from this system, literature now brought it into focus. The fact that literature supplies those possibilities which have been excluded by the prevalent system, may be the reason why many people regard 'fiction' as the opposite of 'reality'; it is, in fact, not the opposite, but the complement.

PERHAPS we can now draw a few general conclusions about the function of the literary repertoire. The field of action in a literary work tends to be on or just beyond the fringes of the particular thought system prevalent at the time. Literature endeavors to counter the problems produced by the system, and so the literary historian should be able not only to gauge which system was in force at the time of the work's creation but also to reconstruct the weaknesses and the historical, human impact of that system and its claims to universal validity. If we wanted to apply Collingwood's question-and-answer logic,[42] we might say that literature answers the questions arising out of the system. Through it, we can reconstruct whatever was concealed or ignored by the philosophy or ideology of the day, pre-

[41] John Locke, *An Essay Concerning Human Understanding,* Book III, Ch. 9 (London, 1961), p. 78. [Au.]

[42] See R. G. Collingwood, *An Autobiography* (Oxford, 1967), pp. 29ff., 107ff. [Au.]

cisely because these neutralized or negated aspects of reality form the focal point of the literary work. At the same time, the text must also implicitly contain the basic framework of the system, as this is what causes the problems that literature is to react to. In other words, the literary work implicitly draws an outline of the prevailing system by explicitly shading in the areas all around that system. And so we can say, as Roland Barthes has put it: "The literary work is essentially paradoxical. It represents history and at the same time resists it. This basic paradox emerges . . . clearly from our histories of literature: everyone feels that the work cannot be pinned down, and that it is something other than its own history, or the sum of its sources, its influences, its models. It forms a solid, irreducible nucleus in the unresolved tangle of events, conditions, and collective mentality."[43]

Out of the interaction between literary work and historical system of thought there emerges a basic component of the literary repertoire. Whatever elements it takes over, thought systems are automatically recoded into a set of signals that will counterbalance the deficiency of those systems. The irreducible nucleus that Barthes spoke of is the aesthetic value of the work or, in other words, its organizing force, and this lies precisely in the recodification of the norms and conventions selected. The repertoire reproduces the familiar, but strips it of its current validity. What it does not do, however, is formulate alternative values, such as one might expect after a process of negation; unlike philosophies and ideologies, literature does not make its selections and its decisions explicit. Instead, it questions or recodes the signals of external reality in such a way that the reader himself is to find the motives underlying the questions, and in doing so he participates in producing the meaning.

If the literary work arises out of the reader's own social or philosophical background, it will serve to detach prevailing norms from their functional context, thus enabling the reader to observe how such social regulators function, and what effect they have on the people subject to them. The reader is thus placed in a position from which he can take a fresh look at the forces which guide and orient him, and which he may hitherto have accepted without question. If these norms have now faded into past history, and the reader is no longer entangled in the system from which they arose, he will be able not only to reconstruct, from their recodification, the historical situation that provided the framework for the text but also to experience for himself the specific deficiencies brought about by those historical norms, and to recognize the answers implicit in the text. And so the literary recodification of social and historical norms has a double function: it enables the participants—or contemporary readers—to see what they cannot normally see in the ordinary process of day-to-day living; and it enables the observers—the subsequent generations of readers—to grasp a reality that was never their own.

The different relations between literature and thought systems bring into focus the different historical situations from which they emerge and, hence, the historical efficacy of the fictional reaction to reality. A typical example of a work directly related to a prevailing system is Sterne's *Tristram Shandy,* which links up with Lockean empiricism. For Locke, the association of ideas represented a fundamental element in man's access to knowledge, as it was the combination of contingent sense data that brought about the extension and consolidation of knowledge. The association of ideas was, then, one of the dominant features of the empirical thought system. In *Tristram Shandy* its presence is only virtual, thrusting into relief those possibilities of knowledge that the Lockean system either rejected or ignored.[44] The problem underlying the association of ideas was its dependence on the principle of pleasure and pain—even though Locke himself regarded innate a priori principles as no longer valid. If knowledge was to be reliable, man must be able to direct the association of ideas—otherwise, this would be independent of human influence. In *Tristram Shandy,* the association of ideas becomes an *idée fixe,* thus demanding a recodifica-

[43] Roland Barthes, *Literatur oder Geschichte,* transl. by Helmut Scheffel (Frankfort, 1969), p. 13. [Au.] On Barthes, see *CTSP,* pp. 1195–99. [Eds.]

[44] As we are only concerned here with an illustration, there is no need to discuss all the references Sterne makes to the system of empiricism. They are, of course, far more numerous than might be supposed just from this consideration of the association of ideas. For further information on Sterne's link with Locke, see Rainer Warning, *Illusion und Wirklichkeit in Tristram Shandy und Jacques le Fataliste* (Munich, 1965), pp. 60ff.; see also John Traugott, *Tristram Shandy's World* (Berkeley and Los Angeles, 1954), pp. 3ff. [Au.]

tion of the whole basis of the empirical system. For Sterne it is something that cannot be stabilized except through verbal cues and hobby-horses. The personal obsessions of the brothers Shandy represent the principle in accordance with which ideas are associated. Although it does lead to a certain degree of stability, this can only apply to the subjective world of the individual character, and so each character associates something quite different with any one idea, with the result that human relations, conduct, and communication become totally unpredictable.[45]

Thus Sterne brings to the fore the human dimension that had been glossed over in Locke's system. Man's habitual propensity for combining ideas was for Locke a natural guarantee for the stabilization of knowledge, but Sterne seizes on this same propensity to show the arbitrariness of such associations—as proved again and again by the meanderings of Walter Shandy and Uncle Toby. Individual explanations of world and life shrink to the level of personal whim. This arbitrariness not only casts doubt on the dominant norm of the Lockean system, but it also reveals the unpredictability and impenetrability of each subjective character. The result is not merely a negation of the Lockean norm but also a disclosure of Locke's hidden reference—namely, subjectivity as the selecting and motivating power behind the association of ideas.

This is only one result of Sterne's recodification of the empirical norm. Once the reliability of human knowledge has been undermined by the revelation of its dependence on personal fixations, the norm under attack itself becomes a background for a new insight: the problematic nature of human relations. This revelation, in turn, leads Sterne to uncover the inherent social disposition of man, which now promises the reliability in human affairs that was shattered by his discrediting of the empirical norms.

Literature need not always refer directly to the prevailing thought system of the day. Fielding's *Tom Jones* is an example of a much more indirect approach. Here the author's avowed intention is to build up a picture of human nature, and this picture incorporates a repertoire that is drawn from many different thought systems. The various norms are presented as the guiding principles behind the conduct of the most important characters. Allworthy embodies the latitudinarian morality of benevolence; Square, one of the hero's tutors, represents the deistic norm of the natural orderliness of things; Thwackum, Tom's other tutor, typifies the orthodox Anglican norm of the corruption of human nature; in Squire Western we find the basic principle of eighteenth-century anthropology: the ruling passion; and Mrs. Western incorporates all the upper-class social conventions concerning the natural superiority of the nobility.[46]

The contrasts between these characters transform their respective norms into different perspectives from which the reader may view first one norm and then another. From these changing perspectives, there emerges one common feature: all the norms reduce human nature to a single principle, thus excluding all those possibilities that do not concur with that principle. The reader himself retains sight both of what the norms represent and of what the representation leaves out. In this respect, the repertoire of the novel may be said to have a horizontal organization, in the sense that it combines and levels out norms of different systems which in real life were kept quite separate from one another. By this selective combination of norms, the repertoire offers information about the systems through which the picture of human nature is to be compiled. The individual norms themselves have to be reassessed to the extent that human nature cannot be reduced to a single hard-and-fast principle, but must be discovered, in all its potential, through the multifarious possibilities that have been excluded by those norms. These possibilities invalidate the universal claims of each selective principle by illustrating its inability to interlink with human experience, and herein lies the true subject matter of the novel. Self-preservation cannot be achieved merely by following principles; it depends on the realization of hu-

[45] See especially the situation between Walter Shandy and Uncle Toby (*Tristram Shandy*, Book V, Ch. 3 [London, 1956], pp. 258ff.), when Walter recites Cicero's lamentation for his daughter. Owing to Uncle Toby's views on the use of language, the recitation produces a chain reaction of unforeseeable utterances and events. [Au.]

[46] In the essay "The Reader's Role in Fielding's *Joseph Andrews* and *Tom Jones*," contained in my book *The Implied Reader: Patterns of Communication from Bunyan to Beckett* (Baltimore and London, 1975), pp. 52ff., I have tried to trace the development of the interplay between the norms represented by these characters, as well as the way in which they are separated from the counter-orientation of the hero. [Au.]

man potentials, and these can only be brought to light by literature, not by systematic discourse.

Tom Jones, then, does not refer directly to one dominant thought system of the eighteenth century; its concern is with the deficiencies produced by a number of systems. It shows the gulf between the rigid confines of principles and the endless fluidity of human experience. Those systems oriented by the power of human reason ignored questions of human conduct in the ever-changing situations of human life. Latitudinarian norms of conduct presupposed that moral inclinations were innate in human nature. The resultant uncertainties affected people's confidence in the orderliness of the world, and so the novel sought to reestablish this confidence by providing a picture of human nature which offered a guarantee of self-preservation through self-correction.[47]

Literature can naturally serve different functions in the context of history. *Tom Jones* dealt with deficiencies in the prevailing systems of thought, and *Tristram Shandy* laid bare the unstable basis of human knowledge as conceived by one particular system, but both examples are linked by the fact that they run counter to the systems of reference incorporated in their repertoires. History, however, is full of situations in which the balancing powers of literature have been used to support prevailing systems. Often such works tend to be of a more trivial nature, as they affirm specific norms with a view to training the reader according to the moral or social code of the day—but this is not always the case.

One serious form of literature that served to confirm the prevailing system was the courtly romance of the Middle Ages. The courtly society was being challenged by changes in the feudal system. In order to reaffirm the courtly values, Chrétien made his knights embark on various quests, in the course of which these values were tested and proven; the knights then returned home, thus stabilizing the courtly society which they had left. Isolation and reintegration form the pattern of all the adventures through which Chrétien presents both the departure of the knights from Arthur's court and their adherence to the values of that court. The adventures embody situations which are no longer covered by the social system of the court. With its pattern of isolation and reintegration, the adventure fortifies the existing system against the challenge of social change.[48] Here, then, the function of literature is to remove a threat to the stability of the system.

In the courtly romance, we again have a balancing operation as in those novels where prevailing norms are undermined, for in both cases literature takes on its function through the weaknesses of the prevailing system—either to break it down or shore it up. The contemporary reader will find himself confronted with familiar conventions in an unfamiliar light, and, indeed, this is the situation that causes him to become involved in the process of building up the meaning of the work. However, readers from a later epoch will also be involved in this process, and so, clearly, a historical gap between text and reader does not necessarily lead to the text losing its innovative character; the difference will only lie in the nature of the innovation. For the contemporary reader, the reassessment of norms contained in the repertoire will make him detach

[47] Although the eighteenth-century novel balanced out the problems of human relations that arose from the prevalent thought systems of the day, this inevitably brought about new problems. The new emphasis on the moral potentiality of human nature led automatically to other sides of man's nature being neglected or ignored. In this respect, we may say that the balancing function of literature itself causes problems, which may even lead to a new reaction from literature, as shown for instance in the Gothic novel and preromantic poetry. Here the darker side of man is brought to the fore, in a manner that had not been possible during the first half of the century owing to the totally different function of the novel and of drama. In the context of history, therefore, one may observe a complex succession of reactions within literature itself, which forms its own history through the problems arising out of its own answers. [Au.]

[48] See Erich Köhler, *Ideal und Wirklichkeit in der höfischen Epik* (Tübingen, 1956), pp. 66–128. However, Köhler regards the relation between literature and reality as a mimetic one between ideal and reality, but not as an interaction between literature and the court system. And so for him the courtly novel represents a mirror image through which society can see itself in its own perfection. Köhler's interesting observations take on a different complexion if one adopts the viewpoint that this mirror image is in fact a reinforcement of threatened norms seen from the perspective of the court system. This is borne out by the fact that the real-life dangers to the court system were collected in the *Renart* cycle, from which the court system was able to distance itself. Thus the counterworld of these dangerous disturbances was brought under control and also relegated to a background position. On the *Renart* cycle as a counter to feudal society, see H. R. Jauss, *Untersuchungen zur mittelalterlichen Tierdichtung* (Tübingen, 1959). [Au.]

these norms from their social and cultural context and so recognize the limitations of their effectiveness. For the later reader, the reassessed norms help to re-create that very social and cultural context that brought about the problems which the text itself is concerned with. In the first instance, the reader is affected as a participant, and in the second as an observer. This again may be borne out by our Fielding example. Fielding's contemporaries were mainly concerned with the problem of human conduct, which led to the fierce debates on the apparent amorality of the hero and his creator. The modern observer is not primarily concerned with these questions of morality so much as with the context of norms from which the repertoire was selected; thus each prevailing thought system of the time is brought into view, together with its deficiencies, which the novel attempts to counteract by providing a frame within which human nature is to be pictured. Here we have two different configurations of meaning, neither of which can in any way be called arbitrary, for the change of perspective is due to the passage of time and not to any deliberate act on the part of the reader. And so we may say that the reassessment of norms is what constitutes the innovative character of the repertoire, but this reassessment may lead to different consequences: the participant will see what he would not have seen in the course of his everyday life; the observer will grasp something which has hitherto never been real for him. In other words, the literary text enables its readers to transcend the limitations of their own real-life situation; it is not a reflection of any given reality, but it is an extension or broadening of their own reality. In Kosík's words: "Every work of art has a unified and indivisible double character: it is an expression of reality, but it also forms the reality that exists, not next to or before the work but actually in the work itself . . . the work of art is not an illustration of *concepts* of reality. As work and as art, it represents reality and so indivisibly and simultaneously *forms* reality."[49]

THE repertoire of a literary text does not consist solely of social and cultural norms; it also incorporates elements and, indeed, whole traditions of past literature that are mixed together with these norms. It may even be said that the proportions of this mixture form the basis of the differences between literary genres. There are texts that lay heavy emphasis on given, empirical factors, thus increasing the proportion of extratextual norms in the repertoire; this is the case with the novel. There are others in which the repertoire is dominated by elements from earlier literature—lyric poetry being the prime example. Striking effects can and have been gained by reversing these proportions, as has happened in the twentieth century, for instance, in the novels of James Joyce, with their countless literary allusions, and in the lyrics of the Beat Generation, who incorporated into their verse a wide range of social and cultural norms drawn from our modern industrial society.

The literary allusions inherent in the repertoire are reduced in the same way as the norms, for again they are functional, not merely imitative. And if the function of the incorporated norms is to bring out the deficiencies of a prevailing system, the function of literary allusions is to assist in producing an answer to the problems set by these deficiencies. Although, like the norms, they open up familiar territory, they also 'quote' earlier answers to the problems—answers which no longer constitute a valid meaning for the present work, but which offer a form of orientation by means of which the new meaning may perhaps be found. The very fact that the allusions are now stripped of their original context makes it clear that they are not intended to be a mere reproduction—they are, so to speak, depragmatized and set in a new context. When, for instance, Fielding 'reproduces' in *Shamela* the virtuous nature of Richardson's Pamela, he virtualizes Richardson's principal, governing norm of steadfastness and releases those possibilities which Richardson had excluded, thus showing that a woman need only be tenacious and persistent to get a good price for her carefully preserved virtue. But the fact that an old context is replaced by a new one does not mean that it disappears altogether. Instead, it is transformed into a virtual background against which the new subject matter can stand out in clear relief.

The different elements of the literary repertoire supply guidelines for the 'dialogue' between text and reader. These guidelines are essential in view of the overall function of the text to provide an answer, and the more complex the problems to be answered, the more differentiated the guidelines

[49] Karel Kosík, *Die Dialektik des Konkreten* (Frankfort, 1967), pp. 123f. [Au.]

should be. The literary text must comprise the complete historical situation to which it is reacting. Now, the social and cultural norms that form this situation need to be organized in such a way that the reason for their selection can be conveyed to the reader, but since this cannot be conveyed explicitly (unless fiction is to be turned into documentary), there has to be a means of generalizing the repertoire, and herein lies the special function of the literary allusions. Fielding, for instance, constructed the plot of *Tom Jones* from elements of the romance and the picaresque novel. The combination of these two hitherto irreconcilable plot structures served a two-fold purpose: (1) the hero, as an outcast on the road, offers the reader a critical perspective on social norms; (2) the romance elements reassures the reader that the hero will not remain a mere outlaw, but will finally triumph. This triumph will, in turn, endorse the criticism inherent in his perspective.[50] In this way, traditional schemata are rearranged to communicate a new picture.

These observations also apply to those genres in which the repertoire consists mainly of literary clichés—for instance, in lyrical poetry, such as Spenser's *Eclogues*. These were designed to bring attention to a specific historical problem, namely, the dangers that would have arisen for England if Queen Elizabeth had gone ahead with her proposed marriage to a Catholic. The only literary store that Spenser could draw from was the pastoral. Although he could count on the fact that the eclogue as a genre would automatically signify for the educated public a reference to reality, the difficulty was to ensure that his readers would grasp the particularity of the reference. This, however, could be represented neither by directly incorporating prevalent social norms and values into the eclogue, nor by merely reproducing the current and familiar pastoral clichés. In order to shape the attitude of his readers, Spenser had to give a new slant to these clichés. The danger arising out of their recodification was that his intentions might be misunderstood by the courtly public, who were to be alerted to an important event precisely by the changes to which the bucolic clichés were subjected. He therefore incorporated in his eclogues various schemata from other genres—such as medieval debate, fable, emblem, and gloss—that enabled him to fade out some of the pastoral meanings and to bring others to the fore. In combining and rearranging various generic features, Spenser succeeded in remoulding bucolic clichés in such a way that they were able to convey the intended message.[51] The literary repertoire can thus be seen to have a two-fold function: it reshapes familiar schemata to form a background for the process of communication, and it provides a general framework within which the message or meaning of the text can be organized.

The social norms and literary allusions that constitute the two basic elements of the repertoire are drawn from two quite different systems: the first from historical thought systems, and the second from past literary reactions to historical problems. The norms and schemata selected for the repertoire are rarely equivalent to one another—and in those few cases where they are, the text will cease to be informative because it will merely repeat the answers offered by an existing text, even though the historical problems will have changed. Generally, however, the two elements of the repertoire are not equivalent to each other precisely in the degree of their familiarity. But the very fact that they have been joined together implies that they are to be related one to the other—even if, as is sometimes the case, they are meant to draw attention to differences. The nonequivalence of these two familiar elements does not mean that the principle of equivalence is absent from the text itself; its presence is signalized by the fact that the familarity of these elements no longer serves to bring about correspondences. According to Merleau-Ponty: "A meaning is always present when the data of the world are subjected by us to a 'coherent deformation'."[52] This is the process brought about by the two different elements of the repertoire. When, for instance, in *Ulysses* Joyce projects all his Homeric and Shakespearean allusions onto everyday life in Dublin, he punctures the illusory self-containment of realistic representation; at the same time, though, the many realistic details of everyday life are related in a kind

[50] On the function of such literary schemata, see the forthcoming publication by G. Birkner, *Wirkungsstrukturen des Romans im 18. und 19. Jahrhundert.* [Au.]

[51] For further details concerning this problem, see W. Iser, *Spensers Arkadien: Fiktion und Geschichte in der englischen Renaissance* (Krefeld, 1970). [Au.]

[52] M. Merleau-Ponty, *Das Auge und der Geist,* transl. by Hans Werner Arndt (Hamburg, 1967), p. 84. [Au.]

of feedback to the Homeric and Shakespearean allusions, so that the relation between past and present no longer seems like a relation of ideal to reality. The projection is two-way, and so there follows a deformation of both elements: the literary repertoire encroaches on everyday life, and the archetype is encroached on by a plethora of unstructured material drawn from the address books and newspapers of the day. Each element acts as an irritant upon the other; they are in no way equivalent to one another, but in their deformations and deforming influences they build up a system of equivalences within the text. Thus the literary allusions impose an unfamiliar dimension of deep-rooted history which shatters the monotonous rhythm of everyday life and 'deforms' its apparent immutability into something illusory; the realistic details, on the other hand, bring out all that the idealized archetype could not have known, so 'deforming' the apparently unattainable ideal into a historical manifestation of what man might be.

The "coherent deformation" points to the existence of a system of equivalences underlying the text. This system is to a large extent identical to what we earlier called aesthetic value. The aesthetic value is that which is not formulated by the text and is not given in the overall repertoire. Its existence is proved by its effect, though this does not mean that it is a part of that which it affects (i.e., the reader, or the reality to be conveyed to the reader). The effect consists of two factors which appear to be heading in different directions but in fact converge. The aesthetic value conditions the selection of the repertoire, and in so doing deforms the given nature of what is selected in order to formulate the system of equivalences peculiar to that one text; in this respect, it constitutes the framework of the text. In addition, however, it constitutes the structural 'drive' necessary for the process of communication. By invalidating correspondences between the elements put together in the repertoire, it prevents the text from corresponding to the repertoires already inherent in all its possible readers; in this respect, the aesthetic value initiates the process whereby the reader assembles the meaning of the text.

This brings us to the effect on the reader of what we might call the 'suspended' equivalences of the repertoire. The reader will have the impression of familiarity through this repertoire, but it is only an impression, for because of the "coherent deformation" in the text, the familiar elements have been deprived of their context, which alone stabilized their original meaning. This leads to two consequences: (1) through the recodification of familiar norms, the reader becomes aware for the first time of the familiar context which had governed the application of that norm; (2) the recodification of the familiar marks a kind of apex in the text, with the familiar sliding back into memory—a memory which does, however, serve to orient the search for the system of equivalences, to the extent that this system must be constituted either in opposition to or in front of the familiar background.

This whole process is conducted along the lines that govern all forms of communication, as described by Moles:

> The basic process of communication between a sender and a recipient . . . consists . . . of the following: taking recognizable signs from the repertoire of the sender, putting them together, and transmitting them along a channel of communication; the recipient then has to identify the signs received with those which he has stored in his own repertoire. Ideas can only be communicated in so far as both repertoires have elements in common. . . . But to the extent to which such a process takes place within systems equipped, like human intelligence, with memory and statistical perception, the observation of . . . similar signs gradually alters the recipient's repertoire and leads ultimately to a complete fusion with that of the sender. . . . Thus acts of communication, in their totality, assume a cumulative character through their continued influence on the repertoire of the recipient. . . . Those semantemes transmitted most frequently by the sender gradually insert themselves into the recipient's repertoire and change it. This is the stimulus of social and cultural circulation.[53]

The repertoires of the text as sender and the reader as recipient will also overlap, and the common elements are an essential precondition for the

[53] Abraham A. Moles, *Informationstheorie und ästhetische Wahrnehmung,* transl. by Hans Ronge (Cologne, 1971), p. 22. [Au.]

"circulation." However, literary communication differs from other forms of communication in that those elements of the sender's repertoire which are familiar to the reader through their application in real-life situations, lose their validity when transplanted into the literary text. And it is precisely this *loss* of validity which leads to the communication of something new.

The extent to which repertoires may overlap can help us to formulate criteria for the effect of literary texts. For instance, the repertoire of rhetorical, didactic, and propagandist literature will generally take over intact the thought system already familiar to its readers. That is to say, it adopts the vertically stabilized validity of the thought system and does not reorganize its elements horizontally, as is always the case when norms are to be reassessed. This observation holds good for medieval mystery plays right through to present-day socialist realism. What such texts set out to communicate is a confirmation of values already known to the public. Such communications are only truly meaningful if these values are being disputed in the real world of the reader, for they are an attempt to stabilize the system and protect it against the attacks resulting from its own weaknesses.

Bolstering up the weaknesses of a system performs the same balancing function as revealing them. The only difference, as far as the selected repertoire of a literary text is concerned, is in the presentation. If the weak points are to be reinforced, there will be a high degree of conformity, or equivalence, between the repertoires of text and reader; if the weak points are to be revealed, the balance will shift toward disparity and reassessment, with the stress laid on those areas where the two repertoires do not coincide.

We may take as an extreme example of this latter technique James Joyce's *Ulysses*. The repertoire of this novel is not only derived from a great number of different systems, but is also presented in such density that the reader finds himself being constantly disoriented. The problem lies not so much in the unfamiliarity of the elements, for these in themselves are not difficult to identify, but in the intermingling and the sheer mass, which cause the repertoire itself to become increasingly amorphous. Not only are the elements themselves recoded, but they all seem devoid of any identifiable frame of reference. And so, even where the repertoires of sender and recipient partially overlap, the incoherence and density of realistic details and literary allusions make all points of contact too tenuous to hold onto. If the overlap, however, is diminished, the repertoire tends to be robbed of one of its usual functions—to provide the framework for the communication of a message—and instead it serves to turn attention to the process of communication itself. Communication depends upon connections, and the repertoire of *Ulysses* is confusing precisely because we cannot establish reliable connections between the diverse elements. Furthermore, although each chapter, through its individual style, seems to offer its own possibilities of connection, the immediate change of style in each subsequent chapter automatically undermines those possibilities.

Two closely related consequences arise from the fact that the communicatory function of the repertoire moves into focus and itself evolves into a theme: first, the lack of any connecting reference produces a gap between the different elements, and this can only be filled by the reader's imagination; second, the different connections suggested by the changing styles of the chapters bring about a continual change in the direction of these imaginings—and, for all the individuality of their contents, this change of concepts remains an intersubjective structure of communication in *Ulysses*. The continual shift from one interpretative pattern to another is the method used by Joyce to enable his reader to experience everyday life. For everyday life itself consists precisely of a series of constantly changing patterns.

The repertoire of this novel both reflects and reveals the rules that govern its own communication. The reader is made aware of the basic features of his mode of perception: porous selectivity, dependence on perspective, habitual reflexes. In order to orient ourselves, we constantly and automatically leave things out, but the density of the repertoire in *Ulysses* prevents us from doing this. Furthermore, the successive changes of style, each restricted to its own perspective, indicate the extent to which perception and interpretation depend upon the standpoint of the observer.

A glance at the extremes on either side of the scale (e.g., socialist realism on the one hand, *Ulysses* on the other) will show that the reader may be called upon to participate in quite different ways. If the text reproduces and confirms familiar norms, he may remain relatively passive, whereas he is forced into intensive activity when the common ground is cut away from under him. In both cases, however, the repertoire organizes his reactions to the text and to the problems it contains. Thus we might say that the repertoire forms an organizational structure of meaning which must be optimized through the reading of the text.[54] This optimization will depend on the reader's own degree of awareness and on his willingness to open himself up to an unfamiliar experience. But it also depends on the strategies of the text, which lay down the lines along which the text is to be actualized. These lines are by no means arbitrary, for the elements of the repertoire are highly determinate.

What is indeterminate—to the extent that it is not formulated—is the system of equivalences, and this can only be discovered by the optimization of the structures offered. As the repertoire is usually characterized by a form of recodification, it supplies its own context of dominant, virtualized, and negated possibilities of meaning, and the meaning becomes the reader's own experience in proportion to the degree of order which he can establish as he optimizes the structure. The meaning must inevitably be pragmatic, in that it can never cover all the semantic potentials of the text, but can only open up one particular form of access to these potentials. As we have seen, this access is not arbitrary, thanks to the repertoire's organization of possibilities into a range of meanings stretching from the dominant through the virtualized to the negated. But the pragmatic meaning can only come into being through a selective realization of this range, and it is in this realization that the reader's own decisions come into play, together with an attitude provoked in him by the text toward the problems thrown up by the repertoire.

The pragmatic meaning is an applied meaning; it enables the literary text to fulfill its function as an answer by revealing and balancing out the deficiencies of the systems that have created the problem. It makes the reader react to his own 'reality', so that this same reality may then be reshaped. Through this process, the reader's own store of past experience may undergo a similar revaluation to that contained within the repertoire, for the pragmatic meaning allows such adaptations and, indeed, encourages them, in order to achieve its intersubjective goal: namely, the imaginary correction of deficient realities.

[54] I use the term *structure* here in the sense outlined by Jan Mukarovsky, *Kapitel aus der Poetik* (Frankfort, 1967), p. 11: "Another basic feature of this structure is its energetic and dynamic character. The energy of the structure is derived from the fact that each of the elements in the overall unity has a specific function which incorporates it into the structural whole and binds it to that whole; the dynamism of the structural whole arises out of the fact that these individual functions and their interacting relationships are subject, by virtue of their energetic character, to continual transformations. The structure as a whole thus finds itself in a ceaseless state of movement, in contrast to a summative whole, which is destroyed by any change." [Au.]

Thomas S. Kuhn

b. 1922

DURING the last two decades, few books have exerted a greater intellectual influence than Thomas S. Kuhn's *The Structure of Scientific Revolutions* (1962; 2d ed., 1970). Indeed, it sometimes appears that it is given the ultimate compliment of being cited even though not read, particularly with reference to the organizing metaphors of the book, the scientific "revolution" and the scientific "paradigm." Kuhn's argument is that scientific change has not been a smooth and steady march from ignorance to knowledge but a much more complex and uneven process, marked by discontinuities, of which "revolutions" are only the most dramatic. Just as Kuhn's view of the history of science has been influential, it has also been profoundly controversial, for reasons that will be discussed briefly. The essay included here, from *The Essential Tension: Selected Studies in Scientific Tradition and Change* (1977), is a general response to several lines of criticism that have been directed at Kuhn's account of the development of science.

A general problem has been that Kuhn's most important term, "paradigm," is used as a metaphor—leading one critic, Margaret Masterman, to observe that the word is used in twenty-two different senses. While Kuhn remarks, in a 1969 "Postscript" to *Structure,* that neither he nor Masterman thinks this so great a problem as it may appear, Kuhn's appropriation of the term itself gives an example of what he means by it, while showing why it is so difficult to give a simple definition: a "paradigm" in natural language is a single exemplifying case of some operation, such as verb conjugation (or the declension of adjectives, etc.) that can be used as an approximate model for conjugating other verbs. In this sense, the single example provides a powerful and efficient point of reference, not only for learning, say, that the third person plural of Latin *amo* (love) is *amant,* in the present indicative, but for using the whole conjugation of *amo* as a model for conjugating other verbs that have some fundamental resemblance to the model. (In this case, the distinguishing mark is the concluding vowel in the stem of the present infinitive—*amā-re.*)

Kuhn's major insight is that scientific developments take place in a similar manner: a particular scientific achievement, ranging from an especially perspicuous experiment to the solution to a perplexing problem and the development of a novel theory, provides a "paradigm" by which other, similar problems are taken up. The application of mathematical formulas to problems of motion, for example, may start with a "paradigmatic" case, the acceleration of a falling body due to gravity, and then be applied to similar cases—for example, the acceleration of a body rolling down an inclined plane, or the motion of a pendulum, to the regularities of planetary motion. It is not merely difficult but would be self-defeating to try to say precisely what a "paradigm" is: one cites examples, in given historical situations, in the expectation that the person contemplating the example will get the point, which is rarely as clear-cut as learning to find the last vowel in the stem of the present infinitive. The point, then, is the recognition and projective exploration of a pattern, not the categorical definition of a term.

In *The Structure of Scientific Revolutions,* Kuhn is principally concerned with the larger pattern that this general process of development has taken historically. Particular disciplines take shape as problem solutions are projectively mapped to domains of nature—and the scope of reference for the term "paradigm" thereby expands to cover physical theories, cosmological models, and so on, which serve to indicate, among other things, what reality contains and what it is "like." The "structure" Kuhn describes can be thought of as a mechanism of change, in which the discipline articulates a "paradigm" as a shared apprehension of some particular domain, the chief symptom of which is that "puzzle solving" becomes the "normal" scientific activity. The pursuit of this activity proceeds so long as the extension of available techniques of inquiry produces the expected results. When, however, scientists encounter "anomalies," particularly anomalies that cannot be attributed to simple errors, the stage for "revolution" is set, so to speak, since it may be that the whole "paradigm" shared by practitioners of the discipline has reached an unexpected limit, bringing on a condition of crisis. Responses to such crises, moreover, are not readily predictable: a whole line of inquiry might be abandoned, or it may happen that a very different "paradigm" emerges. The classic cases of scientific revolutions are the latter, as Copernican astronomy replacing a Ptolemaic model in the Renaissance or the shift from classical to quantum mechanics in this century.

Controversy has followed Kuhn's argument from its first publication as volume 2, number 2 of *The International Encyclopedia of Unified Science*. The *Encyclopedia* was a massive project begun by Otto Neurath and Rudolph Carnap, both members of the Vienna Circle and major figures in the development of modern logical empiricism or positivism. There could be no more stunning irony than that Kuhn's book appeared in this series of monographs, based on the very idea of orderly, incremental progress toward empirical truth that Kuhn's thesis overturns. The irony is sharpened by the fact that as a historian, Kuhn pursues historical research as an empirical problem—to find overwhelming evidence that such issues as theory choice and the shaping of science as a collective enterprise are not strictly empirical problems.

As the essay here attests, the vigor (and occasional obtuseness) of the opposition to this finding becomes itself further evidence counting for Kuhn's argument. As Harold Brown has argued, Kuhn's most determined critics are logical empiricist philosophers of science, who respond within the terms of a particular "paradigm," just as Kuhn's own "paradigm" can be seen as a response to the crisis of logical empiricism over specific problems of logic and verification (see *Isaiah Berlin*). Kuhn's position has been represented as "irrationalist," while his view of the process of paradigm changes has been attacked for being "subjective," or "mystical," or depending on something resembling religious conversion.

With characteristic elegance and lucidity, "Objectivity, Value Judgment, and Theory Choice" provides a response to such objections, while clarifying the sense in which cognizance of questions of value is not opposed to "objectivity" but is part of the conditions for it.

Kuhn's work includes *The Copernican Revolution: Planetary Astronomy and the Development of Western Thought* (1957); *The Structure of Scientific Revolutions* (1962, 1970); *Sources for History of Quantum Physics* (1967); and *The Essential Tension: Selected Studies in Scientific Tradition and Change* (1977). See especially, Kuhn's "Second Thoughts on Paradigms," in *The Essential Tension; Criticism and the Growth of Knowledge,* ed. Imre Lakatos and Alan Musgrave (1970); Harold I. Brown, *Perception, Theory and Commitment: The New Philosophy of Science* (1977); and *Paradigms and Revolutions: Appraisals and Applications of Thomas Kuhn's Philosophy of Science,* ed. Gary Gutting (1980).

OBJECTIVITY, VALUE JUDGMENT, AND THEORY CHOICE

In the penultimate chapter of a controversial book first published fifteen years ago, I considered the ways scientists are brought to abandon one time-honored theory or paradigm in favor of another. Such decision problems, I wrote, "cannot be resolved by proof." To discuss their mechanism is, therefore, to talk "about techniques of persuasion, or about argument and counterargument in a situation in which there can be no proof." Under these circumstances, I continued, "lifelong resistance [to a new theory] . . . is not a violation of scientific standards. . . . Though the historian can always find men—Priestley, for instance—who were unreasonable to resist for as long as they did, he will not find a point at which resistance becomes illogical or unscientific."[1] Statements of that sort obviously raise the question of why, in the absence of binding criteria for scientific choice, both the number of solved scientific problems and the precision of individual problem solutions should increase so markedly with the passage of time. Confronting that issue, I sketched in my closing chapter a number of charcteristics that scientists share by virtue of the training which licenses their membership in one or another community of specialists. In the absence of criteria able to dictate the choice of each individual, I argued, we do well to trust the collective judgment of scientists trained in this way. "What better criterion could there be," I asked rhetorically, "than the decision of the scientific group?"[2]

A number of philosophers have greeted remarks like these in a way that continues to surprise me. My views, it is said, make of theory choice "a matter for mob psychology."[3] Kuhn believes, I am

OBJECTIVITY, VALUE JUDGMENT, AND THEORY CHOICE was originally delivered as a Machette Lecture at Furman University, 30 November 1973. First published in *The Essential Tension: Selected Studies in Scientific Tradition and Change,* copyright 1977. Reprinted by permission of the author and The University of Chicago Press.

[1] *The Structure of Scientific Revolutions,* 2d ed. (Chicago, 1970), pp. 148, 151–52, 159. All the passages from which these fragments are taken appeared in the same form in the first edition, published in 1962. [Au.]

[2] Ibid., p. 170. [Au.]

[3] Imre Lakatos, "Falsification and the Methodology of Scientific Research Programmes," in I. Lakatos and A. Musgrave, eds., *Criticism and the Growth of Knowledge* (Cambridge, 1970), pp. 91–195. The quoted phrase, which appears on p. 178, is italicized in the original. [Au.]

told, that "the decision of a scientific group to adopt a new paradigm cannot be based on good reasons of any kind, factual or otherwise."[4] The debates surrounding such choices must, my critics claim, be for me "mere persuasive displays without deliberative substance."[5] Reports of this sort manifest total misunderstanding, and I have occasionally said as much in papers directed primarily to other ends. But those passing protestations have had negligible effect, and the misunderstandings continue to be important. I conclude that it is past time for me to describe, at greater length and with greater precision, what has been on my mind when I have uttered statements like the ones with which I just began. If I have been reluctant to do so in the past, that is largely because I have preferred to devote attention to areas in which my views diverge more sharply from those currently received than they do with respect to theory choice.

What, I ask to begin with, are the characteristics of a good scientific theory? Among a number of quite usual answers I select five, not because they are exhaustive, but because they are individually important and collectively sufficiently varied to indicate what is at stake. First, a theory should be accurate: within its domain, that is, consequences deducible from a theory should be in demonstrated agreement with the results of existing experiments and observations. Second, a theory should be consistent, not only internally or with itself, but also with other currently accepted theories applicable to related aspects of nature. Third, it should have broad scope: in particular, a theory's consequences should extend far beyond the particular observations, laws, or subtheories it was initially designed to explain. Fourth, and closely related, it should be simple, bringing order to phenomena that in its absence would be individually isolated and, as a set, confused. Fifth—a somewhat less standard item, but one of special importance to actual scientific decisions—a theory should be fruitful of new research findings: it should, that is, disclose new phenomena or previously unnoted relationships among those already known.[6] These five characteristics—accuracy, consistency, scope, simplicity, and fruitfulness—are all standard criteria for evaluating the adequacy of a theory. If they had not been, I would have devoted far more space to them in my book, for I agree entirely with the traditional view that they play a vital role when scientists must choose between an established theory and an upstart competitor. Together with others of much the same sort, they provide *the* shared basis for theory choice.

Nevertheless, two sorts of difficulties are regularly encountered by the men who must use these criteria in choosing, say, between Ptolemy's astronomical theory and Copernicus's, between the oxygen and phlogiston theories of combustion, or between Newtonian mechanics and the quantum theory. Individually the criteria are imprecise: individuals may legitimately differ about their application to concrete cases. In addition, when deployed together, they repeatedly prove to conflict with one another; accuracy may, for example, dictate the choice of one theory, scope the choice of its competitor. Since these difficulties, especially the first, are also relatively familiar, I shall devote little time to their elaboration. Though my argument does demand that I illustrate them briefly, my views will begin to depart from those long current only after I have done so.

Begin with accuracy, which for present purposes I take to include not only quantitative agreement but qualitative as well. Ultimately it proves the most nearly decisive of all the criteria, partly because it is less equivocal than the others but especially because predictive and explanatory powers, which depend on it, are characteristics that scientists are particularly unwilling to give up. Unfortunately, however, theories cannot always be discriminated in terms of accuracy. Copernicus's system, for example, was not more accurate than Ptolemy's until drastically revised by Kepler more than sixty years after Copernicus's death. If Kepler or someone else

[4]Dudley Shapere, "Meaning and Scientific Change," in R. G. Colodny, ed., *Mind and Cosmos: Essays in Contemporary Science and Philosophy*. University of Pittsburgh Series in the Philosophy of Science, vol. 3 (Pittsburgh, 1966), pp. 41–85. The quotation will be found on p. 67. [Au.]

[5]Israel Scheffler, *Science and Subjectivity* (Indianapolis, 1967), p. 81. [Au.]

[6]The last criterion, fruitfulness, deserves more emphasis than it has yet received. A scientist choosing between two theories ordinarily knows that his decision will have a bearing on his subsequent research career. Of course he is especially attracted by a theory that promises the concrete successes for which scientists are ordinarily rewarded. [Au.]

had not found other reasons to choose heliocentric astronomy, those improvements in accuracy would never have been made, and Copernicus's work might have been forgotten. More typically, of course, accuracy does permit discriminations, but not the sort that lead regularly to unequivocal choice. The oxygen theory, for example, was universally acknowledged to account for observed weight relations in chemical reactions, something the phlogiston theory had previously scarcely attempted to do. But the phlogiston theory, unlike its rival, could account for the metals' being much more alike than the ores from which they were formed. One theory thus matched experience better in one area, the other in another. To choose between them on the basis of accuracy, a scientist would need to decide the area in which accuracy was more significant. About that matter chemists could and did differ without violating any of the criteria outlined above, or any others yet to be suggested.

However important it may be, therefore, accuracy by itself is seldom or never a sufficient criterion for theory choice. Other criteria must function as well, but they do not eliminate problems. To illustrate I select just two—consistency and simplicity—asking how they functioned in the choice between the heliocentric and geocentric systems. As astronomical theories both Ptolemy's and Copernicus's were internally consistent, but their relation to related theories in other fields was very different. The stationary central earth was an essential ingredient of received physical theory, a tight-knit body of doctrine which explained, among other things, how stones fall, how water pumps function, and why the clouds move slowly across the skies. Heliocentric astronomy, which required the earth's motion, was inconsistent with the existing scientific explanation of these and other terrestrial phenomena. The consistency criterion, by itself, therefore, spoke unequivocally for the geocentric tradition.

Simplicity, however, favored Copernicus, but only when evaluated in a quite special way. If, on the one hand, the two systems were compared in terms of the actual computational labor required to predict the position of a planet at a particular time, then they proved substantially equivalent. Such computations were what astronomers did, and Copernicus's system offered them no labor-saving techniques; in that sense it was not simpler than Ptolemy's. If, on the other hand, one asked about the amount of mathematical apparatus required to explain, not the detailed quantitative motions of the planets, but merely their gross qualitative features—limited elongation, retrograde motion, and the like—then, as every schoolchild knows, Copernicus required only one circle per planet, Ptolemy two. In that sense the Copernican theory was the simpler, a fact vitally important to the choices made by both Kepler and Galileo and thus essential to the ultimate triumph of Copernicanism. But that sense of simplicity was not the only one available, nor even the one most natural to professional astronomers, men whose task was the actual computation of planetary position.

Because time is short and I have multiplied examples elsewhere, I shall here simply assert that these difficulties in applying standard criteria of choice are typical and that they arise no less forcefully in twentieth-century situations than in the earlier and better-known examples I have just sketched. When scientists must choose between competing theories, two men fully committed to the same list of criteria for choice may nevertheless reach different conclusions. Perhaps they interpret simplicity differently or have different convictions about the range of fields within which the consistency criterion must be met. Or perhaps they agree about these matters but differ about the relative weights to be accorded to these or to other criteria when several are deployed together. With respect to divergences of this sort, no set of choice criteria yet proposed is of any use. One can explain, as the historian characteristically does, why particular men made particular choices at particular times. But for that purpose one must go beyond the list of shared criteria to characteristics of the individuals who make the choice. One must, that is, deal with characteristics which vary from one scientist to another without thereby in the least jeopardizing their adherence to the canons that make science scientific. Though such canons do exist and should be discoverable (doubtless the criteria of choice with which I began are among them), they are not by themselves sufficient to determine the decisions of individual scientists. For that purpose the shared canons must be fleshed out in ways that differ from one individual to another.

Some of the differences I have in mind result from the individual's previous experience as a scientist. In what part of the field was he at work when confronted by the need to choose? How long had he worked there; how successful had he been; and how much of his work depended on concepts and techniques challenged by the new theory? Other factors relevant to choice lie outside the sciences. Kepler's early election of Copernicanism was due in part to his immersion in the Neoplatonic and Hermetic movements of his day; German Romanticism predisposed those it affected toward both recognition and acceptance of energy conservation; nineteenth-century British social thought had a similar influence on the availability and acceptability of Darwin's concept of the struggle for existence. Still other significant differences are functions of personality. Some scientists place more premium than others on originality and are correspondingly more willing to take risks; some scientists prefer comprehensive, unified theories to precise and detailed problem solutions of apparently narrower scope. Differentiating factors like these are described by my critics as subjective and are contrasted with the shared or objective criteria from which I began. Though I shall later question that use of terms, let me for the moment accept it. My point is, then, that every individual choice between competing theories depends on a mixture of objective and subjective factors, or of shared and individual criteria. Since the latter have not ordinarily figured in the philosophy of science, my emphasis upon them has made my belief in the former hard for my critics to see.

WHAT I have said so far is primarily simply descriptive of what goes on in the sciences at times of theory choice. As description, furthermore, it has not been challenged by my critics, who reject instead my claim that these facts of scientific life have philosophic import. Taking up that issue, I shall begin to isolate some, though I think not vast, differences of opinion. Let me begin by asking how philosophers of science can for so long have neglected the subjective elements which, they freely grant, enter regularly into the actual theory choices made by individual scientists? Why have these elements seemed to them an index only of human weakness, not at all of the nature of scientific knowledge?

One answer to that question is, of course, that few philosophers, if any, have claimed to possess either a complete or an entirely well-articulated list of criteria. For some time, therefore, they could reasonably expect that further research would eliminate residual imperfections and produce an algorithm able to dictate rational, unanimous choice. Pending that achievement, scientists would have no alternative but to supply subjectively what the best current list of objective criteria still lacked. That some of them might still do so even with a perfected list at hand would then be an index only of the inevitable imperfection of human nature.

That sort of answer may still prove to be correct, but I think no philosopher still expects that it will. The search for algorithmic decision procedures has continued for some time and produced both powerful and illuminating results. But those results all presuppose that individual criteria of choice can be unambiguously stated and also that, if more than one proves relevant, an appropriate weight function is at hand for their joint application. Unfortunately, where the choice at issue is between scientific theories, little progress has been made toward the first of these desiderata and none toward the second. Most philosophers of science would, therefore, I think, now regard the sort of algorithm which has traditionally been sought as a not quite attainable ideal. I entirely agree and shall henceforth take that much for granted.

Even an ideal, however, if it is to remain credible, requires some demonstrated relevance to the situations in which it is supposed to apply. Claiming that such demonstration requires no recourse to subjective factors, my critics seem to appeal, implicitly or explicitly, to the well-known distinction between the contexts of discovery and of justification.[7] They concede, that is, that the subjective factors I invoke play a significant role in the discovery or invention of new theories, but they also insist that that inevitably intuitive process lies outside of the bounds of philosophy of science and is irrelevant to the question of scientific objectivity. Objectivity enters science, they continue, through the processes by which theories are tested, justified, or judged. Those processes do not, or at least need not, involve subjective factors at all. They can be governed by a set of (objective) criteria shared by the entire group competent to judge.

I have already argued that that position does not fit observations of scientific life and shall now assume that that much has been conceded. What is now at issue is a different point: whether or not this

[7]The least equivocal example of this position is probably the one developed in Scheffler, *Science and Subjectivity*, chap. 4. [Au.]

invocation of the distinction between contexts of discovery and of justification provides even a plausible and useful idealization. I think it does not and can best make my point by suggesting first a likely source of its apparent cogency. I suspect that my critics have been misled by science pedagogy or what I have elsewhere called textbook science. In science teaching, theories are presented together with exemplary applications, and those applications may be viewed as evidence. But that is not their primary pedagogic function (science students are distressingly willing to receive the word from professors and texts). Doubtless *some* of them were *part* of the evidence at the time actual decisions were being made, but they represent only a fraction of the considerations relevant to the decision process. The context of pedagogy differs almost as much from the context of justification as it does from that of discovery.

Full documentation of that point would require longer argument than is appropriate here, but two aspects of the way in which philosophers ordinarily demonstrate the relevance of choice criteria are worth noting. Like the science textbooks on which they are often modelled, books and articles on the philosophy of science refer again and again to the famous crucial experiments: Foucault's pendulum, which demonstrates the motion of earth; Cavendish's demonstration of gravitational attraction; or Fizeau's measurement of the relative speed of sound in water and air. These experiments are paradigms of good reason for scientific choice; they illustrate the most effective of all the sorts of argument which could be available to a scientist uncertain which of two theories to follow; they are vehicles for the transmission of criteria of choice. But they also have another characteristic in common. By the time they were performed no scientist still needed to be convinced of the validity of the theory their outcome is now used to demonstrate. Those decisions had long since been made on the basis of significantly more equivocal evidence. The exemplary crucial experiments to which philosophers again and again refer would have been historically relevant to theory choice only if they had yielded unexpected results. Their use as illustrations provides needed economy to science pedagogy, but they scarcely illuminate the character of the choices that scientists are called upon to make.

Standard philosophical illustrations of scientific choice have another troublesome characteristic. The only arguments discussed are, as I have previously indicated, the ones favorable to the theory that, in fact, ultimately triumphed. Oxygen, we read, could explain weight relations, phlogiston could not; but nothing is said about the phlogiston theory's power or about the oxygen theory's limitations. Comparisons of Ptolemy's theory with Copernicus's proceed in the same way. Perhaps these examples should not be given since they contrast a developed theory with one still in its infancy. But philosophers regularly use them nonetheless. If the only result of their doing so were to simplify the decision situation, one could not object. Even historians do not claim to deal with the full factual complexity of the situations they describe. But these simplifications emasculate by making choice totally unproblematic. They eliminate, that is, one essential element of the decision situations that scientists must resolve if their field is to move ahead. In those situations there are always at least some good reasons for each possible choice. Considerations relevant to the context of discovery are then relevant to justification as well; scientists who share the concerns and sensibilities of the individual who discovers a new theory are ipso facto likely to appear disproportionately frequently among that theory's first supporters. That is why it has been difficult to construct algorithms for theory choice, and also why such difficulties have seemed so thoroughly worth resolving. Choices that present problems are the ones philosophers of science need to understand. Philosophically interesting decision procedures must function where, in their absence, the decision might still be in doubt.

That much I have said before, if only briefly. Recently, however, I have recognized another, subtler source for the apparent plausibility of my critics' position. To present it, I shall briefly describe a hypothetical dialogue with one of them. Both of us agree that each scientist chooses between competing theories by deploying some Bayesian algorithm which permits him to compute a value for $p(T,E)$, i.e., for the probability of a theory T on the evidence E available both to him and to the other members of his professional group at a particular period of time. "Evidence," furthermore, we both interpret broadly to include such considerations as simplicity and fruitfulness. My critic asserts, however, that there is only one such value of p, that corresponding to objective choice, and he believes that all rational members of the group must arrive at it. I assert, on the other hand, for reasons previously given, that the factors he calls objective are insufficient to determine in full any algorithm at all. For the sake of the discussion I have conceded that each individual has an algorithm and that all their algorithms have much in common. Nevertheless, I continue to hold that the algorithms of individuals are all ultimately different by virtue of the subjective considerations with which each must complete the objective criteria before any computations can be done. If my hypothetical critic is liberal, he may now grant that these subjective differences do play a role in determining the hypothetical algorithm on which each individual relies during the early stages of the competition between rival theories. But he is also likely to claim that, as evidence increases with the passage of time, the algorithms of different individuals converge to the algorithm of objective choice with which his presentation began. For him the increasing unanimity of individual choices is evidence for their increasing objectivity and thus for the elimination of subjective elements from the decision process.

So much for the dialogue, which I have, of course, contrived to disclose the non sequitur underlying an apparently plausible position. What converges as the evidence changes over time need only be the values of *p* that individuals compute from their individual algorithms. Conceivably those algorithms themselves also become more alike with time, but the ultimate unanimity of theory choice provides no evidence whatsoever that they do so. If subjective factors are required to account for the decisions that initially divide the profession, they may still be present later when the profession agrees. Though I shall not here argue the point, consideration of the occasions on which a scientific community divides suggests that they actually do so.

MY ARGUMENT has so far been directed to two points. It first provided evidence that the choices scientists make between competing theories depend not only on shared criteria—those my critics call objective—but also on idiosyncratic factors dependent on individual biography and personality. The latter are, in my critics' vocabulary, subjective, and the second part of my argument has attempted to bar some likely ways of denying their philosophic import. Let me now shift to a more positive approach, returning briefly to the list of shared criteria—accuracy, simplicity, and the like—with which I began. The considerable effectiveness of such criteria does not, I now wish to suggest, depend on their being sufficiently articulated to dictate the choice of each individual who subscribes to them. Indeed, if they were articulated to that extent, a behavior mechanism fundamental to scientific advance would cease to function. What the tradition sees as eliminable imperfections in its rules of choice I take to be in part responses to the essential nature of science.

As so often, I begin with the obvious. Criteria that influence decisions without specifying what those decisions must be are familiar in many aspects of human life. Ordinarily, however, they are called, not criteria or rules, but maxims, norms, or values. Consider maxims first. The individual who invokes them when choice is urgent usually finds them frustratingly vague and often also in conflict one with another. Contrast "He who hesitates is lost" with "Look before you leap," or compare "Many hands make light work" with "Too many cooks spoil the broth." Individually maxims dictate different choices, collectively none at all. Yet no one suggests that supplying children with contradictory tags like these is irrelevant to their education. Opposing maxims alter the nature of the decision to be made, highlight the essential issues it presents, and point to those remaining aspects of the decision for which each individual must take responsibility himself. Once invoked, maxims like these alter the nature of the decision process and can thus change its outcome.

Values and norms provide even clearer examples of effective guidance in the presence of conflict and equivocation. Improving the quality of life is a value, and a car in every garage once followed from it as a norm. But quality of life has other aspects, and the old norm has become problematic. Or again, freedom of speech is a value, but so is preservation of life and property. In application, the two often conflict, so that judicial soul-searching, which still continues, has been required to prohibit such behavior as inciting to riot or shouting fire in a crowded theater. Difficulties like these are an appropriate source for frustration, but they rarely result in charges that values have no function or in calls for their abandonment. That response is barred to most of us by an acute consciousness that there are societies with other values and that these value differences result in other ways of life, other decisions about what may and what may not be done.

I am suggesting, of course, that the criteria of choice with which I began function not as rules, which determine choice, but as values, which influence it. Two men deeply committed to the same values may nevertheless, in particular situations, make different choices as, in fact, they do. But that difference in outcome ought not to suggest that the values scientists share are less than critically important either to their decisions or to the development of the enterprise in which they participate. Values like accuracy, consistency, and scope may prove ambiguous in application, both individually and collectively; they may, that is, be an insufficient basis for a *shared* algorithm of choice. But they do specify a great deal: what each scientist must consider in reaching a decision, what he may and may not consider relevant, and what he can legitimately be required to report as the basis for the choice he has made. Change the list, for example by adding social utility as a criterion, and some particular choices will be different, more like those one expects from an engineer. Subtract accuracy of fit to nature from the list, and the enterprise that results may not resemble science at all, but perhaps philosophy instead. Different creative disciplines are characterized, among other things, by different sets of shared values. If philosophy and engineering lie too close to the sciences, think of literature or the plastic arts. Milton's failure to set *Paradise Lost* in a Copernican universe does not indicate that he agreed with Ptolemy but that he had things other than science to do.

Recognizing that criteria of choice can function as values when incomplete as rules has, I think, a number of striking advantages. First, as I have already argued at length, it accounts in detail for aspects of scientific behavior which the tradition has seen as anomalous or even irrational. More important, it allows the standard criteria to function fully in the earliest stages of theory choice, the period when they are most needed but when, on the traditional view, they function badly or not at all. Copernicus was responding to them during the years required to convert heliocentric astronomy from a global conceptual scheme to mathematical machinery for predicting planetary position. Such predictions were what astronomers valued; in their absence, Copernicus would scarcely have been heard, something which had happened to the idea of a moving earth before. That his own version convinced very few is less important than his acknowledgment of the basis on which judgments would have to be reached if heliocentricism were to survive. Though idiosyncrasy must be invoked to explain why Kepler and Galileo were early converts to Copernicus's system, the gaps filled by their efforts to perfect it were specified by shared values alone.

That point has a corollary which may be more important still. Most newly suggested theories do not survive. Usually the difficulties that evoked them are accounted for by more traditional means. Even when this does not occur, much work, both theoretical and experimental, is ordinarily required before the new theory can display sufficient accuracy and scope to generate widespread conviction. In short, before the group accepts it, a new theory has been tested over time by the research of a number of men, some working within it, others within its traditional rival. Such a mode of development, however, *requires* a decision process which permits rational men to disagree, and such disagreement would be barred by the shared algorithm which philosophers have generally sought. If it were at hand, all conforming scientists would make the same decision at the same time. With standards for acceptance set too low, they would move from one attractive global viewpoint to another, never giving traditional theory an opportunity to supply equivalent attractions. With standards set higher, no one satisfying the criterion of rationality would be inclined to try out the new theory, to articulate it in ways which showed its fruitfulness or displayed its accuracy and scope. I doubt that science would survive the change. What from one viewpoint may seem the looseness and imperfection of choice criteria conceived as rules may, when the same criteria are seen as values, appear an indispensable means of spreading the risk which the introduction or support of novelty always entails.

Even those who have followed me this far will want to know how a value-based enterprise of the sort I have described can develop as a science does, repeatedly producing powerful new techniques for prediction and control. To that question, unfortunately, I have no answer at all, but that is only another way of saying that I make no claim to have solved the problem of induction. If science did progress by virtue of some shared and binding algorithm of choice, I would be equally at a loss to explain its success. The lacuna is one I feel acutely, but its presence does not differentiate my position from the tradition.

It is, after all, no accident that my list of the values guiding scientific choice is, as nearly as makes any difference, identical with the tradition's list of rules dictating choice. Given any concrete situation to which the philosopher's rules could be applied, my values would function like his rules, producing the same choice. Any justification of induction, any explanation of why the rules worked, would apply equally to my values. Now consider a situation in which choice by shared rules proves impossible, not because the rules are wrong but because they are, as rules, intrinsically incomplete. Individuals must then still choose and be guided by the rules (now values) when they do so. For that purpose, however, each must first flesh out the rules, and each will do so in a somewhat different way even though the decision dictated by the variously completed rules may prove unanimous. If I now assume, in addition, that the group is large enough so that individual differences distribute on some normal curve, then any argument that justifies the philosopher's choice by rule should be immediately adaptable to my choice by value. A group too small, or a distribution excessively skewed by external historical pressures, would, of course, prevent the argument's transfer.[8] But those are just the circumstances under which scientific progress is itself problematic. The transfer is not then to be expected.

I shall be glad if these references to a normal distribution of individual differences and to the problem of induction make my position appear very close to more traditional views. With respect to theory choice, I have never thought my departures large and have been correspondingly startled by such charges as "mob psychology," quoted at the start. It is worth nothing, however, that the positions are not quite identical, and for that purpose an analogy may be helpful. Many properties of liquids and gases can be accounted for on the kinetic theory by supposing that all molecules travel at the same speed. Among such properties are the regularities known as Boyle's and Charles's law. Other characteristics, most obviously evaporation, cannot be explained in so simple a way. To deal with them one must assume that molecular speeds differ, that they are distributed at random, governed by the laws of chance. What I have been suggesting here is that theory choice, too, can be explained only in part by a theory which attributes the same properties to all the scientists who must do the choosing. Essential aspects of the process generally known as verification will be understood only by recourse to the features with respect to which men may differ while still remaining scientists. The tradition takes it for granted that such features are vital to the process of discovery, which it at once and for that reason rules out of philosophical bounds. That they may have significant functions also in the philosophically central problem of justifying theory choice is what philosophers of science have to date categorically denied.

WHAT remains to be said can be grouped in a somewhat miscellaneous epilogue. For the sake of clarity and to avoid writing a book, I have throughout this paper utilized some traditional concepts and locutions about the viability of which I have elsewhere expressed serious doubts. For those who know the work in which I have done so, I close by indicating three aspects of what I have said which would better represent my views if cast in other terms, simultaneously indicating the main directions in which such recasting should proceed. The areas I have in mind are: value invariance, subjectivity, and partial communication. If my views of scientific development are novel—a matter about which there is legitimate room for doubt—it is in areas such as these, rather than theory choice, that my main departures from tradition should be sought.

Throughout this paper I have implicitly assumed

[8] If the group is small, it is more likely that random fluctuations will result in its members' sharing an atypical set of values and therefore making choices different from those that would be made by a larger and more representative group. External environmental—intellectual, ideological, or economic—must systematically affect the value system of much larger groups, and the consequences can include difficulties in introducing the scientific enterprise to societies with inimical values or perhaps even the end of that enterprise within societies where it had once flourished. In this area, however, great caution is required. Changes in the environment where science is practiced can also have fruitful effects on research. Historians often resort, for example, to differences between national environments to explain why particular innovations were initiated and at first disproportionately pursued in particular countries, e.g., Darwinism in Britain, energy conservation in Germany. At present we know substantially nothing about the minimum requisites of the social milieux within which a sciencelike enterprise might flourish. [Au.]

that, whatever their initial source, the criteria or values deployed in theory choice are fixed once and for all, unaffected by their participation in transitions from one theory to another. Roughly speaking, but only very roughly, I take that to be the case. If the list of relevant values is kept short (I have mentioned five, not all independent) and if their specification is left vague, then such values as accuracy, scope, and fruitfulness are permanent attributes of science. But little knowledge of history is required to suggest that both the application of these values and, more obviously, the relative weights attached to them have varied markedly with time and also with the field of application. Furthermore, many of these variations in value have been associated with particular changes in scientific theory. Though the experience of scientists provides no philosophical justification for the values they deploy (such justification would solve the problem of induction), those values are in part learned from that experience, and they evolve with it.

The whole subject needs more study (historians have usually taken scientific values, though not scientific methods, for granted), but a few remarks will illustrate the sort of variations I have in mind. Accuracy, as a value, has with time increasingly denoted quantitative or numerical agreement, sometimes at the expense of qualitative. Before early modern times, however, accuracy in that sense was a criterion only for astronomy, the science of the celestial region. Elsewhere it was neither expected nor sought. During the seventeenth century, however, the criterion of numerical agreement was extended to mechanics, during the eighteenth and early nineteenth centuries to chemistry and such other subjects as electricity and heat, and in this century to many parts of biology. Or think of utility, an item of value not on my initial list. It too has figured significantly in scientific development, but far more strongly and steadily for chemists than for, say, mathematicians and physicists. Or consider scope. It is still an important scientific value, but important scientific advances have repeatedly been achieved at its expense, and the weight attributed to it at times of choice has diminished correspondingly. What may seem particularly troublesome about changes like these is, of course, that they ordinarily occur in the aftermath of a theory change. One of the objections to Lavoisier's new chemistry was the roadblocks with which it confronted the achievement of what had previously been one of chemistry's traditional goals: the explanation of qualities, such as color and texture, as well as of their changes. With the acceptance of Lavoisier's theory such explanations ceased for some time to be a value for chemists; the ability to explain qualitative variation was no longer a criterion relevant to the evaluation of chemical theory. Clearly, if such value changes had occurred as rapidly or been as complete as the theory changes to which they related, then theory choice would be value choice, and neither could provide justification for the other. But, historically, value change is ordinarily a belated and largely unconscious concomitant of theory choice, and the former's magnitude is regularly smaller than the latter's. For the functions I have here ascribed to values, such relative stability provides a sufficient basis. The existence of a feedback loop through which theory change affects the values which led to that change does not make the decision process circular in any damaging sense.

About a second respect in which my resort to tradition may be misleading, I must be far more tentative. It demands the skills of an ordinary language philosopher, which I do not possess. Still, no very acute ear for language is required to generate discomfort with the ways in which the terms "objectivity" and, more especially, "subjectivity" have functioned in this paper. Let me briefly suggest the respects in which I believe language has gone astray. "Subjective" is a term with several established uses: in one of these it is opposed to "objective," in another to "judgmental." When my critics describe the idiosyncratic features to which I appeal as subjective, they resort, erroneously I think, to the second of these senses. When they complain that I deprive science of objectivity, they conflate that second sense of subjective with the first.

A standard application of the term "subjective" is to matters of taste, and my critics appear to suppose that that is what I have made of theory choice. But they are missing a distinction standard since Kant when they do so. Like sensation reports, which are also subjective in the sense now at issue, matters of taste are undiscussable. Suppose that, leaving a movie theater with a friend after seeing a western, I exclaim: "How I liked that terrible potboiler!" My friend, if he disliked the film, may tell me I have low tastes, a matter about which, in these circumstances, I would readily agree. But, short of saying that I lied, he cannot disagree with my report that I liked the film or try to persuade me that what I said about my reaction was wrong. What is discussable in my remark is not my characterization of my internal state, my exemplification of taste, but rather my *judgment* that the film was a potboiler. Should my friend disagree on that point, we may argue most of the night, each comparing the film with good or great ones we have seen, each revealing, implicitly or explicitly, something about how he *judges* cinematic merit, about his aesthetic. Though one of us may, before retiring, have persuaded the other, he need not have done so to demonstrate that our difference is one of judgment, not taste.

Evaluations or choices of theory have, I think, exactly this character. Not that scientists never say merely, I like such and such a theory, or I do not. After 1926 Einstein said little more than that about his opposition to the quantum theory. But scientists may always be asked to explain their choices, to exhibit the bases for their judgments. Such judgments are eminently discussable, and the man who refuses to discuss his own cannot expect to be taken seriously. Though there are, very occasionally, leaders of scientific taste, their existence tends to prove the rule. Einstein was one of the few, and his increasing isolation from the scientific community in later life shows how very limited a role taste alone can play in theory choice. Bohr, unlike Einstein, did discuss the bases for his judgment, and he carried the day. If my critics introduce the term "subjective" in a sense that opposes it to judgmental—thus suggesting that I make theory choice undiscussable, a matter of taste—they have seriously mistaken my position.

Turn now to the sense in which "subjectivity" is opposed to "objectivity," and note first that it raises issues quite separate from those just discussed. Whether my taste is low or refined, my report that I liked the film is objective unless I have lied. To my judgment that the film was a potboiler, however, the objective-subjective distinction does not apply at all, at least not obviously and directly. When my critics say I deprive theory choice of objectivity, they must, therefore, have recourse to some very different sense of subjective, presumably the one in which bias and personal likes or dislikes function instead of, or in the face of, the actual facts. But that sense of subjective does not fit the process I have been describing any better than the first. Where factors dependent on individual biography or personality must be introduced to make values applicable, no standards of factuality or actuality are being set aside. Conceivably my discussion of theory choice indicates some limitations of objectivity, but not by isolating elements properly called subjective. Nor am I even quite content with the notion that what I have been displaying are limitations. Objectivity ought to be analyzable in terms of criteria like accuracy and consistency. If these criteria do not supply all the guidance that we have customarily expected of them, then it may be the meaning rather than the limits of objectivity that my argument shows.

Turn, in conclusion, to a third respect, or set of respects, in which this paper needs to be recast. I have assumed throughout that the discussions surrounding theory choice are unproblematic, that the facts appealed to in such discussions are independent of theory, and that the discussions' outcome is appropriately called a choice. Elsewhere I have challenged all three of these assumptions, arguing that communication between proponents of different theories is inevitably partial, that what each takes to be facts depends in part on the theory he espouses, and that an individual's transfer of allegiance from theory to theory is often better described as conversion than as choice. Though all these theses are problematic as well as controversial, my commitment to them is undiminished. I shall not now defend them, but must at least attempt to indicate how what I have said here can be adjusted to conform with these more central aspects of my view of scientific development.

For that purpose I resort to an analogy I have developed in other places. Proponents of different theories are, I have claimed, like native speakers of different languages. Communication between them goes on by translation, and it raises all translation's familiar difficulties. That analogy is, of course, incomplete, for the vocabulary of the two theories may be identical, and most words function in the same ways in both. But some words in the basic as well as in the theoretical vocabularies of the two theories—words like "star" and "planet," "mixture" and "compound," or "force" and "matter"—do function differently. Those differences are unexpected and will be discovered and localized, if at all, only by repeated experience of communication breakdown. Without pursuing the matter further, I simply assert the existence of significant limits to what the proponents of different theories can communicate to one another. The same limits make it difficult or, more likely, impossible for an individual to hold both theories in mind together and compare them point by point with each other and with nature. That sort of comparison is, however, the process on which the appropriateness of any word like "choice" depends.

Nevertheless, despite the incompleteness of their communication, proponents of different theories can exhibit to each other, not always easily, the concrete technical results achievable by those who practice within each theory. Little or no translation is required to apply at least some value criteria to those results. (Accuracy and fruitfulness are most immediately applicable, perhaps followed by scope. Consistency and simplicity are far more problematic.) However incomprehensible the new theory may be to the proponents of tradition, the exhibit of impressive concrete results will persuade at least a few of them that they must discover how such results are achieved. For that purpose they must learn to translate, perhaps by treating already published papers as a Rosetta stone or, often more effective, by visiting the innovator, talking with him, watching him and his students at work. Those exposures may not result in the adoption of the theory; some advocates of the tradition may return home and attempt to adjust the old theory to produce equivalent results. But others, if the new theory is to survive, will find that at some point in the language-learning process they have ceased to translate and begun instead to speak the language like a native. No process quite like choice has occurred, but they are practicing the new theory nonetheless. Furthermore, the factors that have led them to risk the conversion they have undergone are just the ones this paper has underscored in discussing a somewhat different process, one which, following the philosophical tradition, it has labelled theory choice.

Hayden White

b. 1928

HAYDEN WHITE'S essay included here provides another example of what *Clifford Geertz* describes as "Blurred Genres"—that is, the recognition in one discipline of a cognitive need for or affinity with another discipline, in the absence of any settled or established way of making the link. This is not readily describable under the notion of "interdisciplinary" studies, much in favor with research foundations during the past two decades, since the actual nature of the need or affinity more often bespeaks a need to transform or re-form the discipline one professes, not simply marry it to another. The dilemma, as White describes it, is a classic double bind: if one wishes to review one's discipline, one way to do so is to consider its history; but when the discipline is history, either the practitioner is already committed to a particular way of doing it so as to be partially disqualified for the job or else, if the reviewer is not a historian (and hence not biased), he is bound to be an incompetent judge of what matters.

In this essay, as elsewhere, White describes metahistory as a critical enterprise wherein the historian addresses reflective questions about the writing of history itself. As a metalanguage requires a set of terms to characterize the language itself, so metahistory as White conceives it uses terms from literary criticism, particularly terms pertaining to narrative form or "emplotment" in writing history. Both in this essay and in *Metahistory: The Historical Imagination in Nineteenth-Century Europe* (1973), White employs a theory of fictions derived from Northrop Frye's *Anatomy of Criticism* (1957), together with a theory of figures derived from Giambattista Vico (*CTSP,* pp. 293–301) as a metalanguage to designate the types of emplotment a historian might choose.

White argues that all historical writing, as narrative, depends on a "non-negatable item," the form of the narrative itself, and, further, that the stories of history are understandable by virtue of their reliance on fictive forms. From the materials of the simple chronicle, as a series of events, a set of facts, the historian provides explanations only by providing formal coherence: the story, that is to say, is never simply there in the facts but must be created. Such presumably elementary matters as what events will be considered as "causes" and which as "effects" depend precisely on how the events are emplotted, just as the mode in which the resulting history will be understood (e.g., as a comedy, tragedy, romance, or satire) depends, among other things, on the structure of the plot.

In *Metahistory,* White documents in detail how such formal determinations affected the writing of history in the nineteenth century and concludes the present essay with his observation that "history as a discipline is in bad shape today because it has lost sight of its origins in the literary imagination." While one could reverse the terms, to say that literary criticism is in bad shape because it has lost sight of its origins in the historical imagination, the risk in either case is the assumption that someone else's house is in better order than one's own. In this particular case, the issue might be differently posed by noting that White's adoption of a formalist account of narrative, energizing though it may be, falls short of accounting for different functions served by narrative forms. The traditional question, posed repeatedly since Aristotle, of the difference in function between "history" and "poetry," might well be replaced by a different set of functional questions, pertaining, for example, to the function of narrative forms wherever they appear—a question by no means resolved in the rather messy mansions of literary criticism.

White's major works include *Metahistory: The Historical Imagination in Nineteenth-Century Europe* (1973) and *The Tropics of Discourse: Essays in Cultural Criticism* (1978).

THE HISTORICAL TEXT AS LITERARY ARTIFACT[1]

One of the ways that a scholarly field takes stock of itself is by considering its history. Yet it is difficult to get an objective history of a scholarly discipline, because if the historian is himself a practitioner of it, he is likely to be a devotee of one or another of its sects and hence biased; and if he is not a practitioner, he is unlikely to have the expertise necessary to distinguish between the significant and the insignificant events of the field's development. One might think that these difficulties would not arise in the field of history itself, but they do and not only for the reasons mentioned above. In order to write the history of any given scholarly discipline or even of a science, one must be prepared to ask questions *about* it of a sort that do not have to be asked in the practice *of* it. One must try to get behind or beneath the presuppositions which sustain a given type of inquiry and ask the questions that can be begged in its practice in the interest of determining why this type of inquiry has been designed to solve the problems it characteristically tries to solve. This is what metahistory seeks to do. It addresses itself to such questions as, What is the structure of a peculiarly *historical* consciousness? What is the epistemological status of historical *explanations,* as compared with other kinds of explanations that might be offered to account for the materials with which historians ordinarily deal? What are the possible *forms* of historical representation and what

THE HISTORICAL TEXT AS LITERARY ARTIFACT was first published in *Clio* 3, no. 3 (1974), reprinted in *The Tropics of Discourse: Essays in Cultural Criticism.* Reprinted by permission of The Johns Hopkins University Press, copyright 1978.

[1] This essay is a revised version of a lecture given before the Comparative Literature Colloquium of Yale University on 24 January 1974. In it I have tried to elaborate some of the themes that I originally discussed in an article, "The Structure of Historical Narrative," *Clio* 1 (1972): 5–20. I have also drawn upon the materials of my book *Metahistory: The Historical Imagination in Nineteenth-Century Europe* (Baltimore, 1973), especially the introduction, entitled "The Poetics of History." The essay profited from conversations with Michael Holquist and Geoffrey Hartman, both of Yale University and both experts in the theory of narrative. The quotations from Claude Lévi-Strauss are taken from his *Savage Mind* (London, 1966) and "Overture to *Le Cru et le cuit,*" in *Structuralism,* ed. Jacques Ehrmann (New York, 1966). The remarks on the iconic nature of metaphor draw upon Paul Henle, *Language, Thought, and Culture* (Ann Arbor, 1966). Jakobson's notions of the tropological nature of style are in "Linguistics and Poetics," in *Style and Language,* ed. Thomas A. Sebeok (New York and London, 1960). In addition to Northrop Frye's *Anatomy of Criticism* (Princeton, 1957), see also his essay on philosophy of history, "New Directions from Old," in *Fables of Identity* (New York, 1963). On story and plot in historical narrative in R. G. Collingwood's thought, see, of course, *The Idea of History* (Oxford, 1956). [Au.]

are their bases? What authority can historical accounts claim as contributions to a secured knowledge of reality in general and to the human sciences in particular?

Now, many of these questions have been dealt with quite competently over the last quarter-century by philosophers concerned to define history's relationships to other disciplines, especially the physical and social sciences, and by historians interested in assessing the success of their discipline in mapping the past and determining the relationship of that past to the present. But there is one problem that neither philosophers nor historians have looked at very seriously and to which literary theorists have given only passing attention. This question has to do with the status of the historical narrative, considered purely as a verbal artifact purporting to be a model of structures and processes long past and therefore not subject to either experimental or observational controls. This is not to say that historians and philosophers of history have failed to take notice of the essentially provisional and contingent nature of historical representations and of their susceptibility to infinite revision in the light of new evidence or more sophisticated conceptualization of problems. One of the marks of a good professional historian is the consistency with which he reminds his readers of the purely provisional nature of his characterizations of events, agents, and agencies found in the always incomplete historical record. Nor is it to say that literary theorists have *never* studied the structure of historical narratives. But in general there has been a reluctance to consider historical narratives as what they most manifestly are: verbal fictions, the contents of which are as much *invented* as *found* and the forms of which have more in common with their counterparts in literature than they have with those in the sciences.

Now, it is obvious that this conflation of mythic and historical consciousness will offend some historians and disturb those literary theorists whose conception of literature presupposes a radical opposition of history to fiction or of fact to fancy. As Northrop Frye has remarked,[2] "In a sense the historical is the opposite of the mythical, and to tell the historian that what gives shape to his book is a myth would sound to him vaguely insulting." Yet Frye himself grants that "when a historian's scheme gets to a certain point of comprehensiveness it becomes mythical in shape, and so approaches the poetic in its structure." He even speaks of different kinds of historical myths: Romantic myths "based on a quest or pilgrimage to a City of God or classless society"; Comic "myths of progress through evolution or revolution"; Tragic myths of "decline and fall, like the works of Gibbon and Spengler"; and Ironic "myths of recurrence or casual catastrophe." But Frye appears to believe that these myths are operative only in such victims of what might be called the "poetic fallacy" as Hegel, Marx, Nietzsche, Spengler, Toynbee, and Sartre—historians whose fascination with the "constructive" capacity of human thought has deadened their responsibility to the "found" data. "The historian works inductively," he says, "collecting his facts and trying to avoid any informing patterns except those he sees, or is honestly convinced he sees, in the facts themselves." He does not work "from" a "unifying form," as the poet does, but "toward" it; and it therefore follows that the historian, like any writer of discursive prose, is to be judged "by the truth of what he says, or by the adequacy of his verbal reproduction of his external model," whether that external model be the actions of past men or the historian's own thought about such actions.

What Frye says is true enough as a statement of the *ideal* that has inspired historical writing since the time of the Greeks, but that ideal presupposes an opposition between myth and history that is as problematical as it is venerable. It serves Frye's purposes very well, since it permits him to locate the specifically "fictive" in the space between the two concepts of the "mythic" and the "historical." As readers of Frye's *Anatomy of Criticism* will remember, Frye conceives fictions to consist in part of sublimates of archetypal myth-structures. These structures have been displaced to the interior of verbal artifacts in such a way as to serve as their latent meanings. The fundamental meanings of all fictions, their thematic content, consist, in Frye's view, of the "pre-generic plot-structures" or *mythoi* derived from the corpora of Classical and Judaeo-Christian religious literature. According to this theory, we understand *why* a particular story has "turned out" as it has when we have identified the archetypal myth, or pregeneric plot structure, of which the story is an exemplification. And we see

[2] See, "New Directions from Old," in *Fables of Identity.* [Eds.]

the "point" of a story when we have identified its theme (Frye's translation of *dianoia*), which makes of it a "parable or illustrative fable." "Every work of literature," Frye insists, "has both a fictional and a thematic aspect," but as we move from "fictional projection" toward the overt articulation of theme, the writing tends to take on the aspect of "direct address, or straight discursive writing and cease[s] to be literature." And in Frye's view, as we have seen, history (or at least "proper history") belongs to the category of "discursive writing," so that when the fictional element—or mythic plot structure—is *obviously* present in it, it ceases to be history altogether and becomes a bastard genre, product of an unholy, though not unnatural, union between history and poetry.

Yet, I would argue, histories gain part of their explanatory effect by their success in making stories out of *mere* chronicles; and stories in turn are made out of chronicles by an operation which I have elsewhere called "emplotment." And by emplotment I mean simply the encodation of the facts contained in the chronicle as components of specific *kinds* of plot structures, in precisely the way that Frye has suggested is the case with "fictions" in general.

The late R. G. Collingwood insisted that the historian was above all a story teller and suggested that historical sensibility was manifested in the capacity to make a plausible story out of a congeries of "facts" which, in their unprocessed form, made no sense at all. In their efforts to make sense of the historical record, which is fragmentary and always incomplete, historians have to make use of what Collingwood[3] called "the constructive imagination," which told the historian—as it tells the competent detective—what "must have been the case" given the available evidence and the formal properties it displayed to the consciousness capable of putting the right question to it. This constructive imagination functions in much the same way that Kant supposed the *a priori* imagination functions when it tells us that even though we cannot perceive both sides of a tabletop simultaneously, we can be certain it has *two* sides if it has one, because the very concept of *one side* entails at least *one other*. Collingwood suggested that historians come to their evidence endowed with a sense of the *possible* forms that different kinds of recognizably human situations *can* take. He called this sense the nose for the "story" contained in the evidence or for the "true" story that was buried in or hidden behind the "apparent" story. And he concluded that historians provide plausible explanations for bodies of historical evidence when they succeed in discovering the story or complex of stories implicitly contained within them.

What Collingwood failed to see was that no given set of casually recorded historical events can in itself constitute a story; the most it might offer to the historian are story *elements*. The events are *made* into a story by the suppression or subordination of certain of them and the highlighting of others, by characterization, motific repetition, variation of tone and point of view, alternative descriptive strategies, and the like—in short, all of the techniques that we would normally expect to find in the emplotment of a novel or a play. For example, no historical event is *intrinsically tragic;* it can only be conceived as such from a particular point of view or from within the context of a structured set of events of which it is an element enjoying a privileged place. For in history what is tragic from one perspective is comic from another, just as in society what appears to be tragic from the standpoint of one class may be, as Marx purported to show of the 18th Brumaire of Louis Buonaparte,[4] only a farce from that of another class. Considered as potential elements of a story, historical events are value-neutral. Whether they find their place finally in a story that is tragic, comic, romantic, or ironic—to use Frye's categories—depends upon the historian's decision to *con*figure them according to the imperatives of one plot structure or mythos rather than another. The same set of events can serve as components of a story that is tragic *or* comic, as the case may be, depending on the historian's choice of the plot structure that he considers most appropriate for ordering events of that kind so as to make them into a comprehensible story.

This suggests that what the historian brings to his

[3] See Collingwood, *The Idea of History*. [Eds.]

[4] See Karl Marx, *The Eighteenth Brumaire of Louis Bonaparte* (1852), in *Surveys from Exile* (New York, 1973), the source of Marx's celebrated remark, "Hegel remarks somewhere that all the great events and characters of world history occur, so to speak, twice. He forgot to add: the first time as tragedy, the second as farce" (p. 146). (The general scholarly opinion is that it was Engels, not Hegel, who first made the provocative remark in a letter to Marx, December 3, 1851.) [Eds.]

consideration of the historical record is a notion of the *types* of configurations of events that can be recognized as stories by the audience for which he is writing. True, he can misfire. I do not suppose that anyone would accept the emplotment of the life of President Kennedy as comedy, but whether it ought to be emplotted romantically, tragically, or satirically is an open question. The important point is that most historical sequences can be emplotted in a number of different ways, so as to provide different interpretations of those events and to endow them with different meanings. Thus, for example, what Michelet[5] in his great history of the French Revolution construed as a drama of Romantic transcendence, his contemporary Tocqueville[6] emplotted as an ironic Tragedy. Neither can be said to have had more knowledge of the "facts" contained in the record; they simply had different notions of the kind of story that best fitted the facts they knew. Nor should it be thought that they told different stories of the Revolution because they had discovered different *kinds* of facts, political on the one hand, social on the other. They sought out different kinds of facts because they had different kinds of stories to tell. But why did these alternative, not to say mutually exclusive, representations of what was substantially the same set of events appear equally plausible to their respective audiences? Simply because the historians shared with their audiences certain preconceptions about how the Revolution might be emplotted, in response to imperatives that were generally extra historical, ideological, aesthetic, or mythical.

Collingwood once remarked that you could never explicate a tragedy to anyone who was not already acquainted with the kinds of situations that are regarded as "tragic" in our culture. Anyone who has taught or taken one of those omnibus courses usually entitled Western Civilization or Introduction to the Classics of Western Literature will know what Collingwood had in mind. Unless you have some idea of the generic attributes of tragic, comic, romantic, or ironic situations, you will be unable to recognize them as such when you come upon them in a literary text. But historical situations do not have built into them intrinsic meanings in the way that literature texts do. Historical situations are not *inherently* tragic, comic, or romantic. They may all be inherently ironic, but they need not be emplotted that way. All the historian needs to do to transform a tragic into a comic situation is to shift his point of view or change the scope of his perceptions. Anyway, we only think of situations as tragic or comic because these concepts are part of our generally cultural and specifically literary heritage. *How* a given historical situation is to be configured depends on the historian's subtlety in matching up a specific plot structure with the set of historical events that he wishes to endow with a meaning of a particular kind. This is essentially a literary, that is to say fiction-making, operation. And to call it that in no way detracts from the status of historical narratives as providing a kind of knowledge. For not only are the pregeneric plot structures by which sets of events can be constituted as stories of a particular kind limited in number, as Frye and other archetypal critics suggest; but the encodation of events in terms of such plot structures is one of the ways that a culture has of making sense of both personal and public pasts.

We can make sense of sets of events in a number of different ways. One of the ways is to subsume the events under the causal laws which may have governed their concatenation in order to produce the particular configuration that the events appear to assume when considered as "effects" of mechanical forces. This is the way of scientific explanation. Another way we make sense of a set of events which appears strange, enigmatic, or mysterious in its immediate manifestations is to encode the set in terms of culturally provided categories, such as metaphysical concepts, religious beliefs, or story forms. The effect of such encodations is to familiarize the unfamiliar; and in general this is the way of historiography, whose "data" are always immediately strange, not to say exotic, simply by virtue of their distance from us in time and their origin in a way of life different from our own.

The historian shares with his audience *general notions* of the *forms* that significant human situations *must* take by virtue of his participation in the specific processes of sense-making which identify him as a member of one cultural endowment rather

[5] Jules Michelet (1798–1874), French historian and writer, author of the massive, multivolume *Histoire de France* (1833–67). [Eds.]

[6] Alexis de Tocqueville (1805–59), French historian and politician, best known for his *Democracy in America* (1835–40). The work referred to is *L'Ancien Régime et la révolution* (1856). [Eds.]

than another. In the process of studying a given complex of events, he begins to perceive the *possible* story form that such events *may* figure. In his narrative account of how this set of events took on the shape which he perceives to inhere within it, he emplots his account as a story of a particular kind. The reader, in the process of following the historian's account of those events, gradually comes to realize that the story he is reading is of one kind rather than another: romance, tragedy, comedy, satire, epic, or what have you. And when he has perceived the class or type to which the story that he is reading belongs, he experiences the effect of having the events in the story explained to him. He has at this point not only successfully *followed* the story; he has grasped the point of it, *understood* it, as well. The original strangeness, mystery, or exoticism of the events is dispelled, and they take on a familiar aspect, not in their details, but in their functions as elements of a familiar kind of configuration. They are rendered comprehensible by being subsumed under the categories of the plot structure in which they are encoded as a story of a particular kind. They are familiarized, not only because the reader now has more *information* about the events, but also because he has been shown how the data conform to an *icon* of a comprehensible finished process, a plot structure with which he is familiar as a part of his cultural endowment.

This is not unlike what happens, or is supposed to happen, in psychotherapy. The sets of events in the patient's past which are the presumed cause of his distress, manifested in the neurotic syndrome, have been defamiliarized, rendered strange, mysterious, and threatening and have assumed a meaning that he can neither accept nor effectively reject. It is not that the patient does not *know* what those events were, does not know the facts; for if he did not in some sense know the facts, he would be unable to recognize them and repress them whenever they arise in his consciousness. On the contrary, he knows them all too well. He knows them so well, in fact, that he lives with them constantly and in such a way as to make it impossible for him to see any other facts except through the coloration that the set of events in question gives to his perception of the world. We might say that, according to the theory of psychoanalysis, the patient has overemplotted these events, has charged them with a meaning so intense that, whether real or merely imagined, they continue to shape both his perceptions and his responses to the world long after they should have become "past history." The therapist's problem, then, is not to hold up before the patient the "real facts" of the matter, the "truth" as against the "fantasy" that obsesses him. Nor is it to give him a short course in psychoanalytical theory by which to enlighten him as to the true nature of his distress by cataloguing it as a manifestation of some "complex." This is what the analyst might do in relating the patient's case to a third party, and especially to another analyst. But psychoanalytic theory recognizes that the patient will resist both of these tactics in the same way that he resists the intrusion into consciousness of the traumatized memory traces in the *form* that he obsessively remembers them. The problem is to get the patient to "reemplot" his whole life history in such a way as to change the *meaning* of those events for him and their *significance* for the economy of the whole set of events that make up his life. As thus envisaged, the therapeutic process is an exercise in the refamiliarization of events that have been defamiliarized, rendered alienated from the patient's life-history, by virtue of their overdetermination as causal forces. And we might say that the events are detraumatized by being removed from the plot structure in which they have a dominant place and inserted in another in which they have a subordinate or simply ordinary function as elements of a life shared with all other men.

Now, I am not interested in forcing the analogy between psychotherapy and historiography; I use the example merely to illustrate a point about the fictive component in historical narratives. Historians seek to refamiliarize us with events which have been forgotten through either accident, neglect, or repression. Moreover, the greatest historians have always dealt with those events in the histories of their cultures which are "traumatic" in nature and the meaning of which is either problematical or overdetermined in the significance that they still have for current life, events such as revolutions, civil wars, large-scale processes such as industrialization and urbanization, or institutions which have lost their original function in a society but continue to play an important role on the current social scene. In looking at the ways in which such structures took shape or evolved, historians *re*familiarize them, not only by providing more information about them, but also by showing how their developments conformed to one or another of the story types that we conventionally invoke to make sense of our own life-histories.

Now, if any of this is plausible as a characterization of the explanatory effect of historical narrative, it tells us something important about the *mimetic* aspect of historical narratives. It is generally maintained—as Frye said—that a history is a verbal model of a set of events external to the mind of the historian. But it is wrong to think of a history as a model similar to a scale model of an airplane or ship, a map, or a photograph. For we can check the adequacy of this latter kind of model by going and looking at the original and, by applying the necessary rules of translation, seeing in what respect the model has actually succeeded in reproducing aspects of the original. But historical structures and processes are not like these originals; we cannot go and look at them in order to see if the historian has adequately reproduced them in his narrative. Nor should we want to, even if we could; for after all it was the very strangeness of the original as it appeared in the documents that inspired the historian's efforts to make a model of it in the first place. If the historian only did that for us, we should be in the same situation as the patient whose analyst merely told him, on the basis of interviews with his parents, siblings, and childhood friends, what the "true facts" of the patient's early life were. We would have no reason to think that anything at all had been *explained* to us.

This is what leads me to think that historical narratives are not only models of past events and processes, but also metaphorical statements which suggest a relation of similitude between such events and processes and the story types that we conventionally use to endow the events of our lives with culturally sanctioned meanings. Viewed in a purely formal way, a historical narrative is not only a *reproduction* of the events reported in it, but also a *complex of symbols* which gives us directions for finding an *icon* of the structure of those events in our literary tradition.

I am here, of course, invoking the distinctions between sign, symbol, and icon which C. S. Peirce[7] developed in his philosophy of language. I think that these distinctions will help us to understand what is fictive in all putatively realistic representations of the world and what is realistic in all manifestly fictive ones. They help us, in short, to answer the question, What are historical representations *representations of?* It seems to me that we must say of histories what Frye seems to think is true only of poetry or philosophies of history, namely that, considered as a system of signs, the historical narrative points in two directions simultaneously: *toward* the events described in the narrative and *toward* the story type or mythos which the historian has chosen to serve as the icon of the structure of the events. The narrative itself is not the icon; what it does is *describe* events in the historical record in such a way as to inform the reader *what to take as an icon* of the events so as to render them "familiar" to him. The historical narrative thus mediates between the events reported in it on the one side and pregeneric plot structures conventionally used in our culture to endow unfamiliar events and situations with meanings, on the other.

The evasion of the implications of the fictive nature of historical narrative is in part a consequence of the utility of the concept "history" for the definition of other types of discourse. "History" can be set over against "science" by virtue of its want of conceptual rigor and failure to produce the kinds of universal laws that the sciences characteristically seek to produce. Similarly, "history" can be set over against "literature" by virtue of its interest in the "actual" rather than the "possible," which is supposedly the object of representation of "literary" works. Thus, within a long and distinguished critical tradition that has sought to determine what is "real" and what is "imagined" in the novel, history has served as a kind of archetype of the "realistic" pole of representation. I am thinking of Frye, Auerbach, Booth, Scholes and Kellogg,[8] and others. Nor is it unusual for literary theorists, when they are speaking about the "context" of a literary work, to suppose that this context—the "historical milieu"—has a concreteness and an accessibility that the work itself can never have, as if it were easier to perceive the reality of a past world put together from a thousand historical documents than it is to probe the depths of a single literary work that is

[7]See *Peirce*. [Eds.]

[8]See Erich Auerbach, *Mimesis: The Representation of Reality in Western Literature* (1968); Wayne Booth, *The Rhetoric of Fiction* (1961); and Robert Scholes and Robert Kellogg, *The Nature of Narrative* (1961). [Eds.]

present to the critic studying it. But the presumed concreteness and accessibility of historical milieux, these contexts of the texts that literary scholars study, are themselves products of the fictive capability of the historians who have studied those contexts. The historical documents are not less opaque than the texts studied by the literary critic. Nor is the world those documents figure more accessible. The one is no more "given" than the other. In fact, the opaqueness of the world figured in historical documents is, if anything, increased by the production of historical narratives. Each new historical work only adds to the number of possible texts that have to be interpreted if a full and accurate picture of a given historical milieu is to be faithfully drawn. The relationship between the past to be analyzed and historical works produced by analysis of the documents is paradoxical; the *more* we know about the past, the more difficult it is to generalize about it.

But if the increase in our knowledge of the past makes it more difficult to generalize about it, it should make it easier for us to generalize about the forms in which that knowledge is transmitted to us. Our knowledge of the past may increase incrementally, but our understanding of it does not. Nor does our understanding of the past progress by the kind of revolutionary breakthroughs that we associate with the development of the physical sciences. Like literature, history progresses by the production of classics, the nature of which is such that they cannot be disconfirmed or negated, in the way that the principal conceptual schemata of the sciences are. And it is their nondisconfirmability that testifies to the essentially *literary* nature of historical classics. There is something in a historical masterpiece that cannot be negated, and this nonnegatable element is its form, the form which is its fiction.

It is frequently forgotten or, when remembered, denied that no given set of events attested by the historical record comprises a *story* manifestly finished and complete. This is as true as the events that comprise the life of an individual as it is of an institution, a nation, or a whole people. We do not *live* stories, even if we give our lives meaning by retrospectively casting them in the form of stories. And so too with nations or whole cultures. In an essay on the "mythical" nature of historiography, Lévi-Strauss remarks on the astonishment that a visitor from another planet would feel if confronted by the thousands of histories written about the French Revolution.[9] For in those works, the "authors do not always make use of the same incidents; when they do, the incidents are revealed in different lights. And yet these are variations which have to do with the same country, the same period, and the same events—events whose reality is scattered across every level of a multilayered structure." He goes on to suggest that the criterion of validity by which historical accounts might be assessed cannot depend on their elements"—that is to say—their putative factual content. On the contrary, he notes, "pursued in isolation, each element shows itself to be beyond grasp. But certain of them derive consistency from the fact that they can be integrated into a system whose terms are more or less credible when set against the overall coherence of the series." But his "coherence of the series" cannot be the coherence of the *chronological* series, that sequence of "facts" organized into the temporal order of their original occurrence. For the "chronicle" of events, out of which the historian fashions his story of "what really happened," already comes preencoded. There are "hot" and "cold" chronologies, chronologies in which more or fewer dates appear to demand inclusion in a full chronicle of what happened. Moreover, the dates themselves come to us already grouped into classes of dates, classes which are constitutive of putative domains of the historical field, domains which appear as problems for the historian to solve if he is to give a full and culturally responsible account of the past.

All this suggests to Lévi-Strauss that, when it is a matter of working up a comprehensive account of the various domains of the historical record in the form of a story, the "alleged historical continuities" that the historian purports to find in the record are "secured only by dint of fraudulent outlines" imposed by the historian on the record. These "fraudulent outlines" are, in his view, a product of "abstraction" and a means of escape from the "threat of an infinite regress" that always lurks at the interior of every complex set of historical "facts." We can construct a comprehensible story of the past, Lévi-Strauss insists, only by a decision to "give up" one or more of the domains of facts offering themselves for inclusion in our accounts. Our *explanations* of historical structures and processes are thus deter-

[9] See Lévi-Strauss, "Overture to *Le Cru et le cuit*" in *Structuralism,* pp. 33–55. [Eds.]

mined more by what we leave out of our representations than by what we put in. For it is in this brutal capacity to exclude certain facts in the interest of constituting others as components of comprehensible stories that the historian displays his tact as well as his understanding. The "overall coherence" of any given "series" of historical facts is the coherence of story, but this coherence is achieved only by a tailoring of the "facts" to the requirements of the story form. And thus Lévi-Strauss concludes: "In spite of worthy and indispensable efforts to bring another moment in history alive and to possess it, a clairvoyant history should admit that it never completely escapes from the nature of myth."

It is this mediative function that permits us to speak of a historical narrative as an extended metaphor. As a symbolic structure, the historical narrative does not *reproduce* the events it describes; it tells us in what direction to think about the events and charges our thought about the events with different emotional valences. The historical narrative does not *image* the things it indicates; it *calls to mind* images of the things it indicates, in the same way that a metaphor does. When a given concourse of events is emplotted as a "tragedy," this simply means that the historian has so described the events as to *remind us* of that form of fiction which we associate with the concept "tragic." Properly understood, histories ought never to be read as unambiguous signs of the events they report, but rather as symbolic structures, extended metaphors, that "liken" the events reported in them to some form with which we have already become familiar in our literary culture.

Perhaps I should indicate briefly what is meant by the *symbolic* and *iconic* aspects of a metaphor. The hackneyed phrase "My love, a rose" is not, obviously, intended to be understood as suggesting that the loved one is *actually* a rose. It is not even meant to suggest that the loved one has the specific attributes of a rose—that is to say, that the loved one is red, yellow, orange, or black, is a plant, has thorns, needs sunlight, should be sprayed regularly with insecticides, and so on. It is meant to be understood as indicating that the beloved shares the *qualities* which the rose has come to *symbolize* in the customary linguistic usages of Western culture. That is to say, considered as a message, the metaphor gives directions for finding an entity that will evoke the images associated *with loved ones and roses alike* in our culture. The metaphor does not *image* the thing it seeks to characterize, *it gives directions* for finding the set of images that are intended to be associated with that thing. It functions as a symbol, rather than as a sign: which is to say that it does not give us either a *description* or an *icon* of the thing it represents, but *tells us* what images to look for in our culturally encoded experience in order to determine how we *should feel* about the thing represented.

So too for historical narratives. They succeed in endowing sets of past events with meanings, over and above whatever comprehension they provide by appeal to putative causal laws, by exploiting the metaphorical similarities between sets of real events and the conventional structures of our fictions. By the very constitution of a set of events in such a way as to make a comprehensible story out of them, the historian charges those events with the symbolic significance of a comprehensible plot structure. Historians may not like to think of their works as translations of fact into fictions; but this is one of the effects of their works. By suggesting alternative emplotments of a given sequence of historical events, historians provide historical events with all of the possible meanings with which the literary art of their culture is capable of endowing them. The real dispute between the proper historian and the philosopher of history has to do with the latter's insistence that events can be emplotted in one and only one story form. History-writing thrives on the discovery of all the possible plot structures that might be invoked to endow sets of events with different meanings. And our understanding of the past increases precisely in the degree to which we succeed in determining how far that past conforms to the strategies of sense-making that are contained in their purest forms in literary art.

Conceiving historical narratives in this way may give us some insight into the crisis in historical thinking which has been under way since the beginning of our century. Let us imagine that the problem of the historian is to make sense of a hypothetical *set* of events by arranging them in a *series* that is at once chronologically *and* syntactically structured, in the way that any discourse from a sentence all the way up to a novel is structured. We can see immediately that the imperatives of chronological arrangement of the events constituting the set must exist in tension with the imperatives of the syntactical strategies alluded to, whether the latter are conceived as those of logic (the syllogism) or those of narrative (the plot structure).

Thus, we have a set of events

(1) *a, b, c, d, e,* . . . . , *n,*

ordered chronologically but requiring description and characterization as elements of plot or argument by which to give them meaning. Now, the series can be emplotted in a number of different ways and thereby endowed with different meanings without violating the imperatives of the chronological arrangement at all. We may briefly characterize some of these emplotments in the following ways:

(2) *A, b, c, d, e,* . . . . , *n*
(3) *a, B, c, d, e,* . . . . , *n*
(4) *a, b, C, d, e,* . . . . , *n*
(5) *a, b, c, D, e,* . . . . , *n*

And so on.

The capitalized letters indicate the privileged status given to certain events or sets of events in the series by which they are endowed with explanatory force, either as causes explaining the structure of the whole series or as symbols of the plot structure of the series considered as a story of a specific kind. We might say that any history which endows any putatively original event (*a*) with the status of a decisive factor (*A*) in the structuration of the whole series of events following after it is "deterministic." The emplotments of the history of "society" by Rousseau in his *Second Discourse,* Marx in the *Manifesto,* and Freud in *Totem and Taboo* would fall into this category. So too, any history which endows the last event in the series (*e*), whether real or only speculatively projected, with the force of full explanatory power (*E*) is of the type of all eschatological or apocalyptical histories. St. Augustine's *City of God* and the various versions of the Joachite notion of the advent of a millenium, Hegel's *Philosophy of History,* and, in general, all Idealist histories are of this sort. In between we would have the various forms of historiography which appeal to plot structures of a distinctively "fictional" sort (Romance, Comedy, Tragedy, and Satire) by which to endow the series with a perceivable form and a conceivable "meaning."

If the series were simply recorded in the order in which the events originally occurred, under the assumption that the ordering of the events in their temporal sequence itself provided a kind of explanation of why they occurred when and where they did, we would have the pure form of the *chronicle.* This would be a "naive" form of chronicle, however, inasmuch as the categories of time and space alone served as the informing interpretative principles. Over against the naive form of chronicle we could postulate as a logical possibility its "sentimental" counterpart, the ironic denial that historical series have any kind of larger significance or describe any imaginable plot structure or indeed can even be construed as a story with a discernible beginning, middle, and end. We could conceive such accounts of history as intending to serve as antidotes to their false or overemplotted counterparts (nos. 2, 3, 4, and 5 above) and could represent them as an ironic return to mere chronicle as constituting the only sense which any cognitively responsible history could take. We could characterize such histories thus:

(6) "*a, b, c, d, e* . . . . , *n*"

with the quotation marks indicating the conscious interpretation of the events as having nothing other than seriality as their meaning.

This schema is of course highly abstract and does not do justice to the possible mixtures of and variations within the types that it is meant to distinguish. But it helps us, I think, to conceive how events might be emplotted in different ways without violating the imperatives of the chronological order of the events (however they are construed) so as to yield alternative, mutually exclusive, and yet, equally plausible interpretations of the set. I have tried to show in *Metahistory* how such mixtures and variations occur in the writings of the master historians of the nineteenth century; and I have suggested in that book that classic historical accounts always represent attempts both to emplot the historical series adequately and implicitly to come to terms with other plausible emplotments. It is this dialectical tension between two or more possible emplotments that signals the element of critical self-consciousness present in any historian of recognizably classical stature.

Histories, then, are not only about events but also about the possible sets of relationships that those events can be demonstrated to figure. These sets of relationships are not, however, immanent in the events themselves; they exist only in the mind of the historian reflecting on them. Here they are present as the modes of relationships conceptualized in the myth, fable, and folklore, scientific knowledge, religion, and literary art, of the historian's own culture. But more importantly, they are, I suggest, immanent in the very language which the historian must use to *describe* events prior to a scientific analysis of them or a fictional emplotment of them. For if the historian's aim is to familiarize us with the unfamiliar, he must use figurative, rather than technical, language. Technical languages are familiarizing only *to* those who have been indoctrinated in their uses and only *of* those sets of events which the practitioners of a discipline have agreed to describe in a uniform terminology. History possesses no such generally accepted technical terminology and in fact no agreement on what kind of events make up its specific subject matter. The historian's characteristic instrument of encodation, communication, and exchange is ordinary educated speech. This implies that the only instruments that he has for endowing his data with meaning, of rendering the strange familiar, and of rendering the mysterious past comprehensible, are the techniques of *figurative* language. All historical narratives presuppose figurative characterizations of the events they purport to represent and explain. And this means that historical narratives, considered purely as verbal artifacts, can be characterized by the mode of figurative discourse in which they are cast.

If this is the case, then it may well be that the kind of emplotment that the historian decides to use to give meaning to a set of historical events is dictated by the dominant figurative mode of the language he has used to *describe* the elements of his account *prior* to his composition of a narrative. Geoffrey Hartman once remarked in my hearing, at a conference on literary history, that he was not sure that he knew what historians of literature might want to do, but he did know that to write a history meant to place an event within a context, by relating it as a part to some conceivable whole. He went on to suggest that as far as he knew, there were only two ways of relating parts to wholes, by metonymy and by synecdoche. Having been engaged for some time in the study of the thought of Giambattista Vico, I was much taken with this thought, because it conformed to Vico's notion that the "logic" of all "poetic wisdom" was contained in the relationships which language itself provided in the four principal modes of figurative representation: metaphor, metonymy, synecdoche, and irony. My own hunch—and it is a hunch which I find confirmed in Hegel's reflections on the nature of nonscientific discourse—is that in any field of study which, like history, has not yet become disciplinized to the point of constructing a formal terminological system for describing its objects, in the way that physics and chemistry have, it is the types of figurative discourse that dictate the fundamental forms of the data to be studied. This means that the *shape* of the *relationships* which will appear to be inherent in the objects inhabiting the field will in reality have been imposed on the field by the investigator in the very *act of identifying and describing* the objects that he finds there. The implication is that historians *constitute* their subjects as possible objects of narrative representation by the very language they use to *describe* them. And if this is the case, it means that the different kinds of historical interpretations that we have of the same set of events, such as the French Revolution as interpreted by Michelet, Tocqueville, Taine, and others, are little more than projections of the linguistic protocols that these historians used to *pre*-figure that set of events prior to writing their narratives of it. It is only a hypothesis, but it seems possible that the conviction of the historian that he has "found" the form of his narrative in the events themselves, rather than imposed it upon them, in the way the poet does, is a result of a certain lack of linguistic self-consciousness which obscures the extent to which descriptions of events *already* constitute interpretations of their nature. As thus envisaged, the difference between Michelet's and Tocqueville's accounts of the Revolution does not reside only in the fact that the former emplotted his story in the modality of a Romance and the latter his in the modality of Tragedy; it resides as well in the tropological mode—metaphorical and metonymic, respectively—with each brought to his apprehension of the facts as they appeared in the documents.

I do not have the space to try to demonstrate the plausibility of this hypothesis, which is the informing principle of my book *Metahistory*. But I hope that this essay may serve to suggest an approach to the study of such discursive prose forms as historiography, an approach that is as old as the study of rhetoric and as new as modern linguistics. Such a story would proceed along the lines laid out by Roman Jakobson in a paper entitled "Linguistics and Poetics,"[10] in which he characterized the difference between Romantic poetry and the various forms of nineteenth-century Realistic prose as residing in the essentially metaphorical nature of the former and the essentially metonymical nature of the latter. I think that this characterization of the difference between poetry and prose is too narrow, because it presupposes that complex macrostructural narratives such as the novel are little more than projections of the "selective" (i.e., phonemic) axis of all speech acts. Poetry, and especially Romantic poetry, is then characterized by Jakobson as a projection of the "combinatory" (i.e., morphemic) axis of language. Such a binary theory pushes the analyst toward a dualistic opposition between poetry and prose which appears to rule out the possibility of a metonymical poetry and a metaphorical prose. But the fruitfulness of Jakobson's theory lies in its suggestion that the various forms of both poetry and prose, all of which have their counterparts in narrative in general and therefore in historiography too, can be characterized in terms of the dominant trope which serves as the paradigm, provided by language itself, of all significant relationships conceived to exist in the world by anyone wishing to represent those relationships in language.

Narrative, or the syntagmatic dispersion of events across a temporal series presented as a prose discourse, in such a way as to display their progressive elaboration as a comprehensible form, would represent the "inward turn" that discourse takes when it tries to *show* the reader the true form of things existing behind a merely apparent formlessness. Narrative *style*, in history as well as in the novel, would then be construed as the modality of the movement from a representation of some original state of affairs to some subsequent state. The primary *meaning* of a narrative would then consist of the destructuration of a set of events (real or imagined) originally encoded in one tropological mode and the progressive restructuration of the set in another tropological mode. As thus envisaged, narrative would be a process of decodation and recodation in which an original perception is clarified by being cast in a figurative mode different from that in which it has come encoded by convention, authority, or custom. And the explanatory force of the narrative would then depend on the contrast between the original encodation and the later one.

For example, let us suppose that a set of experiences comes to us as a grotesque, i.e., as unclassified and unclassifiable. Our problem is to identify the modality of the relationships that bind the discernible elements of the formless totality together in such a way as to make of it a whole of some sort. If we stress the similarities among the elements, we are working in the mode of metaphor; if we stress the differences among them, we are working in the mode of metonymy. Of course, in order to make sense of any set of experiences, we must obviously identify both the parts of a thing that appear to make it up and the nature of the shared aspects of the parts that make them identifiable as a totality. This implies that all original characterizations of anything must utilize *both* metaphor and metonymy in order to "fix" it as something about which we can meaningfully discourse.

In the case of historiography, the attempts of commentators to make sense of the French Revolution are instructive. Burke decodes the events of the Revolution which his contemporaries experience as a grotesque by recoding it in the mode of irony; Michelet recodes these events in the mode of synecdoche; Tocqueville recodes them in the mode of metonymy. In each case, however, the movement from code to recode is narratively described, i.e., laid out on a time-line in such a way as to make the interpretation of the events that made up the "Revolution" a kind of drama that we can recognize as Satirical, Romantic, and Tragic, respectively. This drama can be followed by the reader of the narrative in such a way as to be experienced as a progressive revelation of what the *true* nature of the events consists of. The revelation is not experienced, however, as a restructuring of perception so much as an illumination of a field of occurrence. But actually what has happened is that a set of events originally encoded in one way is simply being decoded by being recoded in another. The events themselves are not substantially changed from one account to another. That is to say, the data that are to be analyzed are not significantly different in the different accounts. What is different are the modalities of their relationships. These modalities, in turn,

[10] See *Style and Language*. [Eds.]

although they *may* appear to the reader to be based on different theories of the nature of society, politics, and history, ultimately have their origin in the figurative characterizations of the whole set of events as representing wholes of fundamentally different sorts. It is for this reason that, when it is a matter of setting different interpretations of the same set of historical phenomena over against one another in an attempt to decide which is the best or most convincing, we are often driven to confusion or ambiguity. This is not to say that we cannot distinguish between good and bad historiography, since we can always fall back on such criteria as responsibility to the rules of evidence, the relative fullness of narrative detail, logical consistency, and the like to determine this issue. But it is to say that the effort to distinguish between good and bad interpretations of a historical event such as the Revolution is not as easy as it might at first appear when it is a matter of dealing with alternative interpretations produced by historians of relatively equal learning and conceptual sophistication. After all, a great historical classic cannot be disconfirmed or nullified either by the discovery of some new datum that might call a specific explanation of some element of the whole account into question or by the generation of new methods of analysis which permit us to deal with questions that earlier historians might not have taken under consideration. And it is precisely because great historical classics, such as works by Gibbon, Michelet, Thucydides, Mommsen, Ranke, Burckhardt, Bancroft,[11] and so on, cannot be definitely disconfirmed that we must look to the specifically literary aspects of their work as crucial, and not merely subsidiary, elements in their historiographical technique.

What all this points to is the necessity of revising the distinction conventionally drawn between poetic and prose discourse in discussion of such narrative forms as historiography and recognizing that the distinction, as old as Aristotle, between history and poetry obscures as much as it illuminates about both. If there is an element of the historical in all poetry, there is an element of poetry in every historical account of the world. And this because in our account of the historical world we are dependent, in ways perhaps that we are not in the natural sciences, on the techniques of *figurative language* both for our *characterization* of the objects of our narrative representations and for the *strategies* by which to constitute narrative accounts of the transformations of those objects in time. And this because history has no stipulatable subject matter uniquely its own; it is always written as part of a contest between contending poetic figurations of what the past *might* consist of.

The older distinction between fiction and history, in which fiction is conceived as the representation of the imaginable and history as the representation of the actual, must give place to the recognition that we can only know the *actual* by contrasting it with or likening it to the *imaginable.* As thus conceived, historical narratives are complex structures in which a world of experience is imagined to exist under at least two modes, one of which is encoded as "real," the other of which is "revealed" to have been illusory in the course of the narrative. Of course, it is a fiction of the historian that the various states of affairs which he constitutes as the beginning, the middle, and the end of a course of development are all "actual" or "real" and that he has merely recorded "what happened" in the transition from the inaugural to the terminal phase. But both the beginning state of affairs and the ending one are inevitably poetic constructions, and as such, dependent upon the modality of the figurative language used to give them the aspect of coherence. This implies that all narrative is not simply a recording of "what happened" in the transition from one state of affairs to another, but a progressive *redescription* of sets of events in such a way as to dismantle a structure encoded in one verbal mode in the beginning so as to justify a recoding of it in another mode at the end. This is what the "middle" of all narratives consist of.

All of this is highly schematic, and I know that this insistence on the fictive element in all historical narratives is certain to arouse the ire of historians who believe that they are doing something fundamentally different from the novelist, by virtue of the fact that they deal with "real," while the novelist

[11] Edward Gibbon (1737–94), English historian, author of *Decline and Fall of the Roman Empire* (1776–88); Michelet, see note 5 above; Thucydides (ca. 460–400 B.C.), Greek historian, author of *The Peloponnesian War*; Theodor Mommsen (1817–1903), German historian, author of *History of Rome* (1854–56); Hubert Howe Bancroft (1832–1918), American historian, author of a 39-volume history of central America, Mexico, and the western United States (1874–90). [Eds.]

deals with "imagined," events. But neither the form nor the explanatory power of narrative derives from the different contents it is presumed to be able to accommodate. In point of fact, history—the real world as it evolves in time—is made sense of in the same way that the poet or novelist tries to make sense of it, i.e., by endowing what originally appears to be problematical and mysterious with the aspect of a recognizable, because it is a familiar, form. It does not matter whether the world is conceived to be real or only imagined; the manner of making sense of it is the same.

So too, to say that we make sense of the real world by imposing upon it the formal coherency that we customarily associate with the products of writers of fiction in no way detracts from the status as knowledge which we ascribe to historiography. It would only detract from it if we were to believe that literature did not teach us anything about reality, but was a product of an imagination which was not of this world but of some other, inhuman one. In my view, we experience the "fictionalization" of history as an "explanation" for the same reason that we experience great fiction as an illumination of a world that we inhabit along with the author. In both we recognize the forms by which consciousness both constitutes and colonizes the world it seeks to inhabit comfortably.

Finally, it may be observed that if historians were to recognize the fictive element in their narratives, this would not mean the degradation of historiography to the status of ideology or propaganda. In fact, this recognition would serve as a potent antidote to the tendency of historians to become captive of ideological preconceptions which they do not recognize as such but honor as the "correct" perception of "the way things *really* are." By drawing historiography nearer to its origins in literary sensibility, we should be able to identify the ideological, because it is the fictive, element in our own discourse. We are always able to see the fictive element in those historians with whose interpretations of a given set of events we disagree; we seldom perceive that element in our own prose. So, too, if we recognized the literary or fictive element in every historical account, we would be able to move the teaching of historiography onto a higher level of self-consciousness than it currently occupies.

What teacher has not lamented his inability to give instruction to apprentices in the *writing* of history? What graduate student of history has not despaired at trying to comprehend and imitate the model which his instructors *appear* to honor but the principles of which remain uncharted? If we recognize that there is a fictive element in all historical narrative, we would find in the theory of language and narrative itself the basis for a more subtle presentation of what historiography consists of than that which simply tells the student to go and "find out the facts" and write them up in such a way as to tell "what really happened."

In my view, history as a discipline is in bad shape today because it has lost sight of its origins in the literary imagination. In the interest of *appearing* scientific and objective, it has repressed and denied to itself its own greatest source of strength and renewal. By drawing historiography back once more to an intimate connection with its literary basis, we should not only be putting ourselves on guard against *merely* ideological distortions; we should be by way of arriving at that "theory" of history without which it cannot pass for a "discipline" at all.

Yurij Lotman

b. 1922

and

B. A. Uspensky

b. 1937

SINCE THE mid-1960s Yurij Lotman, together with his colleagues at Tartu University in Soviet Estonia, has been developing an elaborate theory of semiotics, focusing not merely on literature but, as the title of this essay suggests, on a wide range of cultural phenomena. Lotman's work is influenced most immediately by structural linguistics (through the work of the Prague circle, *de Saussure* and *Emile Benveniste*), just as it belongs in a tradition of literary speculation that includes the Russian formalists and critics such as *Bakhtin.* Partly for this reason, the work of the Tartu School has been somewhat controversial in the Soviet Union; Lotman in particular has been criticized for being too subjective and too schematic and, more generally, for adopting a position (structuralism) that is by nature suspect, as it tends to isolate aesthetic considerations from concerns of praxis.

Lotman's *Lectures on Structural Poetics* (1964), followed by *The Structure of the Artistic Text* (1971), developed an imposing architectonic view of literature as a semiotic system. Lotman's pivotal concept is that semiotic systems operate by the construction of models and that natural language is a primary modeling system as it establishes fundamental, shareable correlations between subjects and objects which are then accessible for the creation of other models. In this view, literature (or art, more generally) is a secondary modeling system that operates in the same way as natural language, though with significant differences of purpose, focus, and immediate content. One might note that this distinction (while in no way directly related) bears some similarity to Coleridge's distinction between the primary and secondary imagination, in *Biographia Literaria* (*CTSP,* pp. 460–71).

The essay included here elaborates this idea in a more expansive register by treating culture as a semiotic process. The approach is not quite what *Clifford Geertz* recommends, that is, treating culture as text, since it is at least logically prior to such a recommendation. By treating "culture" as a limiting, differential concept, Lotman and Uspensky prefigure the conceptual field according to its ability to single out a community of adherents—such that within a nation, for example, one might find many cultures, without assuming that it was intellectually or methodologically necessary to equate nation with culture. Thus, the cultures at issue in Lotman and Uspensky's account exist as they produce texts, and the texts produced function as the collective, nonhereditary memory of the culture in question.

The essay provides illustrations of broad systemic differences when, for example, a culture places greater emphasis upon the permissible rules by which texts are produced, or upon the correctness or permissibility of the texts themselves. This difference can be seen relative to another axis of distinction, whether the culture is concerned more with content or with expression. On this basis, the model would predict that cultures directed toward expression will tend to think in terms of correct texts, while cultures more concerned with content will tend to think in terms of rules. From an analytical point of view, a matrix such as this is especially suggestive, since it puts in focus a broad range of issues that might otherwise never be correlated, such as the relative honor accorded the producer of texts or the regulator (or critic) of texts, and the kinds of taboos or strictures that particular communities may impose upon their members.

While the essay does not attempt to formulate its illustrative principles rigorously, it offers a provocative illustration of a semiotic method by which the "inner workings" of culture, including literary works, can be explored in detail—and, not coincidentally, made intelligible and communicable to a community of scholars.

Lotman's works available in English include *The Structure of the Artistic Text*, trans. Gail Lenhoff and Ronald Vroon (1977), and *Semiotics of Cinéma*, trans. M. Suino (1975). The Tartu School publishes a monograph series, *Trudy po znakovym sistemam* (*Papers on Sign Systems*), in which a variety of studies by members of the school has been presented.

ON THE SEMIOTIC MECHANISM OF CULTURE

There are many ways of defining culture.[1] The difference in the semantic content of the concept *culture* in different historical epochs and among different scholars of our time will not discourage us if we remember that the meaning of the term is derivable from the type of culture: every historically given culture generates some special model of culture peculiar to itself. Therefore, a comparative study of the semantics of the term *culture* over the centuries provides worthwhile material for the construction of typologies.

At the same time, among the variety of definitions one can single out something common to them all that appears to answer to certain features we intuitively attribute to culture in any interpretation of the word. We will consider just two of them here. First, underlying all definitions is the notion that there are certain *specific features of a culture*. Though trivial, this assertion is not without meaning: from it arises the assertion that culture is never a universal set, but always a subset organized in a specific manner. Culture never encompasses *everything*, but forms instead a marked-off sphere. Culture is understood only as a section, a closed-off area against the background of nonculture. The nature of this opposition may vary: nonculture may appear as not belonging to a particular religion, not having access to some knowledge, or not sharing in some type of life and behavior. But culture will always need such an opposition. Indeed, culture stands out as the marked member of this opposition.

Second, the various ways of delimiting culture from nonculture essentially come down to one thing: against the background of nonculture, culture appears as a *system of signs*. In particular, whether we speak of such features of culture as "being man-made" (as opposed to "being natural"), "being conventional" (as opposed to "being spontaneous" and "being nonconventional"), or as the ability to condense human experience (in opposition to the primordial quality of nature)—in each case, we are dealing with different aspects of the semiotic essence of culture.

It is significant that a change of culture (in particular, during epochs of social cataclysms) is usually accompanied by a sharp increase in the degree of semiotic behavior (which may be expressed by the changing of names and designations), and even the fight against the old rituals may itself be ritualized. On the other hand, the introduction of new forms of behavior and the semiotic intensification of old forms can testify to a specific change in the type of culture. Thus, the activities of Peter the Great in Russia largely amount to a struggle with old rituals and symbols, which was expressed in the creation of *new* signs (for example, the absence of the beard became as mandatory as its presence had been earlier; wearing foreign styled clothes became as indispensable as the wearing of Russian clothes earlier, and so on);[2] but the Emperor Paul's activity, on the other hand, was expressed in the semiotic intensification of existing forms, in particular, by in-

ON THE SEMIOTIC MECHANISM OF CULTURE first appeard in *Trudy po znakovym sistemam* V (Tartu, 1971). This translation by George Mihaychuk was first printed in *New Literary History* 9 (1978): 211–32. Reprinted by permission of the editor of *New Literary History* and The Johns Hopkins University Press, copyright 1978.

[1] See A. Kroeber and C. Kluckhohn, "Culture: A Critical Review of Concepts and Definitions," in *Papers of the Peabody Museum* (Cambridge, Mass., 1952); A. Kloskowska, *Kultura masowa* (Warsaw, 1964); R. Benedict, *Patterns of Culture* (Cambridge, Mass., 1934); Stein Rokkan, ed., *Comparative Research across Cultures and Nations* (Paris, 1968); M. Mauss, *Sociologie et anthropologie* (Paris, 1966); Claude Lévi-Strauss, *Anthropologie structurale* (Paris, 1958); and Yvan Simonis, "Claude Lévi-Strauss ou la 'Passion de l'inceste,'" in *Introduction au structuralisme* (Paris, 1968). [Au.]

[2] Compare the special Edicts of Peter on the forms of clothing made mandatory. Thus, in 1700, it was ordered to wear clothes of a Hungarian pattern; in 1701, of a German pattern; in 1702, on celebration days, French caftans. See *Polnoe Sobranie Zakonov* [The complete collection of laws], statutes 1741, 1898, and 1999, according to which, in 1714, any Petersburg merchant who sold Russian clothes of a nondecreed pattern was ordered to be whipped and sentenced to hard labor; and, in 1715, it was decreed to sentence anyone dealing in nails for the shoeing of boots and shoes to hard labor (statutes 2874 and 2929). Compare, on the other hand, the protests against foreign clothing both during the pre-Petrine period and among the Old-Believers who were the carriers of pre-Petrine culture. The Old-Believers, even up to our times, keep the eighteenth-century pattern of clothing and wear it for church services; their funeral clothing appears even more archaic (see the article by N. P. Grinkova on clothing in *Bukhtarminskie staroobryadtsy* [The Old-

creasing their symbolic character. (Compare the increase at that time of genealogical symbolism, of the symbolism of parades, of ceremonial language and similar cases and, on the other hand, the fight against certain words which sounded like symbols of a different ideology. Compare also such symbolic acts as the admonition to the deceased, the challenging of princes to a duel, and so on.)

A KEY question is the relationship of culture to natural language. In the preceding publications of Tartu University (the semiotic series), cultural phenomena were defined as secondary modeling systems, a term which indicated their derivational nature in relation to natural language. Many studies, following the Sapir-Whorf hypothesis, emphasized and examined the influence of language on various manifestations of human culture. Recently Benveniste has emphasized that only natural languages can fulfill a metalinguistic role and that, by virtue of this, they hold a distinct place in the system of human communication.[3] More questionable, however, is the author's proposal in the same article to consider only natural languages as strictly semiotic systems, defining all other cultural models as semantic, that is, not possessing their own systematic semiosis but borrowing it from the sphere of natural languages. Even though it is valuable to contrast primary and secondary modeling systems (without such a contrast it is impossible to single out the distinguishing characteristics of each), it would be appropriate to stress here that in their actual historical functioning, languages are inseparable from culture. No language (in the full sense of the word) can exist unless it is steeped in the context of culture; and no culture can exist which does not have, at its center, the structure of natural language.

As a methodological abstraction, one may imagine language as an isolated phenomenon. However, in its actual functioning, language is molded into a more general system of culture and, together with it, constitutes a complex whole. The fundamental "task" of culture, as we will try to show, is in structurally organizing the world around man. Culture is the generator of structuredness, and in this way it creates a social sphere around man which, like the biosphere, makes life possible; that is, not organic life, but social life.

But in order for it to fulfill that role, culture must have within itself a structural "diecasting mechanism." It is this function that is performed by natural language. It is natural language that gives the members of a social group their intuitive sense of structuredness that with its transformation of the "open" world of realia into a "closed" world of names, forces people to treat as structures those phenomena whose structuredness, at best, is not apparent.[4] Indeed, in many cases it turns out not to matter whether some meaning-forming principle is a structure, in a strict sense, or not. It is sufficient that the participants in an act of communication should *regard* it as a structure and *use* it as such for it to begin to display structurelike qualities. One can well understand how important it is that a system of culture has, at its center, so powerful a source of structuredness as language.

The presumption of structuredness, which has evolved as a result of language intercourse, exerts a powerful organizing force on the entire complex of the means of communication. Thus, the entire system for preserving and communicating human experience is constructed as a concentric system in the center of which are located the most obvious and logical structures, that is, the most structural ones. Nearer to the periphery are found formations whose structuredness is not evident or has not been proved, but which, being included in general sign-communicational situations, *function as structures*. Such quasi structures occupy a large place in human culture. Moreover, it is precisely the fact of their internal lack of orderedness, their incomplete organization, that ensures for human culture the greater inner capacity and the dynamism not known to more ordered systems.

WE UNDERSTAND culture as the *nonhereditary memory of the community*, a memory expressing itself in a system of constraints and prescriptions. This formulation, if accepted, presupposes the following

Believers of Bukhtarminsk] [Leningrad, 1930]). It is not difficult to see that the very nature of the relation to the sign and the general level of the semiotic aspect of culture prior to Peter and during his reign, in the given case, remain one and the same. [Au.]

[3] Emile Benveniste, "Sémiologie de la langue," *Semiotica*, 1, No. 1 (1969). [Au.]

[4] Thus, for example, the structuredness of history constitutes the initial axiom of our approach; otherwise there is no possibility of accumulating historical knowledge. However, this idea cannot be proved or disproved by evidence, as world history is incomplete and we are submerged in it. [Au.]

consequences. First of all, it follows that culture is, by definition, a social phenomenon. This fact does not exclude the possibility of an individual culture in the case where the individual sees himself as a *representative* of the community or in cases of autocommunication, where one person fulfills, in time or space, the functions of various members of the community and in fact forms a group. However, the cases of individual cultures are, of necessity, historically secondary.

On the other hand, depending on the limits placed by the researcher on his material, culture may be treated as common to all mankind, or as the culture of a particular area, or of a particular time, or of a particular social group. Furthermore, insofar as culture is *memory* or, in other words, a record in the memory of what the community has experienced, it is, of necessity, connected to *past* historical experience. Consequently, at the moment of its appearance, culture cannot be recorded as such, for it is only perceived ex post facto. When people speak of the creation of a new culture, they are inevitably looking ahead; that is, they have in mind that which (they presume) *will become* a memory from the point of view of the reconstructable future (of course, the correctness of such an assumption will only be shown by the future itself).

Thus, a program (of behavior) appears as the opposite of a system of culture. The program is directed into the future from a point of view of its author; but culture is turned towards the past from the point of view of the realization of such behavior (of the program). It then follows that the difference between a program of behavior and a culture is a functional one: the same text can be one or the other, functioning variously in the general system of historical life of a particular community.

In general, the definition of culture as the memory of a community raises the question about the system of semiotic rules by which human life experience is changed into culture: these rules can, in their own turn, be treated as a *program*. The very existence of culture implies the construction of a system, of some rules for translating direct experience into text. In order for any historical event to be placed in a specific category, it must first of all be acknowledged as existing; that is, it must be identified with a specific element in the language of the organization which is committing it to memory. Then it has to be evaluated according to all the hierarchic ties of that language. This means that it will be recorded; that is, it will become an element of the text of memory, an element of culture. The implanting of a fact into the collective memory, then, is like a translation from one language into another—in this case, into the "language of culture."

Culture, as a mechanism for organizing and preserving information in the consciousness of the community, raises the specific problem of longevity. It has two aspects: (1) the longevity of the texts of the collective memory and (2) the longevity of the code of the collective memory. In certain cases these two aspects may not be directly related to one another. Thus, for example, superstitions can be seen as elements of a text of an old culture whose code is lost; that is, as a case where the text outlives the code. For example:

> Superstition! a fragment
> Of ancient truth. The temple fell;
> And posterity could never decipher
> The language of its ruins.
> [E. A. Baratynsky]

Every culture creates its own model of the length of its existence, of the continuity of its memory. This model corresponds to the concept a given culture has of the maximum span of time practically comprising its "eternity." Insofar as culture acknowledges itself as existing, only identifying itself with the constant norms of its memory, the continuity of memory and the continuity of existence are usually identified.

Characteristically, many cultures do not allow even the possibility of any kind of substantial change in the realization of the rules formulated by it—in other words, the possibility of any kind of reappraisal of its values. Hence, culture very often is not geared to knowledge about the future, the future being envisaged as time come to a stop, as a stretched out "now"; indeed, this is directly connected to the orientation towards the past, which also ensures the necessary stability, one of the conditions for the existence of culture.

The longevity of texts forms a hierarchy within the culture, one usually identified with the hierarchy of values. The texts considered most valuable are those of a maximum longevity from the point of view, and according to the standard, of the culture in question, or panchronic texts (although "shifted" cultural anomalies are also possible whereby the highest value is ascribed to the momentary). This may correspond to the hierarchy of materials upon which the texts are affixed and to the hierarchy of places and of the means of their preservation.

The longevity of the code is determined by the permanence of its basic structural principles and by its inner dynamism—its capacity for change while still preserving the memory of preceding states and, consequently, of the awareness of its own coherence.

Considering culture as the long-term memory of the community, we can distinguish three ways in which it is filled. First, a quantitative increase in the amount of knowledge—filling the various nodes of the culture's hierarchic system with various texts. Second, a redistribution in the structure of the nodes resulting in a change in the very notion of "a fact to be remembered," and the hierarchic appraisal of what has been recorded in the memory; a continuous reorganization of the coding system which, while remaining itself in its own consciousness and conceiving itself to be continuous, tirelessly reforms separate codes, thus ensuring an increase in the value of the memory by creating "nonactual," yet potentially actualizable, reserves. Third, forgetting. The conversion of a chain of facts into a text is invariably accompanied by selection; that is, by fixing certain events which are translatable into elements of the text and forgetting others, marked as nonessential. In this sense every text furthers not only the remembering process, but forgetting as well. Yet since the selection of memorizable facts is realized every time according to particular semiotic norms of the given culture, one should beware of identifying the events of life with any text, no matter how "truthful" or "artless" or firsthand the text may appear. The text is not reality, but the material for its reconstruction. Therefore, a semiotic analysis of a document should always precede a historical one. Having established the rules for the reconstructing of reality from the text, the researcher will also be able to reckon from the document those elements which, from the point of view of its author, were not "facts" and thus were forgettable, but which might be evaluated quite differently by a historian, for whom, in the light of his own cultural code, they emerge as meaningful events.

However, forgetting takes place in another way as well: culture continually excludes certain texts. The history of the destruction of texts, of the purging of texts from the reserves of the collective memory, proceeds alongside the history of the creation of new texts. Every new movement in art revokes the authority of the texts by which preceding epochs oriented themselves, by transferring them into the category of nontexts, texts of a different level, or by physically destroying them. Culture by its very essence is against forgetting. It overcomes forgetting, turning it into one of the mechanisms of memory.

In the light of the above, one can assume definite *limits to the capacity* of the collective memory, which determines this exclusion of some texts by others. But on the other hand, because of their semantic incompatibility, the nonexistence of some texts becomes a necessary condition for the existence of others.

Despite their apparent similarity, there is a profound difference between forgetting as an element of memory and forgetting as a means of its destruction. In the latter case there takes place the disintegration of culture as a unified collective personality, a personality possessing continued self-consciousness and accumulated experience.

It is worth recalling that one of the sharpest forms of social struggle in the sphere of culture is the obligatory demand to forget certain aspects of historical experience. Epochs of historical regression (the clearest example is the Nazi state culture in the twentieth century), in forcing upon the community highly mythologized schemes of history, end by demanding from society that it forget those texts which do not lend themselves to being so organized. While social formations, during the period of ascent, produce flexible and dynamic models, providing the collective memory with broad possibilities, and aiding its expansion, then social decline, as a rule, is accompanied by an ossifying of the mechanism of the collective memory and by an increasing tendency to contract.

THE SEMIOTIC study of culture does not only consider culture functioning as a system of signs. It is important to emphasize that the very *relation of culture to the sign and to signification* comprises one of its basic typological features.[5]

[5] Compare the remarks on the connection between cultural evolution and the change in relation to the sign in Michel Foucault, *Les mots et les choses, une archéologie du savoir* (Paris, 1966). [Au.]

First of all, it is relevant whether the relation between expression and content is regarded as the only possible one or as an arbitrary (accidental, conventional) one. In the first case the question, what this or that thing is *called*, is crucial, and correspondingly, an incorrect designation may come to be identified with a *different* content (see below). Compare the searches in the Middle Ages for the names of certain hypostases which incidentally became fixed in the Masonic ritual; one should interpret taboos against the uttering of certain names in a similar manner. In the second case the question of designation, and of expression in general, is not an important principle; one can say that expression here appears as an auxiliary and indeed more or less incidental factor with regard to content.

Accordingly, it is possible to distinguish between cultures directed mainly towards expression and those directed chiefly towards content. It is clear that the very fact of emphasis on expression, of strictly ritualized forms of behavior,[6] is usually a consequence either of seeing a one-to-one correlation (rather than an arbitrary one) between the level of expression and the level of content, their inseparability in principle (as is characteristic, in particular, for the ideology of the Middle Ages), or of seeing the influence of expression upon content. (We may note in this respect that, in a sense, *symbol* and *ritual* can be regarded as opposite poles. While a symbol usually presupposes an external, relatively arbitrary expression of some content, ritual is capable of forming content and influencing it.) To a culture directed towards expression that is founded on the notion of *correct* designation and, in particular, correct naming, the entire world can appear as a sort of text consisting of various kinds of signs, where content is predetermined and it is only necessary to know the language; that is, to know the relation between the elements of expression and content. In other words, cognition of the world is equivalent to philological analysis.[7] But in typologically different cultural models, oriented directly towards content, some degree of freedom is assumed both in the choice of content and in its relation to expression.

Culture can be represented as an aggregate of texts; however, from the point of view of the researcher, it is more exact to consider culture as a mechanism creating an aggregate of texts and texts as the realization of culture. An essential feature for the typology of culture is its self-appraisal in this regard. While it is typical of some cultures to regard themselves as an aggregate of normative *texts* (take the *Domostroy*,[8] for example), others model themselves as a system of *rules* that determine the creation of texts. (In other words, in the first case the rules are defined as the sum of precedents; in the

[6] This feature becomes readily apparent in the paradoxical situation where adherence to specific restrictions and requirements comes into conflict with the content which, in fact, produced them. "We kiss thy shackles as those of a saint, but we cannot be helpful to thee," wrote the head of the Russian Church, Metropolitan Makariy, sending his blessings to Maksim Grek, who was languishing in captivity (quoted by A. I. Ivanov, *Literaturnoe nasledie Maksima Greka* [The literary heritage of Maksim the Greek] [Leningrad, 1969], p. 170). Even the holiness of Maksim Grek, admitted by Makariy, and his respect for him cannot bring him to ease the lot of the prisoner; the signs are not subordinate to him. (It makes sense to assume that the head of the Russian Church, Makariy, had in mind not his helplessness in the face of some conditions brought in from outside, but the inner impossibility of transgressing the decision of the *sobor* [church]. His disagreement with the content of the decision did not lower, in his eyes, the authority of the decision as such.) [Au.]

[7] Compare the concept found in various cultures, but most of all in the Middle Ages, of a book as a symbol of the world (or as a model of the world). See E. R. Curtius, "Das Buch als Symbol," in *Europaische Literatur und lateinisches Mittelalter*, 2nd ed. (Bern, 1954); D. Chizhevsky, "Das Buch als Symbol des Kosmos," in *Aus zwei Welten: Beitrage zur Geschichte der slavisch-wetlichen literarischen Beziehungen* ('s-Gravenhage, 1956); P. N. Berkov, "Kniga v poezii Simeona Polotskogo" [The book in the poetry of Simeon Polotsky], in *Literatura i obshchestvennaya mysl' drevney Rusi* [The literature and social thought of Old Rus'], Trudy otdela drevnerusskoy literatury Instituta russkoy literatury AN SSSR [Papers of the department of Old Russian Literature of the Institute of Russian Literature AN SSSR], XXIV (Leningrad, 1969); Yu. M. Lotman and B. A. Uspensky, "Introduzione," in *Ricerche Semiotiche* (Turin, 1973), pp. xiv-xv. Compare also the role of the alphabet in the conceptions of the architectonics of the universe in F. Dornseiff, "Das Alphabet in Mystik und Magie," *Ετοιχεια*, 7 (1922), 33 (see in particular, the remarks on the coincidence of the seven Ionic vowels with the seven planets).

Characteristically, in connection with the above, the Skoptsy sectarians called the Virgin Mary "the living book"; perhaps one can see here the generic tie with the widespread identification among the Orthodox retaining its Byzantine roots, of "Wisdom," that is, of Sophia with the Virgin Mary (see on the question of this identification Uspensky, *Iz istorii russkikh kanonicheskikh imen* [From the history of Russian canonical names] [Moscow, 1969], pp. 48–49). [Au.]

[8] Sixteenth-century Russian book of religious, social, and domestic precepts. [Tr.]

second the precedent exists only where it is described by an appropriate rule.)

Cultures directed primarily towards expression have this conception of themselves as a correct text (or aggregate of texts) whereas cultures directed mainly towards content see themselves as a system of rules. Each type of culture generates its own particular ideal of Book and Manual, including the organization of those texts. Thus, with orientation towards rules, a manual has the appearance of a generative mechanism, while with orientation towards text, one gets the characteristic (question-answer) format of a catechism, and the anthology (book of quotations or selected texts) comes into being.

In contrasting text and rules, as applied to culture, it is also important to keep in mind that, in some cases, the same elements of a culture can serve both functions, that is, both as text and as rules. Thus, for example, taboos which are a component of the general system of a given culture can, on the one hand, be examined as elements (signs) of the *text* reflecting the moral experience of the community and, on the other hand, be regarded as an aggregate of magical *rules* prescribing specific behavior.

The opposition we have formulated between a system of rules and an aggregate of texts can be illustrated by taking literature which is a subsystem of the whole culture.

A clear example of a system explicitly oriented towards rules will be European Neo-Classicism. Although historically the theory of Neo-Classicism was created as a generalization from a particular artistic experience, the picture was somewhat different as seen from within the theory itself: the theoretical models were thought of as eternal and as preceding the actual act of creation. In art, only those texts considered "correct," that is, corresponding to the rules, were recognized as texts, i.e., having significance. It is especially interesting, in light of the above, to see what Boileau, for example, considers as poor works of art. The bad in art is whatever breaks the rules. But even the violation of the rules can be described, in Boileau's opinion, as following certain "incorrect" rules. Therefore, "bad" texts can be classified; any unsatisfactory work of art serves as an example of some typical violation. It is no accident that, for Boileau, the "incorrect" world of art consists of the same elements as the correct but that the difference lies in the system for combining them, prohibited in "good" art.

Another characteristic of this type of culture is the fact that the creator of the rules stands higher in the hierarchy than the creator of the texts. Thus, for example, within the system of Neo-Classicism the critic commands markedly more respect than the writer.

As a contrasting example, one can point to the culture of European Realism of the nineteenth century. The artistic texts that formed part of it were fulfilling their social function directly and did not need an obligatory translation into a metalanguage of theory. The theorist constructed his apparatus following after art. In practice, for example, in Russia after Belinsky, criticism played a most active and independent role. But it is all the more evident that, in assessing his own role, Belinsky, for example, gave priority to Gogol, seeing himself as a mere interpreter.

Although the rules are, in both cases, a necessary minimal condition for the creation of culture, the degree to which they enter into its self-appraisal will vary. This can be compared to the teaching of language as a system of grammatical rules or as a set of usages.[9]

ACCORDING to the distinction formulated above, culture can be opposed both to nonculture and to anticulture. Within the conditions of a culture chiefly oriented towards content and represented as a system of rules, the basic opposition is "organized–nonorganized" (and this opposition can be realized in particular cases as "cosmos–chaos," "ectropy–entropy," "culture–nature," and so on). But within the conditions of a culture oriented primarily towards expression and represented as an aggregate of normative texts, the basic opposition will be "correct–incorrect," i.e., wrong (precisely "incorrect" and not "noncorrect": this opposition may approximate, even coincide with, the opposition "true–false"). In the latter case, culture is opposed not to chaos (entropy) but to a system preceded by a negative sign. Generally, of course, when within a culture directed towards a one-to-one cor-

[9]In connection with this opposition there are various modes of "teaching" culture which we will not consider in detail here since they are the subject of another article (Lotman, "Problema obucheniya kulture kak eë tipologicheskaya kharakteristika" [The problem of teaching a culture as its typological characteristics], *Trudy po znakovym sistemam* [Papers on sign systems], V [Tartu, 1971]). [Au.]

respondence between expression and content and primarily oriented towards expression, the world appears as a text, and the question, what is this or that called, becomes of principal importance. An incorrect designation can be identified with a *different* content (but not with none!), that is, with *different* information and not with a distortion in the information. Thus, for example, the Russian Church Slavonic word *aggel* [angel], written in accordance with the Greek spelling of the corresponding word, was to be read as *angel*; but as it was actually spelled [*angel*], the word was understood in Medieval Russia to signify the devil.[10] Analogously, when, as a result of Patriarch Nikon's reforms, the spelling of Christ's name *Isus* was changed to *Iisus,* the new form was taken to be the name of a different being: not Christ but the Antichrist.[11] Similarly, the distortion of the word *Bog* [God] in the word *spasibo* [thank you] (from *spasi Bog* [save us God]) may, even now, be understood by the Old-Believers as the name of a pagan god, so that the very word *spasibo* is understood as an appeal to the Antichrist (in its place the words *spasi Gospodi* [save us Lord] are usually used by the "priestless" Old-Believers and *spasi Khristos* [save us Christ] by the Old-Believers with priests).[12] The point to note here is that everything opposed to culture (in this case a religious culture) *also has to have its own special expression,* but one that is false (incorrect). In other words, anticulture is constructed here isomorphically to culture, in its own image: it too is understood as a sign system having its own expression. One can say that anticulture is perceived as culture with a negative sign, as a mirror image of culture (where the ties are not broken but are replaced by their opposites). In this kind of situation any other culture with different expressions and ties is seen, from the point of view of the given culture, as anticulture.

This is the source of the natural tendency to interpret all "incorrect" cultures, those opposed to the given ("correct") one, as a *unified* system. Thus, in "The Song of Roland" [*La Chanson de Roland*], Marsiliun turns out to be a pagan, an atheist, a Mohammedan, and a worshipper of Apollo all at the same time:

> Li reis Marsilie la tient, ki Deu nen aimet.
> Mahumet sert e Apollin recleimet: . . .[13]

[10] See Uspensky, *Arkhaicheskaya sistema tserkovnoslavyanskogo proiznosheniya* [The archaic system of Church Slavonic pronunciation] (Moscow, 1968), pp. 51–53, 78–82. [Au.]

[11] See Uspensky, *Iz istorii,* p. 216. [Au.]

[12] There is a legend on this theme, apparently not recorded anywhere, where it is said that the phrase *spasi, Ba!* (going back to the pronunciation of the word *spasibo* with *akanye,* i.e., change of unstressed *o* into *a* [save us Bá]) was shouted by the pagans in Kiev to the pagan idol, floating down the Dnieper, which had been overthrown by St. Vladimir. The very tendency to identify the pagan god with the Antichrist (Satan), that is, incorporating it into the system of Christian ideology, is very characteristic for the type of culture being examined. See, for example, the identification of the pagan Volos-Veles with the demon, who, in other cases, could be identified with St. Vlasiy (Vyach. Vs. Ivanov and V. N. Toporov, "K rekonstruktsii obraza Velesa-Volosa kak protivnika gromoverzhtsa" [Towards a reconstruction of the image of Veles-Volos as an opponent of the thunderer], in *Tezisy dokladov IV Letney shkoly po vtorichnym modeliruyushchim sistemam* [Theses of papers at the fourth summer school on secondary modeling systems] [Tartu, 1970], p. 48); also compare the remark further in this paper about an analogous concept of Apollo. It is characteristic that the eighteenth-century Old-Believers' authority, Feodosiy Vasil'ev, called the devil "wicked leader, unholy lamb," explaining with reference to St. Hyppolitus: "In everything the deceiver wishes to resemble Christ, the Son of God: Christ the lion, the lion Anti-Christ; there appeared Christ the lamb, there appears too the Anti-Christ as a lamb" (see P. S. Smirnov, "Perepiska raskol'nich'ikh deyateley nach. XVIII v." [The correspondence of the leaders of the schism in the beginning of the eighteenth century], *Khristianskoye chtenie* [Christian readings], No. 1 [1909], pp. 48–55).

Inasmuch as in a culture of the kind existing in the Middle Ages there is a given sum of correct texts and a notion of the mirror-image correspondence of the correct and the incorrect, the negative texts may be constructed from the sacral ones as a result of applying systems of antithetical exchanges to them. A striking example of this is the exchange in the Russian admonition of the correct designation *rab bozhiy* [servant of God] for a "black" one, *par bozhiy,* where *par* is the result of a backward (mirrored) reading [*char*] which is the actual pronunciation of the word *rab* (with the change of a voiced consonant into a corresponding voiceless one in the final position). See A. M. Astakhova, "Zaogovornoe iskusstvo na reke Pinege" [Admonitional art on the river Pineg], in *Krest' yanskoe iskustvo SSSR* [Peasant art of the USSR], II (Leningrad, 1928), 50–52, 68. [Au.]

[13] "La Chanson de Roland," in Henri Clouard and Robert Leggewie, eds., *Anthologie de la littérature française* (New York, 1960), 1, 10: "King Marsiliun holds it, who does not love God; he serves Mahomet and confesses Apollin."

For a number of texts the identification of Apollo with

In the Muscovite "Tale of the Defeat of Mamay," Mamay is described as follows: "Being a Hellene by his faith, a worshipper of idols, an iconoclast, and a wicked punisher of Christians."[14] Examples of this kind would not be difficult to multiply.

Also significant in this regard was the antipathy in pre-Petrine Russia to foreign languages, which were viewed as means for expressing alien cultures. Note particularly the special works against Latin and Latinate forms which were identified with Catholic thought and, more widely, with Catholic culture.[15] Typically, when Patriarch Makariy of Antioch arrived in Moscow in the middle of the seventeenth century, he was especially warned of "talking in Turkish." "God forbid," as Tsar Alexey Mikhailovich put it, "that such a holy man should sully his lips and tongue with that impure language."[16] In these words we hear the conviction, so typical for that time, that it is impossible to use alien means of expression and yet stay within one's own ideology (in particular, one could not speak in such an "un-Orthodox" language as Turkish, seen as the means of expression for Mohammedanism, or Latin, seen as the means of expression for Catholicism, and still remain pure in relation to Orthodoxy).

Equally revealing, on the other hand, is the attempt to see all "Orthodox" languages as one language. Thus, during that same period Russian scribes could speak of a single "Helleno-Slavic" language (a grammar of it was even published)[17] and could describe the Slavic languages according to the exact patterns of Greek grammar, seeking in it, indeed, an expression of those grammatical categories which exist only in Greek.

Correspondingly, a culture chiefly directed towards content, one opposed to entropy (chaos), where the main opposition will be "organized–nonorganized," always conceives itself as an active principle which must expand and sees nonculture as the sphere for its potential expansion. On the other hand, in a culture directed mainly towards expression, where the basic opposition is between "correct" and "incorrect," there may be no attempt whatsoever to expand (on the contrary, the culture may strive to limit itself to its own boundaries, to separate itself from all that is opposed to it). Nonculture is here identified with anticulture and therefore, according to its very essence, cannot be a potential area for the expansion of culture.

Examples of how an orientation towards expression and a high degree of ritualization bring with them the tendency to shut oneself off might be Medieval China or the idea "Moscow, the Third Rome." These cases are marked by an urge towards preservation rather than expansion of their system, esoterism, and a lack of missionary zeal.

In one type of culture, knowledge spreads by its expansion into areas not yet known to it, but in the opposite type of culture, the spread of knowledge is possible only as a triumph over falsehood. Naturally, the concept of science, in the modern sense of the word, is connected with culture of the first type. In the second type of culture, science is not opposed so markedly to art, religion, and so on. It is interest-

---

the devil can be explained, besides the general considerations just given, by the identification of the pagan god with the reference to Satan in Revelation 9: 11 as "Apollion." [Au.]

[14] M. N. Tikhomirov, V. F. Rzhiga, and L. A. Dmitriev, eds., *Povesti o Kulikovskoy bitve* [Tales of the battle of Kulikovo Field] (Moscow, 1953), p. 43. [Au.]

[15] See V. V. Vinogradov, *Ocherki po istorii russkogo literaturnogo yazyka XVII–XIX vv.* [Essays on the history of the Russian literary language of the seventeenth-nineteenth centuries] (Moscow, 1938), p. 9; Uspensky, "Vliyanie yzayka na religioznoe soznanie" [The influence of language on religious consciousness], in *Trudy po znakovym sistemam,* IV (Tartu, 1969), 164–65. See also the texts edited by M. Smentsovsky, *Brat'ya Likhudy* [The Likhud brothers] (St. Petersburg, 1899) (appendices); N. F. Kanterev, "O greko-latinskikh shkolakh v Moskve XVII veke do otkrytiya Slavyano-grekolatinskoy Akademii" [On the Greco-Latin schools in Moscow in the seventeenth century up to the opening of the Slavo-Greco-Latin Academy], in *Godichny akt v Moskovskoy Dukhovnoy Akademii l-go oktyabrya 1889 goda* [Yearly act of the Moscow Religious Academy of the first of October 1889] (Moscow, 1889). Even Patriarch Nikon in his polemic with the (Orthodox) Metropolitan Paisiy of Gaza is able to exclaim in answer to the latter's reply in Latin: "O cunning slave, from thine own lips I judge thee not to be an Orthodox since you have addressed us basely in the Latin tongue" (N. Gibbenet, *Isotoricheskoe issledovanie dela patriarkha Nikona* [A historical investigation concerning the case of Patriarch Nikon], Pt. 2 [St. Petersburg, 1884], p. 61). [Au.]

[16] See Pavel Aleppsky, *Puteshestvie Antiokhiyskogo patriarkha Makariya v Rossiyu v polovine XVII v.* [The journey to Russia of Patriarch Makariy of Antioch in the middle of the seventeenth century], tr. from Arabic by G. Murkos (Moscow, 1898), pp. 20–21. [Au.]

[17] See Αδελφοτης *Grammatika dobroglagolivago ellinoslovenskago yazyka* [A grammar of well-spoken Helleno-Slavic] (L'vov, 1591). [Au.]

ing that the opposition of science and art, which is so typical of our time and which sometimes rises to antagonistic levels, only became possible within the conditions of the new, post-Renaissance European culture which had freed itself from the outlook of the Middle Ages and which stood to a great degree in opposition to that outlook (let us remember that the very concept "fine arts," as opposed to science, only appears in the eighteenth century).[18]

This brings to mind the distinction between the Manichaeistic and Augustinian concepts of the devil in Norbert Wiener's brilliant interpretation.[19] According to the Manichaeistic concept, the devil is an essence having evil intentions, that is, consciously and with purpose turning his power against man; but according to the Augustinian concept, the devil is a blind force, an entropy, which is only objectively directed against man because of man's weakness and ignorance. If one accepts a broad enough sense of the term *devil* as that which is opposed to culture (once again, in the broad sense of the word), then it is evident that the difference between the Manichaeistic and the Augustinian approach corresponds to the difference between the two types of cultures which we spoke of earlier.

The opposition "organized–nonorganized" can appear within the very mechanism of culture as well. As we have already stated, the hierarchic structure of culture is constructed as a combination of highly organized systems and of those allowing various degrees of disorganization to the point where, in order to reveal their structure, they must continually be contrasted with the former. If the nuclear structure of a culture mechanism is an ideal semiotic system with structural links realized at all levels (or more correctly, the nearest approximation of such an ideal possible in particular historic situations), then the formations around it are constructed so as to break the various links of such a structure and to require continual comparison with the nucleus of the culture.

This kind of "incompleteness," the incomplete regulatedness of culture as a unified semiotic system, is not a shortcoming but a condition for its normal functioning. The point is that the very function of the cultural assimilation of the world implies assigning to the world a systematic quality. In some cases, as for example in the scientific cognition of the world, the point will be to reveal the system concealed in the object; in others—for example, in education, missionary work, or propaganda—it will be to impart to an unorganized object certain principles of organization. But in order to fulfill this role, culture, and especially its central coding mechanism, must possess certain qualities. Among these, two are essential for our present purposes:

First, it should have a high degree of modeling potential, that is, either the ability to describe as wide a range of objects as possible, which would include as many as yet unknown objects as possible, this being the optimal requirement for cognitive models, or it should have the capability to declare those objects which it cannot be used to describe as nonexistent.

Second, its systematic nature should be acknowledged by the community using it as an instrument for assigning system to what is amorphous. Therefore, the tendency of sign systems to become automatized represents an ever present inner foe of culture against which it continually struggles.

The conflict between the continual attempt to take the systematic to its limits and the continual opposition to the automatization produced thereby within the structure is organically present in every living culture.

This brings us to a problem of primary importance: why is human culture a dynamic system? Why are the semiotic systems that form human culture, with the exception of certain obviously local

[18] See in this regard the observations on the influence of Galileo's aesthetic views on his scholarship in Erwin Panofsky, "Galiley: nauka i iskusstvo (esteticheskie vzglyady i nauchnaya mysl')" [Galileo: science and art (aesthetic opinions and scientific thought)], in *U istokov klassicheskoy nauki* [Among the sources of classical science] (Moscow, 1968), pp. 26–28. Compare Panofsky, *Galileo as a Critic of the Arts* (Hague, 1954), and the remarks on the meaning of artistic form for Galileo in accounting for his scientific conclusions in L. Olyshki, *Geschichte der neusprachlichen wissenschaftlichen Literatur*, Vol. III of *Galilei und seine Zeit* (Halle, 1927), where Olyshki writes: "By means of adapting expression to content, the latter acquires an obligatory and thus artistic form. Poetry and science are for Galileo the spheres which give shape to the world. The problem of content and the problem of form coincide for him." [Au.]

[19] See N. Wiener, *Kibernetika i obshchestvo* [Cybernetics and society] (Moscow, 1958), pp. 47–48. [Au.]

or secondary artificial languages, subject to an obligatory law of evolution? The fact that artificial languages exist convincingly bears witness to the possibility of the existence and successful functioning, within specific limits, of nondeveloping systems. Why then can there exist a unified, nondeveloping language of road signals, while natural language necessarily has a history without which its (real, not theoretical) synchronic functioning is impossible? After all, the existence of diachrony itself is not only not among the minimum conditions necessary for the appearance of semiotic systems but presents the researcher with a theoretical riddle and a practical problem.

The dynamism of the semiotic components of culture is evidently connected with the dynamism of the social life of human society. However, this connection is by itself fairly complicated because we can still ask: "But why must human society be dynamic?" Man is included in a more mobile world than all the rest of nature, and in a very basic way he regards the very notion of movement differently. All organic creatures strive to stabilize their surroundings, all their changeability is a striving for self-preservation without change in a world that is liable to change and contrary to their interests; for man the changeability of his surroundings is a normal condition of living; for him the norm is life within changing conditions, *a change in the way of life*. It is no accident that from the point of view of nature man appears as a destroyer. But it is precisely *culture*, in the broad sense, that distinguishes human society from nonhuman societies. Thus it follows that dynamism is not an outer quality of culture imposed on it by the arbitrariness of external causes but is inseparable from it.

It is another matter that the dynamism of culture is not always acknowledged by its members. As has already been stated, the striving to perpetuate every contemporary (synchronic) condition is typical for many cultures, and the possibility of any substantial change of the rules in force may not be allowed for at all (along with a typical prohibition against their being understood as relative). This is understandable where we are concerned not with observers but with participants, with those within the particular culture: one can only speak of the dynamism of culture from the perspective of an investigator (observer) and not from that of a participant.

On the other hand, the process of gradual change of a culture may not be perceived as continuous, and so the various stages of the process can be taken for different cultures contrasting with one another. (It is exactly in this fashion that language continually changes, but the continuity of this process is not perceived directly by the users of the language themselves since linguistic changes do not occur within a single generation but through the transmission of the language from one generation to the next. In this way, the users of the language tend to see language change as a discrete process; language for them is not an uninterrupted continuum but breaks down into separate strata, the differences between which then acquire *stylistic* meaning.)[20]

The question whether dynamism, the constant need for self-regeneration, is an inner quality of culture or merely the result of the disturbing influence of the material conditions of man's existence on the system of his ideals cannot be resolved simply. Doubtless both processes are relevant.

On the one hand, changes in a culture system are connected with the accumulation of information by the human community and with the inclusion of science into culture as a relatively autonomous system with its own initiatives. Science is enriched not only by positive knowledge but also by developing modeling complexes. The pursuit of inner unification, which is one of the basic tendencies of culture (as we will see below), causes a constant transfer of purely scientific models into the general field of ideas and attempts to ascribe to them the features of the culture as a whole. Therefore, cognition with its initiating tendency and dynamic character will naturally influence the form of the model of the culture.

On the other hand, not everything within the dynamics of semiotic systems can be explained in this manner. It would be difficult to interpret the dynamics of the phonological or grammatical side of language in this way. Whereas the necessity for change in the lexical system can be explained by the need for a different concept of the world to be reflected in the language, phonological change is an

[20] See Uspensky, "Semioticheskie problemy stilya v lingvisticheskom osveshchenii" [Semiotic problems of style in a linguistic interpretation], in *Trudy po znakovym sistemam,* IV (Tartu, 1969), 499. [Au.]

immanent law of the system itself. Or, to take another revealing example, the system of *fashion* can be studied in connection with various external social processes: from the laws of industrial manufacture to social-aesthetic ideals. However, at the same time, fashion is clearly a synchronically closed system with the specific quality that it undergoes change. Fashion is different from a norm in that it regulates a system of directing it not towards permanence but towards change. In so doing, fashion always tries to become the norm, but these concepts are by their very nature in opposition, for hardly does fashion achieve a relative stability approximating the condition of a norm than it quickly seeks to abandon it. The motives for the change in fashion, as a rule, remain incomprehensible to the community regulated by its rules. This nonmotivation of fashion forces one to assume that we are dealing here with pure change; and it is precisely the nonmotivation of change (compare Nekrasov's "fickle fashion" [*izmenchivaja moda*]) that defines the specific social function of fashion. It was no accident that made the forgotten eighteenth-century writer N. Strakhov, the author of *A Correspondence of Fashion, Containing Letters from Sleeveless Modes, Meditations by Inanimate Costumes, Conversations among Speechless Bonnets, the Sentiments of Furnishings, Carriages, Notebooks, Buttons and Ancient Shirt-Fronts, Caftans, Housecoats, Jackets, etc.: A Moral and Critical Composition wherein Are Revealed in Their True Light the Manners, Way of Life and Diverse Comical and Imposing Scenes of a Fashionable Age,* choose Impermanence as his leading Fashion correspondent while among the "Rules of Fashion" in his book we read: "We hereby decree that no color of cloth should remain in use for more than one year."[21] It is quite obvious that the change in the color of cloth is not dictated by any urge to approximate some general ideal of truth, goodness, beauty, or appropriateness. One color is exchanged for another simply because the one was *old* and the other *new.* We are dealing here with a tendency at its purest, one which in a more disguised form appears widely in human culture.

Thus, for example, in Russia in the beginning of the eighteenth century a change took place in the entire system of the cultural life of the ruling social stratum, a change which allowed people of that epoch to call themselves with a certain pride "new." Kantemir wrote of the positive hero of his epoch:

> Wise is he that lets not fall Peter's decrees
> By which we have become at once a people
> new.[22]

In this, as in thousands of other cases, one could point out many interesting reasons for the transformations, dictated by some correlation with other structural orders. However, what is equally clear is that the need for *novelty,* for *systematic change,* is an equally perceptible stimulus for change. Wherein lie the roots of this need? The question could be posed more generally as: "Why does mankind, as distinct from all other creatures of the world, have a history?" One can assume here that mankind lived through a long *prehistoric* period in which duration of time played no part, for there was no development and only at a specific moment did there occur that break which gave birth to a dynamic structure and initiated the history of mankind.

At present the most likely answer to this question appears to be as follows: at a certain moment, the moment, in fact, from which we can begin to speak of culture, man linked his existence to a continually expanding nonhereditary memory; he became a *receiver of information* (during the prehistoric period he was merely a *carrier* of constant and genetically given *information*). But this required the continual actualization of a coding system which had to be constantly present in the consciousness of both the addressee and the addresser as a deautomatized system. The latter made it possible for a particular mechanism to emerge which, on the one hand, would exhibit particular homeostatic functions to such a degree as to preserve the unity of the memory, to remain the same, and on the other, would continually renew itself, deautomatizing itself at every phase and thereby maximizing its ability to absorb information. The necessity for continual self-renewal, to become different and yet remain the same, constitutes one of the chief working mechanisms of culture.

The reciprocal tension between these tendencies justifies the static and the dynamic model of culture,

[21] *Perepiska Mody, . . .* (Moscow, 1791), p. 235. [Au.]

[22] *Satiry i drugie stikhotvorcheskie sochineniya knyazya Antiokha Kantemira* [Satires and other verse compositions of Prince Antiokh Kantemir] (St. Petersburg, 1762), p. 32. [Au.]

the models being defined by the initial axioms of description.

ALONGSIDE this opposition within the system of culture of the old and the new, the unchangeable and the mobile, there is yet another basic opposition, the antithesis of unity and multiplicity. We have already noted that the heterogeneity of the inner organization is a law for the existence of culture. The presence of differently organized structures, and various degrees of organization, is an essential condition for the functioning of the mechanism of culture. We cannot name a single culture in history in which all levels and subsystems were organized on a strictly uniform structural base and synchronized in their historical dynamism. As a result of this need for structural variety, every culture singles out special spheres, *differently* organized, which are valued very highly in an axiological sense although they are outside the general system of organization. Such were the monastery in the medieval world, poetry within the concepts of Romanticism, the world of gypsies, the backstage in the culture of St. Petersburg during the nineteenth century, and many other examples of little islands of "different" organization in the general body of culture, whose aim was to increase the structural variety and to overcome the entropy of structural automatization. Such were the temporary visits by a member of any cultural group into a different social structure—officials entering an artistic environment, landowners coming into Moscow for the winter, townspeople going into the country for the summer, Russian nobles in Paris or Karlsbad. And this, as M. M. Bakhtin has shown, was the function of the carnival in the highly normative life of the Middle Ages.[23]

And yet culture requires unity. In order to fulfill its social function, culture has to appear as a structure subject to unified constructive principles. This unity comes about in the following manner: at a specific stage in the development of culture, there comes a moment when it becomes conscious of itself, when it creates a model of itself. The model defines the unified, the artificially schematized image, that is raised to the level of a structural unity. When imposed onto the reality of this or that culture, it exerts a powerful regulating influence, preordaining the construction of culture, introducing order, and eliminating contradiction. The error of many literary histories is that the self-interpreting models of cultures such as "the concept of Classicism in the works of seventeenth/eighteenth-century theoreticians" or "the concept of Romanticism in the works of the Romantics," which form a special stratum in the system of a culture's evolution, are studied on the same level as the facts of particular writers' works; this is a logical error.

The assertions "everything is different and cannot be described by a single general schema" and "everything is the same and we have to deal with never-ending variations of an invariant model" continually reappear in various guises in the history of culture, from Ecclesiastes and the dialecticians of antiquity to our own day. And this is no accident; they describe various aspects of a single cultural mechanism, and in their reciprocal tension they are part of the essence of culture.

These appear to us to be the basic features of that complicated semiotic system which we define as culture. Its function is to serve as a memory; its basic feature is self-accumulation. At the dawn of European civilization Heraclitus wrote: "Essential to the psyche is the self-generating logos."[24] He grasped the basic characteristic of culture.

SOME OF our observations may be generalized as follows: structure, in nonsemiotic systems (those outside the complex "society-communication-culture"), presupposes some constructive principle of interconnection between elements. It is precisely the realization of this principle that allows one to speak of the given phenomenon as structural. Therefore, once a phenomenon exists, it has no alternative within the limits of its qualitative definition. A phenomenon may have structure, that is, be itself, or not have structure and not be itself. There are no other possibilities. Hence the fact that structure in nonsemiotic systems can only bear a fixed quantity of information.

The semiotic mechanism of culture created by mankind is constructed according to a different principle: opposed and reciprocally alternating

[23] See M. M. Bakhtin, *Tvorchestvo Fransua Rable i narodnaya kul'tura srednevekov' ya i Renessansa* [The works of François Rabelais and the folk culture of the Middle Ages and the Renaissance] (Moscow, 1965). [Au.]

[24] Heraclitus, fragments cited according to *Antichnye filosofy, Svidetel'stva, fragmenty, teksty* [Philosophers of antiquity; certificates, fragments, texts], compiled by A. A. Avitis'yan (Kiev, 1955), p. 27. [Au.]

structural principles are essential. Their *relation to one another,* the disposition of particular elements in the structural field which emerges here, creates that structural regulatedness which allows the system to preserve information. It is crucial here, however, that it is not actually any specific alternatives whose number is finite and constant for the given system that are given, but the very *principle of alternation* itself, and that all the actual oppositions of the given structure are merely interpretations of this principle on a certain level. As a result, any pair of elements, of local regularities, of particular or general structures, or even of whole semiotic systems acquires the significance of being alternatives and forms a structural field which may be filled with information. Hence the system with its ever-increasing information potential.

This snowballing of culture does not exclude the fact that its separate components, sometimes very essential ones, appear stabilized. Thus, for example, the dynamics of natural languages is much slower than the development of other semiotic systems so that compared with any one of them, languages appear as synchronically stabilized systems. Yet culture is able to "squeeze out" information even from this by creating the structural pair "static-dynamic."

The snowballing of culture gave mankind an advantage over all other living beings that exist in conditions where the volume of information is stable. However, this process has a darker side as well: culture devours resources just as greedily as industry and just as readily destroys its environment. The pace of its development is by no means always dictated by man's real needs; there comes into play the inner logic of accelerating change in the working mechanisms of information. In many fields (scientific information, art, information for the masses) crises come about which may bring whole spheres won over by culture to the brink of expulsion from the system of the social memory.

"The self-generating logos" has always been valued positively. Now it is evident that a mechanism has unavoidably come into being which, by its complexity and rate of growth, can smother that very *logos.*

Culture doubtlessly still has many reserves. But for them to be utilized, we need a much clearer notion of its inner workings than we have available at present.

As already noted, language carries out a specific communicative function within which it may be studied as an isolated functioning system, but in the system of culture, language has another role: it provides the collective with *a presumption of communicability.*

Language structure is abstracted from the material of languages; it becomes independent and is transferred to an ever-increasing range of phenomena which begin to behave in the system of human communication as language and thus become elements of culture. Any reality drawn into the sphere of culture begins to function as a sign. But if it already has a sign character (for any quasi sign of this kind is, in a social sense, undoubtedly a reality), then it becomes a sign of a sign. The presumption of language, applied to amorphous material, changes it into language and a language system and generates metalingual phenomena. Thus the twentieth century has produced not only metalanguages of science, but a metaliterature and metapainting (painting about painting) as well, and apparently is creating a metaculture, an all-encompassing metalingual system of a secondary order. Just as scientific metalanguage is not concerned with solving factual problems of a particular science, but has its own aims, so contemporary "metanovels," "metapaintings," and "metacinematography" stand logically on a different hierarchic level than the corresponding first-order phenomena and pursue different ends. Looked at together, they do indeed seem as strange as a logical problem in engineering.

The possibility of self-reduplication of metalanguage formations on an unlimited number of levels, along with the introduction of ever-new objects into the sphere of communication, forms culture's reserve in information.

Paul Ricoeur

b. 1913

THE EARLIER work of Paul Ricoeur, as represented particularly by *The Symbolism of Evil,* displays a variety of intellectual relations but especially phenomenological hermeneutics and its connection to modern theology. The later work on metaphor, while maintaining the same concerns, enters into the more recent language of poststructuralism in order to quarrel with some of its more radical assertions. This development can be seen by comparing Ricoeur's earlier attention to the symbol and its religious associations with emphasis on the metaphor in two later books, *The Rule of Metaphor* and *Interpretation Theory.* In his book on Freud and interpretation, Ricoeur developed a distinction between two types of hermeneutic of the symbol: the hermeneutic of suspicion, where the symbol is regarded as "transparent," through which its determinate meaning is declared to be recovered; and a true hermeneutic in which the symbol is regarded as "opaque," though with an inexhaustible depth. However, Ricoeur also treats the symbol as a sort of miraculous incarnation, and in that sense it too is "bound" or "rooted." By contrast, the metaphor, which Ricoeur regards as "the linguistic procedure—that bizarre form of predication—within which the symbolic power is deposited," may or may not itself be a symbol, which is privileged in all of Ricoeur's work. In *The Rule of Metaphor,* Ricoeur traces the history of the theory of metaphor most eruditely from Aristotle through the history of rhetoric and argues that the Aristotelian notion of metaphor as deviation from *common* usage became changed in an unwarranted way to deviation from *proper* or *original* usage. This change led the way to an erroneous distinction between figurative and proper that Ricoeur sees as having dominated language theory, to its detriment, ever since.

Ricoeur's aim is to shift the idea of the metaphor from that of denomination, where it seems to be a substitution, to predication, which means that a metaphor is not lodged in a noun but in the tension of the copula and that it requires a *semantics* of the sentence for its eventual interpretation. Metaphor's rootedness is in the concrete act of discourse represented by the copula. Predication has always a synthetic character in the act and cannot be understood on the principle of the mere interplay of differences among signifiers. Ricoeur would restore the notion of reference to language theory. The metaphorical activity, he holds, makes possible the creation of new meaning released in interpretation. However, when a metaphor becomes repeated, it loses its "authenticity," and presumably new metaphorical acts must come in its wake. Thus Ricoeur embraces a distinction between living and dead metaphor. Clearly his concern with metaphor and his insistence on a semantics of the sentence and a hermeneutic of the work is opposed to deconstruction, which he claims does not go beyond a semiotics of the word. The essay here, which follows on the two books concerned with metaphor, extends Ricoeur's theory of it. Here he argues for a concept of "indirect reference," in which is involved a "suspension and seemingly an abolition of the ordinary reference attached to descriptive language."

Ricoeur's major work translated into English includes *Fallible Man* (1960, trans. 1966); *The Symbolism of Evil* (1960, trans. 1969); *Freud and Philosophy* (1961 ff., trans. 1970); *The Conflict of Interpretations* (1960–69, trans. 1974); *The Rule of Metaphor* (1975, trans. 1977); *Interpretation Theory: Discourse and the Surplus of Meaning* (1976); *Hermeneutics and the Human Sciences* (1981, trans. 1981); and *Time and Narrative* (1983, trans. 1984). See Don Ihde, *Hermeneutic Phenomenology: The Philosophy of Paul Ricoeur;* Hazard Adams, *Philosophy of the Literary Symbolic* (pp. 372–89).

THE METAPHORICAL PROCESS AS COGNITION, IMAGINATION, AND FEELING

This paper will focus on a specific problem in the somewhat boundless field of metaphor theory. Although this problem may sound merely psychological, insofar as it includes such terms as "image" and "feeling," I would rather characterize it as a problem arising on the boundary between a *semantic* theory of metaphor and a *psychological* theory of imagination and feeling. By a semantic theory, I mean an inquiry into the capacity of metaphor to provide untranslatable information and, accordingly, into metaphor's claim to yield some true insight about reality. The question to which I will address myself is whether such an inquiry may be completed without including as a necessary component a psychological moment of the kind usually described as "image" or "feeling."

THE METAPHORICAL PROCESS AS COGNITION, IMAGINATION, AND FEELING first appeared in *Critical Inquiry* 5 (Autumn 1978). It is reprinted by permission of the University of Chicago Press and Paul Ricoeur, copyright 1978.

At first glance, it seems that it is only in theories in which metaphorical phrases have no informative value and consequently no truth claim that the so-called images or feelings are advocated as substitutive explanatory factors. By substitutive explanation I mean the attempt to derive the alleged significance of metaphorical phrases from their capacity to display streams of images and to elicit feelings that we mistakenly hold for genuine information and for fresh insight into reality. My thesis is that it is not only for theories which deny metaphors any informative value and any truth claim that images and feelings have a *constitutive* function. I want instead to show that the kind of theory of metaphor initiated by I. A. Richards in *Philosophy of Rhetoric,* Max Black in *Models and Metaphors,* Beardsley, Berggren,[1] and others cannot achieve its own goal without including imagining and feeling, that is, without assigning a *semantic* function to what seems to be mere *psychological* features and without, therefore, concerning itself with some accompanying factors extrinsic to the informative kernel of metaphor. This contention seems to run against a well-established—at least since Frege's famous article "Sinn und Bedeutung" and Husserl's *Logical Investigations*[2]—dichotomy, that between *Sinn* or sense and *Vorstellung* or representation, if we understand "sense" as the objective content of an expression and "representation" as its mental actualization, precisely in the form of

[1] For Berggren see n. 22. [Eds.]
[2] See *Frege* and *Husserl.* [Eds.]

image and feeling. But the question is whether the functioning of metaphorical sense does not put to the test and even hold at bay this very dichotomy.

The first articulate account of metaphor, that of Aristotle, already provides some hints concerning what I will call the semantic role of imagination (and by implication, feeling) in the establishment of metaphorical sense. Aristotle says of the *lexis* in general—that is, of diction, elocution, and style, of which metaphor is one of the figures—that it makes discourse (*logos*) *appear* as such and such. He also says that the gift of making good metaphors relies on the capacity to contemplate similarities. Moreover, the vividness of such good metaphors consists in their ability to "set before the eyes" the sense that they display.[3] What is suggested here is a kind of pictorial dimension, which can be called the *picturing function* of metaphorical meaning.

The tradition of rhetoric confirms that hint beyond any specific theory concerning the semantic status of metaphor. The very expression "figure of speech" implies that in metaphor, as in the other tropes or turns, discourse assumes the nature of a body by displaying forms and traits which usually characterize the human face, man's "figure"; it is as though the tropes gave to discourse a quasi-bodily externalization. By providing a kind of figurability to the message, the tropes make discourse appear.

Roman Jakobson suggests a similar interpretation when he characterizes the "poetic" function in his general model of communication as the valorization of the message *for its own sake*. In the same way, Tzvetan Todorov, the Bulgarian theoretician of neo-rhetorics, defines "figure" as the visibility of discourse. Gérard Genette, in *Figures I*, speaks of deviance as an "inner space of language." "Simple and common expressions," he says, "have no form, figures [of speech] have some."

I am quite aware that these are only hints which point toward a problem rather than toward a statement. Furthermore, I am quite aware that they add to this difficulty the fact that they tend to speak metaphorically about metaphor and thus introduce a kind of circularity which obscures the issue. But is not the word "metaphor" itself a metaphor, the metaphor of a displacement and therefore of a transfer in a kind of space? What is at stake is precisely the necessity of these *spatial* metaphors about metaphor included in our talk about "figures" of speech.

Such being the problem, in what direction are we to look for a correct assessment of the *semantic* role of imagination and eventually of feeling? It seems that it is in the *work of resemblance* that a pictorial or iconic moment is implied, as Aristotle suggests when he says that to make good metaphors is to contemplate similarities or (according to some other translations) to have an insight into likeness.

But in order to understand correctly the work of resemblance in metaphor and to introduce the pictorial or iconic moment at the right place, it is necessary briefly to recall the mutation undergone by the theory of metaphor at the level of semantics by contrast with the tradition of classical rhetoric. In this tradition, metaphor was correctly described in terms of *deviance,* but this deviance was mistakenly ascribed to denomination only. Instead of giving a thing its usual common *name,* one designates it by means of a borrowed name, a "foreign" name in Aristotle's terminology. The rationale of this transfer of name was understood as the objective similarity between the things themselves or the subjective similarity between the attitudes linked to the grasping of these things. As concerns the goal of this transfer, it was supposed either to fill up a lexical lacuna, and therefore to serve the principle of economy which rules the endeavor of giving appropriate names to new things, new ideas, or new experiences, or to decorate discourse, and therefore to serve the main purpose of rhetorical discourse, which is to persuade and to please.

The problem of resemblance receives a new articulation in the semantic theory characterized by Max Black as an interaction theory (as opposed to a substitutive theory). The bearer of the metaphorical meaning is no longer the word but the sentence as a whole. The interaction process does not merely consist of the substitution of a word for a word, of a name for a name—which, strictly speaking, defines only metonymy—but in an interaction between a logical subject and a predicate. If metaphor consists in some deviance—this feature is not denied but is described and explained in a new way—this deviance concerns the predicative structure itself. Metaphor, then, has to be described as a deviant predication rather than a deviant denomination. We come closer to what I called the work of resemblance if we ask *how* this deviant predication ob-

[3]See *CTSP,* pp. 60–62. [Eds.]

tains. A French theoretician in the field of poetics, Jean Cohen, in *Structure du langage poétique,* speaks of this deviance in terms of a semantic impertinence, meaning by that the violation of the code of pertinence or relevance which rules the ascription of predicates in ordinary use.[4] The metaphorical statement works as the reduction of this syntagmatic deviance by the establishment of a new semantic pertinence. This new pertinence in turn is secured by the production of a lexical deviance, which is therefore a paradigmatic deviance, that is, precisely the kind of deviance described by classical rhetoricians. Classical rhetoric, in that sense, was not wrong, but it only described the "effect of sense" at the level of the word while it overlooked the production of this semantic twist at the level of sense. While it is true that the effect of sense is focused on the word, the production of sense is borne by the whole utterance. It is in that way that the theory of metaphor hinges on a semantics of the sentence.

Such is the main presupposition of the following analysis. The first question is to understand *how* resemblance works in this production of meaning. The next step will be to connect in the right way the pictorial or iconic moment to this work of resemblance.

As concerns the first step, the work of resemblance as such, it seems to me that we are still only halfway to a full understanding of the semantic innovation which characterizes metaphorical phrases or sentences if we underline only the aspect of deviance in metaphor, even if we distinguish the semantic impertinence which requires the lexical deviance from this lexical deviance itself, as described by Aristotle and all classical rhetoricians. The decisive feature is the semantic innovation, thanks to which a new pertinence, a new congruence, is established in such a way that the utterance "makes sense" as a whole. The *maker* of metaphors is this craftsman with verbal skill *who,* from an inconsistent utterance for a literal interpretation, draws a significant utterance for a new interpretation which deserves to be called metaphorical because it generates the metaphor not only as deviant but as acceptable. In other words, metaphorical meaning does not merely consist of a semantic clash but of the *new* predicative meaning which emerges from the collapse of the literal meaning, that is, from the collapse of the meaning which obtains if we rely only on the common or usual lexical values of our words. The metaphor is not the enigma but the solution of the enigma.

It is here, in the mutation characteristic of the semantic innovation, that similarity and accordingly imagination play a role. But which role? I think that this role cannot be but misunderstood as long as one has in mind the Humean theory of image as a faint impression, that is, as a perceptual residue. It is no better understood if one shifts to the other tradition, according to which imagination can be reduced to the alternation between two modalities of association, either by contiguity or by similarity. Unfortunately, this prejudice has been assumed by such important theoreticians as Jakobson, for whom the metaphoric process is opposed to the metonymic process[5] in the same way as the substitution of one sign for another within a sphere of similarity is opposed to the concatenation between signs along a string of contiguity. What must be understood and underscored is a mode of functioning of similarity and accordingly of imagination which is immanent—that is, nonextrinsic—to the predicative process itself. In other words, the work of resemblance has to be appropriate and homogeneous to the deviance and the oddness and the freshness of the semantic innovation itself.

How is this possible? I think that the decisive problem that an interaction theory of metaphor has helped to delineate but not to solve is the transition from literal incongruence to metaphorical congruence between two semantic fields. Here the metaphor of space is useful. It is as though a change of distance between meanings occurred within a logical space. The *new* pertinence or congruence proper to a meaningful metaphoric utterance proceeds from the kind of semantic proximity which suddenly obtains between terms in spite of their distance. Things or ideas which were remote appear now as close. Resemblance ultimately is nothing else than this rapprochement which reveals a generic kinship between heterogeneous ideas. What Aristotle called the *epiphora* of the metaphor, that is, the transfer of meaning, is nothing else than this

[4] Jean Cohen, *Structure du langage poétique* (Paris, 1966). [Au.]

[5] See *CTSP*, pp. 1113–16. [Eds.]

move or shift in the logical distance, from the far to the near. The lacuna of some recent theories of metaphor, including Max Black's, concerns precisely the innovation proper to this shift.[6]

It is the first task of an appropriate theory of imagination to plug this hole. But this theory of imagination must deliberately break with Hume and draw on Kant, specifically on Kant's concept of productive imagination *as schematizing a synthetic operation.*[7] This will provide us with the first step in our attempt to adjust a psychology of imagination to a semantics of metaphor or, if you prefer, to complete a semantics of metaphor by having recourse to a psychology of imagination. There will be three steps in this attempt of adjustment and of completion.

In the first step, imagination is understood as the "seeing," still homogeneous to discourse itself, which effects the shift in logical distance, the rapprochement itself. The place and the role of productive imagination is there, in the *insight,* to which Aristotle alluded when he said that to make good metaphors is to contemplate likeness—*theorein to omoion.* This insight into likeness is both a thinking and a seeing. It is a thinking to the extent that it effects a restructuration of semantic fields; it is transcategorical because it is categorical. This can be shown on the basis of the kind of metaphor in which the logical aspect of this restructuration is the most conspicuous, the metaphor which Aristotle called metaphor by analogy, that is, the proportional metaphor: A is to B what C is to D. The cup is to Dionysus what the shield is to Ares. Therefore we may say, by shifting terms, Dionysus' shield or Ares' cup. But this thinking is a seeing, to the extent that the insight consists of the instantaneous grasping of the combinatory possibilities offered by the proportionality and consequently the establishment of the proportionality by the rapprochement between the two ratios. I suggest we call this *productive* character of the insight *predicative assimilation.* But we miss entirely its semantic role if we interpret it in terms of the old association by resemblance. A kind of mechanical attraction between mental atoms is thereby substituted for an operation homogeneous to language and to its nuclear act, the predication act. The assimilation consists precisely in *making* similar, that is, semantically proximate, the terms that the metaphorical utterance brings together.

Some will probably object to my ascribing to the imagination this predicative assimilation. Without returning to my earlier critique of the prejudices concerning the imagination itself which may prevent the analysts from doing justice to productive imagination, I want to underscore a trait of predicative assimilation which may support my contention that the rapprochement characteristic of the metaphorical process offers a typical kinship to Kant's *schematism.* I mean the *paradoxical* character of the predicative assimilation which has been compared by some authors to Ryle's concept of "category mistake," which consists in presenting the facts pertaining to one category in the terms appropriate to another.[8] All new rapprochement runs against a previous categorization which resists, or rather which yields while resisting, as Nelson Goodman says.[9] This is what the idea of a semantic impertinence or incongruence preserves. In order that a metaphor obtains, one must continue to identify the previous incompatibility *through* the new compatibility. The predicative assimilation involves, in that way, a specific kind of tension which is not so much between a subject and a predicate as between semantic incongruence and congruence. The insight into likeness is the perception of the conflict between the previous incompatibility and the new compatibility. "Remoteness" is preserved within "proximity." To see *the like* is to see the same in spite of, and through, the different. This tension between sameness and difference characterizes the logical structure of likeness. Imagination, accordingly, is this *ability* to produce new kinds by assimilation and to produce them not *above* the differ-

[6]Black's explanation of the metaphorical process by the "system of associated commonplaces" leaves unsolved the problem of innovation, as the following reservations and qualifications suggest: "Metaphors," he says, "can be supported by specifically constructed systems of implications as well as by accepted commonplaces" (*Models and Metaphors* [Ithaca, N.Y., 1962], p. 43). And further: "These implications usually consist of commonplaces about the subsidiary subject, but may, in suitable cases, consist of deviant implications established *ad hoc* by the writer" (p. 44). How are we to think of these implications that are created on the spot? [Au.]

[7]See Kant, *Critique of Pure Reason.* [Eds.]

[8]*The Concept of Mind* (New York, 1949), pp. 16ff. [Eds.]

[9]*Languages of Art* (Indianapolis, 1976), p. 69. [Eds.]

ences, as in the concept, but in spite of and through the differences. Imagination is this stage in the production of genres where generic kinship has not reached the level of conceptual peace and rest but remains caught in the war between distance and proximity, between remoteness and nearness. In that sense, we may speak with Gadamer[10] of the fundamental metaphoricity of thought to the extent that the figure of speech that we call "metaphor" allows us a glance at the general procedure by which we produce concepts. This is because in the metaphoric process the movement toward the genus is arrested by the resistance of the difference and, as it were, intercepted by the figure of rhetoric.

Such is the first function of imagination in the process of semantic innovation. Imagination has not yet been considered under its sensible, quasi-optic aspect but under its quasi-verbal aspect. However, the latter is the condition of the former. We first have to understand an image, according to Bachelard's remark in the *Poetics of Space,* as "a being pertaining to language."[11] Before being a fading perception, the image is an emerging meaning. Such is, in fact, the tradition of Kant's productive imagination and schematism. What we have above described is nothing else than the schematism of metaphorical attribution.

The next step will be to incorporate into the semantics of metaphor the second aspect of imagination, its *pictorial* dimension. It is this aspect which is at stake in the *figurative* character of metaphor. It is also this aspect which was intended by I. A. Richards' distinction between tenor and vehicle.[12] This distinction is not entirely absorbed in the one Black makes between frame and focus. Frame and focus designate only the contextual setting—say, the sentence as a whole—and the term which is the bearer of the shift of meaning, whereas tenor and vehicle designate the conceptual import and its pictorial envelope. The first function of imagination was to give an account of the frame/focus interplay; its second function is to give an account of the difference of level between tenor and vehicle or, in other words, of the way in which a semantic innovation is not only schematized but pictured. Paul Henle borrows from Charles Sanders Peirce the distinction between sign and icon and speaks of the *iconic* aspect of metaphor.[13] If there are two thoughts in one in a metaphor, there is one which is intended; the other is the concrete aspect *under* which the first one is presented. In Keats' verse "When by my solitary hearth I sit / And hateful thoughts enwrap my soul in gloom," the metaphorical expression "enwrap" consists in presenting sorrow as if it were capable of enveloping the soul in a cloak. Henle comments: "We are led [by figurative discourse] to think of something by a consideration of something like it, and this is what constitutes the iconic mode of signifying."

Someone might object at this point that we are in danger of reintroducing an obsolete theory of the image, in the Humean sense of a weakened sensorial impression. This is therefore the place to recall a remark made by Kant that one of the functions of the schema is to provide images for a concept. In the same vein, Henle writes: "If there is an iconic element in metaphor it is equally clear that the icon is not presented, but merely described." And further: "What is presented is a formula for the construction of icons." What we have therefore to show is that if this new extension of the role of imagination is not exactly included in the previous one, it makes sense for a semantic theory only to the extent that it is controlled by it. What is at issue is the development from schematization to iconic presentation.

The enigma of iconic presentation is the way in which depiction occurs in predicative assimilation: something appears on which we read the new connection. The enigma remains unsolved as long as we treat the image as a mental picture, that is, as the replica of an absent thing. Then the image must remain foreign to the process, extrinsic to predicative assimilation.

We have to understand the process by which a certain production of images channels the schematization of predicative assimilation. By displaying a flow of images, discourse initiates changes of logical distance, generates rapprochement. Imaging or imagining, thus, is the concrete milieu in which and through which we see similarities. To

[10] See *Gadamer.* [Eds.]

[11] Gaston Bachelard, *The Poetics of Space,* trans. Maria Jolas (New York, 1964). [Au.]

[12] I. A. Richards, *The Philosophy of Rhetoric* (1936). [Eds.]

[13] Paul Henle, "Metaphor," in *Language, Thought, and Culture,* ed. Henle (Ann Arbor, Mich., 1958). [Au.] See *Peirce.* [Eds.]

imagine, then, is not to have a mental picture of something but to display relations in a depicting mode. Whether this depiction concerns unsaid and unheard similarities or refers to qualities, structures, localizations, situations, attitudes, or feelings, each time the new intended connection is grasped as what the icon describes or depicts.

It is in this way, I think, that one can do justice within a semantic theory of metaphor to the Wittgensteinian concept of "seeing as." Wittgenstein himself did not extend this analysis beyond the field of perception and beyond the process of interpretation made obvious by the case of ambiguous "Gestalten," as in the famous duck/rabbit drawing.[14] Marcus B. Hester, in his *The Meaning of Poetic Metaphor,* has attempted to extend the concept of "seeing as" to the functioning of poetic images.[15] Describing the experience of *reading,* he shows that the kind of images which are interesting for a theory of poetic language are not those that interrupt reading and distort or divert it. These images—these "wild" images, if I may say so—are properly extrinsic to the fabric of sense. They induce the reader, who has become a dreamer rather than a reader, to indulge himself in the delusive attempt, described by Sartre as fascination, to possess magically the absent thing, body, or person. The kind of images which still belong to the production of sense are rather what Hester calls "bound" images, that is, concrete representations aroused by the verbal element and controlled by it. Poetic language, says Hester, is this language which not only merges sense and sound, as many theoreticians have said, but sense and senses, meaning by that the flow of bound images displayed by the sense. We are not very far from what Bachelard called *retentissement* [reverberation]. In reading, Bachelard says, the verbal meaning generates images which, so to speak, rejuvenate and reenact the traces of sensorial experience. Yet it is not the process of reverberation which expands the schematization and, in Kant's words, provides a concept with an image. In fact, as the experience of reading shows, this display of images ranges from schematization without full-blown images to wild images which distract thought more than they instruct it. The kind of images which are relevant for a semantics of the poetic image are those which belong to the intermediary range of the scale, which are, therefore, the bound images of Hester's theory. These images bring to concrete completion the metaphorical process. The meaning is then depicted under the features of ellipsis. Through this depiction, the meaning is not only schematized but lets itself be read *on* the image in which it is inverted. Or, to put it another way, the metaphorical sense is generated in the thickness of the imagining scene displayed by the verbal structure of the poem. Such is, to my mind, the functioning of the intuitive grasp of a predicative connection.

I do not deny that this second stage of our theory of imagination has brought us to the borderline between pure semantics and psychology or, more precisely, to the borderline between a semantics of productive imagination and a psychology of reproductive imagination. But the metaphorical meaning, as I said in the introduction, is precisely this kind of meaning which denies the well-established distinction between sense and representation, to evoke once more Frege's opposition between *Sinn* and *Vorstellung*. By blurring this distinction, the metaphorical meaning compels us to explore the borderline between the verbal and the nonverbal. The process of schematization and that of the bound images aroused and controlled by schematization obtain precisely on that borderline between a semantics of metaphorical utterances and a psychology of imagination.

The third and final step in our attempt to complete a semantic theory of metaphor with a proper consideration of the role of imagination concerns what I shall call the "suspension" or, if you prefer, the moment of negativity brought by the image in the metaphorical process.

In order to understand this new contribution of the image to this process, we have to come back to the basic notion of meaning as applied to a metaphorical expression. By meaning we may understand—as we have in the preceding as well—the inner functioning of the proposition as a predicative operation, for example, in Black's vocabulary, the "filter" or the "screen" effect of the subsidiary subject on the main subject. Meaning, then, is nothing else than what Frege called *Sinn* [sense], in contradistinction to *Bedeutung* [reference or denotation]. But to ask *about what* a metaphorical

[14] See *Wittgenstein.* [Eds.]

[15] Marcus B. Hester, *The Meaning of Poetic Metaphor* (The Hague, 1967). [Au.]

statement is, is something other and something more than to ask *what* it says.

The question of reference in metaphor is a particular case of the more general question of the truth claim of poetic language. As Goodman says in *Languages of Art,* all symbolic systems are denotative in the sense that they "make" and "remake" reality. To raise the question of the referential value of poetic language is to try to show how symbolic systems *reorganize* "the world in terms of works and works in terms of the world."[16] At that point the theory of metaphor tends to merge with that of models to the extent that a metaphor may be seen as a model for changing our way of looking at things, of perceiving the world. The word "insight," very often applied to the *cognitive* import of metaphor, conveys in a very appropriate manner this move from sense to reference which is no less obvious in poetic discourse than in so-called descriptive discourse. Here, too, we do not restrict ourselves to talking about ideas nor, as Frege says of proper names, "are we satisfied with the sense alone." "We presuppose besides a reference," the "striving for truth," which prompts "our intention in speaking or thinking" and "drives us always to advance from the sense of the reference."[17]

But the paradox of metaphorical reference is that its functioning is as odd as that of the metaphorical sense. At first glance, poetic language refers to nothing but itself. In a classic essay entitled "Word and Language," which defines the poetic function of language in relation to the other functions implied in any communicative transaction, Jakobson bluntly opposes the poetic function of the message to its referential function. On the contrary, the referential function prevails in descriptive language, be it ordinary or scientific. Descriptive language, he says, is not about itself, not inwardly oriented, but outwardly directed. Here language, so to speak, effaces itself for the sake of what is said about reality. "The poetic function—which is more than mere poetry—lays the stress on the palpable side of the signs, underscores the message for its own sake and deepens the fundamental dichotomy between signs and objects."[18] The poetic function and the referential function, accordingly, seem to be polar opposites. The latter directs language toward the nonlinguistic context, the former directs message toward itself.

This analysis seems to strengthen some other classical arguments among literary critics and more specifically in the structuralist camp according to which not only poetry but literature in general implies a mutation in the use of language. This redirects language toward itself to the point that language may be said, in Roland Barthes' words, to "celebrate itself" rather than to celebrate the world.

My contention is that these arguments are not false but give an incomplete picture of the whole process of reference in poetic discourse. Jakobson himself acknowledged that what happens in poetry is not the suppression of the referential function but its profound alteration by the workings of the ambiguity of the message itself. "The supremacy of poetic function over referential function," he says, "does not obliterate the reference but makes it ambiguous. The double-sensed message finds correspondence in a split addresser, in a split addressee, and what is more, in a split reference, as is cogently exposed in the preambles to fairy tales of various people, for instance, in the usual exhortation of the Majorca story tellers: *Aixo era y no era* (it was and it was not)."[19]

I suggest that we take the expression "split reference" as our leading line in our discussion of the referential function of the metaphorical statement. This expression, as well as the wonderful "it was and it was not," contains *in nuce* all that can be said about metaphorical reference. To summarize, poetic language is no less *about* reality than any other use of language but refers to it by the means of a complex strategy which implies, as an essential component, a suspension and seemingly an abolition of the ordinary reference attached to descriptive language. This suspension, however, is only the negative condition of a second-order reference, of an indirect reference built on the ruins of the direct reference. This reference is called second-order reference only with respect to the primacy of the refer-

[16] Nelson Goodman, *op. cit.,* p. 241. [Au.]

[17] As quoted from Frege's "Sense and Reference" in my *The Rule of Metaphor: Multidisciplinary Studies in the Creation of Meaning in Language* (Toronto, 1978), pp. 217–18. [Au.] See *Frege.* [Eds.]

[18] Jakobson, *Selected Writings,* 2 vols. (The Hague, 1962), 2:356. [Au.]

[19] As found in my *The Rule of Metaphor,* p. 224. [Au.]

ence of ordinary language. For, in another respect, it constitutes the primordial reference to the extent that it suggests, reveals, unconceals—or whatever you say—the deep structures of reality to which we are related as mortals who are born into this world and who *dwell* in it for a while.

This is not the place to discuss the ontological implications of this contention nor to ascertain its similarities and dissimilarities with Husserl's concept of *Lebenswelt* or with Heidegger's concept of *In-der-Welt-Sein.*[20] I want to emphasize, for the sake of our further discussion of the role of imagination in the completion of the *meaning* of metaphor, the mediating role of the *suspension*—or *epoché*[21]—of ordinary descriptive reference in connection with the ontological claims of poetic discourse. This mediating role of the *epoché* in the functioning of the reference in metaphor is in complete agreement with the interpretation we have given to the functioning of sense. The sense of a novel metaphor, we said, is the emergence of a new semantic congruence or pertinence from the ruins of the literal sense shattered by semantic incompatibility or absurdity. In the same way as the self-abolition of literal sense is the negative condition for the emergence of the metaphorical sense, the suspension of the reference proper to ordinary descriptive language is the negative condition for the emergence of a more radical way of looking at things, whether it is akin or not to the unconcealing of that layer of reality which phenomenology calls preobjective and which, according to Heidegger, constitutes the horizon of all our modes of dwelling in the world. Once more, what interests me here is the parallelism between the suspension of literal sense and the suspension of ordinary descriptive reference. This parallelism goes very far. In the same way as the metaphorical sense not only abolishes but preserves the literal sense, the metaphorical reference maintains the ordinary vision in tension with the new one it suggests. As Berggren says in "The Use and Abuse of Metaphor": "The possibility or comprehension of metaphorical construing requires, therefore, a peculiar and rather sophisticated intellectual ability which W. Bedell Stanford metaphorically labels 'stereoscopic vision': the ability to entertain two different points of view at the same time. That is to say, the perspective prior to and subsequent to the transformation of the metaphor's principal and subsidiary subjects must both be conjointly maintained."[22]

But what Bedell Stanford called stereoscopic vision is nothing else than what Jakobson called split reference: ambiguity in reference.

My contention now is that one of the functions of imagination is to give a concrete dimension to the suspension or *epoché* proper to split reference. Imagination does not merely *schematize* the predicative assimilation between terms by its synthetic insight into similarities nor does it merely *picture* the sense thanks to the display of images aroused and controlled by the cognitive process. Rather, it contributes concretely to the *epoché* of ordinary reference and to the *projection* of new possibilities of redescribing the world.

In a sense, all *epoché* is the work of the imagination. Imagination *is epoché*. As Sartre emphasized, to imagine is to address oneself to what is not. More radically, to imagine is to make oneself absent to the whole of things. Yet I do not want to elaborate further this thesis of the negativity proper to the image. What I do want to underscore is the solidarity between the *epoché* and the capacity to project new possibilities. Image as absence is the negative side of image as fiction. It is to this aspect of the image as fiction that is attached the power of symbolic systems to "remake" reality, to return to Goodman's idiom. But this productive and projective function of fiction can only be acknowledged if one sharply distinguishes it from the reproductive role of the so-called mental image which merely provides us with a re-presentation of things already perceived. *Fiction* addresses itself to deeply rooted potentialities of reality to the extent that they are absent from the actualities with which we deal in everyday life under the mode of empirical control and manipulation. In that sense, fiction presents under a concrete mode the split structure of the reference pertaining to the metaphorical statement. It both reflects and completes it. It reflects it in the sense that the mediating role of the *epoché* proper

[20] *Lebenswelt:* life-world; *In-der-Welt-Sein*: Being-in-the-world. [Eds.]

[21] A term employed by *Husserl*. [Eds.]

[22] Douglas Berggren, "The Use and Abuse of Metaphor," *Review of Metaphysics* 16 (December 1962): 243. [Au.]

to the image is homogeneous to the paradoxical structure of the cognitive process of reference. The "it was and it was not" of the Majorca storytellers rules both the split reference of the metaphorical statement and the contradictory structure of fiction. Yet, we may say as well that the structure of the fiction not only reflects but completes the logical structure of the split reference. The poet is this genius who generates split references *by* creating fictions. It is in fiction that the "absence" proper to the power of suspending what we call "reality" in ordinary language concretely coalesces and fuses with the *positive insight* into the potentialities of our being in the world which our everyday transactions with manipulatable objects tend to conceal.

You may have noticed that until now I have said nothing concerning feelings in spite of the commitment implied in this paper's title to deal with the problem of the connection between cognition, imagination, *and* feeling. I have no intention to elude this problem.

Imagination and feeling have always been closely linked in classical theories of metaphor. We cannot forget that rhetoric has always been defined as a strategy of discourse aiming at persuading and pleasing. And we know the central role played by pleasure in the aesthetics of Kant. A theory of metaphor, therefore, is not complete if it does not give an account of the place and role of feeling in the metaphorical process.

My contention is that feeling has a place not just in theories of metaphor which deny the *cognitive* import of metaphor. These theories ascribe a substitutive role to image and feeling due to the metaphor's lack of informative value. In addition, I claim that feeling as well as imagination are genuine components in the process described in an interaction theory of metaphor. They both *achieve* the semantic bearing of metaphor.

I have already tried to show the way in which a *psychology* of imagination has to be integrated into a semantics of metaphor. I will now try to extend the same kind of description to feeling. A bad psychology of imagination in which imagination is conceived as a residue of perception prevents us from acknowledging the constructive role of imagination. In the same way, a bad psychology of feeling is responsible for a similar misunderstanding. Indeed, our natural inclination is to speak of feeling in terms appropriate to emotion, that is, to affections conceived as (1) inwardly directed states of mind, and (2) mental experiences closely tied to bodily disturbances, as is the case in fear, anger, pleasure, and pain. In fact both traits come together. To the extent that in emotion we are, so to speak, under the spell of our body, we are delivered to mental states with little intentionality, as though in emotion we "lived" our body in a more intense way.

Genuine feelings are not emotions, as may be shown by feelings which are rightly called *poetic feelings*. Just like the corresponding images which they reverberate, they enjoy a specific kinship with language. They are properly displayed by the poem as a verbal texture. But how are they linked to its meaning?

I suggest that we construe the role of feeling according to the three similar moments which provided an articulation to my theory of imagination.

Feelings, first, accompany and complete imagination in its function of *schematization* of the new predicative congruence. This schematization, as I said, is a kind of insight into the mixture of "like" and "unlike" proper to similarity. Now we may say that this instantaneous grasping of the new congruence is "felt" as well as "seen." By saying that it is felt, we underscore the fact that we are included in the process as knowing subjects. If the process can be called, as I called it, predicative *assimilation*, it is true that *we* are assimilated, that is, made similar, to what is seen as similar. This self-assimilation is a part of the commitment proper to the "illocutionary" force of the metaphor as speech act. We feel *like* what we see *like*.

If we are somewhat reluctant to acknowledge this contribution of feeling to the illocutionary act of metaphorical statements, it is because we keep applying to feeling our usual interpretation of emotion as both inner and bodily states. We then miss the specific structure of feeling. As Stephan Strasser shows in *Das Gemut* [The heart], a feeling is a second-order intentional structure.[23] It is a process of interiorization succeeding a movement of intentional transcendence directed toward some objective state of affairs. To *feel*, in the emotional sense of the word, is to make *ours* what has been put at a distance by thought in its objectifying phase. Feel-

[23] Stephen Strasser, *Das Gemut* (Freiberg, 1956). [Au.]

ings, therefore, have a very complex kind of intentionality. They are not merely inner states but interiorized thoughts. It is as such that they accompany and complete the work of imagination as schematizing a synthetic operation: they make the schematized thought ours. Feeling, then, is a case of *Selbst-Affektion,* in the sense Kant used it in the second edition of *Critique.* This *Selbst-Affektion,* in turn, is a part of what we call poetic feeling. Its function is to abolish the distance between knower and known without canceling the cognitive structure of thought and the intentional distance which it implies. Feeling is not contrary to thought. It is thought made ours. This felt participation is a part of its complete meaning as poem.

Feelings, furthermore, accompany and complete imagination as *picturing* relationships. This aspect of feeling has been emphasized by Northrop Frye in *Anatomy of Criticism* under the designation of "mood." Each poem, he says, structures a mood which is *this* unique mood generated by *this* unique string of words. In that sense, it is coextensive to the verbal structure itself. The mood is nothing other than the way in which the poem affects us as an *icon.* Frye offers strong expression here: "The unity of a poem is the unity of a mood"; the poetic images "express or articulate this mood. This mood is the poem and nothing else behind it."[24] In my own terms, I would say, in a tentative way, that the mood is *the iconic as felt.* Perhaps we could arrive at the same assumption by starting from Goodman's concept of *dense* vs. *discrete* symbols. Dense symbols are felt as dense. That does not mean, once more, that feelings are radically opaque and ineffable. "Density" is a mode of articulation just as discreteness is. Or, to speak in Pascal's terms, the "esprit de finesse" is no less thought than the "esprit géometrique." However, I leave these suggestions open to discussion.

Finally, the most important function of feelings can be construed according to the third feature of imagination, that is, its contribution to the split reference of poetic discourse. The imagination contributes to it, as I said, owing to its own split structure. On the one hand, imagination entails the *epoché,* the suspension, of the direct reference of thought to the objects of our ordinary discourse. On the other hand, imagination provides *models for* reading reality in a new way. This split structure is the structure of imagination as fiction.

What could be the counterpart and the complement of this split structure at the level of feelings? My contention is that feelings, too, display a split structure which completes the split structure pertaining to the cognitive component of metaphor.

On the one hand, feelings—I mean poetic feelings—imply a kind of *epoché* of our bodily emotions. Feelings are negative, suspensive experiences in relation to the literal emotions of everyday life. When we read, we do not literally feel fear or anger. Just as poetic language denies the first-order reference of descriptive discourse to ordinary objects of our concern, feelings deny the first-order feelings which tie us to these first-order objects of reference.

But this denial, too, is only the reverse side of a more deeply rooted operation of feeling which is to insert us within the world in a nonobjectifying manner. That feelings are not merely the denial of emotions but their metamorphosis has been explicitly asserted by Aristotle in his analysis of catharsis. But this analysis remains trivial as long as it is not interpreted in relation to the split reference of the cognitive and the imaginative function of poetic discourse. It is the tragic poem itself, as thought (*dianoia*), which displays specific feelings which are the poetic transposition—I mean the transposition by means of poetic *language*—of fear and compassion, that is, of feelings of the first order, of emotions. The tragic *phobos* and the tragic *eleos* (terror and pity, as some translators say) are both the denial and the transfiguration of the literal feelings of fear and compassion.

On the basis of this analysis of the split structure of poetic feeling, it is possible to do justice to a certain extent to a claim of Heidegger's analytic of the *Dasein* that feelings have *ontological* bearing, that they are ways of "being-there," of "finding" ourselves within the world, to keep something of the semantic intent of the German *Befindlichkeit.* Because of feelings we are "attuned to" aspects of reality which cannot be expressed in terms of the objects referred to in ordinary language. Our entire analysis of the split reference of both language and feeling is in agreement with this claim. But it must be underscored that this analysis of *Befindlichkeit*

[24] Northrop Frye, *Anatomy of Criticism: Four Essays* (Princeton, 1957). [Au.] See *CTSP,* p. 1123. [Eds.]

makes sense only to the extent that it is paired with that of split reference both in verbal and imaginative structures. If we miss this fundamental connection, we are tempted to construe this concept of *Befindlichkeit* as a new kind of intuitionism—and the worst kind!—in the form of a new emotional realism. We miss, in Heidegger's *Daseinanalyse* itself, the close connections between *Befindlichkeit* and *Verstehen,* between situation and project, between anxiety and interpretation. The ontological bearing of feeling cannot be separated from the negative process applied to the first-order emotions, such as fear and sympathy, according to the Aristotelian paradigm of catharsis. With this qualification in mind, we may assume the Heideggerian thesis that it is mainly through feelings that we are attuned to reality. But this attunement is nothing else than the reverberation in terms of feelings of the split reference of both verbal and imaginative structure.

To conclude, I would like to emphasize the points which I submit to discussion:

1. There are three main *presuppositions* on which the rest of my analysis relies: (*a*) metaphor is an act of *predication* rather than of *denomination;* (*b*) a theory of deviance is not enough to give an account of the emergence of a *new congruence* at the predicative level; and (*c*) the notion of metaphorical sense is not complete without a description of the *split reference* which is specific to poetic discourse.
2. On this threefold basis, I have tried to show that imagination and feeling are not extrinsic to the emergence of the metaphorical sense and of the split reference. They are not substitutive for a lack of informative content in metaphorical statements, but they complete their full cognitive intent.
3. *But* the price to pay for the last point is a theory of imagination and of feeling which is still in infancy. The burden of my argument is that the notion of *poetic image* and of *poetic feeling* has to be construed in accordance with the cognitive component, understood itself as a tension between congruence and incongruence at the level of sense, between *epoché* and commitment at the level of reference.
4. My paper suggests that there is a *structural analogy* between the cognitive, the imaginative, and the emotional components of the complete metaphorical act and that the metaphorical process draws its concreteness and its completeness from this structural analogy and this complementary functioning.

M. H. Abrams

b. 1912

WITH THE appearance of his *The Mirror and the Lamp,* a study of critical theory of the romantic period, M. H. Abrams became known as a lucid and thorough scholar of the thought of that age. His second major book, *Natural Supernaturalism,* was an impressive overview of romantic literature. Throughout his career Abrams has produced important essays, mainly on romantic poetry, but in his later work he has entered the contemporary theoretical wars with essays that are openly critical of developments occurring around deconstruction and the question of whether determinate meaning is possible. In a well-known essay "The Deconstructive Angel" (*Critical Inquiry* 3 [1977]), Abrams took as his target in particular the later deconstructive writings of *J. Hillis Miller,* who responded in the essay in this volume.

This selection of Abrams's is a critique of the work of *Jacques Derrida, Stanley Fish,* and *Harold Bloom.* Critical of all three, he is nevertheless able to provide, in his characteristic way, a clear description of the positions they hold. Abrams recognizes their differences, but he sees one overarching similarity among them, and he does not like it. That is their common rejection of presumptions about the meaning of literary texts, indeed of all texts, that have been fairly commonly held by traditional humanists—that authors had something to say which they conveyed in such a way within a tradition of linguistic conventions as to make possible the assumption that their meaning could be construed by a reader. Abrams does not imply that new readings cannot reasonably arise. He holds that we read according to the linguistic strategy employed by the author of the work, and clearly he believes that in situations where a past text provides special difficulties this strategy is theoretically recoverable by the work of humanistic scholarship.

Abrams's principal works are *The Mirror and the Lamp: Romantic Theory and the Critical Tradition* (1953); *Natural Supernaturalism: Tradition and Revolution in Romantic Literature* (1971); and *The Correspondent Breeze* (1984), a collection of essays on romanticism. See Wayne Booth, "M. H. Abrams: Historian as Critic, Critic as Pluralist," *Critical Inquiry* 2 (Spring 1976).

HOW TO DO THINGS WITH TEXTS

The Age of Criticism, which reached its zenith in the mid-decades of this century, has given way to the Age of Reading, and whereas the American new critics and European formalists of the Age of Criticism discovered the work-as-such, current literary theorists have discovered the reader-as-such. This reader, as everyone knows who has kept even cursorily in touch with the latest Paris fashions, is not the man he used to be. He is a wraith of his old self, stripped of everything human, as part of a systematic dehumanizing of all aspects of the traditional view about how a work of literature comes into being, what it is, how it is read, and what it means.

For purpose of comparison, let me sketch the salient and persistent features of the traditional, or humanistic paradigm of the writing and reading of literature. The writer is conceived, in Wordsworth's terms, as "a man speaking to men." Literature, in other words, is a transaction between a human author and his human reader. By his command of linguistic and literary possibilities, the author actualizes and records in words what he undertakes to signify of human beings and actions and about matters of human concern, addressing himself to those readers who are competent to understand what he has written. The reader sets himself to make out what the author has designed and signified, through putting into play a linguistic and literary expertise that he shares with the author. By approximating what the author undertook to signify the reader understands what the language of the work means.

In our Age of Reading, the first casualty in this literary transaction has been the author. To the noninitiate, it is bemusing to observe the complacency with which authors of recent books and essays announce their own demise. "It is about time," says Michel Foucault, "that criticism and philosophy acknowledged the disappearance or the death of the author."[1] "As institution," according to Roland Barthes, "the author is dead: his civil status, his biographical person, have disappeared."[2] The necrology extends to the human reader, and indeed to man himself, who is reduced to an illusion engendered by the play of language, or as Foucault puts it, to "a simple fold in our knowledge," destined to "disappear as soon as that knowledge has found a new form."[3] In these new writings about reading, accordingly, the author deliquesces into writing-as-such and the reader into reading-as-such, and what writing-as-such effects and reading-as-such engages is not a work of literature but a text, writing, *écriture*.[4] In its turn the text forfeits its status as a purposeful utterance about human beings and human concerns, and even its individuality, becoming simply an episode in an all-encompassing textuality—dissolved, as Edward Said has remarked, into "the communal sea of linguicity."[5] Consonantly, the relations between authors which had traditionally been known as "influence" are depersonalized into "intertextuality," a reverberation between ownerless sequences of signs.

It might be expected that, evacuated of its humanity, reading-as-such would become an interplay of bloodless abstractions. Quite to the contrary. We find in French structuralist criticism and its American analogues that reading is a perilous adventure—not of a soul among masterpieces,[6] but of the unsouled reading-process as it engages with the text-as-such. Persistently this inhuman encounter is figured in a rhetoric of extremity, as tense with the awareness of risk and crisis; anguished by doubts about its very possibility; meeting everywhere in the "*action du signifiant*"[7] with violence, disruption, castration, mysterious disappearances, murder, self-destruction; or as overcome by vertigo as the ground falls away and leaves it suspended over an abyss of recessive meanings in a referential void. In this Gothic context of the horrors of reading it is a relief to come upon Roland Barthes's *The Plea-*

HOW TO DO THINGS WITH TEXTS is reprinted from *Partisan Review* (1979) by permission of the author.

[1] See *Foucault* on the subject of the author. [Eds.]

[2] Barthes, *The Pleasure of the Text* (New York: Hill and Wang, 1975), p. 27. On Barthes see *CTSP*, pp. 1195–99. [Eds.]

[3] See Foucault, *The Order of Things* (New York: Pantheon Books, 1971). [Eds.]

[4] *Écriture*, a term employed freely in structuralism and poststructuralism, especially in the work of Barthes and *Derrida*. [Eds.]

[5] *Beginnings: Intention and Method* (New York: Basic Books, 1975), pp. 279–343. [Eds.]

[6] Abrams is quoting from Anatole France. See *CTSP*, p. 671. [Eds.]

[7] "Action of the signifier." [Eds.]

sure of the Text, with its seeming promise to revive the notion, as old as Aristotle and Horace, that the distinctive aim of a literary work is to give pleasure to its readers.[8] But then we find in Barthes's account that the pleasure is not in the artful management of the human agents, interactions, and passions signified by the text, but in the engagement with the text-as-such, and that Barthes adapts the traditional concept to current connoisseurs of textuality by a running conceit sustained by double entendres, in which textual pleasure is assimilated to sexual pleasure; the prime distinction is between the mere *plaisir* effected by a comfortably traditional text and the orgasmic rapture, *jouissance,* in the close encounter with a radical "modern" text which, by foiling the reader's expectations, "brings to a crisis his relations with language." It seems safe to predict that the innocent reader, seduced by Barthes's erotics of the text, who engages with a *nouveau roman* is in for a disappointment.

My concern, however, is with the strategy and the rhetorical tactics of structuralist criticism only as a background for considering three current writers who put forward radical new ways of reading texts. One, Jacques Derrida, is a French philosopher with an increasing following among American critics of literature; by pressing to an extreme the tendencies of structuralism, Derrida proposes a mode of reading which undermines not only the grounds of structuralism itself, but the possibility of understanding language as a medium of decidable meanings.[9] The other two, Stanley Fish and Harold Bloom, are Americans who set their theories of reading in opposition to what they decry as the antihumanism of structuralist procedures.[10] All three are erudite, formidable, and influential innovators who found their strategies of reading on an insight into a neglected aspect of what enters into the interpretation of a text. These theorists differ, we shall see, in essential respects, but they share important features which are distinctive of current radicalism in interpretation. In each, the theory doesn't undertake simply to explain how we in fact read, but to propagate a new way of reading that subverts accepted interpretations and replaces them with unexpected alternatives. Each theory eventuates in a radical scepticism about our ability to achieve a correct interpretation, proposing instead that reading should free itself from illusory linguistic constraints in order to become liberated, creative, producing the meanings that it makes rather than discovers. And all three theories are suicidal; for as the theorist is aware, his views are self-reflexive, in that his subversive process destroys the possibility that a reader can interpret correctly either the expression of his theory or the textual interpretations to which it is applied.

It is worth noting that such Newreading—by which I denote a principled procedure for replacing standard meanings by new meanings—is by no means recent, but had many precedents in Western hermeneutics. We find such a procedure, for example, in ancient Greek and Roman attempts to uncover the deep truths hidden within Homer's surface myths and fictions, and to moralize the immoral tales of Ovid; we find it also in the reinterpretations of the Old Testament by writers of the New Testament, as well as by Jewish Kabbalists; we find a similar procedure in medieval and later exegetes of the many-leveled allegorical meanings in the entire biblical canon. These old reinterpretive enterprises, however diverse, all manifest three procedural moments, or aspects: (1) The interpreter indicates that he understands the standard, or accepted meanings of a text or passage (called by biblical exegetes "the literal meaning"). (2) He replaces, or at least supplements, these standard meanings by new meanings. (3) He mediates between these two systems of signification by setting up a transformational calculus which serves to convert the old meanings into his new meanings. We can, I think, discern a parallel procedure in our current Newreaders. In considering their proposals, I shall ask the following questions. What sort of things does each Newreader undertake to do with texts? By what transformational devices does he manage to do these things? And then there is the general question: What is there about the way language functions that enables a Newreader to accomplish the surprising things he does with texts?

The Science of Nescience: Jacques Derrida

How is one to make entry into the theory of Jacques Derrida, the most elusive, equivocal, and studiously noncommittal of philosophical writers? I shall try

[8] Aristotle, *CTSP,* p. 56; Horace, *CTSP,* pp. 67–75. [Eds.]
[9] See *Derrida.* [Eds.]
[10] See *Fish* and *Bloom.* [Eds.]

to break through with a crashing generalization: As a philosopher of language, Derrida is an absolutist without absolutes.

Derrida proposes that both the Western use of language and philosophies of language are "logocentric"; that they are logocentric because essentially "phonocentric" (that is, giving priority and privilege to speech over writing); and that language is thereby permeated, explicitly and implicitly, by what, in a phrase from Heidegger, he calls "the metaphysics of presence." By "presence"—or in alternative terms, a "transcendental signified" or "ultimate referent"—he designates what I call an absolute; that is, a foundation outside the play of language itself which is immediately and simply present to us as something ultimate, terminal, self-certifying, and thus adequate to "center" the structure of the linguistic system and to guarantee the determinate meaning of an utterance within that system. The positing of some form of presence, it is suggested, is the expression of a desire—which is the motivating desire of metaphysics—to establish a conceptual replacement for the certainty about language and meaning provided by the myth in *Genesis* of language as originated and guaranteed by a divine, hence absolute, authority, or else by the theological view that language is certified by the omnipresence of the Logos. In a remarkable series of readings of diverse texts, philosophical and literary, Derrida subtly uncovers the presupposition that there is an absolute foundation for language, and displays the internal paradoxes and self-contradictions that are attendant upon such a presupposition. The quest for presence, then, is doomed to unsuccess, whether that supposed absolute is the presence of his meaning to the consciousness of the speaker at the instant of his utterance; or Platonic essences that underwrite the significations of verbal names; or a fixed and simple referent, "the thing itself," in the world "outside of language"; or Heidegger's "Being" as the ultimate ground of signification and understanding. But having, in the critical aspect of his reading of texts, dismantled the traditional absolutes, Derrida remains committed to absolutism; for he shares the presupposition of the views he deconstructs that to be determinately understandable, language requires an absolute foundation, and that, since there is no such ground, there is no stop to the play of undecidable meanings: "The absence of a transcendental signified extends the realm and the play of signification to infinity."[11] In this aspect of his dealings with language, Derrida's writings present variations on a Nietzschean theme: Absolutes, though necessary, are dead, therefore free play is permitted.

It should be remarked, however, that the philosophy of language offers an alternative to the supposition that language requires an absolute foundation in order to be determinately meaningful. This alternative sets out from the observation that in practice language often works, that it gets its job done. We live a life in which we have assurance that we are able to mean what we say and know what we mean, and in which our auditors or readers show us by their verbal and actional responses whether or not they have understood us correctly. This alternative stance takes as its task not to explain away these workings of language, but to explain how it is that they happen, and in instances of failure, to inquire what it is that has gone wrong. A prominent recent exemplar of this stance is the *Philosophical Investigations* of Ludwig Wittgenstein.[12] There are similarities between Wittgenstein's views of language and Derrida's, in the critical aspect of Derrida's reading of philosophical texts. Like Derrida, for example, Wittgenstein insists that it is not possible to use language to get outside "the limits of language"; he holds that the concept that language directly represents reality is simply "a picture that holds us captive"; he rejects the account of the meaning of an utterance in terms of the objects or processes to which its words refer, or as equivalent to the conscious state of the speaker of the utterance; and, in his own way, he too deconstructs the traditional absolutes, or "essences," of Western metaphysics. He also rejects as futile the quest for an ultimate foundation for language. Philosophy, he says, "can in the end only describe" the "actual use of language," for it "cannot give it any foundation"; in giving reasons for the working of language, "the spade turns" before we reach an ultimate reason. But Wittgenstein's stance is that language is "a practice" that occurs as part of a shared "form of life," and that this practice works; as he puts it, "this game is played." His *Investigations* are designed to get us to recognize when language works, and when it doesn't—"when language is like an engine idling,

[11] See *Derrida*. [Eds.]
[12] See *Wittgenstein*. [Eds.]

not when it is doing work"—to get us to understand how the slippage occurred.

Derrida of course acknowledges that language works, or as he puts it, that it "functions"—that we constantly perform what we take to be successful speech acts and successful instances of oral communication, and that a written text is *lisible*, "legible," that is, strikes us as having determinably specific meanings. But he accounts for this working as no more than "the *effects* of ideality, of signification, of meaning and of reference"—effects which are engendered by the play of differences within language itself; he then proceeds to "deconstruct" these effects by undertaking to show that, since they lack a ground in presence, their specificity of meaning is only a simulation. Derrida's procedure might be summarized as follows. He agrees that language works, then asks, "But is it possible that it really works?" He concludes that, lacking an ultimate ground, it is absolutely not possible that it works, hence that its working is only a seeming—that, in short, though texts may be legible, they are not intelligible, or determinately significant.

Of each of the traditional terms and distinctions used to analyze the working of language—terms such as "communication," "context," "intention," "meaning," and oppositions such as speech-writing, literal-metaphorical, nonfictional-fictional—Derrida requires not only that they be grounded in absolute presence, but also that they be certified by criteria of what he calls "ideal purity" and "ultimate rigor" if they are to be determinately used and understood. For example: in order to communicate "a determinate content, an identifiable meaning," each of these words must signify a concept "that is unique, univocal, rigorously controllable," and its contextual conditions of use must be "absolutely determinable" and "entirely certain"; while the utterance of a determinate speech act must be tied to "the pure singularity of the event." Of course such analytic words cannot meet these criteria of absolute fixity, purity, and singularity, nor can any words, for it is an essential condition of a language that a finite set of words, manageable in accordance with a finite set of regularities, be capable of generating an unlimited variety of utterances adaptable to an unlimited diversity of circumstances, purposes, and applications. But Derrida's all-or-none principle admits of no alternative: failing to meet absolute criteria which language cannot satisfy without ceasing to do its work, all spoken and written utterances, though they may give the "effect" of determinate significance, are deconstructable into semantic indeterminacy.

Derrida describes his "general strategy of deconstruction" as a mode of "double writing": it first "inverts" the hierarchy of the terms in standard philosophical oppositions such as speech-writing, signifier-signified, then it "displaces" what was the lower term in the hierarchy (or a derivative from that term) "outside the oppositions in which it was held." The latter move generates, in place of the standard terms used to analyze the workings of language, a set of new terms which, he says, are neither words nor concepts, neither signifiers nor signifieds. These invented pseudoterms, however, although "displaced" from their locus within the system of language, nonetheless are capable of producing "conceptual effects"; and these effects operate in two dimensions. On the one side, they account for the fact that texts are "legible," yielding the effects of seemingly determinable meanings. On the other side, they serve as what I have called a set of transformers, which Derrida employs to "disseminate" these effects into their deconstructed alternatives.

The chief transformer is *différance*[13]—Saussure's key term "différence,"[14] twice-born and re-spelled with an "a"—which conflates "difference" and "deferment." In one aspect of its functioning, the "differences" among signs and among the conditions of their use explain how they generate their apparently specific significations; in its deconstructive aspect, it points to the fact that, since these significations can never come to rest in an absolute presence, their specification is deferred from substitute sign to substitute sign in a movement without end. Similarly with the other nonwords for nonentities with which Derrida replaces standard terms for dealing with language; in place of the spoken utterance or written text, the "general text" or "proto-writing"; in place of the word, "mark" or "grapheme"; in place of significance, "dissemination" or a large number of other "nicknames" that Derrida resourcefully coins, or else adapts to his equivocal purpose from common usage. All in their double function account for the legibility of a text at the same time that they "open" the apparent clo-

[13] See *Derrida*. [Eds.]
[14] See *de Saussure*. [Eds.]

sure of the text "*en abyme,*" into the abyss of an endless regress of ever-promised, never-delivered meaning.

Derrida emphasizes that to deconstruct is not to destroy; that his task is to "dismantle the metaphysical and rhetorical structures" operative in a text "not in order to reject or discard them, but to reconstitute them in another way"; that he puts into question the "search for the signified not to annul it, but to understand it within a system to which such a reading is blind." He can in fact be designated as, on principle, a double-dealer in language, working ambidextrously with two semantic orders—the standard and the deconstructed. He writes essays and books, and engages in symposia and in debates, that put forward his deconstructive strategy and exemplify it by deconstructing the texts of other writers. In this deconstruction of logocentric language he assumes the stance that this language works, that he can adequately understand what other speakers and writers mean, and that competent auditors and readers will adequately understand him. In this double process of construing in order to deconstrue he perforce adopts words from the logocentric system; but he does so, he tells us, only "provisionally," or *sous rature,* "under erasure." At times he reminds us of this pervasive procedure by writing a key word but crossing it out, leaving it "legible" yet "effaced"—an ingenious doublespeak, adapted from Heidegger, that enables him to eat his words yet use them too.

Derrida's double-dealing with texts is all-inclusive, for he is aware that his deconstructive reading is self-reflexive; that, although "exorbitant" in intention, it cannot in fact escape the orbit of the linguistic system it deconstructs. "Operating necessarily from the inside," as he says, "the enterprise of deconstruction always in a certain way falls prey to its own work." The invented nonwords which serve as his instruments of deconstruction not only are borrowed from language, but are immediately reappropriated into language in the process of their "iteration" (in Derrida's double sense of being "repeated" and therefore "other" than absolutely self-identical). And the deconstructive reading these instruments effect, he says, is a "production," but "does not leave the text. . . . And what we call production is necessarily a text, the system of a writing and a reading which we know is ordered by its own blind spot." Even as they are put to work on a text, accordingly, the deconstructive instruments deconstruct themselves, as well as the deconstructed translation of the original text which Derrida, as deconstructor, has no option except to write down as still another deconstructible text.

Derrida's critical lexicon, therefore, as Gayatri Spivak, his translator, has said, "is forever on the move." In the consciously vain endeavor to find a point outside the logocentric system on which to plant his deconstructive lever, he leaps from neologism to neologism, as each sinks beneath his feet *en abyme.* His deconstructive enterprise thus is a bootstrap operation, a deliberate exercise in ultimate futility, in a genre of writing he has almost single-handedly invented—the serious philosophy of the absurd. The most earnest and innovative passages in Derrida are those which, on the surface, seem at best playful and at worst embarrassingly arch—passages which deploy grotesque puns, distorted words, false etymologies, genital analogues, and sexual jokes; which insist in our attending to the shapes of printed letters, play endless tricks with Derrida's own name and with his written signature; or collocate wildly incongruous texts. In such passages—extended to the length of a nonbook in his *Glas*—Derrida is the Zen master of Western philosophy, undertaking to shock us out of our habitual linguistic categories in order to show what cannot be told without reappropriation into those categories: what it is to experience a text not as conveying significance, but as simply a chain of marks vibrating with the free and incessant play of *différance.*

Occasionally, however, Derrida ventures the attempt to tell what can't be told, that is, to make his deconstructive concepts, although "in intimate relationship to the machine whose deconstruction they permit," nonetheless "designate the crevice through which the yet unnameable glimmer beyond the closure can be glimpsed." This glimpse is of an apocalyptic new world which, he prophesies, will be effected by the total deconstruction of our logocentric language-world—"the ineluctable world of the future which proclaims itself at present, beyond the closure of knowledge," hence cannot be described but only "proclaimed, *presented,* as a sort of monstrosity."

To realize the inclusiveness of the new world thus

proclaimed, we need to keep in mind what Derrida calls "the axial proposition" in *Of Grammatology,* his basic theoretical work: *Il n'y a pas d' hors-texte,* "there is no outside-the-text." Like all Derrida's key assertions, this sentence is multiple in significance. In one aspect, it says we can't get outside the written text we are reading—it is a closure in which both its seeming author and the people and objects to which the text seems to refer are merely "effects" engendered by the internal action of *différance.* In another aspect, it says that there is nothing in the world which is not itself a text, since we never experience a "thing itself," but only as it is interpreted. In this inclusive rendering, then, all the world's a text, and men and women merely readers—except that the readers, according to Derrida, as "subjects," "egos," "cogitos," are themselves effects which are engendered by an interpretation; so that in the process of undoing texts, we undo our textual selves. The apocalyptic glimpse, it would seem, is of a totally textual universe whose reading is a mode of intertextuality whereby a subject-vortex engages with an object-abyss in infinite regressions of deferred significations.

At the end of his essay "Structure, Sign and Play,"[15] Derrida hazards his most sustained endeavor in the vain attempt to put names to "the as yet unnameable which cannot announce itself except . . . under the formless form, mute, infant, and terrifying, of monstrosity." The annunciation is of "a world of signs without error, without truth, without origin, which is offered to an active interpretation," in which one "plays without security" in a game of "absolute chance, surrendering oneself to *genetic* indeterminacy, the *seminal* chanciness of the trace." Derrida suggests that we at least try to overcome our age-old nostalgia for security, with its hopeless dream of an absolute ground in "full presence, the reassuring foundation, the origin and end of the play," and to assume instead toward this prophecy of deconstruction triumphant the nonchalance of the *Übermensch,* "the Nietzschean *affirmation,* the joyous affirmation of the freeplay of the world." If one cannot share the joy, one can at least acknowledge the vertigo effected by Derrida's vision, yet take some reassurance in the thought that, even in a sign-world of absolute indeterminacy, it will presumably still be possible to achieve the "effect" of telling a hawk from a handsaw, or the "effect," should the need arise, of identifying and warning a companion against an onrushing autobus.

Reading Between the Words: Stanley Fish

Of the deconstructive "interpretation of interpretation" Derrida remarks that it "attempts to pass beyond man and humanism." Stanley Fish represents his theory of reading as a ringing defense against "the dehumanization of meaning" in the "formalism" of current linguistics and stylistics, as well as in structuralist criticism, which raises "the implied antihumanism of other formalist ideologies to a principle." Such theory "is distinguished by what it does away with, and what it does away with are human beings." Fish himself undertakes to explain meaning by reference to "the specifically human activity of reading," proposing as his humanistic "point of departure the interpretive activity (experience) by virtue of which meanings occur." His model for interpretation is that of a reader who confronts the marks on a page and generates meanings by his informed responses to it. In the traditional humanistic view, it will be recalled, there is an author who records what he undertakes to signify, as well as a reader who undertakes to understand what the author has signified. In terms of this paradigm, Fish's rehumanization of reading is only a half-humanism, for it begins by diminishing, and ends by deleting, the part played by the author. In Fish's later writings, we shall see, the reader becomes the only begetter not only of the text's meanings, but also of the author as the intentional producer of a meaningful text.[16]

Fish differs from other systematic Newreaders in that, instead of setting up a matrix of transformers—a set of revisionary terms—he proposes a "method" or "strategy" which is in fact a set of moves to be enacted by the reader in the process of construing a text. These moves are such as to yield meanings which are always surprising, and often

[15] See *Derrida.* [Eds.]

[16] The later essays of *Is There a Text in This Class?* See *Fish.* [Eds.]

antithetic to, what we have hitherto taken a text to mean. As the key to his method, he proposes that we replace our usual question while reading—"What does this sentence (or words, phrase, work) mean?"—by what he calls "the magic question," namely: "What does this sentence do?" The result of this magic question, if persistently applied by readers, is that it "transforms minds."

In all Fish's expositions of his method, however, "the key word," as he himself remarks, "is, of course, experience"; and what in fact works the transformative magic is his major premise, express and implied, "Reading is an experience." On the common assumption that the term "experience" can be predicated of any perception or process of which one is aware, this assertion seems self-evident, and innocent enough; it can, however, lead to dubious consequences when posed as the premise from which to draw philosophical conclusions. Take, for example, one of Fish's favorite sources of sentences to demonstrate his method of reading, Walter Pater's "Conclusion" to *The Renaissance*.[17] In one virtuoso paragraph, Pater begins by casually positing that the perception of all "external objects" is an "experience," then dissolves the experience of each object "into a group of impressions," translates this into "the impression of the individual in his isolation," and reduces it "to a single sharp impression" in a fleeting moment, bearing traces of "moments gone by"; to this, he asserts, "what is real in our life fines itself down." From the premise that everything we perceive is our experience, Pater has taken us headlong down the metaphysical slope to his conclusion of a solipsism of the specious present—that one can validly assert reality only for one's single sense-impression in a fugitive "Now!" The example should make us wary about the consequences for interpretation that Fish deduces from his premise that reading is an experience, and what he proposes as its immediate corollary—that "the meaning of an utterance . . . is the experience—all of it."

One conclusion that Fish draws from this claim that meaning is all of a reader's experience (all the experience, as he qualifies it, of a "competent" or "informed" reader) is that, since the "response includes everything" and is a "total meaning experience," you can't make valid use of the traditional distinction between subject matter and style, "process and product (the how and the what)" in an utterance. Another and related conclusion is that you can't distinguish, within the totality of a declarative sentence, what is being asserted. He excerpts, for example, from Pater's "conclusion" to *The Renaissance:* "That clear perpetual outline of face and limb is but an image of ours." In standard stylistic analysis, he says, this is "a simple declarative of the form X is Y." He then analyzes the experience of reading the sentence in accordance with the question, "What does it do?" and finds that "in fact it is not an assertion at all, although (the promise of) an assertion is one of its components. It is an experience; it occurs; it does something; . . . [and] what it does is what it means." Turn Fish's method of reading back upon his own writing (I find nothing in the method to prevent our doing so) and we get the interesting result that his assertion about Pater's sentence—"In fact it is not an assertion at all . . ."—is in fact not an assertion at all, but only an evolving experience effectuated in a reader.

I want to focus, however, on an important aspect of Fish's strategy for transforming accepted meanings. He supplements his basic equation of meaning with the reader's total response by proposing a start-stop-extrapolate method in reading:

> The basis of the method is a consideration of the *temporal* flow of the reading experience. . . . In an utterance of any length, there is a point at which the reader has taken in only the first word, and then the second, and then the third, and so on, and the report of what happens to the reader is always a report of what has happened *to that point*. (The report includes the reader's set toward future experiences, but not those experiences.)[18]

What happens at each stopping point, then, is that the reader makes sense of the word or words he has so far read, in large part by surmising what will come next. These surmises may, in the text's sequel, turn out to have been right, but they will often turn out to have been wrong; if so, "the resulting mistakes are part of the experience provided by the author's language, and therefore part of its meaning." Thus "the notion of a mistake, at least as something

[17] See Pater, *CTSP*, pp. 642–45. [Eds.]

[18] *Is There a Text in This Class?* (Cambridge: Harvard University Press, 1980). [Eds.]

to be avoided, disappears." And the point at which "the reader hazards interpretive closure" is independent of the "formal units" (such as syntactical phrases or clauses) or "physical features" (such as punctuation or verse lines) in the text written by the author; the method in fact creates what the reader takes to be formal features of the text, "because my model demands (the word is not too strong) perceptual closures and therefore locations at which they occur." In reading the sentence from Pater's *Renaissance,* for example, Fish hazards brief perceptual closures after each of the four opening words: "That clear perpetual outline . . ."

It is apparent that by Fish's start-stop strategy, a large part of a text's meaning consists of the false surmises that the reader generates in the temporal gaps between the words; and this part, it turns out, constitutes many of Fish's new readings. To cite one instance: Fish presents a three-line passage from Milton's *Lycidas* which describes one consequence of Lycidas's death:

> The willows and the hazel copses green
> Shall now no more be seen,
> Fanning their joyous leaves to thy soft lays.

Although, he tells us, it is "*merely* a coincidence" when a perceptual closure coincides with a formal unit or physical feature such as the end of a verse line, it happens in this instance that the reader's process of making sense "will involve the assumption (and therefore the creation) of a completed assertion after the word 'seen'" at the end of the second line; he will then hazard the interpretation that these trees, in sympathy with the death of Lycidas, "will wither and die (will no more be seen by anyone)." And though this interpretation will be undone "in the act of reading the next line," which reverses it by going on to say that they "will in fact be seen, but they will not be seen by Lycidas," the false surmise remains part of the text's meaning.

I recall a new reading of the closing couplet of *Lycidas* which William York Tindall of Columbia proposed to me many years ago. Tindall suggested the following perceptual closures (I cite the first edition of 1637):

> At last he rose, and twitch'd. His mantle
> blew.
> To morrow to fresh Woods, and Pastures
> new.[19]

Those who know Bill Tindall may suspect he was not wholly serious in this proposal. Yet according to Fish's strategy, it is the way a first reader might hazard his perceptual closures. The thought that, even after subsequent correction, this misreading remains an element in the poem's meaning is to me disquieting.

I have myself tried, by way of experiment, to read in accordance with Fish's method. By stern self-discipline, I managed to read word by word and to impose frequent perceptual closures, resisting the compulsion to peek ahead in order to see how the phrases and clauses would work out in the total sentence. And instead of suspending judgment as to meaning until the semantic *Gestalt* was complete, I solicited my invention to anticipate possible meanings and actuated my will to fix on a single one of these possibilities. The result was indeed an evolving sequence of false surmises. I found, however, that the places where I chose to stop rarely coincided with the stopping-places of Stanley Fish, and that my false surmises rarely matched his, especially in the startling degree to which they diverged from what actually followed in the text. What am I to conclude? A possible conjecture is that Fish himself has not always resisted the impulse to peek ahead; that in fact many of his novel readings are not prospective, but retrospective; that in local instances they are the result of a predisposition to generate surprising meanings between the words; and that in large-scale instances, when he presents a new reading of a total literary work, they are the result of a predisposition to generate a system of surprising meanings of a coherent sort.

In his earlier writings, despite some wavering as to what is implied by his use of the term "method," Fish represented his analyses primarily as a description of what competent readers in fact do; its aim was simply to make "available to analytic consciousness the strategies readers perform, independently of whether or not they are aware of having performed them." In his recent theoretical writings, however, Fish asks us to take his method not as "de-

[19]The lines read: "At last he rose, and twitch'd his Mantle blue: / Tomorrow to fresh Woods, and Pastures new." [Eds.]

scriptive" but "prescriptive"; its aim now is to persuade us to give up reading in our customary way and instead to "read in a new or different way." Fish's current views are an extreme form of methodological relativism, in which the initial choice of a method of reading is "arbitrary," and the particular method that the reader elects creates the text and meanings that he mistakenly thinks he finds. "Interpretive strategies" are procedures "not for reading (in the conventional sense) but for writing texts, for constituting their properties and assigning their intentions." "Formal units," and even "the 'facts' of grammar," are "always a function of the interpretive will one brings to bear; they are not 'in' the text." It turns out, indeed, that there is nothing either inside or outside the text except what our elected strategy brings into being, for "everyone is continually executing interpretive strategies and in that act constituting texts, intentions, speakers, and authors." Starting with the premise that the meaning is all of a reader's experience of a text, we have plunged down the metaphysical slope to the conclusion that each reader's optional strategy, by determining his responsive experience, creates everything but the marks on the page, including the author whose intentional verbal acts, we had mistakenly assumed, effectuate the text as meaningful discourse.

From this position Fish draws the consequence that, since all reading strategies are self-confirming, there is no "right reading" of any part of a text; there are only agreements among readers who belong to an "interpretive community" which happens to share the same strategy. And with his usual acumen, Fish acknowledges that the reading strategy he himself proposes is no less "arbitrary" in its adoption and therefore no less a "fiction" than alternative ways of reading; his justification for urging it upon us is that it is "a superior fiction." It is superior because it is "more coherent" in the relation of its practice to its principles, and because "it is also creative." Insistence on a "right reading" and "the real text" are

> the fictions of formalism, and as fictions they have the disadvantage of being confining. My fiction is liberating. It relieves me of the obligation to be right (a standard that simply drops out) and demands only that I be interesting (a standard that can be met without any reference at all to an illusory objectivity). Rather than restoring or recovering texts, I am in the business of making texts and of teaching others to make them by adding to their repertoire of strategies.

In these claims Fish does his own critical practice less than justice. Many of his close readings of literary texts effect in his readers a shock of recognition which is the sign that they are not merely interesting, but that they are right. In such readings, however, he escapes his own theory and reads as other competent readers do, only more expertly than many of us; his orientation to the actual process of reading serves in these instances to sensitize him to nuances effected by the author's choice and order of words that we have hitherto missed. And even when, in conformity with his stated strategy, Fish creates meanings by reading between the words, the new readings are often, as he claims, interesting. They are interesting because they are bravura critical performances by a learned, resourceful, and witty intelligence, and not least, because the new readings never entirely depart from implicit reliance on the old way of reading texts.

I remain unpersuaded, therefore, that the hermeneutic circle is inescapably, as Fish represents it, a vicious circle—a closed interplay between a reader's arbitrary strategy and his interpretive findings. I persist in the assurance that a competent reader of Milton, for example, develops an expertise in reading his sentences in adequate accordance both with Milton's linguistic usage and with the strategy of reading that Milton himself deployed, and assumed that his readers would deploy. This expertise is not an arbitrary strategy—though it remains continuously open to correction and refinement—for it has a sufficient warrant in evidence that we tacitly accumulate in a lifetime of speaking, writing, and reading English, of reading English literature, of reading Milton's contemporaries, and of reading Milton himself. Those who share this assurance set themselves to read Milton's text, not as pretext for a creative adventure in liberated interpretation, but in order to understand what it is that Milton meant, and meant us to understand. For our prepossession is that, no matter how interesting a critic's created text of Milton may be, it will be less interesting than the text that Milton himself wrote for his fit readers though few.

The Scene of Literature: Harold Bloom

Harold Bloom's theory of reading and writing literature centers on the area that Derrida and the structuralists call "intertextuality." Bloom, however, employs the traditional term "influence," and presents his theory in opposition against "the anti-humanistic plain dreariness of all those developments in European criticism that have yet to demonstrate that they can aid in reading any one poem by any poet whatsoever." "Poems," he affirms, "are written by men"; and against "the partisans of *writing* . . . like Derrida and Foucault who imply . . . that language by itself writes the poem and thinks," he insists that only "the human writes, the human thinks." Unlike Stanley Fish, then, Bloom restores the human writer as well as reader to an effective role in the literary transaction. But if Fish's theory is a half-humanism, Bloom's is all-too-human, for it screens out from both the writing and reading of "strong" literature all motives except self-concern and all compunction about giving free rein to one's will to power:

> . . . the living labyrinth of literature is built upon the ruin of every impulse most generous in us. So apparently it is and must be—we are wrong to have founded a humanism directly upon literature itself, and the phrase "humane letters" is an oxymoron. . . . The strong imagination comes to its painful birth through savagery and misrepresentation.[20]

Like many recent critics, Bloom posits a great divide in literary history and locates it in the seventeenth century; his innovation is to account for this division as the change from the relative creative nonchalance of a Homer, Dante, or Shakespeare in "the giant age before the flood" to the acute anxiety of influence suffered by all but a very few poets since the Enlightenment. A modern, and therefore "belated," poet awakens to his calling when irresistibly seized upon by one or more poems of a precursor or father-poet, yet experiences that seizure as an intolerable incursion into his imaginative life-space. The response of the belated writer is to defend himself against the parent-poem by distorting it drastically in the process of reading it; but he cannot escape the precursor, for he inevitably embodies its distorted form into his own attempt at an absolutely original poem.

Bloom's theory, as he points out, is a revision for literary criticism of what Freud sardonically called "the Family Romance." The relation of reader and poet to his parent-precursor, as in Freud's Oedipal relationship, is ambivalent, compounded of love and hate; but in Bloom's detailed descriptions of reading and writing, love enters only to weaken the result of the process, while the aspect of hate, jealousy, and fear is alone given a systematic and creative role to perform. This role is to deploy, with unconscious cunning, a set of defensive tactics, "the revisionary ratios," which are in fact aggressive acts designed to "malform" the precursor in the attempt to disestablish its "priority" over the latecomer, both in time and in creative strength. "Every act of reading is . . . defensive, and as defense it makes of interpretation a necessary misprision. . . . Reading is therefore misprision—or misreading." And since "every poem is a misinterpretation of a parent poem," he concludes that "the meaning of a poem can only be another poem." "There are no right readings"; the sole alternative is between "weak mis-readings and strong mis-readings." A weak misreading attempts, although unavailingly, to get at what a text really means in itself; it is the product of an inhibiting timidity, or at best of an excess of "generosity" toward the parent-poet. A misreading is strong, hence creative and valuable, in proportion to the boldness with which the reader's emotional compulsions are licensed to do violence to the text that he strives to overcome.

It is sometimes argued against Bloom's theory that his claim, "all reading is misreading," is incoherent, on the ground that we cannot know that a text has been misread unless we know what it is to read it correctly. This argument overlooks an interesting feature of Bloom's theory, that is, its quasi-Kantian frame of reference. At times Bloom's idiom corresponds closely enough to Kant's to qualify, in Bloom's terms, as a "deliberate misprision" of Kant's epistemology. Terms which recur on almost every page in which Bloom discusses misreading are "necessity," "necessary," "necessarily," "must be." Such terms are to be taken seriously; they signify an *a priori* necessity. In Bloom's theory, that is, the

[20] *The Anxiety of Influence* (New York: Oxford University Press, 1973), pp. 85–86. [Eds.]

compulsive revisionary ratios through which we experience a poem correspond, in Kant's philosophy, to the cognitive forms of space, time, and the categories that the mind inescapably imposes on all its experience of the world. Consequently Bloom's reader can only know the phenomenal poem constituted by his own revisionary categories; he cannot possibly get outside these categories to know the noumenal *Ding an sich,* or what Bloom calls "the poem-in-itself" or the "poem-as-such."

But Bloom's aim, he says, is not simply to propose "another new poetics," but to establish and convert us to "a newer and starker way of reading poems." The product of this new way of reading is "an antithetical practical criticism, as opposed to all the primary criticisms now in vogue."

> Let us give up the failed enterprise of seeking to "understand" any single poem as an entity in itself. Let us pursue instead the quest of learning to read any poem as its poet's deliberate misinterpretation, *as a poet,* of a precursor poem or of poetry in general.[21]

Bloom therefore, like Derrida and Fish, proposes a way of reading a text that will displace the meanings that "primary," or traditional readers have hitherto found in it. As applied in his reading, Bloom's revisionary ratios in effect function as an inventory of transformers for translating accepted meanings into new meanings; he conveniently presents a one-page table of his transformers which he calls "The Map of Misprision." And such is the virtuosity of these devices that they cannot fail to effect Bloom's antithetic meanings; in his own repeated assertion, "It must be so."

In this analysis I deliberately enact the role which Bloom, in a phrase from Blake, calls "the Idiot Questioner," whose presence as an aspect of his own mind Bloom recognizes but sternly represses. (In the present instance "the Idiot Questioner" can be translated as a stolid inquirer into the credentials of a critic's interpretive procedures.) Pursuing such an inquiry, I note that Bloom, in his tetralogy of books on the theory and practice of antithetic criticism, sets up six revisionary ratios which he names "clinamen," "tessera," "kenosis," and so on. He goes on to assimilate each of these ratios to a variety of other reinterpretive devices—to a Freudian defense-mechanism; to a concept of the Hebrew Kabbalists; to one of the rhetorical tropes such as synecdoche, hyperbole, metaphor; and to a recurrent type of poetic imagery. These amalgamated transformers are not only versatile enough to establish each of Bloom's new readings, but also antithetical enough to convert any possible counter-evidence into a confirmation of his own reading.

Take, for example, the Freudian mechanisms of defense—which Bloom calls "the clearest analogues I have found for the revisionary ratios"—as he applies them to interpret any poem as a distorted version of a precursor-poem. If the belated poem patently echoes the parent-poem, that counts as evidence for the new reading; although, Bloom asserts, "only weak poems, or the weaker elements in strong poems, immediately echo precursor poems, or directly allude to them." If the later poem doesn't contain such "verbal reminders," that counts too, on the basis of the mechanism of repression—the belated poet's anxiety of influence has been strong enough to repress all reference to his predecessor. And if the belated poem differs radically from its proposed precursor, that counts even more decisively, on the basis of the mechanism of "reaction-formation"—the poet's anxiety was so intense as to distort the precursor into its seeming opposite. This power of the negative to turn itself into a stronger positive manifests itself frequently in Bloom's applied criticism. For example, the opening verse paragraph of Tennyson's *Tithonus* has traditionally been read as expressing the aged but immortal protagonist's longing for death. Bloom, however, reads it antithetically as a revision, or

> swerve away from the naturalistic affirmations of Wordsworth and of Keats. What is absent in these opening lines is simply all of nature; what is present is the withered Tithonus. As Tennyson's reaction-formation against his precursors' stance, these lines are a rhetorical irony, denying what they desire, the divination of a poetic survival into strength.[22]

[21] Ibid., pp. 69ff. [Eds.]

[22] *Poetry and Repression* (New Haven: Yale University Press, 1976), pp. 164–65. [Eds.]

Perhaps so; but it will be noted that the reaction-transformer charters the antithetic critic to speak without fear of contradiction, while stranding his Questioner in a no-win position.

Bloom's theory, like that of other Newreaders, is self-referential, for he does not exempt his own interpretations from the assertion that all readings are misreadings. In his recent books on Yeats and Stevens, he often writes brilliant critiques that compel assent from a "primary" critic like myself. The extent of Bloom's own claim for these readings, however, is that they are strong misreadings, in that they do violence to the texts they address, by virtue of his surrender to his need for autonomy and to his anxieties of the influence exerted on him by his critical precursors. And in lieu of any possible criterion of rightness, such readings can be valuable only to the degree that they are "creative or interesting misreadings." By their strength, he says, such readings will provoke his critical successors to react by their own defensive misreadings, and so take their place within the unending accumulation of misreadings of misreadings that constitute the history both of poetry and of criticism, at least since the Enlightenment.

While acknowledging that his theory "may ask to be judged, as argument," Bloom also insists that "a theory *of* poetry must belong *to* poetry, must *be* poetry" and presents his work as "one reader's critical vision" bodied forth in "a severe poem." Let me drop my role as Idiot Questioner of Bloom's evidential procedures to read him in this alternative way, as a prose-poet who expresses a founding vision of the Scene of Literature. In the main, this has been traditionally conceived as a republic of equals composed, in Wordsworth's phrase, of "the mighty living and the mighty dead" whose poetry, as Shelley said, "is the record of the best and happiest moments of the happiest and best minds." In Bloom's bleak re-vision, the Scene of Literature becomes the arena of a savage war for *Lebensraum*[23] waged by the living poet against the oppressive and ever-present dead—a parricidal war, in which each newcomer, in his need to be self-begotten and self-sufficient, undertakes with unconscious cunning to mutilate, murder, and devour his poetic father. The poet's prime compulsions are like those of the Freudian Id, which demands no less than everything at once and is incapable of recognizing any constraints on its satisfactions by moral compunction, logical incompatibility, or empirical impossibility. And the poetic self remains forever fixed at the Oedipal stage of development; for Bloom explicitly denies to the poet "as poet" the Freudian mechanism of sublimation, which allows for the substitution, in satisfying our primordial desires, of higher for lower goals and so makes possible the growth from the infantile stage of total self-concern to the mature recognition of reciprocity with other selves. The war of which each poem is a battleground is ultimately futile, not only because every poet is inescapably fathered by precursors but also because, according to Bloom, his will to priority over his precursors is, in deep psychic fact, a defense against acknowledging his own human mortality. The conflict, furthermore, is doomed to terminate in the death of poetry itself, for the population of strong poets will soon usurp so much of the available living-space that even the illusion of creative originality will no longer be possible.

In Bloom's own idiom of rhetorical tropes, one can say of his critical poem about poetry that it is a sustained synecdoche which puts a part for the whole. By this device, and by his subsidiary device of strong hyperbole, Bloom compels us to face up to aspects of the motivation to write and misread poems—self-assertiveness, lust for power and precedence, malice, envy, revenge—which canonical critics have largely ignored. To those of us who yield ourselves to Bloom's dark and powerful eloquence, the Scene of Literature will never look the same again; such a result is probably the most that any writer compelled by an antithetical vision can hope to achieve. But the part is not the whole. What Bloom's point of vantage cannot take into account is the great diversity of motives for writing poetry, and in the products of that writing, the abundance of subject-matters, characters, genres, and styles, and the range of the passions expressed and represented, from brutality and terror and anguish, indeed, to gaiety, joy, and sometimes sheer fun. In sum, what Bloom's tragic vision of the literary scene systematically omits is almost everything that has hitherto been recognized to constitute the realm of literature.

On Bloom's critical premises, I am of course open

[23] *Lebensraum:* living space. [Eds.]

to the retort that I have misread both his criticism and our heritage of literary texts. But knowing from experience Bloom's geniality to his own critical precursors, I am confident that he will attribute my misreading to an amiable weakness—to my fallacy, that is, of misplaced benevolence.

Newreading and Old Norms

I shall conclude by considering briefly my third question: What makes a text so vulnerable to the diverse things that Newreaders do with it? The chief reason is that our use and understanding of language is not a science but a practice. That is, what we call "knowing a language" is not a matter of knowing that or knowing why, but of knowing how, of having acquired a skill. We are born into a community of speakers and writers who have already acquired this skill, and we in turn acquire it by interplay with these others, in which we learn how to say what we mean and how to understand what others have said by a continuous process of self-correction and refinement, based on what are often very subtle indications of when and in what way we have gone wrong.

The successful practice of language depends on our mastery of linguistic uniformities that we call conventions, or norms, or rules. Linguistic rules, however, differ radically from the rules of chess or of a card-game to which they are often compared. The rules which constitute these games are stipulated in an authoritative code to which we can refer in order to resolve disputes. The use and understanding of language, on the other hand, depends on tacit consensual regularities which are multiplex and fluid; except in very gross ways, these regularities are uncodified, and probably uncodifiable. In our practice, therefore, we must rely not on rules, but on linguistic tact—a tact which is the emergent result of all our previous experience with speaking, hearing, writing, and reading the language.

Stanley Fish seems to me right in his claim that the linguistic meanings we find in a text are relative to the interpretive strategy we employ, and that agreement about meanings depends on membership in a community which shares an interpretive strategy. But if we set out not to create meanings, but to understand what the sequence of sentences in a literary work mean, when we have no choice except to read according to the linguistic strategy the author of the work employed, and expected us to employ. We are capable of doing so, because an immense store of cumulative evidence provides assurance that the authors of literary texts belonged to the linguistic community into which we were later born, and so shared our skill, and the consensual regularities on which that skill depends, with some divergencies—which we have a variety of clues for detecting—which are the result both of the slow change of communal regularities in time and of the limited innovations which can be introduced by the individual author.

When a Newreader, on the basis of his contrived interpretive strategy, asserts that a passage means something radically different from what it has been taken to mean, or else that it means nothing in particular, we lack codified criteria to which we can appeal against the new interpretation; in the last analysis, we can only appeal to our linguistic tact, as supported by the agreement of readers who share that tact. But such an appeal has no probative weight for a reader who has opted out of playing the game of language according to its constitutive regularities; nor is the application of our own inherited practice verifiable by any proof outside its sustainedly coherent working. All we can do is to point out to the Newreader what he already knows—that he is playing a double game, introducing his own interpretive strategy when reading someone else's text, but tacitly relying on communal norms when undertaking to communicate the methods and results of his interpretations to his own readers.

We can't claim that the Newreader's strategy doesn't work, for each of these ways of doing things to texts indubitably works. Allowed his own premises and conversion procedures, Derrida is able to deconstruct any text into a suspension of numberless undecidable significations, Fish can make it the occasion for a creative adventure in false surmises, and Bloom can read it as a perverse distortion of any chosen precursor-text. These substitute strategies in fact have an advantage which is a principal cause of their appeal to students of literature. Our inherited strategy, although it has shown that it can persistently discover new meanings even in a classic text, must operate always under the constraint of communal regularities of usage. Each new strategy, on the other hand, is a discovery procedure which guarantees new meanings. It thus provides freshness of sensation in reading old and familiar texts—at least until we learn to anticipate the limited kind of new meanings it is capable of generating; it also makes it easy for any critical follower to say new and exciting things about a literary work that has been again and again discussed. But we purchase this advantage at a cost, and ultimately the choice between a radical Newreading and the old way of reading is a matter of cultural cost-accounting. We gain a guaranteed novelty, of a kind that makes any text directly relevant to current interests and concerns. What we lose is access to the inexhaustible variety of literature as determinably meaningful texts by, for, and about human beings, as well as access to the enlightening things that have been written about such texts by the humanists and critics who were our precursors, from Aristotle to Lionel Trilling.

J. Hillis Miller

b. 1928

THE WORK OF J. Hillis Miller, somewhat like the work of Roland Barthes (see *CTSP*, pp. 1196–99), frequently occupies a middle ground between critical commentary and theory, proceeding by instance and example to illuminate a current theoretical position. It is, then, a dual observation to say that Miller's work is exemplary. Since the publication of the first book, *Charles Dickens: The World of His Novels* (1958), Miller has displayed a precise and penetrating sense of the text, both as a verbal structure inviting interpretation, and as a reflection of essential social and psychological circumstances. In subsequent work, principally *The Disappearance of God* (1963) and *Poets of Reality* (1965), Miller adopted a generally phenomenological stance, particularly influenced by the work of Geneva critics such as Georges Poulet (see *CTSP*, pp. 1213–22). His later work, as this essay illustrates, is written from the point of view of deconstruction, following *Jacques Derrida* and others.

Miller's account of deconstruction as "neither nihilism nor metaphysics but simply interpretation as such" tends to play down the more radical claims made for deconstruction as a philosophical enterprise devoted to liberating writing (or *écriture*) from a logocentric metaphysics. For Miller, deconstruction appears as an inescapable form of indeterminacy, exemplified in the peculiarity of such relations as host and parasite, where there is always some uncertainty as to which is which. Miller's strategy in the essay here is to respond to M. H. Abrams's somewhat polemical charge that "deconstructionist" readings are parasitical on obvious readings by admitting the charge but deconstructing its intent: there are no "obvious" readings, no "univocal" readings, since the relation between any two texts or acts of writing, whether poems or interpretations, is itself never obvious nor univocal. In discussing Nietzsche, as "one of the patrons" of present-day deconstruction, Miller suggests that contemporary discomfort with deconstruction is only a local example of a fundamental relation between logocentric metaphysics and nihilism, where the former as host elicits the latter as parasite—and vice versa.

By setting the issue in these terms, Miller then proceeds to develop a reading of Shelley's *The Triumph of Life* (with some additional remarks on other poems) as itself an example of the weakly paradoxical relation between parasite and host, nihilism and metaphysics. The unremarked irony (though it may have been anticipated) is that Miller produces a rather "obvious" and "univocal" reading, merely by thematizing his interpretation on the governing trope of the essay, host-parasite.

In this respect, Miller's essay exemplifies at least three problems which have surrounded the appropriation of deconstruction by American critics. First, it is not at all clear that the philosophical presuppositions that led Derrida to develop his version of deconstruction survive translation. By treating the problem as a structural relation between metaphysics and nihilism, for example, Miller appears to presume that at least the truth about *this* matter may be known—which has the effect of converting Derrida's notion of "différ*a*nce" into a wholly parsable difference. The American will to pragmatism is at least suggested by this presumption, but it is more evident in the second problem: the propensity of American practitioners of deconstruction to treat it as another "approach" to criticism, which remains very much the enterprise of developing commentaries about individual texts and only incidentally a philosophical dilemma.

The third problem is exemplified by the progression of Miller's work, from formalism through phenomenology to deconstruction, as yet another example of the host-parasite relation elaborated in Miller's essay. Starting from strategies having their roots not in Hegel and Saussure but in Coleridge and I. A. Richards, each succeeding stage of critical practice effects the conversion of the parasite into the host, as the formalism of the New Criticism hosts phenomenology and structuralism as parasites, which in turn become the hosts for deconstruction. To follow one aspect of the metaphor Miller does not pick up, the genetic identity of these symbiotic couples persists. In the case here, the frustrated search of New Critics for some adequate principle to differentiate literary art from other forms of discourse (which Cleanth Brooks presumed to find in "paradox" or "dramatic irony"—see *CTSP*, pp. 1041–48) persists through its *unheimlich* transformations, to appear in this instance as intertextuality and indeterminacy, subject to the "uneasy joy of interpretation."

Miller's major works include *Charles Dickens: The World of His Novels* (1958); *The Disappearance of God* (1963); *Poets of Reality* (1965); *Thomas Hardy: Desire and Distance* (1970); and *Fiction and Repetition* (1982). See M. H. Abrams's "The Deconstructive Angel," *Critical Inquiry* 3 (1977), for Abrams's response to an earlier version of the following essay. See also Abrams's "How to Do Things with Texts" in this volume.

THE CRITIC AS HOST

> *"Je meurs où je m'attache,"* Mr. Holt said with a polite grin. "The ivy says so in the picture, and clings to the oak like a fond parasite as it is."
> "Parricide, sir!" cries Mrs. Tusher.
> *Henry Esmond,* Bk. I, ch. 3

I

At one point in "Rationality and Imagination in Cultural History" M. H. Abrams cites Wayne Booth's assertion that the "deconstructionist" reading of a given work "is plainly and simply parasitical" on "the obvious or univocal reading."[1] The latter is Abrams' phrase, the former Booth's. My citation of a citation is an example of a kind of chain which it will be part of my intention here to interrogate. What happens when a critical essay extracts a "passage" and "cites" it? Is this different from a citation, echo, or allusion within a poem? Is a citation an alien parasite within the body of the main text, or is the interpretive text the parasite which surrounds and strangles the citation which is its host? The host feeds the parasite and makes its life possible, but at the same time is killed by it, as criticism is often said to kill literature. Or can host and parasite live happily together, in the domicile of the same text, feeding each other or sharing the food?

Abrams, in any case, goes on to add "a more radical reply." If "deconstructionist principles" are taken seriously, he says, "any history which relies on written texts becomes an impossibility" (p. 48). So be it. That's not much of an argument. A certain notion of history or of literary history, like a certain notion of determinable reading, might indeed be an impossibility, and if so, it might be better to know that. That something in the realm of interpretation is a demonstrable impossibility does not, however, prevent it from being "done," as the abundance of histories, literary histories, and readings demonstrates. On the other hand, I should agree that the impossibility of reading should not be taken too lightly. It has consequences, for life and death, since it is incorporated in the bodies of individual human beings and in the body politic of our cultural life and death together.

"Parasitical"—the word suggests the image of "the obvious or univocal reading" as the mighty oak, rooted in the solid ground, endangered by the insidious twining around it of deconstructive ivy. That ivy is somehow feminine, secondary, defective, or dependent. It is a clinging vine, able to live in no other way but by drawing the life sap of its host, cutting off its light and air. I think of Hardy's *The Ivy-Wife* or of the end of Thackeray's *Vanity Fair:* "God bless you, honest William!—Farewell, dear Amelia—Grow green again, tender little parasite, round the rugged old oak to which you cling!"

Such sad love stories of a domestic affection which introduces the parasitical into the closed economy of the home no doubt describe well enough the way some people feel about the relation of a "deconstructive" interpretation to "the obvious or univocal reading." The parasite is destroying the host. The alien has invaded the house, perhaps to kill the father of the family in an act which does not look like parricide, but is. Is the "obvious" reading, though, so "obvious" or even so "univocal"? May it not itself be the uncanny alien which is so close that it cannot be seen as strange, host in the sense of enemy rather than host in the sense of open-handed dispenser of hospitality? Is not the obvious reading perhaps equivocal rather than univocal, most equivocal in its intimate familiarity and in its ability to have got itself taken for granted as "obvious" and single-voiced?

"Parasite" is one of those words which calls up its apparent opposite. It has no meaning without that counte part. There is no parasite without its host. At the same time both word and counterword subdivide. Each reveals itself to be fissured already within itself, to be, like *Unheimlich, unheimlich.*[2] Words in "para," like words in "ana," have this as

THE CRITIC AS HOST first appeared (in a shorter version) in *Critical Inquiry* 3. This version of the essay is from *Deconstruction and Criticism*, published by Seabury Press, reprinted with the permission of Continuum Publishing Corporation, copyright 1979.

[1] *Critical Inquiry*, II, 3 (Spring 1976), 457–58. The first phrase is quoted from Wayne Booth, "M. H. Abrams: Historian as Critic, Critic as Pluralist," *Critical Inquiry,* II, 3 (Spring 1976), 441. The opening pages of the present essay appeared in a preliminary form in *Critical Inquiry,* III, 3 (Spring 1977), 439–47, by permission of The University of Chicago Press. [Au.]

[2] *Unheimlich:* uncanny, literally, un-home-like. [Eds.]

an intrinsic property. "Para" as a prefix in English (sometimes "par") indicates alongside, near or beside, beyond, incorrectly, resembling or similar to, subsidiary to, isomeric or polymeric to. In borrowed Greek compounds "para" indicates beside, to the side of, alongside, beyond, wrongfully, harmfully, unfavorably, and among. Words in "para" form one branch of the tangled labyrinth of words using some form of the Indo-European root *per*. This root is the "base of prepositions and preverbs with the basic meaning of 'forward,' 'through,' and a wide range of extended senses such as 'in front of,' 'before,' 'early,' 'first,' 'chief,' 'toward,' 'against,' 'near,' 'at,' 'around.'"[3]

If words in "para" are one branch of the labyrinth of words in "per," the branch is itself a miniature labyrinth. "Para" is a double antithetical prefix signifying at once proximity and distance, similarity and difference, interiority and exteriority, something inside a domestic economy and at the same time outside it, something simultaneously this side of a boundary line, threshold, or margin, and also beyond it, equivalent in status and also secondary or subsidiary, submissive, as of guest to host, slave to master. A thing in "para," moreover, is not only simultaneously on both sides of the boundary line between inside and out. It is also the boundary itself, the screen which is a permeable membrane connecting inside and outside. It confuses them with one another, allowing the outside in, making the inside out, dividing them and joining them. It also forms an ambiguous transition between one and the other. Though a given word in "para" may seem to choose univocally one of these possibilities, the other meanings are always there as a shimmering in the word which makes it refuse to stay still in a sentence. The word is like a slightly alien guest within the syntactical closure where all the words are family friends together. Words in "para" include: parachute, paradigm, parasol, the French *paravent* (windscreen), and *parapluie* (umbrella), paragon, paradox, parapet, parataxis, parapraxis, parabasis, paraphrase, paragraph, paraph, paralysis, paranoia, paraphernalia, parallel, parallax, parameter, parable, paresthesia, paramnesia, paramorph, paramecium, Paraclete, paramedical, paralegal—and parasite.

"Parasite" comes from the Greek *parasitos,* "beside the grain," *para,* beside (in this case) plus *sitos,* grain, food. "Sitology" is the science of foods, nutrition, and diet. A parasite was originally something positive, a fellow guest, someone sharing the food with you, there with you beside the grain. Later on, "parasite" came to mean a professional dinner guest, someone expert at cadging invitations without ever giving dinners in return. From this developed the two main modern meanings in English, the biological and the social. A parasite is "Any organism that grows, feeds, and is sheltered on or in a different organism while contributing nothing to the survival of its host"; and "A person who habitually takes advantage of the generosity of others without making any useful return." To call a kind of criticism "parasitical" is, in either case, strong language.

A curious system of thought, or of language, or of social organization (in fact all three at once) is implicit in the word parasite. There is no parasite without a host. The host and the somewhat sinister or subversive parasite are fellow guests beside the food, sharing it. On the other hand, the host is himself the food, his substance consumed without recompense, as when one says, "He is eating me out of house and home." The host may then become host in another sense, not etymologically connected. The word "host" is of course the name for the consecrated bread or wafer of the Eucharist, from Middle English *oste,* from Latin *hostia,* sacrifice, victim.

If the host is both eater and eaten, he also contains in himself the double antithetical relation of host and guest, guest in the bifold sense of friendly presence and alien invader. The words "host" and "guest" go back in fact to the same etymological root: *ghos-ti,* stranger, guest, host, properly "someone with whom one has reciprocal duties of hospitality." The modern English word "host" in this alternative sense comes from the Middle English *(h)oste,* from Old French, host, guest, from Latin *hospes* (stem *hospit-*), guest, host, stranger. The "pes" or "pit" in the Latin words and in such modern English words as "hospital" and "hospitality" is from another root, *pot,* meaning "master." The compound or bifurcated root *ghos-pot* meant "master of guests," "one who symbolizes the relationship

[3] All definitions and etymologies in this essay are taken from *The American Heritage Dictionary of the English Language,* William Morris, ed. (Boston: American Heritage Publishing Co., Inc. and Houghton Mifflin Company, 1969). [Au.]

of reciprocal hospitality," as in the Slavic *gospodi,* Lord, sir, master. "Guest," on the other hand, is from Middle English *gest,* from Old Norse *gestr,* from *ghos-ti,* the same root as for "host." A host is a guest, and a guest is a host. A host is a host. The relation of household master offering hospitality to a guest and the guest receiving it, of host and parasite in the original sense of "fellow guest," is inclosed within the word "host" itself.

A host in the sense of a guest, moreover, is both a friendly visitor in the house and at the same time an alien presence who turns the home into a hotel, a neutral territory. Perhaps he is the first emissary of a host of enemies (from Latin *hostis* [stranger, enemy]), the first foot in the door, followed by a swarm of hostile strangers, to be met only by our own host, as the Christian deity is the Lord God of Hosts. The uncanny antithetical relation exists not only between pairs of words in this system, host and parasite, host and guest, but within each word in itself. It reforms itself in each polar opposite when that opposite is separated out. This subverts or nullifies the apparently unequivocal relation of polarity which seems the conceptual scheme appropriate for thinking through the system. Each word in itself becomes divided by the strange logic of the "para," membrane which divides inside from outside and yet joins them in a hymeneal bond, or which allows an osmotic mixing, making the stranger friend, the distant near, the *Unheimlich heimlich,* the homely homey, without, for all its closeness and similarity, ceasing to be strange, distant, and dissimilar.

One of the most frightening versions of the parasite as invading host is the virus. In this case, the parasite is an alien who has not simply the ability to invade a domestic enclosure, consume the food of the family, and kill the host, but the strange capacity, in doing all that, to turn the host into multitudinous proliferating replications of itself. The virus is at the uneasy border between life and death. It challenges that opposition, since, for example, it does not "eat," but only reproduces. It is as much a crystal or a component in a crystal as it is an organism. The genetic pattern of the virus is so coded that it can enter a host cell and violently reprogram all the genetic material in that cell, turning the cell into a little factory for manufacturing copies of itself, so destroying it. This is *The Ivy-Wife* with a vengeance.

Is this an allegory, and if so, of what? The use by modern geneticists of an "analogy" (but what is the ontological status of this analogy?) between genetic reproduction and the social interchanges carried by language or other sign systems may justify a transfer back in the other direction. Is "deconstructive criticism" like a virus which invades the host of an innocently metaphysical text, a text with an "obvious or univocal meaning," carried by a single referential grammar? Does such criticism ferociously reprogram the *gramme* of the host text to make it utter its own message, the "uncanny," the "aporia," "la différance," or what have you? Some people have said so. Could it, on the other hand, be the other way around? Could it be that metaphysics, the obvious or univocal meaning, is the parasitical virus which has for millennia been passed from generation to generation in Western culture in its languages and in the privileged texts of those languages? Does metaphysics enter the language-learning apparatus of each new baby born into that culture and shape the apparatus after its own patterns? The difference might be that this apparatus, unlike the host cell for a virus, does not have its own pre-existing inbuilt genetic code.

Is that so certain, however? Is the system of metaphysics "natural" to man, as it is natural for a cuckoo to sing "cuckoo" or for a bee to build its comb in hexagonal cells? If so, the parasitical virus would be a friendly presence carrying the same message already genetically programmed within its host. The message would predispose all European babies or perhaps all earth babies to read Plato and become Platonists, so that anything else would require some unimaginable mutation of the species man. Is the prison house of language an exterior constraint or is it part of the blood, bones, nerves, and brain of the prisoner? Could that incessant murmuring voice that speaks always within me or constantly weaves the web of language there, even in my dreams, be an uncanny guest, a parasitical virus, and not a member of the family? How could one even ask that question, since it must be asked in words provided by the murmuring voice? Is it not that voice speaking here and now? Perhaps, after all, the analogy with viruses is "only an analogy," a "figure of speech," and need not be taken seriously.

What does this have to do with poems and with the reading of poems? It is meant as an "example" of the deconstructive strategy of interpretation. The procedure is applied, in this case, not to the text of a poem but to the cited fragment of a critical essay containing within itself a citation from another essay, like a parasite within its host. The "example" is a fragment like those miniscule bits of some substance which are put into a tiny test tube and explored by certain techniques of analytical chemistry. To get so far or so much out of a little piece of language, context after context widening out from these few phrases to include as their necessary milieux all the family of Indo-European languages, and all the permutations of our social structures of household economy, gift-giving and gift-receiving—this is an argument for the value of recognizing the equivocal richness of apparently obvious or univocal language, even of the language of criticism. Criticism is in this respect, if in no other, continuous with the language of literature. This equivocal richness, my discussion of "parasite" implies, resides in part in the fact that there is no conceptual expression without figure, and no intertwining of concept and figure without an implied narrative, in this case the story of the alien guest in the home. Deconstruction is an investigation of what is implied by this inherence in one another of figure, concept, and narrative.

My example presents a model for the relation of critic to critic, for the incoherence within a single critic's language, for the asymmetrical relation of critical text to poem, for the incoherence within any single literary text, and for the skewed relation of a poem to its predecessors. To speak of the "deconstructive" reading of a poem as "parasitical" on the "obvious or univocal reading" is to enter willy-nilly into the strange logic of the parasite, to make the univocal equivocal in spite of oneself, according to the law that language is not an instrument or tool in man's hands, a submissive means of thinking. Language rather thinks man and his "world," including poems, if he will allow it to do so.

The system of figurative thought (but what thought is not figurative?) inscribed within the word parasite and its associates, host and guest, invites us to recognize that the "obvious or univocal reading" of a poem is not identical to the poem itself. Both readings, the "univocal" one and the "deconstructive" one, are fellow guests "beside the grain," host and guest, host and host, host and parasite, parasite and parasite. The relation is a triangle, not a polar opposition. There is always a third to whom the two are related, something before them or between them, which they divide, consume, or exchange, across which they meet. The relation in question is always in fact a chain. It is a strange sort of chain without beginning or end, a chain in which no commanding element (origin, goal, or underlying principle) may be identified. In such a chain there is always something earlier or something later to which any link on which one focuses refers and which keeps the series open. The relation between any two contiguous elements in this chain is a strange opposition which is of intimate kinship and at the same time of enmity. It cannot be encompassed by the ordinary logic of polar opposition. It is not open to dialectical synthesis. Each "single element," moreover, far from being unequivocally what it is, subdivides within itself to recapitulate the relation of parasite and host of which, on the larger scale, it appears to be one or the other pole. On the one hand, the "obvious or univocal reading" always contains the "deconstructive reading" as a parasite encrypted within itself as part of itself. On the other hand, the "deconstructive" reading can by no means free itself from the metaphysical reading it means to contest. The poem in itself, then, is neither the host nor the parasite but the food they both need, host in another sense, the third element in this particular triangle. Both readings are at the same table together, bound by a strange relation of reciprocal obligation, of gift or food-giving and gift or food-receiving.

The poem, in my figure, is that ambiguous gift, food, host in the sense of victim, sacrifice. It is broken, divided, passed around, consumed by the critics canny and uncanny who are in that odd relation to one another of host and parasite. Any poem, however, is parasitical in its turn on earlier poems, or it contains earlier poems within itself as enclosed parasites, in another version of the perpetual reversal of parasite and host. If the poem is food and poison for the critics, it must in its turn have eaten. It must have been a cannibal consumer of earlier poems.

Take, for example, Shelley's *The Triumph of Life*. It is inhabited, as its critics have shown, by a long chain of parasitical presences—echoes, allusions, guests, ghosts of previous texts. These are present within the domicile of the poem in that curious phantasmal way, affirmed, negated, sublimated, twisted, straightened out, travestied, which Harold Bloom has begun to study and which it is one major task of literary interpretation today to investigate further and to define. The previous text is both the ground of the new one and something the new poem must annihilate by incorporating it, turning it into ghostly insubstantiality, so that the new poem may perform its possible-impossible task of becoming its own ground. The new poem both needs the old texts and must destroy them. It is both parasitical on them, feeding ungraciously on their substance, and at the same time it is the sinister host which unmans them by inviting them into its home, as the Green Knight invites Gawain. Each previous link in the chain, in its turn, played the same role, as host and parasite, in relation to its predecessors. From the Old to the New Testaments, from Ezekiel to Revelation, to Dante, to Ariosto, to Spenser, to Milton, to Rousseau, to Wordsworth and Coleridge, the chain leads ultimately to *The Triumph of Life*. That poem, in its turn, or Shelley's work generally, is present within the work of Hardy or Yeats or Stevens and forms part of a sequence in the major texts of Romantic "nihilism" including Nietzsche, Freud, Heidegger, and Blanchot. This perpetual re-expression of the relation of host and parasite forms itself again today in current criticism. It is present, for example, in the relation between "univocal" and "deconstructionist" readings of *The Triumph of Life,* between the reading of Meyer Abrams and that of Harold Bloom,[4] or between Abrams' reading of Shelley and the one I am proposing here, or within the work of each one of these critics taken separately. The inexorable law which makes the "alogical" relation of host and parasite re-form itself within each separate entity which had seemed, on the larger scale, to be one or the other, applies as much to critical essays as to the texts they treat. *The Triumph of Life* contains within itself, jostling irreconcilably with one another, both logocentric metaphysics and nihilism. It is no accident that critics have disagreed about it. The meaning of *The Triumph of Life* can never be reduced to any "univocal" reading, neither the "obvious" one nor a single-minded deconstructionist one, if there could be such a thing, which there cannot. The poem, like all texts, is "unreadable," if by "readable" one means a single, definitive interpretation. In fact, neither the "obvious" reading nor the "deconstructionist" reading is "univocal." Each contains, necessarily, its enemy within itself, is itself both host and parasite. The deconstructionist reading contains the obvious one and vice versa. Nihilism is an inalienable alien presence within Occidental metaphysics, both in poems and in the criticism of poems.

[4]See M. H. Abrams, *Natural Supernaturalism: Tradition and Revolution in Romantic Literature* (1971), and Harold Bloom, *Poetry and Repression: Revisionism from Blake to Stevens* (1976). [Eds.]

II

Nihilism—that word has inevitably come up as a label for "deconstruction," secretly or overtly present as the name for what is feared from the new mode of criticism and from its ability to devalue all values, making traditional modes of interpretation "impossible." What is nihilism? Here the analysis may be helped by a chain which goes from Friedrich Nietzsche to Ernst Jünger[5] to Martin Heidegger.[6]

The first book of Nietzsche's *The Will to Power,* in the ordering by his sister of the *Nachlass,* is entitled "European Nihilism." The beginning of the first section of this book is as follows: "Nihilism stands at the door: whence comes this uncanniest of all guests?" (*"Der Nihilismus steht vor der Tür: woher kommt uns dieser unheimlichste aller Gäste?"*)[7]

Heidegger's comment on this comes near the beginning of his essay on Ernst Jünger's *Über die Linie*. The title of Heidegger's essay was later changed to *Zur Seinsfrage, The Question of Being*. Heidegger's essay takes the form of a letter to Jünger:

> It is called the "uncanniest" *[der "unheimlichste"]* because as the unconditional will to will, it wants homelessness as such *[die Heimatlosigkeit als solche]*. Therefore, it does not help to show it the door because it has long since and invisibly been moving around in the house. The important thing is to get a glimpse of the guest and to see through it. You [Jünger] write: "A good definition of nihilism would be comparable to making the cancer bacillus visible. It would not signify a

[5]Ernst Jünger (1895–), German writer. [Eds.]

[6]See *Heidegger*. [Eds.]

[7]Walter Kaufmann and R. J. Hollingdale, trans., *The Will to Power* (New York: Vintage Books, 1968), p. 7; Friedrich Nietzsche, *Werke in Drei Bänden,* ed. Karl Schlechta, III (Munich: Carl Hanser Verlag, 1966), 881. [Au.]

> cure but perhaps the presupposition of it, insofar as men contribute anything toward it." . . . Nihilism itself, as little as the cancer bacillus, is something diseased. In regard to the *essence* of nihilism there is no prospect and no meaningful claim to a cure. . . . The essence of nihilism is neither healable nor unhealable. It is the heal-less *[das Heil-lose]*, but as such a unique relegation into health *[eine einzigartige Verweisung ins Heile]*.[8]

For these three writers, link after link in a chain, the confrontation of nihilism cannot be detached from the system of terms I have been exploring. To put this another way, the system of terms involves inevitably a confrontation with the uncanniest of guests, nihilism. Nihilism is somehow inherent in the relation of parasite and host. Inherent also is the imagery of sickness and health. Health for the parasite, food and the right environment, may be illness, even mortal illness, for the host. On the other hand, there are innumerable cases, in the proliferation of life forms, where the presence of a parasite is absolutely necessary to the health of its host. Moreover, if nihilism is the "heal-less" as such, a wound which may not be closed, an attempt to pretend that this uncanniest of guests is not present in the house might be the worst of all illnesses, the nagging, surly, covert, unidentified kind, there as a general malaise which undermines all activities, depriving them of joy.

The uncanniest guest is nihilism, *"hôte fantôme,"* in Jacques Derrida's phrase, *"hôte qui hante plutôt qu'il n'habite,* guest *et* ghost *d'une inquiétante étrangeté."*[9] Nihilism has already made itself at home with Occidental metaphysics. Nihilism is the latent ghost encrypted within any expression of a logocentric system, for example in Shelley's *The Triumph of Life,* or in any interpretation of such a text, for example in Meyer Abrams' reading of *The Triumph of Life* or in reversed form in Harold Bloom's reading. The two, logocentrism and nihilism, are related to one another in a way which is not antithesis and which may not be synthesized in any dialectical *Aufhebung*.[10] Each defines and is hospitable to the other, host to it as parasite. Yet each is the mortal enemy of the other, invisible to the other, as its phantom unconscious, that is, as something of which it cannot by definition be aware.

If nihilism is the parasitical stranger within the house of metaphysics, "nihilism," as the name for the devaluation or reduction to nothingness of all values, is not the name nihilism has "in itself." It is the name given to it by metaphysics, as the term "unconscious" is given by consciousness to that part of itself which it cannot face directly. In attempting to expel that other than itself contained within itself, logocentric metaphysics deconstitutes itself, according to a regular law which can be demonstrated in the self-subversion of all the great texts of Western metaphysics from Plato onward. Metaphysics contains its parasite within itself, as the "unhealable" which it tries, unsuccessfully, to cure. It attempts to cover over the unhealable by annihilating the nothingness hidden within itself.

Is there any way to break this law, to turn the system around? Would it be possible to approach metaphysics from the standpoint of "nihilism"? Could one make nihilism the host of which metaphysics is the alien guest, so giving new names to both? Nihilism would then not be nihilism but something else, something without a melodramatic aura, perhaps something so innocent-sounding as "rhetoric," or "philology," or "the study of tropes," or even "the trivium." Metaphysics might then be redefined, from the point of view of this trivium, as an inevitable rhetorical or tropological effect. It would not be a cause but a phantom generated within the house of language by the play of language. "Deconstruction" is one current name for this reversal.

The present-day procedure of "deconstruction," of which Nietzsche is one of the patrons, is not, however, new in our own day. It has been repeated regularly in one form or another in all the centuries since the Greek Sophists and rhetoricians, since in fact Plato himself, who in *The Sophist* has enclosed his own self-deconstruction within the canon of his own writing. If deconstruction could liberate us from the prisonhouse of language, it would seem that it should have long since done so, and yet it has not. There must be something wrong with the ma-

[8] Jean T. Wilde and William Kluback, trans., *The Question of Being* [a bilingual text] (New Haven, Conn.: College & University Press, 1958), pp. 36–39. [Au.]

[9] *hôte fantôme:* phantom or spectral host; *hôte . . . étrangeté:* host which haunts more than a house, guest and ghost of a disquieting strangeness. [Eds.]

[10] *Aufhebung:* to lift up, preserve, and cancel or annul, as used by Hegel to describe the effect of dialectic. [Eds.]

chinery of demolition, or some inexpertness in its operator, or perhaps the definition of it as liberating is incorrect. The *fröhliche Wissenschaft*[11] of Nietzsche, his attempt to move beyond metaphysics to an affirmative, life-enhancing, performative act of language, is posited on a dismantling of metaphysics which shows it as leading to nihilism by an inevitable process whereby "the highest values devaluate themselves." The values are not devaluated by something subversive outside themselves. Nihilism is not a social or psychological or even world historical phenomenon. It is not a new or perhaps cyclically reappearing phenomenon in the history of "spirit" or of "Being." The highest values devalue themselves. Nihilism is a parasite always already at home within its host, Western metaphysics. This is stated as a "point of departure" (*Ausgangspunkt*) at the beginning of *Zum Plan* ("Towards an Outline"), at the opening of Book I of *The Will to Power,* just after the sentence defining nihilism as "this uncanniest of all guests":

> . . . It is an error to consider "social distress" or "psychological degeneration" or, worse, corruption as the *cause* of nihilism. . . . Distress, whether of the soul, body, or intellect, cannot of itself give birth to nihilism (i.e. the radical repudiation of value, meaning, and desirability)—Such distress always permits a variety of interpretations. Rather: it is in one particular interpretation, the Christian-moral one, that nihilism is rooted.[12]

Would it be possible, then, to escape from the endless generation out of itself by metaphysics of nihilism, and the endless resubmission of nihilism to the metaphysics which defines it and is the condition of its existence? Is "deconstruction" this new way, a new threefold way out of the labyrinth of human history, which is the history of error, into the sunlit forum of truth and clarity, all ways made straight at last? Can semiotics, rhetoric, and tropology substitute for the old grammar, rhetoric, and logic? Would it be possible to be freed at last from the nightmare of an endless brother battle, Shem replacing Shaun, and Shaun Shem?

I do not think so. "Deconstruction" is neither nihilism nor metaphysics but simply interpretation as such, the untangling of the inherence of metaphysics in nihilism and of nihilism in metaphysics by way of the close reading of texts. This procedure, however, can in no way escape, in its own discourse, from the language of the passages it cites. This language is the expression of the inherence of nihilism in metaphysics and of metaphysics in nihilism. We have no other language. The language of criticism is subject to exactly the same limitations and blind alleys as the language of the works it reads. The most heroic effort to escape from the prisonhouse of language only builds the walls higher.

The deconstructive procedure, however, by reversing the relation of ghost and host, by playing on the play within language, may go beyond the repetitive generation of nihilism by metaphysics and of metaphysics by nihilism. It may reach something like that *fröhliche Wissenschaft* for which Nietzsche called. This would be interpretation as joyful wisdom, the greatest joy in the midst of the greatest suffering, an inhabitation of that gaiety of language which is our seigneur.

Deconstruction does not provide an escape from nihilism, nor from metaphysics, nor from their uncanny inherence in one another. There is no escape. It does, however, move back and forth within this inherence. It makes the inherence oscillate in such a way that one enters a strange borderland, a frontier region which seems to give the widest glimpse into the other land ("beyond metaphysics"), though this land may not by any means be entered and does not in fact exist for Western man. By this form of interpretation, however, the border zone itself may be made sensible, as quattrocento painting makes the Tuscan air visible in its invisibility. The zone may be appropriated in the torsion of the mind's expropriation, its experience of an inability to comprehend logically. This procedure is an attempt to reach clarity in a region where clarity is not possible. In the failure of that attempt, however, something moves, a limit is encountered. This encounter may be compared to the uncanny experience of reaching a frontier where there is no visible barrier, as when Wordsworth found he had crossed the Alps without knowing he was doing so. It is as if the "prisonhouse of language" were like that universe finite but unbounded which some modern cosmologies posit. One may move everywhere freely within this enclosure without ever encountering a

[11] *fröhliche Wissenschaft:* gay science. [Eds.]

[12] Kaufmann and Hollingdale, p. 7; Schlechta, III, 881. [Au.]

wall, and yet it is limited. It is a prison, a milieu without origin or edge. Such a place is therefore all frontier zone without either peaceful homeland, in one direction, land of hosts and domesticity, nor, in the other direction, any alien land of hostile strangers, "beyond the line."

The place we inhabit, wherever we are, is always this in-between zone, place of host and parasite, neither inside nor outside. It is a region of the *Unheimlich,* beyond any formalism, which reforms itself wherever we are, if we know where we are. This "place" is where we are, in whatever text, in the most inclusive sense of that word, we happen to be living. This may be made to appear, however, only by an extreme interpretation of that text, going as far as one can with the terms the work provides. To this form of interpretation, which is interpretation as such, one name given at the moment is "deconstruction."

III

As an "example" of the word "parasite" functioning parasitically within the "body" of work by one author, I turn now to an analysis of the word in Shelley.

The word "parasite" does not appear in *The Triumph of Life.* That poem, however, is structured throughout around the parasitical relationship. *The Triumph of Life* may be defined as an exploration of various forms of the parasitical relation. The poem is governed by the imagery of light and shadow, or of light differentiated within itself. The poem is a series of personifications and scenes each of which gives a figurative "shape" (Shelley's word) to a light which remains the "same" in all its personifications. The figurative shape makes the light a shadow. Any reading of the poem must thread its way through repeated configurations of light and shadow. It must also identify the relation of one scene to the next which replaces it as sunlight puts out the morning star, and the star again the sun. That star is Lucifer, Venus, Vesper, all at once. The polarity constantly reforming itself within a light which turns into shadow in the presence of a novel light is the vehicle which carries, or is carried by, the structure of dream vision within dream vision and of person confronting or replacing precursor person. This structure is repeated throughout the poem. These repetitions make the poem a *mise en abîme* of reflections within reflections or a nest of Chinese boxes. This relation exists within the poem, for example, in the juxtaposition of the poet's vision and the prior vision which is narrated by Rousseau within the poet's vision. Rousseau's vision comes later in the linear sequence of the poem but earlier in "chronological" time. It puts early late, metaleptically, as late's explanatory predecessor. The relation in question also exists in the encapsulation in the poem of echoes and references to a long chain of previous texts in which the emblematic chariot or other figures of the poem have appeared: Ezekiel, Revelation, Virgil, Dante, Spenser, Milton, Rousseau, Wordsworth. Shelley's poem in its turn is echoed by Hardy, by Yeats, and by many others.

This relation inside the poem between one part of it and another, or the relation of the poem to previous and later texts, is a version of the relation of parasite to host. It exemplifies the undecidable oscillation of that relation. It is impossible to decide which element is parasite, which host, which commands or encloses the other. It is impossible to decide whether the series should be thought of as a sequence of elements each external to the next or according to some model of enclosure like that of the Chinese boxes. When the latter model is applied it is impossible to decide which element of any pair is outside, which is inside. In short, the distinction between inside and outside cannot be held to across that strange membrane, wall at once and copulating hymen, which stands between host and parasite. Each element is both exterior to the adjacent one and at the same time encloses and is enclosed by it.

One of the most striking "episodes" of *The Triumph of Life* is the scene of self-destructive erotic love. This scene matches a series of scenes elsewhere in Shelley's poetry in which the word "parasite" is present. The scene shows sexual attraction as one of the most deadly forms of the triumph of life. The triumph of life is in fact the triumph of language. For Shelley this takes the form of the subjection of each man or woman to illusory figures projected by his or her desire. Each of these figures is made of another substitutive shape of light which fades as it is grasped. It fades because it exists only as a transitory metaphor of light. It is a momentary lightbearer. Venus, star of evening, as the poem says, is only another disguise of Lucifer, fallen star of the morning. Vesper becomes Hesper by a change of initial consonant, masculine H for feminine V.

When the infatuated lovers of *The Triumph of Life* rush together, they annihilate one another, like particle and antiparticle, or, in the metaphors Shelley uses, like two thunderclouds colliding in a narrow valley, or like a great wave crashing on the shore. This annihilation, nevertheless, is not complete, since the violent collision leaves always a trace, a remnant, foam on the shore. This is Aphrodite's foam, seed or sperm which starts the cycle all over again in Shelley's drama of endless repetition. The darkest feature of the triumph of life, for Shelley, is that it may not even be ended by death. Life, for him, though it is a living death, may not die. It regenerates itself interminably in ever-new figures of light:

> . . . in their dance round her who dims
> the Sun
>
> Maidens & youths fling their wild arms in air
> As their feet twinkle; they recede, and now
> Bending within each other's atmosphere
>
> Kindle invisibly; and as they glow
> Like moths by light attracted & repelled,
> Oft to new bright destruction come & go.
>
> Till like two clouds into one vale impelled
> That shake the mountains when their
> lightnings mingle
> And die in rain,—the fiery band which held
>
> Their natures, snaps . . . ere the shock
> cease to tingle
> One falls and then another in the path
> Senseless, nor is the desolation single,
>
> Yet ere I can say *where* the chariot hath
> Past over them; nor other trace I find
> But as of foam after the Ocean's wrath
>
> Is spent upon the desert shore.
>
> [ll. 148–64][13]

This magnificent passage is the culmination of a series of passages writing and rewriting the same materials in a chain of repetitions beginning with *Queen Mab*. In the earlier versions the word "parasite" characteristically appears, like a discreet identifying mark woven into the texture of the verbal fabric. The word appears in *Queen Mab* and in the version of one episode of *Queen Mab* called *The Daemon of the World*. It appears then in *Alastor,* in *Laon and Cythna,* in *The Revolt of Islam,* in *Epipsychidion,* and in *The Sensitive Plant,* always with the same surrounding context of motifs and themes. These include narcissism and incest, the conflict of generations, struggles for political power, the motifs of the sun and the moon, the fountain, the brook, the caverned enclosure, ruined tower, or woodland dell, the dilapidation of man's constructions by nature, and the failure of the poetic quest.

That part of *Queen Mab* which Shelley reworked under the title *The Daemon of the World* contains the earliest version of the complex of elements (including the chariot from Ezekiel) which receives its final expression in *The Triumph of Life*. There Ianthe's "golden tresses shade / The bosom's stainless pride, / Twining like tendrils of the parasite / Around a marble column" (ll. 44–47).

In *Alastor* the doomed poet, like Narcissus searching for his lost twin sister, seeks the "veiled maid" (l. 151) who has come to him in dreams. He seeks her in a woodland glen with a "well / Dark, gleaming and of most translucent wave" (ll. 457–58), but he finds only his own eyes reflected there. These eyes, however, are doubled by "two eyes, / Two starry eyes" (ll. 489–90), which meet his eyes when his look rises. They are perhaps actual stars, perhaps the eyes of his evasive beloved. This play of eyes and looks had been prepared a few lines earlier in a description of "parasites, / Starred with ten thousand blossoms" (ll. 439–40), which twine around the trees of the dense forest hiding this well.

In Canto VI of *Laon and Cythna,* then again in the revised version, *The Revolt of Islam* (which veils the theme of incestuous love), Cythna rescues Laon from defeat in battle and takes him for a wild ride on a Tartar's courser to a ruined palace on a mountain top. There they make love, in another scene involving eyes, looks, stars, and Narcissus' well: "her dark and deepening eyes, / Which, as twin phantoms of one star that lies / O'er a dim well, move, though the Star reposes, / Swam in our mute and liquid ecstasies" (ll. 2624–28). This lovemaking takes place in a "natural couch of leaves" in a recess of the ruin. The recess is shaded in spring

[13] *The Triumph of Life* is cited from the text established by Donald H. Reiman in *Shelley's "The Triumph of Life": A Critical Study* (Urbana, Ill.: The University of Illinois Press, 1965). All other citations from Shelley are taken from *Poetical Works,* ed. Thomas Hutchinson, corrected by G. M. Matthews (London, Oxford, New York: Oxford University Press, 1973). [Au.]

by "flowering parasites" which shed their "stars" on the dead leaves when the wandering wind blows (ll. 2578–84).

In *Epipsychidion,* the poet plans to take the lady Emily to an island with a ruined tower where, as he says, "We shall become the same, we shall be one / Spirit within two frames" (ll. 573–74). This ruin too is shaded by "parasite flowers" (l. 502), just as, in *The Sensitive Plant,* the garden which the lady personifies contains "parasite bowers" (l. 47) which die when winter comes.

A special version of the undecidable structure contained within the word "parasite" operates in all these passages. One could say either that the word contains the passages in miniature within itself or that the passages themselves are a dramatization of the word. The passages limit the word's meaning and expand it at the same time, tracing out one special design within the complex system of thought and figuration contained within the word.

These passages might be defined as an attempt to get a complicated group of themes to come out right. Their aim is magical or Promethean. They attempt to describe an act of Narcissistic self-begetting and self-possession which is at the same time an incestuous lovemaking between brother and sister. This lovemaking short-circuits the differences of the sexes and the heterogeneity of families in an unlawful sexual coupling. At the same time this act is a breakdown of the barrier between man and nature. It is also a political act putting an end to a tyranny which is imaged as the familial domination of a bad father over his children and over his progeny in all succeeding generations. It is, finally, an act of poetry which will destroy the barriers between sign and signified. Such poetry will produce an apocalypse of immediacy in which no more poetry will be needed because no more figures will be needed, no metaphors, no substitutions or "standings for," no veils. Man will then stand in the presence of a universal present which will be all light. It will no longer require Luciferic shapes, persons, figures, or images from nature to bear that light and in the bearing hide it.

All these projects fail at once. They fail in a way which *The Triumph of Life* makes clearest in showing that the conjunction of lovers, clouds, wave and shore, or words both destroys what it conjoins and always leaves a remainder. This genetic trace starts the cycle of lovemaking, attempts by the self to possess itself, self-destructive political tyranny, and poetry-writing all over again. Shelley's poetry is the record of a perpetually renewed failure. It is a failure ever to get the right formula and so end the separate incomplete self, end lovemaking, end politics, and end poetry, all at once, in a performative apocalypse in which words will become the fire they have ignited and so vanish as words, in a universal light. The words, however, always remain, there on the page, as the unconsumed traces of each unsuccessful attempt to use words to end words. The attempt must therefore be repeated. The same scene, with the same elements in a slightly different arrangement, is written by Shelley over and over again from *Queen Mab* to *The Triumph of Life,* in a repetition ended only with his death. This repetition mimes the poet's failure ever to get it right and so end the necessity of trying once more with what remains.

The word "parasite," for Shelley, names the bridge, wall, or connecting membrane which at once makes this apocalyptic union possible, abolishing difference, and at the same time always remains as a barrier forbidding it. Like the thin line of Aphrodite's foam on the shore, this remnant starts the process all over again after the vanishing of the previous couple in their violent attempt to end the interminable chain. The parasite is, on the one hand, the barrier and marriage hymen between the horizontal elements which make some binary opposition. This opposition generates forms and generates also a narrative of their interaction. At the same time the parasite is the barrier and connecting screen between elements on different planes vertically, Earth and Heaven, this world and a spiritual one above it. The world above is the white radiance of eternity. This world's opposing pairs, male, for example, against female, both figure forth and hide that white fire.

Parasites for Shelley are always parasite *flowers.* They are vines which twine themselves around the trees of a forest to climb to light and air, or they grow on a ruined palace to cover its stone and make fragrant bowers there. Parasitical flowering vines feed on air and on what they can take from their hosts. Those hosts they join with their stems. Shelley's parasites flower abundantly, making a screen between sky and earth. This screen remains even in winter as a lattice of dried vines.

A final ambiguity of Shelley's version of the system of parasite and host is the impossibility of deciding whether the sister-beloved in these poems is on the same plane as the desiring poet or a transcendent spirit infinitely above him. She is both at once. She is a sister to whom the protagonist might make love, incestuously. At the same time she is an unattainable muse or mother who governs all, as the spirit eyes Alastor pursues are those of no earthly sister, or as the poet's love for Emily in *Epipsychidion* is also an attempt, like that of Prometheus, to steal heavenly fire, or as the scene of erotic love in *The Triumph of Life* is presided over by the devouring female goddess, riding in her triumph, Life, or as, in the first version of this pattern, the earthly Ianthe beloved by Henry is doubled by the female Daemon of the World who presides over their relation and who is present at the end of the poem as the star repeating the heroine's eyes. These star-like eyes are a constant symbol in Shelley of the unattainable transcendent power in its relation to the earthly signs of it, but at the same time they are no more than the beloved's eyes, and also, at the same time, the protagonist's own eyes reflected back to him.

IV

The motif of a relation between the generations in which one generation is related parasitically to another, with the full ambiguity of that relation, appears in *Epipsychidion* in its most complete form. This version makes clearest the relation of this theme to the system of parasite and host, to the theme in Shelley of a repetition generated always by what is left over after an earlier cataclysmic self-destruction, to the political theme which is always present in these passages, to the relation of man's works to nature, and to the dramatization of the power of poetry which is always one of Shelley's themes.

The ruined tower in the Sporades to which the poet will take his Emily in *Epipsychidion* is said, in one of the drafts of the preface, somewhat prosaically, to be "a Saracenic castle which accident has preserved in some repair." In the poem itself this tower is a strange structure which has grown naturally, almost like a flower or stone, saxifrage and saxiform. At the same time it is almost supernatural. It is a house for a god and a goddess, or at any rate for a semi-divine Ocean-King and his sister-spouse. The building brackets the human level. It is above and below that level at once:

> But the chief marvel of the wilderness
> Is a lone dwelling, built by whom or how
> None of the rustic island-people know:
> 'Tis not a tower of strength, though with its
> height
> It overtops the woods; but, for delight,
> Some wise and tender Ocean-King, ere
> crime
> Had been invented, in the world's young
> prime,
> Reared it, a wonder of that simple time,
> An envy of the isles, a pleasure-house
> Made sacred to his sister and his spouse.
> It scarce seems now a wreck of human art,
> But, as it were Titanic; in the heart
> Of Earth having assumed its form, then
> grown
> Out of the mountains, from the living stone,
> Lifting itself in caverns light and high:
> For all the antique and learned imagery
> Has been erased, and in the place of it
> The ivy and the wild-vine interknit
> The volumes of their many-twining stems;
> Parasite flowers illume with dewy gems
> The lampless halls, and when they fade, the
> sky
> Peeps through their winter-woof of tracery
> With moonlight patches, or star atoms keen,
> Or fragments of the day's intense serene;—
> Working mosaic on their Parian floors.
>
> [ll. 483–507]

An "Ocean-King" is, possibly, a human king of this ocean isle and at the same time, possibly, a King of the Ocean, an Olympian or a Titan. In any case, this dwelling was built "in the world's young prime." It was built near the time of origin, when the opposites were confounded or nearly confounded and when incest was not a crime, as it was not for those Egyptian pharaohs who always mated with their sisters, only fit spouses for their earthly divinity. In the same way, in that young time, nature and culture were not opposed. The palace seems at once "Titanic," the work of a superhuman strength, and at the same time human, since it is, after all, "a wreck of human art," though it scarcely seems so. At the same time it is natural, as though it had grown from the rock, not been built by human art at all. Though the building was once adorned with elaborate carved inscriptions and images, those have been effaced by time. Its towers and facades now seem once more natural rock, grown out of the mountains, living stone. The natural, the supernatural, and the human were reconciled in a union whose symbol was brother-sister incest, the same mating with the same, so short-circuiting normal human love with its production of new genetic lines. The prohibition against incest, as Lévi-Strauss[14] has argued, is both human and natural at once. It therefore breaks down the barrier between the two. This breaking was doubly broken by the Ocean-King and his sister. Their copulation kept crime from being invented. It held nature, the supernatural, and the human together—mimicking and maintaining that vision of unity which can be seen from the palace. This seascape-landscape, two in one, makes the particulars of nature seem the ideal dream of a fulfilled sexuality between two great gods, Earth and Ocean:

> And, day and night, aloof, from the high
> towers
> And terraces, the Earth and Ocean seem
> To sleep in one another's arms, and dream
> Of waves, flowers, clouds, woods, rocks, and
> all that we
> Read in their smiles, and call reality.
>
> [ll. 508–12]

To this place the poet plans to bring his Emily, promising a renewal of that ideal sexual union of the prime time. This renewal will magically renew the time itself. It will take them back to a time prior to the invention of crime and reconcile once more, in a performative embrace, nature, supernature, and man.

This performance, however, can never be performed. It remains at the end of *Epipsychidion* a proleptic hope which is forbidden by the words which express it. It can never be performed because in fact this union never existed in the past. It is only a projection backward from the present. It is a "seeming" created by reading the signs or remnants still present in the present. The Ocean-King, wise and tender though he may have been, was human after all. The prohibition against incest precedes the committing of incest. It precedes the division between natural and human while at the same time creating that division. The love-making of the Ocean-King and his spouse was itself the act which "invented crime." Though it was a mating of the same with the same, it did not put a stop to the difference of sexes, families, and generations, as the peopling of the earth, the presence of political and paternal tyranny, the existence of the poet with his unassuaged desire for Emily all demonstrate.

Moreover, the building only seemed to be natural, divine, and human at once. Though its stone is natural enough, its shape was in fact a product of human art, as is demonstrated by the presence on it once of "antique and learned imagery." This imagery was learned because it pointed back still further to a human tradition already immemorial. The "volumes" of the ivy and the wild vine, that screen of parasite flowers, the former making a hieroglyphic pattern on the stone, the latter casting mosaic patterns in tracery on the marble floors, are substitutes for that effaced writing. The purely natural vines and parasites here paradoxically become a kind of writing. They stand for the erased pattern of learned imagery carved in the stone by the Ocean-King's builders. They stand also by implication for writing in general, the writing for example of the poem itself which the reader is at that moment retracing. Yet the pattern of parasite vines is no legible language. It remains "in place of" the erased human language. In this "in place of" all the imaginary unity of "the world's young prime" breaks down. It is dispersed back into irreconcilable compartments separated by the dividing textured membrane which tries to bring them together. Male and female; divine, human, supernatural—all become separate realms. They are realms separated by language itself and by the dependence of language on figure, on the "in place of" of metaphor or allegorical substitution. Any attempt to cross the barrier and unify what have from all time been separated by the language which brings them together (that antique and learned imagery which was already there even for the wise and tender Ocean-King and his sister spouse), leads only to an exacer-

[14]See *Claude Lévi-Strauss*. See also Lévi-Strauss's *Elementary Structures of Kinship* (Boston: Beacon Press, 1969). [Eds.]

bation of the distance. It becomes a transgression which creates the barrier it attempts to efface or ignore. Incest cannot exist without kinship names and is "invented" as a crime not so much in sexual acts between brother and sister as in any imagery for them. This imagery, however, is always there, of immemorial antiquity. It joins nature and culture in what divides them, as the living stone is covered with carved images making it humanly significant, and as the parasite vines or rather the filigrees of their shadows are taken as signs.

In the same way the poet's attempt to repeat with Emily the pleasure of the Ocean-King and his sister only repeats the crime of illicit sexual relations, always at least implicitly incest for Shelley. "Would we two had been twins of the same mother!" (l. 45) says the protagonist to his Emily. The speaker's love only prolongs the divisions. His union with Emily remains always in the future, as is Henri's love in *The Daemon of the World,* or as is the hero's love in *Alastor,* and as the union of Laon and Cythna is paid for when they are burned at the stake. The lovemaking of Laon and Cythna does not in any case produce the political liberation of Islam. In the same way, the poet's attempt in *Epipsychidion* to express in words this union becomes itself the barrier forbidding it. It forbids also the poet's Promethean attempt to scale heaven and seize its fire through language and through erotic love. The passage is one of Shelley's grandest symphonic climaxes, but what it expresses is the failure of poetry and the failure of love. It expresses the destruction of the poet-lover in his attempt to escape his boundaries, the chains at once of selfhood and of language. This failure is Shelley's version of the parasite structure.

Who, however, is "Shelley"? To what does this word refer if any work signed with this name has no identifiable borders, and no interior walls either? It has no edges because it has been invaded from all sides as well as from within by other "names," other powers of writing—Rousseau, Dante, Ezekiel, and the whole host of others, phantom strangers who have crossed the thresholds of the poems, erasing their margins. Though the word "Shelley" may be printed on the cover of a book entitled *Poetical Works,* it must name something without identifiable bounds, since the book incorporates so much outside within its inside. The parasite structure obliterates the frontiers of the texts it enters. For "Shelley," then, the parasite is a communicating screen of figurative language which permanently divides what it would unify in a perpetual "in place of" forbidding union. This screen creates the shadow of that union as an effect of figure, a phantasmal "once was" and "might yet be," never "now" and "here":

Our breath shall intermix, our bosoms
    bound,
And our veins beat together; and our lips
With other eloquence than words, eclipse
The soul that burns between them, and the
    wells
Which boil under our being's inmost cells,
The fountains of our deepest life, shall be
Confused in Passion's golden purity,
As mountain-springs under the morning
    sun.
We shall become the same, we shall be one
Spirit within two frames, oh! wherefore
    two?
One passion in twin-hearts, which grows
    and grew,
Till like two meteors of expanding flame,
Those spheres instinct with it become the
    same,
Touch, mingle, are transfigured; ever still
Burning, yet ever inconsumable:
In one another's substance finding food,
Like flames too pure and light and
    unimbued
To nourish their bright lives with baser prey,
Which point to Heaven and cannot pass
    away:
One hope within two wills, one will beneath
Two overshadowing minds, one life, one
    death,
One Heaven, one Hell, one immortality,
And one annihilation. Woe is me!
The winged words on which my soul would
    pierce
Into the height of Love's rare Universe,
Are chains of lead around its flight of fire—
I pant, I sink, I tremble, I expire!

[ll. 565–91]

No reader of these extraordinary lines can fail to feel that the poet here protests too much. Every repetition of the word "one" only adds another layer to the barrier forbidding oneness. The poet protests too much not only in the attempt in words to produce a union which these words themselves keep from happening, but even in the concluding outcry of woe. Not only does the poet not achieve union through words with his Emily and so climb to Love's fiery heights. He does not even "expire" through the failure of these magic performatives. Words do not make anything happen, nor does their failure to make anything happen either. Though the "Advertisement" to *Epipsychidion* tells the reader the poet died in Florence without ever reaching that isle, "one of wildest of the Sporades," the reader knows that words did not kill him, for "I pant, I sink, I tremble, I expire!" is followed by the relatively calm post-climax dedicatory lines beginning: "Weak Verses, go, kneel at your Sovereign's feet" (l. 591).

The grand climactic passage itself is made of variations on the paradoxical parasite structure. The verbal signs for union necessarily rebuild the barrier they would obliterate. The more the poet says they will be one the more he makes them two by reaffirming the ways they are separated. The lips that speak with an eloquence other than words are doors which are also a liminal barrier between person and person. Those lips may eclipse the soul that burns between them, but they remain as a communicating medium which also is a barrier to union. The lips are the parasite structure once more. Moreover, the voice that speaks of an eloquence beyond words uses eloquent words to speak of this transverbal speech. By naming such speech it keeps the soul from being eclipsed. In the same way, the image of the deep wells reaffirms the notion of cellular enclosure, just as the clash of fire and water in the figure of the mountain-springs being "confused" under the morning sun tells the reader that only by evaporating as entities can lovers become one. The images of two frames with one spirit, the double meteors becoming one floating sphere, the pair each both eater and eaten ("in one another's substance finding food"), are the parasitical relation again. All play variations on "Shelley's" version of the parasite structure, the notion of a unity which yet remains double but in the figurative expression of that unity reveals the impossibility of two becoming one across a parasitic wall and yet remaining two.

This impossibility is mimed in the final *mise en abîme*. This is a cascade of expressions describing a twoness resting on the ground of a oneness which then subdivides once more to rest on a still deeper ground which ultimately reveals itself to be, if it exists at all, the abyss of "annihilation." The vertical wall between cell and cell, lover and beloved, is doubled by a horizontal veil between levels of being. Each veil when removed only reveals another veil, ad infinitum, unless the veil exposes an emptiness. This would be the emptiness of that oneness which is implored into existence in the reiteration of "one," "one," "one," "one": "One hope within two wills, one will beneath / Two overshadowing minds, one life, one death / One Heaven, one Hell, one immortality, / And one annihilation. Woe is me!" The language which tries to efface itself as language to give way to an unmediated union beyond language is itself the barrier which always remains as the woe of an ineffaceable trace. Words are always there as remnant, "chains of lead" which forbid the flight to fiery union they invoke.

This does not mean that love-making and poetry-making are the "same thing" or subject to the same impasses determining their failure as performatives magically transforming the world. In a sense they are antagonists, since lovemaking attempts to do wordlessly what poetry attempts to do with words. No one can doubt that Shelley believed sexual experience "occurs" or that he "describes" it in his poetry, for example in *Laon and Cythna* and in the great passage on erotic love in *The Triumph of Life*. Lovemaking and poetrymaking are not, however, stark opposites in Shelley either. Each is, so to speak, the dramatization of the other or the figure of it. This is an elliptical relation in which whichever of the two the reader focuses on reveals itself to be the metaphorical substitution for the other. The other, however, when the reader moves to it, is not the "original" but a figure of what at first seemed a figure for it. Lovemaking, as *The Triumph of Life* shows, is a way to "experience," as incarnate suffering, the self-destructive effects of signmaking, sign-projecting, and signinterpretation. The wordlessness of lovemaking is only another way of dwelling within signs after all, as is shown in *The Triumph of Life* by the affirmed identity between Venus, evening star of love, and Lucifer, star of morning, "light-bearer," personification of personification and of all the other tropes, all the forms of the "in place of."

Poetrymaking, on the other hand, is for Shelley always a figure of, as well as figured by, the various forms of life—political, religious, familial, and erotic. It does not have priority as an origin but can exist only embodied in one or another of the forms of life it figures. There is, for Shelley, no "sign" without its material carrier, and so the play of substitutions in language can never be a purely ideal interchange. This interchange is always contaminated by its necesary incarnation, the most dramatic form of which is the bodies of lovers. On the other hand, lovemaking is never a purely wordless communion or intercourse. It is in its turn contaminated by language. Lovemaking is a way of living, in the flesh, the aporias of figure. It is also a way of experiencing the way language functions to forbid the perfect union of lovers. Language always remains, after they have exhausted or even annihilated themselves in an attempt to get it right, as the genetic trace starting the cycle all over again.

V

Five times, or seven times if one counts *The Daemon of the World* and *The Revolt of Islam* as separate texts, seven times, or even more than seven if one includes other passages with the same elements where the word "parasite" does not appear—more than seven times, then, throughout his work, Shelley casts himself against the lips of the parasitical gate. Each time he falls back, having failed to make two into one without annihilating both. He falls back as himself the remainder, the power of langauge able to say "Woe is me!" and forced to try again to break the barrier only to fail once more, in repetitions which are terminated only by his death.

The critic, in his turn, like those poets, Browning, Hardy, Yeats, or Stevens who have been decisively "influenced" by Shelley, is a follower who repeats the pattern once again and once again fails to "get it right," just as Shelley repeats himself and repeats his precursors, and just as the poet and Emily follow the Ocean-King and his sister spouse.

The critic's version of the pattern proliferated in this chain of repetitions is as follows. The critic's attempt to untwist the elements in the texts he interprets only twists them up again in another place and leaves always a remnant of opacity, or an added opacity, as yet unraveled. The critic is caught in his own version of the interminable repetitions which determine the poet's career. The critic experiences this as his failure to get his poet right in a final decisive formulation which will allow him to have done with that poet, once and for all. Though each poet is different, each contains his own form of undecidability. This might be defined by saying that the critic can never show decisively whether or not the work of the writer is "decidable," whether or not it is capable of being definitely interpreted. The critic cannot unscramble the tangle of lines of meaning, comb its threads out so they shine clearly side by side. He can only retrace the text, set its elements in motion once more, in that experience of the failure of determinable reading which is decisive here.

The blank wall beyond which rational analysis cannot go arises from the copresence in any text in Western literature, inextricably intertwined, as host and parasite, of some version of logocentric metaphysics and its subversive counterpart. In Shelley's case these are, on the one hand, the "idealism" always present as one possible reading of his poems, even of *The Triumph of Life,* and on the other hand, the putting in question of this in Shelley's "scepticism" by a recognition of the role of projections in human life. This is that law of shadowing which deconstructs idealism. It is most explicitly formulated in *The Triumph of Life:*

> Figures ever new
> Rise on the bubble [of the phenomenal and historical world], paint them how you may;
> We have but thrown, as those before us threw,
> Our shadows on it as it past away.
>
> [ll. 248–51]

The "deconstruction" of metaphysics by an appeal to the figurative nature of language always, however, contains its own impasse, whether this dismantling is performed within the writing of the author himself or in the following of that in repetitive retracing by the critic who comes after, as in my discussion here. This impasse is itself double. On the one hand, the poet and his shadow, the critic, can "deconstruct" metaphysics only with some tool of analysis which is capable of becoming another form of metaphysics in its turn. To put this another way, the differentiation between metaphysics and scepticism reforms itself as a new form of doubleness within "scepticism." Scepticism is not a firm and unequivocal machine of deconstruction. It carries within itself another form of the parasite structure, mirror image with the valences reversed of that within metaphysics itself.

The appeal to language from idealism is an admirable example of this. As is abundantly apparent in criticism at the present time, rhetorical analysis, "semiotics," "structuralism," "narratology," or the interpretation of tropes can freeze into a quasi-scientific discipline promising exhaustive rational certainty in the identification of meaning in a text and in the identification of the way that meaning is produced. The appeal to etymologies can become another archeology. It can become another way to be beguiled by the apparent explanatory power of seeming "origins" and the accompanying explanatory power of the apparently causally determined chains which emerge from a starting point in some "Indo-European root." Insofar as this move in contemporary criticism is motivated by an appeal to Freud's linguistic insights, such critics should perhaps remember Freud's demonstration, in *The Psychopathology of Everyday Life* and in *Jokes and the Unconscious,* of the way wordplay in all its forms is superficial. Wordplay is the repression of something more dangerous. This something, however, interweaves itself with that wordplay and forbids it to be merely verbal or merely play. Rhetorical analysis, the analysis of figure, and even an investigation of etymologies are necessary to put in question a heavily idealist reading of Shelley, but these must be dismantled in their turn in an interminable movement of interrogation which is the life of criticism. Criticism is a human activity which depends for its validity on never being at ease within a fixed "method." It must constantly put its own grounds in question. The critical text and the literary text are each parasite and host for the other, each feeding on the other and feeding it, destroying and being destroyed by it.

The dismantling of the linguistic assumptions necessary to dismantle Shelley's idealism must occur, however, not by a return to idealism, and not by the appeal to some "metalanguage" which will encompass both, but by a movement through rhetorical analysis, the analysis of tropes, and the appeal to etymologies, to something "beyond" language which can yet only be reached by recognition of the linguistic moment in its counter-momentum against idealism or against logocentric metaphysics. By "linguistic moment" I mean the moment in a work of literature when its own medium is put in question. This moment allows the critic to take what remains from the clashing of scepticism and idealism as a new starting place, for example by the recognition of a performative function of language which has entered into my discussion of Shelley. This again, in its reinstating of a new form of referentiality and in its formation of a new clashing, this time between rhetoric as tropes and rhetoric as performative words, must be interrogated in its turn, in a ceaseless movement of interpretation which Shelley himself has mimed in the sequence of episodes in *The Triumph of Life.*

This movement is not subject to dialectical synthesis, nor to any other closure. The undecidable, nevertheless, always has an impetus back into some covert form of dialectical movement, as in my terminology here of the "chain" and the "going beyond." This is constantly countered, however, by the experience of movement in place. The momentary always tends to generate a narrative, even if it is the narrative of the impossibility of narrative, the impossibility of getting from here to there by means of language. The tension between dialectic and undecidability is another way in which this form of criticism remains open, in the ceaseless movement of an "in place of" without resting place.

The word "deconstruction" is in one way a good one to name this movement. The word, like other words in "de," "decrepitude," for example, or "denotation," describes a paradoxical action which is negative and positive at once. In this it is like all words with a double antithetical prefix, words in "ana," like "analysis," or words in "para," like "parasite." These words tend to come in pairs which are not opposites, positive against negative. They are related in a systematic differentiation which requires a different analysis or untying in each case, but which in each case leads, in a different way each time, to the tying up of a double bind. This tying up is at the same time a loosening. It is a paralysis of thought in the face of what cannot be thought rationally: analysis, paralysis; solution, dissolution; composition, decomposition; construction, deconstruction; mantling, dismantling; canny, uncanny; competence, incompetence; apocalyptic, anacalyptic; constituting, deconstituting. Deconstructive criticism moves back and forth between the poles of these pairs, proving in its own activity, for example, that there is no deconstruction which is not at the same time constructive, affirmative. The word says this in juxtaposing "de" and "con."

At the same time, the word "deconstruction" has misleading overtones or implications. It suggests something a bit too external, a bit too masterful and muscular. It suggests the demolition of the helpless text with tools which are other than and stronger than what is demolished. The word "deconstruction" suggests that such criticism is an activity turning something unified back to detached fragments or parts. It suggests the image of a child taking apart his father's watch, reducing it back to useless parts, beyond any reconstitution. A deconstructionist is not a parasite but a parricide. He is a bad son demolishing beyond hope of repair the machine of Western metaphysics.

In fact, insofar as "deconstruction" names the use of rhetorical, etymological, or figurative analysis to demystify the mystifications of literary and philosophical language, this form of criticism is not outside but within. It is of the same nature as what it works against. Far from reducing the text back to detached fragments, it inevitably constructs again in a different form what it deconstructs. It does again as it undoes. It recrosses in one place what it uncrosses in another. Rather than surveying the text with sovereign command from outside, it remains caught within the activity in the text it retraces.

To the action of deconstruction with its implication of an irresistible power of the critic over the text must always be added, as a description of what happens in interpretation, the experience of the impossibility of exercising the power. The dismantler dismantles himself. Far from being a chain which moves deeper and deeper into the text, closer and closer to a definitive interpretation of it, the mode of criticism sometimes now called "deconstruction," which is analytic criticism as such, encounters always, if it is carried far enough, some mode of oscillation. In this oscillation two genuine insights into literature in general and into a given text in particular inhibit, subvert, and undercut one another. This inhibition makes it impossible for either insight to function as a firm resting place, the end point of analysis. My example here has been the copresence in the parasite structure in Shelley of idealism and scepticism, of referentiality which only proleptically refers, in figure, therefore does not refer at all, and of performatives which do not perform. Analysis becomes paralysis, according to the strange necessity which makes these words, or the "experience" or the "procedure," they describe, turn into one another. Each crosses over into its apparent negation or opposite. If the word "deconstruction" names the procedure of criticism, and "oscillation" the impasse reached through that procedure, "undecidability" names the experience of the ceaseless dissatisfied movement in the relation of the critic to the text.

The ultimate justification for this mode of criticism, as of any conceivable mode, is that it works. It reveals hitherto unidentified meanings and ways of having meaning in major literary texts. The hypothesis of a possible heterogeneity in literary texts is more flexible, more open to a given work, than the assumption that a good work of literature is necessarily going to be "organically unified." The latter presupposition is one of the major factors inhibiting recognition of the possibly self-subversive complexity of meanings in a given work. Moreover, "deconstruction" finds in the text it interprets the double antithetical patterns it identifies, for example the relation of parasite and host. It does not claim them as universal explanatory structures, neither for the text in question nor for literature in general. Deconstruction attempts to resist the totalizing and totalitarian tendencies of criticism. It attempts to resist its own tendencies to come to rest in some sense of mastery over the work. It resists these in the name of an uneasy joy of interpretation, beyond nihilism, always in movement, a going beyond which remains in place, as the parasite is outside the door but also always already within, uncanniest of guests.

Julia Kristeva

b. 1941

SINCE HER arrival in Paris from her native Bulgaria in 1966, Julia Kristeva has played an increasingly important and interesting role in the ongoing critique of intellectual traditions that has dominated recent French thought. Kristeva's interests have expanded to include virtually all of the traditional subjects of the human sciences, from her early participation in Lucien Goldmann's seminar and her work as a research assistant at Lévi-Strauss's Laboratory of Social Anthropology to her positions as a member of the editorial board of Philippe Sollers' influential journal, *Tel Quel,* a professor at the University of Paris VII, and a practicing psychoanalyst. At the center of those interests, ranging from literary history and linguistics to social theory and psychoanalysis, is the "speaking subject" and "poetic language," ideas that Kristeva does not relinquish as casualties of the critique of signification but emphasizes as essential postulates of any theory of language or society. More specifically, her work as represented in *Desire in Language* develops what she terms "semanalysis," linking semiotics and psychoanalysis, to show how the speaking subject is shaped by the complex matrix of forces present in and deployed by signifying systems within a culture.

Kristeva's "semanalysis" focuses on "signifying practices," particularly in poetry and art, that reflect the intertwined problems of meaning, the subject, and the idea of structure. Partly under the influence of the Russian formalists (see, for example, *Bahktin* and Boris Eichenbaum, *CTSP,* pp. 829–46), Kristeva singles out poetic language for its distinctive capacity to call attention to polysemy, ambiguity, and undecidability in natural language, making artistic signification therefore a rich arena for exploration and discovery.

While this view is in many respects very traditional, it has radical implications for Kristeva's complex view of feminism, as presented in the essay here. Following Lacan, Kristeva argues that the Freudian castration anxiety is, "in sum, the imaginary construction of a radical operation which constitutes the symbolic field" separating language from a state of nature. Any "signifying practice," in this view, gives a semiotic meaning to the social contract as a "symbolic contract," just as it complicates all social transactions with a sense of loss and desire. In this way, entering into the sociosymbolic contract makes meaning possible, as Kristeva puts it, only in reference "to the *lack* or to the *desire* which constitutes the subject during his or her insertion into the order of language."

By posing her argument in terms of time, Kristeva contrasts two temporal orders, drawing terms from Nietzsche, to distinguish in *linear time* the early phase of modern feminism as tied to the historical moment of the nation or state, and from a more recent phase (after the profound political disturbances of the late 1960s) in which the universalization or deterritorializing of feminist issues belongs to *monumental time*. But while "monumental" time for Nietzsche is virtually mythic, Kristeva treats it as a political "future perfect," just when the traditional means for political (and other) modes of signification are breaking down. Kristeva's analysis is particularly cautious since the symbolic contract at issue can easily be the site for violence. Before the "terror of power," Kristeva reminds us, we may be led to terrorism in the "desire for power."

For similar reasons, Kristeva in this essay (as elsewhere) is somewhat wary of the term "theory," since any analytical discourse can itself be taken up into the signifying structure it seeks to analyze—just as women, given access to positions of power in a male-dominated system, may be taken up into the defense and justification of the system itself. To be thus incorporated is in part to be neutralized or neutered; and the apparently more radical alternative, to inaugurate a countersociety, has ironically the same effect by requiring exclusion and, therefore, scapegoating. As Kristeva observes, feminism may then become "a kind of inverted sexism," insulating itself against criticism.

It is possible that in taking a critical stance, the essay might be regarded as antifeminist (see, for example, *Jardine*); but its crucial point is that for a "new generation" of women, these issues will be insistently present. Kristeva's somber speculation (which she marks as "undoubtedly too Hegelian") is that modern feminism may be "but a moment in the interminable process of coming to consciousness about the implacable violence (separation, castration, etc.) which constitutes any symbolic contract."

The hope held out, however, returns upon the signifying practices of poetry, art, and religion. In Kristeva's view, these are practices that rely on an essentially religious need for speaking beings "to provide themselves with a *representation* (animal, female, male, parental, etc.) in place of what constitutes them as such." Only a critical perspective can bear in mind that the process may turn to "deadly violence" or to "a cultural innovation" and that the aesthetic question is also a question of morality and ethics. Kristeva's speculation in this context is more sanguine, less somber: a new generation may find the means to interiorize the "founding separation of the sociosymbolic contract" and, in so doing, move not only beyond sexism but anthropomorphism in general.

A number of Kristeva's books and essays are available in English. See especially *Desire in Language: A Semiotic Approach to Literature and Art* (1980); *Powers of Horror: An Essay on Abjection* (1980, trans. 1982); and *Revolution in Poetic Language* (1974, trans. 1984). See also Leon S. Roudiez's "Introduction" to *Desire in Language,* and Alice Jardine, "Theories of the Feminine: Kristeva," *Enclitic* (1982).

WOMEN'S TIME

The nation—dream and reality of the nineteenth century—seems to have reached both its apogee and its limits when the 1929 crash and the National-Socialist apocalypse demolished the pillars that, according to Marx, were its essence: economic homogeneity, historical tradition, and linguistic unity.[1] It could indeed be demonstrated that World War II, though fought in the name of national values (in the above sense of the term), brought an end to the nation as a reality: It was turned into a mere illusion which, from that point forward, would be preserved only for ideological or strictly political purposes, its social and philosophical coherence having collapsed. To move quickly toward the specific problematic that will occupy us in this article, let us say that the chimera of economic *homogeneity* gave way to *interdependence* (when not submission to the economic superpowers), while *historical* tradition and *linguistic* unity were recast as a broader and deeper determinant: what might be called a *symbolic denominator*, defined as the cultural and religious memory forged by the interweaving of history and geography. The variants of this memory produce social territories which then redistribute the cutting up into political parties which is still in use but losing strength. At the same time, this memory or symbolic denominator, common to them all, reveals beyond economic globalization and/or uniformization certain characteristics transcending the nation that sometimes embrace an entire continent. A new social ensemble superior to the nation has thus been constituted, within which the nation, far from losing its own traits, rediscovers and accentuates them in a strange temporality, in a kind of "future perfect," where the most deeply repressed past gives a distinctive character to a logical and sociological distribution of the most modern type. For this memory or symbolic common denominator concerns the response that human groupings, united in space and time, have given not to the problems of the *production* of material goods (i.e., the domain of the economy and of the human relationships it implies, politics, etc.) but, rather, to those of *reproduction*, survival of the species, life and death, the body, sex, and symbol. If it is true, for example, that Europe is representative of such a sociocultural ensemble, it seems to me that its existence is based more on this "symbolic denominator," which its art, philosophy, and religions manifest, than on its economic profile, which is certainly interwoven with collective memory but whose traits change rather rapidly under pressure from its partners.

It is clear that a social ensemble thus constituted possesses both a *solidity* rooted in a particular mode of reproduction and its representations through which the biological species is connected to its humanity, which is a tributary of time; as well as a certain *fragility* as a result of the fact that, through its universality, the symbolic common denominator is necessarily echoed in the corresponding symbolic denominator of another sociocultural ensemble. Thus, barely constituted as such, Europe finds itself being asked to compare itself with, or even to recognize itself in, the cultural, artistic, philosophical, and religious constructions belonging to other supranational sociocultural ensembles. This seems natural when the entities involved were linked by history (e.g., Europe and North America, or Europe and Latin America), but the phenomenon also occurs when the universality of this denominator we have called symbolic juxtaposes modes of production and reproduction apparently opposed in both the past and the present (e.g., Europe and India, or Europe and China). In short, with sociocultural ensembles of the European type, we are constantly faced with a double problematic: that of their *identity* constituted by historical sedimentation, and that of their *loss of identity* which is produced by this connection of memories which escape from history only to encounter anthropology. In other words, we confront two temporal dimensions: the time of linear history, or *cursive time* (as Nietzsche called it), and the time of another history, thus another time, *monumental time* (again according to Nietzsche), which englobes these supranational, sociocultural ensembles within even larger entities.

WOMEN'S TIME, originally published as "Le Temps des femmes" in *34/44: Cahiers de recherche des sciences des textes et documents,* no. 5 (Winter 1979), was translated by Alice Jardine and Harry Blake, for publication in *Signs: Journal of Women in Culture and Society* 7 (1981). Reprinted by permission of the University of Chicago Press.

[1]The following discussion emphasizes Europe in a way which may seem superfluous to some American readers given the overall emphasis on deterritorialization. It is, however, essential to the movement of an article that is above all devoted to the necessity of paying attention to the place from which we speak. [Tr.]

I should like to draw attention to certain formations which seem to me to summarize the dynamics of a sociocultural organism of this type. The question is one of sociocultural groups, that is, groups defined according to their place in production, but especially according to their role in the mode of reproduction and its representations, which, while bearing the specific sociocultural traits of the formation in question, are *diagonal* to it and connect it to other sociocultural formations. I am thinking in particular of sociocultural groups which are usually defined as age groups (e.g., "young people in Europe"), as sexual divisions (e.g., "European women"), and so forth. While it is obvious that "young people" or "women" in Europe have their own particularity, it is nonetheless just as obvious that what defines them as "young people" or as "women" places them in a diagonal relationship to their European "origin" and links them to similar categories in North America or in China, among others. That is, insofar as they also belong to "monumental history," they will not be only European "young people" or "women" of Europe but will echo in a most specific way the universal traits of their structural place in reproduction and its representations.

Consequently, the reader will find in the following pages, first, an attempt to situate the problematic of women in Europe within an inquiry on time: that time which the feminist movement both inherits and modifies. Second, I will attempt to distinguish two phases or two generations of women which, while immediately universalist and cosmopolitan in their demands, can nonetheless be differentiated by the fact that the first generation is more determined by the implications of a national problematic (in the sense suggested above), while the second, more determined by its place within the "symbolic denominator," is European *and* trans-European. Finally, I will try, both through the problems approached and through the type of analysis I propose, to present what I consider a viable stance for a European—or at least a European woman—within a domain which is henceforth worldwide in scope.

Which Time?

"Father's time, mother's species," as Joyce put it; and, indeed, when evoking the name and destiny of women, one thinks more of the *space* generating and forming the human species than of *time,* becoming, or history. The modern sciences of subjectivity, of its genealogy and accidents, confirm in their own way this intuition, which is perhaps itself the result of a sociohistorical conjuncture. Freud, listening to the dreams and fantasies of his patients, thought that "hysteria was linked to place."[2] Subsequent studies on the acquisition of the symbolic function by children show that the permanence and quality of maternal love condition the appearance of the first spatial references which induce the child's laugh and then induce the entire range of symbolic manifestations which lead eventually to sign and syntax.[3] Moreover, antipsychiatry and psychoanalysis as applied to the treatment of psychoses, before attributing the capacity for transference and communication to the patient, proceed to the arrangement of new places, gratifying substitutes that repair old deficiencies in the maternal space. I could go on giving examples. But they all converge on the problematic of space, which innumerable religions of matriarchal (re)appearance attribute to "woman," and which Plato, recapitulating in his own system the atomists of antiquity, designated by the aporia of the *chora,* matrix space, nourishing, unnameable, anterior to the One, to God and, consequently, defying metaphysics.[4]

As for time, female[5] subjectivity would seem to

[2] Sigmund Freud and Carl G. Jung, *Correspondence* (Paris: Gallimard, 1975), 1:87. [Au.]

[3] R. Spitz, *La Première année de la vie de l'enfant* [First year of life: a psychoanalytic study of normal and deviant development of object relations] (Paris: PUF, 1958); D. Winnicott, *Jeu et réalité* [Playing and reality] (Paris: Gallimard, 1975); Julia Kristeva, "Noms de lieu" in *Polylogue* (Paris: Editions du Seuil, 1977), translated as "Place Names" in Julia Kristeva, *Desire in Language: A Semiotic Approach to Literature and Art,* ed. Leon S. Roudiez, trans. Thomas Gora, Alice Jardine, and Leon Roudiez (New York: Columbia University Press, 1980) (hereafter cited as *Desire in Language*). [Au. and Tr.]

[4] Plato, *Timaeus* 52: "Indefinitely a place: it cannot be destroyed, but provides a ground for all that can come into being; itself being perceptible, outside of all sensation, by means of a sort of bastard reasoning; barely assuming credibility, it is precisely that which makes us dream when we perceive it, and affirm that all that exists must be somewhere, in a determined place . . ." (my translation). [Au.]

[5] As most readers of recent French theory in translation know, *le féminin* does not have the same pejorative connotations it has come to have in English. It is a term used to speak about women in general, but, as used most often in this article, it probably comes closest to our "female"

provide a specific measure that essentially retains *repetition* and *eternity* from among the multiple modalities of time known through the history of civilizations. On the one hand, there are cycles, gestation, the eternal recurrence of a biological rhythm which conforms to that of nature and imposes a temporality whose stereotyping may shock, but whose regularity and unison with what is experienced as extrasubjective time, cosmic time, occasion vertiginous visions and unnameable *jouissance*.[6] On the other hand, and perhaps as a consequence, there is the massive presence of a monumental temporality, without cleavage or escape, which has so little to do with linear time (which passes) that the very word "temporality" hardly fits: All-encompassing and infinite like imaginary space, this temporality reminds one of Kronos in Hesiod's mythology, the incestuous son whose massive presence covered all of Gea in order to separate her from Ouranos, the father.[7] Or one is reminded of the various myths of resurrection which, in all religious beliefs, perpetuate the vestige of an anterior or concomitant maternal cult, right up to its most recent elaboration, Christianity, in which the body of the Virgin Mother does not die but moves from one spatiality to another within the same time via dormition (according to the Orthodox faith) or via assumption (the Catholic faith).[8]

The fact that these two types of temporality (cyclical and monumental) are traditionally linked to female subjectivity insofar as the latter is thought of as necessarily maternal should not make us forget that this repetition and this eternity are found to be the fundamental, if not the sole, conceptions of time in numerous civilizations and experiences, particularly mystical ones.[9] The fact that certain currents of modern feminism recognize themselves here does not render them fundamentally incompatible with "masculine" values.

In return, female subjectivity as it gives itself up to intuition becomes a problem with respect to a certain conception of time: time as project, teleology, linear and prospective unfolding; time as departure, progression, and arrival—in other words, the time of history.[10] It has already been abundantly demonstrated that this kind of temporality is inherent in the logical and ontological values of any given civilization, that this temporality renders explicit a rupture, an expectation, or an anguish which other temporalities work to conceal. It might also be added that this linear time is that of language considered as the enunciation of sentences (noun + verb; topic-comment; beginning-ending), and that this time rests on its own stumbling block, which is also the stumbling block of that enunciation—death. A psychoanalyst would call this "obsessional time," recognizing in the mastery of time the true structure of the slave. The hysteric (either male or female) who suffers from reminiscences would, rather, recognize his or her self in the anterior temporal modalities: cyclical or monumental. This antinomy, one perhaps embedded in psychic structures, becomes, nonetheless, within a given civilization, an antinomy among social groups and ideologies in which the radical positions of certain feminists would rejoin the discourse of marginal groups of spiritual or mystical inspiration and, strangely enough, rejoin recent scientific preoccupations. Is it not true that the problematic of a time indissociable from space, of a space-time in infinite expansion, or rhythmed by accidents or catastrophes, preoccupies both space science and genetics? And, at another level, is it not true that the contemporary media revolution, which is manifest in the storage and reproduction of information, implies an idea of time as frozen or exploding according to the vagaries of demand, returning to its source but uncontrollable, utterly bypassing its subject and leaving only two preoccupations to those who approve of it: Who is to have power over the origin (the programming) and over the end (the use)?

as defined by Elaine Showalter in *A Literature of Their Own* (Princeton, N.J.: Princeton University Press, 1977). I have therefore used either "women" or "female" according to the context (cf. also n. 9 in "Introduction to Julia Kristeva's 'Women's Time'" in *Signs* 7 [1981], hereafter cited as "Introduction"). "Subjectivity" here refers to the state of being "a thinking, speaking, acting, doing or writing agent" and never, e.g., as opposed to "objectivity" (see the glossary in *Desire in Language*). [Tr.]

[6] I have retained *jouissance*—that word for pleasure which defies translation—as it is rapidly becoming a "believable neologism" in English (see the glossary in *Desire in Language*). [Tr.]

[7] This particular mythology has important implications—equal only to those of the oedipal myth—for current French thought. [Tr.]

[8] See Julia Kristeva, "Hérétique de l'amour," *Tel Quel*, no. 74 (1977), pp. 30–49. [Au.]

[9] See H. C. Peuch, *La Gnose et la temps* (Paris: Gallimard, 1977). [Au.]

[10] See "Introduction." [Tr.]

It is for two precise reasons, within the framework of this article, that I have allowed myself this rapid excursion into a problematic of unheard of complexity. The reader will undoubtedly have been struck by a fluctuation in the term of reference: mother, woman, hysteric. . . . I think that the apparent coherence which the term "woman" assumes in contemporary ideology, apart from its "mass" or "shock" effect for activist purposes, essentially has the negative effect of effacing the differences among the diverse functions or structures which operate beneath this word. Indeed, the time has perhaps come to emphasize the multiplicity of female expressions and preoccupations so that from the intersection of these differences there might arise, more precisely, less commercially, and more truthfully, the real *fundamental difference* between the two sexes: a difference that feminism has had the enormous merit of rendering painful, that is, productive of surprises and of symbolic life in a civilization which, outside the stock exchange and wars, is bored to death.

It is obvious, moreover, that one cannot speak of Europe or of "women in Europe" without suggesting the time in which this sociocultural distribution is situated. If it is true that a female sensibility emerged a century ago, the chances are great that by introducing *its own* notion of time, this sensibility is not in agreement with the idea of an "eternal Europe" and perhaps not even with that of a "modern Europe." Rather, through and with the European past and present, as through and with the ensemble of "Europe," which is the repository of memory, this sensibility seeks its own trans-European temporality. There are, in any case, three attitudes on the part of European feminist movements toward this conception of linear temporality, which is readily labeled masculine and which is at once both civilizational and obsessional.

Two Generations

In its beginnings, the women's movement, as the struggle of suffragists and of existential feminists, aspired to gain a place in linear time as the time of project and history. In this sense, the movement, while immediately universalist, is also deeply rooted in the sociopolitical life of nations. The political demands of women; the struggles for equal pay for equal work; for taking power in social institutions on an equal footing considered feminine or maternal insofar as they are deemed incompatible with insertion in that history—all are part of the *logic of identification*[11] with certain values: not with the ideological (these are combated, and rightly so, as reactionary) but, rather, with the logical and ontological values of a rationality dominant in the nation-state. Here it is unnecessary to enumerate the benefits which this logic of identification and the ensuing struggle have achieved and continue to achieve for women (abortion, contraception, equal pay, professional recognition, etc.); these have already had or will soon have effects even more important than those of the Industrial Revolution. Universalist in its approach, this current in feminism *globalizes* the problems of women of different milieux, ages, civilizations, or simply of varying psychic structures, under the label "Universal Woman." A consideration of *generations* of women can only be conceived of in this global way as a succession, as a progression in the accomplishment of the initial program mapped out by its founders.

In a second phase, linked, on the other hand, to the younger women who came to feminism after May 1968 and, on the other, to women who had an aesthetic or psychoanalytic experience, linear temporality has been almost totally refused, and as a consequence there has arisen an exacerbated distrust of the entire political dimension. If it is true that this more recent current of feminism refers to its predecessors and that the struggle for sociocultural recognition of women is necessarily its main concern, this current seems to think of itself as belonging to another generation—qualitatively different from the first one—in its conception of its own identity and, consequently, of temporality as such. Essentially interested in the specificity of female psychology and its symbolic realizations, these women seek to give a language to the intrasubjective and corporeal experiences left mute by culture in the

[11] The term "identification" belongs to a wide semantic field ranging from everyday language to philosophy and psychoanalysis. While Kristeva is certainly referring in principle to its elaboration in Freudian and Lacanian psychoanalysis, it can be understood here, as a logic, in its most general sense (see the entry on "identification" in Jean LaPlanche and J. B. Pontalis, *Vocabulaire de la psychanalyse* [The language of psychoanalysis] [Paris: Presses Universitaires de France, 1967; rev. ed., 1976]). [Tr.]

past. Either as artists or writers, they have undertaken a veritable exploration of the *dynamic of signs,* an exploration which relates this tendency, at least at the level of its aspirations, to all major projects of aesthetic and religious upheaval. Ascribing this experience to a new generation does not only mean that other, more subtle problems have been added to the demands for sociopolitical identification made in the beginning. It also means that, by demanding recognition of an irreducible identity, without equal in the opposite sex and, as such, exploded, plural, fluid, in a certain way nonidentical, this feminism situates itself outside the linear time of identities which communicate through projection and revindication. Such a feminism rejoins, on the one hand, the archaic (mythical) memory and, on the other, the cyclical or monumental temporality of marginal movements. It is certainly not by chance that the European and trans-European problematic has been posited as such at the same time as this new phase of feminism.

Finally, it is the mixture of the two attitudes—*insertion* into history and the radical *refusal* of the subjective limitations imposed by this history's time on an experiment carried out in the name of the irreducible difference—that seems to have broken loose over the past few years in European feminist movements, particularly in France and in Italy.

If we accept this meaning of the expression "a new generation of women," two kinds of questions might then be posed. What sociopolitical processes or events have provoked this mutation? What are its problems: its contributions as well as dangers?

Socialism and Freudianism

One could hypothesize that if this new generation of women shows itself to be more diffuse and perhaps less conscious in the United States and more massive in Western Europe, this is because of a veritable split in social relations and mentalities, a split produced by socialism and Freudianism. I mean by *socialism* that egalitarian doctrine which is increasingly broadly disseminated and accepted as based on common sense, as well as that social practice adopted by governments and political parties in democratic regimes which are forced to extend the zone of egalitarianism to include the distribution of goods as well as access to culture. By *Freudianism* I mean that lever, inside this egalitarian and socializing field, which once again poses the question of sexual difference and of the difference among subjects who themselves are not reducible one to the other.

Western socialism, shaken in its very beginnings by the egalitarian or differential demands of its women (e.g., Flora Tristan), quickly got rid of those women who aspired to recognition of a specificity of the female role in society and culture, only retaining from them, in the egalitarian and universalistic spirit of Enlightenment Humanism, the idea of a necessary identification between the two sexes as the only and unique means for liberating the "second sex." I shall not develop here the fact that this "ideal" is far from being applied in practice by these socialist-inspired movements and parties and that it was in part from the revolt against this situation that the new generation of women in Western Europe was born after May 1968. Let us just say that in theory, and as put into practice in Eastern Europe, socialist ideology, based on a conception of the human being as determined by its place in *production* and the *relations of production,* did not take into consideration this same human being according to its place in *reproduction,* on the one hand, or in the *symbolic order,* on the other. Consequently, the specific character of women could only appear as nonessential or even nonexistent to the totalizing and even totalitarian spirit of this ideology.[12] We begin to see that this same egalitarian and in fact censuring treatment has been imposed, from Enlightenment Humanism through socialism, on religious specificities and, in particular, on Jews.[13]

What has been achieved by this attitude remains nonetheless of capital importance for women, and I shall take as an example the change in the destiny of women in the socialist countries of Eastern Europe. It could be said, with only slight exaggeration, that the demands of the suffragists and existential

[12] See D. Desanti, "L'Autre Sexe des bolcheviks," *Tel Quel,* no. 76 (1978); Julia Kristeva, *Des Chinoises* (Paris: Editions des femmes, 1975), translated as *On Chinese Women,* trans. Anita Barrows (New York: Urizen Press, 1977). [Au. and Tr.]

[13] See Arthur Hertzberg, *The French Enlightenment and the Jews* (New York: Columbia University Press, 1968); *Les Juifs et la révolution française,* ed. B. Blumenkranz and A. Seboul (Paris: Edition Privat, 1976). [Au.]

feminists have, to a great extent, been met in these countries, since three of the main egalitarian demands of early feminism have been or are now being implemented despite vagaries and blunders: economic, political, and professional equality. The fourth, sexual equality, which implies permissiveness in sexual relations (including homosexual relations), abortion, and contraception, remains stricken by taboo in Marxian ethics as well as for reasons of state. It is, then, this fourth equality which is the problem and which therefore appears *essential* in the struggle of a new generation. But simultaneously and as a consequence of these socialist accomplishments—which are in fact a total deception—the struggle is no longer concerned with the quest for equality but, rather, with difference and specificity. It is precisely at this point that the new generation encounters what might be called the *symbolic* question.[14] Sexual difference—which is at once biological, physiological, and relative to reproduction—is translated by and translates a difference in the relationship of subjects to the symbolic contract which *is* the social contract: a difference, then, in the relationship to power, language, and meaning. The sharpest and most subtle point of feminist subversion brought about by the new generation will henceforth be situated on the terrain of the inseparable conjunction of the sexual and the symbolic, in order to try to discover, first, the specificity of the female, and then, in the end, that of each individual woman.

A certain saturation of socialist ideology, a certain exhaustion of its potential as a program for a new social contract (it is obvious that the effective realization of this program is far from being accomplished, and I am here treating only its system of thought) makes way for . . . Freudianism. I am, of course, aware that this term and this practice are somewhat shocking to the American intellectual consciousness (which rightly reacts to a muddled and normatizing form of psychoanalysis) and, above all, to the feminist consciousness. To restrict my remarks to the latter: Is it not true that Freud has been seen only as a denigrator or even an exploiter of women? as an irritating phallocrat in a Vienna which was at once Puritan and decadent—a man who fantasized women as sub-men, castrated men?

Castrated and/or Subject to Language

Before going beyond Freud to propose a more just or more modern vision of women, let us try, first, to understand his notion of castration. It is, first of all, a question of an *anguish* or *fear* of castration, or of correlative penis *envy;* a question, therefore, of *imaginary* formations readily perceivable in the *discourse* of neurotics of both sexes, men and women. But, above all, a careful reading of Freud, going beyond his biologism and his mechanism, both characteristic of his time, brings out two things. First, as presupposition for the "primal scene," the castration fantasy and its correlative (penis envy) are hypotheses, a priori suppositions intrinsic to the theory itself, in the sense that these are not the ideological fantasies of their inventor but, rather, logical necessities to be placed at the "origin" in order to explain what unceasingly functions in neurotic discourse. In other words, neurotic discourse, in man and woman, can only be understood in terms of its own logic when its fundamental causes are admitted as the fantasies of the primal scene and castration, even if (as may be the case) nothing renders them present in reality itself. Stated in still other terms, the reality of castration is no more real than the hypothesis of an explosion which, according to modern astrophysics, is at the origin of the universe: Nothing proves it, in a sense it is an article of faith, the only difference being that numerous phenomena of life in this "big-bang" universe are explicable only through this initial hypothesis. But one is infinitely more jolted when this kind of intellectual method concerns inanimate matter than when it is applied to our own subjectivity and thus, perhaps, to the fundamental mechanism of our epistemophilic thought.

Moreover, certain texts written by Freud (*The Interpretation of Dreams,* but especially those of the second topic, in particular the *Metapsychology*) and their recent extensions (notably by Lacan),[15]

[14] Here, "symbolic" is being more strictly used in terms of that function defined by Kristeva in opposition to the semiotic: "it involves the thetic phase, the identification of subject and its distinction from objects, and the establishment of a sign system" (see the glossary in *Desire in Language,* and Alice Jardine, "Theories of the Feminine: Kristeva," *Enclitic,* in press). [Tr.]

[15] See, in general, Jacques Lacan, *Ecrits* (Paris: Editions du Seuil, 1966) and, in particular, Jacques Lacan, *Le Séminaire XX: Encore* (Paris: Editions du Seuil, 1975). [Tr.]

imply that castration is, in sum, the imaginary construction of a radical operation which constitutes the symbolic field and all beings inscribed therein. This operation constitutes signs and syntax; that is, language, as a *separation* from a presumed state of nature, of pleasure fused with nature so that the introduction of an articulated network of differences, which refers to objects henceforth and only in this way separated from a subject, may constitute *meaning*. This logical operation of separation (confirmed by all psycholinguistic and child psychology) which preconditions the binding of language which is already syntactical, is therefore the common destiny of the two sexes, men and women. That certain biofamilial conditions and relationships cause women (and notably hysterics) to deny this separation and the language which ensues from it, whereas men (notably obsessionals) magnify both and, terrified, attempt to master them—this is what Freud's discovery has to tell us on this issue.

The analytic situation indeed shows that it is the penis which, becoming the major referent in this operation of separation, gives full meaning to the *lack* or to the *desire* which constitutes the subject during his or her insertion into the order of language. I should only like to indicate here that, in order for this operation constitutive of the symbolic and the social to appear in its full truth and for it to be understood by both sexes, it would be just to emphasize its extension to all that is privation of fulfillment and of totality; exclusion of a pleasing, natural, and sound state: in short, the break indispensable to the advent of the symbolic.

It can now be seen how women, starting with this theoretical apparatus, might try to understand their sexual and symbolic difference in the framework of social, cultural, and professional realization, in order to try, by seeing their position therein, either to fulfill their own experience to a maximum or—but always starting from this point—to go further and call into question the very apparatus itself.

Living the Sacrifice

In any case, and for women in Europe today, whether or not they are conscious of the various mutations (socialist and Freudian) which have produced or simply accompanied their coming into their own, the urgent question on our agenda might be formulated as follows: *What can be our place in the symbolic contract?* If the social contract, far from being that of equal men, is based on an essentially sacrificial relationship of separation and articulation of differences which in this way produces communicable meaning, what is our place in this order of sacrifice and/or of language? No longer wishing to be excluded or no longer content with the function which has always been demanded of us (to maintain, arrange, and perpetuate this sociosymbolic contract as mothers, wives, nurses, doctors, teachers . . .), how can we reveal our place, first as it is bequeathed to us by tradition, and then as we want to transform it?

It is difficult to evaluate what in the relationship of women to the symbolic as it reveals itself now arises from a sociohistorical conjuncture (patriarchal ideology, whether Christian, humanist, socialist or so forth), and what arises from a structure. We can speak only about a structure observed in a sociohistorical context, which is that of Christian, Western civilization and its lay ramifications. In this sense of psychosymbolic structure, women, "we" (is it necessary to recall the warnings we issued at the beginning of this article concerning the totalizing use of this plural?) seem to feel that they are the casualties, that they have been left out of the sociosymbolic contract, of language as the fundamental social bond. They find no affect there, no more than they find the fluid and infinitesimal significations of their relationships with the nature of their own bodies, that of the child, another woman, or a man. This frustration, which to a certain extent belongs to men also, is being voiced today principally by women, to the point of becoming the essence of the new feminist ideology. A therefore difficult, if not impossible, identification with the sacrificial logic of separation and syntactical sequence at the foundation of language and the social code leads to the rejection of the symbolic—lived as the rejection of the paternal function and ultimately generating psychoses.

But this limit, rarely reached as such, produces two types of counterinvestment of what we have termed the sociosymbolic contract. On the one hand, there are attempts to take hold of this contract, to possess it in order to enjoy it as such or to subvert it. How? The answer remains difficult to formulate (since, precisely, any formulation is deemed frustrating, mutilating, sacrificial) or else is in fact formulated using stereotypes taken from extremist and often deadly ideologies. On the other hand, another attitude is more lucid from the beginning, more self-analytical which—without refusing or sidestepping this sociosymbolic order—consists in trying to explore the constitution and functioning of this contract, starting less from the knowledge accumulated about it (anthropology, psychoanalysis, linguistics) than from the very personal affect experienced when facing it as subject and as a woman. This leads to the active research,[16] still rare, undoubtedly hesitant but always dissident, being carried out by women in the human sciences; particularly those attempts, in the wake of contemporary art, to break the code, to shatter language, to find a specific discourse closer to the body and emotions, to the unnameable repressed by the social contract. I am not speaking here of a "woman's language," whose (at least syntactical) existence is highly problematical and whose apparent lexical specificity is perhaps more the product of a social marginality than of a sexual-symbolic difference.[17]

Nor am I speaking of the aesthetic quality of productions by women, most of which—with a few exceptions (but has this not always been the case with both sexes?)—are a reiteration of a more or less euphoric or depressed romanticism and always an explosion of an ego lacking narcissistic gratification.[18] What I should like to retain, nonetheless, as a mark of collective aspiration, as an undoubtedly vague and unimplemented intention, but one which is intense and which has been deeply revealing these past few years, is this: The new generation of women is showing that its major social concern has become the sociosymbolic contract as a sacrificial contract. If anthropologists and psychologists, for at least a century, have not stopped insisting on this in their attention to "savage thought," wars, the discourse of dreams, or writers, women are today affirming—and we consequently face a mass phenomenon—that they are forced to experience this sacrificial contract against their will.[19] Based on this, they are attempting a revolt which they see as a resurrection but which society as a whole understands as murder. This attempt can lead us to a not less and sometimes more deadly violence. Or to a cultural innovation. Probably to both at once. But that is precisely where the stakes are, and they are of epochal significance.

The Terror of Power or the Power of Terrorism

First in socialist countries (such as the USSR and China) and increasingly in Western democracies, under pressure from feminist movements, women are being promoted to leadership positions in government, industry, and culture. Inequalities, devalorizations, underestimations, even persecution of women at this level continue to hold sway in vain. The struggle against them is a struggle against archaisms. The cause has nonetheless been understood, the principle has been accepted.[20] What re-

[16]This work is periodically published in various academic women's journals, one of the most prestigious being *Signs: Journal of Women in Culture and Society*, University of Chicago Press. Also of note are the special issues: "Ecriture, féminité, féminisme," *La Revue des sciences humaines* (Lille III), no. 4 (1977); and "Les Femmes et la philosophie," *Le Doctrinal de sapience* (Editions Solin), no. 3 (1977). [Au.]

[17]See linguistic research on "female language": Robin Lakoff, *Language and Women's Place* (New York: Harper & Row, 1974); Mary R. Key, *Male/Female Language* (Metuchen, N.J.: Scarecrow Press, 1973); A. M. Houdebine, "Les Femmes et la langue," *Tel Quel*, no. 74 (1977), pp. 84–95. The contrast between these "empirical" investigations of women's "speech acts" and much of the research in France on the conceptual bases for a "female language" must be emphasized here. It is somewhat helpful, if ultimately inaccurate, to think of the former as an "external" study of language and the latter as an "internal" exploration of the process of signification. For further contrast, see, e.g., "Part II: Contemporary Feminist Thought in France: Translating Difference" in *The Future of Difference*, ed. Hester Eisenstein and Alice Jardine (Boston: G. K. Hall & Co., 1980); the "Introductions" to *New French Feminisms*, ed. Elaine Marks and Isabelle de Courtivron (Amherst: University of Massachusetts Press, 1980); and for a very helpful overview of the problem of "difference and language" in France, see Stephen Heath, "Difference" in *Screen* 19, no. 3 (Autumn 1978): 51–112. [Tr.]

[18]This is one of the more explicit references to the mass marketing of "écriture féminine" in Paris over the last ten years. [Tr.]

[19]The expression *à leur corps défendant* translates "against their will," but here the emphasis is on women's bodies: literally, "against their bodies." I have retained the former expression in English, partly because of its obvious intertextuality with Susan Brownmiller's *Against Our Will* (New York: Simon & Schuster, 1975). Women are increasingly describing their experience of the violence of the symbolic contract as a form of rape. [Tr.]

[20]Many women in the West who are once again finding all doors closed to them above a certain level of employ-

mains is to break down the resistance to change. In this sense, this struggle, while still one of the main concerns of the new generation, is not, strictly speaking, *its* problem. In relationship to *power*, its problem might rather be summarized as follows: What happens when women come into power and identify with it? What happens when, on the contrary, they refuse power and create a parallel society, a counterpower which then takes on aspects ranging from a club of ideas to a group of terrorist commandos?[21]

The assumption by women of executive, industrial, and cultural power has not, up to the present time, radically changed the nature of this power. This can be clearly seen in the East, where women promoted to decision-making positions suddenly obtain the economic as well as the narcissistic advantages refused them for thousands of years and become the pillars of the existing governments, guardians of the status quo, the most zealous protectors of the established order.[22] This identification by women with the very power structures previously considered as frustrating, oppressive, or inaccessible has often been used in modern times by totalitarian regimes: the German National-Socialists and the Chilean junta are examples of this.[23] The fact that this is a paranoid type of counterinvestment in an initially denied symbolic order can perhaps explain this troubling phenomenon; but an explanation does not prevent its massive propagation around the globe, perhaps in less dramatic forms than the totalitarian ones mentioned above, but all moving toward leveling, stabilization, conformism, at the cost of crushing exceptions, experiments, chance occurrences.

Some will regret that the rise of a libertarian movement such as feminism ends, in some of its aspects, in the consolidation of conformism; others will rejoice and profit from this fact. Electoral campaigns, the very life of political parties, continue to bet on this latter tendency. Experience proves that too quickly even the protest or innovative initiatives on the part of women inhaled by power systems (when they do not submit to them right off) are soon credited to the system's account; and that the long-awaited democratization of institutions as a result of the entry of women most often comes down to fabricating a few "chiefs" among them. The difficulty presented by this logic of integrating the second sex into a value system experienced as foreign and therefore counterinvested is how to avoid the centralization of power, how to detach women from it, and how then to proceed, through their critical, differential, and autonomous interventions, to render decision-making institutions more flexible.

Then there are the more radical feminist currents which, refusing homologation to any role of identification with existing power no matter what the power may be, make of the second sex a *countersociety*. A "female society" is then constituted as a sort of alter ego of the official society, in which all real or fantasized possibilities for *jouissance* take refuge. Against the sociosymbolic contract, both sacrificial and frustrating, this countersociety is imagined as harmonious, without prohibitions, free and fulfilling. In our modern societies which have no hereafter or, at least, which are caught up in a transcendency either reduced to this side of the world (Protestantism) or crumbling (Catholicism and its current challenges), the countersociety remains the only refuge for fulfillment since it is precisely an a-topia, a place outside the law, utopia's floodgate.

As with any society, the countersociety is based on the expulsion of an excluded element, a scapegoat charged with the evil of which the community duly constituted can then purge itself;[24] a purge which will finally exonerate that community of any future criticism. Modern protest movements have often reiterated this logic, locating the guilty one—

ment, especially in the current economic chaos, may find this statement, even qualified, troubling, to say the least. It is accurate, however, *in principle:* whether that of infinite capitalist recuperation or increasing socialist expansion—within both economies, our integration functions as a kind of *operative* illusion. [Tr.]

[21] The very real existence and autonomous activities of both of these versions of women's groups in Europe may seem a less urgent problem in the United States where feminist groups are often absorbed by the academy and/or are forced to remain financially dependent on para-academic/governmental agencies. [Tr.]

[22] See *Des Chinoises*. [Au.]

[23] See M. A. Macciocchi, *Elements pour une analyse du fascisme* (Paris: 10/18, 1976); Michèle Mattelart, "Le Coup d'état au féminin," *Les Temps modernes* (January 1975). [Au.]

[24] The principles of a "sacrificial anthropology" are developed by René Girard in *La Violence et le sacré* [Violence and the sacred] (Paris: Grasset, 1972) and esp. in *Des choses cachées depuis la fondation du monde* (Paris: Grasset, 1978). [Au.] See *Girard*. [Eds.]

in order to fend off criticism—in the foreign, in capital alone, in the other religion, in the other sex. Does not feminism become a kind of inverted sexism when this logic is followed to its conclusion? The various forms of marginalism—according to sex, age, religion, or ideology—represent in the modern world this refuge for *jouissance,* a sort of laicized transcendence. But with women, and insofar as the number of those feeling concerned by this problem has increased, although in less spectacular forms than a few years ago, the problem of the countersociety is becoming massive: It occupies no more and no less than "half of the sky."

It has, therefore, become clear, because of the particular radicalization of the second generation, that these protest movements, including feminism, are not "initially libertarian" movements which only later, through internal deviations or external chance manipulations, fall back into the old ruts of the initially combated archetypes. Rather, the very logic of counterpower and of countersociety necessarily generates, by its very structure, its essence as a simulacrum of the combated society or of power. In this sense and from a viewpoint undoubtedly too Hegelian, modern feminism has only been but a moment in the interminable process of coming to consciousness about the implacable violence (separation, castration, etc.) which constitutes any symbolic contract.

Thus the identification with power in order to consolidate it or the constitution of a fetishist counterpower—restorer of the crises of the self and provider of a *jouissance* which is always already a transgression—seem to be the two social forms which the face-off between the new generation of women and the social contract can take. That one also finds the problem of terrorism there is structurally related.

The large number of women in terrorist groups (Palestinian commandos, the Baader-Meinhoff Gang, Red Brigades, etc.) has already been pointed out, either violently or prudently according to the source of information. The exploitation of women is still too great and the traditional prejudices against them too violent for one to be able to envision this phenomenon with sufficient distance. It can, however, be said from now on that this is the inevitable product of what we have called a denial of the sociosymbolic contract and its counterinvestment as the only means of self-defense in the struggle to safeguard an identity. This paranoid-type mechanism is at the base of any political involvement. It may produce different civilizing attitudes in the sense that these attitudes allow a more or less flexible reabsorption of violence and death. But when a subject is too brutally excluded from this sociosymbolic stratum; when, for example, a woman feels her affective life as a woman or her condition as a social being too brutally ignored by existing discourse or power (from her family to social institutions); she may, by counterinvesting the violence she has endured, make of herself a "possessed" agent of this violence in order to combat what was experienced as frustration—with arms which may seem disproportional, but which are not so in comparison with the subjective or more precisely narcissistic suffering from which they originate. Necessarily opposed to the bourgeois democratic regimes in power, this terrorist violence offers as a program of liberation an order which is even more oppressive, more sacrificial than those it combats. Strangely enough, it is not against totalitarian regimes that these terrorist groups with women participants unleash themselves but, rather, against liberal systems, whose essence is, of course exploitative but whose expanding democratic legality guarantees relative tolerance. Each time, the mobilizaton takes place in the name of a nation, of an oppressed group, of a human essence imagined as good and sound; in the name, then, of a kind of fantasy of archaic fulfillment which an arbitrary, abstract, and thus even bad and ultimately discriminatory order has come to disrupt. While that order is accused of being oppressive, is it not actually being reproached with being too weak, with not measuring up to this pure and good, but henceforth lost, substance? Anthropology has shown that the social order is sacrificial, but sacrifice orders violence, binds it, tames it. Refusal of the social order exposes one to the risk that the so-called good substance, once it is unchained, will explode, without curbs, without law or right, to become an absolute arbitrariness.

Following the crisis of monotheism, the revolutions of the past two centuries, and more recently fascism and Stalinism, have tragically set in action this logic of the oppressed goodwill which leads to massacres. Are women more apt than other social categories, notably the exploited classes, to invest in this implacable machine of terrorism? No categorical response, either positive or negative, can currently be given to this question. It must be pointed out, however, that since the dawn of feminism, and certainly before, the political activity of exceptional women, and thus in a certain sense of liberated women, has taken the form of murder, conspiracy, and crime. Finally, there is also the connivance of the young girl with her mother, her greater difficulty than the boy in detaching herself from the mother in order to accede to the order of signs as invested by the absence and separation constitutive of the paternal function. A girl will never be able to reestablish this contact with her mother—a contact which the boy may possibly rediscover through his relationship with the opposite sex—except by becoming a mother herself, through a child, or through a homosexuality which is in itself extremely difficult and judged as suspect by society; and, what is more, why and in the name of what dubious symbolic benefit would she want to make this detachment so as to conform to a symbolic system which remains foreign to her? In sum, all of these considerations—her eternal debt to the woman-mother—make a woman more vulnerable within the symbolic order, more fragile when she suffers within it, more virulent when she protects herself from it. If the archetype of the belief in a good and pure substance, that of utopias, is the belief in the omnipotence of an archaic, full, total, englobing mother with no frustration, no separation, with no break-producing symbolism (with no castration, in other words), then it becomes evident that we will never be able to defuse the violences mobilized through the counterinvestment necessary to carrying out this phantasm, unless one challenges precisely this myth of the archaic mother. It is in this way that we can understand the warnings against the recent invasion of the women's movements by paranoia,[25] as in Lacan's scandalous sentence "There is no such thing as Woman."[26] Indeed, she does *not* exist with a capital "W," possessor of some mythical unity—a supreme power, on which is based the terror of power and terrorism as the desire for power. But what an unbelievable force for subversion in the modern world! And, at the same time, what playing with fire!

Creatures and Createsses

The desire to be a mother, considered alienating and even reactionary by the preceding generation of feminists, has obviously not become a standard for the present generation. But we have seen in the past few years an increasing number of women who not only consider their maternity compatible with their professional life or their feminist involvement (certain improvements in the quality of life are also at the origin of this: an increase in the number of day-care centers and nursery schools, more active participation of men in child care and domestic life, etc.) but also find it indispensable to their discovery, not of the plenitude, but of the complexity of the female experience, with all that this complexity comprises in joy and pain. This tendency has its extreme: in the refusal of the paternal function by lesbian and single mothers can be seen one of the most violent forms taken by the rejection of the symbolic outlined above, as well as one of the most fervent divinizations of maternal power—all of which cannot help but trouble an entire legal and moral order without, however, proposing an alternative to it. Let us remember here that Hegel distinguished between female right (familial and religious) and male law (civil and political). If our societies know well the uses and abuses of male law, it must also be recognized that female right is designated, for the moment, by a blank. And if these practices of maternity, among others, were to be generalized, women themselves would be responsible for elaborating the appropriate legislation to check the violence to which, otherwise, both their children and men would be subject. But are they capable of doing so? This is one of the important questions that the new generation of women encounters, especially when the members of this new generation refuse to ask those questions, seized by the same rage with which the dominant order originally victimized them.

Faced with this situation, it seems obvious—and feminist groups become more aware of this when

[25] Cf. Micheline Enriquez, "Fantasmes paranoïaques: différences des sexes, homosexualité, loi du père," *Topiques*, no. 13 (1974). [Au.]

[26] See Jacques Lacan, "Dieu et la jouissance de la femme" in *Encore* (Paris: Editions du Seuil, 1975), pp. 61–71, esp. p. 68. This seminar has remained a primary critical and polemical focus for multiple tendencies in the French women's movement. For a brief discussion of the seminar in English, see Heath (n. 17 above). [Tr.]

they attempt to broaden their audience—that the refusal of maternity cannot be a mass policy and that the majority of women today see the possibility for fulfillment, if not entirely at least to a large degree, in bringing a child into the world. What does this desire for motherhood correspond to? This is one of the new questions for the new generation, a question the preceding generation has foreclosed. For want of an answer to this question, feminist ideology leaves the door open to the return of religion, whose discourse, tried and proved over thousands of years, provides the necessary ingredients for satisfying the anguish, the suffering, and the hopes of mothers. If Freud's affirmation—that the desire for a child is the desire for a penis and, in this sense, a substitute for phallic and symbolic dominion—can be only partially accepted, what modern women have to say about this experience should nonetheless be listened to attentively. Pregnancy seems to be experienced as the radical ordeal of the splitting of the subject:[27] redoubling up of the body, separation and coexistence of the self and of an other, of nature and consciousness, of physiology and speech. This fundamental challenge to identity is then accompanied by a fantasy of totality—narcissistic completeness—a sort of instituted, socialized, natural psychosis. The arrival of the child, on the other hand, leads the mother into the labyrinths of an experience that, without the child, she would only rarely encounter: love for an other. Not for herself, nor for an identical being, and still less for another person with whom "I" fuse (love or sexual passion). But the slow, difficult, and delightful apprenticeship in attentiveness, gentleness, forgetting oneself. The ability to succeed in this path without masochism and without annihilating one's affective, intellectual, and professional personality—such would seem to be the stakes to be won through guiltless maternity. It then becomes a creation in the strong sense of the term. For this moment, utopian?

On the other hand, it is in the aspiration toward artistic and, in particular, literary creation that woman's desire for affirmation now manifests itself. Why literature?

Is it because, faced with social norms, literature reveals a certain knowledge and sometimes the truth itself about an otherwise repressed, nocturnal, secret, and unconscious universe? Because it thus redoubles the social contract by exposing the unsaid, the uncanny? And because it makes a game, a space of fantasy and pleasure, out of the abstract and frustrating order of social signs, the words of everyday communication? Flaubert said, "Madame Bovary, c'est moi." Today many women imagine, "Flaubert, c'est moi." This identification with the potency of the imaginary is not only an identification, an imaginary potency (a fetish, a belief in the maternal penis maintained at all costs), as a far too normative view of the social and symbolic relationship would have it. This identification also bears witness to women's desire to lift the weight of what is sacrificial in the social contract from their shoulders, to nourish our societies with a more flexible and free discourse, one able to name what has thus far never been an object of circulation in the community: the enigmas of the body, the dreams, secret joys, shames, hatreds of the second sex.

It is understandable from this that women's writing has lately attracted the maximum attention of both "specialists" and the media.[28] The pitfalls encountered along the way, however, are not to be minimized: For example, does one not read there a relentless belittling of male writers whose books, nevertheless, often serve as "models" for countless productions by women? Thanks to the feminist label, does one not sell numerous works whose naive whining or market-place romanticism would otherwise have been rejected as anachronistic? And does one not find the pen of many a female writer being devoted to phantasmic attacks against Language and Sign as the ultimate supports of phallocratic power, in the name of a semi-aphonic corporality whose truth can only be found in that which is "gestural" or "tonal"?

And yet, no matter how dubious the results of these recent productions by women, the symptom is there—women are writing, and the air is heavy with expectation: What will they write that is new?

[27] The "split subject" (from *Spaltung* as both "splitting" and "cleavage"), as used in Freudian psychoanalysis, here refers directly to Kristeva's "subject in process/in question/on trial" as opposed to the unity of the transcendental ego (see n. 14 in "Introduction"). [Tr.]

[28] Again a reference to *écriture féminine* as generically labeled in France over the past few years and not to women's writing in general. [Tr.]

In the Name of the Father, the Son . . . and the Woman?

These few elements of the manifestations by the new generation of women in Europe seem to me to demonstrate that, beyond the sociopolitical level where it is generally inscribed (or inscribes itself), the women's movement—in its present stage, less aggressive but more artful—is situated within the very framework of the religious crisis of our civilization.

I call "religion" this phantasmic necessity on the part of speaking beings to provide themselves with a *representation* (animal, female, male, parental, etc.) in place of what constitutes them as such, in other words, symbolization—the double articulation and syntactic sequence of language, as well as its preconditions or substitutes (thoughts, affects, etc.). The elements of the current practice of feminism that we have just brought to light seem precisely to constitute such a representation which makes up for the frustrations imposed on women by the anterior code (Christianity or its lay humanist variant). The fact that this new ideology has affinities, often revindicated by its creators, with so-called matriarchal beliefs (in other words, those beliefs characterizing matrilinear societies) should not overshadow its radical novelty. This ideology seems to me to be part of the broader antisacrificial current which is animating our culture and which, in its protest against the constraints of the sociosymbolic contract, is no less exposed to the risks of violence and terrorism. At this level of radicalism, it is the very principle of sociality which is challenged.

Certain contemporary thinkers consider, as is well known, that modernity is characterized as the first epoch in human history in which human beings attempt to live without religion. In its present form, is not feminism in the process of becoming one?

Or is it, on the contrary and as avant-garde feminists hope, that having started with the idea of difference, feminism will be able to break free of its belief in Woman, Her power, Her writing, so as to channel this demand for difference into each and every element of the female whole, and, finally, to bring out the singularity of each woman, and beyond this, her multiplicities, her plural languages, beyond the horizon, beyond sight, beyond faith itself?

A factor for ultimate mobilizaton? Or a factor for analysis?

Imaginary support in a technocratic era where all narcissism is frustrated? Or instruments fitted to these times in which the cosmos, atoms, and cells—our true contemporaries—call for the constitution of a fluid and free subjectivity?

The question has been posed. Is to pose it already to answer it?

Another Generation Is Another Space

If the preceding can be *said*—the question whether all this is *true* belongs to a different register—it is undoubtedly because it is now possible to gain some distance on these two preceding generations of women. This implies, of course, that a *third* generation is now forming, at least in Europe. I am not speaking of a new group of young women (though its importance should not be underestimated) or of another "mass feminist movement" taking the torch passed on from the second generation. My usage of the word "generation" implies less a chronology than a *signifying space,* a both corporeal and desiring mental space. So it can be argued that as of now a third attitude is possible, thus a third generation, which does not exclude—quite to the contrary—the *parallel* existence of all three in the same historical time, or even that they be interwoven one with the other.

In this third attitude, which I strongly advocate—which I imagine?—the very dichotomy man/woman as an opposition between two rival entities may be understood as belonging to *metaphysics.* What can "identity," even "sexual identity," mean in a new theoretical and scientific space where the very notion of identity is challenged?[29] I am not simply suggesting a very hypothetical bisexuality which, even if it existed, would only, in fact, be the aspiration toward the totality of one of the sexes and thus an effacing of difference. What I mean is, first of all, the demassification of the problematic of *difference,* which would imply, in a first phase, an apparent dedramatization of the "fight to the death" between rival groups and thus between the sexes. And this

[29] See Seminar on *Identity* directed by Lévi-Strauss (Paris: Grasset & Fasquelle, 1977). [Au.]

not in the name of some reconciliation—feminism has at least had the merit of showing what is irreducible and even deadly in the social contract—but in order that the struggle, the implacable difference, the violence be conceived in the very place where it operates with the maximum intransigence, in other words, in personal and sexual identity itself, so as to make it disintegrate in its very nucleus.

It necessarily follows that this involves risks not only for what we understand today as "personal equilibrium" but also for social equilibrium itself, made up as it now is of the counterbalancing of aggressive and murderous forces massed in social, national, religious, and political groups. But is it not the unsupportable situation of tension and explosive risk that the existing "equilibrium" presupposes which leads some of those who suffer from it to divest it of its economy, to detach themselves from it, and to seek another means of regulating difference?

To restrict myself here to a personal level, as related to the question of women, I see arising, under the cover of a relative indifference toward the militance of the first and second generations, an attitude of retreat from sexism (male as well as female) and, gradually, from any kind of anthropomorphism. The fact that this might quickly become another form of spiritualism turning its back on social problems, or else a form of repression[30] ready to support all status quos, should not hide the radicalness of the process. This process could be summarized as an *interiorization of the founding separation of the sociosymbolic contract,* as an introduction of its cutting edge into the very interior of every identity whether subjective, sexual, ideological, or so forth. This in such a way that the habitual and increasingly explicit attempt to fabricate a scapegoat victim as foundress of a society or a countersociety may be replaced by the analysis of the potentialities of *victim/executioner* which characterize each identity, each subject, each sex.

What discourse, if not that of a religion, would be able to support this adventure which surfaces as a real possibility, after both the achievements and the impasses of the present ideological reworkings, in which feminism has participated? It seems to me that the role of what is usually called "aesthetic practices" must increase not only to counterbalance the storage and uniformity of information by present-day mass media, data-bank systems, and, in particular, modern communications technology, but also to demystify the identity of the symbolic bond itself, to demystify, therefore, the *community* of language as a universal and unifying tool, one which totalizes and equalizes. In order to bring out—along with the *singularity* of each person and, even more, along with the multiplicity of every person's possible identifications (with atoms, e.g., stretching from the family to the stars)—the *relativity of his/her symbolic as well as biological existence,* according to the variation in his/her specific symbolic capacities. And in order to emphasize the *responsibility* which all will immediately face of putting this fluidity into play against the threats of death which are unavoidable whenever an inside and an outside, a self and an other, one group and another, are constituted. At this level of interiorization with its social as well as individual stakes, what I have called "aesthetic practices" are undoubtedly nothing other than the modern reply to the eternal question of morality. At least, this is how we might understand an ethics which, conscious of the fact that its order is sacrificial, reserves part of the burden for each of its adherents, therefore declaring them guilty while immediately affording them the possibility for *jouissance,* for various productions, for a life made up of both challenges and differences.

Spinoza's question can be taken up again here: Are women subject to ethics? If not to that ethics defined by classical philosophy—in relationship to which the ups and downs of feminist generations seem dangerously precarious—are women not already participating in the rapid dismantling that our age is experiencing at various levels (from wars to drugs to artificial insemination) and which poses the *demand* for a new ethics? The answer to Spinoza's question can be affirmative only at the cost of considering feminism as but a *moment* in the thought of that anthropomorphic identity which currently blocks the horizon of the discursive and scientific adventure of our species.

[30] Repression (*le refoulement* or *Verdrangung*) as distinguished from the foreclosure (*la foreclusion* or *Verwerfung*) evoked earlier in the article (see LaPlanche and Pontalis). [Tr.]

Sandra M. Gilbert

b. 1936

THE WORK OF Sandra Gilbert and her frequent collaborator, Susan Gubar, has had a profound impact on the study of women writers. Their book *The Madwoman in the Attic: The Woman Writer and the Nineteenth-Century Literary Imagination* (1979) provided a paradigmatic example for tracing "a distinctively female literary tradition," just as their more recent *Norton Anthology of Literature by Women* (1985), makes a wide variety of texts conveniently available for students. The essay here (which, in a version expanded to reflect the larger argument of the book, appears as the first chapter of *The Madwoman in the Attic*) provides a powerful illustration of the degree to which the idea of the author and of literary authority has been not only male but oppressively and cripplingly so for women writers.

While one of the major concerns of recent American feminist critics has been to document the portrayal of women in literature by men—and how women writers themselves have acceded to demoralizing or restrictive models—this essay by Gilbert takes a more direct and dramatic route, to show how the most intimate representation of a writer's creative power has been systematically treated as phallic and patriarchal. Unlike continental theorists, Gilbert uses the metaphors and images elected by the writers themselves—finding no need and no compelling reason to refer to Freud, Lacan, or Foucault—to articulate a persistent and preemptive pattern, in which creative power as an active force has been claimed exclusively as male, leaving women always a passive or subservient form of creativity. By treating the problem as historical and empirical, Gilbert gains the considerable advantage of showing that there is no cogent a priori basis for the exclusion of women, suggesting that attempts to construct a theory may offer less in the way of explanation than they offer in the form of cover-up and excuse, since in almost all cases, it has been a man holding the pen, in theoretical writing especially. It is, in this respect, striking to note particularly in French feminist theory (see, for example, *Cixous* and *Kristeva*) the extent to which theoretical arguments are derivative, and in writing *about* women's writing, relatively little use is made of the writing itself.

Both in this essay and in her subsequent collaborations with Gubar, Gilbert is firmly committed to clearing space for women writers to be heard, writing in their own terms, on the principle that the most important starting point is the coherence and continuity of the writing itself. To use a distinction advanced by Noam Chomsky, there can be no theories claiming explanatory adequacy until one can ascertain that theories are descriptively adequate. From this view, the work of women writers has not yet been described, even when it has been read, partly because the problem of writerly authority has not been clearly seen as an idea that is historically saturated with patriarchal assumptions.

In disclosing the pattern and the consequences of that saturation, Gilbert effects a significant clarification of a fundamental descriptive problem, helping to establish that while the exclusion of women is part of an entire system and no mere coincidence, neither is it inevitable. In documenting the pattern both from the works of men who assume it or have presumed to enforce it and from the view of women protesting it, Gilbert does not merely continue or publicize the protest but indicates a number of the ways that women writers have exercised their creative power "to create themselves as characters" and to bring a "secret self to the surface" of their lives.

With Susan Gubar, Gilbert is the author of *The Madwoman in the Attic: The Woman Writer and the Nineteenth-Century Literary Imagination* (1979); and Gubar and Gilbert have edited two important anthologies, *Shakespeare's Sisters: Feminist Essays on Women Poets* (1979) and *The Norton Anthology of Literature by Women* (1985). Gilbert is also the author of *Acts of Attention: The Poems of D. H. Lawrence* (1972) and numerous volumes of poetry, including *In the Fourth World* (1979), *The Summer Kitchen* (1983), and *Emily's Bread* (1984).

LITERARY PATERNITY

Alas! A woman that attempts the pen
Such an intruder on the rights of men,
Such a presumptuous Creature is
esteem'd
The fault can by no vertue be
redeem'd.

—Anne Finch,
Countess of Winchilsea

As to all that nonsense Henry and Larry talked about, the necessity of "I am God" in order to create (I suppose they mean "I am God, I am not a woman"). . . . this "I am God," which makes creation an act of solitude and pride, this image of God alone making sky, earth, sea, it is this image which has confused woman.

—Anaïs Nin[1]

Is a pen a metaphorical penis? Gerard Manley Hopkins seems to have thought so. In a letter to his friend R. W. Dixon in 1886, he confided a crucial feature of his theory of poetry. The artist's "most essential quality," he declared, is "masterly execution, which is a kind of male gift, and especially marks off men from women, the begetting of one's thought on paper, on verse, or whatever the matter is." In addition, he noted that "on better consideration it strikes me that the mastery I speak of is not so much in the mind as a puberty in the life of that quality. The male quality is the creative gift. . . ."[2] Male sexuality, in other words, is not just analogically but actually the

LITERARY PATERNITY was first published in *Cornell Review* (1979). An extended and revised version of the essay comprises the first chapter of *The Madwoman in the Attic* (New Haven: Yale University Press, 1979). Reprinted by permission of the author, copyright © 1979.

[1] "The Introduction," in *The Poems of Anne Countess of Winchilsea,* ed. Myra Reynolds (Chicago: University of Chicago Press, 1903), pp. 4–5; *The Diary of Anaïs Nin, Vol. Two, 1934–1939,* ed. Gunther Stuhlmann (New York: The Swallow Press and Harcourt Brace, 1967), p. 233. [Au.]

[2] *The Correspondence of Gerard Manley Hopkins and Richard Watson Dixon,* ed. C. C. Abbott (London: Oxford University Press, 1935), p. 133. [Au.]

essence of literary power. The poet's pen is in some sense (even more than figuratively) a penis.

Eccentric and obscure though he was, Hopkins was articulating a concept central to that Victorian culture of which he was in this case a representative male citizen. But of course the patriarchal notion that the writer "fathers" his text just as God fathered the world is and has been all-pervasive in Western literary civilization, so much so that, as Edward Said has shown, the metaphor is built into the very word, *author,* with which writer, deity, and *pater familias* are identified. Said's meditation on the word "authority" is worth quoting at length because it summarizes so much that is relevant here:

> *Authority* suggests to me a constellation of linked meanings: not only, as the OED tells us, "a power to enforce obedience," or "a derived or delegated power," or "a power to influence action," or "a power to inspire belief," or "a person whose opinion is accepted"; not only those, but a connection as well with *author*—that is, a person who originates or gives existence to something, a begetter, beginner, father, or ancestor, a person also who sets forth written statements. There is still another cluster of meanings: *author* is tied to the past participle *auctus* of the verb *augere;* therefore *auctor,* according to Eric Partridge, is literally an increaser and thus a founder. *Auctoritas* is production, invention, cause, in addition to meaning a right of possession. Finally, it means continuance, or a causing to continue. Taken together these meanings are all grounded in the following notions: (1) that of the power of an individual to initiate, institute, establish—in short, to begin; (2) that this power and its product are an increase over what had been there previously; (3) that the individual wielding this power controls its issue and what is derived therefore; (4) that authority maintains the continuity of its course.[3]

In conclusion, Said, who is discussing "The Novel as Beginning Intention," remarks that "All four of these [last] abstractions can be used to describe the way in which narrative fiction asserts itself psychologically and aesthetically through the technical efforts of the novelist." But they can also, of course, be used to describe both the author and the authority of any literary text, a point Hopkins's sexual/aesthetic theory seems to have been designed to elaborate. Indeed, Said himself later observes that a convention of most literary texts is "that the unity or integrity of the text is maintained by a series of genealogical connections: author—text, beginning-middle-end, text–meaning, reader–interpretation, and so on. Underneath all these is the imagery of succession, of paternity, or hierarchy."[4]

There is a sense in which the very notion of paternity is itself, as Stephen Dedalus puts it in *Ulysses,* a "legal fiction,"[5] a story requiring imagination if not faith. A man cannot verify his fatherhood by either sense or reason, after all; that his child is *his* is in a sense a tale he tells himself to explain the infant's existence. Obviously, the anxiety implicit in such storytelling urgently needs not only the reassurances of male superiority that patriarchal misogyny implies, but also such compensatory fictions of the Word as those embodied in the genealogical imagery Said describes. Thus it is possible to trace the history of this compensatory, sometimes frankly stated and sometimes submerged imagery that elaborates upon what Stephen Dedalus calls the "mystical estate" of paternity[6] through the works of many literary theoreticians besides Hopkins and Said.

[3] Edward W. Said, *Beginnings: Intention and Method* (New York: Basic Books, 1975), p. 83. [Au.]

[4] *Ibid.,* p. 162. For an analogous use of such imagery of paternity, see Gayatri Spivak's "Translator's Preface" to Jacques Derrida, *Of Grammatology* (Baltimore: The Johns Hopkins University Press, 1976), p. xi: ". . . to use one of Derrida's structural metaphors, [a preface is] the son or seed . . . caused or engendered by the father (text or meaning). . . ." [Au.]

[5] James Joyce, *Ulysses* (New York: The Modern Library, 1934), p. 205. [Au.]

[6] *Ibid.* The whole of this extraordinarily relevant passage develops this notion further: "Fatherhood, in the sense of conscious begetting, is unknown to man," Stephen notes. "It is a mystical estate, an apostolic succession, from only begetter to only begotten. On that mystery and not on the madonna which the cunning Italian intellect flung to the mob of Europe the church is founded and founded irremovably because founded, like the world, macro- and microcosm, upon the void. Upon incertitude, upon unlikelihood. *Amor matris,* subjective and objective genitive, may be the only true thing in life. Paternity may be a legal fiction" (pp. 204–05). [Au.]

Defining poetry as a mirror held up to nature, the mimetic aesthetic that begins with Aristotle and descends through Sidney, Shakespeare, and Jonson, implies that the poet, like a lesser God, has made or engendered an alternative, mirror-universe in which he has as it were enclosed or trapped shadows of reality. Similarly, Coleridge's Romantic concept of the human "imagination or esemplastic power" is of a virile, generative force which, echoing "the eternal act of creation in the infinite I AM . . . dissolves, diffuses, dissipates in order to recreate."[7] In both aesthetics, the poet, like God the Father, is a paternalistic ruler of the fictive world he has created. Shelley called him a "legislator." Keats noted, speaking of writers, that "the ancients were Emperors of vast Provinces" though "each of the moderns" is merely an "Elector of Hanover."[8]

In medieval philosophy, the network of connections among sexual, literary, and theological metaphors is equally complex: God the Father both engenders the cosmos and, as Ernst Robert Curtius notes, writes the Book of Nature: both tropes describe a single act of creation.[9] In addition, the Heavenly Author's ultimate eschatological power is made manifest when, as the *Liber Scriptus* of the traditional Requiem mass indicates, He writes the Book of Judgment. More recently, male artists like the Earl of Rochester in the seventeenth century and Auguste Renoir in the nineteenth, have frankly defined aesthetics based on male sexual delight. "I . . . never Rhym'd, but for my Pintle's [penis's] sake," declares Rochester's witty Timon, and, as the painter Bridget Riley notes, Renoir "said that he painted his paintings with his prick."[10] Clearly, both these artists believe, with Norman O. Brown, that "the penis is the head of the body"; and they would both (to some extent, anyway) agree with John Irwin's suggestion that the relationship "of the masculine self with the feminine-masculine work is also an autoerotic act . . . a kind of creative onanism in which through the use of the phallic pen on the 'pure space' of the virgin page or the chisel on the virgin marble, the self is continually spent and wasted in an act of progressive self-destruction."[11] No doubt it is for all these reasons, moreover, that poets have traditionally used a vocabulary derived from the patriarchal Family Romance to describe their relations with each other. As Harold Bloom has pointed out, "from the sons of Homer to the sons of Ben Jonson, poetic influence had been described as a filial relationship, [a relationship of] *sonship*. . . ." The fierce struggle at the heart of literary history, says Bloom, is a "battle between strong equals, father and son as mighty opposites, Laius and Oedipus at the crossroads. . . ."[12]

Though many of these writers use the metaphor of literary paternity in different ways and for different purposes, all seem overwhelmingly to agree that a literary text is not only speech quite literally embodied, but also power mysteriously made manifest, made flesh. In patriarchal Western culture, therefore, the text's author is a father, a progenitor, a procreator, an aesthetic patriarch whose pen is an instrument of generative power like his penis. More, his pen's power, like his penis's power, is not just the ability to generate life but the power to create a posterity to which he lays claim, as, in Said's paraphrase of Partridge, "an increaser and thus a founder." In this respect, the pen is truly mightier than its phallic counterpart, the sword, and in patriarchy more resonantly sexual. Not only does the writer respond to his muse's quasi-sexual excitation with an outpouring of the aesthetic energy Hopkins called "the fine delight that fathers thought" (in a poem of that title)—a delight poured seminally from pen to page—but as the author of an enduring text the writer engages the attention of the future in exactly the same way that a king (or father) "owns" the homage of the present. No sword-wielding general could rule so long or possess so vast a kingdom.

[7] Coleridge, *Biographia Literaria,* Ch. XIII. [Au.]

[8] Shelley, "A Defense of Poetry," Keats, Letter to John Hamilton Reynolds, Feb. 3, 1818. [Au.]

[9] See E. R. Curtius, *European Literature and the Latin Middle Ages* (New York: Harper Torchbooks, 1963), pp. 305, 306. For further commentary on both Curtius' "The Symbolism of the Book" and the "Book of Nature" metaphor itself, see Derrida, *op. cit.*, pp. 15–17. [Au.]

[10] "Timon, A Satyr," in *Poems by John Wilmot Earl of Rochester,* ed. Vivian de Sola Pinto (London: Routledge and Kegan Paul Ltd., 1953), p. 99. [Au.] Bridget Riley, "The Hermaphrodite," *Art and Sexual Politics,* ed. Thomas B. Hass and Elizabeth C. Baker (London: Collier Books, 1973), p. 82. [Eds.]

[11] Norman O. Brown, *Love's Body* (New York: Vintage Books, 1968), p. 134.; John T. Irwin, *Doubling and Incest, Repetition and Revenge* (Baltimore: Johns Hopkins Univ. Press, 1977), p. 163. Irwin also speaks of "the phallic generative power of the creative imagination" (p. 159). [Au.]

[12] Harold Bloom, *The Anxiety of Influence* (New York: Oxford University Press, 1973), p. 26. [Au.]

Finally, the fact that such a notion of "ownership" or possession is embedded in the metaphor of paternity leads to yet another implication of this complex metaphor. For if the author/father is owner of his text and of his reader's attention, he is also, of course, owner/possessor of the subjects of his text, that is to say of those figures, scenes and events—those brain children—he has both incarnated in black and white and "bound" in cloth or leather. Thus, because he is an *author,* a "man of letters" is simultaneously, like his divine counterpart, a father, a master or ruler, and an owner: the spiritual type of a patriarch, as we understand that term in Western society.

Where does such an implicitly or explicitly patriarchal theory of literature leave literary women? If the pen is a metaphorical penis, with what organ can females generate texts? The question may seem frivolous, but, as my epigraph from Anais Nin indicates, both the patriarchal etiology that defines a solitary Father God as the only creator of all things, and the male metaphors of literary creation that depend upon such an etiology have long "confused" literary women—readers and writers alike. For what if such a proudly masculine cosmic Author is the sole legitimate model for all earthly authors? Or worse, what if the male generative power is not just the only legitimate power but the only power there is? That literary theoreticians from Aristotle to Hopkins seemed to believe this was so no doubt prevented many women from ever "attempting the pen"—to use Anne Finch's phrase—and caused enormous anxiety in generations of those women who were "presumptuous" enough to dare such an attempt. Jane Austen's Anne Elliot understates the case when she decorously observes, toward the end of *Persuasion,* that "men have had every advantage of us in telling their story. Education has been theirs in so much higher a degree; the pen has been in their hands."[13] For, as Anne Finch's complaint suggests, the pen has been defined as not just accidentally but essentially a male "tool," and, therefore, not only inappropriate but actually alien to women. Lacking Austen's demure irony, Finch's passionate protest goes almost as far toward the center of the metaphor of literary paternity as Hopkins's letter to Canon Dixon. Not only is "a woman that attempts the pen" an intrusive and "presumptuous Creature," she is absolutely unredeemable: no virtue can outweigh the "fault" of her presumption because she has grotesquely crossed boundaries dictated by Nature:

> They tell us, we mistake our sex and way;
> Good breeding, fassion, dancing, dressing,
> play
> Are the accomplishments we shou'd desire;
> To write, or read, or think, or to enquire
> Wou'd cloud our beauty, and exaust our
> time,
> And interrupt the conquests of our prime;
> Whilst the dull mannage, of a servile house
> Is held by some, our outmost art and use.[14]

Because they are by definition male activities, this passage implies, writing, reading and thinking are not only alien but also inimical to "female" characteristics. One hundred years later, in a famous letter to Charlotte Bronte, Robert Southey rephrased the same notion: "Literature is not the business of a woman's life, and it cannot be."[15] It cannot be, the metaphor of literary paternity implies, because it is physiologically as well as sociologically impossible. If male sexuality is integrally associated with the assertive presence of literary power, female sexuality is connected with the absence of such power, with the idea—expressed by the nineteenth-century thinker Otto Weininger—that "woman has no share in ontological reality." As we shall see, a further implication of the paternity/creativity metaphor is the notion (implicit both in Weininger and in Southey's letter) that women exist only to be acted on by men, both as literary and as sensual objects. Again one of Anne Finch's poems explores the assumptions submerged in so many literary theories. Addressing three male poets, she exclaims:

> Happy you three! happy the Race of Men!
> Born to inform or to correct the Pen
> To proffitts pleasures freedom and command
> Whilst we beside you but as Cyphers stand
> T'increase your Numbers and to swell
> th'account

[13] Jane Austen, *Persuasion,* Chapter Twenty-Three. [Au.]

[14] Anne Finch, *Poems,* pp. 4–5. [Au.]

[15] Southey, letter to Charlotte Bronte, March 1837. Quoted in Winifred Gerin, *Charlotte Bronte: The Evolution of Genius* (Oxford: Oxford University Press, 1967), p. 110. [Au.]

Of your delights which from our charms
amount
And sadly are by this distinction taught
That since the Fall (by our seducement
wrought)
Ours is the greater losse as ours the greater
fault[16]

Since Eve's daughters have fallen so much lower than Adam's sons, this passage says, *all* females are "Cyphers"—nullities, vacancies—existing merely and punningly to increase male "Numbers" (either poems or persons) by pleasuring either men's bodies or their minds, their penises or their pens.

In that case, however, devoid of what Richard Chase once called "the masculine *élan,*" and implicitly rejecting even the slavish consolations of her "femininity," a literary woman is doubly a "Cypher," for she is really a "eunuch," to use the striking figure Germaine Greer applied to all women in patriarchal society. Thus Anthony Burgess recently declared that Jane Austen's novels fail because her writing "lacks a strong male thrust," and William Gass lamented that literary women "lack that blood congested genital drive which energizes every great style."[17] But the assumptions that underlie their statements were articulated more than a century ago by the nineteenth-century editor-critic Rufus Griswold. Introducing an anthology entitled *The Female Poets of America,* he outlined a theory of literary sex roles which expands, and clarifies, the grim implications of the metaphor of literary paternity.

> It is less easy to be assured of the genuineness of literary ability in women than in men. The moral nature of women, in its finest and richest development, partakes of some of the qualities of genius; it assumes, at least, the similitude of that which in men is the characteristic or accompaniment of the highest grade of mental inspiration. We are in danger, therefore, of mistaking for the efflorescent energy of creative intelligence, that which is only the exuberance of personal 'feelings unemployed.' . . . The most exquisite susceptibility of the spirit, and the capacity to mirror in dazzling variety the effects which circumstances or surrounding minds work upon it, may be accompanied by *no power to originate, nor even, in any proper sense, to reproduce* [ital. mine].[18]

Since Griswold has actually compiled a collection of poems by women, he plainly does not believe that all women lack reproductive or generative literary power all the time. His gender-definitions imply, however, that when such creative energy appears in a woman it may be anomalous, freakish, because as a "male" characteristic it is essentially "unfeminine."

The converse of these explicit and implicit definitions of "femininity" may also be true for those who develop literary theories based upon the "mystical estate" of fatherhood: if a woman lacks generative literary power, then a man who loses or abuses such power becomes like a woman. Significantly, when Hopkins wanted to explain to R. W. Dixon the aesthetic consequences of a *lack* of male mastery, he declared that if "the life" is not "conveyed into the work and . . . displayed there . . . the product is one of those hens' eggs that are good to eat and look just like live ones but never hatch."[19] And when, late in his life, he tried to define his own sense of sterility, his thickening writer's block, he described himself both as an eunuch and *as a woman,* specifically a woman deserted by male power: "the widow of an insight lost," surviving in a diminished

[16] Finch, *Poems,* p. 100. Otto Weininger, *Sex and Character* (London: Heinemann, 1906), p. 286. This sentence is part of an extraordinary passage in which Weininger asserts that "women have no existence and no essence; they are not, they are nothing." This because "woman has no relation to the idea . . . she is neither moral nor anti-moral," whereas "all existence is moral and logical existence." [Au.]

[17] Richard Chase speaks of "the masculine *élan*" throughout "The Brontës, or Myth Domesticated," in *Forms of Modern Fiction,* ed. William V. O'Connor (Minneapolis: Univ. of Minnesota Press, 1948), pp. 102–13. For a discussion of the "female eunuch" see Germaine Greer, *The Female Eunuch.* See also Anthony Burgess, "The Book Is Not For Reading," *New York Times Book Review,* 4 December 1966, pp. 1, 74, and William Gass, Review of Norman Mailer's *Genius and Lust, New York Times Book Review,* 24 October 1976, p. 2. In this connection, too, it is interesting (and depressing) to consider that Virginia Woolf defined *herself* as "a eunuch" (see Noel Annan, "Virginia Woolf Fever," *New York Review of Books,* April 20, 1978, p. 22). [Au.]

[18] Rufus Griswold, Preface to *The Female Poets of America* (Philadelphia: Carey & Hart, 1849), p. 8. [Au.]

[19] Hopkins, *Correspondence,* p. 133. [Au.]

"winter world" that entirely lacks "the roll, the rise, the carol, the creation" of male generative power, whose "strong / Spur" is phallically "live and lancing like the blow pipe flame."[20] And once again some lines from one of Anne Finch's protests against male literary hegemony seem to support Hopkins's image of the powerless and sterile woman artist. Remarking in the conclusion of her "Introduction" to her *Poems* that women are "to be dull / Expected and dessigned" she does not repudiate such expectations, but on the contrary admonishes herself, with bitter irony, to *be* dull:

> Be caution'd then my Muse, and still retir'd;
> Nor be dispis'd, aiming to be admir'd;
> Conscious of wants, still with contracted
> wing,
> To some few friends, and to thy sorrows
> sing;
> For groves of Lawrell, thou wert never
> meant;
> Be dark enough thy shades, and be thou
> there content.[21]

Cut off from generative energy, in a dark and wintry world, Finch seems to be defining herself here not only as a "Cypher" but as "the widow of an insight lost."

Finch's despairing (if ironic) acceptance of male expectations and designs summarizes in a single episode the coercive power not only of cultural constraints but of the literary texts which incarnate them. For it is as much, if not more, from literature as from "life" that literate women learn they are "to be dull / Expected and dessigned." As Leo Bersani puts it, written "language doesn't merely describe identity but actually produces moral and perhaps even physical identity . . . we have to allow for a kind of dissolution or at least elasticity of being induced by an immersion in literature."[22] A century and a half earlier, Jane Austen had Anne Elliot's interlocutor, Captain Harville, make a related point in *Persuasion.* Arguing women's inconstancy over Anne's heated objections, he notes that "all histories are against you—all stories, prose, and verse. . . . I could bring you fifty quotations in a moment on my side of the argument, and I do not think I ever opened a book in my life which had not something to say upon woman's inconstancy. Songs and proverbs, all talk of woman's fickleness."[23] To this Anne responds, as we have seen, that the pen has been in male hands. In the context of Harville's speech, her remark implies that women have not only been excluded from authorship but in addition they have been subject to (and subjects of) male author-ity. With Chaucer's astute Wife of Bath, therefore, Anne might demand "Who peynted the leoun, tel me who?" And, like the Wife's, her own answer to her own rhetorical question would emphasize our culture's historical confusion of literary authorship with patriarchal authority:

> By God, if wommen hadde writen stories,
> As clerkes han withinne hir oratories,
> They wolde han writen of men more
> wikednesse
> Than all the mark of Adam may redresse.

In other words, what Bersani, Austen and Chaucer all imply is that precisely because a writer "fathers" his text, his literary creations (as we saw earlier) are his possession, his property. Having defined them in language and thus generated them, he owns them, controls them, and encloses them on the printed page. Describing his earliest sense of vocation as a writer, Jean-Paul Sartre recalled in *Les Mots* his childhood belief that "to write was to engrave new beings upon [the infinite Tables of the Word] or . . . to catch living things in the trap of phrases. . . ."[24] Naive as such a notion may seem on the face of it, it is not "wholly an illusion, for it is his [Sartre's] truth," as one commentator observes[25]—and indeed it is every writer's "truth," a truth which has traditionally led male authors to assume patriarchal rights of ownership over the female "characters" they engrave upon "the infinite Tables of the Word."

Male authors have also, of course, generated male characters over whom they would seem to have had

[20] See Hopkins, "The fine delight that fathers thought." [Au.]

[21] Finch, *Poems,* p. 5. [Au.]

[22] Leo Bersani, *A Future for Astyanax* (Boston: Little Brown, 1976), p. 194. [Au.]

[23] *Persuasion, loc. cit.* [Au.]

[24] Jean-Paul Sartre, *The Words,* trans. Bernard Frechtman (New York: Braziller, Inc., 1964), p. 114 (paperback edition). [Au.]

[25] Marjorie Grene, *Sartre* (New York: New Viewpoints, 1973), p. 9 [Au.]

similar rights of ownership. But further implicit in the metaphor of literary paternity is the idea that each man, arriving at what Hopkins called the "puberty" of his creative gift, has the ability, even perhaps the obligation, to talk back to other men by generating alternative fictions of his own. Lacking the pen/penis which would enable them similarly to refute one fiction by another, women in patriarchal societies have historically been reduced to *mere* properties, to characters and images imprisoned in male texts because generated solely, as Anne Elliot and Anne Finch observe, by male expectations and designs.

Like the metaphor of literary paternity itself, this corollary notion that the chief creature man has generated is woman has a long and complex history. From Eve, Minerva, Sophia and Galatea onward, after all, patriarchal mythology defines women as created by, from, and for men, the children of male brains, ribs, and ingenuity. For Blake the eternal female was at her best an Emanation of the male creative principle. For Shelley she was an epi-psyche, a soul out of the poet's soul, whose inception paralleled on a spiritual plane the solider births of Eve and Minerva. Throughout the history of Western culture, moreover, male-engendered female figures as superficially disparate as Milton's Sin, Swift's Chloe, and Yeats' Crazy Jane have incarnated men's ambivalence not only toward female sexuality but toward their own (male) physicality. At the same time, male texts, continually elaborating the metaphor of literary paternity, have continually proclaimed that, in Honoré de Balzac's ambiguous words, "woman's virtue is man's greatest invention." A characteristically condensed and oracular comment of Norman O. Brown's perfectly summarizes the assumptions on which all such texts are based:

> Poetry, the creative act, the act of life, the archetypal sexual act. Sexuality is poetry. The lady is our creation, or Pygmalion's statue. The lady is the poem; [Petrarch's] Laura is, really, poetry. . . .

No doubt this complex of metaphors and etiologies simply reflects not just the fiercely patriarchal structure of Western society but also the underpinning of misogyny upon which that severe patriarchy has stood. The roots of "authority" tell us, after all, that if woman is man's property then he must have authored her, just as surely as they tell us that if he authored her she must be his property. As a creation "penned" by man, moreover, woman has been "penned up" or "penned in." As a sort of "sentence" man has spoken, she has herself been "sentenced": fated, jailed, for he has both "indited" her and "indicted" her. As a thought he has "framed," she has been both "framed" (enclosed) in his texts, glyphs, graphics, and "framed up" (found guilty, found wanting) in his cosmologies. For as Humpty Dumpty tells Alice in *Through the Looking Glass,* the "master" of words, utterances, phrases, literary properties, "can manage the whole lot of them!"[26] The etymology and etiology of masculine authority are, it seems, almost necessarily identical. However, for women who felt themselves to be more than, in every sense, the properties of literary texts, the problem posed by such authority was neither metaphysical nor philological, but (as the pain expressed by Anne Finch and Anne Elliot indicates) psychological. Since both patriarchy and its text subordinate and imprison women, before women can even attempt that pen which is so rigorously kept from them, they must escape just those male texts which, defining them as "Cyphers," deny them the autonomy to formulate alternatives to the authority that has imprisoned them and kept them from attempting the pen.

The vicious circularity of this problem helps explain the curious passivity with which Finch responded (or pretended to respond) to male expectations and designs, and it helps explain, too, the centuries-long silence of so many women who must have had talents comparable to Finch's. A final paradox of the metaphor of literary paternity is the fact that, in the same way that an author both generates and imprisons his fictive creatures, he silences them by depriving them of autonomy (that is, of the power of independent speech) even as he gives them life. He silences them and, as Keats' "Ode on a Grecian Urn" suggests, he stills them, or—embedding them in the marble of his art—kills them. As Albert Gelpi neatly puts it, "the artist kills experience into art, for temporal experience can only escape death by dying into the 'immortality' of artistic form. The fixity of 'life' in art and the fluidity of 'life' in nature are incompatible."[27] The pen, therefore, is not only

[26] Lewis Carroll, *Through the Looking Glass,* Chapter VI, "Humpty Dumpty." [Au.]

[27] Albert Gelpi, "Emily Dickinson and the Deerslayer," in *Shakespeare's Sisters,* ed. Sandra Gilbert and Susan Gubar (Bloomington: Indiana University Press, 1979). [Au.]

mightier than the sword, it is also *like* the sword in its power—its need, even—to kill. And this last attribute of the pen once again seems to be associatively linked with its metaphorical maleness. Simone de Beauvoir has commented that the human male's "transcendence" of nature is symbolized by his ability to hunt and kill, just as the human female's identification with nature, her role as a symbol of immanence, is expressed by her central involvement in that life-giving but involuntary birth process which perpetuates the species. Thus, superiority—or authority—"has been accorded in humanity not to the sex that brings forth but to that which kills."[28] In D. H. Lawrence's words, "the Lords of Life are the Masters of Death"—and, therefore, patriarchal poetics implies, they are the masters of art.[29]

Commentators on female subordination from Freud and Horney to de Beauvoir, Wolfgang Lederer, and, most recently, Dorothy Dinnerstein, have of course explored other aspects of the relationship between the sexes that also lead men to want figuratively to "kill" women. What Horney called male "dread" of the female is a phenomenon to which Lederer has devoted a long and scholarly book.[30] Elaborating on de Beauvoir's assertion that as mother of life "woman's first lie, her first treason [seems to be] that of life itself—life which, though clothed in the most attractive forms, is always infested by the ferments of age and death," Lederer remarks upon woman's own tendency to, in effect, kill *herself* into art in order "to appeal to man":

> From the Paleolithic on, we have evidence that woman, through careful coiffure, through adornment and makeup, tried to stress the eternal type rather than the mortal self. Such makeup, in Africa or Japan, may reach the, to us, somewhat estranging degree of a lifeless mask—and yet that is precisely the purpose of it: where nothing is lifelike, nothing speaks of death.[31]

For yet another reason, then, it is no wonder that women have historically hesitated to attempt the pen. Authored by a male God and by a godlike male, killed into a "perfect" image of herself, the woman writer's self-contemplation may be said to have begun with a searching glance into the mirror of the male-inscribed literary text. There she would see at first only those eternal lineaments fixed on her like a mask to conceal her dreadful and bloody link to nature. But looking long enough, looking hard enough, she would see—like Mary Elizabeth Coleridge gazing at "the other side of the mirror"—an enraged and rebellious prisoner: herself. Coleridge's poem describing this vision is central to female (and feminist) poetics:

> I sat before my glass one day,
> And conjured up a vision bare,
> Unlike the aspects glad and gay,
> That erst were found reflected there—
> The vision of a woman, wild
> With more than womanly despair.
>
> Her hair stood back on either side
> A face bereft of loveliness.
> It had no envy now to hide
> What once no man on earth could guess.
> It formed the thorny aureole
> Of hard unsanctified distress.
>
> Her lips were open—not a sound
> Came through the parted lines of red.
> Whate'er it was, the hideous wound
> In silence and in secret bled.
> No sigh relieved her speechless woe,
> She had no voice to speak her dread.
>
> And in her lurid eyes there shone
> The dying flame of life's desire,
> Made mad because its hope was gone,
> And kindled at the leaping fire
> Of jealousy, and fierce revenge,
> And strength that could not change nor tire.
>
> Shade of a shadow in the glass,
> O set the crystal surface free!
> Pass—as the fairer visions pass—

[28] Simone de Beauvoir, *The Second Sex* (New York: Alfred Knopf, 1953), p. 58. [Au.]

[29] D. H. Lawrence, *The Plumed Serpent,* Chapter XXIII, "Huitzilopochtli's Night." [Au.]

[30] See Wolfgang Lederer, M.D., *The Fear of Women* (New York: Harcourt Brace Jovanovich, Inc., 1968); also H. R. Hays, *The Dangerous Sex* (New York: G. P. Putnam's Sons, 1964); Katharine Rogers, *The Troublesome Helpmate* (Seattle: University of Washington Press, 1966); and Dorothy Dinnerstein, *The Mermaid and the Minotaur* (New York: Harper & Row, 1976). [Au.]

[31] Lederer, *op. cit.,* p. 42. [Au.]

Nor ever more return, to be
The ghost of a distracted hour,
That heard me whisper, 'I am she!'[32]

What this poem suggests is that, although the woman who is the prisoner of the mirror/text's images has "no voice to speak her dread," although "no sigh" interrupts "her speechless woe," she has an invincible sense of her own autonomy, her own interiority; she has a sense, to paraphrase Chaucer's Wife of Bath, of the authority of her own experience.[33] The power of metaphor, says Mary Elizabeth Coleridge's poem, can only extend so far. Finally, no human creature can be completely silenced by a text or by an image. Just as stories notoriously have a habit of "getting away" from their authors, human beings since Eden have had a habit of defying author-ity, both divine and literary.[34]

Once more the debate in which Austen's Anne Elliot and her Captain Harville engage is relevant here, for it is surely no accident that the question these two characters are discussing is woman's "inconstancy"—her refusal, that is, to be fixed or "killed" by an author/owner, her stubborn insistence on her own way. That male authors berate her for this refusal even while they themselves generate female characters who perversely display "monstrous" autonomy is one of the ironies of literary art. From a female perspective, however, such "inconstancy" can only be encouraging, for—implying duplicity—it suggests that women themselves have the power to create themselves as characters, even perhaps the power to reach toward the self trapped on the other side of the mirror/text and help her to climb out.

Passages from the works of several other women writers suggest one significant way in which the female artist can bring this secret self to the surface of her own life: against the traditional generative authority of the pen/penis, the literary woman can set the conceptual energy of her own female sexuality. Though our patriarchal culture has tended to sentimentalize and thus trivialize the matriarchal power that, in the view of the nineteenth-century German thinker J. J. Bachofen, once dominated most human societies, a surprising number of literary women seem to have consciously or unconsciously fantasized the rebirth of such power.[35] From Christina Rossetti, who dreamed of a utopian "Mother Country," to Adrienne Rich, whose *Of Woman Born* is (among other things) a metaphorical attempt to map such a land, women writers have almost instinctively struggled to associate their own life-giving sexual energy with their art, opposing both to the deadly force of the swordlike pen/penis.[36]

In Charlotte Bronte's *The Professor,* for instance, the young poet/seamstress Frances Henri celebrates the return of love and liberty after a long interlude of grief and failure by reciting "Milton's invocation to that heavenly muse, who on the 'secret top of Oreb or Sinai' had taught the Hebrew shepherd how in the womb of chaos, the conception of a world had originated and ripened." Though, as Virginia Woolf once suggested, the author of *Paradise Lost* was the "first of the masculinists" in his misogynistic contempt for Eve, the "Mother of Mankind," Bronte drastically revises his imagery, de-emphasizing the generative power of the patriarchal Author and stressing the powerful womb of the matriarchal muse.[37] More directly, in *Shirley* she has her eponymous heroine insist that Milton never "saw" Eve: "it was his cook that he saw." In fact, she declares, the first woman was never, like Milton's Eve, "half doll, half angel" and always potential fiend. Rather, she was a powerful Titan, a woman whose Promethean creative energy gave birth to

[32] Mary Elizabeth Coleridge, "The Other Side of a Mirror," in *Poems by Mary E. Coleridge* (London: Elkin Mathews, 1908), pp. 8–9. [Au.]

[33] See The Wife's Prologue, lines 1–3: "Experience, though noon auctoritee / Were in this world, were right ynough to me / To speke of wo that is in mariage. . ." See also Arlyn Diamond & Lee Edwards, ed., *The Authority of Experience* (Amherst: University of Massachusetts Press, 1977), an anthology of feminist criticism which draws its title from the Wife's speech. [Au.]

[34] In acknowledgement of a point similar to this, Said follows his definition of "authority" with a definition of an accompanying, integrally related concept of "molestation," by which he says he means "that no novelist has ever been unaware that his authority, regardless of how complete, or the authority of a narrator, is a sham" (Said, *Beginnings,* p. 84). [Au.]

[35] J. J. Bachofen, *Myth, Religion, and Mother Right,* tr. Ralph Manheim (Princeton: Bollingen Series, 1967). [Au.]

[36] Rossetti, "Mother Country," in *The Poems of Christina G. Rossetti: Goblin Market and Other Poems* (Boston: Little Brown, 1909), p. 116. Adrienne Rich, *Of Woman Born: Motherhood as Experience and Institution* (New York: W. W. Norton, 1976). [Au.]

[37] See Charlotte Bronte, *The Professor* (New York: Dutton, 1969), p. 155 (Ch. XIX). [Au.]

"the daring which could contend with Omnipotence: the strength which could bear a thousand years of bondage . . . the unexhausted life and uncorrupted excellence, sisters to immortality, which . . . could conceive and bring forth a Messiah."[38] Clearly such a female Author would have maternal powers equal to the paternal energies of any male Titan.

Mary Shelley's fictionalised Author's Introduction to *The Last Man* is based on a similarly revisionary myth of female sexual energy, a covertly feminist Parable of the Cave which implicitly refutes Plato, Milton, and the metaphor of literary paternity. In 1818, Shelley begins, she and "a friend" visited what was said to be "the gloomy cavern of the Cumaean Sibyl." Entering a mysterious, almost inaccessible chamber, they found "piles of leaves, fragments of bark, and a white filmy substance resembling the inner part of the green hood which shelters the grain of the unripe Indian corn." At first, Shelley confesses, she and her male companion (Percy Shelley) were baffled by this discovery, but "At length, my friend . . . exclaimed 'This *is* the Sibyl's cave; these are sibylline leaves!'" Her account continues as follows:

> On examination, we found that all the leaves, bark and other substances were traced with written characters. What appeared to us more astonishing, was that these writings were expressed in various languages: some unknown to my companion . . . some . . . in modern dialects. . . . We could make out little by the dim light, but they seemed to contain prophecies, detailed relations of events but lately passed; names . . . and often exclamations of exultation or woe . . . were traced on their thin scant pages. . . . We made a hasty selection of such of the leaves, whose writing one at least of us could understand, and then . . . bade adieu to the dim hypaethric cavern. . . . Since that period . . . I have been employed in deciphering these sacred remains. . . . I present the public with my latest discoveries in the slight Sibylline pages. Scattered and unconnected as they were, I have been obliged to . . . model the work into a consistent form. But the main substance rests on the divine intuitions which the Cumaean damsel obtained from heaven.[39]

Every feature of this cave journey is significant, especially for the female critic (or writer) who seeks alternatives to the "masculinist" metaphor of literary paternity.

It is obviously important, to begin with, that the cave is a female space, and—more important—a space inhabited not by fettered prisoners (as the famous cave in Plato's *Republic* was) but by a free female hierophant, the lost Sibyl, a prophetess who inscribed her "divine intuitions" on tender leaves and fragments of delicate bark. For Mary Shelley, therefore, it is intimately connected with both her own artistic authority and her own power of self-creation. A male poet or instructor may guide her to this place—as Percy Shelley does, in her fictional narrative—but, as she herself comes to realize, she and she alone can effectively reconstruct the scattered truth of the Sibyl's leaves. Literally the daughter of a dead and dishonored mother—the powerful feminist Mary Wollstonecraft—Mary Shelley portrays herself in this parable as figuratively the daughter of the vanished Sybil, the primordial prophetess who mythically conceived all women artists.

That the Sibyl's leaves are now scattered, fragmented, barely comprehensible is thus the central problem Shelley faces in her own art. Earlier in her introduction, she notes that finding the cave was a preliminary problem. She and her companion were misled and misdirected by native guides, she tells us; left alone in one chamber while the guides went for new torches, they "lost" their way in the darkness; ascending in the "wrong" direction, they accidentally stumbled upon the true cave. But the difficulty of this initial discovery merely foreshadows the difficulty of the crucial task of reconstruction, as Shelley shows. For just as the path to the Sibyl's cave has been forgotten, the coherent truth of her leaves has been shattered and scattered, the body of her art dismembered, and, like Anne Finch, she has become a sort of "Cypher," powerless and enigmatic. But while the way to the cave can be "remembered" by accident, the whole meaning of the Sibylline leaves can only be re-remembered through

[38] Charlotte Bronte, *Shirley* (New York and London: The Haworth Edition, 1900), p. 328. [Au.]

[39] Mary Shelley, *The Last Man* (1826; reprint, Lincoln, Neb.: Univ. of Nebraska Press, 1965), pp. 3–4. [Au.]

painstaking labor: translation, transcription and stitchery, re-vision and re-creation.

The specifically sexual texture of these Sibylline documents, these scattered leaves and leavings, adds to their profound importance for women. Working on leaves, bark and "a white filmy substance," the Sibyl literally wrote, and wrote *upon,* the Book of Nature. She had, in other words, a Goddess' power of maternal creativity, the sexual/artistic strength that is the female equivalent of the male potential for literary paternity. In her "dim hypaerthric cavern"—a dim sea-cave that was nevertheless *open* to the sky—she received her "divine intuitions" through "an aperture" in the "arched dome-like roof" which "let in the light of heaven." On her "raised seat of stone, about the size of a Grecian couch," she *conceived* her art, inscribing it on leaves and bark from the green world outside. And so fierce are her verses, so truthful her "poetic rhapsodies," that even in deciphering them Shelley exclaims that she feels herself "taken . . . out of a world, which has averted its once benignant face from me, to one glowing with imagination and power." For in recovering and reconstructing the Sibyl's scattered artistic/sexual energy, Shelley comes to recognize that she is discovering and recreating—literally *deciphering*—her own creative power. "Sometimes I have thought," she modestly confesses, "that, obscure and chaotic as they are, [these translations from the Sibyl's leaves] owe their present form to me, their decipherer. As if we should give to another artist, the painted fragments which form the mosaic copy of Raphael's Transfiguration in St. Peter's; he would put them together in a form, whose mode would be fashioned by his own peculiar mind and talent."[40]

The quest for creative energy enacted by Charlotte Bronte and Mary Shelley in the passages I have quoted here has been of consuming importance (for obvious reasons) to many other women writers. Emily Dickinson, for instance, sought what Christina Rossetti called a "Mother Country" all her life, and she always envisioned such a country as a land of primordial power. Indeed, though Dickinson's famous "My Life had stood—a Loaded Gun" seems to define sexual/creative energies in terms of a destructive, phallic mechanism, it is important to remember that this almost theatrically reticent literary woman always associated apparently "male" guns with profound "female" volcanoes and mountains.[41] Thus her phallic description of poetic speech in "My Life had stood" is balanced by a characterization of the ("female") volcano as "The Solemn—Torrid—Symbol— / The lips that never lie—." And in one of her lesser known poems of the 1860s she formulated a matriarchal creed of womanly creativity that must surely have given her the strength to sustain her own art through all the doubts and difficulties of her reclusive life:

Sweet Mountains—Ye tell Me no lie—
Never deny Me—Never fly—
Those same unvarying Eyes
Turn on Me—when I fail—or feign,
Or take the Royal names in vain—
Their far—slow—Violet Gaze—
My Strong Madonnas—Cherish still—
The Wayward Nun—beneath the Hill—
Whose service—is to You—
Her latest Worship—When the Day
Fades from the Firmament away—
To lift Her Brows on You—[42]

One of Dickinson's most perceptive admirers, the feminist poet Adrienne Rich, has more recently turned to the same imagery of matriarchal power in what is plainly a similar attempt to confute that metaphor of literary paternity which, as Anais Nin wrote, has "confused" so many women in our society. "Your mother dead and you unborn," she writes in "The Mirror In Which Two Are Seen As One," describing the situation of the female artist, "your two hands [grasp] your head,"

drawing it down against the blade of life
your nerves the nerves of a midwife
learning her trade[43]

[40] *Ibid.* [Au.]

[41] On "My Life Had stood—a Loaded Gun," see Albert Gelpi, "Emily Dickinson's Deerslayer," in Sandra Gilbert and Susan Gubar, ed., *Shakespeare's Sisters: Women Poets, Feminist Critics* (Bloomington: Indiana University Press, 1978). [Au.]

[42] *The Poems of Emily Dickinson,* ed. Thomas H. Johnson (Cambridge, Mass.: Harvard University Press, 1955), #722. [Eds.]

[43] Adrienne Rich, *Poems Selected and New, 1950–1974* (New York: W. W. Norton, 1974), p. 195. [Au.]

Annette Kolodny

b. 1941

Annette Kolodny's earlier work as a literary historian and critic (particularly in *The Lay of the Land,* 1975, and *The Land Before Her,* 1984) illustrates a number of crucial differences in the development of recent feminist theory, primarily in the United States and France. As Kolodny notes in the first part of the essay here, work by North American feminist critics and scholars since the early 1970s has been pursued on a large scale, with professional thoroughness, documenting a tradition of neglect, misreading, and sexual stereotyping that would be, quite literally, criminal if acted out in the marketplace of the 1980s. It is, as Kolodny says, a major accomplishment; but in the context of American literary study in the universities, where a gigantic professional apparatus is in place (and in power), the irony is that work by women, observing the apparent protocols of the profession, has little apparent impact on the professional apparatus itself. Part of the anger to which Kolodny alludes stems from the fact that the reception of the critical and scholarly work itself has tended to confirm a continuing pattern of neglect, misreading, and stereotyping, not just of women poets and writers but now of critics as well. In France, this would not be a crime, but *un scandale;* yet in the context of the Modern Language Association, for example, with more than 30,000 members, teaching in perhaps 4,000 colleges and universities, it is hard to stage a scandal or even, in many cases, to see it.

More is at stake than a difference of scale, to be sure; but the professionalization of literary study in the United States on an unprecedented scale does have a profound effect on how questions of theory are recognized and pursued or even what issues will be acknowledged as consequential. The characteristic profile of criticism by American feminists has generally been the historical study of the representation of women in literature, which can be pursued without directly raising theoretical questions pertaining to "representation," "literature," or even "women." Thematizing these questions in existing forms of critical discourse leads directly to practical issues: what texts will be included on reading and examination lists, who will be allowed to teach what to whom, who will be hired, promoted, or fired, ostensibly on the basis of the professional activities of teaching and publishing?

While these questions of the literary canon and professional ethics are shaped by practical concerns (including the existence of federal statutes prohibiting discrimination based on sex), it remains uncertain what theoretical implications they may have. As *Alice Jardine* observes, much of the work of French feminists has become "antifeminist" (in Jardine's phrase) as it has become more strictly theoretical, since the concept of feminism, as inherited from the rational humanism of the Enlightenment, comes into question when rational humanism itself is questioned. This is not to suggest that "theory" must, perforce, question rational humanism, though that has been the case among many contemporary thinkers. It is, rather, to acknowledge the logical and conceptual problem that arises when it becomes imperative to define and attempt to redress an injustice that appears to be a structural and not an accidental part of a system of thought. Among American feminists, the emergence of gender studies is, in part, a response to this problem, to cast the issues in terms of the effects of culture on identity without reinforcing the categorical ground of biological distinction from which stereotyping also derives.

Kolodny's argument in "Dancing through the Minefield" takes a different approach, staying within the boundaries of literary study per se, to question conventional assumptions about literary history, interpretation, and critical method. The three propositions Kolodny advances, as it were, for navigating the "minefield" have been familiar topics of theoretical debate since the late 1940s: the proposition that "literary history . . . is a fiction" was a central issue in disputes between the New Critics and literary historians, while the contention that as we learn to read "we engage . . . not texts but paradigms" is essential to the arguments of archetypal critics following Northrop Frye (see *CTSP,* pp. 1118–47) as well as to more recent versions of structuralism. Kolodny's third proposition, calling into question the universality of aesthetic judgment and encouraging the reexamination of critical methods, is the very means by which theoretical questions are articulated as such. This is just to say that the institutional structure of academic literary study in North America is based less on articulated speculative or theoretical models than on late-nineteenth-century notions of philology and literary chronology and that courses in criticism and theory, now offered in most universities, were available at only a few major institutions in 1965. At least part of the frustration of American feminist criticism and scholarship stems from the fact that much of it began with the assumption that feminist literary study presented a primarily documentary problem of literary history. From this point of view, the accomplishment of American feminist critics since the late 1960s, exemplified in Kolodny's work, is less in the development of a coherent theory of feminist criticism than in making the issues of feminism and gender an essential and inescapable part of any contemporary theoretical discussion.

Annette Kolodny's work includes *The Lay of the Land: Metaphor as Experience and History in American Life and Letters* (1975) and *The Land before Her: Fantasy and Experience of the American Frontier, 1630–1860* (1984). See also her "A Map for Rereading: Gender and the Interpretation of Literary Texts," *New Literary History* 11 (1980).

DANCING THROUGH THE MINEFIELD:
Some Observations on the Theory, Practice, and Politics of a Feminist Literary Criticism

Had anyone had the prescience, in 1969, to pose the question of defining a "feminist" literary criticism, she might have been told, in the wake of Mary Ellmann's *Thinking About Women*,[1] that it involved exposing the sexual stereotyping of women in both our literature and our literary criticism and, as well, demonstrating the inadequacy of established critical schools and methods to deal fairly or sensitively with works written by women. In broad outline, such a prediction would have stood well the test of time, and, in fact, Ellmann's book continues to be widely read and to point us in useful directions. What could not have been anticipated in 1969, however, was the catalyzing force of an ideology that, for many of us, helped to bridge the gap between the world as we found it and the world as we wanted it to be. For those of us who studied literature, a previously unspoken sense of exclusion from authorship, and a painfully personal distress at discovering whores, bitches, muses, and heroines dead in childbirth where we had once hoped to discover ourselves, could—for the first time—begin to be understood as more than "a set of disconnected, unrealized private emotions."[2] With a renewed courage to make public our otherwise private discontents, what had once been "felt individually as personal insecurity" came at last to be "viewed collectively as structural inconsistency"[3] within the very disciplines we studied. Following unflinchingly the full implications of Ellmann's percipient observations, and emboldened by the liberating energy of feminist ideology—in all its various forms and guises—feminist criticism very quickly moved beyond merely expos[ing] sexism in one work of literature after another,"[4] and promised instead that we might at last "begin to record new choices in a new literary history."[5] So powerful was that impulse that we experienced it, along with Adrienne Rich, as much more than "a chapter in cultural history": it became, rather, "an act of survival."[6] What was at stake was not so much literature or criticism as such, but the historical, social, and ethical consequences of women's participation in, or exclusion from, either enterprise.

The pace of inquiry in the 1970s was fast and furious—especially after Kate Millett's 1970 analysis of the sexual politics of literature[7] added a note of urgency to what had earlier been Ellmann's sardonic anger—while the diversity of that inquiry easily outstripped all efforts to define feminist literary criticism as either a coherent system or a unified set of methodologies. Under its wide umbrella, everything was thrown into question: our established canons, our aesthetic criteria, our interpretative strategies, our reading habits, and most of all, ourselves as critics and as teachers. To delineate its full scope would require nothing less than a book—a book that would be outdated even as it was being composed. For the sake of brevity, therefore, let me attempt only a summary outline.

Perhaps the most obvious success of this new scholarship has been the return to circulation of previously lost or otherwise ignored works by women writers. Following fast upon the initial success of the Feminist Press in reissuing gems such as Rebecca Harding Davis's 1861 novella, *Life in the Iron Mills*, and Charlotte Perkins Gilman's 1892 short story "The Yellow Wallpaper," published in

DANCING THROUGH THE MINEFIELD: SOME OBSERVATIONS ON THE THEORY, PRACTICE AND POLITICS OF A FEMINIST LITERARY CRITICISM was first published in *Feminist Studies* (1980). Copyright 1979 by Annette Kolodny, reprinted by permission of the author. The author made minor editorial changes for this edition.

[1] Mary Ellmann, *Thinking About Women* (New York: Harcourt, Brace & World, 1968). [Au.]

[2] See Clifford Geertz, "Ideology as a Cultural System," *The Interpretation of Cultures: Selected Essays* (New York: Basic Books, 1973), p. 232. [Au.]

[3] Ibid., p. 204. [Au.]

[4] Lillian S. Robinson, "Cultural Criticism and the *Horror Vacui*," *College English* 33 (October 1972); reprinted as "The Critical Task" in her *Sex, Class, and Culture* (Bloomington: Indiana University Press, 1978), p. 51. [Au.]

[5] Elaine Showalter, *A Literature of Their Own: British Women Novelists From Brontë to Lessing* (Princeton, N.J.: Princeton University Press, 1977), p. 36. [Au.]

[6] Adrienne Rich, "When We Dead Awaken: Writing as Re-Vision," *College English* 34 (October 1972); reprinted in *Adrienne Rich's Poetry*, ed. Barbara Charlesworth Gelpi and Albert Gelpi (New York: W. W. Norton, 1975), p. 90. [Au.]

[7] Kate Millett, *Sexual Politics* (Garden City, N.Y.: Doubleday, 1970). [Au.]

1972 and 1973 respectively,[8] commercial trade and reprint houses vied with one another in the reprinting of anthologies of lost texts and, in some cases, in the reprinting of whole series. For those of us in American literature especially, the phenomenon promised a radical reshaping of our concepts of literary history and, at the very least, a new chapter in understanding the development of women's literary traditions. So commercially successful were these reprintings, and so attuned were the reprint houses to the political attitudes of the audiences for which they were offered, that many of us found ourselves wooed to compose critical introductions, which would find in the pages of nineteenth-century domestic and sentimental fictions some signs of either muted rebellions or overt radicalism, in anticipation of the current wave of "New Feminism." In rereading with our students these previously lost works, we inevitably raised perplexing questions as to the reasons for their disappearance from the canons of "major works," and we worried over the aesthetic and critical criteria by which they had been accorded diminished status.

This increased availability of works by women writers led, of course, to an increased interest in what elements, if any, might constitute some sort of unity or connection among them. The possibility that women had developed either a unique or at least a related tradition of their own especially intrigued those of us who specialized in one national literature or another, or in historical periods. Nina Baym's *Woman's Fiction: A Guide to Novels by and about Women in America, 1820–1870*[9] demonstrated the Americanist's penchant for examining what were once the "best-sellers" of their day, the ranks of the popular fiction writers, among which women took a dominant place throughout the nineteenth century, while the feminist studies of British literature emphasized instead the wealth of women writers who have been regarded as worthy of canonization. Not so much building upon one another's work as clarifying, successively, the parameters of the questions to be posed, Sydney Janet Kaplan, Ellen Moers, Patricia Meyer Spacks, and Elaine Showalter, among many others, concentrated their energies on delineating an internally consistent "body of work" by women that might stand as a female counter-tradition. For Kaplan, in 1975, this entailed examining women writers' various attempts to portray feminine consciousness and self-consciousness, not as a psychological category, but as a stylistic or rhetorical device.[10] That same year, arguing essentially that literature publicizes the private, Spacks placed her consideration of a "female imagination" within social and historical frames, to conclude that "for readily discernible historical reasons women have characteristically concerned themselves with matters more or less peripheral to male concerns," and she attributed to this fact an inevitable difference in the literary emphases and subject matters of female and male writers.[11] The next year, Moers's *Literary Women: The Great Writers* focused on the pathways of literary influence that linked the English novel in the hands of women.[12] And finally, in 1977, Showalter took up the matter of a "female literary tradition in the English novel from the generation of the Brontës to the present day" by arguing that because women in general constitute a kind of "subculture within the framework of a larger society," the work of women writers, in particular, would thereby demonstrate a unity of "values, conventions, experiences, and behaviors impinging on each individual" as she found her sources of "self-expression relative to a dominant [and, by implication, male] society."[13]

At the same time that women writers were being reconsidered and reread, male writers were simi-

[8] Rebecca Harding Davis, *Life in the Iron Mills,* originally published in the *Atlantic Monthly,* April 1861; reprinted with "A Biographical Interpretation" by Tillie Olsen (Old Westbury, N.Y.: Feminist Press, 1972). Charlotte Perkins Gilman, "The Yellow Wallpaper," originally published in the *New England Magazine,* May 1892; reprinted with an Afterword by Elaine R. Hedges (Old Westbury, N.Y.: Feminist Press, 1973). [Au.]

[9] Nina Baym, *Woman's Fiction: A Guide to Novels by and about Women in America, 1820–1870* (Ithaca, N.Y.: Cornell University Press, 1978). [Au.]

[10] In her *Feminine Consciousness in the Modern British Novel* (Urbana: University of Illinois Press, 1975), p. 3, Sydney Janet Kaplan explains that she is using the term "feminine consciousness" "not simply as some general attitude of women toward their own femininity, and not as something synonymous with a particular sensibility among female writers. I am concerned with it as a literary device: a method of characterization of females in fiction." [Au.]

[11] Patricia Meyer Spacks, *The Female Imagination* (New York: Avon Books, 1975), p. 6. [Au.]

[12] Ellen Moers, *Literary Women: The Great Writers* (Garden City, N.Y.: Doubleday, 1976). [Au.]

[13] Showalter, *A Literature of Their Own,* p. 11. [Au.]

larly subjected to a new feminist scrutiny. The continuing result—to put years of difficult analysis into a single sentence—has been nothing less than an acute attentiveness to the ways in which certain power relations, usually those in which males wield various forms of influence over females, are inscribed in the texts (both literary and critical) that we have inherited, not merely as subject matter, but as the unquestioned, often unacknowledged *given* of the culture. Even more important than the new interpretations of individual texts are the probings into the consequences (for women) of the conventions that inform those texts. For example, in surveying selected nineteenth- and early-twentieth-century British novels which employ what she calls "the two-suitors convention," Jean E. Kennard sought to understand why and how the structural demands of the convention, even in the hands of women writers, inevitably work to imply "the inferiority and necessary subordination of women." Her 1978 study, *Victims of Convention*, points out that the symbolic nature of the marriage which conventionally concludes such novels "indicates the adjustment of the protagonist to society's values, a condition which is equated with her maturity." Kennard's concern, however, is with the fact that the structural demands of the form too often sacrifice precisely those "virtues of independence and individuality," or, in other words, the very "qualities we have been invited to admire in" the heroines.[14] Kennard appropriately cautions us against drawing from her work any simplistically reductive thesis about the mimetic relations between art and life. Yet her approach nonetheless suggests that what is important about a fiction is not whether it ends in a death or a marriage, but what the symbolic demands of that particular conventional ending imply about the values and beliefs of the world that engendered it.

Her work thus participates in a growing emphasis in feminist literary study on the fact of literature as a social institution, embedded not only within its own literary traditions but also within the particular physical and mental artifacts of the society from which it comes. Adumbrating Millett's 1970 decision to anchor her "literary reflections" to a preceding analysis of the historical, social, and economic contexts of sexual politics,[15] more recent work—most notably Lillian Robinson's—begins with the premise that the process of artistic creation "consists not of ghostly happenings in the head but of a matching of the states and processes of symbolic models against the states and processes of the wider world."[16] The power relations inscribed in the form of conventions within our literary inheritance, these critics argue, reify the encodings of those same power relations in the culture at large. And the critical examination of rhetorical codes becomes, in their hands, the pursuit of ideological codes, because both embody either value systems or the dialectic of competition between value systems. More often than not, these critics insist upon examining not only the mirroring of life in art but also the normative impact of art on life. Addressing herself to the popular art available to working women, for example, Robinson is interested in understanding not only "the forms it uses" but, more important, "the myths it creates, the influence it exerts." "The way art helps people to order, interpret, mythologize, or dispose of their own experience," she declares, may be "complex and often ambiguous, but it is not impossible to define."[17]

Whether its focus be upon the material or the imaginative contexts of literary invention; single texts or entire canons; the relations between authors, genres, or historical circumstances; lost authors or well-known names, the variety and diversity of all feminist literary criticism finally coheres in its stance of almost defensive rereading. What Adrienne Rich had earlier called "revision," that is, "the act of looking back, of seeing with fresh eyes, of entering an old text from a new critical direction,"[18] took on a more actively self-protective coloration in 1978, when Judith Fetterley called upon the woman reader to learn to "resist" the sexist designs a text might make upon her—asking her to identify against herself, so to speak, by manipulating her sympathies on behalf of male heroes but

[14] Jean E. Kennard, *Victims of Convention* (Hamden, Conn.: Archon Books, 1978), pp. 164, 18, 14. [Au.]

[15] See Millett, *Sexual Politics*, pt. 3, "The Literary Reflection," pp. 235–361. [Au.]

[16] The phrase is Geertz's; see "Ideology as a Cultural System," p. 214. [Au.]

[17] Lillian S. Robinson, "Criticism—and Self-Criticism," *College English* 36 (January 1974), and "Criticism: Who Needs It?" in *The Uses of Criticism*, ed. A. P. Foulkes (Bern and Frankfurt: Lang, 1976); both reprinted in *Sex, Class, and Culture*, pp. 67, 80. [Au.]

[18] Rich, "When We Dead Awaken," p. 90. [Au.]

against female shrew or bitch characters.[19] Underpinning a great deal of this critical rereading has been the not-unexpected alliance between feminist literary study and feminist studies in linguistics and language acquisition. Tillie Olsen's commonsense observation of the danger of "perpetuating—by continued usage—entrenched, centuries-old oppressive power realities, early-on incorporated into language,"[20] has been given substantive analysis in the writings of feminists who study "language as a symbolic system closely tied to a patriarchal social structure." Taken together, their work demonstrates "the importance of language in establishing, reflecting, and maintaining an asymmetrical relationship between women and men."[21]

To consider what this implies for the fate of women who essay the craft of language is to ascertain, perhaps for the first time, the real dilemma of the poet who finds her most cherished private experience "hedged by taboos, mined with false-namings."[22] It also explains the dilemma of the male reader who, in opening the pages of a woman's book, finds himself entering a strange and unfamiliar world of symbolic significance. For if, as Nelly Furman insists, neither language use nor language acquisition is "gender-neutral," but is, instead, "imbued with our sex-inflected cultural values;"[23] and if, additionally, reading is a process of "sorting out the structures of signification"[24] in any text, then male readers who find themselves outside of and unfamiliar with the symbolic systems that constitute female experience in women's writings will necessarily dismiss those systems as undecipherable, meaningless, or trivial. And male professors will find no reason to include such works in the canons of "major authors." At the same time, women writers, coming into a tradition of literary language and conventional forms already appropriated, for centuries, to the purposes of male expression, will be forced virtually to "wrestle" with that language in an effort "to remake it as a language adequate to our conceptual processes."[25] To all of this, feminists concerned with the politics of language and style have been acutely attentive. "Language conceals an invincible adversary," observes French critic Hélène Cixous, "because it's the language of men and their grammar."[26] But equally insistent, as in the work of Sandra Gilbert and Susan Gubar, has been the understanding of the need for *all* readers, male and female alike, to learn to penetrate the otherwise unfamiliar universes of symbolic action that comprise women's writings, past and present.[27]

To HAVE attempted so many difficult questions and to have accomplished so much—even acknowledging the inevitable false starts, overlapping, and repetition—in so short a time, should certainly have secured feminist literary criticism an honored berth on that ongoing intellectual journey which we loosely term in academia "critical analysis." Instead of being welcomed onto the train, however, we have been forced to negotiate a minefield. The very energy and diversity of our enterprise have rendered us vulnerable to attack on the grounds that we lack both definition and coherence; while our particular attentiveness to the ways in which literature encodes and disseminates cultural value systems calls down upon us imprecations echoing those heaped upon the Marxist critics of an earlier generation. If we are scholars dedicated to rediscovering a lost body of

[19] Judith Fetterley, *The Resisting Reader: A Feminist Approach to American Fiction* (Bloomington: Indiana University Press, 1978). [Au.]

[20] Tillie Olsen, *Silences* (New York: Delacorte Press, 1978), pp. 239–40. [Au.]

[21] See Cheris Kramer, Barrie Thorne, and Nancy Henley, "Perspectives on Language and Communication," Review Essay, *Signs* 3 (Summer 1978): 646. [Au.]

[22] See Adrienne Rich's discussion of the difficulty in finding authentic language for her experience as a mother in *Of Woman Born: Motherhood as Experience and Institution* (New York: W. W. Norton, 1976), p. 15. [Au.]

[23] Nelly Furman, "The Study of Women and Language: Comment on Vol. 3, no. 3," *Signs* 4 (Fall 1978): 184. [Au.]

[24] Again, my phrasing comes from Geertz, "Thick Description: Toward an Interpretive Theory of Culture," *Interpretation of Cultures*, p. 9. [Au.]

[25] Julia Penelope Stanley and Susan W. Robbins, "Toward a Feminist Aesthetic," *Chrysalis*, no. 6 (1977), p. 63. [Au.]

[26] Hélène Cixous, "The Laugh of the Medusa," trans. Keith Cohen and Paula Cohen, *Signs* 1 (Summer 1976): 887. [Au.]

[27] In *The Madwoman in the Attic: The Woman Writer and the Nineteenth-Century Literary Imagination* (New Haven, Conn.: Yale University Press, 1979), Sandra M. Gilbert and Susan Gubar suggest that women's writings are in some sense "palimpsestic" in that their "surface designs conceal or obscure deeper, less accessible (and less socially acceptable) levels of meaning" (p. 73). It is, in their view, an art designed "both to express and to camouflage" (p. 81). [Au.]

writings by women, then our finds are questioned on aesthetic grounds. And if we are critics determined to practice revisionist readings, it is claimed that our focus is too narrow and our results are only distortions or, worse still, polemical misreadings.

The very vehemence of the outcry, coupled with our total dismissal in some quarters,[28] suggests not our deficiencies, however, but the potential magnitude of our challenge. For what we are asking be scrutinized are nothing less than shared cultural assumptions so deeply rooted and so long ingrained that, for the most part, our critical colleagues have ceased to recognize them as such. In other words, what is really being bewailed in the claims that we distort texts or threaten the disappearance of the great Western literary tradition itself[29] is not so much the disappearance of either text or tradition but, instead, the eclipse of that particular *form* of the text and that particular *shape* of the canon which previously reified male readers' sense of power and significance in the world. Analogously, by asking whether, as readers, we ought to be "really satisfied by the marriage of Dorothea Brooke to Will Ladislaw? of Shirley Keeldar to Louis Moore?" or whether, as Kennard suggests, we must reckon with the ways in which "the qualities we have been invited to admire in these heroines [have] been sacrificed to structural neatness,"[30] is to raise difficult and profoundly perplexing questions about the ethical implications of our otherwise unquestioned aesthetic pleasures. It is, after all, an imposition of high order to ask the viewer to attend to Ophelia's sufferings in a scene where, before, he had always so comfortably kept his eye fixed firmly on Hamlet. To understand all this, then, as the real nature of the challenge we have offered and, in consequence, as the motivation for the often overt hostility we have aroused, should help us learn to negotiate the minefield, if not with grace, then with at least a clearer comprehension of its underlying patterns.

The ways in which objections to our work are usually posed, of course, serve to obscure their deeper motivations. But this may, in part, be due to our own reticence at taking full responsibility for the truly radicalizing premises that lie at the theoretical core of all we have so far accomplished. It may be time, therefore, to redirect discussion, forcing our adversaries to deal with the substantive issues and pushing ourselves into a clearer articulation of what, in fact, we are about. Up until now, I fear, we have dealt only piecemeal with the difficulties inherent in challenging the authority of established canons and then justifying the excellence of women's traditions, sometimes in accord with standards to which they have no intrinsic relation.

At the very point at which we must perforce enter the discourse—that is, claiming excellence or importance for our "finds"—all discussion has already, we discover, long ago been closed. "If Kate Chopin were *really* worth reading," an Oxford-trained colleague once assured me, "she'd have lasted—like Shakespeare"; and he then proceeded to vote against the English department's crediting a women's studies seminar I was offering in American women writers. The canon, for him, conferred excellence; Chopin's exclusion demonstrated only her lesser worth. As far as he was concerned, I could no more justify giving English-department credit for the study of Chopin than I could dare publicly to question Shakespeare's genius. Through hindsight, I have now come to view that discussion as not only having posed fruitless oppositions but also having entirely evaded the much more profound problem lurking just beneath the surface of our disagreement. That is, that the fact of canonization puts any work beyond questions of establishing its merit and, instead, invites students to offer only increas-

[28] Consider, for example, Robert Boyers's reductive and inaccurate generalization that "what distinguishes ordinary books and articles about women from feminist writing is the feminist insistence on asking the same questions of every work and demanding ideologically satisfactory answers to those questions as a means of evaluating it," in "A Case Against Feminist Criticism," *Partisan Review* 43 (1976): 602. It is partly as a result of such misconceptions that we have the paucity of feminist critics who are granted a place in English departments that otherwise pride themselves on the variety of their critical orientations. [Au.]

[29] Ambivalent though he is about the literary continuity that begins with Homer, Harold Bloom nonetheless somewhat ominously prophesies "that the first true break . . . will be brought about in generations to come, if the burgeoning religion of Liberated Woman spreads from its clusters of enthusiasts to dominate the West," in *A Map of Misreading* (New York: Oxford University Press, 1975), p. 33. On p. 36, he acknowledges that while something "as violent [as] a quarrel would ensue if I expressed my judgment" on Robert Lowell and Norman Mailer, "it would lead to something more intense than quarrels if I expressed my judgment upon . . . the 'literature of Women's Liberation.'" [Au.]

[30] Kennard, *Victims of Convention,* p. 14. [Au.]

ingly more ingenious readings and interpretations, the purpose of which is to validate the greatness already imputed by canonization.

Had I only understood it for what it was then, into this circular and self-serving set of assumptions I might have interjected some statement of my right to question why *any* text is revered and my need to know what it tells us about "how we live, how we have been living, how we have been led to imagine ourselves, [and] how our language has trapped as well as liberated us."[31] The very fact of our critical training within the strictures imposed by an established canon of major works and authors, however, repeatedly deflects us from such questions. Instead, we find ourselves endlessly responding to the riposte that the overwhelmingly male presence among canonical authors was only an accident of history and never intentionally sexist, coupled with claims to the "obvious" aesthetic merit of those canonized texts. It is, as I say, a fruitless exchange, serving more to obscure than to expose the territory being protected and dragging us, again and again, through the minefield.

It is my contention that current hostilities might be transformed into a true dialogue with our critics if we at last made explicit what appear, to this observer, to constitute the three crucial propositions to which our special interests inevitably give rise. They are, moreover, propositions which, if handled with care and intelligence, could breathe new life into now moribund areas of our profession: (1) literary history (and with that, the historicity of literature) is a fiction; (2) insofar as we are taught how to read, what we engage are not texts but paradigms; and finally, (3) since the grounds upon which we assign aesthetic value to texts are never infallible, unchangeable, or universal, we must reexamine not only our aesthetics but, as well, the inherent biases and assumptions informing the critical methods which (in part) shape our aesthetic responses. For the sake of brevity, I will not attempt to offer the full arguments for each but, rather, only sufficient elaboration to demonstrate what I see as their intrinsic relation to the potential scope of and present challenge implied by feminist literary study.

1. *Literary history (and with that, the historicity of literature) is a fiction.* To begin with, an established canon functions as a model by which to chart the continuities and discontinuities, as well as the influences upon and the interconnections between works, genres, and authors. That model we tend to forget, however, is of our own making. It will take a very different shape, and explain its inclusions and exclusions in very different ways, if the reigning critical ideology believes that new literary forms result from some kind of ongoing internal dialectic within preexisting styles and traditions or if, by contrast, the ideology declares that literary change is dependent upon societal development and therefore determined by upheavals in the social and economic organization of the culture at large.[32] Indeed, whenever in the previous century of English and American literary scholarship one alternative replaced the other, we saw dramatic alterations in canonical "wisdom."

This suggests, then, that our sense of a "literary history," and, by extension, our confidence in a "historical" canon, is rooted not so much in any definitive understanding of the past as it is in our need to call up and utilize the past on behalf of a better understanding of the present. Thus, to paraphrase David Couzens Hoy, it becomes necessary "to point out that the understanding of art and literature is such an essential aspect of the present's self-understanding that this self-understanding conditions what even gets taken" as constituting that artistic and literary past. To quote Hoy fully, "this continual reinterpretation of the past goes hand in hand with the continual reinterpretation by the present of itself."[33] In our own time, uncertain as to which, if any, model truly accounts for our canonical choices or accurately explains literary history, and pressured further by the feminists' call for some justification of the criteria by which women's writings were largely excluded from both that canon and history, we suffer what Harold Bloom has called "a remarkable dimming" of "our mutual sense of canonical standards."[34]

Into this apparent impasse, feminist literary theorists implicitly introduce the observation that our choices and evaluations of current literature have the effect either of solidifying or of reshaping our

[31] Rich, "When We Dead Awaken," p. 90. [Au.]

[32] The first is a proposition currently expressed by some structuralists and formalist critics; the best statement of the second probably appears in Georg Lukács, *Writer and Critic* (New York: Grosset & Dunlap, 1970), p. 119. [Au.]

[33] David Couzens Hoy, "Hermeneutic Circularity, Indeterminacy, and Incommensurability," *New Literary History* 10 (Fall 1978): 166–67. [Au.]

[34] Bloom, *Map of Misreading*, p. 36. [Au.]

sense of the past. The authority of any established canon, after all, is reified by our perception that current work seems to grow almost inevitably out of it (even in opposition or rebellion), and is called into question when what we read appears to have little or no relation to what we recognize as coming before. So, were the larger critical community to begin to attend seriously to the recent outpouring of fine literature by women, this would surely be accompanied by a concomitant researching of the past, by literary historians, in order to account for the present phenomenon. In that process, literary history would itself be altered: works by seventeenth-, eighteenth-, or nineteenth-century women to which we had not previously attended might be given new importance as "precursors" or as prior influences upon present-day authors; while selected male writers might also be granted new prominence as figures whom women today, or even yesterday, needed to reject. I am arguing, in other words, that the choices we make in the present inevitably alter our sense of the past that led to them.

Related to this is the feminist challenge to that patently mendacious critical fallacy that we read the "classics" in order to reconstruct the past "the way it really was," and that we read Shakespeare and Milton in order to apprehend the meanings that they intended. Short of time machines or miraculous resurrections, there is simply no way to know, precisely or surely, what "really was," what Homer intended when he sang, or Milton when he dictated. Critics more acute than I have already pointed up the impossibility of grounding a reading in the imputation of authorial intention because the further removed the author is from us, so too must be her or his systems of knowledge and belief, points of view, and structures of vision (artistic and otherwise).[35] (I omit here the difficulty of finally either proving or disproving the imputation of intentionality because, inescapably, the only appropriate authority is unavailable: deceased.) What we have really come to mean when we speak of competence in reading historical texts, therefore, is the ability to recognize literary conventions which have survived through time—so as to remain operational in the mind of the reader—and, where these are lacking, the ability to translate (or perhaps transform?) the text's ciphers into more current and recognizable shapes. But we never really reconstruct the past in its own terms. What we gain when we read the "classics," then, is neither Homer's Greece nor George Eliot's England *as they knew it* but, rather, an approximation of an already fictively imputed past made available, through our interpretative strategies, for present concerns. Only by understanding this can we put to rest that recurrent delusion that the "continuing relevance" of the classics serves as "testimony to perennial features of human experience."[36] The only "perennial feature" to which our ability to read and reread texts written in previous centuries testifies to our inventiveness—in the sense that all of literary history is a fiction which we daily re-create as we reread it. What distinguishes feminists in this regard is their desire to alter and extend what we take as historically relevant from out of that vast storehouse of our literary inheritance and, further, feminists' recognition of the storehouse for what it really is: a resource for remodeling our literary history, past, present, and future.

2. *Insofar as we are taught how to read, what we engage are not texts but paradigms.* To pursue the logical consequences of the first proposition leads, however uncomfortably, to the conclusion that we appropriate meaning from a text according to what we need (or desire), or in other words, according to the critical assumptions or predispositions (conscious or not) that we bring to it. And we appropriate different meanings, or report different gleanings, at different times—even from the same text—according to our changed assumptions, circumstances, and requirements. This, in essence, constitutes the heart of the second proposition. For insofar as literature is itself a social institution, so, too, reading is a highly socialized—or learned—activity. What makes it so

[35] John Dewey offered precisely this argument in 1934 when he insisted that a work of art "is recreated every time it is esthetically experienced. . . . It is absurd to ask what an artist 'really' meant by his product: he himself would find different meanings in it at different days and hours and in different stages of his own development." Further, he explained, "It is simply an impossibility that any one today should experience the Parthenon as the devout Athenian contemporary citizen experienced it, any more than the religious statuary of the twelfth century can mean, esthetically, even to a good Catholic today just what it meant to the worshipers of the old period." *Art as Experience* (New York: Capricorn Books, 1958), pp. 108–9. [Au.]

[36] Charles Altieri, "The Hermeneutics of Literary Indeterminacy: A Dissent from the New Orthodoxy," *New Literary History* 10 (Fall 1978): 90. [Au.]

exciting, of course, is that it can be constantly relearned and refined, so as to provide either an individual or an entire reading community, over time, with infinite variations of the same text. It *can* provide that, but, I must add, too often it does not. Frequently our reading habits become fixed, so that each successive reading experience functions, in effect, normatively, with one particular kind of novel stylizing our expectations of those to follow, the stylistic devices of any favorite author (or group of authors) alerting us to the presence or absence of those devices in the works of others, and so on. "Once one has read his first poem," Murray Krieger has observed, "he turns to his second and to the others that will follow thereafter with an increasing series of preconceptions about the sort of activity in which he is indulging. In matters of literary experience, as in other experiences," Krieger concludes, "one is a virgin but once."[37]

For most readers, this is a fairly unconscious process, and not unnaturally, what we are taught to read well and with pleasure when we are young predisposes us to certain specific kinds of adult reading tastes. For the professional literary critic, the process may be no different, but it is at least more conscious. Graduate schools, at their best, are training grounds for competing interpretative paradigms or reading techniques: affective stylistics, structuralism, and semiotic analysis, to name only a few of the more recent entries. The delight we learn to take in the mastery of these interpretative strategies is then often mistakenly construed as our delight in reading specific texts, especially in the case of works that would otherwise be unavailable or even offensive to us. In my own graduate career, for example, with superb teachers to guide me, I learned to take great pleasure in *Paradise Lost,* even though, as both a Jew and a feminist, I can subscribe neither to its theology nor to its hierarchy of sexual valuation. If, within its own terms (as I have been taught to understand them), the text manipulates my sensibilities and moves me to pleasure—as I will affirm it does—then, at least in part, that must be because, in spite of my real-world alienation from many of its basic tenets, I have been able to enter that text through interpretative strategies which allow me to displace less comfortable observations with others to which I have been taught pleasurably to attend. Though some of my teachers may have called this process "learning to read the text properly," I have now come to see it as learning to effectively manipulate the critical strategies which they taught me so well. Knowing, for example, the poem's debt to epic conventions, I am able to discover in it echoes and reworkings of both lines and situations from Virgil and Homer; placing it within the ongoing Christian debate between Good and Evil, I comprehend both the philosophic and the stylistic significance of Satan's ornate rhetoric as compared with God's majestic simplicity in Book III. But in each case, an interpretative model, already assumed, had guided my discovery of the evidence for it.[38]

When we consider the implications of these observations for the processes of canon formation and for the assignment of aesthetic value, we find ourselves locked in a chicken-and-egg dilemma, unable easily to distinguish as primary the importance of *what* we read as opposed to *how* we have learned to read it. For, simply put, we read well, and with pleasure, what we already know how to read; and what we know how to read is to a large extent dependent upon what we have already read (works from which we developed our expectations and learned our interpretative strategies). What we then choose to read—and, by extension, teach and thereby "canonize"—usually follows upon our previous reading. Radical breaks are tiring, demanding, uncomfortable, and sometimes wholly beyond our comprehension.

Though the argument is not usually couched in precisely these terms, a considerable segment of the most recent feminist rereadings of women writers allows the conclusion that, where those authors have dropped out of sight, it may be due not to any lack of merit in the work but, instead, to an incapacity of predominantly male readers to properly interpret and appreciate women's texts—due, in large part, to a lack of prior acquaintance. The fictions that women compose about the worlds they inhabit may owe a debt to prior, influential works by other women or, simply enough, to the daily ex-

[37] Murray Krieger, *Theory of Criticism: A Tradition and Its System* (Baltimore: Johns Hopkins University Press, 1976), p. 6 [Au.]

[38] See Stanley E. Fish, "Normal Circumstances, Literal Language, Direct Speech Acts, the Ordinary, the Everyday, the Obvious, What Goes without Saying, and Other Special Cases," *Critical Inquiry* 4 (Summer 1978): 627–28. [Au.]

perience of the writer herself or, more usually, to some combination of the two. The reader coming upon such fiction with knowledge of neither its informing literary traditions nor its real-world contexts will find himself hard pressed, though he may recognize the words on the page, to competently decipher its intended meanings. And this is what makes the studies by Spacks, Moers, Showalter, Gilbert and Gubar, and others so crucial. For, by attempting to delineate the connections and interrelations that make for a female literary tradition, they provide us invaluable aids for recognizing and understanding the unique literary traditions and sex-related contexts out of which women write.

The (usually male) reader who, both by experience and by reading, has never made acquaintance with those contexts—historically, the lying-in room, the parlor, the nursery, the kitchen, the laundry, and so on—will necessarily lack the capacity to fully interpret the dialogue or action embedded therein; for, as every good novelist knows, the meaning of any character's action or statement is inescapably a function of the specific situation in which it is embedded.[39] Virginia Woolf therefore quite properly anticipated the male reader's disposition to write off what he could not understand, abandoning women's writings as offering "not merely a difference of view, but a view that is weak, or trivial, or sentimental because it differs from his own." In her 1929 essay "Women and Fiction," Woolf grappled most obviously with the ways in which male writers and male subject matter had already preempted the language of literature. Yet she was also tacitly commenting on the problem of (male) audience and conventional reading expectations when she speculated that the woman writer might well "find that she is perpetually wishing to alter the established values [in literature]—to make serious what appears insignificant to a man, and trivial what is to him important."[40] "The 'competence' necessary for understanding [a] literary message . . . depends upon a great number of codices," after all; as Cesare Segre has pointed out, to be competent, a reader must either share or at least be familiar with, "in addition to the code language . . . the codes of custom, of society, and of conceptions of the world"[41] (what Woolf meant by "values"). Males ignorant of women's "values" or conceptions of the world will, necessarily, be poor readers of works that in any sense recapitulate their codes.

The problem is further exacerbated when the language of the literary text is largely dependent upon figuration. For it can be argued, as Ted Cohen has shown, that while "in general, and with some obvious qualifications . . . all literal use of language is accessible to all whose language it is . . . figurative use can be inaccessible to all but those who share information about one another's knowledge, beliefs, intentions, and attitudes."[42] There was nothing fortuitous, for example, in Charlotte Perkins Gilman's decision to situate the progressive mental breakdown and increasing incapacity of the protagonist of "The Yellow Wallpaper" in an upstairs room that had once served as a nursery (with barred windows, no less). But a reader unacquainted with the ways in which women have traditionally inhabited a household might not take the initial description of the setting as semantically relevant, and the progressive infantilization of the adult protagonist would thereby lose some of its symbolic implications. Analogously, the contemporary poet who declares, along with Adrienne Rich, the need for "a whole new poetry beginning here" is acknowledging that the materials available for symbolization and figuration from women's contexts will necessarily differ from those that men have traditionally utilized.

Vision begins to happen in such a life
as if a woman quietly walked away
from the argument and jargon in a room
and sitting down in the kitchen, began
turning in her lap
bits of yarn, calico and velvet scraps,

. . .

pulling the tenets of a life together
with no mere will to mastery,
only care for the many-lived, unending
forms in which she finds herself.[43]

[39] Ibid., p. 643. [Au.]

[40] Virginia Woolf, "Women and Fiction," *Granite and Rainbow: Essays* (London: Hogarth Press, 1958), p. 81. [Au.]

[41] Cesare Segre, "Narrative Structures and Literary History," *Critical Inquiry* 3 (Winter 1976): 272–73. [Au.]

[42] Ted Cohen, "Metaphor and the Cultivation of Intimacy," *Critical Inquiry* 5 (Fall 1978): 9. [Au.]

[43] From Adrienne Rich's "Transcendental Etude," *The Dream of a Common Language: Poems 1974–1977* (New York: W. W. Norton, 1978), pp. 76–77. [Au.]

What, then, is the fate of the woman writer whose competent reading community is composed only of members of her own sex? And what, then, the response of the male critic who, on first looking into Virginia Woolf or Doris Lessing, finds all of the interpretative strategies at his command inadequate to a full and pleasurable deciphering of their pages? Historically, the result has been the diminished status of women's products and their consequent absence from major canons. Nowadays, however, by pointing out that the act of "interpreting language is no more sexually neutral than language use or the language system itself," feminist students of language like Nelly Furman help us better understand the crucial linkage between our gender and our interpretative, or reading, strategies. Insisting upon "the contribution of the . . . reader [in] the active attribution of significance to formal signifiers,"[44] Furman and others promise to shake us all—female and male alike—out of our canonized and conventional aesthetic assumptions.

3. *Since the grounds upon which we assign aesthetic value to texts are never infallible, unchangeable, or universal, we must reexamine not only our aesthetics but, as well, the inherent biases and assumptions informing the critical methods which (in part) shape our aesthetic responses.* I am, on the one hand, arguing that men will be better readers, or appreciators, of women's books when they have read more of them (as women have always been taught to become astute readers of men's texts). On the other hand, it will be noted, the emphasis of my remarks shifts the act of critical judgment from assigning aesthetic valuations to texts and directs it, instead, to ascertaining the adequacy of any interpretative paradigm to a full reading of both female and male writing. My third proposition—and, I admit, perhaps the most controversial—thus calls into question that recurrent tendency in criticism to establish norms for the evaluation of literary works when we might better serve the cause of literature by developing standards for evaluating the adequacy of our critical methods.[45] This does not mean that I wish to discard aesthetic valuation. The choice, as I see it, is not between retaining or discarding aesthetic values; rather, the choice is between having some awareness of what constitutes (at least in part) the bases of our aesthetic responses and going without such an awareness. For it is my view that insofar as aesthetic responsiveness continues to be an integral aspect of our human response system—in part spontaneous, in part learned and educated—we will inevitably develop theories to help explain, formalize, or even initiate those responses.

In challenging the adequacy of received critical opinion or the imputed excellence of established canons, feminist literary critics are essentially seeking to discover how aesthetic value is assigned in the first place, where it resides (in the text or in the reader), and, most important, what validity may really be claimed by our aesthetic "judgments." What ends do those judgments serve, the feminist asks; and what conceptions of the world or ideological stances do they (even if unwittingly) help to perpetuate? In so doing, she points out, among other things, that any response labeled "aesthetic" may as easily designate some immediate experienced moment or event as it may designate a species of nostalgia, a yearning for the components of a simpler past when the world seemed known or at least understandable. Thus the value accorded an opera or a Shakespeare play may well reside in the viewer's immediate viewing pleasure, or it may reside in the play's nostalgic evocation of a once comprehensible and ordered world. At the same time, the feminist confronts, for example, the reader who simply cannot entertain the possibility that women's worlds are symbolically rich, the reader who, like the male characters in Susan Glaspell's 1917 short story "A Jury of Her Peers," has already assumed the innate "insignificance of kitchen things."[46] Such a reader, she knows, will prove himself unable to assign significance to fictions that attend to "kitchen things" and will, instead, judge such fictions as trivial and as aesthetically wanting. For her to take useful issue with such a reader, she must make clear that what appears to be a dispute about aesthetic merit is, in reality, a dispute about the *contexts of*

[44] Furman, "Study of Women and Language," p. 184. [Au.]

[45] "A recurrent tendency in criticism is the establishment of false norms for the evaluation of literary works," notes Robert Scholes in *Structuralism in Literature: An Introduction* (New Haven, Conn.: Yale University Press, 1974), p. 131. [Au.]

[46] For a full discussion of the Glaspell short story that takes this problem into account, please see my "A Map for Rereading: Gender and the Interpretation of Literary Texts," *New Literary History* 11 (Spring 1980): 451–67. [Au.]

judgment; and what is at issue, then, is the adequacy of the prior assumptions and reading habits brought to bear on the text. To put it bluntly: we have had enough pronouncements of aesthetic valuation for a time; it is now our task to evaluate the imputed norms and normative reading patterns that, in part, led to those pronouncements.

By and large, I think I have made my point. Only to clarify it do I add this coda: when feminists turn their attention to the works of male authors which have traditionally been accorded high aesthetic value and, where warranted, follow Olsen's advice that we assert our "right to say: this is surface, this falsifies reality, this degrades,"[47] such statements do not necessarily mean that we will end up with a diminished canon. To question the source of the aesthetic pleaures we have gained from reading Spenser, Shakespeare, Milton, and so on does not imply that we must deny those pleasures. It means only that aesthetic response is once more invested with epistemological, ethical, and moral concerns. It means, in other words, that readings of *Paradise Lost* which analyze its complex hierarchal structures but fail to note the implications of gender within that hierarchy; or which insist upon the inherent (or even inspired) perfection of Milton's figurative language but fail to note the consequences, for Eve, of her specifically gender-marked weakness, which, like the flowers she attends, requires "propping up"; or which concentrate on the poem's thematic reworking of classical notions of martial and epic prowess into Christian (moral) heroism but fail to note that Eve is stylistically edited out of that process—all such readings, however useful, will no longer be deemed wholly adequate. The pleasures we had earlier learned to take in the poem will not be diminished thereby, but they will become part of an altered reading attentiveness.

THESE three propositions I believe to be at the theoretical core of most current feminist literary criticism, whether acknowledged as such or not. If I am correct in this, then that criticism represents more than a profoundly skeptical stance toward all other preexisting and contemporaneous schools and methods, and more than an impassioned demand that the variety and variability of women's literary expression be taken into full account, rather than written off as a caprice and exception, the irregularity in an otherwise regular design. It represents that locus in literary study where, in unceasing effort, female self-consciousness turns in upon itself, attempting to grasp the deepest conditions of its own unique and multiplicitous realities, in the hope, eventually, of altering the very forms through which the culture perceives, expresses, and knows itself. For, if what the larger women's movement looks for in the future is a transformation of the structures of primarily male power which now order our society, then the feminist literary critic demands that we understand the ways in which those structures have been—and continue to be—reified by our literature and by our literary criticism. Thus, along with other "radical" critics and critical schools, though our focus remains the power of the word to both structure and mirror human experience, our overriding commitment is to a radical alteration—an improvement, we hope—in the nature of that experience.

What distinguishes our work from those similarly oriented "social consciousness" critiques, it is said, is its lack of systematic coherence. Pitted against, for example, psychoanalytic or Marxist readings, which owe a decisive share of their persuasiveness to their apparent internal consistency as a system, the aggregate of feminist literary criticism appears woefully deficient in system and painfully lacking in program. It is, in fact, from all quarters, the most telling defect alleged against us, the most explosive threat in the minefield. And my own earlier observation that, as of 1976, feminist literary criticism appeared "more like a set of interchangeable strategies than any coherent school or shared goal orientation" has been taken by some as an indictment, by others as a statement of impatience. Neither was intended. I felt then, as I do now, that this would "prove both its strength *and* its weakness,"[48] in the sense that the apparent disarray would leave us vulnerable to the kind of objection I have just alluded to; while the fact of our diversity would finally place us securely where, all along, we should have been: camped out, on the far side of the minefield, with the other pluralists and pluralisms.

In our heart of hearts, of course, most critics are really structuralists (whether or not they accept the

[47] Olsen, *Silences,* p. 45. [Au.]

[48] Annette Kolodny, "Literary Criticism," Review Essay, *Signs* 2 (Winter 1976): 420. [Au.]

label) because what we are seeking are patterns (or structures) that can order and explain the otherwise inchoate; thus, we invent, or believe we discover, relational patternings in the texts we read which promise transcendence from difficulty and perplexity to clarity and coherence. But, as I have tried to argue in these pages, to the imputed "truth" or "accuracy" of these findings the feminist must oppose the painfully obvious truism that what is attended to in a literary work, and hence what is reported about it, is often determined not so much by the work itself as by the critical technique or aesthetic criteria through which it is filtered or, rather, read and decoded. All the feminist is asserting, then, is her own equivalent right to liberate new (and perhaps different) significances from these same texts; and at the same time, her right to choose which features of a text she takes as relevant because she is, after all, asking new and different questions of it. In the process, she claims neither definitiveness nor structural completeness for her different readings and reading systems, but only their usefulness in recognizing the particular achievements of woman-as-author and their applicability in conscientiously decoding woman-as-sign.

That these alternate foci of critical attentiveness will render alternate readings or interpretations of the same text—even among feminists—should be no cause for alarm. Such developments illustrate only the pluralist contention that "in approaching a text of any complexity . . . the reader must choose to emphasize certain aspects which seem to him crucial," and that "in fact, the variety of readings which we have for many works is a function of the selection of crucial aspects made by the variety of readers." Robert Scholes, from whom I have been quoting, goes so far as to assert that "there is no single 'right' reading for any complex literary work," and, following the Russian formalist school, he observes that "we do not speak of readings that are simply true or false, but of readings that are more or less rich, strategies that are more or less appropriate."[49] Because those who share the term "feminist" nonetheless practice a diversity of critical strategies, leading, in some cases, to quite different readings, we must acknowledge among ourselves that sister critics, "having chosen to tell a different story, may in their interpretation identify different aspects of the meanings conveyed by the same passage."[50]

Adopting a "pluralist" label does not mean, however, that we cease to disagree; it means only that we entertain the possibility that different readings, even of the same text, may be differently useful, even illuminating, within different contexts of inquiry. It means, in effect, that we enter a dialectical process of examining, testing, even trying out the contexts—be they prior critical assumptions or explicitly stated ideological stances (or some combination of the two)—that led to the disparate readings. Not all will be equally acceptable to every one of us, of course, and even those prior assumptions or ideologies that are acceptable may call for further refinement or clarification. But at the very least, because we will have grappled with the assumptions that led to it, we will be better able to articulate *why* we find a particular reading or interpretation adequate or inadequate. This kind of dialectical process, moreover, not only makes us more fully aware of what criticism is, and how it functions; it also gives us access to its future possibilities, making us conscious, as R. P. Blackmur put it, "of what we have done," "of what can be done next, or done again;"[51] or, I would add, of what can be done differently. To put it still another way: just because we will no longer tolerate the specifically sexist omissions and oversights of earlier critical schools and methods does not mean that, in their stead, we must establish our own "party line."

In my view, our purpose is not and should not be the formulation of any single reading method or potentially Procrustean set of critical procedures nor, even less, the generation of prescriptive catego-

[49] Scholes, *Structuralism in Literature*, pp. 144–45. These comments appear within his explication of Tzvetan Todorov's theory of reading. [Au.]

[50] I borrow this concise phrasing of pluralistic modesty from M. H. Abrams's "The Deconstructive Angel," *Critical Inquiry* 3 (Spring 1977): 427. Indications of the pluralism that was to mark feminist inquiry were to be found in the diversity of essays collected by Susan Koppelman Cornillon for her early and groundbreaking anthology, *Images of Women in Fiction: Feminist Perspectives* (Bowling Green, Ohio: Bowling Green University Popular Press, 1972). [Au.]

[51] R. P. Blackmur, "A Burden for Critics," *Hudson Review* 1 (Summer 1948): 171. Blackmur, of course, was referring to the way in which criticism makes us conscious of how art functions; I use his wording here because I am arguing that that same awareness must also be focused on the critical act itself. "Consciousness," he avers, "is the way we feel the critic's burden." [Au.]

ries for some dreamed-of-nonsexist literary canon.[52] Instead, as I see it, our task is to initiate nothing less than a playful pluralism, responsive to the possibilities of multiple critical schools and methods, but captive of none, recognizing that the many tools needed for our analysis will necessarily be largely inherited and only partly of our own making. Only by employing a plurality of methods will we protect ourselves from the temptation of so oversimplifying any text—and especially those particularly offensive to us—that we render ourselves unresponsive to what Scholes has called "its various systems of meaning and their interaction."[53] Any text we deem worthy of our critical attention is usually, after all, a locus of many and varied kinds of (personal, thematic, stylistic, structural, rhetorical) relationships. So, whether we tend to treat a text as a *mimesis,* in which words are taken to be re-creating or representing viable worlds; or whether we prefer to treat a text as a kind of equation of communication, in which decipherable messages are passed from writers to readers; and whether we locate meaning as inherent in the text, in the act of reading, or in some collaboration between reader and text—whatever our predilection, let us not generate from it a straightjacket that limits the scope of possible analysis. Rather, let us generate an ongoing dialogue of competing potential possibilities—among feminists and, as well, between feminists and nonfeminist critics.

The difficulty of what I describe does not escape me. The very idea of pluralism seems to threaten a kind of chaos for the future of literary inquiry while, at the same time, it seems to deny the hope of establishing some basic conceptual model which can organize all data—the hope which always begins any analytical exercise. My effort here, however, has been to demonstrate the essential delusions that inform such objections: if literary inquiry has historically escaped chaos by establishing canons, then it has only substituted one mode of arbitrary action for another—and in this case, at the expense of half the population. And if feminists openly acknowledge ourselves as pluralists, then we do not give up the search for patterns of opposition and connection—probably the basis of thinking itself; what we give up is simply the arrogance of claiming that our work is either exhaustive or definitive. (It is, after all, the identical arrogance we are asking our nonfeminist colleagues to abandon.) If this kind of pluralism appears to threaten both the present coherence of and the inherited aesthetic criteria for a canon of "greats," then, as I have earlier argued, it is precisely that threat which alone can free us from the prejudices, the strictures, and the blind spots of the past. In feminist hands, I would add, it is less a threat than a promise.

What unites and repeatedly invigorates feminist literary criticism, then, is neither dogma nor method but an acute and impassioned *attentiveness* to the ways in which primarily male structures of power are inscribed (or encoded) within our literary inheritance; the consequences of that encoding for women—as characters, as readers, and as writers; and, with that, a shared analytic *concern* for the implications of that encoding not only for a better understanding of the past but also for an improved reordering of the present and future. If that concern identifies feminist literary criticism as one of the many academic arms of the larger women's movement, then that attentiveness, within the halls of academe, poses no less a challenge for change, generating as it does the three propositions explored here. The critical pluralism that inevitably follows upon those three propositions, however, bears little resemblance to what Robinson has called "the greatest bourgeois theme of all, the myth of pluralism, with its consequent rejection of ideological commitment as 'too simple' to embrace the (necessarily complex) truth."[54] Only ideological commitment could have gotten us to enter the minefield, putting in jeopardy our careers and our livelihood. Only the power of ideology to transform our conceptual worlds, and the inspiration of that ideology to liberate long-suppressed energies and emotions, can account for our willingness to take on critical tasks that, in an earlier decade, would have been "abandoned in despair or apathy."[55] The fact of dif-

[52] I have earlier elaborated my objection to prescriptive categories for literature in "The Feminist as Literary Critic," Critical Response, *Critical Inquiry* 2 (Summer 1976): 827–28. [Au.]

[53] Scholes, *Structuralism in Literature,* pp. 151–52. [Au.]

[54] Lillian S. Robinson, "Dwelling in Decencies: Radical Criticism and the Feminist Perspective," *College English* 32 (May 1971); reprinted in *Sex, Class, and Culture,* p. 11. [Au.]

[55] "Ideology bridges the emotional gap between things as they are and as one would have them be, thus ensuring the performance of roles that might otherwise be aban-

ferences among us proves only that, despite our shared commitments, we have nonetheless refused to shy away from complexity, preferring to disagree openly rather than to give up either intellectual honesty or hard-won insights.

Finally, I would argue, pluralism informs feminist literary inquiry not simply as a description of what already exists but, more importantly, as the only critical stance consistent with the current status of the larger women's movement. Segmented and variously focused, the different women's organizations neither espouse any single system of analysis nor, as a result, express any wholly shared, consistently articulated ideology. The ensuing loss in effective organization and political clout is a serious one, but it has not been paralyzing; in spite of our differences, we have united to act in areas of clear mutual concern. The trade-off, as I see it, has made possible an ongoing and educative dialectic of analysis and proffered solutions, protecting us thereby from the inviting traps of reductionism and dogma. And so long as this dialogue remains active, both our politics and criticism will be free of dogma—but never, I hope, of feminist ideology, in all its variety. For, "whatever else ideologies may be—projections of unacknowledged fears, disguises for ulterior motives, phatic expressions of group solidarity" (and the women's movement, to date, has certainly been all of these, and more)—whatever ideologies express, they are, as Geertz astutely observes, "most distinctively, maps of problematic social reality and matrices for the creation of collective conscience." And despite the fact that "ideological advocates . . . tend as much to obscure as to clarify the true nature of the problems involved," as Geertz notes, "they at least call attention to their existence and, by polarizing issues, make continued neglect more difficult. Without Marxist attack, there would have been no labor reform; without Black Nationalists, no deliberate speed."[56] Without Seneca Falls, I would add, no enfranchisement of women, and without "consciousness raising," no feminist literary criticism nor, even less, women's studies.

Ideology, however, only truly manifests its power by ordering the *sum* of our actions.[57] If feminist criticism calls anything into question, it must be that dog-eared myth of intellectual neutrality. For what I take to be the underlying spirit or message of any consciously ideologically premised criticism—that is, that ideas are important *because* they determine the ways we live, or want to live, in the world—is vitiated by confining those ideas to the study, the classroom, or the pages of our books. To write chapters decrying the sexual stereotyping of women in our literature, while closing our eyes to the sexual harassment of our women students and colleagues; to display Katherine Hepburn and Rosalind Russell in our courses on "The Image of the Independent Career Woman in Film," while managing not to notice the paucity of female woman administrators on our own campus; to study the women who helped make universal enfranchisement a political reality, while keeping silent about our activist colleagues who are denied promotion or tenure; to include segments on "Women in the Labor Movement" in our American studies or women's studies courses, while remaining willfully ignorant of the department secretary fired for her efforts to organize a clerical workers' union; to glory in the delusions of "merit," "privilege," and "status" which accompany campus life in order to insulate ourselves from the millions of women who labor in poverty—all this is not merely hypocritical; it destroys both the spirit and the meaning of what we are about. It puts us, however unwittingly, in the service of those who laid the minefield in the first place. In my view, it is a fine thing for many of us, individually, to have traversed the minefield; but that happy circumstance will only prove of lasting importance if, together, we expose it for what it is (the male fear of sharing power and significance with women) and deactivate its components, so that others, after us, may literally dance through the minefield.

doned in despair or apathy," Geertz comments in "Ideology as a Cultural System," p. 205. [Au.]

[56] Ibid., pp. 220, 205. [Au.]

[57] I here follow Frederic Jameson's view in *The Prison-House of Language: A Critical Account of Structuralism and Russian Formalism* (Princeton, N.J.: Princeton University Press, 1974), p. 107: "Ideology would seem to be that grillwork of form, convention, and belief which orders our actions." [Au.]

Clifford Geertz

b. 1926

THE INCLUSION of "Blurred Genres" by Clifford Geertz, an anthropologist and professor of social science at the Institute for Advanced Study at Princeton, is itself an example of the phenomenon the essay describes. The work of Geertz and other anthropologists (such as Marcel Mauss, *Claude Lévi-Strauss,* Victor Turner, Edmund Leach, and others) has been of compelling interest to critics uneasy with the theoretical constraints of aesthetic formalism or the perceived sterility of traditional "approaches" to literature. The irony that the essay also describes is that anthropologists (such as, for example, Geertz, Turner, Leach, and others) have been prey to similar dissatisfactions with methods and theories in the social sciences, leading to an interest in the interpretive, text-based disciplines of literary study and criticism. Thus there is a mutuality of interest—and perhaps puzzlement, if not alarm—in the convergence of the social and literary disciplines.

Geertz is of special interest for several reasons, not the least of which is his remarkable gift for lively, interesting prose. It seems natural enough that with his writerly sense of the text, he should find it congenial to treat cultural phenomena as texts. As he says in defense of the general strategy, treating such things as a cockfight as a text instead of a rite or a pastime brings out an important feature: "its use of emotion for cognitive ends" (*The Interpretation of Cultures* [1973], p. 449). While this remark highlights a feature of critical practice (and literary texts) that can easily be taken for granted, it also indicates one of the reasons why anthropological methods may be appealing to critics. At least from the outside, anthropology appears as a comprehensive, totalizing discipline, in intent if not in practice, free to examine the range of human behavior and institutions from the cockfight to the College of Cardinals, and to do so in the manner that strives to eliminate prejudice (or prejudicial ideology) by the intimate acquaintance of fieldwork. In this respect, the work of the anthropologist appears to serve cognitive ends that are frequently blocked when the text is already given as such, inasmuch as the anthropologist in the field must first constitute affairs of culture *as* texts in which the emotive and cognitive are joined. As Geertz notes elsewhere (*Times Literary Supplement,* June 7, 1985), this very presumption is, within the professional ranks, a worrisome point indeed—on the grounds that fieldwork ("me anthropologist, you native," as Geertz deftly puts it) may be neither rigorous nor even *decent.*

While there may be other cautions (such as the reservations expressed by Fredric Jameson in "The Ideology of the Text," *Salmagundi* 31–32 [1975]), the "blurring of genres" Geertz describes in this essay represents an important circumstance for contemporary theory in the humanities and social sciences. Geertz's account of the "refiguration" of social thought uses the mild rhetoric of worry and ironic amusement, where one might say the same things in the mood of crisis. The difference is that, in the latter case, one might be tempted to take desperate measures, or at least premature steps to resolution before the true shape of the situation was clear.

When Geertz suggests in this essay, for example, that "a challenge is being mounted to some of the central assumptions of mainstream social science" by advocates of interpretive text-analogical methods, the "sea change" he predicts if present trends continue has no predictable shape—partly because some of the central assumptions of mainstream interpretive disciplines are being called into question precisely because they have ignored issues of social structure and social change. Indeed, as Geertz says, "It will take the wariest of wary reasonings, on all sides of the divide, to get it clearer."

Geertz's major works include *The Interpretation of Cultures* (1973); *Kinship in Bali* (with Hildred Geertz) (1975); and *Local Knowledge: Selected Essays in Interpretive Anthropology* (1983).

BLURRED GENRES: THE REFIGURATION OF SOCIAL THOUGHT

I

Certain truths about the social sciences today seem self-evident. One is that in recent years there has been an enormous amount of genre mixing in social science, as in intellectual life generally, and such blurring of kinds is continuing apace. Another is that many social scientists have turned away from a laws-and-instances ideal of explanation toward a cases-and-interpretations one, looking less for the sort of thing that connects planets and pendulums and more for the sort that connects chrysanthemums and swords. Yet another truth is that analogies drawn from the humanities are coming to play the kind of role in sociological understanding that analogies drawn from the crafts and technology have long played in physical understanding. I not only think these things are true, I think they are true together; and the culture shift that makes them so is the subject of this essay: the refiguration of social thought.

This genre blurring is more than just a matter of Harry Houdini or Richard Nixon turning up as characters in novels or of midwestern murder sprees described as though a gothic romancer had imagined them. It is philosophical inquiries looking like literary criticism (think of Stanley Cavell[1] on Beckett or Thoreau, Sartre on Flaubert), scientific discussions looking like belles lettres *morceaux* (Lewis Thomas, Loren Eiseley), baroque fantasies presented as deadpan empirical observations (Borges, Barthelme), histories that consist of equations and tables or law court testimony (Fogel and Engerman, Le Roi Ladurie), documentaries that read like true confessions (Mailer), parables posing as ethnographies (Castenada), theoretical treatises set out as travelogues (Lévi-Strauss),[2] ideological arguments cast as historiographical inquiries (Edward Said),[3] epistemological studies constructed like political tracts (Paul Feyerabend), methodological polem-

BLURRED GENRES: THE REFIGURATION OF SOCIAL THOUGHT first appeared in *The American Scholar* 49 (Spring 1980),

[1] See *Cavell*. [Eds.]

[2] See *Lévi-Strauss*. [Eds.]

[3] See *Said*. [Eds.]

ics got up as personal memoirs (James Watson). Nabokov's *Pale Fire,* that impossible object made of poetry and fiction, footnotes and images from the clinic, seems very much of the time; one waits only for quantum theory in verse or biography in algebra.

Of course, to a certain extent this sort of thing has always gone on—Lucretius, Mandeville, and Erasmus Darwin[4] all made their theories rhyme. But the present jumbling of varieties of discourse has grown to the point where it is becoming difficult either to label authors (What *is* Foucault[5]—historian, philosopher, political theorist? What Thomas Kuhn[6]—historian, philosopher, sociologist of knowledge?) or to classify works (What is George Steiner's *After Babel*—linguistics, criticism, culture history? What William Gass's *On Being Blue*—treatise, causerie, apologetic?). And thus it is more than a matter of odd sports and occasional curiosities, or of the admitted fact that the innovative is, by definition, hard to categorize. It is a phenomenon general enough and distinctive enough to suggest that what we are seeing is not just another redrawing of the cultural map—the moving of a few disputed borders, the marking of some more picturesque mountain lakes—but an alteration of the principles of mapping. Something is happening to the way we think about the way we think.

We need not accept hermetic views of *écriture* as so many signs signing signs, or give ourselves so wholly to the pleasure of the text that its meaning disappears into our responses, to see that there has come into our view of what we read and what we write a distinctly democratical temper. The properties connecting texts with one another, that put them, ontologically anyway, on the same level, are coming to seem as important in characterizing them as those dividing them; and rather than face an array of natural kinds, fixed types divided by sharp qualitative differences, we more and more see ourselves surrounded by a vast, almost continuous field of variously intended and diversely constructed works we can order only practically, relationally, and as our purposes prompt us. It is not that we no longer have conventions of interpretation; we have more than ever, built—often enough jerry-built—to accommodate a situation at once fluid, plural, uncentered, and ineradicably untidy.

So far as the social sciences are concerned, all this means that their oft-lamented lack of character no longer sets them apart. It is even more difficult than it always has been to regard them as underdeveloped natural sciences, awaiting only time and aid from more advanced quarters to harden them, or as ignorant and pretentious usurpers of the mission of the humanities, promising certainties where none can be, or as comprising a clearly distinctive enterprise, a third culture between Snow's canonical two. But that is all to the good: freed from having to become taxonomically upstanding, because nobody else is, individuals thinking of themselves as social (or behavioral or human or cultural) scientists have become free to shape their work in terms of its necessities rather than received ideas as to what they ought or ought not to be doing. What Clyde Kluckhohn once said about anthropology—that it's an intellectual poaching license—not only seems more true now than when he said it, but true of a lot more than anthropology. Born omniform, the social sciences prosper as the condition I have been describing becomes general.

It has thus dawned on social scientists that they did not need to be mimic physicists or closet humanists or to invent some new realm of being to serve as the object of their investigations. Instead they could proceed with their vocation, trying to discover order in collective life, and decide how what they were doing was connected to related enterprises when they managed to get some of it done; and many of them have taken an essentially hermeneutic—or, if that word frightens, conjuring up images of biblical zealots, literary humbugs, and Teutonic professors, an "interpretive"—approach to their task. Given the new genre dispersion, many have taken other approaches: structuralism, neo-positivism, neo-Marxism, micro-micro descriptivism, macro-macro system building, and that curious combination of common sense and common nonsense, sociobiology. But the move toward conceiving the social life as organized in terms of symbols (signs, representations, *signifiants; Darstell-*

[4]Titus Lucretius Carus (ca. 99–55 B.C.), Roman philosopher, wrote *On the Nature of Things* in verse; Bernard Mandeville (1670–1733), English author and physician, author of *The Fable of the Bees* (1714); Erasmus Darwin (1731–1802), English physician and writer, expounded the botanical system of Linnaeus in a long poem, *The Botanical Garden* (1789–91). [Eds.]

[5]See *Foucault.* [Eds.]

[6]See *Kuhn.* [Eds.]

ungen . . . the terminology varies), whose meaning (sense, import, *signification, Bedeutung* . . .) we must grasp if we are to understand that organization and formulate its principles, has grown by now to formidable proportions. The woods are full of eager interpreters.

Interpretive explanation—and it is a form of explanation, not just exalted glossography—trains its attention on what institutions, actions, images, utterances, events, customs, all the usual objects of social-scientific interest, mean to those whose institutions, actions, customs, and so on they are. As a result, it issues not in laws like Boyle's, or forces like Volta's, or mechanisms like Darwin's, but in constructions like Burckhardt's, Weber's, or Freud's: systematic unpackings of the conceptual world in which *condottiere,* Calvinists, or paranoids live.

The manner of these constructions itself varies: Burckhardt portrays, Weber models, Freud diagnoses. But they all represent attempts to formulate how this people or that, this period or that, this person or that, makes sense to itself and, understanding that, what we understand about social order, historical change, or psychic functioning in general. Inquiry is directed toward cases or sets of cases, and toward the particular features that mark them off; but its aims are as far-reaching as those of mechanics or physiology: to distinguish the materials of human experience.

With such aims and such a manner of pursuing them come as well some novelties in analytical rhetoric, the tropes and imageries of explanation. As theory, scientific or otherwise, moves mainly by analogy, a "seeing-as" comprehension of the less intelligible by the more (the earth is a magnet, the heart is a pump, light is a wave, the brain is a computer, and space is a balloon), when its course shifts, the conceits in which it expresses itself shift with it. In the earlier stages of the natural sciences, before the analogies became so heavily intramural—and in those (cybernetics, neurology) in which they still have not—it has been the world of the crafts and, later, of industry that has for the most part provided the well-understood realities (well-understood because, *certum quod factum,* as Vico said, man had made them)[7] with which the ill-understood ones (ill-understood because he had not) could be brought into the circle of the known. Science owes more to the steam engine than the steam engine owes to science; without the dyer's art there would be no chemistry; metallurgy is mining theorized. In the social sciences, or at least in those that have abandoned a reductionist conception of what they are about, the analogies are coming more and more from the contrivances of cultural performance than from those of physical manipulation—from theater, painting, grammar, literature, law, play. What the lever did for physics, the chess move promises to do for sociology.

Promises are not always kept, of course, and when they are, they often turn out to have been threats; but the casting of social theory in terms more familiar to gamesters and aestheticians than to plumbers and engineers is clearly well under way. The recourse to the humanities for explanatory analogies in the social sciences is at once evidence of the destabilization of genres and of the rise of "the interpretive turn," and their most visible outcome is a revised style of discourse in social studies. The instruments of reasoning are changing and society is less and less represented as an elaborate machine or a quasi-organism than as a serious game, a sidewalk drama, or a behavioral text.

II

All this fiddling around with the proprieties of composition, inquiry, and explanation represents, of course, a radical alteration in the sociological imagination, propelling it in directions both difficult and unfamiliar. And like all such changes in fashions of the mind, it is about as likely to lead to obscurity and illusion as it is to precision and truth. If the result is not to be elaborate chatter or the higher nonsense, a critical consciousness will have to be developed; and as so much more of the imagery, method, theory, and style is to be drawn from the humanities than previously, it will mostly have to come from humanists and their apologists rather than from natural scientists and theirs. That humanists, after years of regarding social scientists as technologists, or interlopers, are ill equipped to do this is something of an understatement.

Social scientists, having just freed themselves, and then only partially, from dreams of social physics—covering laws, unified science, operationalism, and all that—are hardly any better equipped. For

[7]See *CTSP,* pp. 294–301. [Eds.]

them, the general muddling of vocational identities could not have come at a better time. If they are going to develop systems of analysis in which such conceptions as following a rule, constructing a representation, expressing an attitude, or forming an intention are going to play central roles—rather than such conceptions as isolating a cause, determining a variable, measuring a force, or defining a function—they are going to need all the help they can get from people who are more at home among such notions than they are. It is not interdisciplinary brotherhood that is needed, nor even less highbrow eclecticism. It is recognition on all sides that the lines grouping scholars together into intellectual communities, or (what is the same thing) sorting them out into different ones, are these days running at some highly eccentric angles.

The point at which the reflections of humanists on the practices of social scientists seems most urgent is with respect to the deployment in social analysis of models drawn from humanist domains—that "wary reasoning from analogy," as Locke called it, that "leads us often into the discovery of truths and useful productions, which would otherwise lie concealed." (Locke was talking about rubbing two sticks together to produce fire and the atomic-friction theory of heat, though business partnership and the social contract would have served him as well.) Keeping the reasoning wary, thus useful, thus true, is, as we say, the name of the game.

The game analogy is both increasingly popular in contemporary social theory and increasingly in need of critical examination. The impetus for seeing one or another sort of social behavior as one or another sort of game has come from a number of sources (not excluding, perhaps, the prominence of spectator sports in mass society). But the most important are Wittgenstein's conception of forms of life as language games, Huizinga's ludic view of culture, and the new strategies of von Neumann's and Morgenstern's *Theory of Games and Economic Behavior.* From Wittgenstein has come the notion of intentional action as "following a rule"; from Huizinga, of play as the paradigm form of collective life; from von Neumann and Morgenstern, of social behavior as a reciprocative maneuvering toward distributive payoffs. Taken together they conduce to a nervous and nervous-making style of interpretation in the social sciences that mixes a strong sense of the formal orderliness of things with an equally strong sense of the radical arbitrariness of that order: chessboard inevitability that could as well have worked out otherwise.

The writings of Erving Goffman—perhaps the most celebrated American sociologist right now, and certainly the most ingenious—rest, for example, almost entirely on the game analogy. (Goffman also employs the language of the stage quite extensively, but as his view of the theater is that it is an oddly mannered kind of interaction game—Ping-Pong in masks—his work is not, at base, really dramaturgical.) Goffman applies game imagery to just about everything he can lay his hands on, which, as he is no respecter of property rights, is a very great deal. The to-and-fro of lies, meta-lies, unbelievable truths, threats, tortures, bribes, and blackmail that comprises the world of espionage is construed as an "expression game"; a carnival of deceptions rather like life in general, because, in a phrase that could have come from Conrad or Le Carré, "agents [are] a little like us all and all of us [are] a little like agents." Etiquette, diplomacy, crime, finance, advertising, law, seduction, and the everyday "realm of bantering decorum" are seen as "information games"—mazy structures of players, teams, moves, positions, signals, information states, gambles, and outcomes, in which only the "game-worthy"—those willing and able "to dissemble about anything"—prosper.

What goes on in a psychiatric hospital, or any hospital or prison or even a boarding school in Goffman's work is a "ritual game of having a self," where the staff holds most of the face cards and all of the trumps. A tête-à-tête, a jury deliberation, "a task jointly pursued by persons physically close to one another," a couple dancing, lovemaking, or boxing—indeed all face-to-face encounters—are games in which, "as every psychotic and comic ought to know, any accurately improper move can poke through the thin sleeve of immediate reality." Social conflict, deviance, entrepreneurship, sex roles, religious rites, status ranking, and the simple need for human acceptance get the same treatment. Life is just a bowl of strategies.

Or, perhaps better, as Damon Runyon once remarked, it is three-to-two against. For the image of society that emerges from Goffman's work, and from that of the swarm of scholars who in one way or another follow or depend on him, is of an unbroken stream of gambits, ploys, artifices, bluffs, disguises, conspiracies, and outright impostures as individuals and coalitions of individuals struggle—sometimes cleverly, more often comically—to play enigmatical games whose structure is clear but whose point is not. Goffman's is a radically unromantic vision of things, acrid and bleakly knowing, and one which sits rather poorly with traditional humanistic pieties. But it is no less powerful for that. Nor, with its uncomplaining play-it-as-it-lays ethic, is it all that inhumane.

However that may be, not all gamelike conceptions of social life are quite so grim, and some are positively frolicsome. What connects them all is the view that human beings are less driven by forces than submissive to rules, that the rules are such as to suggest strategies, the strategies are such as to inspire actions, and the actions are such as to be self-rewarding—*pour le sport*. As literal games—baseball or poker or Parcheesi—create little universes of meaning, in which some things can be done and some cannot (you can't castle in dominoes), so too do the analogical ones of worship, government, or sexual courtship (you can't mutiny in a bank). Seeing society as a collection of games means seeing it as a grand plurality of accepted conventions and appropriate procedures—tight, airless worlds of move and countermove, life *en règle*. "I wonder," Prince Metternich is supposed to have said when an aide whispered into his ear at a royal ball that the czar of all the Russians was dead, "I wonder what his motive could have been."

The game analogy is not a view of things that is likely to commend itself to humanists, who like to think of people not as obeying the rules and angling for advantage but as acting freely and realizing their finer capacities. But that it seems to explain a great deal about a great many aspects of modern life, and in many ways to catch its tone, is hardly deniable. ("If you can't stand the Machiavellianism," as a recent *New Yorker* cartoon said, "get out of the cabal.") Thus if it is to be countered it cannot be by mere disdain, refusing to look through the telescope, or by passioned restatements of hallowed truths, quoting scripture against the sun. It is necessary to get down to the details of the matter, to examine the studies and to critique the interpretations—whether Goffman's of crime as character gambling, Harold Garfinkel's of sex change as identity play, Gregory Bateson's of schizophrenia as rule confusion, or my own of the complicated goings-on in a mideastern bazaar as an information contest. As social theory turns from propulsive metaphors (the language of pistons) toward ludic ones (the language of pastimes), the humanities are connected to its arguments not in the fashion of skeptical bystanders but, as the source of its imagery, chargeable accomplices.

III

The drama analogy for social life has of course been around in a casual sort of way—all the world's a stage and we but poor players who strut and so on—for a very long time. And terms from the stage, most notably "role," have been staples of sociological discourse since at least the 1930s. What is relatively new—new, not unprecedented—are two things. First, the full weight of the analogy is coming to be applied extensively and systematically, rather than being deployed piecemeal fashion—a few allusions here, a few tropes there. And second, it is coming to be applied less in the depreciatory "mere show," masks and mummery mode that has tended to characterize its general use, and more in a constructional, genuinely dramaturgical one—making, not faking, as the anthropologist Victor Turner has put it.

The two developments are linked, of course. A constructionalist view of what theater is—that is, poiesis—implies that a dramatistic perspective in the social sciences needs to involve more than pointing out that we all have our entrances and exits, we all play parts, miss cues, and love pretense. It may or may not be a Barnum and Bailey world and we may or may not be walking shadows, but to take the drama analogy seriously is to probe behind such familiar ironies to the expressive devices that make collective life seem anything at all. The trouble with analogies—it is also their glory—is that they connect what they compare in both directions. Having trifled with theater's idiom, some social scientists find themselves drawn into the rather tangled coils of its aesthetic.

Such a more thoroughgoing exploitation of the drama analogy in social theory—as an analogy, not an incidental metaphor—has grown out of sources in the humanities not altogether commensurable. On the one hand, there has been the so-called ritual theory of drama associated with such diverse figures as Jane Harrison, Francis Fergusson, T. S. Eliot,[8] and Antonin Artaud. On the other, there is the symbolic action—"dramatism," as he calls it—of the American literary theorist and philosopher Kenneth Burke,[9] whose influence is, in the United States anyway, at once enormous and—because almost no one actually uses his baroque vocabulary, with its reductions, ratios, and so on—elusive. The trouble is, these approaches pull in rather opposite directions: the ritual theory toward the affinities of theater and religion—drama as communion, the temple as stage; the symbolic action theory toward those of theater and rhetoric—drama as persuasion, the platform as stage. And this leaves the basis of the analogy—just what in the theatron is like what in the agora—hard to focus. That liturgy and ideology are histrionic is obvious enough, as it is that etiquette and advertising are. But just what that means is a good deal less so.

Probably the foremost proponent of the ritual theory approach in the social sciences right now is Victor Turner. A British formed, American reformed anthropologist, Turner, in a remarkable series of works trained on the ceremonial life of a Central African tribe, has developed a conception of "social drama" as a regenerative process that, rather like Goffman's of "social gaming" as strategic interaction, has drawn to it such a large number of able researchers as to produce a distinct and powerful interpretive school.

For Turner, social dramas occur "on all levels of social organization from state to family." They arise out of conflict situations—a village falls into factions, a husband beats a wife, a region rises against the state—and proceed to their denouements through publicly performed conventionalized behavior. As the conflict swells to crisis and the excited fluidity of heightened emotion, where people feel at once more enclosed in a common mood and loosened from their social moorings, ritualized forms of authority—litigation, feud, sacrifice, prayer—are invoked to contain it and render it orderly. If they succeed, the breach is healed and the status quo, or something resembling it, is restored; if they do not, it is accepted as incapable of remedy and things fall apart into various sorts of unhappy endings: migrations, divorces, or murders in the cathedral. With differing degrees of strictness and detail, Turner and his followers have applied this schema to tribal passage rites, curing ceremonies, and judicial processes; to Mexican insurrections, Icelandic sagas, and Thomas Becket's difficulties with Henry II; to picaresque narrative, millenarian movements, Caribbean carnivals, and Indian peyote hunts; and to the political upheaval of the sixties. A form for all seasons.

This hospitableness in the face of cases is at once the major strength of the ritual theory version of the drama analogy and its most prominent weakness. It can expose some of the profoundest features of social process, but at the expense of making vividly disparate matters look drably homogeneous.

Rooted as it is in the repetitive performance dimensions of social action—the reenactment and thus the reexperiencing of known form—the ritual theory not only brings out the temporal and collective dimensions of such action and its inherently public nature with particular sharpness; it brings out also its power to transmute not just opinions, but, as the British critic Charles Morgan has said with respect to drama proper, the people who hold them. "The great impact [of the theater]," Morgan writes, "is neither a persuasion of the intellect nor a beguiling of the senses. . . . It is the enveloping movement of the whole drama on the soul of man. We surrender and are changed." Or at least we are when the magic works. What Morgan, in another fine phrase, calls "the suspense of form . . . the incompleteness of a known completion," is the source of the power of this "enveloping movement," a power, as the ritual theorists have shown, that is hardly less forceful (and hardly less likely to be seen as otherworldly) when the movement appears in a female initiation rite, a peasant revolution, a national epic, or a star chamber.

Yet these formally similar processes have different content. They say, as we might put it, rather different things, and thus have rather different implications for social life. And though ritual theorists are hardly incognizant of that fact, they are, precisely because they are so concerned with the general movement of things, ill-equipped to deal with it. The great dramatic rhythms, the commanding forms of theater, are perceived in social processes of all sorts, shapes, and significances (though ritual theorists in fact do much better with the cyclical, restorative pe-

[8] See *CTSP*, pp. 784–90. [Eds.]
[9] See *CTSP*, pp. 942–47. [Eds.]

riodicities of comedy than the linear, consuming progressions of tragedy, whose ends tend to be seen as misfires rather than fulfillments). Yet the individuating details, the sort of thing that makes *A Winter's Tale* different from *Measure for Measure, Macbeth* from *Hamlet,* are left to encyclopedic empiricism: massive documentation of a single proposition—*plus ça change, plus c'est le même changement.* If dramas are, to adapt a phrase of Susanne Langer's, poems in the mode of action, something is being missed: what exactly, socially, the poems say.

This unpacking of performed meaning is what the symbolic action approaches are designed to accomplish. Here there is no single name to cite, just a growing catalogue of particular studies, some dependent on Kenneth Burke, some on Ernst Cassirer,[10] Northrop Frye,[11] Michel Foucault, or Emile Durkheim, concerned to say what some bit of acted saying—a coronation, a sermon, a riot, an execution—says. If ritual theorists, their eye on experience, tend to be hedgehogs, symbolic action theorists, their eye on expression, tend to be foxes.

Given the dialectical nature of things, we all need our opponents, and both sorts of approach are essential. What we are most in want of right now is some way of synthesizing them. In my own about-to-be-published analysis of the traditional Indic polity in Bali as a "theater state"—cited here not because it is exemplary, but because it is mine—I have tried to address this problem. In this analysis I am concerned, on the one hand (the Burkean one), to show how everything from kin group organization, trade, customary law, and water control, to mythology, architecture, iconography, and cremation combines to a dramatized statement of a distinct form of political theory, a particular conception of what status, power, authority, and government are and should be: namely, a replication of the world of the gods that is at the same time a template for that of men. The state enacts an image of order that—a model for its beholders, in and of itself—orders society. On the other hand (the Turner one), as the populace at large does not merely view the state's expressions as so many gaping spectators but is caught up bodily in them, and especially in the great, mass ceremonies—political operas of Burgundian dimensions—which form their heart, the sort of "we surrender and are changed" power of drama to shape experience is the strong force that holds the polity together. Reiterated form, staged and acted by its own audience, makes (to a degree, for no theater ever wholly works) theory fact.

But my point is that some of those fit to judge work of this kind ought to be humanists who reputedly know something about what theater and mimesis and rhetoric are, and not just with respect to my work but to that of the whole steadily broadening stream of social analyses in which the drama analogy is, in one form or another, governing. At a time when social scientists are chattering about actors, scenes, plots, performances, and personae, and humanists are mumbling about motives, authority, persuasion, exchange, and hierarchy, the line between the two, however comforting to the puritan on the one side and the cavalier on the other, seems uncertain indeed.

IV

The text analogy now taken up by social scientists is, in some ways, the broadest of the recent refigurations of social theory, the most venturesome, and the least well developed. Even more than "game" or "drama," "text" is a dangerously unfocused term, and its application to social action, to people's behavior toward other people, involves a thoroughgoing conceptual wrench, a particularly outlandish bit of "seeing-as." Describing human conduct in the analogy of player and counterplayer, or of actor and audience, seems, whatever the pitfalls, rather more natural than describing it in that of writer and reader. Prima facie, the suggestion that the activities of spies, lovers, witch doctors, kings, or mental patients are moves or performances is surely a good deal more plausible than the notion that they are sentences.

But prima facie is a dubious guide when it comes to analogizing; were it not, we should still be thinking of the heart as a furnace and the lungs as bellows. The text analogy has some unapparent advantages still insufficiently exploited, and the surface dissimilarity of the here-we-are-and-there-we-are of social interaction to the solid composure of lines on a page is what gives it—or can when the disaccordance is rightly aligned—its interpretive force.

The key to the transition from text to text ana-

[10] See *CTSP*, pp. 994–1013. [Eds.]

[11] See *CTSP*, pp. 1118–47 and *Frye.* [Eds.]

logue, from writing as discourse to action as discourse, is, as Paul Ricoeur[12] has pointed out, the concept of "inscription": the fixation of meaning. When we speak, our utterances fly by as events like any other behavior; unless what we say is inscribed in writing (or some other established recording process), it is as evanescent as what we do. If it is so inscribed, it of course passes, like Dorian Gray's youth, anyway; but at least its meaning—the *said*, not the *saying*—to a degree and for a while remains. This too is not different for action in general: its meaning can persist in a way its actuality cannot.

The great virtue of the extension of the notion of text beyond things written on paper or carved into stone is that it trains attention on precisely this phenomenon: on how the inscription of action is brought about, what its vehicles are and how they work, and on what the fixation of meaning from the flow of events—history from what happened, thought from thinking, culture from behavior—implies for sociological interpretation. To see social institutions, social customs, social changes as in some sense "readable" is to alter our whole sense of what such interpretation is toward modes of thought rather more familiar to the translator, the exegete, or the iconographer than to the test giver, the factor analyst, or the pollster.

All this comes out with exemplary vividness in the work of Alton Becker, a comparative linguist, on Javanese shadow puppetry, or the *wayang* as it is called. Wayang-ing (there is no other suitable verb) is, Becker says, a mode of text building, a way of putting symbols together to construct an expression. To construe it, to understand not just what it means but how it does so, one needs, he says, a new philology.

Philology, the text-centered study of language, as contrasted to linguistics, which is speech centered, has of course traditionally been concerned with making ancient or foreign or esoteric documents accessible to those for whom they are ancient or foreign or esoteric. Terms are glossed, notes appended, commentaries written, and, where necessary, transcriptions made and translations effected—all toward the end of producing an annotated edition as readable as the philologist can make it. Meaning is fixed at a meta-level; essentially what a philologist, a kind of secondary author, does is re-inscribe: interpret a text with a text.

Left at this, matters are straightforward enough, however difficult they may turn out to be in practice. But when philological concern goes beyond routinized craft procedures (authentication, reconstruction, annotation) to address itself to conceptual questions concerning the nature of texts as such—that is, to questions about their principles of construction—simplicity flees. The result, Becker notes, has been the shattering of philology, itself by now a near obsolescent term, into disjunct and rivalrous specialties, and most particularly the growth of a division between those who study individual texts (historians, editors, critics—who like to call themselves humanists), and those who study the activity of creating texts in general (linguists, psychologists, ethnographers—who like to call themselves scientists). The study of inscriptions is severed from the study of inscribing, the study of fixed meaning is severed from the study of the social processes that fix it. The result is a double narrowness. Not only is the extension of text analysis to non-written materials blocked, but so is the application of sociological analysis to written ones.

The repair of this split and the integration of the study of how texts are built, how the said is rescued from its saying, into the study of social phenomena—Apache jokes, English meals, African cult sermons, American high schools, Indian caste, or Balinese widow burning, to mention some recent attempts aside from Becker's—is what the "new philology," or whatever else it eventually comes to be called, is all about. "In a multicultured world," Becker writes, "a world of multiple epistemologies, there is need for a new philologist—a specialist in contextual relations—in all areas of knowledge in which text-building . . . is a central activity: literature, history, law, music, politics, psychology, trade, even war and peace."

Becker sees four main orders of semiotic connection in a social text for his new philologist to investigate: the relation of its parts to one another; the relation of it to others culturally or historically associated with it; the relation of it to those who in some sense construct it; and the relation of it to realities conceived as lying outside of it. Certainly there are others—its relation to its *materia*, for one; and, more certainly yet, even these raise profound methodological issues so far only hesitantly

[12] See *Ricoeur*. [Eds.]

addressed. "Coherence," "inter-textuality," "intention," and "reference"—which are what Becker's four relations more or less come down to—all become most elusive notions when one leaves the paragraph or page for the act or institution. Indeed, as Nelson Goodman has shown, they are not all that well-defined for the paragraph or page, to say nothing of the picture, the melody, the statue, or the dance. Insofar as the theory of meaning implied by this multiple contextualization of cultural phenomena (some sort of symbolic constructivism) exists at all, it does so as a catalogue of wavering intimations and half-joined ideas.

How far this sort of analysis can go beyond such specifically expressive matters as puppetry, and what adjustments it will have to make in doing so, is, of course, quite unclear. As "life is a game" proponents tend to gravitate toward face-to-face interaction, courtship and cocktail parties, as the most fertile ground for their sort of analysis, and "life is a stage" proponents are attracted toward collective intensities, carnivals and insurrections, for the same reason, so "life is a text" proponents incline toward the examination of imaginative forms: jokes, proverbs, popular arts. There is nothing either surprising or reprehensible in this; one naturally tries one's analogies out where they seem most likely to work. But their long-run fates surely rest on their capacity to move beyond their easier initial successes to harder and less predictable ones—of the game idea to make sense of worship, the drama idea to explicate humor, or the text idea to clarify war. Most of these triumphs, if they are to occur at all, are, in the text case even more than the others, still to come. For the moment, all the apologist can do is what I have done here: offer up some instances of application, some symptoms of trouble, and some pleas for help.

V

So much, anyway, for examples. Not only do these particular three analogies obviously spill over into one another as individual writers tack back and forth between ludic, dramatistic, and textualist idioms, but there are other humanistic analogies on the social science scene at least as prominent as they: speech act analyses following Austin and Searle;[13] discourse models as different as those of Habermas's "communicative competence" and Foucault's "archaeology of knowledge"; representationalist approaches taking their lead from the cognitive aesthetics of Cassirer, Langer, Gombrich, or Goodman; and of course Lévi-Strauss's higher cryptology. Nor are they as yet internally settled and homogeneous: the divisions between the play-minded and the strategy-minded to which I alluded in connection with the game approach, and between the ritualists and the rhetoricians in connection with the drama approach, are more than matched in the text approach by the collisions between the against-interpretation mandarins of deconstructionism and the symbolic-domination tribunes of neo-Marxism. Matters are neither stable nor consensual, and they are not likely soon to become so. The interesting question is not how all this muddle is going to come magnificently together, but what does all this ferment mean.

One thing it means is that, however raggedly, a challenge is being mounted to some of the central assumptions of mainstream social science. The strict separation of theory and data, the "brute fact" idea; the effort to create a formal vocabulary of analysis purged of all subjective reference, the "ideal language" idea; and the claim to moral neutrality and the Olympian view, the "God's truth" idea—none of these can prosper when explanation comes to be regarded as a matter of connecting action to its sense rather than behavior to its determinants. The refiguration of social theory represents, or will if it continues, a sea change in our notion not so much of what knowledge is, but of what it is we want to know. Social events do have causes and social institutions effects; but it just may be that the road to discovering what we assert in asserting this lies less through postulating forces and measuring them than through noting expressions and inspecting them.

The turn taken by an important segment of social scientists, from physical process analogies to symbolic form ones, has introduced a fundamental debate into the social science community concerning not just its methods but its aims. It is a debate that grows daily in intensity. The golden age (or perhaps it was only the brass) of the social sciences when, whatever the differences in theoretical positions

[13] See *Austin* and *Searle*. [Eds.]

and empirical claims, the basic goal of the enterprise was universally agreed upon—to find out the dynamics of collective life and alter them in desired directions—has clearly passed. There are too many social scientists at work today for whom the anatomization of thought is wanted, not the manipulation of behavior.

But it is not only for the social sciences that this alteration in how we think about how we think has disequilibrating implications. The rising interest of sociologists, anthropologists, psychologists, political scientists, and even now and then a rogue economist in the analysis of symbol systems poses—implicitly anyway, explicitly sometimes—the question of the relationship of such systems to what goes on in the world; and it does so in a way both rather different from what humanists are used to and rather less evadable—with homilies about spiritual values and the examined life—than many of them, so it seems, would at all like.

If the social technologist notion of what a social scientist is is brought into question by all this concern with sense and signification, even more so is the cultural watchdog notion of what a humanist is. The specialist without spirit dispensing policy nostrums goes, but the lectern sage dispensing approved judgments does as well. The relation between thought and action in social life can no more be conceived of in terms of wisdom than it can in terms of expertise. How it is to be conceived, how the games, dramas, or texts which we do not just invent or witness but live, have the consequence they do remains very far from clear. It will take the wariest of wary reasonings, on all sides of all divides, to get it clearer.

Stanley Fish

b. 1938

IN HIS introduction to the book in which the essay included here is the title piece, Fish reviews the development, over the course of more than a decade, of the theory he sets forth. This development he treats as a shift in questions asked. The question that first occupied him involved whether the reader or the text was the source of meaning. His program at that time was to attack the theory of the "affective fallacy" as offered by Monroe Beardsley and W. K. Wimsatt (see *CTSP*, pp. 1022–31) and the accompanying theory of the self-sufficiency of the text. In his early work, including books on Milton and seventeenth-century poetry, Fish located meaning in the structure of the reader's progress through the text, emphasizing the activity of reading itself, even though he continued to regard the text as a stable entity that controlled what the reader could experience. At this stage, for Fish, the whole progress of reading embodies meaning; nothing is discarded. This view proposed to locate the reader in the Chomskian idea of linguistic competence (see *Chomsky*), though this did not successfully account for divergences of interpretation among the competent. The commonality of reading experience was anchored in the text, and Fish found himself, by his own account, back with those very same New Critics from whom his emphasis on reading was designed to separate him.

Gradually Fish came to conclude that "linguistic and textual facts, rather than being the objects of interpretation, are its products"; but first he had to rid himself of the assumption that without the text as object containing these facts, the only alternative was a solipsistic subjectivity. Ultimately he found the ground for his theory in the notion of an "interpretive community" which declares what is or is not literature at any time, all texts whatever having the potentiality for being included. In Fish's next phase the object is constituted as literary; the subject is both a determiner of its world and "informed by conventional notions." But soon the idea of both text and reader had to be further qualified because neither had an independent status. What remain are texts that emerge as the consequence of the interpretive man-made models that have called them into being. Interpretive strategies thus precede and make texts rather than arising from them. Such strategies arise from the interpretive community, and all interpreters belong to one or another of these. It follows, if this is inevitable, that subjectivity is an illusion and need not concern us and that criticism's business is to "establish by political and persuasive means . . . the set of interpretive assumptions from the vantage of which the evidence (and the facts and the intentions and everything else) will hereafter be specifiable." In the end, Fish's theory leads to the study of social and institutional power, the power to impose meaning.

Fish's books are *Surprised by Sin* (1971), *Self-Consuming Artifacts* (1972), and *Is There a Text in This Class?* (1980), a collection of essays written over the previous decade.

IS THERE A TEXT IN THIS CLASS?

On the first day of the new semester a colleague at Johns Hopkins University was approached by a student who, as it turned out, had just taken a course from me. She put to him what I think you would agree is a perfectly straightforward question: "Is there a text in this class?" Responding with a confidence so perfect that he was unaware of it (although in telling the story, he refers to this moment as "walking into the trap"), my colleague said, "Yes; it's the *Norton Anthology of Literature,*" whereupon the trap (set not by the student but by the infinite capacity of language for being appropriated) was sprung: "No, no," she said, "I mean in this class do we believe in poems and things, or is it just us?" Now it is possible (and for many tempting) to read this anecdote as an illustration of the dangers that follow upon listening to people like me who preach the instability of the text and the unavailability of determinate meanings; but in what follows I will try to read it as an illustration of how baseless the fear of these dangers finally is.

Of the charges levied against what Meyer Abrams has recently called the New Readers (Derrida, Bloom, Fish) the most persistent is that these apostles of indeterminacy and undecidability ignore, even as they rely upon, the "norms and possibilities" embedded in language, the "linguistic meanings" words undeniably have, and thereby invite us to abandon "our ordinary realm of experience in speaking, hearing, reading and understanding" for a world in which "no text can mean anything in particular" and where "we can never say just what anyone means by anything he writes."[1] The charge is that literal or normative meanings are overriden by the actions of willful interpreters. Suppose we examine this indictment in the context of the present example. What, exactly, is the normative or literal or linguistic meaning of "Is there a text in this class?"

Within the framework of contemporary critical debate (as it is reflected in the pages, say, of *Critical Inquiry*) there would seem to be only two ways of answering this question: either there *is* a literal meaning of the utterance and we should be able to say what it is, or there are as many meanings as there are readers and no one of them is literal. But the answer suggested by my little story is that the utterance has *two* literal meanings: within the circumstances assumed by my colleague (I don't mean that he took the step of assuming them, but that he was already stepping within them) the utterance is obviously a question about whether or not there is a required textbook in this particular course; but within the circumstances to which he was alerted by his student's corrective response, the utterance is just as obviously a question about the instructor's position (within the range of positions available in contemporary literary theory) on the status of the text. Notice that we do not have here a case of indeterminacy or undecidability but of a determinacy and decidability that do not always have the same shape and that can, and in this instance do, change. My colleague was not hesitating between two (or more) possible meanings of the utterance; rather, he immediately apprehended what seemed to be an inescapable meaning, given his prestructured understanding of the situation, and then he immediately

IS THERE A TEXT IN THIS CLASS? is the title essay from the book published by Harvard University Press. It is reprinted here by permission of the publishers, copyright 1980 by the President and Fellows of Harvard College.

[1] M. H. Abrams, "The Deconstructive Angel," *Critical Inquiry*, 3, no. 3 (Spring 1977), 431, 434. [Au.] See *Abrams; Derrida; Bloom.* [Eds.]

apprehended another inescapable meaning when that understanding was altered. Neither meaning was imposed (a favorite word in the anti-new-reader polemics) on a more normal one by a private, idiosyncratic interpretive act; both interpretations were a function of precisely the public and constituting norms (of language and understanding) invoked by Abrams. It is just that these norms are not embedded in the language (where they may be read out by anyone with sufficiently clear, that is, unbiased, eyes) but inhere in an institutional structure within which one hears utterances as already organized with reference to certain assumed purposes and goals. Because both my colleague and his student are situated in that institution, their interpretive activities are not free, but what constrains them are the understood practices and assumptions of the institution and not the rules and fixed meanings of a language system.

Another way to put this would be to say that neither reading of the question—which we might for convenience's sake label as "Is there a text in this class?"$_1$ and "Is there a text in this class?"$_2$—would be immediately available to any native speaker of the language. "Is there a text in this class?"$_1$ is interpretable or readable only by someone who already knows what is included under the general rubric "first day of class" (what concerns animate students, what bureaucratic matters must be attended to before instruction begins) and who therefore hears the utterance under the aegis of that knowledge, which is not applied after the fact but is responsible for the shape the fact immediately has. To someone whose consciousness is not already informed by that knowledge, "Is there a text in this class?"$_1$ would be just as unavailable as "Is there a text in this class?"$_2$ would be to someone who was not already aware of the disputed issues in contemporary literary theory. I am not saying that for some readers or hearers the question would be wholly unintelligible (indeed, in the course of this essay I will be arguing that unintelligibility, in the strict or pure sense, is an impossibility), but that there are readers and hearers for whom the intelligibility of the question would have neither of the shapes it had, in a temporal succession, for my colleague. It is possible, for example, to imagine someone who would hear or intend the question as an inquiry about the location of an object, that is, "I think I left my text in this class; have you seen it?" We would then have an "Is there a text in this class?"$_3$ and the possibility, feared by the defenders of the normative and determinate, of an endless succession of numbers, that is, of a world in which every utterance has an infinite plurality of meanings. But that is not what the example, however it might be extended, suggests at all. In any of the situations I have imagined (and in any that I might be able to imagine) the meaning of the utterance would be severely constrained, not after it was heard but in the ways in which it *could*, in the first place, be heard. An infinite plurality of meanings would be a fear only if sentences existed in a state in which they were not already embedded in, and had come into view as a function of, some situation or other. That state, if it could be located, would be the normative one, and it would be disturbing indeed if the norm were free-floating and indeterminate. But there is no such state; sentences emerge only in situations, and within those situations, the normative meaning of an utterance will always be obvious or at least accessible, although within another situation that same utterance, no longer the same, will have another normative meaning that will be no less obvious and accessible. (My colleague's experience is precisely an illustration.) This does not mean that there is no way to discriminate between the meanings an utterance will have in different situations, but that the discrimination will already have been made by virtue of our being in a situation (we are never not in one) and that in another situation the discrimination will also have already been made, but differently. In other words, while at any one point it is always possible to order and rank "Is there a text in this class?"$_1$ and "Is there a text in this class?"$_2$ (because they will always have already been ranked), it will never be possible to give them an immutable once-and-for-all ranking, a ranking that is independent of their appearance or nonappearance in situations (because it is only in situations that they do or do not appear).

Nevertheless, there is a distinction to be made between the two that allows us to say that, in a limited sense, one is more normal than the other: for while each is perfectly normal in the context in which their literalness is immediately obvious (the successive contexts occupied by my colleague), as things stand now, one of those contexts is surely more available, and therefore more likely to be the perspective within which the utterance is heard, than the other. Indeed, we seem to have here an instance of what I would call "institutional nesting": if "Is there a text in this class?"$_1$ is hearable only by those who know what is included under the rubric "first day of class," and if "Is there a text in this class?"$_2$ is hearable only by those whose categories of understanding include the concerns of contemporary literary theory, then it is obvious that in a random population presented with the utterance, more people would "hear" "Is there a text in this class?"$_1$ than "Is there a text in this class?"$_2$; and, moreover, that while "Is there a text in this class?"$_1$ could be immediately hearable by someone for whom "Is there a text in this class?"$_2$ would have to be laboriously explained, it is difficult to imagine someone capable of hearing "Is there a text in this class?"$_2$ who was not already capable of hearing "Is there a text in this class."$_1$ (One is hearable by anyone in the profession and by most students and by many workers in the book trade, and the other only by those in the profession who would not think it peculiar to find, as I did recently, a critic referring to a phrase "made popular by Lacan.")[2] To admit as much is not to weaken my argument by reinstating the category of the normal, because the category as it appears in that argument is not transcendental but institutional; and while no institution is so universally in force and so perdurable that the meanings it enables will be normal for ever, some institutions or forms of life are so widely lived in that for a great many people the meanings they enable seem "naturally" available and it takes a special effort to see that they are the products of circumstances.

The point is an important one, because it accounts for the success with which an Abrams or an E. D. Hirsch can appeal to a shared understanding of ordinary language and argue from that understanding to the availability of a core of determinate meanings. When Hirsch offers "The air is crisp" as an example of a "verbal meaning" that is accessible to all speakers of the language, and distinguishes what is sharable and determinate about it from the associations that may, in certain circumstances, accompany it (for example, "I should have eaten less at supper." "Crisp air reminds me of my childhood in Vermont"),[3] he is counting on his readers to agree so completely with his sense of what that shared and normative verbal meaning is that he does not bother even to specify it; and although I have not taken a survey, I would venture to guess that his optimism, with respect to this particular example, is well founded. That is, most, if not all, of his readers immediately understand the utterance as a rough meteorological description predicting a certain quality of the local atmosphere. But the "happiness" of the example, far from making Hirsch's point (which is always, as he has recently reaffirmed, to maintain "the stable determinacy of meaning")[4] makes mine. The obviousness of the utterance's meaning is not a function of the values its words have in a linguistic system that is independent of context; rather, it is because the words are heard as already embedded in a context that they have a meaning that Hirsch can then cite as obvious. One can see this by embedding the words in another context and observing how quickly another "obvious" meaning emerges. Suppose, for example, we came upon "The air is crisp" (which you are even now hearing as Hirsch assumes you hear it) in the middle of a discussion of music ("When the piece is played correctly the air is crisp"); it would immediately be heard as a comment on the performance by an instrument or instruments of a musical air. Moreover, it would *only* be heard that way, and to hear it in Hirsch's way would require an effort on the order of a strain. It could be objected that in Hirsch's text "The air is crisp"$_1$ has no contextual setting at all; it is merely presented, and therefore any agreement as to its meaning must be because of the utterance's acontextual properties. But there *is* a contextual setting and the sign of its presence is precisely the absence of any reference to it. That is, it is impossible even to think of a sentence independently of a context, and when we are asked to consider a sentence for which no context has been specified, we will automatically hear it in the context in which it has been most often encountered. Thus Hirsch invokes a context by not invoking it; by not surrounding the utterance with circum-

[2] See *Lacan*. [Eds.]

[3] E. D. Hirsch, *Validity in Interpretation* (New Haven: Yale University Press, 1967), pp. 218–219. [Au.] See *CTSP*, pp. 1176–94. [Eds.]

[4] E. D. Hirsch, *The Aims of Interpretation* (Chicago: University of Chicago Press, 1976), p. 1. [Au.]

stances, he directs us to imagine it in the circumstances in which it is most likely to have been produced; and to so imagine it is already to have given it a shape that seems at the moment to be the only one possible.

What conclusions can be drawn from these two examples? First of all, neither my colleague nor the reader of Hirsch's sentence is constrained by the meanings words have in a normative linguistic system; and yet neither is free to confer on an utterance any meaning he likes. Indeed, "confer" is exactly the wrong word because it implies a two stage procedure in which a reader or hearer first scrutinizes an utterance and *then* gives it a meaning. The argument of the preceding pages can be reduced to the assertion that there is no such first stage, that one hears an utterance within, and not as preliminary to determining, a knowledge of its purposes and concerns, and that to so hear it is already to have assigned it a shape and given it a meaning. In other words, the problem of how meaning is determined is only a problem if there is a point at which its determination has not yet been made, and I am saying that there is no such point.

I am *not* saying that one is never in the position of having to self-consciously figure out what an utterance means. Indeed, my colleague is in just such a position when he is informed by his student that he has not heard her question as she intended it ("No, No, I mean in this class do we believe in poems and things, or is it just us?") and therefore must now figure it out. But the "it" in this (or any other) case is not a collection of words waiting to be assigned a meaning but an utterance whose already assigned meaning has been found to be inappropriate. While my colleague has to begin all over again, he does not have to begin from square one; and indeed he never was at square one, since from the very first his hearing of the student's question was informed by his assumption of what its concerns could possibly be. (That is why he is not "free" even if he is unconstrained by determinate meanings.) It is that assumption rather than his performance within it that is challenged by the student's correction. She tells him that he has mistaken her meaning, but this is not to say that he has made a mistake in combining her words and syntax into a meaningful unit; it is rather that the meaningful unit he immediately discerns is a function of a mistaken identification (made before she speaks) of her intention. He was prepared as she stood before him to hear the kind of thing students ordinarily say on the first day of class, and therefore that is precisely what he heard. He has not misread the text (his is not an error in calculation) but mis*pre*read the text, and if he is to correct himself he must make another (pre)determination of the structure of interests from which her question issues. This, of course, is exactly what he does and the question of how he does it is a crucial one, which can best be answered by first considering the ways in which he *didn't* do it.

He didn't do it by attending to the literal meaning of her response. That is, this is not a case in which someone who has been misunderstood clarifies her meaning by making more explicit, by varying or adding to her words in such a way as to render their sense inescapable. Within the circumstances of utterance as he has assumed them her words are perfectly clear, and what she is doing is asking him to imagine other circumstances in which the same words will be equally, but differently, clear. Nor is it that the words she does add ("No, No, I mean . . .") direct him to those circumstances by picking them out from an inventory of all possible ones. For this to be the case there would have to be an inherent relationship between the words she speaks and a particular set of circumstances (this would be a higher level literalism) such that any competent speaker of the language hearing those words would immediately be referred to that set. But I have told the story to several competent speakers of the language who simply didn't get it, and one friend—a professor of philosophy—reported to me that in the interval between his hearing the story and my explaining it to him (and just how I was able to do that is another crucial question) he found himself asking "What kind of joke is this and have I missed it?" For a time at least he remained able only to hear "Is there a text in this class" as my colleague first heard it; the student's additional words, far from leading him to another hearing, only made him aware of his distance from it. In contrast, there are those who not only get the story but get it before I tell it; that is, they know in advance what is coming as soon as I say that a colleague of mine was recently asked, "Is there a text in this class?" Who are these people and what is it that makes their comprehension of the story so immediate and easy? Well, one could say, without being the least bit facetious, that they are the people who come to hear me speak because they are the people who already know my position on certain matters (or know that I will *have* a position). That is, they hear, "Is there a text in this class?" even as it appears at the beginning of the anecdote (or for that matter as a title of an essay) in the light of their knowledge of what I am likely to do with it. They hear it coming from *me,* in circumstances which have committed me to declaring myself on a range of issues that are sharply delimited.

My colleague was finally able to hear it in just that way, as coming from me, not because I was there in his classroom, nor because the words of the student's question pointed to me in a way that would have been obvious to any hearer, but because he was able to think of me in an office three doors down from his telling students that there are no determinate meanings and that the stability of the text is an illusion. Indeed, as he reports it, the moment of recognition and comprehension consisted of his saying to himself, "Ah, there's one of Fish's victims!" He did not say this because her words identified her as such but because his ability to see her as such informed his perception of her words. The answer to the question "How did he get from her words to the circumstances within which she intended him to hear them?" is that he must already be thinking within those circumstances in order to be able to hear her words as referring to them. The question, then, must be rejected, because it assumes that the construing of sense leads to the identification of the context of utterance rather than the other way around. This does not mean that the context comes first and that once it has been identified the construing of sense can begin. This would be only to reverse the order of precedence, whereas precedence is beside the point because the two actions it would order (the identification of context and the making of sense) occur simultaneously. One does not say "Here I am in a situation; now I can begin to determine what these words mean." To be in a situation is to see the words, these or any other, as already meaningful. For my colleague to realize that he may be confronting one of my victims is *at the same time* to hear what she says as a question about his theoretical beliefs.

But to dispose of one "how" question is only to raise another: if her words do not lead him to the context of her utterance, how does he get there? Why did he think of me telling students that there were no determinate meanings and not think of someone or something else? First of all, he might well have. That is, he might well have guessed that she was coming from another direction (inquiring, let us say, as to whether the focus of this class was to be the poems and essays or our responses to them, a question in the same line of country as hers but quite distinct from it) or he might have simply been stymied, like my philosopher friend, confined, in the absence of an explanation, to his first determination of her concerns and unable to make any sense of her words other than the sense he originally made. How, then, did he do it? In part, he did it because he *could* do it; he was able to get to this context because it was already part of his repertoire for organizing the world and its events. The category "one of Fish's victims" was one he already had and didn't have to work for. Of course, *it* did not always have *him,* in that his world was not always being organized by it, and it certainly did not have him at the beginning of the conversation; but it was available to him, and he to it, and all he had to do was to recall it or be recalled to it for the meanings it subtended to emerge. (Had it not been available to him, the career of his comprehension would have been different and we will come to a consideration of that difference shortly.)

This, however, only pushes our inquiry back further. How or why was he recalled to it? The answer to this question must be probabilistic and it begins with the recognition that when something changes, not everything changes. Although my colleague's understanding of his circumstances is transformed in the course of this conversation, the circumstances are still understood to be academic ones, and within that continuing (if modified) understanding, the directions his thought might take are already severely limited. He still presumes, as he did at first, that the student's question has something to do with university business in general, and with English literature in particular, and it is the organizing rubrics associated with these areas of experience that are likely to occur to him. One of those rubrics is "what-goes-on-in-other-classes" and one of those other classes is mine. And so, by a route that is neither entirely unmarked nor wholly determined, he comes to me and to the notion "one of Fish's victims" and to a new construing of what his student has been saying.

Of course that route would have been much more

circuitous if the category "one of Fish's victims" was not already available to him as a device for producing intelligibility. Had that device not been part of his repertoire, had he been incapable of being recalled to it because he never knew it in the first place, how would he have proceeded? The answer is that he could not have proceeded at all, which does not mean that one is trapped forever in the categories of understanding at one's disposal (or the categories at whose disposal one is), but that the introduction of new categories or the expansion of old ones to include new (and therefore newly seen) data must always come from the outside or from what is perceived, for a time, to be the outside. In the event that he was unable to identify the structure of her concerns because it had never been his (or he its), it would have been her obligation to explain it to him. And here we run up against another instance of the problem we have been considering all along. She could not explain it to him by varying or adding to her words, by being more explicit, because her words will only be intelligible if he already has the knowledge they are supposed to convey, the knowledge of the assumptions and interests from which they issue. It is clear, then, that she would have to make a new start, although she would not have to start from scratch (indeed, starting from scratch is never a possibility); but she would have to back up to some point at which there was a shared agreement as to what was reasonable to say so that a new and wider basis for agreement could be fashioned. In this particular case, for example, she might begin with the fact that her interlocutor already knows what a text is; that is, he has a way of thinking about it that is responsible for his hearing of her first question as one about bureaucratic classroom procedures. (You will remember that "he" in these sentences is no longer my colleague but someone who does not have his special knowledge.) It is that way of thinking that she must labor to extend or challenge, first, perhaps, by pointing out that there are those who think about the text in other ways, and then by trying to find a category of his own understanding which might serve as an analogue to the understanding he does not yet share. He might, for example, be familiar with those psychologists who argue for the constitutive power of perception, or with Gombrich's theory of the beholder's share, or with that philosophical tradition in which the stability of objects has always been a matter of dispute. The example must remain hypothetical and skeletal, because it can only be fleshed out after a determination of the particular beliefs and assumptions that would make the explanation necessary in the first place; for whatever they were, they would dictate the strategy by which she would work to supplant or change them. It is when such a strategy has been successful that the import of her words will become clear, not because she has reformulated or refined them but because they will now be read or heard within the same system of intelligibility from which they issue.

In short, this hypothetical interlocutor will in time be brought to the same point of comprehension my colleague enjoys when he is able to say to himself, "Ah, there's one of Fish's victims," although presumably he will say something very different to himself if he says anything at all. The difference, however, should not obscure the basic similarities between the two experiences, one reported, the other imagined. In both cases the words that are uttered are immediately heard within a set of assumptions about the direction from which they could possibly be coming, and in both cases what is required is that the hearing occur within another set of assumptions in relation to which the same words ("Is there a text in this class?") will no longer be the same. It is just that while my colleague is able to meet that requirement by calling to mind a context of utterance that is already a part of his repertoire, the repertoire of his hypothetical stand-in must be expanded to include that context so that should he some day be in an analogous situation, he would be able to call it to mind.

The distinction, then, is between already having an ability and having to acquire it, but it is not finally an essential distinction, because the routes by which that ability could be exercised on the one hand, and learned on the other, are so similar. They are similar first of all because they are similarly *not* determined by words. Just as the student's words will not direct my colleague to a context he already has, so will they fail to direct someone not furnished with that context to its discovery. And yet in neither case does the absence of such a mechanical determination mean that the route one travels is randomly found. The change from one structure of understanding to another is not a rupture but a modification of the interests and concerns that are already in place; and because they are already in place, they constrain the direction of their own modification. That is, in both cases the hearer is already in a situation informed by tacitly known purposes and goals, and in both cases he ends up in another situation whose purposes and goals stand in some elaborated relation (of contrast, opposition, expansion, extension) to those they supplant. (The one relation in which they could not stand is no relation at all.) It is just that in one case the network of elaboration (from the text as an obviously physical object to the question of whether or not the text is a physical object) has already been articulated (although not all of its articulations are in focus at one time; selection is always occurring), while in the other the articulation of the network is the business of the teacher (here the student) who begins, necessarily, with what is already given.

The final similarity between the two cases is that in neither is success assured. It was no more inevitable that my colleague tumble to the context of his student's utterance than it would be inevitable that she could introduce that context to someone previously unaware of it; and, indeed, had my colleague remained puzzled (had he simply not thought of me), it would have been necessary for the student to bring him along in a way that was finally indistinguishable from the way she would bring someone to a new knowledge, that is, by beginning with the shape of his present understanding.

I have lingered so long over the unpacking of this anecdote that its relationship to the problem of authority in the classroom and in literary criticism may seem obscure. Let me recall you to it by recalling the contention of Abrams and others that authority depends upon the existence of a determinate core of meaning because in the absence of such a core there is no normative or public way of construing what anyone says or writes, with the result that interpretation becomes a matter of individual and private construings none of which is subject to challenge or correction. In literary criticism this means that no interpretation can be said to be better or worse than any other, and in the classroom this means that we have no answer to the student who says my interpretation is as valid as yours. It is only if there is a shared basis of agreement at once guiding interpretation and providing a mechanism for deciding between interpretations that a total debilitating relativism can be avoided.

But the point of my analysis has been to show that while "Is there a text in this class?" does not have a determinate meaning, a meaning that survives the sea change of situations, in any situation we might imagine the meaning of the utterance is either perfectly clear or capable, in the course of time, of being clarified. What is it that makes this possible, if it is not the "possibilities and norms" already encoded in language? How does communication ever occur if not by reference to a public and stable norm? The answer, implicit in everything I have already said, is that communication occurs within situations and that to be in a situation is already to be in possession of (or to be possessed by) a structure of assumptions, of practices understood to be relevant in relation to purposes and goals that are already in place; and it is within the assumption of these purposes and goals that any utterance is *immediately* heard. I stress immediately because it seems to me that the problem of communication, as someone like Abrams poses it, is a problem only because he assumes a distance between one's receiving of an utterance and the determination of its meaning—a kind of dead space when one has only the words and then faces the task of construing them. If there were such a space, a moment before interpretation began, then it would be necessary to have recourse to some mechanical and algorithmic procedure by means of which meanings could be calculated and in relation to which one could recognize mistakes. What I have been arguing is that meanings come already calculated, not because of norms embedded in the language but because language is always perceived, from the very first, within a structure of norms. That structure, however, is not abstract and independent but social; and therefore it is not a single structure with a privileged relationship to the process of communication as it occurs in any situation but a structure that changes when one situation, with its assumed background of practices, purposes, and goals, has given way to another. In other words, the shared basis of agreement sought by Abrams and others is never not already found, although it is not always the same one.

Many will find in this last sentence, and in the argument to which it is a conclusion, nothing more than a sophisticated version of the relativism they fear. It will do no good, they say, to speak of norms and standards that are context specific, because this is merely to authorize an infinite plurality of norms and standards, and we are still left without any way of adjudicating between them and between the competing systems of value of which they are functions. In short, to have many standards is to have no standards at all.

On one level this counterargument is unassailable, but on another level it is finally beside the point. It is unassailable as a general and theoretical conclusion: the positing of context- or institution-specific norms surely rules out the possibility of a norm whose validity would be recognized by everyone, no matter what his situation. But it is beside the point for any particular individual, for since everyone is situated somewhere, there is no one for whom the absence of an asituational norm would be of any practical consequence, in the sense that his performance or his confidence in his ability to perform would be impaired. So that while it is generally true that to have many standards is to have none at all, it is not true for anyone in particular (for there is no one in a position to speak "generally"), and therefore it is a truth of which one can say "it doesn't matter."

In other words, while relativism is a position one can entertain, it is not a position one can occupy. No one can *be* a relativist, because no one can achieve the distance from his own beliefs and assumptions which would result in their being no more authoritative *for him* than the beliefs and assumptions held by others, or, for that matter, the beliefs and assumptions he himself used to hold. The fear that in a world of indifferently authorized norms and values the individual is without a basis for action is groundless because no one is indifferent to the norms and values that enable his consciousness. It is in the name of personally held (in fact they are doing the holding) norms and values that the individual acts and argues, and he does so with the full confidence that attends belief. When his beliefs change, the norms and values to which he once gave unthinking assent will have been demoted to the status of opinions and become the objects of an analytical and critical attention; but that attention will itself be enabled by a new set of norms and values that are, for the time being, as unexamined and undoubted as those they displace. The point is that there is never a moment when one believes nothing, when consciousness is innocent of any and all categories of thought, and whatever categories of thought are operative at a given moment will serve as an undoubted ground.

Here, I suspect, a defender of determinate meaning would cry "solipsist" and argue that a confidence that had its source in the individual's categories of thought would have no public value. That is, unconnected to any shared and stable system of meanings, it would not enable one to transact the verbal business of everyday life; a shared intelligibility would be impossible in a world where everyone was trapped in the circle of his own assumptions and opinions. The reply to this is that an individual's assumptions and opinions are not "his own" in any sense that would give body to the fear of solipsism. That is, *he* is not their origin (in fact it might be more accurate to say that they are his); rather, it is their prior availability which delimits in advance the paths that his consciousness can possibly take. When my colleague is in the act of construing his student's question ("Is there a text in this class?"), none of the interpretive strategies at his disposal are uniquely his, in the sense that he thought them up; they follow from his preunderstanding of the interests and goals that could possibly animate the speech of someone functioning within the institution of academic America, interests and goals that are the particular property of no one in particular but which link everyone for whom their assumption is so habitual as to be unthinking. They certainly link my colleague and his student, who are able to communicate and even to reason about one another's intentions, not, however, because their interpretive efforts are constrained by the shape of an independent language but because their shared understanding of what could possibly be at stake in a classroom situation results in language appearing to them in the same shape (or successions of shapes). That shared understanding is the basis of the confidence with which they speak and reason, but its categories are their own only in the sense that as actors within an institution they automatically fall heir to the institution's way of making sense, its systems of intelligibility. That is why it is so hard for someone whose very being is defined by his position within an institution (and if not this one, then some other) to explain to someone outside it a practice or a meaning that seems to him to require no explanation, because he regards it as natural. Such a person, when pressed, is likely to say, "but that's just the way it's done" or "but isn't it obvious" and so testify that the practice or meaning in question is community property, as, in a sense, he is too.

We see then that (1) communication does occur,

despite the absence of an independent and context-free system of meanings, that (2) those who participate in this communication do so confidently rather than provisionally (they are not relativists), and that (3) while their confidence has its source in a set of beliefs, those beliefs are not individual-specific or idiosyncratic but communal and conventional (they are not solipsists).

Of course, solipsism and relativism are what Abrams and Hirsch fear and what lead them to argue for the necessity of determinate meaning. But if, rather than acting on their own, interpreters act as extensions of an institutional community, solipsism and relativism are removed as fears because they are not possible modes of being. That is to say, the condition required for someone to be a solipsist or relativist, the condition of being independent of institutional assumptions and free to originate one's own purposes and goals, could never be realized, and therefore there is no point in trying to guard against it. Abrams, Hirsch, and company spend a great deal of time in a search for the ways to limit and constrain interpretation, but if the example of my colleague and his student can be generalized (and obviously I think it can be), what they are searching for is never not already found. In short, my message to them is finally not challenging, but consoling—not to worry.

Murray Krieger

b. 1923

Murray Krieger's recent work (for his earlier see *CTSP*, pp. 1223–49) has been an effort to mediate between the earlier New Criticism, of which he was a student and shrewd analyst, and contemporary poststructuralism. It has always been his tendency to seek to enlarge his own theoretical position in order to encompass those most recent insights worth maintaining. If the New Criticism implied a theory of the "presence" of the signified in the signifier, even of the referent, in its treatment of the poem as an aesthetically closed object, the poststructuralists held for "absence" and radical openness. Krieger's new argument is (as in fact the earlier one had implied) a paradox combining both presence and absence, closure and openness. The poem, for him, manages the momentary illusion of self-identity "in the teeth of the principle of difference." This illusion does not obliterate difference but rather recognizes difference within itself. The New Critics had made much of irony and paradox (see Brooks, *CTSP*, pp. 1041–48), and Krieger retains irony in the form of the paradox of presence/absence. Krieger's irony is that of the conscious fiction purposely rent by its own awareness of tentative presence and threatening absence. In a more recent essay than the one below, Krieger builds a defense of the symbol against the attack of *Paul de Man*. Taking his title from Keats's "Ode to a Nightingale," Krieger treats the poem as a "waking dream": "As a dream, the symbol creates for us a surrogate reality, claiming the completeness of an irreducible domain within its eccentric terms; although it also stimulates a wakefulness that undercuts its metaphoric extravagances and threatens to reduce symbol to allegory." Thus the poem contains the vision of its own paradox and is "self-demystifying," remaining within the symbolist aesthetic while at the same time fully aware of the void. This awareness Krieger has always appreciated as far back as his *The Tragic Vision* with its existentialist roots. Now the awareness is transformed into the terms of linguistically oriented thought. The qualities that Krieger gives to the poem he does not wish to accord to other verbal forms, holding to a traditional distinction between poetry and other discourse and thus writing an apology for the existence of "poetics."

Krieger's later works include *The Classic Vision* (1971); *Theory of Criticism* (1976); *Poetic Presence and Illusion* (1979); and *Arts on the Level: The Fall of the Elite Object* (1981). He has also edited (with L. S. Dembo) and written the introduction to *Directions for Criticism: Structuralism and Its Alternatives* (1977). The essay quoted above, "A Waking Dream; The Symbolic Alternative to Allegory," appeared in *Allegory, Myth, and Symbol*, ed. M. W. Bloomfield (1981). See *Murray Krieger and Contemporary Critical Theory*, ed. Bruce Henricksen, a collection of essays about Krieger's work.

AN APOLOGY FOR POETICS

First I should like to place my theory between the New Criticism and certain elements of post-Structuralism by revealing those assumptions it seems to share with each of these positions, which I see as radically opposed to one another. Despite the fact that my early work was largely fashioned by New-Critical predispositions and despite a lingering sympathy with some of their central literary objectives, I have in at least two ways sought to differentiate my thinking from the New Critics'. Perhaps these modifications were performed in part to immunize this theoretical tradition from the assaults of those who would see in it undeniable tendencies toward mystification, but I like to think that my own transformations of the New Criticism borrowed from—if they did not anticipate—assumptions about language which post-Structuralism has now made commonplace among us.

The New-Critical aesthetic rested totally on a prior commitment to formal closure as the primary characteristic of the successful literary object. Its dedication to organicism, or to the peculiar sort of "contextualism" which I have described in many places elsewhere, gave to the poem the objective of self-sufficiency or of microcosmic perfection which, New Critics would claim, was the ultimate realization of the formalistic tradition from Aristotle to Kant to Coleridge and the organicists who followed. All borrowings from the world of actions, values, and language—as well as the borrowings from earlier poems—were to be radically transformed by the poet working in, as well as through, his medium into a world of its own finality sealed from his personal interests as from ours. Indeed, those venerable terms, "disinterestedness," "detachment," and "impersonality," all could be invoked as assurances of the work's capacity to come to terms with itself. And yet, in its casuistic perfection, the world of the poem was to guide our vision by making itself normative of it. Consequently, although the existential was to be re-formed into aesthetic terms, through the work there was to be an existential projection after all.

AN APOLOGY FOR POETICS is reprinted from *American Criticism in the Poststructuralist Age,* ed. Ira Konigsberg copyright 1981 by the University of Michigan Press. By permission.

It has now been a number of years and a number of writings of my own since I have come to reject an exclusive commitment to aesthetic closure of the New-Critical kind. The New-Critical position derived much of its strength from the claim that organicism is all or none and not a matter of degree; consequently, the poem could not be considered part open and part closed, so that an anti-New-Critical adjustment could not be achieved simply by moving from the emphasis on closure to the emphasis on openness. Instead, through the introduction of notions like self-reference, illusion, and metaphorical duplicity, I argued for a paradoxical simultaneity of utter closure and utter openness.

The argument proceeded in the following way: those moments during which the fictional world betrays a self-consciousness about itself as fiction remind us of the illusionary nature of that "reality" which seeks to enclose us. By a kind of negative reference, this reminder implicitly points to the world which the poem explicitly excludes in order to affirm its own closure. The world may be reduced to the stage in front of us, but so long as we are aware that it is only the stage in front of us, there is a world outside threatening to break in. Thus the work of art, as its own metaphorical substitution for the world of experience beyond, is a metaphor that at once affirms its own integrity and yet, by negative implication, denies itself, secretly acknowledging that it is but an artful evasion of the world. This claim to duplicity permitted me to allow the work to celebrate its own ways and the ways of its language unencumbered, without denying the ways of the world and *its* language. The work's very retreat from referentiality acted paradoxically to point it, through negative reference, to the world it so self-consciously excluded.

The second essential assumption of the New Criticism was its preestablished commitment to the poem as fixed object—a commitment which has effectively been attacked by much post-New Criticism as mere fetishism. The arguments against such reification as an act of uncritical spatializing of the language process have been often enough rehearsed and are well known. We are by now well aware of the extent to which the New Critics neglected the relation of art to the social process as well as to the psychological processes of human creation and response as these are defined by the flow of language as a governing force in human experiencing.

I would hope that my own theorizing has reflected these concerns. I have increasingly tried to dwell upon the poem as an "intentional object" only, an illusion of a single entity created through the complicity of the reader who, sharing the author's habit of seeking closure, allows the work—even as he does his share in creating it—to lead him toward the act of sealing it off within the aesthetic or fictional frame that his perceptual training leads him to impose. The metaphorical habits he has learned—from childhood, from religion, from previous traffic with the arts—lead him to seek an apocalypse, an end to history, in the work as he seeks in it to bring chronological time to a stop.

Such has been the human use of myth—the quest for the myths we need—in the western aesthetic since Aristotle formulated the distinction between history and poetry as they relate to time and to beginnings, middles, and ends. In thus emphasizing the poem as a will-o'-the-wisp, I have meant to reintroduce the temporal element, the element of process and of human experience, into our understanding of the literary work as it is created by the poet and created complicitously by us. Because I want to see the work as functioning within the metaphorical apocalypse we allow it to create for us even while it remains the unexceptional piece of language (running back into the past and forward into the future) which it would be were it *not* for us as aesthetically conscious readers, I am necessarily tempted to look for evidence of a self-conscious duplicity in the work as we come upon it and as we, in effect, ask it to do these things.

But I do not suggest that through these workings the aesthetic becomes a game of now you see it, now you don't. Rather I see the work as touching and unlocking in us the anthropological quest for that which marks and defines every moment of a culture's vision as well as of its inner skepticism that undoes its visionary reality with a "real" reality which is no less illusionary. The making and unmaking of our metaphors, our mythic equations, in experience as in art only reveal the primacy of the operation of the aesthetic in us all—and perhaps explain the extent to which our drive for art is accompanied by a cognitive itch which even the experience of art itself never quite eases, so that the need to experience more art happily remains.

These differences from the New Criticism allow me, I hope, to escape the difficulties arising out of its epistemological naiveté, leaving me less uncomfortable as I contemplate currently more fashionable theories about language with which I share large areas of agreement. Since the ascendancy of Structuralism more than a decade ago, critics in this country have had to come to terms with the Saussurean notion of verbal signs as arbitrary and as based upon the principle of differentiation. Thus what used to seem to be the simple matter of representation in language—the presence of a fixed signified in the signifier—is converted into a problematic. In the view of Structuralism, signifiers operate in a dynamic field of differentiation and have only arbitrary relations with their presumed signifieds.[1] A culture's confidence in the identity and inevitability of its verbal meanings, rather than its confronting their differentiation and arbitrariness, only testifies to that culture's self-mystifications as it falls prey to the metaphysical habit of logocentrism.[2] The wistful imposition of identity is accompanied by the ontological claim of presence, now to be undone by a shrewder philosophy of language that reminds us of the field of absence upon which the system of differences plays. Hence we have the rejection of metaphor for metonymy, and with the rejection of metaphor the removal of the ground on which the New Criticism rested. After all, how can one retain the central requirement of unity in metaphor—the overcoming of verbal differences by the fusion that overwhelms all boundaries that set words apart from one another—if the very basis on which words function subjects them indiscriminately to the Structuralist's "all-purpose differentiating machine" of which René Girard[3] has contemptuously spoken?

Though I may be persuaded about language as the marshalling of arbitrary and differentiated signifiers, I would hold out for the possibility that a single verbal structure can convert its elements so that we read them under the aegis of metaphorical identity with its claim to presence. It is this hold-out claim to what the poem can persuade us its language is doing which ties me still to the New-Critical tradition despite my concessions to Struc-

[1] See *de Saussure*. [Eds.]
[2] A term made popular by *Jacques Derrida*. [Eds.]
[3] See *Girard*. [Eds.]

turalist theory. I seek to maintain this power for creating poetic identity in language despite language's normal incapacities, so that I do not see Structuralism or post-Structuralism as precluding a poetics such as the tradition since Kant and Coleridge has been seeking to construct. I grant that the conception of metaphor, with its illusion of presence, may well be a secular conversion of the religious myth of transubstantiation, so that we may wish to reduce it at once to nostalgic mystification. And we may then see such mystification operating in all our spatializing of verbal relations which would bring linguistic temporality to a stop in its attempt to redeem time. By confessing the illusionary nature of this metaphorical operation we help perform on ourselves, I am suggesting a sophisticated view of language that knows of its metonymic condition and yet generates an internal play among its elements which appears to create a metaphorical identity that exists in the teeth of the principle of difference. It is an identity that knows the world of difference, a metaphor that has known metonymy, a spatial vision which sustains itself only through the acknowledgment that all may be finally nothing but time. If it functions as what I have elsewhere called a "miracle," it can do so because it proclaims itself as miracle only while acknowledging that it cannot occur.

Clearly, what is at stake is whether there can be any claim for distinctions within the realm of signifiers, whether we can break off segments of language called poems as if they have something special in them. One of the ironies of Structuralism, it has often been pointed out, is the undifferentiating way in which it asserts its principle of difference (it was just this problem which prompted the Derridean critique of Lévi-Strauss).[4] Eventually any poetics, but especially one like mine, must create its own ground by seeking discontinuities within textuality, at least for the momentary purpose of our aesthetic experience at the hands of a poem. This recurrent need, in our history, to establish a poetics perhaps accounts for the persistence with which theorists resort to a deviationist principle for distinguishing poems from other texts. And what for them sets poems apart must somehow be related to the power of converting differences into identities, the arbitrary into the inevitable—in short, verbal absence into verbal presence.

But these last years there have been assaults from several directions on the theoretical deviationism which for many decades had been a basic assumption for the dominant aesthetic. Some of these newer directions overlap one another significantly, and this is about what we should expect since most of them are related, one way or another, to that version of Structuralism which—in an anti-hierarchical spirit—rejects the literary work as an elite object and, consequently, rejects any collection of such works as a duly constituted canon.

First, the application of "information theory" is used by some as a monolithic model of interpretation which reduces all varieties of discourse to itself, searching out the cues for encoding (by the author) and decoding (by the reader) of the message which, as programmed discourse, the text presumably exists to communicate.

Second, the analysis of the process of signification leads others to apply their conclusions about the emptiness of signifiers—the absence of all signifieds from them—to words in poems as in non-poems. They judge the deviationist's claim to find a privileged fullness in poetic language to be a delusion and a fetish, a mystification. In poetry as in philosophy, they would deconstruct the metaphysical assumption that ontologizes verbal meanings.

Third, there are those who see all varieties of language as playing a similar role in culture's history, its way of meaning and of conceiving its reality. One can use what Foucault calls discursive formations to uncover the several archeological stages in our development.[5] And there are no exceptions among those discourses contributing to, or reflecting, those formations.

Fourth, theorists may seek to deny the apparent meanings intended by all texts, reducing them to rationalizations of the author's "will to power." These critics are not satisfied with stopping the deconstructive process once assumed stable meanings have been changed into a textual play among signifiers; they rather pursue that process beyond all texts—until textual pretensions are traced to the political or psychological motive that puts them forward as its verbal disguise. For these critics,

[4] Derrida's critiques of *Lévi-Strauss* appear in "Structure, Sign, and Play" (this volume) and *Of Grammatology*. [Eds.]

[5] Foucault, *The Archeology of Knowledge*. [Eds.]

whether they derive from Marx or Nietzsche or Freud, there is no innocent text, no disinterestedness in its production or its reception: instead, though the text offers itself and its fiction as all there is, the author means to use it to manipulate the actual world, to imperialize the world his way. And poems, again, are no exception.

Fifth, there are those who analyze all texts as originating in tropes or in narrative structures. Such analysis bestows literary categories upon nonliterary as upon literary texts, so that all texts are treated as similarly figured and similarly fictional. Consequently, there is no normal discourse from which poetic language could deviate, no neutral sequence of events on which we have not already imposed narrative and tropological shape. In effect, all language is deviation and there is no norm. Thus there is no neutral reference, so that we all speak in fictions, whatever truths we deludedly think we mouth. We have gone beyond Molière's Monsieur Jourdain who was surprised (and impressed) to learn that he had been speaking prose all his life; for in this view we have indeed, like all our fellows, been speaking—and writing—creative literature: poetry, fictions which we had been taking for sober referentiality. Where all are poems, there need be no special gift of poem-making.

Sixth, finally (and this also overlaps some of the others) theorists can consider all speaking and writing—or even, more broadly, all human activity—as indifferent parts of what I have earlier referred to as the seamless fabric of textuality, of course without distinctions within it: the world of words as text or even the world itself as text (the journal *Semiotexte* or the new, more radical journal, *Social Text*). We cannot, in this view, escape from experience, worldly and verbal or worldly *as* verbal, as a single capacious room composed of wall-to-wall discourse (to borrow Edward Said's phrase): the world as text, all of it just one hermeneutic challenge. Here is the farthest move away from any notion of the poem as a potentially discrete entity.

In all of these cases, the distinction-making power which would create a poetry and a poetics has been cut off. And, in light of the convergence of the several lines of recent theory upon these Structuralist or near-Structuralist notions, there would seem to be good reason to be persuaded by what they have taught us about the deceptive nature of sign-functioning and about the unified character of our apparently varied discourses at given moments in our culture. But I propose that we still worry about whether we wish to include literary discourse within this monolithic construct. Or, on the other hand, do we rather wish to see literary discourse as achieving a self-privileging exemption from that construct by manipulating all its generic linguistic elements until they are forced to subvert their own natures and do precisely what a Structuralist view of language would preclude them from doing: from functioning as signifiers that create and fill themselves with their own signifieds as they go, thereby setting this text apart from textuality-at-large as its own unique, self-made system? Without some such notion, are we capable of accounting for all that our greatest works perform for us? Do we not, further, have to recognize the peculiarly fictional, and even self-consciously fictional—which is to say self-referential—character of our most highly valued literature, even if we wish to grant to non-literature a fictionality and reflexivity which less sophisticated readings of would-be "referential" discourse did not used to grant? And are not literary fictions, with their peculiar self-reference, sufficient to separate the work which they characterize from the rest of discourse?

By urging the reflexivity of all discourse upon us, Structuralists and post-Structuralists have perhaps not leveled literature into common *écriture* so much as they have raised all *écriture* into literature. If these critics argue against the exclusiveness of poetry (that is, fictions, "imaginative literature") and rather seek to include a wide range of works by essayists, historians, philosophers, and even social scientists, they do so by treating these works as texts to which techniques of analysis appropriate to literary criticism may be applied. Even more, their techniques of deconstructing their non-literary texts, stripping them of their pretensions and reducing them to their naked fictionality, are to a great extent echoes of what poems have always been doing to themselves and teaching their critics to do to them. It is for this reason I suggest that, instead of the concept of literature being deconstructed into *écriture, écriture* has been constructed into literature. As a consequence, everything has become a "text," and texts—as well as the very notion of textuality—have become as ubiquitous as writing itself, with each text now to be accorded the privileged mode of interpretation which used to be reserved for discourse with the apparent internal self-justification of poetry.

I think, for example, of the work of Hayden White[6] on history writing, in which he sets forth a number of models of narrative structure based on the several tropes (or master figures), modes of discourse which he treats as reflecting the modes of human consciousness. Obviously, his reduction of every historian's truth claim to be the illusions of the poet's fictions, his obliteration of the realm of neutral fact and of discursive reference, will not please many historians who take their truth-claiming function seriously. Indeed, it may well seem to condescend to non-poetic humanistic texts for us to cut them off from any truth claim by restricting them to the realm of fiction and to the metaphorical swerve of private consciousness. Whatever the deconstructive mood may suggest, the historian may well want us to believe his version of history over the versions of others, or the philosopher to make us accept his claims about the nature of language or of reality, so that either may well resent our turning him into a poet *malgré lui*. The literary humanist should understand that it may not be taken exclusively as flattery if he brings historians, philosophers, and other humanists under the literary tent, especially since they are so intent on their more direct objectives. Words like "fiction" and "illusion" should teach us that there is a negative side (from the cognitive point of view) as well as a positive side (from the aesthetic point of view) to being a maker of literary fictions, and others may not be as comfortable with the designation as we literary people are. The sober scholar in the non-literary disciplines, who does his careful work and makes his claims to its justness, may well feel that his discipline and its distinctive ambition are being trivialized by being treated as a fiction shaped by his tropological bent. And such attitudes, that would protect the distinction between—say—history and poetry, have had the history of literary criticism on their side since Aristotle initiated the distinction between history and poetry in Chapter Nine of the *Poetics*. Indeed, even earlier, Plato had inherited and severely contributed to the war between the philosophers and the poets in many places in his work, beginning most notably, perhaps, in Book Two of the *Republic*.[7]

Such questions as those, for example, about the boundary between history or biography on the one side and the novel on the other, and about the applicability of narratological analysis to each of them probably remain serious questions, despite efforts to collapse all discourse into undifferentiated textuality and all textuality into trope and fiction. Surely, even after we have granted that some fictional obfuscation, with its rhetorical swerving, takes place outside the realm of literary fictions, we may allow some remnant of the free play of fictional reflexivity to be left to the literary intent, and may allow it to be replaced by more precise and clearly aimed objectives in, say, historical studies. Our temptation to tell the historian what he is doing ought to subside, at least a little, before his own perhaps less subtle sense of what he is about. And the finally free-floating inventiveness of self-conscious make-believe in the literary text should also in the end be acknowledged as a thing apart, despite our best efforts to see in what ways these differing kinds of texts, produced in response to such varying purposes, may reflect on one another. Aesthetic foregrounding may well go on outside poems, but we do condescend to our writers in all the disciplines when we ignore, or deprecate, the several responses which the body of their works appears to be soliciting from their different readers.

So I suggest we respond critically to the enterprise, currently so common among us, that would undermine the poem's differentness from other discourse. What this enterprise has been seeking to accomplish is a deconstruction of the metaphysical assumptions behind the traditional aesthetic and its resulting claim about the poem's ontology: the claim that the poem is a totalized structure, a self-realized teleological closure, a microcosm whose mutually dependent elements are cooperatively present in the fulfillment of their centripetal potentialities. Instead, the deconstructive move reduces the poem to a play of centrifugal forces such as characterizes general non-poetic discourse. Gaps appear everywhere—absences and emptiness—and we are to acknowledge these gaps for what they are, resisting our constructive tendency, imposed on us by centuries of self-deceiving habits of literary interpretation with their ontological assumptions, of trying at all costs to fill those gaps. For what we have taken to be the self-fulfilling and self-sealing poem is, like all discourse, mere vacancy, acknowledging an absence of substance, fleeing all presence as it leads us down the lines moving outward to the intertextual forces which become the code, but

[6] See *White*. [Eds.]
[7] See *CTSP*, pp. 19–23. [Eds.]

which permit no integrity, no free-standing sovereignty, to any would-be body operating within them. In this sense, the poem, as a construction of elements manipulated by art into a presence (according to the traditional older aesthetic), has been deconstructed into absences that can be made to point only to the code of writing itself.

But what of the need for closure, an aesthetic need felt by the human imagination, and the imagination's search for it in the objects of its experience? Should we not value, and set aside for separate treatment, those specially constructed objects that seem addressed to that aesthetic need? A criticism that preserves its own referential obligation to its literary object can treat poems as dislocations of language that enable language to create itself as a medium that can close off what Structuralists have shown to be normally open. The persistent impulse both on the poet's part to close the form he creates and on our part to close the form we perceive accounts for the internal purposiveness that, for Immanuel Kant, characterizes the aesthetic mode. Presumably it is this need to make or to find closure which leads us to the myth-making and, with it, the privileging of objects that recent deconstructionists would undermine.

The imagination's need to find closure may largely account for the role of the story—like that of the picture frame or the proscenium arch—in the history of culture. The inherent nature of narrative structure surely reveals a responsiveness to what Frank Kermode has called our "sense of an ending."[8] The satisfying ending is one that fulfills internally aroused expectations, that realizes the purposes immanent in the story. From Aristotle's concept of denouement or falling action to the formal finality called for by Kant, and in the formalistic tradition that is indebted to both, we find the imposition of a mythic ending, a structural apocalypse, which cuts off the fiction from history. It acts, in effect, as an intrusion of the spatial imagination on the radical temporality of pure sequence, shaping time into the separateness of fiction. Linear sequence is suspended, transformed into circularity.

But there is something in literature that also keeps it open to the world, to language at large, and to the reader. As we contemplate the verbal object through our culturally imposed habits of perceiving what is presented to us as aesthetic, we must deal with the two-sided nature of its words, now that they have been, in spite of their normal tendencies, shaped into a poetic medium: they try to work their way into a self-sufficient presence, and yet they remain transient and empty signifiers. This is the paradoxical nature of language as aesthetic medium, and both sides must be exploited. Language is able to create itself into a self-justified fiction, but, because it is also no more than language—just words after all—it is able to display a self-consciousness about its illusionary character. Language seems in our best poetry to be both full of itself and empty, both totally here as itself and pointing elsewhere, away from itself. It permits its reader at once to cherish its creation as a closed object, one that comes to terms with itself, and to recognize its necessarily incomplete nature in its dependence on us as its readers, on literary history, on the general language system, and on the way of the world. We can see its words as uniquely apart from the world and the world of language, while we see them also as blending into those worlds.

Not that I am claiming these special characteristics to be *in* literary works so much as they are products of our aesthetic habits of perception—when dealing with such works—which seek to find them there. And part of our aesthetic habit of dealing with fictions is its self-consciousness about the occasion that sponsors it. In other words, the literary work persuades us of itself as a special object even as we retain an awareness of the rather extraordinary activity we are performing in contributing to our own persuasion. It is not fetishism when we recognize the tentative conditions that encourage the closure we celebrate, and when we accept the openness that surrounds the moment of our commitment to the closed object.

It is under these provisional conditions that we have learned to commit ourselves to the aesthetic response and to project upon the poem our grounds for it. Thus these conditions also qualify and complicate our sense of presence—of signifiers that have filled themselves with the signifieds they have created within themselves—within the play of words before us. And, despite arguments of both Structuralists and post-Structuralists, the illusion of presence emerges for us from the written as well as the spoken words before us. But it is always a presence sponsored *pour l'occasion* and co-existing with our

[8] See *Kermode*. [Eds.]

awareness of the lurking absences that haunt both writing and speech (*écriture* and *parole*).

As has been suggested in post-Structuralist semiotics, the speaking voice may make us too ready to conceive the presence of the speaker, so that we concede too little to the anonymity of speech as it enters the network of all that is spoken or can be spoken; in consequence, so the argument runs, we would concede more if we were confronted by the silence of the apparently anonymous written page. But, on the other hand, a counter-argument might claim, speech may seem to be the more firmly tied to absence—the continuing fadings-away linked to temporal sequence—as the sounds dissipate in the air as they are spoken; further, the orphaned page, composed of visible (and invisible) traces left by an absent speaker, may nevertheless persuade us of a spatial simultaneity among its words as it takes its place within the physically co-present book. Let me turn the matter around again by adding that even speech, considered as a sequence of sounds, suggests a sensuous presence in its auditory phenomena that belie our sense of them as fleeting transparencies. As the poet dwells upon those characteristics, heard and seen, which turn words into sensory things, the signifiers can take on the weightiness of substance. In these ways, with the knowing cooperation of the reader-hearer, the word on the page *or* on the tongue can be made the occasion for our assigning a tentative spatial presence to it. But in remembering it also as being no more than word—the trace on the page, the buzz in the ear—we do not deny its temporality within the flow of our experience, worldly and linguistic: its elusive *un*presence despite our attempts to seize upon and fix it.

As I contemplate the possibility of conceiving speech as more likely to sponsor the feeling of absence than writing is, as well as the possibility of conceiving them the opposite way, I am aware that it has been my interest to dwell upon the poet's attempt to persuade us to break through to presence, whichever of the two is the case. I am aware, further, that in my career I have been concerned more with the presence of texts as discontinuous entities than with the speaking presence *in* texts of the authorial consciousness which is their point of origin. This fact only reveals my inheritance from the New Criticism and its obsession with isolated texts as well as my inheritance from the Anglo-American tradition dating from Bacon, which seeks to respond to empirical phenomena, rather than the French inheritance from Descartes, whose concern with the *cogito* and the resulting concern with consciousness can never long be shaken. It may be that the New Criticism has, after all, even shaped my differences from it just as, perhaps, critics of consciousness like Georges Poulet[9] have helped shape the thinking of the post-Structuralists who have excluded consciousness as a controlling origin for the text.

There is yet another emendation I would make to the post-Structuralist's critique as it affects my claim—an unmystified claim—to poetic presence. I would argue that there is a major difference—not noted in post-Structuralist theory—between the generic difficulty with presence in our logocentrism and the special difficulty with presence in the language of poetry. It is not noted because one must distinguish poetic from other discourse (by means of a deviationist aesthetic) before being able to see the different sort of presence constructed by the poem. I have pointed out the usual assumptions about transparent representation—a signified fixed into presence within its signifier—assumptions which, according to post-Structuralists, we see our language as making, thanks to its implicit metaphysical assumptions. It is this presence which is to fall victim to the post-Structuralist's deconstructive enterprise. As a proponent of a deviationist theory of poetry, I could join in this enterprise while holding out for a special presence which a poem can build into itself by subverting and reworking the materials left it by those discourses which post-Structuralists have deconstructed in order to reveal the absences within them. The metonymic character of the usual sequence of signifiers, with their differentiations, can be transformed by the poet (so I would claim), who manipulates his verbal elements so that they may function as metaphorical identities, creating a presentation of signifieds through the generating powers of the signifiers with which those signifieds are perceived as being one. This poetic presentation feeds itself into a fullness out of the gaps of the failed *re*presentations in non-poetic discourse. If Derrida calls attention to our need to correct the naive feeling of presence in all texts constructed in the logocentric tradition of the West, de Man complains of the poet's arrogant effort to

[9]See *CTSP*, pp. 1212–22. [Eds.]

achieve the monistic presence of symbolism instead of accepting the allegory which is the appropriate way of language.[10] Each of these denies simple presence by seeing all language as functioning in a similar way, but though neither would grant to poetry any privilege within the general realm of discourse, de Man's critique does attack verbal presence on rather different grounds, within the province of the self-privileging poet or the overreaching theorist who takes up the fight for privilege on behalf of the poet. And these are the grounds on which my own argument for poetic presence, without challenging Derrida's, can stand as an alternative to de Man's.

But the dream of unity, of formal repetitions that are seen as the temporal equivalent of juxtapositions, that convert the temporal into the spatial through the miracle of simultaneity—this dream persists, reinforced by every aesthetic illusion which we help create and to which we succumb. We cultivate the mode of identity, the realm of metaphor, within an aesthetic frame that acknowledges its character as momentary construct and thereby its frailty as illusion. But it allows us a glimpse of our own capacity for vision before the bifurcations of language have struck. The dream of unity may be entertained tentatively and is hardly to be granted cognitive power, except for the secret life-without-language or life-before-language which it suggests, the very life which the language of difference precludes. In poetry we grasp at the momentary possibility that this can be a life-in-language.

Let me suggest that, in our anxiety to resist the mystification of ourselves, we may concede too much to temporality when we grant it a "reality" which we deny to its rival category, space. Space, presumably, is an invention of the reifying act of mind in flight from confrontation with the world of fact which *is* the world of time. So the mystifications of the spatial imagination are, in the work of Paul de Man, deconstructed by our introduction of temporal facts. But we must wonder whether this deconstructive act is not a privileging of time that sets it outside the realm of mind and language while giving it ultimate control over both in spite of all our inventions. Is time any less a human category than space, to be given a secure ontological space which its own very meaning contradicts? Yet the spatial, as that which redeems time, must be taken as a delusion when considered from the temporal perspective, though—let us grant—this perspective may be no less fictional than the spatial. So the poem as language may well have a dual character, being seen at once as canonized text and as just more textuality, as words at once shaped into a palpable form of art and playing an undistinguished role in the network of discourse. This duality should not be broken up into separate choices: either a metaphorical delusion—the spatial simultaneity of the I AM—or the open flow of time which is to set the delusion straight. Instead, it is to be seen as two illusionary ways in which poetic texts seem at the same time to force us to see them as functioning. It is this self-conscious duplicity within both response and poem which leads me—despite whatever other changes my theory has undergone—to persist in seeing poetry still as a form of discourse whose functioning separated it from the rest.

In the original "Apology for Poetry," Sir Philip Sidney[11] sought to maintain the place of poetry though it was being threatened by an austere philosophy that shut it off from the truth and would allow it no other proper function. This attack would exclude poetry from the rest of discourse, while our current theoretical movements would too readily absorb it into the rest of discourse. Any theory devoted to poetry must today argue for a separate definition of the poem, thereby justifying its own right, within the realm of language theory, to function as a maker of claims for its subject. Thus my apology is not for poetry, but for poetics, the theoretical discourse whose existence, resting on the assumption that there *is* a poetry, is threatened with every denial of poetry's separate place. In this way, having begun my career by commenting on the "New Apologists for Poetry,"[12] I now find myself an apologist—I hope not altogether an older apologist—for poetics. I can make my apology, I am now convinced, only by making the tentative, self-undercutting moves that separate me from those older new apologists and may seem at moments to align me with those who refuse to grant a separate definition to poetry *or* poetics. But my hold-out separatist tendencies invariably win out, so that, with whatever phenomenological concessions, I remain an apologist after all.

[10] See *de Man*. [Eds.]

[11] See *CTSP*, pp. 154–77. [Eds.]

[12] The title of Krieger's first book (1956). [Eds.]

Charles Altieri

b. 1942

In *Act and Quality*, from which the selection here is taken, Charles Altieri develops a complex and sophisticated theory of literature, most strongly influenced by ordinary language philosophy and speech act theory. He begins with Wittgenstein's view that all affairs of language present us with "forms of life," learned in action and that what expressions "mean" is always conditioned by the means of expression or the method of projection actually employed. Altieri argues that writers and readers exhibit particular forms of competence, discernible in "procedures" that writers employ and readers must acknowledge as the very condition for recognizing that expressions are, in fact, significant and that the potential relation between writing and reading communities depends upon a "grammar" comprised of specific but flexible procedures. From this point of view, the condition of understanding a text or utterance is a knowledge of the relevant grammar by which ordered relations are established.

More specifically, Altieri argues that literature, viewed as a kind of action, characteristically involves an exemplary (and exemplifying) performance that makes a specific possibility of action, character, or evaluation publicly available. By thus making Wittgenstein's metaphor literal, literature is seen as a method of projecting "forms of life," with a distinctive grammar and sets of procedures by which valued qualities are exemplified. Altieri similarly adapts the distinction between linguistic competence and performance (see *Chomsky*) for specific literary use. Just as sentences recognized as belonging to a language may be evaluated according to degrees of grammaticality, they may also be evaluated according to degrees of acceptability; and in a similar way, we distinguish between texts and readings of texts both in their capacity to exemplify value and as performances that may be more or less perspicuous, felicitous, or interesting.

While Altieri's position requires complex critical analyses, it has the advantage of avoiding metaphysical arguments which presume either that literature must have a definable "essence" or that, because literature is fictive, it is therefore ontologically empty (and semantically indeterminate). Since a literary work is an institutional fact that comes into being in a complex but still definite set of relations, its mode of "being" is neither parasitic on an imitated model nor reduced to a single process of substitution under the notion of signification.

In the selection here, Altieri offers a critique of three characteristic arguments that maintain or imply that literature is inherently indeterminate. In each instance, his arguments offer shrewd appraisals of why the arguments themselves turn out to be indeterminate or self-defeating, while advancing his own case for a performative and procedural theory of literature. The three cases of psychological arguments (primarily "reader response" criticism), textualist arguments (primarily deconstruction), and historical arguments based on changing models of "literariness" all have similar problems that stem from inadequate conceptions of the relations that literary experience presupposes and makes possible. The first instance—the assumption that the "meaning" of a text is constituted by a reader—Altieri shows to be, first, trivially true inasmuch as texts only have meaning *for someone* but, second, following only from mistaking the experience of reading for the meaning of the experience. Wittgenstein shows that in the case of pain (or any immediate experience), to postulate "private language" is a non sequitur, since any language, as expressible, is by that fact public, just as the ability to relate the terms of the language to the experience is the condition of expressibility. Thus, the meaning of anything that can be expressed is not determined "subjectively," and, as Altieri notes, "The relevant opposition is not between the personally subjective and the objective, but between the personal and the impersonal, both of which admit public determinations." Similarly, textualist arguments create the illusion of indeterminacy by applying particular analytical procedures (most notably, a Saussurean analysis of signification as purely differential and arbitrary) without respect for situations and contexts in which the determination of meaning actually arises. In the final case, where indeterminacy seems to stem from historical changes, Altieri argues that the main problem is that the critic does not sufficiently acknowledge the complex structure of action in the text but assumes that ambiguity is indeterminacy, on the tacit view that determinate meaning must be expressed as thematic coherence.

What is perhaps most characteristic of Altieri's argument in *Act and Quality* is his insistence that one need not (and probably should not) abandon too quickly collections of critical practices, most notably the ideas of the New Critics about the dramatic particularity of literary texts, when they can be recovered as valuable analytical procedures, even (or especially) when they are dissociated from premature theoretical and ideological claims. It is on similar grounds that he argues on behalf of traditional humanism and its "classic" texts as offering paradigmatic examples, thereby creating "classes" of texts in which valued qualities in human experience remain available.

Altieri's work includes *Enlarging the Temple: New Directions in American Poetry during the 1960's* (1979); *Act and Quality: A Theory of Literary Meaning and Humanistic Understanding* (1981); and *Self and Sensibility in Contemporary American Poetry* (1984).

LITERARY PROCEDURES AND THE QUESTION OF INDETERMINACY

1. Three Indeterminacy Theories I Shall Criticize

If there is any doctrine that constitutes a shared ideology in recent literary studies, it must be the belief that substantial aspects of literary meaning are indeterminate. Where twenty years ago virtually every good graduate student could spin out intricate arguments demonstrating how verbal and image patterns articulated paradoxical themes in a literary text, his counterpart now learns to show how texts respond to perennial problems of language and authority by declaring their own indeterminacy or at least by rewarding a wide variety of different reading approaches.

My general discussion of semantic issues has obviously been directed against this position. Still, the risk of repetition is worth facing in order to take on the theoretical versions of indeterminacy that have shaped this climate.[1] I consider it an important test of my perspective that it can disclose and combat serious flaws in these arguments, and I find confronting them a useful contrastive strategy for exhibiting the values in a procedural approach, especially in the description it establishes of literariness as a specific way of focussing the performance of concrete actions for empathic and qualitative reflection.

Our efforts to establish a procedural definition of literariness give us a sense of what an alternative to indeterminacy might look like. Indeterminacy theorists rarely describe in a rigorous way what they oppose. At most, one garners a loose sense that their antagonists are either badly stated versions of organicism or reductions of meaning to thematic patterns. Let this discussion, then, be at least a challenge for them to test their weapons. But let me also clarify the target. In defending a concept of determinacy, I shall not argue that there is a single correct reading for every literary text, even if one takes *literary* in the restricted sense developed above. Determinacy is, as we shall see, a matter of degree and a function of possible communal agreement about assessment procedures. It is a matter of degree because for theory, at least, we must concentrate on probabilistic grounds and on discussions of the general shape of authorial purposes. There will always be indeterminate aspects of texts, like the meaning of Milton's "two-handed engine." But we can consider a text reasonably determinate if we can show that clear public constraints apply to the kinds of evidence that will make a difference for a community, and if there are grounds for agreeing on the level of specific details and on the hierarchy of relationships that establish authorial and dramatic purpose. A general case for determinacy, moreover, must show that in most cases we either have a basic sense of informing purpose or we know the kind of evidence (which may not be easy to get or to prove) which would resolve competing interpretations.

Determinacy is neither certainty nor propositional adequacy to facts. But there remain two theoretical ways of testing for it. Both are matters of judgment. A viable argument for explaining determinacy must describe a basic model of interpretation which postulates a more abstract or general form of synthetic operations than those which foster the conflicts used to justify indeterminacy theories. This shall be the role I ask the concept of performance to play, and this is why I need to contrast this concept to typical discussions of indeterminacy. There is, moreover, strong warrant for relying on a notion like performance because, as we have seen,

LITERARY PROCEDURES AND THE QUESTION OF INDETERMINACY is reprinted from *Act and Quality: A Theory of Literary Meaning and Humanistic Understanding*, by permission of the University of Massachusetts Press, copyright 1981.

[1] E. D. Hirsch is a cautionary example here. His *Aims of Criticism* (Chicago: University of Chicago Press, 1976), pp. 17–49, offers a convincing case against the most general indeterminacy arguments, by showing that if all discourse is indeterminate, there is no possible truth in saying so, because that statement too would be indeterminate. Hirsch has had little effect, however, partially because he does not take on the specific formulations of those theories which have some bite for literary issues and which can take subtle Nietzschean forms, stressing the critic's will to power. [Au.]

some semantic operation must be available which frees us from the tautological equation—only textuality, therefore no purpose and no determinacy. The second test involves negative judgments. One can claim a sufficient general model of determinacy with respect to literary texts if one describes a series of fundamental operations which competent readers take as basic to defeating an accepted reading. For, in knowing what counts against a reading, a community reveals implicit criteria it might not be able to articulate fully.

With these matters to contend with, I shall have to ignore arguments for indeterminacy based on considerations of historical change and cultural relativity. The basic theoretical issues involved have already been discussed with respect to meaning and significance and to questions of the limitations of cultural foreunderstanding. Moreover, a grammatical perspective on meaning easily handles specific matters of changes in genre conventions or in the meaning of words, because it insists that awareness of the historical dimensions of a text is a necessary feature of literary education. One is simply not a competent reader who does not know what "vegetable love" meant in the seventeenth century, or who is ignorant of the stylistic conflict between Williams and Eliot.[2]

Those theories I shall consider gain a good deal of their power from confusing and contradictory aspects of the New Criticism. The New Critics greatly expanded our sense of the semantic complexity of a text, but they did not develop adequate ways of showing how this information might be coherently processed.[3] As practical interpreters, they stressed rhetorical and formal features of literary discourse, while as spokesmen for the humanities, they insisted on literature as a special form of intense, complex, concrete experience. The claims to form seemed to give determinate status to a romantic, and ultimately unintelligible, sense of immediate experience, while the claims about experience seemed to circumvent the problems of circularity that attend formal, autotelic criteria for interpretation. We are now witnessing the inevitable breakdown of this unstable synthesis, with each pole claiming its own interpretive methods which necessarily lead to indeterminacy. Each of the models of indeterminacy I shall deal with derives a good deal of its authority from this condition. Psychological versions of indeterminacy, for example, emphasize the difficulty of attributing objective status to the complex experiential impact of literary language. Textualist versions of literary meaning, on the other hand, depend on notions of rhetorical form and the constitutive properties of language, which overdetermine appropriate interpretive contexts and render meanings logically, rather than empirically, unstable. The final model of indeterminacy takes as its focus the way texts themselves respond to dilemmas of correlating formal and experiential aspects of meaning, and, thus, present themselves as "writerly," or subject to a variety of incompatible thematic structures. Each theory in turn tests and clarifies a basic element in my argument—the status of the reading subject, the conditions for contextualizing evidence in order to attribute formal intentions, and the relative priority of action to theme as grounds for establishing meanings.

2. The Problem with Psychological Versions of Indeterminacy

There are two distinctive types of psychological indeterminacy theory with a surprising degree of congruence. There are self-consciously empirical developments of I. A. Richards' response theories, which insist that meanings for objects which are imaginatively experienced must be in large part created by the individual reader. The position is clear in the work of Norman Holland and Walter Slatoff and, I think, logically required by Stanley Fish's arguments about affective stylistics, although he denies

[2] On the determinate quality of historical features of style, see Nelson Goodman, "The Status of Style," *Critical Inquiry* 1 (1975): 799–811. On the limits of pluralist versions of indeterminacy with respect to historical issues, see Meyer Abrams, "The Deconstructive Angel: The Limits of Pluralism," *Critical Inquiry* 3 (1977): 425–38. [Au.]

[3] Paul de Man makes exactly this argument as justification for indeterminacy claims in the second chapter of *Blindness and Insight* (New York: Oxford University Press, 1971), abbreviated BI. For a very good description of how contemporary criticism still repeats the themes of New Critical theory which it claims to reject, see Gerald Graff, "What Was New Criticism," *Salmagundi*, no. 27 (1974): 72–93. [Au.]

it.[4] What these critics root in empirical psychology, Paul de Man's earlier writings derive from a phenomenological description of the manner in which an intentional consciousness constitutes meanings from physical signs. Here are Holland and Fish generalizing about literary meaning:

> Meaning—whether we are talking simply of putting black marks together to form words or the much more complex process of putting words together to form themes—does not inhere in the words-on-the-page but, like beauty, in the eye of the beholder. (PIP, 98)

> The stylisticians proceed as if there were observable facts that could first be described and then interpreted. What I am suggesting is that an interpreting entity, endowed with purposes and concerns, is, by virtue of its very operation, determining what counts as the facts to be observed; and moreover, that since this determining is not a neutral marking out of a valueless area, but the extension of an already existing field of interests, it *is* an interpretation.[5]

These generalizations depend on three assumptions: (1) that signs are truly objective only as physical data—"A poem taken purely objectively is nothing but specks of carbon on dried wood pulp" (PIP, 2);[6] (2) that the less scientific and referential an utterance is the more its emotive properties can only be reconstituted in individual experience—"a being with a character experiences reality only to the extent he can give it life within that character" (PIP, 161); and (3) that criticism is not objectively asssessable but rhetorically expresses individual desires, and consequently is most authentic when seen as self-analysis—"A reader uses the fine, subtle listening 'new' critics have taught these last decades to listen to himself and to others with the same attention to detail and nuance that formerly was reserved for literature as a separate entity" (PIP, 134).

What Holland takes as empirical, de Man derives from Nietzsche, Freud, and Marx: all representations or interpretations are essentially symptomatic epiphenomena of underlying primary structures of desire. Both Holland and de Man, then, place the individual at the center of meaning, but only de Man is sufficiently ironic to recognize that the determining force played by desire threatens our fictions of identity as well as our dreams of objectivity about literary works. De Man's "radical relativist" position on indeterminacy takes its departure from a phenomenological distinction between natural and human meanings that echoes Slatoff on scientific versus imaginative utterances and both Holland and Fish on the necessary imaginative recreation of mere objective marks on a page. Natural signs always have clear and repeatable meanings, because they hide nothing and follow established laws, while human utterances are always intentional, al-

[4] I have used as my basic text for psychological indeterminacy theories Norman Holland, *Poems in Persons: An Introduction to the Psychoanalysis of Literature* (New York: Norton, 1973), abbreviated PIP, and Paul de Man, BI. Also basic to this position is Walter Slatoff, *With Respect to Readers: Dimensions of Literary Response* (Ithaca: Cornell University Press, 1970). For further readings in Holland and later refinements of his position, see *5 Readers Reading* (New Haven: Yale University Press, 1975); "Unity Identity Text Self," *PMLA* 90 (1975): 813–22; and "The New Paradigm: Subjective or Transitive?" *New Literary History* 7 (1976): 335–46. Holland repeatedly denies that his view is a subjectivism and prefers the word *transactive,* but he certainly claims texts are indeterminate and locates the source of the indeterminacy in what he calls a reader's *identity theme,* a position I find hard finally to distinguish from subjectivism. [Au.]

[5] Stanley Fish, "What Is Stylistics and Why Are They Saying Such Terrible Things About It," in Seymour Chatman, ed., *Approaches to Poetics* (New York: Columbia University Press, 1973), pp. 148–49. Fish's other basic statement of indeterminacy principles is "Literature in the Reader: Affective Stylistics," *New Literary History* 2 (1970): 123–62. Fish, like Holland, refuses the kind of labels I apply here, but if readers create *what count as the facts,* we are pretty close to psychological subjectivism, however transactional. I quote here from his response to Ralph Rader's devastating critique of his work, both in "Fact, Theory and Literary Explanation," *Critical Inquiry* 1 (1974): 262–72, and in his response to Fish's response, "Explaining Our Literary Understanding," *Critical Inquiry* 1 (1974): 960 ff. Rader's work makes it unnecessary to consider Fish here, but I should point out that Rader's basic attack on Fish, for ignoring the conventional procedures by which we construct units of meaning, parallels my general concerns. [Au.] See *Fish.* [Eds.]

[6] This view of meaning as constructions from signs and therefore subjective is one of the fundamental themes shared by psychological and phenomenological approaches. See, for example, Fish, "Affective Stylistics," p. 140, and Georges Poulet, "Phenomenology of Reading," *New Literary History* 1 (1969): 53–68. [Au.]

ways both uttered from a point of view not entirely evident in the signs and dependent on the intentions of the interpreter, and therefore always problematic (BI, 10).[7] Intentionality, for him, is not, he says, simply a procedure that transfers content from a mind to a text and then to a reader, as it is for E. D. Hirsch. Rather, intentionality signs a verbal object with the presence of a desire that can never be determinately recovered (BI, 25), for intentionality means that the signs emanate from a point of view, or what Sartre called a surpassing of the object, that can only be recovered from other points of view. Claims about the unity of a text, for example, reside "not in the poetic text as such," for then intention would have the status of a natural sign; rather, they must be proposed "in the act of interpreting this text" (BI, 29). Neither author nor critic has a privileged position on the text, for each has a different spatio-temporal perspective on it and is caught up in one of the two kinds of infinite regress contained in the hermeneutical circle. First, hypotheses about the whole text must continually be modified and displaced by further experience of particulars, and, second, the self who interprets is continually being modified by his changing grasp of both his and the author's intentions (BI, 29–32).

I find these psychological theories of literary meaning extremely useful for elaborating the different ways in which the act of reading is conceived by a procedural approach that emphasizes competence. Questions of procedural competence arise here on the most fundamental epistemological level, and involve us in questions of what *subjectivity* and *objectivity* can mean. For it does not make sense to distinguish sharply between marks on a page as objective content and meanings which are then added by subjects—at least, when the procedure being discussed is the activity of reading. There need be no quarrel that from certain perspectives the fundamental objectivity of a sign resides in its physical properties. These perspectives, however, are usually specialized ones, remote from the kind of objectivity signs have in ordinary experience. Take a picture of a lion in a newspaper. How sensible is it to claim that objectively all we see are certain arrangements of dots and lines which we then subjectively interpret? What if the dots and lines are not substances at all, then do we objectively see only atoms and electrical forces? *Objectivity*, then, may be less an ontological term than one referring to what is fundamental and publicly shared in different modes of inquiry.[8] The kind of objectivity a scientist requires is different from that needed in ordinary behavior, but that does not make ordinary behavior more subjective; it simply makes it less precise, and therefore not an adequate standard for certain purposes. It is not the ordinary purpose of reading to be clear about the physical properties of words on a page. This is why simple reflection tells us that when we read, we do not ordinarily construe words from letters and empty spaces, nor meanings from words, but take the letters as direct signs of meaningful utterances (assuming, of course, that problematic cases do not arise). It is more difficult not to take letters as objects not transferring meaning than it is simply to read them, and there is obviously quite a gap between our ordinary sense of reading and the kind of behavior we notice when we feel we are subjectively construing such signs (perhaps as reminding us of pictures or hieroglyphs). Our usual meanings of *subjective* and *objective* do not apply to such primary processes as reading ordinary sentences.

The implications of this initial point become crucial when we recognize how a similar notion of objectivity leads Holland and Slatoff to base their analysis on an empiricism that ignores distinctions between natural and institutional facts. They assume that one can establish a theory of meaning by simply observing what readers do in reading. In a rough way, this observation procedure is adequate

[7] De Man stresses the subjective construction of meanings in large part because he is led to that position by his early work attacking Romantic dreams of a language that could parallel natural structures. See especially "The Intentionality of the Romantic Image," in Harold Bloom, ed., *Romanticism and Consciousness* (New York: Norton, 1970). De Man's later writings have shifted the forms of indeterminacy from intention to the metaphoric quality of literary texts, that is, from phenomenological psychology to semantics. This is clearest in "Semiology and Rhetoric," *Diacritics* 3 (Fall, 1973): 27–33, and "Theory of Metaphor in Rousseau's Second Discourse," in David Thorburn, ed., *Romanticism: Vistas, Instances, Continuities* (Ithaca: Cornell University Press, 1973), hereafter abbreviated TMR. [Au.]

[8] The clearest philosophical attack on the idea that words are objective signs which we then interpret is J. L. Austin's *Sense and Sensibilia* (New York: Oxford, 1962), pp. 84–142. For the notion of objectivity as procedurally or situationally determined, see chapter eleven of Austin's *How to Do Things With Words*. [Au.] See *Austin*. [Eds.]

for a physical science working within established paradigms. However, as soon as the phenomena in question involve education and the corollary possibilities of behavior being judged as inadequate, one must observe not only what people do, but the ways in which what they do is judged or defined by the relevant procedures. It follows from our earlier discussion of institutional facts that a scientist from another world could not explain the game of chess by simply observing how people play; he would need to know the traditions and purposes of the game and understand the possible and the good ways of playing it. It seems certain that this scientist could not learn what a promise is by observing a representative sample of promises. He might learn something about promising behavior, but it would be ludicrous to define a promise as a pledge which people seem to keep about seventy percent of the time.

I have made enough abstract claims about competence and procedures. Holland's methods enable us to put the case in concrete terms, for his questions and analyses obviously ignore the relevant issues needed in a description of reading and in understanding the grounds on which we judge the adequacy of such a description. There is, first of all, something very odd in asking one's subjects in an experiment intended to measure the reading of complex texts, "Well, how did you respond?" and "How does the thing make you feel?" (PIP, 70, 91). Not only are these questions heavily theory-laden, they ignore the kinds of considerations that distinguish meanings from simple associative responses. Again, imagine defining chess, or promises, or the enterprise Holland himself is engaged in by correlating answers to questions like these.

The complexities clarified by what Holland does not consider are most obvious in his analysis of one particular respondent, Saul, whose answers derive not from affective states but from his acceptance of aesthetic norms that sound very much like Ezra Pound (PIP, 90–95). Saul's responses, in short, are not immediate, but are mediated by a set of values he has derived from the institutions of literary discourse. Yet while these mediated responses are too complex for Holland's empiricism, they would be judged by most competent readers as naive reliance on a limited moment in the history of taste. We come around again to the complex issue of the nature and the levels of convention. If direct observations of reading activity could tell us the status of literary texts, there would be little point to locating Saul's ideology. But not only can we recognize it, we can see both why he says what he does and what he overlooks. In other words, we confront the facts that there is a history of taste and that there are recursive procedures based on more general conventions which enable us to criticize and to comprehend historical changes. This does not mean that there is a metaphysical essence of reading, for we probably never completely escape our culture. But it does suggest, once again, how flexible that culture is in allowing us to develop a self-conscious critical awareness of our limitations.

De Man is no empiricist. Nonetheless, his Sartrean view of intentionality allies him with Holland on a central thesis of psychological indeterminacy theories—an equation of the intensely personal with the subjective play of desires. De Man recognizes the irony of speaking about *self* at all in this context, since the self is probably a cultural construct, certainly not an empirical entity one can directly experience. Yet the same cultural assumption remains. As Holland puts it, "A being with a character experiences reality only to the extent he can give it life within that character" (PIP, 161).

The force of this claim derives from taking a tautology for a significant truth. Of course, for me to experience *x*, I must have the experience, but it does not follow that I make the meaning. I must personally attribute a meaning, but it is not I who determine what the meaning is. For if each agent determined what meanings to give words and situations, meaning would be entirely private. Holland and de Man confuse having a feeling (which is the act of a subject) with knowing what a feeling is.[9]

There are difficult issues of empirical psychology here, but they do not affect the semantic point made by the private language argument: to be able to speak about a feeling at all involves publicly determinate knowledge of how to relate linguistic con-

[9]I take this distinction from Stuart Hampshire, *Thought and Action* (London: Chatto and Windus, 1959), pp. 121–22. Hampshire's book and Anthony Kenny, *Action, Emotion and Will* (New York: Humanities Press, 1963) provide full explanations of how the philosophical attack on the positivist's referential/emotive dichotomy gives us nonsubjective ways of talking about emotional experiences. For another analogue of Hampshire's distinction, consider the intuitive differences between describing a literary work and describing one's response to it. [Au.]

ventions to overt situational details we learn to recognize in grammatical terms.[10] After all, we often redescribe emotions as we do intentions, a procedure only intelligible if we identify emotions from public contexts. Similar insights led Husserl to insist that intentionality is not a feature of personal relations to situations, but of a consciousness to a noematic object. In other words, Husserl flirted with idealism to preserve a distinction between the determinate relationships an active consciousness has to its objects and the necessarily negative or "unreal" features of subjective intentions later to be stressed by Sartre.

However, it is important to insist that denying the subjective base of our knowledge of emotions does not entail denying that emotions are deeply experienced by persons. The relevant opposition is not between the personally subjective and the objective, but between the personal and the impersonal, both of which admit public determinations. *Personal* is a term that measures involvement, not degrees of hermeneutic objectivity. Again, the relevant structures for the theorist are not ontological subjectivity and objectivity, but the different procedures evoked by different kinds of situations. Moreover, when we are dealing with institutional facts, we must recognize that structures of competence make our experience in large part rule-governed; actors assume internalized roles and do not merely express subjective biases. (The subjective may create particular ways of playing the roles, but these, too, if knowable at all, are publicly determinable.) The roles, nonetheless, can be performed with great personal intensity. One might argue, in fact, that the attack on subjectivity in Eliot's, and especially in Yeats', poetic derives from a sense that personal intensity increases in direct ratio to the subjective baggage one can jettison when he performs the conventions of reading.

3. Textualist, Semantic Models of Indeterminacy

De Man's recent work brings us to the second type of indeterminacy theory based on descriptions of the semantically overdetermined quality of linguistic acts. His vision of the failure of the New Critics to control the complexities they revealed leads to complex meditations on the instability of any context an interpreter might pose as an image of controlling form or purpose. For signification, especially in metaphoric discourse, complicates purpose by invoking endless possible paradigmatic sets and affective contexts. These multiplicities are doubled again by the contexts, metaphoric chains, and performative forces inscribed in the interpreter's discourse. To put de Man in the larger textualist frame needed to elaborate the general structure of this model: formalism bred the dream of complex informing structures, which we now must recognize, instead, as aspects of what Derrida calls *structurality,* the capacity to disseminate continual possibilities of structure that never resolve into a determinate context.[11] The simplest, and in some ways the most rigorous, case for reversing New Critical doctrine into visions of textualist structurality is presented by Arthur Moore's critique of *organic form.*[12] Form, he argues, can serve to delimit meaning only if we establish our notion of form independently of a given text. If I mean by form a *sonnet* or a *comedy,* then I have a fixed concept to apply to a text, a concept whose meaning does not depend on

[10] I cannot resist pointing out an obvious case of the dangers inherent in denying the link between the personal and established procedures. It turns out that in "The Significance of Frank O'Hara," *Iowa Review* 4 (1973): 102–04, I published a reading of "The Day Lady Died" which almost exactly parallels the one Holland gives the poem to show how his identity theme psychologically conditions his reading (PIP, 110–34). We can, in fact, easily separate in the reading Holland the professional critic from Holland the psychological subject. But the more interesting fact is the difficulty a psychological theory would have explaining both why our readings of the poem are so similar and why, nonetheless, our literary theories are so different. The similarity is easy to handle if one assumes we both know how to read poetry, and that the theorist using a poem as Holland does has no professional obligation to read the specific criticism (that would spoil what he is trying to demonstrate in the reading). [Au.]

[11] See Derrida's "Structure, Sign, Play," in Richard Macksey and Eugenio Donato, eds., *The Structuralist Controversy* (Baltimore: Johns Hopkins University Press, 1970), pp. 247–64. [Au.] Reprinted in this volume. [Eds.]

[12] *Contestable Concepts in Literary Theory* (Baton Rouge: Louisiana State University Press, 1973), pp. 155–232. It should be noted that Rader, in the essay cited above, makes essentially the same argument against formalism, but in the service of a sophisticated model for verifying interpretive procedures through the use of facts independent of formal analysis. The quote at the end of the paragraph comes from p. 174. [Au.]

what I take the text to mean. But as soon as we try a more organic notion of form, as a concept that establishes what is semantically relevant in a text, we enter a vicious hermeneutical circle that no phenomenological magic can make benign. Organic form is established by our sense of relevant particulars, and we have no facts independent of those we construct in our interpretation with which to control our hypotheses of semantical relevance. We combine advocate and jury, or, as Moore puts it, form becomes "no less and no more than the means by which" a critic "literally recreates the work of art from the potentialities of language."

If I am to represent the logic of textualist indeterminacy adequately, however, I cannot avoid returning once more to Derrida. It is, after all, only appropriate that a position ironically mirroring positivist criteria for secure names should repeat in semantic terms the dichotomy between reference and emotive, or, in this case, associative, discourse that inspired Richards' position.[13] Here I shall presume my earlier discussion of unstable names and concentrate on Derrida's argument that the iterability of writing makes context indeterminate and renders intentions unrecoverable:

> A written sign carries with it a force that breaks with its context, that is with the collectivity of presences organizing the moment of its inscription. . . . By virtue of its essential iterability, a written syntagma can always be detached from the chain in which it is inserted or given without causing it to lose all possibility of functioning, if not all possibility of "communicating" precisely. One can perhaps come to recognize other possibilities in it by inscribing it or grafting it onto other chains. No context can entirely enclose it.[14]
>
> In order for a context to be *exhaustively* determinable, in the sense required by Austin, conscious intention would at the very least have to be *totally* present and *immediately* transparent to itself and to others, since it is a determining center of context. (SEC, 192; italics mine)

Derrida's claims threaten the center of my arguments, since one can deny his radical opposition between certainty and scepticism only by arguing for probability conditions based on procedures—which in turn require that contexts and intentions be sufficiently determinate to indicate appropriate procedures. Without determinable intentions and contexts, there is no way to affirm a distinction between the ascriptive level of textuality and the purposes that characterize pragmatic uses of language.

Because we are dealing with a specific conceptual issue here, I will assume that one can take Derrida's statements as philosophical claims. Then I will try to show that Derrida poses the issues in ways that have very little relationship to the features of experience where problems of determinate meaning arise. Thus, when we do test his claims against common practices they are neither perspicuous nor accurate. Notice, first, the phrases I have underlined in the quotation above. These reinforcing adverbs insist on absolute criteria, which in effect put questions of meaning in a purely logical universe. Here Derrida (out of context) is his own best commentator: ". . . I become suspicious. This is especially so when an adverb, apparently redundant, is used to reinforce the declaration. Like a warning light, it signals an uneasiness that demands to be followed up."[15] I am not sure that Derrida is masking uneasiness, but there is certainly cause for suspicion of his adverbial claims. These claims insure the truth of his version of indeterminacy, but they also effectively banish his claims from any practical or testable discourse about meaning. It is tautologically true that all discourse has some degree of indeterminacy—to prevent this, each statement would have to catalogue all the facts, desires, and laws that might impinge upon it. But questions of indeterminate meaning, as they relate to the description of actual language behavior, must concern themselves with degrees of indeterminacy, and, consequently, with purposes and

[13] See Jacques Derrida, "White Mythology: Metaphor in the Text of Philosophy," *New Literary History* 6 (1974): 5–74, esp. p. 45, and "Différance," in this volume. [Eds.] The ironic positivism in Derrida has not gone unnoticed. See Warner Berthoff, "The Way We Think Now: Protocols for Deprivation," *New Literary History* 7 (1976): 599–618. [Au.]

[14] Jacques Derrida, "Signature, Event, and Context," *Glyph One* (Baltimore: The Johns Hopkins University Press, 1977), p. 182, hereafter abbreviated SEC. [Eds.]

[15] Jacques Derrida, "Limited, Inc.," *Glyph Two* (Baltimore: The Johns Hopkins University Press, 1977), p. 174, hereafter abbreviated LI. [Eds.] I note in SEC seven separate sentences relying on these reinforcing adverbs: pp. 174, 181, 182, 183, 186, 192, 194. [Au.]

contexts that create specific needs for intelligibility. Statements do not fail because they are not absolutely determinate, but because they are not sufficiently determinate for specific tasks.

Derrida's understanding of intention and context suffers from a similar idealization for the purpose of sceptical reversals. If intentions could ever be "totally present" and "immediately transparent," they would have to have the ontological status of the single objects Derrida and Russell demand as anchors for descriptive names. But who has ever seen a totally present intention? Again, Derrida asks us to suppose that meanings and contexts depend on the most problematic of properties, and, thus, he justifies a tautological scepticism. Yet his view of intention is neither plausible nor intelligible (nor accurate to Austin's).[16] A meaningful attack on intention would have to address the arguments of those, like Anscombe, who show how intention is not a psychological event, but a property we attribute to certain kinds of behavior. From this perspective, Derrida has the relationship between intention and context reversed. As John Searle points out in his powerful critique of what can be abstracted as philosophical claims in Derrida, conventions and contexts enable someone to form intentions to himself and to have them recognized. The intention to write a poem is less a locatable psychic event than a series of choices in a context to which reasons may be attributed.

Derrida cannot recognize the correlation between intention and context, because he has a similarly abstract view of context. For Derrida, contexts are essentially arbitrary frames for a discourse, independent of the speaker's purposes. Thus, he argues as if an utterance can evoke or be placed in an infinite variety of contexts, with no qualifying conditions. He claims, correctly, that an ordinarily senseless expression, like "the green is either," is not absolutely determinate as senseless, because it could make sense in some contexts, say as an example of agrammaticality: "The possibility of disengagement and citational graft" exists for every sign (SEC, 185). But possibility is not a normal consideration in interpretation. We do not determine meanings by treating sentences and contexts as independent of one another; nor are contexts necessarily carried along to other contexts simply because a statement is iterable. Contexts are part of the ways sentences come to mean in the first place. We consider "the green is either" to be senseless not in some absolute metaphysical world, but in terms of the ordinary contexts in which we imagine sentences occurring. The fact that the sentence can make sense in some contexts is a sign that we always read its sense through assumptions about appropriate contexts. Indeed, it is a strong argument against Derrida that he can so easily posit the contexts needed for giving sense to the utterance, and that he clearly recognizes how changes in context involve specific changes in what counts as determinate discourse. That different contexts are always possible simply makes no difference to the argument that in given situations we can be reasonably sure of what the relevant contexts are for establishing a sufficient degree of determinacy.

Let me try to link questions of intention, appropriate context, and iterability by developing a simple concrete example. Suppose I write a letter saying, "I will come next week." As a set of linguistic terms this statement is infinitely repeatable and "next week" not a specific temporal reference. Yet a reasonable person would only use this abbreviated statement if he thought the particular context of the letter sufficient for his purposes. He could always specify the date if he felt it necessary. More important, in order to gain an understanding of this letter adequate to act upon its message, there are many contexts and aspects of intention we do not need to know. We do not need to know other cases where the speaker has used the utterance, nor the contexts which made him the kind of person who might make this journey, nor the complex motives he might have in going. There are situations where these might be relevant, but usually not if we wish to understand the basic meaning. The statement is not indeterminate, even though its motives, causes,

[16] John Searle's attempt to refute Derrida, "Reiterating the Differences," *Glyph One*, pp. 198–211, is especially useful on the subject of intention and the problematic notions of writing and absence that support Derrida's claims. There is room, however, also to note the literary mythology informing, or at least leaving traces, in Derrida's speech acts about intention. The absolute demands for presence pose intentions as pure psychic moments of virginal innocence, in which the self might observe itself directly. But then writing comes like Satan to violate the bower with the rude strokes of convention and iterability. See especially SEC, pp. 191–92. [Au.]

and possible consequences might be and probably are. Imagine how long one could function in a human community, which is founded on probabilities, not certainties, if each time he received this message he didn't bother to pick the person up, because, after all, he doesn't see it as *exhaustively determinable* and is not sure of all the person's motives. Imagine how we could decide that the context is not sufficient—only by assuming that another probable context is the relevant one. It is true that, if we found this letter ten years later, it would be indeterminate as a speech act, though not as a semantic unit. This would be so not because the context is indeterminate, but because there is no relevant context at all. That is, the very conditions of uncertainty clarify the simple probability on which sense depends.

What we adduce about context pertains also to Derridean arguments about the displacing power of metaphor. Derrida claims, for example, that philosophical discourse is inherently unstable, because many of its central terms, like *idea, theory,* and *propre sens,* are inherently metaphorical and multiply contexts. But this assumes that metaphoricity is a property of words, rather than of uses. It ignores the possibility that contexts or conventions can give appropriate fixed senses to these terms, so that their metaphoric qualities are either placed or ignored. The examples I mentioned are by now dead metaphors: philosophers disagree not because the terms are inherently unstable but because they desire to employ them in different kinds of argumentative contexts, like behaviorist or mentalist ones. The terms are defined differently not because of their inherent properties, but because of their generality, which makes their specific meanings depend on an argumentative structure. Moreover, when we consider live metaphors, there need be no indeterminacy. Metaphors cannot easily be elements in referring propositions, but we can understand them as features of a specific expressive speech act. When metaphors displace or complicate reference, they usually do so for an expressive or hermeneutic purpose, and that purpose can normally be inferred from the situation. Metaphors are expressions of an action taking place through the utterance, and if we understand the situation we normally see why the metaphor is used. (In cases where the metaphor cannot be paraphrased, we understand its purpose as creating a certain kind of effect and we assess how effective it is—and here expressive success, not truth, is the relevant dimension of understanding.[17]

Let me demonstrate the determinacy of metaphor by exercising a bit of counterperversity on Paul de Man's brilliant reading of metaphor in Rousseau (TMR). Rousseau, he argues, claimed that speech originates from one man seeing another and describing him as a giant. Later, the man might recognize his similarity with the other and shift to a generic abstraction like *man.* But, de Man goes on, the expression *man* is actually less accurately referential than the metaphor, because it covers over all sorts of potential differences between the men. The metaphor *giant,* on the other hand, tells us nothing about the realm of objective facts, but, then, it does not pretend to and does not catch us up in bad faith as does the putative description *man.* The metaphor gives an honest expression of a mental state of a given man in a given situation, an expression which does not tempt us to false generalizations, because it is so clear as a particular action.

4. Indeterminacy Based on Changing Ideas of "Literariness"

I hope I have made it clear that there are no general reasons why contexts are not sufficiently determinate to allow public agreement on the basic nature of speech acts. One need not so much refute Derrida for this purpose as point out how his claims are largely tautological and self-enclosed. His arguments about meaning are ultimately empty, because they simply do not address the differences between linguistic possibilities and actual linguistic choices. He shows that language as language is indeterminate, because it admits of possible choices, but he does not show that once choices are made there are

[17] For support of my view of metaphor, see Donald Stewart, "Metaphor, Truth, and Definition," *Journal of Aesthetics and Art Criticism* 32 (1973): 205–18; Ted Cohen, "Notes on Metaphor," *Journal of Aesthetics and Art Criticism* 34 (1976): 249–59; and L. Jonathan Cohen, "The Role of Inductive Reasoning in the Interpretation of Metaphor," in Donald Davidson and Gilbert Harman, eds., *Semantics of Natural Language* (Boston: David Reidel, 1972), pp. 722–40. [Au.]

not probabilistic grounds for deciding what the immediately relevant choices and contexts are. However, while one can dismiss Derrida's relevance for general semantics, the case is not so clear for specifically literary issues. Here we must show that literary texts provide sufficient probabilistic contexts for determining meanings in both the worlds they represent and in the authorial act. Indeterminacy theories specifically devoted to literary matters are likely to prove more perplexing than those based on general psychological and semantic arguments. One must locate principles for synthesizing into a single hierarchy of relationships extremely dense semantic units organized by internal, self-referential contexts. Nonetheless, I have argued that there are procedural considerations that enable us to reconstruct these contexts by naturalizing the text as concrete performance for reflective purpose. The pressure of a third group of indeterminacy theories should allow me to clarify the provenance of this claim and to prepare for the next chapter's discussion of an intensional text grammar.

Because this third group of theories is concerned primarily with practical questions, it does not manifest the clear conceptual organization of the other groups. Thematic claims for indeterminacy may derive from a wide variety of contexts, for example, from a sense of modernity developed out of the conjunction of Nietzsche, Freud, and Marx (as in Edward Said's *Beginnings* and in Roland Barthes' more historical pronouncements), from Paul de Man's insistence that self-conscious writers use indeterminacy to mark the gap between the life of consciousness and the demands of the empirical world, or from Frank Kermode's claims for the inherent plenitude of classic texts that allows them to be reinterpreted according to the demands of different cultures.[18]

I have chosen as a representative example of these theories a recent essay by Frank Kermode on Hawthorne. The essay combines aspects of all the forms of thematic indeterminacy I have just mentioned, and it succinctly exemplifies the way Derridean concerns are domesticated, historicized, and psychologized in some of our best recent practical criticism. Kermode's theme is that Hawthorne is essentially a modern writer, because he recognizes that the very process of representing life in a fiction undermines the possibility of the writer's authoritatively interpreting his materials. Hawthorne employs the conventional typological structures which give an illusion of a writer's authority, but he carefully deconstructs any single thematic coherence within the typology—thus, he suggests that the experience presented can only be given coherence by an individual reader in effect creating his own text. The following comment, on *The House of Seven Gables,* suggests how Hawthorne's metacommentary self-consciously reinforces his awareness of the new hermeneutic world opened up by American scepticism about authority and historical recurrence:

> The text of the novel imitates him in this; its Gothic materials—lost maps, inherited courses [*sic*]—its magic, its confusion of the "traditionary" and the historical, its allegories cunningly too clear or too obscure—are all evasions of narrative authority, and imply that each man must make his own reading. The types inscribed on it are shifting, unstable, varying in force, to be fulfilled only by the determinations of the reader; in strong contrast, then, to the old Puritan types. So the text belongs to its moment and implicitly declares that the modern classic is not, like the book of God or the old book of nature, or the old accommodated classic, of which the senses, though perhaps hidden, are fully determined, there in full before the interpreter. In the making of it the reader must take his share. (HM, 436)

It is crucial to this sense of modernity that Hawthorne is not simply a complex writer; rather, he is

[18] Said gives a very nice formulation of the five expectations that characterize the classical models of meaning which modern views of intertextuality reject. See *Beginnings,* p. 162. Paul de Man's essay on Derrida in *Blindness and Insight* provides a good example of a critic trying to subsume Derrida's logical treatment of meaning into a historical and purposive view of the author's thematic awareness of the problems. De Man, in short, makes indeterminacy a possible authorial perspective, and, thus, implies that we can understand it as the action of the implied author. For Kermode, I will concentrate on one essay, "Hawthorne's Modernity," *Partisan Review* 41 (1974), 428–41, where his theory is less qualified than in his recent book *The Classic* (New York: Viking, 1975). I will abbreviate this essay as HM. [Au.] See *Said* and *Kermode.* [Eds.]

a consciously indeterminate one, refusing to give his materials any secure interpretations and forcing readers to make "the book according to the order and disorder of our own imagination" (HM, 439). It seems that authors, as well as critics, are trapped between an impossible dream of objective interpretations of experience, on the one hand, and, on the other, a hopelessly solipsistic process of generating fictions which can at best be honest about their own incapacity to understand how other minds make sense of the world.

Kermode's claims are based on a very interesting, and (for my purpose) useful, confusion. He fails to distinguish between an indeterminate text and a quite determinate textual act, which explores tensions that arise from attempting to interpret complex events by simple thematic categories or an insufficient typological grammar. Kermode does not ask whether difficulties of determining the text derive from his model of coherence or from the action presented, and he ignores the fact that it is consistent to offer a coherent, determinate account of a literary text as exploring or postulating an essential indeterminacy in its dramatic situation. What remains determinable is the nature and quality of the acts by which the author develops his claims and suggests their significance—this, at least, is what we buy when we stress competence as the capacity to naturalize a text in terms of a performance we reflect upon for its representative qualities.

In fact, if we look at what Kermode actually does in this essay, we will find strong confirmation for my hypothesis about competence. For, despite his explicit position, he, in effect, demonstrates how to construct a text as a performance. While he takes a share in making the text (an expression that reminds us of Holland's tautology about character), he does not, therefore, arbitrarily impose his own categories. Instead, he offers a very persuasive description of Hawthorne's authorial action that constitutes a comprehensive reading of the textual details. Kermode recognizes the limits of simple moral interpretations of Hawthorne's actions, and shows, instead, how the strands of Hawthorne's fiction make sense as a dramatization of the difficulty of making moral judgments in a social context torn between religious and secular schemes of interpretation. The real power of Kermode's reading is not to release us into subjective readings, but to show how subjective moral allegories only capture us in the hermeneutic trap Hawthorne is depicting. Kermode claims that the reader as interpreter must make his own arrangement of the text's shifting play of signifiers, but, by forgoing moral interpretation for description of Hawthorne's action, he manages to achieve a position where a kind of objectivity is possible, and where the inadequacy of other readings is clearly established. He does this by showing how Hawthorne's problems with typology themselves typify a recurrent human problem.

Kermode, too, typifies a recurrent problem that leads to and informs much of the current interest in indeterminacy. A variety of cultural and academic forces—the enervation of the New Criticism, the desire for relevance, a distrust of formal and aesthetic issues as not sufficiently absorbing for critical work—has led to equating determinate meaning with the possibility of coherent thematic interpretations of a text's details. This emphasis, in turn, fosters discoveries that literary texts are indeterminate. Thematic expectations lead interpreters to concentrate on whether an abstract conceptual model will fit the complexity of event and verbal texture in a work. The results are predictable, especially in a literary culture so aware of the tensions which I have discussed between representation and its other. Moreover, thematic analyses encourage indeterminacy theories, because in their straight form they make it difficult to claim distinctive cognitive properties in literary experience. What depth literary themes provide one can find better stated elsewhere, so it is tempting to root the value of literary experience in other properties—especially in literature's capacity to make themes ironic and to dramatize their inadequacy to concrete situations. (This move ironically repeats New Critical versions of paradox from different epistemological perspectives.) Then there are more subtle pressures at work. Good critics want to stress the complex and intense energies involved in reading a text—both out of respect for the text and out of the desire to perform their own talents. However, if one equates meaning with theme, there is little room now (after decades of interpretation) for the full play of a reader's energies, unless he concentrates on showing how the details contradict any easy generalizations and invite endless reinterpretation. We find this evident in Kermode's reading of the perennial modernism of the *classic* as permanently vital, because always capable of being reinterpreted. This emphasis on reinterpretation preserves the energy of classic texts by denying two of their central features—the necessary *pastness* of the classic, which makes its continuing relevance a testimony to perennial features of human experience, and the relationship between the qualitative depth of classic treatments of actions and their continuing power. It may well be that the term *classic* is significant because the works to which we apply it have the power of generating classes; that is, they become prototypes of basic recurrent modes for imaginatively organizing experience. What matters, then, is less the openness in semantic texture that allows reinterpretation than the depth with which actions are rendered and engage our energies. A text like the *Aeneid* can be read in much the same way Kermode reads Hawthorne—less because it is open to thematic reinterpretation, than because its action typifies perennial problems inherent in interpreting historical change. The implied author must come to terms with the contradictions between the Augustan ideal of the Pax Romana and the danger that the means needed to achieve that ideal threaten to undermine it by repeating the violence endemic to the cultures it wants to supplant; Aeneas himself must continually grapple with reading signs that invoke two contradictory symbolic codes (or texts, in Derrida's formulation), one based on the Trojan values on which he had formed himself, the other requiring faith in a destined new order.

Those very features which lead thematic criticism toward indeterminacy become essentially determinate properties in readings that emphasize dramatistic performative qualities. By contrasting a performance model to Kermode's theses, we can begin to see both what that model can account for and the implications it has for practical criticism. The basic terms for that contrast derive from Kant's attempt to distinguish the status of ideas or themes in art from their status in other modes of discourse: "By an aesthetical idea I understand that representation of the imagination which occasions much thought, without however any definite thought, i.e., any *concept*, being capable of being adequate to it."[19] One cannot be sure exactly how much formalism lies beyond Kant's claim, but it is possible to insist, as Wittgenstein does, that this different status of concepts stems from the fact that, in ordinary experiences, art works are not so much analyzed and interpreted as described and treated as performances. Performances, in turn, cannot be reduced either to verbal constructs or to their informing ideas. These alternatives both serve as means rather than ends, because they make it possible for an interpreter to reconstruct dimensions of an action in a situation. The reader needs interpretive strategies, but these are provisional ways into appreciation of the performance. They are neither substitutes for the concrete enactment nor its goal. Interpretive concepts function more as themes do in music than as explanations do in science or ethics. These concepts become what Whitehead called "lures for feeling"; they are means for bringing large matters to bear in intensifying aspects of a specific irreducible event or situation. One cannot rule out subjective contexts as possible lures for feeling, but for criticism, and ultimately for the reader who internalizes public standards, there remains the procedural test of convincing others that a particular way of conceiving the performance in the text articulates the fullest possibilities inherent in the words, situations, and formal patterns. The criteria for describing a performance, in short, are essentially those by which Kermode persuades us to include Hawthorne's metafictional concerns in our reading of his novels. A text, then, may be conceptually indeterminate because, as Kant says, it admits the interplay of many concepts. But this does not mean we choose among these concepts; rather, we try to establish the action in such a way that we can see how each might affect the nature and quality of what remains a single purposive performance.

Themes, then, contribute to the meaning of a literary text, but do not constitute the meaning. In one sense, this is obvious, because we treat texts as particulars, important as specific organizations of details rather than as primarily instances of generalizations. These texts depend on principles of organization and evaluation which are of a different

[19] *Critique of Judgment,* trans. J. H. Bernard (New York: Hafner, 1968), sec. 49, p. 157. For Wittgenstein's position, see *Lectures and Conversations on Aesthetics, Psychology and Religious Belief,* ed. Cyril Barrett (Berkeley: University of California Press, 1972), 28–40, and John Casey, *The Language of Criticism* (London: Methuen, 1966). The New Critics often tried to define a denotative referent for aesthetic ideas, and, thus, produced claims about truth to nondiscursive experiences. [Au.]

order of being, and are capable of organizing and using themes. In concrete cases, even with texts whose main purpose is to articulate or defend an idea, this means that as long as we view the text in literary terms—that is, as a significant, self-organizing particular—our largest category of explanation will be *act,* not *theme.* Thus, even with texts based on single organizing ideas, our concern is less with the determinate nature of the organizing ideas than with the purposes the ideas serve. We attend to the qualities of thought by which the ideas are articulated or applied to the abstract and concrete dimensions of the situation. We often find that the nature of the theme—say the idea of justice in *Paradise Lost* or of nature in the *Prelude*—cannot be abstracted from the text. Justice in *Paradise Lost* means the relationships drawn by the text among the various situations in which the concept is used. This, indeed, is why literary texts, as performed correlations among aspects of an idea, so readily transcend the ideological limitations of their historical genesis.

When we insist on the qualitative aspects of even heavily thematic texts, we see that there need not be much difference between classic or readerly texts and self-conscious modernist treatments of indeterminacy. Most literary texts matter because of the properties they hold in tension. These may be dramatic instances, where an author performs a capacity to make fixed ideas resonate in situations—as, say, in Donne's "Holy Sonnets" or in a novel like *Middlemarch*—or they may be situations where ideas themselves conflict and will not be reconciled with one another or with events. In both cases, the texts have determinate and vital existence to the extent that they focus our sympathies and our reflective beings on intense relationships between a human agent and a situation. Thematic criticism can deepen our awareness of that situation, so long as it does not propose too simple a conceptual substitute for it. Then, among other things, it encourages claims about indeterminacy as soon as other features are recognized. These claims are, virtually by definition, reductions of both the dramatic and the conceptual tensions which characterize the power of most texts to move us deeply while rewarding the mind's ability to understand what it is moved by.

5. How a Performance Model Can Claim to Resolve These Problems: The Authority of Actions

Much of my last argument may have seemed only a rehash of New Critical doctrines. It was that—determinedly and determinately—but with what I take to be the crucial difference that now this doctrine can be put on a concrete basis. Texts have properties of particularity, dramatic tension, and depth because we construe them as specific performances in situations which unfold in time for our sympathy and reflection. Moreover, we now have an imperative for returning to New Critical generalizations about the text as dramatic work, because we can see where the alternative emphasis on thematic content has led. With an essentially Burkean restatement of New Critical views, we can clearly handle what becomes problematic in Kermode's essay. Now we have another way of understanding how a reader's energies might be absorbed. Reading is only partially thematic interpretation. Equally significant are processes of making qualitative distinctions, assessing acts, and trying to deepen one's grasp of the agents' relationships to their specific and conceptual situations. If theme is central, energies are all connected with decoding operations. But these operations, as we have seen, have nowhere to go but into refined ironies, because the theory provides no other focus for sympathetic and reflective engagement. With action as our center, even the simplest themes can provide place and play for the most intense energies.

A stress on performance can also establish terms for locating and resolving the more general problems that lead to an easy reliance on notions of indeterminacy. Kermode's observations about Hawthorne, for example, can be shown to derive from a basic determinable feature of literary texts which modern writers tend to emphasize. A literary text typically blends two levels of action—a dramatic course of events, and a process of interpretation and judgment carried on by an implicit author, whom Geoffrey Hartman calls "the voice in the shuttle." Modern writers take advantage of this situation by calling attention to complex aspects of voice which can be set in conflict with the mimetic level. *Madame Bovary* here is the quintessential modern text, for it nicely plays off the authorial voice against Emma's dramatic plight. While she tragically pursues her banal desires, the authorial voice coldly distances itself from that tragic world by using elaborate artifice, grotesque plot manipulations, and obvious control over the dramatic, fictive subjects it creates in order to insist on its freedom from the ironic realm of desire. *Madame Bovary* is not open or pluralistic, but it demands of a reader who is to appreciate it fully that she remain open to the complex interrelationships between the two levels of action. The tensions Flaubert articulates, Kafka brings to one radical extreme, an extreme where indeterminacy is an important concept. For with Kafka, the authorial desire for an adequate stance from which to evaluate, or at least to handle, his dramatic materials becomes the basic action of the novel. There are always more allegorical possibilities arising on the expressive level than can be satisfactorily and coherently applied to the events of the story. But even here the point of Kafka's fables is not to elicit a variety of readings, but to dramatize consequences deriving from the difficulty of determining meanings for events.

Finally—once we can distinguish acts of performing problems involving indeterminacy from indeterminate texts—we can give an adequate description of what is at stake in the fashionable topic of a writer's authority. Kermode is typical of contemporary critics in assuming that authority depends on a writer's ability to make a determinate and accurate interpretation of his materials. It seems more probable, however, that a writer's authority resides less in his generalizations than in the qualities of human concern his text displays. What gives Hawthorne, Flaubert, and Tolstoy authority—and what denies it to Beaumont and Fletcher or Scribe or Vachel Lindsay—is the fact that the members of the former group make a world serious people can imaginatively inhabit, concern themselves with, and take delight in. Literary authority derives from making problems believable, not from solving them.[20] Indeed, had Hawthorne taken literally the only remarks Kermode seems to think are not indeterminate, had he really believed that "the reader may choose among these theories" (HM, 438), his rendering of the hermeneutic problems which perplex modern man would be far less compelling and his authority that much diminished. On matters like these it is not simply Kermode's authority, but that of literary traditions in general, which is ultimately at stake. So long as we insist that readers can choose freely among alternatives, we simplify and trivialize both hermeneutic activities and the objects that authorize our concern with that activity.

[20] There is a simple test for the superiority of a qualitative and question-oriented model of authority, as opposed to a thematic one. In *Beginnings*, Said does brilliant readings of the tension between a writer trying to authorize his text as an interpretation of experience and the pressure or molestation of that authority by the intractable facts of the world or pulls of connotative language. Yet his image of authority cannot handle the basic fact that we can distinguish different degrees of respect for a writer's authority precisely in the honesty and depth with which he presents the ironic forces that molest his desired projection of thematic meaning. [Au.]

Alice A. Jardine

b. 1951

Alice A. Jardine works at the juncture of Anglo-American and French feminist thought. The essay here became parts of the first two chapters of her *Gynesis: Configurations of Woman and Modernity* (1985), in which she expands the concerns of the essay into lengthy considerations of questions of the subject, representation, and fictions. She then proceeds to discuss the thought of Jacques Lacan, Jacques Derrida, and Gilles Deleuze, all three of whom have been involved in developing a language that has helped to shape French feminist thought. Following that, she studies a number of modern literary works in connection with this thought.

Jardine takes particular note at the outset of the important differences between Anglo-American and French feminism. Anglo-American feminist criticism has been concerned with the sex of the author, with "narrative destinies," the image of woman projected in texts, and gender stereotyping, gender being the term employed to describe the pressure of culture on sexual identity, while sexuality refers to biological identity only. French feminism has followed poststructuralist thought in its proclamation of the disappearance of the author (see especially *Foucault*) and the teleological narrative (as in the French *nouvel roman*). Characters have become merely name functions; the image has been unsettled, and sexual identity itself has been deconstructed. Indeed, as we shall see, there is question whether French feminism has not gone beyond feminism entirely and is not actually antifeminist. Clearly the scene of French feminism (if that is what it any longer can be said to be) is a scene of language study. American feminist studies of language have tended to examine language "externally," that is to say, empirically. In France the effort has been to explore signification "internally" by way of examination of such questions as the subject, the real, identity, and meaning. In addition to having a sexual identity, the author as a speaking subject is in question. Representation itself becomes a fantasy of Western thought. *Truth* and humanism are rejected, though there remains belief in a world from which *Truth* has disappeared.

Jardine suggests for the future, rather than a turn toward silence or religion in the face of all this, a "continual attention—historical, ideological, and affective—to the place from which we speak." She has concluded that we cannot pursue the question of sexual difference *within* the legacy of representation and its "comfortable conception of the speaking subject." In this she definitely sides with French feminism, but she is also aware of a certain practical worldliness in the Anglo-American feminist movement, though she is unable to accept the tacit assumptions about language and the subject which she thinks are made by American feminist critics and language scholars.

Jardine's term "gynesis" is the "putting into discourse of 'woman'." This is a process which she declares is beyond the subject, representation, and man's "truth." It is, the more we see it in operation in her writing, modernity or what Derrida called *écriture* and *différance*, itself. Indeed, "woman," being itself a word, is subject to the play of difference that detaches it from representation (in this view) and enters it into the chain of signification. "Woman" is, as a result, a metaphor of writing and of reading in the poststructuralist sense, the process that disrupts Western symbolic structures and logics. It is in the sense that this line of thought dispenses with the author and representation that Jardine's "gynesis" is possibly *beyond* feminism, at least feminism as it is inherited from the humanist and rationalist tradition.

In addition to "Gynesis," Alice A. Jardine has edited (with Hester Eisenstein) *The Future of Difference* (1980), a collection of feminist studies. She is also cotranslator of Julia Kristeva's *Desire in Language* (1980) and "Women's Time" (in this volume).

GYNESIS

In a discussion of the problems involved when "observing others," Paul de Man mentions in passing that, when addressing two cultures, "the distressing question as to who should be exploiting whom is bound to arise."[1]

In Paris, after almost three years of working closely with feminists and others, I am no longer sure either whom I am "observing," or who my "others" are. Given that in-between state, I would like to begin with the title of the MLA Special Session for which this paper was originally written: "New Directions in Feminist Critical Theories in France and the Francophone World."[2]

I will be sharing with you here some of my reflections on theories developed in France (I should say in Paris) over the past two decades. That much is clear. But the words "new directions," "feminist," and "critical" pose a problem for me. First, it is unclear that there are any "new directions" in French feminist thought right now—for *feminists in France* at least. After the outburst of theoretical enthusiasm and energy during the late 1960's and early 1970's, the French *Mouvement de libération des femmes* (MLF) experienced a series of splits, rivalries, and disappointments which have led them to stop, go back, think, read, and write again. In fact, the term "MLF" now legally belongs to only one group in France—"Psychoanalysis and Politics." And this group, according to its own literature and public stance, is most definitely opposed to feminism—as are many of the other women theorists, writing in France today, whose names are beginning to circulate in the United States. Who, then, do we mean by "feminist"? That word, too, poses a serious problem. Not that we would want to end up by demanding a definition of what feminism is and, therefore, of what one must do, say, and be, if one is to acquire that epithet; dictionary meanings are suffocating, to say the least. But if we were to take "feminism" for a moment as referring only to those in France who qualify themselves as feminists in their life and work, our task would be greatly simplified. For example, if I were to talk about feminist theorists in France, I would want to insist on what might be called the "invisible feminists," those younger women as yet not "famous" who are working quietly behind the scenes, in study groups and special seminars, trying to sort out and pick up the pieces left in the wake of the both theoretical and practical disputes of the last few years. Or I might invoke the feminists who are attempting to map out

GYNESIS first appeared in *Diacritics* 12 (1982). It is reprinted here by permission of Johns Hopkins University Press and Alice A. Jardine.

[1] *Blindness and Insight* (New York: Oxford University Press, 1971), p. 10. The context for this remark is provided by Claude Lévi-Strauss. [Au.]

[2] My thanks to Marguerite LeClézio for inviting me to present this paper at the 1981 MLA.[Au.]

some very new and long awaited directions under Mitterand's government; or the ones who have left France to work at the Université des Femmes in Belgium, or in the United States. But, increasingly, when in the United States one refers to "feminist theories in France" or to "French feminisms," it is not those women one has in mind. Perhaps this is because they are not, or are not primarily, working in feminist critical or literary theory, whereas theory is currently a locus of interest for American feminism. Feminist (literary) criticism, as such, does not really exist as a genre in France. To my knowledge, only three books published in France over the past few years could be categorized as feminist literary criticism: Anne-Marie Dardigna's *Les châteaux d'éros,* Claudine Herrmann's *Les voleuses de langue,* and Marcelle Marini's *Les territoires du féminin avec Marguerite Duras.*[3] Other women theorists whose work has had or is beginning to have a major impact on theories of reading, and who at one level or another are writing about women, at the very least do not qualify themselves either privately or in their writing as feminists and, at the most, identify themselves and their work as hostile to, or "beyond," feminism as a concept. Hélène Cixous, Sarah Kofman, Julia Kristeva, Eugénie Lemoine-Luccioni, for instance, belong to this group and their names are heard in the United States.[4]

I would even go so far as to say that the major new directions in French theory over the past two decades—whether articulated by men or women—posit themselves as profoundly, that is to say conceptually and in praxis, anti-feminist. That does not mean that they should be rejected or ignored by feminists. On the contrary.

But it does mean that those American feminists, including myself, whose reading habits have been deeply changed by contemporary French thought must remain attentive to what are, ultimately, some very complex problems of translation—in the most literal sense of the word as well as in its broader and more difficult sense, as the inter-cultural exchange of ideas: the specific problems inherent to the importation and exportation of thought.[5]

What follows may be seen as a gesture towards thinking through some of those problems. First I will attempt to clarify what I mean by the "anti-feminism" of contemporary French thought and, in so doing, explicate my own title. Then I will complicate things further by outlining briefly what I see as the three major topographies of that French thought—as explored by the male theorists there. Why insist on "the men" instead of "the women"? Because all of the women theorists in France whose names I have mentioned are, to one degree or another, in the best French tradition and not unproblematically, direct disciples of those men. That is not meant as a criticism, but, at the same time, those women cannot be read as if they were working in isolation—especially in France where the tradition of the "school of thought" or the "literary salon" is still strong. I should also mention that the questions and problems I am raising are grounded in a hypothesis that the "new directions" in contemporary French thought are, in their "inspiration" and "conclusions," an attempt to delimit and think through what is now loosely called "modernity" or, more problematically in the United States, "post-modernism." My feeling is that any "detour" of feminism through contemporary French thought is a voyage into that as yet still vague territory of *modernity* completely avoided, in my opinion, by Anglo-American feminist thought. The generic term "contemporary French theory" designates for me the first group of writers after the Frankfurt School to try to come to terms with the (threatened?) collapse of the dialectic and its representations which *is* modernity. Ultimately, the question I would want to put into circulation here would be this: are feminism and modernity oxymoronic in their terms and

[3] Claudine Herrmann, *Les Voleuses de langue* (Paris: des Femmes, 1976); Anne-Marie Dardigna, *Les Châteaux d'éros* (Paris: Maspero, 1980); and Marcelle Marini, *Les Territoires du féminin avec Marguerite Duras* (Paris: Editions de Minuit, 1977). [Au.]

[4] Luce Irigaray is a special case, one we will not be able to discuss in this essay, but will reserve for attention at a later date. [Au.]

[5] During the discussion following my presentation of this paper at the MLA, there was a lot of energy expended over the words "feminist" and "anti-feminist." It was almost as if the problems of translation addressed here could be resolved if everyone in the room could just come to an agreement about what feminism is—or is not. The problems with that (primarily Anglo-American) approach to interpretation are, of course, made abundantly clear by many of the French theorists mentioned here. What is important, they might say, is not to decide who is or isn't a feminist, but, rather, to examine how and why feminism—as both word and concept—may itself be problematic. [Au.]

terminology? If so, how and why? If not, what new ruse of reason has made them appear—at least in France—to be so?

Not long ago, Annette Kolodny wrote that "As yet, no one has formulated any exacting definition of the term 'feminist criticism'."[6] Like Elaine Showalter, she distinguishes between those women who write about "men's books" and those who write about "women's books." (Kolodny also mentions a third category—"any criticism written by a woman, no matter what the subject,"—but she does not pursue it, implying its inadmissibility to any feminist.) Feminist criticism, within those parameters, is as multiple and heterogeneous as the "methodologies" available for use. She adds: "[These investigations] have allowed us to better define the portrayal of and attitudes toward female characters in a variety of authors and, where appropriate, helped us to expose the ways in which sexual bias and/or stereotyped formulations of women's roles in society become codified in literary texts" [p. 75]. This short statement by Kolodny summarizes well, I think, feminist criticism in its most fundamental gesture: an analysis (and critique) of fictional representations of women (characters) in men's and women's writing.

If the author is male, one finds that the female destiny (at least in the novel) rarely deviates from one or two seemingly irreversible, dualistic teleologies: monster and/or angel, she is condemned to death (or sexual mutilation or disappearance) and/or to happy-ever-after marriage. Her plot is not her own and the feminist critic is at her best when drawing the painful analogies between those written plots and their mimetic counterparts in "real life."

Increasingly, women feminist readers reach the point where they can no longer read "the men." That is, they begin to find the repetition unbearable. This is true of both kinds of male fictions—"fiction" and "criticism." This limit, when reached, is particularly relevant in the case of criticism, however, when one realizes that the majority of male critics (in all of their incarnations) seem not to have read (or taken seriously) what feminist criticism has produced. They continue either to ignore gender or else to incorporate it into an untransformed reading system, with an ironic wink of the eye, a guilty humanistic benevolence, or a bold stroke of "male feminism."

This is perhaps one of the reasons why the focus on women writers (and critics) has given such fresh energy to feminist criticism: focusing on women writers, feminist critics can leave this repetition behind, feel that they are charting an unknown territory which, at the same time, is strangely familiar. This mixture of unfamiliarity and intimate, identificatory reading seems, indeed, to be the key to a new creative feminist style. This change in focus has, at the very least and undoubtedly, produced some of the most important feminist criticism to date.

Let this stand, then, as a brief outline of primarily Anglo-American feminist concerns: the sex of the author, narrative destinies, images of women, and gender stereotypes, are the touchstones of feminist literary criticism as it has developed, most particularly, in the United States.

When one turns to France, however, one learns that this bedrock of feminist inquiry has been dislodged: there, in step with what are seen as the most important fictional texts of modernity, the "author" (and his or her intentionalities) has disappeared; the "narrative" has no teleology; "characters" are little more than proper name functions; the "image" as icon must be rendered unrecognizable; and the framework of sexual identity, recognized as intrinsic to all of those structures, is to be dismantled.

We will be looking here at this new kind of inquiry where it intersects with what I am calling the fundamental feminist gesture. Of these intersections, there are three that seem to me particularly relevant.

The first concerns the word, "author," and more generally, the problem of the speaking subject. Lacanian psychoanalysis, Nietzschean and neo-Heideggerian philosophies in France, have shaken this concept apart. As Michel Foucault reminds us, "None of this is recent: criticism and philosophy took note of the disappearance—or death—of the author some time ago. But the consequences of their discovery of it have not been sufficiently examined, nor has its impact been accurately measured."[7] First, the "I" and the "we" have been

[6] "Some Notes on Defining a 'Feminist Criticism'," *Critical Inquiry,* Vol. 2, No. 1 (Autumn 1975), p. 75. [Au.]

[7] "What Is an Author?" (in this volume). [Eds.]

utterly confused: the "I" is several, psychoanalysis has shown; and, further, one of the major ruses of Western metaphysics' violence has been the appropriation of a "we" by an imperialistic if imaginary "I" (whole individual with an interior and exterior, etc.) The notion of the "Self"—so intrinsic to Anglo-American thought—becomes absurd. It is not something called the "Self" which speaks, but language, the unconscious, the textuality of the text. If nothing else, there is only a "splendid anonymity" or a plural and neuter "they." Contemporary fiction enacts this anonymity within a lottery of constantly shifting pronouns.

The assurance of an author's sex within this whirlpool of de-centering is problematized beyond recognition. The "policing of sexual identity" is henceforth seen as being complicitous with the appropriations of representation; gender (masculine, feminine) is separate from identity (female, male). The question of whether a "man" or "woman" wrote a text (a game feminists know well at the level of literary history) becomes nonsensical. A man becomes a woman [*devient femme*] when he writes, or, if not, he does not "write" (in the radical sense of *écriture*) what he writes, or, at least, does not know what he's writing. . . . No-one writes. "And behind all of these questions we hear hardly anything but the stirring of an *indifference:* 'What difference does it make who is speaking?'"[8] The feminist's initial incredulity faced with this complex "beyonding" of sexual identity is largely based on *common sense* (after all, *someone* wrote it?!). But is it not that very *sense* ("common to all," i.e. humanism) that the feminist is attempting to undermine? On the other hand, when you problematize "Man" (as being at the foundations of Western notions of the Self) to the extent that French thought has, you're bound to find "Woman"—no matter who's speaking—and *that* most definitely concerns feminist criticism.[9]

The second major intersection of importance here is the status and stakes of representations, where the tools of representation (and of feminist criticism)—narrative, characters—are recognized as existing only at the level of the fantasies which have entrapped us. To endlessly analyze those fantasies is to ask for repetition. It is the *process* which moves beyond/behind/through those fantasies—the enunciation and disposition of phantasies[10]—which must be examined. That "process" is attached to no self, no stable psychological entity, no content. And, here again, "theory" is presented as in step with a certain kind of contemporary "fiction."

The third intersection, and the most problematic for me personally, is the radical French requestioning of the status of fiction and, intrinsically, of the status of truth. One of the oldest metaphysical problems, this is the newest and most fundamental problem for modernity. What does the radical requestioning of the status of truth and/or fictions in theory (and fiction) in France imply for feminist criticism? The feminist critic is concerned about the relationship between "fiction" and "reality" (truth)—with how the two interact, mime each other, and reinforce cultural patterns.

These "new directions"—beyond the "Self," the Dialectics of Representation," and beyond (Man's) "Truth"—have not emerged in a void. Over the past century, those master (European) narratives—history, religion—which have determined our sense of legitimacy in the West have undergone a series of crises in legitimation. Legitimacy is part of that judicial domain which, historically, has determined the right to govern, the succession of kings, the link between the father and son, the necessary paternal fiction, the ability to decide who is the father—in patriarchal culture. The crises experienced by the major Western narratives have not, therefore, been gender-neutral. They are crises in the narratives invented by men.

To go back and try to analyze those narratives and their crises means going back to the Greek philosophies in which they are grounded and, most particularly, to the originary relationships posited between the *technè* and *physis, time* and *space,* and all the dualistic couples which determine our ways of thinking. And rethinking those dualistic couples means, among other things, putting their "obligatory connotations" into discursive circulation, making those connotations explicit in order, one hopes, to put them into question. For example, the *technè*

[8] Ibid. [Eds.]

[9] See *Cixous.* [Eds.]

[10] Here I maintain the distinction in English between "fantasies" (conscious) and "phantasies" (unconscious). [Au.]

and time have always connoted the male; *physis* and space the female. To think new relationships between the *technè* and *physis, time* and *space,* within an atmosphere of crisis, requires a backing away from all that has defined their relationships in the history of Western philosophy, a requestioning of the major topics of that philosophy: Man, the Subject, Truth, History, Meaning. At the forefront of this rethinking is a rejection by/within those narratives of what seem to have been the strongest pillars of their history: Anthropomorphism, Humanism, and Truth. And again, it is in France where, in my opinion, this rethinking has taken its strongest conceptual leaps, as "philosophy," "history," and "literature" attempt to account for the crisis-in-narrative which is modernity.

In France, such rethinking has involved, above all, a reincorporation and reconceptualization of that which has been the master narratives' own "non-knowledge," what has eluded them, what has engulfed them. This other than themselves is almost always a "space" of some kind, over which the narrative has lost control, *a space coded as feminine.* To designate that process, I have suggested a new name, what I hope to be a believable neologism: *gynesis*—the putting into discourse of "woman" as that process beyond the Cartesian Subject, the Dialectics of Representation, or Man's Truth. The object produced by this process is neither a person nor a thing, but a horizon, that towards which the process is tending: a *gynema.* This *gynema* is a reading effect, a woman-in-effect, never stable, without identity. Its appearance in a written text is perhaps noticed only by the woman (feminist) reader—either at the point where it becomes insistently "feminine" or where women (as defined metaphysically, historically) seem magically to reappear within the discourse. The feminist reader's eye comes to a halt at this tear in the fabric, producing a state of uncertainty and sometimes of distrust—especially when the faltering narrative in which it is embedded has been articulated by a man from within a nonetheless still existent discipline. When it appears in women theorists' discourse, it would seem to be less troubling. The still existent slippages in signification among feminine/woman/women and what we are calling *gynesis* and *gynema* are dismissed as "unimportant" because it is a woman speaking.

What I mean by the "anti-feminism" of contemporary French thought may now seem clearer. For feminism, as a concept, as inherited from the humanist and rationalist eighteenth century, is traditionally about a group of human beings in history whose identity is defined by that history's representation of sexual decidability. And every term of that definition has been put into question by contemporary French thought. In the writings of those French theorists participating in *gynesis,* "woman" may become intrinsic to entire conceptual systems, without being "about" women—much less "about" feminism.

First, this is the case, literally, insofar as contemporary thought in France is based almost entirely on men's writing and, most importantly, on fiction written by men. For example, a survey of such disparate writers as Jacques Lacan, Jacques Derrida, Gilles Deleuze—or Hélène Cixous, Luce Irigaray, Julia Kristeva—yields remarkably few references to women writers. (To women, yes; one even finds passing remarks on women theorists—Lou Andreas Salomé, Marie Bonaparte, Melanie Klein—but to women writers, no.) Lacan has much advice for women analysts, but only focuses once on a woman writer (Marguerite Duras)—as having understood his theory![11] Derrida, to my knowledge, never explicitly mentions a woman writer.[12] Deleuze and Guattari refer to Virginia Woolf as having incorporated the process of what they call *le devenir femme* in her writing—but "not to the same extent"[13] as Henry James, D. H. Lawrence, or Henry Miller.

The leading figure of "Psychoanalysis and Politics" and its women's bookstore *Des Femmes,* Cixous is perhaps the foremost theoretician in France on the specificity of "feminine writing" (which does *not* mean written by a woman). Yet it is not women

[11] Jacques Lacan, "Hommage à Marguerite Duras," in *Marguerite Duras* (Paris: Albatros, 1979). [Au.]

[12] Excluding Marie Bonaparte—essential to Derrida's critique of Lacan in *Le Facteur de la vérité*—I can find only three oblique exceptions to this observation. Oblique in that a *particular woman* is never named in any of the three references: a footnote to "Violence et métaphysique" in *L'Écriture et la différance* (Paris: Seuil, 1967) p. 228; his references to an article by Barbara Johnson in "Envois," *La Carte postale* (Paris: Flammarion, 1980), pp. 162–164; and his dialogue with Barbara Johnson à propos of her paper on Mary Shelley's *Frankenstein* in *Les Fins de l'homme* (Paris: Galilée, 1981), pp. 75–88. [Au.]

[13] Gilles Deleuze and Claire Parnet, *Dialogues* (Paris: Flammarion, 1977), pp. 55–60. [Au.]

writers who are the focus of her work. Her focus is on the male poets (Genet, Hölderlin, Kafka, Kleist, Shakespeare) and on the male theoreticians (Derrida, Heidegger, Kierkegaard, Lacan, Nietzsche). Because in the past women have always written "as men," Cixous hardly ever alludes to women writers; one recent exception has been her reading and public praise of Clarisse Lispector, whose narrative is more "traditional" than one might have expected.[14] Irigaray and Kristeva are uniquely concerned with analyzing the male tradition: from Freud to the philosophers to the avant-garde. The kind of empirical text-picking I have just indulged in is perhaps ultimately not very useful. But this textual lack of reference should at least be pointed out given our "intersections." For the second reason that *gynesis* is not necessarily "about" women is more abstract: women can (have) exist(ed) only as opposed to men within traditional categories of thought. Indeed, women (especially feminists) who continue to think within those categories are, henceforth, seen as being men. . . .

Let me now again briefly enumerate these three intersections, this time emphasizing the "sources" of *gynesis,* so that we may begin to see more closely why this accusation is made. Then I will discuss one male theorist who has had a profound influence on both feminist and anti-feminist thinking in France: Jacques Lacan. I will be emphasizing his work, in such a brief way, less as written by the man named Lacan than as read by a new generation of men and women theorists in France.

The Speaking Subject: The Positivities of Alienation[15]

The "Other" has been the major preoccupation of French thought for the last fifty years. In the United States, at least until very recently, that term has most often evoked Sartrean phenomenology and the inevitability of inter-subjective warfare. But while Americans were busy reading Sartre, French intellectuals were re-reading Heidegger and Nietzsche, becoming obsessed with Mallarmé, and the texts of such writers as Georges Bataille and Maurice Blanchot, and re-questioning Hegel's master/slave dialectic as elaborated in Kojève's reading.[16] These rereadings and the theoretical outburst of what is loosely called "structuralist theory" interlocked unevenly, but progressed together steadily towards a radical redefinition of "alterity" which directly refuted that of Sartre. The phenomenological "Self" and "Other" came to be seen as belonging with all of those Cartesian models of rational and scientific knowledge where "certainty" is located in the Ego—as "predator of the Other." And it is this Ego, no matter what its sex or ideological position, that came to be seen as responsible for our modern technological nightmare. It is also this Ego that the fictions of modernity (Artaud, Joyce, Mallarmé, Beckett) have been seen as attempting to explode. The result of this recognition has been an accelerating exploration of Man's Non-Coincidence-With-Himself through new theories of alterity. And parallel to this retreat of the All-Too-Human-Subject (both male and female), there has been a regenderization of the space where alterity is to be re-explored in language. The space "outside of" the conscious subject has always connoted the feminine in the history of Western thought—and any movement into alterity is a movement into that female space; any attempt to give a place to that alterity within discourse involves a *mise en discours de la femme.*[17] If an autonomous "I" or "he" can no longer exist then only an anonymous "she" will be seen to—as Heidegger might say—ex-sist.

[14] See Hélène Cixous, "L'Approche de Clarisse Lispector" in *Poétique,* No. 40 (1979). The reader might also want to refer to her brief interview with Michel Foucault on Marguerite Duras; "A propos de Marguerite Duras" in *Cahiers Renaud Barrault,* No. 89. [Au.]

[15] I am aware of the scandalous nature of using these "old words"—"positivities" and "alienation"—to qualify a general philosophical movement intent on abolishing positivism and phenomenological theories of alienation (*Entaüsserung* in Hegel). I am not sure whether the fact that these two words seem best to qualify a "certain teleology" of contemporary French thought is due to an extreme case of *paléonymie* (cf. Derrida, *Marges, La Dissémination,* and *Positions*) or whether the fact of such a general emphasis could seem obvious only to the feminist reader. [Au.]

[16] Alexandre Kojève, *Introduction to the Reading of Hegel: Lectures on the Phenomenology of Spirit,* assembled by Raymond Queneau, ed. Allan Bloom, trans. James H. Nichols, Jr. (New York: Basic Books, 1969). [Eds.]

[17] "put into the discourse of woman." [Eds.]

THINKING THE UNREPRESENTABLE: THE DISPLACEMENT OF DIFFERENCE

Representation is the condition that confirms the possibility of an imitation (mimesis) based on the dichotomy of presence and absence, the dichotomies of dialectical thinking (negativity). Representation, mimesis, and the dialectic are inseparable; they designate together a way of thinking as old as the West, a way of thinking which French thought, through German philosophy, has been attempting to re-think since the turn of the century. Between 1930–1960, the dialectic (and its modes of representation), as elaborated by the neo-Hegelians and redefined by the phenomenologists, was the major focus of French intellectuals and represented a major hope for reconstructing the world. An understanding of negativity—either as represented by the "idealist" or as redefined by the "Marxist"—would bring about the possibility of building a general science of contradiction. But there soon surfaced in France a movement towards redefining the functions of mediation elaborated by traditional Hegelians and Marxists, as well as a quickening sense of urgency about looking again at the relationship between those two systems of thought. That movement, which came into its full maturity after 1968, still pursues its quest for a conceptuality which would be non-dialectical, non-representational, and non-mimetic.

The destruction of the dialectic in France is, for our purposes here, where the process of *gynesis* becomes the clearest. For to de-structure or attempt to subvert the dialectic is to put the function of mediation into question. Lacan was the first to displace, slightly, the mediator in patriarchal culture—the father—from "reality" to the "symbolic," as well as the first to reconceptualize and re-emphasize new spaces "exceeding" the dialectic, twisting the dialectic into a knot. The philosophers-after-Lacan, especially Derrida, Deleuze, and Lyotard,[18] were to displace mediation even further. The *Aufhebung,*[19] recognized as mediating between Culture and Nature, Difference and Identity, is also seen as that which fundamentally defines Male and Female through hierarchization. Those philosophers will, therefore, in their radical displacement of mediation, set about a total reconceptualization of difference (beyond contradiction), self-consciously throwing both sexes into a metonymic confusion of gender. And, as with the demise of the Cartesian Ego, that which is "beyond the Father,"[20]—overflowing the dialectics of representation, unrepresentable—will be gendered as feminine.

[18] Jean-François Lyotard, author of *The Postmodern Condition* and other works. [Eds.]

[19] Usually translated into French as *relève* and into English as "sublation." [Eds.]

THE DEMISE OF EXPERIENCE: FICTION AS STRANGER THAN TRUTH?

Disarmed of the cogito and the dialectic, lost in a maze of delegitimized narratives, any question of "Truth" in/for modernity can only be a tentative one. It will therefore only concern us here to the extent that a certain definition of truth, based in an experience of reality, is intrinsic to feminism as a hermeneutic. That is, the notion that women's truth-in-experience-and-reality is and has always been different from men's and has consequently been devalued and always already delegitimized in patriarchal culture. And that if men are experiencing that delegitimation today, it can only be a positive step towards demystifying the politics of male sexuality. . . .

The major battle, in the wake of Freud, Nietzsche, and Heidegger, has been to unravel the illusion that there exists a universal truth which can be proven by any so-called universal experience and/or logic. Truth, therefore, can equal neither "experience" nor "reality" as those words have been traditionally understood; and therefore any discourse basing itself in either one is, in truth, an age-old fiction.

Henceforth, the theorists of/in modernity will begin a search for the potential spaces of a "truth" which would be neither true nor false; for a "truth" which would be *in-vrai-semblable.* For *vraisemblance* is the code word of our metaphysical heritage.[21] "Truth" can thus only be thought through

[20] A reference to Lacan's phrase "law of the father." [Eds.]

[21] From a psychoanalytical perspective, Jean-Michel Ribettes has maintained that it is also particularly male, belonging as it does to an obsessional rather than hysterical economy. Cf.: "Le Phalsus (Vrai/semblant/vraisemblance du texte obsessional" in *La Folle vérité,* ed. Julia Kristeva (Paris: Seuil, 1979), pp. 116–170. [Au.]

that which subverts it. The true must be thought strangely, outside of the metaphysical categories of opposition—or between them.

This approach involves, first and foremost, a relinquishing of mastery—indeed, a valorization of non-mastery. Secondly, the *true,* to be isolated in those processes anterior to, or in some cases, beyond the Truth as produced by the *Technè,* is that which can never be seen, which never presents itself as such but rather captures, points, withdraws, hides itself in its veils: and that true is "woman"—the "non-truth" or "partial truth" of Truth. Or, for others, "woman" is precisely that element which disturbs even *that* presupposition (Truth as castrated).

Whatever the strange intricacies of these new wanderings through the demise of Truth-In-Experience, "woman" is that element most *discursively present.* Julia Kristeva has called this new element a *vréel*[22]—a kind of "she-truth."

This "she-truth" has been put into discourse in new ways in France—hence the *gynesis* whose potential spaces I have had to outline so schematically here. The demise of the Subject, of the Dialectic, and of Truth has left thinkers-in-modernity with a *void* which they are vaguely aware must be spoken differently, and strangely. As "woman." Or *gynema . . .*

AMONG Cartesian orphans, Lacan is one of the best known explorers of the spatial contours of *gynesis.* In his Seminar XX, entitled *Encore,*[23] he elaborates, elaborately, how and why "woman" is that which escapes any form of universal logic, how and why "woman is not All." That is, he shows how, as opposed to Universal Man (the Self of Humanist thought), "woman" may be seen as the anti-universal *par excellence.* Woman is not All; she is excluded by the nature of words and things. There is something *chez elle* which "escapes" discourse.

But Lacan does not stop there. For if woman is not All, she nevertheless has access to what he calls a "supplementary jouissance"—beyond Man, beyond the Phallus. This "extra jouissance" is a substance, different from but not unrelated to "the quite expansive substance, complement of the other" described as "modern space": a "pure space, just as one says pure spirit" [p. 25]. Most importantly, this *substance jouissante* is of the order of the infinite; it cannot be understood consciously, dialectically, or in terms of Man's Truth—for it is what we have always called "God . . ."

"Feminine *jouissance*" will, therefore, be posited as the ultimate limit to any discourse articulated by Man. It is, however, only the first of a series of such limits, which, through metonymy, will all be gendered as feminine. For example, the limit of any discourse for Lacan is also the "true." Truth (capital T) can/could only exist as long as there is/was a belief in Universal Woman. The "true," like woman, is not All. And this "true," *inter-dit,* located as it is between words, between-the-lines, provides an access to what is perhaps the most important discursive limit for Lacan: the Real.

The Real must be treated carefully. For not to treat it carefully is to misjudge the force of Lacan's twisting of the dialectic and to return to a nineteenth century Freud through the back door. In Lacanian literature, the Real has no ontological foundation. It "is" neither Reality, nor History, nor a Text. The Real designates that which is categorically unrepresentable, non-human, at the limits of the known; it is emptiness, the scream, the "zero-point" of death, the proximity of feminine *jouissance.*

Further, the Real—like "feminine *jouissance*" and like the "true"—is *imprévisible.* Unseen and unforeseeable, it surges out of the unconscious, as terrifying as any God no matter what name the latter carries.

Is the unconscious, then, going to be gendered as being as feminine as the other limits of the symbolic which it seems to hold in store for us? Yes. Woman as Other is "in relationship to what can be said of the unconscious, radically the Other, [. . .] that which has to do with this Other" [p. 75].

But if Man's unconscious is "woman," what about women's unconscious? Here we arrive inevitably at a question addressed to Lacan by a feminist, Luce Irigaray's "scandalous question": is woman the unconscious, or does she have one?[24] Lacan will reply: "Both"—but only with regard to the male subject. Irigaray will not be satisfied with

[22] *La Folle vérité,* p. 11. [Au.]

[23] Paris: Editions de Seuil, 1975. [Au.] Page references to this work appear in brackets in the text. [Eds.]

[24] Cf. Luce Irigaray, *Speculum de l'autre femme* (Paris: Editions de Minuit, 1974), and *Ce Sexe qui n'en est pas un* (Paris: Editions de Minuit, 1977). [Au.]

that answer. But other women analysts will begin with this supposition in their attempt to define the "female subject"—at the coordinates of writing by men and feminine *jouissance*.

It is no accident that those analysts will confront that question through "literature." For is the modern question put to the literary text not the same as that asked about woman? Is literature our unconscious or does it have one? Lacan will again answer: "both." It has one to the extent that it does not know what it is saying. It is our unconscious to the extent that it is the space of literarity itself: *lalangue,* as the "cloud of language [which] makes [up] writing" [Lacan, p. 109]. Writing is that letter which escapes discourse as its "effect," just as *lalangue* is that which "is at the service of completely other things than communication" [p. 126]. Like the unconscious, the written text is a *savoir faire* with *lalangue* [p. 127].

This succession of feminine spaces is enough to make the woman reader dizzy. Is writing then going to be gendered as being as feminine as "feminine jouissance," the "true," the "Real," and the "unconscious"? Here Lacan stops. Beyond the realm of intersubjectivity, for Lacan, there can be no understanding. Lacan will call a halt to his feminine metonymy faced with literature itself—except to the extent that *lalangue* is necessarily maternal and that the "letter" always has what he calls a "feminizing effect."[25] In spite of Lacan's irritating paternalism, we must not forget that he consistently shied away from going beyond his own early warning that "the images and symbols *chez la femme* can never be separated from the images and symbols *de la femme.*"[26] If "woman" in his thought designates that which subverts the Subject, Representation, and Truth, it is because "she" does so in the history of Western thought. To assert that is perhaps to uncritically continue it. In any case, psychoanalysis alone can go no further than that recognition without rephenomenologizing its original conception. The next link in the feminine chain will be left to Lacan's Others.

One of those is Eugénie Lemoine-Luccioni.[27] She begins with Lacan's barring of universal woman (the woman): woman is not All. Woman is divided, partitioned; that is her specificity. Further, that this division-in-herself marks woman's specificity means that alienation is fundamental to her being-in-the-world (rather than merely fundamental to culture). For Lemoine-Luccioni—and this is the core of her argument—it is only this intrinsic partitioning in/of woman that is capable of explaining what we have known about women from the beginning of time. Hers is an extreme Lacanian case of "The man will always . . . the woman will always" as Stephen Heath points out.[28] This division-in-herself explains woman's narcissism [*Partage des femmes,* p. 35]; why she can't create, "even as a painter" [p. 165]; why it is men who are the philosophers and poets "We've known that since Dante" [p. 10]. It, in fact, explains everything—from woman's lack of talent for mathematics [p. 80] to her perennial modesty: "It is not in the nature of woman to expose herself" [p. 70].

In her second book, *Le rêve du cosmonaute,* Lemoine-Luccioni goes even further. There, she insists on how women in fact incarnate Lacan's woman-spaces. Women exist within his "feminine *jouissance*";[29] they attain the Real "more surely" than men [p. 61]. It is, above all, women who engender *lalangue* upon which the symbolic order is founded and upon which it will always depend.

Within this context, it comes as no surprise that feminism is denounced by Lemoine-Luccioni as a danger to the social contract itself. For if "woman" were to disappear, "so too would the symptom of man, as Lacan says. And with no more symptom, no more language, and therefore no more man either" [p. 10]. The only hope, therefore, is for women to revindicate, not their right to a discourse or to a look of their own, but rather to their difference-as-not-all.

What then would be women's place in the world? If women incarnate "woman" as the problem of identity, the discontinuity of the social contract, the symptom of Man, then "why not count on them to assume the irreducible difference that resists unification, since woman is there, and the sexual difference is there as well, and since woman alone can be the figure of division?" [p. 182]. Saving the world would seem to be up to women . . .

[25] Cf. "Litturaterre" in *Littérature,* No. 3, 1971. [Au.]

[26] Lacan, *Ecrits* (Paris: Seuil, 1966), p. 728. [Au.]

[27] Cf. Eugénie Lemoine-Luccioni, *Partage des femmes* (Paris: Seuil, 1976), and *Le Rêve du cosmonaute* (Paris, Seuil, 1980). [Au.]

[28] "Difference" in *Screen,* Vol. 19, No. 3 (Autumn 1978). [Au.]

[29] *Le Rêve du cosmonaute,* p. 49. [Au.]

Another woman analyst, Michèle Montrelay, while sharing the curious logical mixture of pessimism and optimism apparent in Lemoine-Luccioni, is less dogmatically Lacanian.[30] Her analysis, while remaining strictly loyal to the Lacanian doxa, does not fall into the same anthropological commonplaces as does that of Lemoine-Luccioni. This is in part because she is not primarily writing about women, but about something called "femininity." But it is also because she is closer to the literary text that Lemoine-Luccioni. Montrelay would seem to want to render Lacan's "woman" incarnate in a different way. Her "woman" is not partitioned, divided, in the world, but rather the locus of a "primary imaginary" dedicated to "feminine *jouissance*." And women are not necessarily closer to this primary imaginary than men. In fact, "Women's books [only] speak of this 'feminine' imaginary which men—poets, among others—possess" [p. 155]. According to Montrelay, it is the male poets, not women, who have provided us with an access to that imaginary—through writing.

Here is where Montrelay completes Lacan's feminine metonymy more thoroughly than Lemoine-Luccioni: "feminine *jouissance* can be understood as writing [. . .] this jouissance and the literary text (which is also written like an orgasm produced within discourse) are the effect of the same murder of the signifier [. . .] Is it not for this reason that, with Bataille, Jarry, Jabès, writing portrays itself as the *jouissance* of a woman?" [pp. 80-81].

The list of male writers continues throughout Montrelay's book. Women, writing, "do not leave this feminine substance on the page"—as men do. In any case, it would seem encouraging that woman writers are gradually becoming "less feminist." For, ultimately, Montrelay shares the same apocalyptic sentiment as Lemoine-Luccioni. Somehow humanity must avoid the inevitable trauma of doing away with "woman" as man's symptom—if we are to avoid bringing the social order, the order of language, crashing down.

Here we have reached a point where, if space permitted, we would want to 1. trace the trajectory of Lacan's "woman spaces" as unfolded by other male French theorists, even by those most overtly opposed to Lacanian analysis; and 2. follow how other women theorists, whatever their posture towards analysis, have, in varying degrees and from different political stances, insistently posited that women somehow incarnate those spaces. For example, if we were to return for a moment to the notion of writing-as-feminine, we would most certainly want to treat, at length, the work of the foremost theoretician of *écriture* in France: Jacques Derrida.[31] For there, Lacan's "feminine *jouissance*" (as not all, in excess, invisible, half-said), as "supplement," will be found to be intrinsic to a new, non-human, denaturalized body: not that of woman, but of the text as *écriture*.

For Derrida and his disciples, the questions of how women might accede to subjecthood, write surviving texts, or acquire a signature of their own are the wrong questions—eminently phallogocentric questions.

Rather, woman must be released from her metaphysical bondage and it is writing, as the locus of the "feminine question," that can and does subvert the history of that metaphysics. The attributes of writing are the attributes of "woman"—that which disturbs the Subject, the Dialectic, and Truth is feminine in its essence.

We would also want to look at the ways in which women theorists of *écriture,* like those of Lacan's "feminine *jouissance,*" have not hesitated to incarnate Derrida's "feminine operation" by/in women, if in very different ways. Hélène Cixous names Derrida's "writing-as-feminine-locus-and-operation": *l'écriture féminine.*[32] And she goes on to posit that if "feminine writing" does not require the signature of a woman, women, today, nonetheless, do have a privileged access to it. For Sarah Kofman,[33] women already incarnate Derrida's "feminine operation" (as undecidability, oscillation), an operation that will eventually put an end to all metaphysical oppositions, including that of men/women, and move towards a generalized feminine *jouissance*.

[30] Michèle Montrelay, *L'Ombre et le nom* (Paris: Minuit, 1977). [Au.]

[31] For Derrida's most extensive presentation of writing as "feminine operation," see his *Eperons: les styles de Nietzsche* (Paris: Flammarion, 1978). It has been translated into English as *Spurs* in the quatrilingual edition (Venice: Corbo e Fiore, 1976). [Au.] Also by the University of Chicago Press in a French/English version. [Eds.]

[32] Cixous' most extensive developments of *écriture féminine* as a concept have been in her seminars in Paris. But glimpses of the concept's debt to Derrida's work may be found, most particularly, in her "Le Sexe ou la tête", *Les Cahiers du GRIF* 13 (October 1976). [Au.]

[33] Cf., in particular, Sarah Kofman's "Ça Cloche" in *Les Fins de l'homme,* op. cit., pp. 89–116. [Au.]

For these women, feminism is hopelessly anachronistic, grounded in a (male) metaphysical logic which modernity has already begun to overthrow.

I HAVE tried to outline here some of the reasons why we might not want to qualify the "new directions" in contemporary French thought as feminist and, most especially, as feminist only when and because they are being developed by women. At the same time, I feel that French thought can be an extremely important interlocutor for what we call feminist literary criticism in the United States. For if, as I have only been able to suggest here, modernity represents a new kind of discursivity on/about/as woman (and women), a valorization and/or speaking of "woman"; and if we, as American feminists, are going to take modernity and its theorists seriously; then feminist criticism has some new and complex questions to address itself to.

Are *gynesis* and feminism in contradiction, or do they overlap and participate with each other in some way? In what ways might the text of *gynesis* be reintroducing certain very familiar representations of women "in spite of themselves"? That is, to what extent is that process designated as feminine absolutely dependent on those representations? Might it be that to posit that process—beyond the Subject, the Dialectics of Representation, and Man's Truth—as a process incarnated by women is to fall back into the very anthropomorphic (or gynomorphic?) images that the thinkers of modernity are trying to disintegrate?

Most importantly, if modernity and feminism are not to become mutually exclusive—and, at the same time, if feminism is not to compromise the quality of its attention to female stereotyping of whatever kind—what will be our strategy for asking those questions, and others?

New directions indeed . . .

Lillian S. Robinson

b. 1941

LILLIAN S. ROBINSON'S work is revolutionary, Marxist, and feminist. She was an activist student in the late sixties and early seventies, and in one of the essays in her collection, *Sex, Class, and Culture,* she alludes to being arrested for protest activities in that period. The activist background remains in her conception of criticism and of the cultural role of literature and the arts. She is critical of *Max Horkheimer* and *Theodor Adorno* for what she regards as an aestheticist and formalist (therefore bourgeois) rejection of popular art; she tirelessly advocates a criticism that will "serve the forces of change." In her 1976 essay "Criticism: Who Needs It?" she argues that such a criticism "assumes that to be a radical does not consist in holding certain opinions, but in learning to make these views the basis of concrete action."

It follows that Robinson's survey and critique of various forms of feminist criticism express dissatisfaction with feminist attempts merely to enlarge the "canon" in order to include women writers. Nor does she wish to stop with the development of alternative readings of literary tradition that reinterpret women or point out sexist ideology in canonized works. Rather, she would call in question, presumably by way of a Marxist critique, the notion of canonicity itself, implying that the categories of value themselves are outmoded and false, that the standards of literary value are themselves the problem that leads to exclusion not only of works by women but also of works of minority or oppressed peoples. What is important is that the experience of such people have a voice in literature. One of the ways this can come about is to call in question the division between fine and popular art (thus her dissatisfaction with Horkheimer and Adorno, who should know better). She projects a study of television that will attempt to "put together the pieces of what television tells about everyday life."

It may be added here that the problem of canonicity has not been the concern only of feminists. Indeed, as a literary concern it is an aspect of that powerful social thrust of our times in which many groups seek modes of self-identification and expression.

Lillian S. Robinson's essays through 1977 are collected in *Sex, Class, and Culture* (1978). She is author with four others of *Feminist Scholarship: Kindling in the Groves of Academe* (1985).

TREASON OUR TEXT: FEMINIST CHALLENGES TO THE LITERARY CANON

Successful plots have often had gunpowder in them. Feminist critics have gone so far as to take treason to the canon as our text.[1]

JANE MARCUS

THE LOFTY SEAT OF CANONIZED BARDS (Pollok, 1827)

As with many other restrictive institutions, we are hardly aware of it until we come into conflict with it; the elements of the literary canon are simply absorbed by the apprentice scholar and critic in the normal course of graduate education, without anyone's ever seeming to inculcate or defend them. Appeal, were any necessary, would be to the other meaning of "canon," that is, to established standards of judgment and of taste. Not that either definition is presented as rigid and immutable—far from it, for lectures in literary history are full of wry references to a benighted though hardly distant past when, say, the metaphysical poets were insufficiently appreciated or Vachel Lindsay was the most modern poet recognized in American literature. Whence the acknowledgment of a subjective dimension, sometimes generalized as "sensibility," to the category of taste. Sweeping modifications in the canon are said to occur because of changes in collective sensibility, but individual admissions and elevations from "minor" to "major" status tend to be achieved by successful critical promotion, which is to say, demonstration that a particular author does meet generally accepted criteria of excellence.

The results, moreover, are nowhere codified: they are neither set down in a single place, nor are they absolutely uniform. In the visual arts and in music, the cold realities of patronage, purchase, presentation in private and public collections, or performance on concert programs create the conditions for a work's canonical status or lack of it. No equivalent set of institutional arrangements exists for literature, however. The fact of publication and even the feat of remaining in print for generations, which are at least analogous to the ways in which pictures and music are displayed, are not the same sort of indicators; they represent less of an investment and hence less general acceptance of their canonicity. In the circumstances, it may seem somewhat of an exaggeration to speak of "the" literary canon, almost paranoid to call it an institution, downright hysterical to characterize that institution as restrictive. The whole business is so much more informal, after all, than any of these terms implies, the concomitant processes so much more gentlemanly. Surely, it is more like a gentlemen's agreement than a repressive instrument—isn't it?

But a gentleman is inescapably—that is, by definition—a member of a privileged class and of the male sex. From this perspective, it is probably quite accurate to think of the canon as an entirely gentlemanly artifact, considering how few works by nonmembers of that class and sex make it into the informal agglomeration of course syllabi, anthologies, and widely commented-upon "standard authors" that constitutes the canon as it is generally understood. For, beyond their availability on bookshelves, it is through the teaching and study—one might even say the habitual teaching and study—of certain works that they become institutionalized as canonical literature. Within that broad canon, moreover, those admitted but read only in advanced courses, commented upon only by more or less narrow specialists, are subjected to the further tyranny of "major" versus "minor."

For more than a decade now, feminist scholars

TREASON OUR TEXT: FEMINIST CHALLENGES TO THE LITERARY CANON is reprinted by permission of *Tulsa Studies in Women's Literature*, copyright 1983.

[1] Jane Marcus, "Gunpowder Treason and Plot," talk delivered at the School of Criticism and Theory, Northwestern University, colloquium "The Challenge of Feminist Criticism," November 1981. Seeking authority for the sort of creature a literary canon might be, I turned, like many another, to the *Oxford English Dictionary*. The tags that head up the several sections of this essay are a by-product of that effort rather than of any more exact and laborious scholarship. [Au.]

have been protesting the apparently systematic neglect of women's experience in the literary canon, neglect that takes the form of distorting and misreading the few recognized female writers and excluding the others. Moreover, the argument runs, the predominantly male authors in the canon show us the female character and relations between the sexes in a way that both reflects and contributes to sexist ideology—an aspect of these classic works about which the critical tradition remained silent for generations. The feminist challenge, although intrinsically (and, to my mind, refreshingly) polemical, has not been simply a reiterated attack, but a series of suggested alternatives to the male-dominated membership and attitudes of the accepted canon. In this essay, I propose to examine these feminist alternatives, assess their impact on the standard canon, and propose some directions for further work. Although my emphasis in each section is on the substance of the challenge, the underlying polemic is, I believe, abundantly clear.

The presence of canonized forefathers (Burke, 1790)

Start with the Great Books, the traditional desert-island ones, the foundation of courses in the Western humanistic tradition. No women authors, of course, at all, but within the works thus canonized, certain monumental female images: Helen, Penelope, and Clytemnestra, Beatrice and the Dark Lady of the Sonnets, Bérénice, Cunégonde, and Margarete. The list of interesting female characters is enlarged if we shift to the Survey of English Literature and its classic texts; here, moreover, there is the possible inclusion of a female author or even several, at least as the course's implicit "historical background" ticks through and past the Industrial Revolution. It is a possibility that is not always honored in the observance. "*Beowulf* to Virginia Woolf" is a pleasant enough joke, but though lots of surveys begin with the Anglo-Saxon epic, not all that many conclude with *Mrs. Dalloway*. Even in the nineteenth century, the pace and the necessity of mass omissions may mean leaving out Austen, one of the Brontës, or Eliot. The analogous overview of American literary masterpieces, despite the relative brevity and modernity of the period considered, is likely to yield a similarly all-male pantheon; Emily Dickinson may be admitted—but not necessarily—and no one else even comes close.[2] Here again, the male-authored canon contributes to the body of information, stereotype, inference, and surmise about the female sex that is generally in the culture.

Once this state of affairs has been exposed, there are two possible approaches for feminist criticism. It can emphasize alternative readings of the tradition, readings that reinterpret women's character, motivations, and actions and that identify and challenge sexist ideology. Or it can concentrate on gaining admission to the canon for literature by women writers. Both sorts of work are being pursued, although, to the extent that feminist criticism has defined itself as a subfield of literary studies—as distinguished from an approach or method—it has tended to concentrate on writing by women.

In fact, however, the current wave of feminist theory began as criticism of certain key texts, both literary and paraliterary, in the dominant culture.

[2] In a survey of 50 introductory courses in American literature offered at 25 U.S. colleges and universities, Emily Dickinson's name appeared more often than that of any other woman writer: 20 times. This frequency puts her in a fairly respectable twelfth place. Among the 61 most frequently taught authors, only 7 others are women; Edith Wharton and Kate Chopin are each mentioned 8 times, Sarah Orne Jewett and Anne Bradstreet 6 each, Flannery O'Connor 4 times, Willa Cather and Mary Wilkins Freeman each 3 times. The same list includes 5 black authors, all of them male. Responses from other institutions received too late for compilation only confirmed these findings. See Paul Lauter, "A Small Survey of Introductory Courses in American Literature," *Women's Studies Quarterly* 9 (Winter 1981): 12. In another study, 99 professors of English responded to a survey asking which works of American literature published since 1941 they thought should be considered classics and which books should be taught to college students. The work mentioned by the most respondents (59 citations) was Ralph Ellison's *Invisible Man*. No other work by a black appears among the top 20 that constitute the published list of results. Number 19, *The Complete Stories of Flannery O'Connor*, is the only work on this list by a woman. (*Chronicle of Higher Education*, September 29, 1982.) For British literature, the feminist claim is not that Austen, the Brontës, Eliot, and Woolf are habitually omitted, but rather that they are by no means always included in courses that, like the survey I taught at Columbia some years ago, had room for a single nineteenth-century novel. I know, however, of no systematic study of course offerings in this area more recent than Elaine Showalter's "Women in the Literary Curriculum," *College English* 32 (May 1971): 855–62. [Au.]

Kate Millett, Eva Figes, Elizabeth Janeway, Germaine Greer, and Carolyn Heilbrun all use the techniques of essentially literary analysis on the social forms and forces surrounding those texts.[3] The texts themselves may be regarded as "canonical" in the sense that all have had significant impact on the culture as a whole, although the target being addressed is not literature or its canon.

In criticism that is more strictly literary in its scope, much attention has been concentrated on male writers in the American tradition. Books like Annette Kolodny's *The Lay of the Land* and Judith Fetterley's *The Resisting Reader* have no systematic, comprehensive equivalent in the criticism of British or European literature.[4] Both of these studies identify masculine values and imagery in a wide range of writings, as well as the alienation that is their consequence for women, men, and society as a whole. In a similar vein, Mary Ellmann's *Thinking About Women* examines ramifications of the tradition of "phallic criticism" as applied to writers of both sexes.[5] These books have in common with one another and with overarching theoretical manifestos like *Sexual Politics* a sense of having been betrayed by a culture that was supposed to be elevating, liberating, and one's own.

By contrast, feminist work devoted to that part of the Western tradition which is neither American nor contemporary is likelier to be more evenhanded. "Feminist critics," declare Lenz, Greene, and Neely in introducing their collection of essays on Shakespeare, "recognize that the greatest artists do not necessarily duplicate in their art the orthodoxies of their culture; they may exploit them to create character or intensify conflict, they may struggle with, criticize, or transcend them.[6] From this perspective, Milton may come in for some censure, Shakespeare and Chaucer for both praise and blame, but the clear intention of a feminist approach to these classic authors is to enrich our understanding of what is going on in the texts, as well as how—for better, for worse, or for both—they have shaped our own literary and social ideas.[7] At its angriest, none of this reinterpretation offers a fundamental challenge to the canon *as canon;* although it posits new values, it never suggests that, in the light of those values, we ought to reconsider whether the great monuments are really so great, after all.

SUCH IS ALL THE WORLDE HATHE CONFIRMED AND AGREED UPON, THAT IT IS AUTHENTIQUE AND CANONICAL (T. Wilson, 1553)

In an evolutionary model of feminist studies in literature, work on male authors is often characterized as "early," implicitly primitive, whereas scholarship on female authors is the later development, enabling us to see women—the writers themselves and the women they write about—as active agents rather than passive images or victims. This implicit characterization of studies addressed to male writers is as inaccurate as the notion of an inexorable evolution. In fact, as the very definition of feminist

[3] Kate Millett, *Sexual Politics* (Garden City, N.Y.: Doubleday, 1970); Eva Figes, *Patriarchal Attitudes* (New York: Stein & Day, 1970); Elizabeth Janeway, *Man's World, Woman's Place: A Study in Social Mythology* (New York: William Morrow, 1971); Germaine Greer, *The Female Eunuch* (New York: McGraw-Hill, 1971); Carolyn G. Heilbrun, *Toward a Recognition of Androgyny* (New York: Harper & Row, 1974). The phenomenon these studies represent is discussed at greater length in a study of which I am a co-author; see Ellen Carol DuBois, Gail Paradise Kelly, Elizabeth Lapovsky Kennedy, Carolyn W. Korsmeyer, and Lillian S. Robinson, *Feminist Scholarship: Kindling in the Groves of Academe* (Urbana: University of Illinois Press, 1985). [Au.]

[4] Annette Kolodny, *The Lay of the Land: Metaphor as Experience and History in American Life and Letters* (Chapel Hill: University of North Carolina Press, 1975); Judith Fetterley, *The Resisting Reader: A Feminist Approach to American Fiction* (Bloomington: Indiana University Press, 1978). [Au.]

[5] Mary Ellmann, *Thinking about Women* (New York: Harcourt, Brace & World, 1968). [Au.]

[6] Carolyn Ruth Swift Lenz, Gayle Greene, and Carol Thomas Neely, eds. *The Woman's Part: Feminist Criticism of Shakespeare* (Urbana: University of Illinois Press, 1980), p. 4. In this vein, see also Juliet Dusinberre, *Shakespeare and the Nature of Woman* (London: Macmillan, 1975); Irene G. Dash, *Wooing, Wedding, and Power: Women in Shakespeare's Plays* (New York: Columbia University Press, 1981). [Au.]

[7] Sandra M. Gilbert, "Patriarchal Poetics and the Woman Reader: Reflections on Milton's Bogey," *PMLA* 93 (May 1978): 368–82. The articles on Chaucer and Shakespeare in *The Authority of Experience: Essays in Feminist Criticism*, ed. Arlyn Diamond and Lee R. Edwards (Amherst: University of Massachusetts Press, 1977), reflect the complementary tendency. [Au.]

criticism has come increasingly to mean scholarship and criticism devoted to women writers, work on the male tradition has continued. By this point, there has been a study of the female characters or the views on the woman question of every major—perhaps every known—author in Anglo-American, French, Russian, Spanish, Italian, German, and Scandinavian literature.[8]

Nonetheless, it is an undeniable fact that most feminist criticism focuses on women writers, so that the feminist efforts to humanize the canon have usually meant bringing a woman's point of view to bear by incorporating works by women into the established canon. The least threatening way to do so is to follow the accustomed pattern of making the case for individual writers one by one. The case here consists in showing that an already recognized woman author has been denied her rightful place, presumably because of the general devaluation of female efforts and subjects. More often than not, such work involves showing that a woman already securely established in the canon belongs in the first rather than the second rank. The biographical and critical efforts of R. W. B. Lewis and Cynthia Griffin Wolff, for example, have attempted to enhance Edith Wharton's reputation in this way.[9] Obviously, no challenge is presented to the particular notions of literary quality, timelessness, universality, and other qualities that constitute the rationale for canonicity. The underlying argument, rather, is that consistency, fidelity to those values, requires recognition of at least the few best and best-known women writers. Equally obviously, this approach does not call the notion of the canon itself into question.

We acknowledge it Canonlike, but not Canonicall (Bishop Barlow, 1601)

Many feminist critics reject the method of case-by-case demonstration. The wholesale consignment of women's concerns and productions to a grim area bounded by triviality and obscurity cannot be compensated for by tokenism. True equity can be attained, they argue, only by opening up the canon to a much larger number of female voices. This is an endeavor that eventually brings basic aesthetic questions to the fore.

Initially, however, the demand for wider representation of female authors is substantiated by an extraordinary effort of intellectual reappropriation. The emergence of feminist literary study has been characterized, at the base, by scholarship devoted to the discovery, republication, and reappraisal of "lost" or undervalued writers and their work. From Rebecca Harding Davis and Kate Chopin through Zora Neale Hurston and Mina Loy to Meridel LeSueur and Rebecca West, reputations have been reborn or remade and a female counter-canon has come into being, out of components that were largely unavailable even a dozen years ago.[10]

In addition to constituting a feminist alternative to the male-dominated tradition, these authors also

[8] As I learned when surveying fifteen years' worth of *Dissertation Abstracts* and MLA programs, much of this work has taken the form of theses or conference papers rather than books and journal articles. [Au.]

[9] See R. W. B. Lewis, *Edith Wharton: A Biography* (New York: Harper & Row, 1975); Cynthia Griffin Wolff, *A Feast of Words: The Triumph of Edith Wharton* (New York: Oxford University Press, 1977); see also Marlene Springer, *Edith Wharton and Kate Chopin: A Reference Guide* (Boston: G. K. Hall, 1976). [Au.]

[10] See, for instance, Rebecca Harding Davis, *Life in the Iron Mills* (Old Westbury, N.Y.: Feminist Press, 1972), with a biographical and critical Afterword by Tillie Olsen; Kate Chopin, *The Complete Works,* ed. Per Seyersted (Baton Rouge: Louisiana State University Press, 1969); Alice Walker, "In Search of Zora Neale Hurston," *Ms.*, March 1975, pp. 74-75; Robert Hemenway, *Zora Neale Hurston* (Urbana: University of Illinois Press, 1978): Zora Neale Hurston, *I Love Myself When I Am Laughing and Also When I Am Looking Mean and Impressive* (Old Westbury: Feminist Press, 1979), with introductory material by Alice Walker and Mary Helen Washington; Carolyn G. Burke, "Becoming Mina Loy," *Women's Studies* 7 (1979): 136–50; Meridel LeSueur, *Ripening* (Old Westbury: Feminist Press, 1981); on LeSueur, see also Mary McAnally, ed., *We Sing Our Struggle: A Tribute to Us All* (Tulsa, Okla.: Cardinal Press, 1982); *The Young Rebecca: Writings of Rebecca West, 1911–1917,* selected and introduced by Jane Marcus (New York: Viking Press, 1982).

The examples cited are all from the nineteenth and twentieth centuries. Valuable work has also been done on women writers before the Industrial Revolution. See Joan Goulianos, ed., *By a Woman Writt: Literature from Six Centuries by and About Women* (Indianapolis: Bobbs-Merrill, 1973); Mary R. Mahl and Helene Koon, eds., *The Female Spectator: English Women Writers before 1800* (Bloomington: Indiana University Press, 1977). [Au.]

have a claim to representation in "the" canon. From this perspective, the work of recovery itself makes one sort of *prima facie* case, giving the lie to the assumption, where it has existed, that aside from a few names that are household words—differentially appreciated, but certainly well known—there simply has not been much serious literature by women. Before any aesthetic arguments have been advanced either for or against the admission of such works to the general canon, the new literary scholarship on women has demonstrated that the pool of potential applicants is far larger than anyone has hitherto suspected.

WOULD AUGUSTINE, IF HE HELD ALL THE BOOKS TO HAVE AN EQUAL RIGHT TO CANONICITY . . . HAVE PREFERRED SOME TO OTHERS? (W. Fitzgerald, trans. Whitaker, 1849)

But the aesthetic issues cannot be forestalled for very long. We need to understand whether the claim is being made that many of the newly recovered or validated texts by women meet existing criteria or, on the other hand, that those criteria themselves intrinsically exclude or tend to exclude women and hence should be modified or replaced. If this polarity is not, in fact, applicable to the process, what are the grounds for presenting a large number of new female candidates for (as it were) canonization?

The problem is epitomized in Nina Baym's introduction to her study of American women's fiction between 1820 and 1870:

> Reexamination of this fiction may well show it to lack the esthetic, intellectual and moral complexity and artistry that we demand of great literature. I confess frankly that, although I have found much to interest me in these books, I have not unearthed a forgotten Jane Austen or George Eliot or hit upon the one novel that I would propose to set alongside *The Scarlet Letter.* Yet I cannot avoid the belief that "purely" literary criteria, as they have been employed to identify the best American works, have inevitably had a bias in favor of things male—in favor of, say, a whaling ship, rather than a sewing circle as a symbol of the human community. . . . While not claiming any literary greatness for any of the novels . . . in this study, I would like at least to begin to correct such a bias by taking their content seriously. And it is time, perhaps—though this task lies outside my scope here—to reexamine the grounds upon which certain hallowed American classics have been called great.[11]

Now, if students of literature may be allowed to confess to one Great Unreadable among the Great Books, my own *bête noire* has always been the white whale; I have always felt I was missing something in *Moby Dick* that is clearly there for many readers and that is there for me when I read, say, Aeschylus or Austen. So I find Baym's strictures congenial, at first reading. Yet the contradictory nature of the position is also evident on the face of it. Am I or am I not being invited to construct a (feminist) aesthetic rationale for my impatience with *Moby Dick?* Do Baym and the current of thought she represents accept "esthetic, intellectual and moral complexity and artistry" as the grounds of greatness, or are they challenging those values as well?

As Myra Jehlen points out most lucidly, this attractive position will not bear close analysis: "[Baym] is having it both ways, admitting the artistic limitations of the women's fiction . . . and at the same time denying the validity of the rulers that measure these limitations, disdaining any ambition to reorder the literary canon and, on second thought, challenging the canon after all, or rather challenging not the canon itself but the grounds for its selection.[12] Jehlen understates the case, however, in calling the duality a paradox, which is, after all, an intentionally created and essentially rhetorical phenomenon. What is involved here is more like the *agony* of feminist criticism, for it is the champions of women's literature who are torn between defending the quality of their discoveries and radically redefining literary quality itself.

Those who are concerned with the canon as a

[11] Nina Baym, *Women's Fiction: A Guide to Novels By and About Women in America, 1820–70* (Ithaca: Cornell University Press, 1978), pp. 14-15. [Au.]

[12] Myra Jehlen, "Archimedes and the Paradox of Feminist Criticism," *Signs* 6 (Summer 1981): 592. [Au.]

pragmatic instrument rather than a powerful abstraction—the compilers of more equitable anthologies or course syllabi, for example—have opted for an uneasy compromise. The literature by women that they seek—as well as that by members of excluded racial and ethnic groups and by working people in general—conforms as closely as possible to the traditional canons of taste and judgment. Not that it reads like such literature as far as content and viewpoint are concerned, but the same words about artistic intent and achievement may be applied without absurdity. At the same time, the rationale for a new syllabus or anthology relies on a very different criterion: that of truth to the culture being represented, the *whole* culture and not the creation of an almost entirely male white elite. Again, no one seems to be proposing—aloud—the elimination of *Moby Dick* or *The Scarlet Letter,* just squeezing them over somewhat to make room for another literary reality, which, joined with the existing canon, will come closer to telling the (poetic) truth.

The effect is pluralist, at best, and the epistemological assumptions underlying the search for a more fully representative literature are strictly empiricist: by including the perspective of women (who are, after all, half-the-population), we will know more about the culture as it actually was. No one suggests that there might be something in this literature itself that challenges the values and even the validity of the previously all-male tradition. There is no reason why the canon need speak with one voice or as one man on the fundamental questions of human experience. Indeed, even as an elite white male voice, it can hardly be said to do so. Yet a commentator like Baym has only to say "it is time, perhaps . . . to reexamine the grounds," *while not proceeding to do so,* for feminists to be accused of wishing to throw out the entire received culture. The argument could be more usefully joined, perhaps, if there *were* a current within feminist criticism that went beyond insistence on representation to consideration of precisely how inclusion of women's writing alters our view of the tradition. Or even one that suggested some radical surgery on the list of male authors usually represented.

After all, when we turn from the construction of pantheons, which have no *prescribed* number of places, to the construction of course syllabi, then something does have to be eliminated each time something else is added, and here ideologies, aesthetic and extra-aesthetic, do necessarily come into play. Is the canon and hence the syllabus based on it to be regarded as the compendium of excellence or as the record of cultural history? For there comes a point when the proponent of making the canon recognize the achievement of both sexes has to put up or shut up; either a given woman writer is good enough to replace some male writer on the prescribed reading list or she is not. If she is not, then either she should replace him anyway, in the name of telling the truth about the culture, or she should not, in the (unexamined) name of excellence. This is the debate that will have to be engaged and that has so far been broached only in the most "inclusionary" of terms. It is ironic that in American literature, where attacks on the male tradition have been most bitter and the reclamation of women writers so spectacular, the appeal has still been only to pluralism, generosity, and guilt. It is populism without the politics of populism.

To canonize your owne writers (Polimanteria, 1595)

Although I referred earlier to a feminist counter-canon, it is only in certain rather restricted contexts that literature by women has in fact been explicitly placed "counter" to the dominant canon. Generally speaking, feminist scholars have been more concerned with establishing the existence, power, and significance of a specially female tradition. Such a possibility is adumbrated in the title of Patricia Meyer Spacks's *The Female Imagination;* however, this book's overview of selected themes and stages in the female life-cycle as treated by some women writers neither broaches nor (obviously) suggests an answer to the question whether there is a female imagination and what characterizes it.[13]

Somewhat earlier, in her anthology of British and American women poets, Louise Bernikow had made a more positive assertion of a continuity and connection subsisting among them.[14] She leaves it to

[13] Patricia Meyer Spacks, *The Female Imagination* (New York: Alfred A. Knopf, 1975). [Au.]

[14] *The World Split Open: Four Centuries of Women Poets In England and America, 1552-1950,* ed. and intro. Louise Bernikow (New York: Vintage Books, 1974). [Au.]

the poems, however, to forge their own links, and, in a collection that boldly and incisively crosses boundaries between published and unpublished writing, literary and anonymous authorship, "high" art, folk art, and music, it is not easy for the reader to identify what the editor believes it is that makes women's poetry specifically *"women's."*

Ellen Moers centers her argument for a (transhistorical) female tradition upon the concept of "heroinism," a quality shared by women writers over time with the female characters they created.[15] Moers also points out another kind of continuity, documenting the way that women writers have read, commented on, and been influenced by the writings of other women who were their predecessors or contemporaries. There is also an unacknowledged continuity between the writer and her female reader. Elaine Showalter conceives the female tradition, embodied particularly in the domestic and sensational fiction of the nineteenth century, as being carried out through a kind of subversive conspiracy between author and audience.[16] Showalter is at her best in discussing this minor "women's fiction." Indeed, without ever making a case for popular genres as serious literature, she bases her arguments about a tradition more solidly on them than on acknowledged major figures like Virginia Woolf. By contrast, Sandra Gilbert and Susan Gubar focus almost exclusively on key literary figures, bringing women writers and their subjects together through the theme of perceived female aberration—in the act of literary creation itself, as well as in the behavior of the created persons or personae.[17]

Moers's vision of a continuity based on "heroinism" finds an echo in later feminist criticism that posits a discrete, perhaps even autonomous "women's culture." The idea of such a culture has been developed by social historians studying the "homosocial" world of nineteenth-century women.[18] It is a view that underlies, for example, Nina Auerbach's study of relationships among women in selected novels, where strong, supportive ties among mothers, daughters, sisters, and female friends not only constitute the real history in which certain women are conceived as living but function as a normative element as well.[19] That is, fiction in which positive relations subsist to nourish the heroine comes off much better, from Auerbach's point of view, than fiction in which such relations do not exist.

In contrast, Judith Lowder Newton sees the heroines of women's fiction as active, rather than passive, precisely because they do live in a man's world, not an autonomous female one.[20] Defining their power as "ability" rather than "control," she perceives "both a preoccupation with power and subtle power strategies" being exercised by the women in novels by Fanny Burney, Jane Austen, Charlotte Brontë, and George Eliot. Understood in this way, the female tradition, whether or not it in fact reflects and fosters a "culture" of its own, provides an alternative complex of possibilities for women, to be set beside the pits and pedestals offered by all too much of the Great Tradition.

Canonize such a multifarious Genealogie of Comments (Nashe, 1593)

Historians like Smith-Rosenberg and Cott are careful to specify that their generalizations extend only to white middle- and upper-class women of the

[15] Ellen Moers, *Literary Women: The Great Writers* (Garden City, N.Y.: Doubleday, 1976). [Au.]

[16] Elaine Showalter, *A Literature of Their Own: British Women Novelists from Brontë to Lessing* (Princeton, N.J.: Princeton University Press, 1977). [Au.]

[17] Sandra M. Gilbert and Susan Gubar, *The Madwoman in the Attic: The Woman Writer and the Nineteenth-Century Literary Imagination* (New Haven, Conn.: Yale University Press, 1979). [Au.]

[18] Carroll Smith-Rosenberg, "The Female World of Love and Ritual: Relations Between Women in Nineteenth-Century America," *Signs* 1 (Fall 1975):1–30; Nancy F. Cott, *The Bonds of Womanhood: "Woman's Sphere" in New England, 1780-1830* (New Haven, Conn.: Yale University Press, 1977). [Au.]

[19] Nina Auerbach, *Communities of Women: An Idea in Fiction* (Cambridge, Mass.: Harvard University Press, 1979). See also Janet M. Todd, *Women's Friendship in Literature* (New York: Columbia University Press, 1980); Louise Bernikow, *Among Women* (New York: Crown, 1980). [Au.]

[20] Judith Lowder Newton, *Women, Power, and Subversion: Social Strategies in British Fiction* (Athens: University of Georgia Press, 1981). [Au.]

nineteenth century. Although literary scholars are equally scrupulous about the national and temporal boundaries of their subject, they tend to use the gender term comprehensively. In this way, conclusions about "women's fiction" or "female consciousness" have been drawn or jumped to from considering a body of work whose authors are all white and comparatively privileged. Of the critical studies I have mentioned, only Bernikow's anthology, *The World Split Open,* brings labor songs, black women's blues lyrics, and anonymous ballads into conjunction with poems that were written for publication by professonal writers, both black and white. The other books, which build an extensive case for a female tradition that Bernikow only suggests, delineate their subject in such a way as to exclude not only black and working-class authors but any notion that race and class might be relevant categories in the definition and apprehension of "women's literature." Similarly, even for discussions of writers who were known to be lesbians, this aspect of the female tradition often remains unacknowledged; worse yet, some of the books that develop the idea of a female tradition are openly homophobic, employing the word "lesbian" only pejoratively.[21]

Black and lesbian scholars, however, have directed much less energy to polemics against the feminist "mainstream" than to concrete, positive work on the literature itself. Recovery and reinterpretation of a wealth of unknown or undervalued texts has suggested the existence of both a black women's tradition and a lesbian tradition. In a clear parallel with the relationship between women's literature in general and the male-dominated tradition, both are by definition part of women's literature, but they are also distinct from and independent of it.

There are important differences, however, between these two traditions and the critical effort surrounding them. Black feminist criticism has the task of demonstrating that, in the face of all the obstacles a racist and sexist society has been able to erect, there is a continuity of black women who have written and written well. It is a matter of gaining recognition for the quality of the writing itself and respect for its principal subject, the lives and consciousness of black women. Black women's literature is also an element of black literature as a whole, where the recognized voices have usually been male. A triple imperative is therefore at work: establishing a discrete and significant black female tradition, then situating it within black literature and (along with the rest of that literature) within the common American literary heritage.[22] So far, unfortunately, each step toward integration has met with continuing exclusion. A black women's tradition has been recovered and revaluated chiefly through the efforts of black feminist scholars. Only some of that work has been accepted as part of either a racially mixed women's literature or a two-sex black literature. As for the gatekeepers of American literature in general, how many of them are willing to swing open the portals even for Zora Neale Hurston or Paule Marshall? How many have heard of them?

The issue of "inclusion," moreover, brings up questions that echo those raised by opening the male-dominated canon to women. How do generalizations about women's literature "as a whole" change when the work of black women is not merely added to but fully incorporated into that tradition? How does our sense of black literary history change? And what implications do these changes have for reconsideration of the American canon?

[21] On the failings of feminist criticism with respect to black and lesbian writers, see Barbara Smith, "Toward a Black Feminist Criticism," ***Conditions: Two,*** **1, 2 (Oct. 1977); Mary Helen Washington, "New Lives and New Letters: Black Women Writers at the End of the Seventies,"** ***College English*** **43 (January 1981); Bonnie Zimmerman, "What Has Never Been: An Overview of Feminist Lesbian Criticism,"** ***Feminist Studies*** **7, 3 (1981).**

[22] See, e.g., Smith, "Toward a Black Feminist Criticism"; Barbara Christian, *Black Women Novelists: The Development of a Tradition, 1892–1976* (Westport, Conn.: Greenwood Press, 1980); Erlene Stetson, ed., *Black Sister: Poetry by Black American Women, 1764-1980* (Bloomington: Indiana University Press, 1981) and its forthcoming sequel; Gloria Hull, "Black Women Poets from Wheatley to Walker," in *Sturdy Black Bridges: Visions of Black Women in Literature,* ed. Roseann P. Bell et al. (Garden City, N.Y.: Anchor Books, 1979); Mary Helen Washington, "Introduction: In Pursuit of Our Own History," *Midnight Birds: Stories of Contemporary Black Women Writers* (Garden City, N.Y.: Anchor Books, 1980); the essays and bibliographies in *But Some of Us Are Brave: Black Women's Studies,* ed. Gloria Hull, Patricia Bell Scott, and Barbara Smith (Old Westbury: Feminist Press, 1982). [Au.]

Whereas many white literary scholars continue to behave as if there were no major black woman writers, most are prepared to admit that certain well-known white writers were lesbians for all or part of their lives. The problem is getting beyond a position that says either "so *that's* what was wrong with her!" or, alternatively, "it doesn't matter who she slept with—we're talking about literature." Much lesbian feminist criticism has addressed theoretical questions about *which* literature is actually part of the lesbian tradition, all writing by lesbians, for example, or all writing by women about women's relations with one another. Questions of class and race enter here as well, both in their own guise and in the by now familiar form of "aesthetic standards." Who speaks for the lesbian community: the highly educated experimentalist with an unearned income or the naturalistic working-class autobiographer? Or are both the *same kind* of foremother, reflecting the community's range of cultural identities and resistance?[23]

A cheaper way of Canon-making in a corner (Baxter, 1639)

It is not only members of included social groups, however, who have challenged the fundamentally elite nature of the existing canon. "Elite" is a literary as well as a social category. It is possible to argue for taking all texts seriously as texts without arguments based on social oppression or cultural exclusion, and popular genres have therefore been studied as part of the female literary tradition. Feminists are not in agreement as to whether domestic and sentimental fiction, the female Gothic, the women's sensational novel functioned as instruments of expression, repression, or subversion, but they have successfully revived interest in the question as a legitimate cultural issue.[24] It is no longer automatically assumed that literature addressed to the mass female audience is necessarily bad because it is sentimental, or for that matter, sentimental because it is addressed to that audience. Feminist criticism has examined without embarrassment an entire literature that was previously dismissed solely because it was popular with women and affirmed standards and values associated with femininity. And proponents of the "continuous tradition" and "women's culture" positions have insisted that this material be placed beside women's "high" art as part of the articulated and organic female tradition.

This point of view remains controversial within the orbit of women's studies, but the real problems start when it comes into contact with the universe of canon formation. Permission may have been given the contemporary critic to approach a wide range of texts, transcending and even ignoring the traditional canon. But in a context where the ground of struggle—highly contested, moreover—concerns Edith Wharton's advancement to somewhat more major status, fundamental assumptions have changed very little. Can Hawthorne's "d——d mob of scribbling women" *really* be invading the realms so long sanctified by Hawthorne himself and his brother geniuses? Is this what feminist criticism or even feminist cultural history means? Is it—to apply some outmoded and deceptively simple categories—a good development or a bad one? If these questions have not been raised, it is because women's literature and the female tradition tend to be evoked as an autonomous cultural experience, not impinging on the rest of literary history.

Wisdome under a ragged coate is seldome canonicall (Crosse, 1603)

Whether dealing with popular genres or high art, commentary on the female tradition usually has

[23] See Zimmerman, "What Has Never Been"; Adrienne Rich, "Jane Eyre: Trials of a Motherless Girl," *Lies, Secrets, and Silence: Selected Prose, 1966-1978* (New York: W. W. Norton, 1979); Lillian Faderman, *Surpassing the Love of Men: Romantic Friendship and Love Between Women from the Renaissance to the Present* (New York: William Morrow, 1981); the literary essays in *Lesbian Studies*, ed. Margaret Cruikshank (Old Westbury, N.Y.: Feminist Press, 1982). [Au.]

[24] Some examples on different sides of the question are: Ann Douglas, *The Feminization of American Culture* (New York: Alfred A. Knopf, 1976); Elaine Showalter, *A Literature of Their Own* and her article "Dinah Mulock Craik and the Tactics of Sentiment: A Case Study in Victorian Female Authorship," *Feminist Studies* 2 (May 1975): 5–23; Katherine Ellis, "Paradise Lost: The Limits of Domesticity in the Nineteenth-Century Novel," *Feminist Studies* 2 (May 1975): 55–65. [Au.]

been based on work that was published at some time and was produced by professional writers. But feminist scholarship has also pushed back the boundaries of literature in other directions, considering a wide range of forms and styles in which women's writing—especially that of women who did not perceive themselves as writers—appears. In this way, women's letters, diaries, journals, autobiographies, oral histories, and private poetry have come under critical scrutiny as evidence of women's consciousness *and expression.*

Generally speaking, feminist criticism has been quite open to such material, recognizing that the very conditions that gave many women the impetus to write made it impossible for their culture to define them as writers. This acceptance has expanded our sense of possible forms and voices, but it has challenged our received sense of appropriate style. What it amounts to is that if a woman writing in isolation and with no public audience in view nonetheless had "good"—that is, canonical—models, we are impressed with the strength of her text when she applies what she has assimilated about writing to her own experiences as a woman. If, however, her literary models were chosen from the same popular literature that some critics are now beginning to recognize as part of the female tradition, then she has not got hold of an expressive instrument that empowers her.

At the Modern Language Association meeting in 1976, I included in my paper the entire two-page autobiography of a participant in the Summer Schools for Women Workers held at Bryn Mawr in the first decades of the century. It is a circumstantial narrative in which events from the melancholy to the melodramatic are accumulated in a serviceable, somewhat hackneyed style. The anonymous "Seamer on Men's Underwear" had a unique sense of herself both as an individual and as a member of the working class. But was she a writer? Part of the audience was as moved as I was by the narrative, but the majority was outraged at the piece's failure to meet the criteria—particularly, the "complexity" criteria—of good art.

When I developed my remarks for publication, I wrote about the problems of dealing with an author who is trying too hard to write elegantly, and attempted to make the case that clichés or sentimentality need not be signals of meretricious prose and that ultimately it is honest writing for which criticism should be looking.[25] Nowadays, I would also address the question of the female tradition, the role of popular fiction within it, and the influence of that fiction on its audience. It seems to me that, if we accept the work of the professional "scribbling woman," we have also to accept its literary consequences, not drawing the lines at the place where that literature may have been the force that enabled an otherwise inarticulate segment of the population to grasp a means of expression and communication.

Once again, the arena is the female tradition itself. If we are thinking in terms of canon formation, it is the alternative canon. Until the aesthetic arguments can be fully worked out in the feminist context, it will be impossible to argue, in the general marketplace of literary ideas, that the novels of Henry James ought to give place—a *little* place, even—to the diaries of his sister Alice. At this point, I suspect most of our male colleagues would consider such a request, even in the name of Alice James, much less the Seamer on Men's Underwear, little more than a form of "reverse discrimination"—a concept to which some of them are already overly attached. It is up to feminist scholars, when we determine that this is indeed the right course to pursue, to demonstrate that such an inclusion would constitute a genuinely affirmative action for all of us.

The development of feminist literary criticism and scholarship has already proceeded through a number of identifiable stages. Its pace is more reminiscent of the survey course than of the slow processes of canon formation and revision, and it has been more successful in defining and sticking to its own intellectual turf, the female counter-canon, than in gaining general canonical recognition for Edith Wharton, Fanny Fern, or the female diarists of the Westward Expansion. In one sense, the more coherent our sense of the female tradition is, the stronger will be our eventual case. Yet the longer we wait, the more comfortable the women's literature ghetto—separate, apparently autonomous, and far from equal—may begin to feel.

At the same time, I believe the challenge cannot come only by means of the patent value of the work of women. We must pursue the questions certain of

[25] Lillian S. Robinson, "Working/Women/Writing," *Sex, Class, and Culture* (Bloomington: Indiana University Press, 1978), p. 252. [Au.]

us have raised and retreated from as to the eternal verity of the received standards of greatness or even goodness. And, while not abandoning our new-found female tradition, we have to return to confrontation with "the" canon, examining it as a source of ideas, themes, motifs, and myths about the two sexes. The point in so doing is not to label and hence dismiss even the most sexist literary classics, but to enable all of us to apprehend them, finally, in all their human dimensions.

Hazard Adams

b. 1926

SINCE his first book, *Blake and Yeats: The Contrary Vision* (1955), Hazard Adams's approach to the role and work of criticism has been remarkably consistent: to apprehend and understand imaginative work from its own point of view. For just that reason, his critical position is difficult to characterize. As he asserts of criticism itself in the selection here, Adams's position is ironic, in maintaining a tension between competing alternatives. He develops Blake's distinction between "negations," where one term of an opposition denies or negates the other, and a "contrary," where there is no presumption that opposing terms are in mortal conflict and one must be the victor.

As with Northrop Frye, Adams's work on Blake has informed his critical speculations, with the important difference that Frye, in *Anatomy of Criticism,* with perhaps less irony than the case may have required, took Blake's Los at his word—"I must create a System or be Enslav'd by Another Man's." As Blake understood, the risk of this imperative is the creation of a "mill with complicated wheels," which may be "revolutionary," chiefly in the sense of starting "the same dull round over again." Adams has not produced a system, at least not as one might find it in Blake's prophetic books, Yeats's *A Vision,* or Frye's *Anatomy;* but as these selections from *Philosophy of the Literary Symbolic* show, he proceeds systematically to represent the need and the difficulty of apprehending anything "from its own point of view."

In the scheme outlined here, modes of discourse and knowledge are represented along a continuum of cultural creation, taking the poetic as the normative, not the abnormal case. As Adams explains in the first selection here, from the "Introduction" to *Philosophy of the Literary Symbolic,* the root idea of the poetic (as developed both by Vico and by Blake) is an inclusive and creative gesture, constituting a world by giving it imaginative form—and thereby making oneself a "circumference," containing a world, as opposed to a "center," viewing that world (including one's own body and actions) as external and opposed to a self or subject. In this view, poetry and mathematics are the limits of the continuum, just as "myth" and "antimyth," as contraries, converge, for example, when mathematicians proceed from the claims that mathematics represents reality to the claim that reality is mathematical—or when poets, like Blake or Yeats, create "systems." Adams refers to diverse forms of creation along the continuum as "fictions," not as a term of opposition to "truth" but as an acknowledgment that forms of knowledge and expression are constituted by human acts, not given or passively "discovered."

Criticism Adams places in the middle, along with the writing of history, with myth and poetry on the one side and religion and science on the other. So situated, the critic and historian are involved in the creation of fictions, self-consciously contingent and mediatory, having the status neither of myth nor of doctrine, but with the implicit task of indicating how (and with what effect) myth becomes doctrine or vice versa. This is partly why Adams conceives of criticism as ironic, recalling Wallace Stevens's well-known lines about "the finer knowledge of belief," that "what it believes in is not true." From the middle ground Adams reserves for criticism, one would also add, "but neither is it false."

It is partly for this reason that Adams engages recent work in the history and philosophy of science, in the second excerpt here from the last chapter of *Philosophy of the Literary Symbolic.* Especially in the work of Gerald Holton and *Thomas Kuhn,* Adams finds analogous concerns as when, for example, Gerald Holton (in *Thematic Origins of Scientific Thought*) distinguishes between science as a nascent activity of imagination and conception (S_1) and science as an institution of collective agreements (S_2), or in Kuhn's notion of the scientific "paradigm" as a disciplinary matrix. In both cases, the problem of the historian of science becomes a problem of criticism (in a Kantian sense), as historical evidence fails with sublime regularity to confirm the view that the progress of science is a steady though incremental march to absolute truth. The critical dilemma closely resembles what confronts the literary analyst and historian: by what model can one explain the creation of opposing models without turning the opposition into a negation—or, alternatively, simply dissolving the opposition? In the case of natural science, a metaphysically or ontologically grounded notion of truth provides a ready justification for a historiography of "progress," just as it provides an implicit teleology: one conducts such inquiries precisely because they lead to Truth. When historical evidence shows a radically more complex picture, the status of oppositions used to generate pivotal terms comes into question.

One might argue (with Northrop Frye, for example) that literature never progresses, since it is a structure of potentialities that can be represented as a synchronic or mythic structure; but then it appears that the activity of constructing a critical model for that structure has either become a part of what it describes or becomes not a description of a system of potentialities but a set of limiting conditions in its own right. In the first case, "criticism" and "poetry" become, as it were, indifferent; in the second case, "criticism" ceases to serve a reflective role to become a source of doctrine itself. In this case, the postulate that literature is mythic serves to maintain the difference between literature and science but only vexes the status of criticism. Can it make claims that are "true," and, if not, are its claims mythic or merely dogmatic? Since it is obvious that both literature and criticism change, just as science and philosophy of science change, are the changes themselves indifferent?

The particular interest of this problem is that any dialectical strategy (whether Hegelian or Blakean) that depends on oppositions to generate the functional terms for discourse is liable to assume a condition of stability in the oppositions themselves. When it turns out that the opposition is either oversimplified or subject to dynamic alteration, the confidence in a set of distinctions made as if they were logically a priori is undermined by historical change.

As Adams constructs his model primarily after Blake and Vico, for example, it is notable that he interprets the model by deploying one axis of opposition against another. On one axis are three thematic oppositions, difference/indifference, subject/object, and symbol/allegory; the other axis opposes the notion of the "contrary" to the notion of the "negation," such that any of the thematic oppositions could be treated as either contraries or negations. The strategy is indeed powerful, but it stops short of accepting the historical interpretation that was vital for both Blake and Vico. Whereas Vico used his notion of "poetic logic" and "imaginative universals" to explain the development of Roman law, Blake used his notion of the "ancient poets" as "reprobate" in the service of an apocalyptic vision of resurrection from a fall. The similarity between Vico and Blake in this instance reflects not so much a common view of history as teleological but rather the more stubborn expectation that differences, and specifically historical differences, will *count* for something.

If one adopts a position of radical historicism (as Kuhn sometimes seems to do), then it may appear a matter of indifference, for example, which physical theory one endorses—which is precisely why Kuhn's work has been controversial in any domain where practitioners are convinced that it makes a great difference which theory one chooses—and why, not coincidentally, Kuhn qualifies the historicism of his notion of paradigms with speculations on problems of value (see *Kuhn*). Similarly, Gerald Holton's appeal to "themata" as ordering elements in the history of science provides an indirect means for explaining fundamental choices in theory or investigative strategy that are not transparently derived from evidence but have to do with recognizing "evidence" as such.

In all three cases, Kuhn, Holton, and Adams, the tension, in Adams's terms, is between oppositions as negations or as contraries; and the choice is made all the more problematic because of the historical fact of a common metaphysical heritage that presumes that knowledge must be a disclosure of being. On this account, Vico and Blake are on the same ground, as it were, with Bacon, Newton, and Locke, Blake's unholy trinity of scientists, in assuming that history will disclose being as truth. Instead, history discloses being as active, indeed, restless, in the propagation of choices.

For Blake, this dilemma took shape in the difficulty of finishing an apocalyptic epic, where the very form of teleological narrative undermined the poetic insight that oppositions need not be negations. Blake's solution was to invent a new form, in *Jerusalem,* where painting, verse, and critical commentary are integrated. For Adams's argument, the main difficulty is that a third term is required to prevent thematic oppositions from being, by metaphysical default, negations that generate static hierarchies. In the concluding section of *Philosophy of the Literary Symbolic* (not included here), Adams argues for a concept of "identity" as the contrary to "difference/indifference" and "subject/object" and a concept of the "secular symbolic" as the contrary of "symbol/allegory." This view provides, in a way, a critical contrary for poetic creation, not requiring a new form of critical discourse, or even a new "approach," but rather an act of historical recuperation in which the study of the history of criticism constructs the appropriate context for choice—and enough evidence to see that choices are profoundly consequential.

Adams's work includes *Blake and Yeats: The Contrary Vision* (1955); *William Blake: A Reading of the Shorter Poems* (1963); *The Contexts of Poetry* (1963);

The Interests of Criticism (1969); *Lady Gregory* (1973); *Philosophy of the Literary Symbolic* (1983); *Joyce Cary's Trilogies: Pursuit of the Particular Real* (1983). Adams is also the editor of *Critical Theory Since Plato* (1971), the author of two novels, *The Horses of Instruction* (1968) and *The Truth About Dragons* (1970), and an ironic account of academic life and politics, *The Academic Tribes* (1976).

FROM

PHILOSOPHY OF THE LITERARY SYMBOLIC

Introduction

1. SOME BLAKEAN AND VICHEAN VIEWS

In the chapter that is devoted wholly to Blake's views, I shall make a distinction between "myth" and "antimyth" that will carry over to the book's conclusion. Please make no assumptions yet about what these words mean, for the meanings rise out of the later discussions of Blake. I now offer four fundamental Blakean notions, and overlap them with three fundamental notions found in the writings of Vico. Though Blake, to my knowledge, had never heard of Vico, he might as well have.

1. Blake wrote in *The Marriage of Heaven and Hell:*

> The ancient Poets animated all sensible objects with Gods or Geniuses, calling them by the names and adorning them with the properties of woods, rivers, mountains, lakes, cities, nations, and whatever their enlarged and numerous senses could perceive.
>
> And particularly they studied the genius of each city and country, placing it under its mental deity.
>
> Till a system was formed, which some took advantage of, and enslaved the vulgar by attempting to realize or abstract the mental deities from their objects: Thus began priesthood.
>
> Choosing forms of worship from poetic tales.[1]

This is a complicated passage, which I shall examine again later. Here I want to note Blake's idea that the poetic capacity, which he identifies with primordial naming, is the source of language and culture. This means that the true model of language is trope and not the abstract ideal form of symbolic logic. This is not a unique view. It had been enunciated by Vico; it was picked up by Herder;[2] and it became a popular notion in romanticism. But with respect to the culture at large it has always been, I think, what Blake would call a "reprobate" view. Blake drew his notion of the "reprobate" from the biblical image of the visionary crying in the wilderness; it is an ironic reversal of the Calvinist meaning. For Blake, greater and greater forms of linguistic abstraction arise from poetic sources and in turn generate need for interpreters, or what Blake calls "priesthood," which would include those we now call critics. He goes on to remark that in this historical process something is lost:

> And at length they [the priests] pronounced that the gods had ordained such things. Thus men forgot that all deities reside in the human breast. [p. 153]

Reprinted here are selections from chapter one, "Introduction," and chapter twelve, "Conclusions," in PHILOSOPHY OF THE LITERARY SYMBOLIC, by permission of the author and the publisher, University Presses of Florida, copyright © 1983.

[1] *The Complete Writings of William Blake,* ed. Geoffrey Keynes (London: Nonesuch; New York: Random House, 1957), p. 153 (plate 11). [Au.]

[2] Giambattista Vico (1668–1744), Italian philosopher and historian (see *CTSP,* pp. 294–301); Johann Gottfried von Herder (1744–1803), German philosopher and critic, an important influence on the development of German Romanticism. [Eds.]

Blake implies that his "primitive and original ways"[3] are designed to restore a golden age before the fall into separation of words from their contained objects, of man from his gods.

2. Blake also wrote in the *Marriage* a sentence that I have chosen as the epigraph for this book:

> . . . one portion of being is the Prolific, the other the Devouring: to the Devourer it seems as if the producer was in his chains; but it is not so, he only takes portions of existence and fancies that the whole. [p. 155]

Here the "prolific," with which Blake connects the naming power of the "ancient poets," is made a constant social force, from which emanates cultural food, so to speak. The food is *devoured* by an abstracting, interpreting, using, hungering society. It is easy enough for the devourers to become deluded into thinking that the prolific are merely their captives. The history of the arts in the nineteenth century suggests that many prolifics came to feel that this was their fate. But Blake says it is never really so, which is at worst a defiant remark, or at best a truth.

3. Blake offers in his longer poems a notion involving his own special use of the terms "center" and "circumference."[4] If you are at a center or are a center, everything is outside you in the form of nature or matter. When you study yourself analytically you put yourself outside yourself in this material field. If you are at a circumference your experiences are inside you and a part of yourself. You contain the world in the form your imagination, including your power of language, gives it. You become an ancient poet. On the other hand, at a center you are a priest or alien interpreter of an outer world.

4. Finally, Blake made in *Milton* and *Jerusalem* an important distinction between "contraries" and "negations," which is the basis for his un-Hegelian dialectic.[5] A negation is a situation in which, in an opposition like soul/body or good/evil, one side is privileged over the other, that is, one side negates the reality or authority of the other, attempting to suppress it. This is, in Blake, definitely a historical notion. Blake's example in the *Marriage,* where the term "contrary" is first introduced, is the opposition soul/body: In the history of religion the soul has negated the body, connecting it with evil. This is a process that developed from original visionary acts toward priesthood, which bureaucratizes the interpretation of the act into law. In the Christian "church," a term indicating an era for Blake, the law is that of "chastity" or sexual repression. The process turns soul/body into good/evil. A "contrary" would be an opposition in which the distinction itself (or the reasoning that creates it) is on one side, and on the other is the denial of the distinction in favor of the identity of the two things in the term "energy," with neither side negated.

"Identity" is a tricky word applied to Blake. More will be said about it. Here let me state that "identity" is not indifference, but instead the contrary of the distinction difference/indifference.[6] This is the first of three negations, the contraries of which I shall seek. The second, subject/object, concerned Blake himself pretty directly, though he did not employ the terms. The third is symbol/allegory and is deeply involved with the first two. To con-

[3] Letter to Butts, January 10, 1802, *Complete Writings,* p. 812. [Au.]

[4] Blake's imagery is full of instances of expansions and contractions, circumferences and centers. See, for example, *Jerusalem,* plate 71, ibid., p. 709. [Au.]

[5] For example, *Jerusalem,* plate 10, ibid., p. 629. [Au.]

[6] René Girard, *Violence and the Sacred,* trans. Patrick Gregory (Baltimore: Johns Hopkins University Press, 1972), p. 159 [*La Violence et le sacré* (Paris: Bernard Grasset, 1972)] argues that inside a cultural system only differences are perceived. Outside, all the antagonists seem alike. Further, "wherever differences are lacking, violence threatens" (p. 57). I seek a stance beyond Girard's inside/outside, beyond his difference/indifference, which can be the contrary to that negation. Girard also remarks, "The rite selects a form of violence as 'good,' as necessary to the unity of the community" (p. 115). This differentiating form of violence is perhaps preferable to the undifferentiating form that Girard sees the culture terrified of and managing in this way. But clearly both are Blakean "negations," corresponding to the opposition of Orc/Urizen in Blake's poetry. A contrary is needed, which would imply the possibility of a higher form of culture, not a return to a primitive state. Blake offers his figure Los as a contrary form. I offer the as-yet-undeveloped notion of "identity." Where identity is lacking, alienation reigns.

Angus Fletcher remarks with pertinence: "Moral fables assert, symbolically, that some objects are sacred and some are sinful, and the true believer should avoid the one and embrace the other. . . . But when we seek the true meaning of 'sacred' [that is, the 'contrary' meaning] in religious usage, we meet a paradox, for it turns out that 'sacred' means both good and evil": *Allegory: The Theory of a Symbolic Mode* (Ithaca: Cornell University Press, 1964), p. 225. [Au.] See *Girard.* [Eds.]

sider this and romantic and postromantic efforts to find a contrary to the negation to which Goethe and others gave the name is my historical theme. I have not, however, tried to write a history as such, either of the distinction between symbol and allegory or of the symbolic. In his book, *Allegory,* Angus Fletcher wisely declined to write a history of his subject. It would have been impossible, because as he treats his subject he discovers that there is really no end to it.[7] I am in the same situation and have therefore chosen moments of exemplary importance to my theoretical theme, which is centered on the pursuit of contraries to the three negations I have mentioned above.

I come now to the three overlapping notions in Vico. He has been much written about in recent years by both theoreticians of history and semioticians, and his views have been digested and clearly presented along with those of J. G. Herder by Isaiah Berlin.[8] The first two notions involve two distinctions Vico makes. The first distinction is between "poetic logic" and conceptual logic, and the second is between "imaginative universals" and abstract universals. Both "poetic logic" and "imaginative universals" he connects with primitive people.

1. "Poetic Logic": The keys to Vico's new science of man are his claims that in the childhood of the world men were by necessity "sublime poets" and that the first science to be mastered before more can be known about man is that of mythology.[9] The first wisdom of the gentile world was what Vico calls "poetic wisdom" operating by "poetic logic"—"a metaphysics not rational and abstract like that of learned men now, but felt and imagined as that of the first men must have been, who, without power of ratiocination, were all robust sense and vigorous imagination" [p. 116 (1:145–46)]. The fundamental difference here between Vico and others who held similar views[10] is that Vico does not consistently denigrate as hopeless because they are irrational the qualities he mentions above; in some moods he even celebrates them. Nor does he try to rationalize examples of "poetic logic" by claiming that myths hide rational statements by allegory. The term "poetic" in Vico refers to a mode of thought that does not work toward abstract concepts, but in Blake's terms toward the expansion of centers. "Poetic logic" gave rise first to history, not poetry (in the sense of imitation and feigning, at least); and the first history was created by poets, for "all gentile histories have their beginnings in fables" [p. 314 (2:21)]. Mythologies are really "civil histories of the first peoples, who were everywhere naturally poets" [p. 105 (1:130)]. This view of Vico's differs from most allegorical euhemerism in that it does not claim myths to be early impressions of historical fact corrupted into fable over time, but events formulated originally in the mode of "poetic logic." In him there is no notion of an original enlightened condition of Deistic reasonableness before a Fall into debased religion. Jove by the "poetic logic" of metaphor is the sky *and* the first of the gods. One does not *stand for* the other. This all follows from the nature of primitive thought, which for Vico is never far divorced from primitive language, which is animistic, incapable of abstraction, and fundamentally tropological. Indeed, language is the form of thought. Ideas and words are a twin birth.[11] Vico goes so far as to say, anticipating modern struc-

[7] Ibid., p. 1. [Au.]

[8] Isaiah Berlin, *Vico and Herder: Two Studies in the History of Ideas* (London: Hogarth, 1976), particularly pp. 42–55. The standard Italian commentary is that of Fausto Nicolini, *Commento storico all seconda scienza nouva,* 2 vols. (Rome: 1949–50). [Au.]

[9] *The New Science of Giambattista Vico,* rev. trans. of the 3d ed., 1774, trans. Thomas Goddard Bergin and Max Harold Fisch (Ithaca: Cornell University Press, 1968), pp. 71, 33 [*La scienza nouva,* ed. Fausto Nicolini, 2 vols. (Bari: Gius. Laterza & Figli, 1928), 1:87, 42]. For this, a study of the Hebraic biblical tradition will not do because of the miraculous incursion of the deity into the history of the Hebrews, which makes them a special case. (Thus Vico avoids religious disputation.) They received their law direct from God and never went through the long historical process that the gentile tribes—dispersed descendants of Noah—experienced. The gentiles, therefore, had to discover and make laws for themselves by a long process of development which everywhere began in religion. The similarities among myths arose not because of a common historical and geographical origin but because of a common human nature. [Au.]

[10] See, for example, Antoine Court de Gebelin, *Monde primitif analysé et comparé avec le monde moderne* (Paris, 1773). Gebelin is under the domineering influence of Cartesianism with its supreme confidence in the mathematical structure of reality. A good rationalist, he makes no distinction between allegory and symbolism. [Au.]

[11] Berlin, *Vico and Herder,* points out that Joseph de Maistre's remark "la pensée et la parole sont un magnifique synonyme" [thought and language are a magnificent synonym] one hundred years later probably comes from Vico (p. 42). [Au.]

turalist thought, that minds are formed by the nature of language, not vice versa.[12]

Fundamental to Vico's notion of the origins of language in the concrete and poetic are three of the four major tropes: metaphor, metonymy, and synecdoche. (Irony appears somewhat later.) These tropes, which are treated by classical thought simply as devices of rhetoric spread upon a fabric of conceptual logic, Vico treats as the fundamental "corollaries" of "poetic logic," the "necessary modes of expression" [p. 131 (1:167)], thereby implicitly joining thought to language. He expresses his important reversal of the classical view of tropes as follows:

> By means of these three divinities [Jove, Cybele, and Neptune] . . . they [primitive men] explained everything appertaining to the sky, the earth, and the sea. And similarly by means of the other divinities they signified the other kinds of things appertaining to each, denoting all flowers, for instance, by Flora, and all fruits by Pomona. We nowadays reverse this practice in respect of spiritual things, such as the faculties of the human mind, the passions, the virtues, vices, sciences, and arts; for the most part the ideas we form of them are so many feminine personifications, to which we refer all the causes, properties and effects that severally appertain to them. For when we wish to give utterance to our understanding of spiritual things, we must seek aid from our imagination to explain them and, like painters, form human images of them. But these theological poets, unable to make use of the understanding, did the opposite and more sublime thing: they attributed senses and passions, as we saw not long since, to bodies, and to bodies as vast as sky, sea, and earth. Later, as these vast imaginations shrank and the power of abstraction grew, the personifications were reduced to diminutive signs [p. 128 (1:162)].

There appears here the idea of a primordial "sympathetic nature," as well as that of shrinkage to a Blakean center. Modern man's mind is "so detached from the senses, even in the vulgar, by abstractions corresponding to all the abstract terms our language abounds in" that we cannot form any image of such a nature, at least not without an immense effort [p. 118 (1:148)]. The tropes are "corollaries" of a "poetic logic" identical to that exercised by Blake's "ancient poets."

2. "Imaginative Universals": According to Vico, the earliest people did not possess "intelligible class concepts of things," but they nevertheless had to move in thought and expression from particulars to some sort of universals, "to which, as to certain models or ideal portraits" they could "reduce all the particular species which resembled them" [p. 74 (1:91)]. A Vichean "imaginative universal," the special product of "poetic logic," remains animate in its universality by retaining all the qualities of any particular referred to it. "It is an eternal property of the fables always to enlarge the ideas of particulars" [p. 312 (2:18)] and, I might add, to insist on the "identity" with the particular of that enlargement.

We are not surprised, therefore, to find that metaphor is the "most necessary and frequent" corollary of "poetic logic" by which the first poets "attributed to bodies the being of animate substances, with capacities measured by their own, namely sense and passion, and in this way made fables of them" [p. 129 (1:164)]. Vico notes how many inanimate things are verbally formed by metaphors from the human body, its parts, senses, or passions, and concludes that "as rational metaphysics teaches that man becomes all things by understanding them (*homo intelligendo fit omnia*), this imaginative metaphysics [poetic logic] shows that man becomes all things by *not* understanding them (*homo non intelligendo fit omnia*); and perhaps the latter proposition is truer than the former, for when man understands he extends his mind and takes in things; but when he does not understand he makes the things out of himself and becomes them by transforming himself into them" [p. 130 (1:165)]. Like metaphor, each metonymy and synecdoche creates a fable in miniature. Vico classes the gods and some traditional heroes as "imaginative universals"—Hercules, Homer, Aesop, Horatio, and Orlando, for example. Homer, the heroic character of Grecian men "insofar as they told their histories in song," is an "imaginative universal." All the inconsistencies that surround Homer as a singular indi-

[12] See Berlin, ibid., who quotes from *De nostre temporis studiorum ratione* (1708). [Au.]

vidual during a particular period are made consistent by this view, which Vico develops to some length, anticipating Blake's remark in the annotations to Reynolds's *Discourses,* "Every class is individual."

3. The third Vichean notion is that of "fictions": If myth and poetry developed in the way Vico describes, so originally did jurisprudence. The most ancient laws of the gentiles arose out of single instances and were only later given general application. They were not conceived before the acts occurred that made them necessary. Vico introduces the idea of "fictions" into his account of Roman law, which he calls as a whole a "serious poem." By this he means a historical development out of the practice of "poetic logic." His treatment of law as fictions in which "what had happened was taken as not having happened, and what had not happened as having happened" anticipates Hans Vaihinger's[13] theory of "as if" (which I shall discuss in chapter 7) by two centuries, even down to the type of illustration used, and it emphasizes not the untruth of a fiction but the notion of a fiction as a making, implicit in the Blakean idea of the "prolific" activity of the "ancient poets."

There is in Vico, however, a latent positivism, with which a theory of symbolic cannot go along. He seems to regard "poetic logic" as principally and perhaps only a necessary precursor to philosophy. He writes that in fables,

> as in embryos or matrices, we have discovered the outlines of all esoteric wisdom. And it may be said that in the fables the nations have in a rough way and in the language of the human senses described the beginnings of this world of sciences, which the specialized studies of scholars have since clarified for us by reasoning and generalizations. [p. 297 (1:380)]

For Vico, the early poets were the "sense" and the philosophers the "intellect" of human wisdom. The latter, working upon the crude and confused accomplishments of the former, made humanity "complete" [p. 167 (1:213)]. It would seem that each metaphor or "fable in brief" provides the materials for abstract thought, but once abstract thought assimilates metaphor, the metaphor's formative power is lost and there is decay into a "false" figure of speech, useful for illustrative purposes perhaps, but dangerous when extended beyond its now diminished realm. At the same time, Vico remarks that it was the very "deficiency of human reasoning power" that gave rise to the great sublime poetry of the heroic age and that "the philosophies which came afterward, the arts of poetry and of criticism, have produced none equal or better, and have even prevented its production [p. 120 (1:151)]. This sounds nostalgic, like Blake's story of the "ancient poets" and the subsequent "priesthood." As an antidote to that nostalgia Vico offers not a theory of the persistence of "poetic logic" in art but only the *recorso,* the theory of the growth, maturity, and decline of a civilization, whose apotheosis seems to occur as the "abstract" mind gains complete ascendancy over the "poetic." The growth of the "abstract" marks the decadence of the "poetic," but the supreme dominance of the abstract marks also the decadence of the culture.

Vico offers a theory based on a keen appreciation of the facts of flux, and this enables him to search back into origins, to find the dynamic character of myth and language. But his sensitivity to change leads him to an inner conflict. On the one hand, he demonstrates sympathy for "poetic logic" as a mode of thought. It seems to provide a Blakean contrary to that excess of abstraction which leads man away from his own life in the world. On the other hand, he seems to regard "poetic logic" as a stage in human development to be passed through. His third great age—the Age of Man—liberates man from myth. Vico offers to a philosophy of the literary symbolic a view of language that makes "poetic logic" more fundamental than abstract conceptualization and thereby tends, as Croce said of him, to "suppress the dualism between poetry and language" that has long dogged our civilization.[14] Further, his attempt to distinguish "imaginative universals" from abstract ones shows him grounding the poetic in a process that is clearly not the mode of romantic allegory as I shall soon describe it. But Vico does not take the crucial step to a

[13]Hans Vaihinger (1852–1933), German philosopher. [Eds.]

[14]Benedetto Croce, *The Philosophy of Giambattista Vico,* trans. R. G. Collingwood (New York: Russell and Russell, 1964), p. 50. [Au.]

view of language as fully creative and symbolic. He cannot free himself entirely from certain assumptions about human progress that make him at times seem to denigrate the poetic almost as much as did the Cartesianism he sought to revise. This failure allows us to read him as a supreme historical ironist, with civilization buffeted between the poles of poetry and abstract thought in an endless cyclical movement. What he needs is a Blakean notion of "prolific" contrariety to oppose to the cyclicity which negates now "poetic logic," now "conceptual logic." The contrary must also oppose the idea of straight-line progress from "poetic logic" to a culture of the pure concept.

FROM

PHILOSOPHY OF THE LITERARY SYMBOLIC
Conclusions

In an effort to clarify a role for criticism among the liberal arts and sciences, I now return to the distinction betwen myth and antimyth and the Blakean principles with which this book began. On the basis of these principles I shall attempt to distinguish a philosophy of the literary symbolic from a variety of structuralist, phenomenological, and poststructuralist positions. The conclusions reached I identify with the tradition of the symbolic as I have constructed it in a selection of its many transformations—from the romantic distinction between symbolism and allegory through to a true contrary opposing "miraculous" symbol/allegory to "secular" symbolic.

1. Dialectic of Fictive Cultural Forms

A similarity among differences between structuralist and phenomenological positions is the refusal of both to make any sort of fundamental distinction—or sometimes even practical distinction—between kinds of language, as was made by, say, Wheelwright[15] or some theorists of the American New Criticism. Yet on the nature of this one undifferentiated form of language, phenomenologists and structuralists generally disagree. The rejection of such distinctions is also made by certain critics who belong to neither group. For example, E. D. Hirsch, Jr.:

> No literary theorist from Coleridge to the present has succeeded in formulating a viable distinction between the nature of ordinary written speech and the nature of literary written speech. . . . I believe the distinction can never be successfully formulated, and the futility of attempting the distinction will come to be generally recognized.[16]

Not himself a structuralist, and in certain ways harshly critical of them, Hirsch is nevertheless with the structuralists on this point, for his model of discourse is that of symbolic logic. He treats all writing in its terms and thus tends toward a romantically allegoric concept of all verbal structures. Phenomenologists tend to approach the matter from a quite different direction, reasserting variations of the "miraculous" concept of the symbol.

My design is, of course, to argue for the concept of the poem as "secular" symbolic form, identifying language fundamentally with poetry, but recognizing a progression of antimythical emanations from it. In this, I *seem* to be like the phenomenologists, but my conception of language as creative, as I shall try to show, differs from their concept of all language as hermeneutic. At the same time, I am not prepared to claim any absolute fissure between poetic language and any such language as may be set up in opposition to it. In this, I seem to be like Hirsch, the symbolic logicians, and the structuralists. However, my model of language is not the mathematical one, nor is my normative description of it a term such as "logical discourse." As we have seen, Frye has speculated about the relation of poetry to mathematics, and Yeats before him mused on mathematic form as myth. I propose a linguistic continuum that runs from a mythic pole outward

[15] Philip Wheelwright; see *CTSP*, pp. 1103–12. [Eds.]

[16] E. D. Hirsch, Jr., *The Aims of Interpretation* (Chicago: University of Chicago Press, 1976), pp. 90–91. [Au.]

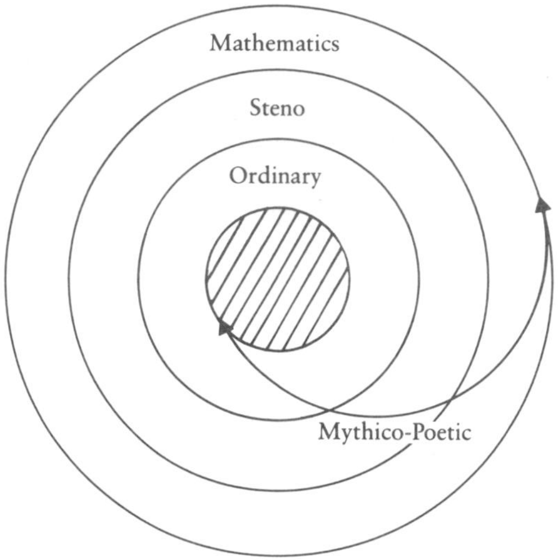

Figure 12.1

through the fictive zones that some philosophers have tried to call "ordinary" language (if it exists) and Wheelwright's "steno language" to mathematical symbolism, which marks the outer limit of symbolic creativity (fig. 12.1). Blake's identification of centers with circumferences applies here. The mythic center is actually a container of all the possibilities implicit in the totality, becoming a circumference, as my diagram (fig. 12.1) attempts to show, the circle turning inside out in the way that Frye's "center" of literary merges with circumferential anagogy in any particular work. There can finally be no lines measuring off these zones, so my diagram is misleading; but unlike Hirsch, I do not believe that because we cannot logically formulate or "measure" where one mode ceases and another begins, we should not make fictive distinctions helpful to our understanding. The principle is a contrary to one requiring a choice between indifference and difference. It states that any verbal structure has *identity*. It will take this chapter to indicate just what I mean by the term.

It should be clear that this notion of identity does not offer the mythic as a necessarily historical origin, as does Vico and as Blake seems to do (though, I think, does not have to do). But it does deny as fundamental the assumptions about language upon which behavioral social science has based its methodologies. With its quantitative methods, behavioral social science makes mathematics the origin, building abstract behavioral models outward from it. In such a system there is declared to be no containing circumference, all language pointing outward, though one can say, at a higher level, that quantitative social science ends up trying to contain human behavior in a mathematic form. Structuralism, which claims to be a "human" science, or the basis of such a science, is in the end not much different in this matter.

If we are to make the effort as critics to acknowledge (since adoption is finally impossible) the point of view of the poem, we can hardly declare tropes to be deviations from some norm, since they have as much right as anything else to be declared the norm. Metaphor is hardly a transgressive activity, as in some of the headier structuralist flights, unless we are perversely to identify transgression with normality. The idea of discourse that eliminates all tropes from a norm is really an ideal of pure mathematic abstraction.

When the mathematical ideal negates the poetic the result is twofold: (1) All language is regarded as "outward" pointing; it is either transparently mimetic or arbitrarily significatory (allegorical) of a "primary" mathematized universe, that is, it goes to a center and stays there; (2) tropes are regarded as merely devices to lend vividness to discourse or to entertain, or figures to be allegorically interpreted, and poetry becomes decorated outward-pointing language. The idea of such purification toward the bare bones of logic is derived from a positivistic assumption about how the mind works that from the poetic point of view turns things inside out: Rather than computers being regarded as copies of mind, it is implied that the mind is a copy of a computer. Under these conditions "ordinary language" becomes simply a term for how language deviates from a mathematical norm. The argument that there is no ordinary language has been cleverly made by Stanley Fish, who attacks the distinction between ordinary and literary language by declaring the nonexistence of both.[17] Ordinary language seems to me a misleading fiction useless to criticism as long as it is employed to declare poetry as in some way deviant from it. Fish argues that the dis-

[17] Stanley Fish, "How Ordinary Is Ordinary Language?" *New Literary History* 5, no. 1 (Autumn 1973): 41–54. [Au.]

tinction has forced criticism to claim that poetry is either more than language ("message plus"), which leads to a concept of decorative form, or less than language ("message minus"), which eliminates content and eventuates in theories of "pure poetry." The plus and minus characterizations are simplistic, but in any case Fish's analysis does not focus on the issue that is fundamental in this book. That issue is whether we can give to language an expansive, creative character or only an imitative and/or significatory one, whether it is only a dead center, and not a center that is always becoming a circumference.

With that said, I want to locate the arts, history, and criticism as cultural forms of symbolic in their appropriate dialectical positions on a continuum. My dialectic, like Yeats's, does not provide for Hegelian synthesis, but for the constantly renewed conflict of Heraclitus; the notion of identity requires conflict as well as continuum when it is rationally formulated. The dialectic is that of myth and antimyth. Table 12.1 organizes this opposition.

The side of myth is the side of a paradox harbored by the word "identity." Identity is a harbor of individuality *and* relationship. One has an identity, and one can be identical *with* something. A tribe of primitive people can claim that they are crocodiles but do not make the error of jumping in the river that flows by their huts and cavorting with those creatures with which they have established identity. The side of antimyth eschews paradox (as it eschews the identity present in a trope) and abstracts toward general law. In both cases, I shall claim (because I deliberately seek to acknowledge myth's point of view) that what we have are fictions, not untruths, but creations. I say this, even as (indeed, because) I recognize that from antimyth's point of view the antimythic creation is not creation but a correspondence with an external reality. In the end, however, we shall have to say that this too is a fiction—a making.

Table 12.1. Dialectic of fictive cultural forms

	Myth	*Antimyth*
Mode:	Sympathy	Analysis
Direction:	Particularity	General or universal law
Movement:	To a circumference	To a center
End:	Individual	Abstract Unity
Paradox:	The particular encompasses the whole	None
Anti-paradox:	None	The particular is inside the aggregate whole
Contrary:	Identity	Difference/ Indifference

Let us now imagine these contraries as two extremes or limits. At the antimythical pole we have a vision of the world as external to us, the world of nature and her mathematical laws as object to our subject. Our own bodies are *outside* us, objectified like the world and treatable wholly in terms of behavioristic assumptions. We define ourselves as natural or at least social objects. This is, of course, a myth itself, though what I have chosen, to avoid equivocation, to call a fiction. Antimyth accepts the fiction that the thing to be demythologized is external, in the sense of being an object to a subject. Part of the fiction is that the particular is determined *by* and *in* the world. Extended into religion it is the fiction of man in relation to a sky god, an alien god, or a moral law, external to, usually above, him.

As a limit, antimyth represents the fiction of complete division into primary externality and secondary internality and the consequent privileging of the external. The explicit invention of the division in the history of science, which is usually pushed back to Galileo, is denied by the historian of science Gerald Holton to have been a "wanton act of dehumanization." Rather, he claims it to have been a "strategic decision to reach a worthy human goal, that of understanding nature (including, ultimately, man's nature) in a new way."[18] This is certainly true, but as a pole or limit, it is precisely a dehumanization in that it externalizes man from himself by making man (or at least as much of man as can be gotten hold of in that form) a nature. We might call the notion of antimyth a "category," to use Kantian language, but it would be better to say that it is a pure form (indeed, *the* pure form) of scientific thought. It is not the form of the *process* of scientific thought. It is only a normative concept and as such readily illustrates how normative concepts taken as absolutes can spread over the whole

[18] Gerald Holton, *Thematic Origins of Scientific Thought: Kepler to Einstein* (Cambridge, Mass.: Harvard University Press, 1973), p. 440. [Au.]

range of a subject and corrupt our understanding of it. The *process* of science is an emergence from myth into antimythical form. Antimyth as a concept contains only "normal science" in Thomas Kuhn's sense or "public science" (S_2) in Holton's.[19]

Both Kuhn and Holton attempt to expand our notions of the process of science by their ideas of paradigms and themata respectively. Holton treats themata as preconceptions in scientific activity that are not verifiable or falsifiable. He treats them as a third (really a primordial) dimension of science in addition to the dimension of the empirical and phenomenal and the dimension of the heuristic-analytic. These latter two alone compose what he calls "public science" or S_2. What is lacking there is part of the process: ". . . the dimension of fundamental presuppositions, notions, terms, methodological judgments, and decisions . . . which are themselves neither directly evolved from, nor resolvable into, objective observation on the one hand, or logical, mathematical, and other formal analytical ratiocination on the other hand."[20] I take it that themata are those fictive acts out of which scientific theories emerge in the process we think of as doing science. "Public science" cannot explain the role of these themata. There is a relation between a public science and the time in which it is practiced that evades scientific explanation. Holton remarks of contemporary science's world: ". . . it is now a profoundly egalitarian rather than hierarchical universe, so much so that a whole theory of relativity (Milne's) has been built around the so-called cosmological principle, the principle that any observer anywhere in the universe interprets data in exactly the same way as any other observer elsewhere."[21] This appears to be an example of the emergence of scientific theory from myth, though not, perhaps, without a doubling back through antimyth to the culture in general. In any case, we can treat it as an emergence into antimyth, because it appears that before a thema can function scientifically in a "public" or "normal" sense it must be shaped into antimythical form.

Holton seems to treat the primary/secondary or subject/object division as a thema, like, say, the thema of fundamental probabilism in physical nature or the notion of the thing-in-itself as a mathematical structure (Heisenberg). His notion of themata as "preconceptions that appear to be unavoidable for scientific thought"[22] would cover the division into primary and secondary qualities. But subject/object is in one sense deeper than a thema and in another sense subsequent to themata. It is deeper in that it is the structure of the pure form to which all themata must accommodate themselves. It is subsequent in that thematic processes of thought that produce science (S_2) go on, or at least can begin, independent of it. Like what Michael Polanyi calls "tacit knowing," the "nature" of such a process is unspecifiable.[23]

Kuhn's notion of paradigms stands in relation to antimyth in the same way that themata do, though in Holton's view themata come more from the individual than from the community. Kuhn's notion of paradigms has been modified considerably since *The Structure of Scientific Revolutions* appeared in 1962. Originally it was very broad, but Margaret Masterman's analysis, in which she showed that Kuhn used the term in at least twenty-one different senses, which she then divided into three basic groups, led Kuhn to redefine down to two fundamental senses.[24] Originally Kuhn offered paradigms of three types: metaphysical (sometimes "quasi-metaphysical," as in Kuhn's description of Descartes' corpuscular theory, which told many scientists "what many of their research problems should be"), sociological, and artificial. Masterman's argument was that though most commentators treated Kuhn's paradigms as metaphysical, their fundamental sense was not that at all; they represented sets of scientific habits prior to theory in their development, sociologically describable and above all con-

[19] Thomas Kuhn, *The Structure of Scientific Revolutions,* 2d ed. (Chicago: University of Chicago Press, 1970), pp. 10–42; Holton, *Thematic Origins*, pp. 19ff. [Au.]

[20] Holton, *Thematic Origins,* p. 57. [Au.]

[21] Ibid., p. 103. [Au.]

[22] Ibid., p. 23. [Au.]

[23] See Polanyi, *Personal Knowledge* (1958) (Chicago: University of Chicago Press, 1962), and Polanyi and Harry Prosch, *Meaning* (Chicago: University of Chicago Press, 1975). [Au.]

[24] Margaret Masterman, "The Nature of a Paradigm," in *Criticism and the Growth of Knowledge* (1970), ed. Imri Lakatos and Alan Musgrave (Cambridge: Cambridge University Press, 1972), pp. 59–89. Kuhn's response, "Reflections on My Critics," occupies pp. 231–78. [Au.] See also, Kuhn, "Second Thoughts on Paradigms" in *The Essential Tension: Selected Studies in Scientific Traditions and Change* (Chicago: University of Chicago Press, 1977), pp. 293–319. [Eds.]

crete and observable. The fundamental form was what she called the "artifact or construct" paradigm that could be a piece of apparatus or anything bringing about puzzle-solving or normal science.[25] Kuhn conspired in this retreat from metaphysics in his postscript of 1969.[26] It is clear, however, that Kuhn's theory must admit paradigms of the metaphysical sort because many of his examples are of that sort. But it is probably true that when they are admitted they are admitted *as* construct paradigms. This is because Kuhn himself has a perfectly natural antimythical bias, as his interest in science might lead us to assume in the first place, though his theory raises all kinds of problems for purely antimythical *beliefs*. Kuhn's abandonment of metaphysics, following Masterman's cue, makes his social science that much harder, a condition which has been devoutly, if on occasion mistakenly, wished for. (In fact, Kuhn eventually drops the term "paradigm" and substitutes for it the term "disciplinary matrix," which he describes as an "entire constellation of beliefs, values, techniques, and so on shared by members of a given community.")[27] For Kuhn, there is always a concrete situation in which a paradigm comes into play. Scientists don't learn concepts, laws, and theories "in the abstract and by themselves." They encounter these tools "in a historically and pedagogically prior unit that displays them with and through their applications."[28] This means that paradigms are relatively silent in the way that the Aristotelian notion of matter can become silent because of its "omnipresence and qualitative neutrality" in Aristotelian physics.[29] But I doubt that because it is omnipresent it can quite be dispensed with. It is, still, paradigmatic. Antimyth is more than paradigmatic, for it is never overthrowable without denying science itself. Except, of course, that we are speaking at this point of public science. It is interesting to see how the notion of necessary externality appears even as Holton, for example, speaks of

> . . . the process of removing the discourse from the personal level . . . to a second level, that of public science, where the discourse is more unambiguously understandable, being predominantly about phenomena and analytical schemes. . . . This is a process which every scientist unquestionably accepts, a process that may be termed externalization or projection.[30]

It is what I call emergence toward antimyth.

What Kuhn calls "normal science" involves acceptance of paradigms and the making of community that this implies. Acceptance of a paradigm limits as well as liberates, since it tends to select the problems that will be regarded as scientific at any given time. But we can see, as Holton points out, it is in the nature of science, when limited to only two rather than his three dimensions, that certain questions cannot be asked. They are not scientific questions. This is true at a broader and deeper level than Holton indicates—at the metaphysical level that Kuhn abandons, the level nearing antimyth, which defines the limit of scientific projections.

The antimyth of externality is in the end something that the philosophy of science must recognize as the structure of scientific fictions. Once it is assumed that paradigms are fictive, the temptation is to reinvoke antimythical principle and consider each successive paradigm nearer to an objective (external) truth. That is, the antimyth is invoked at a higher level than the current paradigm. Kuhn, as a philosopher of science, tries to step out of paradigms, and perhaps even out of the antimyth (though his retreat from metaphysics is a contrary act), and it is this move that causes him to differ with Karl Popper. Kuhn claims: "We may . . . have to relinquish the notion, explicit or implicit, that changes of paradigm carry scientists and those who learn from them closer and closer to the truth."[31] From the point of view of the *philosopher* of science, Kuhn sees the notion of a teleology in science itself as a vacuous concept. His view has outraged many scientists and philosophers—to the degree that they accept the absolute dominance of an antimythical world-view and reject so-called "metaphysical" issues. More precisely, Kuhn refuses to

[25] Masterman, "The Nature of a Paradigm," p. 65. [Au.]
[26] Kuhn, *The Structure of Scientific Revolutions*, pp. 174–210. [Au.]
[27] Ibid., pp. 182, 175. [Au.]
[28] Ibid., p. 46. [Au.]
[29] Kuhn, "Reflections on My Critics," p. 269. [Au.]
[30] Holton, *Thematic Origins*, p. 101. [Au.]
[31] Kuhn, *The Structure of Scientific Revolutions*, p. 170; Karl Popper, *The Logic of Scientific Discovery* (London: Hutchinson, 1935). [Au.]

> compare theories as representations of nature, as statements about "what is really out there." Granting that neither theory of a historical pair is true, [many thinkers] nevertheless seek a sense in which the latter is a better approximation to the truth. I believe nothing of that sort can be found.[32]

For Kuhn, to posit an ontological limit, as Popper does, is to imply a neutral observation language, which he says has never been achieved (and, in my view, can never be achieved), or implies knowledge of the limit already, which makes the whole search unnecessary. Kuhn goes so far as to consider abandoning the cherished notions that sensory experience is fixed and neutral and that theories are simply man-made interpretations of given data.

The same notion is expressed by Holton in his rejection of ". . . the idea of a perfect entity . . . easily recognizable in scientific thought, from the beginning to this day, as the conception—a haunting and apparently irresistible one despite all evidence to the contrary—of the final, single, perfect object of knowledge to which the current state of scientific knowledge is widely thought to lead us."[33] Holton goes on to speak of it as inexpressible in ordinary language, but the truth must be that it is inexpressible in any language or symbolic form. Yet a positing of such an external limit is so pervasive in science that one must entertain the notion of its necessity as a fiction to the whole enterprise. This means not that the scientist doing Holton's S_1—the unspecifiable imaginative process—need *believe* it, but that normal science adopts it as part of the structure of antimyth. One can argue appropriately that the historian or philosopher of science cannot adopt it, at least not fully. The historian and philosopher perform in the realm of the ironic, and indeed *must* maintain a certain distance from science. Kuhn's quarrel with Popper seems definable in terms of Kuhn's ironic withdrawal. Of course, it ought to be clear enough that for a scientist to adopt the antimythical as a *belief* beyond the activity of S_2 itself is error.

The structures which operate under the aegis of antimyth can be materials for myth and can themselves have fiction-making power. They can create words and images which help to shape the culture, but always from or within an antimythical base. Thus the power is properly called antimythopoeic, but no less therefore fictive. As such it skews things in a certain way. Albert Einstein remarked that experience remains the sole criterion of the utility of a mathematical construct, but he also observed that a creative principle resides in mathematics. In criticizing Mach he wanted to go beyond "phenomenological physics" to achieve a theory, as Holton remarks, "whose basis may be further from direct experience, but which in return has more unity in the foundation."[34] The desire to connect to experience may, indeed, be the scientist's desire to return to a pre-antimythic condition, the place of myth, the origin of making or poesis in the broadest sense, where things are "simple" again. We see this in Einstein's attitude toward his own theories, and his connecting them with classic purity. We see also returns to a sort of image-making. Holton notes a tendency among physicists to evoke visual images of what one would see if it were seeable, which it is not once it becomes assimilated to the form of antimyth.

Michael Polanyi has sought to look beneath what our models of knowing are and invents the idea of tacit knowing. This idea speaks of something deeper than antimyth—something, as Polanyi says, "unspecifiable."[35] This is radically "personal" knowledge not grounded in explicit operations of logic. We can never get antimythically *to* such knowledge because when we try to establish *rules* of tacit knowing we discover that beneath them is always another tacit form and thus an infinite regress. This is perhaps what Yeats offers at the end of *A Vision,* where his ironic language reaches the end of its tether:

> The particulars are the work of the thirteenth sphere or cycle, which is in every man and called by every man his freedom. Doubtless, for it can do all things and knows all things, it knows what it will do with its own freedom but it has kept the secret.[36]

[32] Kuhn, "Reflections on My Critics," p. 265. [Au.]

[33] Holton, *Thematic Origins,* p. 104. [Au.]

[34] Gerald Holton, *The Scientific Imagination* (Cambridge: Cambridge University Press, 1978), p. 145. [Au.]

[35] Polanyi, *Meaning,* p. 39. [Au.]

[36] W. B. Yeats, *A Vision* (New York: Macmillan, 1938), p. 183. [Au.]

This is a necessarily ironic description of the ground of antimythical fiction-making.

Polanyi goes on to an account of metaphor as an integrative act of tacit knowing or personal knowledge that creates a meaning unspecifiable by recourse to subsidiaries, because it itself is the meaning of the subsidiaries. Meaning here is always located ahead rather than behind the fictive act and thus can never be allegorically recovered. There are some interesting connections here to the Kantian notion of "internal purposiveness" in art and aesthetic experience. If we consider Kuhn's retreat from antimyth and note that it involves refusal to posit an ontological limit, we may come to conclude that Kant's aesthetic theory unintentionally encompasses his critique of pure reason, just as Schiller seems to have tried to make it encompass his ethical theory. Kuhn's retreat is, in these terms, a disestablishment of external purposiveness in science and turns science in the direction of art.

At the mythical pole we have the contrary to the duality of subject/object. The world is part of us, but we are also extended into the world. John Butler Yeats wrote that the poet is involved in a "continual progress in identifying himself with everything that lives, and that does not live, not merely men and women or animals and birds but even trees and plants and rocks and stones."[37] The fundamental quality of mythical thought, as I use the term here, is the drive toward identity, the contrary of difference/indifference. The condition of pure myth would be the successful taking of everything into one's own imagination and the identification of all the elements once inside *with* the whole, yet the maintenance of the individual identity *of* everything so that it is *let be,* to use a phrase of Heidegger. The condition of pure antimyth would be the externalization and objectification of everything except at a central unmoving point, an isolated, purely subjective and totally passive consciousness, alien to everything else. But then there is the turn—the drift back to myth, the yearning for some form of total unification.

Of course, if we try to transcend the opposition I have posed and gain a more spacious view, the antimyth reveals itself as a fiction: The antimyth, the subject surrounded by an alien object, is itself a human creation—something *inside* and emanating from the human imagination. In this light, a shift in my own metaphor is necessary; for my continuum appears to be a sort of fountain whose source is myth and whose jet reaches toward complete analytic or externalizing power but which returns cyclically to its source for replenishment. If this is correct, we can declare that the intellectual life feeds on myth, as Blake's "devourer" feeds on his "prolific," and that the proper organization of the liberal arts and sciences is vertical, the fine arts and literature at the foundation, the pure sciences at the top, with the various humanistic disciplines and social sciences in between. Except, of course, that there is always a flow back, with antimyth at the top returning, often as potentiality for myth.

But full absorption into myth would be impossible to cultural man, as is phase 15 of Yeats's wheel. Yeats calls it a "supernatural incarnation" and thus introduces a "miraculous" though unachievable space. I prefer to call it a fictive limit we never reach. The limit we can reach at this end of the continuum is art. Myth is a term indicating a limit being approached by all symbolic activity that would claim to make, not merely copy or signify. Approaching the limit, language asserts its freedom from antimythical strictures about language. It brings the qualities of myth into action as a contrary to antimythical power. Pure indifference, in the Yeatsian sense of phase 15, impossible in his system, would be unable to grant antimyth its place; and if antimyth is not granted its place, all of the potential vicious social possibilities of myth would be unleashed, and the world would become unlivable, as it threatened to be under Nazism. By the same token, pure antimyth is reduction to an unlivable center of alienation.

Recently, Northrop Frye, continuing his expansion of the terms "myth" and "mythology" beyond the confines of "literature" to designate larger social verbal structures, has remarked:

> A mythological universe is a vision of reality in terms of human concerns and hopes and anxieties; it is not a primitive form of science. Unfortunately, human nature being what it is, man first acquires a mythological universe and then pretends as long as he can that it is also the actual universe. All mythological universes are by definition centered on man,

[37] *Further Letters of John Butler Yeats,* ed. Lennox Robinson (Dundrum: The Cuala Press, 1920), p. 22. [Au.]

> therefore the actual universe was also assumed to be centered on man.[38]

This passage touches on many of the issues with which I have been concerned. The appearance of science, the creator of Frye's "actual universe," did not destroy or render unnecessary a "mythological universe." Frye makes a very interesting point about this where he suggests that at one time technology seemed to promise a marriage with myth that would produce one dominant structure:

> . . . but poets have dragged their feet in its celebration. Blake, D. H. Lawrence, Morris, Yeats, Pound, are only a few of those who have shown marked hostility to technology and have refused to believe that its peaceful and destructive aspects can be separated. The poets see nothing imaginative in a domination of nature which expresses no love for it, in an activity founded on will, which always overreacts, in a way of life marked by a constant increase in speed, which means also an increase in introversion and the breaking down of genuine personal relationships.[39]

Frye goes on to suggest that for these reasons science fiction began as celebration ("hardware fantasy") of technology but has quickly become "software philosophical romance."[40]

It must always be so. Science is always a movement out of myth and inevitably tends to the contrary end of a continuum. It can never successfully force on society complete victory of what is therefore antimyth without perpetrating its own form of disaster. Frye's remarks point to how a myth that has closed itself and has become a doctrine, demanding subservience, can be the vehicle of terror. Under such conditions, the contrary is not admitted, as for so long the Copernican theory was rejected because it was not compatible with a man-centered myth that had closed itself into doctrine. Curiously, then, a man-centered myth that closes itself decenters man. Frye points to the opposite terror above, where the antimyth negates the human center and alienates nature.

[38] Northrop Frye, *The Secular Scripture: A Study of the Structure of Romance* (Cambridge, Mass.: Harvard University Press, 1976), p. 14. [Au.]
[39] Ibid., p. 180. [Au.]
[40] Ibid. [Au.]

Figure 12.2 illustrates an attempt to build a dialectical continuum on which can be placed two of the forms that constitute what we call the humanistic disciplines, for the myth/antimyth contrary does not divide up all human activity. Indeed, I have already collapsed it into a more fundamental metaphor of the fountain. The fountain generates a cyclical movement by virtue of a constant return of antimyth to myth. Still the notion of a continuum between contraries is useful for a while longer. There is a ground all along the continuum, to say nothing of a middle ground. All the so-called academic disciplines are somewhere on the continuum, usually described in the more general forms of the fine arts, the humanities, the social sciences, and natural sciences. To read recent philosophy and history of science is to recognize that the ground of scientific activity in its largest sense is unspecifiable and is not a hypothetical-empirical model with an ontological limit, which is the appearance of Holton's S_2. To recognize this offers perhaps some solace to the so-called social scientist, who seems in practice torn between the model of S_2 and various forms of supposedly subjective expression. Talcott Parsons's brief outline of the history of the social sciences describes ideological struggles among competing views of the disciplines. It was not until Weber, he concludes, that a social science balancing contending forces was evolved. Parsons makes a claim for the social sciences as an autonomous disciplinary category, emerging from the contending forces of empiricist-utilitarian monism and idealistic dualism. He defends the tripartite academic division of humanities, social sciences, and natural sciences:

> [the social sciences] are not natural sciences in the sense of excluding the categories of subjective meaning, that is, they must consider knowing subjects as objects. Nor are they humanistic-cultural in the sense that the individuality of particular meanings must take complete precedence over analytical generalities and such categories as causality.[41]

This is almost a fair statement. But one could say a good deal more, since clearly the statement implies

[41] Talcott Parsons, "Unity and Diversity in the Modern Intellectual Disciplines: The Role of the Social Sciences," *Daedalus* 94, no. 1 (Winter 1965): 63. [Au.]

Fig. 12.2. The Cyclical Fiction of Cultural Forms

Mythic Pole ← Toward Myth → THE IRONIC — Toward Anti-Myth → Anti-Mythic Pole

Language and Myths	*Art*	*Criticism*	*History*	*Religion*	*Mathematics and Science*
unity of feeling	radical creation	creation/ description	past as presence/ past as past	upper/lower	object/subject
synthesis	particular	interpretation	ideality of recollection	ethical meaning	numerical determinism
sympathy of relationship (identity)	freedom	art/science	determinism/ freedom	God/man	Nature/man
URTHONA	(Los)	LUVAH (Orc)		THARMAS (covering cherub)	URIZEN (Satan)

(indifference/difference is opposed by identity.) ⟵ Return of anti-myth to myth, of mathematics to art, of religion to myth, of differentiation to poetry in the fictive act. ⟵ (indifference and difference are opposed, and indifference is negated.)

that social science always *externalizes* the knowing subject. Accepting the notion of internal/external or subject/object, the statement is grounded in anti-myth. Because of the externalization of the knowing subject into an object, the ideal form of social science here is behavioral. (I use this term not in opposition to "instinct" psychology, as it is sometimes used, but to cover both modes as deterministic.) The behavioral form can be thought of as a displacement of the ideal mathematical form of anti-myth. Periodically in the social sciences, and most recently with the advent of highly sophisticated computers, there is an ebullient attempt to adopt pure mathematical form in the discipline. But then there is a tendency to pull back. Holton remarks:

> . . . disciplines such as psychology (and certainly history) are so constructed that they are wrong to imitate the habit in the modern physical sciences to depress or project the discussion forcibly to the x/y plane [S_2]. When the thematic component is as strong and as explicitly needed as it is in these fields, the criteria of acceptability should be able to remain explicitly in three-dimensional proposition space.[42]

[42] Holton, *Thematic Origins,* p. 65. [Au.]

Social science's relation to mathematics is ironic and not entirely different from natural science's flirtation with an ontological limit. On the other hand, to move toward the mythical passing some point of balance turns a social science into something of recognizably other dimensions. Too often the disciplines of history and literary criticism, placed in the area of the "ironic" on figure 12.2, are battlefields in which opposing sides make efforts to drag the discipline toward the extreme either of myth or of antimyth. If pulled in either direction, these disciplines lose their reason for being. The purely empirical or antimythical historian tends to make no distinction between the writing of history (history as a symbolic discipline) and the flow of events. One simply copies or signifies the other. I have actually known historians who have been unable to distinguish the two or to recognize that there is some sort of problem implicit in this naïvely empiricist notion. This breed ought to be on the decline, given the recent invasion of historical study by analysts of language; but the solution to the problem of the place of history is not to flee to the opposite and identify it as an art, which is only to loosen it from qualities of empiricism that all historical writing must have.

The important thing to recognize at this point is that an empirical act is a constitutive act. Both criticism and history must constitute something as an "object" of study, even as they know that they are "constituting" it, that is, creating a fiction according to certain antimythical categories. *At the same time,* they must reach out toward mythic identification with that object *as if* it were not yet constituted. In a few versions of recent reader-oriented criticism this has been acknowledged, though more often such criticism refuses to constitute the object (even as a fictive object). Blake said that the inexplicit can "rouse the faculties to act," and Keats insisted on art's bringing about a "momentous depth of speculation." Both of these observations insist on an "object" of some sort that is doing these things, but they also require a constitutive act of the reader or viewer before the work can be said to have any value. Neither statement is as sophisticated as we would want it to be today, but with some extension either could be used to show that a text is *there* as potentiality, but that we must always constitute it as there with a certain independence from us, even as we must insist on our involvement with it. It is both/and, as are all activities in relation to whatever they constitute. Recently some critics have seemed to want to become more important than the potentialities from which they constitute their readings; for a while, the style was to claim to be transparent interpreters of superior texts. This is part of the *politics* of critical theory, which appears to be cyclical: either there is a flight from objectification of meaning, even as it seems to be established; or there is a flight from subjectivity, even as it is practiced. Blake describes this sort of cyclicity (on a considerably grander scale than I have here) in the struggle of Orc and Urizen, which goes nowhere; and he has to bring in his character Los as a contrary. It is this cyclical situation that I believe Stanley Fish is attempting to avoid in the last chapters of *Is There a Text in This Class?* There he makes no claim (or almost no claim) that the ways of criticism will change as a result of his arguments, only that one ought to know what kind of game one is playing (and perhaps square one's language with the facts of it: a task that is not easy).[43] It is this cyclicity that I am trying to provide a contrary to.

I am claiming that both criticism and history are creative cultural forms. Their constitutive acts are "ironic" because (from the point of view of a commentary on them) they must maintain both mythical and antimythical stances at the same time. Not to go too far in the direction of either pole as an authority produces the virtue we call scholarly restraint. The growth of literary theory and historiography as separate subjects has recently been accelerated by a greater appreciation of the problems of expression in the two fields that this ironic situation generates.

In figure 12.1 both historical writing and literary criticism would have to be placed somewhere between center and circumference—between where language claims to create and where it claims to "copy" or to describe analytically. I should like to return to the implications of that chart for criticism and for poetry: At the mythico-poetic pole tropes are not tropes in the classical sense, but integrative, creative acts. In the classical rhetorical view there must always be a gap between word and concept; there is always conceivably a better word for the concept. But, if we regard language in action as generating concepts, from a source of unspecifiable subsidiaries, the concept is not an otherness but an emanation (but *not* a lost Blakean one), and the word does not "signify" an externality in the ordinary antimythical sense of the term.

According to this view, language generates out of itself antimyth, and antimyth then demands the verbal fiction of the nonverbal concept or pure idea, or in science the ontological limit. But this fiction, apart from language, has no external substance; it is always created symbolically.

The most radical form of phenomenology would tell us we must get back to things and free ourselves of the tyrannical abstractness of all words and ideas. This, too, would presume the existence of a norm of language distant from the mythic pole. It sets up an idea of signifier and signified and concludes that no poem can connect itself to a signified in the sense of a referent. Therefore, the argument goes, we must abandon language or work through it to the object. This position finds language a prison house from which there is a radical escape through the negation of language.

On the contrary, we must affirm that the imagination and language have a hand in constructing things for culture. From the point of view of the poetic, which is language-centered, therefore

[43] Stanley Fish, *Is There a Text in This Class?* (Cambridge, Mass., and London: Harvard University Press, 1981), pp. 303–71. [Au.]

imagination-centered, therefore man-centered, a world prior to human culture, which is always proceeding from myth, lacks full reality or is mere potentiality. It is always only subsidiary and unspecifiable because not here yet. The world of culture is something we are *always proceeding to make* rather than *referring back or outward toward.* From the point of view of antimyth, of course, the world is an objective *out there;* it is what Frye has called the "actual universe" to be described by science: But as we think about it, or in any form of our thinking about it, that too is a creation of antimyth. It quickly becomes an abstract idea as fictive as Locke's "primary" qualities were to Blake.

What I have been seeking is a theory of secular creativity in language that gives priority, but not the power that Blake called negation, to the fictive. In this attempt I have chosen to adopt the term "symbolic." Benedetto Croce was quite right to ask what a symbol, used in this sense, symbolizes. I employ symbolization to indicate an act of linguistic creativity. For the symbolic, in my usage, there is no symbolized, only the realm of the potential to be worked up into the symbolic. In Croce's terms, this would involve not the identity of intuition and expression, but the unspecifiability of intuition *outside* of expression. Being is not prior to but *in* the field of language. As such, it is, of course, cultural being and moral being. It does not say there is no world there, but it also does claim that the world there is not the world of the "object." It is a potentiality for the human imagination to work upon, and it throws moral responsibility radically on man. This is why that wise author Joyce Cary said he feared what man would do with imagination and freedom, though he celebrated them in all his books.

Man, then, is not only a devourer of language but is also a constant creator of forms in language in the manner of Blake's "ancient poets," whom Blake declares to have confronted a potentiality and set about making (by naming) the world of culture. Each of us, however, grows up in a language that, like Blake's eternal London, is constantly decaying even as it is being built. True, as continental criticism likes to tell us, we cannot recapture an original undifferentiated innocence. Nor is it important whether it ever existed or not. We have instead the endless task of retrieving language from its own tendency toward ruin or exhaustion. If creation does not go on as decay takes place, the world of human culture becomes Hell. Hell is the diminishment of culture, the result of adoption of the antimyth of human passivity as dogma and the negation of linguistic imagination. But it can also be the result of the negation of antimyth and a seeking for solace in the primitive.

This view directs us radically toward the future, not toward the nothingness and individual death that is the fundamental reality of the existentialists, but toward the continuing act of linguistic creation, toward a passing along of the cultural role. It suggests that the poet's materials are always for him a potentiality to be worked up into form. Every poet begins the day as did Blake's ancients. Each such beginning restores the literal root meaning of "poet." However, as I have suggested, the maker of fictions is not merely the poet as conventionally conceived but everyone who symbolizes, including those opposite makers who seem to be taking apart or "copying" but actually are constructing antimyth. It becomes clear, from this point of view, for example, that history, which seems directed toward copying an outward past, is also the act of creating that past, a symbolic past, which is the only past we have. We are always thus on the threshold of history in an entirely different sense from the common one. We are always making it. Yet, belonging to the "ironic," historians are also hypostatizing a past and "copying" it.

The difference between *signifiant* and *signifié* is itself a fictive creation of language as it operates at a distance from the mythic pole, beyond that unlocatable point where what Vico called "poetic logic" has turned into antimyth. To look back to the poem from a vantage beyond the turning point is to submit it to a mode of thought that is the poem's negation, where the poem is merely its analyzed structure or is only a romantic allegory. But these are all characterizations finally not of the poem but of the limitations of this point of view toward the poem. This allegoric vantage is in the area of antimyth, where language has extended itself to invent the dislocations that we, when we stand *there,* thrust back upon poems.

But one must beware of simply located points of difference on the continuum. That is to be thrust back into an awkward distinction between ordinary and literary, steno and depth language, and overspatializes and quantifies the unmeasurable continuum between center and circumference. The whole continuum is creative. As we pass further and further outward (really, of course, inward, creating more and more externality as we go), what we create is the fiction or antimyth of externality—until we reach mathematics, where something very strange happens—for mathematics proceeds to assert its power to contain, claims that the world is mathematical rather than that mathematics represents the world. Our continuum, by turning inside out, defies measurement, which belongs to antimyth. Heisenberg's notion of the thing-in-itself as a mathematical structure can be read as the assertion of a fictive containment of antimyth.

I have said that the place of criticism on this continuum of language is ironic. Because it must project itself farther out on the radius (or farther inward—therefore pointing outward) than any so-called literary text it treats, it must employ the categories of analysis and reduction, even as it must at some point reject those categories. This is why Frye was compelled in his *Anatomy* to begin by claiming criticism to be a science, but in the end to make his work an anatomy, thus fictively containing his science or antimyth.[44] From this odd perch, irony is one of the things criticism projects back into poetry when critical language cannot hold the poem together in any other way. Certain critics, marveling sweetly over their own condition, imagine that criticism may well be more interesting than poetry today. It should be no surprise that this self-regarding activity should valorize allegory. But this takes us back to a conclusion already reached that criticism is finally, like all symbolic forms, at least partly a *making* of its own. From its ironic area, it produces an antimyth of bifurcations even while it protects the poem's myth. The danger to criticism is to lose the only area where it is distinctly something other than either myth or antimyth, though always in irresolution and always having to be done again.

This theory of "secular" creativity, then, though it refuses to draw a line measuring off poetry from other forms of discourse, and though it argues for the creativity of all language, does not quarrel with our needs as critics to create the dialectical contrariety of myth and antimyth—for the whole system is a creation of criticism—where a continuum is what we apparently have created. The fiction includes the antimyth of difference/indifference and of nature as mathematical law. Blake called antimyth the "starry floor" beneath which, through God's mercy, man could not fall any further than he already had.[45] I do not believe in a fall, but I do believe in a limit.

Criticism, under the ironic condition I have outlined, would seem to be a struggle of radical creation with descriptive analysis, in which neither can be allowed full sway. History would seem to be the product of the historian's mediation between the past regarded as a presence (that is, constructed) and the past regarded as a past (reconstructed or "copied"). We see in both criticism and history an oscillation, at times, between these two poles. A movement to either extreme tends to vitiate the critic's or the historian's ironic strength. At the creative extreme we find par excellence Walter Pater's treatment of the Mona Lisa, which W. B. Yeats quite appropriately turned into verse for his *Oxford Book of Modern Verse*.[46] At the other extreme are a variety of reductive processes, the emphasis on critical "methodologies" and "approaches" and empirical modes.

The diagram of cultural forms (fig. 12.2) converts itself into a circle by virtue of what I call the return of antimyth to myth. This illustrates the point I have made about the creativity of antimyth even as its creation denies creativity. This is a paradox after all, so figure 12.2 must be amended to show that, as a creative force, antimyth in the end (in returning to myth) finally regains possession of its own paradox. The return of antimyth to myth, in this sense, is also the return of mathematics, the language of science, to art, where Frye placed it as a containing form. It is also a return of religion to myth.

It may seem odd that I have placed religion on the antimythical side, and I admit that it often does not

[44] Frye's naming of his book as he did calls for some thought. The anatomy as a literary genre might well be regarded as an evoker of irony in my sense of the term. I claim irony to be the product of the relation of or difference between the poem and the commentary. Frye's work is "literary" but at the same time it stands outward from the poetic center (though not so far outward as to be "science" after all) because it hypostatizes an object, "literature," and is a commentary on that object. Yeats's *A Vision* has similar qualities, but I place it closer to the poetic center because it doesn't really have an object. It ends up commenting on itself. Of course, when I say center above, I really mean circumference. [Au.]

[45] In Blake's "Introduction to *Songs of Experience*," *Complete Writings*, p. 210. [Au.]

[46] *Oxford Book of Modern Verse*, ed. W. B. Yeats (New York: Oxford University Press, 1936), p. 1. [Au.]

want to stay there. There is little question that religion has its sources in and returns to myth; in the process of emanation it develops two antimythical characteristics. First, it acknowledges a threshold, in Wheelwright's sense—a form of otherness, which it then modifies in some versions with the notion of incarnation or "miraculous" symbol, which in turn implies a Fall. Second, it works toward development of the moral law, an external model of human action that is given supernatural sanction. But though it asserts these differences and posits an ideal realm of indifference, it also returns to myth via its own antimythical form: It tries to create through that form a vision of potential identity—the coexistence of freedom of individual moral choice with the law and the identicality of each individuality with all others. At the level with which we are now concerned, we can find a paradoxical creativity here—a creativity which involves a deliberate discipline of annihilation of the isolated selfhood and the flowing in of the fullness of a vision that is revelation in absence. In the end, such acts are chosen acts from the point of view of the artist. This is, in part, what I think Blake meant when from the point of view of the artist he wrote:

> Prayer is the Study of Art.
> Praise is the Practise of Art.
> Fasting &c., all relate to Art.
> The outward Ceremony is Antichrist.
> The Eternal Body of Man is The
> Imagination, that is,
> God himself
> The Divine Body[47]

On the other hand, from the point of view of the theologian, art ought to be a form of prayer.

I have somewhat frivolously connected various of the cultural forms with Blake's Zoas and (in parentheses) their "time forms." A fanciful essay could be written on these relationships. I am unable, however, to find a Zoa or other form to represent criticism. Perhaps this is because there ought to be something a little disembodied about the critical act. In Blake's poem it would have to be a ghostly fifth creature never quite anywhere—mediating, educating, and celebrating—somewhat fussy, perhaps, and regarded as rather a noxious vapor by the author.

[47] Blake, "The Laocoön," *Complete Writings*, p. 776. [Au.]

Edward W. Said

b. 1935

In its development, Edward W. Said's work has become more and more concerned with the relation of criticism to political questions, which are in his case always large questions and always moral questions. His views are deliberately meant to be impossible to classify—for reasons having to do with his sense of the social role of criticism itself. "Texts are worldly," he says, and criticism must treat of their worldliness. Said attacks a form of professionalism in criticism that removes texts from the world, and he looks very critically on the domestication of poststructuralist thought that tends to isolate texts in "textuality" or some system hermetically sealed from human politics. It is as if, for Said, deconstruction, once professionalized, has forgotten that language itself is "worldly." He insists that criticism must study the realities of power and authority in which texts come to be and exist. This requires of the critic a certain distance and yet at the same time involvement. The distance may be characterized as a "knowledge of history, a recognition of the importance of social circumstance, an analytical capacity for making distinctions." It appears that Said has displaced Kant's aesthetic judgment (see *CTSP*, pp. 377–99) back into the world from which it seemed to have been divorced. But Said wants not merely aesthetic disinterest or disinterest in the sense in which Matthew Arnold advocated it (see *CTSP*, pp. 583–95). He would certainly fault the notion of aesthetic judgment as being without a center or beginning in the world. As he says, his book *Beginnings: Intention and Method* "argued the practical and theoretical necessity of a reasoned point of departure for any intellectual and creative job of work." But he knows also that such positions are dangerous, because they inevitably shut out something. Arnold's "disinterest" was clearly affiliated with a narrow culture and thus had severe limitations. So, for the critic, Said posits a position of perpetual marginality. The critic has two choices: complicity with the ruling culture and willingness to exclude everything not "natural" to it, including its dominant political practices; and the attempt to study what Said calls the difference between "instinctual filiation" (nature) and "social affiliation" (culture) in the actual world. This distinction itself raises crucial questions of which Said is aware: Is "filiation" primordial, or is it but the received mode of "affiliation"? Was there a beginning we can possibly call natural filiation or is that in any case always already lost in the past? Either way, the proper role of the critic is both inside and outside of "affiliation": "Always situated, it is skeptical, secular, reflectively open to its own failings." It can never be value-free, which is to say it cannot be without an ethical "beginning."

Said's books are *Joseph Conrad and the Fiction of Autobiography* (1966); *Beginnings: Intention and Method* (1975); *Orientalism* (1978); *The Question of Palestine* (1979); *Covering Islam* (1981); and *The World, the Text, and the Critic* (1983).

SECULAR CRITICISM

Literary criticism is practiced today in four major forms. One is the practical criticism to be found in book reviewing and literary journalism. Second is academic literary history, which is a descendant of such nineteenth-century specialties as classical scholarship, philology, and cultural history. Third is literary appreciation and interpretation, principally academic but, unlike the other two, not confined to professionals and regularly appearing authors. Appreciation is what is taught and performed by teachers of literature in the university and its beneficiaries in a literal sense are all those millions of people who have learned in a classroom how to read a poem, how to enjoy the complexity of a metaphysical conceit, how to think of literature and figurative language as having characteristics that are unique and not reducible to a simple moral or political message. And the fourth form is literary theory, a relatively new subject. It appeared as an eye-catching topic for academic and popular discussion in the United States later than it did in Europe: people like Walter Benjamin and the young Georg Lukacs,[1] for instance, did their theoretical work in the early years of this century, and they wrote in a known, if not universally uncontested, idiom. American literary theory, despite the pioneering studies of Kenneth Burke[2] well before World War Two, came of age only in the 1970s, and that because of an observably deliberate attention to prior European models (structuralism, semiotics, deconstruction). . . .

Now the prevailing situation of criticism is such that the four forms represent in each instance specialization (although literary theory is a bit eccentric) and a very precise division of intellectual labor. Moreover, it is supposed that literature and the humanities exist generally within the culture ("our" culture, as it is sometimes known), that the culture is ennobled and validated by them, and yet that in the version of culture inculcated by professional humanists and literary critics, the approved practice of high culture is marginal to the serious political concerns of society.

This has given rise to a cult of professional expertise whose effect in general is pernicious. For the intellectual class, expertise has usually been a service rendered, and sold, to the central authority of society. This is the *trahison des clercs* of which Julien Benda spoke in the 1920s.[3] Expertise in foreign affairs, for example, has usually meant legitimization of the conduct of foreign policy and, what is more to the point, a sustained investment in revalidating the role of experts in foreign affairs.[4] The same sort of thing is true of literary critics and professional humanists, except that their expertise is based upon noninterference in what Vico[5] grandly calls the world of nations but which prosaically might just as well be called "the world." We tell our students and our general constituency that we defend the classics, the virtues of a liberal education, and the precious pleasures of literature even as we also show ourselves to be silent (perhaps incompetent) about the historical and social world in which all these things take place.

The degree to which the cultural realm and its expertise are institutionally divorced from their real

[1] See *Benjamin* and *Lukács*. [Eds.]

[2] Kenneth Burke (b. 1897) (see *CTSP*, pp. 942–47). [Eds.]

[3] Julien Benda (1867–1956), French author of *The Treason of the Intellectuals* (1927). [Eds.]

[4] There is a good graphic account of the problem in Noam Chomsky, *Language and Responsibility* (New York: Pantheon, 1977), p. 6; See also Edward W. Said, *Covering Islam* (New York: Pantheon, 1981), pp. 147–64. [Au.]

[5] Giovanni Battista Vico (1668–1744), *The New Science*; see *CTSP*, pp. 293–301. [Eds.]

connections with power was wonderfully illustrated for me by an exchange with an old college friend who worked in the Department of Defense for a period during the Vietnam war. The bombings were in full course then, and I was naively trying to understand the kind of person who could order daily B-52 strikes over a distant Asian country in the name of the American interest in defending freedom and stopping communism. "You know," my friend said, "the Secretary is a complex human being: he doesn't fit the picture you may have formed of the cold-blooded imperialist murderer. The last time I was in his office I noticed Durrell's *Alexandria Quartet* on his desk." He paused meaningfully, as if to let Durrell's presence on that desk work its awful power alone. The further implication of my friend's story was that no one who read and presumably appreciated a novel could be the cold-blooded butcher one might suppose him to have been.[6] Many years later this whole implausible anecdote (I do not remember my response to the complex conjunction of Durrell with the ordering of bombing in the sixties) strikes me as typical of what actually obtains: humanists and intellectuals accept the idea that you can read classy fiction as well as kill and maim because the cultural world is available for that particular sort of camouflaging, and because cultural types are not supposed to interfere in matters for which the social system has not certified them. What the anecdote illustrates is the approved separation of high-level bureaucrat from the reader of novels of questionable worth and definite status.

During the late 1960s, however, literary theory presented itself with new claims. The intellectual origins of literary theory in Europe were, I think it is accurate to say, insurrectionary. The traditional university, the hegemony of determinism and positivism, the reification of ideological bourgeois "humanism," the rigid barriers between academic specialties: it was powerful responses to all these that linked together such influential progenitors of today's literary theorist as Saussure, Lukacs, Bataille, Lévi-Strauss, Freud, Nietzsche, and Marx.[7] Theory proposed itself as a synthesis overriding the petty fiefdoms within the world of intellectual production, and it was manifestly to be hoped as a result that all the domains of human activity could be seen, and lived, as a unity.

And yet something happened, perhaps inevitably. From being a bold interventionary movement across lines of specialization, American literary theory of the late seventies had retreated into the labyrinth of "textuality," dragging along with it the most recent apostles of European revolutionary textuality—Derrida and Foucault[8]—whose trans-Atlantic canonization and domestication they themselves seemed sadly enough to be encouraging. It is not too much to say that American or even European literary theory now explicitly accepts the principle of noninterference, and that its peculiar mode of appropriating its subject matter (to use Althusser's[9] formula) is *not* to appropriate anything that is worldly, circumstantial, or socially contaminated. "Textuality" is the somewhat mystical and disinfected subject matter of literary theory.

Textuality has therefore become the exact antithesis and displacement of what might be called history. Textuality is considered to take place, yes, but by the same token it does not take place anywhere or anytime in particular. It is produced, but by no one and at no time. It can be read and interpreted, although reading and interpreting are routinely understood to occur in the form of misreading and misinterpreting. The list of examples could be extended indefinitely, but the point would remain the same. As it is practiced in the American academy today, literary theory has for the most part isolated textuality from the circumstances, the events, the physical senses that made it possible and render it intelligible as the result of human work.

Even if we accept (as in the main I do) the arguments put forward by Hayden White—that there is no way to get past texts in order to apprehend "real" history directly[10]—it is still possible to say

[6]The example of the Nazi who read Rilke and then wrote out genocidal orders to his concentration-camp underlings had not yet become well known. Perhaps then the Durrell–Secretary of Defense anecdote might not have seemed so useful to my enthusiastic friend. [Au.]

[7]Georges Bataille (1897–1962), French writer; see *de Saussure, Lukács, Lévi-Strauss;* Freud (see *CTSP,* pp. 748–53); Nietzsche (see *CTSP,* pp. 635–41); Marx (see *CTSP,* pp. 631–34). [Eds.]

[8]See *Derrida* and *Foucault.* [Eds.]

[9]See *Althusser.* [Eds.]

[10]See Hayden White, *Metahistory: The Historical Imagination in Nineteenth-Century Europe* (Baltimore: Johns Hopkins University Press, 1973), and his *Tropics of Dis-*

that such a claim need not also eliminate interest in the events and the circumstances entailed by and expressed in the texts themselves. Those events and circumstances are textual too (nearly all of Conrad's tales and novels present us with a situation—say a group of friends sitting on a ship's deck listening to a story—giving rise to the narrative that forms the text), and much that goes on in texts alludes to them, *affiliates* itself directly to them. My position is that texts are worldly, to some degree they are events, and, even when they appear to deny it, they are nevertheless a part of the social world, human life, and of course the historical moments in which they are located and interpreted.

Literary theory, whether of the Left or of the Right, has turned its back on these things. This can be considered, I think, the triumph of the ethic of professionalism. But it is no accident that the emergence of so narrowly defined a philosophy of pure textuality and critical noninterference has coincided with the ascendancy of Reaganism, or for that matter with a new cold war, increased militarism and defense spending, and a massive turn to the right on matters touching the economy, social services, and organized labor.[11] In having given up the world entirely for the aporias and unthinkable paradoxes of a text,[12] contemporary criticism has retreated from its constituency, the citizens of modern society, who have been left to the hands of "free" market forces, multinational corporations, the manipulations of consumer appetites. A precious jargon has grown up, and its formidable complexities obscure the social realities that, strange though it may seem, encourage a scholarship of "modes of excellence" very far from daily life in the age of declining American power.

Criticism can no longer cooperate in or pretend to ignore this enterprise. It is not practicing criticism either to validate the status quo or to join up with a priestly caste of acolytes and dogmatic metaphysicians. Each essay in this book[13] affirms the connection between texts and the existential actualities of human life, politics, societies, and events. The realities of power and authority—as well as the resistances offered by men, women, and social movements to institutions, authorities, and orthodoxies—are the realities that make texts possible, that deliver them to their readers, that solicit the attention of critics. I propose that these realities are what should be taken account of by criticism and the critical consciousness.

It should be evident by now that this sort of criticism can only be practiced outside and beyond the consensus ruling the art today in the four accepted forms I mentioned earlier. Yet if this is the function of criticism at the present time, to be between the dominant culture and the totalizing forms of critical systems, then there is some comfort in recalling that this has also been the destiny of critical consciousness in the recent past.

No reader of Erich Auerbach's *Mimesis,* one of the most admired and influential books of literary criticism ever written, has failed to be impressed by the circumstances of the book's actual writing. These are referred to almost casually by Auerbach in the last lines of his epilogue, which stands as a very brief methodological explanation for what is after all a monumental work of literary intelligence. In remarking that for so ambitious a study as "the representation of reality in Western Literature" he could not deal with everything that had been written in and about Western literature. Auerbach then adds:

> I may also mention that the book was written during the war and at Istanbul, where the libraries are not equipped for European studies. International communications were impeded; I had to dispense with almost all periodicals, with almost all the more recent investigations, and in some cases with reliable critical editions of my texts. Hence it is possible and even probable that I overlooked things which I ought to have considered and that I occasionally assert something that modern research has disproved or modified. . . . On the other hand, it is quite possible that the book owes its existence to just this lack of a rich and specialized library. If it had been possible for me to acquaint myself with all the work that has been done on so

course: Essays in Cultural Criticism (Baltimore: Johns Hopkins University Press, 1978). [Au.] See *White.* [Eds.]

[11] See my article "Opponents, Audiences, Constituencies, and Community," *Critical Inquiry* (Fall 1982), for an analysis of the liaison between the cult of textuality and the ascendancy of Reaganism. [Au.]

[12] See *de Man.* [Eds.]

[13] This essay is the introduction to thirteen essays. [Eds.]

> many subjects, I might never have reached the point of writing.[14]

The drama of this little bit of modesty is considerable, in part because Auerbach's quiet tone conceals much of the pain of his exile. He was a Jewish refugee from Nazi Europe, and he was also a European scholar in the old tradition of German Romance scholarship. Yet now in Istanbul he was hopelessly out of touch with the literary, cultural, and political bases of that formidable tradition. In writing *Mimesis,* he implies to us in a later work, he was not merely practicing his profession despite adversity: he was performing an act of cultural, even civilizational, survival of the highest importance. What he had risked was not only the possibility of appearing in his writing to be superficial, out of date, wrong, and ridiculously ambitious (who in his right mind would take on as a project so vast a subject as Western literature in its entirety?). He had also risked, on the other hand, the possibility of *not* writing and thus falling victim to the concrete dangers of exile: the loss of texts, traditions, continuities that make up the very web of a culture. And in so losing the authentic presence of the culture, as symbolized materially by libraries, research institutes, other books and scholars, the exiled European would become an exorbitantly disoriented outcast from sense, nation, and milieu.

That Auerbach should choose to mention Istanbul as the place of his exile adds yet another dose of drama to the actual fact of *Mimesis.* To any European trained principally, as Auerbach was, in medieval and renaissance Roman literatures, Istanbul does not simply connote a place outside Europe. Istanbul represents the terrible Turk, as well as Islam, the scourge of Christendom, the great Oriental apostasy incarnate. Throughout the classical period of European culture Turkey was the Orient, Islam its most redoubtable and aggressive representative.[15] This was not all, though. The Orient and Islam also stood for the ultimate alienation from and opposition to Europe, the European tradition of Christian Latinity, as well as to the putative authority of ecclesia, humanistic learning, and cultural community. For centuries Turkey and Islam hung over Europe like a gigantic composite monster, seeming to threaten Europe with destruction. To have been an exile in Istanbul at that time of fascism in Europe was a deeply resonating and intense form of exile from Europe.

Yet Auerbach explicitly makes the point that it was precisely his distance from home—in all senses of that word—that made possible the superb undertaking of *Mimesis.* How did exile become converted from a challenge or a risk, or even from an active impingement on his European selfhood, into a positive mission, whose success would be a cultural act of great importance?

The answer to this question is to be found in Auerbach's autumnal essay, "Philologie der Weltliteratur." The major part of the essay elaborates on the notion first explicitly announced in *Mimesis,* but already recognizable in Auerbach's early interest in Vico, that philological work deals with humanity at large and transcends national boundaries. As he says, "our philological home is the earth: it can no longer be the nation." His essay makes clear, however, that his earthly home is European culture. But then, as if remembering the period of his extra-European exile in the Orient, he adds: "The most priceless and indispensable part of a philologist's heritage is still his own nation's culture and heritage. Only when he is first separated from this heritage, however, and then transcends it does it become truly effective."[16] In order to stress the salutary value of separation from home, Auerbach cites a passage from Hugo of St. Victor's *Didascalicon:*

> It is, therefore, a great source of virtue for the practiced mind to learn, bit by bit, first to change about in visible and transitory things, so that afterwards it may be able to leave them behind altogether. The man who finds his homeland sweet is still a tender beginner; he to whom every soil is as his native one is already strong; but he is perfect to whom the entire world is as a foreign land [the Latin text is more explicit here—*perfectus vero cui mundus totus exilium est*].

[14] Erich Auerbach, *Mimesis: The Representation of Reality in Western Literature,* trans. Willard Trask (1953; rpt. Princeton: Princeton University Press, 1968), p. 557. [Au.]

[15] See the evidence in Samuel C. Chew, *The Crescent and the Rose: Islam and England During the Renaissance* (New York: Oxford University Press, 1937). [Au.]

[16] Auerbach, "Philology and *Weltliteratur,*" trans. M. and E. W. Said, *Centennial Review,* 13 (Winter 1969), p. 17. [Au.]

This is all that Auerbach quotes from Hugo; the rest of the passage continues along the same lines.

> The tender soul has fixed his love on one spot in the world; the strong man has extended his love to all places; the perfect man has extinguished his. From boyhood I have dwelt on foreign soil, and I know with what grief sometimes the mind takes leave of the narrow hearth of a peasant's hut, and I know, too, how frankly it afterwards disdains marble firesides and panelled halls.[17]

Auerbach associates Hugo's exilic credo with the notions of *paupertas* and *terra aliena,*[18] even though in his essay's final words he maintains that the ascetic code of willed homelessness is "a good way also for one who wishes to earn a proper love for the world." At this point, then, Auerbach's epilogue to *Mimesis* suddenly becomes clear: "it is quite possible that the book owes its existence to just this lack of a rich and specialized library." In other words, the book owed its existence to the very fact of Oriental, non-Occidental exile and homelessness. And if this is so, then *Mimesis* itself is not, as it has so frequently been taken to be, only a massive reaffirmation of the Western cultural tradition, but also a work built upon a critically important alienation from it, a work whose conditions and circumstances of existence are not immediately derived from the culture it describes with such extraordinary insight and brilliance but built rather on an agonizing distance from it. Auerbach says as much when he tells us in an earlier section of *Mimesis* that, had he tried to do a thorough scholarly job in the traditional fashion, he could never have written the book: the culture itself, with its authoritative and authorizing agencies, would have prevented so audacious a one-man task. Hence the executive value of exile, which Auerbach was able to turn into effective use.

Let us look again at the notion of place, the notion by which during a period of displacement someone like Auerbach in Istanbul could feel himself to be out of place, exiled, alienated. The readiest account of place might define it as the nation, and certainly in the exaggerated boundary drawn between Europe and the Orient—a boundary with a long and often unfortunate tradition in European thought[19]—the idea of the nation, of a national-cultural community as a sovereign entity and place set against other places, has its fullest realization. But this idea of place does not cover the nuances, principally of reassurance, fitness, belonging, association, and community, entailed in the phrase *at home* or *in place*. In this book I shall use the word *culture* to suggest an environment, process, and hegemony in which individuals (in their private circumstances) and their works are embedded, as well as overseen at the top by a superstructure and at the base by a whole series of methodological attitudes. It is in culture that we can seek out the range of meanings and ideas conveyed by the phrases *belonging to* or *in a* place, being *at home in a place.*

The idea of culture of course is a vast one. As a systematic body of social and political as well as historical significance, "culture" is similarly vast; one index of it is the Kroeber-Kluckhohn thesaurus on meanings of the word "culture" in social science.[20] I shall avoid the details of these proliferating meanings, however, and go straight to what I think can best serve my purposes here. In the first place, culture is used to designate not merely something to which one belongs but something that one possesses and, along with that proprietary process, culture also designates a boundary by which the concepts of what is extrinsic or intrinsic to the culture come into forceful play. These things are not controversial: most people employing *culture* would assent to them, as Auerbach does in the epilogue when he speaks of being in Istanbul, away from his habitual cultural environment, within its research materials and familiar environment.

But, in the second place, there is a more interesting dimension to this idea of culture as possessing possession. And that is the power of culture by virtue of its elevated or superior position to authorize, to dominate, to legitimate, demote, interdict, and validate: in short, the power of culture to be an agent of, and perhaps the main agency for, powerful differentiation within its domain and beyond it too.

[17] Hugo of St. Victor, *Didascalicon,* trans. Jerome Taylor (New York: Columbia University Press, 1961), p. 101. [Au.]

[18] *paupertas:* poverty; *terra aliena:* alien land. [Eds.]

[19] See my *Orientalism* (New York: Pantheon, 1978), esp. chap. 1. [Au.]

[20] A. L. Kroeber and Clyde Kluckhohn, *Culture: A Critical Review of Concepts and Definitions* (1952; rprt. New York: Vintage Books, 1963). [Au.]

It is this idea that is evident in French Orientalism, for example, as distinguished from English Orientalism, and this in turn plays a major role in the work of Ernest Renan, Louis Massignon, and Raymond Schwab, major scholars whose work is assessed in the last part of this book.[21]

When Auerbach speaks of not being able to write such a book as *Mimesis* had he remained in Europe, he refers precisely to that grid of research techniques and ethics by which the prevailing culture imposes on the individual scholar its canons of how literary scholarship is to be conducted. Yet even this sort of imposition is a minor aspect of culture's power to dominate and authorize work. What is more important in culture is that it is a system of values *saturating* downward almost everything within its purview; yet, paradoxically, culture dominates from above without at the same time being available to everything and everyone it dominates. In fact, in our age of media-produced attitudes, the ideological insistence of a culture drawing attention to itself as superior has given way to a culture whose canons and standards are invisible to the degree that they are "natural," "objective," and "real."

Historically one supposes that culture has always involved hierarchies; it has separated the elite from the popular, the best from the less than best, and so forth. It has also made certain styles and modes of thought prevail over others. But its tendency has always been to move downward from the height of power and privilege in order to diffuse, disseminate, and expand itself in the widest possible range. In its beneficent form this is the culture of which Matthew Arnold speaks in *Culture and Anarchy* as stimulating in its adherents a powerful zeal:

> The great men of culture are those who have had a passion for diffusing, for making prevail, for carrying from one end of society to the other, the best knowledge, the best ideas of their time; who have laboured to divest knowledge of all that was harsh, uncouth, difficult, abstract, professional, exclusive; to humanise it, to make it efficient outside the clique of the cultivated and learned, yet still remaining the *best* knowledge and thought of the time [Arnold's definition of culture of course] and a true source, therefore, of sweetness and light.[22]

The question raised by Arnold's passion for culture here is the relationship between culture and society. He argues that society is the actual, material base over which culture tries, through the great men of culture, to extend its sway. The optimum relationship between culture and society then is *correspondence,* the former covering the latter. What is too often overlooked by Arnold's readers is that he views this ambition of culture to reign over society as essentially combative: "the best that is known and thought" must contend with competing ideologies, philosophies, dogmas, notions, and values, and it is Arnold's insight that what is at stake in society is not merely the cultivation of individuals, or the development of a class of finely tuned sensibilities, or the renaissance of interest in the classics, but rather the assertively achieved and *won* hegemony of an identifiable set of ideas, which Arnold honorifically calls culture, over all other ideas in society.

Yet it is still pertinent to ask Arnold where this struggle for hegemony takes place. If we say "in society" we will approach the answer, I think, but we will still have to specify *where* in society. In other words, Arnold's attention is to society defined grossly as, let us say, a nation—England, France, Germany—but more interestingly he seems also to be viewing society as a process and perhaps also an entity capable of being guided, controlled, even taken over. What Arnold always understood is that to be able to set a force or a system of ideas called "culture" over society is to have understood that the stakes played for are an identification of society with culture, and consequently the acquisition of a very formidable power. It is no accident that in his conclusion to *Culture and Anarchy* Arnold resolutely identifies a triumphant culture with the State, insofar as culture is man's best self and the State its realization in material reality. Thus the power of culture is potentially nothing less than the power of the State: Arnold is unambiguous on this point. He tells first of his unqualified opposition to such things as strikes and demonstrations, no matter how noble the cause, and then goes on to prove that such "anarchy" as strikes and demonstrations chal-

[21] Ernest Renan (1823–92), French historian; Louis Massignon (1883–1962), French orientalist; Raymond Schwab (1884–1956), French man of letters. [Eds.]

[22] Matthew Arnold, *Culture and Anarchy,* ed. J. Dover Wilson (1869; rpt. Cambridge: Cambridge University Press, 1969), p. 70. [Au.]

lenge the authority of the State, which is what morally, politically, and aesthetically they are:

> Because a State in which law is authoritative and sovereign, a firm and settled course of public order, is requisite if man is to bring to maturity anything precious and lasting now, or to found anything precious and lasting for the future.
>
> Thus in our eyes, the very framework and exterior order of the State, whoever may administer the State, is sacred; and culture is the most resolute enemy of anarchy, because of the great hopes and designs for the State which culture teaches us to nourish.[23]

The interdependence in Arnold's mind between culture, the sustained suzerainty of culture over society (anything precious and lasting), and the framework and quasi-theological exterior order of the State is perfectly clear. And it signifies a coincidence of power, which Arnold's entire rhetoric and thought constantly elaborates. To be for and in culture is to be in and for a State in a compellingly loyal way. With this assimilation of culture to the authority and exterior framework of the State go as well such things as assurance, confidence, the majority sense, the entire matrix of meanings we associate with "home," belonging and community. Outside this range of meanings—for it is the outside that partially defines the inside in this case—stand anarchy, the culturally disfranchised, those elements opposed to culture and State: the homeless, in short.

It is not my intention here to discuss in detail the profoundly important implications of Arnold's concluding remarks on culture. But it is worth insisting on at least a few of those implications in a broader setting than Arnold's. Even as an ideal for Arnold, culture must be seen as much for what it is not and for what it triumphs over when it is consecrated by the State as for what it positively is. This means that culture is a system of discriminations and evaluations—perhaps mainly aesthetic, as Lionel Trilling has said, but no less forceful and tyrannical for that[24]—for a particular class in the State able to identify with it; and it also means that culture is a system of exclusions legislated from above but enacted throughout its polity, by which such things as anarchy, disorder, irrationality, inferiority, bad taste, and immorality are identified, then deposited outside the culture and kept there by the power of the State and its institutions. For if it is true that culture is, on the one hand, a positive doctrine of the best that is thought and known, it is also on the other a differentially negative doctrine of all that is not best. If with Michel Foucault we have learned to see culture as an institutionalized process by which what is considered appropriate to it is kept appropriate, we have also seen Foucault demonstrating how certain alterities, certain Others, have been kept silent, outside or—in the case of his study of penal discipline and sexual repression—domesticated for use inside the culture.

Even if we wish to contest Foucault's findings about the exclusions by classical European culture of what it constituted as insane or irrational, and even if we are not convinced that the culture's paradoxical encouragement and repression of sexuality has been as generalized as he believes, we cannot fail to be convinced that the dialectic of self-fortification and self-confirmation by which culture achieves its hegemony over society and the State is based on a constantly practiced differentiation of self from what it believes to be not itself. And this differentiation is frequently performed by setting the valorized culture over the Other. This is by no means a metaphysical point, as two nineteenth-century English examples will demonstrate quickly. Both are related to the point I made earlier about Auerbach, that culture often has to do with an aggressive sense of nation, home, community, and belonging. First there is Macaulay's famous Minute of 1835 on Indian education:

> I have no knowledge of either Sanskrit or Arabic. But I have done what I could to form a correct estimate of their value. I have read translations of the most celebrated Arabic and Sanskrit works. I have conversed, both here and at home, with men distinguished by their proficiency in the Eastern tongues. I am quite ready to take the oriental learning at the valuation of the orientalists themselves. I have never found one among them who could deny that a single shelf of a good European library was worth the whole native literature of India and Arabia. The intrinsic superiority

[23] Ibid., p. 204. [Au.]

[24] Lionel Trilling, *Beyond Culture: Essays on Learning and Literature* (New York: Viking Press, 1965), p. 175. [Au.]

> of the Western literature is indeed fully admitted by those members of the committee who support the oriental plan of education . . . It is, I believe, no exaggeration to say that all the historical information which has been collected in the Sanscrit language is less valuable than what may be found in the paltry abridgements used at preparatory schools in England. In every branch of physical or moral philosophy, the relative position of the two nations is nearly the same.[25]

This is no mere expression of an opinion. Neither can it be dismissed, as in his *Grammatology* Derrida has dismissed Lévi-Strauss, as a textual instance of ethnocentrism. For it is that and more. Macaulay's was an ethnocentric opinion with ascertainable results. He was speaking from a position of power where he could translate his opinions into the decision to make an entire subcontinent of natives submit to studying in a language not their own. This in fact is what happened. In turn this validated the culture to itself by providing a precedent, and a case, by which superiority and power are lodged both in a rhetoric of belonging, or being "at home," so to speak, and in a rhetoric of administration: the two become interchangeable.

A second instance also concerns India. With admirable perspicacity Eric Stokes has studied the importance of utilitarian philosophy to British rule in India. What is striking in Stokes's *The English Utilitarians and India* is how a relatively small body of thinkers—among them Bentham, of course, and both Mills—were able to argue and implement a philosophic doctrine for India's governance, a doctrine in some respects bearing an unmistakable resemblance to Arnold's and Macaulay's views of European culture as superior to all others. John Stuart Mill among the India House Utilitarians has today a higher cultural status, so much so that his views on liberty and representative government have for generations passed as the advanced liberal culture statement on these matters. Yet of Mill, Stokes has this to say: "In his essay *On Liberty* John Stuart Mill had carefully stated that its doctrines were only meant to apply to those countries which were sufficiently advanced in civilization to be capable of settling their affairs by rational discussion. He was faithful to his father in holding to the belief that India could still be governed only despotically. But although he himself refused to apply the teachings of *Liberty* or *Representative Government* to India, a few Radical Liberals and a growing body of educated Indians made no such limitations."[26] A quick glance at the last chapter of *Representative Government*—to say nothing of the passage in the third volume of *Dissertations and Discussions* where he speaks of the absence of rights for barbarians—makes absolutely clear Mill's view that what he has to say about the matter cannot really apply to India, mainly because in his culture's judgment India's civilization has not attained the requisite degree of development.

The entire history of nineteenth-century European thought is filled with such discriminations as these, made between what is fitting for us and what is fitting for them, the former designated as inside, in place, common, belonging, in a word *above,* the latter, who are designated as outside, excluded, aberrant, inferior, in a word *below.* From these distinctions, which were given their hegemony by the culture, no one could be free, not even Marx—as a reading of his articles on India and the Orient will immediately reveal.[27] The large cultural-national designation of European culture as the privileged norm carried with it a formidable battery of other distinctions between ours and theirs, between proper and improper, European and non-European, higher and lower: they are to be found everywhere in such subjects and quasi-subjects as linguistics, history, race theory, philosophy, anthropology, and even biology. But my main reason for mentioning them here is to suggest how in the transmission and persistence of a culture there is a continual process of reinforcement, by which the hegemonic culture will add to itself the prerogatives given it by its sense of national identity, its power as an implement, ally, or branch of the state, its rightness, its exterior forms and assertions of itself: and most important, by its vindicated power as a victor over everything not itself.

[25] Quoted in Philip D. Curtin, ed., *Imperialism* (New York: Walker and Company, 1971), p. 182. [Au.]

[26] Eric Stokes, *The English Utilitarians and India* (Oxford: Clarendon Press, 1959), p. 298. [Au.]

[27] See *Orientalism,* pp. 153–156; also the important study by Bryan Turner, *Marx and the End of Orientalism* (London: Allen and Unwin, 1978). [Au.]

There is no reason to doubt that all cultures operate in this way or to doubt that on the whole they tend to be successful in enforcing their hegemony. They do this in different ways, obviously, and I think it is true that some tend to be more efficient than others, particularly when it comes to certain kinds of police activities. But this is a topic for comparative anthropologists and not one about which broad generalizations should be risked here. I am interested, however, in noting that if culture exerts the kinds of pressure I have mentioned, and if it creates the environment and the community that allows people to feel they belong, then it must be true that resistance to the culture has always been present. Often that resistance takes the form of outright hostility for religious, social, or political reasons (one aspect of this is well described by Eric Hobsbawm in *Primitive Rebels*). Often it has come from individuals or groups declared out of bounds or inferior by the culture (here of course the range is vast, from the ritual scapegoat to the lonely prophet, from the social pariah to the visionary artist, from the working class to the alienated intellectual). But there is some very compelling truth to Julien Benda's contention that in one way or the other it has often been the intellectual, the *clerc*, who has stood for values, ideas, and activities that transcend and deliberately interfere with the collective weight imposed by the nation-state and the national culture.

Certainly what Benda says about intellectuals (who, in ways specific to the intellectual vocation itself, are responsible for defiance) resonates harmoniously with the personality of Socrates as it emerges in Plato's *Dialogues*, or with Voltaire's opposition to the Church, or more recently with Gramsci's notion of the organic intellectual allied with an emergent class against ruling-class hegemony.[28] Even Arnold speaks of "aliens" in *Culture and Anarchy*, "persons who are mainly led, not by their class spirit, but by a general humane spirit," which he connects directly with ideal culture and not, it would appear, with that culture he was later to identify with the State. Benda is surely wrong, on the other hand, to ascribe so much social power to the solitary intellectual whose authority, according to Benda, comes from his individual voice and from his opposition to organized collective passions. Yet if we allow that it has been the historical fate of such collective sentiments as "my country right or wrong" and "we are whites and therefore belong to a higher race than blacks" and "European or Islamic or Hindu culture is superior to all others" to coarsen and brutalize the individual, then it is probably true that an isolated individual consciousness, going against the surrounding environment as well as allied to contesting classes, movements, and values, is an isolated voice out of place but very much *of* that place, standing consciously against the prevailing orthodoxy and very much for a professedly universal or humane set of values, which has provided significant local resistance to the hegemony of one culture. It is also the case, both Benda and Gramsci agree, that intellectuals are eminently useful in making hegemony work. For Benda this of course is the *trahison des clercs* in its essence; their unseemly participation in the perfection of political passions is what he thinks is dispiritingly the very essence of their contemporary mass sellout. For Gramsci's more complex mind, individual intellectuals like Croce[29] were to be studied (perhaps even envied) for making their ideas seem as if they were expressions of a collective will.

All this, then, shows us the individual consciousness placed at a sensitive nodal point, and it is this consciousness at that critical point which this book attempts to explore in the form of what I call *criticism*. On the one hand, the individual mind registers and is very much aware of the collective whole, context, or situation in which it finds itself. On the other hand, precisely because of this awareness—a worldly self-situating, a sensitive response to the dominant culture—that the individual consciousness is not naturally and easily a mere child of the culture, but a historical and social actor in it. And because of that perspective, which introduces circumstance and distinction where there had only been conformity and belonging, there is distance, or what we might also call criticism. A knowledge of history, a recognition of the importance of social circumstance, an analytical capacity for making distinctions: these trouble the quasi-religious authority of being comfortably at home, at home among one's people, supported by known powers

[28] Antonio Gramsci (1891–1937), Italian Marxist philosopher. [Eds.]

[29] Benedetto Croce (1866–1952), Italian philosopher (see *CTSP*, pp. 726–35). [Eds.]

and acceptable values, protected against the outside world.

But to repeat: the critical consciousness is a part of its actual social world and of the literal body that the consciousness inhabits, not by any means an escape from either one or the other. Although as I characterized him, Auerbach was away from Europe, his work is steeped in the reality of Europe, just as the specific circumstances of his exile enabled a concrete critical recovery of Europe. We have in Auerbach an instance both of filiation with his natal culture and, because of exile, *affiliation* with it through critical consciousness and scholarly work. We must look more closely now at the cooperation between filiation and affiliation that is located at the heart of critical consciousness.

RELATIONSHIPS of filiation and affiliation are plentiful in modern cultural history. One very strong three-part pattern, for example, originates in a large group of late nineteenth- and early twentieth-century writers, in which the failure of the generative impulse—the failure of the capacity to produce or generate children—is portrayed in such a way as to stand for a general condition afflicting society and culture together, to say nothing of individual men and women. *Ulysses* and *The Waste Land* are two especially well-known instances, but there is a similar evidence to be found in *Death in Venice* or *The Way of All Flesh, Jude the Obscure, À la recherche du temps perdu,* Mallarmé's and Hopkins' poetry, much of Wilde's writing, and *Nostromo.* If we add to this list the immensely authoritative weight of Freud's psychoanalytic theory, a significant and influential aspect of which posits the potentially murderous outcome of bearing children, we will have the unmistakable impression that few things are as problematic and as universally fraught as what we might have supposed to be the mere natural continuity between one generation and the next. Even in a great work that belongs intellectually and politically to another universe of discourse—Lukacs' *History and Class Consciousness*—there is much the same thesis being advanced about the difficulties and ultimately the impossibility of natural filiation: for, Lukacs says, reification is the alienation of men from what they have produced, and it is the starkly uncompromising severity of his vision that he means by this all the products of human labor, children included, which are so completely separated from each other, atomized, and hence frozen into the category of ontological objects as to make even natural relationships virtually impossible.[30]

Childless couples, orphaned children, aborted childbirths, and unregenerately celibate men and women populate the world of high modernism with remarkable insistence, all of them suggesting the difficulties of filiation.[31] But no less important in my opinion is the second part of the pattern, which is immediately consequent upon the first, the pressure to produce new and different ways of conceiving human relationships. For if biological reproduction is either too difficult or too unpleasant, is there some other way by which men and women can create social bonds between each other that would substitute for those ties that connect members of the same family across generations?

A typical answer is provided by T. S. Eliot during the period right after the appearance of *The Waste Land.* His model now is Lancelot Andrewes, a man whose prose and devotional style seem to Eliot to have transcended the personal manner of even so fervent and effective a Christian preacher as Donne. In the shift from Donne to Andrewes,[32] which I believe underlies the shift in Eliot's sensibility from the world-view of *Prufrock, Gerontion,* and *The Waste Land* to the conversion poetry of *Ash Wednesday* and the *Ariel Poems,* we have Eliot saying something like the following: the aridity, wastefulness, and sterility of modern life make filiation an unreasonable alternative at least, an unattainable one at most. One cannot think about continuity in biological terms, a proposition that may have had urgent corroboration in the recent failure of Eliot's first marriage but to which Eliot's mind gave a far wider application.[33] The only other alternatives seemed to be provided by institutions, associations, and communities whose social existence was not in fact guaranteed by biology, but by affiliation. Thus according to Eliot Lancelot Andrewes conveys in his writing the enfolding presence of the English

[30] See *Lukács.* [Eds.]

[31] See my *Beginnings: Intention and Method* (New York: Basic Books, 1975), pp. 81–88 and passim. [Au.]

[32] John Donne (1572–1631), English poet and divine; Lancelot Andrewes (1555–1626), English divine. [Eds.]

[33] This information is usefully provided by Lyndall Gordon, *Eliot's Early Years* (Oxford and New York: Oxford University Press, 1977). [Au.]

church, "something representative of the finest spirit of England of the time [and] . . . a masterpiece of ecclesiastical statesmanship." With Hooker, then, Andrewes invoked an authority beyond simple Protestantism. Both men were

> on terms of equality with their Continental antagonists and [were able] to elevate their Church above the position of a local heretical sect. They were fathers of a national Church and they were Europeans. Compare a sermon of Andrewes with a sermon by another earlier master, Latimer. It is not merely that Andrewes knew Greek, or that Latimer was addressing a far less cultivated public, or that the sermons of Andrewes are peppered with allusion and quotation. It is rather that Latimer, the preacher of Henry VIII and Edward VI, is merely a Protestant; but the voice of Andrewes is the voice of a man who has a formed visible Church behind him, who speaks with the old authority and the new culture.[34]

Eliot's reference to Hooker and Andrewes is figurative, but it is meant with a quite literal force, just as that second "merely" (Latimer is merely a Protestant) is an assertion by Eliot of "the old authority and the new culture." If the English church is not in a direct line of filiation stemming from the Roman church, it is nevertheless something more than a mere local heresy, more than a mere protesting orphan. Why? Because Andrewes and others like him to whose antecedent authority Eliot has now subscribed were able to harness the old paternal authority to an insurgent Protestant and national culture, thereby creating a new institution based not on direct genealogical descent but on what we may call, barbarously, *horizontal affiliation.* According to Eliot, Andrewes' language does not simply express the anguished distance from an originating but now unrecoverable father that a protesting orphan might feel; on the contrary, it converts that language into the expression of an emerging affiliative corporation—the English church—which commands the respect and the attention of its adherents.

In Eliot's poetry much the same change occurs. The speakers of *Prufrock* and *Gerontion* as well as the characters of *The Waste Land* directly express the plight of orphanhood and alienation, whereas the personae of *Ash Wednesday* and *Four Quartets* speak the common language of other communicants within the English church. For Eliot the church stands in for the lost family mourned throughout his earlier poetry. And of course the shift is publicly completed in *After Strange Gods* whose almost belligerent announcement of a credo of royalism, classicism, and catholicism form a set of affiliations achieved by Eliot outside the filial (republican, romantic, protestant) pattern given him by the facts of his American (and outlandish) birth.

The turn from filiation to affiliation is to be found elsewhere in the culture and embodies what Georg Simmel calls the modern cultural process by which life "incessantly generates forms for itself," forms that, once they appear, "demand a validity which transcends the moment, and is emancipated from the pulse of life. For this reason, life is always in a latent opposition to the form."[35] One thinks of Yeats going from the blandishments of "the honey of generation" to the Presences who are "self-born mockers of man's enterprise," which he set down in *A Vision* according to a spacious affiliative order he invented for himself and his work. Or, as Ian Watt has said about Conrad's contemporaries, writers like Lawrence, Joyce, and Pound, who present us with "the breaking of ties with family, home, class, country, and traditional beliefs as necessary stages in the achievement of spiritual and intellectual freedom": these writers "then invite us to share the larger transcendental [affiliative] or private systems of order and value which they have adopted and invented."[36] In his best work Conrad shows us the futility of such private systems of order and value (say the utopian world created by Charles and Amelia Gould in *Nostromo*), but no less than his contemporaries he too took on in his own life (as did Eliot and Henry James) the adopted identity of an emigré-turned-English-gentleman. On the other side of the spectrum we find Lukacs suggesting that only class consciousness, itself an insurrectionary form of an attempt at affiliation, could possibly break through the antinomies and atomizations of

[34] T. S. Eliot, *Selected Essays* (1932, rpt. London: Faber and Faber, 1953), pp. 343–44. [Au.]

[35] Georg Simmel, *The Conflict of Modern Culture and Other Essays,* trans. and ed. K. Peter Etzkorn (New York: Teachers College Press, 1968), p. 12. [Au.]

[36] Ian Watt, *Conrad in the Nineteenth Century* (Berkeley: University of California Press, 1979), p. 32. [Au.]

reified existence in the modern capitalist world-order.

What I am describing is the transition from a failed idea or possibility of filiation to a kind of compensatory order that, whether it is a party, an institution, a culture, a set of beliefs, or even a world-vision, provides men and women with a new form of relationship, which I have been calling affiliation but which is also a new system. Now whether we look at this new affiliative mode of relationship as it is to be found among conservative writers like Eliot or among progressive writers like Lukacs and, in his own special way, Freud, we will find the deliberately explicit goal of using that new order to reinstate vestiges of the kind of authority associated in the past with filiative order. This, finally, is the third part of the pattern. Freud's psychoanalytic guild and Lukacs' notion of the vanguard party are no less providers of what we might call a restored authority. The new hierarchy or, if it is less a hierarchy than a community, the new community is greater than the individual adherent or member, just as the father is greater by virtue of seniority than the sons and daughters; the ideas, the values, and the systematic totalizing world-view validated by the new affiliative order are all bearers of authority too, with the result that something resembling a cultural system is established. Thus if a filial relationship was held together by natural bonds and natural forms of authority—involving obedience, fear, love, respect, and instinctual conflict—the new affiliative relationship changes these bonds into what seem to be transpersonal forms—such as guild consciousness, consensus, collegiality, professional respect, class, and the hegemony of a dominant culture. The filiative scheme belongs to the realms of nature and of "life," whereas affiliation belongs exclusively to culture and society.

It is worth saying incidentally that what an estimable group of literary artists have adumbrated in the passage from filiation to affiliation parallels similar observations made by sociologists and records corresponding developments in the structure of knowledge. Tönnies' notion of the shift from *Gemeinschaft* to *Gesellschaft*[37] can easily be reconciled with the idea of filiation replaced by affiliation. Similarly, I believe, the increased dependence of the modern scholar upon the small, specialized guild of people in his or her field (as indeed the very idea of a field itself), and the notion within fields that the originating human subject is of less importance than transhuman rules and theories, accompany the transformation of naturally filiative into systematically affiliative relationships. The loss of the subject, as it has commonly been referred to, is in various ways the loss as well of the procreative, generational urge authorizing filiative relationships.

The three-part pattern I have been describing—and with it the processes of filiation and affiliation as they have been depicted—can be considered an instance of the passage from nature to culture, as well as an instance of how affiliation can easily become a system of thought no less orthodox and dominant than culture itself. What I want abruptly to talk about at this juncture are the effects of this pattern as they have affected the study of literature today, at a considerable remove from the early years of our century. The structure of literary knowledge derived from the academy is heavily imprinted with the three-part pattern I have illustrated here. This imprinting has occurred in ways that are impressive so far as critical thought (according to my notion of what it ought to be) is concerned. Let me pass directly now to concrete examples.

Ever since Eliot, and after him Richards and Leavis,[38] there has been an almost unanimously held view that it is the duty of humanistic scholars in our culture to devote themselves to the study of the great monuments of literature. Why? So that they may be passed on to younger students, who in turn become members, by affiliation and formation, of the company of educated individuals. Thus we find the university experience more or less officially consecrating the pact between a canon of works, a band of initiate instructors, a group of younger affiliates; in a socially validated manner all this reproduces the filiative discipline supposedly transcended by the educational process. This has almost always been the case historically within what might be called the cloistral world of the traditional Western, and certainly of the Eastern, university. But we are now, I think, in a period of world history when for the first time the compensatory affiliative relationships interpreted during the academic course of study in the Western university actually exclude more than they include. I mean quite simply that,

[37] Ferdinand Tönnies (1855–1936), German sociologist. *Gemeinschaft:* community; *Gesellschaft:* society. [Eds.]

[38] I. A. Richards (see *CTSP*, pp. 847–59); F. R. Leavis (1895–1978), English critic. [Eds.]

for the first time in modern history, the whole imposing edifice of humanistic knowledge resting on the classics of European letters, and with it the scholarly discipline inculcated formally into students in Western universities through the forms familiar to us all, represents only a fraction of the real human relationships and interactions now taking place in the world. Certainly Auerbach was among the last great representatives of those who believed that European culture could be viewed coherently and importantly as unquestionably central to human history. There are abundant reasons for Auerbach's view being no longer tenable, not the least of which is the diminishing acquiescence and deference accorded to what has been called the Natopolitan world long dominating peripheral regions like Africa, Asia, and Latin America. New cultures, new societies, and emerging visions of social, political, and aesthetic order now lay claim to the humanist's attention, with an insistence that cannot long be denied.

But for perfectly understandable reasons they are denied. When our students are taught such things as "the humanities" they are almost always taught that these classic texts embody, express, represent what is best in our, that is, the only, tradition. Moreover they are taught that such fields as the humanities and such subfields as "literature" exist in a relatively neutral political element, that they are to be appreciated and venerated, that they define the limits of what is acceptable, appropriate, and legitimate so far as culture is concerned. In other words, the affiliative order so presented surreptitiously duplicates the closed and tightly knit family structure that secures generational hierarchical relationships to one another. Affiliation then becomes in effect a literal form of *re-presentation*, by which what is ours is good, and therefore deserves incorporation and inclusion in our programs of humanistic study, and what is not ours in this ultimately provincial sense is simply left out. And out of this representation comes the systems from Northrop Frye's[39] to Foucault's, which claim the power to show how things work, once and for all, totally and predictively. It should go without saying that this new affiliative structure and its systems of thought more or less directly reproduce the skeleton of family authority supposedly left behind when the family was left behind. The curricular structures holding European literature departments make that perfectly obvious: the great texts, as well as the great teachers and the great theories, have an authority that compels respectful attention not so much by virtue of their content but because they are either old or they have power, they have been handed on in time or seem to have no time, and they have traditionally been revered, as priests, scientists, or efficient bureaucrats have taught.

It may seem odd, but it is true, that in such matters as culture and scholarship I am often in reasonable sympathy with conservative attitudes, and what I might object to in what I have been describing does not have much to do with the activity of conserving the past, or with reading great literature, or with doing serious and perhaps even utterly conservative scholarship as such. I have no great problem with those things. What I am criticizing is two particular assumptions. There is first the almost unconsciously held ideological assumption that the Eurocentric model for the humanities actually represents a natural and proper subject matter for the humanistic scholar. Its authority comes not only from the orthodox canon of literary monuments handed down through the generations, but also from the way this continuity reproduces the filial continuity of the chain of biological procreation. What we then have is a substitution of one sort of order for another, in the process of which everything that is nonhumanistic and nonliterary and non-European is deposited outside the structure. If we consider for a minute that most of the world today is non-European, that transactions within what the UNESCO/McBride Report calls the world information order are therefore not literary, and that the social sciences and the media (to name only two modes of cultural production in ascendancy today over the classically defined humanities) dominate the diffusion of knowledge in ways that are scarcely imaginable to the traditional humanistic scholar, then we will have some idea of how ostrichlike and retrograde assertions about Eurocentric humanities really are. The process of representation, by which filiation is reproduced in the affiliative structure and made to stand for what belongs to us (as we in turn belong to the family of our languages and traditions), reinforces the known at the expense of the knowable.

Second is the assumption that the principal relationships in the study of literature—those I have identified as based on representation—ought to

[39] See *Frye* and *CTSP*, pp. 1117–47. [Eds.]

obliterate the traces of other relationships within literary structures that are based principally upon acquisition and appropriation. This is the great lesson of Raymond Williams' *The Country and the City*. His extraordinarily illuminating discussion there of the seventeenth-century English country-house poems does not concentrate on what those poems represent, but on what they *are* as the result of contested social and political relationships. Descriptions of the rural mansion, for example, do not at bottom entail only what is to be admired by way of harmony, repose, and beauty; they should also entail for the modern reader what in fact has been excluded from the poems, the labor that created the mansions, the social processes of which they are the culmination, the dispossessions and theft they actually signified. Although he does not come out and say it, Williams' book is a remarkable attempt at a dislodgement of the very ethos of system, which has reified relationships and stripped them of their social density. What he tries to put in its place is the great dialectic of acquisition and representation, by which even realism—as it is manifest in Jane Austen's novels—has gained its durable status as the result of contests involving money and power. Williams teaches us to read in a different way and to remember that for every poem or novel in the canon there is a social fact being requisitioned for the page, a human life engaged, a class suppressed or elevated—none of which can be accounted for in the framework rigidly maintained by the processes of representation and affiliation doing above-ground work for the conservation of filiation. And for every critical system grinding on there are events, heterogeneous and unorthodox social configurations, human beings and texts disputing the possibility of a sovereign methodology of system.

Everything I have said is an extrapolation from the verbal echo we hear between the words "filiation" and "affiliation." In a certain sense, what I have been trying to show is that, as it has developed through the art and critical theories produced in complex ways by modernism, filiation gives birth to affiliation. Affiliation becomes a form of representing the filiative processes to be found in nature, although affiliation takes validated nonbiological social and cultural forms. Two alternatives propose themselves for the contemporary critic. One is organic complicity with the pattern I have described. The critic enables, indeed transacts, the transfer of legitimacy from filiation to affiliation; literally a midwife, the critic encourages reverence for the humanities and for the dominant culture served by those humanities. This keeps relationships within the narrow circle of what is natural, appropriate, and valid for "us," and thereafter excludes the non-literary, the non-European, and above all the political dimension in which all literature, all texts, can be found. It also gives rise to a critical system or theory whose temptation for the critic is that it resolves all the problems that culture gives rise to. As John Fekete has said, this "expresses the modern disaffection for reality, but progressively incorporates and assimilates it within the categories of prevailing social (and cultural) rationality. This endows it with a double appeal, and the expanding scope of the theory, corresponding to the expanding mode of the production and reproduction of social life, gives it authority as a major ideology."[40]

The second alternative is for the critic to recognize the difference between instinctual filiation and social affiliation, and to show how affiliation sometimes reproduces filiation, sometimes makes its own forms. Immediately, then, most of the political and social world becomes available for critical and secular scrutiny, as in *Mimesis* Auerbach does not simply admire the Europe he has lost through exile but sees it anew as a composite social and historical enterprise, made and remade unceasingly by men and women in society. This secular critical consciousness can also examine those forms of writing affiliated with literature but excluded from consideration with literature as a result of the ideological capture of the literary text within the humanistic curriculum as it now stands. My analysis of recent literary theory in this book focuses on these themes in detail, especially on the way critical systems—even of the most sophisticated kind—can succumb to the inherently representative and reproductive relationship between a dominant culture and the domains it rules.

WHAT does it mean to have a critical consciousness if, as I have been trying to suggest, the intellectual's situation is a worldly one and yet, by virtue of that worldliness itself, the intellectual's social identity

[40] John Fekete, *The Critical Twilight: Explorations in the Ideology of Anglo-American Literary Theory from Eliot to McLuhan* (London: Routledge and Kegan Paul, 1977), pp. 193–94. [Au.]

should involve something more than strengthening those aspects of the culture that require mere affirmation and orthodox compliancy from its members?

The whole of this book is an attempt to answer this question. My position, again, is that the contemporary critical consciousness stands between the temptations represented by two formidable and related powers engaging critical attention. One is the culture to which critics are bound filiatively (by birth, nationality, profession); the other is a method or system acquired affiliatively (by social and political conviction, economic and historical circumstances, voluntary effort and willed deliberation). Both of these powers exert pressures that have been building toward the contemporary situation for long periods of time: my interest in eighteenth-century figures like Vico and Swift, for example, is premised on their knowledge that their era also made claims on them culturally and systematically, and it was their whole enterprise therefore to resist these pressures in everything they did, albeit of course, that they were worldly writers and materially bound to their time.

As it is now practiced and as I treat it, criticism is an academic thing, located for the most part far away from the questions that trouble the reader of a daily newspaper. Up to a certain point this is as it should be. But we have reached the stage at which specialization and professionalization, allied with cultural dogma, barely sublimated ethnocentrism and nationalism, as well as a surprisingly insistent quasi-religious quietism, have transported the professional and academic critic of literature—the most focused and intensely trained interpreter of texts produced by the culture—into another world altogether. In that relatively untroubled and secluded world there seems to be no contact with the world of events and societies, which modern history, intellectuals, and critics have in fact built. Instead, contemporary criticism is an institution for publicly affirming the values of our, that is, European, dominant elite culture, and for privately setting loose the unrestrained interpretation of a universe defined in advance as the endless misreading of a misinterpretation. The result has been the regulated, not to say calculated, irrelevance of criticism, except as an adornment to what the powers of modern industrial society transact: the hegemony of militarism and a new cold war, the depoliticization of the citizenry, the overall compliance of the intellectual class to which critics belong. The situation I attempt to characterize in modern criticism (not excluding "Left" criticism) has occurred in parallel with the ascendancy of Reaganism. The role of the Left, neither repressed nor organized, has been important for its complaisance.

I do not wish to be misunderstood as saying that the flight into method and system on the part of critics who wish to avoid the ideology of humanism is altogether a bad thing. Far from it. Yet the dangers of method and system are worth noting. Insofar as they become sovereign and as their practitioners lose touch with the resistance and the heterogeneity of civil society, they risk becoming wall-to-wall discourses, blithely predetermining what they discuss, heedlessly converting everything into evidence for the efficacy of the method, carelessly ignoring the circumstances out of which all theory, system, and method ultimately derive.

Criticism in short is always situated; it is skeptical, secular, reflectively open to its own failings. This is by no means to say that it is value-free. Quite the contrary, for the inevitable trajectory of critical consciousness is to arrive at some acute sense of what political, social, and human values are entailed in the reading, production, and transmission of every text. To stand between culture and system is therefore to stand *close to*—closeness itself having a particular value for me—a concrete reality about which political, moral, and social judgments have to be made and, if not only made, then exposed and demystified. If, as we have recently been told by Stanley Fish, every act of interpretation is made possible and given force by an interpretive community, then we must go a great deal further in showing what situation, what historical and social configuration, what political interests are concretely entailed by the very existence of interpretive communities.[41] This is an especially important task when these communities have evolved camouflaging jargons.

I hope it will not seem a self-serving thing to say that all of what I mean by criticism and critical consciousness is directly reflected not only in the subjects of these essays but in the essay form itself. For if I am to be taken seriously as saying that secular

[41] For an extended analysis of the role of interpretive communities, see Stanley Fish, *Is There a Text in This Class?* (Cambridge: Harvard University Press, 1980). [Au.] See *Fish*. [Eds.]

criticism deals with local and worldly situations, and that it is constitutively opposed to the production of massive, hermetic systems, then it must follow that the essay—a comparatively short, investigative, radically skeptical form—is the principal way in which to write criticism. Certain themes, naturally enough, recur in the essays that make up this book. Given a relatively wide selection of topics, the book's unity, however, is also a unity of attitude and of concern. With two exceptions, all of the essays collected here were written during the period immediately following the completion of my book *Beginnings: Intention and Method,* which argued the practical and theoretical necessity of a reasoned point of departure for any intellectual and creative job of work, given that we exist in secular history, in the "always-already" begun realm of continuously human effort. Thus each essay presupposes that book. Yet it is more important to point out that (again with two exceptions) all of these essays were written as I was working on three books dealing with the history of relations between East and West: *Orientalism* (1978), *The Question of Palestine* (1979), and *Covering Islam* (1981), books whose historical and social setting is political and cultural in the most urgent way. On matters having to do with the relationship between scholarship and politics, between a specific situation and the interpretation and the production of a text, between textuality itself and social reality, the connection of some essays here to those three books will be evident enough.

The essays collected here are arranged in three interlinked ways. First I look at the worldly and secular world in which texts take place and in which certain writers (Swift, Hopkins, Conrad, Fanon) are exemplary for their attention to the detail of everyday existence defined as situation, event, and the organization of power. For the critic, the challenge of this secular world is that it is not reducible to an explanatory or originating theory, much less to a collection of cultural generalities. There are instead a small number of perhaps unexpected characteristics of worldliness that play a role in making sense of textual experience, among them filiation and affiliation, the body and the senses of sight and hearing, repetition, and the sheer heterogeneity of detail. Next I turn to the peculiar problems of contemporary critical theory as it either confronts or ignores issues raised for the study of texts (and textuality) by the secular world. Finally, I treat the problem of what happens when the culture attempts to understand, dominate, or recapture another, less powerful one.

A word is in order about the special role played by Swift in this book. There are two essays on him, both of them stressing the resistances he offers to the modern critical theorist (resistance being a matter of central relevance to my argument in this book). The reasons for this are not only that Swift cannot easily be assimilated to current ideas about "writers," "the text," or "the heroic author," but that his work is at once occasional, powerful, and—from the point of view of systematic textual practice—incoherent. To read Swift seriously is to try to apprehend a series of events in all their messy force, not to admire and then calmly to decode a string of high monuments. In addition, his own social role was that of the critic involved with, but never possessing, power: alert, forceful, undogmatic, ironic, unafraid of orthodoxies and dogmas, respectful of settled uncoercive community, anarchic in his sense of the range of alternatives to the status quo. Yet he was tragically compromised by his time and his worldly circumstances, a fact alluded to by E. P. Thompson and Perry Anderson in their dispute over his real (progressive or reactionary) political commitments. For me he represents the critical consciousness in a raw form, a large-scale model of the dilemmas facing the contemporary critical consciousness that has tended to be too cloistered and too attracted to easy systematizing. He stands so far outside the world of contemporary critical discourse as to serve as one of its best critics, methodologically unarmed though he may have been. In its energy and unparalleled verbal wit, its restlessness, its agitational and unacademic designs on its political and social context, Swift's writing supplies modern criticism with what it has sorely needed since Arnold covered critical writing with the mantle of cultural authority and reactionary political quietism.

It is an undoubted exaggeration to say, on the other hand, that these essays make absolutely clear what my critical position—only implied by *Orientalism* and my other recent books—really is. To some this may seem like a failing of rigor, honesty, or energy. To others it may imply some radical uncertainty on my part as to what I do stand for, especially given the fact that I have been accused by colleagues of intemperate and even unseemly polemicism. To still others—and this concerns me more—it may seem that I am an undeclared Marxist, afraid of losing respectability and concerned by the contradictions entailed by the label "Marxist."

Without wishing to answer all the questions raised by these matters, I would like my views to be as clear as possible. On the question of government and foreign policy that particularly involve me, nothing more should be added here than what is said in the last four essays in this book. But on the important matter of a critical position, its relationship to Marxism, liberalism, even anarchism, it needs to be said that criticism modified in advance by labels like "Marxism" or "liberalism" is, in my view, an oxymoron. The history of thought, to say nothing of political movements, is extravagantly illustrative of how the dictum "solidarity before criticism" means the end of criticism. I take criticism so seriously as to believe that, even in the very midst of a battle in which one is unmistakably on one side against another, there should be criticism, because there must be critical consciousness if there are to be issues, problems, values, even lives to be fought for. Right now in American cultural history, "Marxism" is principally an academic, not a political, commitment. It risks becoming an academic subspecialty. As corollaries of this unfortunate truth there are also such things to be mentioned as the absence of an important socialist party (along the lines of the various European parties), the marginalized discourse of "Left" writing, the seeming incapacity of professional groups (scholarly, academic, regional) to organize effective Left coalitions with political-action groups. The net effect of "doing" Marxist criticism or writing at the present time is of course to declare political preference, but it is also to put oneself outside a great deal of things going on in the world, so to speak, and in other kinds of criticism.

Perhaps a simpler way of expressing all this is to say that I have been more influenced by Marxists than by Marxism or any other *ism*. If the arguments going on within twentieth-century Marxism have had any meaning, it is this: as much as any discourse, Marxism is in need of systematic decoding, demystifying, rigorous clarification. Here the work of non-Marxist radicals (Chomsky's, say, or I. F. Stone's)[42] is valuable, especially if the doctrinal walls keeping out nonmembers have not been put up to begin with. The same is true of criticism deriving from a profoundly conservative outlook, Auerbach's own, for example; at its best, this work also teaches us how to be critical, rather than how to be good members of a school. The positive uses of affiliation are many after all, which is not to say that authoritarianism and orthodoxy are any less dangerous.

Were I to use one word consistently along with *criticism* (not as a modification but as an emphatic) it would be *oppositional.* If criticism is reducible neither to a doctrine nor to a political position on a particular question, and if it is to be in the world and self-aware simultaneously, then its identity is its difference from other cultural activities and from systems of thought or of method. In its suspicion of totalizing concepts, in its discontent with reified objects, in its impatience with guilds, special interests, imperialized fiefdoms, and orthodox habits of mind, criticism is most itself and, if the paradox can be tolerated, most unlike itself at the moment it starts turning into organized dogma. "Ironic" is not a bad word to use along with "oppositional." For in the main—and here I shall be explicit—criticism must think of itself as life-enhancing and constitutively opposed to every form of tyranny, domination, and abuse; its social goals are noncoercive knowledge produced in the interests of human freedom. If we agree with Raymond Williams, "that however dominant a social system may be, the very meaning of its domination involves a limitation or selection of the activities it covers, so that by definition it cannot exhaust all social experience, which therefore always potentially contains space for alternative acts and alternative intentions which are not yet articulated as a social institution or even project,"[43] then criticism belongs in that potential space inside civil society, acting on behalf of those alternative acts and alternative intentions whose advancement is a fundamental human and intellectual obligation.

There is a danger that the fascination of what's

[42] See *Chomsky;* I. F. Stone (b. 1907), American journalist. [Eds.]

[43] Raymond Williams, *Politics and Letters: Interviews with New Left Review* (London: New Left Books, 1979), p. 252. [Au.]

difficult—criticism being one of the forms of difficulty—might take the joy out of one's heart. But there is every reason to suppose that the critic who is tired of management and the day's war is, like Yeats's narrator, quite capable at least of finding the stable, pulling out the bolt, and setting creative energies free. Normally, however, the critic can but entertain, without fully expressing, the hope. This is a poignant irony, to be recalled for the benefit of people who maintain that criticism is art, and who forget that, the moment anything acquires the status of a cultural idol or a commodity, it ceases to be interesting. That at bottom is a *critical* attitude, just as doing criticism and maintaining a critical position are critical aspects of the intellectual's life.

APPENDIX

Gottlob Frege

1848–1925

GOTTLOB FREGE, born six years before the death of F. W. Schelling, was for most of his professional life a professor of philosophy at the University of Jena. But unlike his more illustrious predecessors there (including Fichte, Hegel, and Schelling), Frege remained little known and evidently little read during his lifetime. Most of his major philosophical works focused scrupulously, if not to say relentlessly, on mathematical logic.

His *Begriffsschrift, eine der arithmetischen nachgebildete* (1879) is arguably the first important work in the development of modern symbolic logic, and in this work Frege developed a remarkably expressive formalism for representing logical propositions and judgments. While generally neglected, his reputation and influence (especially among English-speaking philosophers) has grown steadily since Russell and Whitehead acknowledged his pioneering efforts in the formalization of logic.

Ironically, Frege had an important, albeit indirect, influence on the development of modern European philosophy in his penetrating (and somewhat scathing) critique of Edmund Husserl's *Philosophy of Arithmetic* (1891). *Husserl's* response to Frege's critique (according to Joseph Kockelmans) was at least to abandon the psychologism in the book, to which Frege had objected; but this took Husserl in the direction of transcendental psychology and phenomenology—surely not a response that Frege would have approved. In Husserl's later attempt to make philosophy into a rigorous science, the entire matter of representation and expression is subsumed under the notion of a cognitive or perceptual intention, presuming that anything cognizable (including cognition itself) must immediately appear to consciousness as present.

While in itself this contrast between Frege and Husserl may be only incidental, it indicates a fundamental conflict in the development of modern critical and philosophical thought. In rejecting transcendental metaphysics and both nominalist and formalist accounts of logic and mathematics, Frege narrowed his philosophical alternatives but radically clarified the importance of language and logic for all philosophical issues. First, he made it clear that how any term or proposition is understood is not necessarily the same as its use to designate some thing or entity; but, second, he showed why it is not obvious what can or will count as an "entity" to be designated. Particularly in the realm of concepts and functions, both "sense" (*Sinn*) and "meaning" (*Bedeutung*) are intimately bound up with modes of representation and expression—which, in a philosophical orientation (such as Husserl's) that assumes one can eliminate mediation to arrive at some originary intuition, can scarcely be acknowledged at all.

Frege's essay "On Sense and Meaning" (1892) is doubly important as it illuminates a fundamental problem while illustrating an analytical method that, as developed by such philosophers and logicians as Bertrand Russell, Ludwig Wittgenstein, W. V. Quine, Alonzo Church, and others, has been rich and fruitful. While the essay is written with a logical problem in mind (that is, the relation of "equality"), it is one of the earliest examples of philosophical analysis to show that the problem pervades natural language and is not restricted to mathematics or formal logic alone. From this point of view, Frege, like *C. S. Peirce,* anticipates the concern of later philosophers and critics with problems of language and meaning, particularly where semantic and epistemological issues overlap but require differentiation.

An earlier translation of the essay here was titled "Sense and Reference," rendering *Bedeutung* as "reference." But for Frege, the issue is not "reference" as such, or "representation," but the logical condition under which a statement of equality could be asserted. In the relation "a = b," "a" and "b" are presumed to be the names of relata which can be equated because they are names for the same "object." In cases such as that of the planet Venus, where a single object is being called both "morning star" and "evening star," the expressions would have a different sense but the same meaning by virtue of singling out only one object. While such "objects" of expressions need not be physical bodies but could include numbers and the truth values of propositions, the distinction is, as Frege notes, problematic in the case of a work of art, which has, in his use of the terms, *Sinn* or sense but not *Bedeutung.* While one could say that "morning star" and "evening star" both mean "the planet Venus," or "a" and "b" both mean the number 1, one would not say that Richard Burton and Hamlet both mean the same thing, since there is no commonly agreed upon way to single out what that "thing" might be. Frege was obviously intrigued by the peculiarity of the case, suggesting only that expressions with sense but not meaning (*Sinn* but not *Bedeutung*) are "representations" (see note 8); but some philosophers and logicians influenced by Frege evidently found such cases merely otiose—as when, for example, Rudolph Carnap employed Frege's distinction to declare that expressions with *Sinn* but not *Bedeutung,* like works of metaphysics and poems, were "meaningless" and without cognitive value.

While part of the problem in this case is that the characteristic use of the word "meaning" in English more nearly approximates Frege's notion of *Sinn,* there is then no word that is not misleading to translate his notion of *Bedeutung.* It remains that the relation between "reference" and "representation" still resists convincing analysis, by either logical empiricism, following Frege, or phenomenology, following Husserl, since it poses a problem for metaphysics that is categorically peculiar whenever there is a representation without a referent. If one equates these terms ("reference" and "representation"), then either term has sense *or* meaning only in relation to objects, either empirical or transcendental. Whether one opts to destroy metaphysics or merely deconstruct it, the first alternative deprives it of meaning (in Frege's sense), while the second deprives it of both sense and meaning, but neither does away with the problem.

Several major works by Frege have been translated into English: *The Foundations of Arithmetic,* trans. J. L. Austin (1953); *The Basic Laws of Arithmetic,* trans. M. Furth (1964); and *Translations from the Philosophical Writings of Gottlob Frege,* ed. P. Geach and M. Black (1960). Translations of several other essays are included in E. D. Klemke's important collection of critical and interpretive articles, *Essays on Frege* (1968). For an important essay on related issues, see Saul Kripke, "Naming and Necessity," in *Semantics of Natural Language,* ed. Gilbert Harman and Donald Davidson (1972).

ON SENSE AND MEANING

Equality[1] gives rise to challenging questions which are not altogether easy to answer. Is it a relation? A relation between objects, or between names or signs of objects? In my *Begriffsschrift*[2] I assumed the latter. The reasons which seem to favour this are the following: $a=a$ and $a=b$ are obviously statements of differing cognitive value; $a=a$ holds *a priori* and, according to Kant, is to be labelled analytic, while statements of the form $a=b$ often contain very valuable extensions of our knowledge and cannot always be established *a priori.* The discovery that the rising sun is not new every morning, but always the same, was one of the most fertile astronomical discoveries. Even to-day the reidentification of a small planet or a comet is not always a matter of course. Now if we were to regard equality as a relation between that which the names 'a' and 'b' designate, it would seem that $a=b$ could not differ from $a=a$ (i.e., provided $a=b$ is true). A relation would thereby be expressed of a thing to itself, and indeed one in which each thing stands to itself but to no other thing. What we apparently want to state by $a=b$ is that the signs or names 'a' and 'b' designate the same thing, so that those signs themselves would be under discussion; a relation between them would be asserted. But this relation would hold between the names or signs only in so far as they named or designated something. It would be mediated by the connexion of each of the two signs with the same designated thing. But this is arbitrary. Nobody can be forbidden to use any arbitrarily producible event or object as a sign for something. In that case the sentence $a=b$ would no longer refer to the subject matter but only to its mode of designation; we would express no proper knowledge by its means. But in many cases this is just what we want to do. If the sign 'a' is distinguished from the sign 'b' only as an object (here, by means of its shape), not as a sign (i.e. not by the manner in which it designates something), the cognitive value of $a=a$ becomes essentially equal to that of $a=b$, provided $a=b$ is true. A difference can arise only if the difference between the signs corresponds to a difference in the mode of presentation of the thing designated. Let a, b, c be the lines connecting the vertices of a triangle with the midpoints of the opposite sides. The point of intersection of a and b is then the same as the point of intersection of b and c. So we have different designations for the same point, and these names ('point of intersection of a and b,' 'point of intersection of b and c') likewise indicate the mode of presentation; and hence the statement contains actual knowledge.

It is natural, now, to think of there being connected with a sign (name, combination of words, written mark), besides that which the sign desig-

ON SENSE AND MEANING was first published in *Zeitschrift für Philosophie und philosophische Kritik* 100 (1892): 25–50. This translation by Max Black is reprinted from *Translations from the Philosophical Writings of Gottlob Frege,* ed. Peter Geach and Max Black, 3d ed. (1980), by permission of the publisher, Basil Blackwell.

[1] I use this word in the sense of identity and understand 'a=b' to have the sense of 'a is the same as b' or 'a and b coincide.' [Au.]

[2] The reference is to Frege's *Begriffsschrift, eine der arithmetischen nachgebildete Formelsprache des reinen Denkens* (Halle, 1879). [Tr.]

nates, which may be called the meaning of the sign, also what I should like to call the *sense* of the sign, wherein the mode of presentation is contained. In our example, accordingly, the meaning of the expressions 'the point of intersection of *a* and *b*' and 'the point of intersection of *b* and *c*' would be the same, but not their sense. The meaning of 'evening star' would be the same as that of 'morning star,' but not the sense.

It is clear from the context that by sign and name I have here understood any designation figuring as a proper name, which thus has as its meaning a definite object (this word taken in the widest range), but not a concept or a relation, which shall be discussed further in another article.[3] The designation of a single object can also consist of several words or other signs. For brevity, let every such designation be called a proper name.

The sense of a proper name is grasped by everybody who is sufficiently familiar with the language or totality of designations to which it belongs;[4] but this serves to illuminate only a single aspect of the thing meant, supposing it to have one. Comprehensive knowledge of the thing meant would require us to be able to say immediately whether any given sense attaches to it. To such knowledge we never attain.

The regular connexion between a sign, its sense, and what it means is of such a kind that to the sign there corresponds a definite sense and to that in turn a definite thing meant, while to a given thing meant (an object) there does not belong only a single sign. The same sense has different expressions in different languages or even in the same language. To be sure, exceptions to this regular behaviour occur. To every expression belonging to a complete totality of signs, there should certainly correspond a definite sense; but natural languages often do not satisfy this condition, and one must be content if the same word has the same sense in the same context. It may perhaps be granted that every grammatically well-formed expression figuring as a proper name always has a sense. But this is not to say that to the sense there also corresponds a thing meant. The words 'the celestial body most distant from the Earth' have a sense, but it is very doubtful if there is also a thing they mean. The expression 'the least rapidly convergent series' has a sense but demonstrably there is nothing it means, since for every given convergent series, another convergent, but less rapidly convergent, series can be found. In grasping a sense, one is not certainly assured of meaning anything.

If words are used in the ordinary way, what one intends to speak of is what they mean. It can also happen, however, that one wishes to talk about the words themselves or their sense. This happens, for instance, when the words of another are quoted. One's own words then first designate words of the other speaker, and only the latter have their usual meaning. We then have signs of signs. In writing, the words are in this case enclosed in quotation marks. Accordingly, a word standing between quotation marks must not be taken as having its ordinary meaning.

In order to speak of the sense of an expression 'A' one may simply use the phrase 'the sense of the expression "A"'. In indirect speech one talks about the sense, e.g., of another person's remarks. It is quite clear that in this way of speaking words do not have their customary meaning but designate what is usually their sense. In order to have a short expression, we will say: In indirect speech, words are used *indirectly* or have their *indirect* meaning. We distinguish accordingly the *customary* from the *indirect* meaning of a word; and its *customary* sense from its *indirect* sense. The indirect meaning of a word is accordingly its customary sense. Such exceptions must always be borne in mind if the mode of connexion between sign, sense, and meaning in particular cases is to be correctly understood.

The meaning and sense of a sign are to be distinguished from the associated idea. If what a sign means is an object perceivable by the senses, my idea of it is an internal image,[5] arising from memo-

[3]See his 'Ueber Begriff und Gegenstand' (*Vierteljahrsschrift für wissenschaftliche Philosophie* XVI [1892], 192–205); in *Translations*, pp. 42–55. [Tr.]

[4]In the case of an actual proper name such as 'Aristotle' opinions as to the sense may differ. It might, for instance, be taken to be the following: the pupil of Plato and teacher of Alexander the Great. Anybody who does this will attach another sense to the sentence 'Aristotle was born in Stagira' than will a man who takes as the sense of the name: the teacher of Alexander the Great who was born in Stagira. So long as the thing meant remains the same, such variations of sense may be tolerated, although they are to be avoided in the theoretical structure of a demonstrative science and ought not to occur in a perfect language. [Au.]

[5]We may include with ideas direct experiences: here, sense-impressions and acts themselves take the place of the traces which they have left in the mind. The distinction is unimportant for our purpose, especially since

ries of sense impressions which I have had and acts, both internal and external, which I have performed. Such an idea is often imbued with feeling; the clarity of its separate parts varies and oscillates. The same sense is not always connected, even in the same man, with the same idea. The idea is subjective: one man's idea is not that of another. There result, as a matter of course, a variety of differences in the ideas associated with the same sense. A painter, a horseman, and a zoologist will probably connect different ideas with the name 'Bucephalus.' This constitutes an essential distinction between the idea and sign's sense, which may be the common property of many people, and so is not a part of a mode of the individual mind. For one can hardly deny that mankind has a common store of thoughts which is transmitted from one generation to another.[6]

In the light of this, one need have no scruples in speaking simply of *the* sense, whereas in the case of an idea one must, strictly speaking, add whom it belongs to and at what time. It might perhaps be said: Just as one man connects this idea, and another that idea, with the same word, so also one man can associate this sense and another that sense. But there still remains a difference in the mode of connexion. They are not prevented from grasping the same sense; but they cannot have the same idea. *Si duo idem faciunt, non est idem.* If two persons picture the same thing, each still has his own idea. It is indeed sometimes possible to establish differences in the ideas, or even in the sensations, of different men; but an exact comparison is not possible, because we cannot have both ideas together in the same consciousness.

The meaning of a proper name is the object itself which we designate by using it; the idea which we have in that case is wholly subjective; in between lies the sense, which is indeed no longer subjective like the idea, but is yet not the object itself. The following analogy will perhaps clarify these relationships. Somebody observes the Moon through a telescope. I compare the Moon itself to the meaning; it is the object of the observation, mediated by the real image projected by the object glass in the interior of the telescope, and by the retinal image of the observer. The former I compare to the sense, the latter is like the idea or experience. The optical image in the telescope is indeed one-sided and dependent upon the standpoint of observation; but it is still objective, inasmuch as it can be used by several observers. At any rate it could be arranged for several to use it simultaneously. But each one would have his own retinal image. On account of the diverse shapes of the observers' eyes, even a geometrical congruence could hardly be achieved, and an actual coincidence would be out of the question. This analogy might be developed still further, by assuming A's retinal image made visible to B; or A might also see his own retinal image in a mirror. In this way we might perhaps show how an idea can itself be taken as an object, but as such is not for the observer what it directly is for the person having the idea. But to pursue this would take us too far afield.

We can now recognize three levels of difference between words, expressions, or whole sentences. The difference may concern at most the ideas, or the sense but not the meaning, or, finally, the meaning as well. With respect to the first level, it is to be noted that, on account of the uncertain connexion of ideas with words, a difference may hold for one person, which another does not find. The difference between a translation and the original text should properly not overstep the first level. To the possible difference here belong also the colouring and shading which poetic eloquence seeks to give to the sense. Such colouring and shading are not objective, and must be evoked by each hearer or reader according to the hints of the poet or the speaker. Without some affinity in human ideas art would certainly be impossible; but it can never be exactly determined how far the intentions of the poet are realized.

In what follows there will be no further discussion of ideas and experiences; they have been mentioned here only to ensure that the idea aroused in the hearer by a word shall not be confused with its sense or its meaning.

To make short and exact expressions possible, let the following phraseology be established:

A proper name (word, sign, sign combination, expression) *expresses* its sense, *means* or *designates* its meaning. By employing a sign we express its sense and designate its meaning.

Idealists or sceptics will perhaps long since have

---

memories of sense-impressions and acts always go along with such impressions and acts themselves to complete the perpetual image. One may on the other hand understand direct experience as including any object in so far as it is sensibly perceptible or spatial. [Au.]

[6] Hence it is inadvisable to use the word 'idea' to designate something so basically different. [Au.]

objected: 'You talk, without further ado, of the Moon as an object; but how do you know that the name "the Moon" has any meaning? How do you know that anything whatsoever has a meaning?' I reply that when we say 'the Moon,' we do not intend to speak of our idea of the Moon, nor are we satisfied with the sense alone, but we presuppose a meaning. To assume that in the sentence 'The Moon is smaller than the Earth' the idea of the Moon is in question, would be flatly to misunderstand the sense. If this is what the speaker wanted, he would use the phrase 'my idea of the Moon.' Now we can of course be mistaken in the presupposition, and such mistakes have indeed occurred. But the question whether the presupposition is perhaps always mistaken need not be answered here; in order to justify mention of that which a sign means it is enough, at first, to point our intention in speaking or thinking. (We must then add the reservation: provided such a meaning exists.)

So far we have considered the sense and meaning only of such expressions, words, or signs as we have called proper names. We now inquire concerning the sense and meaning of an entire assertoric sentence. Such a sentence contains a thought.[7] Is this thought, now, to be regarded as its sense or its meaning? Let us assume for the time being that the sentence does mean something. If we now replace one word of the sentence by another having the same meaning, but a different sense, this can have no effect upon the meaning of the sentence. Yet we can see that in such a case the thought changes; since, e.g., the thought in the sentence 'The morning star is a body illuminated by the Sun' differs from that in the sentence 'The evening star is a body illuminated by the Sun.' Anybody who did not know that the evening star is the morning star might hold the one thought to be true, the other false. The thought, accordingly, cannot be what is meant by the sentence, but must rather be considered as its sense. What is the position now with regard to the meaning? Have we a right even to inquire about it? Is it possible that a sentence as a whole has only a sense, but no meaning? At any rate, one might expect that such sentences occur, just as there are parts of sentences having sense but no meaning. And sentences which contain proper names without meaning will be of this kind. The sentence 'Odysseus was set ashore at Ithaca while sound asleep' obviously has a sense. But since it is doubtful whether the name 'Odysseus,' occurring therein, means anything, it is also doubtful whether the whole sentence does. Yet it is certain, nevertheless, that anyone who seriously took the sentence to be true or false would ascribe to the name 'Odysseus' a meaning, not merely a sense; for it is of what the name means that the predicate is affirmed or denied. Whoever does not admit the name has meaning can neither apply nor withhold the predicate. But in that case it would be superfluous to advance to what the name means; one could be satisfied with the sense, if one wanted to go no further than the thought. If it were a question only of the sense of the sentence, the thought, it would be needless to bother with what is meant by a part of the sentence; only the sense, not the meaning, of the part is relevant to the sense of the whole sentence. The thought remains the same whether 'Odysseus' means something or not. The fact that we concern ourselves at all about what is meant by a part of the sentence indicates that we generally recognize and expect a meaning for the sentence itself. The thought loses value for us as soon as we recognize that the meaning of one of its parts is missing. We are therefore justified in not being satisfied with the sense of a sentence, and in inquiring also as to its meaning. But now why do we want every proper name to have not only a sense, but also a meaning? Why is the thought not enough for us? Because, and to the extent that, we are concerned with its truth-value. This is not always the case. In hearing an epic poem, for instance, apart from the euphony of the language we are interested only in the sense of the sentences and the images and feelings thereby aroused. The question of truth would cause us to abandon aesthetic delight for an attitude of scientific investigation. Hence it is a matter of no concern to us whether the name 'Odysseus,' for instance, has meaning, so long as we accept the poem as a work of art.[8] It is the striving for truth that drives us always to advance from the sense to the thing meant.

[7]By a thought I understand not the subjective performance of thinking but its objective content, which is capable of being the common property of several thinkers. [Au.]

[8]It would be desirable to have a special term for signs having only sense. If we name them, say, representations, the words of the actors on the stage would be representations; indeed the actor himself would be a representation. [Au.]

We have seen that the meaning of a sentence may always be sought, whenever the meaning of its components is involved; and that this is the case when and only when we are inquiring after the truth-value.

We are therefore driven into accepting the *truth-value* of a sentence as constituting what it means. By the truth-value of a sentence I understand the circumstance that it is true or false. There are no further truth-values. For brevity I call the one the True, the other the False. Every assertoric sentence concerned with what its words mean is therefore to be regarded as a proper name, and its meaning, if it has one, is either the True or the False. These two objects are recognized, if only implicitly, by everybody who judges something to be true—and so even by a sceptic. The designation of the truth values as objects may appear to be an arbitrary fancy or perhaps a mere play upon words, from which no profound consequences could be drawn. What I am calling an object can be more exactly discussed only in connexion with concept and relation. I will reserve this for another article.[9] But so much should already be clear, that in every judgment,[10] no matter how trivial, the step from the level of thoughts to the level of meaning (the objective) has already been taken.

One might be tempted to regard the relation of the thought to the True not as that of sense to meaning, but rather as that of subject to predicate. One can, indeed, say: 'The thought that 5 is a prime number is true.' But closer examination shows that nothing more has been said than in the simple sentence '5 is a prime number.' The truth claim arises in each case from the form of the assertoric sentence, and when the latter lacks its usual force, e.g., in the mouth of an actor upon the stage, even the sentence 'The thought that 5 is a prime number is true' contains only a thought, and indeed the same thought as the simple '5 is a prime number.' It follows that the relation of the thought to the True may not be compared with that of subject to predicate.

Subject and predicate (understood in the logical sense) are just elements of thought; they stand on the same level for knowledge. By combining subject and predicate, one reaches only a thought, never passes from sense to meaning, never from a thought to its truth-value. One moves at the same level but never advances from one level to the next. A truth-value cannot be a part of a thought, any more than, say, the Sun can, for it is not a sense but an object.

If our supposition that the meaning of a sentence is its truth-value is correct, the latter must remain unchanged when a part of the sentence is replaced by an expression with the same meaning. And this is in fact the case. Leibniz gives the definition: '*Eadem sunt, quae sibi mutuo substitui possunt, salva veritate.*' If we are dealing with sentences for which the meaning of their component parts is at all relevant, then what feature except the truth-value can be found that belongs to such sentences quite generally and remains unchanged by substitutions of the kind just mentioned?

If now the truth-value of a sentence is its meaning, then on the one hand all true sentences have the same meaning and so, on the other hand, do all false sentences. From this we see that in the meaning of the sentence all that is specific is obliterated. We can never be concerned only with the meaning of a sentence; but again the mere thought alone yields no knowledge, but only the thought together with its meaning, i.e. its truth-value. Judgments can be regarded as advances from a thought to a truth-value. Naturally this cannot be a definition. Judgment is something quite peculiar and incomparable. One might also say that judgments are distinctions of parts within truth-values. Such distinction occurs by a return to the thought. To every sense attaching to a truth-value would correspond its own manner of analysis. However, I have here used the word 'part' in a special sense. I have in fact transferred the relation between the parts and the whole of the sentence to its meaning, by calling the meaning of a word part of the meaning of the sentence, if the word itself is a part of the sentence. This way of speaking can certainly be attacked, because the total meaning and one part of it do not suffice to determine the remainder, and because the word 'part' is already used of bodies in another sense. A special term would need to be invented.

The supposition that the truth value of a sentence is what it means shall now be put to further test. We have found that the truth-value of a sentence remains unchanged when an expression is replaced by another with the same meaning: but we have not yet considered the case in which the expression to be replaced is itself a sentence. Now if our view is

[9] See his 'Ueber Begriff und Gegenstand' (1892), in *Translations*, pp. 42–45. [Tr.] See note 3 above. [Eds.]

[10] A judgment, for me, is not the mere grasping of a thought, but the admission of its truth. [Au.]

correct, the truth-value of a sentence containing another as part must remain unchanged when the part is replaced by another sentence having the same truth-value. Exceptions are to be expected when the whole sentence or its part is direct or indirect quotation; for in such cases as we have seen, the words do not have their customary meaning. In direct quotation, a sentence designates another sentence, and in indirect speech a thought.

We are thus led to consider subordinate sentences or clauses. These occur as parts of a sentence complex, which is, from the logical standpoint, likewise a sentence—a main sentence. But here we meet the question whether it is also true of the subordinate sentence that its meaning is a truth-value. Of indirect speech we already know the opposite. Grammarians view the subordinate clauses as representatives of parts of sentences and divide them accordingly into noun clauses, adjective clauses, adverbial clauses. This might generate the supposition that the meaning of a subordinate clause was not a truth-value but rather of the same kind as the meaning of a noun or adjective or adverb—in short, of a part of a sentence, whose sense was not a thought but only a part of a thought. Only a more thorough investigation can clarify the issue. In so doing, we shall not follow the grammatical categories strictly, but rather group together what is logically of the same kind. Let us first search for cases in which the sense of the subordinate clause, as we have just supposed, is not an independent thought.

The case of an abstract[11] noun clause, introduced by 'that,' includes the case of indirect quotation, in which we have seen the words to have their indirect meaning, coincident with what is customarily their sense. In this case, then, the subordinate clause has for its meaning a thought, not a truth-value; as sense not a thought, but the sense of the words 'the thought that (etc.),' which is only a part of the thought in the entire complex sentence. This happens after 'say,' 'hear,' 'be of the opinion,' 'be convinced,' 'conclude,' and similar words.[12] There is a different, and indeed somewhat complicated, situation after words like 'perceive,' 'know,' 'fancy,' which are to be considered later.

That in the cases of the first kind the meaning of the subordinate clause is in fact the thought can also be recognized by seeing that it is indifferent to the truth of the whole whether the subordinate clause is true or false. Let us compare, for instance, the two sentences 'Copernicus believed that the planetary orbits are circles' and 'Copernicus believed that the apparent motion of the sun is produced by the real motion of the Earth.' One subordinate clause can be substituted for the other without harm to the truth. The main clause and the subordinate clause together have as their sense only a single thought, and the truth of the whole includes neither the truth nor the untruth of the subordinate clause. In such cases it is not permissible to replace one expression in the subordinate clause by another having the same customary meaning, but only by one having the same indirect meaning, i.e. the same customary sense. Somebody might conclude: The meaning of a sentence is not its truth-value, for in that case it could always be replaced by another sentence of the same truth-value. But this proves too much; one might just as well claim that the meaning of 'morning star' is not Venus, since one may not always say 'Venus' in place of 'morning star.' One has the right to conclude only that the meaning of a sentence is not *always* its truth value, and that 'morning star' does not always mean the planet Venus, viz. when the word has its indirect meaning. An exception of such a kind occurs in the subordinate clause just considered which has a thought as its meaning.

If one says 'It seems that . . .' one means 'It seems to me that . . .' or 'I think that . . .' We therefore have the same case again. The situation is similar in the case of expressions such as 'to be pleased,' 'to regret,' 'to approve,' 'to blame,' 'to hope,' 'to fear.' If, toward the end of the battle of Waterloo,[13] Wellington was glad that the Prussians were coming, the basis for his joy was a conviction. Had he been deceived, he would have been no less pleased so long as his illusion lasted; and before he became so convinced he could not have been pleased that the Prussians were coming—even though in fact they might have been already approaching.

Just as a conviction or a belief is the ground of a

[11] Frege probably means clauses grammatically replaceable by an abstract noun-phrase; e.g., 'Smith denies *that dragons exist*' = 'Smith denies *the existence of dragons*'; or again, in this context after 'denies', 'that Brown is wise' is replaceable by 'the wisdom of Brown.' [Tr.]

[12] In 'A lied in saying he had seen B,' the subordinate clause designates a thought which is said (1) to have been asserted by A (2) while A was convinced of its falsity. [Au.]

[13] Frege uses the Prussian name for the battle—'Belle Alliance.' [Tr.]

feeling, it can, as in inference, also be the ground of a conviction. In the sentence: 'Columbus inferred from the roundness of the Earth that he could reach India by travelling towards the west,' we have as the meanings of the parts two thoughts, that the Earth is round, and that Columbus by travelling to the west could reach India. All that is relevant here is that Columbus was convinced of both, and that the one conviction was a ground for the other. Whether the Earth is really round and Columbus could really reach India by travelling west, as he thought, is immaterial to the truth of our sentence; but it is not immaterial whether we replace 'the Earth' by 'the planet which is accompanied by a moon whose diameter is greater than the fourth part of its own.' Here also we have the indirect meaning of the words.

Adverbial final clauses beginning 'in order that' also belong here; for obviously the purpose is a thought; therefore: indirect meaning for the words, subjunctive mood.

A subordinate clause with 'that' after 'command,' 'ask,' 'forbid,' would appear in direct speech as an imperative. Such a sentence has no meaning but only a sense. A command, a request, are indeed not thoughts, but they stand on the same level as thoughts. Hence in subordinate clauses depending upon 'command,' 'ask,' etc., words have their indirect meaning. The meaning of such a clause is therefore not a truth-value but a command, a request, and so forth.

The case is similar for the dependent question in phrases such as 'doubt whether' 'not to know what.' It is easy to see that here also the words are to be taken to have their indirect meaning. Dependent clauses expressing questions and beginning with 'who,' 'what,' 'where,' 'when,' 'how,' 'by what means,' etc., seem at times to approximate very closely to adverbial clauses in which words have their customary meanings. These cases are distinguished linguistically [in German] by the mood of the verb. With the subjunctive, we have a dependent question and indirect meanings of the words, so that a proper name cannot in general be replaced by another name of the same object.

In the cases so far considered the words of the subordinate clauses had their indirect meaning, and this made it clear that the meaning of the subordinate clause itself was indirect, i.e. not a truth-value but a thought, a command, a request, a question. The subordinate clause could be regarded as a noun, indeed one could say: as a proper name of that thought, that command, etc., which it represented in the context of the sentence structure.

We now come to other subordinate clauses, in which the words do have their customary meaning without however a thought occurring as sense and a truth-value as meaning. How this is possible is best made clear by examples.

> Whoever discovered the elliptic form of the planetary orbits died in misery.

If the sense of the subordinate clause were here a thought, it would have to be possible to express it also in a separate sentence. But it does not work, because the grammatical subject 'whoever' has no independent sense and only mediates the relation with the consequent clause 'died in misery.' For this reason the sense of the subordinate clause is not a complete thought, and what it means is Kepler, not a truth value. One might object that the sense of the whole does contain a thought as part, viz. that there was somebody who first discovered the elliptic form of the planetary orbits; for whoever takes the whole to be true cannot deny this part. This is undoubtedly so; but only because otherwise the dependent clause 'whoever discovered the elliptic form of the planetary orbits' would have nothing to mean. If anything is asserted there is always an obvious presupposition that the simple or compound proper names used have meaning. If therefore one asserts 'Kepler died in misery,' there is a presupposition that the name 'Kepler' designates something; but it does not follow that the sense of the sentence 'Kepler died in misery' contains the thought that the name 'Kepler' designates something. If this were the case the negation would have to run not

> Kepler did not die in misery

but

> Kepler did not die in misery, or the name 'Kepler' has no reference.

That the name 'Kepler' designates something is just as much a presupposition for the assertion

> Kepler died in misery

as for the contrary assertion. Now languages have the fault of containing expressions which fail to designate an object (although their grammatical form seems to qualify them for that purpose) because the truth of some sentence is a prerequisite. Thus it depends on the truth of the sentence:

> There was someone who discovered the elliptic form of the planetary orbits

whether the subordinate clause

> Whoever discovered the elliptic form of the planetary orbits

really designates an object, or only seems to do so while in fact there is nothing for it to mean. And thus it may appear as if our subordinate clause contained as a part of its sense the thought that there was somebody who discovered the elliptic form of the planetary orbits. If this were right the negation would run:

> Either whoever discovered the elliptic form of the planetary orbits did not die in misery or there was nobody who discovered the elliptic form of the planetary orbits.

This arises from an imperfection of language, from which even the symbolic language of mathematical analysis is not altogether free; even there combinations of symbols can occur that seem to mean something but (at least so far) do not mean anything, e.g. divergent infinite series. This can be avoided, e.g., by means of the special stipulation that divergent infinite series shall mean the number 0. A logically perfect language (*Begriffsschrift*) should satisfy the conditions, that every expression grammatically well constructed as a proper name out of signs already introduced shall in fact designate an object, and that no new sign shall be introduced as a proper name without being secured a meaning. The logic books contain warnings against logical mistakes arising from the ambiguity of expressions. I regard as no less pertinent a warning against apparent proper names without any meaning. The history of mathematics supplies errors which have arisen in this way. This lends itself to demagogic abuse as easily as ambiguity—perhaps more easily. 'The will of the people' can serve as an example; for it is easy to establish that there is at any rate no generally accepted meaning for this expression. It is therefore by no means unimportant to eliminate the source of these mistakes, at least in science, once and for all. Then such objections as the one discussed above would become impossible, because it could never depend upon the truth of a thought whether a proper name had meaning.

With the consideration of these noun clauses may be coupled that of types of adjective and adverbial clauses which are logically in close relation to them.

Adjective clauses also serve to construct compound proper names, though, unlike noun clauses, they are not sufficient by themselves for this purpose. These adjective clauses are to be regarded as equivalent to adjectives. Instead of 'the square root of 4 which is smaller than 0,' one can also say 'the negative square root of 4.' We have here the case of a compound proper name constructed from the expression for a concept with the help of the singular definite article. This is at any rate permissible if the concept applies to one and only one single object.[14]

Expressions for concepts can be so constructed that marks of a concept are given by adjective clauses as, in our example, by the clause 'which is smaller than 0.' It is evident that such an adjective clause cannot have a thought as sense or a truth-value as meaning, any more than the noun clause could. Its sense, which can also in many cases be expressed by a single adjective, is only a part of a thought. Here, as in the case of the noun clause, there is no independent subject and therefore no possibility of reproducing the sense of the subordinate clause in an independent sentence.

Places, instants, stretches of time, logically considered, are objects; hence the linguistic designation of a definite place, a definite instant, or a stretch of time is to be regarded as a proper name. Now adverbial clauses of place and time can be used to construct such a proper name in much the same way as we have seen noun and adjective clauses can. In the same way, expressions for concepts that apply to places, etc., can be constructed. It is to be noted here also that the sense of these subordinate clauses cannot be reproduced in an independent sentence, since an essential component, viz. the determina-

[14] In accordance with what was said before, an expression of the kind in question must actually always be assured of meaning, by means of a special stipulation, e.g. by the convention that it shall count as meaning 0 when the concept applies to no object or to more than one. [Au.]

tion of place or time, is missing and is just indicated by a relative pronoun or a conjunction.[15]

In conditional clauses, also, there most often recognizably occurs an indefinite indicator, with a correlative indicator in the dependent clause. (We have already seen this occur in noun, adjective, and adverbial clauses.) In so far as each indicator relates to the other, both clauses together form a connected whole, which as a rule expresses only a single thought. In the sentence

> If a number is less than 1 and greater than 0, its square is less than 1 and greater than 0

the component in question is 'a number' in the antecedent clause and 'its' in the consequent clause. It is by means of this very indefiniteness that the sense acquires the generality expected of a law. It is this which is responsible for the fact that the antecedent clause alone has no complete thought as its sense and in combination with the consequent clause expresses one and only one thought, whose parts are no longer thoughts. It is, in general, incorrect to say that in the hypothetical judgment two judgments are put in reciprocal relationship. If this or something similar is said, the word 'judgment' is used in the same sense as I have connected with the word 'thought,' so that I would use the formulation: 'A hypothetical thought establishes a reciprocal relationship between two thoughts.' This could be true only if an indefinite indicator is absent;[16] but in such a case there would also be no generality.

If an instant of time is to be indefinitely indicated in both the antecedent and the consequent clause, this is often achieved merely by using the present tense of the verb, which in such a case however does not indicate the temporal present. This grammatical form is then the indefinite indicator in the main and subordinate clauses. An example of this is: 'When the Sun is in the tropic of Cancer, the longest day in the northern hemisphere occurs.' Here, also, it is impossible to express the sense of the subordinate clause in a full sentence, because this sense is not a complete thought. If we say: 'The Sun is in the tropic of Cancer,' this would refer to our present time and thereby change the sense. Neither is the sense of the main clause a thought; only the whole, composed of main and subordinate clauses, has such a sense. It may be added that several common components may be indefinitely indicated in the antecedent and consequent clauses.

It is clear that noun clauses with 'who' or 'what' and adverbial clauses with 'where,' 'when,' 'wherever,' 'whenever' are often to be interpreted as having the sense of antecedent clauses, e.g. 'who touches pitch, defiles himself.'

Adjective clauses can also take the place of conditional clauses. Thus the sense of the sentence previously used can be given in the form 'The square of a number which is less than 1 and greater than 0 is less than 1 and greater than 0.'

The situation is quite different if the common component of the two clauses is designated by a proper name. In the sentence:

> Napoleon, who recognized the danger to his right flank, himself led his guards against the enemy position

two thoughts are expressed:

> 1. Napoleon recognized the danger to his right flank
> 2. Napoleon himself led his guards against the enemy position.

[15] In the case of these sentences, various interpretations are easily possible. The sense of the sentence, 'After Schleswig-Holstein was separated from Denmark, Prussia and Austria quarrelled' can be rendered in the form 'After the separation of Schleswig-Holstein from Denmark, Prussia and Austria quarrelled.' In this version, it is surely sufficiently clear that the sense is not to be taken as having as a part the thought that Schleswig-Holstein was once separated from Denmark, but that this is the necessary presupposition in order for the expression 'after the separation of Schleswig-Holstein from Denmark' to have any meaning at all. To be sure, our sentence can also be interpreted as saying that Schleswig-Holstein was once separated from Denmark. We then have a case which is to be considered later. In order to understand the difference more clearly, let us project ourselves into the mind of a Chinese who, having little knowledge of European history, believes it to be false that Schleswig-Holstein was ever separated from Denmark. He will take our sentence, in the first version, to be neither true nor false but will deny it to have any meaning, on the ground that its subordinate clause lacks a meaning. This clause would only apparently determine a time. If he interpreted our sentence in the second way, however, he would find a thought expressed in it which he would take to be false, beside a part which would be without meaning for him. [Au.]

[16] At times there is no linguistically explicit indicator and one must be read off from the entire context. [Au.]

When and where this happened is to be fixed only by the context, but is nevertheless to be taken as definitely determined thereby. If the entire sentence is uttered as an assertion, we thereby simultaneously assert both component sentences. If one of the parts is false, the whole is false. Here we have the case that the subordinate clause by itself has a complete thought as sense (if we complete it by indication of place and time). The meaning of the subordinate clause is accordingly a truth-value. We can therefore expect that it may be replaced, without harm to the truth-value of the whole, by a sentence having the same truth-value. This is indeed the case; but it is to be noticed that for purely grammatical reasons, its subject must be 'Napoleon,' for only then can it be brought into the form of an adjective clause attaching to 'Napoleon.' But if the demand that it be expressed in this form is waived, and the connexion shown by 'and,' this restriction disappears.

Subsidiary clauses beginning with 'although' also express complete thoughts. This conjunction actually has no sense and does not change the sense of the clause but only illuminates it in a peculiar fashion.[17] We could indeed replace the concessive clause without harm to the truth of the whole by another of the same truth-value; but the light in which the clause is placed by the conjunction might then easily appear unsuitable, as if a song with a sad subject were to be sung in a lively fashion.

In the last cases the truth of the whole included the truth of the component clauses. The case is different if an antecedent clause expresses a complete thought by containing, in place of an indefinite indicator, a proper name or something which is to be regarded as equivalent. In the sentence

> If the Sun has already risen, the sky is very cloudy

the time is the present, that is to say, definite. And the place is also to be thought of as definite. Here it can be said that a relation between the truth-values of antecedent and consequent clauses has been asserted, viz. that the case does not occur in which the antecedent means the True and the consequent the False. Accordingly, our sentence is true if the Sun has not yet risen, whether the sky is very cloudy or not, and also if the Sun has risen and the sky is very cloudy. Since only truth-values are here in question, each component clause can be replaced by another of the same truth-value without changing the truth-value of the whole. To be sure, the light in which the subject then appears would usually be unsuitable; the thought might easily seem distorted; but this has nothing to do with its truth-value. One must always observe that there are overtones of subsidiary thoughts, which are however not explicitly expressed and therefore should not be reckoned in the sense. Hence, also, no account need be taken of their truth-values.[18]

The simple cases have now been discussed. Let us review what we have learned.

The subordinate clause usually has for its sense not a thought, but only a part of one, and consequently no truth-value is being meant. The reason for this is either that the words in the subordinate clause have indirect meaning, so that the meaning, not the sense, of the subordinate clause is a thought; or else that, on account of the presence of an indefinite indicator, the subordinate clause is incomplete and expresses a thought only when combined with the main clause. It may happen, however, that the sense of the subsidiary clause is a complete thought, in which case it can be replaced by another of the same truth value without harm to the truth of the whole—provided there are no grammatical obstacles.

An examination of all the subordinate clauses which one may encounter will soon provide some which do not fit well into these categories. The reason, so far as I can see, is that these subordinate clauses have no such simple sense. Almost always, it seems, we connect with the main thoughts expressed by us subsidiary thoughts which, although not expressed, are associated with our words, in accordance with psychological laws, by the hearer. And since the subsidiary thought appears to be connected with our words on its own account, almost like the main thought itself, we want it also to be expressed. The sense of the sentence is thereby enriched, and it may well happen that we have more simple thoughts than clauses. In many cases the

[17] Similarly in the case of 'but,' 'yet.' [Au.]

[18] The thought of our sentence might also be expressed thus: 'Either the Sun has not risen yet or the sky is very cloudy'—which shows how this kind of sentence connexion is to be understood. [Au.]

sentence must be understood in this way, in others it may be doubtful whether the subsidiary thought belongs to the sense of the sentence or only accompanies it.[19] One might perhaps find that the sentence

> Napoleon, who recognized the danger to his right flank, himself led his guards against the enemy position

expresses not only the two thoughts shown above, but also the thought that the knowledge of the danger was the reason why he led the guards against the enemy position. One may in fact doubt whether this thought is just slightly suggested or really expressed. Let the question be considered whether our sentence is false if Napoleon's decision had already been made before he recognized the danger. If our sentence could be true in spite of this, the subsidiary thought should not be understood as part of the sense. One would probably decide in favour of this. The alternative would make for a quite complicated situation: We would have more simple thoughts than clauses. If the sentence

> Napoleon recognized the danger to his right flank

were now to be replaced by another having the same truth value, e.g.

> Napoleon was already more than 45 years old

not only would our first thought be changed, but also our third one. Hence the truth-value of the latter might change—viz. if his age was not the reason for the decision to lead the guards against the enemy. This shows why clauses of equal truth-value cannot always be substituted for one another in such cases. The clause expresses more through its connexion with another than it does in isolation.

Let us now consider cases where this regularly happens. In the sentence:

> Bebel fancies that the return of Alsace-Lorraine would appease France's desire for revenge

two thoughts are expressed, which are not however shown by means of antecedent and consequent clauses, viz.:

> (1) Bebel believes that the return of Alsace-Lorraine would appease France's desire for revenge
>
> (2) the return of Alsace-Lorraine would not appease France's desire for revenge.

In the expression of the first thought, the words of the subordinate clause have their indirect meaning, while the same words have their customary meaning in the expression of the second thought. This shows that the subordinate clause in our original complex sentence is to be taken twice over, with different meanings: once for a thought, once for a truth value. Since the truth-value is not the total meaning of the subordinate clause, we cannot simply replace the latter by another of equal truth-value. Similar considerations apply to expressions such as 'know,' 'discover,' 'it is known that.'

By means of a subordinate causal clause and the associated main clause we express several thoughts, which however do not correspond separately to the original clauses. In the sentence: 'Because ice is less dense than water, it floats on water' we have

> (1) Ice is less dense than water;
>
> (2) If anything is less dense than water, it floats on water;
>
> (3) Ice floats on water.

The third thought, however, need not be explicitly introduced, since it is contained in the remaining two. On the other hand, neither the first and third nor the second and third combined would furnish the sense of our sentence. It can now be seen that our subordinate clause

> because ice is less dense than water

expresses our first thought, as well as a part of our second. This is how it comes to pass that our subsidiary clause cannot be simply replaced by another of equal truth value; for this would alter our second thought and thereby might well alter its truth value.

The situation is similar in the sentence

[19] This may be important for the question whether an assertion is a lie, or an oath a perjury. [Au.]

> If iron were less dense than water, it would float on water.

Here we have the two thoughts that iron is not less dense than water, and that something floats on water if it is less dense than water. The subsidiary clause again expresses one thought and a part of the other.

If we interpret the sentence already considered

> After Schleswig-Holstein was separated from Denmark, Prussia and Austria quarrelled

in such a way that it expresses the thought that Schleswig-Holstein was once separated from Denmark, we have first this thought, and secondly the thought that, at a time more closely determined by the subordinate clause, Prussia and Austria quarrelled. Here also the subordinate clause expresses not only one thought but also a part of another. Therefore it may not in general be replaced by another of the same truth-value.

It is hard to exhaust all the possibilities given by language; but I hope to have brought to light at least the essential reasons why a subordinate clause may not always be replaced by another of equal truth value without harm to the truth of the whole sentence structure. These reasons arise:

(1) when the subordinate clause does not have a truth-value as its meaning, inasmuch as it expresses only a part of a thought;

(2) when the subordinate clause does have a truth-value as its meaning but is not restricted to so doing, inasmuch as its sense includes one thought and part of another.

The first case arises:

(a) for words having indirect meaning

(b) if a part of the sentence is only an indefinite indicator instead of a proper name.

In the second case, the subsidiary clause may have to be taken twice over, viz. once in its customary meaning, and the other time in indirect meaning; or the sense of a part of the subordinate clause may likewise be a component of another thought, which, taken together with the thought directly expressed by the subordinate clause, makes up the sense of the whole sentence.

It follows with sufficient probability from the foregoing that the cases where a subordinate clause is not replaceable by another of the same value cannot be brought in disproof of our view that a truth-value is the meaning of a sentence that has a thought as its sense.

Let us return to our starting point.

When we found '$a=a$' and '$a=b$' to have different cognitive values, the explanation is that for the purpose of knowledge, the sense of the sentence, viz., the thought expressed by it, is no less relevant than its meaning, i.e. its truth-value. If now $a=b$, then indeed what is meant by 'b' is the same as what is meant by 'a,' and hence the truth-value of '$a=b$' is the same as that of '$a=a$.' In spite of this, the sense of 'b' may differ from that of 'a,' and thereby the thought expressed in '$a=b$' differs from that of $a=a$.' In that case the two sentences do not have the same cognitive value. If we understand by 'judgment' the advance from the thought to its truth-value, as in the present paper, we can also say that the judgments are different.

Charles Sanders Peirce

1839–1914

WHILE Charles Sanders Peirce (pronounced "purse") is widely acknowledged as the founder of pragmatism, he expressed his own mild disapproval of what "pragmatism" had become as William James and others had developed it and, typically, made matters slightly difficult by characterizing his own view as "pragmaticism." In Peirce's original formulation, pragmatism was presented as a way of conceiving objects according to their effects; but his later view changed the emphasis from the object to the symbol. The pragmaticist maxim is that "The entire intellectual purport of a symbol consists in the totality of all general modes of rational conduct which . . . would ensue upon the acceptance of the symbol" (see "Issues of Pragmaticism," *The Monist* 15 [October 1905]: 481–99). Whereas James had interpreted pragmatism psychologically, Peirce treated it logically and semiotically—and in fact coined the word "semiotics" several decades before *Ferdinand de Saussure* predicted the emergence of "semiology" as the general study of signs.

Like *Gottlob Frege,* Peirce was profoundly interested in the foundations of logic; and, also like Frege, he developed a representational formalism (which he called "existential graphs") of considerable expressiveness—but notorious obscurity. William James is reported to have viewed Peirce as perhaps the only one of his fellow students and colleagues at Harvard with genuine philosophical genius; but Peirce's difficulties in receiving and keeping academic appointments left him professionally isolated, and, for the most part, living in genuine misery.

A major difficulty faced by modern students of Peirce is the apparently miscellaneous character of his papers. Apart from several series of articles in *The Journal of Speculative Philosophy* (1868), *Popular Science Monthly* (1877–78), and *The Monist* (1891–92, 1905) and several articles written for *Baldwin's Dictionary* (1902), the great bulk of Peirce's writing was not published in his lifetime. He did not write any single book but did leave, in manuscript, an extraordinary collection of loosely connected papers, developing a philosophical position that is difficult to characterize.

It is important that Peirce's interest in signs, having emerged from his reflections on classical problems of nominalism, realism, and representation, is hardly evident at all in his published writings but appears dominant in the unpublished manuscripts.

An important, though difficult, clue lies in Peirce's early essay, "On a New List of Categories" (1867). The essay is unusual in many respects, not least of which is its style, which is simultaneously reminiscent of Duns Scotus, Kant, and Hegel;

in this context, see John E. Boler's *Charles Peirce and Scholastic Realism* (1963). Peirce's argument is equally strange, starting with the premise that the cognition of an object is always dependent on reducing impressions to the unity of a proposition, whereas the capacity to determine the identity of an object is always dependent on the "indefinite determinability" of predicates. "Being," in this scheme, is just the copula, the "is" of predication, and as such the concept of "Being" has no content. Thus, according to Peirce, if we say, "'The stove is black,' the stove is the *substance*, from which its blackness has not been differentiated, and the *is*, while it leaves the substance just as it was seen, explains its confusedness, by the application to it of *blackness* as a predicate" (*Collected Papers*, 1 : 548).

If this manner of argument leaves a reader in some state of "confusedness," it is because Peirce discriminates in this way between "substance" and "being": "Substance is inapplicable to a predicate, and being is equally so to a subject." The essential point is this: the very conception of a "being" depends on the formation of a proposition, linking subject and predicate; but any *object* is then itself a mediating representation that is intelligible only by the mental activity of a consciousness constructing another mediating representation which Peirce calls the "interpretant." The result is that the "substance" of subjects and the "being" of predicates join in objects which are propositions, and the highest "reality" belongs to the *sign* or *symbol.*

While one might observe that this is an ingenious way to effect a resolution between nominalism and realism, it is also the beginning of a massive speculative project in the study of signs, or "semiotics." In the letter to Lady Welby included here, Peirce explains his theory of the categories of "Firstness," "Secondness," and "Thirdness," linking these ideas to his theory of signs as consisting of "Icons," "Indices," and "Symbols."

Most of Peirce's papers have been published in *The Collected Papers of Charles Sanders Peirce*, ed. Arthur Burks, Charles Hartshorne, and Paul Weiss, 8 vols. (1931–58). A new chronological edition of the papers is now being published by Indiana University Press. Several shorter selections are available: see especially *Charles Sanders Peirce Selected Writings: Values in a Universe of Chance*, ed. Philip P. Weiner (1958), and *Charles S. Peirce: The Essential Writings*, ed. Edward C. Moore (1972). See also Bruce Kuklick, *The Rise of American Philosophy: Cambridge, Massachusetts, 1860–1930* (1977), and John Boler, *Charles Peirce and Scholastic Realism* (1963).

FROM

LETTERS TO LADY WELBY

P.O. Milford, Pa.
1904, Oct. 12

My dear Lady Welby:

Not a day has passed since I received your last letter that I have not lamented the circumstances that prevented me from writing that very day the letter that I was intent upon writing to you, without my promising myself that it should soon be done. . . .

For one thing, I wanted to express my surprise at finding you rather repelled the designation of a "rationalist," and said that as a woman you were naturally conservative. Of course, the lady of the house is usually the minister of foreign affairs (barring those of money and law) and as an accomplished diplomat, is careful and conservative. But when a woman takes up an idea my experience is that she does so with a singleness of heart that distinguishes her. Some of my very best friends have been very radical women. I do not know that I don't think your recommending a serious consideration of changing the base of numeration is a bit radical.

But I wanted to write to you about signs, which in your opinion and mine, are matters of so much concern. More in mine, I think, than in yours. For in mine, the highest grade of reality is only reached by signs; that is, by such ideas as those of Truth and Right and the rest. It sounds paradoxical; but when I have devolved to you my whole theory of signs, it will seem less so. I think that I will today explain the outlines of my classification of signs.

You know that I particularly approve of inventing new words for new ideas. I do not know that the study I call *Ideoscopy* can be called a new idea, but the word *phenomenology* is used in a different sense. *Ideoscopy* consists in describing and classifying the ideas that belong to ordinary experience or that naturally arise in connection with ordinary life, without regard to their being valid or invalid or to their psychology. In pursuing this study I was long ago (1867) led, after only three or four years' study, to throw all ideas into the three classes of Firstness, of Secondness, and of Thirdness.[1] This sort of notion is as distasteful to me as to anybody; and for years, I endeavored to pooh-pooh and refute it; but it long ago conquered me completely. Disagreeable as it is to attribute such meaning to numbers, & to a triad above all, it is as true as it is disagreeable. The ideas of Firstness, Secondness, and Thirdness are simple enough. Giving to being the broadest possible sense, to include ideas as well as things, and ideas that we fancy we have just as much as ideas we do have, I should define Firstness, Secondness, and Thirdness thus:

Firstness is the mode of being of that which is such as it is, positively and without reference to anything else.

Secondness is the mode of being of that which is such as it is, with respect to a second but regardless of any third.

Thirdness is the mode of being of that which is such as it is, in bringing a second and third into relation to each other.

I call these three ideas the cenopythagorean[2] categories.

The typical ideas of Firstness are qualities of feeling, or mere appearances. The scarlet of your royal liveries, the quality itself, independently of its being perceived or remembered, is an example, by which I do not mean that you are to imagine that you *do not* perceive or remember it, but that you are to drop out of account that which may be attached to it in perceiving or in remembering, but which does not belong to the quality. For example, when you remember it, your idea is said to be *dim* and when it is before your eyes, it is *vivid*. But dimness or vividness do not belong to your idea of the quality. They *might* no doubt, if considered simply as a feeling; but when you think of vividness you do not consider it from that point of view. You think of it as a degree of disturbance of your consciousness. The

This letter was written on October 12, 1904. It originally appeared in *Charles S. Peirce's Letters to Lady Welby*, ed. Irwin C. Lieb (New Haven, 1953) and is reprinted here from *Charles S. Peirce Selected Writings: Values in a Universe of Chance*, ed. Philip P. Weiner (1958), by permission of Dover Publications.

[1] See "On a New List of Categories" (1867), in *The Collected Papers of Charles Sanders Peirce*, 1:287–99. [Eds.]

[2] A term coined by Peirce, from Greek *kenos*, "empty," and Pythagorean, after the pre-Socratic Greek philosopher and mathematician Pythagoras (ca. 582–507 B.C.). [Eds.]

quality of red is not thought of as belonging to you, or as attached to liveries. It is simply a peculiar positive possibility regardless of anything else. If you ask a mineralogist what hardness is, he will say that it is what one predicates of a body that one cannot scratch with a knife. But a simple person will think of hardness as a simple positive possibility the *realization* of which causes a body to be like a flint. That idea of hardness is an idea of Firstness. The unanalyzed total impression made by any manifold not thought of as actual fact, but simply as a quality as simple positive possibility of appearance is an idea of Firstness. Notice the *naïveté* of Firstness. The cenopythagorean categories are doubtless another attempt to characterize what Hegel sought to characterize as his three stages of thought.[3] They also correspond to the three categories of each of the four triads of Kant's table.[4] But the fact that these different attempts were independent of one another (the resemblance of these Categories to Hegel's stages was not remarked for many years after the list had been under study, owing to my antipathy to Hegel) only goes to show that there really are three such elements. The idea of the present instant, which, whether it exists or not, is naturally thought as a point of time in which no thought can take place or any detail be separated, is an idea of Firstness.

The type of an idea of Secondness is the experience of effort, prescinded[5] from the idea of a purpose. It may be said that there is no such experience, that a purpose is always in view as long as the effort is cognized. This may be open to doubt; for in sustained effort we soon let the purpose drop out of view. However, I abstain from psychology which has nothing to do with ideoscopy. The existence of the word *effort* is sufficient proof that people think they have such an idea; and that is enough. The experience of effort cannot exist without the experience of resistance. Effort only is effort by virtue of its being opposed; and no third element enters. Note that I speak of the *experience,* not of the *feeling,* of effort. Imagine yourself to be seated alone at night in the basket of a balloon, far above earth, calmly enjoying the absolute calm and stillness. Suddenly the piercing shriek of a steam-whistle breaks upon you, and continues for a good while. The impression of stillness was an idea of Firstness, a quality of feeling. The piercing whistle does not allow you to think or do anything but suffer. So that too is absolutely simple. Another Firstness. But the breaking of the silence by the noise was an experience. The person in his inertness identifies himself with the precedent state of feeling, and the new feeling which comes in spite of him is the non-ego. He has a two-sided consciousness of an ego and a non-ego. That consciousness of the action of a new feeling in destroying the old feeling is what I call an *experience.* Experience generally is what the course of life has *compelled* me to think. Secondness is either *genuine* or *degenerate.* There are many degrees of genuineness. Generally speaking genuine secondness consists in one thing acting upon another, brute action. I say brute, because so far as the idea of any *law* or *reason* comes in, Thirdness comes in. When a stone falls to the ground, the law of gravitation does not act to make it fall. The law of gravitation is the judge upon the bench who may pronounce the law till doomsday, but unless the strong arm of the law, the brutal sheriff, gives effect to the law, it amounts to nothing. True, the judge can create a sheriff if need be; but he must have one. The stone's actually falling is purely the affair of the stone and the earth at the time. This is a case of *reaction.* So is *existence* which is the mode of being of that which reacts with other things. But there is also action without reaction. *Such is the action of the previous upon the subsequent.* It is a difficult question whether the idea of this one-sided determination is a pure idea of secondness or whether it involves thirdness. At present, the former view seems to me correct. I suppose that when Kant made Time a form of the internal sense alone, he was influenced by some such considerations as the following. The relation between the previous and the subsequent consists in the previous being determinate and fixed for the subsequent, and the subsequent being indeterminate for the previous. But indeterminacy belongs only to ideas; the existent is determinate in every respect; and this is just what the law of causation consists in. Accordingly, the relation of time

[3] Georg Wilhelm Friedrich Hegel (1770–1831), German philosopher. See in this context Hegel's *The Phenomenology of Mind,* trans. George Lichtheim (1931; rpt. 1967). [Eds.]

[4] Immanuel Kant (1724–1804), German philosopher. See *The Critique of Pure Reason,* trans. Norman Kemp Smith (1929; rpt. 1964), p. 113. [Eds.]

[5] *Prescind,* to detach or abstract. See Peirce's discussion of this concept in "On a New List of Categories." [Eds.]

concerns only ideas. It may also be argued that, according to the law of the conservation of energy, there is nothing in the physical universe corresponding to our idea that the previous determines the subsequent in any way in which the subsequent does not determine the previous. For, according to that law, all that happens in the physical universe consists in the exchange of just so much *vis viva* $\frac{1}{2}m\,(ds/dt)^2$ for so much displacement. Now the square of a negative quantity being positive, it follows that if all the velocities were reversed at any instant, everything would go on just the same, only time going backward as it were. Everything that had happened would happen again in reverse order. These seem to me to be strong arguments to prove that temporal causation (a very different thing from physical dynamic action) is an action upon ideas and not upon existents. But since our idea of the past is precisely the idea of that which is absolutely determinate, fixed, *fait accompli,* and dead, as against the future which is living, plastic, and determinable, it appears to me that the idea of one-sided action, in so far as it concerns the being of the determinate, is a pure idea of Secondness; and I think that great errors of metaphysics are due to looking at the future as something that will have been past. I cannot admit that the idea of the future can be so translated into the Secundal ideas of the past. To say that a given Kind of event never will happen is to deny that there is any date at which its happening will be past; but it is not equivalent to any affirmation about a past relative to any assignable date. When we pass from the idea of an event to saying that it never will happen, or will happen in endless repetition, or introduce in any way the idea of endless repetition, I will say the idea is *mellonized* (*méllon,* about to be, do, or suffer). When I conceive a fact as acting but not capable of being acted upon, I will say that it is *parelélythose* (past) and the mode of being which consists in such action I will call *parelelythosine* (-ine = einai, being). I regard the former as an idea of Thirdness, the latter as an idea of Secondness. I consider the idea of any dyadic relation not involving any third as an idea of Secondness; and I should not call any completely degenerate except the relation of identity. But similarity which is the only possible identity of Firsts is very near to that. Dyadic relations have been classified by me in a great variety of ways; but the most important are first with regard to the nature of the Second in itself and second with regard to the nature of its first. The Second, or *Relate* is, in itself, either a *Referate,* if it is intrinsically a possibility, such as a Quality or it is a *Revelate* if it is of its own nature an Existent. In respect to its first, the Second is divisible either in regard to the dynamic first or to the immediate first. In regard to its dynamic first, a Second is determined either by virtue of its own intrinsic nature, or by virtue of a real relation to that second (an action). Its immediate second is either a Quality or an Existent.

I now come to Thirdness. To me, who have for forty years considered the matter from every point of view that I could discover, the inadequacy of Secondness to cover all that is in our minds is so evident that I scarce know how to begin to persuade any person of it who is not already convinced of it. Yet I see a great many thinkers who are trying to construct a system without putting any thirdness into it. Among them are some of my best friends who acknowledge themselves indebted to me for ideas but have never learned the principal lesson. Very well. It is highly proper that Secondness should be searched to its very bottom. Thus only can the indispensableness and irreducibility of thirdness be made out, although for him who has the mind to grasp it, it is sufficient to say that no branching of a line can result from putting one line on the end of another. My friend Schröder[6] fell in love with my algebra of dyadic relations. The few pages I gave to it in my Note B in the "Studies in Logic by Members of the Johns Hopkins University" were proportionate to its importance.[7] His book is profound,[8] but its profundity only makes it more clear that Secondness cannot compass Thirdness. (He is careful to avoid ever saying that it can, but he does go so far as to say that Secondness is the more important. So it is, considering that Thirdness cannot be understood without Secondness. But as to its application, it is so inferior to Thirdness as to be in that aspect quite in a different world.) Even in the most degen-

[6] The Schröder to whom Peirce refers was a German professor of logic with whom Peirce had corresponded, in reference to Peirce's *Studies in Logic* (1883; rpt. 1983). [Eds.]

[7] *Studies in Logic by Members of the Johns Hopkins University,* edited by Charles S. Peirce (Boston: Little, Brown & Company, 1883). Peirce's "Note B" is reprinted in *Collected Papers,* vol. 3. [Eds.]

[8] *Vorlesungen über die Algebra der Logik* (Leipzig: B. G. Teubner, 1890–1905). [Eds.]

erate form of Thirdness, and Thirdness has two grades of degeneracy, something may be detected which is not mere secondness. If you take any ordinary triadic relation, you will always find a *mental* element in it. Brute action is secondness, any mentality involves thirdness. Analyze for instance the relation involved in "A gives B to C." Now what is giving? It does not consist in A's putting B away from him and C's subsequently taking B up. It is not necessary that any material transfer should take place. It consists in A's making C the possessor according to *Law*. There must be some kind of law before there can be any kind of giving—be it but the law of the strongest. But now suppose that giving *did* consist merely in A's laying down the B which C subsequently picks up. That would be a degenerate form of Thirdness in which the thirdness is externally appended. In A's putting away B, there is no thirdness. In C's taking B, there is no thirdness. But if you say that these two acts constitute a single operation by virtue of the identity of the B, you transcend the mere brute fact, you introduce a mental element. As to my algebra of dyadic relations, Russell in his book which is superficial to nauseating me, has some silly remarks, about my "relative addition" etc., which are mere nonsense.[9] He says, or Whitehead says, that the need for it seldom occurs. The need for it *never* occurs if you bring in the same mode of connection in any other way. It is part of a system which does not bring in that mode of connection in any other way. In that system, it is indispensable. But let us leave Russell and Whitehead to work out their own salvation. The criticism which I make on that algebra of dyadic relations, with which I am by no means in love, though I think it is a pretty thing, is that the very triadic relations which it does not recognize, it does itself employ. For every combination of relatives to make a new relative is a triadic relation irreducible to dyadic relations. Its *inadequacy* is shown in other ways, but in this way it is in a conflict with itself *if it be regarded,* as I never did regard it, *as sufficient for the expression of all relations.* My universal algebra of relations, with the subjacent indices and Σ and Π is susceptible of being enlarged so as to comprise everything and so, still better, though not to ideal perfection, is the system of existential graphs.[10] I have not sufficiently applied myself to the study of the degenerate forms of Thirdness, though I think I see that it has two distinct grades of degeneracy. In its genuine form, Thirdness is the triadic relation existing between a sign, its object, and the interpreting thought, itself a sign, considered as constituting the mode of being of a sign. A sign mediates between the *interpretant* sign and its object. Taking sign in its broadest sense, its interpretant is not necessarily a sign. Any concept is a sign, of course. Ockham, Hobbes, and Leibniz[11] have sufficiently said that. But we may take a sign in so broad a sense that the interpretant of it is not a thought, but an action or experience, or we may even so enlarge the meaning of sign that its interpretant is a mere quality of feeling. A *Third* is something which brings a First into relation to a Second. A sign is a sort of Third. How shall we characterize it? Shall we say that a Sign brings a Second, its Object, into *cognitive* relation to a Third? That a Sign brings a Second into the same relation to a first in which it stands itself to that First? If we insist on *consciousness,* we must say what we mean by consciousness of an object. Shall we say we mean Feeling? Shall we say we mean association, or Habit? These are, on the face of them, psychological distinctions, which I am particular to avoid. What is the essential difference between a sign that is communicated to a mind, and one that is not so communicated? If the question were simply what we *do* mean by a sign, it might soon be resolved. But that is not the point. We are in the situation of a zoologist who wants to know what ought to be the meaning of "fish" in order to make fishes one of the great classes of vertebrates. It appears to me that the essential function of a sign is to render inefficient relations efficient—not to set them into action, but to establish a habit or general rule whereby they will act on occasion. According to the physical doctrine, nothing ever happens but the continued rectilinear velocities with the accelerations that accompany different relative positions of the particles. All other relations, of which we know so many, are inefficient. Knowledge in some way renders them efficient; and a sign is something by knowing which we know

[9] See Bertrand Russell, *The Principles of Mathematics* (1903), p. 24. [Eds.]

[10] See *Collected Papers,* vol. 4. [Eds.]

[11] William of Ockham (or Occam) (ca. 1285–ca. 1349), English scholastic philosopher, an earlier proponent of nominalism; Thomas Hobbes (1588–1679), English philosopher and political theorist; Gottfried Wilhelm Leibniz (1646–1716), German philosopher and mathematician. [Eds.]

something more. With the exception of knowledge, in the present instant, of the contents of consciousness in that instant (the existence of which knowledge is open to doubt) all our thought & knowledge is by signs. A sign therefore is an object which is in relation to its object on the one hand and to an interpretant on the other in such a way as to bring the interpretant into a relation to the object, corresponding to its own relation to the object. I might say "similar to its own," for a correspondence consists in a similarity; but perhaps correspondence is narrower.

I am now prepared to give my division of signs, as soon as I have pointed out that a sign has two objects, its object as it is represented and its object in itself. It has also three interpretants, its interpretant as represented or meant to be understood, its interpretant as it is produced, and its interpretant in itself. Now signs may be divided as to their own material nature, as to their relations to their objects, and as to their relations to their interpretants.[12]

As it is in itself, a sign is either of the nature of an appearance, when I call it a *qualisign;* or secondly, it is an individual object or event, when I call it a *sinsign* (the syllable *sin* being the first syllable of *se*mel, *sim*ul, *sin*gular, etc.); or thirdly, it is of the nature of a general type, when I call it a *legisign*. As we use the term "word" in most cases, saying that "the" is one "word" and "an" is a second "word," a "word" is a legisign. But when we say of a page in a book, that it has 250 "words" upon it, of which twenty are "the's," the "word" is a sinsign. A sinsign so embodying a legisign, I term a "replica" of the legisign. The difference between a legisign and a qualisign, neither of which is an individual thing, is that a legisign has a definite identity, though usually admitting a great variety of appearances. Thus, &, *and,* and the sound are all one word. The qualisign, on the other hand, has no identity. It is the mere quality of an appearance & is not exactly the same throughout a second. Instead of identity, it has *great similarity,* & cannot differ much without being called quite another qualisign.

In respect to their relations to their dynamic objects, I divide signs into Icons, Indices, and Symbols (a division I gave in 1867).[13] I define an Icon as a sign which is determined by its dynamic object by virtue of its own internal nature. Such is any qualisign, like a vision—or the sentiment excited by a piece of music considered as representing what the composer intended. Such may be a sinsign, like an individual diagram; say, a curve of the distribution of errors. I define an Index as a sign determined by its Dynamic object by virtue of being in a real relation to it. Such is a Proper Name (a legisign); such is the occurrence of a symptom of a disease (the Symptom itself is a legisign, a general type of a definite character. The occurrence in a particular case is a sinsign). I define a Symbol as a sign which is determined by its dynamic object only in the sense that it will be so interpreted. It thus depends either upon a convention, a habit, or a natural disposition of its interpretant, or of the field of its interpretant (that of which the interpretant is a determination). Every symbol is necessarily a legisign, for it is inaccurate to call a replica of a legisign a symbol.

In respect to its immediate object a sign may either be a sign of a quality, of an existent, or of a law.

In regard to its relation to its signified interpretant, a sign is either a Rheme, a Dicent, or an Argument. This corresponds to the old triune Term, Proposition, & Argument, modified so as to be applicable to signs generally. A *Term* is simply a class-name or proper-name. I do not regard the common noun as an essentially necessary part of speech. Indeed, it is only fully developed as a separate part of speech in the Aryan languages & the Basque—possibly in some other out-of-the-way tongues. In the Shemitic languages it is generally in form a verbal affair, & usually is so in substance too. As well as I can make out, such it is in most languages. In my universal algebra of logic there is no common noun. A rheme is any sign that is not true nor false, like almost any single word except "yes" and "no," which are almost peculiar to modern languages. A *proposition* as I use that term, is a dicent symbol. A dicent is not an assertion, but is a sign *capable* of being asserted. But an assertion is a dicent. According to my present view (I may see more light in future) the act of assertion is not a pure act of signification. It is an exhibition of the fact that one subjects oneself to the penalties visited on a liar if the proposition asserted is not true. An act of judgment is the self-recognition of a belief; and a belief consists in the acceptance of a proposition as a basis of conduct deliberately. But I think this posi-

[12] See *Collected Papers,* vol. 2, for a fuller exposition of Peirce's classification of trichotomies and signs. See also Appendix B in Lieb, *Charles S. Peirce's Letters to Lady Welby.* [Eds.]

[13] See "On a New List of Categories," p. 295. [Eds.]

tion is open to doubt. It is simply a question of which view gives the simplest view of the nature of the proposition. Holding, then, that a Dicent does not assert, I naturally hold that an Argument need not actually be submitted or urged. I therefore define an argument as a sign which is represented in its signified interpretant not as a Sign of that interpretant (the conclusion) (for that would be to urge or submit it) but *as if* it were a Sign of the Interpretant or perhaps as if it were a Sign of the state of the universe to which it refers, in which the premisses are taken for granted. I define a dicent as a sign represented in its signified interpretant *as if it were* in a Real Relation to its Object. (Or as being so, if it is asserted.) A rheme is defined as a sign which is represented in its signified interpretant as *if it were* a character or mark (or as being so).

According to my present view, a sign may appeal to its dynamic interpretant in three ways:

1st, an argument only may be *submitted* to its interpretant, as something the reasonableness of which will be acknowledged.
2nd, an argument or dicent may be *urged* upon the interpretant by an act of insistence.
3rd, argument or dicent may be and a rheme can only be, presented to the interpretant for *contemplation*.

Finally, in its relation to its immediate interpretant, I would divide signs into three classes as follows:

1st, those which are interpretable in thoughts or other signs of the same kind in infinite series,
2nd, those which are interpretable in actual experiences,
3rd, those which are interpretable in qualities or feelings or appearances.

Now if you think on the whole (as I do) that there is much valuable truth in all this, I should be gratified if you cared to append it to the next edition of your book, after editing it & of course cutting out personalities of a disagreeable kind *especially if accompanied by one or more* (running or other) *close criticisms;* for I haven't a doubt there is more or less error involved. . . .

Ferdinand de Saussure

1857–1913

THE NOTION of the arbitrary relation of signifier to signified, or the "arbitrary nature of the sign," as Ferdinand de Saussure puts it, was not invented by him; the issue was raised as early as Plato's *Cratylus*. However, de Saussure is generally regarded as having developed the idea, which has had subsequent important implications for, first, linguistic and, later, anthropological and psychoanalytical and literary theory. This idea and the correlative one of the differential nature of language provides the ground for the modern movement known as structuralism (see Barthes, *CTSP*, pp. 1195–99). A structure is a system of differences, to be studied independently of what it or its parts might refer to outside the system. In structuralist linguistics, one studies words regarded as units solely by virtue of their difference from other words. Thus a word is known by what it is *not* more than by what it is; the system is totally "negative," even though, as de Saussure also argues, the combination of words is a "positive fact." In the *Course in General Linguistics,* de Saussure introduced a synchronic or atemporal treatment of language in contrast to his other mainly historical and diachronic studies. Another important distinction made by de Saussure but not discussed in this selection (it is mentioned by *Claude Lévi-Strauss*) is that between *langue* and *parole, langue* being the system of language in general, *parole* any particular usage within it. In a piece of structuralist literary criticism, a literary text is a *parole.*

De Saussure's *Course in General Linguistics* was not published in the author's lifetime, nor did he leave behind him a manuscript or even notes that might be gathered into a text. Rather, the book is a reconstruction by his students from their own notes of lectures he gave at the University of Geneva between 1906 and 1911. As a result, there has been some criticism of the text by linguists, and at least one has gone so far as to describe the text as by the Pseudo-Saussure. Indeed, as *Émile Benveniste* points out in his essay "The Nature of the Linguistic Sign," there is some confusion in the *Course* about the extent to which the sign is arbitrary. Despite all of this, the *Course* has been immensely influential, one of the most important texts representing the advent of the linguistic world. In a variety of fields, analogies of the differential sign have been dominant. Thus we find in the anthropological work of *Lévi-Strauss* the assertion that the true units of a myth are "bundles" of "relations" or, in Saussurean terms, differences. Even among his so-called postructuralist critics de Saussure remains a major influence. In *Of Grammatology,* which ushered in the poststructuralist movement by subjecting the *Course* to critique, *Jacques Derrida* merely extends de Saussure's thought to logical conclusions that de Saussure did not anticipate.

De Saussure is often regarded as having established linguistics as a science by minimizing the importance of the concept of reference, to view language as an independent system. This radical notion has often been the basis of complaint about the structuralist position. Other views of the relation of language to externality abound, though in recent years the Saussurean view has tended to be most popular among literary theorists. This has not been the case, however, among philosophers and linguists in America and England.

De Saussure published relatively little in his lifetime: about 600 pages in essays on such subjects as Phrygian inscriptions and Lithuanian dialects. *Course in General Linguistics* (1913) first appeared in English translation in 1959. De Saussure's writings are found in French in *Recueil des publications scientifique de F. de Saussure* (1922). See Rulon S. Wells, "De Saussure's System of Linguistics," *Word* 3 (1947), and the introduction by Manuel Mourette-Lema to *A Geneva School Reader in Linguistics,* ed. R. Goedel (1969).

FROM

COURSE IN GENERAL LINGUISTICS

NATURE OF THE LINGUISTIC SIGN

1. *Sign, Signified, Signifier*

Some people regard language, when reduced to its elements, as a naming-process only—a list of words, each corresponding to the thing that it names. For example:

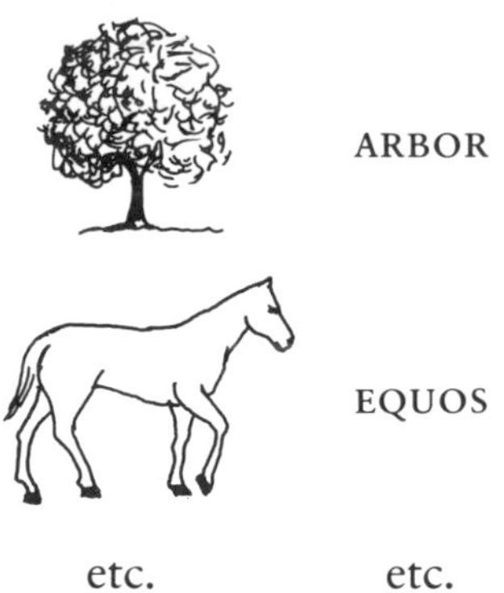

COURSE IN GENERAL LINGUISTICS is a translation by Wade Baskins of *Cours de linguistique générale* (1913). The selection reprinted here is done so by permission of The Philosophical Library, copyright 1959.

This conception is open to criticism at several points. It assumes that ready-made ideas exist before words; it does not tell us whether a name is vocal or psychological in nature (*arbor,* for instance, can be considered from either viewpoint); finally, it lets us assume that the linking of a name and a thing is a very simple operation—an assumption that is anything but true. But this rather naive approach can bring us near the truth by showing us that the linguistic unit is a double entity, one formed by the associating of two terms.

We have seen in considering the speaking-circuit that both terms involved in the linguistic sign are psychological and are united in the brain by an associative bond. This point must be emphasized.

The linguistic sign unites, not a thing and a name, but a concept and a sound-image. The latter is not the material sound, a purely physical thing, but the psychological imprint of the sound, the impression that it makes on our senses. The sound-image is sensory, and if I happen to call it "material," it is only in that sense, and by way of opposing it to the other term of the association, the concept, which is generally more abstract.

The psychological character of our sound-images becomes apparent when we observe our own speech. Without moving our lips or tongue, we can talk to ourselves or recite mentally a selection of verse. Because we regard the words of our language as sound-images, we must avoid speaking of the "phonemes" that make up the words. This term, which suggests vocal activity, is applicable to the spoken word only, to the realization of the inner image in discourse. We can avoid that misunderstanding by speaking of the *sounds* and *syllables* of a word provided we remember that the names refer to the sound-image.

The linguistic sign is then a two-sided psychological entity that can be represented by the drawing:

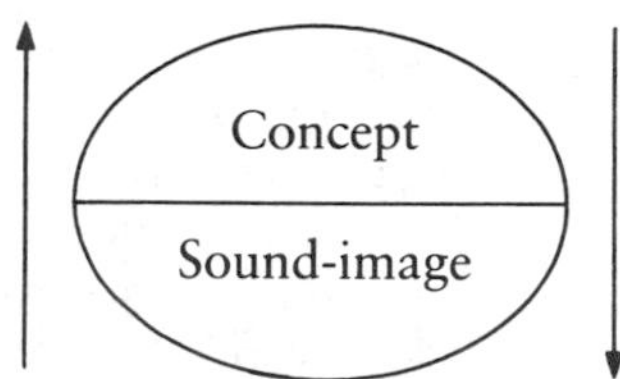

The two elements are intimately united, and each recalls the other. Whether we try to find the meaning of the Latin word *arbor* or the word that Latin uses to designate the concept "tree," it is clear that only the associations sanctioned by that language appear to us to conform to reality, and we disregard whatever others might be imagined.

Our definition of the linguistic sign poses an important question of terminology. I call the combination of a concept and a sound-image a *sign,* but in current usage the term generally designates only a sound-image, a word, for example (*arbor,* etc.). One tends to forget that *arbor* is called a sign only because it carries the concept "tree," with the result that the idea of the sensory part implies the idea of the whole.

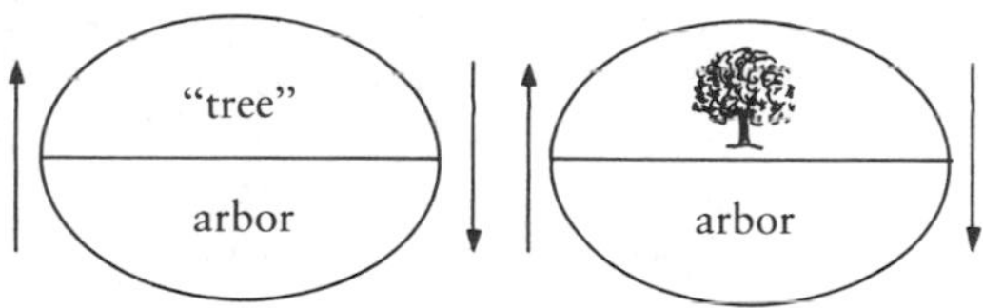

Ambiguity would disappear if the three notions involved here were designated by three names, each suggesting and opposing the others. I propose to retain the word *sign* [*signe*] to designate the whole and to replace *concept* and *sound-image* respectively by *signified* [*signifié*] and *signifier* [*signifiant*]; the last two terms have the advantage of indicating the opposition that separates them from each other and from the whole of which they are parts. As regards *sign,* if I am satisfied with it, this is simply because I do not know of any word to replace it, the ordinary language suggesting no other.

The linguistic sign, as defined, has two primordial characteristics. In enunciating them I am also positing the basic principles of any study of this type.

2. *Principle I: The Arbitrary Nature of the Sign*

The bond between the signifier and the signified is arbitrary. Since I mean by sign the whole that results from the associating of the signifier with the signified, I can simply say: *the linguistic sign is arbitrary.*

The idea of "sister" is not linked by any inner relationship to the succession of sounds *s-ö-r* which serves as its signifier in French; that it could be represented equally by just any other sequence is proved by differences among languages and by the very existence of different languages: the signified "ox" has as its signifier *b-ö-f* on one side of the border and *o-k-s* (*Ochs*) on the other.

No one disputes the principle of the arbitrary nature of the sign, but it is often easier to discover a truth than to assign to it its proper place. Principle I dominates all the linguistics of language; its consequences are numberless. It is true that not all of them are equally obvious at first glance; only after many detours does one discover them, and with them the primordial importance of the principle.

One remark in passing: when semiology becomes organized as a science, the question will arise whether or not it properly includes modes of expression based on completely natural signs, such as pantomime. Supposing that the new science welcomes them, its main concern will still be the whole group of systems grounded on the arbitrariness of the sign. In fact, every means of expression used in society is based, in principle, on collective behavior or—what amounts to the same thing—on convention. Polite formulas, for instance, though often imbued with a certain natural expressiveness (as in the case of a Chinese who greets his emperor by bowing down to the ground nine times), are nonetheless fixed by rule; it is this rule and not the intrinsic value of the gestures that obliges one to use them. Signs that are wholly arbitrary realize better than the others the ideal of the semiological process; that is why language, the most complex and universal of all systems of expression, is also the most characteristic; in this sense linguistics can become the master-pattern for all branches of semiology although language is only one particular semiological system.

The word *symbol* has been used to designate the linguistic sign, or more specifically, what is here called the signifier. Principle I in particular weighs against the use of this term. One characteristic of the symbol is that it is never wholly arbitrary; it is not empty, for there is the rudiment of a natural bond between the signifier and the signified. The symbol of justice, a pair of scales, could not be replaced by just any other symbol, such as a chariot.

The word *arbitrary* also calls for comment. The term should not imply that the choice of the signifier is left entirely to the speaker (we shall see below that the individual does not have the power to change a sign in any way once it has become established in the linguistic community); I mean that it is unmotivated, i.e. arbitrary in that it actually has no natural connection with the signified.

In concluding let us consider two objections that might be raised to the establishment of Principle I:

1) *Onomatopoeia* might be used to prove that the choice of the signifier is not always arbitrary. But onomatopoeic formations are never organic elements of a linguistic system. Besides, their number is much smaller than is generally supposed. Words like French *fouet* 'whip' or *glas* 'knell' may strike certain ears with suggestive sonority, but to see that they have not always had this property we need only examine their Latin forms (*fouet* is derived from *fāgus* 'beech-tree,' *glas* from *classicum* 'sound of a trumpet'). The quality of their present sounds, or rather the quality that is attributed to them, is a fortuitous result of phonetic evolution.

As for authentic onomatopoeic words (e.g., *glug-glug, tick-tock,* etc.), not only are they limited in number, but also they are chosen somewhat arbitrarily, for they are only approximate and more or less conventional imitations of certain sounds (cf. English *bow-bow* and French *ouaoua*). In addition, once these words have been introduced into the language, they are to a certain extent subjected to the same evolution—phonetic, morphological, etc.—that other words undergo (cf. *pigeon,* ultimately from Vulgar Latin *pīpiō,* derived in turn from an onomatopoeic formation): obvious proof that they lose something of their original character in order to assume that of the linguistic sign in general, which is unmotivated.

2) *Interjections,* closely related to onomatopoeia, can be attacked on the same grounds and come no closer to refuting our thesis. One is tempted to see in them spontaneous expressions of reality dictated, so to speak, by natural forces. But for most interjections we can show that there is no fixed bond between their signified and their signifier. We need only compare two languages on this point to see how much such expressions differ from one language to the next (e.g. the English equivalent of French *aïe!* is *ouch!*). We know, moreover, that many interjections were once words with specific meanings (cf. French *diable!* 'darn!' *mordieu!* 'golly!' from *mort Dieu* 'God's death,' etc.).

Onomatopoeic formations and interjections are of secondary importance, and their symbolic origin is in part open to dispute.

3. *Principle II: The Linear Nature of the Signifier*

The signifier, being auditory, is unfolded solely in time from which it gets the following characteristics: (a) it represents a span, and (b) the span is measurable in a single dimension; it is a line.

While Principle II is obvious, apparently linguists have always neglected to state it, doubtless because they found it too simple; nevertheless, it is fundamental, and its consequences are incalculable. Its importance equals that of Principle I; the whole mechanism of language depends upon it. In contrast to visual signifiers (nautical signals, etc.) which can offer simultaneous groupings in several dimensions, auditory signifiers have at their command only the dimension of time. Their elements are presented in succession; they form a chain. This feature becomes readily apparent when they are represented in writing and the spatial line of graphic marks is substituted for succession in time.

Sometimes the linear nature of the signifier is not obvious. When I accent a syllable, for instance, it seems that I am concentrating more than one significant element on the same point. But this is an illusion; the syllable and its accent constitute only one phonational act. There is no duality within the act but only different oppositions to what precedes and what follows.

Linguistic Value

1. *Language as Organized Thought Coupled with Sound*

To prove that language is only a system of pure values, it is enough to consider the two elements involved in its functioning: ideas and sounds.

Psychologically our thought—apart from its expression in words—is only a shapeless and indistinct mass. Philosophers and linguists have always agreed in recognizing that without the help of signs we would be unable to make a clear-cut, consistent distinction between two ideas. Without language, thought is a vague, uncharted nebula. There are no pre-existing ideas, and nothing is distinct before the appearance of language.

Against the floating realm of thought, would sounds by themselves yield predelimited entities? No more so than ideas. Phonic substance is neither more fixed nor more rigid than thought; it is not a mold into which thought must of necessity fit but a plastic substance divided in turn into distinct parts to furnish the signifiers needed by thought. The linguistic fact can therefore be pictured in its totality—i.e. language—as a series of contiguous subdivisions marked off on both the indefinite plane of jumbled ideas (*A*) and the equally vague plane of sounds (*B*). The following diagram gives a rough idea of it:

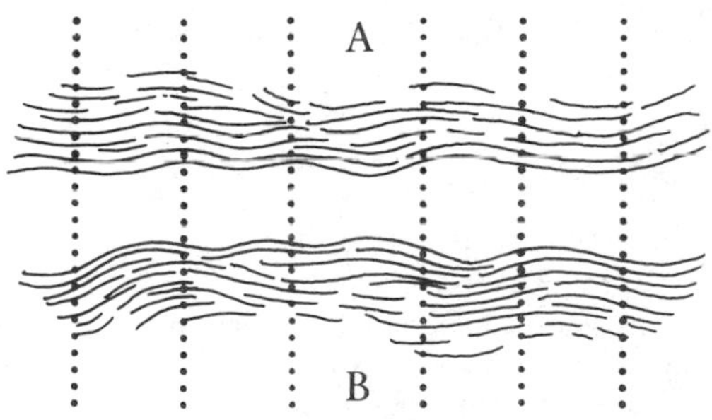

The characteristic role of language with respect to thought is not to create a material phonic means for expressing ideas but to serve as a link between thought and sound, under conditions that of necessity bring about the reciprocal delimitations of units. Thought, chaotic by nature, has to become ordered in the process of its decomposition. Neither are thoughts given material form nor are sounds transformed into mental entities; the somewhat mysterious fact is rather that "thought-sound" implies division, and that language works out its units while taking shape between two shapeless masses. Visualize the air in contact with a sheet of water; if the atmospheric pressure changes, the surface of the water will be broken up into a series of divisions, waves; the waves resemble the union or coupling of thought with phonic substance.

Language might be called the domain of articulations, using the word as it was defined earlier. Each linguistic term is a member, an *articulus* in which an idea is fixed in a sound and a sound becomes the sign of an idea.

Language can also be compared with a sheet of paper: thought is the front and the sound the back; one cannot cut the front without cutting the back at the same time; likewise in language, one can neither divide sound from thought nor thought from sound; the division could be accomplished only abstractedly, and the result would be either pure psychology or pure phonology.

Linguistics then works in the borderland where the elements of sound and thought combine; *their combination produces a form, not a substance.*

These views give a better understanding of what was said before about the arbitrariness of signs. Not only are the two domains that are linked by the linguistic fact shapeless and confused, but the choice of a given slice of sound to name a given idea is completely arbitrary. If this were not true, the notion of value would be compromised, for it would include an externally imposed element. But actually values remain entirely relative, and that is why the bond between the sound and the idea is radically arbitrary.

The arbitrary nature of the sign explains in turn why the social fact alone can create a linguistic system. The community is necessary if values that owe their existence solely to usage and general acceptance are to be set up; by himself the individual is incapable of fixing a single value.

In addition, the idea of value, as defined, shows that to consider a term as simply the union of a certain sound with a certain concept is grossly misleading. To define it in this way would isolate the term from its system; it would mean assuming that one can start from the terms and construct the system by adding them together when, on the contrary, it is from the interdependent whole that one must start and through analysis obtain its elements.

To develop this thesis, we shall study value successively from the viewpoint of the signified or concept, the signifier, and the complete sign.

Being unable to seize the concrete entities or units of language directly, we shall work with words. While the word does not conform exactly to the definition of the linguistic unit, it at least bears a rough resemblance to the unit and has the advantage of being concrete; consequently, we shall use words as specimens equivalent to real terms in a synchronic system, and the principles that we evolve with respect to words will be valid for entities in general.

2. *Linguistic Value from a Conceptual Viewpoint*

When we speak of the value of a word, we generally think first of its property of standing for an idea, and this is in fact one side of linguistic value. But if this is true, how does *value* differ from *signification?* Might the two words be synonyms? I think not, although it is easy to confuse them, since the confusion results not so much from their similarity as from the subtlety of the distinction that they mark.

From a conceptual viewpoint, value is doubtless one element in signification, and it is difficult to see how signification can be dependent upon value and still be distinct from it. But we must clear up the issue or risk reducing language to a simple naming-process.

Let us first take signification as it is generally understood and as it was pictured previously. As the arrows in the drawing show, it is only the counterpart of the sound-image. Everything that occurs concerns only the sound-image and the concept when we look upon the word as independent and self-contained.

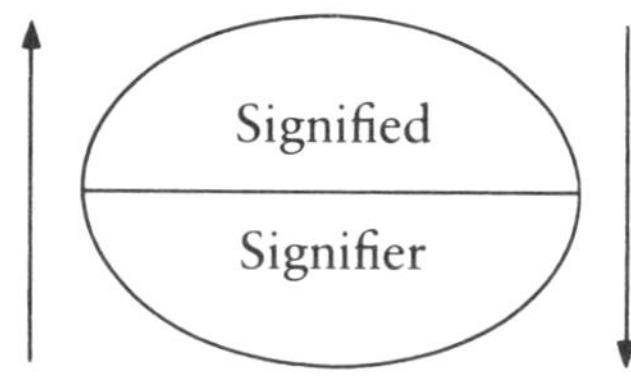

But here is the paradox: on the one hand the concept seems to be the counterpart of the sound-image, and on the other hand the sign itself is in turn the counterpart of the other signs of language.

Language is a system of interdependent terms in which the value of each term results solely from the simultaneous presence of the others, as in the diagram:

How, then, can value be confused with signification, i.e. the counterpart of the sound-image? It seems impossible to liken the relations represented here by horizontal arrows to those represented above by vertical arrows. Putting it another way—and again taking up the example of the sheet of paper that is cut in two—it is clear that the observable relation between the different pieces A, B, C, D, etc. is distinct from the relation between the front and back of the same piece as in A/A′, B/B′, etc.

To resolve the issue, let us observe from the outset that even outside language all values are apparently governed by the same paradoxical principle. They are always composed:

(1) of a *dissimilar* thing that can be *exchanged* for the thing of which the value is to be determined; and

(2) of *similar* things that can be *compared* with the thing of which the value is to be determined.

Both factors are necessary for the existence of a value. To determine what a five-franc piece is worth one must therefore know: (1) that it can be exchanged for a fixed quantity of a different thing, e.g. bread; and (2) that it can be compared with a similar value of the same system, e.g. a one-franc piece, or with coins of another system (a dollar, etc.). In the same way a word can be exchanged for something dissimilar, an idea; besides, it can be compared with something of the same nature, another word. Its value is therefore not fixed so long as one simply states that it can be "exchanged" for a given concept, i.e. that it has this or that signification: one must also compare it with similar values, with other words that stand in opposition to it. Its content is really fixed only by the concurrence of everything that exists outside it. Being part of a system, it is endowed not only with a signification but also and especially with a value, and this is something quite different.

A few examples will show clearly that this is true.

Modern French *mouton* can have the same signification as English *sheep* but not the same value, and this for several reasons, particularly because in speaking of a piece of meat ready to be served on the table, English uses *mutton* and not *sheep*. The difference in value between *sheep* and *mouton* is due to the fact that *sheep* has beside it a second term while the French word does not.

Within the same language, all words used to express related ideas limit each other reciprocally; synonyms like French *redouter* 'dread' *craindre* 'fear,' and *avoir peur* 'be afraid' have value only through their opposition: if *redouter* did not exist, all its content would go to its competitors. Conversely, some words are enriched through contact with others: e.g. the new element introduced in *décrépit* (un vieillard *décrépit*) results from the coexistence of *décrépi* (un mur *décrépi*). The value of just any term is accordingly determined by its environment; it is impossible to fix even the value of the word signifying "sun" without first considering its surroundings: in some languages it is not possible to say "sit in the *sun*."

Everything said about words applies to any term of language, e.g. to grammatical entities. The value of a French plural does not coincide with that of a Sanskrit plural even though their signification is usually identical; Sanskrit has three numbers instead of two (*my eyes, my ears, my arms, my legs,* etc. are dual); it would be wrong to attribute the same value to the plural in Sanskrit and in French; its value clearly depends on what is outside and around it.

If words stood for pre-existing concepts, they would all have exact equivalents in meaning from one language to the next; but this is not true. French uses *louer* (*une maison*) 'let (a house)' indifferently to mean both "pay for" and "receive payment for," whereas German uses two words, *mieten* and *vermieten;* there is obviously no exact correspondence of values. The German verbs *schätzen* and *urteilen* share a number of significations, but that correspondence does not hold at several points.

Inflection offers some particularly striking examples. Distinctions of time, which are so familiar to us, are unknown in certain languages. Hebrew does not recognize even the fundamental distinctions between the past, present, and future. Proto-Germanic has no special form for the future; to say that the future is expressed by the present is wrong, for the value of the present is not the same in Germanic as in languages that have a future along with the present. The Slavic languages regularly single out two aspects of the verb: the perfective represents action as a point, complete in its totality; the imperfective represents it as taking place, and on the line of time. The categories are difficult for a Frenchman to understand, for they are unknown in French; if they were predetermined, this would not be true. Instead of pre-existing ideas then, we find in all the foregoing examples *values* emanating from the system. When they are said to correspond to concepts, it is understood that the concepts are purely differential and defined not by their positive content but negatively by their relations with the other terms of the system. Their most precise characteristic is in being what the others are not.

Now the real interpretation of the diagram of the signal becomes apparent. Thus

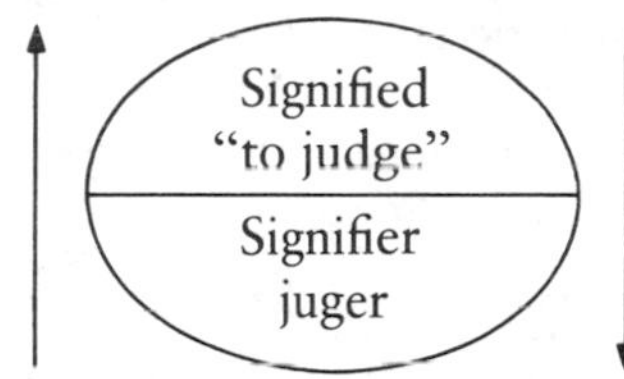

means that in French the concept "to judge" is linked to the sound-image *juger;* in short, it symbolizes signification. But it is quite clear that initially the concept is nothing, that is only a value determined by its relations with other similar values, and that without them the signification would not exist. If I state simply that a word signifies something when I have in mind the associating of a sound-image with a concept, I am making a statement that may suggest what actually happens, but by no means am I expressing the linguistic fact in its essence and fullness.

3. *Linguistic Value from a Material Viewpoint*

The conceptual side of value is made up solely of relations and differences with respect to the other terms of language, and the same can be said of its material side. The important thing in the word is not the sound alone but the phonic differences that make it possible to distinguish this word from all others, for differences carry signification.

This may seem surprising, but how indeed could

the reverse be possible? Since one vocal image is no better suited than the next for what it is commissioned to express, it is evident, even *a priori,* that a segment of language can never in the final analysis be based on anything except its noncoincidence with the rest. *Arbitrary* and *differential* are two correlative qualities.

The alteration of linguistic signs clearly illustrates this. It is precisely because the terms *a* and *b* as such are radically incapable of reaching the level of consciousness—one is always conscious of only the *a/b* difference—that each term is free to change according to laws that are unrelated to its signifying function. No positive sign characterizes the genitive plural in Czech *žen;* still the two forms *žena: žen* function as well as the earlier forms *žena: ženb; žen* has value only because it is different.

Here is another example that shows even more clearly the systematic role of phonic differences: in Greek, éphēn is an imperfect and *éstēn* an aorist although both words are formed in the same way; the first belongs to the system of the present indicative of *phēmī* 'I say,' whereas there is no present **stēmi;* now it is precisely the relation *phēmī: éphēn* that corresponds to the relation between the present and the imperfect (cf. *déiknūmi: edéiknūn,* etc.). Signs function, then, not through their intrinsic value but through their relative position.

In addition, it is impossible for sound alone, a material element, to belong to language. It is only a secondary thing, substance to be put to use. All our conventional values have the characteristic of not being confused with the tangible element which supports them. For instance, it is not the metal in a piece of money that fixes its value. A coin nominally worth five francs may contain less than half its worth of silver. Its value will vary according to the amount stamped upon it and according to its use inside or outside a political boundary. This is even more true of the linguistic signifier, which is not phonic but incorporeal—constituted not by its material substance but by the differences that separate its sound-image from all others.

The foregoing principle is so basic that it applies to all the material elements of language, including phonemes. Every language forms its words on the basis of a system of sonorous elements, each element being a clearly delimited unit and one of a fixed number of units. Phonemes are characterized not, as one might think, by their own positive quality but simply by the fact that they are distinct. Phonemes are above all else opposing, relative, and negative entities.

Proof of this is the latitude that speakers have between points of convergence in the pronunciation of distinct sounds. In French, for instance, general use of a dorsal *r* does not prevent many speakers from using a tongue-tip trill; language is not in the least disturbed by it; language requires only that the sound be different and not, as one might imagine, that it have an invariable quality. I can even pronounce the French *r* like German *ch* in *Bach, doch,* etc., but in German I could not use *r* instead of *ch,* for German gives recognition to both elements and must keep them apart. Similarly, in Russian there is no latitude for *t* in the direction of *t'* (palatalized *t*), for the result would be the confusing of two sounds differentiated by the language (cf. *govorit'* 'speak' and *goverit* 'he speaks'), but more freedom may be taken with respect to *th* (aspirated *t*) since this sound does not figure in the Russian system of phonemes.

Since an identical state of affairs is observable in writing, another system of signs, we shall use writing to draw some comparisons that will clarify the whole issue. In fact:

1) The signs used in writing are arbitrary; there is no connection, for example, between the letter *t* and the sound that it designates.

2) The value of letters is purely negative and differential. The same person can write *t,* for instance, in different ways: The only requirement is that the sign for *t* not be confused in his script with the signs used for *l, d,* etc.

3) Values in writing function only through reciprocal opposition within a fixed system that consists of a set number of letters. This third characteristic, though not identical to the second, is closely related to it, for both depend on the first. Since the graphic sign is arbitrary, its form matters little or rather matters only within the limitations imposed by the system.

4) The means by which the sign is produced is completely unimportant, for it does not affect the system (this also follows from characteristic 1). Whether I make the letters in white or black, raised or engraved, with pen or chisel—all this is of no importance with respect to their signification.

4. *The Sign Considered in Its Totality*

Everything that has been said up to this point boils down to this: in language there are only differences.

Even more important: a difference generally implies positive terms between which the difference is set up; but in language there are only differences *without positive terms.* Whether we take the signified or the signifier, language has neither idea nor sounds that existed before the linguistic system, but only conceptual and phonic differences that have issued from the system. The idea or phonic substance that a sign contains is of less importance than the other signs that surround it. Proof of this is that the value of a term may be modified without either its meaning or its sound being affected, solely because a neighboring term has been modified.

But the statement that everything in language is negative is true only if the signified and the signifier are considered separately; when we consider the sign in its totality, we have something that is positive in its own class. A linguistic system is a series of differences of sound combined with a series of differences of ideas; but the pairing of a certain number of acoustical signs with as many cuts made from the mass of thought engenders a system of values; and this system serves as the effective link between the phonic and psychological elements within each sign. Although both the signified and the signifier are purely differential and negative when considered separately, their combination is a positive fact; it is even the sole type of facts that language has, for maintaining the parallelism between the two classes of differences is the distinctive function of the linguistic institution.

Certain diachronic facts are typical in this respect. Take the countless instances where alteration of the signifier occasions a conceptual change and where it is obvious that the sum of the ideas distinguished corresponds in principle to the sum of the distinctive signs. When two words are confused through phonetic alteration (e.g. French *décrépit* from *dēcrepitus* and *décrépi* from *crispus*), the ideas that they express will also tend to become confused if only they have something in common. Or a word may have different forms (cf. *chaise* 'chair' and *chaire* 'desk'). Any nascent difference will tend invariably to become significant but without always succeeding or being successful on the first trial. Conversely, any conceptual difference perceived by the mind seeks to find expression through a distinct signifier, and two ideas that are no longer distinct in the mind tend to merge into the same signifier.

When we compare signs—positive terms—with each other, we can no longer speak of difference; the expression would not be fitting, for it applies only to the comparing of two sound-images, e.g. *father* and *mother,* or two ideas, e.g. the idea "father" and the idea "mother"; two signs, each having a signified and signifier, are not different but only distinct. Between them there is only *opposition.* The entire mechanism of language, with which we shall be concerned later, is based on oppositions of this kind and on the phonic and conceptual differences that they imply.

What is true of value is true also of the unit. A unit is a segment of the spoken chain that corresponds to a certain concept; both are by nature purely differential.

Applied to units, the principle of differentiation can be stated in this way: *the characteristics of the unit blend with the unit itself.* In language, as in any semiological system, whatever distinguishes one sign from the others constitutes it. Difference makes character just as it makes value and the unit.

Another rather paradoxical consequence of the same principle is this: in the last analysis what is commonly referred to as a "grammatical fact" fits the definition of the unit, for it always expresses an opposition of terms; it differs only in that the opposition is particularly significant (e.g. the formation of German plurals of the type *Nacht: Nächte*). Each term present in the grammatical fact (the singular without umlaut or final *e* in opposition to the plural with umlaut and *-e*) consists of the interplay of a number of oppositions within the system. When isolated, neither *Nacht* nor *Nächte* is anything: thus everything is opposition. Putting it another way, the *Nacht: Nächte* relation can be expressed by an algebraic formula a/b in which a and b are not simple terms but result from a set of relations. Language, in a manner of speaking, is a type of algebra consisting solely of complex terms. Some of its oppositions are more significant than others; but units and grammatical facts are only different names for designating diverse aspects of the same general fact: the functioning of linguistic oppositions. This statement is so true that we might very well approach the problem of units by starting from grammatical facts. Taking an opposition like *Nacht: Nächte,* we might ask what are the units involved in it. Are they only the two words, the whole series of similar words, *a* and *ä*, or all singulars and plurals, etc.?

Units and grammatical facts would not be confused if linguistic signs were made up of something besides differences. But language being what it is, we shall find nothing simple in it regardless of our approach; everywhere and always there is the same complex equilibrium of terms that mutually condition each other. Putting it another way, *language is a form and not a substance*. This truth could not be overstressed, for all the mistakes in our terminology, all our incorrect ways of naming things that pertain to language, stem from the involuntary supposition that the linguistic phenomenon must have substance.

SYNTAGMATIC AND ASSOCIATIVE RELATIONS

1. *Definitions*

In a language-state everything is based on relations. How do they function?

Relations and differences between linguistic terms fall into two distinct groups, each of which generates a certain class of values. The opposition between the two classes gives a better understanding of the nature of each class. They correspond to two forms of our mental activity, both indispensable to the life of language.

In discourse, on the one hand, words acquire relations based on the linear nature of language because they are chained together. This rules out the possibility of pronouncing two elements simultaneously. The elements are arranged in sequence on the chain of speaking. Combinations supported by linearity are *syntagms*. The syntagm is always composed of two or more consecutive units (e.g. French *re-lire* 're-read,' *contre tous* 'against everyone,' *la vie humaine* 'human life,' *Dieu est bon* 'God is good,' *s'il fait beau temps, nous sortirons* 'if the weather is nice, we'll go out,' etc.). In the syntagm a term acquires its value only because it stands in opposition to everything that precedes or follows it, or to both.

Outside discourse, on the other hand, words acquire relations of a different kind. Those that have something in common are associated in the memory, resulting in groups marked by diverse relations. For instance, the French word *enseignement* 'teaching' will unconsciously call to mind a host of other words (*enseigner* 'teach,' *renseigner* 'acquaint,' etc.; or *armement* 'armament,' *changement* 'amendment,' etc.; or *éducation* 'education,' *apprentissage* 'apprenticeship,' etc.). All those words are related in some way.

We see that the co-ordinations formed outside discourse differ strikingly from those formed inside discourse. Those formed outside discourse are not supported by linearity. Their seat is in the brain; they are a part of the inner storehouse that makes up the language of each speaker. They are *associative relations*.

The syntagmatic relation is *in praesentia*. It is based on two or more terms that occur in an effective series. Against this, the associative relation unites terms *in absentia* in a potential mnemonic series.

From the associative and syntagmatic viewpoint a linguistic unit is like a fixed part of a building, e.g. a column. On the one hand, the column has a certain relation to the architrave that it supports; the arrangement of the two units in space suggests the syntagmatic relation. On the other hand, if the column is Doric, it suggests a mental comparison of this style with others (Ionic, Corinthian, etc.) although none of these elements is present in space: the relation is associative.

Each of the two classes of co-ordination calls for some specific remarks.

2. *Syntagmatic Relations*

The examples have already indicated that the notion of syntagm applies not only to words but to groups of words, to complex units of all lengths and types (compounds, derivatives, phrases, whole sentences).

It is not enough to consider the relation that ties together the different parts of syntagms (e.g. French *contre* 'against' and *tous* 'everyone' in *contre tous*, *contre* and *maître* 'master' in *contremaître* 'foreman'), one must also bear in mind the relation that links the whole to its parts (e.g. *contre tous* in opposition on the one hand to *contre* and on the other *tous*, or *contremaître* in opposition to *contre* and *maître*).

An objection might be raised at this point. The sentence is the ideal type of syntagm. But it belongs to speaking, not to language. Does it not follow that the syntagm belongs to speaking? I do not think so. Speaking is characterized by freedom of combinations; one must therefore ask whether or not all syntagms are equally free.

It is obvious from the first that many expressions

belong to language. These are the pat phrases in which any change is prohibited by usage, even if we can single out their meaningful elements (cf. *à quoi bon?* 'what's the use?' *allons donc!* 'nonsense!'). The same is true, though to a lesser degree, of expressions like *prendre la mouche* 'take offense easily,' *forcer la main à quelqu'un* 'force someone's hand,' *rompre une lance* 'break a lance,' or even *avoir mal* (*à la tête,* etc.) 'have (a headache, etc.),' *à force de* (*soins,* etc.) 'by dint of (care, etc.),' *que vous en semble?* 'how do you feel about it?' *pas n'est besoin de . . .* 'there's no need for. . . ,' etc., which are characterized by peculiarities of signification or syntax. These idiomatic twists cannot be improvised; they are furnished by tradition. There are also words which, while lending themselves perfectly to analysis, are characterized by some morphological anomaly that is kept solely by dint of usage (cf. *difficulté* 'difficulty' beside *facilité* 'facility,' etc., and *mourrai* '[I] shall die' beside *dormirai* '[I] shall sleep').

There are further proofs. To language rather than to speaking belong the syntagmatic types that are built upon regular forms. Indeed, since there is nothing abstract in language, the types exist only if language has registered a sufficient number of specimens. When a word like *indécorable* arises in speaking, its appearance supposes a fixed type, and this type is in turn possible only through remembrance of a sufficient number of similar words belonging to language (*impardonable* 'unpardonable,' *intolérable* 'intolerable,' *infatigable* 'indefatigable,' etc.). Exactly the same is true of sentences and groups of words built upon regular patterns. Combinations like *la terre tourne* 'the world turns,' *que vous dit-il?* 'what does he say to you?' etc. correspond to general types that are in turn supported in the language by correct remembrances.

But we must realize that in the syntagm there is no clear-cut boundary between the language fact, which is a sign of collective usage, and the fact that belongs to speaking and depends on individual freedom. In a great number of instances it is hard to class a combination of units because both forces have combined in producing it, and they have combined in indeterminable proportions.

3. *Associative Relations*

Mental association creates other groups besides those based on the comparing of terms that have something in common; through its grasp of the nature of the relations that bind the terms together, the mind creates as many associative series as there are diverse relations. For instance, in *enseignement* 'teaching,' *enseigner* 'teach,' *enseignons* '(we) teach,' etc., one element, the radical, is common to every term; the same word may occur in a different series formed around another common element, the suffix (cf. *enseignement, armement, changement,* etc.); or the association may spring from the analogy of the concepts signified (*enseignement, instruction, apprentissage, éducation,* etc.); or again, simply from the similarity of the sound-images (e.g. *enseignement* and *justement* 'precisely'). Thus there is at times a double similarity of meaning and form, at times similarity only of form or of meaning. A word can always evoke everything that can be associated with it in one way or another.

Whereas a syntagm immediately suggests an order of succession and a fixed number of elements, terms in an associative family occur neither in fixed numbers nor in a definite order. If we associate *painful, delightful, frightful,* etc. we are unable to predict the number of words that the memory will suggest or the order in which they will appear. A particular word is like the center of a constellation; it is the point of convergence of an indefinite number of co-ordinated terms.

But of the two characteristics of the associative series—indeterminate order and indefinite number—only the first can always be verified; the second may fail to meet the test. This happens in the case of inflectional paradigms, which are typical of associative groupings. Latin *dominus, dominī, dominō,* etc. is obviously an associative group formed around a common element, the noun theme *domin-,* but the series

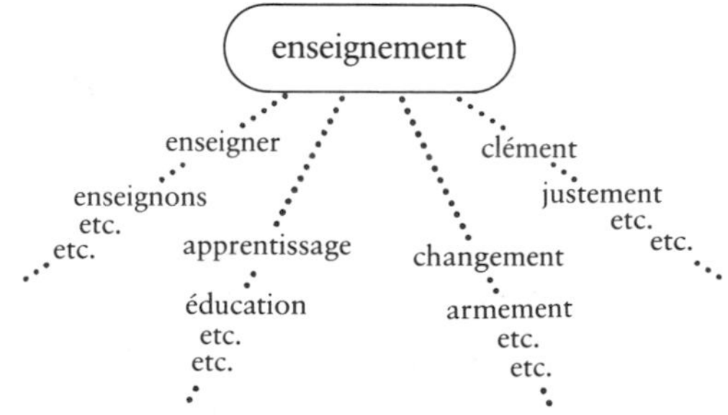

is not indefinite as in the case of *enseignement, changement,* etc.; the number of cases is definite.

Against this, the words have no fixed order of succession, and it is by a purely arbitrary act that the grammarian groups them in one way rather than in another; in the mind of speakers the nominative case is by no means the first one in the declension, and the order in which terms are called depends on circumstances.

Edmund Husserl

1859–1938

Edmund Husserl is generally acknowledged as the founder of modern phenomenology. His early philosophical work included a major treatise on the philosophy of arithmetic (a work that drew sharp criticism from *Gottlob Frege*) in which he articulated a theme dominant throughout his philosophical career: concepts are commonly defined according to their extensions, not their content. Definitions so derived obscure the importance of the mode or manner of perceiving and thinking by concentrating attention exclusively on agreement (or disagreement) about the extension of terms. Husserl's position is that everything "given" in perception is necessarily constituted in and through a specific mode of consciousness and that the philosophical exploration and critique of cognition cannot be restricted to merely logical or empirical considerations.

In his later work, Husserl emphasized the importance of intention—in the sense that every thought is a thought of something and therefore actively intends its object. In *Ideas,* he traced the development of a distinctive philosophical outlook achieved by a process of reduction: one removes from consideration all the content of a thought or perception that could be represented as external or extensional. What remains is not nothing but rather the pure stream of thinking or perceiving itself, in which all intentional objects are constituted.

According to Husserl, this reduction to the intentional core of perception and cognition (which he calls the "*epoché*") brings the "natural standpoint" to a crisis, just as it creates a phenomenological standpoint, from which cognition appears as the pure function or activity of the ego or self. Husserl does not, however, propose an empirical or psychologistic account of the ego. For Husserl, the "ego" discovered through the phenomenological *epoché* is not empirical but transcendental.

In the selection below, an essay written for *The Encyclopedia Britannica* (14th edition), Husserl offers a global account of phenomenology as, first, a radical alternative to ordinary empirical psychology and, second, the basis for a universal philosophical method. He sees the latter aspect of phenomenology as deriving from Descartes' program of universal doubt, with the difference that Husserl universalizes the methodology of the *epoché* or "bracketing" to locate a transcendental *cogito* as the universal power of consciousness.

While Husserl's influence on European philosophy has been significant and widespread, both in the development of phenomenological method and in the emergence of existentialism, his impact on English-speaking philosophy and philosophers has been relatively slight. This may be partly attributable to the fact that (like Hegel before him) he presumed that introspective meditation was a sufficient analytical tool, which in turn may partly explain why neither Husserl nor Hegel developed precise theories of language or philosophies of science that reflected current scientific practices.

Husserl's influence on literary theorists and critics has been more pronounced, however, because the phenomenological method as a critique of consciousness and perception (particularly as developed by later phenomenologists such as *Martin Heidegger* and Maurice Merleau-Ponty) encourages and supports close attention to complex processes associated with reading and writing—just as its transcendental metaphysical claims invite deconstruction (see *Derrida*).

While many of Husserl's writings have not been translated, most of his major works are available in English translation. *Ideas: General Introduction to Pure Phenomenology,* trans. W. R. Boyce Gibson (1931, rpt. 1962), is the most complete presentation of Husserl's position. Several shorter volumes of lectures have appeared in a series of translations published by Martinus Nijhoff; see especially *Cartesian Meditations: An Introduction to Phenomenology,* trans. Dorion Cairns (1970); *The Idea of Phenomenology,* trans. William P. Alston and George Nakhnikian (1964); and *The Paris Lectures,* trans. Peter Koestenbaum (1970). For critical and interpretive studies of a wide range of topics in Husserl's philosophy and his influence on other phenomenologists and existentialists, see *Phenomenology: The Philosophy of Edmund Husserl and Its Interpretation,* ed. Joseph J. Kockelmans (1967).

PHENOMENOLOGY

Phenomenology denotes a new, descriptive, philosophical method, which, since the concluding years of the last century, has established (1) an a priori psychological discipline, able to provide the only secure basis on which a strong empirical psychology can be built, and (2) a universal philosophy, which can supply an organum for the methodical revision of all the sciences.

I. Phenomenological Psychology

Present-day psychology, as the science of the "psychical" in its concrete connection with spatio-temporal reality, regards as its material whatever is present in the world as "ego-istic"; *i.e.,* "living," perceiving, thinking, willing, etc., actual, potential and habitual. And as the psychical is known as a certain stratum of existence, proper to men and beasts, psychology may be considered as a branch of anthropology and zoology. But animal nature is a part of physical reality, and that which is concerned with physical reality is natural science. Is it, then, possible to separate the psychical cleanly enough from the physical to establish a pure psychology parallel to natural science? That a purely psychological investigation is practicable within limits is shown by our obligation to it for our fundamental conceptions of the psychical, and most of those of the psycho-physical.

But before determining the question of an unlimited psychology, we must be sure of the characteristics of psychological experience and the psychical data it provides. We turn naturally to our immediate experiences. But we cannot discover the psychical in any experience, except by a "reflection," or perversion of the ordinary attitude. We are accustomed to concentrate upon the matters, thoughts, and values of the moment, and not upon the psychical "act of experience" in which these are apprehended. This "act" is revealed by a "reflec-

PHENOMENOLOGY first appeared in *The Encyclopedia Britannica,* 14th ed. (1929). Reprinted with the permission of The Encyclopedia Britannica, Inc.

tion"; and a reflection can be practised on every experience. Instead of the matters themselves, the values, goals, utilities, etc., we regard the subjective experiences in which these "appear." These "appearances" are phenomena, whose nature is to be a "consciousness-of" their object, real or unreal as it be. Common language catches this sense of "relativity," saying, I was thinking *of* something, I was frightened *of* something, etc. Phenomenological psychology takes its name from the "phenomena," with the psychological aspect of which it is concerned: and the word "intentional" has been borrowed from the scholastic to denote the essential "reference" character of the phenomena. All consciousness is "intentional."

In unreflective consciousness we are "directed" upon objects, we "intend" them; and reflection reveals this to be an immanent process characteristic of all experience, though infinitely varied in form. To be conscious of something is no empty having of that something in consciousness. Each phenomenon has its own intentional structure, which analysis shows to be an ever-widening system of individually intentional and intentionally related components. The perception of a cube, for example, reveals a multiple and synthesized intention: a continuous variety in the "appearance" of the cube, according to differences in the points of view from which it is seen, and corresponding differences in "perspective," and all the difference between the "front side" actually seen at the moment and the "backside" which is not seen, and which remains, therefore, relatively "indeterminate," and yet is supposed equally to be existent. Observation of this "stream" of "appearance-aspects" and of the manner of their synthesis, shows that every phase and interval is already in itself a "consciousness-of" something, yet in such a way that with the constant entry of new phases the total consciousness, at any moment, lacks not synthetic unity, and is, in fact, a consciousness of one and the same object. The intentional structure of the train of a perception must conform to a certain type, if any physical object is to be perceived as there! And if the same object be intuited in other modes, if it be imagined, or remembered, or copied, all its intentional forms recur, though modified in character from what they were in the perception, to correspond to their new modes. The same is true of every kind of psychical experience. Judgment, valuation, pursuit, these also are no empty experiences having in consciousness of judgments, values, goals and means, but are likewise experiences compounded of an intentional stream, each conforming to its own fast type.

Phenomenological psychology's comprehensive task is the systematic examination of the types and forms of intentional experience, and the reduction of their structures to the prime intentions, learning thus what is the nature of the psychical, and comprehending the being of the soul.

The validity of these investigations will obviously extend beyond the particularity of the psychologist's own soul. For psychical life may be revealed to us not only in self-consciousness but equally in our consciousness of other selves, and this latter source of experience offers us more than a reduplication of what we find in our self-consciousness, for it establishes the differences between "own" and "other" which we experience, and presents us with the characteristics of the "social-life." And hence the further task accrues to psychology of revealing the intentions of which the "social life" consists.

Phenomenological-psychological and Eidetic Reductions

The Phenomenological psychology must examine the self's experience of itself and its derivative experience of other selves and of society, but whether, in so doing, it can be free of all psycho-physical admixture, is not yet clear. Can one reach a really pure self-experience and purely psychical data? This difficulty, even since Brentano's discovery of intentionality, as the fundamental character of the psychical, has blinded psychologists to the possibilities of phenomenological psychology. The psychologist finds his self-consciousness mixed everywhere with "external" experience, and non-psychical realities. For what is experienced as external belongs not to the intentional "internal," though our experience of it belongs there as an experience of the external. The phenomenologist, who will only notice phenomena, and know purely his own "life," must practice an ἐποχή.[1] He must inhibit every ordinary objective "position," and partake in no judgment concerning the objective world. The experience itself will remain what it was, an experience of this

[1] *epoché:* Greek term meaning a check or suspension of judgment, first introduced by the Greek skeptical philosophers. [Eds.]

house, of this body, of this world in general, in its particular mode. For one cannot describe any intentional experience, even though it be "illusory," a self-contradicting judgment and the like, without describing what in the experience is, as such, the object of consciousness.

Our comprehensive ἐποχή puts, as we say, the world between brackets, excludes the world which is simply there! from the subject's field, presenting in its stead the so-and-so-experienced-perceived-remembered-judged-thought-valued-etc., world, as such, the "bracketed" world. Not the world or any part of it appears, but the "sense" of the world. To enjoy phenomenological experience we must retreat from the objects posited in the natural attitude to the multiple modes of their "appearance," to the "bracketed" objects.

The phenomenological reduction to phenomena, to the purely psychical, advances by two steps: (1) systematic and radical ἐποχή of every objectifying "position" in an experience, practised both upon the regard of particular objects and upon the entire attitude of mind, and (2) expert recognition, comprehension and description of the manifold "appearances" of what are no longer "objects" but "unities" of "sense." So that the phenomenological description will comprise two parts, description of the "noetic" (νόεω) or "experiencing" and description of the "noematic" (νόημα) or the "experienced." Phenomenological experience, is the only experience which may properly be called "internal" and there is no limit to its practice. And as a similar "bracketing" of objective, and description of what then "appears" ("noema" in "noesis"), can be performed upon the "life" of another self which we represent to ourselves, the "reductive" method can be extended from one's own self-experience to one's experience of other selves. And, further, that society, which we experience in a common consciousness, may be reduced not only to the intentional fields of the individual consciousness, but also by the means of an inter-subjective reduction, to that which unites these, namely the phenomenological unity of the social life. Thus enlarged, the psychological concept of internal experience reaches its full extent.

But it takes more than the unity of a manifold "intentional life," with its inseparable complement of "sense-unities," to make a "soul." For from the individual life that "ego-subject" cannot be disjoined, which persists as an identical ego or "pole," to the particular intentions, and the "habits" growing out of these. Thus the "inter-subjective," phenomenologically reduced and concretely apprehended, is seen to be a "society" of "persons," who share a conscious life.

Phenomenological psychology can be purged of every empirical and psycho-physical element, but, being so purged, it cannot deal with "matters of fact." Any closed field may be considered as regards its "essence," its εἴδος,[2] and we may disregard the factual side of our phenomena, and use them as "examples" merely. We shall ignore individual souls and societies, to learn their a priori, their "possible" forms. Our thesis will be "theoretical," observing the invariable through variation, disclosing a typical realm of a priori. There will be no psychical existence whose "style" we shall not know. Psychological phenomenology must rest upon eidetic phenomenology.

The phenomenology of the perception of bodies, for example, will not be an account of actually occurring perceptions, or those which may be expected to occur, but of that invariable "structure," apart from which no perception of a body, single or prolonged, can be conceived. The phenomenological reduction reveals the phenomena of actual internal experience; the eidetic reduction, the essential forms constraining psychical existence.

Men now demand that empirical psychology shall conform to the exactness required by modern natural science. Natural science, which was once a vague, inductive empiric, owes its modern character to the a priori system of forms, nature as it is "conceivable," which its separate disciplines, pure geometry, laws of motion, time, etc., have contributed. The methods of natural science and psychology are quite distinct, but the latter, like the former, can only reach "exactness" by a rationalization of the "essential."

The psycho-physical has an a priori which must be learned by any complete psychology, this a priori is not phenomenological, for it depends no less upon the essence of physical, or more particularly organic nature.

[2] *eidos:* Greek term meaning form or idea. [Eds.]

II. Transcendental Phenomenology

Transcendental philosophy may be said to have originated in Descartes, and phenomenological psychology in Locke, Berkeley and Hume, although the latter did not grow up primarily as a method or discipline to serve psychology, but to contribute to the solution of the transcendental problematic which Descartes had posed. The theme propounded in the *Meditations* was still dominant in a philosophy which it had initiated. All reality, so it ran, and the whole of the world which we perceive as existent, may be said to exist only as the content of our own representations, judged in our judgments, or, at best, proved by our own knowing. There lay impulse enough to rouse all the legitimate and illegitimate problems of transcendence, which we know. Descartes' "Doubting" first disclosed "transcendental subjectivity," and his "Ego Cogito" was its first conceptual handling. But the Cartesian transcendental "Mens" became the "Human Mind," which Locke undertook to explore; and Locke's exploration turned into a psychology of the internal experience. And since Locke thought his psychology could embrace the transcendental problems, in whose interest he had begun his work, he became the founder of a false psychologistical philosophy which has persisted because men have not analysed their concept of "subjective" into its two-fold significance. Once the transcendental problem is fairly stated, the ambiguity of the sense of the "subjective" becomes apparent, and establishes the phenomenological psychology to deal with its one meaning, and the transcendental phenomenology with its other.

Phenomenological psychology has been given the priority in this article, partly because it forms a convenient stepping-stone to the philosophy and partly because it is nearer to the common attitude than is the transcendental. Psychology, both in its eidetic and empirical disciplines, is a "positive" science, promoted in the "natural attitude" with the world before it for the ground of all its themes, while transcendental experience is difficult to realize because it is "supreme" and entirely "unworldly." Phenomenological psychology, although comparatively new, and completely new as far as it uses intentional analysis, can be approached from the gates of any of the positive sciences: and, being once reached, demands only a re-employment, in a more stringent mode, of its formal mechanism of reduction and analysis, to disclose the transcendental phenomena.

But it is not to be doubted that transcendental phenomenology could be developed independently of all psychology. The discovery of the double relativity of consciousness suggests the practice of both reductions. The psychological reduction does not reach beyond the psychical in animal realities, for psychology subserves real existence, and even its eidetic is confined to the possibilities of real worlds. But the transcendental problem will include the entire world and all its sciences, to "doubt" the whole. The world "originates" in us, as Descartes led men to recognize, and within us acquires its habitual influence. The general significance of the world, and the definite sense of its particulars, is something of which we are conscious within our perceiving, representing, thinking, valuing life, and therefore something "constituted" in some subjective genesis.

The world and its property, "in and for itself," exists as it exists, whether I, or we, happen, or not, to be conscious of it. But let once this general world, make its "appearance" in consciousness as "the" world, it is thenceforth related to the subjective, and all its existence and the manner of it, assumes a new dimension, becoming "incompletely intelligible," "questionable." Here, then, is the transcendental problem; this "making its appearance," this "being for us" of the world, which can only gain its significance "subjectively," what is it? We may call the world "internal" because it is related to consciousness, but how can this quite "general" world, whose "immanent" being is as shadowy as the consciousness wherein it "exists," contrive to appear before us in a variety of "particular" aspects, which experience assures us are the aspects of an independent, self-existent world? The problem also touches every "ideal" world, the world of pure number, for example, and the world of "truths in themselves." And no existence, or manner of existence, is less wholly intelligible than ourselves. Each by himself, and in society, we, in whose consciousness the world is valid, being men, belong ourselves to the world. Must we, then, refer ourselves to ourselves to gain a worldly sense, a worldly being? Are we both psychologically to be called men, subjects of a psychical life, and yet be transcendental to ourselves and the whole world, being subjects of a transcendental world-constituting life? Psychical subjectivity, the "I" and "we" of everyday intent, may be experienced as it is in itself under the phenomenological-psychological reduction, and being eidetically treated, may establish a phenomenological psychology. But the transcendental subjectivity, which for want of language we can only call again, "I myself," "we ourselves," cannot be found under the attitude of psychological or natural science, being no part at all of the objective world, but that subjective conscious life itself, wherein the world and all its content is made for "us," for "me." We that are, indeed, men, spiritual and bodily, existing in the world, are, therefore, "appearances" unto ourselves, parcel of what "we" have constituted, pieces of the significance "we" have made. The "I" and "we," which we apprehend, presuppose a hidden "I" and "we" to whom they are "present."

To this transcendental subjectivity, transcendental experience gives us direct approach. As the psychical experience was purified, so is the transcendental, by a reduction. The transcendental reduction may be regarded as a certain further purification of the psychological interest. The universal is carried to a further stage. Henceforth the "bracketing" includes not the world only but its "souls" as well. The psychologist reduces the ordinarily valid world to a subjectivity of "souls," which are a part of the world which they inhabit. The transcendental phenomenologist reduces the already psychologically purified to the transcendental, that most general, subjectivity, which makes the world and its "souls," and confirms them.

I no longer survey my perception experiences, imagination-experiences, the psychological data which my psychological experience reveals: I learn to survey transcendental experience. I am no longer interested in my own existence. I am interested in the pure intentional life, wherein my psychically real experiences have occurred. This step raises the transcendental problem (the transcendental being defined as the quality of that which is consciousness) to its true level. We have to recognize that relativity to consciousness is not only an actual quality of our world, but, from eidetic necessity, the quality of every conceivable world. We may, in a free fancy, vary our actual world, and transmute it to any other which we can imagine, but we are obliged with the world to vary ourselves also, and ourselves we cannot vary except within the limits prescribed to us by the nature of subjectivity. Change worlds as we may, each must ever be a world such as we could experience, prove upon the evidence of our theories and inhabit with our practice. The transcendental problem is eidetic. My psychological experiences, perceptions, imaginations and the like remain in form and content what they were, but I see them as "structures" now, for I am face to face at last with the ultimate structure of consciousness.

It is obvious that, like every other intelligible problem, the transcendental problem derives the means of its solution from an existence-stratum, which it presupposes and sets beyond the reach of its enquiry. This realm is no other than the bare subjectivity of consciousness in general, while the realm of its investigation remains not less than every sphere which can be called "objective," which considered in its totality, and at its root, is the conscious life. No one, then, can justly propose to solve the transcendental problem by psychology either empirical or eidetic-phenomenological, without *petitio principii,* for psychology's "subjectivity" and "consciousness" are not that subjectivity and consciousness, which our philosophy will investigate. The transcendental reduction has supplanted the psychological reduction. In the place of the psychological "I" and "we," the transcendental "I" and "we" are comprehended in the concreteness of transcendental consciousness. But though the transcendental "I" is not my psychological "I," it must not be considered as if it were a second "I," for it is no more separated from my psychological "I" in the conventional sense of separation, than it is joined to it in the conventional sense of being joined.

Transcendental self-experience may, at any moment, merely by a change of attitude, be turned back into psychological self-experience. Passing, thus, from the one to the other attitude, we notice a certain "identity" about the ego. What I saw under the psychological reflection as "my" objectification, I see under the transcendental reflection as self-objectifying, or, as we may also say, as objectified by the transcendental "I." We have only to recognize that what makes the psychological and transcendental spheres of experience parallel is an "identity" in their significance, and that what differentiates them is merely a change of attitude, to realize that the psychological and transcendental phenomenologies will also be parallel. Under the more stringent ἐποχή the psychological subjectivity is transformed into the transcendental subjectivity, and the psychological inter-subjectivity into the transcendental inter-subjectivity. It is this last which is the concrete, ultimate ground, whence all that transcends consciousness, including all that is real in the world, derives the sense of its existence. For all objective existence is essentially "relative," and owes its nature to a unity of intention, which being established according to transcendental laws, produces consciousness with its habit of belief and its conviction.

Phenomenology, the Universal Science

Thus, as phenomenology is developed, the Leibnitzian foreshadowing of a universal ontology, the unification of all conceivable a priori sciences, is improved, and realized upon the new and non-dogmatic basis of a phenomenological method. For phenomenology as the science of all concrete phenomena proper to subjectivity and inter-subjectivity, is *eo ipso* an a priori science of all possible existence and existences. Phenomenology is universal in its scope, because there is no a priori which does not depend upon its intentional constitution, and derive from this its power of engendering habits in the consciousness that knows it, so that the establishment of any a priori must reveal the subjective process by which it is established.

Once the a priori disciplines, such as the mathematical sciences, are incorporated within phenomenology, they cannot thereafter be beset by "paradoxes" or disputes concerning principles: and those sciences which have become a priori independently of phenomenology, can only hope to set their methods and premises beyond criticism, by founding themselves upon it. For their very claim to be positive, dogmatic sciences bears witness to their dependency, as branches, merely, of that universal, eidetic ontology, which is phenomenology.

The endless task, this exposition of the universum of the a priori, by referring all objectives to their transcendental "origin," may be considered as one function in the construction of a universal science of fact, where every department, including the positive, will be settled on its a priori. So that our last division of the complete phenomenology is thus: eidetic phenomenology, or the universal ontology, for a first philosophy; and a second philosophy as the science of the transcendental inter-subjectivity or universum of fact.

Thus the antique conception of philosophy as the universal science, philosophy in the Platonic, philosophy in the Cartesian, sense, that shall embrace all knowledge, is once more justly restored. All rational problems, and all those problems, which for one reason or another, have come to be known as "philosophical," have their place within phenomenology, finding from the ultimate source of transcendental experience or eidetic intuition, their proper form and the means of their solution. Phenomenology itself learns its proper function of transcendental human "living" from an entire relationship to "self." It can intuit life's absolute norms and learn life's original teleological structure. Phenomenology is not less than man's whole occupation with himself in the service of the universal reason. Revealing life's norms, he does, in fact, set free a stream of new consciousness intent upon the infinite idea of entire humanity, humanity in fact and truth.

Metaphysical, teleological, ethical problems, and problems of the history of philosophy, the problem of judgment, all significant problems in general, and the transcendental bonds uniting them, lie within phenomenology's capability.

Phenomenological philosophy is but developing the mainsprings of old Greek philosophy, and the supreme motive of Descartes. These have not died. They split into rationalism and empiricism. They stretch over Kant and German idealism, and reach the present, confused day. They must be reassumed, subject to methodical and concrete treatment. They can inspire a science without bounds.

Phenomenology demands of phenomenalists that they shall forgo particular closed systems of philosophy, and share decisive work with others toward persistent philosophy.

Mikhail M. Bakhtin

1895–1975

Except for *Problems of Dostoyevsky's Poetics* (1929), where his concept of the dialogical is developed, Bakhtin's work was not published under his own name until the sixties. Certain works of his under the names of Volosinov and Medvedev appeared in Russia in the thirties, however. Bakhtin spent six years in exile in that decade, during which he wrote the long essay "Discourse in the Novel" and much else. Because of suppression of his writings, the disappearance of a book-length manuscript during World War II, and refusal of the authorities to grant him the doctorate for his eventually influential dissertation on Rabelais, submitted first in 1940 and rejected finally in 1949, his work did not become well known until recent translations into English, occurring mainly in the seventies. Bakhtin's thought seems, nevertheless, amazingly timely and has had a powerful recent influence, particularly in the theory of narrative. If the criterion of placement were the time at which his work gained fame, he would belong in the main body of this text.

Above all, Bakhtin is a theorist of genre, particularly of the novel, the history and nature of which (the two are one for him) he describes in a new way, contrasting the novel with the poem, emphasizing the "freedom for the point of view of others to reveal themselves" in it (polyphony) against the monological poem. In essays other than the one here, he sees in literary history the gradual "novelization" of the poem. The novel and its tendency toward polyphony and the dialogical (par excellence in Dostoyevsky) he traces back into a "carnivalistic" sense of the world that leads in literature through its "joyful relativity" and "vitality" to emphasis on free heterogenic invention and multiple styles in a single work. The novelistic (and carnivalistic) runs in its early forms from the Socratic dialogue through the so-called Menippean satire. Its notion of truth is that of something born between people rather than possessed and then expressed by an author. Such texts are products of differences (though Bakhtin does not use this structuralist term) that are cultural and historical. There is always a dialogical *making* in the novel. The author is there but in a special sort of relation to the characters, text, or truth. Bakhtin makes his concept of the novelistic spread eventually over all literary art.

Finally, Bakhtin's historical view emphasizes the individual as always multiple, governed by what he calls "heteroglossia": all those conditions that impinge in any moment on a human event, affecting meaning. These conditions contribute to the idea that truth comes to us only dialogically.

The major works of Bakhtin in English translation are *Rabelais and His World* (1965, trans. 1968); *Problems of Dostoyevsky's Poetics* (1929; rev. 1963; trans.

1973, 1984); [V. N. Volosinov], *Marxism and the Philosophy of Language* (1929, 1930, trans. 1973); [V. N. Volosinov], *Freudianism: A Marxist Critique* (1927, trans. 1976); [P. N. Medvedev], *The Formal Method in Literary Scholarship* (1928; trans. 1978); *The Dialogic Imagination* (essays written in the 1930s, trans. 1981). See Katerina Clark and Michael Holquist, *Mikhail Bakhtin* (1984).

FROM

DISCOURSE IN THE NOVEL

Modern Stylistics and the Novel

The current state of questions posed by a stylistics of the novel reveals, fully and clearly, that all the categories and methods of traditional stylistics remain incapable of dealing effectively with the artistic uniqueness of discourse in the novel, or with the specific life that discourse leads in the novel. "Poetic language," "individuality of language," "image," "symbol," "epic style" and other general categories worked out and applied by stylistics, as well as the entire set of concrete stylistic devices subsumed by these categories (no matter how differently understood by individual critics), are all equally oriented toward the single-languaged and single-styled genres, toward the poetic genres in the narrow sense of the word. Their connection with this exclusive orientation explains a number of the particular features and limitations of traditional stylistic categories. All these categories, and the very philosophical conception of poetic discourse in which they are grounded, are too narrow and cramped, and cannot accommodate the artistic prose of novelistic discourse.

Thus stylistics and the philosophy of discourse indeed confront a dilemma: either to acknowledge the novel (and consequently all artistic prose tending in that direction) an unartistic or quasi-artistic genre, or to radically reconsider that conception of poetic discourse in which traditional stylistics is grounded and which determines all its categories.

This excerpt from DISCOURSE IN THE NOVEL is reprinted from *The Dialogic Imagination,* edited by Michael Holquist, translated by Caryl Emerson and Michael Holquist, by permission of the University of Texas Press, copyright 1981.

This dilemma, however, is by no means universally recognized. Most scholars are not inclined to undertake a radical revision of the fundamental philosophical conception of poetic discourse. Many do not even see or recognize the philosophical roots of the stylistics (and linguistics) in which they work, and shy away from any fundamental philosophical issues. They utterly fail to see behind their isolated and fragmented stylistic observations and linguistic descriptions any theoretical problems posed by novelistic discourse. Others—more principled—make a case for consistent individualism in their understanding of language and style. First and foremost they seek in the stylistic phenomenon a direct and unmediated expression of authorial individuality, and such an understanding of the problem is least likely of all to encourage a reconsideration of basic stylistic categories in the proper direction.

However, there is another solution of our dilemma that does take basic concepts into account: one need only consider oft-neglected rhetoric, which for centuries has included artistic prose in its purview. Once we have restored rhetoric to all its ancient rights, we may adhere to the old concept of poetic discourse, relegating to "rhetorical forms" everything in novelistic prose that does not fit the Procrustean bed of traditional stylistic categories.[1]

Gustav Shpet,[2] in his time, proposed such a solution to the dilemma, with all due rigorousness and consistency. He utterly excluded artistic prose and its ultimate realization—the novel—from the realm

[1] Such a solution to the problem was especially tempting to adherents of the formal method in poetics: in fact, the re-establishment of rhetoric, with all its rights, greatly strengthens the Formalist position. Formalist rhetoric is a necessary addition to Formalist poetics. Our Formalists were being completely consistent when they spoke of the necessity of reviving rhetoric alongside poetics (on this, see B. M. Eichenbaum, *Literature* [*Literatura;* Leningrad, 1927], pp. 147–148). [Au.]

[2] Gustav Shpet (1879–1937), professor, University of Moscow. [Eds.]

of poetry, and assigned it to the category of purely rhetorical forms.[3]

Here is what Shpet says about the novel: "The recognition that contemporary forms of moral propaganda—i.e., the *novel*—do not spring from *poetic creativity* but are purely rhetorical compositions, is an admission, and a conception, that apparently cannot arise without immediately confronting a formidable obstacle in the form of the universal recognition, despite everything, that the novel *does* have a certain aesthetic value."[4]

Shpet utterly denies the novel any aesthetic significance. The novel is an extra-artistic rhetorical genre, "the contemporary form of moral propaganda"; artistic discourse is exclusively poetic discourse (in the sense we have indicated above).

Viktor Vinogradov[5] adopted an analogous point of view in his book *On Artistic Prose,* assigning the problem of artistic prose to rhetoric. While agreeing with Shpet's basic philosophical definitions of the "poetic" and the "rhetorical," Vinogradov was, however, not so paradoxically consistent: he considered the novel a syncretic, mixed form ("a hybrid formation") and admitted that it contained, along with rhetorical elements, some purely poetic ones.[6]

The point of view that completely excludes novelistic prose, as a rhetorical formation, from the realm of poetry—a point of view that is basically false—does nevertheless have a certain indisputable merit. There resides in it an acknowledgment in principle and in substance of the inadequacy of all contemporary stylistics, along with its philosophical and linguistic base, when it comes to defining the specific distinctive features of novelistic prose. And what is more, the very reliance on rhetorical forms has a great heuristic significance. Once rhetorical discourse is brought into the study with all its living diversity, it cannot fail to have a deeply revolutionizing influence on linguistics and on the philosophy of language. It is precisely those aspects of any discourse (the internally dialogic quality of discourse, and the phenomena related to it), not yet sufficiently taken into account and fathomed in all the enormous weight they carry in the life of language, that are revealed with great external precision in rhetorical forms, provided a correct and unprejudiced approach to those forms is used. Such is the general methodological and heuristic significance of rhetorical forms for linguistics and for the philosophy of language.

The special significance of rhetorical forms for understanding the novel is equally great. The novel, and artistic prose in general, has the closest genetic, family relationship to rhetorical forms. And throughout the entire development of the novel, its intimate interaction (both peaceful and hostile) with living rhetorical genres (journalistic, moral, philosophical and others) has never ceased; this interaction was perhaps no less intense than was the novel's interaction with the artistic genres (epic, dramatic, lyric). But in this uninterrupted interrelationship, novelistic discourse preserved its own qualitative uniqueness and was never reducible to rhetorical discourse.

The novel is an artistic genre. Novelistic discourse is poetic discourse, but one that does not fit within the frame provided by the concept of poetic discourse as it now exists. This concept has certain underlying presuppositions that limit it. The very concept—in the course of its historical formulation from Aristotle to the present day—has been oriented toward the specific "official" genres and connected with specific historical tendencies in verbal ideological life. Thus a whole series of phenomena remained beyond its conceptual horizon.

Philosophy of language, linguistics and stylistics [i.e., such as they have come down to us] have all postulated a simple and unmediated relation of speaker to his unitary and singular "own" language, and have postulated as well a simple realization of this language in the monologic utterance of the individual. Such disciplines actually know only two poles in the life of language, between which are located all the linguistic and stylistic phenomena they know: on the one hand, the system of a *unitary language,* and on the other the *individual* speaking in this language.

Various schools of thought in the philosophy of language, in linguistics and in stylistics have, in different periods (and always in close connection with the diverse concrete poetic and ideological styles of a given epoch), introduced into such concepts as "system of language," "monologic utterance," "the speaking *individuum,*" various differing nu-

[3] Originally in his *Aesthetic Fragments* [*Estetičeskie fragmenty*]; in a more complete aspect in the book *The Inner Form of the Word* [*Vnutrennjaja forma slova*] (M., 1927). [Au.]

[4] *Vnutrennjaja forma slova,* p. 215. [Au.]

[5] Viktor Vinogradov (1895–1969), linguist and theorist. [Eds.]

[6] V. V. Vinogradov, *On Artistic Prose* [*O xudožestvennom proze*], Moscow-Leningrad, 1930, pp. 75–106. [Au.]

ances of meaning, but their basic content remains unchanged. This basic content is conditioned by the specific sociohistorical destinies of European languages and by the destinies of ideological discourse, and by those particular historical tasks that ideological discourse has fulfilled in specific social spheres and at specific stages in its own historical development.

These tasks and destinies of discourse conditioned specific verbal-ideological movements, as well as various specific genres of ideological discourse, and ultimately the specific philosophical concept of discourse itself—in particular, the concept of poetic discourse, which had been at the heart of all concepts of style.

The strength and at the same time the limitations of such basic stylistic categories become apparent when such categories are seen as conditioned by specific historical destinies and by the task that an ideological discourse assumes. These categories arose from and were shaped by the historically *aktuell* forces at work in the verbal-ideological evolution of specific social groups; they comprised the theoretical expression of actualizing forces that were in the process of creating a life for language.

These forces are *the forces that serve to unify and centralize the verbal-ideological world.*

Unitary language constitutes the theoretical expression of the historical processes of linguistic unification and centralization, an expression of the centripetal forces of language. A unitary language is not something given [*dan*] but is always in essence posited [*zadan*]—and at every moment of its linguistic life it is opposed to the realities of heteroglossia. But at the same time it makes its real presence felt as a force for overcoming this heteroglossia, imposing specific limits to it, guaranteeing a certain maximum of mutual understanding and crystalizing into a real, although still relative, unity—the unity of the reigning conversational (everyday) and literary language, "correct language."

A common unitary language is a system of linguistic norms. But these norms do not constitute an abstract imperative; they are rather the generative forces of linguistic life, forces that struggle to overcome the heteroglossia[7] of language, forces that unite and centralize verbal-ideological thought, creating within a heteroglot national language the firm, stable linguistic nucleus of an officially recognized literary language, or else defending an already formed language from the pressure of growing heteroglossia.

What we have in mind here is not an abstract linguistic minimum of a common language, in the sense of a system of elementary forms (linguistic symbols) guaranteeing a *minimum* level of comprehension in practical communication. We are taking language not as a system of abstract grammatical categories, but rather language conceived as ideologically saturated, language as a world view, even as a concrete opinion, insuring a *maximum* of mutual understanding in all spheres of ideological life. Thus a unitary language gives expression to forces working toward concrete verbal and ideological unification and centralization, which develop in vital connection with the processes of sociopolitical and cultural centralization.

Aristotelian poetics, the poetics of Augustine, the poetics of the medieval church, of "the one language of truth," the Cartesian poetics of neoclassicism, the abstract grammatical universalism of Leibniz (the idea of a "universal grammar"), Humboldt's insistence on the concrete—all these, whatever their differences in nuance, give expression to the same centripetal forces in socio-linguistic and ideological life; they serve one and the same project of centralizing and unifying the European languages. The victory of one reigning language (dialect) over the others, the supplanting of languages, their enslavement, the process of illuminating them with the True Word, the incorporation of barbarians and lower social strata into a unitary language of culture and truth, the canonization of ideological systems, philology with its methods of studying and teaching dead languages, languages that were by that very fact "unities," Indo-European linguistics with its focus of attention, directed away from language plurality to a single proto-language—all this determined the content and power of the category of "unitary language" in linguistic and stylistic thought, and determined its creative, style-shaping role in the majority of the poetic genres that coalesced in the channel formed by those same centripetal forces of verbal-ideological life.

But the centripetal forces of the life of language, embodied in a "unitary language," operate in the midst of heteroglossia. At any given moment of its evolution, language is stratified not only into linguis-

[7]Heteroglossia: those conditions, the converging of internal and external forces, that control the meaning of an utterance. [Eds.]

tic dialects in the strict sense of the word (according to formal linguistic markers, especially phonetic), but also—and for us this is the essential point—into languages that are socio-ideological: languages of social groups, "professional" and "generic" languages, languages of generations and so forth. From this point of view, literary language itself is only one of these heteroglot languages—and in its turn is also stratified into languages (generic, period-bound and others). And this stratification and heteroglossia, once realized, is not only a static invariant of linguistic life, but also what insures its dynamics: stratification and heteroglossia widen and deepen as long as language is alive and developing. Alongside the centripetal forces, the centrifugal forces of language carry on their uninterrupted work; alongside verbal-ideological centralization and unification, the uninterrupted processes of decentralization and disunification go forward.

Every concrete utterance of a speaking subject serves as a point where centrifugal as well as centripetal forces are brought to bear. The processes of centralization and decentralization, of unification and disunification, intersect in the utterance; the utterance not only answers the requirements of its own language as an individualized embodiment of a speech act, but it answers the requirements of heteroglossia as well; it is in fact an active participant in such speech diversity. And this active participation of every utterance in living heteroglossia determines the linguistic profile and style of the utterance to no less a degree than its inclusion in any normative-centralizing system of a unitary language.

Every utterance participates in the "unitary language" (in its centripetal forces and tendencies) and at the same time partakes of social and historical heteroglossia (the centrifugal, stratifying forces).

Such is the fleeting language of a day, of an epoch, a social group, a genre, a school and so forth. It is possible to give a concrete and detailed analysis of any utterance, once having exposed it as a contradiction-ridden, tension-filled unity of two embattled tendencies in the life of language.

The authentic environment of an utterance, the environment in which it lives and takes shape, is dialogized heteroglossia, anonymous and social as language, but simultaneously concrete, filled with specific content and accented as an individual utterance.

At the time when major divisions of the poetic genres were developing under the influence of the unifying, centralizing, centripetal forces of verbal-ideological life, the novel—and those artistic-prose genres that gravitate toward it—was being historically shaped by the current of decentralizing, centrifugal forces. At the time when poetry was accomplishing the task of cultural, national and political centralization of the verbal-ideological world in the higher official socio-ideological levels, on the lower levels, on the stages of local fairs and at buffoon spectacles, the heteroglossia of the clown sounded forth, ridiculing all "languages" and dialects; there developed the literature of the *fabliaux* and *Schwänke* of street songs, folksayings, anecdotes, where there was no language-center at all, where there was to be found a lively play with the "languages" of poets, scholars, monks, knights and others, where all "languages" were masks and where no language could claim to be an authentic, incontestable face.

Heteroglossia, as organized in these low genres, was not merely heteroglossia vis-à-vis the accepted literary language (in all its various generic expressions), that is, vis-à-vis the linguistic center of the verbal-ideological life of the nation and the epoch, but was a heteroglossia consciously opposed to this literary language. It was parodic, and aimed sharply and polemically against the official languages of its given time. It was heteroglossia that had been dialogized.

Linguistics, stylistics and the philosophy of language that were born and shaped by the current of centralizing tendencies in the life of language have ignored this dialogized heteroglossia, in which is embodied the centrifugal forces in the life of language. For this very reason they could make no provision for the dialogic nature of language, which was a struggle among socio-linguistic points of view, not an intra-language struggle between individual wills or logical contradictions. Moreover, even intra-language dialogue (dramatic, rhetorical, cognitive or merely casual) has hardly been studied linguistically or stylistically up to the present day. One might even say outright that the dialogic aspect of discourse and all the phenomena connected with it have remained to the present moment beyond the ken of linguistics.

Stylistics has been likewise completely deaf to dialogue. A literary work has been conceived by stylistics as if it were a hermetic and self-sufficient whole, one whose elements constitute a closed system presuming nothing beyond themselves, no other utterances. The system comprising an artistic work was thought to be analogous with the system of a language, a system that could not stand in a dialogic interrelationship with other languages. From the point of view of stylistics, the artistic work as a whole—whatever that whole might be—is a self-sufficient and closed authorial monologue, one that presumes only passive listeners beyond its own boundaries. Should we imagine the work as a rejoinder in a given dialogue, whose style is determined by its interrelationship with other rejoinders in the same dialogue (in the totality of the conversation)—then traditional stylistics does not offer an adequate means for approaching such a dialogized style. The sharpest and externally most marked manifestations of this stylistic category—the polemical style, the parodic, the ironic—are usually classified as rhetorical and not as poetic phenomena. Stylistics locks every stylistic phenomenon into the monologic context of a given self-sufficient and hermetic utterance, imprisoning it, as it were, in the dungeon of a single context; it is not able to exchange messages with other utterances; it is not able to realize its own stylistic implications in a relationship with them; it is obliged to exhaust itself in its own single hermetic context.

Linguistics, stylistics and the philosophy of language—as forces in the service of the great centralizing tendencies of European verbal-ideological life—have sought first and foremost for *unity* in diversity. This exclusive "orientation toward unity" in the present and past life of languages has concentrated the attention of philosophical and linguistic thought on the firmest, most stable, least changeable and most mono-semic aspects of discourse—on the *phonetic* aspects first of all—that are furthest removed from the changing socio-semantic spheres of discourse. Real ideologically saturated "language consciousness," one that participates in actual heteroglossia and multi-languagedness, has remained outside its field of vision. It is precisely this orientation toward unity that has compelled scholars to ignore all the verbal genres (quotidian, rhetorical, artistic-prose) that were the carriers of the decentralizing tendencies in the life of language, or that were in any case too fundamentally implicated in heteroglossia. The expression of this hetero- as well as polyglot consciousness in the specific forms and phenomena of verbal life remained utterly without determinative influence on linguistics and stylistic thought.

Therefore proper theoretical recognition and illumination could not be found for the specific feel for language and discourse that one gets in stylizations, in *skaz,*[8] in parodies and in various forms of verbal masquerade, "not talking straight," and in the more complex artistic forms for the organization of contradiction, forms that orchestrate their themes by means of languages—in all characteristic and profound models of novelistic prose, in Grimmelshausen, Cervantes, Rabelais, Fielding, Smollett, Sterne and others.

The problem of stylistics for the novel inevitably leads to the necessity of engaging a series of fundamental questions concerning the philosophy of discourse, questions connected with those aspects in the life of discourse that have had no light cast on them by linguistic and stylistic thought—that is, we must deal with the life and behavior of discourse in a contradictory and multi-languaged world.

Discourse in Poetry and Discourse in the Novel

For the philosophy of language, for linguistics and for stylistics structured on their base, a whole series of phenomena have therefore remained almost entirely beyond the realm of consideration: these include the specific phenomena that are present in discourse and that are determined by its dialogic orientation, first, amid others' utterances inside a *single* language (the primordial dialogism of discourse), amid other "social languages" within a single *national* language and finally amid different national languages within the same *culture,* that is, the same socio-ideological conceptual horizon.[9]

In recent decades, it is true, these phenomena have begun to attract the attention of scholars in language and stylistics, but their fundamental and wide-ranging significance in all spheres of the life of discourse is still far from acknowledged.

The dialogic orientation of a word among other words (of all kinds and degrees of otherness) creates new and significant artistic potential in discourse, creates the potential for a distinctive art of prose,

[8] *Skaz*: a technique of narration imitating the speech of a narrator. [Eds.]

[9] Linguistics acknowledges only a mechanical reciprocal influencing and intermixing of languages, (that is, one that is unconscious and determined by social conditions) which is reflected in abstract linguistic elements (phonetic and morphological). [Au.]

which has found its fullest and deepest expression in the novel.

We will focus our attention here on various forms and degrees of dialogic orientation in discourse, and on the special potential for a distinctive prose-art.

As treated by traditional stylistic thought, the word acknowledges only itself (that is, only its own context), its own object, its own direct expression and its own unitary and singular language. It acknowledges another word, one lying outside its own context, only as the neutral word of language, as the word of no one in particular, as simply the potential for speech. The direct word, as traditional stylistics understands it, encounters in its orientation toward the object only the resistance of the object itself (the impossibility of its being exhausted by a word, the impossibility of saying it all), but it does not encounter in its path toward the object the fundamental and richly varied opposition of another's word. No one hinders this word, no one argues with it.

But no living word relates to its object in a *singular* way: between the word and its object, between the word and the speaking subject, there exists an elastic environment of other, alien words about the same object, the same theme, and this is an environment that it is often difficult to penetrate. It is precisely in the process of living interaction with this specific environment that the word may be individualized and given stylistic shape.

Indeed, any concrete discourse (utterance) finds the object at which it was directed already as it were overlain with qualifications, open to dispute, charged with value, already enveloped in an obscuring mist—or, on the contrary, by the "light" of alien words that have already been spoken about it. It is entangled, shot through with shared thoughts, points of view, alien value judgments and accents. The word, directed toward its object, enters a dialogically agitated and tension-filled environment of alien words, value judgments and accents, weaves in and out of complex interrelationships, merges with some, recoils from others, intersects with yet a third group: and all this may crucially shape discourse, may leave a trace in all its semantic layers, may complicate its expression and influence its entire stylistic profile.

The living utterance, having taken meaning and shape at a particular historical moment in a socially specific environment, cannot fail to brush up against thousands of living dialogic threads, woven by socio-ideological consciousness around the given object of an utterance; it cannot fail to become an active participant in social dialogue. After all, the utterance arises out of this dialogue as a continuation of it and as a rejoinder to it—it does not approach the object from the sidelines.

The way in which the word conceptualizes its object is a complex act—all objects, open to dispute and overlain as they are with qualifications, are from one side highlighted while from the other side dimmed by heteroglot social opinion, by an alien word about them.[10] And into this complex play of light and shadow the word enters—it becomes saturated with this play, and must determine within it the boundaries of its own semantic and stylistic contours. The way in which the word conceives its object is complicated by a dialogic interaction within the object between various aspects of its socio-verbal intelligibility. And an artistic representation, an "image" of the object, may be penetrated by this dialogic play of verbal intentions that meet and are interwoven in it; such an image need not stifle these forces, but on the contrary may activate and organize them. If we imagine the *intention* of such a word, that is, its *directionality toward the object,* in the form of a ray of light, then the living and unrepeatable play of colors and light on the facets of the image that it constructs can be explained as the spectral dispersion of the ray-word, not within the object itself (as would be the case in the play of an image-as-trope, in poetic speech taken in the narrow sense, in an "autotelic word"), but rather as its spectral dispersion in an atmosphere filled with the alien words, value judgments and accents through which the ray passes on its way toward the object; the social atmosphere of the word, the atmosphere that surrounds the object, makes the facets of the image sparkle.

The word, breaking through to its own meaning and its own expression across an environment full of alien words and variously evaluating accents, harmonizing with some of the elements in this environ-

[10] Highly significant in this respect is the struggle that must be undertaken in such movements as Rousseauism, Naturalism, Impressionism, Acmeism, Dadaism, Surrealism and analogous schools with the "qualified" nature of the object (a struggle occasioned by the idea of a return to primordial consciousness, to original consciousness, to the object itself in itself, to pure perception and so forth). [Au.]

ment and striking a dissonance with others, is able, in this dialogized process, to shape its own stylistic profile and tone.

Such is the *image in artistic prose* and the image of *novelistic prose* in particular. In the atmosphere of the novel, the direct and unmediated intention of a word presents itself as something impermissibly naive, something in fact impossible, for naiveté itself, under authentic novelistic conditions, takes on the nature of an internal polemic and is consequently dialogized (in, for example, the work of the Sentimentalists, in Chateaubriand and in Tolstoy). Such a dialogized image can occur in all the poetic genres as well, even in the lyric (to be sure, without setting the tone).[11] But such an image can fully unfold, achieve full complexity and depth and at the same time artistic closure, only under the conditions present in the genre of the novel.

In the poetic image narrowly conceived (in the image-as-trope), all activity—the dynamics of the image-as-word—is completely exhausted by the play between the word (with all its apsects) and the object (in all its aspects). The word plunges into the inexhaustible wealth and contradictory multiplicity of the object itself, with its "virginal," still "unuttered" nature; therefore it presumes nothing beyond the borders of its own context (except, of course, what can be found in the treasure-house of language itself). The word forgets that its object has its own history of contradictory acts of verbal recognition, as well as that heteroglossia that is always present in such acts of recognition.

For the writer of artistic prose, on the contrary, the object reveals first of all precisely the socially heteroglot multiplicity of its names, definitions and value judgments. Instead of the virginal fullness and inexhaustibility of the object itself, the prose writer confronts a multitude of routes, roads and paths that have been laid down in the object by social consciousness. Along with the internal contradictions inside the object itself, the prose writer witnesses as well the unfolding of social heteroglossia *surrounding* the object, the Tower-of-Babel mixing of languages that goes on around any object; the dialectics of the object are interwoven with the social dialogue surrounding it. For the prose writer, the object is a focal point for heteroglot voices among which his own voice must also sound; these voices create the background necessary for his own voice, outside of which his artistic prose nuances cannot be perceived, and without which they "do not sound."

The prose artist elevates the social heteroglossia surrounding objects into an image that has finished contours, an image completely shot through with dialogized overtones; he creates artistically calculated nuances on all the fundamental voices and tones of this heteroglossia. But as we have already said, every extra-artistic prose discourse—in any of its forms, quotidian, rhetorical, scholarly—cannot fail to be oriented toward the "already uttered," the "already known," the "common opinion" and so forth. The dialogic orientation of discourse is a phenomenon that is, of course, a property of *any* discourse. It is the natural orientation of any living discourse. On all its various routes toward the object, in all its directions, the word encounters an alien word and cannot help encountering it in a living, tension-filled interaction. Only the mythical Adam, who approached a virginal and as yet verbally unqualified world with the first word, could really have escaped from start to finish this dialogic inter-orientation with the alien word that occurs in the object. Concrete historical human discourse does not have this privilege: it can deviate from such inter-orientation only on a conditional basis and only to a certain degree.

It is all the more remarkable that linguistics and the philosophy of discourse have been primarily oriented precisely toward this artificial, preconditioned status of the word, a word excised from dialogue and taken for the norm (although the primacy of dialogue over monologue is frequently proclaimed). Dialogue is studied merely as a compositional form in the structuring of speech, but the internal dialogism of the word (which occurs in a monologic utterance as well as in a rejoinder), the dialogism that penetrates its entire structure, all its semantic and expressive layers, is almost entirely ignored. But it is precisely this internal dialogism of the word, which does not assume any external compositional forms of dialogue, that cannot be isolated as an independent act, separate from the word's ability to form a concept [*koncipirovanie*] of its object—it is precisely this internal dialogism that has such enormous power to shape style. The

[11] The Horatian lyric, Villon, Heine, Laforgue, Annenskij and others—despite the fact that these are extremely varied instances. [Au.]

internal dialogism of the word finds expression in a series of peculiar features in semantics, syntax and stylistics that have remained up to the present time completely unstudied by linguistics and stylistics (nor, what is more, have the peculiar semantic features of ordinary dialogue been studied).

The word is born in a dialogue as a living rejoinder within it; the word is shaped in dialogic interaction with an alien word that is already in the object. A word forms a concept of its own object in a dialogic way.

But this does not exhaust the internal dialogism of the word. It encounters an alien word not only in the object itself: every word is directed toward an *answer* and cannot escape the profound influence of the answering word that it anticipates.

The word in living conversation is directly, blatantly, oriented toward a future answer-word: it provokes an answer, anticipates it and structures itself in the answer's direction. Forming itself in an atmosphere of the already spoken, the word is at the same time determined by that which has not yet been said but which is needed and in fact anticipated by the answering word. Such is the situation in any living dialogue.

All rhetorical forms, monologic in their compositional structure, are oriented toward the listener and his answer. This orientation toward the listener is usually considered the basic constitutive feature of rhetorical discourse.[12] It is highly significant for rhetoric that this relationship toward the concrete listener, taking him into account, is a relationship that enters into the very internal construction of rhetorical discourse. This orientation toward an answer is open, blatant and concrete.

This open orientation toward the listener and his answer in everyday dialogue and in rhetorical forms has attracted the attention of linguists. But even where this has been the case, linguists have by and large gotten no further than the compositional forms by which the listener is taken into account; they have not sought influence springing from more profound meaning and style. They have taken into consideration only those aspects of style determined by demands for comprehensibility and clarity—that is, precisely those aspects that are deprived of any internal dialogism, that take the listener for a person who passively understands but not for one who actively answers and reacts.

The listener and his response are regularly taken into account when it comes to everyday dialogue and rhetoric, but every other sort of discourse as well is oriented toward an understanding that is "responsive"—although this orientation is not particularized in an independent act and is not compositionally marked. Responsive understanding is a fundamental force, one that participates in the formulation of discourse, and it is moreover an *active* understanding, one that discourse senses as resistance or support enriching the discourse.

Linguistics and the philosophy of language acknowledge only a passive understanding of discourse, and moreover this takes place by and large on the level of common language, that is, it is an understanding of an utterance's *neutral signification* and not its *actual meaning*.

The linguistic significance of a given utterance is understood against the background of language, while its actual meaning is understood against the background of other concrete utterances on the same theme, a background made up of contradictory opinions, points of view and value judgments—that is, precisely that background that, as we see, complicates the path of any word toward its object. Only now this contradictory environment of alien words is present to the speaker not in the object, but rather in the consciousness of the listener, as his apperceptive background, pregnant with responses and objections. And every utterance is oriented toward this apperceptive background of understanding, which is not a linguistic background but rather one composed of specific objects and emotional expressions. There occurs a new encounter between the utterance and an alien word, which makes itself felt as a new and unique influence on its style.

A passive understanding of linguistic meaning is no understanding at all, it is only the abstract aspect of meaning. But even a more concrete *passive* understanding of the meaning of the utterance, an understanding of the speaker's intention insofar as that understanding remains purely passive, purely receptive, contributes nothing new to the word under consideration, only mirroring it, seeking, at its most ambitious, merely the full reproduction of that which is already given in the word—even such an understanding never goes beyond the boundaries of

[12] Cf. V. Vinogradov's book *On Artistic Prose*, the chapter "Rhetoric and Poetics," pp. 75ff., where definitions taken from the older rhetorics are introduced. [Au.]

the word's context and in no way enriches the word. Therefore, insofar as the speaker operates with such a passive understanding, nothing new can be introduced into his discourse; there can be no new aspects in his discourse relating to concrete objects and emotional expressions. Indeed the purely negative demands, such as could only emerge from a passive understanding (for instance, a need for greater clarity, more persuasiveness, more vividness and so forth), leave the speaker in his own personal context, within his own boundaries; such negative demands are completely immanent in the speaker's own discourse and do not go beyond his semantic or expressive self-sufficiency.

In the actual life of speech, every concrete act of understanding is active: it assimilates the word to be understood into its own conceptual system filled with specific objects and emotional expressions, and is indissolubly merged with the response, with a motivated agreement or disagreement. To some extent, primacy belongs to the response, as the activating principle: it creates the ground for understanding, it prepares the ground for an active and engaged understanding. Understanding comes to fruition only in the response. Understanding and response are dialectically merged and mutually condition each other; one is impossible without the other.

Thus an active understanding, one that assimilates the word under consideration into a new conceptual system, that of the one striving to understand, establishes a series of complex interrelationships, consonances and dissonances with the word and enriches it with new elements. It is precisely such an understanding that the speaker counts on. Therefore his orientation toward the listener is an orientation toward a specific conceptual horizon, toward the specific world of the listener; it introduces totally new elements into his discourse; it is in this way, after all, that various different points of view, conceptual horizons, systems for providing expressive accents, various social "languages" come to interact with one another. The speaker strives to get a reading on his own word, and on his own conceptual system that determines this word, within the alien conceptual system of the understanding receiver; he enters into dialogical relationships with certain aspects of this system. The speaker breaks through the alien conceptual horizon of the listener, constructs his own utterance on alien territory, against his, the listener's, apperceptive background.

This new form of internal dialogism of the word is different from that form determined by an encounter with an alien word within the object itself: here it is not the object that serves as the arena for the encounter, but rather the subjective belief system of the listener. Thus this dialogism bears a more subjective, psychological and (frequently) random character, sometimes crassly accommodating, sometimes provocatively polemical. Very often, especially in the rhetorical forms, this orientation toward the listener and the related internal dialogism of the word may simply overshadow the object: the strong point of any concrete listener becomes a self-sufficient focus of attention, and one that interferes with the word's creative work on its referent.

. . . .

In those examples of the internal dialogization of discourse that we have chosen (the internal, as contrasted with the external, compositionally marked, dialogue) the relationship of the alien word, to an alien utterance enters into the positing of the style. Style organically contains within itself indices that reach outside itself, a correspondence of its own elements and the elements of an alien context. The internal politics of style (how the elements are put together) is determined by its external politics (its relationship to alien discourse). Discourse lives, as it were, on the boundary between its own context and another, alien, context.

In any actual dialogue the rejoinder also leads such a double life: it is structured and conceptualized in the context of the dialogue as a whole, which consists of its own utterances ("own" from the point of view of the speaker) and of alien utterances (those of the partner). One cannot excise the rejoinder from this combined context made up of one's own words and the words of another without losing its sense and tone. It is an organic part of a heteroglot unity.

The phenomenon of internal dialogization, as we have said, is present to a greater or lesser extent in all realms of the life of the word. But if in extra-artistic prose (everyday, rhetorical, scholarly) dialogization usually stands apart, crystallizes into a special kind of act of its own and runs its course in ordinary dialogue or in other, compositionally clearly marked forms for mixing and polemicizing with the discourse of another—then in *artistic* prose, and especially in the novel, this dialogization penetrates from within the very way in which the word conceives its object and its means for expressing itself, reformulating the semantics and syntactical structure of discourse. Here dialogic inter-orientation becomes, as it were, an event of discourse itself, animating from within and dramatizing discourse in all its aspects.

In the majority of poetic genres (poetic in the narrow sense), as we have said, the internal dialogization of discourse is not put to artistic use, it does not enter into the work's "aesthetic object," and is artificially extinguished in poetic discourse. In the novel, however, this internal dialogization becomes one of the most fundamental aspects of prose style and undergoes a specific artistic elaboration.

But internal dialogization can become such a crucial force for creating form only where individual differences and contradictions are enriched by social heteroglossia, where dialogic reverberations do not sound in the semantic heights of discourse (as happens in the rhetorical genres) but penetrate the deep strata of discourse, dialogize language itself and the world view a particular language has (the internal form of discourse)—where the dialogue of voices arises directly out of a social dialogue of "languages," where an alien utterance begins to sound like a socially alien language, where the orientation of the word among alien utterances changes into an orientation of a word among socially alien languages within the boundaries of one and the same national language.

In genres that are poetic in the narrow sense, the natural dialogization of the word is not put to artistic use, the word is sufficient unto itself and does not presume alien utterances beyond its own boundaries. Poetic style is by convention suspended from any mutual interaction with alien discourse, any allusion to alien discourse.

Any way whatever of alluding to alien languages, to the possibility of another vocabulary, another semantics, other syntactic forms and so forth, to the possibility of other linguistic points of view, is equally foreign to poetic style. It follows that any sense of the boundedness, the historicity, the social determination and specificity of one's own language is alien to poetic style, and therefore a critical qualified relationship to one's own language (as merely one of many languages in a heteroglot world) is foreign to poetic style—as is a related phenomenon, the incomplete commitment of oneself, of one's full meaning, to a given language.

Of course this relationship and the relationship to his own language (in greater or lesser degree) could never be foreign to a historically existent poet, as a human being surrounded by living hetero- and polyglossia; but this relationship could not find a place in the *poetic style* of his work without destroying that style, without transposing it into a prosaic key and in the process turning the poet into a writer of prose.

In poetic genres, artistic consciousness—understood as a unity of all the author's semantic and expressive intentions—fully realizes itself within its own language; in them alone is such consciousness fully immanent, expressing itself in it directly and without mediation, without conditions and without distance. The language of the poet is *his* language, he is utterly immersed in it, inseparable from it, he makes use of each form, each word, each expression according to its unmediated power to assign meaning (as it were, "without quotation marks"), that is, as a pure and direct expression of his own intention. No matter what "agonies of the word" the poet endured in the process of creation, in the finished work language is an obedient organ, fully adequate to the author's intention.

The language in a poetic work realizes itself as something about which there can be no doubt, something that cannot be disputed, something all-encompassing. Everything that the poet sees, understands and thinks, he does through the eyes of a given language, in its inner forms, and there is nothing that might require, for its expression, the help of any other or alien language. The language of the poetic genre is a unitary and singular Ptolemaic world outside of which nothing else exists and nothing else is needed. The concept of many worlds of language, all equal in their ability to conceptualize and to be expressive, is organically denied to poetic style.

The world of poetry, no matter how many contradictions and insoluble conflicts the poet develops within it, is always illumined by one unitary and indisputable discourse. Contradictions, conflicts and doubts remain in the object, in thoughts, in living experiences—in short, in the subject matter—but they do not enter into the language itself. In poetry, even discourse about doubts must be cast in a discourse that cannot be doubted.

To take responsibility for the language of the work as a whole at all of its points as *its* language, to assume a full solidarity with each of the work's aspects, tones, nuances—such is the fundamental prerequisite for poetic style; style so conceived is fully adequate to a single language and a single linguistic consciousness. The poet is not able to oppose his own poetic consciousness, his own intentions to the language that he uses, for he is completely within it and therefore cannot turn it into an object to be perceived, reflected upon or related to. Language is present to him only from inside, in the work it does to effect its intention, and not from outside, in its objective specificity and boundedness. Within the limits of poetic style, direct unconditional intentionality, language at its full weight and the objective display of language (as a socially and historically limited linguistic reality) are all simultaneous, but incompatible. The unity and singularity of language are the indispensable prerequisites for a realization of the direct (but not objectively typifying) intentional individuality of poetic style and of its monologic steadfastness.

This does not mean, of course, that heteroglossia or even a foreign language is completely shut out of a poetic work. To be sure, such possibilities are limited: a certain latitude for heteroglossia exists only in the "low" poetic genres—in the satiric and comic genres and others. Nevertheless, heteroglossia (other socio-ideological languages) can be introduced into purely poetic genres, primarily in the speeches of characters. But in such a context it is objective. It appears, in essence, as a *thing*, it does not lie on the *same* plane with the real language of the work: it is the depicted gesture of one of the characters and does not appear as an aspect of the word doing the depicting. Elements of heteroglossia enter here not in the capacity of another language carrying its own particular points of view, about which one can say things not expressible in one's own language, but rather in the capacity of a depicted thing. Even when speaking of alien things, the poet speaks in his own language. To shed light on an alien world, he never resorts to an alien language, even though it might in fact be more adequate to that world. Whereas the writer of prose, by contrast—as we shall see—attempts to talk about even his *own* world in an alien language (for example, in the nonliterary language of the teller of tales, or the representative of a specific socio-ideological group); he often measures his own world by alien linguistic standards.

As a consequence of the prerequisites mentioned above, the language of poetic genres, when they approach their stylistic limit,[13] often becomes authoritarian, dogmatic and conservative, sealing itself off from the influence of extraliterary social dialects. Therefore such ideas as a special "poetic language," a "language of the gods," a "priestly language of poetry" and so forth could flourish on poetic soil. It is noteworthy that the poet, should he not accept the given literary language, will sooner resort to the artificial creation of a new language specifically for poetry than he will to the exploitation of actual available social dialects. Social languages are filled with specific objects, typical, socially localized and limited, while the artificially created language of poetry must be a directly intentional language, unitary and singular. Thus, when Russian prose writers at the beginning of the twentieth century began to show a profound interest in dialects and *skaz,* the Symbolists (Bal'mont, V. Ivanov) and later the Futurists dreamed of creating a special "language of poetry," and even made experiments directed toward creating such a language (those of V. Khlebnikov).

The idea of a special unitary and singular language of poetry is a typical utopian philosopheme of poetic discourse: it is grounded in the actual conditions and demands of poetic style, which is always a style adequately serviced by one directly intentional language from whose point of view other languages (conversational, business and prose languages, among others) are perceived as objects that are in no way its equal.[14] The idea of a "poetic language" is yet another expression of that same Ptolemaic conception of the linguistic and stylistic world.

. . . .

The poet is a poet insofar as he accepts the idea of a unitary and singular language and a unitary, monologically sealed-off utterance. These ideas are

[13] It goes without saying that we continually advance as typical the extreme to which poetic genres aspire; in concrete examples of poetic works it is possible to find features fundamental to prose, and numerous hybrids of various generic types exist. These are especially widespread in periods of shift in literary poetic languages. [Au.]

[14] Such was the point of view taken by Latin toward national languages in the Middle Ages. [Au.]

immanent in the poetic genres with which he works. In a condition of actual contradiction, these are what determine the means of orientation open to the poet. The poet must assume a complete single-personed hegemony over his own language, he must assume equal responsibility for each one of its aspects and subordinate them to his own, and only his own, intentions. Each word must express the poet's *meaning* directly and without mediation; there must be no distance between the poet and his word. The meaning must emerge from language as a single intentional whole: none of its stratification, its speech diversity, to say nothing of its language diversity, may be reflected in any fundamental way in his poetic work.

To achieve this, the poet strips the word of others' intentions, he uses only such words and forms (and only in such a way) that they lose their link with concrete intentional levels of language and their connection with specific contexts. Behind the words of a poetic work one should not sense any typical or reified images of genres (except for the given poetic genre), nor professions, tendencies, directions (except the direction chosen by the poet himself), nor world views (except for the unitary and singular world view of the poet himself), nor typical and individual images of speaking persons, their speech mannerisms or typical intonations. *Everything that enters the work must immerse itself in Lethe, and forget its previous life in any other contexts: language may remember only its life in poetic contexts (in such contexts, however, even concrete reminiscences are possible).*

Of course there always exists a limited sphere of more or less concrete contexts, and a connection with them must be deliberately evidenced in poetic discourse. But these contexts are purely semantic and, so to speak, accented in the abstract; in their linguistic dimension they are impersonal or at least no particularly concrete linguistic specificity is sensed behind them, no particular manner of speech and so forth, no socially typical linguistic face (the possible personality of the narrator) need peek out from behind them. Everywhere there is only one face—the linguistic face of the author, answering for every word as if it were his own. No matter how multiple and varied these semantic and accentual threads, associations, pointers, hints, correlations that emerge from every poetic word, one language, one conceptual horizon, is sufficient to them all; there is no need of heteroglot social contexts. What is more, the very movement of the poetic symbol (for example, the unfolding of a metaphor) presumes precisely this unity of language, an unmediated correspondence with its object. Social diversity of speech, were it to arise in the work and stratify its language, would make impossible both the normal development and the activity of symbols within it.

The very rhythm of poetic genres does not promote any appreciable degree of stratification. *Rhythm, by creating an unmediated involvement between every aspect of the accentual system of the whole* (via the most immediate rhythmic unities), destroys in embryo those social worlds of speech and of persons that are potentially embedded in the word: in any case, rhythm puts definite limits on them, does not let them unfold or materialize. Rhythm serves to strengthen and concentrate even further the unity and hermetic quality of the surface of poetic style, and of the unitary language that this style posits.

As a result of this work—stripping all aspects of language of the intentions and accents of other people, destroying all traces of social heteroglossia and diversity of language—a tension-filled unity of language is achieved in the poetic work. This unity may be naive, and present only in those extremely rare epochs of poetry, when poetry had not yet exceeded the limits of a closed, unitary, undifferentiated social circle whose language and ideology were not yet stratified. More often than not, we experience a profound and conscious tension through which the unitary poetic language of a work rises from the heteroglot and language-diverse chaos of the literary language contemporary to it.

This is how the poet proceeds. The novelist working in prose (and almost any prose writer) takes a completely different path. He welcomes the heteroglossia and language diversity of the literary and extraliterary language into his own work not only not weakening them but even intensifying them (for he interacts with their particular self-consciousness). It is in fact out of this stratification of language, its speech diversity and even language diversity, that he constructs his style, while at the same time he maintains the unity of his own creative personality and the unity (although it is, to be sure, unity of another order) of his own style.

The prose writer does not purge words of intentions and tones that are alien to him, he does not destroy the seeds of social heteroglossia embedded in words, he does not eliminate those language characterizations and speech mannerisms (potential narrator-personalities) glimmering behind the words and forms, each at a different distance from the ultimate semantic nucleus of his work, that is, the center of his own personal intentions.

The language of the prose writer deploys itself according to degrees of greater or lesser proximity to the author and to his ultimate semantic instantiation: certain aspects of language directly and unmediatedly express (as in poetry) the semantic and expressive intentions of the author, others refract these intentions; the writer of prose does not meld completely with any of these words, but rather accents each of them in a particular way—humorously, ironically, parodically and so forth;[15] yet another group may stand even further from the author's ultimate semantic instantiation, still more thoroughly refracting his intentions; and there are, finally, those words that are completely denied any authorial intentions: the author does not express *himself* in them (as the author of the word)—rather, he *exhibits* them as a unique speech-thing, they function for him as something completely reified. Therefore the stratification of language—generic, professional, social in the narrow sense, that of particular world views, particular tendencies, particular individuals, the social speech diversity and language-diversity (dialects) of language—upon entering the novel establishes its own special order within it, and becomes a unique artistic system, which orchestrates the intentional theme of the author.

Thus a prose writer can distance himself from the language of his own work, while at the same time distancing himself, in varying degrees, from the different layers and aspects of the work. He can make use of language without wholly giving himself up to it, he may treat it as semi-alien or completely alien to himself, while compelling language ultimately to serve all his own intentions. The author does not speak in a given language (from which he distances himself to a greater or lesser degree), but he speaks, as it were, *through* language, a language that has somehow more or less materialized, become objectivized, that he merely ventriloquates.

The prose writer as a novelist does not strip away the intentions of others from the heteroglot language of his works, he does not violate those socio-ideological cultural horizons (big and little worlds) that open up behind heteroglot languages—rather, he welcomes them into his work. The prose writer makes use of words that are already populated with the social intentions of others and compels them to serve his own new intentions, to serve a second master. Therefore the intentions of the prose writer are refracted, and refracted *at different angles,* depending on the degree to which the refracted, heteroglot languages he deals with are socio-ideologically alien, already embodied and already objectivized.

The orientation of the word amid the utterances and languages of others, and all the specific phenomena connected with this orientation, takes on *artistic* significance in novel style. Diversity of voices and heteroglossia enter the novel and organize themselves within it into a structured artistic system. This constitutes the distinguishing feature of the novel as a genre.

Any stylistics capable of dealing with the distinctiveness of the novel as a genre must be a *sociological stylistics.* The internal social dialogism of novelistic discourse requires the concrete social context of discourse to be exposed, to be revealed as the force that determines its entire stylistic structure, its "form" and its "content," determining it not from without, but from within; for indeed, social dialogue reverberates in all aspects of discourse, in those relating to "content" as well as the "formal" aspects themselves.

The development of the novel is a function of the deepening of dialogic essence, its increased scope and greater precision. Fewer and fewer neutral, hard elements ("rock bottom truths") remain that are not drawn into dialogue. Dialogue moves into the deepest molecular and, ultimately, subatomic levels.

Of course, even the poetic word is social, but poetic forms reflect lengthier social processes, i.e., those tendencies in social life requiring centuries to unfold. The novelistic word, however, registers with extreme subtlety the tiniest shifts and oscillations of the social atmosphere; it does so, moreover, while registering it as a whole, in all of its aspects.

When heteroglossia enters the novel it becomes

[15] That is to say, the words are not his if we understand them as direct words, but they are his as things that are being transmitted ironically, exhibited and so forth, that is, as words that are understood from the distances appropriate to humor, irony, parody, etc. [Au.]

subject to an artistic reworking. The social and historical voices populating language, all its words and all its forms, which provide language with its particular concrete conceptualizations, are organized in the novel into a structured stylistic system that expresses the differentiated socio-ideological position of the author amid the heteroglossia of his epoch.

Walter Benjamin

1892–1940

WALTER BENJAMIN displayed throughout his life the vocation of literary criticism, as it might be distinguished from the profession. One might say that Benjamin was always an amateur, though not always happily so: he wrote for love of the activity, realizing with characteristic irony that he would probably never be able to earn a living at it. "There are places in which I can earn a minimum," he wrote, "and places in which I can live on a minimum, but there is no place where I can do both" (*Illuminations,* p. 25). At the same time, however, Benjamin brought a candor and an intellectual independence to critical writing that is rare. Without genuine colleagues, and therefore without the institutional support upon which professions depend, he wrote passionately about writing as an activity essential to all civilizing institutions.

Until his tragic suicide in 1940, precipitated by his unsuccessful attempt to leave Nazi Germany, Benjamin was known primarily for his penetrating and frequently controversial essays and reviews. Like other German-Jewish intellectuals, fascism and national socialism presented him with not only the aspect of obscene barbarism but a profound dilemma touching the institutionalization of tradition: the oppressed live in a perpetual "state of emergency" partly because the ruling classes preemptively capture the idea of history to justify their own right to rule. The dilemma, simply stated, is that anyone who seeks a historical justification for the right to rule thereby becomes the oppressor. Writing self-consciously from a position of marginality, Benjamin is therefore uncommonly wary about positive claims to rightness, virtue, and correct thinking, since these are not in themselves positive attributes of policies, people, or modes of thought but the results of a critical dialectic.

Thus Benjamin might be described as a historical materialist, vigilantly concerned with the relation of writing to political reality, but it would be radically insufficient to say he is a Marxist. In the selection here, his very manner of theoretical vigilance calls theory itself into question as a potential instrument of oppression. The writer is always engaged in the material, historical conditions of which he writes, and the presumption that the theorist could occupy a position above and removed from the historical scene of conflict is a position that Benjamin sees as not only deluded but dangerous.

Despite his marginality—or perhaps, because of it—Benjamin has been influential in shaping subsequent conceptions of criticism, most notably through his influence on *Theodor Adorno, Max Horkheimer,* and other founders of the Frankfurt School.

Benjamin's writings translated into English include two collections of essays,

Illuminations (1969) and *Reflections* (1978), and *The Origins of German Tragic Drama* (1977). See especially Hannah Arendt's introductory essay in *Illuminations* and Geoffrey Hartman, *Criticism in the Wilderness*. For further discussion of the critical theorists of the Frankfurt School, see Martin Jay, *The Dialectical Imagination: A History of the Frankfurt School and the Institute for Social Research, 1923–1950* (1972).

THESES ON THE PHILOSOPHY OF HISTORY

I

The story is told of an automaton constructed in such a way that it could play a winning game of chess, answering each move of an opponent with a countermove. A puppet in Turkish attire and with a hookah in its mouth sat before a chessboard placed on a large table. A system of mirrors created the illusion that this table was transparent from all sides. Actually, a little hunchback who was an expert chess player sat inside and guided the puppet's hand by means of strings. One can imagine a philosophical counterpart to this device. The puppet called "historical materialism" is to win all the time. It can easily be a match for anyone if it enlists the services of theology, which today, as we know, is wizened and has to keep out of sight.

II

"One of the most remarkable characteristics of human nature," writes Lotze,[1] "is, alongside so much selfishness in specific instances, the freedom from envy which the present displays toward the future." Reflection shows us that our image of happiness is thoroughly colored by the time to which the course of our own existence has assigned us. The kind of happiness that could arouse envy in us exists only in the air we have breathed, among people we could have talked to, women who could have given themselves to us. In other words, our image of happiness is indissolubly bound up with the image of redemption. The same applies to our view of the past, which is the concern of history. The past carries with it a temporal index by which it is referred to redemption. There is a secret agreement between past generations and the present one. Our coming was expected on earth. Like every generation that preceded us, we have been endowed with a *weak* Messianic power, a power to which the past has a claim. That claim cannot be settled cheaply. Historical materialists are aware of that.

III

A chronicler who recites events without distinguishing between major and minor ones acts in accordance with the following truth: nothing that has ever happened should be regarded as lost for history. To be sure, only a redeemed mankind receives the fullness of its past—which is to say, only for a redeemed mankind has its past become citable in all its moments. Each moment it has lived becomes a *citation à l'ordre du jour*[2]—and that day is Judgment Day.

IV

> *Seek for food and clothing first, then the Kingdom of God shall be added unto you.*
>
> —Hegel, 1807

The class struggle, which is always present to a historian influenced by Marx, is a fight for the crude

[1] Rudolph Hermann Lotze (1817–1881), German philosopher and psychologist, who attempted to reconcile the principles of romantic idealism with mechanistic science. [Eds.]

[2] "summons to the order of the day." [Eds.]

and material things without which no refined and spiritual things could exist. Nevertheless, it is not in the form of the spoils which fall to the victor that the latter make their presence felt in the class struggle. They manifest themselves in this struggle as courage, humor, cunning, and fortitude. They have retroactive force and will constantly call in question every victory, past and present, of the rulers. As flowers turn toward the sun, by dint of a secret heliotropism the past strives to turn toward that sun which is rising in the sky of history. A historical materialist must be aware of this most inconspicuous of all transformations.

V

The true picture of the past flits by. The past can be seized only as an image which flashes up at the instant when it can be recognized and is never seen again. "The truth will not run away from us": in the historical outlook of historicism these words of Gottfried Keller[3] mark the exact point where historical materialism cuts through historicism. For every image of the past that is not recognized by the present as one of its own concerns threatens to disappear irretrievably. (The good tidings which the historian of the past brings with throbbing heart may be lost in a void the very moment he opens his mouth.)

VI

To articulate the past historically does not mean to recognize it "the way it really was" (Ranke).[4] It means to seize hold of a memory as it flashes up at a moment of danger. Historical materialism wishes to retain that image of the past which unexpectedly appears to man singled out by history at a moment of danger. The danger affects both the content of the tradition and its receivers. The same threat hangs over both: that of becoming a tool of the ruling classes. In every era the attempt must be made anew to wrest tradition away from a conformism that is about to overpower it. The Messiah comes not only as the redeemer, he comes as the subduer of Antichrist. Only that historian will have the gift of fanning the spark of hope in the past who is firmly convinced that *even the dead* will not be safe from the enemy if he wins. And this enemy has not ceased to be victorious.

VII

> *Consider the darkness and the great*
> *cold*
> *In this vale which resounds with*
> *mystery.*
>
> —Brecht, THE THREEPENNY OPERA

To historians who wish to relive an era, Fustel de Coulanges[5] recommends that they blot out everything they know about the later course of history. There is no better way of characterizing the method with which historical materialism has broken. It is a process of empathy whose origin is the indolence of the heart, *acedia,* which despairs of grasping and holding the genuine historical image as it flares up briefly. Among medieval theologians it was regarded as the root cause of sadness. Flaubert, who was familiar with it, wrote: "*Peu de gens devineront combien il a fallu être triste pour ressusciter Carthage.*"[6] The nature of this sadness stands out more clearly if one asks with whom the adherents of historicism actually empathize. The answer is inevitable: with the victor. And all rulers are the heirs of those who conquered before them. Hence, empathy with the victor invariably benefits the rulers. Historical materialists know what that means. Whoever has emerged victorious participates to this day in the triumphal procession in which the present rulers step over those who are lying prostrate. According to traditional practice, the spoils are carried along in the procession. They are called cultural treasures, and a historical materialist views them with cautious detachment. For without exception the cultural treasures he surveys have an origin which he cannot contemplate without horror. They owe their existence not only to the efforts of the great minds and talents who have created them, but also to the anonymous toil of their contempo-

[3] Gottfried Keller (1819–1890), Swiss novelist, short-story writer, and poet. [Eds.]

[4] Leopold von Ranke (1795–1886), German historian. [Eds.]

[5] Numa Denis Fustel de Coulanges (1830–1889), French historian and professor of antiquities at the University of Strasbourg, who argued against the presumed Germanic origins of feudalism and the manorial system in favor of primarily Roman influences. [Eds.]

[6] "Few will be able to guess how sad one had to be in order to resuscitate Carthage." [Tr.]

raries. There is no document of civilization which is not at the same time a document of barbarism. And just as such a document is not free of barbarism, barbarism taints also the manner in which it was transmitted from one owner to another. A historical materialist therefore dissociates himself from it as far as possible. He regards it as his task to brush history against the grain.

VIII

The tradition of the oppressed teaches us that the "state of emergency" in which we live is not the exception but the rule. We must attain to a conception of history that is in keeping with this insight. Then we shall clearly realize that it is our task to bring about a real state of emergency, and this will improve our position in the struggle against Fascism. One reason why Fascism has a chance is that in the name of progress its opponents treat it as a historical norm. The current amazement that the things we are experiencing are "still" possible in the twentieth century is *not* philosophical. This amazement is not the beginning of knowledge—unless it is the knowledge that the view of history which gives rise to it is untenable.

IX

> *Mein Flügel ist zum Schwung bereit,*
> *ich kehrte gern zurück,*
> *denn blieb ich auch lebendige Zeit,*
> *ich hätte wenig Glück.*
>
> —Gerhard Scholem, "Gruss vom Angelus"[7]

A Klee[8] painting named "Angelus Novus" shows an angel looking as though he is about to move away from something he is fixedly contemplating. His eyes are staring, his mouth is open, his wings are spread. This is how one pictures the angel of history. His face is turned toward the past. Where we perceive a chain of events, he sees one single catastrophe which keeps piling wreckage upon wreckage and hurls it in front of his feet. The angel would like to stay, awaken the dead, and make whole what has been smashed. But a storm is blowing from Paradise; it has got caught in his wings with such violence that the angel can no longer close them. This storm irresistibly propels him into the future to which his back is turned, while the pile of debris before him grows skyward. This storm is what we call progress.

X

The themes which monastic discipline assigned to friars for meditation were designed to turn them away from the world and its affairs. The thoughts which we are developing here originate from similar considerations. At a moment when the politicians in whom the opponents of Fascism had placed their hopes are prostrate and confirm their defeat by betraying their own cause, these observations are intended to disentangle the political worldlings from the snares in which the traitors have entrapped them. Our consideration proceeds from the insight that the politicians' stubborn faith in progress, their confidence in their "mass basis," and, finally, their servile integration in an uncontrollable apparatus have been three aspects of the same thing. It seeks to convey an idea of the high price our accustomed thinking will have to pay for a conception of history that avoids any complicity with the thinking to which these politicians continue to adhere.

XI

The conformism which has been part and parcel of Social Democracy from the beginning attaches not only to its political tactics but to its economic views as well. It is one reason for its later breakdown. Nothing has corrupted the German working class so much as the notion that it was moving with the current. It regarded technological developments as the fall of the stream with which it thought it was moving. From there it was but a step to the illusion that the factory work which was supposed to tend toward technological progress constituted a political achievement. The old Protestant ethics of work was resurrected among German workers in secularized form. The Gotha Program[9] already bears

[7]Gershom Gerhard Scholem (1897–), Jewish scholar and translator, born in Berlin, later librarian of the Hebrew University of Jerusalem (1923–27) and National Library (1925–32), lecturer and professor of Jewish mysticism at Hebrew University (1933–65). [Eds.] "My wing is ready for flight,/ I would like to turn back./ If I stayed timeless time,/ I would have little luck." [Tr.]

[8]Paul Klee (1879–1940), Swiss painter and artist, who taught at the Bauhaus from 1922 to 1931, until forced to resign by the Nazis. [Eds.]

[9]The Gotha Congress of 1875 united the two German Socialist parties, one led by Ferdinand Lassalle, the other by Karl Marx and Wilhelm Liebknecht. The program, drafted by Liebknecht and Lassalle, was severely attacked by

traces of this confusion, defining labor as "the source of all wealth and all culture." Smelling a rat, Marx countered that ". . . the man who possesses no other property than his labor power" must of necessity become "the slave of other men who have made themselves the owners. . . ." However, the confusion spread, and soon thereafter Josef Dietzgen[10] proclaimed: "The savior of modern times is called work. The . . . improvement . . . of labor constitutes the wealth which is now able to accomplish what no redeemer has ever been able to do." This vulgar-Marxist conception of the nature of labor bypasses the question of how its products might benefit the workers while still not being at their disposal. It recognizes only the progress in the mastery of nature, not the retrogression of society; it already displays the technocratic features later encountered in Fascism. Among these is a conception of nature which differs ominously from the one in the Socialist utopias before the 1848 revolution. The new conception of labor amounts to the exploitation of nature, which with naïve complacency is contrasted with the exploitation of the proletariat. Compared with this positivistic conception, Fourier's fantasies, which have so often been ridiculed, prove to be surprisingly sound. According to Fourier, as a result of efficient cooperative labor, four moons would illuminate the earthly night, the ice would recede from the poles, sea water would no longer taste salty, and beasts of prey would do man's bidding. All this illustrates a kind of labor which, far from exploiting nature, is capable of delivering her of the creations which lie dormant in her womb as potentials. Nature, which, as Dietzgen puts it, "exists gratis," is a complement to the corrupted conception of labor.

XII

> *We need history, but not the way a spoiled loafer in the garden of knowledge needs it.*
>
> —Nietzsche, OF THE USE AND ABUSE OF HISTORY

Not man or men but the struggling, oppressed class itself is the depository of historical knowledge. In Marx it appears as the last enslaved class, as the avenger that completes the task of liberation in the name of generations of the downtrodden. This conviction, which had a brief resurgence in the Spartacist group,[11] has always been objectionable to Social Democrats. Within three decades they managed virtually to erase the name of Blanqui, though it had been the rallying sound that had reverberated through the preceding century. Social Democracy thought fit to assign to the working class the role of the redeemer of future generations, in this way cutting the sinews of its greatest strength. This training made the working class forget both its hatred and its spirit of sacrifice, for both are nourished by the image of enslaved ancestors rather than that of liberated grandchildren.

XIII

> *Every day our cause becomes clearer and people get smarter.*
>
> —Wilhelm Dietzgen, DIE RELIGION DER SOZIALDEMOKRATIE

Social Democratic theory, and even more its practice, have been formed by a conception of progress which did not adhere to reality but made dogmatic claims. Progress as pictured in the minds of Social Democrats was, first of all, the progress of mankind itself (and not just advances in men's ability and knowledge). Secondly, it was something boundless, in keeping with the infinite perfectibility of mankind. Thirdly, progress was regarded as irresistible, something that automatically pursued a straight or spiral course. Each of these predicates is controversial and open to criticism. However, when the chips are down, criticism must penetrate beyond these predicates and focus on something that they have in common. The concept of the historical progress of mankind cannot be sundered from the concept of its progression through a homogeneous, empty time. A critique of the concept of such a progression must be the basis of any criticism of the concept of progress itself.

Marx in London. See his "Critique of the Gotha Program." [Tr.]

[10] Josef Dietzgen (1828–88), German philosopher. [Eds.]

[11] Leftist group, founded by Karl Liebknecht and Rosa Luxemburg at the beginning of World War I in opposition to the pro-war policies of the German Socialist party, later absorbed by the Communist party. [Tr.]

XIV

Origin is the goal.

—Karl Kraus,[12]
WORTE IN VERSEN, Vol. I

History is the subject of a structure whose site is not homogeneous, empty time, but time filled by the presence of the now [*Jetztzeit*].[13] Thus, to Robespierre ancient Rome was a past charged with the time of the now which he blasted out of the continuum of history. The French Revolution viewed itself as Rome reincarnate. It evoked ancient Rome the way fashion evokes costumes of the past. Fashion has a flair for the topical, no matter where it stirs in the thickets of long ago; it is a tiger's leap into the past. This jump, however, takes place in an arena where the ruling class gives the commands. The same leap in the open air of history is the dialectical one, which is how Marx understood the revolution.

XV

The awareness that they are about to make the continuum of history explode is characteristic of the revolutionary classes at the moment of their action. The great revolution introduced a new calendar. The initial day of a calendar serves as a historical time-lapse camera. And, basically, it is the same day that keeps recurring in the guise of holidays, which are days of remembrance. Thus the calendars do not measure time as clocks do; they are monuments of a historical consciousness of which not the slightest trace has been apparent in Europe in the past hundred years. In the July revolution an incident occurred which showed this consciousness still alive. On the first evening of fighting it turned out that the clocks in towers were being fired on simultaneously and independently from several places in Paris. An eye-witness, who may have owed his insight to the rhyme, wrote as follows:

Qui le croirait! on dit, qu'irrités contre
l'heure
De nouveaux Josués au pied de chaque tour,
Tiraient sur les cadrans pour arrêter le
jour.[14]

XVI

A historical materialist cannot do without the notion of a present which is not a transition, but in which time stands still and has come to a stop. For this notion defines the present in which he himself is writing history. Historicism gives the "eternal" image of the past; historical materialism supplies a unique experience with the past. The historical materialist leaves it to others to be drained by the whore called "Once upon a time" in historicism's bordello. He remains in control of his powers, man enough to blast open the continuum of history.

XVII

Historicism rightly culminates in universal history. Materialistic historiography differs from it as to method more clearly than from any other kind. Universal history has no theoretical armature. Its method is additive; it musters a mass of data to fill the homogeneous, empty time. Materialistic historiography, on the other hand, is based on a constructive principle. Thinking involves not only the flow of thoughts, but their arrest as well. Where thinking suddenly stops in a configuration pregnant with tensions, it gives that configuration a shock, by which it crystallizes into a monad. A historical materialist approaches a historical subject only where he encounters it as a monad. In this structure he recognizes the sign of a Messianic cessation of happening, or, put differently, a revolutionary chance in the fight for the oppressed past. He takes cognizance of it in order to blast a specific era out of the homogeneous course of history—blasting a specific life out of the era or a specific work out of the lifework. As a result of this method the lifework is preserved in this work and at the same time canceled;[15] in the lifework, the era; and in the era, the entire course of history. The nourishing fruit of the historically understood contains time as a precious but tasteless seed.

[12] Karl Kraus (1874–1936), Austrian writer. [Eds.]

[13] Benjamin says "Jetztzeit" and indicates by the quotation marks that he does not simply mean an equivalent to *Gegenwart*, that is, present. He clearly is thinking of the mystical *nunc stans*. [Tr.]

[14] "Who would have believed it! we are told that new Joshuas / at the foot of every tower, as though irritated with / time itself, fired at the dials in order to stop the day." [Tr.]

[15] The Hegelian term *aufheben* in its threefold meaning: to preserve, to elevate, to cancel. [Tr.]

XVIII

"In relation to the history of organic life on earth," writes a modern biologist, "the paltry fifty millennia of *homo sapiens* constitute something like two seconds at the close of a twenty-four-hour day. On this scale, the history of civilized mankind would fill one-fifth of the last second of the last hour." The present, which, as a model of messianic time, comprises the entire history of mankind in an enormous abridgment, coincides exactly with the stature which the history of mankind has in the universe.

A

Historicism contents itself with establishing a causal connection between various moments in history. But no fact that is a cause is for that very reason historical. It became historical post-humously, as it were, through events that may be separated from it by thousands of years. A historian who takes this as his point of departure stops telling the sequence of events like the beads of a rosary. Instead, he grasps the constellation which his own era has formed with a definite earlier one. Thus he establishes a conception of the present as the "time of the now" which is shot through with chips of Messianic time.

B

The soothsayers who found out from time what it had in store certainly did not experience time as either homogeneous or empty. Anyone who keeps this in mind will perhaps get an idea of how past times were experienced in remembrance—namely, in just the same way. We know that the Jews were prohibited from investigating the future. The Torah and the prayers instruct them in remembrance, however. This stripped the future of its magic, to which all those succumb who turn to the soothsayers for enlightenment. This does not imply, however, that for the Jews the future turned into homogeneous, empty time. For every second of time was the strait gate through which the Messiah might enter.

Max Horkheimer

1895–1973

In 1930, Max Horkheimer became the director of the Institute for Social Research in Frankfurt, and under his leadership the so-called Frankfurt School took shape around an ambitious intellectual (and political) program of philosophical criticism. Horkheimer's own philosophical work was based on a rigorous critique of positivism and a pervasive commitment to examining the historical and social conditions under which modern industrial society has emerged. In 1933, the institute moved to Paris and later to Columbia University, just before the Nazi occupation of France.

Together with *Theodor Adorno,* Erich Fromm, Franz Neumann, and others, Horkheimer proposed a far-reaching model of "theory" that called into question the traditional view that a theory is contained in the logical structure of propositions about a subject. "Critical theory," in Horkheimer's model, differs most notably in positing a social totality within which theory is primarily an activity. Thus, when the human sciences (including what in American universities are called the social sciences and humanities) attempt to pattern their explanatory and philosophical discourse on the physical sciences, they lose sight of the fact that a theory of sociology, for example, cannot be separated out from the social totality within which the theory is formulated by individuals, for particular reasons.

According to Horkheimer, this leads to an intellectual alienation akin to the alienation of the working class in the modern capitalist state, with the distinction that it "finds expression in philosophical terminology as the separation of value and research, knowledge and action" (*Critical Theory,* p. 208). "Critical theory," by contrast, represents an attempt to include within the activity of theory at once the excluded subjects and topics—value, interest, belief, ideology—and the theorist's own complex and sometimes inchoate relation to the same matters.

In the essay here, Horkheimer outlines his critique of positivism, as it has developed since Plato and through the great critiques of Kant, on the assumption that philosophy ought to produce positive or "scientific" knowledge itself. Here, Horkheimer is at odds with both *Husserl,* for example, and *Wittgenstein,* as the first sought to make philosophy a rigorous science without presuppositions, and the second sought to make philosophy a rigorously analytical enterprise. In Horkheimer's view, philosophy, unlike other disciplines, does not have an external subject matter from which "data" derive but rather produces its subject matter by falling back upon itself, "upon its own theoretical activity." For this reason, the vitality of philosophy is its inherently critical character: philosophy provides "criticism of what is prevalent," through the distinctive (and dialectical) activity of reflection; and the distinctive subject matter of philosophy is then seen to be precisely "the development of critical and dialectical thought."

Many of Horkheimer's essays are available in English in *Critical Theory: Selected Essays,* trans. Matthew J. O'Connell and others (1972). See also Martin Jay, "The Frankfurt School and the Genesis of Cultural Theory," in Dick Howard and K. E. Klare, eds., *The Unknown Dimension: European Marxism since Lenin* (1972). See also Martin Jay's *The Dialectical Imagination: A History of the Frankfurt School and the Institute of Social Research, 1923–1950* (1972).

THE SOCIAL FUNCTION OF PHILOSOPHY

When the words physics, chemistry, medicine, or history are mentioned in a conversation, the participants usually have something very definite in mind. Should any difference of opinion arise, we could consult an encyclopedia or accepted textbook or turn to one or more outstanding specialists in the field in question. The definition of any one of these sciences derives immediately from its place in present-day society. Though these sciences may make the greatest advances in the future, though it is even conceivable that several of them, physics and chemistry for example, may some day be merged, no one is really interested in defining these concepts in any other way than by reference to the scientific activities now being carried on under such headings.

It is different with philosophy. Suppose we ask a professor of philosophy what philosophy is. If we are lucky and happen to find a specialist who is not averse to definitions in general, he will give us one. If we then adopt this definition, we should probably soon discover that it is by no means the universally accepted meaning of the word. We might then appeal to other authorities, and pore over textbooks, modern and old. The confusion would only increase. Many thinkers, accepting Plato and Kant as their authorities, regard philosophy as an exact science in its own right, with its own field and subject matter. In our epoch this conception is chiefly represented by the late Edmund Husserl.[1] Other thinkers, like Ernst Mach,[2] conceive philosophy as the critical elaboration and synthesis of the special sciences into a unified whole. Bertrand Russell, too, holds that the task of philosophy is "that of logical analysis, followed by logical synthesis."[3] He thus fully agrees with L. T. Hobhouse, who declares that "Philosophy . . . has a synthesis of the sciences as its goal."[4] This conception goes back to Auguste Comte and Herbert Spencer,[5] for whom philosophy constituted the total system of human knowledge. Philosophy, therefore, is an independent science for some, a subsidiary or auxiliary discipline for others.

If most writers of philosophical works agree on the scientific character of philosophy, a few, but by no means the worst, have emphatically denied it. For the German poet Schiller[6] whose philosophical essays have had an influence perhaps even more

THE SOCIAL FUNCTION OF PHILOSOPHY (1939) is reprinted from *Critical Theory: Selected Essays* by Max Horkheimer, trans. Matthew J. O'Connell and others (New York: Seabury Press, 1972). The essay appeared originally in English and is reprinted with the permission of Continuum Publication Corporation, copyright 1972.

[1] Edmund Husserl (1859–1938), German philosopher, founder of modern phenomenology. See *Husserl.* [Eds.]

[2] Ernst Mach (1838–1916), Austrian physicist and philosopher, a strict empiricist who argued for the elimination of all metaphysical or religious elements in science. [Eds.]

[3] Bertrand Russell, "Logical Atomism," in: *Contemporary British Philosophy,* ed. by J. H. Muirhead, I (1925), p. 379. [Au.]

[4] L. T. Hobhouse, "The Philosophy of Development," in: *Contemporary British Philosophy,* ed. by J. H. Muirhead, I (1925), p. 152. [Au.]

[5] Auguste Comte (1798–1857), French philosopher, founder of the philosophical movement known as positivism; Herbert Spencer (1820–1903), English philosopher. [Eds.]

[6] Friedrich von Schiller (1759–1805), German poet, dramatist, and historian. See *CTSP,* 418–31. [Eds.]

profound than his dramas, the purpose of philosophy was to bring aesthetic order into our thoughts and actions. Beauty was the criterion of its results. Other poets, like Hölderlin and Novalis,[7] held a similar position, and even pure philosophers, Schelling for instance, came very close to it in some of their formulations. Henri Bergson,[8] at any rate, insists that philosophy is closely related to art, and is not a science.

As if the different views on the general character of philosophy were not enough, we also find the most diverse notions about its content and its methods. There are still some thinkers who hold that philosophy is concerned exclusively with the highest concepts and laws of Being, and ultimately with the cognition of God. This is true of the Aristotelian and Neo-Thomist schools. Then there is the related view that philosophy deals with the so-called *a priori.* Alexander describes philosophy as "the experiential or empirical study of the non-empirical or *a priori,* and of such questions as arise out of the relation of the empirical to the *a priori*" (space, time and deity).[9] Others, who derive from the English sensualists and the German school of Fries and Apelt,[10] conceive of it as the science of inner experience. According to logical empiricists like Carnap[11] philosophy is concerned essentially with scientific language; according to the school of Windelband and Rickert[12] (another school with many American followers), it deals with universal values, above all with truth, beauty, goodness, and holiness.

Finally, everyone knows that there is no agreement in method. The Neo-Kantians all believe that the procedure of philosophy must consist in the analysis of concepts and their reduction to the ultimate elements of cognition. Bergson and Max Scheler[13] consider intuition ("*Wesensschau, Wesenserschauung*") to be the decisive philosophical act. The phenomenological method of Husserl and Heidegger[14] is flatly opposed to the empirio-criticism of Mach and Avenarius.[15] The logistic of Bertrand Russell, Whitehead,[16] and their followers, is the avowed enemy of the dialectic of Hegel. The kind of philosophizing one prefers depends, according to William James,[17] on one's character and experience.

These definitions have been mentioned in order to indicate that the situation in philosophy is not the same as in other intellectual pursuits. No matter how many points of dispute there may be in those fields, at least the general line of their intellectual work is universally recognized. The prominent representatives more or less agree on subject matter and methods. In philosophy, however, refutation of one school by another usually involves complete rejection, the negation of the substance of its work as fundamentally false. This attitude is not shared by all schools, of course. A dialectical philosophy, for example, in keeping with its principles, will tend to extract the relative truths of the individual points of view and introduce them in its own comprehensive theory. Other philosophical doctrines, such as modern positivism, have less elastic principles, and they simply exclude from the realm of knowledge a very large part of the philosophical literature, especially the great systems of the past. In short, it cannot be taken for granted that anyone who uses the term "philosophy" shares with his audience more than a few very vague conceptions.

The individual sciences apply themselves to problems which must be treated because they arise out of the life process of present-day society. Both the individual problems and their allotment to specific disciplines derive, in the last analysis, from the

[7] Friedrich Hölderlin (1770–1843), German poet; Novalis, pseudonym of Friedrich von Hardenberg (1772–1801), German poet and writer. [Eds.]

[8] Henri Bergson (1859–1941), French philosopher, winner of Nobel Prize in literature for 1927; see T. E. Hulme, "Bergson's Theory of Art" in *CTSP,* pp. 774–81. [Eds.]

[9] S[amuel] Alexander, *Space, Time and Deity,* vol. I (1920), p. 4. [Au.] See *CTSP,* pp. 860–69. [Eds.]

[10] Jacob Frederick Fries (1773–1843), German philosopher; Ernst Friedrich Apelt (1812–59), German philosopher. [Eds.]

[11] Rudolf Carnap (1891–1970), German-American philosopher, member of the Vienna Circle, a principal figure in the development of Logical Positivism. [Eds.]

[12] Wilhelm Windelband (1848–1915), German philosopher and historian of philosophy; Heinrich Rickert (1863–1936), German philosopher and historiographer. [Eds.]

[13] Max Scheler (1874–1928), German moral philosopher, influenced by Husserl. [Eds.]

[14] See *Edmund Husserl* and *Martin Heidegger.* [Eds.]

[15] Richard Heinrich Ludwig Avenarius (1843–96), German philosopher. [Eds.]

[16] Bertrand Russell (1872–1970), British philosopher, mathematician; Alfred North Whitehead (1861–1947), British philosopher and mathematician. The principal work referred to here is Russell and Whitehead's *Principia Mathematica* (1910–13). [Eds.]

[17] William James (1842–1910), American philosopher and psychologist. [Eds.]

needs of mankind in its past and present forms of organization. This does not mean that every single scientific investigation satisfies some urgent need. Many scientific undertakings produced results that mankind could easily do without. Science is no exception to that misapplication of energy which we observe in every sphere of cultural life. The development of branches of science which have only a dubious practical value for the immediate present is, however, part of that expenditure of human labor which is one of the necessary conditions of scientific and technological progress. We should remember that certain branches of mathematics, which appeared to be mere playthings at first, later turned out to be extraordinarily useful. Thus, though there are scientific undertakings which can lead to no immediate use, all of them have some potential applicability within the given social reality, remote and vague as it may be. By its very nature, the work of the scientist is capable of enriching life in its present form. His fields of activity are therefore largely marked out for him, and the attempts to alter the boundaries between the several domains of science, to develop new disciplines, as well as continuously to differentiate and integrate them, are always guided by social need, whether consciously or not. This need is also operative, though indirectly, in the laboratories and lecture halls of the university, not to mention the chemical laboratories and statistical departments of large industrial enterprises and in the hospitals.

Philosophy has no such guide. Naturally, many desires play upon it; it is expected to find solutions for problems which the sciences either do not deal with or treat unsatisfactorily. But the practice of social life offers no criterion for philosophy; philosophy can point to no successes. Insofar as individual philosophers occasionally do offer something in this respect, it is a matter of services which are not specifically philosophical. We have, for example, the mathematical discoveries of Descartes and Leibniz, the psychological researches of Hume,[18] the physical theories of Ernst Mach, and so forth. The opponents of philosophy also say that insofar as it has value, it is not philosophy but positive science. Everything else in philosophical systems is mere talk, they claim, occasionally stimulating, but usually boring and always useless. Philosophers, on the other hand, show a certain obstinate disregard for the verdict of the outside world. Ever since the trial of Socrates, it has been clear that they have a strained relationship with reality as it is, and especially with the community in which they live. The tension sometimes takes the form of open persecution; at other times merely failure to understand their language. They must live in hiding, physically or intellectually. Scientists, too, have come into conflict with the societies of their time. But here we must resume the distinction between the philosophical and the scientific elements of which we have already spoken, and reverse the picture, because the reasons for the persecution usually lay in the philosophical views of these thinkers, not in their scientific theories. Galileo's bitter persecutors among the Jesuits admitted that he would have been free to publish his heliocentric theory if he had placed it in the proper philosophical and theological context. Albertus Magnus[19] himself discussed the heliocentric theory in his *Summa,* and he was never attacked for it. Furthermore, the conflict between scientists and society, at least in modern times, is not connected with fundamentals but only with individual doctrines, not tolerated by this or that authority in one country at one time, tolerated and even celebrated in some other country at the same time or soon afterwards.

The opposition of philosophy to reality arises from its principles. Philosophy insists that the actions and aims of man must not be the product of blind necessity. Neither the concepts of science nor the form of social life, neither the prevailing way of thinking nor the prevailing mores should be accepted by custom and practiced uncritically. Philosophy has set itself against mere tradition and resignation in the decisive problems of existence, and it has shouldered the unpleasant task of throwing the light of consciousness even upon those human relations and modes of reaction which have become so deeply rooted that they seem natural, immutable, and eternal. One could reply that the sciences, too,

[18] René Descartes (1596–1650), French philosopher and mathematician, developed the field of analytical geometry; Gottfried Wilhelm Leibniz (1646–1716), German philosopher and mathematician, made major contributions to the development of calculus; David Hume (1711–76), Scottish philosopher and historian. [Eds.]

[19] Albertus Magnus (also Saint Albert the Great) (ca. 1193–1280), scholastic philosopher, sought to reconcile apparent contradictions of Aristotelian and Christian thought. [Eds.]

and particularly their inventions and technological changes, save mankind from the deep-worn grooves of habit. When we compare present-day life with that thirty, fifty, or a hundred years ago, we cannot truthfully accept the notion that the sciences have not disturbed human habits and customs. Not only industry and transportation, but even art, has been rationalized. A single illustration will suffice. In former years a playwright would work out his individual conception of human problems in the seclusion of his personal life. When his work finally reached the public, he thereby exposed his world of ideas to conflict with the existing world and thus contributed to the development of his own mind and of the social mind as well. But today both the production and reception of works of art on the screen and the radio have been completely rationalized. Movies are not prepared in a quiet studio; a whole staff of experts is engaged. And from the outset the goal is not harmony with some idea, but harmony with the current views of the public, with the general taste, carefully examined and calculated beforehand by these experts. If, sometimes, the pattern of an artistic product does not harmonize with public opinion, the fault usually does not lie in an intrinsic disagreement, but in an incorrect estimate by the producers of the reaction of public and press. This much is certain: no sphere of industry, either material or intellectual, is ever in a state of complete stability; customs have no time in which to settle down. The foundations of present-day society are constantly shifting through the intervention of science. There is hardly an activity in business or in government which thought is not constantly engaged in simplifying and improving.

But if we probe a little deeper, we discover that despite all these manifestations, man's way of thinking and acting is not progressing as much as one might be led to believe. On the contrary, the principles now underlying the actions of men, at least in a large portion of the world, are certainly more mechanical than in other periods when they were grounded in living consciousness and conviction. Technological progress has helped to make it even easier to cement old illusions more firmly, and to introduce new ones into the minds of men without interference from reason. It is the very diffusion and industrialization of cultural institutions which cause significant factors of intellectual growth to decline and even disappear, because of shallowness of content, dullness of the intellectual organs, and elimination of some of man's individualistic creative powers. In recent decades, this dual aspect of the triumphal procession of science and technology has been repeatedly noted by both romantic and progressive thinkers. The French writer Paul Valéry[20] has recently formulated the situation with particular cogency. He relates how he was taken to the theater as a child to see a fantasy in which a young man was pursued by an evil spirit who used every sort of devilish device to frighten him and make him do his bidding. When he lay in bed at night, the evil spirit surrounded him with hellish fiends and flames; suddenly his room would become an ocean and the bedspread a sail. No sooner did one ghost disappear, than a new one arrived. After a while these horrors ceased to affect the little boy, and finally, when a new one began, he exclaimed: Voilà les bêtises qui recommencent! (Here comes some more of that nonsense!) Some day, Valéry concludes, mankind might react in the same way to the discoveries of science and the marvels of technology.

Not all philosophers, and we least of all, share Paul Valéry's pessimistic conception of scientific progress. But it is true that neither the achievements of science by themselves, nor the advance in industrial method, are immediately identical with the real progress of mankind. It is obvious that man may be materially, emotionally, and intellectually impoverished at decisive points despite the progress of science and industry. Science and technology are only elements in an existing social totality, and it is quite possible that, despite all their achievements, other factors, even the totality itself, could be moving backwards, that man could become increasingly stunted and unhappy, that the individual could be ruined and nations headed toward disaster. We are fortunate that we live in a country which has done away with national boundaries and war situations over half a continent. But in Europe, while the means of communication became more rapid and complete, while distances decreased, while the habits of life became more and more alike, tariff walls grew higher and higher, nations feverishly piled up armaments, and both foreign relations and internal political conditions approached and eventually arrived at a state of war. This antagonistic situation asserts itself in other parts of the world, too, and

[20] Paul Valéry (1871–1945), French poet and writer. [Eds.]

who knows whether, and for how long, the remainder of the world will be able to protect itself against the consequences in all their intensity. Rationalism in details can readily go with a general irrationalism. Actions of individuals, correctly regarded as reasonable and useful in daily life, may spell waste and even destruction for society. That is why in periods like ours, we must remember that the best will to create something useful may result in its opposite, simply because it is blind to what lies beyond the limits of its scientific specialty or profession, because it focuses on what is nearest at hand and misconstrues its true nature, for the latter can be revealed only in the larger context. In the New Testament, "They know not what they do" refers only to evildoers. If these words are not to apply to all mankind, thought must not be merely confined within the special sciences and to the practical learning of the professions, thought which investigates the material and intellectual presuppositions that are usually taken for granted, thought which impregnates with human purpose those relationships of daily life that are almost blindly created and maintained.

When it was said that the tension between philosophy and reality is fundamental, unlike the occasional difficulties against which science must struggle in social life, this referred to the tendency embodied in philosophy, not to put an end to thought, and to exercise particular control over all those factors of life which are generally held to be fixed, unconquerable forces or eternal laws. This was precisely the issue in the trial of Socrates. Against the demand for submission to the customs protected by the gods and unquestioning adaptation to the traditional forms of life, Socrates asserted the principle that man should know what he does, and shape his own destiny. His god dwells within him, that is to say, in his own reason and will. Today the conflicts in philosophy no longer appear as struggles over gods, but the situation of the world is no less critical. We should indeed be accepting the present situation if we were to maintain that reason and reality have been reconciled, and that man's autonomy was assured within this society. The original function of philosophy is still very relevant.

It may not be incorrect to suppose that these are the reasons why discussions within philosophy, and even discussions about the concept of philosophy, are so much more radical and unconciliatory than discussions in the sciences. Unlike any other pursuit, philosophy does not have a field of action marked out for it within the given order. This order of life, with its hierarchy of values, is itself a problem for philosophy. While science is still able to refer to given data which point the way for it, philosophy must fall back upon itself, upon its own theoretical activity. The determination of its object falls within its own program much more than is the case with the special sciences, even today when the latter are so deeply engrossed with problems of theory and methodology. Our analysis also gives us an insight into the reason why philosophy has received so much more attention in European life than in America. The geographical expansion and historical development have made it possible for certain social conflicts, which have flared up repeatedly and sharply in Europe because of the existing relationships, to decline in significance in this continent under the strain of opening up the country and of performing the daily tasks. The basic problems of societal life found a temporary practical solution, and so the tensions which give rise to theoretical thought in specific historical situations, never became so important. In this country, theoretical thought usually lags far behind the determination and accumulation of facts. Whether that kind of activity still satisfies the demands which are justly made upon knowledge in this country too, is a problem which we do not have the time to discuss now.

It is true that the definitions of many modern authors, some of which have already been cited, hardly reveal that character of philosophy which distinguishes it from all the special sciences. Many philosophers throw envious glances at their colleagues in other faculties who are much better off because they have a well-marked field of work whose fruitfulness for society cannot be questioned. These authors struggle to "sell" philosophy as a particular kind of science, or at least, to prove that it is very useful for the special sciences. Presented in this way, philosophy is no longer the critic, but the servant of science and the social forms in general. Such an attitude is a confession that thought which transcends the prevailing forms of scientific activity, and thus transcends the horizon of contemporary society, is impossible. Thought should rather be content to accept the tasks set for it by the ever renewed needs of government and industry, and to deal with these tasks in the form in which they are received. The extent to which the form and content of these tasks are the correct ones for mankind at the present historical moment, the question whether the social organization in which they arise is still suitable for mankind—such problems are neither scientific nor philosophical in the eyes of those humble philosophers; they are matters for personal decision, for subjective evaluation by the individual who has surrendered to his taste and temper. The only philosophical position which can be recognized in such a conception is the negative doctrine that there really is no philosophy, that systematic thought must retire at the decisive moments of life, in short, philosophical skepticism and nihilism.

Before proceeding further, it is necessary to distinguish the conception of the social function of philosophy presented here from another view, best represented in several branches of modern sociology, which identifies philosophy with one general social function, namely ideology.[21] This view maintains that philosophical thought, or, more correctly, thought as such, is merely the expression of a specific social situation. Every social group—the German Junkers,[22] for example—develops a conceptual apparatus, certain methods of thought and a specific style of thought adapted to its social position. For centuries the life of the Junkers has been associated with a specific order of succession; their relationship to the princely dynasty upon which they were dependent and to their own servants had patriarchal features. Consequently, they tended to base their whole thought on the forms of the organic, the ordered succession of generations, on biological growth. Everything appeared under the aspect of the organism and natural ties. Liberal bourgeoisie, on the other hand, whose happiness and unhappiness depend upon business success, whose experience has taught them that everything must be reduced to the common denominator of money, have developed a more abstract, more mechanistic way of thinking. Not hierarchical but leveling tendencies are characteristic of their intellectual style, of their philosophy. The same approach applies to other groups, past and present. With the philosophy of Descartes, for example, we must ask whether his notions corresponded to the aristocratic and Jesuit groups of the court, or to the noblesse de robe, or to the lower bourgeoisie and the masses. Every pattern of thought, every philosophical or other cultural work, belongs to a specific social group, with which it originates and with whose existence it is bound up. Every pattern of thought is "ideology."

There can be no doubt that there is some truth in this attitude. Many ideas prevalent today are revealed to be mere illusions when we consider them from the point of view of their social basis. But it is not enough merely to correlate these ideas with some one social group, as that sociological school does. We must penetrate deeper and develop them out of the decisive historical process from which the social groups themselves are to be explained. Let us take an example. In Descartes' philosophy, mechanistic thinking, particularly mathematics, plays an important part. We can even say that this whole philosophy is the universalization of mathematical thought. Of course, we can now try to find some group in society whose character is correlative with this viewpoint, and we shall probably find some such definite group in the society of Descartes' time. But a more complicated, yet more adequate, approach is to study the productive system of those days and to show how a member of the rising middle class, by force of his very activity in commerce and manufacture, was induced to make precise calculations if he wished to preserve and increase his power in the newly developed competitive market, and the same holds true of his agents, so to speak, in science and technology whose inventions and other scientific work played so large a part in the constant struggle between individuals, cities, and nations in the modern era. For all these subjects, the given approach to the world was its consideration in mathematical terms. Because this class, through the development of society, became characteristic of the whole of society, that approach was widely diffused far beyond the middle class itself. Sociology is not sufficient. We must have a comprehensive theory of history if we wish to avoid serious errors. Otherwise we run the risk of relating important philosophical theories to accidental, or at any rate, not decisive groups, and of misconstruing the significance of the specific group in the whole of society, and, therefore, of misconstruing the culture pattern in question. But this is not the chief objec-

[21] Cf. Karl Mannheim, *Ideology and Utopia* (London, 1937). [Eds.]

[22] German Junkers, generally a term of reproach, derived from "jung" and "Herr," or "young lord," applied to the Prussian nobility. [Eds.]

tion. The stereotyped application of the concept of ideology to every pattern of thought is, in the last analysis, based on the notion that there is no philosophical truth, in fact no truth at all for humanity, and that all thought is *seinsgebunden* (situationally determined). In its methods and results it belongs only to a specific stratum of mankind and is valid only for this stratum. The attitude to be taken to philosophical ideas does not comprise objective testing and practical application, but a more or less complicated correlation to a social group. And the claims of philosophy are thus satisfied. We easily recognize that this tendency, the final consequence of which is the resolution of philosophy into a special science, into sociology, merely repeats the skeptical view which we have already criticized. It is not calculated to explain the social function of philosophy, but rather to perform one itself, namely, to discourage thought from its practical tendency of pointing to the future.

The real social function of philosophy lies in its criticism of what is prevalent. That does not mean superficial fault-finding with individual ideas or conditions, as though a philosopher were a crank. Nor does it mean that the philosopher complains about this or that isolated condition and suggests remedies. The chief aim of such criticism is to prevent mankind from losing itself in those ideas and activities which the existing organization of society instills into its members. Man must be made to see the relationship between his activities and what is achieved thereby, between his particular existence and the general life of society, between his everyday projects and the great ideas which he acknowledges. Philosophy exposes the contradiction in which man is entangled in so far as he must attach himself to isolated ideas and concepts in everyday life. My point can easily be seen from the following. The aim of Western philosophy in its first complete form, in Plato, was to cancel and negate onesidedness in a more comprehensive system of thought, in a system more flexible and better adapted to reality. In the course of some of the dialogues, the teacher demonstrates how his interlocutor is inevitably involved in contradictions if he maintains his position too onesidedly. The teacher shows that it is necessary to advance from this one idea to another, for each idea receives its proper meaning only within the whole system of ideas. Consider, for example, the discussion of the nature of courage in the *Laches*. When the interlocutor clings to his definition that courage means not running away from the battlefield, he is made to realize that in certain situations, such behavior would not be a virtue but foolhardiness, as when the whole army is retreating and a single individual attempts to win the battle all by himself. The same applies to the idea of *Sophrosyne*, inadequately translated as temperance or moderation. *Sophrosyne* is certainly a virtue, but it becomes dubious if it is made the sole end of action and is not grounded in knowledge of all the other virtues. *Sophrosyne* is conceivable only as a moment of correct conduct within the whole. Nor is the case less true for justice. Good will, the will to be just, is a beautiful thing. But this subjective striving is not enough. The title of justice does not accrue to actions which were good in intention but failed in execution. This applies to private life as well as to State activity. Every measure, regardless of the good intentions of its author, may become harmful unless it is based on comprehensive knowledge and is appropriate for the situation. *Summum jus*, says Hegel in a similar context, may become *summa injuria*. We may recall the comparison drawn in the *Gorgias*. The trades of the baker, the cook, and the tailor are in themselves very useful. But they may lead to injury unless hygienic considerations determine their place in the lives of the individual and of mankind. Harbors, shipyards, fortifications, and taxes are good in the same sense. But if the happiness of the community is forgotten, these factors of security and prosperity become instruments of destruction.

Thus, in Europe, in the last decades before the outbreak of the present war, we find the chaotic growth of individual elements of social life: giant economic enterprises, crushing taxes, an enormous increase in armies and armaments, coercive discipline, one-sided cultivation of the natural sciences, and so on. Instead of rational organization of domestic and international relations, there was the rapid spread of certain portions of civilization at the expense of the whole. One stood against the other, and mankind as a whole was destroyed thereby. Plato's demand that the state should be ruled by philosophers does not mean that these rulers should be selected from among the authors of textbooks on logic. In business life, the *Fachgeist*, the spirit of the specialist, knows only profit, in military life power, and even in science only success in a special discipline. When this spirit is left unchecked, it typifies an anarchic state of society. For Plato, philosophy meant the tendency to bring and maintain the various energies and branches of knowledge in a unity which would transform these partially destructive elements into productive ones in the fullest sense. This is the meaning of his demand that the philosophers should rule. It means lack of faith in the prevailing popular thought. Unlike the latter, reason never loses itself in a single idea, though that idea might be the correct one at any given moment. Reason exists in the whole system of ideas, in the progression from one idea to another, so that every idea is understood and applied in its true meaning, that is to say, in its meaning within the whole of knowledge. Only such thought is rational thought.

This dialectical conception has been applied to the concrete problems of life by the great philosophers; indeed, the rational organization of human existence is the real goal of their philosophies. Dialectical clarification and refinement of the conceptual world which we meet in daily and scientific life, education of the individual for right thinking and acting, has as its goal the realization of the good, and, during the flourishing periods of philosophy at least, that meant the rational organization of human society. Though Aristotle, in his *Metaphysics,* regards the self-contemplation of the mind, theoretical activity, as the greatest happiness, he expressly states that this happiness is possible only on a specific material basis, that is, under certain social and economic conditions. Plato and Aristotle did not believe with Antisthenes[23] and the Cynics that reason could forever continue to develop in people who literally led a dog's life, nor that wisdom could go hand in hand with misery. An equitable state of affairs was for them the necessary condition for the unfolding of man's intellectual powers, and this idea lies at the basis of all of Western humanism.

Anyone who studies modern philosophy, not merely in the standard compendia, but through his own historical researches, will perceive the social problem to be a very decisive motive. I need only mention Hobbes and Spinoza.[24] The *Tractatus Theologico-Politicus* of Spinoza was the only major work which he published during his lifetime. With other thinkers, Leibniz and Kant for instance, a more penetrating analysis reveals the existence of social and historical categories in the foundations of the most abstract chapters of their works, their metaphysical and transcendental doctrines. Without those categories, it is impossible to understand or solve their problems. A basic analysis of the content of purely theoretical philosophical doctrines is therefore one of the most interesting tasks of modern research in the history of philosophy. But this task has little in common with the superficial correlation to which reference has already been made. The historian of art or literature has corresponding tasks.

Despite the important part played in philosophy by the examination of social problems, expressed or unexpressed, conscious or unconscious, let us again emphasize that the social function of philosophy is not to be found just there, but rather in the development of critical and dialectical thought. Philosophy is the methodical and steadfast attempt to bring reason into the world. This precarious and controversial position results from this. Philosophy is inconvenient, obstinate, and with all that, of no immediate use—in fact it is a source of annoyance. Philosophy lacks criteria and compelling proofs. Investigation of facts is strenuous, too, but one at least knows what to go by. Man is naturally quite reluctant to occupy himself with the confusion and entanglements of his private and public life: he feels insecure and on dangerous ground. In our present division of labor, those problems are assigned to the philosopher or theologian. Or, man consoles himself with the thought that the discords are merely transient and that fundamentally everything is all right. In the past century of European history, it has been shown conclusively that, despite a semblance of security, man has not been able to arrange his life in accordance with his conceptions of humanity. There is a gulf between the ideas by which men judge themselves and the world on the one hand, and the social reality which they reproduce through their actions on the other hand. Because of this circumstance, all their conceptions and judgments are two-sided and falsified. Now man sees himself head-

[23] Antisthenes (ca. 444–ca. 371 B.C.), Greek philosopher, argued that virtue should be pursued for its own sake, and to that end one should renounce the external world and live in poverty. [Eds.]

[24] Baruch (or Benedict) Spinoza (1632–77), Dutch philosopher, whose *Ethics* set forth the now classic argument for pantheism. His *Tractatus Theologico-Politicus* was based on work by René Descartes. [Eds.]

ing for disaster or already engulfed in it, and in many countries he is so paralyzed by approaching barbarism that he is almost completely unable to react and protect himself. He is the rabbit before the hungry stoat. There are times perhaps when one can get along without theory, but his deficiency lowers man and renders him helpless against force. The fact that theory may rise into the rarefied atmosphere of a hollow and bloodless idealism or sink into tiresome and empty phrasemongering, does not mean that these forms are its true forms. As far as tedium and banality are concerned, philosophy often finds its match in the so-called investigation of facts. Today, at any event, the whole historical dynamic has placed philosophy in the center of social actuality, and social actuality in the center of philosophy.

Attention should be drawn to a particularly important change which has taken place along these lines since classical antiquity. Plato held that Eros enables the sage to know the ideas. He linked knowledge with a moral or psychological state, Eros, which in principle may exist at every historical moment. For this reason, his proposed State appeared to him as an eternal ideal of reason, not bound up with any historical condition. The dialogue on the *Laws,* then, was a compromise, accepted as a preliminary step which did not affect the eternal ideal. Plato's State is an Utopia, like those projected at the beginning of the modern era and even in our own days. But Utopia is no longer the proper philosophic form for dealing with the problem of society. It has been recognized that the contradictions in thought cannot be resolved by purely theoretical reflection. That requires an historical development beyond which we cannot leap in thought. Knowledge is bound up not only with psychological and moral conditions, but also with social conditions. The enunciation and description of perfect political and social forms out of pure ideas is neither meaningful nor adequate.

Utopia as the crown of philosophical systems is therefore replaced by a scientific description of concrete relationships and tendencies, which can lead to an improvement of human life. This change has the most far-reaching consequences for the structure and meaning of philosophical theory. Modern philosophy shares with the ancients their high opinion of the potentialities of the human race, their optimism over man's potential achievements. The proposition that man is by nature incapable of living a good life or of achieving the highest levels of social organization, has been rejected by the greatest thinkers. Let us recall Kant's famous remarks about Plato's Utopia: "The Platonic Republic has been supposed to be a striking example of purely imaginary perfection. It has become a byword, as something that could exist in the brain of an idle thinker only, and Bruckner thinks it ridiculous that Plato could have said that no prince could ever govern well, unless he participated in the ideas. We should do better, however, to follow up this thought and endeavor (where that excellent philosopher leaves us without his guidance) to place it in a clearer light by our own efforts, rather than to throw it aside as useless, under the miserable and very dangerous pretext of its impracticability. For nothing can be more mischievous and more unworthy a philosopher than the vulgar appeal to what is called adverse experience, which possibly might never have existed, if at the proper time institutions had been framed according to those ideas, and not according to crude concepts, which, because they were derived from experience only, have marred all good intentions."[25]

Since Plato, philosophy has never deserted the true idealism that it is possible to introduce reason among individuals and among nations. It has only discarded the *false* idealism that it is sufficient to set up the picture of perfection with no regard for the way in which it is to be attained. In modern times, loyalty to the highest ideas has been linked, in a world opposed to them, with the sober desire to know how these ideas can be realized on earth.

Before concluding, let us return once more to a misunderstanding which has already been mentioned. In philosophy, unlike business and politics, criticism does not mean the condemnation of a thing, grumbling about some measure or other, or mere negation and repudiation. Under certain conditions, criticism may actually take this destructive turn; there are examples in the Hellenistic age. By criticism, we mean that intellectual, and eventually practical, effort which is not satisfied to accept the prevailing ideas, actions, and social conditions unthinkingly and from mere habit; effort which aims to coordinate the individual sides of social life with

[25] I. Kant, *Critique of Pure Reason,* trans. by F. Max Müller (New York, 1920), pp. 257–258. [Au.]

each other and with the general ideas and aims of the epoch, to deduce them genetically, to distinguish the appearance from the essence, to examine the foundations of things, in short, really to know them. Hegel, the philosopher to whom we are most indebted in many respects, was so far removed from any querulous repudiation of specific conditions, that the King of Prussia called him to Berlin to inculcate the students with the proper loyalty and to immunize them against political opposition. Hegel did his best in that direction, and declared the Prussian state to be the embodiment of the divine Idea on earth. But thought is a peculiar factor. To justify the Prussian state, Hegel had to teach man to overcome the onesidedness and limitations of ordinary human understanding and to see the interrelationship between all conceptual and real relations. Further, he had to teach man to construe human history in its complex and contradictory structure, to search out the ideas of freedom and justice in the lives of nations, to know how nations perish when their principle proves inadequate and the time is ripe for new social forms. The fact that Hegel thus had to train his students in theoretical thought, had highly equivocal consequences for the Prussian state. In the long run, Hegel's work did more serious harm to that reactionary institution than all the use the latter could derive from his formal glorification. Reason is a poor ally of reaction. A little less than ten years after Hegel's death (his chair remained unoccupied that long), the King appointed a successor to fight the "dragon's teeth of Hegelian pantheism," and the "arrogance and fanaticism of his school."

We cannot say that, in the history of philosophy, the thinkers who had the most progressive effect were those who found most to criticize or who were always on hand with so-called practical programs. Things are not that simple. A philosophical doctrine has many sides, and each side may have the most diverse historical effects. Only in exceptional historical periods, such as the French Enlightenment, does philosophy itself become politics. In that period, the word philosophy did not call to mind logic and epistemology so much as attacks on the church hierarchy and on an inhuman judicial system. The removal of certain preconceptions was virtually equivalent to opening the gates of the new world. Tradition and faith were two of the most powerful bulwarks of the old regime, and the philosophical attacks constituted an immediate historical action. Today, however, it is not a matter of eliminating a creed, for in the totalitarian states, where the noisiest appeal is made to heroism and a lofty *Weltanschauung*, neither faith nor *Weltanschauung* rule, but only dull indifference and the apathy of the individual towards destiny and to what comes from above. Today our task is rather to ensure that, in the future, the capacity for theory and for action which derives from theory will never again disappear, even in some coming period of peace when the daily routine may tend to allow the whole problem to be forgotten once more. Our task is continually to struggle, lest mankind become completely disheartened by the frightful happenings of the present, lest man's belief in a worthy, peaceful and happy direction of society perish from the earth.

Isaiah Berlin

b. 1909

As a historian, philosopher, and social-political theorist, Sir Isaiah Berlin has been most widely recognized for individual essays (such as "The Hedgehog and the Fox," elaborated from the aphorism attributed to Archilochus, "The fox knows many things, but the hedgehog knows one big thing") that exemplify a distinctive mode of critical thinking. Berlin's essays are typically based on particularly apposite and telling metaphors, figures, or examples that not only facilitate his own explanation of a topic or problem but provide paradigms for other, similar analyses.

The essay here displays Berlin's characteristic lucidity and penetration, but it is included for other reasons. As attention in many fields shifted to language early in this century, a number of vexing problems quickly appeared: how does one connect "reference" and "meaning" (see, for example, *Frege*); how can a "fact" be connected to a "proposition" (cf. *Wittgenstein*); what does a "sign" "signify," or how is it connected to "reality" (cf. *Saussure, Benveniste, Peirce,* and *Whorf*)? All of these issues took an unusually controversial focus in the problem of verification. When Wittgenstein proposed in the *Tractatus* that language provided a picture of the logical structure of a fact, it was assumed that either directly or indirectly one could ascertain the adequacy of the representation. Most notably, philosophers of the Vienna Circle (as well as other positivists) argued that the "meaning" of a proposition was functionally identical with the method of its verification and, in moving to expunge metaphysical issues from the language of philosophy, insisted that for any proposition to be meaningful, it had to be verifiable by some means.

This position led to a number of philosophical embarrassments. If, for example, the language of natural science is reconstructed into a deductive logical formalism (derived from Frege, Russell and Whitehead, and Wittgenstein), it then appears that "observation statements" can be isolated and treated as confirmation or verification of deductive predictions, derived from the logically reconstructed scientific theory. When this doctrine was presented in A. J. Ayer's *Language, Truth, and Logic* (1936), reviewers were quick to point out that a peculiarity of the logical formalism employed to represent implication rendered the requirement of verification radically ambiguous: any statement, it appears, could be interpreted to verify any prediction. (For a more technical treatment of this dilemma, see Harold Brown, *Perception, Theory, and Commitment: The New Philosophy of Science* [Chicago: University of Chicago Press, 1977], pp. 25–33.)

Berlin's essay provides both an elegant review of this problem and an exemplary clarification of different contexts in which the problem may appear by distinguishing between sentences, observing rules of grammar; statements, obeying rules of logic; and propositions, subject to judgments of truth or adequacy.

For other essays on this and related topics, see G. H. Parkinson, ed. *Theory of Meaning* (1965). Other major works by Berlin include *The Hedgehog and the Fox* (1935); *Vico and Herder: Two Studies in the History of Ideas* (1976); and *Russian Thinkers,* ed. Henry Hardy and Aileen Kelly (1978).

VERIFICATION

This paper is an attempt to estimate how far the principle of verification fulfils the purpose for which it is employed by many contemporary empiricist philosophers. The general truth of their doctrines I shall not call into question. The thesis which I shall try to establish is that the principle of verifiability or verification after playing a decisive role in the history of modern philosophy, by clearing up confusions, exposing major errors and indicating what were and what were not questions proper for philosophers to ask, which has enabled it to exercise in our day a function not unlike that which Kant's critical method performed for his generation, cannot, for all that, be accepted as a final criterion of empirical significance, since such acceptance leads to wholly untenable consequences. I shall consequently urge that after due homage has been paid to its therapeutic influence, it needs to be abandoned or else considerably revised, if it is to be prevented from breeding new fallacies in place of those which it eradicates.

I propose to begin by assuming that what the principle sets out to do both can and should be done; and to consider whether it can do this alone and unassisted. I shall seek to show that it cannot, and that to maintain the opposite entails a view of empirical propositions too paradoxical to deserve serious notice.

As is well known, its supporters claim that the function which it fulfils is that of acting as a criterion for determining whether assertions of a certain type mean in fact what they purport to mean. The pressing need for such a criterion arises out of the view on which much modern empiricism rests, according to which all truly significant assertions must be concerned either with the facts of experience, in the sense in which they are the subject matter of the judgements of common sense and of empirical science, or else with the verbal means used to symbolize such facts. The task in question is to find some infallible criterion by which to distinguish assertions of the first, i.e. experiential type, from all other possible modes of employing symbols. I must begin by making clear my use of certain essential terms: by a sentence I propose to mean any arrangement of words which obeys the rules of grammar; by a statement any sentence which obeys the rules of logic; and finally, by a proposition any sentence which conveys to someone that something is or is not the case. And this seems on the whole to accord with common usage. In addition I propose, at any rate in the first section of the argument, to mean by the term experience only what phenomenalists[1] say they mean by it, that is, only such actual or possible data as are provided by observation and introspection. I do not wish to assert that phenomenalism is self-evidently true. On the contrary, no method yet suggested of translating the propositions about material objects into propositions about observation and introspection data seems wholly satisfactory. But for the purpose of my thesis it will be sufficient to confine myself to the latter, i.e. to propositions concerned solely with objects of immediate acquaintance; since if the verification criterion is inadequate in dealing with them it will *a fortiori* fail to apply to the much more complex

VERIFICATION was originally published in *Proceedings of the Aristotelian Society* 39 (1938–39): 225–48. Reprinted by permission of the Aristotelian Society and Sir Isaiah Berlin.

[1] Phenomenalism is the general philosophical view that knowledge is restricted to phenomena or empirical appearance. It may include the view that "appearance" is the whole of reality or that "noumena," presumed to underlie or inform appearances, are not knowable. [Eds.]

case of statements about material objects. If this is true it will tend to show that historical connexion between phenomenalism and 'verificationism' is not a logical one, and that the failure of the latter does not necessarily invalidate the former. This conclusion I should like to believe to be true, since the opposite would prove fatal to the view which seems to me to be true on other grounds, as I shall urge in the last section of this paper, that whereas the phenomenalist analysis of statements of common sense is fundamentally correct, and has not proved convincing more on account of insufficient ingenuity in the formulation of specific analyses, or of the vagueness of the analysandum, than because of some fatal defect in the method itself, the principle of verification, in spite of its undoubted efficacy in the past in detecting and destroying unreal puzzles, has now begun to yield diminishing returns, and even to create new spurious problems of its own. This, I shall argue, is due to the fact that it is not in principle capable of being applied to the whole field of empirical belief and knowledge, but only to a limited portion of it—a fact which is brought out particularly clearly by the examination of that version of it, sometimes called operationalism, according to which the different logical or epistemological categories to which a given proposition may belong are determined by the differences in the kind of tests normally employed to discover its truth or falsity.

The essence of the principle of verification will appear clearly if one considers its progressive modification in the face of difficulties. The bare assertion that all significant statements were concerned either with facts about experience or with the symbolic means of expressing them was too vague and excluded too little. Metaphysicians and theologians could claim that they, too, reported facts of experience, although facts of a very different order from those which were of interest to empirical scientists, arrived at by non-empirical processes of cognition, and thus wholly outside the range of any evidence drawn from the data of observation or introspection. A stricter criterion of significance seemed therefore to be required, at any rate in the case of propositions claiming to describe experience. To supply it (I do not vouch for the historical accuracy of this account) the principle of verification was adopted, a test, which, so it is claimed, made it possible to determine without further ado whether a given collocation of words was or was not significant in the above sense. In its earliest and most uncompromising form it declared that the meaning of a proposition resided in the means of its verification; the questions 'What does the statement *p* mean?' and 'What must one do to discover whether *p* is true?' were logically equivalent—the answer to one was the answer to the other. The most obvious objection to this doctrine, which critics were not slow to urge, was that this formulation involved a glaring hysteron proteron;[2] for before I could think of possible ways of verifying a given statement I first must know what the statement means, otherwise there could be nothing for me to verify. How can I ask whether a group of symbols asserts a truth or a falsehood if I am not certain of what it means, or indeed whether it means anything at all? Surely, therefore, understanding what the sentence means—what proposition it expresses—must in some sense be prior to the investigation of its truth, and cannot be defined in terms of the possibility of such an investigation—on the contrary the latter must be defined in terms of it. But this objection is not as formidable as it looks. A supporter to the theory may reply that what he means by the expression 'to know the means of the verification of *p*' is knowing in what circumstances one would judge the group of symbols '*p*' to convey something which was or was not the case; adding that what one means by saying that one understands a given sentence, or that the sentence has meaning, is precisely this, that one can conceive of a state of affairs such that if it is the case—exists—the sentence in question is the proper, conventionally correct description of it, i.e. the proposition expressed by the sentence is true, while if it is not the case, the proposition expressed is false. To understand a sentence—to certify it as expressing a given proposition—is thus equivalent to knowing how I should set about to look for the state of affairs which, if the state of affairs exists, it correctly describes. To say that a sentence is intelligible, i.e. that it expresses a proposition, without specifying what the proposition is, is to say that I know that I could set about to look for the relevant situation without saying what kind of situation it is. It follows that any sentence such that I can conceive of no experience of which it is the correct descrip-

[2] "Hysteron proteron," the logical fallacy of assuming to be true as a premise that which is to be proved as the conclusion; i.e., begging the question. [Eds.]

tion, is for me meaningless. The limits of what I can conceive are set by experience—that is, I can conceive only whatever is either identical with, or else in some respect similar to the kind of situation which I have already met with or imagined; the possible is a logical alternative of, and conceivable only by reference to, the actual; whatever is wholly different from it is wholly inconceivable. The actual, on this view, consists of the data of observation, sensible and introspective, and what can be inferred from them. The logically possible is conceived only by analogy with it; sentences which purport to refer to something outside this are therefore meaningless. If nevertheless I claim that they mean something to me I am using the term 'meaning' ambiguously or loosely: I may wish to say that they suggest, or are evidence for, a situation, without formally describing it, as tears are evidence of distress without being a statement about it; or else that they evoke an emotion in me, convey or induce a mood or an attitude, stimulate behaviour, or even that no more is occurring than that I am acquainted with the normal use of the individual words in the sentences to which I attribute meaning and that they are grouped in accordance with the rules of grammar and of logic, as in certain types of nonsense verse. This seems prima facie plausible enough, and successfully eliminates whole classes of expressions as being meaningless in the strict sense because they seem to describe no conceivable experience, and can therefore, as Hume[3] recommended, be safely rejected as so much metaphysical rubbish. Whatever survives this drastic test can then be classified exhaustively as being either direct statements about possible experience, that is empirical propositions, or second or higher order statements about the relations of types of such statements to each other, i.e. propositions of logic and other formal sciences. And this was as much as the anti-metaphysical party had ever claimed. It was soon seen however that as it stood this position was wholly untenable.

To begin with the conception of 'means of verification' was far too narrow. If it was interpreted literally it always referred to the present or the immediate future in which alone sensible verification of what I was asserting could take place. This gave all statements about the past, and a great many about the present and future, a meaning which was prima facie very different from that which they seemed to have. Such a sentence for example as 'It was raining half an hour ago' had to be regarded as equivalent to one or more of such statements as 'I am now having a moderately fresh memory image of falling rain', 'My shoes look fairly, but not very, wet', 'I am looking at the chart of a recording barometer and observe an undulating line of a certain shape', 'I expect, if I ask you "Was it raining half an hour ago?" to hear the answer "Yes"' and the like. This is unsatisfactory on two grounds both equally fatal. In the first place by translating all propositions about the past (and about the future) into propositions about experience in the present (which alone I can conclusively verify) it gives two senses of the word 'present'; the sense in which it is distinguishable from 'past' and 'future', i.e. the normal sense, and the sense in which it includes them; the second sense, being contrastable with nothing, adds nothing to any statement in which it occurs; to say in this sense that all significant statements refer only to the present is thus to utter a pointless tautology. Yet the sense in which alone it was relevant to say that all conclusively verifiable propositions were concerned only with the present, was the first, not the second, sense; the sense in which to speak of the present state of something is to distinguish it from past and future states. Moreover, the translation feels wrong. One does not usually mean by the sentence 'It rained yesterday' the present empirical evidence for it, not even the total sum of such evidence. For the relation 'being evidence of' not being that of logical implication, the evidential proposition may be true and the proposition which it claims to establish false; the two therefore cannot be equivalent. What I mean to assert is that it was raining yesterday, not that events which are now occurring make it unreasonable to doubt that it did: the rain I speak of is the rain of yesterday, whatever may or may not be happening today. To verify yesterday's rain conclusively (the verificandum[4] being taken in a phenomenalist sense as a logical construction out of observation data), one has to have lived through yesterday and to have observed whether it rained or not. To do this now is in some sense of the word impossible: yet the meaning of the sentence is not seriously in doubt. It follows that ei-

[3] David Hume (1711–76), Scottish philosopher and historian. [Eds.]

[4] "Verificandum," that which is to be verified. [Eds.]

ther all propositions save those about the immediate present are meaningless: or that meaning cannot depend on conclusive verifiability.

To this the defenders of the theory can answer that in saying that the meaning of *p* resides in (*liegt in*) the means of its verification they did not literally mean to assert any such equivalence: they meant only that '*p* is significant' entails that some means of verifying is possible. The proposition is never equivalent to the sum of evidence for it; but unless one can say that there could be a situation in which an observer could verify it, one cannot say that the sentence has any meaning. Thus '*p* is significant' where *p* is empirical entails and is entailed by '*p* is verifiable', but is not equivalent to any specific group of actual propositions cited as evidence for it. Moreover by verifiability what is meant is verifiability not in practice, but in principle; this last being needed to eliminate not only the objection that some propositions e.g. that there are mountains on the other side of the moon are clearly significant and yet cannot be verified on account of technical difficulties which observers with more luck and skill than ourselves might overcome, but to secure plausible analyses of propositions about the past, which we are prevented from verifying by the accident of our position in time as well as space. We *might* have been born earlier than we were, and lived in countries other than those which in fact we inhabit; I cannot now, do what I will, verify the proposition 'Julius Caesar was bald' by direct inspection, but there is no *logical* reason why I should not have been born in ancient Rome in time to have observed Caesar's head; the reason is causal, unless indeed I define myself as having been born in the twentieth century, in which case some other observer could have carried out this observation. For there is no reason why '*p* is verifiable' should mean '*p* is verifiable by me.'[5] Solipsism even of the so-called methodological variety is a wholly gratuitous assumption. I can conceive of other observers by analogy with my own self, however the notion of a particular self is to be analysed. So much has been pointed out by Berkeley.[6] To verify the proposition that such observers actually exist, and have experiences which are not ours, is of course a very different and much more difficult task. Thus '"*p*" is significant' has now come to mean 'it is conceivable (i.e. there is no logical contradiction in supposing) that someone should observe or should have observed what is correctly described by "*p*"'. In this watered-down form the principle does seem to acquire a much wider sphere of application and attempts at 'silly' analyses can be successfully foiled. But the position is still far from secured.

For all that can be accounted for on this hypothesis are such singular categorical propositions as are conclusively verifiable, at any rate in principle, by a suitably situated observer. This leaves three classes of propositions unaccounted for, and these by far the most commonly used:—(1) Propositions which are not singular:—(2) Propositions which are not categorical:—(3) Propositions which seem to be both singular and categorical, but not to be conclusively verifiable by observation.

(1) General propositions offer the most obvious difficulty. No sentence of the form 'all *s* is *p*', whether taken in extension or intension, where *s* denotes an infinite set (or at any rate does not *explicitly* denote a finite one) can be verified by any finite number of observations. That is to say it is not conclusively verifiable at all. The same applies to all propositions containing 'any' or 'every' as components. The attempt made by Ramsey[7] and those who accept his view to treat them as rules or prescriptions, logical or empirical, and therefore neither true nor false, cannot be defended since, as they are used, they are held to be refutable by a single negative instance, and it is nonsense to say of rules that they have instances or can be refuted. Yet they have clear empirical meaning, particularly when taken in extension, and cannot be left out of account. To meet this difficulty the principle of verification was revised and two types of it distinguished: the first, called verification in the strong sense, was the familiar version. The second, or 'weak' verification was invented to apply to general propositions and to singular-seeming propositions about material objects, in so far as these were thought to entail general propositions about sense data—a view which it has proved far from easy to hold. Two versions of 'weak' verifiability are given by Mr. Ayer:[8] accord-

[5] *vide* 'Unverifiable-by-me', by G. Ryle, *Analysis*, 4, 1. [Au.]

[6] George Berkeley (1685–1753), Irish philosopher and bishop. [Eds.]

[7] Frank P. Ramsey (1903–30), British mathematician and logician. [Eds.]

[8] *Language, Truth and Logic*, p. 26. [Au.]

ing to the first we ask about a given proposition 'Would any observations be relevant to the determination of its truth or falsehood?' If so the proposition is significant. This may well be true, but as it stands the suggested criterion is far too vague to be of use.[9] Relevance is not a precise logical category, and fantastic metaphysical systems may choose to claim that observation data are 'relevant' to their truth. Such claims cannot be rebutted unless some precise meaning is assigned to the concept of relevance, which, because the word is used to convey an essentially vague idea, cannot be done. Thus 'weak' verification, designed to admit only general, and material object, statements, cannot be prevented from opening the gates for any statement, however meaningless, to enter, provided that someone can be found to claim that observation is in some sense relevant to it. As a criterion for distinguishing sense from nonsense relevance plainly does not work: indeed to accept it is in effect to abrogate the principle of verification altogether. Mr. Ayer, conscious of this perhaps, attempts to provide another far more rigorous formulation of 'weak' verification, which at first seems to fit our needs more adequately.[10] He says, 'To make our position clearer we may formulate it in another way . . . we may say that it is the mark of a genuine factual proposition . . . that some experiential [i.e. strongly verifiable] propositions can be deduced from it in conjunction with certain other premises without being deducible from those other premises alone. This criterion seems liberal enough.' Unfortunately it is a good deal too liberal, and does not guarantee us against nonsense any better than the previous test. What it appears to assert is this: given three propositions p, q, r, where r is conclusively verifiable in principle, then p is weakly verified, and therefore significant, if r follows from p and q, and does not follow from q alone. Thus 'all men are mortal' is 'weakly' verifiable, because 'Socrates will die' which does not follow from 'Socrates is a man' by itself, follows from the two in conjunction. It may be noted that 'verifiable' seems here to have lost its sense of 'rendered true' or 'established beyond doubt,' and is equivalent to something much looser, like 'made probable' or 'plausible', itself an obscure and unexamined concept. However, even in this diluted form the principle will not do. For if I say

> This logical problem is bright green,
> I dislike all shades of green,
> Therefore I dislike this problem,

I have uttered a valid syllogism whose major premise has satisfied the definition of weak verifiability as well as the rules of logic and of grammar, yet it is plainly meaningless. One cannot reply to this that it is put out of court by the confusion of categories which it contains, or some such answer, since this entails the direct applicability of a criterion of significance other than 'weak' verification, which makes the latter otiose. No criterion which is powerless in the face of such nonsense as the above is fit to survive. 'Weak' verifiability is a suspicious device in any case, inasmuch as it bears the name without fulfilling the original function of verification proper, and appears to suggest that there is more than one sense of empirical truth. The chief argument in its favour seems to be that unless it is valid, any theory which entails it must be false. Since the contrary instance cited above is fatal to it, this consequence must be accepted. Weak verification has thus failed to provide the needed criterion.

By far the most ingenious attempt to solve the difficulty is that made by Dr. Karl Popper[11] who suggests that a proposition is significant if and only if it can be conclusively falsified by the conclusive verification of a singular proposition which contradicts it—as when a law is refuted by the occurrence of one negative instance. But while this may provide a valid criterion of significance for general propositions about observation data, it throws no light on whether the sense in which they are called true is or is not identical with that in which singular propositions are so called. The implication which one may be tempted to draw from this is that propositions of different logical types are true or false, verifiable and falsifiable, each in its own specific fashion: indeed that this is what is meant by saying that they belong to different categories; that is to say that the logical (and epistemological) character of a proposition is determined by the way in which it is verifi-

[9] On this *vide* 'Meaninglessness', by Dr. A. C. Ewing, *Mind*, N.S., Vol. XLVL, No. 183, particularly pp. 352–3. [Au.]

[10] Ibid., a few lines later. [Au.]

[11] In his book *Logik der Forschung*. [Au.] Revised version published in English as *The Logic of Scientific Discovery* (1959). [Eds.]

able (or falsifiable), the two being alternative ways of saying the same thing about it. This view which if true would solve many difficulties cannot, however, be accepted, as I hope to show in the next section of the argument. It should further be noted that Popper's criterion of falsifiability, while it may deal successfully with general propositions of observation, does not apply equally well to propositions about material objects for whose benefit it was originally introduced. But as we have agreed to accept phenomenalism this is beside the issue, and the criterion may therefore be provisionally accepted.

(2) The second type of proposition not covered by the original 'strong' verifiability criterion consists of those which are not categorical. These are highly relevant to the whole issue, and repay exceptionally close attention. It has too often been assumed by logicians that all hypothetical propositions are general, and all general propositions are hypothetical: 'all *s* is *p*' is equivalent to 'if *s* then *p*' and vice versa. Nothing could be further from the truth. While some hypothetical propositions are general, others are not. The commonest of all propositions which occur in the writings of contemporary positivists, the propositions indispensable to any discussion of meaning or verification, the familiar 'if I look up I shall observe a blue patch', are indubitably hypothetical, but in no sense general. To show this one need only point out that they are conclusively verifiable. Indeed it was because an attempt was made to reduce all other statements to verifiable propositions of this type that absurdities resulted. I verify the proposition mentioned above by looking up and observing a blue patch: if conclusive verification ever occurs, it occurs in this case. It must be noted that I have actually proved more than I have asserted: not merely the hypothetical but a conjunctive proposition 'I shall look up and I shall see a blue patch' has been verified. This is unavoidable from the nature of the case. But although the conjunctive proposition entails the hypothetical, it is not entailed by it, and the two are therefore not equivalent. The conjunction is falsified if (*a*) I do not look up and see a blue patch, (*b*) I do not look up and do not see a blue patch, (*c*) I look up and see no blue patch. The hypothetical proposition is falsified by the occurrence of (*c*) alone. If either (*a*) or (*b*) is the case, the hypothetical proposition is rendered neither true nor false, and may be either. It is essential to note firstly that the relation between the protasis 'I shall look up' and the apodosis[12] 'I shall see a blue patch' is not one of material implication, otherwise the whole would be falsified by denying the protasis. Secondly, that it is not one of strict implication, since the antecedent may be affirmed and the consequent denied without a formal contradiction. Thirdly, that it is not necessarily causal: I may, of course, when I declare that if I look up I shall see a blue patch, say this because I believe that there is causal connexion between the two events, but equally I may not believe this, and decide to bet that this will happen because I am by temperament a passionate gambler, and all the more stimulated if I believe that the weight of inductive evidence is against me; or I may say it because it is an exception which disproves one causal law, without necessarily regarding it as being itself an instance of another law; or I may say it out of sheer contrariness, or any other motive whatever. My *rational* ground for saying what I do would doubtless take the form of a general causal proposition which entails the proposition on whose truth I am betting, but I may choose to behave irrationally, or use the proposition in an *ad absurdum* argument to prove its opposite: the general proposition 'observers in conditions similar to these normally see blue patches if they look up' entails, but is not entailed by, the proposition 'if A looks up he will observe a blue patch': the latter proposition, so far from being equivalent to the former, may be true where the other is false, and, as we said above, may be conclusively verifiable—a condition which the general proposition is logically incapable of attaining. The proposition is therefore both singular and hypothetical, its subject being not a hypothetical variable, but a nameable particular. So far all seems clear. The difficulty arises when the antecedent is not fulfilled: When I assert, for example, that if I look up I shall see a blue patch, and then fail to look up. The proposition appears now to be no longer conclusively verifiable. The opportunity for that has been missed and cannot be recovered. I must now resort to the roundabout method of producing evidence for it, i.e. 'weakly' verifying the general causal proposition of which the proposition to be verified is an instance; nor can the instantial propo-

[12] "Protasis" is the clause expressing the conditional in a conditional sentence, while "apodosis" is the clause expressing the conclusion or result. [Eds.]

sition be made more probable than the general proposition which entails it. But clearly the statement 'if I look up I shall see a blue patch', which now becomes 'if I had looked up I should have seen a blue patch', expresses a proposition which is still true or false in precisely the same sense as before, although the means of its verification have altered; yet clearly the statement cannot have changed in meaning because I did not in fact look up. Yet if it were true that the impossibility of strongly verifying a given proposition entailed that it had a logical character different from propositions which can be strongly verified, the proposition in question would alter in character solely because I did or did not choose to act in a certain fashion. This would mean that the kind of meaning possessed by singular hypothetical sentences or statements would depend on the empirical fact that their protases did or did not actually come true, which is patently absurd. It seems to me to follow that neither the meaning, nor the logical character, of a statement can possibly depend on what steps one would naturally take to ascertain its truth: and in so far as operationalists assert this without qualification, they are mistaken.

At this point someone might reply that although an unfulfilled singular hypothetical statement (or for that matter a hypothetical statement whose protasis is not known to be fulfilled) cannot be verified conclusively in actual fact, it can be so verified in principle. I did not in fact look up and so I cannot know for certain what would have happened if I did; but I might have looked up: or rather it is not self-contradictory to assert that an observer could or did look up; and such an observer, possible in principle, is in a position to verify the proposition conclusively. And so such propositions are, after all, no worse off than categorical statements about the vanished past: they too may not in fact have been verified conclusively; but they could have been so verified; and so are verifiable conclusively in principle. This argument, plausible though it is, is ultimately untenable, for the reason that were I situated favourably for verifying these unverified hypotheses, I should *ipso facto* not have been able to verify some of those which I in fact did: and I could not, in the logical sense of 'could not', have done both. An eternal omnisentient being, which is in all places at all times can, if it chooses, verify all categorical propositions about past, present and future phenomena: but even it cannot verify what did not occur; that which might have occurred had not that happened which in fact did. And if it is omniscient as well as omnisentient, and if there is any sense in which it could be said to know this too, it knows it by means other than sensible verification. A simple example will, I hope, make it clear. Suppose that instead of asserting one singular hypothetical proposition, I assert two such propositions in the form of the premises of a dilemma, such that the protasis of each is incompatible with the protasis of the other. For instance: 'if I remain here I shall have a headache. If I do not remain here I shall be bored'. Each of these propositions may itself be verifiable in principle: the conjunction of both cannot be verified conclusively, even in principle, since it involves me in the logical impossibility of being in a certain state and not being in it at the same time. Of course I can adduce the evidence of various observers for what would happen under these two logically incompatible sets of conditions. But such inductive evidence verifies only 'weakly' (whatever meaning may be attached to that unfortunate phrase). 'If I were now at the North Pole I should feel colder than I do' cannot in principle be strongly verified, since I cannot even in principle be simultaneously here and at the North Pole and compare the different temperatures. It is beside the point to say that this arises only if I am defined as capable of being situated here or at the North Pole but not at both; whereas I might have been a giant with one foot on the North Pole and the other in this room, in which case I might have verified the proposition conclusively. I could myself be defined differently, but the same problem would still arise whatever the defined scope of my powers; a proposition asserting an unfulfilled possibility can always be constructed to contradict whatever is the case, and this can be made the protasis of a second singular hypothetical proposition whose verifiability is incompatible with that of the first. To put it semi-formally: given that for every empirical proposition p at least one contradictory *not-p* is constructable; then for every singular hypothetical proposition of the form 'if p then q' (let us call it pq), a second proposition 'if not p then r' may be constructed (let us call it pr), where r may or may not be equivalent to q. Then it is the case that where pq and pr are propositions describing the possible data of a given observer, the conclusive verification of pq and pr is not compossible, and the truth of either is compatible with the falseness of the other.

And yet each of the two alternatives of the disjunction is in its own right a proposition which in suitable circumstances could be conclusively verified; either may be true and the other false, either probable and the other improbable; their only logical relation is that of unco-verifiability—they cannot both be conclusively verified even in principle. And this plainly cannot alter the meaning which either has in its own right. If this conclusion is correct it follows that the meaning of a proposition need not be affected—let alone determined—by the fact that a given means of verification is or is not logically possible in its case. I have emphasized the case of singular hypotheticals because they seem to bring out particularly clearly that if meaning depends on the relevant type of verifiability, then in order to know what one of these conjunctions of propositions means one requires to know whether both the protases are true. And this is self-evidently false. Yet these are the very propositions which occur in all philosophical analyses of empirical statements, the stuff of which logical constructions are built, the basic propositions to which propositions about the public world are commonly reduced by phenomenalists of all shades and hues.

Perhaps another example will make this even clearer. Supposing that I have a bet with you that all persons seen entering this room will appear to be wearing black shoes. Let the term 'this room' be defined as anything recognized by both of us as being correctly described as this room in virtue of certain observable characteristics, such that if either of us certifies their disappearance from his sense field, the entity described as this room shall be deemed to have ceased to exist. Under what conditions can such a bet be lost or won? We may begin by affirming the truth of the analytic proposition that the room will last either for a finite time or forever. In either case the set of persons observed to enter it, is similarly either finite or infinite. Only if it is the case that the observed set of visitors is finite, that the room visibly comes to the end of its existence, and that each of the persons who are seen to enter appears to wear black shoes, can I win the bet. When, on the other hand, it is the case either that the room lasts for ever, or that the set of persons seen to enter it is without limit, or both these, but at least one person appears to wear shoes of some other colour than black, or no shoes at all, I lose the bet. There are however further possibilities: when, for example, either the room lasts for ever or the number of persons seen to enter is limitless, or both, and every person entering appears to wear black shoes; in that event the bet is undecided since the proposition on whose truth or falsity it turns, has been neither verified nor falsified conclusively. In all possible cases it could in principle be falsified by seeing the arrival of a person not wearing black shoes. But whereas in some cases it could also be verified conclusively, in others it can not. Yet when we arrange the bet neither of us need know whether I am in principle capable of winning or not. Nevertheless the proposition in terms of which the bet is stated is not in the least ambiguous. It is not the case that the words 'all persons . . .' must if the proposition is to have a definite meaning be used to refer *either* to a finite set (in which case conclusive verifiability is possible), *or* an infinite set (in which case it may not be), but not to both. Yet if the meaning of a proposition always depended upon the type of verifiability of which it is capable, the above would be systematically ambiguous: we should have to be regarded as having made two separate bets, one on the behaviour of a finite set, the other on that of an infinite one. Yet we are under the impression that only one bet had been made because we attributed to the proposition beginning with the words 'all persons will . . .' not many senses but one, namely, that in which it is equivalent to 'no one person will not. . . .' And we are right.

Like the previous example this tends to show that if one wishes to understand a sentence which purports to express a proposition when it is asserted by someone, while it is doubtless generally useful to discover under what conditions he would consider its truth as established, to regard its meaning as dependent on what kind of conditions these would be, is to hold a false doctrine of what constitutes meaning. Of course I do not wish to deny that in general I can only discover the difference between sentences of different kinds, e.g. between those used to refer to visual data and those concerning auditory ones, or between propositions concerning persons and propositions about physical objects or about sense data, by observing in what kind of experience verification for them is sought. But it does not follow from this that the kind of verification which a given proposition can in principle obtain, determines the type of meaning which it possesses, and so can act as a principle of logical or epistemological classification, such that the propositions belonging to two different classes defined in this way, cannot for that reason belong to one and the same logical or epistemological category, or be answers to questions of the same logical type. And yet this is the fallacy which seems to me to underlie much that is said by upholders of theories of verification and operationalism. That significance is connected with verifiability I have no wish to deny. But not in this direct fashion, by a kind of one-to-one correspondence.

(3) This brings us to the third type of propositions mentioned above: the apparently categorical, but not conclusively verifiable propositions, as for example those about material objects or other selves. The scope of this paper does not permit an adequate discussion of the merits and defects of phenomenalism; but even if we conceive it to be in principle correct, however inadequate all existing formulations of it, we must allow that among the experiential propositions into which a proposition asserting the existence of a material object must be analysed, there must inevitably be some which describe how the object would appear to an observer, were conditions different from those which in fact obtain; if in other words he were not observing what he is. The proposition 'I am holding a brown pencil in my hand' may or may not entail propositions about past and future actual and hypothetical data presented to me; analysts differ on this point; some hold these to be part of what is meant by 'this pencil', others maintain them to be only evidence for the existence of, but not elements in the analysis of it. And this holds equally of the actual and hypothetical data of observers other than myself. What is common however to all phenomenalist accounts, is that part, at any rate, of what I mean by saying that it is an actual pencil that is now before me, and not the phantom of one, is that the datum which I am now observing belongs to a group of visual, tactual, auditory etc. data some of whose members are the subject matter of hypothetical propositions which describe what I should be experiencing if I were not at this moment in the circumstances in which in fact I am. These propositions are, as was shown above, not coverifiable with the propositions which describe what I am actually observing, and this fact alone is quite sufficient to make propositions about physical objects not conclusively verifiable in principle, whether or not they are held to contain, telescoped with them, various causal and general propositions as, according to some philosophers, they do. Indeed the assertion that general propositions enter into the analysis of prima facie singular propositions about material objects seems to me a good deal more dubious than that these last are not conclusively verifiable; if this seems certain, that is due to the unco-verifiability of some of the singular propositions which are true of the object, not as it is in the past or in the future, but at any given moment. Indeed when anti-phenomenalists maintain that every suggested translation of a given common sense statement into sense datum language, however richly it is equipped with general and hypothetical propositions, fails to render in full the meaning of the original, because material objects possess attributes which necessarily elude observation, when for example, Prof. G. F. Stout[13] in discussing what we mean by the solidity of material objects as conceived by common sense, observes that we think of it not as a permanent possibility but as a permanent impossibility of sensation, what gives such objections apparent plausibility and Prof. Stout's epigram its point, is that there is indeed something which must for logical reasons elude verification by the most exhaustive conceivable series of observations, carried out by any number of possible observers, namely, propositions about what I, or some other given observer, could verify, were we not situated as we are. And this the most thorough going phenomenalism must do justice to, however successfully it may have exorcised the last remaining vestiges of the concept of matter as an invisible, intangible, dimly conceived substratum.

If what I have urged above is true, verification whether 'strong' or 'weak' fails to perform its task even within the framework of pure phenomenalism which must not therefore be so formulated as to entail it as its primary criterion of significance. And to establish this negative conclusion was the main purpose of my thesis. In conclusion I should like to add a few remarks on what this seems to suggest with regard to the question of the proper analysis of physical objects and other selves. If following the view suggested by Prof. C. D. Broad[14] we look upon our concept of a given material object as a finite

[13] *Studies in Philosophy and Psychology*, p. 136. [Au.]

[14] Discussed by Mr. John Wisdom in *Metaphysics and Verification* (I), *Mind* N.S., Vol. XLVII, No. 188, pp. 480–1. [Au.]

complex of sensible characteristics (to be referred to as *m*) selected more or less arbitrarily and unselfconsciously from the wider set of uniformly covariant characteristics *n*, then *m* which is constitutive of the object for a given observer, will differ for different individuals, times and cultures, although a certain minimum of overlapping common reference is needed for the possibility of communication in the present, and of understanding records of the past. The set of characteristics *m*, if it is affirmed to have an instance, will turn out to render true a finite number of categorical and a potentially infinite number of hypothetical propositions; and the paradoxical fact often urged against phenomenalism that any given proposition or set of propositions recording observations may be false, and yet the relevant proposition about a material object which is 'based' upon them may remain true—that in other words the latter type of proposition cannot be shown either to entail or be entailed by the former—is explained by the fact that *m* is vague and *n* (for all we know) infinite, and consequently however much of *m* you falsify it will never demonstrate that *n* has been exhausted. But when *m*, which represents your personal selection out of *n*, is progressively falsified, a point will arise at which you will probably abandon your belief in the existence of the material object in question, since your experience does not present a sufficient number of characteristics defined as *m*. But where this point will arise for a given individual is a purely psychological or sociological question; and I, who carve an *m* which differs from yours, out of the common totality *n*, will understand you only to the extent to which our respective *m*'s overlap; and therefore what will seem to you evidence adverse to your proposition will seem to weaken mine at the very most only to the extent to which your *m* overlaps with mine. Even if 'a case of *m* exists' were far more precisely formulated than it ever is in ordinary life, as a collection of singular propositions, it would still not be conclusively verifiable because some of its components are hypothetical and unco-verifiable; but as words are commonly used it is always fluid and vague, and so cannot be conclusively falsified either. Thus the verification criterion which was intended to eliminate metaphysical propositions in order to save those of science and common sense, cannot deal with these even in its loosest and most enfeebled form.

Other selves are more recalcitrant still. The strict verification principle seems to demand a behaviourist analysis of selves other than that of the observer, introspection data being confined to, because conclusively verifiable by, him alone. Even if, as was argued above, this be rejected and the existence of other selves, conceived by analogy with the given observer's own, be conceded at least the same obscure status as is, in the present state of philosophical discussion, enjoyed by material objects, each self being allowed to verify at any rate its own experience, it still seems difficult to explain, even in terms of the falsifiability criterion, what could show that the sentences 'My toothache is more violent than yours' or 'Smith thinks faster than Jones' are not meaningless. Each observer, we say, can vouch for the occurrence or the non-occurrence only of events in his own experience. Whatever may be said about the meaning of such terms as 'privacy' and 'publicity' as applied to data which are evidence for material objects, introspected states must, as language is ordinarily used, be declared to be private in some sense in which material objects are not: an inter-subjective observer who perceives my thoughts and feelings as well as his own seems a self-contradictory concept: otherwise it would be no more absurd to say that he and I experience the same headache as that we see the same table. Here, once again, the verification principle does not apply in either of its forms; and yet the propositions comparing the experiences of several observers seem at once intelligible, empirical, and as often as not precise and true.

The conclusion which follows if the above account of the matter is correct, is this: that the criterion provided by 'strong' verification at best applies to a very narrow range of observation propositions; while 'weak' verification either fails to act as a criterion of sense altogether or, if made equivalent to 'strong' falsification, and in that form made sole arbiter of meaning, entails a brand of phenomenalism which provides unsatisfactory analyses of propositions about material objects and other selves. It follows *a fortiori* that the criterion of types of verifiability cannot act as the basis of classification of empirical propositions into logical categories. For it can neither distinguish statements recording observations from other categories of empirical propositions, nor enable us to distinguish different types of observation statements from each other. In view of this complete failure to satisfy our demand for a criterion, are we to abandon our search for a criterion altogether, or even declare the demand itself to be senseless, saying that meaning is meaning—an unanalysable concept—that to understand is an ultimate form of activity like seeing or hearing, that 'empirical' is an ultimate category, and can not be explained or defined otherwise than ostensively, that is by examples? This is perhaps the case. But if so, statements like the above express the fact too baldly and obscurely. What one ought rather to say is that verifiability depends on intelligibility and not vice versa; only sentences which are constructed in accordance with the rules of logic and of grammar, and describe what can logically be conceived as existing, are significant, are empirical statements, express genuinely empirical propositions. The notion of the logically conceivable must not be misunderstood. It must not be confused with the view ultimately derived from Russell, and sometimes offered as a substitute for verification theories, according to which a sentence has empirical meaning when every variable which occurs in it is such that one at least of its values denote an actual or possible object of sensible or introspective knowledge; or, as it is sometimes put, when all the concepts in a judgement are *a posteriori* concepts; or, if a more familiar formulation is preferred, when understanding a proposition entails actual or possible acquaintance with at least one instance of every universal which occurs in it. Even if we ignore the difficulties of the phenomenalism which this entails it can only be a necessary, never a sufficient condition of empirical significance, at most a negative test. For I can formulate a sentence correct by the rules of logic and of grammar and containing as variables only the names of observable characteristics, which yet may turn out to be meaningless, as for example 'red hours are not more passionate than his ambition': this would doubtless involve a glaring confusion of categories, but the criterion, like that of 'weak' verification and for the same reason, is powerless to prevent this. The notion of significance cannot be determined by any such mechanical test: to say of a sentence that it means something, that I and others understand it, in other words that it conveys a proposition, is to say no more and no less than that we can conceive what would be the case if it were true. As for the meaning of 'I can conceive', only that is conceivable by me, which in some respect resembles my actual experience, as it occurs in observation or introspection, memory or imagination, or any other form of direct acquaintance, which can be described only by reference to it, as a determinate however logically distant from its source, of some determinable with at least one of whose determinates I am acquainted; much as a man born blind may understand propositions of visual experience by analogy with the senses which he possesses. The proposition that what is conceivable is necessarily similar to actual experience is analytic, being part of what is meant by the word 'conceivable'. To speak therefore of conceiving an experience dissimilar in all respects, wholly different, from my own, is to advance a self-contradictory concept, suggesting as it does that I both can apply my habitual logical categories to it, inasmuch as it is called experience, and that I cannot do so, inasmuch that it is declared to be wholly and utterly different from it. Statements which are metaphysical in the bad sense are meaningless not because they are unverifiable—but because they purport, in the language which resembles that which we normally use to describe situations which we regard as capable of being empirically experienced, to describe something which is alleged to transcend such experience, and to be incommunicable by any kind of analogy with it. Since, so far as we mean anything by these words, the limits of what can be conceived are set by analogy to what we are acquainted with, to deny such resemblance is tantamount to saying that what the proposition affects to describe is inconceivable; and this is to say that it is not a genuine proposition, but, in the empirical sense of meaning as descriptive, and not, e.g. emotive or evocative, a meaningless statement, linguistically similar to significant ones. Such a statement is unverifiable because, when examined, it turns out to be meaningless and not vice versa, and it is meaningless, because although words are being used in it in accordance with the accepted conventions of logic and of grammar, they represent the result either of genuine confusion, or of a pursuit of obscurity from whatever cause or motive, since they are used in a fashion different from that in which words are used when they are intended to describe the experienced world. And so, while they may resemble genuinely descriptive expressions, whatever else they may or may not be doing, they literally describe nothing.

Benjamin Lee Whorf

1897–1941

BENJAMIN LEE WHORF is best known for his thesis concerning linguistic relativity, an idea also developed by Edward Sapir, Whorf's teacher and sometime colleague. In its most general form, the "Whorf-Sapir" hypothesis is that human perception, cognition, and behavior are structured and in part determined by language. Whorf's own development of this thesis was based primarily on his research on North American Indian languages, notably Hopi. While there appears to be a superficial similarity between Whorf's research and *Saussure*'s claims concerning the arbitrariness of the sign, Whorf pursues the idea of linguistic relativity as precisely motivated by the distinctive circumstances of a particular culture. In the essay here, he also argues that verbal and grammatical structures are directly connected to behavior, to emphasize the practical consequence of his general thesis. In a well-known example, one may find several words for "snow" in the language of an Alaskan tribe but only one word for "bird," "airplane," and "aviator" in Hopi, since in both cases common experience of the world is segmented according to prevailing interests and needs. How "reality" appears is then reflected in language and, reciprocally, affects how the world is perceived.

Among the most striking implications of this thesis is that terms and concepts that appear to be self-evident primitives in European languages (or, as Whorf says, "Standard Average European" or "SAE"), especially terms that pertain to time, space, measurement, and counting, appear to be highly dependent on linguistic conventions. From this point of view, claims of universality for certain philosophical methods (as, for example, *Husserl*'s idea of phenomenology) are immediately suspect.

Whorf posits a "thought world" as the linguistically shaped "microcosm that each man carries about within himself, by which he measures and understands what he can of the macrocosm." Moreover, the relation between two different languages, as each may shape a different "thought world," presents an obvious difficulty of commensurability: if fundamental concepts (such as the idea of an "entity" or "event") differ, it is not certain that adequate translation can be made.

In this context, it is important to note that Whorf's thesis had an important effect on the development of a particular variant of structuralist linguistics in American universities that is quite different from structuralism following *Saussure*, *Lévi-Strauss*, or Roland Barthes (see *CTSP*, pp. 1195–1211). Among American linguists, "structuralism" is most commonly identified with the work of G. L. Trager, H. L. Smith, Charles Fries, or R. B. Lees, for example, and is taken to refer to grammatical/syntactical structures presumed to be derivable from empirical observation and expressible in so-called slot-and-substitution representations of syntactical relations. Thus, *Chomsky*'s idea of transformational-generative grammar and his espousal of linguistic universals or Cartesian "innate ideas" is in sharp opposition to both the "structural" linguistics (i.e., "slot-and-substitution" grammars) and the linguistic relativism of Whorf.

Whorf's most important papers are collected in *Language, Thought, and Reality: Selected Writings of Benjamin Lee Whorf*, ed. John B. Carroll (1956). See also Harry Hoijer, ed., *Language in Culture: Conference on the Interrelations of Language and Other Aspects of Culture* (1954).

THE RELATION OF HABITUAL THOUGHT AND BEHAVIOR TO LANGUAGE

> Human beings do not live in the objective world alone, nor alone in the world of social activity as ordinarily understood, but are very much at the mercy of the particular language which has become the medium of expression for their society. It is quite an illusion to imagine that one adjusts to reality essentially without the use of language and that language is merely an incidental means of solving specific problems of communication or reflection. The fact of the matter is that the "real world" is to a large extent unconsciously built up on the language habits of the group. . . . We see and hear and otherwise experience very largely as we do because the language habits of our community predispose certain choices of interpretation.
>
> —Edward Sapir

THE RELATION OF HABITUAL THOUGHT AND BEHAVIOR TO LANGUAGE first appeared in *Language, Culture, and Personality: Essays in Memory of Edward Sapir,* ed. Leslie Spier (Menasha, WI: Sapir Memorial Publication Fund, 1941), pp. 75–93. It was reprinted in *Language, Thought, and Reality: Selected Writings of Benjamin Lee Whorf,* ed. John B. Carroll (Cambridge, MA: M.I.T. Press, 1956) and is reprinted here by permission of the M.I.T. Press.

There will probably be general assent to the proposition that an accepted pattern of using words is often prior to certain lines of thinking and forms of behavior, but he who assents often sees in such a statement nothing more than a platitudinous recognition of the hypnotic power of philosophical and learned terminology on the one hand or of catchwords, slogans, and rallying cries on the other. To see only thus far is to miss the point of one of the important interconnections which Sapir saw between language, culture, and psychology, and succinctly expressed in the introductory quotation. It is not so much in these special uses of language as in its constant ways of arranging data and its most ordinary everyday analysis of phenomena that we need to recognize the influence it has on other activities, cultural and personal.

The Name of the Situation as Affecting Behavior

I came in touch with an aspect of this problem before I had studied under Dr. Sapir, and in a field usually considered remote from linguistics. It was in the course of my professional work for a fire insurance company, in which I undertook the task of analyzing many hundreds of reports of circumstances surrounding the start of fires, and in some cases, of explosions. My analysis was directed toward purely physical conditions, such as defective wiring, presence or lack of air spaces between metal flues and woodwork, etc., and the results were presented in these terms. Indeed it was undertaken with no thought that any other significances would or could be revealed. But in due course it became evident that not only a physical situation *qua* physics, but the meaning of that situation to people, was sometimes a factor, through the behavior of the people, in the start of the fire. And this factor of meaning was clearest when it was a LINGUISTIC MEANING, residing in the name or the linguistic description commonly applied to the situation. Thus, around a storage of what are called "gasoline drums," behavior will tend to a certain type, that is, great care will be exercised; while around a storage of what are called "empty gasoline drums," it will tend to be different—careless, with little repression of smoking or of tossing cigarette stubs about. Yet the "empty" drums are perhaps the more dangerous, since they contain explosive vapor. Physically the situation is hazardous, but the linguistic analysis according to regular analogy must employ the word 'empty,' which inevitably suggests lack of hazard. The word 'empty' is used in two linguistic patterns: (1) as a virtual synonym for 'null and void, negative, inert,' (2) applied in analysis of physical situations without regard to, e.g., vapor, liquid vestiges, or stray rubbish, in the container. The situation is named in one pattern (2) and the name is then "acted out" or "lived up to" in another (1), this being a general formula for the linguistic conditioning of behavior into hazardous forms.

In a wood distillation plant the metal stills were insulated with a composition prepared from limestone and called at the plant "spun limestone." No attempt was made to protect this covering from excessive heat or the contact of flame. After a period of use, the fire below one of the stills spread to the "limestone," which to everyone's great surprise burned vigorously. Exposure to acetic acid fumes from the stills had converted part of the limestone (calcium carbonate) to calcium acetate. This when heated in a fire decomposes, forming inflammable acetone. Behavior that tolerated fire close to the covering was induced by use of the name "limestone," which because it ends in "stone" implies noncombustibility.

A huge iron kettle of boiling varnish was observed to be overheated, nearing the temperature at which it would ignite. The operator moved it off the fire and ran it on its wheels to a distance, but did not cover it. In a minute or so the varnish ignited. Here the linguistic influence is more complex; it is due to the metaphorical objectifying (of which more later) of "cause" as contact or the spatial juxtaposition of "things"—to analyzing the situation as 'on' versus 'off' the fire. In reality, the stage when the external fire was the main factor had passed; the overheating was now an internal process of convection in the varnish from the intensely heated kettle, and still continued when 'off' the fire.

An electric glow heater on the wall was little used, and for one workman had the meaning of a convenient coathanger. At night a watchman entered and snapped a switch, which action he verbalized as 'turning on the light.' No light appeared, and this result he verbalized as 'light is burned out.' He could not see the glow of the heater because of the old coat hung on it. Soon the heater ignited the coat, which set fire to the building.

A tannery discharged waste water containing animal matter into an outdoor settling basin partly roofed with wood and partly open. This situation is one that ordinarily would be verbalized as 'pool of water.' A workman had occasion to light a blowtorch near by, and threw his match into the water. But the decomposing waste matter was evolving gas under the wood cover, so that the setup was the reverse of 'watery.' An instant flare of flame ignited the woodwork, and the fire quickly spread into the adjoining building.

A drying room for hides was arranged with a blower at one end to make a current of air along the room and thence outdoors through a vent at the other end. Fire started at a hot bearing on the blower which blew the flames directly into the hides and fanned them along the room, destroying the entire stock. This hazardous setup followed naturally from the term 'blower' with its linguistic equivalence to 'that which blows,' implying that its function necessarily is to 'blow.' Also its function is verbalized as 'blowing air for drying,' overlooking that it can blow other things, e.g., flames and sparks. In reality, a blower simply makes a current of air and can exhaust as well as blow. It should have been installed at the vent end to DRAW the air over the hides, then through the hazard (its own casing and bearings), and thence outdoors.

Beside a coal-fired melting pot for lead reclaiming was dumped a pile of "scrap lead"—a misleading verbalization, for it consisted of the lead sheets of old radio condensers, which still had paraffin paper between them. Soon the paraffin blazed up and fired the roof, half of which was burned off.

Such examples, which could be greatly multiplied, will suffice to show how the cue to a certain line of behavior is often given by the analogies of the linguistic formula in which the situation is spoken of, and by which to some degree it is analyzed, classified, and allotted its place in that world which is "to a large extent unconsciously built up on the language habits of the group." And we always assume that the linguistic analysis made by our group reflects reality better than it does.

Grammatical Patterns as Interpretations of Experience

The linguistic material in the above examples is limited to single words, phrases, and patterns of limited range. One cannot study the behavioral compulsiveness of such material without suspecting a much more far-reaching compulsion from large-scale patterning of grammatical categories, such as plurality, gender and similar classifications (animate, inanimate, etc.), tenses, voices, and other verb forms, classifications of the type of "parts of speech," and the matter of whether a given experience is denoted by a unit morpheme, an inflected word, or a syntactical combination. A category such as number (singular vs. plural) is an attempted interpretation of a whole large order of experience, virtually of the world or of nature; it attempts to say how experience is to be segmented, what experience is to be called "one" and what "several." But the difficulty of appraising such a far-reaching influence is great because of its background character, because of the difficulty of standing aside from our own language, which is a habit and a cultural *non est disputandum,* and scrutinizing it objectively. And if we take a very dissimilar language, this language becomes a part of nature, and we even do to it what we have already done to nature. We tend to think in our own language in order to examine the exotic language. Or we find the task of unraveling the purely morphological intricacies so gigantic that it seems to absorb all else. Yet the problem, though difficult, is feasible; and the best approach is through an exotic language, for in its study we are at long last pushed willy-nilly out of our ruts. Then we find that the exotic language is a mirror held up to our own.

In my study of the Hopi language, what I now see as an opportunity to work on this problem was first thrust upon me before I was clearly aware of the problem. The seemingly endless task of describing the morphology did finally end. Yet it was evident, especially in the light of Sapir's lectures on Navaho, that the description of the LANGUAGE was far from complete. I knew for example the morphological formation of plurals, but not how to use plurals. It was evident that the category of plural in Hopi was not the same thing as in English, French, or German. Certain things that were plural in these languages were singular in Hopi. The phase of investigation which now began consumed nearly two more years.

The work began to assume the character of a comparison between Hopi and western European languages. It also became evident that even the grammar of Hopi bore a relation to Hopi culture, and the grammar of European tongues to our own "Western" or "European" culture. And it appeared that the interrelation brought in those large subsumations of experience by language, such as our own terms 'time,' 'space,' 'substance,' and 'matter.' Since, with respect to the traits compared, there is little difference between English, French, German, or other European languages with the POSSIBLE (but doubtful) exception of Balto-Slavic and non-Indo-European, I have lumped these languages into one group called SAE, or "Standard Average European."

That portion of the whole investigation here to be reported may be summed up in two questions: (1) Are our own concepts of 'time,' 'space,' and 'matter' given in substantially the same form by experience to all men, or are they in part conditioned by the structure of particular languages? (2) Are there traceable affinities between (*a*) cultural and behavioral norms and (*b*) large-scale linguistic patterns? (I should be the last to pretend that there is anything so definite as "a correlation" between culture and language, and especially between ethnological rubrics such as 'agricultural, hunting,' etc., and linguistic ones like 'inflected,' 'synthetic,' or 'isolating.'[1] When I began the study, the problem was by no means so clearly formulated, and I had little notion that the answers would turn out as they did.)

[1] We have plenty of evidence that this is not the case. Consider only the Hopi and the Ute, with languages that on the overt morphological and lexical level are as similar as, say, English and German. The idea of "correlation" between language and culture, in the generally accepted sense of correlation, is certainly a mistaken one. [Au.]

Plurality and Numeration in SAE and Hopi

In our language, that is SAE, plurality and cardinal numbers are applied in two ways: to real plurals and imaginary plurals. Or more exactly if less tersely: perceptible spatial aggregates and metaphorical aggregates. We say 'ten men' and also 'ten days.' Ten men either are or could be objectively perceived as ten, ten in one group perception[2]—ten men on a street corner, for instance. But 'ten days' cannot be objectively experienced. We experience only one day, today; the other nine (or even all ten) are something conjured up from memory or imagination. If 'ten days' be regarded as a group it must be as an "imaginary," mentally constructed group. Whence comes this mental pattern? Just as in the case of the fire-causing errors, from the fact that our language confuses the two different situations, has but one pattern for both. When we speak of 'ten steps forward, ten strokes on a bell,' or any similarly described cyclic sequence, "times" of any sort, we are doing the same thing as with 'days.' CYCLICITY brings the response of imaginary plurals. But a likeness of cyclicity to aggregates is not unmistakably given by experience prior to language, or it would be found in all languages, and it is not.

Our AWARENESS of time and cyclicity does contain something immediate and subjective—the basic sense of "becoming later and later." But, in the habitual thought of us SAE people, this is covered under something quite different, which though mental should not be called subjective. I call it OBJECTIFIED, or imaginary, because it is patterned on the OUTER world. It is this that reflects our linguistic usage. Our tongue makes no distinction between numbers counted on discrete entities and numbers that are simply "counting itself." Habitual thought then assumes that in the latter the numbers are just as much counted on "something" as in the former. This is objectification. Concepts of time lose contact with the subjective experience of "becoming later" and are objectified as counted QUANTITIES, especially as lengths, made up of units as a length can be visibly marked off into inches. A 'length of time' is envisioned as a row of similar units, like a row of bottles.

In Hopi there is a different linguistic situation. Plurals and cardinals are used only for entities that form or can form an objective group. There are no imaginary plurals, but instead ordinals used with singulars. Such an expression as 'ten days' is not used. The equivalent statement is an operational one that reaches one day by a suitable count. 'They stayed ten days' becomes 'they stayed until the eleventh day' or 'they left after the tenth day.' 'Ten days is greater than nine days' becomes 'the tenth day is later than the ninth.' Our "length of time" is not regarded as a length but as a relation between two events in lateness. Instead of our linguistically promoted objectification of that datum of consciousness we call 'time,' the Hopi language has not laid down any pattern that would cloak the subjective "becoming later" that is the essence of time.

Nouns of Physical Quantity in SAE and Hopi

We have two kinds of nouns denoting physical things: individual nouns, and mass nouns, e.g., 'water, milk, wood, granite, sand, flour, meat.' Individual nouns denote bodies with definite outlines: 'a tree, a stick, a man, a hill.' Mass nouns denote homogeneous continua without implied boundaries. The distinction is marked by linguistic form; e.g., mass nouns lack plurals,[3] in English drop articles, and in French take the partitive article *du, de la, des*. The distinction is more widespread in language than in the observable appearance of things. Rather few natural occurrences present themselves as unbounded extents; 'air' of course, and often 'water, rain, snow, sand, rock, dirt, grass.' We do not encounter 'butter, meat, cloth, iron, glass' or

[2] As we say, 'ten at the SAME TIME,' showing that in our language and thought we restate the fact of group perception in terms of a concept 'time,' the large linguistic component of which will appear in the course of this paper. [Au.]

[3] It is no exception to this rule of lacking a plural that a mass noun may sometimes coincide in lexeme with an individual noun that of course has a plural; e.g., 'stone' (no pl.) with 'a stone' (pl. 'stones'). The plural form denoting varieties, e.g., 'wines' is of course a different sort of thing from the true plural; it is a curious outgrowth from the SAE mass nouns, leading to still another sort of imaginary aggregates, which will have to be omitted from this paper. [Au.]

most "materials" in such kind of manifestation, but in bodies small or large with definite outlines. The distinction is somewhat forced upon our description of events by an unavoidable pattern in language. It is so inconvenient in a great many cases that we need some way of individualizing the mass noun by further linguistic devices. This is partly done by names of body-types: 'stick of wood, piece of cloth, pane of glass, cake of soap'; also, and even more, by introducing names of containers though their contents be the real issue: 'glass of water, cup of coffee, dish of food, bag of flour, bottle of beer.' These very common container formulas, in which 'of' has an obvious, visually perceptible meaning ("contents"), influence our feeling about the less obvious type-body formulas: 'stick of wood, lump of dough,' etc. The formulas are very similar: individual noun plus a similar relator (English 'of'). In the obvious case this relator denotes contents. In the inobvious one it "suggests" contents. Hence the 'lumps, chunks, blocks, pieces,' etc., seem to contain something, a "stuff," "substance," or "matter" that answers to the 'water,' 'coffee,' or 'flour' in the container formulas. So with SAE people the philosophic "substance" and "matter" are also the naïve idea; they are instantly acceptable, "common sense." It is so through linguistic habit. Our language patterns often require us to name a physical thing by a binomial that splits the reference into a formless item plus a form.

Hopi is again different. It has a formally distinguished class of nouns. But this class contains no formal subclass of mass nouns. All nouns have an individual sense and both singular and plural forms. Nouns translating most nearly our mass nouns still refer to vague bodies or vaguely bounded extents. They imply indefiniteness, but not lack, of outline and size. In specific statements, 'water' means one certain mass or quantity of water, not what we call "the substance water." Generality of statement is conveyed through the verb or predicator, not the noun. Since nouns are individual already, they are not individualized by either type-bodies or names of containers, if there is no special need to emphasize shape or container. The noun itself implies a suitable type-body or container. One says, not 'a glass of water' but *kə·yi* 'a water,' not 'a pool of water' but *pa·hə*,[4] not 'a dish of cornflour' but *ŋəmni* 'a (quantity of) cornflour,' not 'a piece of meat' but *sikʷi* 'a meat.' The language has neither need for nor analogies on which to build the concept of existence as a duality of formless item and form. It deals with formlessness through other symbols than nouns.

PHASES OF CYCLES IN SAE AND HOPI

Such terms as 'summer, winter, September, morning, noon, sunset' are with us nouns, and have little formal linguistic difference from other nouns. They can be subjects or objects, and we say 'at sunset' or 'in winter' just as we say 'at a corner' or 'in an orchard.'[5] They are pluralized and numerated like nouns of physical objects, as we have seen. Our thought about the referents of such words hence becomes objectified. Without objectification, it would be a subjective experience of real time, i.e., of the consciousness of "becoming later and later"—simply a cyclic phase similar to an earlier phase in that ever-later-becoming duration. Only by imagination can such a cyclic phase be set beside another and another in the manner of a spatial (i.e. visually perceived) configuration. But such is the power of linguistic analogy that we do so objectify cyclic phasing. We do it even by saying 'a phase' and 'phases' instead of, e.g., 'phasing.' And the pattern of individual and mass nouns, with the resulting binomial formula of formless item plus form, is so general that it is implicit for all nouns, and hence our very generalized formless items like 'substance, matter,' by which we can fill out the binomial for an enormously wide range of nouns. But even these are not quite generalized enough to take in our phase nouns. So for the phase nouns we have made a formless item, 'time.' We have made it by using 'a time,' i.e., an occasion or a phase, in the pattern of a mass noun, just as from 'a summer' we make 'sum-

[4]Hopi has two words for water quantities; *kə·yi* and *pa·hə*. The difference is something like that between 'stone' and 'rock' in English, *pa·hə* implying greater size and "wildness"; flowing water, whether or not outdoors or in nature, is *pa·hə;* so is 'moisture.' But, unlike 'stone' and 'rock,' the difference is essential, not pertaining to a connotative margin, and the two can hardly ever be interchanged. [Au.]

[5]To be sure, there are a few minor differences from other nouns, in English for instance in the use of the articles. [Au.]

mer' in the pattern of a mass noun. Thus with our binomial formula we can say and think 'a moment of time, a second of time, a year of time.' Let me again point out that the pattern is simply that of 'a bottle of milk' or 'a piece of cheese.' Thus we are assisted to imagine that 'a summer' actually contains or consists of such-and-such a quantity of 'time.'

In Hopi however all phase terms, like 'summer, morning,' etc., are not nouns but a kind of adverb, to use the nearest SAE analogy. They are a formal part of speech by themselves, distinct from nouns, verbs, and even other Hopi "adverbs." Such a word is not a case form or a locative pattern, like 'des Abends' or 'in the morning.' It contains no morpheme like one of 'in the house' or 'at the tree.'[6] It means 'when it is morning' or 'while morning-phase is occurring.' These "temporals" are not used as subjects or objects, or at all like nouns. One does not say 'it's a hot summer' or 'summer is hot'; summer is not hot, summer is only WHEN conditions are hot, WHEN heat occurs. One does not say 'THIS summer,' but 'summer now' or 'summer recently.' There is no objectification, as a region, an extent, a quantity, of the subjective duration-feeling. Nothing is suggested about time except the perpetual "getting later" of it. And so there is no basis here for a formless item answering to our 'time.'

Temporal Forms of Verbs in SAE and Hopi

The three-tense system of SAE verbs colors all our thinking about time. This system is amalgamated with that larger scheme of objectification of the subjective experience of duration already noted in other patterns—in the binomial formula applicable to nouns in general, in temporal nouns, in plurality and numeration. This objectification enables us in imagination to "stand time units in a row." Imagination of time as like a row harmonizes with a system of THREE tenses; whereas a system of TWO, an earlier and a later, would seem to correspond better to the feeling of duration as it is experienced. For if we inspect consciousness we find no past, present, future, but a unity embracing complexity. EVERYTHING is in consciousness, and everything in consciousness IS, and is together. There is in it a sensuous and nonsensuous. We may call the sensuous—what we are seeing, hearing, touching—the 'present' while in the nonsensuous the vast image-world of memory is being labeled 'the past' and another realm of belief, intuition, and uncertainty 'the future'; yet sensation, memory, foresight, all are in consciousness together—one is not "yet to be" nor another "once but no more." Where real time comes in is that all this in consciousness is "getting later," changing certain relations in an irreversible manner. In this "latering" or "durating" there seems to me to be a paramount contrast between the newest, latest instant at the focus of attention and the rest—the earlier. Languages by the score get along well with two tenselike forms answering to this paramount relation of "later" to "earlier." We can of course CONSTRUCT AND CONTEMPLATE IN THOUGHT a system of past, present, future, in the objectified configuration of points on a line. This is what our general objectification tendency leads us to do and our tense system confirms.

In English the present tense seems the one least in harmony with the paramount temporal relation. It is as if pressed into various and not wholly congruous duties. One duty is to stand as objectified middle term between objectified past and objectified future, in narration, discussion, argument, logic, philosophy. Another is to denote inclusion in the sensuous field: 'I SEE him.' Another is for nomic, i.e. customarily or generally valid, statements: 'We SEE with our eyes.' These varied uses introduce confusions of thought, of which for the most part we are unaware.

Hopi, as we might expect, is different here too. Verbs have no "tenses" like ours, but have validity-forms ("assertions"), aspects, and clause-linkage forms (modes), that yield even greater precision of speech. The validity-forms denote that the speaker (not the subject) reports the situation (answering to our past and present) or that he expects it (answering to our future)[7] or that he makes a nomic state-

[6] 'Year' and certain combinations of 'year' with name of season, rarely season names alone, can occur with a locative morpheme 'at,' but this is exceptional. It appears like historical detritus of an earlier different patterning, or the effect of English analogy, or both. [Au.]

[7] The expective and reportive assertions contrast according to the "paramount relation." The expective expresses anticipation existing EARLIER than objective fact, and coinciding with objective fact LATER than the status quo of the speaker, this status quo, including all the subsummation of the past therein, being expressed by the reportive. Our notion "future" seems to represent at once the ear-

ment (answering to our nomic present). The aspects denote different degrees of duration and different kinds of tendency "during duration." As yet we have noted nothing to indicate whether an event is sooner or later than another when both are REPORTED. But need for this does not arise until we have two verbs: i.e. two clauses. In that case the "modes" denote relations between the clauses, including relations of later to earlier and of simultaneity. Then there are many detached words that express similar relations, supplementing the modes and aspects. The duties of our three-tense system and its tripartite linear objectified "time" are distributed among various verb categories, all different from our tenses; and there is no more basis for an objectified time in Hopi verbs than in other Hopi patterns; although this does not in the least hinder the verb forms and other patterns from being closely adjusted to the pertinent realities of actual situations.

Duration, Intensity, and Tendency in SAE and Hopi

To fit discourse to manifold actual situations, all languages need to express durations, intensities, and tendencies. It is characteristic of SAE and perhaps of many other language types to express them metaphorically. The metaphors are those of spatial extension, i.e. of size, number (plurality), position, shape, and motion. We express duration by 'long, short, great, much, quick, slow,' etc.; intensity by 'large, great, much, heavy, light, high, low, sharp, faint,' etc.; tendency by 'more, increase, grow, turn, get, approach, go, come, rise, fall, stop, smooth, even, rapid, slow'; and so on through an almost inexhaustible list of metaphors that we hardly recognize as such, since they are virtually the only linguistic media available. The nonmetaphorical terms in this field, like 'early, late, soon, lasting, intense, very, tending,' are a mere handful, quite inadequate to the needs.

It is clear how this condition "fits in." It is part of our whole scheme of OBJECTIFYING—imaginatively spatializing qualities and potentials that are quite nonspatial (so far as any spatially perceptive senses can tell us). Noun-meaning (with us) proceeds from physical bodies to referents of far other sort. Since physical bodies and their outlines in PERCEIVED SPACE are denoted by size and shape terms and reckoned by cardinal numbers and plurals, these patterns of denotation and reckoning extend to the symbols of nonspatial meanings, and so suggest an IMAGINARY SPACE. Physical shapes 'move, stop, rise, sink, approach,' etc., in perceived space; why not these other referents in their imaginary space? This has gone so far that we can hardly refer to the simplest nonspatial situation without constant resort to physical metaphors. I "grasp" the "thread" of another's arguments, but if its "level" is "over my head" my attention may "wander" and "lose touch" with the "drift" of it, so that when he "comes" to his "point" we differ "widely," our "views" being indeed so "far apart" that the "things" he says "appear" "much" too arbitrary, or even "a lot" of nonsense!

The absence of such metaphor from Hopi speech is striking. Use of space terms when there is no space involved is NOT THERE—as if on it had been laid the taboo teetotal! The reason is clear when we know that Hopi has abundant conjugational and lexical means of expressing duration, intensity, and tendency directly as such, and that major grammatical patterns do not, as with us, provide analogies for an imaginary space. The many verb "aspects" express duration and tendency of manifestations, while some of the "voices" express intensity, tendency, and duration of causes or forces producing manifestations. Then a special part of speech, the "tensors," a huge class of words, denotes only intensity, tendency, duration, and sequence. The function of the tensors is to express intensities, "strengths," and how they continue or vary, their rate of change; so that the broad concept of intensity, when considered as necessarily always varying and/or continuing, includes also tendency and duration. Tensors convey distinctions of degree, rate, constancy, repetition, increase and decrease of intensity, immediate sequence, interruption or sequence after an interval, etc., also QUALITIES of strengths, such as we should express metaphorically as smooth, even, hard, rough. A striking feature is their lack of resemblance to the terms of real space and movement that to us "mean the same." There is not even more than a trace of apparent derivation

lier (anticipation) and the later (afterwards, what will be), as Hopi shows. This paradox may hint of how elusive the mystery of real time is, and how artificially it is expressed by a linear relation of past-present-future. [Au.]

from space terms.[8] So, while Hopi in its nouns seems highly concrete, here in the tensors it becomes abstract almost beyond our power to follow.

Habitual Thought in SAE and Hopi

The comparison now to be made between the habitual thought worlds of SAE and Hopi speakers is of course incomplete. It is possible only to touch upon certain dominant contrasts that appear to stem from the linguistic differences already noted. By "habitual thought" and "thought world" I mean more than simply language, i.e., than the linguistic patterns themselves. I include all the analogical and suggestive value of the patterns (e.g., our "imaginary space" and its distant implications), and all the give-and-take between language and the culture as a whole, wherein is a vast amount that is not linguistic but yet shows the shaping influence of language. In brief, this "thought world" is the microcosm that each man carries about within himself, by which he measures and understands what he can of the macrocosm.

The SAE microcosm has analyzed reality largely in terms of what it calls "things" (bodies and quasibodies) plus modes of extensional but formless existence that it calls "substances" or "matter." It tends to see existence through a binomial formula that expresses any existent as a spatial form plus a spatial formless continuum related to the form, as contents is related to the outlines of its container. Nonspatial existents are imaginatively spatialized and charged with similar implications of form and continuum.

The Hopi microcosm seems to have analyzed reality largely in terms of EVENTS (or better "eventing"), referred to in two ways, objective and subjective. Objectively, and only if perceptible physical experience, events are expressed mainly as outlines, colors, movements, and other perceptive reports. Subjectively, for both the physical and nonphysical, events are considered the expression of invisible intensity factors, on which depend their stability and persistence, or their fugitiveness and proclivities. It implies that existents do not "become later and later" all in the same way; but some do so by growing like plants, some by diffusing and vanishing, some by a procession of metamorphoses, some by enduring in one shape till affected by violent forces. In the nature of each existent able to manifest as a definite whole is the power of its own mode of duration: its growth, decline, stability, cyclicity, or creativeness. Everything is thus already "prepared" for the way it now manifests by earlier phases, and what it will be later, partly has been, and partly is in act of being so "prepared." An emphasis and importance rests on this preparing or being prepared aspect of the world that may to the Hopi correspond to that "quality of reality" that 'matter' or 'stuff' has for us.

Habitual Behavior Features of Hopi Culture

Our behavior, and that of Hopi, can be seen to be coordinated in many ways to the linguistically conditioned microcosm. As in my fire casebook, people act about situations in ways which are like the ways they talk about them. A characteristic of Hopi behavior is the emphasis on preparation. This includes announcing and getting ready for events well beforehand, elaborate precautions to insure persistence of desired conditions, and stress on good will as the preparer of right results. Consider the analogies of the day-counting pattern alone. Time is mainly reckoned "by day" (*taLk, -tala*) or "by night" (*tok*), which words are not nouns but tensors, the first formed on a root "light, day," the second on a root "sleep." The count is by ORDINALS. This is not the pattern of counting a number of different men or things, even though they appear successively, for, even then, they COULD gather into an assemblage. It is the pattern of counting successive

[8] One such trace is that the tensor 'long in duration,' while quite different from the adjective 'long' of space, seems to contain the same root as the adjective 'large' of space. Another is that 'somewhere' of space used with certain tensors means 'at some indefinite time.' Possibly however this is not the case and it is only the tensor that gives the time element, so that 'somewhere' still refers to space and that under these conditions indefinite space means simply general applicability, regardless of either time or space. Another trace is that in the temporal (cycle word) 'afternoon' the element meaning 'after' is derived from the verb 'to separate.' There are other such traces, but they are few and exceptional, and obviously not like our own spatial metaphorizing. [Au.]

reappearances of the SAME man or thing, incapable of forming an assemblage. The analogy is not to behave about day-cyclicity as to several men ("several days"), which is what WE tend to do, but to behave as to the successive visits of the SAME MAN. One does not alter several men by working upon just one, but one can prepare and so alter the later visits of the same man by working to affect the visit he is making now. This is the way the Hopi deal with the future—by working within a present situation which is expected to carry impresses, both obvious and occult, forward into the future event of interest. One might say that Hopi society understands our proverb 'Well begun is half done,' but not our 'Tomorrow is another day.' This may explain much in Hopi character.

This Hopi preparing behavior may be roughly divided into announcing, outer preparing, inner preparing, covert participation, and persistence. Announcing, or preparative publicity, is an important function in the hands of a special official, the Crier Chief. Outer preparing is preparation involving much visible activity, not all necessarily directly useful within our understanding. It includes ordinary practicing, rehearsing, getting ready, introductory formalities, preparing of special food, etc. (all of these to a degree that may seem overelaborate to us), intensive sustained muscular activity like running, racing, dancing, which is thought to increase the intensity of development of events (such as growth of crops), mimetic and other magic, preparations based on esoteric theory involving perhaps occult instruments like prayer sticks, prayer feathers, and prayer meal, and finally the great cyclic ceremonies and dances, which have the significance of preparing rain and crops. From one of the verbs meaning "prepare" is derived the noun for "harvest" or "crop": *na'twani* 'the prepared' or the 'in preparation.'[9]

Inner preparing is use of prayer and meditation, and at lesser intensity good wishes and good will, to further desired results. Hopi attitudes stress the power of desire and thought. With their "microcosm" it is utterly natural that they should. Desire and thought are the earliest, and therefore the most important, most critical and crucial, stage of preparing. Moreover, to the Hopi, one's desires and thoughts influence not only his own actions, but all nature as well. This too is wholly natural. Consciousness itself is aware of work, of the feel of effort and energy, in desire and thinking. Experience more basic than language tells us that, if energy is expended, effects are produced. WE tend to believe that our bodies can stop up this energy, prevent it from affecting other things until we will our BODIES to overt action. But this may be so only because we have our own linguistic basis for a theory that formless items like "matter" are things in themselves, malleable only by similar things, by more matter, and hence insulated from the powers of life and thought. It is no more unnatural to think that thought contacts everything and pervades the universe than to think, as we all do, that light kindled outdoors does this. And it is not unnatural to suppose that thought, like any other force, leaves everywhere traces of effect. Now, when WE think of a certain actual rosebush, we do not suppose that our thought goes to that actual bush, and engages with it, like a searchlight turned upon it. What then do we suppose our consciousness is dealing with when we are thinking of that rosebush? Probably we think it is dealing with a "mental image" which is not the rosebush but a mental surrogate of it. But why should it be NATURAL to think that our thought deals with a surrogate and not with the real rosebush? Quite possibly because we are dimly aware that we carry about with us a whole imaginary space, full of mental surrogates. To us, mental surrogates are old familiar fare. Along with the images of imaginary space, which we perhaps secretly know to be only imaginary, we tuck the thought-of actually existing rosebush, which may be quite another story, perhaps just because we have that very convenient "place" for it. The Hopi thought-world has no imaginary space. The corollary to this is that it may not locate thought dealing with real space anywhere but in real space, nor insulate real space from the effects of thought. A Hopi would naturally suppose that his thought (or he himself) traffics with the actual rosebush—or more likely, corn plant—that he is thinking about. The thought then should leave some trace of itself with the plant in the field. If it is a good thought, one about health and growth, it is good for the plant; if a bad thought, the reverse.

The Hopi emphasize the intensity-factor of

[9]The Hopi verbs of preparing naturally do not correspond neatly to our "prepare"; so that *na'twani* could also be rendered 'the practiced-upon, the tried-for,' and otherwise. [Au.]

thought. Thought to be most effective should be vivid in consciousness, definite, steady, sustained, charged with strongly felt good intentions. They render the idea in English as 'concentrating, holding it in your heart, putting your mind on it, earnestly hoping.' Thought power is the force behind ceremonies, prayer sticks, ritual smoking, etc. The prayer pipe is regarded as an aid to "concentrating" (so said my informant). Its name, *na'twanpi,* means 'instrument of preparing.'

Covert participation is mental collaboration from people who do not take part in the actual affair, be it a job of work, hunt, race, or ceremony, but direct their thought and good will toward the affair's success. Announcements often seek to enlist the support of such mental helpers as well as of overt participants, and contain exhortations to the people to aid with their active good will.[10] A similarity to our concepts of a sympathetic audience or the cheering section at a football game should not obscure the fact that it is primarily the power of directed thought, and not merely sympathy or encouragement, that is expected of covert participants. In fact these latter get in their deadliest work before, not during, the game! A corollary to the power of thought is the power of wrong thought for evil; hence one purpose of covert participation is to obtain the mass force of many good wishers to offset the harmful thought of ill wishers. Such attitudes greatly favor cooperation and community spirit. Not that the Hopi community is not full of rivalries and colliding interests. Against the tendency to social disintegration in such a small, isolated group, the theory of "preparing" by the power of thought, logically leading to the great power of the combined, intensified, and harmonized thought of the whole community, must help vastly toward the rather remarkable degree of cooperation that, in spite of much private bickering, the Hopi village displays in all the important cultural activities.

Hopi "preparing" activities again show a result of their linguistic thought background in an emphasis on persistence and constant insistent repetition. A sense of the cumulative value of innumerable small momenta is dulled by an objectified, spatialized view of time like ours, enhanced by a way of thinking close to the subjective awareness of duration, of the ceaseless "latering" of events. To us, for whom time is a motion on a space, unvarying repetition seems to scatter its force along a row of units of that space, and be wasted. To the Hopi, for whom time is not a motion but a "getting later" of everything that has ever been done, unvarying repetition is not wasted but accumulated. It is storing up an invisible change that holds over into later events.[11] As we have seen, it is as if the return of the day were felt as the return of the same person, a little older but with all the impresses of yesterday, not as "another day," i.e., like an entirely different person. This principle joined with that of thought-power and with traits of general Pueblo culture is expressed in the theory of the Hopi ceremonial dance for furthering rain and crops, as well as in its short, piston-like tread, repeated thousands of times, hour after hour.

Some Impresses of Linguistic Habit in Western Civilization

It is harder to do justice in few words to the linguistically conditioned features of our own culture than in the case of the Hopi, because of both vast scope and difficulty of objectivity—because of our deeply ingrained familiarity with the attitudes to be analyzed. I wish merely to sketch certain characteristics adjusted to our linguistic binomialism of form

[10] See, *e.g.*, Ernest Beaglehole, *Notes on Hopi economic life* (Yale University Publications in Anthropology, no. 15, 1937), especially the reference to the announcement of a rabbit hunt, and on p. 30, description of the activities in connection with the cleaning of Toreva Spring—announcing, various preparing activities, and finally, preparing the continuity of the good results already obtained and the continued flow of the spring. [Au.]

[11] This notion of storing up power, which seems implied by much Hopi behavior, has an analog in physics: acceleration. It might be said that the linguistic background of Hopi thought equips it to recognize naturally that force manifests not as motion or velocity, but as cumulation or acceleration. Our linguistic background tends to hinder in us this same recognition, for having legitimately conceived force to be that which produces change, we then think of change by our linguistic metaphorical analog, motion, instead of by a pure motionless changingness concept, i.e., accumulation or acceleration. Hence it comes to our naïve feeling as a shock to find from physical experiments that it is not possible to define force by motion, that motion and speed, as also "being at rest," are wholly relative, and that force can be measured only by acceleration. [Au.]

plus formless item or "substance," to our metaphoricalness, our imaginary space, and our objectified time. These, as we have seen, are linguistic.

From the form-plus-substance dichotomy the philosophical views most traditionally characteristic of the "Western world" have derived huge support. Here belong materialism, psychophysical parallelism, physics—at least in its traditional Newtonian form—and dualistic views of the universe in general. Indeed here belongs almost everything that is "hard, practical common sense." Monistic, holistic, and relativistic views of reality appeal to philosophers and some scientists, but they are badly handicapped in appealing to the "common sense" of the Western average man—not because nature herself refutes them (if she did, philosophers could have discovered this much), but because they must be talked about in what amounts to a new language. "Common sense," as its name shows, and "practicality" as its name does not show, are largely matters of talking so that one is readily understood. It is sometimes stated that Newtonian space, time, and matter are sensed by everyone intuitively, whereupon relativity is cited as showing how mathematical analysis can prove intuition wrong. This, besides being unfair to intuition, is an attempt to answer offhand question (1) put at the outset of this paper, to answer which this research was undertaken. Presentation of the findings now nears its end, and I think the answer is clear. The offhand answer, laying the blame upon intuition for our slowness is discovering mysteries of the Cosmos, such as relativity, is the wrong one. The right answer is: Newtonian space, time, and matter are no intuitions. They are receipts from culture and language. That is where Newton got them.

Our objectified view of time is, however, favorable to historicity and to everything connected with the keeping of records, while the Hopi view is unfavorable thereto. The latter is too subtle, complex, and ever-developing, supplying no ready-made answer to the question of when "one" event ends and "another" begins. When it is implicit that everything that ever happened still is, but is in a necessarily different form from what memory or record reports, there is less incentive to study the past. As for the present, the incentive would be not to record it but to treat it as "preparing." But OUR objectified time puts before imagination something like a ribbon or scroll marked off into equal blank spaces, suggesting that each be filled with an entry. Writing has no doubt helped toward our linguistic treatment of time, even as the linguistic treatment has guided the uses of writing. Through this give-and-take between language and the whole culture we get, for instance:

1. Records, diaries, bookkeeping, accounting, mathematics stimulated by accounting.
2. Interest in exact sequence, dating, calendars, chronology, clocks, time wages, time graphs, time as used in physics.
3. Annals, histories, the historical attitude, interest in the past, archaeology, attitudes of introjection toward past periods, e.g., classicism, romanticism.

Just as we conceive our objectified time as extending in the future in the same way that it extends in the past, so we set down our estimates of the future in the same shape as our records of the past, producing programs, schedules, budgets. The formal equality of the spacelike units by which we measure and conceive time leads us to consider the "formless item" or "substance" of time to be homogeneous and in ratio to the number of units. Hence our prorata allocation of value to time, lending itself to the building up of a commercial structure based on time-prorata values: time wages (time work constantly supersedes piece work), rent, credit, interest, depreciation charges, and insurance premiums. No doubt this vast system, once built, would continue to run under any sort of linguistic treatment of time; but that it should have been built at all, reaching the magnitude and particular form it has in the Western world, is a fact decidedly in consonance with the patterns of the SAE languages. Whether such a civilization as ours would be possible with widely different linguistic handling of time is a large question—in our civilization, our linguistic patterns and the fitting of our behavior to the temporal order are what they are, and they are in accord. We are of course stimulated to use calendars, clocks, and watches, and to try to measure time ever more precisely; this aids science, and science in turn, following these well-worn cultural grooves, gives back to culture an ever-growing store of applications, habits, and values, with which culture again directs science. But what lies outside this spiral? Science is beginning to find that there is something in the Cosmos that is not in accord with the concepts we have formed in mounting the spiral. It is trying to frame a NEW LANGUAGE by which to adjust itself to a wider universe.

It is clear how the emphasis on "saving time" which goes with all the above and is very obvious objectification of time, leads to a high valuation of "speed," which shows itself a great deal in our behavior.

Still another behavioral effect is that the character of monotony and regularity possessed by our image of time as an evenly scaled limitless tape measure persuades us to behave as if that monotony were more true of events than it really is. That is, it helps to routinize us. We tend to select and favor whatever bears out this view, to "play up to" the routine aspects of existence. One phase of this is behavior evincing a false sense of security or an assumption that all will always go smoothly, and a lack in foreseeing and protecting ourselves against hazards. Our technique of harnessing energy does well in routine performance, and it is along routine lines that we chiefly strive to improve it—we are, for example, relatively uninterested in stopping the energy from causing accidents, fires, and explosions, which it is doing constantly and on a wide scale. Such indifference to the unexpectedness of life would be disastrous to a society as small, isolated, and precariously poised as the Hopi society is, or rather once was.

Thus our linguistically determined thought world not only collaborates with our cultural idols and ideals, but engages even our unconscious personal reactions in its patterns and gives them certain typical characters. One such character, as we have seen, is CARELESSNESS, as in reckless driving or throwing cigarette stubs into waste paper. Another of different sort is GESTURING when we talk. Very many of the gestures made by English-speaking people at least, and probably by all SAE speakers, serve to illustrate, by a movement in space, not a real spatial reference but one of the nonspatial references that our language handles by metaphors of imaginary space. That is, we are more apt to make a grasping gesture when we speak of grasping an elusive idea than when we speak of grasping a doorknob. The gesture seeks to make a metaphorical and hence somewhat unclear reference more clear. But, if a language refers to nonspatials without implying a spatial analogy, the reference is not made any clearer by gesture. The Hopi gesture very little, perhaps not at all in the sense we understand as gesture.

It would seem as if kinesthesia, or the sensing of muscular movement, though arising before language, should be made more highly conscious by linguistic use of imaginary space and metaphorical images of motion. Kinesthesia is marked in two facets of European culture: art and sport. European sculpture, an art in which Europe excels, is strongly kinesthetic, conveying great sense of the body's motions; European painting likewise. The dance in our culture expresses delight in motion rather than symbolism or ceremonial, and our music is greatly influenced by our dance forms. Our sports are strongly imbued with this element of the "poetry of motion." Hopi races and games seem to emphasize rather the virtues of endurance and sustained intensity. Hopi dancing is highly symbolic and is performed with great intensity and earnestness, but has not much movement or swing.

Synesthesia, or suggestion by certain sense receptions of characters belonging to another sense, as of light and color by sounds and vice versa, should be made more conscious by a linguistic metaphorical system that refers to nonspatial experiences by terms for spatial ones, though undoubtedly it arises from a deeper source. Probably in the first instance metaphor arises from synesthesia and not the reverse; yet metaphor need not become firmly rooted in linguistic pattern, as Hopi shows. Nonspatial experience has one well-organized sense, HEARING—for smell and taste are but little organized. Nonspatial consciousness is a realm chiefly of thought, feeling, and SOUND. Spatial consciousness is a realm of light, color, sight, and touch, and presents shapes and dimensions. Our metaphorical system, by naming nonspatial experiences after spatial ones, imputes to sounds, smells, tastes, emotions, and thoughts qualities like the colors, luminosities, shapes, angles, textures, and motions of spatial experience. And to some extent the reverse transference occurs; for, after much talking about tones as high, low, sharp, dull, heavy, brilliant, slow, the talker finds it easy to think of some factors in spatial experience as like factors of tone. Thus we speak of "tones" of color, a gray "monotone," a "loud" necktie, a "taste" in dress: all spatial metaphor in reverse. Now European art is distinctive in the way it seeks deliberately to play with synesthesia. Music tries to suggest scenes, color, movement, geometric design; painting and sculpture are often consciously guided by the analogies of music's rhythm; colors are conjoined with feeling for the analogy to concords and discords. The European theater and opera seek a synthesis of many arts. It may be that in this way our metaphorical language that is in some sense a confusion of thought is producing, through art, a result of far-reaching value—a deeper esthetic sense leading toward a more direct apprehension of underlying unity behind the phenomena so variously reported by our sense channels.

Historical Implications

How does such a network of language, culture, and behavior come about historically? Which was first: the language patterns or the cultural norms? In main they have grown up together, constantly influencing each other. But in this partnership the nature of the language is the factor that limits free plasticity and rigidifies channels of development in the more autocratic way. This is so because a language is a system, not just an assemblage of norms. Large systematic outlines can change to something really new only very slowly, while many other cultural innovations are made with comparative quickness. Language thus represents the mass mind; it is affected by inventions and innovations, but affected little and slowly, whereas TO inventors and innovators it legislates with the decree immediate.

The growth of the SAE language-culture complex dates from ancient times. Much of its metaphorical reference to the nonspatial by the spatial was already fixed in the ancient tongues, and more especially in Latin. It is indeed a marked trait of Latin. If we compare, say Hebrew, we find that, while Hebrew has some allusion to not-space as space, Latin has more. Latin terms for nonspatials, like *educo, religio, principia, comprehendo,* are usually metaphorized physical references: lead out, tying back, etc. This is not true of all languages—it is quite untrue of Hopi. The fact that in Latin the direction of development happened to be from spatial to nonspatial (partly because of secondary stimulation to abstract thinking when the intellectually crude Romans encountered Greek culture) and that later tongues were strongly stimulated to mimic Latin, seems a likely reason for a belief, which still lingers on among linguists, that this is the natural direction of semantic change in all languages, and for the persistent notion in Western learned circles (in strong contrast to Eastern ones) that objective experience is prior to subjective. Philosophies make out a weighty case for the reverse, and certainly the direction of development is sometimes the reverse. Thus the Hopi word for "heart" can be shown to be a late formation within Hopi from a root meaning think or remember. Or consider what has happened to the word "radio" in such a sentence as "he bought a new radio," as compared to its prior meaning "science of wireless telephony."

In the Middle Ages the patterns already formed in Latin began to interweave with the increased mechanical invention, industry, trade, and scholastic and scientific thought. The need for measurement in industry and trade, the stores and bulks of "stuffs" in various containers, the typebodies in which various goods were handled, standardizing of measure and weight units, invention of clocks and measurement of "time," keeping of records, accounts, chronicles, histories, growth of mathematics and the partnership of mathematics and science, all cooperated to bring our thought and language world into its present form.

In Hopi history, could we read it, we should find a different type of language and a different set of cultural and environmental influences working together. A peaceful agricultural society isolated by geographic features and nomad enemies in a land of scanty rainfall, arid agriculture that could be made successful only by the utmost perseverance (hence the value of persistence and repetition), necessity for collaboration (hence emphasis on the psychology of teamwork and on mental factors in general), corn and rain as primary criteria of value, need of extensive PREPARATIONS and precautions to assure crops in the poor soil and precarious climate, keen realization of dependence upon nature favoring prayer and a religious attitude toward the forces of nature, especially prayer and religion directed toward the ever-needed blessing, rain—these things interacted with Hopi linguistic patterns to mold them, to be molded again by them, and so little by little to shape the Hopi world outlook.

To sum up the matter, our first question asked in the beginning is answered thus: Concepts of "time" and "matter" are not given in substantially the same form by experience to all men but depend upon the nature of the language or languages through the use of which they have been developed. They do not depend so much upon ANY ONE SYSTEM (e.g., tense, or nouns) within the grammar as upon the ways of analyzing and reporting experience which have become fixed in the language as integrated "fashions of speaking" and which cut across the typical grammatical classifications, so that such a "fashion" may include lexical, morphological, syntactic, and otherwise systemically diverse means coordinated in a certain frame of consistency. Our own "time" differs markedly from Hopi "duration." It is conceived as like a space of strictly limited dimensions, or sometimes as like a motion upon such a space, and employed as an intellectual tool accordingly. Hopi "duration" seems to be inconceivable in terms of space or motion, being the mode in which life differs from form, and consciousness *in toto* from the spatial elements of consciousness. Certain ideas born of our own time-concept, such as that of absolute simultaneity, would be either very difficult to express or impossible and devoid of meaning under the Hopi conception, and would be replaced by operational concepts. Our "matter" is the physical subtype of "substance" or "stuff," which is conceived as the formless extensional item that must be joined with form before there can be real existence. In Hopi there seems to be nothing corresponding to it; there are no formless extensional items; existence may or may not have form, but what it also has, with or without form, is intensity and duration, these being nonextensional and at bottom the same.

But what about our concept of "space," which was also included in our first question? There is no such striking difference between Hopi and SAE about space as about time, and probably the apprehension of space is given in substantially the same form by experience irrespective of language. The experiments of the Gestalt psychologists with visual perception appear to establish this as a fact. But the CONCEPT OF SPACE will vary somewhat with language, because, as an intellectual tool,[12] it is so closely linked with the concomitant employment of other intellectual tools, of the order of "time" and "matter," which are linguistically conditioned. We see things with our eyes in the same space forms as the Hopi, but our idea of space has also the property of acting as a surrogate of nonspatial relationships like time, intensity, tendency, and as a void to be filled with imagined formless items, one of which may even be called 'space.' Space as sensed by the Hopi would not be connected mentally with such surrogates, but would be comparatively "pure," unmixed with extraneous notions.

As for our second question: There are connections but not correlations or diagnostic correspondences between cultural norms and linguistic patterns. Although it would be impossible to infer the existence of Crier Chiefs from the lack of tenses in Hopi, or vice versa, there is a relation between a language and the rest of the culture of the society which uses it. There are cases where the "fashions of speaking" are closely integrated with the whole general culture, whether or not this be universally true, and there are connections within this integration, between the kind of linguistic analyses employed and various behavioral reactions and also the shapes taken by various cultural developments. Thus the importance of Crier Chiefs does have a connection, not with tenselessness itself, but with a system of thought in which categories different from our tenses are natural. These connections are to be found not so much by focusing attention on the typical rubrics of linguistic, ethnographic, or sociological description as by examining the culture and the language (always and only when the two have been together historically for a considerable time) as a whole in which concatenations that run across these departmental lines may be expected to exist, and, if they do exist, eventually to be discoverable by study.

[12] Here belong "Newtonian" and "Euclidean" space, etc. [Au.]

Emile Benveniste

1902–1976

The collection of Emile Benveniste's essays in linguistics written from the thirties to the late fifties covers a variety of subjects, from consideration of Aristotle to the relation of the behavior of bees to language. The two essays printed here, one published in 1939 and one in 1958, have in common a concern for the question of the referent. In "The Nature of the Linguistic Sign," Benveniste points out that there is a fruitful contradiction in *de Saussure*'s idea of the sign. On the one hand, de Saussure regards the sign as containing an arbitrary relation of signifier to signified. Yet at the same time he tacitly admits that the French and German words for ox apply to the same "reality" or referent. Benveniste's point about de Saussure is that there is a tacit notion of a referent present after all. The very arbitrariness on which de Saussure insists is dependent on the presence of the real object to which two entirely different signs refer. Furthermore, the sound image, or signifier, and the signified are inextricably one and can hardly be regarded as in an arbitrary relation if it is not possible to think the concept apart from the word, as de Saussure avers.

Clearly Benveniste thinks of language as fundamental to thought. In "Subjectivity in Language" he pursues this notion further by making a distinction between language and speech; by the latter term he means communication. His point is that communication is a property of language but not its fundamental nature or essence. Language is "constituent" and constitutes man as subject. The "I" of discourse is a linguistic creation, the polarity of "I-you" a product of language, prior to communication, which must be, one supposes, a consequence of it. It is Benveniste's view that the "I" and the other are dependent on each other and are nothing apart from this opposition, that reality is linguistically constituted as dialectical.

One sees in Benveniste an approach to linguistics more philosophically oriented than that of his predecessor de Saussure. There are obviously links between him and the earlier neo-Kantians back to Wilhelm von Humboldt. In his discussion of verbs in the later part of "Subjectivity in Language" one detects an affinity with the speech-act theorizing of *J. L. Austin* and *John Searle.*

Benveniste's *Problems in General Linguistics,* a translation of his major essays, appeared in English in 1971. Untranslated works include *Origine de la formation des noms en indo-européen* (1935); *Nom d'agent et noms d'actions en indo-européen* (1948); *Hittite et indo-européen* (1962); and *Le vocabulaire des institutions indo-européen* (1969–70). Despite considerable reference to him by recent literary theorists, little has been written about Benveniste's work, though remarks by him are quoted as authoritative in such works as Robert Scholes's *Structuralism in Literature* (1974) and Edward W. Said's *Beginnings* (1975).

THE NATURE OF THE LINGUISTIC SIGN

The idea of the linguistic sign, which is today asserted or implied in most works of general linguistics, came from Ferdinand de Saussure. And it was as an obvious truth, not yet explicit but nevertheless undeniable in fact, that Saussure taught that the nature of the sign is *arbitrary*. The formula immediately commanded attention. Every utterance concerning the essence of language or the modalities of discourse begins with a statement of the arbitrary character of the linguistic sign. The principle is of such significance that any thinking bearing upon any part of linguistics whatsoever necessarily encounters it. That it is cited everywhere and always granted as obvious are two good reasons for seeking at least to understand the sense in which Saussure took it and the nature of the proofs which show it.

In the *Cours de linguistique générale,*[1] this definition is explained in very simple statements. One calls *sign* "the total resultant of the association of a signifier [=sound image] and what is signified [=concept] . . ." "The idea of 'sister' is not linked by any inner relationship to the succession of sounds *s-ö-r* which serves as its signifier in French; that it could be represented equally by just any other sequence is proved by differences among languages and by the very existence of different languages: the signified 'ox' has as its signifier *b-ö-f* on one side of the border and *o-k-s* (Ochs) on the other." This ought to establish that "The bond between the signifier and the signified is arbitrary," or, more simply, that "the linguistic sign is arbitrary." By "arbitrary," the author means that "it is *unmotivated,* i.e., arbitrary in that it actually has no natural connection with the signified." This characteristic ought then to explain the very fact by which it is verified: namely, that expressions of a given notion vary in time and space and in consequence have no necessary relationship with it.

We do not contemplate discussing this conclusion in the name of other principles or by starting with different definitions. The question is whether it is consistent and whether, having accepted the bipartite nature of the sign (and we do accept it), it follows that the sign should be characterized as arbitrary. It has just been that Saussure took the linguistic sign to be made up of a signifier and signified. Now—and this is essential—he meant by "signifier," the *concept.* He declared in so many words that the "linguistic sign unites, not a thing and a name, but a concept and a sound image." But immediately afterward he stated that the nature of the sign is arbitrary because it "actually has no natural connection with the signified." It is clear that the argument is falsified by an unconscious and surreptitious recourse to a third term which was not included in the initial definition. This third term is the thing itself, the reality. Even though Saussure said that the idea of "sister" is not connected to the signifier *s-ö-r,* he was not thinking any the less of the *reality* of the notion. When he spoke of the difference between *b-ö-f* and *o-k-s,* he was referring in spite of himself to the fact that these two terms applied to the same *reality.* Here, then, is the *thing,* expressly excluded at first from the definition of the sign, now creeping into it by a detour, and permanently installing a contradiction there. For if one states in principle—and with reason—that language is *form,* not *substance*, it is necessary to admit—and Saussure asserted it plainly—that linguistics is exclusively a science of forms. Even more imperative is the necessity for leaving the "substance," *sister* or *ox,* outside the realm of the sign. Now it is only if one thinks of the animal *ox* in its concrete and "substantial" particularity, that one is justified in considering "arbitrary" the relationship between *böf* on the one hand and *oks* on the other to the same reality. There is thus a contradiction between the way in which Saussure defined the linguistic sign and the fundamental nature which he attributed to it.

Such an anomaly in Saussure's close reasoning does not seem to me to be imputable to a relaxation of his critical attention. I would see instead a distinctive trait of the historical and relativist thought of the end of the nineteenth century, an inclination often met with in the philosophical reflection of comparative thought. Different people react differently to the same phenomenon. The infinite diversity of attitudes and judgments leads to the consideration

THE NATURE OF THE LINGUISTIC SIGN originally appeared in *Acta Linguistica* (Copenhagen, 1939). Reprinted from *Problems in General Linguistics,* trans. Mary Elizabeth Meek, by permission of the University of Miami Press,

[1]See *de Saussure.* [Eds.]

that apparently nothing is necessary. From the universal dissimilarity, a universal contingency is inferred. The Saussurian concept is in some measure dependent on this system of thought. To decide that the linguistic sign is arbitrary because the same animal is called *bœuf* in one country and *Ochs* elsewhere, is equivalent to saying that the notion of mourning is arbitrary because in Europe it is symbolized by black, in China by white. Arbitrary, yes, but only under the impassive regard of Sirius or for the person who limits himself to observing from outside the bond established between an objective reality and human behavior and condemns himself thus to seeing nothing in it but contingency. Certainly with respect to a same reality, all the denominations have equal value; that they exist is thus the proof that none of them can claim that the denomination in itself is absolute. This is true. It is only too true and thus not very instructive. The real problem is far more profound. It consists in discerning the inner structure of the phenomenon of which only the outward appearance is perceived, and in describing its relationship with the ensemble of manifestations on which it depends.

And so it is for the linguistic sign. One of the components of the sign, the sound image, makes up the signifier; the other, the concept, is the signified. Between the signifier and the signified, the connection is not arbitrary; on the contrary, it is *necessary*. The concept (the "signified") *bœuf* is perforce identical in my consciousness with the sound sequence (the "signifier") *böf*. How could it be otherwise? Together the two are imprinted on my mind, together they evoke each other under any circumstance. There is such a close symbiosis between them that the concept of *bœuf* is like the soul of the sound image *böf*. The mind does not contain empty forms, concepts without names. Saussure himself said:

> Psychologically our thought—apart from its expression in words—is only a shapeless and indistinct mass. Philosophers and linguists have always agreed in recognizing that without the help of signs we would be unable to make a clear-cut, consistent distinction between two ideas. Without language, thought is a vague, uncharted nebula. There are no preexisting ideas, and nothing is distinct before the appearance of language.

Conversely, the mind accepts only a sound form that incorporates a representation identifiable for it; if it does not, it rejects it as unknown or foreign. The signifier and the signified, the mental representation and the sound image, are thus in reality the two aspects of a single notion and together make up the ensemble as the embodier and the embodiment. The signifier is the phonic translation of a concept; the signified is the mental counterpart of the signifier. This consubstantiality of the signifier and the signified assures the structural unity of the linguistic sign. Here again we appeal to Saussure himself for what he said of language:

> Language can also be compared with a sheet of paper: thought is the front and the sound the back; one cannot cut the front without cutting the back at the same time; likewise in language, one can neither divide sound from thought nor thought from sound; the division could be accomplished only abstractedly, and the result would be either pure psychology or pure phonology.

What Saussure says here about language holds above all for the linguistic sign in which the primary characteristics of language are incontestably fixed.

One now sees the zone of the "arbitrary," and one can set limits to it. What is arbitrary is that one certain sign and no other is applied to a certain element of reality, and not to any other. In this sense, and only in this sense, is it permissible to speak of contingency, and even in so doing we would seek less to solve the problem than to point it out and then to take leave of it temporarily. For the problem is none other than the famous *φύσει* or *θέσει?* and can only be resolved by decree. It is indeed the metaphysical problem of the agreement between the mind and the world transposed into linguistic terms, a problem which the linguist will perhaps one day be able to attack with results but which he will do better to put aside for the moment. To establish the relationship as arbitrary is for the linguist a way of defending himself against this question and also against the solution which the speaker brings instinctively to it. For the speaker there is a complete equivalence between language and reality. The sign overlies and commands reality; even better, it *is* that reality (*nomen/omen*, speech taboos, the magic power of the word, etc.). As a matter of fact, the point of view of the speaker and of the linguist are so different in this regard that the assertion of the linguist as to the arbitrariness of designations does not refute the contrary feeling of the speaker. But, whatever the case may be, the nature of the linguistic sign is not at all involved if one defines it as Saussure did, since the essence of this definition is precisely to consider only the relationship of the signifier and the signified. The domain of the arbitrary is thus left outside the extension of the linguistic sign.

It is thus rather pointless to defend the principle of the "arbitrariness of the sign" against the objection which could be raised from onomatopoeia and expressive words. Not only because their range of use is relatively limited and because expressivity is an essentially transitory, subjective, and often secondary effect, but especially because, here again, whatever the reality is that is depicted by the onomatopoeia or the expressive word, the allusion to that reality in most cases is not immediate and is only admitted by a symbolic convention analogous to the convention that sanctions the ordinary signs of the system. We thus get back to the definition and the characteristics which are valid for all signs. The arbitrary does not exist here either, except with respect to the phenomenon or to the *material* object, and does not interfere with the actual composition of the sign.

Some of the conclusions which Saussure drew from the principle here discussed and which had wide effect should now be briefly considered. For instance, he demonstrated admirably that one can speak at the same time of the mutability and immutability of the sign; mutability, because since it is arbitrary it is always open to change, and immutability, because being arbitrary it cannot be challenged in the name of rational norm. "Language is radically powerless to defend itself against the forces which from one moment to the next are shifting the relationship between the signified and the signifier. This is one of the consequences of the arbitrary nature of the sign." The merit of this analysis is in no way diminished, but on the contrary is reinforced, if one states more precisely the relationship to which it in fact applies. It is not between the signifier and the signified that the relationship is modified and at the same time remains immutable; it is between the sign and the object; that is, in other terms, the objective *motivation* of the designation, submitted, as such, to the action of various historical factors. What Saussure demonstrated remains true, but true of the *signification,* not the sign.

Another problem, no less important, which the definition of the sign concerns directly, is that of *value,* in which Saussure thought to find a confirmation of his views: ". . . the choice of a given slice of sound to name a given idea is completely arbitrary. If this were not true, the notion of value would be compromised, for it would include an externally imposed element. But actually values remain entirely relative, and that is why the bond between the sound and the idea is radically arbitrary." It is worth the trouble to take up in succession the several parts of this argument. The choice that invokes a certain sound slice for a certain idea is not at all arbitrary; this sound slice would not exist without the corresponding idea and vice versa. In reality, Saussure was always thinking of the representation of the *real object* (although he spoke of the "idea") and of the evidently unnecessary and unmotivated character of the bond which united the sign to the *thing* signified. The proof of this confusion lies in the following sentence in which I have underlined the characteristic part: "If this were not true, the notion of value would be compromised *since it would include an externally imposed element.*" It is indeed an "externally imposed element," that is, the *objective* reality which this argument takes as a pole of reference. But if one considers the sign in itself and insofar as it is the carrier of value, the arbitrary is necessarily eliminated. For—the last proposition is the one which most clearly includes its own refutation—it is quite true that values remain entirely "relative" but the question is how and with respect to what. Let us state this at once: value is an element of the sign; if the sign taken in itself is not arbitrary, as we think to have shown, it follows that the "relative" character of the value cannot depend on the "arbitrary" nature of the sign. Since it is necessary to leave out of account the conformity of the sign to reality, all the more should one consider the value as an attribute only of the *form,* not of the substance. From then on, to say that the values are "relative" means that they are relative *to each other.* Now, is that not precisely the proof of their *necessity?* We deal no longer here with the isolated sign but with language as a system of signs, and no one has conceived of and described the systematic economy of language as forcefully as Saussure. Whoever says system says arrangement or conformity of parts in a structure which transcends and explains its elements. Everything is so *necessary* in it that modifications of the whole and of details reciprocally condition one another. The relativity of values is the best proof that they depend closely upon one another in the synchrony of a system which is always being threatened, always being restored. The point is that all values are values of opposition and are defined only by their difference. Opposed to each other, they maintain themselves in a mutual relationship of necessity. An opposition is, owing to the force of circumstances, subtended by necessity, as it is necessity which gives shape to the opposition. If language is something other than a fortuitous conglomeration of erratic notions and sounds uttered at random, it is because necessity is inherent in its structure as in all structure.

It emerges, then, that the role of contingency inherent in language affects denomination insofar as denomination is a phonic symbol of reality and affects it in its relationship with reality. But the sign, the primordial element in the linguistic system, includes a signifier and a signified whose bond has to be recognized as *necessary,* these two components being consubstantially the same. *The absolute character of the linguistic sign* thus understood commands in its turn the dialectical *necessity* of values of constant opposition, and forms the structural principle of language. It is perhaps the best evidence of the fruitfulness of a doctrine that it can engender a contradiction which promotes it. In restoring the true nature of the sign in the internal conditioning of the system, we go beyond Saussure himself to affirm the rigor of Saussure's thought.

SUBJECTIVITY IN LANGUAGE

If language is, as they say, the instrument of communication, to what does it owe this property? The question may cause surprise, as does everything that seems to challenge an obvious fact, but it is sometimes useful to require proof of the obvious. Two answers come to mind. The one would be that language is *in fact* employed as the instrument of communication, probably because men have not found a better or more effective way in which to communicate. This amounts to stating what one wishes to understand. One might also think of replying that language has such qualities as make it suited to serve as an instrument; it lends itself to transmitting what I entrust to it—an order, a question, an announcement—and it elicits from the interlocutor a behavior which is adequate each time. Developing a more technical aspect of this idea, one might add that the behavior of language admits of a behaviorist description, in terms of stimulus and response, from which one might draw conclusions as to the intermediary and instrumental nature of language. But is it really language of which we are speaking here? Are we not confusing it with discourse? If we posit that discourse is language put into action, and necessarily between partners, we show amidst the confusion, that we are begging the question, since the nature of this "instrument" is explained by its situation as an "instrument." As for the role of transmission that language plays, one should not fail to observe, on the one hand, that this role can devolve upon nonlinguistic means—gestures and mimicry—and, on the other hand, that, in speaking here of an "instrument," we are letting ourselves be deceived by certain processes of transmission which in human societies without exception come after language and imitate its functioning. All systems of signals, rudimentary or complex, are in this situation.

In fact, the comparison of language to an instrument—and it should necessarily be a material instrument for the comparison to even be comprehensible—must fill us with mistrust, as should every simplistic notion about language. To speak of an instrument is to put man and nature in opposition. The pick, the arrow, and the wheel are not in nature. They are fabrications. Language is in the nature of man, and he did not fabricate it. We are always inclined to that naïve concept of a primordial period in which a complete man discovered another one, equally complete, and between the two of them language was worked out little by little. This is pure fiction. We can never get back to man separated from language and we shall never see him inventing it. We shall never get back to man reduced to himself and exercising his wits to conceive of the exis-

SUBJECTIVITY IN LANGUAGE originally appeared in *Journal de psychologie* (1958). Reprinted from *Problems in General Linguistics,* trans. Mary Elizabeth Meek, by permission of the University of Miami Press, copyright 1971.

tence of another. It is a speaking man whom we find in the world, a man speaking to another man, and language provides the very definition of man.

All the characteristics of language, its immaterial nature, its symbolic functioning, its articulated arrangement, the fact that it has *content,* are in themselves enough to render suspect this comparison of language to an instrument, which tends to dissociate the property of language from man. Certainly in everyday practice the give and take of speaking suggests an exchange, hence a "thing" which we exchange, and speaking seems thus to assume in instrumental or vehicular function which we are quick to hypostasize as an "object." But, once again, this role belongs to the individual act of speech.

Once this function is seen as belonging to the act of speech, it may be asked what predisposition accounts for the fact that the act of speech should have it. In order for speech to be the vehicle of "communication," it must be so enabled by language, of which it is only the actualization. Indeed, it is in language that we must search for the condition of this aptitude. It seems to us that it resides in a property of language barely visible under the evidence that conceals it, which only sketchily can we yet characterize.

It is in and through language that man constitutes himself as a *subject,* because language alone establishes the concept of "ego" in reality, in *its* reality which is that of the being.

The "subjectivity" we are discussing here is the capacity of the speaker to posit himself as "subject." It is defined not by the feeling which everyone experiences of being himself (this feeling, to the degree that it can be taken note of, is only a reflection) but as the psychic unity that transcends the totality of the actual experiences it assembles and that makes the permanence of the consciousness. Now we hold that that "subjectivity," whether it is placed in phenomenology or in psychology, as one may wish, is only the emergence in the being of a fundamental property of language. "Ego" is he who *says* "ego." That is where we see the foundation of "subjectivity," which is determined by the linguistic status of "person."

Consciousness of self is only possible if it is experienced by contrast. I use *I* only when I am speaking to someone who will be a *you* in my address. It is this condition of dialogue that is constitutive of *person,* for it implies that reciprocally *I* becomes *you* in the address of the one who in his turn designates himself as *I*. Here we see a principle whose consequences are to spread out in all directions. Language is possible only because each speaker sets himself up as a *subject* by referring to himself as *I* in his discourse. Because of this, *I* posits another person, the one who, being, as he is, completely exterior to "me," becomes my echo to whom I say *you* and who says *you* to me. This polarity of persons is the fundamental condition in language, of which the process of communication, in which we share, is only a mere pragmatic consequence. It is a polarity, moreover, very peculiar in itself, as it offers a type of opposition whose equivalent is encountered nowhere else outside of language. This polarity does not mean either equality or symmetry: "ego" always has a position of transcendence with regard to *you*. Nevertheless, neither of the terms can be conceived of without the other; they are complementary, although according to an "interior/exterior" opposition, and, at the same time, they are reversible. If we seek a parallel to this, we will not find it. The condition of man in language is unique.

And so the old antinomies of "I" and "the other," of the individual and society, fall. It is a duality which it is illegitimate and erroneous to reduce to a single primordial term, whether this unique term be the "I," which must be established in the individual's own consciousness in order to become accessible to that of the fellow human being, or whether it be, on the contrary, society, which as a totality would preexist the individual and from which the individual could only be disengaged gradually, in proportion to his acquisition of self-consciousness. It is in a dialectic reality that will incorporate the two terms and define them by mutual relationship that the linguistic basis of subjectivity is discovered.

But must this basis be linguistic? By what right does language establish the basis of subjectivity?

As a matter of fact, language is responsible for it in all its parts. Language is marked so deeply by the expression of subjectivity that one might ask if it could still function and be called language if it were constructed otherwise. We are of course talking of language in general, not simply of particular languages. But the concordant facts of particular languages give evidence for language. We shall give only a few of the most obvious examples.

The very terms we are using here, *I* and *you,* are not to be taken as figures but as linguistic forms indicating "person." It is a remarkable fact—but who would notice it, since it is so familiar?—that the "personal pronouns" are never missing from among the signs of a language, no matter what its type, epoch, or region may be. A language without the expression of person cannot be imagined. It can only happen that in certain languages, under certain circumstances, these "pronouns" are deliberately omitted; this is the case in most of the Far Eastern societies, in which a convention of politeness imposes the use of periphrases or of special forms between certain groups of individuals in order to replace the direct personal references. But these usages only serve to underline the value of the avoided forms; it is the implicit existence of these pronouns that gives social and cultural value to the substitutes imposed by class relationships.

Now these pronouns are distinguished from all other designations a language articulates in that *they do not refer to a concept or to an individual.*

There is no concept "I" that incorporates all the *I*'s that are uttered at every moment in the mouths of all speakers, in the sense that there is a concept "tree" to which all the individual uses of *tree* refer. The "I," then, does not denominate any lexical entity. Could it then be said that *I* refers to a particular individual? If that were the case, a permanent contradiction would be admitted into language, and anarchy into its use. How could the same term refer indifferently to any individual whatsoever and still at the same time identify him in his individuality? We are in the presence of a class of words, the "personal pronouns," that escape the status of all the other signs of language. Then, what does *I* refer to? To something very peculiar which is exclusively linguistic: *I* refers to the act of individual discourse in which it is pronounced, and by this it designates the speaker. It is a term that cannot be identified except in what we have called elsewhere an instance of discourse and that has only a momentary reference. The reality to which it refers is the reality of the discourse. It is in the instance of discourse in which *I* designates the speaker that the speaker proclaims himself as the "subject." And so it is literally true that the basis of subjectivity is in the exercise of language. If one really thinks about it, one will see that there is no other objective testimony to the identity of the subject except that which he himself thus gives about himself.

Language is so organized that it permits each speaker to *appropriate to himself* an entire language by designating himself as *I*.

The personal pronouns provide the first step in this bringing out of subjectivity in language. Other classes of pronouns that share the same status depend in their turn upon these pronouns. These other classes are the indicators of *deixis,* the demonstratives, adverbs, and adjectives, which organize the spatial and temporal relationships around the "subject" taken as referent: "this, here, now," and their numerous correlatives, "that, yesterday, last year, tomorrow," etc. They have in common the feature of being defined only with respect to the instances of discourse in which they occur, that is, in dependence upon the *I* which is proclaimed in the discourse.

It is easy to see that the domain of subjectivity is further expanded and must take over the expression of temporality. No matter what the type of language, there is everywhere to be observed a certain linguistic organization of the notion of time. It matters little whether this notion is marked in the inflection of the verb or by words of other classes (particles, adverbs, lexical variations, etc.); that is a matter of formal structure. In one way or another, a language always makes a distinction of "tenses"; whether it be a past and a future, separated by a "present," as in French [or English], or, as in various Amerindian languages, of a preterite-present opposed to a future, or a present-future distinguished from a past, these distinctions being in their turn capable of depending on variations of aspect, etc. But the line of separation is always a reference to the "present." Now this "present" in its turn has only a linguistic fact as temporal reference: the coincidence of the event described with the instance of discourse that describes it. The temporal referent of the present can only be internal to the discourse. The *Dictionnaire générale* defines the "present" as "le temps du verbe qui exprime le temps où l'on est." But let us beware of this; there is no other criterion and no other expression by which to indicate "the time at which one *is*" except to take it as "the time at which one *is speaking*." This is the eternally "present" moment, although it never relates to the same events of an "objective" chronology because it is determined for each speaker by each of the instances of discourse related to it. Linguistic time is *self-referential.* Ultimately, human temporality with all its linguistic apparatus reveals the subjectivity inherent in the very using of language.

Language is accordingly the possibility of subjectivity because it always contains the linguistic forms appropriate to the expression of subjectivity, and discourse provokes the emergence of subjectivity because it consists of discrete instances. In some way language puts forth "empty" forms which each speaker, in the exercise of discourse, appropriates to himself and which he relates to his "person," at the same time defining himself as *I* and a partner as *you.* The instance of discourse is thus constitutive of all the coordinates that define the subject and of which we have briefly pointed out only the most obvious.

THE ESTABLISHMENT of "subjectivity" in language creates the category of person—both in language and also, we believe, outside of it as well. Moreover, it has quite varied effects in the very structure of languages, whether it be in the arrangement of the forms or in semantic relationships. Here we must necessarily have particular languages in view in order to illustrate some effects of the change of perspective which "subjectivity" can introduce. We cannot say what the range of the particular phenomena we are pointing out may be in the universe of real languages; for the moment it is less important to delimit them than to reveal them. English provides several convenient examples.

In a general way, when I use the present of a verb with three persons (to use the traditional nomenclature), it seems that the difference in person does not lead to any change of meaning in a conjugated verb form. *I eat, you eat,* and *he eats* have in common and as a constant that the verb form presents a description of an action, attributed respectively and in an identical fashion to "I," "you," and "he." Similarly, *I suffer, you suffer, he suffers* have the description of the same state in common. This gives the impression of being an obvious fact and even the formal alignment in the paradigm of the conjugation implies this.

Now a number of verbs do not have this permanence of meaning in the changing of persons, such as those verbs with which we denote dispositions or mental operations. In saying *I suffer,* I describe my present condition. In saying *I feel (that the weather is going to change),* I describe an impression which I feel. But what happens if, instead of *I feel (that the weather is going to change),* I say *I believe (that the weather is going to change)?* The formal symmetry between *I feel* and *I believe* is complete. Is it so for the meaning? Can I consider *I believe* to be a description of myself of the same sort as *I feel?* Am I describing myself believing when I say *I believe (that . . .)?* Surely not. The operation of thought is not at all the object of the utterance; *I believe (that . . .)* is equivalent to a mitigated assertion. By saying *I believe (that . . .),* I convert into a subjective utterance the fact asserted impersonally, namely, *the weather is going to change,* which is the true proposition.

Let us consider further the following utterances: "You are Mr. X., *I suppose.*" "*I presume* that John received my letter." "He has left the hospital, from which *I conclude* that he is cured." These sentences contain verbs that are verbs of operation: *suppose, presume,* and *conclude* are all logical operations. But *suppose, presume,* and *conclude,* put in the first person, do not behave the way, for example, *reason* and *reflect* do, which seem, however, to be very close. The forms *I reason* and *I reflect* describe me as reasoning and reflecting. Quite different are *I suppose, I presume,* and *I conclude.* In saying *I conclude (that . . .),* I do not describe myself as occupied in concluding; what could the activity of "concluding" be? I do not represent myself as being in the process of supposing and presuming when I say *I suppose, I presume. I conclude* indicates that, in the situation set forth, I extract a relationship of conclusion touching on a given fact. It is this logical relationship which is materialized in a personal verb. Similarly, *I suppose* and *I presume,* are very far from *I pose* and *I resume.* In *I suppose* and *I presume,* there is an indication of attitude, not a description of an operation. By including *I suppose* and *I presume* in my discourse, I imply that I am taking a certain attitude with regard to the utterance that follows. It will have been noted that all the verbs cited are followed by *that* and a proposition; this proposition is the real utterance, not the personal verb form that governs it. But on the other hand, that personal form is, one might say, the indicator of subjectivity. It gives the assertion that follows the subjective context—doubt, presumption, inference—suited to characterize the attitude of the speaker with respect to the statement he is making. This manifestation of subjectivity does not stand out except in the first person. One can hardly imagine similar verbs in the second person except for taking up an argument again *verbatim*; thus, *you suppose that he has left* is only a way of repeating what "you" has just said: "*I suppose* that he has left." But if one removes the expression of person, leaving only "*he supposes that* . . . ," we no longer have, from the point of view of *I* who utters it, anything but a simple statement.

We will perceive the nature of this "subjectivity" even more clearly if we consider the effect on the meaning produced by changing the person of certain verbs of speaking. These are verbs that by their meaning denote an individual act of social import: *swear, promise, guarantee, certify,* with locutional variants like *pledge to . . . , commit (oneself) to. . . .* In the social conditions in which a language is exercised, the acts denoted by these verbs are regarded as binding. Now here the difference between the "subjective" utterance and the "nonsubjective" is fully apparent as soon as we notice the nature of the opposition between the "persons" of the verb. We must bear in mind that the "third person" is the form of the verbal (or pronominal) paradigm that does *not* refer to a person because it refers to an object located outside direct address. But it exists and is characterized only by its opposition to the person *I* of the speaker who, in uttering it, situates it as "non-person." Here is its status. The form *he* . . . takes its value from the fact that it is necessarily part of a discourse uttered by "I."

Now *I swear* is a form of peculiar value in that it places the reality of the oath upon the one who says *I*. This utterance is a *performance;* "to swear" consists exactly of the utterance *I swear,* by which Ego is bound. The utterance *I swear* is the very act which pledges me, not the description of the act that I am performing. In saying *I promise, I guarantee,* I am actually making a promise or a guarantee. The consequences (social, judicial, etc.) of my swearing, of my promise, flow from the instance of discourse containing *I swear, I promise.* The utterance is identified with the act itself. But this condition is not given in the meaning of the verb, it is the "subjectivity" of discourse which makes it possible. The difference will be seen when *I swear* is replaced by *he swears.* While *I swear* is a pledge, *he swears* is simply a description, on the same plane as *he runs, he smokes.* Here it can be seen that, within the conditions belonging to these expressions, the same verb, according as it is assumed by a "subject" or is placed outside "person," takes on a different value. This is a consequence of the fact that the instance of discourse that contains the verb establishes the act at the same time that it sets up the subject. Hence the act is performed by the instance of the utterance of its "name" (which is "swear") at the same time that the subject is established by the instance of the utterance of its indicator (which is "I").

Many notions in linguistics, perhaps even in psychology, will appear in a different light if one reestablishes them within the framework of discourse. This is language in so far as it is taken over by the man who is speaking and within the condition of intersubjectivity, which alone makes linguistic communication possible.

Jacques Lacan

1901–1981

Jacques Lacan was for some time known as the *enfant terrible* of the psychoanalytical movement, partly for his unconventional analytical methods and partly for his reading of Freud. His "deviance" caused a break with the International Psychoanalytic Association in 1953, the year of his famous *Discours de Rome,* which appears in the English translation of *Ecrits* as "The Function and Field of Speech and Language in Psychoanalysis"; it is perhaps best consulted in Anthony Wilden's *The Language of the Self* (1968) with notes and a far-ranging commentary connecting Lacan to twentieth-century thought.

Lacan reads Freud through structuralism, particularly *de Saussure*'s theory of the signifier and *Lévi-Strauss*'s anthropology. However, he also displays the influence of phenomenology and, particularly in his early work, Hegel's *Phenomenology of Mind.* He harshly criticizes American psychoanalysis for its tendencies toward behaviorism, empiricism, and ego psychology. He seizes on the texts of Freud that are particularly concerned with language and reads them through the lens of structuralist linguistics. For Lacan, the unconscious is "structured like a language." He proceeds to interpret de Saussure's text as privileging the signifier over the signified, dominating linguistic structure. This model gives language (and the unconscious) a sort of autonomy, which decenters both language and the unconscious with respect to externality or the referent. By an irony familiar since structuralism, the unconscious is centered on lack or absence of the desired object.

Although Lacan says that human beings are always already enmeshed in the chain of signifiers, he also offers a story of entrance into that chain in his theory of three stages of human development, which he occasionally treats as if they actually occur diachronically but more often sees as synchronous or at least overlapping: the mirror stage, the imaginary, and the symbolic. Lacan's theory of subjectivity, based on these stages, displays phenomenological influence. The mirror stage, symbolized as the child's discovery of its image, establishes the idea of subjectivity by introducing the idea of alienation of the subject in the image, which becomes other to the self. The imaginary involves the child's simple dualistic relation with this mirror image. The symbolic is the entrance into language, where the subject is constantly deferred along the chain of signifiers. Thus the old "know thyself" becomes a naive simplification of a situation in which the subject is linguistically constituted elsewhere but never adequately. This concept of the subject is beyond the simple Cartesian subject and suggests that subjectivity is always (after entrance into the symbolic via the mirror stage) really an intersubjectivity formed in and as dialogue. This dialogue, which appears to be a version of structuralist difference, cannot end, except with death, because it is predicated on absence or lack and therefore desire. It is, in Freudian terms, "overdetermined."

Lacan's writings now translated include *Ecrits: A Selection* (1977); *The Four Fundamental Concepts of Psychoanalysis* (the eleventh seminar of 1964, published in France in 1973, trans. 1978); *Feminine Sexuality* (published in France between 1966 and 1975, trans. 1982); *The Language of the Self* (1968); "Seminar on the Purloined Letter," *Yale French Studies* 48 (1972). A number of the other seminars have been published in French. In addition to Wilden's commentary mentioned, see Edith Kurzweil, *The Age of Structuralism*; Stuart Schneiderman, *The Death of an Intellectual Hero*; R. Coward and J. Ellis, *Language and Materialism*; Gary Handwerk, *Irony and Ethics in Narrative: From Schlegel to Lacan*; Catherine Clement, *The Lives and Legends of Jacques Lacan*; and Michael Clark, *Jacques Lacan: A Bibliography.*

THE MIRROR STAGE as Formative of the Function of the I as Revealed in Psychoanalytic Experience

The conception of the mirror stage that I introduced at our last congress, thirteen years ago, has since become more or less established in the practice of the French group. However, I think it worthwhile to bring it again to your attention, especially today, for the light it sheds on the formation of the *I* as we experience it in psychoanalysis. It is an experience that leads us to oppose any philosophy directly issuing from the *Cogito*.

Some of you may recall that this conception originated in a feature of human behaviour illuminated by a fact of comparative psychology. The child, at an age when he is for a time, however short, outdone by the chimpanzee in instrumental intelligence, can nevertheless already recognize as such his own image in a mirror. This recognition is indicated in the illuminative mimicry of the *Aha-Erlebnis,* which Köhler[1] sees as the expression of situational apperception, an essential stage of the act of intelligence.

This act, far from exhausting itself, as in the case of the monkey, once the image has been mastered and found empty, immediately rebounds in the case of the child in a series of gestures in which he experiences in play the relation between the movements assumed in the image and the reflected environment, and between this virtual complex and the reality it reduplicates—the child's own body, and the persons and things, around him.

This event can take place, as we have known since Baldwin, from the age of six months, and its repetition has often made me reflect upon the startling spectacle of the infant in front of the mirror. Unable as yet to walk, or even to stand up, and held tightly as he is by some support, human or artificial (what, in France, we call a *'trotte-bébé'*), he nevertheless overcomes, in a flutter of jubilant activity, the obstructions of his support and, fixing his attitude in a slightly leaning-forward position, in order to hold it

THE MIRROR STAGE AS FORMATIVE OF THE FUNCTION OF THE I AS REVEALED IN PSYCHOANALYTIC EXPERIENCE was first delivered as a lecture in 1936. An early version appeared in *The International Journal of Psychoanalysis* in 1937. A later version was delivered as a lecture in 1949 (at the International Congress of Psychoanalysis in Zurich) and published in *Revue française de psychanalyse* in the same year. Reprinted from *Ecrits* (trans. Alan Sheridan) by permission of W. W. Norton & Company, Inc., and Tavistock Publications, Ltd.

[1]Wolfgang Köhler (1887–1967), American psychologist. [Eds.]

in his gaze, brings back an instantaneous aspect of the image.

For me, this activity retains the meaning I have given it up to the age of eighteen months. This meaning discloses a libidinal dynamism, which has hitherto remained problematic, as well as an ontological structure of the human world that accords with my reflections on paranoiac knowledge.

We have only to understand the mirror stage *as an identification,* in the full sense that analysis gives to the term: namely, the transformation that takes place in the subject when he assumes an image—whose predestination to this phase-effect is sufficiently indicated by the use, in analytic theory, of the ancient term *imago.*

This jubilant assumption of his specular image by the child at the *infans* stage, still sunk in his motor incapacity and nursling dependence, would seem to exhibit in an exemplary situation the symbolic matrix in which the *I* is precipitated in a primordial form, before it is objectified in the dialectic of identification with the other, and before language restores to it, in the universal, its function as subject.

This form would have to be called the Ideal-I,[2] if we wished to incorporate it into our usual register, in the sense that it will also be the source of secondary identifications, under which term I would place the functions of libidinal normalization. But the important point is that this form situates the agency of the ego, before its social determination, in a fictional direction, which will always remain irreducible for the individual alone, or rather, which will only rejoin the coming-into-being (*le devenir*) of the subject asymptotically, whatever the success of the dialectical syntheses by which he must resolve as *I* his discordance with his own reality.

The fact is that the total form of the body by which the subject anticipates in a mirage the maturation of his power is given to him only as *Gestalt,* that is to say, in an exteriority in which this form is certainly more constituent than constituted, but in which it appears to him above all in a constrasting size (*un relief de stature*) that fixes it and in a symmetry that inverts it, in contrast with the turbulent movements that the subject feels are animating him. Thus, this *Gestalt*—whose pregnancy should be regarded as bound up with the species, though its motor style remains scarcely recognizable—by these two aspects of its appearance, symbolizes the mental permanence of the *I,* at the same time as it prefigures its alienating destination; it is still pregnant with the correspondences that unite the *I* with the statue in which man projects himself, with the phantoms that dominate him, or with the automaton in which, in an ambiguous relation, the world of his own making tends to find completion.

Indeed, for the *imagos*—whose veiled faces it is our privilege to see in outline in our daily experience and in the penumbra of symbolic efficacity[3]—the mirror-image would seem to be the threshold of the visible world, if we go by the mirror disposition that the *imago of one's own body* presents in hallucinations or dreams, whether it concerns its individual features, or even its infirmities, or its object-projections; or if we observe the role of the mirror apparatus in the appearances of the *double,* in which psychical realities, however heterogeneous, are manifested.

That a *Gestalt* should be capable of formative effects in the organism is attested by a piece of biological experimentation that is itself so alien to the idea of psychical causality that it cannot bring itself to formulate its results in these terms. It nevertheless recognizes that it is a necessary condition for the maturation of the gonad of the female pigeon that it should see another member of its species, of either sex; so sufficient in itself is this condition that the desired effect may be obtained merely by placing the individual within reach of the field of reflection of a mirror. Similarly, in the case of the migratory locust, the transition within a generation from the solitary to the gregarious form can be obtained by exposing the individual, at a certain stage, to the exclusively visual action of a similar image, provided it is animated by movements of a style sufficiently close to that characteristic of the species. Such facts are inscribed in an order of homeomorphic identification that would itself fall within the larger question of the meaning of beauty as both formative and erogenic.

But the facts of mimicry are no less instructive when conceived as cases of heteromorphic identification, in as much as they raise the problem of the

[2]Throughout this article I leave in its peculiarity the translation I have adopted for Freud's *Ideal-Ich* [i.e., '*je-idéal*'], without further comment, other than to say that I have not maintained it since. [Au.]

[3]Cf. Claude Lévi-Strauss, *Structural Anthropology,* Chapter X. [Au.] See *Lévi-Strauss.* [Eds.]

signification of space for the living organism—psychological concepts hardly seem less appropriate for shedding light on these matters than ridiculous attempts to reduce them to the supposedly supreme law of adaptation. We have only to recall how Roger Caillois[4] (who was then very young, and still fresh from his breach with the sociological school in which he was trained) illuminated the subject by using the term *'legendary psychasthenia'* to classify morphological mimicry as an obsession with space in its derealizing effect.

I have myself shown in the social dialectic that structures human knowledge as paranoiac[5] why human knowledge has greater autonomy than animal knowledge in relation to the field of force of desire, but also why human knowledge is determined in that 'little reality' (*ce peu de réalité*), which the Surrealists, in their restless way, saw as its limitation. These reflections lead me to recognize in the spatial captation manifested in the mirror-stage, even before the social dialectic, the effect in man of an organic insufficiency in his natural reality—in so far as any meaning can be given to the word 'nature'.

I am led, therefore, to regard the function of the mirror-stage as a particular case of the function of the *imago,* which is to establish a relation between the organism and its reality—or, as they say, between the *Innenwelt* and the *Umwelt.*

In man, however, this relation to nature is altered by a certain dehiscence at the heart of the organism, a primordial Discord betrayed by the signs of uneasiness and motor unco-ordination of the neonatal months. The objective notion of the anatomical incompleteness of the pyramidal system and likewise the presence of certain humoral residues of the maternal organism confirm the view I have formulated as the fact of a real *specific prematurity of birth* in man.

It is worth noting, incidentally, that this is a fact recognized as such by embryologists, by the term *foetalization,* which determines the prevalence of the so-called superior apparatus of the neurax, and especially of the cortex, which psycho-surgical operations lead us to regard as the intraorganic mirror.

This development is experienced as a temporal dialectic that decisively projects the formation of the individual into history. The *mirror stage* is a drama whose internal thrust is precipitated from insufficiency to anticipation—and which manufactures for the subject, caught up in the lure of spatial identification, the succession of phantasies that extends from a fragmented body-image to a form of its totality that I shall call orthopaedic—and, lastly, to the assumption of the armour of an alienating identity, which will mark with is rigid structure the subject's entire mental development. Thus, to break out of the circle of the *Innenwelt* into the *Umwelt* generates the inexhaustible quadrature of the ego's verifications.

This fragmented body—which term I have also introduced into our system of theoretical references—usually manifests itself in dreams when the movement of the analysis encounters a certain level of aggressive disintegration in the individual. It then appears in the form of disjointed limbs, or of those organs represented in exoscopy, growing wings and taking up arms for intestinal persecutions—the very same that the visionary Hieronymus Bosch[6] has fixed, for all time, in painting, in their ascent from the fifteenth century to the imaginary zenith of modern man. But this form is even tangibly revealed at the organic level, in the lines of 'fragilization' that define the anatomy of phantasy, as exhibited in the schizoid and spasmodic symptoms of hysteria.

Correlatively, the formation of the *I* is symbolized in dreams by a fortress, or a stadium—its inner arena and enclosure, surrounded by marshes and rubbish-tips, dividing it into two opposed fields of contest where the subject flounders in quest of the lofty, remote inner castle whose form (sometimes juxtaposed in the same scenario) symbolizes the id in a quite startling way. Similarly, on the mental plane, we find realized the structures of fortified works, the metaphor of which arises spontaneously, as if issuing from the symptoms themselves, to designate the mechanisms of obsessional neurosis—inversion, isolation, reduplication, cancellation and displacement.

But if we were to build on these subjective givens alone—however little we free them from the condition of experience that makes us see them as partaking of the nature of a linguistic technique—our theoretical attempts would remain exposed to the

[4] Roger Caillois (1913–78), French critic and poet. [Eds.]
[5] Cf. 'Aggressivity in Psychoanalysis', p. 8 and *Ecrits,* p. 180. [Au.]

[6] Hieronymus Bosch (1462?–1516), Flemish painter. [Eds.]

charge of projecting themselves into the unthinkable of an absolute subject. This is why I have sought in the present hypothesis, grounded in a conjunction of objective data, the guiding grid for a *method of symbolic reduction.*

It establishes in the *defences of the ego* a genetic order, in accordance with the wish formulated by Miss Anna Freud,[7] in the first part of her great work, and situates (as against a frequently expressed prejudice) hysterical repression and its returns at a more archaic stage than obsessional inversion and its isolating processes, and the latter in turn as preliminary to paranoic alienation, which dates from the deflection of the specular *I* into the social *I*.

This moment in which the mirror-stage comes to an end inaugurates, by the identification with the *imago* of the counterpart and the drama of primordial jealousy (so well brought out by the school of Charlotte Bühler[8] in the phenomenon of infantile *transitivism*), the dialectic that will henceforth link the *I* to socially elaborated situations.

It is this moment that decisively tips the whole of human knowledge into mediatization through the desire of the other, constitutes its objects in an abstract equivalence by the co-operation of others, and turns the I into that apparatus for which every instinctual thrust constitutes a danger, even though it should correspond to a natural maturation—the very normalization of this maturation being henceforth dependent, in man, on a cultural mediation as exemplified, in the case of the sexual object, by the Oedipus complex.

In the light of this conception, the term primary narcissism, by which analytic doctrine designates the libidinal investment characteristic of that moment, reveals in those who invented it the most profound awareness of semantic latencies. But it also throws light on the dynamic opposition between this libido and the sexual libido, which the first analysts tried to define when they invoked destructive and, indeed, death instincts, in order to explain the evident connection between the narcissistic libido and the alienating function of the *I*, the aggressivity it releases in any relation to the other, even in a relation involving the most Samaritan of aid.

In fact, they were encountering that existential negativity whose reality is so vigorously proclaimed by the contemporary philosophy of being and nothingness.

But unfortunately that philosophy grasps negativity only within the limits of a self-sufficiency of consciousness, which, as one of its premises, links to the *méconnaissances* that constitute the ego, the illusion of autonomy to which it entrusts itself. This flight of fancy, for all that it draws, to an unusual extent, on borrowings from psychoanalytic experience, culminates in the pretention of providing an existential psychoanalysis.

At the culmination of the historical effort of a society to refuse to recognize that it has any function other than the utilitarian one, and in the anxiety of the individual confronting the 'concentrational'[9] form of the social bond that seems to arise to crown this effort, existentialism must be judged by the explanations it gives of the subjective impasses that have indeed resulted from it; a freedom that is never more authentic than when it is within the walls of a prison; a demand for commitment, expressing the impotence of a pure consciousness to master any situation; a voyeuristic–sadistic idealization of the sexual relation; a personality that realizes itself only in suicide; a consciousness of the other that can be satisfied only by Hegelian murder.

These propositions are opposed by all our experience, in so far as it teaches us not to regard the ego as centered on the *perception–consciousness system,* or as organized by the 'reality principle'—a principle that is the expression of a scientific prejudice most hostile to the dialectic of knowledge. Our experience shows that we should start instead from the *function of méconnaissance* that characterizes the ego in all is structures, so markedly articulated by Miss Anna Freud. For, if the *Verneinung*[10] represents the patent form of that function, its effects will, for the most part, remain latent, so long as they are not illuminated by some light reflected on

[7] Anna Freud, Austro-English (b. 1895), psychoanalyst, daughter of Sigmund Freud. [Eds.]

[8] Charlotte Bühler (1893–1974), German psychologist. [Eds.]

[9] 'Concentrationnaire', an adjective coined after World War II (this article was written in 1949) to describe the life of the concentration-camp. In the hands of certain writers it became, by extension, applicable to many aspects of 'modern' life. [Tr.]

[10] *Verneinung*: negation. [Eds.]

to the level of fatality, which is where the id manifests itself.

We can thus understand the inertia characteristic of the formations of the *I*, and find there the most extensive definition of neurosis—just as the captation of the subject by the situation gives us the most general formula for madness, not only the madness that lies behind the walls of asylums, but also the madness that deafens the world with its sound and fury.

The sufferings of neurosis and psychosis are for us a schooling in the passions of the soul, just as the beam of the psychoanalytic scales, when we calculate the tilt of its threat to entire communities, provides us with an indication of the deadening of the passions in society.

At this junction of nature and culture, so persistently examined by modern anthropology, psychoanalysis alone recognizes this knot of imaginary servitude that love must always undo again, or sever.

For such a task, we place no trust in altruistic feeling, we who lay bare the aggressivity that underlies the activity of the philanthropist, the idealist, the pedagogue, and even the reformer.

In the recourse of subject to subject that we preserve, psychoanalysis may accompany the patient to the ecstatic limit of the *'Thou art that'*, in which is revealed to him the cipher of his mortal destiny, but it is not in our mere power as practitioners to bring him to that point where the real journey begins.

THE AGENCY OF THE LETTER IN THE UNCONSCIOUS OR REASON SINCE FREUD

'Of Children in Swaddling Clothes

O cities of the sea, I behold in you your citizens, women as well as men tightly bound with stout bonds around their arms and legs by folk who will not understand your language; and you will only be able to give vent to your griefs and sense of loss of liberty by making tearful complaints, and sighs, and lamentations one to another; for those who bind you will not understand your language nor will you understand them.'

Leonardo da Vinci[1]

Although the nature of this contribution was determined by the theme of the third volume of *La Psychanalyse*,[2] I owe to what will be found there to insert it at a point somewhere between writing *(l'écrit)* and speech—it will be half-way between the two.

Writing is distinguished by a prevalence of the *text* in the sense that this factor of discourse will assume in this essay a factor that makes possible the kind of tightening up that I like in order to leave the reader no other way out than the way in, which I prefer to be difficult. In that sense, then, this will not be writing.

Because I always try to provide my seminars each time with something new, I have refrained so far from giving such a text, with one exception, which is not particularly outstanding in the context of the series, and which I refer to at all only for the general level of its argument.

For the urgency that I now take as a pretext for leaving aside such an aim only masks the difficulty that, in trying to maintain it at the level at which I ought to present my teaching here, I might push it too far from speech, whose very different techniques are essential to the formative effect I seek.

That is why I have taken the expedient offered me by the invitation to lecture to the philosophy group of the Fédération des étudiants ès lettres[3] to pro-

THE AGENCY OF THE LETTER IN THE UNCONSCIOUS OR REASON SINCE FREUD was originally delivered as a lecture in 1957 and published in *Psychanalyse* in 1958. It is reprinted here from *Ecrits* (trans. Alan Sheridan) by permission of W. W. Norton & Company, Inc., and Tavistock Publications, Ltd.

[1] *Codice Atlantico* 145. [Au.]

[2] *Psychanalyse et sciences de l'homme.* [Au.]

[3] The lecture took place on 9 May, 1957, in the Amphithéâtre Descartes of the Sorbonne, and the discussion was continued afterwards over drinks. [Au.]

duce an adaptation suitable to what I have to say: its necessary generality matches the exceptional character of the audience, but its sole object encounters the collusion of their common training, a literary one, to which my title pays homage.

Indeed, how could we forget that to the end of his days Freud constantly maintained that such a training was the prime requisite in the formation of analysts, and that he designated the eternal *universitas litterarum* as the ideal place for its institution.[4]

Thus my recourse (in rewriting) to the movement of the (spoken) discourse, restored to its vitality, by showing whom I meant it for, marks even more clearly those for whom it is not intended.

I mean that it is not intended for those who, for any reason whatever, in psychoanalysis, allow their discipline to avail itself of some false identity—a fault of habit, but its effect on the mind is such that the true identity may appear as simply one alibi among others, a sort of refined reduplication whose implications will not be lost on the most subtle minds.

So one observes with a certain curiosity the beginnings of a new direction concerning symbolization and language in the *International Journal of Psychoanalysis*, with a great many sticky fingers leafing through the pages of Sapir and Jespersen.[5] These exercises are still somewhat unpractised, but it is above all the tone that is lacking. A certain 'seriousness' as one enters the domain of veracity cannot fail to raise a smile.

And how could a psychoanalyst of today not realize that speech is the key to that truth, when his whole experience must find in speech alone its instrument, its context, its material, and even the background noise of its uncertainties.

I. The Meaning of the Letter

As my title suggests, beyond this 'speech', what the psychoanalytic experience discovers in the unconscious is the whole structure of language. Thus from the outset I have alerted informed minds to the extent to which the notion that the unconscious is merely the seat of the instincts will have to be rethought.

But how are we to take this 'letter' here? Quite simply, literally.[6]

By 'letter' I designate the material support that concrete discourse borrows from language.

This simple definition assumes that language is not to be confused with the various psychical and somatic functions that serve it in the speaking subject—primarily because language and its structure exist prior to the moment at which each subject at a certain point in his mental development makes his entry into it.

Let us note, then, that aphasias, although caused by purely anatomical lesions in the cerebral apparatus that supplies the mental centre for these functions, prove, on the whole, to distribute their deficits between the two sides of the signifying effect of what we call here 'the letter' in the creation of signification.[7] A point that will be clarified later.

Thus the subject, too, if he can appear to be the slave of language is all the more so of a discourse in the universal movement in which his place is already inscribed at birth, if only by virtue of his proper name.

Reference to the experience of the community, or to the substance of this discourse, settles nothing. For this experience assumes its essential dimension in the tradition that this discourse itself establishes. This tradition, long before the drama of history is inscribed in it, lays down the elementary structures of culture. And these very structures reveal an ordering of possible exchanges which, even if unconscious, is inconceivable outside the permutations authorized by language.

With the result that the ethnographic duality of nature and culture is giving way to a ternary concept of the human condition—nature, society, and culture—the last term of which could well be reduced to language, or that which essentially distinguishes human society from natural societies.

But I shall not make of this distinction either a point or a point of departure, leaving to its own obscurity the question of the original relations be-

[4] *Die Frage der Laienanalyse, G. W.*, XIV: 281–3. [Au.]

[5] Edward Sapir (1884–1939), American anthropological linguist; Otto Jespersen (1860–1943), Danish linguist. [Eds.]

[6] '*À la lettre*'. [Tr.]

[7] This aspect of aphasia, so useful in overthrowing the concept of 'psychological function', which only obscures every aspect of the question, becomes quite clear in the purely linguistic analysis of the two major forms of aphasia worked out by one of the leaders of modern linguistics, Roman Jakobson. See the most accessible of his works, the *Fundamentals of Language* (with Morris Halle), Mouton, 's Gravenhage, part II, Chapters 1 to 4. [Au.]

tween the signifier and labour. I shall be content, for my little jab at the general function of *praxis* in the genesis of history, to point out that the very society that wished to restore, along with the privileges of the producer, the causal hierarchy of the relations between production and the ideological superstructure to their full political rights, has none the less failed to give birth to an esperanto in which the relations of language to socialist realities would have rendered any literary formalism radically impossible.[8]

For my part, I shall trust only those assumptions that have already proven their value by virtue of the fact that language through them has attained the status of an object of scientific investigation.

For it is by virtue of this fact that linguistics[9] is seen to occupy the key position in this domain, and the reclassification of the sciences and a regrouping of them around it signals, as is usually the case, a revolution in knowledge; only the necessities of communication made me inscribe it at the head of this volume under the title 'the sciences of man'—despite the confusion that is thereby covered over.[10]

To pinpoint the emergence of linguistic science we may say that, as in the case of all sciences in the modern sense, it is contained in the constitutive moment of an algorithm that is its foundation. This algorithm is the following:

$$\frac{S}{s}$$

which is read as: the signifier over the signified, 'over' corresponding to the bar separating the two stages.

This sign should be attributed to Ferdinand de Saussure[11] although it is not found in exactly this form in any of the numerous schemas, which none the less express it, to be found in the printed version of his lectures of the years 1906–7, 1908–9, and 1910–11, which the piety of a group of his disciples caused to be published under the title, *Cours de linguistique générale,* a work of prime importance for the transmission of a teaching worthy of the name, that is, that one can come to terms with only in its own terms.

That is why it is legitimate for us to give him credit for the formulation S/*s* by which, in spite of the differences among schools, the beginning of modern linguistics can be recognized.

The thematics of this science is henceforth suspended, in effect, at the primordial position of the signifier and the signified as being distinct orders separated initially by a barrier resisting signification. And that is what was to make possible an exact study of the connections proper to the signifier, and of the extent of their function in the genesis of the signified.

For this primordial distinction goes well beyond the discussion concerning the arbitrariness of the sign, as it has been elaborated since the earliest reflections of the ancients, and even beyond the impasse which, through the same period, has been encountered in every discussion of the bi-univocal correspondence between the word and the thing, if only in the mere act of naming. All this, of course, is quite contrary to the appearances suggested by the importance often imputed to the role of the index finger pointing to an object in the learning process of the *infans* subject learning his mother tongue, or the use in foreign language teaching of so-called 'concrete' methods.

One cannot go further along this line of thought than to demonstrate that no signification can be sustained other than by reference to another signification[12]: in its extreme form this amounts to the proposition that there is no language *(langue)* in existence for which there is any question of its inability to cover the whole field of the signified, it being an effect of its existence as language *(langue)* that it necessarily answers all needs. If we try to grasp in language the constitution of the object, we cannot fail to notice that this constitution is to be

[8] We may recall that the discussion of the need for a new language in communist society did in fact take place, and Stalin, much to the relief of those who adhered to his philosophy, put an end to it with the following formulation: language is not a superstructure. [Au.]

[9] By 'linguistics' I mean the study of existing languages (*langues*) in their structure and in the laws revealed therein; this excludes any theory of abstract codes sometimes included under the heading of communication theory, as well as the theory, originating in the physical sciences, called information theory, or any semiology more or less hypothetically generalized. [Au.]

[10] *Psychanalyse et sciences de l'homme.* [Au.]

[11] See *de Saussure.* [Eds.]

[12] Cf. the *De Magistro* of St. Augustine, especially the chapter 'De significatione locutionis' which I analysed in my seminar of 23 June, 1954. [Au.]

found only at the level of concept, a very different thing from a simple nominative, and that the *thing*, when reduced to the noun, breaks up into the double, divergent beam of the 'cause' *(causa)* in which it has taken shelter in the French word *chose*, and the nothing *(rien)* to which it has abandoned its Latin dress *(rem)*.

These considerations, important as their existence is for the philosopher, turn us away from the locus in which language questions us as to its very nature. And we will fail to pursue the question further as long as we cling to the illusion that the signifier answers to the function of representing the signified, or better, that the signifier has to answer for its existence in the name of any signification whatever.

For even reduced to this latter formulation, the heresy is the same—the heresy that leads logical positivism in search of the 'meaning of meaning',[13] as its objective is called in the language of its devotees. As a result, we can observe that even a text highly charged with meaning can be reduced, through this sort of analysis, to insignificant bagatelles, all that survives being mathematical algorithms that are, of course, without any meaning.[14]

To return to our formula S/*s*: if we could infer nothing from it but the notion of the parallelism of its upper and lower terms, each one taken in its globality, it would remain the enigmatic sign of a total mystery. Which of course is not the case.

In order to grasp its function I shall begin by reproducing the classic, yet faulty illustration by which its usage is normally introduced, and one can see how it opens the way to the kind of error referred to above.

In my lecture, I replaced this illustration with another, which has no greater claim to correctness than that it has been transplanted into that incongruous dimension that the psychoanalyst has not

yet altogether renounced because of his quite justified feeling that his conformism takes its value entirely from it. Here is the other diagram:

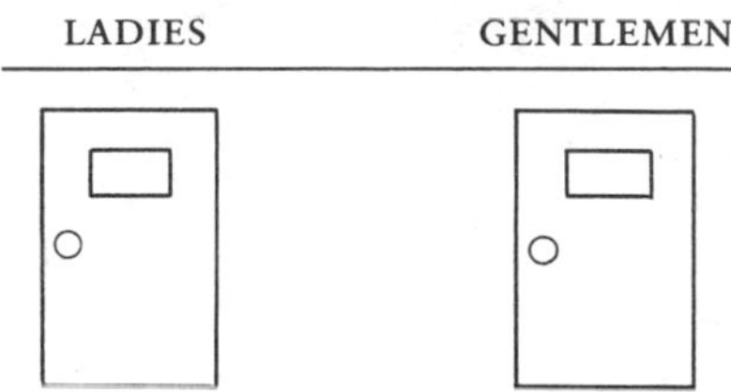

where we see that, without greatly extending the scope of the signifier concerned in the experiment, that is, by doubling a noun through the mere juxtaposition of two terms whose complementary meanings ought apparently to reinforce each other, a surprise is produced by an unexpected precipitation of an unexpected meaning: the image of twin doors symbolizing, through the solitary confinement offered Western Man for the satisfaction of his natural needs away from home, the imperative that he seems to share with the great majority of primitive communities by which his public life is subjected to the laws of urinary segregation.

It is not only with the idea of silencing the nominalist debate with a low blow that I use this example, but rather to show how in fact the signifier enters the signified, namely, in a form which, not being immaterial, raises the question of its place in reality. For the blinking gaze of a short sighted person might be justified in wondering whether this was indeed the signifier as he peered closely at the little enamel signs that bore it, a signifier whose signified would in this call receive its final honours

[13] English in the original. [Tr.]

[14] So, Mr. I. A. Richards, author of a work precisely in accord with such an objective, has in another work shown us its application. He took for his purposes a page from Mong-tse (Mencius, to the Jesuits) and called the piece, *Mencius on the Mind*. The guarantees of the purity of the experiment are nothing to the luxury of the approaches. And our expert on the traditional Canon that contains the text is found right on the spot in Peking where our demonstration-model mangle has been transported regardless of cost.

But we shall be no less transported, if less expensively, to see a bronze that gives out bell-tones at the slightest contact with thought, transformed into a rag to wipe the blackboard of the most dismaying British psychologism. And not without eventually being identified with the meninx of the author himself—all that remains of him or his object after having exhausted the meaning of the latter and the good sense of the former. [Au.]

from the double and solemn procession from the upper nave.

But no contrived example can be as telling as the actual experience of truth. So I am happy to have invented the above, since it awoke in the person whose word I most trust a memory of childhood, which having thus happily come to my attention is best placed here.

A train arrives at a station. A little boy and a little girl, brother and sister, are seated in a compartment face to face next to the window through which the buildings along the station platform can be seen passing as the train pulls to a stop. 'Look', says the brother, 'we're at Ladies!'; 'Idiot!' replies his sister, 'Can't you see we're at Gentlemen'.

Besides the fact that the rails in this story materialize the bar in the Saussurian algorithm (and in a form designed to suggest that its resistance may be other than dialectical), we should add that only someone who didn't have his eyes in front of the holes (it's the appropriate image here) could possibly confuse the place of the signifier and signified in this story, or not see from what radiating centre the signifier sends forth its light into the shadow of incomplete significations.

For this signifier will now carry a purely animal Dissension, destined for the usual oblivion of natural mists, to the unbridled power of ideological warfare, relentless for families, a torment to the Gods. For these children, Ladies and Gentlemen will be henceforth two countries towards which each of their souls will strive on divergent wings, and between which a truce will be the more impossible since they are actually the same country and neither can compromise on its own superiority without detracting from the glory of the other.

But enough. It is beginning to sound like the history of France. Which it is more human, as it ought to be, to evoke here than that of England, destined to tumble from the Large to the Small End of Dean Swift's egg.

It remains to be conceived what steps, what corridor, the S of the signifier, visible here in the plurals[15] in which it focuses its welcome beyond the window, must take in order to rest its elbows on the ventilators through which, like warm and cold air, indignation and scorn come hissing out below.

[15] Not, unfortunately, the case in the English here—the plural of 'gentleman' being indicated other than by the addition of an 's'. [Tr.]

One thing is certain: if the algorithm S/*s* with its bar is appropriate, access from one to the other cannot in any case have a signification. For in so far as it is itself only pure function of the signifier, the algorithm can reveal only the structure of a signifier in this transfer.

Now the structure of the signifier is, as it is commonly said of language itself, that it should be articulated.

This means that no matter where one starts to designate their reciprocal encroachments and increasing inclusions, these units are subjected to the double condition of being reducible to ultimate differential elements and of combining them according to the laws of a closed order.

These elements, one of the decisive discoveries of linguistics, are *phonemes*; but we must not expect to find any *phonetic* constancy in the modulatory variability to which this term applies, but rather the synchronic system of differential couplings necessary for the discernment of sounds in a given language. Through this, one sees that an essential element of the spoken word itself was predestined to flow into the mobile characters which, in a jumble of lower-case Didots or Garamonds,[16] render validly present what we call the 'letter', namely, the essentially localized structure of the signifier.

With the second property of the signifier, that of combining according to the laws of a closed order, is affirmed the necessity of the topological substratum of which the term I ordinarily use, namely, the signifying chain, gives an approximate idea: rings of a necklace that is a ring in another necklace made of rings.

Such are the structural conditions that define grammar as the order of constitutive encroachments of the signifier up to the level of the unit immediately superior to the sentence, and lexicology as the order of constitutive inclusions of the signifier to the level of the verbal locution.

In examining the limits by which these two exercises in the understanding of linguistic usage are determined, it is easy to see that only the correlations between signifier and signifier provide the standard for all research into signification, as is indicated by the notion of 'usage' of a taxeme or semanteme which in fact refers to the context just above that of the units concerned.

But it is not because the undertakings of gram-

[16] Names of different type-faces. [Tr.]

mar and lexicology are exhausted within certain limits that we must think that beyond those limits signification reigns supreme. That would be an error.

For the signifier, by its very nature, always anticipates meaning by unfolding its dimension before it. As is seen at the level of the sentence when it is interrupted before the significant term: 'I shall never . . .', 'All the same it is . . .', 'And yet there may be. . .'. Such sentences are not without meaning, a meaning all the more oppressive in that it is content to make us wait for it.[17]

But the phenomenon is no different which by the mere recoil of a 'but' brings to the light, comely as the Shulamite, honest as the dew, the negress adorned for the wedding and the poor woman ready for the auction-block.[18]

From which we can say that it is in the chain of the signifier that the meaning 'insists' but that none of its elements 'consists' in the signification of which it is at the moment capable.

We are forced, then, to accept the notion of an incessant sliding of the signified under the signifier—which Ferdinand de Saussure illustrates with an image resembling the wavy lines of the upper and lower Waters in miniatures from manuscripts of *Genesis*; a double flux marked by fine streaks of rain, vertical dotted lines supposedly confining segments of correspondence.

All our experience runs counter to this linearity, which made me speak once, in one of my seminars on psychosis, of something more like 'anchoring points' *('points de capiton')* as a schema for taking into account the dominance of the letter in the dramatic transformation that dialogue can effect in the subject.[19]

The linearity that Saussure holds to be constitutive of the chain of discourse, in conformity with its emission by a single voice and with its horizontal position in our writing—if this linearity is necessary, in fact, it is not sufficient. It applies to the chain of discourse only in the direction in which it is orientated in time, being taken as a signifying factor in all languages in which 'Peter hits Paul' reverses its time when the terms are inverted.

But one has only to listen to poetry, which Saussure was no doubt in the habit of doing,[20] for a polyphony to be heard, for it to become clear that all discourse is aligned along the several staves of a score.

There is in effect no signifying chain that does not have, as if attached to the punctuation of each of its units, a whole articulation of relevant contexts suspended 'vertically', as it were, from that point.

Let us take our word 'tree' again, this time not as an isolated noun, but at the point of one of these punctuations, and see how it crosses the bar of the Saussurian algorithm. (The anagram of *'arbre'* and *'barre'* should be noted.)

For even broken down into the double spectre of its vowels and consonants, it can still call up with the robur and the plane tree the significations it takes on, in the context of our flora, of strength and majesty. Drawing on all the symbolic contexts suggested in the Hebrew of the Bible, it erects on a barren hill the shadow of the cross. Then reduces to the capital Y, the sign of dichotomy which, except for the illustration used by heraldry, would owe nothing to the tree however genealogical we may think it. Circulatory tree, tree of life on the cerebellum, tree of Saturn, tree of Diana, crystals formed in a tree struck by lightning, is it your figure that traces our destiny for us in the tortoise-shell cracked by the fire, or your lightning that causes that slow shift in the axis of being to surge up from an unnamable night into the Ἑν πάντα of language:

> No! says the Tree, it says No! in the shower
> of sparks
> Of its superb head

lines that require the harmonics of the tree just as much as their continuation:

[17] To which verbal hallucination, when it takes this form, opens a communicating door with the Freudian structure of psychosis—a door until now unnoticed (cf. 'On a Question Preliminary to any Possible Treatment of Psychosis', pp. 179–225). [Au.]

[18] The allusions are to the 'I am black, but comely . . .' of the *Song of Solomon,* and to the nineteenth-century cliché of the 'poor, but honest' woman. [Tr.]

[19] I spoke in my seminar of 6 June, 1956, of the first scene of *Athalie,* incited by an allusion—tossed off by a highbrow critic in the *New Statesman and Nation*—to the 'high whoredom' of Racine's heroines, to renounce reference to the savage dramas of Shakespeare, which have become compulsional in analytic circles where they play the role of status-symbol for the Philistines. [Au.]

[20] The publication by Jean Starobinski, in *Le Mercure de France* (February 1964) of Saussure's notes on anagrams and their hypogrammatical use, from the Saturnine verses to the writings of Cicero, provide the corroboration that I then lacked (note 1966). [Au.]

Which the storm treats as universally
As it does a blade of grass.[21]

For this modern verse is ordered according to the same law of the parallelism of the signifier that creates the harmony governing the primitive Slavic epic or the most refined Chinese poetry.

As is seen in the fact that the tree and the blade of grass are chosen from the same mode of the existent in order for the signs of contradiction—saying 'No!' and 'treat as'—to affect them, and also so as to bring about, through the categorical contrast of the particularity of 'superb' with the 'universally' that reduces it, in the condensation of the 'head' *(Tête)* and the 'storm' *(tempête),* the indiscernible shower of sparks of the eternal instant.

But this whole signifier can only operate, it may be said, if it is present in the subject. It is the objection that I answer by supposing that it has passed over to the level of the signified.

For what is important is not that the subject know anything whatsoever. (If LADIES and GENTLEMEN were written in a language unknown to the little boy and girl, their quarrel would simply be the more exclusively a quarrel over words, but no less ready to take on signification.)

What this structure of the signifying chain discloses is the possibility I have, precisely in so far as I have this language in common with other subjects, that is to say, in so far as it exists as a language, to use it in order to signify *something quite other* than what it says. This function of speech is more worth pointing out than that of 'disguising the thought' (more often than not indefinable) of the subject; it is no less than the function of indicating the place of this subject in the search for the true.

I have only to plant my tree in a locution; climb the tree, even project on to it the cunning illumination a descriptive context gives to a word; raise it *(arborer)* so as not to let myself be imprisoned in some sort of *communiqué* of the facts, however official, and if I know the truth, make it heard, in spite of all the *between-the-lines* censures by the only signifier my acrobatics through the branches of the tree can constitute, provocative to the point of burlesque, or perceptible only to the practised eye, according to whether I wish to be heard by the mob or by the few.

The properly signifying function thus depicted in language has a name. We learned this name in some grammar of our childhood, on the last page, where the shade of Quintilian,[22] relegated to some phantom chapter concerning 'final considerations on style', seemed suddenly to speed up his voice in an attempt to get in all he had to say before the end.

It is among the figures of style, or tropes—from which the verb 'to find' *(trouver)* comes to us—that this name is found. This name is *metonymy.*

I shall refer only to the example given there: 'thirty sails'. For the disquietude I felt over the fact that the word 'ship', concealed in this expression, seemed, by taking on its figurative sense, through the endless repetition of the same old example, only to increase its presence, obscured *(voilait)* not so much those illustrious sails *(voiles)* as the definition they were supposed to illustrate.

The part taken for the whole, we said to ourselves, and if the thing is to be taken seriously, we are left with very little idea of the importance of this fleet, which 'thirty sails' is precisely supposed to give us: for each ship to have just one sail is in fact the least likely possibility.

By which we see that the connexion between ship and sail is nowhere but in the signifier, and that it is in the *word-to-word* connexion that metonymy is based.[23]

[21] 'Non! dit l'Arbre, il dit: Non! dans l'étincellement
De sa tête superbe
Que la tempête traite universellement
Comme elle fait une herbe.'
(Paul Valéry, 'Au Platane', *Les Charmes*). [Au.]

[22] Marcus Fabius Quintilianus (c. 40–c. 118), Roman rhetorician. [Eds.]

[23] I pay homage here to the works of Roman Jakobson—to which I owe much of this formulation; works to which a psychoanalyst can constantly refer in order to structure his own experience, and which render superfluous the 'personal communications' of which I could boast as much as the next fellow.

Indeed, one recognizes in this oblique form of allegiance the style of that immortal couple, Rosencrantz and Guildenstern, who are virtually indistinguishable, even in the imperfection of their destiny, for it survives by the same method as Jeannot's knife, and for the same reason for which Goethe praised Shakespeare for presenting the character in double form: they represent, in themselves alone, the whole *Gesellschaft,* the Association itself (*Wilhelm Meisters Lehrjahre,* ed. Trunz, Christian Wegner Verlag, Hamburg, V (5): 299)—I mean the International Psychoanalytical Association.

We should savour the passage from Goethe as a whole: 'Dieses leise Auftreten dieses Schmiegen und Biegen, dies Jasagen, Streicheln und Schmeicheln, dieses

I shall designate as metonymy, then, the one side *(versant)* of the effective field constituted by the signifier, so that meaning can emerge there.

The other side is *metaphor*. Let us immediately find an illustration; Quillet's dictionary seemed an appropriate place to find a sample that would not seem to be chosen for my own purposes, and I didn't have to go any further than the well known line of Victor Hugo:

> His sheaf was neither miserly nor
> spiteful . . .[24]

under which aspect I presented metaphor in my seminar on the psychoses.

It should be said that modern poetry and especially the Surrealist school have taken us a long way in this direction by showing that any conjunction of two signifiers would be equally sufficient to constitute a metaphor, except for the additional requirement of the greatest possible disparity of the images signified, needed for the production of the poetic spark, or in other words for metaphoric creation to take place.

It is true this radical position is based on the experiment known as automatic writing, which would not have been attempted if its pioneers had not been reassured by the Freudian discovery. But it remains a confused position because the doctrine behind it is false.

The creative spark of the metaphor does not spring from the presentation of two images, that is, of two signifiers equally actualized. It flashes between two signifiers one of which has taken the place of the other in the signifying chain, the occulted signifier remaining present through its (metonymic) connexion with the rest of the chain.

One word for another: that is the formula for the metaphor and if you are a poet you will produce for your own delight a continuous stream, a dazzling tissue of metaphors. If the result is the sort of intoxication of the dialogue that Jean Tardieu[25] wrote under this title, that is only because he was giving us a demonstration of the radical superfluousness of all signification in a perfectly convincing representation of a bourgeois comedy.

It is obvious that in the line of Hugo cited above, not the slightest spark of light springs from the proposition that the sheaf was neither miserly nor spiteful, for the reason that there is no question of the sheaf's having either the merit or demerit of these attributes, since the attributes, like the sheaf, belong to Booz, who exercises the former in disposing of the latter and without informing the latter of his sentiments in the case.

If, however, his sheaf does refer us to Booz, and this is indeed the case, it is because it has replaced him in the signifying chain at the very place where he was to be exalted by the sweeping away of greed and spite. But now Booz himself has been swept away by the sheaf, and hurled into the outer darkness where greed and spite harbour him in the hollow of their negation.

But once *his* sheaf has thus usurped his place, Booz can no longer return there; the slender thread of the little word *his* that binds him to it is only one more obstacle to his return in that it links him to the notion of possession that retains him at the heart of greed and spite. So *his* generosity, affirmed in the passage, is yet reduced to *less than nothing* by the munificence of the sheaf which, coming from nature, knows neither our reserve nor our rejections, and even in its accumulation remains prodigal by our standards.

But if in this profusion the giver has disappeared along with his gift, it is only in order to rise again in what surrounds the figure of speech in which he was annihilated. For it is the figure of the burgeoning of fecundity, and it is this that announces the surprise that the poem celebrates, namely, the promise that the old man will receive in the sacred context of his accession to paternity.

So, it is between the signifier in the form of the

Behendigkeit, dies Schwänzein, diese Allheit und Leerheit, diese rechtliche Schurkerei, diese Unfähigkeit, wie kann sie durch einen Menschen ausgedruckt werden? Es sollten ihrer wenigstens ein Dutzend sein, wenn man sie haben könnte; denn sie bloss in Gesellschaft etwas, sie sind die Gesellschaft . . .'

Let us thank also, in this context, the author R. M. Loewenstein of 'Some Remarks on the Role of Speech in Psychoanalytic Technique' (*I. J. P.*, Nov.–Dec., 1956, XXXVII (6): 467) for taking the trouble to point out that his remarks are 'based on' work dating from 1952. This is no doubt the explanation for the fact that he has learned nothing from work done since then, yet which he is not ignorant of, as he cites me as their 'editor' (sic). [Au.]

[24] 'Sa gerbe n'était pas avare ni haineuse', a line from 'Booz endormi'. [Tr.]

[25] Jean Tardieu (b. 1903), French writer. [Eds.]

proper name of a man and the signifier that metaphorically abolishes him that the poetic spark is produced, and it is in this case all the more effective in realizing the signification of paternity in that it reproduces the mythical event in terms of which Freud reconstructed the progress, in the unconscious of all men, of the paternal mystery.

Modern metaphor has the same structure. So the line *Love is a pebble laughing in the sunlight,* recreates love in a dimension that seems to me most tenable in the face of its imminent lapse into the mirage of narcissistic altruism.

We see, then that, metaphor occurs at the precise point at which sense emerged from non-sense, that is, at that frontier which, as Freud discovered, when crossed the other way produces the word that in French is *the* word *par excellence,* the word that is simply the signifier *'esprit'*;[26] it is at this frontier that we realize that man defies his very destiny when he derides the signifier.

But to come back to our subject, what does man find in metonymy if not the power to circumvent the obstacles of social censure? Does not this form, which gives its field a truth in its very oppression, manifest a certain servitude inherent in its presentation?

One may read with profit a book by Leo Strauss, from the land that traditionally offers asylum to those who choose freedom, in which the author reflects on the relation between the art of writing and persecution.[27] By pushing to its limits the sort of connaturality that links this art to that condition, he lets us glimpse a certain something which in this matter imposes its form, in the effect of truth on desire.

But haven't we felt for some time now that, having followed the ways of the letter in search of Freudian truth, we are getting very warm indeed, that it is burning all about us?

Of course, as it is said, the letter killeth while the spirit giveth life. We can't help but agree, having had to pay homage elsewhere to a noble victim of the error of seeking the spirit in the letter; but we should also like to know how the spirit could live without the letter. Even so, the pretentions of the spirit would remain unassailable if the letter had not shown us that it produces all the effects of truth in man without involving the spirit at all.

It is none other than Freud who had this revelation, and he called his discovery the unconscious.

II. The Letter in the Unconscious

In the complete works of Freud, one out of every three pages is devoted to philological references, one out of every two pages to logical inferences, everywhere a dialectical apprehension of experience, the proportion of analysis of language increasing to the extent that the unconscious is directly concerned.

Thus in 'The Interpretation of Dreams' every page deals with what I call the letter of the discourse, in its texture, its usage, its immanence in the matter in question. For it is with this work that the work of Freud begins to open the royal road to the unconscious. And Freud gave us notice of this; his confidence at the time of launching this book in the early days of this century[28] only confirms what he continued to proclaim to the end: that he had staked the whole of his discovery on this essential expression of his message.

The first sentence of the opening chapter announces what for the sake of the exposition could not be postponed: that the dream is a rebus. And Freud goes on to stipulate what I have said from the start, that it must be understood quite literally. This derives from the agency in the dream of that same literal (or phonematic) structure in which the signifier is articulated and analysed in discourse. So the unnatural images of the boat on the roof, or the man with a comma for a head, which are specifically mentioned by Freud, are examples of dream-images that are to be taken only for their value as

[26] *'Mot',* in the broad sense, means 'word'. In the narrower sense, however, it means 'a witticism'. The French *'esprit'* is translated, in this context, as 'wit', the equivalent of Freud's *Witz.* [Tr.]

'Esprit' is certainly the equivalent of the German *Witz* with which Freud marked the approach of his third fundamental work on the unconscious. The much greater difficulty of finding this equivalent in English is instructive: 'wit', burdened with all the discussion of which it was the object from Davenant and Hobbes to Pope and Addison, abandoned its essential virtues to 'humour', which is something else. There only remains the 'pun', but this word is too narrow in its connotation. [Au.]

[27] Leo Strauss, *Persecution and the Art of Writing,* The Free Press, Glencoe, Illinois. [Au.]

[28] Cf. the correspondence, namely letters 107 and 109. [Au.]

signifiers, that is to say, in so far as they allow us to spell out the 'proverb' presented by the rebus of the dream. The linguistic structure that enables us to read dreams is the very principle of the 'significance of the dream', the *Traumdeutung*.

Freud shows us in every possible way that the value of the image as signifier has nothing whatever to do with its signification, giving as an example Egyptian hieroglyphics in which it would be sheer buffoonery to pretend that in a given text the frequency of a vulture, which is an *aleph*, or of a chick, which is a *vau*, indicating a form of the verb 'to be' or a plural, prove that the text has anything at all to do with these ornithological specimens. Freud finds in this writing certain uses of the signifier that are lost in ours, such as the use of determinatives, where a categorical figure is added to the literal figuration of a verbal term; but this is only to show us that even in this writing, the so-called 'ideogram' is a letter.

But it does not require the current confusion on this last term for there to prevail in the minds of psychoanalysts lacking linguistic training the prejudice in favour of a symbolism deriving from natural analogy, or even of the image as appropriate to the instinct. And to such an extent that, outside the French school, which has been alerted, a distinction must be drawn between reading coffee grounds and reading hieroglyphics, by recalling to its own principles a technique that could not be justified were it not directed towards the unconscious.

It must be said that this is admitted only with difficulty and that the mental vice denounced above enjoys such favour that today's psychoanalyst can be expected to say that he decodes before he will come around to taking the necessary tour with Freud (turn at the statue of Champollion,[29] says the guide) that will make him understand that what he does is decipher; the distinction is that a cryptogram takes on its full dimension only when it is in a lost language.

Taking the tour is simply continuing in the *Traumdeutung*.

Entstellung, translated as 'distortion' or 'transposition', is what Freud shows to be the general precondition for the functioning of the dream, and it is what I designated above, following Saussure, as the sliding of the signified under the signifier, which is always active in discourse (its action, let us note, is unconscious).

But what we call the two 'sides' of the effect of the signifier on the signified are also found here.

Verdichtung, or 'condensation', is the structure of the superimposition of the signifiers, which metaphor takes as its field, and whose name, condensing in itself the word *Dichtung*, shows how the mechanism is connatural with poetry to the point that it envelops the traditional function proper to poetry.

In the case of *Verschiebung*, 'displacement', the German term is closer to the idea of that veering off of signification that we see in metonymy, and which from its first appearance in Freud is represented as the most appropriate means used by the unconscious to foil censorship.

What distinguishes these two mechanisms, which play such a privileged role in the dream-work *(Traumarbeit)*, from their homologous function in discourse? Nothing, except a condition imposed upon the signifying material, called *Rücksicht auf Darstellbarkeit*, which must be translated by 'consideration of the means of representation'. (The translation by 'role of the possibility of figurative expression' being too approximative here.) But this condition constitutes a limitation operating *within* the system of writing; this is a long way from dissolving the system into a figurative semiology on a level with phenomena of natural expression. This fact could perhaps shed light on the problems involved in certain modes of pictography which, simply because they have been abandoned in writing as imperfect, are not therefore to be regarded as mere evolutionary stages. Let us say, then, that the dream is like the parlour-game in which one is supposed to get the spectators to guess some well known saying or variant of it solely by dumb-show. That the dream uses speech makes no difference since for the unconscious it is only one among several elements of the representation. It is precisely the fact that both the game and the dream run up against a lack of taxematic material for the representation of such logical articulations as causality, contradiction, hypothesis, etc., that proves they are a form of writing rather than of mime. The subtle processes that the dream is seen to use to represent these logical articulations, in a much less artificial way than games usually employ, are the object of a

[29] Jean-François Champollion (1790–1832), the first scholar to decipher the Ancient Egyptian hieroglyphics. [Tr.]

special study in Freud in which we see once more confirmed that the dream-work follows the laws of the signifier.

The rest of the dream-elaboration is designated as secondary by Freud, the nature of which indicates its value: they are phantasies or daydreams *(Tagtraum)* to use the term Freud prefers in order to emphasize their function of wish-fulfillment *(Wunscherfüllung)*. Given the fact that these phantasies may remain unconscious, their distinctive feature is in this case their signification. Now, concerning these phantasies, Freud tells us that their place in the dream is either to be taken up and used as signifying elements for the statement of the unconscious thoughts *(Traumgedanke)*, or to be used in the secondary elaboration just mentioned, that is to say, in a function not to be distinguished from our waking thought *(von unserem wachen Denken nicht zu unterschieden)*. No better idea of the effects of this function can be given than by comparing it to areas of colour which, when applied here and there to a stencilplate, can make the stencilled figures, rather forbidding in themselves, more reminiscent of hieroglyphics or of a rebus, look like a figurative painting.

Forgive me if I seem to have to spell out Freud's text; I do so not only to show how much is to be gained by not cutting it about, but also in order to situate the development of psychoanalysis according to its first guide-lines, which were fundamental and never revoked.

Yet from the beginning there was a general *méconnaissance* of the constitutive role of the signifier in the status that Freud from the first assigned to the unconscious and in the most precise formal manner.

There are two reasons for this, of which the least obvious, of course, is that this formalization was not sufficient in itself to bring about a recognition of the agency of the signifier because the *Traumdeutung* appeared long before the formalizations of linguistics for which one could no doubt show that it paved the way by the sheer weight of its truth.

The second reason, which is after all only the reverse side of the first, is that if psychoanalysts were fascinated exclusively by the significations revealed in the unconscious, it is because these significations derived their secret attraction from the dialectic that seemed to be immanent in them.

I have shown in my seminars that it is the need to counteract the continuously accelerating effects of this bias that alone explains the apparent changes of direction or rather changes of tack, which Freud, through his primary concern to preserve for posterity both his discovery and the fundamental revisions it effected in our knowledge, felt it necessary to apply to his doctrine.

For, I repeat, in the situation in which he found himself, having nothing that corresponded to the object of his discovery that was at the same level of scientific development—in this situation, at least he never failed to maintain this object on the level of its ontological dignity.

The rest was the work of the gods and took such a course that analysis today takes its bearings in those imaginary forms that I have just shown to be drawn 'resist-style' *(en reserve)* on the text they mutilate—and the analyst tries to accommodate his direction to them, confusing them, in the interpretation of the dream, with the visionary liberation of the hieroglyphic aviary, and seeking generally the control of the exhaustion of the analysis in a sort of 'scanning'[30] of these forms whenever they appear, in the idea that they are witnesses of the exhaustion of the regressions and of the remodelling of the object relation from which the subject is supposed to derive his 'character-type.'[31]

The technique that is based on such positions can be fertile in its various effects, and under the aegis of therapy, difficult to criticize. But an internal criticism must none the less arise from the flagrant disparity between the mode of operation by which the technique is justified—namely the analytic rule, all the instruments of which, beginning with 'free association', depend on the conception of the unconscious of its inventor—and, on the other hand, the general *méconnaissance* that reigns regarding this conception of the unconscious. The most ardent adherents of this technique believe themselves to be freed of any need to reconcile the two by the merest pirouette: the analytic rule (they say) must be all the more religiously observed since it is only the result of a lucky accident. In other words, Freud never knew what he was doing.

A return to Freud's text shows on the contrary the

[30] That is the process by which the results of a piece of research are assured through a mechanical exploration of the entire extent of the field of its object. [Au.]

[31] By referring only to the development of the organism, the typology fails to recognize (*méconnaît*) the structure in which the subject is caught up respectively in phantasy, in drive, in sublimation. I am at present developing the theory of this structure (note 1966). [Au.]

absolute coherence between his technique and his discovery, and at the same time this coherence allows us to put all his procedures in their proper place.

That is why any rectification of psychoanalysis must inevitably involve a return to the truth of that discovery, which, taken in its original moment, is impossible to obscure.

For in the analysis of dreams, Freud intends only to give us the laws of the unconscious in their most general extension. One of the reasons why dreams were most propitious for this demonstration is exactly, Freud tells us, that they reveal the same laws whether in the normal person or in the neurotic.

But in either case, the efficacy of the unconscious does not cease in the waking state. The psychoanalytic experience does nothing other than establish that the unconscious leaves none of our actions outside its field. The presence of the unconscious in the psychological order, in other words in the relation-functions of the individual, should, however, be more precisely defined: it is not coextensive with that order, for we know that if unconscious motivation is manifest in conscious psychical effects, as well as in unconscious ones, conversely it is only elementary to recall to mind that a large number of psychical effects that are quite legitimately designated as unconscious, in the sense of excluding the characteristic of consciousness, are nonetheless without any relation whatever to the unconscious in the Freudian sense. So it is only by an abuse of the term that unconscious in that sense is confused with psychical, and that one may thus designate as psychical what is in fact an effect of the unconscious, as on the somatic for instance.

It is a matter, therefore, of defining the topography of this unconscious. I say that it is the very topography defined by the algorithm:

$$\frac{S}{s}$$

What we have been able to develop concerning the effects of the signifier on the signified suggests its transformation into:

$$f(S)\frac{I}{s}$$

We have shown the effects not only of the elements of the horizontal signifying chain, but also of its vertical dependencies in the signified, divided into two fundamental structures called metonymy and metaphor. We can symbolize them by, first:

$$f(S \ldots S')S \cong S(—)s$$

that is to say, the metonymic structure, indicating that it is the connexion between signifier and signifier that permits the elision in which the signifier installs the lack-of-being in the object relation, using the value of 'reference back' possessed by signification in order to invest it with the desire aimed at the very lack it supports. The sign—placed between ( ) represents here the maintenance of the bar — which, in the original algorithm, marked the irreducibility in which, in the relations between signifier and signified, the resistance of signification is constituted.[32]

Secondly,

$$f\left(\frac{S'}{S}\right)S \cong S(+)s$$

the metaphoric structure indicating that it is in the substitution of signifier for signifier that an effect of signification is produced that is creative or poetic, in other words, which is the advent of the signification in question.[33] The sign + between ( ) represents here the crossing of the bar — and the constitutive value of this crossing for the emergence of signification.

This crossing expresses the condition of passage of the signifier into the signified that I pointed out above, although provisionally confusing it with the place of the subject.

It is the function of the subject, thus introduced, that we must now turn to since it lies at the crucial point of our problem.

'I think, therefore I am' *(cogito ergo sum)* is not merely the formula in which is constituted, with the historical high point of reflection on the conditions of science, the link between the transparency of the transcendental subject and his existential affirmation.

Perhaps I am only object and mechanism (and so nothing more than phenomenon), but assuredly in

[32] The sign ≅ here designates congruence. [Au.]

[33] S′ designating here the term productive of the signifying effect (or significance); one can see that the term is latent in metonymy, patent in metaphor. [Au.]

so far as I think so, I am — absolutely. No doubt philosophers have brought important corrections to this formulation, notably that in that which thinks *(cogitans),* I can never constitute myself as anything but object *(cogitatum).* Nonetheless it remains true that by way of this extreme purification of the transcendental subject, my existential link to its project seems irrefutable, at least in its present form, and that: *'cogito ergo sum' ubi cogito, ibi sum,* overcomes this objection.

Of course, this limits me to being there in my being only in so far as I think that I am in my thought; just how far I actually think this concerns only myself and if I say it, interests no one.[34]

Yet to elude this problem on the pretext of its philosophical pretensions is simply to admit one's inhibition. For the notion of subject is indispensable even to the operation of a science such as strategy (in the modern sense) whose calculations exclude all 'subjectivism'.

It is also to deny oneself access to what might be called the Freudian universe—in a way that we speak of the Copernican universe. It was in fact the so-called Copernican revolution to which Freud himself compared his discovery, emphasizing that it was once again a question of the place man assigns to himself at the centre of a universe.

Is the place that I occupy as the subject of a signifier concentric or excentric, in relation to the place I occupy as subject of the signified?—that is the question.

It is not a question of knowing whether I speak of myself in a way that conforms to what I am, but rather of knowing whether I am the same as that of which I speak. And it is not at all inappropriate to use the word 'thought' here. For Freud uses the term to designate the elements involved in the unconscious, that is the signifying mechanisms that we now recognize as being there.

It is nonetheless true that the philosophical *cogito* is at the centre of the mirage that renders modern man so sure of being himself even in his uncertainties about himself, and even in the mistrust he has learned to practise against the traps of self-love.

Furthermore, if, turning the weapon of metonymy against the nostalgia that it serves, I refuse to seek any meaning beyond tautology, if in the name of 'war is war' and 'a penny's a penny' I decide to be only what I am, how even here can I elude the obvious fact that I am in that very act?

And it is no less true if I take myself to the other, metaphoric pole of the signifying quest, and if I dedicate myself to becoming what I am, to coming into being, I cannot doubt that even if I lose myself in the process, I am in that process.

Now it is on these very points, where evidence will be subverted by the empirical, that the trick of the Freudian conversion lies.

This signifying game between metonymy and metaphor, up to and including the active edge that splits my desire between a refusal of the signifier and a lack of being, and links my fate to the question of my destiny, this game, in all its inexorable subtlety, is played until the match is called, there where I am not, because I cannot situate myself there.

That is to say, what is needed is more than these words with which, for a brief moment I disconcerted my audience: I think where I am not, therefore I am where I do not think. Words that render sensible to an ear properly attuned with what elusive ambiguity[35] the ring of meaning flees from our grasp along the verbal thread.

What one ought to say is: I am not wherever I am the plaything of my thought; I think of what I am where I do not think to think.

This two-sided mystery is linked to the fact that the truth can be evoked only in that dimension of alibi in which all 'realism' in creative works takes its virtue from metonymy; it is likewise linked to this other fact that we accede to meaning only through the double twist of metaphor when we have the one and only key: the S and the *s* of the Saussurian algorithm are not on the same level, and man only deludes himself when he believes his true place is at their axis, which is nowhere.

Was nowhere, that is, until Freud discovered it; for if what Freud discovered isn't that, it isn't anything.

THE CONTENTS of the unconscious with all their disappointing ambiguities give us no reality in the

[34] It is quite otherwise if by posing a question such as 'Why philosophers?' I become more candid than nature, for then I am asking not only the question that philosophers have been asking themselves for all time, but also the one in which they are perhaps most interested. [Au.]

[35] *'Ambiguité de furet'*—literally, 'ferret-like ambiguity'. This is one of a number of references in Lacan to the game 'hunt-the-slipper' (*jeu du furet*). [Tr.]

subject more consistent than the immediate; their virtue derives from the truth and in the dimension of being: *Kern unseres Wesen*[36] are Freud's own terms.

The double-triggered mechanism of metaphor is the very mechanism by which the symptom, in the analytic sense, is determined. Between the enigmatic signifier of the sexual trauma and the term that is substituted for it in an actual signifying chain there passes the spark that fixes in a symptom the signification inaccessible to the conscious subject in which that symptom may be resolved—a symptom being a metaphor in which flesh or function is taken as a signifying element.

And the enigmas that desire seems to pose for a 'natural philosophy'—its frenzy mocking the abyss of the infinite, the secret collusion with which it envelops the pleasure of knowing and of dominating with *jouissance*, these amount to no other derangement of instinct than that of being caught in the rails—eternally stretching forth towards the *desire for something else*—of metonymy. Hence its 'perverse' fixation at the very suspension-point of the signifying chain where the memory-screen is immobilized and the fascinating image of the fetish is petrified.

There is no other way of conceiving the indestructibility of unconscious desire—in the absence of a need which, when forbidden satisfaction, does not sicken and die, even if it means the destruction of the organism itself. It is in a memory, comparable to what is called by that name in our modern thinking-machines (which are in turn based on an electronic realization of the composition of signification), it is in this sort of memory that is found the chain that *insists* on reproducing itself in the transference, and which is the chain of dead desire.

It is the truth of what this desire has been in his history that the patient cries out through his symptom, as Christ said that the stones themselves would have cried out if the children of Israel had not lent them their voice.

And that is why only psychoanalysis allows us to differentiate within memory the function of recollection. Rooted in the signifier, it resolves the Platonic aporias of reminiscence through the ascendancy of history in man.

One has only to read the 'Three Essays on Sexuality' to observe, in spite of the pseudo-biological glosses with which it is decked out for popular consumption, that Freud there derives all accession to the object from a dialectic of return.

Starting from Hölderlin's νοστος, Freud arrives less than twenty years later at Kierkegaard's repetition; that is, in submitting his thought solely to the humble but inflexible consequences of the 'talking cure',[37] he was unable ever to escape the living servitudes that led him from the sovereign principle of the Logos to re-thinking the Empedoclean antinomies of death.

And how else are we to conceive the recourse of a man of science to a *Deus ex machina* than on that 'other scene' he speaks of as the locus of the dream, a *Deus ex machina* only less derisory for the fact that it is revealed to the spectator that the machine directs the director? How else can we imagine that a scientist of the nineteenth century, unless we realize that he had to bow before the force of evidence that went well beyond his prejudices, valued more highly than all his other works his *Totem and Taboo*, with its obscene, ferocious figure of the primordial father, not to be exhausted in the expiation of Oedipus' blindness, and before which the ethnologists of today bow as before the growth of an authentic myth?

So that imperious proliferation of particular symbolic creations, such as what are called the sexual theories of the child, which supply the motivation down to the smallest detail of neurotic compulsions, these reply to the same necessities as do myths.

Thus, to speak of the precise point we are treating in my seminars on Freud, little Hans, left in the lurch at the age of five by his symbolic environment, and suddenly forced to face the enigma of his sex and his existence, developed, under the direction of Freud and of his father, Freud's disciple, in mythic form, around the signifying crystal of his phobia, all the permutations possible on a limited number of signifiers.

The operation shows that even on the individual level the solution of the impossible is brought within man's reach by the exhaustion of all possible forms of the impossibilities encountered in solution by recourse to the signifying equation. It is a striking demonstration that illuminates the labyrinth of

[36] 'The nucleus of our being'. [Tr.]

[37] English in the original. [Tr.]

a case which so far has only been used as a source of demolished fragments. We should be struck, too, by the fact that it is in the coextensivity of the development of the symptom and of its curative resolution that the nature of the neurosis is revealed: whether phobic, hysterical, or obsessive, the neurosis is a question that being poses for the subject 'from where it was before the subject came into the world' (Freud's phrase, which he used in explaining the Oedipal complex to little Hans).

The 'being' referred to is that which appears in a lightning moment in the void of the verb 'to be' and I said that it poses its question for the subject. What does that mean? It does not pose it *before* the subject, since the subject cannot come to the place where it is posed, but it poses it *in place* of the subject, that is to say, in that place it poses the question *with* the subject, as one poses a problem *with* a pen, or as Aristotle's man thought *with* his soul.

Thus Freud introduced the ego into his doctrine,[38] by defining it according to the resistances that are proper to it. What I have tried to convey is that these resistances are of an imaginary nature much in the same sense as those coaptative lures that the ethology of animal behaviour shows us in display or combat, and that these lures are reduced in man to the narcissistic relation introduced by Freud, which I have elaborated in my essay on the mirror stage. I have tried to show that by situating in this ego the synthesis of the perceptual functions in which the sensorimotor selections are integrated, Freud seems to abound in that delegation that is traditionally supposed to represent reality for the ego, and that this reality is all the more included in the suspension of the ego.

For this ego, which is notable in the first instance for the imaginary inertias that it concentrates against the message of the unconscious, operates solely with a view to covering the displacement constituted by the subject with a resistance that is essential to the discourse as such.

That is why an exhaustion of the mechanisms of defence, which Fenichel[39] the practitioner shows us so well in his studies of analytic technique (while his whole reduction on the theoretical level of neuroses and psychoses to genetic anomalies in libidinal development is pure platitude), manifests itself, without Fenichel's accounting for it or realizing it himself, as simply the reverse side of the mechanisms of the unconscious. Periphrasis, hyperbaton, ellipsis, suspension, anticipation, retraction, negation, digression, irony, these are the figures of style (Quintilian's *figurae sententiarum*); as catachresis, litotes, antonomasia, hypotyposis are the tropes, whose terms suggest themselves as the most proper for the labelling of these mechanisms. Can one really see these as mere figures of speech when it is the figures themselves that are the active principle of the rhetoric of the discourse that the analysand in fact utters?

By persisting in describing the nature of resistance as a permanent emotional state, thus making it alien to the discourse, today's psychoanalysts have simply shown that they have fallen under the blow of one of the fundamental truths that Freud rediscovered through psychoanalysis. One is never happy making way for a new truth, for it always means making our way into it: the truth is always disturbing. We cannot even manage to get used to it. We are used to the real. The truth we repress.

Now it is quite specially necessary to the scientist, to the seer, even to the quack, that he should be the only one to *know*. The idea that deep in the simplest (and even sickest) of souls there is something ready to blossom is bad enough! But if someone seems to know as much as they about what we ought to make of it . . . then the categories of primitive, prelogical, archaic, or even magical thought, so easy to impute to others, rush to our aid! It is not right that these nonentities keep us breathless with enigmas that prove to be only too unreliable.

To interpret the unconscious as Freud did, one would have to be as he was, an encyclopedia of the arts and muses, as well as an assiduous reader of the *Fliegende Blätter*.[40] And the task is made no easier by the fact that we are at the mercy of a thread woven with allusions, quotations, puns, and equivocations. And is that our profession, to be antidotes to trifles?

Yet that is what we must resign ourselves to. The unconscious is neither primordial nor instinctual; what it knows about the elementary is no more than the elements of the signifier.

The three books that one might call canonical

[38] This and the next paragraph were rewritten solely with a view to greater clarity of expression (note 1968). [Au.]

[39] Otto Fenichel (1899–1946), Austrian psychoanalyst. [Eds.]

[40] A German comic newspaper of the late nineteenth and early twentieth centuries. [Tr.]

with regard to the unconscious—'The Interpretation of Dreams', 'The Psychopathology of Everyday Life', and 'Jokes and their Relation to the Unconscious'—are simply a web of examples whose development is inscribed in the formulas of connexion and substitution (though carried to the tenth degree by their particular complexity—diagrams of them are sometimes provided by Freud by way of illustration); these are the formulas we give to the signifier in its *transference*-function. For in 'The Interpretation of Dreams' it is in the sense of such a function that the term *Übertragung*, or transference, is introduced, which later gave its name to the mainspring of the intersubjective link between analyst and analysand.

Such diagrams are not only constitutive of each of the symptoms in a neurosis, but they alone make possible the understanding of the thematic of its course and resolution. The great case-histories provided by Freud demonstrate this admirably.

To fall back on a more limited incident, but one more likely to provide us with the final seal on our proposition, let me cite the article on fetishism of 1927,[41] and the case Freud reports there of a patient who, to achieve sexual satisfaction, needed a certain shine on the nose *(Glanz auf der Nase)*; analysis showed that his early, English-speaking years had seen the displacement of the burning curiosity that he felt for the phallus of his mother, that is to say, for that eminent *manque-à-être*, for that want-to-be, whose privileged signifier Freud revealed to us, into a *glance at the nose*[42] in the forgotten language of his childhood, rather than a *shine on the nose*.[43]

It is the abyss opened up at the thought that a thought should make itself heard in the abyss that provoked resistance to psychoanalysis from the outset. And not, as is commonly said, the emphasis on man's sexuality. This latter has after all been the dominant object in literature throughout the ages. And in fact the more recent evolution of psychoanalysis has succeeded by a bit of comical legerdemain in turning it into a quite moral affair, the cradle and trysting-place of oblativity and attraction. The Platonic setting of the soul, blessed and illuminated, rises straight to paradise.

The intolerable scandal in the time before Freudian sexuality was sanctified was that it was so 'intellectual'. It was precisely in that that it showed itself to be the worthy ally of all those terrorists whose plottings were going to ruin society.

At a time when psychoanalysts are busy remodelling psychoanalysis into a right-thinking movement whose crowning expression is the sociological poem of the *autonomous ego*, I would like to say, to all those who are listening to me, how they can recognize bad psychoanalysts; this is by the word they use to deprecate all technical or theoretical research that carries forward the Freudian experience along its authentic lines. That word is *'intellectualization'*—execrable to all those who, living in fear of being tried and found wanting by the wine of truth, spit on the bread of men, although their slaver can no longer have any effect other than that of leavening.

III. The Letter, Being and the Other[44]

Is what thinks in my place, then, another I? Does Freud's discovery represent the confirmation, on the level of psychological experience, of Manicheism?[45]

In fact, there is no confusion on this point: what Freud's researches led us to is not a few more or less curious cases of split personality. Even at the heroic epoch I have been describing, when, like the animals in fairy stories, sexuality talked, the demonic atmosphere that such an orientation might have given rise to never materialized.[46]

The end that Freud's discovery proposes for man was defined by him at the apex of his thought in these moving terms: *Wo es war, soll Ich werden*. I must come to the place where that was.

This is one of reintegration and harmony, I could even say of reconciliation *(Versöhnung)*.

[41] *Fetischismus, G. W.* XIV: 311; "Fetishism', *Collected Papers*, V: 198; *Standard Edition* XXI: 149. [Au.]

[42] English in the original. [Tr.]

[43] English in the original. [Tr.]

[44] *La lettre l'être et l'autre*. [Au.]

[45] One of my colleagues went so far in this direction as to wonder if the id (*Es*) of the last phase wasn't in fact the 'bad ego'. (It should now be obvious whom I am referring to—1966.) [Au.]

[46] Note, nonetheless, the tone with which one spoke in that period of the 'elfin pranks' of the unconscious; a work of Silberer's is called *Der Zufall und die Koboldstreiche des Unbewussten* (Chance and the Elfin Tricks of the Unconscious)—completely anachronistic in the context of our present soul-managers. [Au.]

But if we ignore the self's radical ex-centricity to itself with which man is confronted, in other words, the truth discovered by Freud, we shall falsify both the order and methods of psychoanalytic mediation; we shall make of it nothing more than the compromise operation that it has, in effect, become, namely, just what the letter as well as the spirit of Freud's work most repudiates. For since he constantly invoked the notion of compromise as supporting all the miseries that his analysis is supposed to assuage, we can say that any recourse to compromise, explicit or implicit, will necessarily disorient psychoanalytic action and plunge it into darkness.

But neither does it suffice to associate oneself with the moralistic tartufferies of our time or to be forever spouting something about the 'total personality' in order to have said anything articulate about the possibility of mediation.

The radical heteronomy that Freud's discovery shows gaping within man can never again be covered over without whatever is used to hide it being profoundly dishonest.

Who, then, is this other to whom I am more attached than to myself, since, at the heart of my assent to my own identity it is still he who agitates me?

His presence can be understood only at a second degree of otherness, which already places him in the position of mediating between me and the double of myself, as it were with my counterpart.

If I have said that the unconscious is the discourse of the Other (with a capital O), it is in order to indicate the beyond in which the recognition of desire is bound up with the desire for recognition.

In other words this other is the Other that even my lie invokes as a guarantor of the truth in which it subsists.

By which we can also see that it is with the appearance of language the dimension of truth emerges.

Prior to this point, we can recognize in the psychological relation, which can be easily isolated in the observation of animal behaviour, the existence of subjects, not by means of some projective mirage, the phantom of which a certain type of psychologist delights in hacking to pieces, but simply on account of the manifested presence of intersubjectivity. In the animal hidden in his lookout, in the well-laid trap of certain others, in the feint by which an apparent straggler leads a predator away from the flock, something more emerges than in the fascinating display of mating or combat ritual. Yet there is nothing even there that transcends the function of lure in the service of a need, or which affirms a presence in that beyond-the-veil where the whole of Nature can be questioned about its design.

For there even to be a question (and we know that it is one Freud himself posed in 'Beyond the Pleasure Principle'), there must be language.

For I can lure my adversary by means of a movement contrary to my actual plan of battle, and this movement will have its deceiving effect only in so far as I produce it in reality and for my adversary.

But in the propositions with which I open peace negotiations with him, what my negotiations propose to him is situated in a third locus which is neither my speech nor my interlocutor.

This locus is none other than the locus of signifying convention, of the sort revealed in the comedy of the sad plaint of the Jew to his crony: 'Why do you tell me you are going to Cracow so I'll believe you are going to Lvov, when you really are going to Cracow?'

Of course the flock-movement I just spoke of could be understood in the conventional context of game-strategy, where it is a rule that I deceive my adversary, but in that case my success is evaluated within the connotation of betrayal, that is to say, in relation to the Other who is the guarantor of Good Faith.

Here the problems are of an order the heteronomy of which is completely misconstrued *(méconnue)* if reduced to an 'awareness of others', or whatever we choose to call it. For the 'existence of the other' having once upon a time reached the ears of the Midas of psychoanalysis through the partition that separates him from the secret meetings of the phenomenologists, the news is now being whispered through the reeds: 'Midas, King Midas, is the other of his patient. He himself has said it.'

What sort of breakthrough is that? The other, what other?

The young André Gide,[47] defying the landlady to whom his mother had confided him to treat him as a responsible person, opening with a key (false only in that it opened all locks of the same make) the lock that this lady took to be a worthy signifier of her educational intentions, and doing it quite ob-

[47] André Gide (1869–1951), French novelist. [Eds.]

viously for her benefit—what 'other' was he aiming at? She who was supposed to intervene and to whom he would then say: 'Do you think my obedience can be secured with a ridiculous lock?'. But by remaining out of sight and holding her peace until that evening in order, after primly greeting his return, to lecture him like a child, she showed him not just another with the face of anger, but another André Gide who is no longer sure, either then or later in thinking back on it, of just what he really meant to do—whose own truth has been changed by the doubt thrown on his good faith.

Perhaps it would be worth our while pausing a moment over this empire of confusion which is none other than that in which the whole human opera-buffa plays itself out, in order to understand the ways in which analysis can proceed not just to restore an order but to found the conditions for the possibility of its restoration.

Kern unseres Wesen, the nucleus of our being, but it is not so much that Freud commands us to seek it as so many others before him have with the empty adage 'Know thyself'—as to reconsider the ways that lead to it, and which he shows us.

Or rather that which he proposes for us to attain is not that which can be the object of knowledge, but that (doesn't he tell us as much?) which creates our being and about which he teaches us that we bear witness to it as much and more in our whims, our aberrations, our phobias and fetishes, as in our more or less civilized personalities.

Madness, you are no longer the object of the ambiguous praise with which the sage decorated the impregnable burrow of his fear; and if after all he finds himself tolerably at home there, it is only because the supreme agent forever at work digging its tunnels is none other than reason, the very Logos that he serves.

So how do you imagine that a scholar with so little talent for the 'commitments' that solicited him in his age (as they do in all ages), that a scholar such as Erasmus held such an eminent place in the revolution of the Reformation in which man has as much of a stake in each man as in all men?

The answer is that the slightest alteration in the relation between man and the signifier, in this case in the procedures of exegesis, changes the whole course of history by modifying the moorings that anchor his being.

It is precisely in this that Freudianism, however misunderstood it has been, and however confused its consequences have been, to anyone capable of perceiving the changes we have lived through in our own lives, is seen to have founded an intangible but radical revolution. There is no point in collecting witnesses to the fact:[48] everything involving not just the human sciences, but the destiny of man, politics, metaphysics, literature, the arts, advertising, propaganda, and through these even economics, everything has been affected.

Is all this anything more than the discordant effects of an immense truth in which Freud traced for us a clear path? What must be said, however, is that any technique that bases its claim on the mere psychological categorization of its object is not following this path, and this is the case of psychoanalysis today except in so far as we return to the Freudian discovery.

Furthermore, the vulgarity of the concepts by which it recommends itself to us, the embroidery of pseudo-Freudianism *(frofreudisme)* which is no longer anything but decoration, as well as the bad repute in which it seems to prosper, all bear witness to its fundamental betrayal of its founder.

By his discovery, Freud brought within the circle of science the boundary between the object and being that seemed to mark its outer limit.

That this is the symptom and the prelude of a reexamination of the situation of man in the existent such as has been assumed up to the present by all our postulates of knowledge—don't be content, I beg of you, to write this off as another case of Heideggerianism,[49] even prefixed by a neo- that adds nothing to the dustbin style in which currently, by the use of his ready-made mental jetsam, one excuses oneself from any real thought.

When I speak of Heidegger, or rather when I translate him, I at least make the effort to leave the speech he proffers us its sovereign significance.

[48] To pick the most recent in date, François Mauriac, in the *Figaro littéraire* of 25 May, apologizes for refusing 'to tell the story of his life'. If no one these days can undertake to do that with the old enthusiasm, the reason is that, 'a half century since, Freud, whatever we think of him' has already passed that way. And after being briefly tempted by the old saw that this is only the 'history of our body', Mauriac returns to the truth that his sensitivity as a writer makes him face: to write the history of oneself is to write the confession of the deepest part of our neighbours' souls as well. [Au.]

[49] See *Martin Heidegger.* [Eds.]

If I speak of being and the letter, if I distinguish the other and the Other, it is because Freud shows me that they are the terms to which must be referred the effects of resistance and transference against which, in the twenty years I have engaged in what we all call after him the impossible practice of psychoanalysis, I have done unequal battle. And it is also because I must help others not to lose their way there.

It is to prevent the field of which they are the inheritors from becoming barren, and for that reason to make it understood that if the symptom is a metaphor, it is not a metaphor to say so, any more than to say that man's desire is a metonymy. For the symptom *is* a metaphor whether one likes it or not, as desire *is* a metonymy, however funny people may find the idea.

Finally, if I am to rouse you to indignation over the fact that, after so many centuries of religious hypocrisy and philosophical bravado, nothing has yet been validly articulated as to what links metaphor to the question of being and metonymy to its lack, there must be an object there to answer to that indignation both as its instigator and its victim: that object is humanistic man and the credit, hopelessly affirmed, which he has drawn over his intentions.

14–26 May, 1957

Martin Heidegger

1889–1976

MARTIN HEIDEGGER, the famous philosopher of *Being and Time* and many other important works, is especially important to literary criticism for his theory and practice of phenomenological hermeneutics. "Hermeneutics" is usually translated as "interpretation," but Heidegger's theory of interpretation is complicated by his awareness of a variety of problems frequently ignored by his predecessors. The term comes, Heidegger informs us, from the Greek verb *hermeneuein,* related to the name of Hermes, bringer of messages. But Heidegger asserts that the bringing of a message is always a listening as well and is therefore a sort of intersubjective dialogue between interpreter and interpretant, in which being emerges. Thus Heidegger emphasizes the remark "we have been a conversation" in the essay on the German poet J. C. F. Hölderlin (1770–1843) that follows here. It is an excellent example of Heidegger's way with a text.

For Heidegger, all interpretations are in time, and the temporal situation governs and is part of the interpretation itself. Another word for this is "fore-sight" or the position from which one interprets. At the same time, interpretation is not a subjective domination of the text. It is a striving to let the text be, or to listen. The medium of all of this is language, which Heidegger regards as a power rather than a tool, and a power in which man lives. To discover the origin of language is impossible, for it is in one sense previous to man, being what composes him or in which he lives. Heidegger therefore claims that not only does man speak language, language speaks man. For Heidegger, the usual analytic procedures on the analogy of science and the production of technology do not let be and listen but instead dominate. This sort of subjective mastery, or subjectism, Heidegger's hermeneutics opposes.

The result is a mode of interpretation that verges on the poetic, for the poetic is for Heidegger the hermeneutic. There is no real difference between philosophy and poetry. Both are hermeneutic, and Heidegger's own discourse about poetry or poems has characteristics of the poems he is apparently discussing—except that "discussion" is hardly the word. The aim is to open up by performing a linguistic mediation, conversing with the text. Heidegger is one of those responsible for a notion that has frequently been uttered in recent critical theory that criticism is itself literature (see, for example, *Hartman*). This view tends to assimilate all language to poetry rather than declaring poetry some special and curious form of language, conceived of in its purity on the model of symbolic logic or mathematics. The latter view may be traced back as far as Socrates' remark in the *Republic* (*CTSP,* p. 38) that one ought to give up poetry and trust mathematics if one wants to approach the truth. The former view is held by Vico and a number of poets in the romantic period.

Important translated works by Heidegger, particularly for literary theory, are *Being and Time* (1927, trans. 1962); *Kant and the Problem of Metaphysics* (1925–26, trans. 1972); *An Introduction to Metaphysics* (1953, trans. 1974); *Identity and Difference* (1957, trans. 1957); *The End of Philosophy* (1969, trans. 1972); *On the Way to Language* (1971); and *Poetry, Language, Thought* (1971), which contains the well-known essay "The Origin of the Work of Art" (1936). See Michael Murray, ed., *Heidegger and Modern Philosophy*, which includes a bibliography of Heidegger's work and works about him.

HÖLDERLIN AND THE ESSENCE OF POETRY

THE FIVE POINTERS

1. Writing poetry: "That most innocent of all occupations." (III, 377)
2. "Therefore has language, most dangerous of possessions, been given to man . . . so that he may affirm what he is. . . ." (IV, 246)
3. "Much has man learnt.
   Many of the heavenly ones has he named,
   Since we have been a conversation
   And have been able to hear from one another."
   (IV,343)
4. "But that which remains, is established by the poets." (IV, 63)
5. "Full of merit, and yet poetically, dwells Man on this earth." (VI, 25)

Why has Hölderlin's work been chosen for the purpose of showing the essence of poetry? Why not Homer or Sophocles, why not Virgil or Dante, why not Shakespeare or Goethe? The essence of poetry is realized in the works of these poets too, and more richly even, than in the creative work of Hölderlin, which breaks off so early and abruptly.

This may be so. And yet Hölderlin has been chosen, and he alone. But generally speaking is it possible for the universal essence of poetry to be read off from the work of one single poet? Whatever is universal, that is to say, what is valid for many, can only be reached through a process of comparison. For this, one requires a sample containing the greatest possible diversity of poems and kinds of poetry. From this point of view Hölderlin's poetry is only one among many others. By itself it can in no way suffice as a criterion for determining the essence of poetry. Hence we fail in our purpose at the very outset. Certainly—so long as we take "essence of poetry" to mean what is gathered together into a universal concept, which is then valid in the same way for every poem. But this universal which thus applies equally to every particular, is always the indifferent, that essence which can never become essential.

Yet it is precisely this essential element of the essence that we are searching for—that which compels use to decide whether we are going to take poetry seriously and if so how, whether and to what extent we can bring with us the presuppositions necessary if we are to come under the sway of poetry.

Hölderlin has not been chosen because his work, one among many, realizes the universal essence of poetry, but solely because Hölderlin's poetry was borne on by the poetic vocation to write expressly of the essence of poetry. For us Hölderlin is in a pre-eminent sense *the poet of the poet*. That is why he compels a decision.

But—to write about the poet, is this not a symp-

HÖLDERLIN AND THE ESSENCE OF POETRY is from *Erlautenungen zu Hölderlins Dichtung* (1951) and is reprinted from *Existence and Being,* ed. Werner Broch, by permission of the publishers, Regnery Gateway, Inc., copyright 1967.

tom of a perverted narcissism and at the same time a confession of inadequate richness of vision? To write about the poet, is that not a senseless exaggeration, something decadent and a blind alley?

The answer will be given in what follows. To be sure, the path by which we reach the answer is one of expediency. We cannot here, as would have to be done, expound separately each of Hölderlin's poems one after the other. Instead let us take only five pointers which the poet gave on the subject of poetry. The necessary order in these sayings and their inner connectedness ought to bring before our eyes the essential essence of poetry.

1.

In a letter to his mother in January, 1799, Hölderlin calls the writing of poetry "that most innocent of all occupations" (III, 377). To what extent is it the "most innocent"? Writing poetry appears in the modest guise of *play*. Unfettered, it invents its world of images and remains immersed in the realm of the imagined. This play thus avoids the seriousness of decisions, which always in one way or another create guilt. Hence writing poetry is completely harmless. And at the same time it is ineffectual, since it remains mere saying and speaking. It has nothing about it of action, which grasps hold directly of the real and alters it. Poetry is like a dream, and not reality; a playing with words, and not the seriousness of action. Poetry is harmless and ineffectual. For what can be less dangerous than mere speech? But in taking poetry to be the "most innocent of all occupations," we have not yet comprehended its essence. At any rate this gives us an indication of where we must look for it. Poetry creates its works in the realm and out of the "material" of language. What does Hölderlin say about language? Let us hear a second saying of the poet.

2.

In a fragmentary sketch, dating from the same period (1800) as the letter just quoted, the poet says:

> But man dwells in huts and wraps himself in the bashful garment, since he is more fervent and more attentive too in watching over the spirit, as the priestess the divine flame; this is his understanding. And therefore he has been given arbitrariness, and to him, godlike, has been given higher power to command and to accomplish, and therefore has language, most dangerous of possessions, been given to man, so that creating, destroying, and perishing and returning to the everliving, to the mistress and mother, he may affirm what he is—that he has inherited, learned from thee, thy most divine possession, all-preserving love. (IV, 246)

Language, the field of the "most innocent of all occupations," is the "most dangerous of possessions." How can these two be reconciled? Let us put this question aside from the moment and consider the three preliminary questions: 1. Whose possession is language? 2. To what extent is it the most dangerous of possessions? 3. In what sense is it really a possession?

First of all we notice where this saying about language occurs: in the sketch for a poem which is to describe who man is, in contrast to the other beings of nature; mention is made of the rose, the swans, the stag in the forest (IV, 300 and 385). So, distinguishing plants from animals, the fragment begins: "But man dwells in huts."

And who then is man? He who must affirm what he is. To affirm means to declare; but at the same time it means: to give in the declaration a guarantee of what is declared. Man is *he* who he *is*, precisely in the affirmation of his own existence. This affirmation does not mean here an additional and supplementary expression of human existence, but it does in the process make plain the existence of man. But what must man affirm? That he belongs to the earth. This relation of belonging to consists in the fact that man is heir and learner in all things. But all these things are in conflict. That which keeps things apart in opposition and thus at the same time binds them together, is called by Hölderlin "intimacy." The affirmation of belonging to this intimacy occurs through the creation of a world and its ascent, and likewise through the destruction of a world and its decline. The affirmation of human existence and hence its essential consummation occurs through freedom of decision. This freedom lays hold of the necessary and places itself in the bonds of a supreme obligation. This bearing witness of belonging to all that is existent becomes actual as history. In order that history may be possible, language has been given to man. It is one of man's possessions.

But to what extent is language the "most dangerous of possessions"? It is the danger of all dangers, because it creates initially the possibility of a danger. Danger is the threat to existence from what is existent. But now it is only by virtue of language at all that man is exposed to something manifest, which, *as* what is existent, afflicts and enflames man in his existence, and as what is nonexistent deceives and disappoints. It is language which first creates the manifest conditions for menace and confusion to existence, and thus the possibility of the loss of existence, that is to say—danger. But language is not only the danger of dangers, but necessarily conceals in itself a continual danger for itself. Language has the task of making manifest in its work the existent, and of preserving it as such. In it, what is purest and what is most concealed, and likewise what is complex and ordinary, can be expressed in words. Even the essential word, if it is to be understood and so become a possession in common, must make itself ordinary. Accordingly it is remarked in another fragment of Hölderlin's: "Thou spokest to the Godhead, but this you have all forgotten, that the first-fruits are never for mortals, they belong to the gods. The fruit must become more ordinary, more everyday, and then it will be mortals' own" (IV, 238). The pure and the ordinary are both equally something said. Hence the word as word never gives any direct guarantee as to whether it is an essential word or a counterfeit. On the contrary—an essential word often looks in its simplicity like an unessential one. And on the other hand that which is dressed up to look like the essential is only something recited by heart or repeated. Therefore language must constantly present itself in an appearance which it itself attests, and hence endanger what is most characteristic of it, the genuine saying.

In what sense however is this most dangerous thing one of man's possessions? Language is his own property. It is at his disposal for the purpose of communicating his experiences, resolutions and moods. Language serves to give information. As a fit instrument for this, it is a "possession." But the essence of language does not consist entirely in being a means of giving information. This definition does not touch its essential essence, but merely indicates an effect of its essence. Language is not a mere tool, one of the many which man possesses; on the contrary, it is only language that affords the very possibility of standing in the openness of the existent. Only where there is language, is there world, i.e., the perpetually altering circuit of decision and production, of action and responsibility, but also of commotion and arbitrariness, of decay and confusion. Only where world predominates, is there history. Language is a possession in a more fundamental sense. It is good for the fact that (i.e., it affords a guarantee that) man can *exist* historically. Language is not a tool at his disposal, rather it is that event which disposes of the supreme possibility of human existence. We must first of all be certain of this essence of language, in order to comprehend truly the sphere of action of poetry and with it poetry itself. How does language become actual? In order to find the answer to this question, let us consider a third saying of Hölderlin's.

3.

We come across this saying in a long and involved sketch for the unfinished poem which begins "Versöhnender, der du nimmergeglaubt . . ." (IV, 162ff. and 339ff):

Much has man learnt.
Many of the heavenly ones has he named,
Since we have been a conversation
And have been able to hear from one
another.

(IV,343)

Let us first pick out from these lines the part which has a direct bearing on what we have said so far: "Since we have been a conversation . . ." We—mankind—are a conversation. The being of men is founded in language. But this only becomes actual in *conversation*. Nevertheless the latter is not merely a manner in which language is put into effect, rather it is only as conversation that language is essential. What we usually mean by language, namely, a stock of words and syntactical rules, is only a threshold of language. But now what is meant by "a conversation"? Plainly, the act of speaking with others about something. Then speaking also brings about the process of coming together. But Hölderlin says: "Since we have been a conversation and have been able to hear from one another." Being able to hear is not a mere consequence of speaking with one another, on the contrary it is rather presupposed in the latter process. But even the ability to hear is itself also adapted to the possibility of the word and makes use of it. The ability to speak and the ability to hear are equally fundamental. We are a conversation—and that means: we can hear from one another. We are a conversation, that always means at the same time: we are a *single* conversation. But the unity of a conversation consists in the fact that in the essential word there is always manifest that one and the same thing on which we agree, and on the basis of which we are united and so are essentially ourselves. Conversation and its unity support our existence.

But Hölderlin does not say simply: we are a conversation—but: "Since we have been a conversation . . ." Where the human faculty of speech is present and is exercised, that is not by itself sufficient for the essential actualization of language—conversation. Since when have we been a conversation? Where there is to be a *single* conversation, the essential word must be constantly related to the one and the same. Without this relation an argument too is absolutely impossible. But the one and the same can only be manifest in the light of something perpetual and permanent. Yet permanence and perpetuity only appear when what persists and is present begins to shine. But that happens in the moment when time opens out and extends. After man has placed himself in the presence of something perpetual, then only can he expose himself to the changeable, to that which comes and goes; for only the persistent is changeable. Only after "ravenous time" has been riven into present, past and future, does the possibility arise of agreeing on something permanent. We have been a single conversation since the time when it "is time." Ever since time arose, we have *existed* historically. Both—existence as a *single* conversation and historical existence—are alike ancient, they belong together and are the same thing.

Since we have been a conversation—man has learnt much and named many of the heavenly ones. Since language really became actual as conversation, the gods have acquired names and a world has appeared. But again it should be noticed: the presence of the gods and the appearance of the world are not merely a consequence of the actualization of language, they are contemporaneous with it. And this to the extent that it is precisely in the naming of the gods, and in the transmutation of the world into word, that the real conversation, which we ourselves are, consists.

But the gods can acquire a name only by addressing and, as it were, claiming us. The word which names the gods is always a response to such a claim. This response always springs from the responsibility of a destiny. It is in the process by which the gods bring our existence to language that we enter the sphere of the decision as to whether we are to yield ourselves to the gods or withhold ourselves from them.

Only now can we appreciate in its entirety what is meant by: "Since we have been a conversation . . ." Since the gods have led us into conversation, since time has been time, ever since then the basis of our existence has been a conversation. The proposition that language is the supreme event of human existence has through it acquired its meaning and foundation.

But the question at once arises: how does this conversation, which we are, begin? Who accomplishes this naming of the gods? Who lays hold of something permanent in ravenous time and fixes it in the word? Hölderlin tells us with the sure simplicity of the poet. Let us hear a fourth saying.

4.

This saying forms the conclusion of the poem "Remembrance" and runs:

> But that which remains, is established by the
> poets.
>
> (IV, 63)

This saying throws light on our question about the essence of poetry. Poetry is the act of establishing by the word and in the word. What is established in this manner? The permanent. But can the permanent be established then? Is it not that which has always been present? No! Even the permanent must be fixed so that it will not be carried away, the simple must be wrested from confusion, proportion must be set before what lacks proportion. That which supports and dominates the existent in its entirety must become manifest. Being must be opened out, so that the existent may appear. But this very permanent is the transitory. "Thus, swiftly passing is everything heavenly; but not in vain" (IV, 163f.). But that this should remain, is "Entrusted to the poets as a care and a service" (IV, 145). The poet names the gods and names all things in that which they are. This naming does not consist merely in something already known being supplied with a name; it is rather that when the poet speaks the essential word, the existent is by this naming nominated as what it is. So it becomes known *as* existent. Poetry is the establishing of being by means of the word. Hence that which remains is never taken from the transitory. The simple can never be picked out immediately from the intricate. Proportion does not lie in what lacks proportion. We never find the foundation in what is bottomless. Being is never an existent. But, because being and essence of things can never be calculated and derived from what is present, they must be freely created, laid down and given. Such a free act of giving is establishment.

But when the gods are named originally and the essence of things receives a name, so that things for the first time shine out, human existence is brought into a firm relation and given a basis. The speech of the poet is establishment not only in the sense of the free act of giving, but at the same time in the sense of the firm basing of human existence on its foundation.

If we conceive this essence of poetry as the establishing of being by means of the word, then we can have some inkling of the truth of that saying which Hölderlin spoke long after he had been received into the protection of the night of lunacy.

5.

We find this fifth pointer in the long and at the same time monstrous poem which begins:

> In the lovely azure there flowers with its
> Metallic roof the church-tower.
>
> (VI, 24ff)

Here Hölderlin says (line 32f.):

> Full of merit, and yet poetically, dwells
> Man on this earth.

What man works at and pursues is through his own endeavors earned and deserved. "Yet"—says Hölderlin in sharp antithesis, all this does not touch the essence of his sojourn on this earth, all this does not reach the foundation of human existence. The latter is fundamentally "poetic." But we now understand poetry as the inaugural naming of the gods and of the essence of things. To "dwell poetically" means: to stand in the presence of the gods and to be involved in the proximity of the essence of things. Existence is "poetical" in its fundamental aspect—which means at the same time: in so far as it is established (founded), it is not a recompense, but a gift.

Poetry is not merely an ornament accompanying existence, not merely a temporary enthusiasm or nothing but an interest and amusement. Poetry is the foundation which supports history, and therefore it is not a mere appearance of culture, and absolutely not the mere "expression" of a "culture-soul."

That our existence is fundamentally poetic, this cannot in the last resort mean that it is really only a harmless game. But does not Hölderlin himself, in the first pointer which we quoted, call poetry "That most innocent of all occupations"? How can this be reconciled with the essence of poetry as we are now revealing it? This brings us back to the question which we laid aside in the first instance. In now proceeding to answer this question, we will try at the same time to summarize and bring before the inner eye the essence of poetry and of the poet.

First of all it appeared that the field of action of poetry is language. Hence the essence of poetry must be understood through the essence of language. Afterwards it became clear that poetry is the inaugural naming of being and of the essence of all things—not just any speech, but that particular kind which for the first time brings into the open all that which we then discuss and deal with in everyday language. Hence poetry never takes language as a raw material ready to hand, rather it is poetry which first makes language possible. Poetry is the primitive language of a historical people. Therefore, in just the reverse manner, the essence of language must be understood through the essence of poetry.

The foundation of human existence is conversation, in which language does truly become actual. But primitive language is poetry, in which being is established. Yet language is the "most dangerous of possessions." Thus poetry is the most dangerous work—and at the same time the "most innocent of all occupations."

In fact—it is only if we combine these two definitions and conceive them as one that we fully comprehend the essence of poetry.

But is poetry then truly the most dangerous work? In a letter to a friend, immediately before leaving on his last journey to France, Hölderlin writes: "O Friend! The world lies before me brighter than it was, and more serious. I feel pleasure at how it moves onward, I feel pleasure when in summer 'the ancient holy father with calm hand shakes lightnings of benediction out of the rosy clouds.' For amongst all that I can perceive of God, this sign has become for me the chosen one. I used to be able to exult over a new truth, a better insight into that which is above us and around us, now I am frightened lest in the end it should happen with me as with Tantalus of old, who received more from the gods than he was able to digest" (V,321).

The poet is exposed to the divine lightnings. This is spoken of in the poem which we must recognize as the purest poetry about the essence of poetry, and which begins:

> When on festive days a countryman goes
> To gaze on his field, in the morning . . .
>
> (IV, 151ff)

There, the last stanza says:

> Yet it behoves us, under the storms of God,
> Ye poets! with uncovered head to stand,
> With our own hand to grasp the very
> lightning-flash
> Paternal, and to pass, wrapped in song,
> The divine gift to the people.

And a year later, when he had returned to his mother's house, struck down with madness, Hölderlin wrote to the same friend, recalling his stay in France:

"The mighty element, the fire of heaven and the stillness of men, their life amid nature, and their limitation and contentment, have constantly seized me, and, as it is told of the heroes, I can truly say that I have been struck by Apollo" (V, 327). The excessive brightness has driven the poet into the dark. Is any further evidence necessary as to the extreme danger of his "occupation"? The very destiny itself of the poet tells everything. The passage in Hölderlin's "Empedocles" rings like a premonition:

> He, through whom the spirit speaks, must
> leave betimes.
>
> (III, 154)

And nevertheless: poetry is the "most innocent of all occupations," Hölderlin writes to this effect in his letter, not only in order to spare his mother, but because he knows that this innocent fringe belongs to the essence of poetry, just as the valley does to the mountain; for how could this most dangerous work be carried on and preserved, if the poet were not "cast out" ("Empedocles" III, 191) from everyday life and protected *against* it by the apparent harmlessness of his occupation?

Poetry looks like a game and yet it is not. A game does indeed bring men together, but in such a way that each forgets himself in the process. In poetry on the other hand, man is reunited on the foundation of his existence. There he comes to rest; not indeed to the seeming rest of inactivity and emptiness of thought, but to that infinite state of rest in which all powers and relations are active (cf. the letter to his brother, dated 1st January, 1799. III, 368f).

Poetry rouses the appearance of the unreal and of dream in the face of the palpable and clamorous reality, in which we believe ourselves at home. And yet in just the reverse manner, what the poet says and undertakes to be, is the real. So Pathea, with the clairvoyance of a friend, declares of "Empedocles" (III, 78):

> That he himself should be, is
> What is life, and the rest of us are dreams
> of it.

So in the very appearance of its outer fringe the essence of poetry seems to waver and yet stands firm. In fact it is itself essentially establishment—that is to say: an act of firm foundation.

Yet every inaugural act remains a free gift, and Hölderlin hears it said: "Let poets be free as swallows" (IV, 168). But this freedom is not undisciplined arbitrariness and capricious desire, but supreme necessity.

Poetry, as the act of establishing being, is subject to a *twofold* control. In considering these integral laws we first grasp the essence entire.

The writing of poetry is the fundamental naming of the gods. But the poetic word only acquires its power of naming when the gods themselves bring us to language. How do the gods speak?

> . . . . And signs to us from antiquity are the
> language of the gods.
>
> (IV, 135)

The speech of the poet is the intercepting of these signs, in order to pass them on to his own people. This intercepting is an act of receiving and yet at the same time a fresh act of giving; for "in the first signs" the poet catches sight already of the completed message and in his word boldly presents what he has glimpsed, so as to tell in advance of the not-yet-fulfilled. So:

> . . . the bold spirit, like an eagle
> Before the tempests, flies prophesying
> In the path of his advancing gods.
>
> (IV, 135)

The establishment of being is bound to the signs of the gods. And at the same time the poetic word is only the interpretation of the "voice of the people." This is how Hölderlin names the sayings in which a people remembers that it belongs to the totality of all that exists. But often this voice grows dumb and weary. In general even it is not capable of saying of itself what is true, but has need of those who explain it. The poem which bears the title "Voice of the People," has been handed down to us in two versions. It is above all the concluding stanzas which are different, but the difference is such that they supplement one another. In the first version the ending runs:

> Because it is pious, I honor for love of the
> heavenly ones
> The people's voice, the tranquil,
> Yet for the sake of gods and men
> May it not always be tranquil too willingly!
>
> (IV,141)

And the second version is:

> . . . and truly
> Sayings are good, for they are a reminder
> Of the Highest, yet something is also needed
> To explain the holy sayings.
>
> (IV,144)

In this way the essence of poetry is joined onto the laws of the signs of the gods and of the voice of the people, laws which tend toward and away from each other. The poet himself stands between the former—the gods, and the latter—the people. He is one who has been cast out—out into that *Between*, between gods and men. But only and for the first time in this Between is it decided, who man is and where he is settling his existence. "Poetically, dwells man on this earth."

Unceasingly and ever more securely, out of the fullness of the images pressing about him and always more simply, did Hölderlin devote his poetic word to this realm of Between. And this compels us to say that he is the poet of the poet.

Can we continue now to suppose that Hölderlin is entangled in an empty and exaggerated narcissism due to inadequate richness of vision? Or must we recognize that this poet, from an excess of impetus, reaches out with poetic thought into the foundation and the midst of being. It is to *Hölderlin himself* that we must apply what he said of Oedipus in the late poem "In the lovely azure there flowers . . .":

> King Oedipus has one
> Eye too many perhaps.
>
> (VI,26)

Hölderlin writes poetry about the essence of poetry—but not in the sense of a timelessly valid concept. This essence of poetry belongs to a determined time. But not in such a way that it merely conforms to this time, as to one which is already in existence. It is that Hölderlin, in the act of establishing the essence of poetry, first determines a new time. It is the time of the gods that have fled *and* of the god that is coming. It is the time *of need,* because it lies under a double lack and a double Not: the No-more of the gods that have fled and the Not-yet of the god that is coming.

The essence of poetry, which Hölderlin establishes, is in the highest degree historical, because it anticipates a historical time; but as a historical essence it is the sole essential essence.

The time is needy and therefore its poet is extremely rich—so rich that he would often like to relax in thoughts of those that have been and in eager waiting for that which is coming and would like only to sleep in this apparent emptiness. But he holds his ground in the Nothing of this night. Whilst the poet remains thus by himself in the supreme isolation of his mission, he fashions truth, vicariously and therefore truly, for his people. The seventh stanza of the elegy "Bread and Wine" (IV, 123f.) tells of this. What it has only been possible to analyze here intellectually, is expressed there poetically.

> "But Friend! we come too late. The gods are
> alive, it is true,

But up there above one's head in another
world.
Eternally they work there and seem to pay
little heed
To whether we live, so attentive are the
Heavenly Ones.
For a weak vessel cannot always receive
them,
Only now and then does man endure divine
abundance.
Life is a dream of them. But madness
Helps, like slumber and strengthens need
and night.
Until heroes enough have grown in the iron
cradle,
Hearts like, as before, to the Heavenly in
power.
Thundering they come. Meanwhile it often
seems
Better to sleep than to be thus without
companions,
To wait thus, and in the meantime what to
do and say
I know not, and what use are poets in a time
of need?
But, thou sayest, they are like the wine-god's
holy priests,
Who go from land to land in the holy
night."

Ludwig Wittgenstein

1889–1951

LUDWIG WITTGENSTEIN'S importance for modern philosophy and criticism lies not just in a set of concepts and doctrines but in a distinctive view of the purpose of philosophy. Under the influence of Russell, Whitehead, and Frege, Wittgenstein developed the view that philosophy was not and could not be a "science" as physics or mathematics are sciences but had, instead, the distinctive task of elucidating the logical form of propositions. While his account of logical form altered significantly from his first published work, the *Tractatus Logico-Philosophicus* (1921), to the posthumously published *Philosophical Investigations* (1953), his view of the essentially critical function of philosophy remained remarkably constant.

In the *Tractatus,* Wittgenstein developed what has been characterized as a "picture theory" of meaning, based on the principle that what a logical proposition offers is a picture of the logical structure of a fact. "The world is all that is the case," Wittgenstein asserts, in the famous first proposition in that early work, but he continues, in the second (and notably less famous second proposition), "The world is the totality of facts not things." In this account, Wittgenstein maintained that propositions could represent "the whole of reality" but could only show or display the logical form propositions must share with reality in order to represent it (cf. #4.12). In this respect, the "pictures" in question in the theory are the result of a method of projection or depiction in which logical structures are the relevant "objects."

In the preface to *Philosophical Investigations,* Wittgenstein expressed the desire to republish his earlier work so as to ensure that his later view be seen "in the right light." The *Investigations,* for example, appear to abandon the picture theory of meaning, since further work on language had made it clear that as language is acquired and used, the method of projection or depiction cannot be adequately elucidated as if it were concerned only with the truth value of propositions. One might say that the difference is a broadening of scope for the philosopher's activity: language is deployed for many more purposes than making true or false statements. As his attention shifted to the multifarious deployments of language, Wittgenstein elaborated his notion of the "language game" to show the intimate and pervasive links between language and "forms of life."

The *Investigations* begin with a quotation from Augustine's *Confessions* that expresses the traditional view of language that Wittgenstein had tacitly adopted in the *Tractatus:* that words name objects and that sentences are combinations of such names. Wittgenstein then proceeds to show the gross oversimplification of this premise, in showing that expressions in a language do not have a common essence by virtue of which they are all included in "language" but rather present a complex network of relations in which similarities (like "family resemblances") permit us to traverse the network and see connections without the requirement that words and objects always correspond.

Wittgenstein's influence has been exceptionally wide, as he has been claimed as an ancestor or progenitor for sometimes mutually incompatible views of philosophy. The *Tractatus,* for example, was especially important for the early work of philosophers in the so-called Vienna Circle, including Moritz Schlick, Rudolph Carnap, and Herbert Feigl, who elaborated the radical program of logical positivism to eliminate metaphysical statements as meaningless and to unify empirical science by a critique of the logical structure of its language. Work that led to the *Investigations,* on the other hand, was equally influential in the development of linguistic and "ordinary language" philosophy and the theory of "speech acts" in the work of Friedrich Waismann, Gilbert Ryle, *J. L. Austin, Stanley Cavell,* and others. For literary critics (such as *Charles Altieri,* for example), Wittgenstein provides both exemplary arguments and methodological paradigms for explicating language as action and criticism as itself a "form of life."

Only the *Tractatus* was published during Wittgenstein's lifetime, but his notebooks and other works have appeared steadily since his death, including *Philosophical Investigations,* trans. G. E. M. Anscombe (New York: Macmillan Company, 1953); *On Certainty,* ed. G. E. M. Anscombe and G. H. von Wright, trans. Denis Paul and G. E. M. Anscombe (Oxford: Basil Blackwell, 1969); and *Lectures & Conversations on Aesthetics, Psychology, and Religious Belief,* ed. Cyril Barrett (Berkeley: University of California Press, 1972). See also Anthony Kenny, *Wittgenstein* (Cambridge, MA: Harvard University Press, 1973).

FROM

PHILOSOPHICAL INVESTIGATIONS

1. "Cum ipsi (majores homines) appellabant rem aliquam, et cum secundum eam vocem corpus ad aliquid movebant, videbam, et tenebam hoc ab eis vocari rem illam, quod sonabant, cum eam vellent ostendere. Hoc autem eos velle ex motu corporis aperiebatur: tamquam verbis naturalibus omnium gentium, quae fiunt vultu et nutu oculorum, ceterorumque membrorum actu, et sonitu vocis indicante affectionem animi in petendis, habendis, rejiciendis, fugiendisve rebus. Ita verba in variis sententiis locis suis posita, et crebro audita, quarum rerum signa essent, paulatim colligebam, measque jam voluntates, edomito in eis signis ore, per haec enuntiabam." (Augustine, *Confessions,* I. 8.)[1]

These words, it seems to me, give us a particular picture of the essence of human language. It is this: the individual words in language name objects—sentences are combinations of such names.——In

[1] "When they (my elders) named some object, and accordingly moved towards something, I saw this and I grasped that the thing was called by the sound they uttered when they meant to point it out. Their intention was shewn by their bodily movements, as it were the natural language of all peoples: the expression of the face, the play of the eyes, the movement of other parts of the body, and the tone of voice which expresses our state of mind in seeking, having, rejecting, or avoiding something. Thus, as I heard words repeatedly used in their proper places in various sentences, I gradually learnt to understand what objects they signified; and after I had trained my mouth to form these signs, I used them to express my own desires." [Tr.]

this picture of language we find the roots of the following idea: Every word has a meaning. This meaning is correlated with the word. It is the object for which the word stands.

Augustine does not speak of there being any difference between kinds of words. If you describe the learning of language in this way you are, I believe, thinking primarily of nouns like "table", "chair", "bread", and of people's names, and only secondarily of the names of certain actions and properties; and of the remaining kinds of word as something that will take care of itself.

Now think of the following use of language: I send someone shopping. I give him a slip marked "five red apples". He takes the slip to the shopkeeper, who opens the drawer marked "apples"; then he looks up the word "red" in a table and finds a colour sample opposite it; then he says the series of cardinal numbers—I assume that he knows them by heart—up to the word "five" and for each number he takes an apple of the same colour as the sample out of the drawer.——It is in this and similar ways that one operates with words.——"But how does he know where and how he is to look up the word 'red' and what he is to do with the word 'five'?"——Well, I assume that he *acts* as I have described. Explanations come to an end somewhere.—But what is the meaning of the word "five"?—No such thing was in question here, only how the word "five" is used.

2. That philosophical concept of meaning has its place in a primitive idea of the way language functions. But one can also say that it is the idea of a language more primitive than ours.

Let us imagine a language for which the description given by Augustine is right. The language is meant to serve for communication between a builder A and an assistant B. A is building with building-stones; there are blocks, pillars, slabs and beams. B has to pass the stones, and that in the order in which A needs them. For this purpose they use a language consisting of the words "block", "pillar", "slab", "beam". A calls them out;—B brings the stone which he has learnt to bring at such-and-such a call.——Conceive this as a complete primitive language.

3. Augustine, we might say, does describe a system of communication; only not everything that we call language is this system. And one has to say this in many cases where the question arises "Is this an appropriate description or not?" The answer is: "Yes, it is appropriate, but only for this narrowly circumscribed region, not for the whole of what you were claiming to describe."

It is as if someone were to say: "A game consists in moving objects about on a surface according to certain rules . . ."—and we replied: You seem to be thinking of board games, but there are others. You can make your definition correct by expressly restricting it to those games.

4. Imagine a script in which the letters were used to stand for sounds, and also as signs of emphasis and punctuation. (A script can be conceived as a language for describing sound-patterns.) Now imagine someone interpreting that script as if there were simply a correspondence of letters to sounds and as if the letters had not also completely different functions. Augustine's conception of language is like such an over-simple conception of the script.

5. If we look at the example in §1, we may perhaps get an inkling how much this general notion of the meaning of a word surrounds the working of language with a haze which makes clear vision impossible. It disperses the fog to study the phenomena of language in primitive kinds of application in which one can command a clear view of the aim and functioning of the words.

A child uses such primitive forms of language when it learns to talk. Here the teaching of language is not explanation, but training.

6. We could imagine that the language of §2 was the *whole* language of A and B; even the whole language of a tribe. The children are brought up to perform *these* actions, to use *these* words as they do so, and to react in *this* way to the words of others.

An important part of the training will consist in the teacher's pointing to the objects, directing the child's attention to them, and at the same time uttering a word; for instance, the word "slab" as he points to that shape. (I do not want to call this "ostensive definition", because the child cannot as yet *ask* what the name is. I will call it "ostensive teaching of words".—I say that it will form an important part of the training, because it is so with human beings; not because it could not be imagined otherwise.) This ostensive teaching of words can be said to establish an association between the word and the thing. But what does this mean? Well, it may mean various things; but one very likely thinks first of all that a picture of the object comes before the child's mind when it hears the word. But now, if this does happen—is it the purpose of the word?—Yes, it *may* be the purpose.—I can imagine such a use of words (of series of sounds). (Uttering a word is like striking a note on the keyboard of the imagination.) But in the language of §2 it is *not* the purpose of the words to evoke images. (It may, of course, be discovered that that helps to attain the actual purpose.)

But if the ostensive teaching has this effect,—am I to say that it effects an understanding of the word? Don't you understand the call "Slab!" if you act upon it in such-and-such a way?—Doubtless the ostensive teaching helped to bring this about; but only together with a particular training. With different training the same ostensive teaching of these words would have effected a quite different understanding.

"I set the brake up by connecting up rod and lever."—Yes, given the whole of the rest of the mechanism. Only in conjunction with that is it a brake-lever, and separated from its support it is not even a lever; it may be anything, or nothing.

7. In the practice of the use of language (2) one party calls out the words, the other acts on them. In instruction in the language the following process will occur: the learner *names* the objects; that is, he utters the word when the teacher points to the stone.—And there will be this still simpler exercise: the pupil repeats the words after the teacher—both of these being processes resembling language.

We can also think of the whole process of using words in (2) as one of those games by means of which children learn their native language. I will call these games "language-games" and will sometimes speak of a primitive language as a language-game.

And the processes of naming the stones and of repeating words after someone might also be called language-games. Think of much of the use of words in games like ring-a-ring-a-roses.

I shall also call the whole, consisting of language and the actions into which it is woven, the "language-game".

8. Let us now look at an expansion of language (2). Besides the four words "block", "pillar", etc., let it contain a series of words used as the shopkeeper in (1) used the numerals (it can be the series of letters of the alphabet); further let there be two words, which may as well be "there" and "this" (because this roughly indicates their purpose), that are used in connexion with a pointing gesture; and finally a number of colour samples. A gives an order like: "d—slab—there". At the same time he shews the assistant a colour sample, and when he says "there" he points to a place on the building site. From the stock of slabs B takes one for each letter of the alphabet up to "d", of the same colour as the sample, and brings them to the place indicated by A.—On other occasions A gives the order "this—there". At "this" he points to a building stone. And so on.

9. When a child learns this language, it has to learn the series of 'numerals' a, b, c, . . . by heart. And it has to learn their use.—Will this training include ostensive teaching of the words?—Well, people will, for example, point to slabs and count: "a, b, c slabs".—Something more like the ostensive teaching of the words "block", "pillar", etc. would be the ostensive teaching of numerals that serve not to count but to refer to groups of objects that can be taken in at a glance. Children do learn the use of the first five or six cardinal numerals in this way.

Are "there" and "this" also taught ostensively?—Imagine how one might perhaps teach their use. One will point to places and things—but in this case the pointing occurs in the *use* of the words too and not merely in learning the use.—

10. Now what do the words of this language *signify?*—What is supposed to shew what they signify, if not the kind of use they have? And we have already described that. So we are asking for the expression "This word signifies *this*" to be made a part of the description. In other words the description ought to take the form: "The word . . . . signifies . . . .".

Of course, one can reduce the description of the use of the word "slab" to the statement that this word signifies this object. This will be done when, for example, it is merely a matter of removing the mistaken idea that the word "slab" refers to the shape of building-stone that we in fact call a "block"—but the kind of '*referring*' this is, that is to say the use of these words for the rest, is already known.

Equally one can say that the signs "a", "b", etc.

signify numbers; when for example this removes the mistaken idea that "a", "b", "c", play the part actually played in language by "block", "slab", "pillar". And one can also say that "c" means this number and not that one; when for example this serves to explain that the letters are to be used in the order a, b, c, d, etc. and not in the order a, b, d, c.

But assimilating the descriptions of the uses of words in this way cannot make the uses themselves any more like one another. For, as we see, they are absolutely unlike.

11. Think of the tools in a tool-box: there is a hammer, pliers, a saw, a screw-driver, a rule, a glue-pot, glue, nails and screws.—The functions of words are as diverse as the functions of these objects. (And in both cases there are similarities.)

Of course what confuses us is the uniform appearance of words when we hear them spoken or meet them in script and print. For their *application* is not presented to us so clearly. Especially when we are doing philosophy!

12. It is like looking into the cabin of a locomotive. We see handles all looking more or less alike. (Naturally, since they are all supposed to be handled.) But one is the handle of a crank which can be moved continuously (it regulates the opening of a valve); another is the handle of a switch, which has only two effective positions, it is either off or on; a third is the handle of a brake-lever, the harder one pulls on it, the harder it brakes; a fourth, the handle of a pump: it has an effect only so long as it is moved to and fro.

13. When we say: "Every word in language signifies something" we have so far said *nothing whatever;* unless we have explained exactly *what* distinction we wish to make. (It might be, of course, that we wanted to distinguish the words of language (8) from words 'without meaning' such as occur in Lewis Carroll's poems, or words like "Lilliburlero" in songs.)

14. Imagine someone's saying: "*All* tools serve to modify something. Thus the hammer modifies the position of the nail, the saw the shape of the board, and so on."—And what is modified by the rule, the glue-pot, the nails?—"Our knowledge of a thing's length, the temperature of the glue, and the solidity of the box."—Would anything be gained by this assimilation of expressions?—

15. The word "to signify" is perhaps used in the most straight-forward way when the object signified is marked with the sign. Suppose that the tools A uses in building bear certain marks. When A shews his assistant such a mark, he brings the tool that has that mark on it.

It is in this and more or less similar ways that a name means and is given to a thing.—It will often prove useful in philosophy to say to ourselves: naming something is like attaching a label to a thing.

16. What about the colour samples that A shews to B: are they part of the *language?* Well, it is as you please. They do not belong among the words; yet when I say to someone: "Pronounce the word 'the'", you will count the second "the" as part of the sentence. Yet it has a role just like that of a colour-sample in language-game (8); that is, it is a sample of what the other is meant to say.

It is most natural, and causes least confusion, to reckon the samples among the instruments of the language.

((Remark on the reflexive pronoun "*this* sentence".))

17. It will be possible to say: In language (8) we have different *kinds of word.* For the function of the word "slab" and the word "block" are more alike than those of "slab" and "d". But how we group words into kinds will depend on the aim of the classification,—and on our own inclination.

Think of the different points of view from which one can classify tools or chess-men.

18. Do not be troubled by the fact that languages (2) and (8) consist only of orders. If you want to say that this shews them to be incomplete, ask yourself whether our language is complete;—whether it was so before the symbolism of chemistry and the notation of the infinitesimal calculus were incoporated in it; for these are, so to speak, suburbs of our language. (And how many houses or streets does it take before a town begins to be a town?) Our language can be seen as an ancient city: a maze of little streets and squares, of old and new houses, and of houses with additions from various periods; and this surrounded by a multitude of new boroughs with straight regular streets and uniform houses.

19. It is easy to imagine a language consisting only of orders and reports in battle.—Or a language consisting only of questions and expressions for answering yes and no. And innumerable others.—

And to imagine a language means to imagine a form of life.

But what about this: is the call "Slab!" in example (2) a sentence or a word?—If a word, surely it has not the same meaning as the like-sounding word of our ordinary language, for in §2 it is a call. But if a sentence, it is surely not the elliptical sentence: "Slab!" of our language.—As far as the first question goes you can call "Slab!" a word and also a sentence; perhaps it could be appropriately called a 'degenerate sentence' (as one speaks of a degenerate hyperbola); in fact it *is* our 'elliptical' sentence.—But that is surely only a shortened form of the sentence "Bring me a slab", and there is no such sentence in example (2).—But why should I not on the contrary have called the sentence "Bring me a slab" a *lengthening* of the sentence "Slab!"?—Because if you shout "Slab!" you really mean: "Bring me a slab".—But how do you do this: how do you *mean that* while you *say* "Slab!"? Do you say the unshortened sentence to yourself? And why should I translate the call "Slab!" into a different expression in order to say what someone means by it? And if they mean the same thing—why should I not say: "When he says 'Slab!' he means 'Slab!'"? Again, if you can mean "Bring me the slab", why should you not be able to mean "Slab!"?—But when I call "Slab!", then what I want is, *that he should bring me a slab!*—Certainly, but does 'wanting this' consist in thinking in some form or other a different sentence from the other you utter?—

20. But now it looks as if when someone says "Bring me a slab" he could mean this expression as *one* long word corresponding to the single word "Slab!"—Then can one mean it sometimes as one word and sometimes as four? And how does one usually mean it?—I think we shall be inclined to say: we mean the sentence as *four* words when we use it in contrast with other sentences such as "*Hand* me a slab", "Bring *him* a slab", "Bring *two* slabs", etc.; that is, in contrast with sentences containing the separate words of our command in other combinations.—But what does using one sentence in contrast with others consist in? Do the others, perhaps, hover before one's mind? *All* of them? And *while* one is saying the one sentence, or before, or afterwards?—No. Even if such an explanation rather tempts us, we need only think for a moment of what actually happens in order to see that we are going astray here. We say that we use the command in contrast with other sentences because *our language* contains the possibility of those other sentences. Someone who did not understand our language, a foreigner, who had fairly often heard someone giving the order: "Bring me a slab!", might believe that this whole series of sounds was one word corresponding perhaps to the word for "building-stone" in his language. If he himself had then given this order perhaps he would have pronounced it differently, and we should say: he pronounces it so oddly because he takes it for a *single* word.—But then, is there not also something different going on in him when he pronounces it,—something corresponding to the fact that he conceives the sentence as a *single* word?—Either the same thing may go on in him, or something different. For what goes on in you when you give such an order? Are you conscious of its consisting of four words *while* you are uttering it? Of course you have a *mastery* of this language—which contains those other sentences as well—but is this having a mastery something that *happens* while you are uttering the sentence?—And I have admitted that the foreigner will probably pronounce a sentence differently if he conceives it differently; but what we call his wrong concept *need* not lie in anything that accompanies the utterance of the command.

The sentence is 'elliptical', not because it leaves out something that we think when we utter it, but because it is shortened—in comparison with a particular paradigm of our grammar.—Of course one might object here: "You grant that the shortened and the unshortened sentence have the same sense.—What is this sense, then? Isn't there a verbal expression for this sense?"—But doesn't the fact that sentences have the same sense consist in their having the same *use?*—(In Russian one says "stone red" instead of "the stone is red"; do they feel the copula to be missing in the sense, or attach it in *thought?*)

21. Imagine a language-game in which A asks and B reports the number of slabs or blocks in a pile, or the colours and shapes of the building-stones that are stacked in such-and-such a place.—such a report might run: "Five slabs". Now what is the difference between the report or statement "Five slabs" and the order "Five slabs!"?—Well, it is the part which uttering these words plays in the language-game. No doubt the tone of voice and the look with which they are uttered, and much else besides, will also be different. But we could also imag-

ine the tone's being the same—for an order and a report can be spoken in a *variety* of tones of voice and with various expressions of face—the difference being only in the application. (Of course, we might use the words "statement" and "command" to stand for grammatical forms of sentence and intonations; we do in fact call "Isn't the weather glorious to-day?" a question, although it is used as a statement.) We could imagine a language in which *all* statements had the form and tone of rhetorical questions; or every command the form of the question "Would you like to . . .?". Perhaps it will then be said: "What he says has the form of a question but is really a command",—that is, has the function of a command in the technique of using the language. (Similarly one says "You will do this" not as a prophecy but as a command. What makes it the one or the other?)

22. Frege's idea that every assertion contains an assumption, which is the thing that is asserted, really rests on the possibility found in our language of writing every statement in the form: "It is asserted that such-and-such is the case."—But "that such-and-such is the case" is *not* a sentence in our language—so far it is not a *move* in the language-game. And if I write, not "It is asserted that. . . .", but "It is asserted: such-and-such is the case", the words "It is asserted" simply become superfluous.

We might very well also write every statement in the form of a question followed by a "Yes"; for instance: "Is it raining? Yes!" Would this shew that every statement contained a question?

Of course we have the right to use an assertion sign in contrast with a question-mark, for example, or if we want to distinguish an assertion from a fiction or a supposition. It is only a mistake if one thinks that the assertion consists of two actions, entertaining and asserting (assigning the truth-value, or something of the kind), and that in performing these actions we follow the propositional sign roughly as we sing from the musical score. Reading the written sentence loud or soft is indeed comparable with singing from a musical score, but *'meaning'* (thinking) the sentence that is read is not.

Frege's assertion sign marks the *beginning of the sentence*. Thus its function is like that of the full-stop. It distinguishes the whole period from a clause *within* the period. If I hear someone say "it's raining" but do not know whether I have heard the beginning and end of the period, so far this sentence does not serve to tell me anything.

23. But how many kinds of sentence are there? Say assertion, question, and command?—There are *countless* kinds: countless different kinds of use of what we call "symbols", "words", "sentences". And this multiplicity is not something fixed, given once for all; but new types of language, new language-games, as we may say, come into existence, and others become obsolete and get forgotten. (We can get a *rough picture* of this from the changes in mathematics.)

Here the term "language-*game*" is meant to bring into prominence the fact that the *speaking* of language is part of an activity, or of a form of life.

Review the multiplicity of language-games in the following examples, and in others:

Giving orders, and obeying them—
Describing the appearance of an object, or giving its measurements—
Constructing an object from a description (a drawing)—
Reporting an event—
Speculating about an event—

Imagine a picture representing a boxer in a particular stance. Now, this picture can be used to tell someone how he should stand, should hold himself; or how he should not hold himself; or how a particular man did stand in such-and-such a place; and so on. One might (using the language of chemistry) call this picture a propositional-radical. This will be how Frege thought of the "assumption".

Forming and testing a hypothesis—
Presenting the results of an experiment in tables and diagrams—
Making up a story; and reading it—
Play-acting—
Singing catches—
Guessing riddles—
Making a joke; telling it—
Solving a problem in practical arithmetic—
Translating from one language into another—
Asking, thanking, cursing, greeting, praying.

—It is interesting to compare the multiplicity of the tools in language and of the ways they are used, the multiplicity of kinds of word and sentence, with what logicians have said about the structure of language. (Including the author of the *Tractatus Logico-Philosophicus*.)

24. If you do not keep the multiplicity of language-games in view you will perhaps he inclined to ask questions like: "What is a question?"—Is it the statement that I do not know such-and-such, or the statement that I wish the other person would tell me. . . .? Or is it the description of my mental state of uncertainty?—And is the cry "Help!" such a description?

Think how many different kinds of thing are called "description": description of a body's position by means of its co-ordinates; description of a facial expression; description of a sensation of touch; of a mood.

Of course it is possible to substitute the form of statement or description for the usual form of question: "I want to know whether . . . ." or "I am in doubt whether . . . ."—but this does not bring the different language-games any closer together.

The significance of such possibilities of transformation, for example of turning all statements into sentences beginning "I think" or "I believe" (and thus, as it were, into descriptions of *my* inner life) will become clearer in another place. (Solipsism.)

25. It is sometimes said that animals do not talk because they lack the mental capacity. And this means: "they do not think, and that is why they do not talk." But—they simply do not talk. Or to put it better: they do not use language—if we except the most primitive forms of language.—Commanding, questioning, recounting, chatting, are as much a part of our natural history as walking, eating, drinking, playing.

26. One thinks that learning language consists in giving names to objects. Viz, to human beings, to shapes, to colours, to pains, to moods, to numbers, etc. To repeat—naming is something like attaching a label to a thing. One can say that this is preparatory to the use of a word. But *what* is it a preparation *for?*

27. "We name things and then we can talk about them: can refer to them in talk."—As if what we did next were given with the mere act of naming. As if there were only one thing called "talking about a thing". Whereas in fact we do the most various things with our sentences. Think of exclamations alone, with their completely different functions.

Water!
Away!
Ow!
Help!
Fine!
No!

Are you inclined still to call these words "names of objects"?

In languages (2) and (8) there was no such thing as asking something's name. This, with its correlate, ostensive definition, is, we might say, a language-game on its own. That is really to say: we are brought up, trained, to ask: "What is that called?"—upon which the name is given. And there is also a language-game of inventing a name for something, and hence of saying, "This is . . . ." and then using the new name. (Thus, for example, children give names to their dolls and then talk about them and to them. Think in this connexion how singular is the use of a person's name to *call* him!)

. . . .

40. Let us first discuss *this* point of the argument: that a word has no meaning if nothing corresponds to it.—It is important to note that the word "meaning" is being used illicitly if it is used to signify the thing that 'corresponds' to the word. That is to confound the meaning of a name with the *bearer* of the name. When Mr. N. N. dies one says that the bearer of the name dies, not that the meaning dies. And it would be nonsensical to say that, for if the name ceased to have meaning it would make no sense to say "Mr. N. N. is dead."

41. In §15 we introduced proper names into language (8). Now suppose that the tool with the name "N" is broken. Not knowing this, A gives B the sign "N". Has this sign meaning now or not?—What is B to do when he is given it?—We have not settled anything about this. One might ask: what *will* he do? Well, perhaps he will stand there at a loss, or shew A the pieces. How one *might* say: "N" has become meaningless; and this expression would mean that the sign "N" no longer had a use in our language-game (unless we gave it a new one). "N" might also become meaningless because, for whatever reason, the tool was given another name and the sign "N" no longer used in the language-game.—But we could also imagine a convention whereby B has to shake his head in reply if A gives him the sign belonging to a tool that is broken.—In

this way the command "N" might be said to be given a place in the language-game even when the tool no longer exists, and the sign "N" to have meaning even when its bearer ceases to exist.

42. But has for instance a name which has *never* been used for a tool also got a meaning in that game?—Let us assume that "X" is such a sign and that A gives this sign to B—well, even such signs could be given a place in the language-game, and B might have, say, to answer them too with a shake of the head. (One could imagine this as a sort of joke between them.)

43. For a *large* class of cases—though not for all—in which we employ the word "meaning" it can be defined thus: the meaning of a word is its use in the language.

And the *meaning* of a name is sometimes explained by pointing to its *bearer.*

44. We said that the sentence "Excalibur has a sharp blade" made sense even when Excalibur was broken in pieces. Now this is so because in this language-game a name is also used in the absence of its bearer. But we can imagine a language-game with names (that is, with signs which we should certainly include among names) in which they are used only in the presence of the bearer; and so could *always* be replaced by a demonstrative pronoun and the gesture of pointing.

45. The demonstrative "this" can never be without a bearer. It might be said: "so long as there is a *this,* the word 'this' has a meaning too, whether *this* is simple or complex."—But that does not make the word into a name. On the contrary: for a name is not used with, but only explained by means of, the gesture of pointing.

46. What lies behind the idea that names really signify simples?—Socrates says in the *Theaetetus:* "If I make no mistake, I have heard some people say this: there is no definition of the primary elements—so to speak—out of which we and everything else are composed; for everything exists[2] in its own right can only be *named,* no other determination is possible, neither that it *is* nor that it *is not* . . . . . But what exists in its own right has to be . . . . . named without any other determination. In consequence it is impossible to give an account of any primary element; for it, nothing is possible but the bare name; its name is all it has. But just as what consists of these primary elements is itself complex, so the names of the elements become descriptive language by being compounded together. For the essence of speech is the composition of names."

Both Russell's 'individuals' and my 'objects' (*Tractatus Logico-Philosophicus*) were such primary elements.

47. But what are the simple constituent parts of which reality is composed?—What are the simple constituent parts of a chair?—The bits of wood of which it is made? Or the molecules, or the atoms?—"Simple" means: not composite. And here the point is: in what sense 'composite'? It makes no sense at all to speak absolutely of the 'simple parts of a chair'.

Again: Does my visual image of this tree, of this chair, consist of parts? And what are its simple component parts? Multi-colouredness is one kind of complexity; another is, for example, that of a broken outline composed of straight bits. And a curve can be said to be composed of an ascending and a descending segment.

If I tell someone without any further explanation: "What I see before me now is composite", he will have the right to ask: "What do you mean by 'composite'? For there are all sorts of things that that can mean!"—The question "Is what you see composite?" makes good sense if it is already established what kind of complexity—that is, which particular use of the word—is in question. If it had been laid down that the visual image of a tree was to be called "composite" if one saw not just a single trunk, but also branches, then the question "Is the visual image of this tree simple or composite?", and the question "What are its simple component parts?", would have a clear sense—a clear use. And of course the answer to the second question is not "The branches" (that would be an answer to the *grammatical* question: "What are here called 'simple component parts'?") but rather a description of the individual branches.

But isn't a chessboard, for instance, obviously, and absolutely, composite?—You are probably thinking of the composition out of thirty-two white and thirty-two black squares. But could we not also say, for instance, that it was composed of the colours black and white and the schema of squares? And if there are quite different ways of looking at it, do you still want to say that the chessboard is absolutely 'composite'?—Asking "Is this object com-

[2] I have translated the German translation which Wittgenstein used rather than the original. [Tr.]

posite?" *outside* a particular language-game is like what a boy once did, who had to say whether the verbs in certain sentences were in the active or passive voice, and who racked his brains over the question whether the verb "to sleep" meant something active or passive.

We use the word "composite" (and therefore the word "simple") in an enormous number of different and differently related ways. (Is the colour of a square on a chessboard simple, or does it consist of pure white and pure yellow? And is white simple, or does it consist of the colours of the rainbow?—Is this length of 2 cm. simple, or does it consist of two parts, each 1 cm. long? But why not of one bit 3 cm. long, and one bit 1 cm. long measured in the opposite direction?)

To the *philosophical* question: "Is the visual image of this tree composite, and what are its component parts?" the correct answer is: "That depends on what you understand by 'composite'." (And that is of course not an answer but a rejection of the question.)

48. Let us apply the method of §2 to the account in the *Thaeaetetus*. Let us consider a language-game for which this account is really valid. The language serves to describe combinations of coloured squares on a surface. The squares form a complex like a chessboard. There are red, green, white and black squares. The words of the language are (correspondingly) "R", "G", "W", "B", and a sentence is a series of these words. They describe an arrangement of squares in the order:

1	2	3
4	5	6
7	8	9

And so for instance the sentence "RRBGGGRWW" describes an arrangement of this sort:

red	red	black
green	green	green
red	white	white

Here the sentence is a complex of names, to which corresponds a complex of elements. The primary elements are the coloured squares. "But are these simple?"—I do not know what else you would have me call "the simples", what would be more natural in this language-game. But under other circumstances I should call a monochrome square "composite", consisting perhaps of two rectangles, or of the elements colour and shape. But the concept of complexity might also be so extended that a smaller area was said to be 'composed' of a greater area and another one subtracted from it. Compare the 'composition of forces', the 'division' of a line by a point outside it; these expressions shew that we are sometimes even inclined to conceive the smaller as the result of a composition of greater parts, and the greater as the result of a division of the smaller.

But I do not know whether to say that the figure described by our sentence consists of four or of nine elements! Well, does the sentence consist of four letters or of nine?—And which are *its* elements, the types of letter, or the letters? Does it matter which we say, so long as we avoid misunderstandings in any particular case?

49. But what does it mean to say that we cannot define (that is, describe) these elements, but only name them? This might mean, for instance, that when in a limiting case a complex consists of only *one* square, its description is simply the name of the coloured square.

Here we might say—though this easily leads to all kinds of philosophical superstition—that a sign "R" or "B", etc. may be sometimes a word and sometimes a proposition. But whether it 'is a word or a proposition' depends on the situation in which it is uttered or written. For instance, if A has to describe complexes of coloured squares to B and he uses the word "R" *alone,* we shall be able to say that the word is a description—a proposition. But if he is memorizing the words and their meanings, or if he is teaching someone else the use of the words and uttering them in the course of ostensive teaching, we shall not say that they are propositions. In this situation the word "R", for instance, is not a description; it *names* an element—but it would be queer to make that a reason for saying that an element can *only* be named! For naming and describing do not stand on the same level: naming is a preparation for description. Naming is so far not a move in the language-game—any more than putting a piece in its place on the board is a move in chess. We may say: *nothing* has so far been done, when a thing has been named. It has not even *got* a name except in the language-game. This was what Frege meant too, when he said that a word had meaning only as part of a sentence.

50. What does it mean to say that we can attribute neither being nor non-being to elements?—One might say: if everything that we call "being" and "non-being" consists in the existence and non-existence of connexions between elements, it makes no sense to speak of an element's being (non-being); just as when everything that we call "destruction" lies in the separation of elements, it makes no sense to speak of the destruction of an element.

One would, however, like to say: existence cannot be attributed to an element, for if it did not *exist,* one could not even name it and so one could say nothing at all of it.—But let us consider an analogous case. There is *one* thing of which one can say neither that it is one metre long, nor that it is not one metre long, and that is the standard metre in Paris.—But this is, of course, not to ascribe any extraordinary property to it, but only to mark its peculiar role in the language-game of measuring with a metre-rule.—Let us imagine samples of colour being preserved in Paris like the standard metre. We define: "sepia" means the colour of the standard sepia which is there kept hermetically sealed. Then it will make no sense to say of this sample either that it is of this colour or that it is not.

We can put it like this: This sample is an instrument of the language used in ascriptions of colour. In this language-game it is not something that is represented, but is a means of representation.—And just this goes for an element in language-game (48) when we name it by uttering the word "R": this gives this object a role in our language-game; it is now a *means* of representation. And to say "If it did not *exist,* it could have no name" is to say as much and as little as: if this thing did not exist, we could not use it in out language-game.—What looks as if it *had* to exist, is part of the language. It is a paradigm in our language-game; something with which comparison is made. And this may be an important observation; but it is none the less an observation concerning our language-game—our method of representation.

51. In describing language-game (48) I said that the words "R", "B", etc. corresponded to the colours of the squares. But what does this correspondence consist in; in what sense can one say that certain colours of squares correspond to these signs? For the account in (48) merely set up a connexion between those signs and certain words of our language (the names of colours).—Well, it was presupposed that the use of the signs in the language-game would be taught in a different way, in particular by pointing to paradigms. Very well; but what does it mean to say that in the *technique of using the language* certain elements correspond to the signs?—Is it that the person who is describing the complexes of coloured squares always says "R" where there is a red square; "B" when there is a black one, and so on? But what if he goes wrong in the description and mistakenly says "R" where he sees a black square—what is the criterion by which this is a *mistake?*—Or does "R"s standing for a red square consist in this, that when the people whose language it is use the sign "R" a red square always comes before their minds?

In order to see more clearly, here as in countless similar cases, we must focus on the details of what goes on; must look at them *from close to.*

52. If I am inclined to suppose that a mouse has come into being by spontaneous generation out of grey rags and dust, I shall do well to examine those rags very closely to see how a mouse may have hidden in them, how it may have got there and so on. But if I am convinced that a mouse cannot come into being from these things, then this investigation will perhaps be superfluous.

But first we must learn to understand what it is that opposes such an examination of details in philosophy.

53. Our language-game (48) has *various* possibilities; there is a variety of cases in which we should say that a sign in the game was the name of a square of such-and-such a colour. We should say so if, for instance, we knew that the people who used the language were taught the use of the signs in such-and-such a way. Or if it were set down in writing, say in the form of a table, that this element corresponded to this sign, and if the table were used in teaching the language and were appealed to in certain disputed cases.

We can also imagine such a table's being a tool in the use of the language. Describing a complex is then done like this: the person who describes the complex has a table with him and looks up each element of the complex in it and passes from this to the sign (and the one who is given the description may also use a table to translate it into a picture of coloured squares). This table might be said to take over here the role of memory and association in other cases. (We do not usually carry out the order "Bring me a red flower" by looking up the colour red in a table of colours and then bringing a flower of the colour that we find in the table; but when it is a question of choosing or mixing a particular shade of red, we do sometimes make use of a sample or table.)

If we call such a table the expression of a rule of the language-game, it can be said that what we call a rule of a language-game may have very different roles in the game.

54. Let us recall the kinds of case where we say that a game is played according to a definite rule.

The rule may be an aid in teaching the game. The learner is told it and given practice in applying it.—Or it is an instrument of the game itself.—Or a rule is employed neither in the teaching nor in the game itself; nor is it set down in a list of rules. One learns the game by watching how others play. But we say that it is played according to such-and-such rules because an observer can read these rules off from the practice of the game—like a natural law governing the play.—But how does the observer distinguish in this case between players' mistakes and correct play?—There are characteristic signs of it in the players' behaviour. Think of the behaviour characteristic of correcting a slip of the tongue. It would be possible to recognize that someone was doing so even without knowing his language.

55. "What the names in language signify must be indestructible; for it must be possible to describe the state of affairs in which everything destructible is destroyed. And this description will contain words; and what corresponds to these cannot then be destroyed, for otherwise the words would have no meaning." I must not saw off the branch on which I am sitting.

One might, of course, object at once that this description would have to except itself from the destruction.—But what corresponds to the separate words of the description and so cannot be destroyed if it is true, is what gives the words their meaning—is that without which they would have no meaning.—In a sense, however, this man is surely what corresponds to his name. But he is destructible, and his name does not lose its meaning when the bearer is destroyed.—An example of something corresponding to the name, and without which it would have no meaning, is a paradigm that is used in connexion with the name in the language-game.

56. But what if no such sample is part of the language, and we *bear in mind* the colour (for instance) that a word stands for?—"And if we bear it in mind then it comes before our mind's eye when we utter the word. So, if it is always supposed to be possible for us to remember it, it must be in itself indestructible."—But what do we regard as the criterion for remembering it right?—When we work with a sample instead of our memory there are circumstances in which we say that the sample has changed colour and we judge of this by memory. But can we not sometimes speak of a darkening (for example) of our memory-image? Aren't we as much at the mercy of memory as of a sample? (For someone might feel like saying: "If we had no memory we should be at the mercy of a sample".)—Or perhaps of some chemical reaction. Imagine that you were supposed to paint a particular colour "C", which was the colour that appeared when the chemical substances X and Y combined.—Suppose that the colour struck you as brighter on one day than on another; would you not sometimes say: "I must be wrong, the colour is certainly the same as yesterday"? This shews that we do not always resort to what memory tells us as the verdict of the highest court of appeal.

57. "Something red can be destroyed, but red cannot be destroyed, and that is why the meaning of the word 'red' is independent of the existence of a red thing."—Certainly it makes no sense to say that the colour red is torn up or pounded to bits. But don't we say "The red is vanishing"? And don't clutch at the idea of our always being able to bring red before our mind's eye even when there is nothing red any more. That is just as if you chose to say that there would still always be a chemical reaction producing a red flame.—For suppose you cannot remember the colour any more?—When we forget which colour this is the name of, it loses meaning for us; that is, we are no longer able to play a particular language-game with it. And the situation then is comparable with that in which we have lost a paradigm which was an instrument of our language.

. . . .

65. Here we come up against the great question that lies behind all these considerations.—For some-

one might object against me: "You take the easy way out! You talk about all sorts of language-games, but have nowhere said what the essence of a language-game, and hence of language, is: what is common to all these activities, and what makes them into language or parts of language. So you let yourself off the very part of the investigation that once gave you yourself most headache, the part about the *general form of propositions* and of language."

And this is true.—Instead of producing something common to all that we call language, I am saying that these phenomena have no one thing in common which makes us use the same word for all,—but that they are *related* to one another in many different ways. And it is because of this relationship, or these relationships, that we call them all "language". I will try to explain this.

66. Consider for example the proceedings that we call "games". I mean board-games, card-games, ball-games, Olympic games, and so on. What is common to them all?—Don't say: "There *must* be something common, or they would not be called 'games'"—but *look and see* whether there is anything common to all.—For if you look at them you will not see something that is common to *all*, but similarities, relationships, and a whole series of them at that. To repeat: don't think, but look!—Look for example at board-games, with their multifarious relationships. Now pass to card-games; here you find many correspondences with the first group, but many common features drop out, and others appear. When we pass next to ball-games, much that is common is retained, but much is lost.—Are they all 'amusing'? Compare chess with noughts and crosses. Or is there always winning and losing, or competition between players? Think of patience. In ball games there is winning and losing; but when a child throws his ball at the wall and catches it again, this feature has disappeared. Look at the parts played by skill and luck; and at the difference between skill in chess and skill in tennis. Think now of games like ring-a-ring-a-roses; here is the element of amusement, but how many other characteristic features have disappeared! And we can go through the many, many other groups of games in the same way; can see how similarities crop up and disappear.

And the result of this examination is: we see a complicated network of similarities overlapping and criss-crossing: sometimes overall similarities, sometimes similarities of detail.

67. I can think of no better expression to characterize these similarities than "family resemblances"; for the various resemblances between members of a family: build, features, colour of eyes, gait, temperament, etc. etc. overlap and criss-cross in the same way.—And I shall say: 'games' form a family.

And for instance the kinds of number form a family in the same way. Why do we call something a "number"? Well, perhaps because it has a—direct—relationship with several things that have hitherto been called number; and this can be said to give it an indirect relationship to other things we call the same name. And we extend our concept of number as in spinning a thread we twist fibre on fibre. And the strength of the thread does not reside in the fact that some one fibre runs through its whole length, but in the overlapping of many fibres.

But if someone wished to say: "There is something common to all these constructions—namely the disjunction of all their common properties"—I should reply: Now you are only playing with words. One might as well say: "Something runs through the whole thread—namely the continuous overlapping of those fibres".

68. "All right: the concept of number is defined for you as the logical sum of these individual interrelated concepts: cardinal numbers, rational numbers, real numbers, etc.; and in the same way the concept of a game as the logical sum of a corresponding set of sub-concepts."—It need not be so. For I *can* give the concept 'number' rigid limits in this way, that is, use the word "number" for a rigidly limited concept, but I can also use it so that the extension of the concept is *not* closed by a frontier. And this is how we do use the word "game". For how is the concept of a game bounded? What still counts as a game and what no longer does? Can you give the boundary? No. You can *draw* one; for none has so far been drawn. (But that never troubled you before when you used the word "game".)

"But then the use of the word is unregulated, the 'game' we play with it is unregulated."—It is not everywhere circumscribed by rules; but no more are there any rules for how high one throws the ball in tennis, or how hard; yet tennis is a game for all that and has rules too.

69. How should we explain to someone what a game is? I imagine that we should describe *games* to

him, and we might add: "This *and similar things* are called 'games'". And do we know any more about it ourselves? Is it only other people whom we cannot tell exactly what a game is?—But this is not ignorance. We do not know the boundaries because none have been drawn. To repeat, we can draw a boundary—for a special purpose. Does it take that to make the concept usable? Not at all! (Except for that special purpose.) No more than it took the definition: 1 pace = 75 cm. to make the measure of length 'one pace' usable. And if you want to say "But still, before that it wasn't an exact measure", then I reply: very well, it was an inexact one.—Though you still owe me a definition of exactness.

70. "But if the concept 'game' is uncircumscribed like that, you don't really know what you mean by a 'game'."—When I give the description: "The ground was quite covered with plants"—do you want to say I don't know what I am talking about until I can give a definition of a plant?

My meaning would be explained by, say, a drawing and the words "The ground looked roughly like this". Perhaps I even say "it looked *exactly* like this."—Then were just *this* grass and *these* leaves there, arranged just like this? No, that is not what it means. And I should not accept any picture as exact in *this* sense.

Someone says to me: "Shew the children a game." I teach them gaming with dice, and the other says "I didn't mean that sort of game." Must the exclusion of the game with dice have come before his mind when he gave me the order?

71. One might say that the concept 'game' is a concept with blurred edges.—"But is a blurred concept a concept at all?"—Is an indistinct photograph a picture of a person at all? Is it even always an advantage to replace an indistinct picture by a sharp one? Isn't the indistinct one often exactly what we need?

Frege compares a concept to an area and says that an area with vague boundaries cannot be called an area at all. This presumably means that we cannot do anything with it.—But is it senseless to say: "Stand roughly there"? Suppose that I were standing with someone in a city square and said that. As I say it I do not draw any kind of boundary, but perhaps point with my hand—as if I were indicating a particular *spot*. And this is just how one might explain to someone what a game is. One gives examples and intends them to be taken in a particular way.—I do not, however, mean by this that he is supposed to see in those examples that common thing which I—for some reason—was unable to express; but that he is now to *employ* those examples in a particular way. Here giving examples is not an *indirect* means of explaining—in default of a better. For any general definition can be misunderstood too. The point is that *this* is how we play the game. (I mean the language-game with the word "game".)

72. *Seeing what is common.* Suppose I shew someone various multicoloured pictures, and say: "The colour you see in all these is called 'yellow ochre'".—This is a definition, and the other will get to understand it by looking for and seeing what is common to the pictures. Then he can look *at*, can point *to*, the common thing.

Compare with this a case in which I shew him figures of different shapes all painted the same colour, and say: "What these have in common is called 'yellow ochre'".

And compare this case: I shew him samples of different shades of blue and say: "The colour that is common to all these is what I call 'blue'".

73. When someone defines the names of colours for me by pointing to samples and saying "This colour is called 'blue', this 'green' . . . . ." this case can be compared in many respects to putting a table in my hands, with the words written under the colour-samples.—Though this comparison may mislead in many ways.—One is now inclined to extend the comparison: to have understood the definition means to have in one's mind an idea of the thing defined, and that is a sample or picture. So if I am shewn various different leaves and told "This is called a 'leaf'", I get an idea of the shape of a leaf, a picture of it in my mind.—But what does the picture of a leaf look like when it does not shew us any particular shape, but 'what is common to all shapes of leaf'? Which shade is the 'sample in my mind' of the colour green—the sample of what is common to all shades of green?

"But might there not be such 'general' samples? Say a schematic leaf, or a sample of *pure* green?"—Certainly there might. But for such a schema to be understood as a *schema*, and not as the shape of a particular leaf, and for a slip of pure green to be understood as a sample of all that is greenish and not as a sample of pure green—this in turn resides in the way the samples are used.

Ask yourself: what *shape* must the sample of the

colour green be? Should it be rectangular? Or would it then be the sample of a green rectangle?—So should it be 'irregular' in shape? And what is to prevent us then from regarding it—that is, from using it—only as a sample of irregularity of shape?

74. Here also belongs the idea that if you see this leaf as a sample of 'leaf shape in general' you *see* it differently from someone who regards it as, say, a sample of this particular shape. Now this might well be so—though it is not so—for it would only be to say that, as a matter of experience, if you *see* the leaf in a particular way, you use it in such-and-such a way or according to such-and-such rules. Of course, there is such a thing as seeing in *this* way or *that;* and there are also cases where whoever sees a sample like *this* will in general use it in *this* way, and whoever sees it otherwise in another way. For example, if you see the schematic drawing of a cube as a plane figure consisting of a square and two rhombi you will, perhaps, carry out the order "Bring me something like this" differently from someone who sees the picture three-dimensionally.

75. What does it mean to know what a game is? What does it mean, to know it and not be able to say it? Is this knowledge somehow equivalent to an unformulated definition? So that if it were formulated I should be able to recognize it as the expression of my knowledge? Isn't my knowledge, my concept of a game, completely expressed in the explanations that I could give? That is, in my describing examples of various kinds of game; shewing how all sorts of other games can be constructed on the analogy of these; saying that I should scarcely include this or this among games; and so on.

76. If someone were to draw a sharp boundary I could not acknowledge it as the one that I too always wanted to draw, or had drawn in my mind. For I did not want to draw one at all. His concept can then be said to be not the same as mine, but akin to it. The kinship is that of two pictures, one of which consists of colour patches with vague contours, and the other of patches similarly shaped and distributed, but with clear contours. The kinship is just as undeniable as the difference.

77. And if we carry this comparison still further it is clear that the degree to which the sharp picture *can* resemble the blurred one depends on the latter's degree of vagueness. For imagine having to sketch a sharply defined picture 'corresponding' to a blurred one. In the latter there is a blurred red rectangle: for it you put down a sharply defined one. Of course—several such sharply defined rectangles can be drawn to correspond to the indefinite one.—But if the colours in the original merge without a hint of any outline won't it become a hopeless task to draw a sharp picture corresponding to the blurred one? Won't you then have to say: "Here I might just as well draw a circle or heart as a rectangle, for all the colours merge. Anything—and nothing—is right."—And this is the position you are in if you look for definitions corresponding to our concepts in aesthetics or ethics.

In such a difficulty always ask yourself: How did we *learn* the meaning of this word ("good" for instance)? From what sort of examples? in what language-games? Then it will be easier for you to see that the word must have a family of meanings.

. . . .

489. Ask yourself: On what occasion, for what purpose, do we say this?

What kind of actions accompany these words? (Think of a greeting.) In what scenes will they be used; and what for?

490. How do I know that *this line of thought* has led me to this action?—Well, it is a particular picture: for example, of a calculation leading to a further experiment in an experimental investigation. It looks like *this*—and now I could describe an example.

491. Not: "without language we could not communicate with one another"—but for sure: without language we cannot influence other people in such-and-such ways; cannot build roads and machines, etc. And also: without the use of speech and writing people could not communicate.

492. To invent a language could mean to invent an instrument for a particular purpose on the basis of the laws of nature (or consistently with them); but it also has the other sense, analogous to that in which we speak of the invention of a game.

Here I am stating something about the grammar of the word "language" by connecting it with the grammar of the word "invent".

493. We say: "The cock calls the hens by crowing"—but doesn't a comparison with our language lie at the bottom of this?—Isn't the aspect quite altered if we imagine the crowing to set the hens in motion by some kind of physical causation?

But if it were shewn how the words "Come to me" act on the person addressed, so that finally, given certain conditions, the muscles of his legs are innervated, and so on—should we feel that that sentence lost the character of a *sentence?*

494. I want to say: It is *primarily* the apparatus of our ordinary language, of our word-language, that we call language; and then other things by analogy or comparability with this.

495. Clearly, I can establish by experience that a human being (or animal) reacts to one sign as I want him to, and to another not. That, e.g., a human being goes to the right at the sign "—>" and goes to the left at the sign "<—"; but that he does not react to the sign "o—|", as to "<—".

I do not even need to fabricate a case, I only have to consider what is in fact the case; namely, that I can direct a man who has learned only German, only by using the German language. (For here I am looking at learning German as adjusting a mechanism to respond to a certain kind of influence; and it may be all one to us whether someone else has learned the language, or was perhaps from birth constituted to react to sentences in German like a normal person who has learned German.)

496. Grammar does not tell us how language must be constructed in order to fulfil its purpose, in order to have such-and-such an effect on human beings. It only describes and in no way explains the use of signs.

497. The rules of grammar may be called "arbitrary", if that is to mean that the *aim* of the grammar is nothing but that of the language.

If someone says "If our language had not this grammar, it could not express these facts"—it should be asked what "*could*" means here.

498. When I say that the orders "Bring me sugar" and "Bring me milk" make sense, but not the combination "Milk me sugar", that does not mean that the utterance of this combination of words has no effect. And if its effect is that the other person stares at me and gapes, I don't on that account call it the order to stare and gape, even if that was precisely the effect that I wanted to produce.

499. To say "This combination of words makes no sense" excludes it from the sphere of language and thereby bounds the domain of language. But when one draws a boundary it may be for various kinds of reason. If I surround an area with a fence or a line or otherwise, the purpose may be to prevent someone from getting in or out; but it may also be part of a game and the players be supposed, say, to jump over the boundary; or it may shew where the property of one man ends and that of another begins; and so on. So if I draw a boundary line that is not yet to say what I am drawing it for.

500. When a sentence is called senseless, it is not as it were its sense that is senseless. But a combination of words is being excluded from the language, withdrawn from circulation.

. . . .

Two uses of the word "see".

The one: "What do you see there?"—"I see *this*" (and then a description, a drawing, a copy). The other: "I see a likeness between these two faces"—let the man I tell this to be seeing the faces as clearly as I do myself.

The importance of this is the difference of category between the two 'objects' of sight.

The one man might make an accurate drawing of the two faces, and the other notice in the drawing the likeness which the former did not see.

I contemplate a face, and then suddenly notice its likeness to another. I *see* that it has not changed; and yet I see it differently. I call this experience "noticing an aspect".

Its *causes* are of interest to psychologists.

We are interested in the concept and its place among the concepts of experience.

You could imagine the illustration

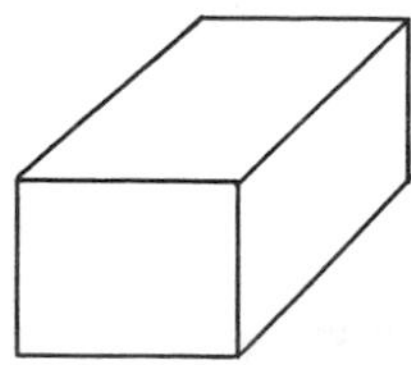

appearing in several places in a book, a text-book for instance. In the relevant text something different is in question every time: here a glass cube, there an inverted open box, there a wire frame of that shape, there three boards forming a solid angle. Each time the text supplies the interpretation of the illustration.

But we can also *see* the illustration now as one thing now as another.—So we interpret it, and *see* it as we *interpret* it.

Here perhaps we should like to reply: The description of what is got immediately, i.e. of the visual experience, by means of an interpretation—is an indirect description. "I see the figure as a box" means: I have a particular visual experience which I have found that I always have when I interpret the figure as a box or when I look at a box. But if it meant this I ought to know it. I ought to be able to refer to the experience directly, and not only indirectly. (As I can speak of red without calling it the colour of blood.)

I shall call the following figure, derived from Jastrow,[3] the duck-rabbit. It can be seen as a rabbit's head or as a duck's.

And I must distinguish between the 'continuous seeing' of an aspect and the 'dawning' of an aspect.

The picture might have been shewn me, and I never have seen anything but a rabbit in it.

Here it is useful to introduce the idea of a picture-object. For instance

would be a 'picture-face'.

In some respects I stand towards it as I do towards a human face. I can study its expression, can react to it as to the expression of the human face. A child can talk to picture-men or picture-animals, can treat them as it treats dolls.

I may, then, have seen the duck-rabbit simply as a picture-rabbit from the first. That is to say, if asked "What's that?" or "What do you see here?" I should have replied: "A picture-rabbit". If I had further been asked what that was, I should have explained by pointing to all sorts of pictures of rabbits, should perhaps have pointed to real rabbits, talked abut their habits, or given an imitation of them.

I should not have answered the question "What do you see here?" by saying: "Now I am seeing it as a picture-rabbit". I should simply have described my perception: just as if I had said "I see a red circle over there."—

Nevertheless someone else could have said of me: "He is seeing the figure as a picture-rabbit."

It would have made as little sense for me to say "Now I am seeing it as . . ." as to say at the sight of a knife and fork "Now I am seeing this as a knife and fork". This expression would not be understood.—And more than: "Now it's a fork" or "It can be a fork too".

One doesn't '*take*' what one knows as the cutlery at a meal *for* cutlery; any more than one ordinarily tries to move one's mouth as one eats, or aims at moving it.

If you say "Now it's a face for me", we can ask: "What change are you alluding to?"

I see two pictures, with the duck-rabbit surrounded by rabbits in one, by ducks in the other. I do not notice that they are the same. Does it *follow* from this that I *see* something different in the two cases?—It gives us a reason for using this expression here.

"I saw it quite differently, I should never have recognized it!" Now, that is an exclamation. And there is also a justification for it.

I should never have thought of superimposing the heads like that, of making *this* comparison between them. For they suggest a different mode of comparison.

Nor has the head seen like *this* the slightest similarity to the head seen like *this*—although they are congruent.

I am shewn a picture-rabbit and asked what it is; I say "It's a rabbit". Not "Now it's a rabbit". I am reporting my perception.—I am shewn the duck-rabbit and asked what it is; I *may* say "It's a duck-rabbit". But I may also react to the question quite differently.—The answer that it is a duck-rabbit is again the report of a perception; the answer "Now

[3] *Fact and Fable in Psychology.* [Au.]

it's a rabbit" is not. Had I replied "It's a rabbit", the ambiguity would have escaped me, and I should have been reporting my perception.

The change of aspect. "But surely you would say that the picture is altogether different now!"

But what is different: my impression? my point of view?—Can I say? I *describe* the alteration like a perception; quite as if the object had altered before my eyes.

"Now I am seeing *this*", I might say (pointing to another picture, for example). This has the form of a report of a new perception.

The expression of a change of aspect is the expression of a *new* perception and at the same time of the perception's being unchanged.

I suddenly see the solution of a puzzle-picture. Before, there were branches there; now there is a human shape. My visual impression has changed and now I recognize that it has not only shape and colour but also a quite particular 'organization'.—My visual impression has changed;—what was it like before and what is it like now?—If I represent it by means of an exact copy—and isn't that a good representation of it?—no change is shewn.

And above all do *not* say "After all my visual impression isn't the *drawing*; it is *this*—which I can't shew to anyone."—Of course it is not the drawing, but neither is it anything of the same category, which I carry within myself.

The concept of the 'inner picture' is misleading, for this concept uses the '*outer* picture' as a model; and yet the uses of the words for these concepts are no more like one another than the uses of 'numeral' and 'number'. (And if one chose to call numbers 'ideal numerals', one might produce a similar confusion.)

If you put the 'organization' of a visual impression on a level with colours and shapes, you are proceeding from the idea of the visual impression as an inner object. Of course this makes this object into a chimera; a queerly shifting construction. For the similarity to a picture is now impaired.

If I know that the schematic cube has various aspects and I want to find out what someone else sees, I can get him to make a model of what he sees, in addition to a copy, or to point to such a model; even though *he* has no idea of my purpose in demanding two accounts.

But when we have a changing aspect the case is altered. Now the only possible expression of our experience is what before perhaps seemed, or even was, a useless specification when once we had the copy.

And this by itself wrecks the comparison of 'organization' with colour and shape in visual impressions.

If I saw the duck-rabbit as a rabbit, then I saw: these shapes and colours (I give them in detail)—and I saw besides something like this: and here I point to a number of different pictures of rabbits.—This shews the difference between the concepts.

'Seeing as . . . .' is not part of perception. And for that reason it is like seeing and again not like.

I look at an animal and am asked: "What do you see?" I answer: "A rabbit".—I see a landscape; suddenly a rabbit runs past. I exclaim "A rabbit!"

Both things, both the report and the exclamation, are expressions of perception and of visual experience. But the exclamation is so in a different sense from the report: it is forced from us.—It is related to the experience as a cry is to pain.

But since it is the description of a perception, it can also be called the expression of thought.—If you are looking at the object, you need not think of it; but if you are having the visual experience expressed by the exclamation, you are also *thinking* of what you see.

Hence the flashing of an aspect on us seems half visual experience, half thought.

Someone suddenly sees an appearance which he does not recognize (it may be a familiar object, but in an unusual position or lighting); the lack of recognition perhaps lasts only a few seconds. Is it correct to say he has a different visual experience from someone who knew the object at once?

For might not someone be able to describe an unfamiliar shape that appeared before him just as *accurately* as I, to whom it is familiar? And isn't that the answer?—Of course it will not generally be so. And his description will run quite differently. (I say, for example, "The animal had long ears"—he: "There were two long appendages", and then he draws them.)

I meet someone whom I have not seen for years; I see him clearly, but fail to know him. Suddenly I know him, I see the old face in the altered one. I believe that I should do a different portrait of him now if I could paint.

Now, when I know my acquaintance in a crowd, perhaps after looking in his direction for quite a while,—is this a special sort of seeing? Is it a case of both seeing and thinking? or an amalgam of the two, as I should almost like to say?

The question is: *why* does one want to say this?

The very expression which is also a report of what is seen, is here a cry of recognition.

What is the criterion of the visual experience?—The criterion? What do you suppose?

The representation of 'what is seen'.

The concept of a representation of what is seen, like that of a copy, is very elastic, and so *together with it* is the concept of what is seen. The two are intimately connected. (Which is *not* to say that they are alike.)

How does one tell that human beings *see* three-dimensionally?—I ask someone about the lie of the land (over there) of which he has a view. "Is it like *this*?" (I shew him with my hand)—"Yes."—"How do you know?"—"It's not misty, I see it quite clear."—He does not give reasons for the surmise. The only thing that is natural to us is to represent what we see three-dimensionally; special practice and training are needed for two-dimensional representation whether in drawing or in words. (The queerness of children's drawings.)

If someone sees a smile and does not know it for a smile, does not understand it as such, does he see it differently from someone who understands it?—He mimics it differently, for instance.

Hold the drawing of a face upside down and you can't recognize the expression of the face. Perhaps you can see that it is smiling, but not exactly what *kind* of smile it is. You cannot imitate the smile or describe it more exactly.

And yet the picture which you have turned round may be a most exact representation of a person's face.

The figure (a)

is the reverse of the figure (b)

As (c)

is the reverse of (d)

Pleasure

But—I should like to say—there is a different difference between my impressions of (c) and (d) and between those of (a) and (b). (d), for example, looks neater than (c). (Compare a remark of Lewis Carroll's.) (d) is easy, (c) hard to copy.

Imagine the duck-rabbit hidden in a tangle of lines. Now I suddenly notice it in the picture, and notice it simply as the head of a rabbit. At some later time I look at the same picture and notice the same figure, but see it as the duck, without necessarily realizing that it was the same figure both times.—If I later see the aspect change—can I say that the duck and rabbit aspects are now seen quite differently from when I recognized them separately in the tangle of lines? No.

But the change produces a surprise not produced by the recognition.

If you search in a figure (1) for another figure (2), and then find it, you see (1) in a new way. Not only can you give a new kind of description of it, but noticing the second figure was a new visual experience.

But you would not necessarily want to say "Figure (1) looks quite different now; it isn't even in the least like the figure I saw before, though they are congruent!"

There are here hugely many interrelated phenomena and possible concepts.

Then is the copy of the figure an *incomplete* description of my visual experience? No.—But the circumstances decide whether, and what, more detailed specifications are necessary.—It *may* be an incomplete description; if there is still something to ask.

Of course we can say: There are certain things which fall equally under the concept 'picture-rabbit' and under the concept 'picture-duck'. And a picture, a drawing, is such a thing.—But the *impression* is not simultaneously of a picture-duck and a picture-rabbit.

"What I really *see* must surely be what is produced in me by the influence of the object"—Then what is produced in me is a sort of copy, something that in its turn can be looked at, can be before one; almost something like a *materialization*.

And this materialization is something spatial and it must be possible to describe it in purely spatial terms. For instance (if it is a face) it can smile; the concept of friendliness, however, has no place in an account of it, but is *foreign* to such an account (even though it may subserve it).

If you ask me what I saw, perhaps I shall be able to make a sketch which shews you; but I shall mostly have no recollection of the way my glance shifted in looking at it.

The concept of 'seeing' makes a tangled impression. Well, it is tangled.—I look at the landscape, my gaze ranges over it, I see all sorts of distinct and indistinct movement; *this* impresses itself sharply on me, *that* is quite hazy. After all, how completely ragged what we see can appear! And now look at all that can be meant by "description of what is seen".—But this just is what is called description of what is seen. There is not *one genuine* proper case of such description—the rest being just vague, something which awaits clarification, or which must just be swept aside as rubbish.

Here we are in enormous danger of wanting to make fine distinctions.—It is the same when one tries to define the concept of a material object in terms of 'what is really seen'.—What we have rather to do is to *accept* the everyday language-game, and to note *false* accounts of the matter *as* false. The primitive language-game which children are taught needs no justification; attempts at justification need to be rejected.

Take as an example the aspects of a triangle. This triangle

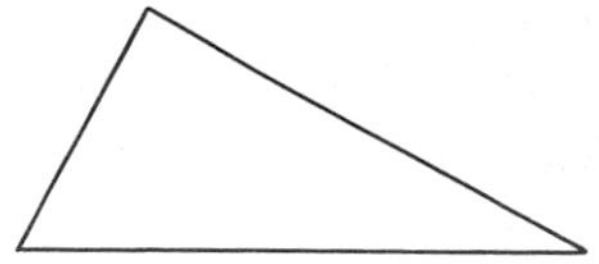

can be seen as a triangular hole, as a solid, as a geometrical drawing; as standing on its base, as hanging from its apex; as a mountain, as a wedge, as an arrow or pointer, as an overturned object which is meant to stand on the shorter side of the right angle, as a half parallelogram, and as various other things.

"You can think now of *this* now of *this* as you look at it, can regard it now as *this* now as *this*, and then you will see it now *this* way, now *this*."—*What* way? There *is* no further qualification.

But how is it possible to *see* an object according to an *interpretation?*—The question represents it as a queer fact; as if something were being forced into a form it did not really fit. But no squeezing, no forcing took place here.

When it looks as if there were no room for such a form between other ones you have to look for it in another dimension. If there is no room here, there *is* room in another dimension.

. . . .

Do I really see something different each time, or do I only interpret what I see in a different way? I am inclined to say the former. But why?—To interpret is to think, to do something; seeing is a state.

Now it is easy to recognize cases in which we are *interpreting*. When we interpret we form hypotheses, which may prove false.—"I am seeing this figure as a . . . . ." can be verified as little as (or in the same sense as) "I am seeing bright red". So there is a similarity in the use of "seeing" in the two contexts. Only do not think you knew in advance what the "*state* of seeing" means here! Let the use *teach* you the meaning.

We find certain things about seeing puzzling, because we do not find the whole business of seeing puzzling enough.

If you look at a photograph of people, houses and trees, you do not feel the lack of the third dimension in it. We should not find it easy to describe a photograph as a collection of colour-patches on a flat surface; but what we see in a stereoscope looks three-dimensional in a different way again.

(It is anything but a matter of course that we see 'three-dimensionally' with two eyes. If the two visual images are amalgamated, we might expect a blurred one as a result.)

The concept of an aspect is akin to the concept of an image. In other words: the concept 'I am now seeing it as . . . .' is akin to 'I am now having *this* image'.

Doesn't it take imagination to hear something as a variation on a particular theme? And yet one is perceiving something in so hearing it.

"Imagine this changed like this, and you have this other thing." One can use imagining in the course of proving something.

Seeing an aspect and imagining are subject to the will. There is such an order as "Imagine *this*", and also: "Now see the figure like *this*"; but not: "Now see this leaf green".

The question now arises: Could there be human beings lacking in the capacity to see something *as something*—and what would that be like? What sort of consequences would it have?—Would this defect be comparable to colour-blindness or to not having absolute pitch?—We will call it "aspect-blindness"—and will next consider what might be meant by this. (A conceptual investigation.) The aspect-blind man is supposed not to see the aspects A change. But is he also supposed not to recognize that the double cross contains both a black and a white cross? So if told "Shew me figures containing a black cross among these examples" will he be unable to manage it? No, he should be able to do that; but he will not be supposed to say: "Now it's a black cross on a white ground!"

Is he supposed to be blind to the similarity between two faces?—And so also to their identity or approximate identity? I do not want to settle this. (He ought to be able to execute such orders as "Bring me something that looks like *this*.")

Ought he to be unable to see the schematic cube as a cube?—It would not follow from that that he could not recognize it as a representation (a working drawing for instance) of a cube. But for him it would not jump from one aspect to the other.—Question: Ought he to be able to *take* it as a cube in certain circumstances, as we do?—If not, this could not very well be called a sort of blindness.

The 'aspect-blind' will have an altogether different relationship to pictures from ours.

(Anomalies of *this* kind are easy for us to imagine.)

Aspect-blindness will be *akin* to the lack of a 'musical ear'.

The importance of this concept lies in the connexion between the concepts of 'seeing an aspect' and 'experiencing the meaning of a word'. For we want to ask "What would you be missing if you did not *experience* the meaning of a word?"

What would you be missing, for instance, if you did not understand the request to pronounce the word "till" and to mean it as a verb,—or if you did not feel that a word lost its meaning and became a mere sound if it was repeated ten times over?

In a law-court, for instance, the question might be raised how someone meant a word. And this can be inferred from certain facts.—It is a question of *intention*. But could how he experienced a word—the word "bank" for instance—have been significant in the same way?

Suppose I had agreed on a code with someone; "tower" means bank. I tell him "Now go to the tower"—he understands me and acts accordingly, but he feels the word "tower" to be strange in this use, it has not yet 'taken on' the meaning.

"When I read a poem or narrative with feeling, surely something goes on in me which does not go on when I merely skim the lines for information."—What processes am I alluding to?—The sentences have a different *ring*. I pay careful attention to my intonation. Sometimes a word has the wrong intonation, I emphasize it too much or too little. I notice this and shew it in my face. I might later talk about my reading in detail, for example about the mistakes in my tone of voice. Sometimes a picture, as it were an illustration, comes to me. And this seems to help me to read with the correct expression. And I could mention a good deal more of the same kind.—I can also give a word a tone of voice which brings out the meaning of the rest, almost as if this word were a picture of the whole thing. (And this may, of course, depend on sentence-formation.)

When I pronounce this word while reading with expression it is completely filled with its meaning.—"How can this be, if meaning is the use of the word?" Well, what I said was intended figuratively. Not that I chose the figure: it forced itself on me.—But the figurative employment of the word can't get into conflict with the original one.

Perhaps it could be explained why precisely *this* picture suggests itself to me. (Just think of the expression, and the meaning of the expression: "the word that hits it off".)

But if a sentence can strike me as like a painting in words, and the very individual word in the sentence as like a picture, then it is no such marvel that a word uttered in isolation and without purpose can seem to carry a particular meaning in itself.

Think here of a special kind of illusion which throws light on these matters.—I go for a walk in the environs of a city with a friend. As we talk it comes out that I am imagining the city to lie on our right. Not only have I *no* conscious reason for this assumption, but some quite simple consideration was enough to make me realize that the city lay rather to the left ahead of us. I can at first give no answer to the question *why* I imagine the city in *this* direction. I had *no reason* to think it. But though I see no reason still I seem to see certain psychological causes for it. In particular, certain associations and memories. For example, we walked along a canal, and once before in similar circumstances I had followed a canal and that time the city lay on our right.—I might try as it were psychoanalytically to discover the causes of my unfounded conviction.

"But what is this queer experience?"—Of course it is not queerer than any other; it simply differs in kind from those experiences which we regard as the most fundamental ones, our sense impressions for instance.

"I feel as if I knew the city lay over there."—"I feel as if the name 'Schubert' fitted Schubert's works and Schubert's face."

You can say the word "March" to yourself and mean it at one time as an imperative at another as the name of a month. And now say "March!"—and then "March *no further!*"—Does the *same* experience accompany the word both times—are you sure?

If a sensitive ear shews me, when I am playing this game, that I have now *this* now *that* experience of the word—doesn't it also shew me that I often do not have *any* experience of it in the course of talking?—For the fact that I then also mean it, intend it, now like *this* now like *that*, and maybe also say so later is, of course, not in question.

But the question now remains why, in connexion with this *game* of experiencing a word, we also speak of 'the meaning' and of 'meaning it'.—This is a different kind of question.—It is the phenomenon which is characteristic of this language-game that in *this* situation we use this expression: we say we pronounced the word with *this* meaning and take this expression over from that other language-game.

Call it a dream. It does not change anything.

Given the two ideas 'fat' and 'lean', would you be rather inclined to say that Wednesday was fat and Tuesday lean, or *vice versa?* (I incline decisively towards the former.) Now have "fat" and "lean" some different meaning here from their usual one?—They have a different use.—So ought I really to have used different words? Certainly not that.—I want to use *these* words (with their familiar meanings) *here.*—Now, I say nothing about the causes of this phenomenon. They *might* be associations from my childhood. But that is a hypothesis. Whatever the explanation,—the inclination is there.

Asked "What do you really mean here by 'fat' and 'lean'?"—I could only explain the meanings in the usual way. I could *not* point to the examples of Tuesday and Wednesday.

Here one might speak of a 'primary' and 'secondary' sense of a word. It is only if the word has the primary sense for you that you use it in the secondary one.

Only if you have learnt to calculate—on paper or out loud—can you be made to grasp, by means of this concept, what calculating in the head is.

The secondary sense is not a 'metaphorical' sense. If I say "For me the vowel *e* is yellow" I do not mean: 'yellow' in a metaphorical sense,—for I could not express what I want to say in any other way than by means of the idea 'yellow'.

Someone tells me: "Wait for me by the bank". Question: Did you, *as you were saying the word,* mean this bank?—This question is of the same kind as "Did you intend to say such-and-such to him on your way to meet him?" It refers to a definite time (the time of walking, as the former question refers to the time of speaking)—but not to an *experience* during that time. Meaning is as little an experience as intending.

But what distinguishes them from experience?—They have no experience-content. For the contents (images for instance) which accompany and illustrate them are not the meaning or intending.

The intention *with which* one acts does not 'accompany' the action any more than the thought 'accompanies' speech. Thought and intention are neither 'articulated' nor 'non-articulated'; to be compared neither with a single note which sounds during the acting or speaking, nor with a tune.

'Talking' (whether out loud or silently) and 'thinking' are not concepts of the same kind; even though they are in closest connexion.

The *interest* of the experiences one has while speaking and of the intention is not the same. (The experiences might perhaps inform a psychologist about the '*unconscious*' intention.)

"At that word we both thought of him." Let us assume that each of us said the same words to himself—and how can it mean MORE than that?—But wouldn't even those words be only a *germ?* They must surely belong to a language and to a context, in order really to be the expression of the thought *of* that man.

If God had looked into our minds he would not have been able to see there whom we were speaking of.

"Why did you look at me at that word, were you thinking of . . . .?"—So there is a reaction at a certain moment and it is explained by saying "I thought of . . . . ." or "I suddenly remembered . . . ."

In saying this you refer to that moment in the time you were speaking. It makes a difference whether you refer to this or to that moment.

Mere explanation of a word does not refer to an occurrence at the moment of speaking.

The language-game "I mean (or meant) *this*" (subsequent explanation of a word) is quite different from this one: "I thought of . . . . as I said it." The latter is akin to "It reminded me of . . . ."

"I have already remembered three times today that I must write to him." Of what importance is it what went on in me then?—On the other hand what is the importance, what the interest, of the statement itself?—It permits certain conclusions.

"At these words *he* occurred to me."—What is the primitive reaction with which the language-game begins—which can then be translated into these words? How do people get to use these words?

The primitive reaction may have been a glance or a gesture, but it may also have been a word.

"Why did you look at me and shake your head?"—"I wanted to give you to understand that you . . . . ." This is supposed to express not a symbolic convention but the purpose of my action.

Meaning it is not a process which accompanies a word. For no *process* could have the consequences of meaning.

(Similarly, I think, it could be said: a calculation is not an experiment, for no experiment could have the peculiar consequences of a multiplication.)

There are important accompanying phenomena of talking which are often missing when one talks without thinking, and this is characteristic of talking without thinking. But *they* are not the thinking.

"Now I know!" What went on here?———So did I *not* know, when I declared that now I knew?

You are looking at it wrong.

(What is the signal for?)

And could the 'knowing' be called an accompaniment of the exclamation?

The familiar physiognomy of a word, the feeling that it has taken up its meaning into itself, that it is an actual likeness of its meaning—there could be human beings to whom all this was alien. (They would not have an attachment to their words.)—And how are these feelings manifested among us?—By the way we choose and value words.

Georg Lukács

1885–1971

WHILE Georg Lukács's earliest works, *Soul and Form* (1910) and *Theory of the Novel* (1920), written before he joined the Communist party in 1918, are both works that he later criticized severely, they provide an important reflection of the underlying continuity of development in his aesthetic thought. As one of the most important Marxist aesthetic theorists of the century, Lukács was also a major political figure in Hungary, having served in the cabinet of Béla Kun (in 1919), and as an intellectual leader in the Hungarian Communist party. His earlier works, deeply influenced by Hegel, present literary production as the expression of immanent principles in the soul and in nature, treated not as abstract entities or ideas but as practical will to action.

Lukács's acceptance of the historical materialism of Marx, Engels, and Lenin provided, from this point of view, a context within which to articulate that will to action as both aesthetic and engaged with the realm of political praxis. His well-known objection to modernism in art as a form of bourgeois degeneracy, based on the indulgence of individual subjectivity and a retreat from reality, follows from his conception of art as a reflection of reality. In the essay here, Lukács provides an explanation of Lenin's epistemological theory of "reflection" with emphasis on two particulars: first, Lenin's insistence on the fact that phenomena are always richer than the laws propounded to explain them; second, that "objective" nature includes partisan commitment within itself. While Lukács's praise of Lenin's position is already obviously partisan, reflecting one of the principal liabilities of the argument—namely, by what means does one discriminate which (or whose) consciousness of the partisanship intrinsic in the "objective" is "false" consciousness?"—Lukács's deployment of the argument is masterful.

By positing as part of the objective reality—indeed, as its deepest impulse—an "element of partisanship," Lukács can argue directly from a teleological point of view. Significantly, the teleology in question need not be Marx's vision of the dictatorship of the proletariat or, for that matter, any historiological doctrine. Rather, the end and purpose of the work of art is just to reflect the underlying principles of reality in concrete universals: "The universal appears as a quality of the individual and the particular, reality becomes manifest and can be experienced within appearance, the general principle is exposed as the specific impelling cause for the individual case being specially depicted." It follows that the telos of the work of art, being consonant with its mode of operation, entails formal self-sufficiency for the work itself. That is, as the work of art successfully reflects reality, it does so by separating itself formally, since the condition under which the work of art can actually do its work is precisely that the reflection be recognized as intending concrete universals and not a snapshot of some circumstance or event. From this point of view, the objectivity of the work of art is a function of its formal self-sufficiency.

It is striking that Lukács's position, as developed in this essay, closely resembles Aristotle's argument in the *Poetics* (*CTSP*, pp. 44–66)—though perhaps even more ironically it resembles James Joyce's interpretation of Aristotle as arguing that art imitates nature not in objects or actions so much as in the underlying law of which both objects and actions are the expressions. In any case, Lukács's argument depends on maintaining a dialectical unity of form and content and an opposition to all forms of "subjectivism" which would make of the work of art merely the expression of the "creative" individual or the superficial propaganda of an author's individual views. While Lukács therefore opposes most varieties of modern critical formalism (as they violate Lenin's dictum that "the categories of thought are not tools for men but the expression of the order governing nature and men"), the objectivity of artistic form remains a serious problem, treated in the last section of the essay.

The main difficulty for Lukács is that claims for formal "objectivity" run the immediate risk of a "relapse into bourgeois aestheticism" in which form, as a putative category, is abstracted from content, as if it were a separate question or object for critical examination—a position developed in a different context in Fredric Jameson's "The Ideology of the Text." Lukács's solution, consonant with his interpretation of the nature of objectivity, is to insist that form and content not be separated, any more than the concrete universal be separated into a universal plus a particular, since the objectivity of artistic form is always dialectical.

Lukács's major works include *Soul and Form*, (1910, trans. 1971); *The Theory of the Novel* (1920, trans. 1971); *The Historical Novel*, (1955, trans. 1962); and *Aesthetik*, 2 vols. (1962). His political writings include *History and Class Consciousness* (1923) and *Political Writings, 1919–1929* (1972). See George Lichtheim, *George Lukács* (1970), and Fredric Jameson, *Marxism and Form* (1971), chap. 3, pp. 160–205.

ART AND OBJECTIVE TRUTH

I. The Objectivity of Truth in Marxist-Leninist Epistemology

The basis for any correct cognition of reality, whether of nature or society, is the recognition of the objectivity of the external world, that is, its existence independent of human consciousness. Any apprehension of the external world is nothing more than a reflection in consciousness of the world that exists independently of consciousness. This basic fact of the relationship of consciousness to being also serves, of course, for the artistic reflection of reality.

The theory of reflection provides the common basis for *all* forms of theoretical and practical mastery of reality through consciousness. Thus it is also the basis for the theory of the artistic reflection of reality. In this discussion, we will seek to elaborate the *specific* aspects of artistic reflection within the scope of the general theory.

A valid, comprehensive theory of reflection first arose with dialectical materialism, in the works of Marx, Engels and Lenin. For the bourgeois mind a correct theory of objectivity and of the reflection in consciousness of a reality existing independent of consciousness, a materialist, dialectical theory, is an impossibility. Of course, in practice, in bourgeois science and art there are countless instances of an accurate reflection of reality, and there have even been a number of attempts at a correct theoretical posing and solution of the question. Once the question is elevated, however, into a question of epistemology, bourgeois thinkers become trapped in mechanistic materialism or sink into philosophic idealism. Lenin characterized and exposed the limitations of both directions of bourgeois thinking with unsurpassed clarity. Of mechanistic materialism he declared: "Its chief failure lies in its incapacity to apply dialectics to the theory of images, to the process and evolution of knowledge." Philosophic idealism he went on to characterize thus: "Contrarily, from the standpoint of *dialectical* materialism, philosophical idealism is a *one-sided,* exaggerated, extravagant . . . development, a pompous inflation of one aspect, of one side, of one frontier of knowledge to a sanctified absolute divorced from matter, from nature. . . . Single-dimensionality, one-sidedness, frigidity, subjectivism and subjective blindness, *voilà,* the epistemological roots of idealism."

This double-faceted inadequacy of bourgeois epistemology appears in all areas and in all problems of the reflection of reality through consciousness. In this connection we cannot investigate the entire realm of epistemology or trace the history of human knowledge. We must limit ourselves to a few important aspects of the epistemology of Marxism-Leninism which are especially significant for the *problem of objectivity* in the *artistic reflection of reality.*

The first problem to deal with is that of the direct reflections of the external world. All knowledge rests on them; they are the foundation, the point of departure for all knowledge. But they are *only* the point of departure and not all there is to the process of knowing. Marx expressed himself with unmistakable clarity on this question, declaring: "Science would be superfluous if there were an immediate coincidence of the appearance and reality of things." And in his study of Hegel's logic, Lenin analysed this question and arrived at this formulation: "Truth is not to be found at the beginning but at the end, more particularly within the process. Truth is not the *initial impression.*" Following Marx he illustrated this observation with an example from political economy: "Value is a category which deprives goods of their materiality, but it is *truer* than the law of supply and demand." From this introductory observation Lenin goes on to define the function of abstract terms, concepts, laws, etc., in the total human comprehension of reality and to define their place in the over-all theory of reflection and of the objective knowledge of reality. "Just as the simple incorporation of value, the single act of exchanging goods, includes in microcosm, in embryo, *all* the principal contradictions of capitalism—so the simplest generalization, the initial and simplest formulation of *concepts* (judgments, conclusions) implies man's ever-expanding apprehension of the *ob-*

ART AND OBJECTIVE TRUTH was published in 1954, reprinted in *Writer and Critic, and Other Essays,* ed. and trans. Arthur D. Kahn (New York: Grosset & Dunlap, 1971). Reprinted by permission of The Merlin Press.

jective macrocosm." On this basis he is able to state in summary: "The abstractions of matter, natural *law,* value, etc., in a word, *all* scientific (accurate, seriously considered, not irrational) abstractions reflect nature more profoundly, more faithfully, more *completely.* From active observation to abstract thought and from there to practical activity—such is the dialectical path of apprehending truth and objective reality."

By analysing the place of various abstractions in epistemology, Lenin underscores with the greatest precision the dialectical dichotomy within them. He says: "The significance of the *universal* is contradictory: it is inert, impure, incomplete, etc., but it is also a *stage* in the cognition of the concrete, for we never apprehend the concrete completely. The infinite sum of general concepts, laws, etc., provides the concrete in its completeness." This dichotomy alone clarifies the dialectic of appearance and reality. Lenin says: "The phenomenon is *richer* than the law." And he goes on to comment on a definition of Hegel's: "That (the word 'passive') is an excellent materialist and remarkably apt description. Every law deals with the passive—and that is why a law, every law, is restricted, incomplete, approximate."

With this profound insight into the incompleteness of the intellectual reproduction of reality, both in the direct mirroring of phenomena as well as in concepts and laws (when they are considered one-sidedly, undialectically, outside the infinite process of dialectical interaction), Lenin arrived as a materialist elimination of all false formulations of bourgeois epistemology. For every bourgeois epistemology has one-sidedly emphasized the priority of one approach to apprehending reality, one mode in the conscious reproduction of reality. Lenin concretely presents the dialectical interaction in the process of cognition. "Is the perceptual image *closer* to reality than thought? Both yes and no. The perceptual image cannot entirely comprehend motion; for example, it cannot comprehend speed of three hundred thousand kilometres per second, but *thought* can and should do so. Thus thought derived from perception mirrors reality." In this way the idealistic depreciation of the "lower" faculties of cognition is overcome through dialectics. With the strict materialism of his epistemology and his unwavering insistence on the principle of objectivity, Lenin is able to grasp the correct dialectical relationship of the modes of human perception of reality in their dynamics. Regarding the role of fantasy in cognition, he says: "The approach of human reason to the individual thing, obtaining an impression (a concept) of it is no simple, direct, lifeless mirroring but a complicated, dichotomous, zigzag act which by its very nature encompasses the possibility that imagination can soar away from life. . . . For even in the simplest generalization of the most elementary universal idea (like the idea of a table) there lurks a shred of imagination (vice versa, it is foolish to deny the role of imagination in the most exact science)."

Only through dialectics is it possible to overcome the incompleteness, the rigidity and the barrenness of any one-sided conception of reality. Only through the correct and conscious application of dialectics can we overcome the incompleteness in the infinite process of cognition and bring our thinking closer to the dynamic infinity in objective reality. Lenin says: "We cannot imagine motion, we cannot express it, measure it, imitate it without interrupting its continuity, without simplifying, vulgarizing, disintegrating and stifling its dynamism. The intellectual representation of motion is always vulgarized and devitalized and not only through thoughts but through the senses as well and not only of motion, but of any concept at all. And precisely in this is the essence of dialectics. *Precisely this essence* is to be expressed through the formula: unity, identity of opposites."

The union of materialist dialectics with *practice,* its derivation from practice, its control through practice, its directive role in practice, rest on this profound conception of the dialectical nature of objective reality and of the dialectic of its reflection in consciousness. Lenin's theory of revolutionary practice rests on his recognition of the fact that reality is always richer and more varied than the best and most comprehensive theory that can be developed to apprehend it, and at the same time, however, on the consciousness that with the active application of dialectics one can learn from reality, apprehend important new factors in reality and apply them in practice. "History," Lenin said, "especially the history of revolution, was always richer in content, more complex, more dynamic, subtler than the most effective parties, the most class-conscious vanguard of the most progressive classes ever imagined." The extraordinary elasticity in Lenin's tactics, his ability to adapt himself swiftly to sudden changes in history and to derive the maximum from these changes rested on his profound grasp of objective dialectics.

This relationship between the strict objectivity in epistemology[1] and its integral relationship to practice is one of the significant aspects of the materialist dialectic of Marxism-Leninism. The objectivity of the external world is no inert, rigid objectivity fatalistically determining human activity; because of its very independence of consciousness it stands in the most intimate indissoluble interaction with practice. In his early youth Lenin had already rejected any mere fatalistic, abstract, undialectical conception of objectivity as false and conducive to apologetics. In his struggle against Michailowsky's subjectivism he also criticized Struve's blatantly apologetic materialism correctly and profoundly as an objectivism of practice, of *partisanship*. Materialism implies, Lenin said in summarizing his objections against Struve, "so to speak the element of partisanship within itself in setting itself the task of evaluating any event directly and openly from the standpoint of a particular social group."

II. The Theory of Reflection in Bourgeois Aesthetics

This contradictory basis in man's apprehension of the external world, this immanent contradiction in the structure of the reflection of the eternal world in consciousness appears in all theoretical concepts regarding the artistic reproduction of reality. When we investigate the history of aesthetics from the standpoint of Marxism-Leninism, we discover everywhere the one-sidedness of the two tendencies so profoundly analysed by Lenin: on the one hand, the incapacity of mechanical materialism "to apply dialectics to the theory of images", and on the other hand, the basic error inherent in idealism: "the universal (the concept, the idea) as a *peculiar entity in itself*." Naturally, these two tendencies rarely appear as absolutes in the history of aesthetics. Mechanical materialism, whose strength lies in its insistence upon the concept of the reflection of objective reality and in its maintenance of this view in aesthetics, is transformed into idealism, as a result of its incapacity to comprehend motion, history, etc., as Engels so convincingly demonstrated. In the history of aesthetics, as in epistemology generally, objective idealists (Aristotle, Hegel) made heroic attempts at overcoming dialectically the inadequacy, one-sidedness and rigidity of idealism. But since their attempts were made on an idealistic basis, they achieved individual astute formulations regarding objectivity, but their systems as a whole fall victim to the one-sidedness of idealism.

To expose the contradictory, one-sided and inadequate approaches of mechanical materialism and idealism, we can cite in this discussion only one classical illustration of each. We refer to the works of the classics because they expressed their opinions with a straightforward, honest frankness, quite in contrast to the aestheticians of the decadence of bourgeois ideology with their eclectic and apologetic temporizing and chicanery.

In his novel *Les bijoux indiscrets,* Diderot,[2] a leading exponent of the mechanistic theory of the direct imitation of nature, expressed this theory in its crassest form. His heroine, the spokesman for his own points of view, offers the following critique of French classicism: "But I know that only truth pleases and moves. Besides, I know that the perfection in a play consists in such a precise imitation of an action that the audience is deceived into believing that they are present at the action." And to eliminate any doubt that he means by this deception the photographic imitation of reality, Diderot has his heroine imagine a case where a person is told the plot of a tragedy as though it were a real court intrigue; then he goes to the theatre to witness the continuation of this actual event: "I conduct him to his loge behind a grille in the theatre; from it he sees the stage, which he takes to be the palace of the Sultan. Do you believe that the man will let himself be deceived for a moment even if I put on a serious face? On the contrary." For Diderot this comment represents an annihilating aesthetic judgment on this drama. Clearly, on the basis of such a theory, which strives for the ultimate in objectivity

[1] Objectivity not in the sense of a pretension to non-partisan tolerance of all positions but in the sense of the conviction of the strict objectivity in nature and society and their laws. [Au.]

[2] Denis Diderot (1713–84), French philosopher, encyclopedist, and critic. *Les bijoux indiscrets* (1748) may be roughly translated as "The indiscreet young things." It should be noted that this work was published anonymously, evidently in circumstances of financial exigency. [Eds.]

in art, not a single real problem of specifically artistic objectivity can be resolved. (That Diderot does formulate and resolve a whole series of problems both in his theory and more especially in his creative work is beside the point, for he resolves them solely by departing from this crude theory.)

For the opposite extreme, we can examine Schiller's[3] aesthetics. In the very interesting preface to his *Braut von Messina,* Schiller provides an impressive critique of the inadequacy of the aesthetic theory of imitation. He correctly poses the task of art—"not to be content simply with the appearances of truth," but to build its edifices "on truth itself". As a thorough idealist, however, Schiller considers truth not as a more profound and comprehensive reflection of objective reality than is given in mere appearance; instead he isolates truth from material reality and makes it an autonomous entity, contrasting it crudely and exclusively with reality. He says: "Nature itself is only an idea of the Spirit, which is never captured by the senses." That is why the product of artistic fantasy in Schiller's eyes is "truer than reality and more real than experience." This idealistic attenuation and petrification of what is normal and beyond immediate experience undermines all Schiller's correct and profound insights. Although in principle he expresses a correct insight when he says "that the artist cannot utilize a single element of reality just as he finds it", he carries this correct observation too far, considering only what is immediately at hand as real and holding truth to be a supernatural principle instead of a more incisive, comprehensive reflection of objective reality—opposing the two idealistically and absolutely. Thus from correct initial insights he arrives at false conclusions, and through the very theoretical approach by which he establishes a basis for objectivity in art more profound than that provided by mechanical materialism, he eliminates all objectivity from art.

In the contemporary evolution of aesthetics we find the same two extremes: on the one hand, the insistence on immediate reality; on the other hand, the isolation from material reality of any aspects reaching beyond immediate reality. As a result of the general turn in ideology in bourgeois decadence, however, to a hypocritical, foggy idealism, both theoretical approaches suffer considerable modification. The theory of the direct reproduction of reality more and more loses its mechanical materialist character as a theory of the reflection of the external world. Direct experience becomes even more strongly subjectivized, more firmly conceived as an independent and autonomous function of the individual (as impression, emotional response, etc., abstractly divorced from the objective reality which generates it). Naturally, in actual practice the outstanding realists even of this period continue to create on the basis of an artistic imitation of reality, no longer, however, with the subtlety and (relative) consequence of the realists of the period of bourgeois ascendency. More and more, theories become permeated with an eclecticism of a false objectivism and a false subjectivism. They isolate objectivity from practice, eliminate all motion and vitality and set it in crass, fatalistic, romantic opposition to an equally isolated subjectivity. Zola's famous definition of art, "un coin de la nature vu à travers un tempérament,"[4] is a prime example of such eclecticism. A scrap of reality is to be reproduced mechanically and thus with a false objectivity, and is to become poetic by being viewed in the light of the observer's subjectivity, a subjectivity divorced from practice and from interaction with practice. The artist's subjectivity is no longer what it was for the old realists, the means for achieving the fullest possible reflection of motion of a totality, but a garnish to a mechanical reproduction of a chance scrap of experience.

The resultant subjectivizing of the direct reproduction of reality reaches its ultimate extension in naturalism and enjoys the most varied theoretical exposition. The most famous and influential of these theories is the so-called theory of "empathy." This theory denies any imitation of reality independent of consciousness. The leading modern exponent of this theory, Lipps,[5] declares, for example: "The form of an object is always determined by me, through my inner activity." And he concludes, "Aesthetic pleasure is objectivized self-gratification." Ac-

[3] Friedrich von Schiller (1759–1805), German dramatist, poet and historian (see *CTSP*, pp. 417–431). [Eds.]

[4] Émile Zola (1840–1902), French novelist (see *CTSP*, pp. 646–59). "un coin . . ."—a piece of nature seen through a temperament. [Eds.]

[5] Theodor Lipps (1851–1914), German philosopher. [Eds.]

cording to this view, the essence of art is the introduction of human thoughts, feelings, etc., into an external world regarded as unknowable. This theory faithfully mirrors the ever-intensifying subjectivization in artistic practice apparent in the transition from naturalism to impressionism, etc., in the growing subjectivization of subject matter and of creative method and in the increasing alienation of art from great social problems.

Thus the theory of realism of the imperialist period reveals an intensifying dissolution and disintegration of the ideological preconditions for realism. And it is clear that with the undisguised reactions against realism, idealistic subjectivism attains a theoretical extremism unknown to earlier idealism. The extreme idealistic rigidity is further intensified insofar as idealism under imperialism has become an idealism of imperialist parasitism. Whereas the great exponents of classical idealism sought an effective intellectual mastery of the great problems of their time, even if in their idealism their formulations were distorted and inverted, this new idealism is an ideology of reaction, of flight from the great issues of the era, a denial of reality by "abstracting it out of existence." The well-known, influential aesthetician Worringer,[6] founder and theoretician of the so-called "theory of abstraction", derives the need for abstraction from man's "spiritual space-phobia" (*geistige Raumscheu*), his "overwhelming need for tranquillity" (*ungeheures Ruhebeduerfnis*). Accordingly, he rejects modern realism as too imitative, as too close to reality. He bases his theory on an "absolute will to art", by which he means "a potential inner drive completely independent of the object . . . existing for itself and acting as will to form". The faddish pretension of this theory to the highest artistic objectivity is characteristic of the theories of the imperialist period; they never come out in the open but always mask their intentions. In his characterization of the "struggle" of the Machians against idealism, Lenin exposed this manœuvre of imperialist idealism. The theory of abstraction, which subsequently provided the theoretical base for expressionism, represented a culmination of the subjectivist elimination of all content from aesthetics; it is a theory of the subjectivist petrification and decay of artistic forms in the period of capitalist degeneration.

[6] Wilhelm Worringer (1881–1965), German philosopher, [Eds.]

III. The Artistic Reflection of Reality

The artistic reflection of reality rests on the same contradiction as any other reflection of reality. What is specific to it is that it pursues another resolution of these contradictions than science. We can best define the specific character of the artistic reflection of reality by examining first in the abstract the goal it sets itself, in order then to illuminate the preconditions for attaining this goal. The goal for all great art is to provide a picture of reality in which the contradiction between appearance and reality, the particular and the general, the immediate and the conceptual, etc., is so resolved that the two converge into a spontaneous integrity in the direct impression of the work of art and provide a sense of an inseparable integrity. The universal appears as a quality of the individual and the particular, reality becomes manifest and can be experienced within appearance, the general principle is exposed as the specific impelling cause for the individual case being specially depicted. Engels characterized this essential mode of artistic creation clearly in a comment about characterization in a novel: "Each is simultaneously a type and a particular individual, a 'this one' (*Dieser*), as old Hegel expressed it, and so it must be."

It follows then that every work of art must present a circumscribed, self-contained and complete context with its own *immediately* self-evident movement and structure. The necessity for the immediate obviousness of the special context is clearest in literature. The true, fundamental interrelationships in any novel or drama can be disclosed only at the end. Because of the very nature of their construction and effect, only the conclusion provides full clarification of the beginning. Furthermore, the composition would fail utterly and have no impact if the path to this culmination were not clearly demarcated at every stage. The motivating factors in the world depicted in a literary work of art are revealed in an artistic sequence and climaxing. But this climaxing must be accomplished within a direct unity of appearance and reality present from the very beginning; in the intensifying concretizing of both aspects, it must make their unity ever more integral and self-evident.

This self-contained immediacy in the work of art presupposes that every work of art evolve within itself all the preconditions for its characters, situations, events, etc. The unity of appearance and reality can become direct experience only if the reader experiences every important aspect of the growth or change with all their primary determining factors, if the outcome is never simply handed to him but he is conducted to the outcome and directly experiences the process leading to the outcome. The basic materialism of all great artists (no matter whether their ostensible philosophy is partly or completely idealistic) appears in their clear depiction of the pertinent preconditions and motivations out of which the consciousness of their characters arises and develops.

Thus every significant work of art creates its "own world". Characters, situations, actions, etc., in each have a unique quality unlike that in any other work of art and entirely distinct from anything in everyday reality. The greater the artist, the more intensely his creative power permeates all aspects of his work of art and the more pregnantly his fictional "world" emerges through all the details of the work. Balzac[7] said of his *Comédie Humaine:* "My work has its own geography as well as its own genealogy and its own families, its places and its objects, its people and its facts; even as it possesses its heraldry, its aristocracy and its bourgeoisie, its workmen and its peasants, its politicians and its dandies and its army—in short, its world."

Does not the establishment of such particularity in a work of art preclude the fulfilment of its function as a reflection of reality? By no means! It merely affirms the special character, the peculiar kind of reflection of reality there is in art. The apparently circumscribed world in the work of art and its apparent non-correspondence is merely an illusion, though a necessary one, essential and intrinsic to art. The effect of art, the immersion of the receptant in the action of the work of art, his complete penetration into the special "world" of the work of art, results from the fact that the work by its very nature offers a truer, more complete, more vivid and more dynamic reflection of reality than the receptant otherwise possesses, that it conducts him on the basis of his own experiences and on the basis of the organization and generalization of his previous reproduction of reality beyond the bounds of his experiences toward a more concrete insight into reality. It is therefore only an illusion—as though the work itself were not a reflection of reality, as though the reader did not conceive of the special "world" as a reflection of reality and did not compare it with his own experiences. He acts consistently in accordance with this pretence, and the effect of the work of art ceases once the reader becomes aware of a contradiction, once he senses that the work of art is not an accurate reflection of reality. But this illusion is in any case necessary. For the reader does not consciously compare an individual experience with an isolated event of the work of art but surrenders himself to the general effect of the work of art on the basis of his own assembled general experience. And the comparison between both reflections of reality remains unconscious so long as the reader is engrossed, that is, so long as his experiences regarding reality are broadened and deepened by the fiction of the work of art. Thus Balzac is not contradicting his statement about his "own world" when he says, "To be productive one needs only to study. French society should be the historian, I only its amanuensis."

The self-containment of a work of art is therefore the reflection of the process of life in motion and in concrete dynamic context. Of course, science sets itself the same goal. It achieves dialectical concreteness by probing more profoundly into the laws of motion. Engels says: "The universal law of the transformation of form is far more concrete than any individual 'concrete' example of it." This progression in the scientific cognition of reality is endless. That is, objective reality is correctly reflected in any accurate scientific cognition; to this extent this cognition is absolute. Since, however, reality is always richer, more multifaceted than any law, it is in the nature of knowledge that knowledge must always be expanded, deepened, enriched, and that the absolute always appears as relative and as an approximation. Artistic concreteness too is a unity of the absolute and the relative, but a unity which cannot go beyond the framework of the work of art. Objective progress in the historical process and the

[7]Honoré de Balzac (1799–1850), French novelist. Balzac's *La Comédie humaine* extends to 40 volumes. [Eds.]

further development of our knowledge of this process do not eliminate the artistic value, the validity and effect of great works of art which depict their times correctly and profoundly.

There is a second and more important difference between the scientific and the artistic reflections of reality in that individual scientific cognitions (laws, etc.) are not independent of each other but form an integral system. And this context becomes the more intensive the more science develops. Every work of art, however, must stand on its own. Naturally, there is development in art, and this development follows an objective pattern with laws that can be analysed. But the fact that this objective pattern in the development of art is a part of the general social development does not eliminate the fact that a work of art becomes such by possessing this self-containment, this capacity to achieve its effect on its own.

The work of art must therefore reflect correctly and in proper proportion all important factors objectively determining the area of life it represents. It must so reflect these that this area of life becomes comprehensible from within and from without, re-experiencable, that it appears as a totality of life. This does not mean that every work of art must strive to reflect the objective, extensive totality of life. On the contrary, the extensive totality of reality necessarily is beyond the possible scope of any artistic creation; the totality of reality can only be reproduced intellectually in ever-increasing approximation through the infinite process of science. The totality of the work of art is rather intensive: the circumscribed and self-contained order of those factors which objectively are of decisive significance for the portion of life depicted, which determine its existence and motion, its specific quality and its place in the total life process. In this sense the briefest song is as much an intensive totality as the mightiest epic. The objective character of the area of life represented determines the quantity, quality, proportion, etc., of the factors that emerge in interaction with the specific laws of the literary form appropriate for the representation of this portion of life.

The self-containment implies first of all that the goal of the work of art is depicting that subtlety, richness and inexhaustibility of life about which we have quoted Lenin, and bringing it dynamically and vividly to life. No matter whether the intention in the work of art is the depiction of the whole of society or only an artificially isolated incident, the aim will still be to depict the intensive inexhaustibility of the subject. This means that it will aim at involving creatively in its fiction all important factors which in objective reality provide the basis for a particular event or complex of events. And artistic involvement means that all these factors will appear as personal attributes of the persons in the action, as the specific qualities of the situations depicted, etc.; thus in a directly perceptible unity of the individual and the universal. Very few people are capable of such an experience of reality. They achieve knowledge of general determinants in life only through the abandonment of the immediate, only through abstraction, only through generalized comparison of experiences. (In this connection, the artist himself is no exception. His work consists rather in elevating the experiences he obtains ordinarily to artistic form, to a representation of the unity of the immediate and the universal.) In representing individual men and situations, the artist awakens the illusion of life. In depicting them as exemplary men and situations (the unity of the individual and the typical), in bringing to life the greatest possible richness of the objective conditions of life as the particular attributes of individual people and situations, he makes his "own world" emerge as the reflection of life in its total motion, as process and totality, in that it intensifies and surpasses in its totality and in its particulars the common reflection of the events of life.

This depiction of the subtlety of life, of a richness beyond ordinary experience, is only one side in the special mode of the artistic representation of reality. If a work of art depicted only the overflowing abundance of new concepts, only those aspects which provide new insights, only the subtlety beyond the common generalization about ordinary experience, then the reader would merely be confused instead of being involved, for the appearance of such aspects in life generally confuses people and leaves them at a loss. It is therefore necessary that *within* this richness and subtlety the artist introduce a new order of things which displaces or modifies the old abstractions. This is also a reflection of objective reality. For such a new order is never simply imposed on life but is derived from the new phenomena of life through reflection, comparison, etc. But in life itself it is always a question of two steps; in the first place, one is surprised by the new facts and sometimes even overwhelmed by them and then only does one need to deal with them intellectually by applying the dialectical method. In art these two steps coincide, not in the sense of a mechanical unity (for then the newness of the individual phenomena would again be annihilated) but in the sense of a process in which from the outset the order within the new phenomena manifesting the subtlety of life is sensed and emerges in the course of the artistic climaxing ever more sharply and clearly.

This representation of life, structured and ordered more richly and strictly than ordinary life experience, is in intimate relation to the active social function, the propaganda effect of the genuine work of art. Such a depiction cannot possibly exhibit the lifeless and false objectivity of an "impartial" imitation which takes no stand or provides no call to action. From Lenin, however, we know that this partisanship is not introduced into the external world arbitrarily by the individual but is a motive force inherent in reality which is made conscious through the correct dialectical reflection of reality and introduced into practice. This partisanship of objectivity must therefore be found intensified in the work of art—intensified in clarity and distinctness, for the subject matter of a work of art is consciously arranged and ordered by the artist toward this goal, in the sense of this partisanship; intensified, however, in objectivity too, for a genuine work of art is directed specifically toward depicting this partisanship as a quality in the subject matter, presenting it as a motive force inherent in it and growing organically out of it. When Engels approves of tendentiousness in literature he always means, as does Lenin after him, this "partisanship of objectivity" and emphatically rejects any subjective superimposed tendentiousness: "But I mean that the tendentiousness must spring out of the situation and action without being expressly pointed out."

All bourgeois theories treating the problem of the aesthetic illusion allude to this dialectic in the artistic reflection of reality. The paradox in the effect of a work of art is that we surrender ourselves to the work as though it presented reality to us, accept it as reality and immerse ourselves in it although we are always aware that it is not reality but simply a special form of reflecting reality. Lenin correctly observes: "Art does not demand recognition as *reality*." The illusion in art, the aesthetic illusion, depends therefore on the self-containment we have examined in the work of art and on the fact that the work of art in its totality reflects the full process of life and does not represent in its details reflections of particular phenomena of life which can be related individually to aspects of actual life on which they are modelled. Non-correspondence in this respect is the precondition of the artistic illusion, an illusion absolutely divorced from any such correspondence. On the other hand and inseparable from it is the fact that the aesthetic illusion is only possible when the work of art reflects the total objective process of life with *objective accuracy*.

This objective dialectic in the artistic reflection of reality is beyond the ken of bourgeois theory, and bourgeois theory always degenerates into subjectivism at least in specific points, if not in totality. Philosophic idealism must, as we have seen, isolate this characteristic of self-containment in a work of art and its elevation above ordinary reality, from material and objective reality; it must oppose the self-containment, the perfection of form in the work of art, to the theory of reflection. When objective idealism seeks to rescue and establish the objectivity of art abstractly, it inevitably falls into mysticism. It is by no means accidental that the Platonic theory of art as the reflection of "ideas" exerts such a powerful historical influence right up to Schelling and Schopenhauer. And when the mechanical materialists fall into idealism because of the inadequacy of their philosophic conception of social phenomena, they usually go from a mechanical photographic theory of imitation to Platonism, to a theory of the artistic imitation of "ideas". (This is especially apparent with Shaftesbury[8] and at times evident with Diderot.) But this mystical objectivism is always and inevitably transformed into subjectivism. The more the aspects of the self-containment of a work and of the dynamic character of the artistic elaboration and reshaping of reality are opposed to the theory of reflection instead of being derived from it dialectically, the more the principle of form, beauty and artistry is divorced from life; the more it becomes an unclear, subjective and mystical principle. The Platonic "ideas" occasionally inflated and attenuated in the idealism of the period of bourgeois ascendancy, though artificially isolated from social

[8] Anthony Ashley Cooper, 3d earl of Shaftesbury (1671–1713), English philosopher. [Eds.]

reality, were reflections of decisive social problems and thus for all their idealistic distortion were full of content and were not without relevance; but with the decline of the class they more and more lose content. The social isolation of the personally dedicated artist in a declining society is mirrored in this mystical, subjective inflation of the principle of form divorced from any connection with life. The original despair of genuine artists over this situation passes to parasitic resignation and the self-complacency of "art for art's sake" and its theory of art. Baudelaire sings of beauty in a tone of despondent subjective mysticism: "Je trône dans l'azure comme un sphinx incompris."[9] In the later art for art's sake of the imperialist period such subjectivism evolves into a theory of a contemptuous, parasitic divorce of art from life, into a denial of any objectivity in art, a glorification of the "sovereignty" of the creative individual and a theory of indifference to content and arbitrariness in form.

We have already seen that mechanical materialism tends toward an opposite direction. Sticking to the mechanical imitation of life as it is immediately perceived in all its superficial detail, it must deny the special character of the artistic reflection of reality or fall into idealism with all its distortions and subjectivism. The pseudo-objectivity of mechanical materialism, of the mechanical, direct imitation of the immediate world of phenomena, is thus inevitably transformed into idealistic subjectivism since it does not acknowledge the objectivity of the underlying laws and relationships that cannot immediately be perceived and since it sees in these laws and relationships no reflection of objective reality but simply technical means for superficial groupings of sense data. The weakness of the direct imitation of life in its particularity must intensify and develop further into subjective idealism without content as the general ideological development of the bourgeoisie transforms the philosophic materialist basis of this sort of artistic imitation of reality into agnostic idealism (the theory of empathy).

The objectivity of the artistic reflection of reality depends on the correct reflection of the totality. The artistic correctness of a detail thus has nothing to do with whether the detail corresponds to any similar detail in reality. The detail in a work of art is an accurate reflection of life when it is a necessary aspect of the accurate reflection of the total process of objective reality, no matter whether it was observed by the artist in life or created through imagination out of direct or indirect experience. On the other hand, the artistic truth of a detail which corresponds photographically to life is purely accidental, arbitrary and subjective. When, for example, the detail is not directly and obviously necessary to the context, then it is incidental to a work of art, its inclusion is arbitrary and subjective. It is therefore entirely possible that a collage of photographic material may provide an incorrect, subjective and arbitrary reflection of reality. For merely arranging thousands of chance details in a row never results in artistic necessity. In order to discipline accident into a proper context with artistic necessity, the necessity must be latent within the details themselves. The detail must be so selected and so depicted from the outset that its relationship with the totality may be organic and dynamic. Such selection and ordering of details depends solely on the artistic, objective reflection of reality. The isolation of details from the general context and their selection on the basis of a photographic correspondence with reality imply a rejection of the more profound problem of objective necessity, even a denial of the existence of this necessity. Artists who create thus, choose and organize material not out of the objective necessity in the subject matter but out of pure subjectivity, a fact which is manifested in the work as an objective anarchy in the selection and arrangement of their material.

Ignoring deeper objective necessity in the reflection of reality is manifested also in creative art as annihilation of objectivity. We have already seen how for Lenin and Engels partisanship in the work of art is a component of objective reality and of a correct, objective artistic reflection of life. The tendency in the work of art speaks forth from the objective context of the world depicted within the work; it is the language of the work of art transmitted through the reflection of reality and therefore the speech of reality itself, not the subjective opinion of the writer exposed baldly or explicitly in a personal commentary or in a subjective, ready-made conclusion. The concept of art as *direct* propaganda, a concept particularly exemplified in recent

[9]Charles Baudelaire (1821–67), French poet and critic (see *CTSP*, pp. 627–30). "*Je trône* . . . : I sit enthroned in the blue like an unappreciated sphinx." (Note that "l'azure" is used to suggest the aura of benificent, sometimes uncanny calm.) [Eds.]

art by Upton Sinclair, rejects the deeper, objective propaganda potential of art in the Leninist conception of partisanship and substitutes pure personal propaganda which does not grow organically out of the logic of the subject matter but remains a mere subjective expression of the author's views.

IV. The Objectivity of Artistic Form

Both the tendencies to subjectivism just analysed disrupt the dialectical unity of form and content in art. In principle it is not decisive whether the form or the content is wrenched out of the dialectical unity and inflated to an autonomy. In either case the concept of the objectivity of form is abandoned. Either means that the form becomes a "device" to be manipulated subjectively and wilfully; in either case form loses its character as a specific mode of the reflection of reality. Of similar tendencies in logic Lenin declared sharply and unequivocally: "Objectivism: the categories of thought are not tools for men but the expression of the order governing nature and men." This rigorous and profound formulation provides a natural basis for the investigation of form in art, with the emphasis, naturally, on the specific, essential characteristics of artistic reflection; always within the framework of the dialectical materialist conception of the nature of form.

The question of the objectivity of form is among the most difficult and least investigated in Marxist aesthetics. Marxist-Leninist epistemology indicates unequivocally indeed, as we have seen, the direction in which the solution of the problem is to be sought. But contemporary bourgeois concepts have so influenced our Marxist theory of literature and our literary practice as to introduce confusion and reserve in the face of a correct Marxist formulation and even a hesitation about recognizing an objective principle in artistic form. The fear that to emphasize objectivity of form in art will mean a relapse into bourgeois aestheticism has its epistemological base in the failure to recognize the dialectical unity of content and form. Hegel defines this unity thus: ". . . content is nothing but the conversion of form into content, and form is nothing but the conversion of content into form." Though this concept seems abstractly expressed, we will see as we proceed that Hegel did indeed correctly define the interrelationship of form and content.

Of course, merely in connection with their interrelationship. Hegel must be "turned upside down" materialistically in that the mirroring quality of both content and form must be established as the key to our investigation. The difficulty consists in grasping the fact that artistic form is just as much a mode of reflecting reality as the terminology of logic (as Lenin demonstrated so convincingly). Just as in the process of the reflection of reality through thought, the categories that are most general, the most abstracted from the surface of the world of phenomena, from sense data, therefore, express the most abstract laws governing nature and men; so is it with the forms of art. It is only a question of making clear what this highest level of abstraction signifies in art.

That the artistic forms carry out the process of abstraction, the process of generalization, is a fact long recognized. Aristotle contrasted poetry and history from this point of view (it should be noted by the contemporary reader that Aristotle understood by history a narrative chronicle of loosely related events in the manner of Herodotus).[10] Aristotle says: "Historians and poets do not differ in the fact that the latter write in verse, the former in prose. . . . The difference lies rather in fact that the one reports what actually happened, the other what could happen. Thus poetry is more philosophical than history, for poetry tends to express the universal, history the particular." Aristotle obviously meant that because poetry expresses the universal it is more philosophical than history. He meant that poetry (fiction) in its characters, situations and plots not merely imitates individual characters, situations and actions but expresses simultaneously the regular, the universal and the typical. In full agreement Engels declares the task of realism to be to create "typical characters under typical conditions". The difficulty in grasping abstractly what great art of all time has achieved in practice is twofold: in the first place, the error must be avoided of opposing the typical, the universal and the regular to the individual, of disrupting intellectually the inseparable unity of the individual and universal

[10] Herodotus [484?–425? B.C.], Greek historian, often called the father of history; author of *The Persian Wars*. [Eds.]

which determines the practice of all great poets from Homer to Gorki. In the second place, it must be understood that this unity of the particular and the universal, of the individual and the typical, is not a quality of literary content that is considered in isolation, a quality for the expression of which the artistic form is merely a "technical aid", but that it is a product of that interpenetration of form and content defined abstractly by Hegel.

The first difficulty can only be resolved from the standpoint of the Marxist conception of the concrete. We have seen that mechanical materialism as well as idealism—each in its own way, and, in the course of historical development, in different forms—bluntly oppose the direct reflection of the external world, the foundation for any understanding of reality, to the universal and the typical, etc. As a result, the typical appears as the product of a merely subjective intellectual operation, as a mere intellectual, abstract and thus ultimately purely subjective accessory to the world of immediate experience; not as a component of objective reality. From such a counterposing of opposites it is impossible to arrive at a conception of the unity of the individual and the typical in a work of art. Either a false conception of the concrete or an equally false conception of the abstract becomes the key to the aesthetic, or at most an eclectic one-or-the-other is propounded. Marx defined the concrete with extraordinary incisiveness: "The concrete is concrete because it is the synthesis of many determinants, the unity within diversity. In our thinking the concrete thus appears as the process of synthesis, as the result, not as the point of departure, although it is really the point of departure and hence also the point of departure for perception and conception." In our introductory remarks we noted how Lenin defines the dialectical approach to the intellectual reflection of the concrete in Marxist epistemology.

The task of art is the reconstitution of the concrete—in this Marxist sense—in a direct, perceptual self-evidence. To that end those factors must be discovered in the concrete and rendered perceptible whose unity makes the concrete concrete. Now in reality every phenomenon stands in a vast, infinite context with all other simultaneous and previous phenomena. A work of art, considered from the point of view of its content, provides only a greater or lesser extract of reality. Artistic form therefore has the responsibility of preventing this extract from giving the effect of an extract and thus requiring the addition of an environment of time and space; on the contrary, the extract must seem to be a self-contained whole and to require no external extension.

When the artist's intellectual disciplining of reality before he begins a work of art does not differ in principle from any other intellectual ordering of reality, the more likely the result will be a work of art.

Since the work of art has to act as a self-contained whole and since the concreteness of objective reality must be reconstituted in perceptual immediacy in the work of art, all those factors which objectively make the concrete concrete must be depicted in their interrelation and unity. In reality itself these conditions emerge quantitatively as well as qualitatively in extraordinary variety and dispersion. The concreteness of a phenomenon depends directly upon this extensive, infinite total context. In the work of art, any extract, any event, any individual or any aspect of the individual's life must represent such a context in its concreteness, thus in the unity of all its inherent important determinants. These determinants must in the first place be present from the start of the work; secondly, they must appear in their greatest purity, clarity and typicality; thirdly, the proportions in the relationships of the various determinants must reflect that objective partisanship with which the work is infused; fourthly, despite the fact that they are present in greater purity, profundity and abstraction than is found in any individual instance in actual life, these determinants may not offer any abstract contrast to the world of phenomena that is directly perceptible, but, contrarily, must appear as concrete, direct, perceptible qualities of individual men and situations. Any artistic process conforming to the intellectual reflection of reality through the aid of abstractions, etc., which seems artistically to "overload" the particular with typical aspects intensified to the utmost quantitatively and qualitatively requires a consequent artistic intensification of concreteness. No matter how paradoxical it may sound, an intensification of concreteness in comparison with life must therefore accompany the process of developing artistic form and the path to generalization.

Now when we pass to our second question, the role of form in the establishment of this concreteness, the reader will perhaps no longer consider Hegel's quotation regarding the transformation of content into form and form into content so abstract. Consider the determinants in a work of art we have so far derived exclusively from the most general conception of artistic form—the self-containment of a work of art: on the one hand, the intensive infinity, the apparent inexhaustibility of a work of art and the subtlety of the development by which it recalls life in its most intensive manifestation; on the other hand, the fact that it discloses simultaneously within this inexhaustibility and life-like subtlety the laws of life in their freshness, inexhaustibility and subtlety. All these factors seem merely to be factors of content. They are. But they are at the same time, and even primarily, factors emerging and becoming apparent through artistic form. They are the result of the transformation of content into form and result in the transformation of form into content.

Let us illustrate this very important fact of art with a few examples. Take a simple example, one might almost say a purely quantitative example. Whatever objections one might level against Gerhart Hauptmann's[11] *Weavers* as a drama, there is no question that it succeeds in awakening an illusion that we are not involved merely with individuals but with the grey, numberless masses of Silesian weavers. The depiction of the masses as masses is the artistic achievement of this drama. When we investigate how many characters Hauptmann actually used to depict these masses, we are surprised to discover that he used scarcely ten to a dozen weavers, a number much smaller than is to be found in many other dramas which do not even begin to provide an impression of great masses of people. The effect arises from the fact that the few characters depicted are so selected and characterized and set in such situations and in such relationships that within the context and in the formal proportionality in the aesthetic illusion, we have the impression of a great mass. How little this aesthetic illusion depends on the actual number of characters is clear from the same author's drama of the peasants' revolt, *Florian Geyer,* where Hauptmann creates an incomparably greater cast of characters, some of which are even very clearly delineated as individuals; nevertheless the audience only intermittently has the sense of a real mass, for here Hauptmann did not succeed in representing a relationship of the characters to each other which would give the sense of a mass and would endow the mass with its own artistic physiognomy and its own capacity to act.

This significance of form emerges even more clearly in more complicated cases. Take the depiction of the typical in Balzac's *Père Goriot.* In this novel Balzac exposes the contradictions in bourgeois society, the inevitable inner contradictions appearing in every institution in bourgeois society, the varied forms of conscious and unconscious rebellion against the enslavement and crippling of the institutions in which men are imprisoned. Every manifestation of these contradictions in an individual or a situation is intensified to an extreme by Balzac and with merciless consequence. Among his characters he depicts men representing ultimate extremes: being lost or in revolt, thirsting for power or degenerate: Goriot and his daughters, Rastignac, Vautrin, the Viscountess de Beauséant, Maxime de Trailles. The events through which these characters expose themselves follow upon each other in an avalanche that appears incredible if the content is considered in isolation—an avalanche impelled by scarcely credible explosions. Consider what happens in the course of the action: the final tragedy of Goriot's family, the tragedy of Mme de Beauséant's love affair, the exposure of Vautrin, the tragedy arranged by Vautrin in the Taillefer house, etc. And yet, or rather precisely on account of this rush of events, the novel provides the effect of a terrifyingly accurate and typical picture of bourgeois society. The basis for its effectiveness is Balzac's accurate exposure of the typical aspects of the basic contradiction in bourgeois society—a necessary precondition to the effect but not in itself the effect. The effect itself results from the composition, from the context provided by the relationships of the extreme cases, a context in which the apparent outlandishness of the individual cases is eliminated. Extract any one of the conflicts from the general context and you discover a fantastic, melodramatic, improbable tale. But it is just because of the exaggeration in the individual events, in the characterization and even in the language within the relationships established among those extreme events through Balzac's composition that the common social background emerges. Only with such an extreme intensification of improbable events could Balzac depict how Vautrin and Goriot are similarly

[11] Gerhart Hauptmann (1862–1942), German dramatist, poet, and novelist. *The Weavers* was published in 1892. Hauptmann received the Nobel Prize for literature in 1912. [Eds.]

victims of capitalist society and rebels against its consequences, how Vautrin and Mme de Beauséant are motivated by a similar incomplete conception of society and its contradictions, how the genteel salon and the prison differ only quantitatively and incidentally and resemble each other in profound respects and how bourgeois morality and open crime shade into each other imperceptibly. And furthermore—through the piling up of extreme cases and on the basis of the accurate reflection of the social contradictions which underlie them in their extremeness, an atmosphere arises which eliminates any sense of their being extreme and improbable, an atmosphere in which the social reality of capitalist society emerges out of these instances and through them in a crassness and fullness that could not otherwise be realized.

Thus the content of the work of art must be transformed into a form through which it can achieve its full artistic effectiveness. Form is nothing but the highest abstraction, the highest mode of condensation of content, of the extreme intensification of motivations, of constituting the proper proportion among the individual motivations and the hierarchy of importance among the individual contradictions of the life mirrored in the work of art.

It is, of course, necessary to study this characteristic form in individual categories of form, not simply generally in composition, as we have done so far. We cannot investigate the particular categories since our task is more general—to define form and to investigate its objective existence. We will select only one example, plot, which has been considered central in discussions of literary form since Aristotle.

It is a formal principle of epic and drama that their construction be based on a plot. Is this *merely* a formal requirement, abstracted from content? Not at all. When we analyse this formal requirement precisely in its formal abstractness, we come to the conclusion that only through plot can the dialectic of human existence and consciousness be expressed, that only through a character's action can the contrast between what he is objectively and what he imagines himself to be, be expressed in a process that the reader can experience. Otherwise the writer would either be forced to take his characters as they take themselves to be and to present them from their own limited subjective perspective, or he would have to merely assert the contrast between their view of themselves and the reality and would not be able to make his readers perceive and experience the contrast. The requirement for representing the artistic reflection of social reality through plot is therefore no mere invention of aestheticians; it derives from the basic materialist dialectical practice of the great poets (regardless of their frequent idealist ideologies) formulated by aesthetics and established as a formal postulate—without being recognized as the most general, abstract reflection of a fundamental fact of objective reality. It will be the task of Marxist aesthetics to reveal the quality of the formal aspects of art concretely as modes of reflecting reality. Here we can merely point to the problem, which even in regard to plot alone is far too complicated for adequate treatment in this essay. (Consider, for example, the significance of the plot as a means for depicting process.)

The dialectic of content and form, the transformation from the one into the other, can naturally be studied in all the stages of origin, development and effect of a work of art. We will merely allude to a few important aspects here. When we take the problem of subject matter, we seem at first glance to be dealing again with a problem of content. If we investigate more closely, however, we see that breadth and depth of subject matter convert into decisive problems of form. In the course of investigating the history of individual forms, one can see clearly how the introduction and mastery of new thematic material calls forth a new form with significantly new principles within the form, governing everything from composition to diction. (Consider the struggle for bourgeois drama in the eighteenth century and the birth of an entirely new type of drama with Diderot, Lessing and the young Schiller.)

When we follow this process over a long period of history, the conversion of content into form and vice versa in the effect of works of art is even more impressive. Precisely in those works in which this conversion of one into the other is most developed, does the resultant new form attain the fullest consummation and seem entirely "natural" (one thinks of Homer, Cervantes, Shakespeare, etc.). This "artlessness" in the greatest masterpieces illuminates not only the problem of the mutual conversion of content and form into each other but also the significance of this conversion: the establishment of the objectivity of the work of art itself. The more "artless" a work of art, the more it gives the effect of life and nature, the more clearly it exemplifies an actual concentrated reflection of its times and the more clearly it demonstrates that the only function of its form is the expression of this objectivity, this reflection of life in the greatest concreteness and clarity and with all its motivating contradictions. On the other hand, every form of which the reader is conscious as form, in its very independence of the content and in its incomplete conversion into content necessarily gives the effect of a subjective expression rather than a full reflection of the subject matter itself (Corneille and Racine in contrast to the Greek tragedians and Shakespeare). That content which emerges as an independent entity (like its antithesis, form as an independent entity) also has a subjective character, we have already seen.

This interrelationship of form and content did not escape the important aestheticians of earlier periods, of course. Schiller, for example, recognized one side of this dialectic and acutely formulated it, viewing the role of art as the annihilation of subject matter through form. In this statement, however, he provided an idealistic and one-sided subjectivist formulation of the problem. For the simple transfer of content into form without the dialectical counteraction necessarily leads to an artificial independence of form, to the subjectivizing of form, as is often the case not only in Schiller's theory but in his creative practice as well.

It would be the task of a Marxist aesthetic to demonstrate concretely how objectivity of form is an aspect of the creative process. The comments of great artists of the past provide an almost inexhaustible source for this investigation, an investigation we have hardly begun. Bourgeois aesthetics can scarcely begin any study of this material, for when it recognizes the objectivity of forms, it conceives of this objectivity only in some mystical fashion and makes of objectivity of form a sterile mystique about form. It becomes the responsibility of a Marxist aesthetic in developing the concept of form as a mode of reflection to demonstrate how this objectivity emerges in the creative process as objectivity, as truth independent of the artist's consciousness.

This objective independence from the artist's consciousness begins immediately with a selection of the subject matter. In all subject matter there are certain artistic possibilities. The artist, of course, is "free" to select any one of these or to use the subject matter as the springboard to a different sort of artistic expression. In the latter case a contradiction inevitably arises between the thematic content and the artistic elaboration, a contradiction which cannot be eliminated no matter how skilfully the artist may manipulate. (One recalls Maxim Gorki's striking critique of Leonid Andreyev's *Darkness*.)[12] This objectivity reaches beyond the relationship of content, theme and artistic form.

When we obtain a Marxist theory of genres, we will then be able to see that every genre has its own specific, objective laws which no artist can ignore without peril. When Zola, for example, in his novel *The Masterpiece* adopted the basic structure of Balzac's masterly short story "The Unknown Masterpiece", extending the work to novel length, he demonstrated in his failure Balzac's profound artistic insight in selecting the short story to represent the tragedy of an artist.

With Balzac the short-story form grows out of the essential quality of the theme and subject matter. Balzac compressed into the narrowest form the tragedy of the modern artist, the tragic impossibility of creating a classical work of art with the specific means of expression of modern art—means of expression which themselves merely reflect the specific character of modern life and its ideology. He simply depicted the collapse of such an artist and contrasted him with two other important, less dedicated (therefore not tragic) artists. Thus he concentrated everything on the single, decisive problem, adequately expressed in a tight and fast-moving plot of artistic disintegration through an artist's suicide and destruction of his work. To treat this theme in a novel instead of a short story would require entirely different subject matter and an entirely different plot. In a novel the writer would have to expose and develop in breadth the entire process arising out of the social conditions of modern life and leading to these artistic problems. (Balzac had followed such an approach in analysing the relationship of literature to journalism in *Lost Illusions*.) To accomplish this task the novelist would have to go beyond the bounds of the short story with its single and restricted climax and would have to find subject matter suitable for transforming the additional

[12] Maxim Gorki (or Gorky), pseudonym of Aleksey Pyeshkov (1868–1936), Russian writer, generally considered the founder of Soviet Realism; Leonid N. Andreyev (1871–1919), Russian writer. Gorky was an early supporter of Andreyev, until the latter rejected Bolshevism. [Eds.]

breadth and diversity in motivations into a dynamic plot. Such a transformation is missing from Zola's work. He did indeed introduce a series of traditional motivations in an attempt at providing novelistic breadth to the short-story material. But the new motivations (the struggle of the artist with society, the struggle between the dedicated and the opportunistic artists, etc.) do not arise out of the inner dialectic of the original short-story material but remain unrelated and superficial in the development and do not provide the broad, varied complex necessary for the construction of a novel.

Once sketched, characters and plots show the same independence of the artist's consciousness. Although originating in the writer's head, they have their own dialectic, which the writer must obey and pursue consequently if he does not want to destroy his work. Engels noted the objective independent existence of Balzac's characters and their life careers when he pointed out that the dialectics of the world depicted by Balzac led the author to conclusions in opposition to his own conscious ideology. Contrary examples are to be found in such strongly subjective writers as Schiller or Dostoyevski.[13] In the struggle between the writer's ideology and the inner dialectic of his characters, the writer's subjectivity is often victorious with the result that he dissipates the significant material he has projected. Thus Schiller distorts the profound conflict he had planned between Elizabeth and Mary Stuart (the struggle between the Reformation and the Counter-Reformation) out of Kantian moralizing; thus Dostoyevski, as Gorki once acutely remarked, ends by slandering his own characters.

The objective dialectic of form because of its very objectivity is an *historical* dialectic. The idealistic inflation of form becomes most obvious in the transformation of forms not merely into mystical and autonomous but even "eternal" entities. Such idealistic de-historicizing of form eliminates any concreteness and all dialectic. Form becomes a fixed model, a schoolbook example, for mechanical imitation. The leading aestheticians of the classical period often advanced beyond this undialectical conception. Lessing,[14] for example, recognized clearly the profound truths in Aristotle's Poetics as the expression of definite laws of tragedy. At the same time he saw clearly that what was important was the living essence, the ever-new, ever-modified application of these laws without mechanical subservience to them. He revealed sharply and vividly how Shakespeare, who ostensibly did not follow Aristotle and probably did not even know Aristotle, consistently fulfilled afresh Aristotle's important prescriptions, which Lessing considered the most profound laws of the drama; while the servile, dogmatic students of Aristotle's words, the French classicists, ignored the essential issues in Aristotle's vital legacy.

But a truly historical, dialectical and systematic formulation of the objectivity of form and its specific application to ever-changing historical reality only became possible with a materialist dialectic. In the fragmentary introduction to his *A Critique of Political Economy*, Marx defined precisely the two great problems in the historical dialectic of the objectivity of form in regard to the epic. He showed first that every artistic form is the outgrowth of definite social conditions and of ideological premises of a particular society and that only on these premises can subject matter and formal elements emerge which cause a particular form to flourish (mythology as the foundation of the epic). For Marx the concept of the objectivity of artistic forms here too offered the basis for the analysis of the historical and social factors in the generation of artistic forms. His emphasis on the law of uneven development, on the fact "that certain flourishing periods (of art) by no means stand in direct relation to the general social development", shows that he saw in those periods of extraordinary creative activity (the Greeks, Shakespeare) objective culminations in the development of art and that he considered artistic value as objectively recognizable and definable. Transformation of this profound dialectical theory into relativistic, vulgar sociology means the degradation of Marxism into the mire of bourgeois ideology.

The dialectical objectivity in Marx's second formulation regarding the development of art is even more striking. It is an indication of the primitive level of Marxist aesthetics and of our lag behind the general development of Marxist theory that this second formulation has enjoyed little currency among Marxist aestheticians and was practically never applied concretely before the appearance of Stalin's work on questions of linguistics. Marx said: "But the difficulty does not lie in understanding that Greek art and epic were related to certain

[13] Fyodor Dostoyevski (1821–81), Russian novelist. [Eds.]

[14] Gotthold Ephraim Lessing (1729–81), German philosopher, playwright, and critic (see *CTSP*, pp. 348–52). [Eds.]

forms of social development. The difficulty is that they still provide us with aesthetic pleasure and serve in certain measure as norms and unattainable models." Here the problem of the objectivity of artistic form is posed with great clarity. If Marx dealt in the first question with the genesis of artistic form, form *in statu nascendi,*[15] here he deals with the question of the objective validity of a finished work of art, of the artistic form, and he does so in such a way that he sets the investigation of this objectivity as the task at hand but leaves no doubt of the objectivity itself—of course, within the framework of a concrete historical dialectic. Marx's manuscript unfortunately breaks off in the middle of his profound exposition. But his extant remarks show that for him Greek art forms spring out of the specific content of Greek life and that form arises out of social and historical content and has the function of raising this content to the level of objectivity in artistic representation.

Marxist aesthetics must set out from this concept of the dialectical objectivity of artistic form as seen in its historical concreteness. It must reject any attempt at making artistic forms either sociologically relative, at transforming dialectics into sophistry or at effacing the difference between periods of flourishing creativity and of decadence, between serious art and mere dabbling, to the elimination of the objectivity of artistic form. Marxist aesthetics must decisively reject, in addition, any attempt at assigning artistic forms an abstract formalistic pseudo-objectivity in which artistic form and distinction among formal genres are construed abstractly as independent of the historical process and as mere formal considerations.

This concretizing of the principle of objectivity within artistic form can be achieved by Marxist aesthetics only in constant struggle against bourgeois currents dominant today in aesthetics and against their influence on our aestheticians. Simultaneous with the dialectical and critical reinvestigation of the great heritage from the periods of history when artistic theory and practice flourished, a relentless struggle against the subjectivization of art dominant in contemporary bourgeois aesthetics must be waged. In the end it makes no difference whether form is eliminated subjectively and transformed into the mere expression of a so-called great personality (the Stefan George[16] school), whether it is exaggerated into a mystical objectivity and inflated to an independent reality (neo-classicism) or denied and eliminated with mechanistic objectivity (the stream-of-consciousness theory). All these directions ultimately lead to the separation of form from content, to the blunt opposition of one to the other and thus to the destruction of the dialectical basis for the objectivity of form. We must recognize and expose in these tendencies the same imperialistic parasitism which Marxist-Leninist epistemology exposed long ago in the philosophy of the imperialist period. (In this respect the development of a concrete Marxist aesthetic lags behind the general development of Marxism.) Behind the collapse of artistic form in bourgeois decadence, behind the aesthetic theories glorifying the subjectivist disintegration or petrification of forms, there is to be found the same rot of bourgeois decadence as in other ideological areas. One would be distorting Marx's profound theory of the uneven development of art into a relativistic caricature if on the basis of this Marxist insight one were to mistake this collapse for the genesis of new form.

Especially significant because it is such a widely disseminated and misleading aspect of the trend to the subjectivization of art is the confusion of form with technique which is so fashionable today. Recently too a technological concept of thought has become dominant in bourgeois logic, a theory of logic as a formalist instrument. Marxist-Leninist epistemology has exposed such tendencies as idealist and agnostic. The identification of technique and form, the conception of aesthetics as mere technology of art, is on the same epistemological level as these subjectivist, agnostic ideological tendencies. That art has a technical side, that this technique must be mastered (indeed can be mastered only by true artists) has nothing to do with the question—the supposed identity of technique and form. Logical thinking requires schooling, too, and is a technique that can be learned and mastered; but that the categories of logic have merely a technical and auxiliary character is a subjective and agnostic deduction from this fact. Every artist must possess a highly developed technique by which he can repre-

[15] being born. [Eds.]

[16] Stefan George (1868–1933), German poet, opposed traditional realism, strongly influenced by the French Symbolists. [Eds.]

sent the world that shimmers before him, with artistic conviction. Acquiring and mastering this technique are extraordinarily important tasks.

To eliminate any confusion, however, one must define the place of technique in aesthetics correctly, from a dialectical materialist point of view. In his remarks about the dialectics of intentions and subjective intentional activity Lenin gave a clear response and exposed subjectivist illusions about this relationship. He wrote: "In reality human intentions are created by an objective world and presuppose it—accept it as given, existing. But to man it *appears* that his intentions come from beyond and are independent of the world." Technician theories identifying technique with form arise exclusively out of this subjectivist illusion, which fails to see the dialectical interrelationship of reality, content, form and technique or how the quality and efficacy of technique are necessarily determined by these objective factors; or that technique is a means for expressing the reflection of objective reality through the alternating conversion of content and form; or that technique is *merely* a means to this end and can only be correctly understood in this context, in its dependence upon this context. When one defines technique thus, in its proper dependence upon the objective problem of content and form, its necessarily subjective character is seen as a necessary aspect of the dialectical general context of aesthetics.

Only when technique is rendered autonomous, when in this artificial independence it replaces objective form, does the danger arise of subjectivization of the problems of aesthetics, and in a two-fold respect: in the first place, technique considered in isolation becomes divorced from the objective problems of art and appears as an independent instrument at the service of the artist's subjectivity, an independent instrument with which one can approach any subject matter and produce any form. Rendering technique independent can easily lead to a degeneration into an ideology of subjectivist virtuosity of form, to the cult of "perfection of form" for its own sake, into aestheticism. Secondly, and closely related to this, the exaggeration of the relevance of purely technical problems in artistic representation obscures the more profound problems of artistic form that are much more difficult to comprehend. Such obscurantism in bourgeois ideology accompanies the disintegration and congelation of artistic forms and the loss of a sense for the special problems of artistic form. The great aestheticians of the past always put the decisive problem of form in the foreground and thus maintained a proper hierarchy within aesthetics. Aristotle said that the poet must demonstrate his power rather in the action than in verse. And it is very interesting to see that Marx's and Engels' aversion to the "petty clever defecations" (Engels) of contemporary virtuosos of form without content, of the banal "masters of technique" went so far that they treated the bad verse of Lassalle's[17] *Sickingen* with indulgence because Lassalle had at least dared in this tragedy—admittedly a failure and considered so by them—to grapple with real, basic problems of dramatic content and form. The same Marx praised this attempt who in his correspondence with Heine showed that he had so steeped himself in the fundamental problems of art as well as in the details of artistic technique that he was able to offer the great poet specific technical suggestions to improve his poetry.

[17] Ferdinand Lassalle (1825–64), German socialist, an early associate of Marx, who later developed an opposing theory of state socialism; one of the founders of the General German Workers' Association. [Eds.]

Claude Lévi-Strauss

b. 1908

THE MOST famous of structural anthropologists, Claude Lévi-Strauss, remarks in an important essay, "Structural Analysis in Linguistics and in Anthropology," "The error of traditional anthropology, like that of traditional linguistics, was to consider the terms, and not the relations between them." Thus he declares his debt to the preceding structural linguists. In that essay he calls N. S. Troubetskoy the father of structural linguistics, but elsewhere in his writings it is *Ferdinand de Saussure*. Whoever it may be, Lévi-Strauss holds that the advent of structuralist linguistics represents in the social sciences the same sort of revolution that nuclear physics did in the physical sciences. The main advances made by Troubetskoy, de Saussure, et al., were to establish these principles: (1) one must study the unconscious infrastructure of linguistic phenomena rather than the conscious structure; (2) terms are not independent entitites; one must study their relations (or in Saussurean terms "differences"); (3) one must establish the concept of system and elucidate the structure of systems (the Saussurean emphasis on synchronic linguistics); (4) one must seek out general laws of structure. Lévi-Strauss accepts this program and applies it, in the essay mentioned and in *The Elementary Structures of Kinship* (1949, trans. 1969), to the question of kinship. He holds in these works that, like phonemes in linguistics, kinship terms are elements of meaning but that the meaning inheres in the structure of relations among the terms rather than in the terms *as such*. The importance of the uncle on the maternal side, for example, is to be understood only in a larger system of relations among father, mother, sister, brother, and the incest taboo. To understand the avunculate we have to grasp it as one relation in a systematic whole.

In the essay here Lévi-Strauss applies yet again principles brought over from linguistics finally to analyze the Oedipal myth as having a fundamental structure in all its so-called variants. He argues that this structure is not a pattern with a certain signification as, say, Carl Jung (*CTSP*, pp. 809–19) would have it. Rather the mythic structure reveals a relational set, and this set produces stories resolving in structure a logically unresolvable problem in the culture. At least it is unresolvable according to logic as we usually think of it. However, Lévi-Strauss's argument is that myths do have a logic based on binary oppositions, and this logic is the myth's structure. He parallels this mode of thought to the behavior of the French "bricoleur," a rather primitive autodidactical worker, who solves problems by devious means, employing a heterogeneous repertoire of what happens to be at hand.

Lévi-Strauss's emphasis on relationality or differential structure has had a considerable influence on literary criticism. It is therefore worthwhile to examine his treatment of a literary text (for him, literary texts and myths are different, though in some respects related). This examination occurs in collaboration with Roman Jakobsen (*CTSP*, pp. 1113–16) in "Charles Baudelaire's 'Les Chats'" (1962) and is available in English in a number of collections. See *Jacques Derrida's* critique of Lévi-Strauss's concept of structure on the ground that his concept implies but does not imply a "center."

Principal works by Lévi-Strauss translated into English are *Structural Anthropology* (1958, trans. 1963); *Mythologiques*, 3 vols. (1964–68, trans. 1969 ff.); *The Savage Mind* (1962, trans. 1966); *Race and History* (1952, trans. 1958); *The Elementary Structures of Kinship* (1949, trans. 1969); *Tristes Tropiques* (1955, trans. 1961). See Edmund Leach, *Claude Lévi-Strauss;* E. N. Hayes and T. Hayes, eds., *Claude Lévi-Strauss: The Anthropologist as Hero;* James A. Boone, *From Symbolism to Structuralism: Lévi-Strauss in a Literary Tradition.*

THE STRUCTURAL STUDY OF MYTH

"It would seem that mythological worlds have been built up only to be shattered again, and that new worlds were built from the fragments."

—Franz Boas[1]

Despite some recent attempts to renew them, it seems that during the past twenty years anthropology has increasingly turned from studies in the field of religion. At the same time, and precisely because the interest of professional anthropologists has withdrawn from primitive religion, all kinds of amateurs who claim to belong to other disciplines have seized this opportunity to move in, thereby turning into their private playground what we had left as a wasteland. The prospects for the scientific study of religion have thus been undermined in two ways.

The explanation for this situation lies to some extent in the fact that the anthropological study of religion was started by men like Tylor, Frazer, and Durkheim,[2] who were psychologically oriented although not in a position to keep up with the progress of psychological research and theory. Their interpretations, therefore, soon became vitiated by the outmoded psychological approach which they used as their basis. Although they were undoubtedly right in giving their attention to intellectual processes, the way they handled these remained so crude that it discredited them altogether. This is much to be regretted, since, as Hocart so profoundly noted in his introduction to a posthumous book recently published,[3] psychological interpretations were withdrawn from the intellectual field only to be introduced again in the field of affectivity, thus adding to "the inherent defects of the psychological school . . . the mistake of deriving clear-cut ideas . . . from vague emotions." Instead of trying to enlarge the framework of our logic to include processes which, whatever their apparent differences, belong to the same kind of intellectual operation, a naïve attempt was made to reduce them to inarticulate emotional drives, which resulted only in hampering our studies.

THE STRUCTURAL STUDY OF MYTH first appeared in *Journal of American Folklore* 68, no. 270 (October–December 1955): 428–44, published by the American Folklore Society. It is reproduced here from *Structural Anthropology* by Claude Lévi-Strauss, copyright 1963 by Basic Books, Inc., Publishers. Reprinted by permission of both publishers.

[1]In Boas' Introduction to James Teit, "Traditions of the Thompson River Indians of British Columbia," *Memoirs of the American Folklore Society*, VI (1898), p. 18. [Au.]

[2]Edward Burnett Tylor (1832–1917), English anthropologist; James George Frazer (1854–1941), Scottish anthropologist, author of *The Golden Bough* and other influential writings; Emile Durkheim, (1858–1917), French sociologist, author of *The Elementary Forms of Religious Life* and other works. [Eds.]

[3]A. M. Hocart, *Social Origins* (London, 1954), p. 7. [Au.]

Of all the chapters of religious anthropology probably none has tarried to the same extent as studies in the field of mythology. From a theoretical point of view the situation remains very much the same as it was fifty years ago, namely, chaotic. Myths are still widely interpreted in conflicting ways: as collective dreams, as the outcome of a kind of esthetic play, or as the basis of ritual. Mythological figures are considered as personified abstractions, divinized heroes, or fallen gods. Whatever the hypothesis, the choice amounts to reducing mythology either to idle play or to a crude kind of philosophic speculation.

In order to understand what a myth really is, must we choose between platitude and sophism? Some claim that human societies merely express, through their mythology, fundamental feelings common to the whole of mankind, such as love, hate, or revenge or that they try to provide some kind of explanations for phenomena which they cannot otherwise understand—astronomical, meteorological, and the like. But why should these societies do it in such elaborate and devious ways, when all of them are also acquainted with empirical explanations? On the other hand, psychoanalysts and many anthropologists have shifted the problems away from the natural or cosmological toward the sociological and psychological fields. But then the interpretation becomes too easy: If a given mythology confers prominence on a certain figure, let us say an evil grandmother, it will be claimed that in such a society grandmothers are actually evil and that mythology reflects the social structure and the social relations; but should the actual data be conflicting, it would be as readily claimed that the purpose of mythology is to provide an outlet for repressed feelings. Whatever the situation, a clever dialectic will always find a way to pretend that a meaning has been found.

Mythology confronts the student with a situation which at first sight appears contradictory. On the one hand it would seem that in the course of a myth anything is likely to happen. There is no logic, no continuity. Any characteristic can be attributed to any subject; every conceivable relation can be found. With myth, everything becomes possible. But on the other hand, this apparent arbitrariness is belied by the astounding similarity between myths collected in widely different regions. Therefore the problem: If the content of a myth is contingent, how are we going to explain the fact that myths throughout the world are so similar?

It is precisely this awareness of a basic antinomy pertaining to the nature of myth that may lead us toward its solution. For the contradiction which we face is very similar to that which in earlier times brought considerable worry to the first philosophers concerned with linguistic problems; linguistics could only begin to evolve as a science after this contradiction had been overcome. Ancient philosophers reasoned about language the way we do about mythology. On the one hand, they did notice that in a given language certain sequences of sounds were associated with definite meanings, and they earnestly aimed at discovering a reason for the linkage between those *sounds* and that *meaning*. Their attempt, however, was thwarted from the very beginning by the fact that the same sounds were equally present in other languages although the meaning they conveyed was entirely different. The contradiction was surmounted only by the discovery that it is the combination of sounds, not the sounds themselves, which provides the significant data.

It is easy to see, moreover, that some of the more recent interpretations of mythological thought originated from the same kind of misconception under which those early linguists were laboring. Let us consider, for instance, Jung's idea that a given mythological pattern—the so-called archetype—possesses a certain meaning. This is comparable to the long-supported error that a sound may possess a certain affinity with a meaning: for instance, the "liquid" semi-vowels with water, the open vowels with things that are big, large, loud, or heavy, etc., a theory which still has its supporters.[4] Whatever emendations the original formulation may now call for,[5] everybody will agree that the Saussurean principle of the *arbitrary character of linguistic signs* was a prerequisite for the accession of linguistics to the scientific level.[6]

To invite the mythologist to compare his precarious situation with that of the linguist in the prescientific stage is not enough. As a matter of fact we may thus be led only from one difficulty to another. There is a very good reason why myth cannot simply

[4] See, for instance, Sir R. A. Paget, "The Origin of Language," *Journal of World History,* I, No. 2 (UNESCO, 1953). [Au.]

[5] See Emile Benveniste, "Nature du signe linguistique," *Acta Linguistica,* I, No. 1 (1939); and Chapter V in *Structuralist Anthropology.* [Au.] See *Benveniste.* [Eds.]

[6] See *de Saussure.* [Eds.]

be treated as language if its specific problems are to be solved; myth *is* language: to be known, myth has to be told; it is a part of human speech. In order to preserve its specificity we must be able to show that it is both the same thing as language, and also something different from it. Here, too, the past experience of linguists may help us. For language itself can be analyzed into things which are at the same time similar and yet different. This is precisely what is expressed in Saussure's distinction between *langue* and *parole,* one being the structural side of language, the other the statistical aspect of it, *langue* belonging to a reversible time, *parole* being non-reversible. If those two levels already exist in language, then a third one can conceivably be isolated.

We have distinguished *langue* and *parole* by the different time referents which they use. Keeping this in mind, we may notice that myth uses a third referent which combines the properties of the first two. On the one hand, a myth always refers to events alleged to have taken place long ago. But what gives the myth an operational value is that the specific pattern described is timeless; it explains the present and the past as well as the future. This can be made clear through a comparison between myth and what appears to have largely replaced it in modern societies, namely, politics. When the historian refers to the French Revolution, it is always as a sequence of past happenings, a non-reversible series of events the remote consequences of which may still be felt at present. But to the French politician, as well as to his followers, the French Revolution is both a sequence belonging to the past—as to the historian—and a timeless pattern which can be detected in the contemporary French social structure and which provides a clue for its interpretation, a lead from which to infer future developments. Michelet, for instance, was a politically minded historian. He describes the French Revolution thus: "That day . . . everything was possible. . . . Future became present . . . that is, no more time, a glimpse of eternity."[7] It is that double structure, altogether historical and ahistorical, which explains how myth, while pertaining to the realm of *parole* and calling for an explanation as such, as well as to that of *langue* in which it is expressed, can also be an absolute entity on a third level which, though it remains linguistic by nature, is nevertheless distinct from the other two.

A remark can be introduced at this point which will help to show the originality of myth in relation to other linguistic phenomena. Myth is the part of language where the formula *traduttore, tradittore*[8] reaches its lowest truth value. From that point of view it should be placed in the gamut of linguistic expressions at the end opposite to that of poetry, in spite of all the claims which have been made to prove the contrary. Poetry is a kind of speech which cannot be translated except at the cost of serious distortions; whereas the mythical value of the myth is preserved even through the worst translation. Whatever our ignorance of the language and the culture of the people where it originated, a myth is still felt as a myth by any reader anywhere in the world. Its substance does not lie in its style, its original music, or its syntax, but in the *story* which it tells. Myth is language, functioning on an especially high level where meaning succeeds practically at "taking off" from the linguistic ground on which it keeps on rolling.

To sum up the discussion at this point, we have so far made the following claims: (1) If there is a meaning to be found in mythology, it cannot reside in the isolated elements which enter into the composition of a myth, but only in the way those elements are combined. (2) Although myth belongs to the same category as language, being, as a matter of fact, only part of it, language in myth exhibits specific properties. (3) Those properties are only to be found *above* the ordinary linguistic level, that is, they exhibit more complex features than those which are to be found in any other kind of linguistic expression.

If the above three points are granted, at least as a working hypothesis, two consequences will follow: (1) Myth, like the rest of language, is made up of constituent units. (2) These constituent units presuppose the constituent units present in language when analyzed on other levels—namely, phonemes, morphemes, and sememes—but they, nevertheless, differ from the latter in the same way as the latter differ among themselves; they belong to a higher and more complex order. For this reason, we shall call them *gross constituent units.*

How shall we proceed in order to identify and isolate these gross constituent units or mythemes?

[7] Jules Michelet, *Histoire de la Revolution française,* IV, 1. I took this quotation from M. Merleau-Ponty, *Les Aventures de la dialectique* (Paris, 1955), p. 273. [Au.]

[8] *Traduttore, tradittore:* to translate is to betray. [Eds.]

We know that they cannot be found among phonemes, morphemes, or sememes, but only on a higher level; otherwise myth would become confused with any other kind of speech. Therefore, we should look for them on the sentence level. The only method we can suggest at this stage is to proceed tentatively, by trial and error, using as a check the principles which serve as a basis for any kind of structural analysis: economy of explanation; unity of solution; and ability to reconstruct the whole from a fragment, as well as later stages from previous ones.

The technique which has been applied so far by this writer consists in analyzing each myth individually, breaking down its story into the shortest possible sentences, and writing each sentence on an index card bearing a number corresponding to the unfolding of the story.

Practically each card will thus show that a certain function is, at a given time, linked to a given subject. Or, to put it otherwise, each gross constituent unit will consist of a *relation*.

However, the above definition remains highly unsatisfactory for two different reasons. First, it is well known to structural linguists that constituent units on all levels are made up of relations, and the true difference between our *gross* units and the others remains unexplained; second, we still find ourselves in the realm of a non-reversible time, since the numbers of the cards correspond to the unfolding of the narrative. Thus the specific character of mythological time, which as we have seen is both reversible and non-reversible, synchronic and diachronic, remains unaccounted for. From this springs a new hypothesis, which constitutes the very core of our argument: The true constituent units of a myth are not the isolated relations but *bundles of such relations,* and it is only as bundles that these relations can be put to use and combined so as to produce a meaning. Relations pertaining to the same bundle may appear diachronically at remote intervals, but when we have succeeded in grouping them together we have reorganized our myth according to a time referent of a new nature, corresponding to the prerequisite of the initial hypothesis, namely a two-dimensional time referent which is simultaneously diachronic and synchronic, and which accordingly integrates the characteristics of *langue* on the one hand, and those of *parole* on the other. To put it in even more linguistic terms, it is as though a phoneme were always made up of all its variants.

Two comparisons may help to explain what we have in mind.

Let us first suppose that archaeologists of the future coming from another planet would one day, when all human life had disappeared from the earth, excavate one of our libraries. Even if they were at first ignorant of our writing, they might succeed in deciphering it—an undertaking which would require, at some early stage, the discovery that the alphabet, as we are in the habit of printing it, should be read from left to right and from top to bottom. However, they would soon discover that a whole category of books did not fit the usual pattern—these would be the orchestra scores on the shelves of the music division. But after trying, without success, to decipher staffs one after the other, from the upper down to the lower, they would probably notice that the same patterns of notes recurred at intervals, either in full or in part, or that some patterns were strongly reminiscent of earlier ones. Hence the hypothesis: What if patterns showing affinity, instead of being considered in succession, were to be treated as one complex pattern and read as a whole? By getting at what we call *harmony,* they would then see that an orchestra score, to be meaningful, must be read diachronically along one axis—that is, page after page, and from left to right—and synchronically along the other axis, all the notes written vertically making up one gross constituent unit, that is, one bundle of relations.

The other comparison is somewhat different. Let us take an observer ignorant of our playing cards, sitting for a long time with a fortune-teller. He would know something of the visitors: sex, age, physical appearance, social situation, etc., in the same way as we know something of the different cultures whose myths we try to study. He would also listen to the séances and record them so as to be able to go over them and make comparisons—as we do when we listen to myth-telling and record it. Mathematicians to whom I have put the problem agree that if the man is bright and if the material available to him is sufficient, he may be able to reconstruct the nature of the deck of cards being used, that is, fifty-two or thirty-two cards according to the case, made up of four homologous sets consisting of the same units (the individual cards) with only one varying feature, the suit.

Now for a concrete example of the method we propose. We shall use the Oedipus myth, which is well known to everyone. I am well aware that the

Oedipus myth has only reached us under late forms and through literary transmutations concerned more with esthetic and moral preoccupations than with religious or ritual ones, whatever these may have been. But we shall not interpret the Oedipus myth in literal terms, much less offer an explanation acceptable to the specialist. We simply wish to illustrate—and without reaching any conclusions with respect to it—a certain technique, whose use is probably not legitimate in this particular instance, owing to the problematic elements indicated above. The "demonstration" should therefore be conceived, not in terms of what the scientist means by this term, but at best in terms of what is meant by the street peddler, whose aim is not to achieve a concrete result, but to explain, as succinctly as possible, the functioning of the mechanical toy which he is trying to sell to the onlookers.

The myth will be treated as an orchestra score would be if it were unwittingly considered as a unilinear series; our task is to re-establish the correct arrangement. Say, for instance, we were confronted with a sequence of the type: 1,2,4,7,8,2,3,4,6,8,1,4,5,7,8,1,2,5,7,3,4,5,6,8 . . . , the assignment being to put all the 1's together, all the 2's, the 3's, etc.; the result is a chart:

1	2		4			7	8
	2	3	4		6		8
1			4	5		7	8
1	2			5		7	
		3	4	5	6		8

We shall attempt to perform the same kind of operation on the Oedipus myth, trying out several arrangements of the mythemes until we find one which is in harmony with the principles enumerated above. Let us suppose, for the sake of argument, that the best arrangement is the following (although it might certainly be improved with the help of a specialist in Greek mythology):

Cadmos seeks his sister Europa, ravished by Zeus			
		Cadmos kills the dragon	
	The Spartoi kill one another		
			Labdacos (Laios' father) = *lame*(?)
	Oedipus kills his father, Laios		Laios (Oedipus's father) = *left-sided* (?)
		Oedipus kills the Sphinx	
			Oedipus = *swollen-foot* (?)
Oedipus marries his mother, Jocasta			
	Eteocles kills his brother, Polynices		
Antigone buries her brother, Polynices, despite prohibition			

We thus find ourselves confronted with four vertical columns, each of which includes several relations belonging to the same bundle. Were we to *tell* the myth, we would disregard the columns and read the rows from left to right and from top to bottom. But if we want to *understand* the myth, then we will have to disregard one half of the diachronic dimension (top to bottom) and read from left to right, column after column, each one being considered as a unit.

All the relations belonging to the same column exhibit one common feature which it is our task to discover. For instance, all the events grouped in the first column on the left have something to do with blood relations which are overemphasized, that is, are more intimate than they should be. Let us say, then, that the first column has as its common feature the *overrating of blood relations*. It is obvious that the second column expresses the same thing, but inverted: *underrating of blood relations*. The third column refers to monsters being slain. As to the fourth, a few words of clarification are needed. The remarkable connotation of the surnames in Oedipus' father-line has often been noticed. However, linguists usually disregard it, since to them the only way to define the meaning of a term is to investigate all the contexts in which it appears, and personal names, precisely because they are used as such, are not accompanied by any context. With the method we propose to follow the objection disappears, since the myth itself provides its own context. The significance is no longer to be sought in the eventual meaning of each name, but in the fact that all the names have a common feature: All the hypothetical meanings (which may well remain hypothetical) refer to *difficulties in walking straight and standing upright.*

What then is the relationship between the two columns on the right? Column three refers to monsters. The dragon is a chthonian being which has to be killed in order that mankind be born from the Earth; the Sphinx is a monster unwilling to permit men to live. The last unit reproduces the first one, which has to do with the *autochthonous origin* of mankind. Since the monsters are overcome by men, we may thus say that the common feature of the third column is *denial of the autochthonous origin of man.*[9]

This immediately helps us to understand the meaning of the fourth column. In mythology it is a universal characteristic of men born from the Earth that at the moment they emerge from the depth they either cannot walk or they walk clumsily. This is the case of the chthonian beings in the mythology of the Pueblo: Muyingwu, who leads the emergence, and the chthonian Shumaikoli are lame ("bleeding-foot," "sore-foot"). The same happens to the Koskimo of the Kwakiutl after they have been swallowed by the chthonian monster, Tsiakish: when they returned to the surface of the earth "they limped forward or tripped sideways." Thus the common feature of the fourth column is *the persistence of the autochthonous origin of man.* It follows that column four is to column three as column one is to column two. The inability to connect two kinds of relationships is overcome (or rather replaced) by the assertion that contradictory relationships are identical inasmuch as they are both self-contradictory in a similar way. Although this is still a provisional formulation of the structure of mythical thought, it is sufficient at this stage.

Turning back to the Oedipus myth, we may now see what it means. The myth has to do with the inability, for a culture which holds the belief that mankind is autochthonous (see, for instance, Pausanias, VIII, xxix, 4: plants provide a *model* for humans), to find a satisfactory transition between this theory and the knowledge that human beings are actually born from the union of man and woman. Although the problem obviously cannot be solved, the Oedipus myth provides a kind of logical tool which relates the original problem—born from one or born from two?—to the derivative problem: born from different or born from same? By a correlation of this type, the overrating of blood relations is to the underrating of blood relations as the

[9] We are not trying to become involved with specialists in an argument; this would be presumptuous and even meaningless on our part. Since the Oedipus myth is taken here merely as an example treated in arbitrary fashion, the chthonian nature ascribed to the Sphinx might seem surprising; we shall refer to the testimony of Marie Delcourt: "In the archaic legends, [she is] certainly born of the Earth itself" (*Oedipe ou la légende du conquérant* [Liège: 1944], p. 108). No matter how remote from Delcourt's our method may be (and our conclusions would be, no doubt, if we were competent to deal with the problem in depth), it seems to us that she has convincingly established the nature of the Sphinx in the archaic tradition, namely, that of a female monster who attacks and rapes young men; in other words, the personification of a female being with an inversion of the sign. This explains why, in the handsome iconography compiled by Delcourt at the end of her work, men and women are always found in an inverted "sky/earth" relationship.

As we shall point out below, we selected the Oedipus myth as our first example because of the striking analogies that seem to exist between certain aspects of archaic Greek thought and that of the Pueblo Indians, from whom we have borrowed the examples that follow. In this respect it should be noted that the figure of the Sphinx, as reconstructed by Delcourt, coincides with two figures of North American mythology (who probably merge into one). We are referring, on the one hand, to "the old hag," a repulsive witch whose physical appearance presents a "problem" to the young hero. If he "solves" this problem—that is, if he responds to the advances of the abject creature—he will find in his bed, upon awakening, a beautiful young woman who will confer power upon him (this is also a Celtic theme). The Sphinx, on the other hand, recalls even more "the child-protruding woman" of the Hopi Indians, that is, a phallic mother par excellence. This young woman was abandoned by her group in the course of a difficult migration, just as she was about to give birth. Henceforth she wanders in the desert as the "Mother of Animals," which she withholds from hunters. He who meets her in her bloody clothes "is so frightened that he has an erection," of which she takes advantage to rape him, after which she rewards him with unfailing success in hunting. See H. R. Voth, "The Oraibi Summer Snake Ceremony," *Field Columbian Museum,* Publication No. 83, Anthropological Series, Vol. III, No. 4 (Chicago: 1903), pp. 352–3 and p. 353, *n* 1. [Au.]

attempt to escape autochthony is to the impossibility to succeed in it. Although experience contradicts theory, social life validates cosmology by its similarity of structure. Hence cosmology is true.

Two remarks should be made at this stage.

In order to interpret the myth, we left aside a point which has worried the specialists until now, namely, that in the earlier (Homeric) versions of the Oedipus myth, some basic elements are lacking, such as Jocasta killing herself and Oedipus piercing his own eyes. These events do not alter the substance of the myth although they can easily be integrated, the first one as a new case of autodestruction (column three) and the second as another case of crippledness (column four). At the same time there is something significant in these additions, since the shift from foot to head is to be correlated with the shift from autochthonous origin to self-destruction.

Our method thus eliminates a problem which has, so far, been one of the main obstacles to the progress of mythological studies, namely, the quest for the *true* version, or the *earlier* one. On the contrary, we define the myth as consisting of all its versions; or to put it otherwise, a myth remains the same as long as it is felt as such. A striking example is offered by the fact that our interpretation may take into account the Freudian use of the Oedipus myth and is certainly applicable to it. Although the Freudian problem has ceased to be that of autochthony *versus* bisexual reproduction, it is still the problem of understanding how *one* can be born from *two:* How is it that we do not have only one procreator, but a mother plus a father? Therefore, not only Sophocles, but Freud himself, should be included among the recorded versions of the Oedipus myth on a par with earlier or seemingly more "authentic" versions.

An important consequence follows. If a myth is made up of all its variants, structural analysis should take all of them into account. After analyzing all the known variants of the Theban version, we should thus treat the others in the same way: first, the tales about Labdacos' collateral line including Agave, Pentheus, and Jocasta herself: the Theban variant about Lycos with Amphion and Zetos as the city founders; more remote variants concerning Dionysus (Oedipus' matrilateral cousin); and Athenian legends where Cecrops takes the place of Cadmos, etc. For each of them a similar chart should be drawn and then compared and reorganized according to the findings: Cecrops killing the serpent with the parallel episode of Cadmos; abandonment of Dionysus with abandonment of Oedipus; "Swollen Foot" with Dionysus' *loxias,* that is, walking obliquely; Europa's quest with Antiope's; the founding of Thebes by the Spartoi or by the brothers Amphion and Zetos; Zeus kidnapping Europa and Antiope and the same with Semele; the Theban Oedipus and the Argian Perseus, etc. We shall then have several two-dimensional charts, each dealing with a variant, to be organized in a three-dimensional order, as shown in the figure, so that three different readings become possible: left to right, top to bottom, front to back (or vice versa). All of these charts cannot be expected to be identical; but experience shows that any difference to be observed may be correlated with other differences, so that a logical treatment of the whole will allow simplifications, the final outcome being the structural law of the myth.

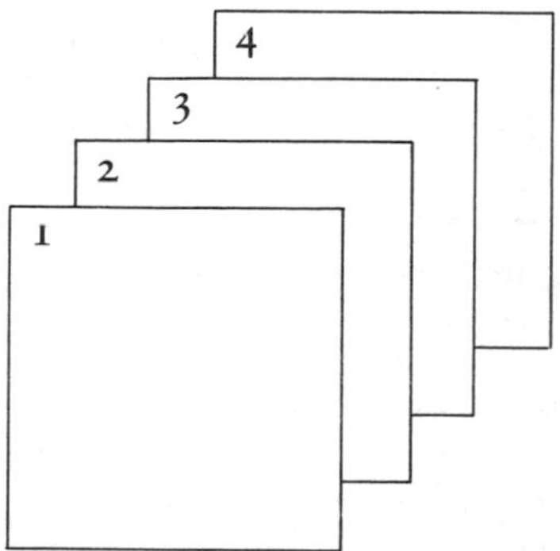

At this point the objection may be raised that the task is impossible to perform, since we can only work with known versions. Is it not possible that a new version might alter the picture? This is true enough if only one or two versions are available, but the objection becomes theoretical as soon as a reasonably large number have been recorded. Let us make this point clear by a comparison. If the furniture of a room and its arrangement were known to us only through its reflection in two mirrors placed on opposite walls, we should theoretically dispose of an almost infinite number of mirror images which would provide us with a complete knowledge. However, should the two mirrors be obliquely set, the number of mirror images would become very small; nevertheless, four or five such images would very likely give us, if not complete information, at least a sufficient coverage so that we would feel sure that no large piece of furniture is missing in our description.

On the other hand, it cannot be too strongly emphasized that all available variants should be taken into account. If Freudian comments on the Oedipus complex are a part of the Oedipus myth, then questions such as whether Cushing's version of the Zuni origin myth should be retained or discarded become irrelevant. There is no single "true" version of which all the others are but copies or distortions. Every version belongs to the myth.

The reason for the discouraging results in works on general mythology can finally be understood. They stem from two causes. First, comparative mythologists have selected preferred versions instead of using them all. Second, we have seen that the structural analysis of *one* variant of *one* myth belonging to *one* tribe (in some cases, even *one* village) already requires two dimensions. When we use several variants of the same myth for the same tribe or village, the frame of reference becomes three-dimensional, and as soon as we try to enlarge the comparison, the number of dimensions required increases until it appears quite impossible to handle them intuitively. The confusions and platitudes which are the outcome of comparative mythology can be explained by the fact that multi-dimensional frames of reference are often ignored or are naïvely replaced by two- or three-dimensional ones. Indeed, progress in comparative mythology depends largely on the cooperation of mathematicians who would undertake to express in symbols multi-dimensional relations which cannot be handled otherwise.

To check this theory,[10] an attempt was made from 1952 to 1954 toward an exhaustive analysis of all the known versions of the Zuni origin and emergence myth: Cushing, 1883 and 1896; Stevenson, 1904; Parsons, 1923; Bunzel, 1932; Benedict, 1934.[11] Furthermore, a preliminary attempt was made at a comparison of the results with similar myths in other Pueblo tribes, Western and Eastern. Finally, a test was undertaken with Plains mythology. In all cases, it was found that the theory was sound; light was thrown, not only on North American mythology, but also on a previously unnoticed kind of logical operation, or one known so far only in a wholly different context. The bulk of material which needs to be handled practically at the outset of the work makes it impossible to enter into details, and we shall have to limit ourselves here to a few illustrations.

A simplified chart of the Zuni emergence myth would read:

CHANGE			DEATH
mechanical value of plants (used as ladders to emerge from lower world)	emergence led by Beloved Twins	sibling incest (origin of water)	gods kill children of men (by drowning)
food value of wild plants	migration led by the two Newekwe (ceremonial clowns)		magical contest with People of the Dew (collecting wild food *versus* cultivation)
		brother and sister sacrificed (to gain victory)	
food value of cultivated plants			
		brother and sister adopted (in exchange for corn)	

[10] See *Annuaire de l'École pratique des Hautes Études,* Section des Sciences religieuses, 1952–1953, pp. 19–21, and 1953–1954, pp. 27–9. Thanks are due here to an unrequested but deeply appreciated grant from the Ford Foundation. [Au.]

[11] F. H. Cushing, *Zuni Fetiches,* Bureau of American Ethnology, 2nd Annual report (1880–1881), Washington, D.C.: 1883; *Outlines of Zuni Creation Myths,* Bureau of American Ethnology, 13th Annual Report, Washington, D.C.: 1896. M. C. Stevenson, *The Zuni Indians,* Bureau of American Ethnology, 23rd Annual Report, Washington, D.C.: 1905. E. C. Parsons, "The Origin Myth of Zuni," *Journal of American Folklore,* XXXVI, 1923. R. L. Bunzel, *Introduction to Zuni Ceremonialism,* Bureau of American Ethnology, 47th Annual Report, Washington, D.C.: 1930. R. Benedict, *Zuni Mythology,* 2 vols., Columbia University Contributions to Anthropology, no. 21, New York, 1934. [Au.]

periodical character of agricultural work			
			war against the Kyanakwe (gardeners *versus* hunters)
food value of game (hunting)			
	war led by the two War-Gods		
inevitability of warfare			salvation of the tribe (center of the World found)
		brother and sister sacrificed to avoid the Flood)	
DEATH			PERMANENCE

As the chart indicates, the problem is the discovery of a life-death mediation. For the Pueblo, this is especially difficult; they understand the origin of human life in terms of the model of plant life (emergence from the earth). They share that belief with the ancient Greeks, and it is not without reason that we chose the Oedipus myth as our first example. But in the American Indian case, the highest form of plant life is to be found in agriculture which is periodical in nature, that is, which consists in an alternation between life and death. If this is disregarded, the contradiction appears elsewhere: Agriculture provides food, therefore life; but hunting provides food and is similar to warfare which means death. Hence there are three different ways of handling the problem. In the Cushing version, the difficulty revolves around an opposition between activities yielding an immediate result (collecting wild food) and activities yielding a delayed result—death has to become integrated so that agriculture can exist. Parsons' version shifts from hunting to agriculture, while Stevenson's version operates the other way around. It can be shown that all the differences between these versions can be rigorously correlated with these basic structures.

Thus the three versions describe the great war waged by the ancestors of the Zuni against a mythical population, the Kyanakwe, by introducing into the narrative significant variations which consist (1) in the friendship or hostility of the gods; (2) in the granting of final victory to one camp or the other; (3) in the attribution of the symbolic function to the Kyanakwe, described sometimes as hunters (whose bows are strung with animal sinews) and sometimes as gardeners (whose bows are strung with plant fibers).

CUSHING	PARSONS	STEVENSON
Gods, Kyanakwe } allied, use fiber string on their bows (gardeners)	Kyanakwe, alone, use fiber string	Gods, Men } allied, use fiber string
VICTORIOUS OVER	VICTORIOUS OVER	VICTORIOUS OVER
Men, alone, use sinew (until they shift to fiber)	Gods, Men } allied, use sinew string	Kyanakwe, alone, use sinew string

Since fiber string (agriculture) is always superior to sinew string (hunting), and since (to a lesser extent) the gods' alliance is preferable to their antagonism, it follows that in Cushing's version, men are seen as doubly underprivileged (hostile gods, sinew string); in the Stevenson version, doubly privileged (friendly gods, fiber string); while Parsons' version confronts us with an intermediary situation (friendly gods, but sinew strings, since men begin by being hunters). Hence:

OPPOSITIONS	CUSHING	PARSONS	STEVENSON
gods/men	–	+	+
fiber/sinew	–	–	+

Bunzel's version is of the same type as Cushing's from a structural point of view. However, it differs from both Cushing's and Stevenson's, inasmuch as the latter two explain the emergence as the result of man's need to evade his pitiful condition, while Bunzel's version makes it the consequence of a call from the higher powers—hence the inverted sequences of the means resorted to for the emergence:

In both Cushing and Stevenson, they go from plants to animals; in Bunzel, from mammals to insects, and from insects to plants.

Among the Western Pueblo the logical approach always remains the same; the starting point and the point of arrival are simplest, whereas the intermediate stage is characterized by ambiguity:

LIFE (=INCREASE)

(Mechanical) value of the plant kingdom, taking growth alone into account		ORIGINS
Food value of the plant kingdom, limited to wild plants		FOOD-GATHERING
Food value of the plant kingdom, including wild and cultivated plants		AGRICULTURE
Food value of the animal kingdom, limited to animals	*(but there is a contradiction here, owing to the negation of life = destruction, hence:)*	
Destruction of the animal kingdom, extended to human beings		HUNTING WARFARE

↓ DEATH (= DECREASE)

The fact that contradiction appears in the middle of the dialectical process results in a double set of dioscuric pairs, the purpose of which is to mediate between conflicting terms:

1. 2 divine messengers	2 ceremonial clowns		2 war-gods
2. homogeneous pair: dioscuri (2 brothers)	siblings (brother and sister)	couple (husband and wife)	heterogeneous pair: (grandmother and grandchild)

We have here combinational variants of the same function in different contexts (hence the war attribute of the clowns, which has given rise to so many queries).

The problem, often regarded as insoluble, vanishes when it is shown that the clowns—gluttons who may with impunity make excessive use of agricultural products—have the same function in relation to food production as the war-gods. (This function appears, in the dialectical process, as *overstepping the boundaries* of hunting, that is, hunting for men instead of for animals for human consumption.)

Some central and Eastern Pueblos proceed the other way around. They begin by stating the identity of hunting and cultivation (first corn obtained by Game-Father sowing deer-dewclaws), and they try to derive both life and death from that central notion. Then, instead of extreme terms being simple and intermediary ones duplicated as among the Western groups, the extreme terms become duplicated (i.e., the two sisters of Eastern Pueblo) while a simple mediating term comes to the foreground (for instance, the Poshaiyanne of the Zia), but endowed with equivocal attributes. Hence the attributes of this "messiah" can be deduced from the place it occupies in the time sequence: good when at the beginning (Zuni, Cushing), equivocal in the middle (Central Pueblo), bad at the end (Zia), except in Bunzel's version, where the sequence is reversed as has been shown.

By systematically using this kind of structural analysis it becomes possible to organize all the known variants of a myth into a set forming a kind of permutation group, the two variants placed at the far ends being in a symmetrical, though inverted, relationship to each other.

Our method not only has the advantage of bringing some kind of order to what was previously chaos; it also enables us to perceive some basic logical processes which are at the root of mythical thought.[12] Three main processes should be distinguished.

The trickster of American mythology has re-

[12] For another application of this method, see our study "Four Winnebago Myths: A Structural Sketch," in Stanley Diamond (ed.), *Culture in History: Essays in Honor of Paul Radin* (New York: 1960), pp. 351–62. [Au.]

mained so far a problematic figure. Why is it that throughout North America his role is assigned practically everywhere to either coyote or raven? If we keep in mind that mythical thought always progresses from the awareness of oppositions toward their resolution, the reason for these choices becomes clearer. We need only assume that two opposite terms with no intermediary always tend to be replaced by two equivalent terms which admit of a third one as a mediator; then one of the polar terms and the mediator become replaced by a new triad, and so on. Thus we have a mediating structure of the following type:

INITIAL PAIR	FIRST TRIAD	SECOND TRIAD
Life		
	Agriculture	
		Herbivorous animals
		Carrion-eating animals (raven: coyote)
	Hunting	
		Beasts of prey
	Warfare	
Death		

The unformulated argument is as follows: carrion-eating animals are like beasts of prey (they eat animal food), but they are also like food-plant producers (they do not kill what they eat). Or to put it otherwise, Pueblo style (for Pueblo agriculture is more "meaningful" than hunting): ravens are to gardens as beasts of prey are to herbivorous animals. But it is also clear that herbivorous animals may be called first to act as mediators on the assumption that they are like collectors and gatherers (plant-food eaters), while they can be used as animal food though they are not themselves hunters. Thus we may have mediators of the first order, of the second order, and so on, where each term generates the next by a double process of opposition and correlation.

This kind of process can be followed in the mythology of the Plains, where we may order the data according to the set:

Unsuccessful mediator between Earth and Sky
(Star-Husband's wife)

Heterogeneous pair of mediators
(grandmother and grandchild)

Semi-homogeneous pair of mediators
(Lodge-Boy and Thrown-away)
↓

While among the Pueblo (Zuni) we have the corresponding set:

Successful mediator between Earth and Sky
(Poshaiyanki)

Semi-homogeneous pair of mediators
(Uyuyewi and Matsailema)

Homogeneous pair of mediators
(the two Ahaiyuta)
↓

On the other hand, correlations may appear on a horizontal axis (this is true even on the linguistic level; see the manifold connotation of the root *pose* in Tewa according to Parsons: coyote, mist, scalp, etc.). Coyote (a carrion-eater) is intermediary between herbivorous and carnivorous just as mist between Sky and Earth; as scalp between war and agriculture (scalp is a war crop); as corn smut between wild and cultivated plants; as garments between "nature" and "culture"; as refuse between village and outside; and as ashes (or soot) between roof (sky vault) and hearth (in the ground). This chain of mediators, if one may call them so, not only throws light on entire parts of North American mythology—why the Dew-God may be at the same time the Game-Master and the giver of raiments and be personified as an "Ash-Boy"; or why scalps are mist-producing; or why the Game-Mother is associated with corn smut; etc.—but it also probably corresponds to a universal way of organizing daily experience. See, for instance, the French for plant smut (*nielle,* from Latin *nebula*); the luck-bringing power attributed in Europe to refuse (old shoe) and ashes (kissing chimney sweeps); and compare the American Ash-Boy cycle with the Indo-European Cinderella: Both are phallic figures (mediators between male and female); masters of the dew and the game; owners of fine raiments; and social mediators (low class marrying into high class); but they are impossible to interpret through recent diffusion, as has been contended, since Ash-Boy and Cinderella are symmetrical but inverted in every detail (while the borrowed Cinderella tale in America—Zuni Turkey-Girl—is parallel to the prototype). Hence the chart:

	EUROPE	AMERICA
Sex	female	male
Family Status	double family (remarried father)	no family (orphan)
Appearance	pretty girl	ugly boy
Sentimental status	nobody likes her	unrequited love for girl
Transformation	luxuriously clothed with supernatural help	stripped of ugliness with supernatural help

Thus, like Ash-Boy and Cinderella, the trickster is a mediator. Since his mediating function occupies a position halfway between two polar terms, he must retain something of that duality—namely an ambiguous and equivocal character. But the trickster figure is not the only conceivable form of mediation; some myths seem to be entirely devoted to the task of exhausting all the possible solutions to the problem of bridging the gap betwen *two* and *one*. For instance, a comparison between all the variants of the Zuni emergence myth provides us with a series of mediating devices, each of which generates the next one by a process of opposition and correlation:

messiah > dioscuri > trickster > bisexual being > sibling pair > married couple > grandmother-grandchild > four-term group > triad

In Cushing's version, this dialectic is associated with a change from a spatial dimension (mediation between Sky and Earth) to a temporal dimension (mediation between summer and winter, that is, between birth and death). But while the shift is being made from space to time, the final solution (triad) re-introduces space, since a triad consists of a dioscuric pair *plus* a messiah, present simultaneously; and while the point of departure was ostensibly formulated in terms of a space referent (Sky and Earth), this was nevertheless implicitly conceived in terms of a time referent (first the messiah calls, *then* the dioscuri descend). Therefore the logic of myth confronts us with a double, reciprocal exchange of functions to which we shall return shortly.

Not only can we account for the ambiguous character of the trickster, but we can also understand another property of mythical figures the world over, namely, that the same god is endowed with contradictory attributes—for instance, he may be *good* and *bad* at the same time. If we compare the variants of the Hopi myth of the origin of Shalako, we may order them in terms of the following structure:

$$(\text{Masauwu}: x) \cong (\text{Muyingwu}: \text{Masauwu}) \cong (\text{Shalako}: \text{Muyingwu}) \cong (y: \text{Masauwu})$$

where x and y represent arbitrary values corresponding to the fact that in the two "extreme" variants the god Masauwu, while appearing alone rather than associated with another god, as in variant two, or being absent, as in variant three, still retains intrinsically a relative value. In variant one, Masauwu (alone) is depicted as helpful to mankind (though not as helpful as he could be), and in version four, harmful to mankind (though not as harmful as he could be). His role is thus defined—at least implicitly—in contrast with another role which is possible but not specified and which is represented here by the values x and y. In version two, on the other hand, Muyingwu is relatively more helpful than Masauwu, and in version three, Shalako more helpful than Muyingwu. We find an identical series when ordering the Keresan variants:

$$(\text{Poshaiyanki}: x) \cong (\text{Lea}: \text{Poshaiyanki}) \cong (\text{Poshaiyanki}: \text{Tiamoni}) \cong (y: \text{Poshaiyanki})$$

This logical framework is particularly interesting, since anthropologists are already acquainted with it on two other levels—first, in regard to the problem of the pecking order among hens, and second, to what this writer has called *generalized exchange* in the field of kinship. By recognizing it also on the level of mythical thought, we may find ourselves in a better position to appraise its basic importance in anthropological studies and to give it a more inclusive theoretical interpretation.

Finally, when we have succeeded in organizing a whole series of variants into a kind of permutation group, we are in a position to formulate the law of that group. Although it is not possible at the present stage to come closer than an approximate formulation which will certainly need to be refined in the future, it seems that every myth (considered as the aggregate of all its variants) corresponds to a formula of the following type:

$$F_x(a): F_y(b) \cong F_x(b): F_{a-1}(y)$$

Here, with two terms, *a* and *b*, being given as well as two functions, *x* and *y*, of these terms, it is assumed that a relation of equivalence exists between two situations defined respectively by an inversion of *terms* and *relations*, under two conditions: (1) that one term be replaced by its opposite (in the above formula, *a* and $a - 1$); (2) that an inversion be made between the *function value* and the *term value* of two elements (above, *y* and *a*).

This formula becomes highly significant when we recall that Freud considered that *two traumas* (and not one, as is so commonly said) are necessary in order to generate the individual myth in which a neurosis consists. By trying to apply the formula to the analysis of these traumas (and assuming that they correspond to conditions 1 and 2 respectively) we should not only be able to provide a more precise and rigorous formulation of the genetic law of the myth, but we would find ourselves in the much desired position of developing side by side the anthropological and the psychological aspects of the theory; we might also take it to the laboratory and subject it to experimental verification.

At this point it seems unfortunate that with the limited means at the disposal of French anthropological research no further advance can be made. It should be emphasized that the task of analyzing mythological literature, which is extremely bulky, and of breaking it down into its constituent units, requires team work and technical help. A variant of average length requires several hundred cards to be properly analyzed. To discover a suitable pattern of rows and columns for those cards, special devices are needed, consisting of vertical boards about six feet long and four and a half feet high, where cards can be pigeon-holed and moved at will. In order to build up three-dimensional models enabling one to compare the variants, several such boards are necessary, and this in turn requires a spacious workshop, a commodity particularly unavailable in Western Europe nowadays. Furthermore, as soon as the frame of reference becomes multi-dimensional (which occurs at an early stage, as has been shown above) the board system has to be replaced by perforated cards, which in turn require IBM equipment, etc.

THREE final remarks may serve as conclusion.

First, the question has often been raised why myths, and more generally oral literature, are so much addicted to duplication, triplication, or quadruplication of the same sequence. If our hypotheses are accepted, the answer is obvious: The function of repetition is to render the structure of the myth apparent. For we have seen that the synchronic-diachronic structure of the myth permits us to organize it into diachronic sequences (the rows in our tables) which should be read synchronically (the columns). Thus, a myth exhibits a "slated" structure, which comes to the surface, so to speak, through the process of repetition.

However, the slates are not absolutely identical. And since the purpose of myth is to provide a logical model capable of overcoming a contradiction (an impossible achievement if, as it happens, the contradiction is real), a theoretically infinite number of slates will be generated, each one slightly different from the others. Thus, myth grows spiral-wise until the intellectual impulse which has produced it is exhausted. Its *growth* is a continuous process, whereas its *structure* remains discontinuous. If this is the case, we should assume that it closely corresponds, in the realm of the spoken word, to a crystal in the realm of physical matter. This analogy may help us to better understand the relationship of myth to both *langue* on the one hand and *parole* on the other. Myth is an intermediary entity between a statistical aggregate of molecules and the molecular structure itself.

Prevalent attempts to explain alleged differences between the so-called primitive mind and scientific thought have resorted to qualitative differences between the working processes of the mind in both cases, while assuming that the entities which they were studying remained very much the same. If our interpretation is correct, we are led toward a completely different view—namely, that the kind of logic in mythical thought is as rigorous as that of modern science, and that the difference lies, not in the quality of the intellectual process, but in the nature of the things to which it is applied. This is well in agreement with the situation known to prevail in the field of technology: What makes a steel ax superior to a stone ax is not that the first one is better made than the second. They are equally well made, but steel is quite different from stone. In the same way we may be able to show that the same logical processes operate in myth as in science, and that man has always been thinking equally well; the improvement lies, not in an alleged progress of man's mind, but in the discovery of new areas to which it may apply its unchanged and unchanging powers.

Maurice Blanchot

b. 1907

MAURICE BLANCHOT'S career has stretched over the decades from the thirties. Best known for his difficult, elusive novels, he has nevertheless produced a prodigious amount of theoretical criticism, most of it having first appeared in French literary journals and much of it having some connection to his own concerns as a novelist. Knowledge of him in American critical circles has not been great, though he has been the subject of essays by both *Paul de Man* and *Geoffrey Hartman,* and Georges Poulet discusses him briefly (*CTSP,* pp. 1212–22) in a well-known article, where Blanchot's work is seen, not favorably, as a "'derealization' of being through language" by means of a "process of rigorous intellectualization." Little is known about Blanchot personally: there are no photographs; biographical dictionaries give only the sketchiest data; he has never granted interviews, nor has he appeared as a lecturer at symposia or conferences.

This reclusiveness is of a piece with his concept of the author, which is set forth in the essay here, where the author's relation to the book is one of lack of comprehension, inevitable alienation, inevitable failure, and the continued need, therefore, to repeat, to write yet again. So, while the author is detached and unimportant to the book he has produced (thus, the author's anxiety and even horror at writing), at the same time the author's plight is of great interest to the author Blanchot. It is not simply a matter, as it usually was among the New Critics, of theoretically eliminating the author from one's critical thought; it is a matter of considering the curious alienation and solitude of the author.

Blanchot is also interested in the reader. In the essay "Reading" from his collection of essays *L'Espace littéraire* (1955), he observes the other end of the critical spectrum and finds there no anxiety or terror. Rather, there is a struggle with the author (though unknown to the reader as a struggle) in order to "give the work back to itself." The reader is fundamentally anonymous, endowing the book with a sudden existence. This activity is not for Blanchot "constitutive" in the Kantian sense but is rather a letting be, an affirmation. It is here in the later work of Blanchot that the influence of *Heidegger* is evident. Earlier, Blanchot's main interests included Kierkegaard, Kafka, Mallarmé, and Hegel. In one of his most important essays, "Literature and the Right to Death," the figures of Mallarmé and Hegel play major roles behind the scenes, though Blanchot's way with his predecessors is to carry on a sort of hidden dialogue with them that is more oblique and allusive than direct. In that essay Blanchot looks principally at language, distinguishing literary from everyday language, and he observes of the former that it is made of uneasiness and contradiction. Its interest is in the meaning, the absence of the thing, and "it would like to attain this absence absolutely in itself and for itself." Thus Blanchot seems to go beyond Hegel's notion of negation, which he identifies with the activity of everyday language, and even beyond the famous statement of Mallarmé about producing the flower that is absent from all bouquets—the flower conjured by the poet. Blanchot's poem is without the author, with an anonymous reader; it is an absence of absence, an existence without being.

Blanchot's major essays have been translated as *The Gaze of Orpheus and Other Literary Essays* (1981). The book includes a selection of essays from *Faux Pas* (1943), *La Part de feu* (1949), *L'Espace littéraire* (1955), *Le Livre à venir* (1959), and *L'Entretien fini* (1969). Blanchot's novels *Thomas the Obscure, Death Sentence,* and *The Madness of the Day* are available in English translation. See Sarah N. Lawall, *Critics of Consciousness* (1968); Paul de Man, *Blindness and Insight* (1971, 1983); and Geoffrey Hartman, *Beyond Formalism* (1970), all of which contain essays on Blanchot.

THE ESSENTIAL SOLITUDE

It seems we have learned something about art when we experience what the word solitude designates. This word has been tossed around much too freely. Yet what does it mean to "be alone"? When is one alone? As we ask ourselves this question, we should not simply return to thoughts that we find moving. Solitude on the level of the world is a wound we do not need to comment on here.

Nor do we have in mind the solitude of the artist, the solitude which he is said to need if he is to practice his art. When Rilke writes to the Comtesse de Solms-Laubach (August 3, 1907): "Except for two short interruptions, I have not pronounced a single word for weeks; at last my solitude has closed in and I am in my work like a pit in its fruit,"[1] the solitude he speaks of is not essentially solitude: it is self-communion.

THE ESSENTIAL SOLITUDE comes from Blanchot's *L'Espace littéraire* (1955). It is reprinted from *The Gaze of Orpheus and Other Literary Essays,* ed. P. Adams Sitney, trans. Lydia Davis, by permission of the publisher, Station Hill Press, copyright 1981.

[1]Rainer Maria Rilke (1875–1926), German poet. [Eds.]

The Solitude of the Work

In the solitude of the work—the work of art, the literary work—we see a more essential solitude. It excludes the self-satisfied isolation of individualism, it is unacquainted with the search for difference; it is not dissipated by the fact of sustaining a virile relationship in a task that covers the mastered extent of the day. The person who is writing the work is thrust to one side, the person who has written the work is dismissed. What is more, the person who is dismissed does not know it. This ignorance saves him, diverts him and allows him to go on. The writer never knows if the work is done. What he has finished in one book, he begins again or destroys in another. Valéry,[2] who celebrates this privilege of the infinite in the work, still sees only its easiest aspect: the fact that the work is infinite means (to him) that although the artist is not capable of ending it, he is nevertheless capable of turning it into the enclosed space of an endless task whose incompleteness develops mastery of the spirit, expresses that mastery, expresses it by developing it in the form of power. At a certain point, circumstances—that is, history—in the form of an editor, financial demands, social duties, pronounce the missing end and the

[2]See *CTSP*, pp. 914–26. [Eds.]

artist, freed by a purely compulsory outcome, pursues the incomplete elsewhere.

According to this point of view, the infinity of the work is simply the infinity of the spirit. The spirit tries to accomplish itself in a single work, instead of realizing itself in the infinity of works and the movement of history. But Valéry was in no way a hero. He chose to talk about everything, to write about everything: thus, the scattered whole of the world diverted him from the rigor of the unique whole of the work—he amiably allowed himself to be turned away from it. The *etc.* was hiding behind the diversity of thoughts, of subjects.

Nevertheless, the work—the work of art, the literary work—is neither finished nor unfinished: it is. What it says is exclusively that: that it is—and nothing more. Outside of that, it is nothing. Anyone who tries to make it express more finds nothing, finds that it expresses nothing. Anyone who lives in dependence on the work, whether because he is writing it or reading it, belongs to the solitude of something that expresses only the word *being:* a word that the language protects by hiding it or that the language causes to appear by disappearing into the silent void of the work.

The first framework of the solitude of the work is this absence of need which never permits it to be called finished or unfinished. The work can have no proof, just as it can have no use. It cannot be verified—truth can lay hold of it, renown illuminate it: this existence concerns it not at all, this obviousness makes it neither certain nor real, nor does it make it manifest.

The work is solitary: that does not mean that it remains incommunicable, that it lacks a reader. But the person who reads it enters into that affirmation of the solitude of the work, just as the one who writes it belongs to the risk of that solitude.

The Work, the Book

If we want to examine more closely what such statements suggest, perhaps we should look for their source. The writer writes a book, but the book is not yet the work, the work is not a work until the word *being* is pronounced in it, in the violence of a beginning which is its own; this event occurs when the work is the innermost part of someone writing it and of someone reading it. We can therefore ask ourselves this: if solitude is the writer's risk, doesn't it express the fact that he is turned, oriented towards the open violence of the work, never grasping more than its substitute, its approach, and its illusion in the form of the book? The writer belongs to the work, but what belongs to him is only a book, a mute accumulation of sterile words, the most meaningless thing in the world. The writer who experiences this void simply believes that the work is unfinished, and he believes that with a little more effort and the luck of some favorable moments, he—and only he—will be able to finish it. And so he sets back to work. But what he wants to finish, by himself, remains something interminable, it ties him to an illusory labor. And in the end, the work ignores him, it closes on his absence, in the impersonal, anonymous statement that it is—and nothing more. Which we express by remarking that the artist, who only finishes his work at the moment he dies, never knows his work. And we may have to reverse that remark, because isn't the writer dead as soon as the work exists, as he himself sometimes foresees, when he experiences a very strange kind of worklessness.[3]

"Noli me legere"[4]

The same situation can also be described this way: a writer never reads his work. For him, it is the unreadable, a secret, and he cannot remain face to face with it. A secret, because he is separated from

[3] This is not the situation of the man who works and accomplishes his task and whose task escapes him by transforming itself in the world. What this man makes is transformed, but in the world, and he recaptures it through the world, at least if he can recapture it, if alienation is not immobilized, if it is not diverted to the advantage of a few, but continues until the completion of the world. On the contrary, what the writer has in view is the work, and what he writes is a book. The book, as such, can become an active event in the world (an action, however, that is always reserved and insufficient), but it is not action the artist has in view, but the work, and what makes the book a substitute for the work is enough to make it a thing that, like the work, does not arise from the truth of the world; and it is an almost frivolous thing, if it has neither the reality of the work nor the seriousness of real labor in the world. [Au.]

[4] "Read me not." [Eds.]

it. Yet this impossibility of reading is not a purely negative movement, rather it is the only real approach the author can have to what we call a work. Where there is still only a book, the abrupt *Noli me legere* already causes the horizon of another power to appear. An experience that is fleeting, though immediate. It does not have the force of a prohibition, it is a statement that emerges from the play and the meaning of the words—the insistent, harsh and poignant statement that what is there, in the inclusive presence of a definitive text, still rejects—is the rude and caustic emptiness of rejection—or else excludes, with the authority of indifference, the person who has written it and now wants to recapture it by reading it. The impossibility of reading is the discovery that now, in the space opened by creation, there is no more room for creation—and no other possibility for the writer than to keep on writing the same work. No one who has written the work can live near it, dwell near it. This is the very decision that dismisses him, that cuts him off, that turns him into the survivor, the workless, unemployed, inert person on whom art does not depend.

The writer cannot dwell near the work: he can only write it, and once it is written he can only discern the approach to it in the abrupt *Noli me legere* that distances him, that moves him away or forces him to return to that "remove" where he first came in, to become the understanding of what he had to write. So that now he finds himself back again, in some sense at the beginning of his task, and he rediscovers the neighborhood of the outside, the errant intimacy of the outside, which he was not able to make into a dwelling.

Perhaps this ordeal points us in the direction of what we are looking for. The writer's solitude, then, this condition that is his risk, arises from the fact that in the work he belongs to what is always before the work. Through him the work arrives, is the firmness of a beginning, but he himself belongs to a time dominated by the indecision of beginning again. The obsession that ties him to a privileged theme, that makes him repeat what he has already said, sometimes with the power of enriched talent, but sometimes with the prolixity of an extraordinarily impoverishing repetition, less and less forcefully, more and more monotonously, illustrates his apparent need to come back to the same point, to retrace the same paths, to persevere and begin again what, for him, never really begins, to belong to the shadow of events instead of the object, to what allows the words themselves to become images, appearances—instead of signs, values, the power of truth.

Persecutive Prehension

It occurs that a man who is holding a pencil may want very much to let go of it, but his hand will not let go: quite the opposite—it tightens, it has no intention of opening. The other hand intervenes with more success, but then we see the hand that we may call sick slowly gesturing, trying to recapture the object that is moving away. What is strange is the slowness of this gesture. The hand moves through a time that is hardly human, that is neither the time of viable action nor the time of hope, but rather the shadow of time which is itself the shadow of a hand slipping in an unreal way towards an object that has become its shadow. At certain moments, this hand feels a very great need to grasp: it must take the pencil, this is necessary, this is an order, an imperious requirement. The phenomenon is known as "persecutive prehension."

The writer seems to be master of his pen, he can become capable of great mastery over words, over what he wants to make them express. But this mastery only manages to put him in contact, keep him in contact, with a fundamental passivity in which the word, no longer anything beyond its own appearance, the shadow of a word, can never be mastered or even grasped; it remains impossible to grasp, impossible to relinquish, the unsettled moment of fascination.

The writer's mastery does not lie in the hand that writes, the "sick" hand that never lets go of the pencil, that cannot let it go because it does not really hold what it is holding; what it holds belongs to shadow, and the hand itself is a shadow. Mastery is always the achievement of the other hand, the one that does not write, the one that can intervene just when it has to, grasp the pencil and take it away. Mastery, then, consists of the power to stop writing, to interrupt what is being written, giving its rights and its exclusive cutting edge back to the instant.

We must resume our questions. We have said: the writer belongs to the work, but what belongs to him—what he finishes alone—is only a book. The restriction of "only" responds to the expression "alone." The writer never stands before the work, and where there is a work, he does not know it, or more exactly, he is ignorant of his very ignorance, it is only present in the impossibility of reading, an ambiguous experience that sends him back to work.

The writer sets back to work. Why doesn't he stop writing? If he breaks with the work, as Rimbaud[5] did, why does that break strike us as a mysterious impossibility? Is it simply that he wants a perfect work, and if he keeps on working at it, is this only because the perfection is never perfect enough? Does he even write for the sake of a work? Is he preoccupied by it as the thing that will put an end to his task, as a goal worthy of all his efforts? Not at all. And the work is never that for the sake of which one is able to write (that for the sake of which one might relate to what is written as to the exercise of a power).

The fact that the writer's task comes to an end when he dies is what hides the fact that because of this task his life slips into the unhappiness of infinity.

The Interminable, the Incessant

The solitude that comes to the writer through the work of literature is revealed by this: the act of writing is now interminable, incessant. The writer no longer belongs to the authoritative realm where expressing oneself means expressing the exactness and certainty of things and of values depending on the meaning of their limits. What is written consigns the person who must write to a statement over which he has no authority, a statement that is itself without consistency, that states nothing, that is not the repose, the dignity of silence, because it is what is still speaking when everything has been said, what does not precede speech because it instead prevents it from being a beginning of speech, just as it withdraws from speech the right and the power to interrupt itself. To write is to break the bond uniting the speech to myself, to break the relationship that makes me talk towards "you" and gives me speech within the understanding that this speech receives from you, because it addresses you, it is the address that begins in me because it ends in you. To write is to break this link. What is more, it withdraws language from the course of the world, it deprives it of what makes it a power such that when I speak, it is the world that is spoken, it is the day that is built by work, action and time.

The act of writing is interminable, incessant. The writer, they say, stops saying "I." Kafka[6] observes with surprise, with enchantment and delight, that as soon as he was able to substitute "he" for "I" he entered literature. This is true, but the transformation is much more profound. The writer belongs to a language no one speaks, a language that is not addressed to anyone, that has no center, that reveals nothing. He can believe he is asserting himself in this language, but what he is asserting is completely without a self. To the extent that, as a writer, he accedes to what is written, he can never again express himself and he cannot appeal to you either, nor yet let anyone else speak. Where he is, only being speaks, which means that speech no longer speaks, but simply is—dedicates itself to the pure passivity of being.

When to write means to consign oneself to the interminable, the writer who agrees to sustain its essence loses the power to say "I." He then loses the power to make others say "I." Thus it is impossible for him to give life to characters whose freedom would be guaranteed by his creative force. The idea of a character, like the traditional form of the novel, is only one of the compromises that a writer—drawn out of himself by literature in search of its essence—uses to try to save his relations with the world and with himself.

To write is to make oneself the echo of what cannot stop talking—and because of this, in order to become its echo, I must to a certain extent impose silence on it. To this incessant speech I bring the decisiveness, the authority of my own silence. Through my silent mediation, I make perceptible the uninterrupted affirmation, the giant murmur in which language, by opening, becomes image, becomes imaginary, an eloquent depth, an indistinct fullness that is empty. The source of this silence is the self-effacement to which the person who writes is invited. Or, this silence is the resource of his mastery, the right to intervene maintained by the hand that does not write—the part of himself that can always say no, and, when necessary, appeals to time, restores the future.

[5] Arthur Rimbaud (1854–91), French poet. [Eds.]

[6] Franz Kafka (1883–1924), Czech novelist. [Eds.]

When we admire the tone of a work, responding to the tone as what is most authentic about it, what are we referring to? Not the style, and not the interest and the quality of the language, but precisely the silence, the virile force through which the person who writes, having deprived himself of himself, having renounced himself, has nevertheless maintained within his effacement the authority of a power, the decision to be silent, so that in this silence what speaks without beginning or end can take on form, coherence and meaning.

Tone is not the voice of the writer, but the intimacy of the silence he imposes on speech, which makes this silence still *his own,* what remains of himself in the discretion that sets him to one side. Tone makes the great writers, but perhaps the work is not concerned about what makes them great.

In the effacement to which he is invited, the "great writer" still restrains himself: what speaks is no longer himself, but it is not the pure slipping of the speech of no one. Of the effaced "I," it retains the authoritarian, though silent affirmation. It retains the cutting edge, the violent rapidity of active time, of the instant. This is how he is preserved inside the work, is contained where there is no more restraint. But because of this the work, too, retains a content; it is not completely interior to itself.

The writer we call classic—at least in France[7]—sacrifices the speech that is his own within him, but in order to give voice to the universal. The calm of a form governed by rules, the certainty of a speech freed from caprice, in which impersonal generality speaks, assures him a relationship with truth. Truth that is beyond person and would like to be beyond time. Literature then has the glorious solitude of reason, that rarified life at the heart of the whole that would require resolution and courage—if that reason were not in fact the equilibrium of an orderly aristocratic society, that is, the noble contentment of a section of society that concentrates the whole in itself, by isolating itself and maintaining itself above what permits it to live.

When to write is to discover the interminable, the writer who enters this region does not go beyond himself towards the universal. He does not go towards a world that is more sure, more beautiful, better justified, where everything is arranged in the light of a just day. He does not discover the beautiful language that speaks honorably for everyone. What speaks in him is the fact that in one way or another he is no longer himself, he is already no longer anyone. The "he" that is substituted for "I"—this is the solitude that comes to the writer through the work. "He" does not indicate objective disinterest, creative detachment. "He" does not glorify the consciousness of someone other than me, the soaring of a human life that, within the imaginary space of the work of art, keeps its freedom to say "I." "He" is myself having become no one, someone else having become the other; it is the fact that there, where I am, I can no longer address myself to myself, and that the person who addresses himself to me does not say "I," is not himself.

RECOURSE TO THE "JOURNAL"

It is perhaps striking that the moment the work becomes the pursuit of art, becomes literature, the writer feels a growing need to preserve a relationship with himself. He feels an extreme reluctance to relinquish himself in favor of that neutral power, formless, without a destiny, which lies behind everything that is written, and his reluctance and apprehension are revealed by the concern, common to so many authors, to keep what he calls his *Journal.* This is quite unlike the so-called romantic complacencies. The Journal is not essentially a confession, a story about oneself. It is a Memorial. What does the writer have to remember? Himself, who he is when he is not writing, when he is living his daily life, when he is alive and real, and not dying and without truth. But the strange thing is that the means he uses to recall himself to himself is the very element of forgetfulness: the act of writing. Yet this is why the truth of the Journal does not lie in the interesting and literary remarks to be found in it, but in the insignificant details that tie it to everyday reality. The Journal represents the series of reference points that a writer establishes as a way of recognizing himself, when he anticipates the dangerous metamorphosis he is vulnerable to. It is a path that is still viable, a sort of parapet walk that runs alongside the other path, overlooks it and sometimes coincides with it, the other being the one where the endless task is wandering. Here, real things are still

[7]See Sainte-Beuve's "What Is a Classic?" (*CTSP,* pp. 555–62) for part of the history of the "classic" in France. [Eds.]

spoken of. Here, the one who speaks retains his name and speaks in his name, and the date inscribed belongs to a common time in which what happens really happens. The Journal—this book that is apparently completely solitary—is often written out of fear and dread in the face of the solitude that comes to the writer through the work.

Recourse to the Journal indicates that the person writing does not want to break with the happiness, the decorum of days that are really days and that really follow one another. The Journal roots the movement of writing in time, in the humbleness of the everyday, dated and preserved by its date. Perhaps what is written there is already only insincerity, perhaps it is said without concern for what is true, but it is said under the safeguard of the event, it belongs to the affairs, the incidents, the commerce of the world, to an active present, to a stretch of time that is perhaps completely worthless and insignificant, but that at least cannot turn back; it is the work of something that goes beyond itself, goes toward the future, goes there definitively.

The Journal shows that already the person writing is no longer capable of belonging to time through ordinary firmness of action, through the community created by work, by profession, through the simplicity of intimate speech, the force of thoughtlessness. Already he does not really belong to history anymore, but he does not want to lose time either, and since he no longer knows how to do anything but write, at least he writes at the demand of his day-to-day story and in keeping with his everyday preoccupations. Often writers who keep journals are the most literary of all writers, but perhaps this is precisely because in doing so they avoid the extreme of literature, if literature is in fact the fascinating domain of the absence of time.

The Fascination of the Absence of Time

To write is to surrender oneself to the fascination of the absence of time. Here we are undoubtedly approaching the essence of solitude. The absence of time is not a purely negative mode. It is the time in which nothing begins, in which initiative is not possible, where before the affirmation there is already the recurrence of the affirmation. Rather than a purely negative mode, it is a time without negation, without decision, when *here* is also *nowhere*, when each thing withdraws into its image and the "I" that we are recognizes itself as it sinks into the neutrality of a faceless "he." The time of the absence of time is without a present, without a presence. This "without a present," however, does no refer to a past. *Formerly* had the dignity and the active force of *now;* memory still bears witness to this active force, memory which frees me from what would otherwise recall me, frees me from it by giving me the means to summon it freely, to dispose of it according to my present intention. Memory is the freedom from the past. But what is without a present does not accept the present of a memory either. Memory says of an event: that was, once, and now never again. The irremediable nature of what is without a present, of what is not even there as having been, says: that has never occurred, never a single first time, and yet it is resuming, again, again, infinitely. It is without end, without beginning. It is without a future.

The time of the absence of time is not dialectical. What appears in it is the fact that nothing appears, the being that lies deep within the absence of being, the being that is when there is nothing, that is no longer when there is something—as though there were beings only through the loss of being, when being is lacking. The reversal that constantly refers us back, in the absence of time, to the presence of absence, but to this presence of absence, to absence as affirmation of itself, affirmation in which nothing is affirmed, in which nothing ceases to be affirmed, in the aggravation of the indefinite—this movement is not dialectical. Contradictions do not exclude one another there, nor are they reconciled there; only time, for which negation becomes our power, can be the "unity of incompatible things." In the absence of time, what is new does not renew anything; what is present is not contemporary; what is present presents nothing, represents itself, belongs now and henceforth and at all times to recurrence. This is not, but comes back, comes as already and always past, so that I do not know it, but I recognize it, and this recognition destroys the power in me to know, the right to grasp, makes what cannot be grasped into something that cannot be relinquished, the inaccessible that I cannot cease attaining, what I cannot take but can only take back—and never give up.

This time is not the ideal immobility that is glorified under the name of the eternal. In the region we are trying to approach, here is submerged in nowhere, but nowhere is nevertheless here, and dead time is a real time in which death is present, in which it arrives but does not stop arriving, as though by arriving it rendered sterile the time that permits it to arrive. The dead present is the impossibility of realizing a presence—an impossibility that is present, that is there as that which doubles every present, the shadow of the present, which the present carries and hides in itself. When I am alone, in this present, I am not alone, but am already returning to myself in the form of Someone. Someone is there, where I am alone. The fact of being alone is that I belong to this dead time that is not my time, nor yours, nor common time, but the time of Someone. Someone is what is still present when no one is there. In the place where I am alone, I am not there, there is no one there, but the impersonal is there: the outside as what anticipates, precedes, dissolves all possibility of personal relationship. Someone is the faceless He, the One of which one is a part, but who is a part of it? No one is part of the One. "One" belongs to a region that cannot be brought into the light—not because it conceals a secret alien to all revelation, not even because it is radically dark, but because it transforms everything that has access to it, even light, into anonymous, impersonal being, the Not-true, the Not-real and yet always there. In this sense, the "One" is what appears closest to one when one dies.[8]

Where I am alone, day is no longer anything but the loss of an abode, it is an intimacy with the outside, the outside that is placeless and without repose. The act of coming here causes the one who comes to be part of the dispersal, the fissure in which the exterior is a stifling intrusion, the nakedness and cold of that in which one remains exposed, where space is the dizziness of being spaced. Then fascination reigns.

The Image

Why fascination? Seeing implies distance, the decision that causes separation, the power not to be in contact and to avoid the confusion of contact. Seeing means that this separation has nevertheless become an encounter. But what happens when what you see, even though from a distance, seems to touch you with a grasping contact, when the manner of seeing is a sort of touch, when seeing is a *contact* at a distance? What happens when what is seen imposes itself on your gaze, as though the gaze had been seized, touched, put in contact with appearance? Not an active contact, not the initiative and action that might still remain in a true touch; rather, the gaze is drawn, absorbed into an immobile movement and a depth without depth. What is given to us by contact at a distance is the image, and fascination is passion for the image.

What fascinates us, takes away our power to give it a meaning, abandons its "perceptible" nature, abandons the world, withdraws to the near side of the world and attracts us there, no longer reveals itself to us and yet asserts itself in a presence alien to the present in time and to presence in space. The split, which had been the possibility of seeing, solidifies, right inside the gaze, into impossibility. In this way, in the very thing that makes it possible, the gaze finds the power that neutralizes it—that does not suspend it or arrest it, but on the contrary prevents it from ever finishing, cuts it off from all beginning, makes it into a neutral, wandering glimmer that is not extinguished, that does not illuminate: the circle of the gaze, closed on itself. Here we have an immediate expression of the inversion that is the essence of solitude. Fascination is the gaze of solitude, the gaze of what is incessant and interminable, in which blindness is still vision, vision that is no longer the possibility of seeing, but the impossibility of not seeing, impossibility that turns into seeing, that perseveres—always and always—in a vision that does not end: a dead gaze, a gaze that has become the ghost of an eternal vision.

It can be said that a person who is fascinated does not perceive any real object, any real form, because what he sees does not belong to the world of reality, but to the indeterminate realm of fascination. A realm that is so to speak absolute. Distance is not excluded from it, but it is excessive, being the unlimited depth that lies behind the image, a depth that is not alive, not tractable, absolutely present though not provided, where objects sink when they become separated from their meaning, when they subside into their image. This realm of fascination, where what we see seizes our vision and makes it inter-

[8] When I am alone, I am not the one who is here and you are not the one I am far away from, nor other people, nor the world. At this point we begin to ponder the idea of "essential solitude and solitude in the world." [Au.] See Blanchot's four pages entitled "La solitude essentielle et la solitude dans le monde" in the appendix to *L'Espace littéraire* (Gallimard, 1955). [Tr.]

minable, where our gaze solidifies into light, where light is the absolute sheen of an eye that we do not see, that we nevertheless do not leave off seeing because it is the mirror image of our own gaze, this realm is supremely attractive, fascinating: light that is also the abyss, horrifying and alluring, light in which we sink.

Our childhood fascinates us because it is the moment of fascination, it is fascinated itself, and this golden age seems bathed in a light that is splendid because it is unrevealed, but the fact is that this light is alien to revelation, has nothing to reveal, is pure reflection, a ray that is still only the radiance of an image. Perhaps the power of the maternal figure derives its brilliance from the very power of fascination, and one could say that if the Mother exerts this fascinating attraction, it is because she appears when the child lives completely under the gaze of fascination, and so concentrates in herself all the powers of enchantment. It is because the child is fascinated that the mother is fascinating, and this is also why all the impressions of our earliest years have a fixed quality that arises from fascination.

When someone who is fascinated sees something, he does not see it, properly speaking, but it touches him in his immediate proximity, it seizes him and monopolizes him, even though it leaves him absolutely at a distance. Fascination is tied in a fundamental way to the neutral, impersonal presence, the indeterminate One, the immense and faceless Someone. It is the relationship—one that is itself neutral and impersonal—that the gaze maintains with the depths that have no gaze and no contour, the absence that one sees beyond it is blinding.

The Act of Writing

To write is to enter into the affirmation of solitude where fascination threatens. It is to yield to the risk of the absence of time, where eternal recommencement holds sway. It is to pass from the I to the He, so that what happens to me happens to no one, is anonymous because of the fact that it is my business, repeats itself in an infinite dispersal. To write is to arrange language under fascination and, through language, in language, remain in contact with the absolute milieu, where the thing becomes an image again, where the image, which had been allusion to a figure, becomes an allusion to what is without figure, and having been a form sketched on absence, becomes the unformed presence of that absence, the opaque and empty opening on what is when there is no more world, when there is no world yet.

Why this? Why should the act of writing have anything to do with this essential solitude, the essence of which is that in it, concealment appears?[9]

[9] We will not try to answer this question directly here. We will simply ask: just as a statue glorifies marble—and if all art tries to draw out into the daylight the elemental depths that the world denies and drives back as it asserts itself—isn't language in the poem, in literature, related to ordinary language in the same way that the image is related to the thing? We are apt to think that poetry is a language which, more than any other, does justice to images. Probably this is an allusion to a much more essential transformation: the poem is not a poem because it includes a certain number of figures, metaphors, comparisons. On the contrary, what is special about a poem is that nothing in it strikes a vivid image. We must therefore express what we are looking for in another way: in literature, doesn't language itself become entirely image, not a language containing images or putting reality into figures, but its own image, the image of language—and not a language full of imagery—or an imaginary language, a language no one speaks—that is to say, spoken from its own absence—in the same way that the image appears on the absence of the thing, a language that is also addressed to the shadow of events, not to their reality, because of the fact that the words that express them are not signs, but images, images of words and words in which things become images?

What are we trying to describe by saying this? Aren't we headed in a direction that will force us to return to opinions we were happy to relinquish, opinions similar to the old idea that art was an imitation, a copy of the real? If the language in a poem becomes its own image, doesn't that mean that poetic speech is always second, secondary? According to the customary analysis, an image exists after an object: it follows from it; we see, then we imagine. After the object comes the image. "After" seems to indicate a subordinate relationship. We speak in a real way, then we speak in an imaginary way, or we imagine ourselves speaking. Isn't poetic speech nothing more than a tracing, a weakened shadow, the transposition of the unique speaking language into a space where the requirements for effectiveness are attenuated? But perhaps the customary analysis is wrong. Perhaps, before we go any further, we should ask ourselves: but what is the image? (See the essay entitled "The Two Versions of the Imaginary.") [Au.]

J. L. Austin

1911–1960

At Oxford, J. L. Austin exerted a major influence on the development of modern Anglo-American analytical philosophy, as one of the principal figures in the development of what is commonly known as "ordinary language philosophy." While Austin, like *Wittgenstein* before him, was influenced by the work of *Frege* (Austin translated Frege's *Begriffsschrift*), he was not drawn to the development of logical formalism. On the contrary, he took the view that "ordinary language" is only "ordinary" in that it is generally used without critical or analytical scrutiny. For philosophy, Austin thought no subject more auspicious than the reflective examination of ordinary language, for the subtlety it represents and conveys.

Austin's philosophical approach is distinguished by the combination of great logical acuity and scrupulous attention to everyday verbal behavior. One of his most important insights was that human utterances, while they may seem transparent, are also acts of extraordinary complexity. Against the common philosophical view that language is imprecise or imperfect, he argued that not only was ordinary language precise but that, by careful, collective attention, philosophers could reach consensus on a broad range of issues pertaining to language. From his early work, the philosophy of "Speech Acts" developed (as exemplified in the work of *John Searle* and J. O. Urmson, for example) by following out the implications of the distinctions Austin elaborated in the William James lectures he delivered at Harvard University in 1955, published as *How to Do Things with Words*.

As *Stanley Cavell* has warned, however, it would be an error to assume that Austin's concern with "ordinary language" makes of his work an extension of applied linguistics: his concern with ordinary language was a concern with how facts about the world and facts of human action conjoin (or collide) on the field of language. In this respect, Austin as a philosopher was more directly and profoundly attuned to traditional philosophical concerns than may at first appear—in part because his essays and lectures do not present avowedly architectonic arguments. Austin is disarming because, in looking at a subject matter so intimately familiar, one sometimes may not notice the immense erudition or the intellectual subtlety that informs Austin's philosophical strategies, including digressions, cautions, and passing remarks.

In the selection here, Austin expounds his argument that in issuing an utterance, we also commit acts and that some among those acts are in fact constituted by producing an utterance. (For a fuller discussion of "Speech Acts," see *John Searle*). Austin first distinguishes between "constative" and "performative" aspects of language use: the first makes statements or otherwise conveys information; the latter involves us in (or constitutes) actions of specific kinds. Austin argues that performatives are likely to be ignored by philosophers, as if language were involved only in making true or false statements. Austin contends that language, viewed in terms of acts, discloses a rich and significant structure of implication, not well explicated (if even acknowledged) by the conventional logical analysis of propositions. Thus, any utterance can (at least in principle) be viewed as involving three kinds of acts: *locutionary* acts, in making the utterance; *illocutionary* acts, in which the completed utterance completes an intentional act; and *perlocutionary* acts, by which illocutionary acts have some specific consequence—as, for example, when by saying, "Please shut the door" (locutionary), "I make a *request*" (illocutionary), "with the consequence that you do, in fact, shut the door" (perlocutionary).

While in one respect these are obvious distinctions to make, in another it is by no means obvious how language functions to facilitate or even constitute such chains of action. What Austin shows is that language, as an index to such action, is a philosophical resource of extraordinary depth and subtlety.

Austin's major works (most of which were published posthumously) include *Philosophical Papers,* ed. J. O. Urmson and G. J. Warnock (1961); *Sense and Sensibilia,* reconstructed from manuscript notes by G. J. Warnock (1962); and *How to Do Things with Words,* ed. J. O. Urmson and Marina Sbisà (1962). See also C. Caton, ed., *Philosophy and Ordinary Language* (1963), and K. T. Fann, ed., *Symposium on J. L. Austin* (1969).

FROM

HOW TO DO THINGS WITH WORDS

In embarking on a programme of finding a list of explicit performative verbs, it seemed that we were going to find it not always easy to distinguish performative utterances from constative,[1] and it therefore seemed expedient to go farther back for a while to fundamentals—to consider from the ground up how many senses there are in which to say something *is* to do something, or *in* saying something we do something, and even *by* saying something we do something. And we began by distinguishing a whole group of senses of 'doing something' which are all included together when we say, what is obvious, that to say something is in the full normal sense to do something—which includes the utterance of certain noises, the utterance of certain words in a certain construction, and the utterance of them with a certain 'meaning' in the favourite philosophical sense of that word, i.e. with a certain sense and with a certain reference.

The act of 'saying something' in this full normal sense I call, i.e. dub, the performance of a locutionary act, and the study of utterances thus far and in these respects the study of locutions, or of the full units of speech. Our interest in the locutionary act is, of course, principally to make quite plain what it is, in order to distinguish it from other acts with which we are going to be primarily concerned. Let me add merely that, of course, a great many further

This is Lecture VIII of HOW TO DO THINGS WITH WORDS, first delivered in 1955. It is reprinted by permission of the publishers from *How to Do Things with Words* by J. L. Austin, Cambridge, MA: Harvard University Press, copyright 1962 by the President and Fellows of Harvard College.

[1] By "constative," Austin means uses of language to make statements, including statements that establish some set of facts, indicate contextual conditions, or embody assertions. See *How To do Things with Words,* pp. 3, 6, 133–50. [Eds.]

refinements would be possible and necessary if we were to discuss it for its own sake—refinements of very great importance not merely to philosophers but to, say, grammarians and phoneticians.

We had made three rough distinctions between the phonetic act, the phatic act, and the rhetic act. The phonetic act is merely the act of uttering certain noises. The phatic act is the uttering of certain vocables or words, i.e. noises of certain types, belonging to and as belonging to, a certain vocabulary, conforming to and as conforming to a certain grammar. The rhetic act is the performance of an act of using those vocables with a certain more-or-less definite sense and reference. Thus 'He said "The cat is on the mat"', reports a phatic act, where 'He said that the cat was on the mat' reports a rhetic act. A similar contrast is illustrated by the pairs:

> 'He said "The cat is on the mat"', 'He said (that) the cat was on the mat';
> 'He said "I shall be there"', 'He said he would be there';
> 'He said "Get out"', 'He told me to get out';
> 'He said "Is it in Oxford or Cambridge?"'; 'He asked whether it was in Oxford or Cambridge'.

To pursue this for its own sake beyond our immediate requirements, I shall mention some general points worth remembering:

(1) Obviously, to perform a phatic I must perform a phonetic act, or, if you like, in performing one I am performing the other (not, however, that phatic acts are a sub-class of phonetic acts; we defined the phatic act as the uttering of vocables *as* belonging to a certain vocabulary): but the converse is not true, for if a monkey makes a noise indistinguishable from 'go' it is still not a phatic act.

(2) Obviously in the definition of the phatic act two things were lumped together: vocabulary and grammar. So we have not assigned a special name to the person who utters, for example, 'cat thoroughly the if' or 'the slithy toves did gyre.' Yet a further point arising is the intonation as well as grammar and vocabulary.

(3) The phatic act, however, like the phonetic, is essentially mimicable, reproducible (including intonation, winks, gestures, &c.). One can mimic not merely the statement in quotation marks 'She has lovely hair', but also the more complex fact that he said it like this: 'She has lovely *hair*' (shrugs).

This is the 'inverted commas' use of 'said' as we get it in novels: every utterance can be just reproduced in inverted commas, or in inverted commas with 'said he' or, more often, 'said she', &c., after it.

But the rhetic act is the one we report, in the case of assertions, by saying 'He said that the cat was on the mat', 'He said he would go', 'He said I was to go' (his words were 'You are to go'). This is the so-called 'indirect speech'. If the sense or reference is *not* being taken as clear, then the whole or part is to be in quotation marks. Thus I might say: 'He said I was to go to "the minister", but he did not say which minister' or 'I said that he was behaving badly and he replied that "the higher you get the fewer"'. We cannot, however, always use 'said that' easily: we would say 'told to', 'advise to', &c., if he used the imperative mood, or such equivalent phrases as 'said I was to', 'said I should', &c. Compare such phrases as 'bade me welcome' and 'extended his apologies'.

I add one further point about the rhetic act: of course sense and reference (naming and referring) themselves are here ancillary acts performed in performing the rhetic act. Thus we may say 'I meant by "bank" . . .' and we say 'by "he" I was referring to. . .'. Can we perform a rhetic act without referring or without naming? In general it would seem that the answer is that we cannot, but there are puzzling cases. What is the reference in 'all triangles have three sides'? Correspondingly, it is clear that we can perform a phatic act which is not a rhetic act, though not conversely. Thus we may repeat someone else's remark or mumble over some sentence, or we may read a Latin sentence without knowing the meaning of the words.

The question when one pheme or one rheme is the *same* as another, whether in the 'type' or 'token' sense, and the question what is one single pheme or rheme, do not so much matter here. But, of course, it is important to remember that the same pheme, e.g., sentence, that is, tokens of the same type, may be used on different occasions of utterance with a different sense or reference, and so be a different rheme. When different phemes are used with the same sense and reference, we might speak of rhetically equivalent acts ('the same statement' in one sense) but not of the same rheme or rhetic acts (which are the same statement in another sense which involves using the same words).

The pheme is a unit of *language:* its typical fault is to be nonsense—meaningless. But the rheme is a unit of *speech;* its typical fault is to be vague or void or obscure, &c.

But though these matters are of much interest, they do not so far throw any light at all on our problem of the constative as opposed to the performative utterance. For example, it might be perfectly possible, with regard to an utterance, say 'It is going to charge', to make entirely plain 'what we were saying' in issuing the utterance, in all the senses so far distinguished, and yet not at all to have cleared up whether or not in issuing the utterance I was performing the act of *warning* or not. It may be perfectly clear what I mean by 'It is going to charge' or 'Shut the door', but not clear whether it is meant as a statement or warning, &c.

To perform a locutionary act is in general, we may say, also and *eo ipso* to perform an *illocutionary* act, as I propose to call it. Thus in performing a locutionary act we shall also be performing such an act as:

> asking or answering a question,
> giving some information or an assurance or a warning,
> announcing a verdict or an intention,
> pronouncing sentence,
> making an appointment or an appeal or a criticism,
> making an identification or giving a description,

and the numerous like. (I am not suggesting that this is a clearly defined class by any means.) There is nothing mysterious about our *eo ipso* here. The trouble rather is the number of different senses of so vague an expression as 'in what way are we using it'—this may refer even to a locutionary act, and further to perlocutionary acts to which we shall come in a minute. When we perform a locutionary act, we use speech: but in what way precisely are we using it on this occasion? For there are very numerous functions of or ways in which we use speech, and it makes a great difference to our act in some sense—sense (B)[2]—in which way and which *sense* we were on this occasion 'using' it. It makes a great difference whether we were advising, or merely suggesting, or actually ordering, whether we were strictly promising or only announcing a vague intention, and so forth. These issues penetrate a little but not without confusion into grammar (see above), but we constantly do debate them, in such terms as whether certain words (a certain locution) *had the force of* a question, or *ought to have been taken as* an estimate and so on.

I explained the performance of an act in this new and second sense as the performance of an 'illocutionary' act, i.e. performance of an act *in* saying something as opposed to performance of an act *of* saying something; I call the act performed an 'illocution' and shall refer to the doctrine of the different types of function of language here in question as the doctrine of 'illocutionary forces'.

It may be said that for too long philosophers have neglected this study, treating all problems as problems of locutionary usage', and indeed that the 'descriptive fallacy' mentioned in Lecture I commonly arises through mistaking a problem of the former kind for a problem of the latter kind. True, we are now getting out of this; for some years we have been realizing more and more clearly that the occasion of an utterance matters seriously, and that the words used are to some extent to be 'explained' by the 'context' in which they are designed to be or have actually been spoken in a linguistic interchange. Yet still perhaps we are too prone to give these explanations in terms of 'the meanings of words'. Admittedly we can use 'meaning' also with reference to illocutionary force—'He meant it as an order', &c. But I want to distinguish *force* and meaning in the sense in which meaning is equivalent to sense and reference, just as it has become essential to distinguish sense and reference.

Moreover, we have here an illustration of the different uses of the expression, 'uses of language', or 'use of a sentence', &c.—'use' is a hopelessly ambiguous or wide word, just as is the word 'meaning', which it has become customary to deride. But 'use', its supplanter, is not in much better case. We may entirely clear up the 'use of a sentence' on a particular occasion, in the sense of the locutionary act, without yet touching upon its use in the sense of an *illocutionary* act.

Before refining any further on this notion of the illocutionary act, let us contrast both the locution-

[2] See below, p. 836. [Au.]

ary *and* the illocutionary act with yet a third kind of act.

There is yet a further sense (C) in which to perform a locutionary act, and therein an illocutionary act, may also be to perform an act of another kind. Saying something will often, or even normally, produce certain consequential effects upon the feelings, thoughts, or actions of the audience, or of the speaker, or of other persons: and it may be done with the design, intention, or purpose of producing them; and we may then say, thinking of this, that the speaker has performed an act in the nomenclature of which reference is made either (C. *a*), only obliquely, or even (C. *b*), not at all, to the performance of the locutionary or illocutionary act. We shall call the performance of an act of this kind the performance of a 'perlocutionary' act, and the act performed, where suitable—essentially in cases falling under (C. *a*)—a 'perlocution'. Let us not yet define this idea any more carefully—of course it needs it—but simply give examples:

(E. 1)

Act (A) or Locution

He said to me 'Shoot her!' meaning by 'shoot' shoot and referring by 'her' to *her*.

Act (B) or Illocution

He urged (or advised, ordered, &c.) me to shoot her.

Act (C. *a*) or Perlocution

He persuaded me to shoot her.

Act (C. *b*)

He got me to (or made me, &c.) shoot her.

(E. 2)

Act (A) or Locution

He said to me, 'You can't do that'.

Act (B) or Illocution

He protested against my doing it.

Act (C. *a*) or Perlocution

He pulled me up, checked me.

Act (C. *b*)

He stopped me, he brought me to my senses, &c.

He annoyed me.

We can similarly distinguish the locutionary act 'he said that . . .' from the illocutionary act 'he argued that . . .' and the perlocutionary act 'he convinced me that . . .'

It will be seen that the 'consequential effects' here mentioned (see C. *a* and C. *b*) do not include a particular kind of consequential effects, those achieved, e.g., by way of committing the speaker as in promising, which come into the illocutionary act. Perhaps restrictions need making, as there is clearly a difference between what we feel to be the real production of real effects and what we regard as mere conventional consequences; we shall in any case return later to this.

We have here then roughly distinguished three kinds of acts—the locutionary, the illocutionary, and the perlocutionary. Let us make some general comments on these three classes, leaving them still fairly rough. The first three points will be about 'the use of language' again.

(1) Our interest in these lectures is essentially to fasten on the second, illocutionary act and contrast it with the other two. There is a constant tendency in philosophy to elide this in favour of one or other of the other two. Yet it is distinct from both. We have already seen how the expressions 'meaning' and 'use of sentence' can blur the distinction between locutionary and illocutionary acts. We now notice that to speak of the 'use' of language can likewise blur the distinction between the illocutionary and perlocutionary act—so we will distinguish them more carefully in a minute. Speaking of the 'use of "language" for arguing or warning' looks just like speaking of 'the use of "language" for persuading, rousing, alarming'; yet the former may, for rough contrast, be said to be *conventional,* in the sense that at least it could be made explicit by the performative formula; but the latter could not. Thus we can say 'I argue that' or 'I warn you that' but we cannot say 'I convince you that' or 'I alarm you that'. Further, we may entirely clear up whether someone was arguing or not without touching on the question whether he was convincing anyone or not.

(2) To take this farther, let us be quite clear that the expression 'use of language' can cover other matters even more diverse than the illocutionary and perlocutionary acts and obviously quite diverse from any with which we are here concerned. For example, we may speak of the 'use of language' *for* something, e.g. for joking; and we may use 'in' in a way different from the illocutionary 'in', as when

we say 'in saying "p" I was joking' or 'acting a part' or 'writing poetry'; or again we may speak of 'a poetical use of language' as distinct from 'the use of language in poetry'. These references to 'use of language' have nothing to do with the illocutionary act. For example, if I say 'Go and catch a falling star', it may be quite clear what both the meaning and the force of my utterance is, but still wholly unresolved which of these other kinds of things I may be doing. There are aetiolations, parasitic uses, etc., various 'not serious' and 'not full normal' uses. The normal conditions of reference may be suspended, or no attempt made at a standard perlocutionary act, no attempt to make you do anything, as Walt Whitman does not seriously incite the eagle of liberty to soar.

(3) Furthermore, there may be some things we 'do' in some connexion with saying something which do not seem to fall, intuitively at least, exactly into any of these roughly defined classes, or else seem to fall vaguely into more than one; but any way we do not at the outset feel so clear that they are as remote from our three acts as would be joking or writing poetry. For example, *insinuating*, as when we insinuate something in or by issuing some utterance, seems to involve some convention, as in the illocutionary act; but we cannot *say* 'I insinuate . . .', and it seems like implying to be a clever effect rather than a mere act. A further example is evincing emotion. We may evince emotion in or by issuing an utterance, as when we swear; but once again we have no use here for performative formulas and the other devices of illocutionary acts. We might say that we use swearing[3] *for* relieving our feelings. We must notice that the illocutionary act is a conventional act: an act done as conforming to a convention.

The next three points that arise do so importantly because our acts are *acts*.

(4) Acts of all our three kinds necessitate, since they are the performing of actions, allowance being made for the ills that all action is heir to. We must systematically be prepared to distinguish between 'the act of doing *x*'', i.e. achieving *x*, and 'the act of attempting to do *x*'.

In the case of illocutions we must be ready to draw the necessary distinction, not noticed by ordinary language except in exceptional cases, between

(*a*) the act of attempting or purporting (or affecting or professing or claiming or setting up or setting out) to perform a certain illocutionary act, and

(*b*) the act of successfully achieving or consummating or bringing off such an act.

This distinction is, or should be, a commonplace of the theory of our language about 'action' in general. But attention has been drawn earlier to its special importance in connexion with performatives: it is always possible, for example, to try to thank or inform somebody yet in different ways to fail, because he doesn't listen, or takes it as ironical, or wasn't responsible for whatever it was, and so on. This distinction will arise, as over any act, over locutionary acts too; but failures here will not be unhappinesses as there, but rather failures to get the words out, to express ourselves clearly, etc.

(5) Since our acts are actions, we must always remember the distinction between producing effects or consequences which are intended or unintended; and (i) when the speaker intends to produce an effect it may nevertheless not occur, and (ii) when he does not intend to produce it or intends not to produce it it may nevertheless occur. To cope with complication (i) we invoke as before the distinction between attempt and achievement; to cope with complication (ii) we invoke the normal linguistic devices of disclaiming (adverbs like 'unintentionally' and so on) which we hold ready for general use in all cases of doing actions.[4]

(6) Furthermore, we must, of course, allow that as actions they may be things that we do not exactly *do*, in the sense that we did them, say, under duress or in any other such way. Other ways besides in which we may not fully do the action are given in (2) above. We may, perhaps, add the cases given in (5) where we produce consequences by mistake, did not intend to do so.

(7) Finally we must meet the objection about our illocutionary and perlocutionary acts—namely that

[3]'Swearing' is ambiguous: 'I swear by Our Lady' *is* to swear by Our Lady; but 'Bloody' is not to swear by Our Lady. [Au.]

[4]This complication (ii), it may be pointed out, can of course also arise in the cases of both locutionary and illocutionary acts. I may say something or refer to something without meaning to, or commit myself unintentionally to a certain undertaking; for example, I may order someone to do something, when I did not intend to order him to do so. But it is in connexion with perlocution that it is most prominent, as is also the distinction between attempt and achievement. [Au.]

the notion of an act is unclear—by a general doctrine about action. We have the idea of an 'act' as a fixed physical thing that we do, as distinguished from conventions and as distinguished from consequences. But

(*a*) the illocutionary act and even the locutionary act too involve conventions: compare with them the act of doing obeisance. It is obeisance only because it is conventional and it is done only because it is conventional. Compare also the distinction between kicking a wall and kicking a goal;

(*b*) the perlocutionary act always includes some consequences, as when we say 'By doing *x* I was doing *y*': we do bring in a greater or less stretch of 'consequences' always, some of which may be 'unintentional'. There is no restriction to the minimum physical act at all. That we can import an arbitrarily long stretch of what might also be called the 'consequences' of our act into the nomenclature of the act itself is, or should be, a fundamental commonplace of the theory of our language about all 'action' in general. Thus if asked 'What did he do?', we may reply either 'He shot the donkey' or 'He fired a gun' or 'He pulled the trigger' or 'He moved his trigger finger', and all may be correct. So, to shorten the nursery story of the endeavours of the old woman to drive her pig home in time to get her old man's supper, we may in the last resort say that the cat drove or got the pig, or made the pig get, over the stile. If in such cases we *mention* both a B act (illocution) and a C act (perlocution) we shall say '*by* B-ing he C-ed' rather than '*in*-B-ing . . .' This is the reason for calling C a *per*locutionary act as distinct from an illocutionary act.

Next time we shall revert to the distinction between our three kinds of act, and to the expressions 'in' and 'by doing *x* I am doing *y*', with a view to getting the three classes and their members and non-members somewhat clearer. We shall see that just as the locutionary act embraces doing many things at once to be complete, so may the illocutionary and perlocutionary acts.

Hans-Georg Gadamer

b. 1900

HANS-GEORG GADAMER'S theory of interpretation begins with acknowledgment of the "hermeneutic circle" as set forth by the German theologian Friedrich Schleiermacher (1768–1834) and later by *Martin Heidegger* in *Being and Time.* This concept places interpretation in an apparently impossible situation, in which one must have an understanding of the whole of a text before one can grasp the meaning of the parts, while at the same time this understanding must be predicated on an understanding of the parts. Neither Heidegger nor Gadamer believes this puzzle to be impossible of solution. Rather, they regard it as the necessary condition of interpretation. The point that both make is that all acts of interpretation are embedded thoroughly in history, and no interpretation can escape its own "horizon" of understanding. A hermeneutic act is, therefore, a "conversation" (see *Heidegger*), a meeting of the text's historicity with that of the interpreter. This relation, which might be called in structuralist parlance "difference," is in the end what the interpretation produced amounts to. The interpreter's horizon is called a "fore-project" or "prejudice" but not in the sense we usually attribute to the latter term. Interpretation, because radically thrown into history, is inevitably a constant, never ending process, for the interpretive horizon is ever changing.

Clearly, Gadamer's view is opposed to the efforts of historicist thought to objectify history and discredit all "prejudice." To do so, for Gadamer, is itself to express the historicist prejudice. All prejudice cannot be reasoned away, for reason itself is *in* history and is not its own master. Efforts to find a ground for absolute and unchanging meaning in a text Gadamer regards as wrongheaded. Thus he is in disagreement with E. D. Hirsch's effort (*CTSP,* pp. 1176–94) to locate a ground for meaning in the scholarly reconstruction of authorial intention. Writing, though it seems to be a phenomenon secondary to speech, is not really that and involves an alienation from authorial intention. Nor can interpretation be grounded in a historical reconstruction of the contemporary addressee, as in some forms of reception theory (see *Jauss*). The problem here is partly where to draw the line between contemporary and noncontemporary. Indeed, is not the ideality of the text its openness to new relationships?

Gadamer has been criticized on the ground that his recourse to tradition in his idea of prejudice is reactionary, but his concept of interpretation as a process seems to counter this view to some extent. In any case, his position is that the understanding of a text always means a "present involvement with what is said." In a sense, Gadamer has adapted Heidegger's idea of "conversation" to the historical condition.

Gadamer's books translated into English are *Truth and Method* (1960, trans. 1975); *Philosophical Hermeneutics* (1967–72, trans. 1976), a collection of his essays from *Kleine Schriften* plus an essay on Heidegger which appeared elsewhere; *Dialogue and Dialectic* (1942–72, trans. 1980); and *Philosophical Apprenticeship* (1977, trans. 1985). See James S. Hans, "Hans-Georg Gadamer and Hermeneutic Phenomenology," *Philosophy Today* (Spring 1978), and David Couzens Hoy, *The Critical Circle: Literature and History in Contemporary Hermeneutics.*

FROM

TRUTH AND METHOD

1 THE ELEVATION OF THE HISTORICALITY OF UNDERSTANDING TO THE STATUS OF HERMENEUTICAL PRINCIPLE

(A) THE HERMENEUTIC CIRCLE AND THE PROBLEM OF PREJUDICES

(i) Heidegger's disclosure of the fore-structure of understanding

Heidegger went into the problems of historical hermeneutics and criticism only in order to develop from it, for the purposes of ontology, the fore-structure of understanding. Contrariwise, our question is how hermeneutics, once freed from the ontological obstructions of the scientific concept of objectivity, can do justice to the historicality of understanding. The way in which hermeneutics has traditionally understood itself is based on its character as art or technique.[1] This is true even of Dilthey's[2] extension of hermeneutics to become an organon of the human sciences. It may be asked whether there is such a thing as this art or technique of understanding—we shall come back to the point. But at any rate we may enquire into the consequences that Heidegger's fundamental derivation of the circular structure of understanding from the temporality of There-being has for the hermeneutics of the human sciences. These consequences do not need to be such that a theory is applied to practice and the latter now be performed differently, ie in a way that is technically correct. They could also consist in a correction (and purification of inadequate manners) of the way in which constantly exercised understanding understands itself—a procedure that would benefit the art of understanding at most only indirectly.

Hence we shall examine once more Heidegger's description of the hermeneutical circle in order to use, for our own purpose, the new fundamental significance acquired here by the circular structure. Heidegger writes: 'It is not to be reduced to the level of a vicious circle, or even of a circle which is merely tolerated. In the circle is hidden a positive possibility of the most primordial kind of knowing. To be sure, we genuinely take hold of this possibility only when, in our interpretation, we have understood that our first, last and constant task is never to allow our fore-having, fore-sight, and fore-conception to be presented to us by fancies and popular conceptions, but rather to make the scientific theme secure by working out these fore-structures in terms of the things themselves'.[3]

What Heidegger works out here is not primarily a demand on the practice of understanding, but is a description of the way in which interpretation through understanding is achieved. The point of Heidegger's hermeneutical thinking is not so much to prove that there is a circle as to show that this

This selection from TRUTH AND METHOD, originally published as *Wahrheit und Methode* in Germany in 1960, is reprinted here from *Truth and Method,* New York: The Seabury Press, 1975, by permission of the Continuum Publishing Corporation, publishers, copyright 1975.

[1] Cf. Schleiermacher's *Hermeneutik* (ed. H. Kimmerle in *Abhandlungen der Heidelberger Akademie,* 1959, 2nd *Abhandlung*), which is explicitly committed to the old ideal of technique (p. 127, note: 'I . . . hate it when a theory does not go beyond nature and the bases of art, whose object it is.') [Au.] Friedrich Schleiermacher (1768–1834), German theologian. [Eds.]

[2] Wilhelm Dilthey (1833–1911), German philosopher. [Eds.]

[3] *Being and Time,* trans. J. Macquarrie and Edward Robinson (Oxford: Basil Blackwell, 1967), p. 195. [Eds.]

circle possesses an ontologically positive significance. The description as such will be obvious to every interpreter who knows what he is about.[4] All correct interpretation must be on guard against arbitrary fancies and the limitations imposed by imperceptible habits of thought and direct its gaze 'on the things themselves' (which, in the case of the literary critic, are meaningful texts, which themselves are again concerned with objects). It is clear that to let the object take over in this way is not a matter for the interpreter of a single decision, but is 'the first, last and constant task'. For it is necessary to keep one's gaze fixed on the thing throughout all the distractions that the interpreter will constantly experience in the process and which originate in himself. A person who is trying to understand a text is always performing an act of projecting. He projects before himself a meaning for the text as a whole as soon as some initial meaning emerges in the text. Again, the latter emerges only because he is reading the text with particular expectations in regard to a certain meaning. The working out of this fore-project, which is constantly revised in terms of what emerges as he penetrates into the meaning, is understanding what is there.

This description is, of course, a rough abbreviation of the whole. The process that Heidegger describes is that every revision of the fore-project is capable of projecting before itself a new project of meaning, that rival projects can emerge side by side until it becomes clearer what the unity of meaning is, that interpretation begins with fore-conceptions that are replaced by more suitable ones. This constant process of new projection is the movement of understanding and interpretation. A person who is trying to understand is exposed to distraction from fore-meanings that are not borne out by the things themselves. The working-out of appropriate projects, anticipatory in nature, to be confirmed 'by the things' themselves, is the constant task of understanding. The only 'objectivity' here is the confirmation of a fore-meaning in its being worked out. The only thing that characterises the arbitrariness of inappropriate fore-meanings is that they come to nothing in the working-out. But understanding achieves its full potentiality only when the fore-meanings that it uses are not arbitrary. Thus it is quite right for the interpreter not to approach the text directly, relying solely on the fore-meaning at once available to him, but rather to examine explicitly the legitimacy, ie the origin and validity, of the fore-meanings present within him.

This fundamental requirement must be seen as the radicalisation of a procedure that in fact we exercise whenever we understand anything. Every text presents the task of not simply employing unexamined our own linguistic usage—or in the case of a foreign language the usage that we are familiar with from writers or from daily intercourse. We regard our task as rather that of deriving our understanding of the text from the linguistic usage of the time of the author. The question is, of course, to what extent this general requirement can be fulfilled. In the field of semantics, in particular, we are confronted with the problem of the unconscious nature of our own use of language. How do we discover that there is a difference between our own customary usage and that of the text?

I think we must say that it is generally the experience of being pulled up short by the text. Either it does not yield any meaning or its meaning is not compatible with what we had expected. It is this that makes us take account of possible difference in usage. It is a general presupposition that can be questioned only in particular cases that someone who speaks the same language as I do uses the words in the sense familiar to me. The same thing is true in the case of a foreign language, ie that we all think we have a normal knowledge of it and assume this normal usage when we are reading a text.

What is true of the fore-meaning of usage, however, is equally true of the fore-meanings with regard to content with which we read texts, and which make up our fore-understanding. Here one must likewise ask how one can possibly escape from the circularity of one's fore-understanding. Certainly it is not a general presumption that what is said to us in a text adapts flawlessly to one's own ideas and expectations. On the contrary, what another person tells me, whether in conversation, letter, book or whatever, is generally thought automatically to be his own and not my opinion; and it

[4] Cf. E. Staiger's description, which is in accord with that of Heidegger, in *Die Kunst der Interpretation,* p. 11 ff. I do not, however, agree that the work of a literary critic begins only 'when we are in the situation of a contemporary reader'. This is something we never are, and yet we are capable of understanding, although we can never achieve a definite 'personal or temporal identity' with, the author. [Au.]

is this that I am to take note of without necessarily having to share it. But this presupposition is not something that makes understanding easier, but harder, in that the fore-meanings that determine my own understanding can go entirely unnoticed. If they give rise to misunderstandings, how can misunderstandings of a text be recognised at all if there is nothing else to contradict? How can a text be protected from misunderstanding from the start?

If we examine the situation more closely, however, we find that meanings cannot be understood in an arbitrary way. Just as we cannot continually misunderstand the use of a word without its affecting the meaning of the whole, so we cannot hold blindly to our own fore-meaning of the thing if we would understand the meaning of another. Of course this does not mean that when we listen to someone or read a book we must forget all our fore-meanings concerning the content, and all our own ideas. All that is asked is that we remain open to the meaning of the other person or of the text. But this openness always includes our placing the other meaning in a relation with the whole of our own meanings or ourselves in a relation to it. Now it is the case that meanings represent a fluid variety of possibilities (when compared with the agreement presented by a language and a vocabulary), but it is still not the case that within this variety of what can be thought, ie of what a reader can find meaningful and hence expect to find, everything is possible, and if a person fails to hear what the other person is really saying, he will not be able to place correctly what he has misunderstood within the range of his own various expectations of meaning. Thus there is a criterion here also. The hermeneutical task becomes automatically a questioning of things and is always in part determined by this. This places hermeneutical work on a firm basis. If a person is trying to understand something, he will not be able to rely from the start on his own chance previous ideas, missing as logically and stubbornly as possible the actual meaning of the text until the latter becomes so persistently audible that it breaks through the imagined understanding of it. Rather, a person trying to understand a text is prepared for it to tell him something. That is why a hermeneutically trained mind must be, from the start, sensitive to the text's quality of newness. But this kind of sensitivity involves neither 'neutrality' in the matter of the object nor the extinction of one's self, but the conscious assimilation of one's own fore-meanings and prejudices. The important thing is to be aware of one's own bias, so that the text may present itself in all its newness and thus be able to assert its own truth against one's own fore-meanings.

When Heidegger showed that what we call the 'reading of what is there' is the fore-structure of understanding, this was, phenomenologically, completely correct. He also showed by an example the task that arises from this. In *Being and Time* he gave a concrete example, in the question of being, of the general statement that was, for him, a hermeneutical problem.[5] In order to explain the hermeneutical situation of the question of being in regard to fore-having, fore-sight and fore-conception, he critically applied his question, directed at metaphysics, to important turning-points in the history of metaphysics. Here he was actually doing simply what the historical, hermeneutical consciousness requires in every case. Methodologically conscious understanding will be concerned not merely to form anticipatory ideas, but to make them conscious, so as to check them and thus acquire right understanding from the things themselves. This is what Heidegger means when he talks about 'securing' our scientific theme by deriving our fore-having, fore-sight and fore-conceptions from the things themselves.

It is not, then, at all a case of safeguarding ourselves against the tradition that speaks out of the text but, on the contrary, to keep everything away that could hinder us in understanding it in terms of the thing. It is the tyranny of hidden prejudices that makes us deaf to the language that speaks to us in tradition. Heidegger's demonstration that the concept of consciousness in Descartes and of spirit in Hegel[6] is still influenced by Greek substance-ontology, which sees being in terms of what is present and actual, undoubtedly goes beyond the self-understanding of modern metaphysics, yet not in an arbitrary, wilful way, but on the basis of a fore-having that in fact makes this tradition intelligible by revealing the ontological premises of the concept of subjectivity. On the other hand, Heidegger discovers in Kant's critique of 'dogmatic' metaphysics the idea of a metaphysics of the finite which is a

[5] *Being and Time*, pp. 359ff. [Au.]

[6] René Descartes (1596–1650), French philosopher; G. W. F. Hegel (1770–1831), German philosopher (see *CTSP*, pp. 517–31). [Eds.]

challenge to his own ontological scheme. Thus he 'secures' the scientific theme by framing it within the understanding of tradition and so putting it, in a sense, at risk. This is the concrete form of the historical consciousness that is involved in understanding.

This recognition that all understanding inevitably involves some prejudice gives the hermeneutical problem its real thrust. By the light of this insight it appears that historicism, despite its critique of rationalism and of natural law philosophy, is based on the modern enlightenment and unknowingly shares its prejudices. And there is one prejudice of the enlightenment that is essential to it: the fundamental prejudice of the enlightenment is the prejudice against prejudice itself, which deprives tradition of its power.

Historical analysis shows that it is not until the enlightenment that the concept of prejudice acquires the negative aspect we are familiar with. Actually 'prejudice' means a judgment that is given before all the elements that determine a situation have been finally examined. In German legal terminology a 'prejudice' is a provisional legal verdict before the final verdict is reached. For someone involved in a legal dispute, this kind of judgment against him affects his chances adversely. Accordingly, the French préjudice, as well as the Latin praejudicium, means simply 'adverse effect', 'disadvantage', 'harm'. But this negative sense is only a consecutive one. The negative consequence depends precisely on the positive validity, the value of the provisional decision as a prejudgment, which is that of any precedent.

Thus 'prejudice' certainly does not mean a false judgment, but it is part of the idea that it can have a positive and a negative value. This is due clearly to the influence of the Latin praejudicium. There are such things as préjugés légitimes. This seems a long way from our current use of the word. The German Vorurteil, like English 'prejudice' and even more than the French préjugé, seems to have become limited in its meaning, through the enlightenment and its critique of religion, and have the sense simply of an 'unfounded judgment'.[7] It is only its having a basis, a methodological justification (and not the fact that it may be actually correct) that gives a judgment its dignity. The lack of such a basis does not mean, for the enlightenment, that there might be other kinds of certainty, but rather that the judgment does not have any foundation in the facts themselves, ie that it is 'unfounded'. This is a conclusion only in the spirit of rationalism. It is the reason for the discrediting of prejudices and the claim by scientific knowledge completely to exclude them.

Modern science, in adopting this principle, is following the rule of Cartesian doubt of accepting nothing as certain which can in any way be doubted, and the idea of the method that adheres to this requirement. In our introductory observations we have already pointed out how difficult it is to harmonise the historical knowledge that helps to shape our historical consciousness with this ideal and how difficult it is, for that reason, for the modern concept of method to grasp its true nature. This is the place to turn these negative statements into positive ones. The concept of the 'prejudice' is where we can make a beginning.

(ii) The discrediting of prejudice by the enlightenment

If we pursue the view that the enlightenment developed in regard to prejudices we find it makes the following fundamental division: a distinction must be made between the prejudice due to human authority and that due to over-hastiness.[8] The basis of this distinction is the origin of prejudices in regard to the persons who have them. It is either the respect in which we hold others and their authority, that leads us into error, or else it is an over-hastiness in ourselves. That authority is a source of prejudices accords with the well-known principle of the enlightenment that Kant formulated: Have the courage to make use of your own understanding.[9] Although this distinction is certainly not limited to the role that prejudices play in the understanding of texts, its chief application is still in the sphere of hermeneutics. For the critique of the enlightenment is directed primarily against the religious tradition

[7] Cf. Leo Strauss, *Die Religionskritik Spinozas,* p. 163: 'The word "prejudice" is the most suitable expression for the great aim of the enlightenment, the desire for free, untrammeled verification; the *Vorurteil* is the unambiguous polemical correlate of the very ambiguous word "freedom"'. [Au.]

[8] *Praeiudicium auctoritatis et precipitantiae,* which we find as early as Christian Thomasius's *Lectiones de praeiudiciis* (1689/90) and his *Einleitung der Vernunftlehre,* ch 13, §§ 39/40. Cf the article in Walch's *Philosophisches Lexikon* (1726), p. 2794ff. [Au.]

[9] At the beginning of his essay, 'Beantwortung der Frage: Was ist Aufklärung?' (1784). [Au.]

of christianity, ie the bible. By treating the latter as an historical document, biblical criticism endangers its own dogmatic claims. This is the real radicality of the modern enlightenment as against all other movements of enlightenment: it must assert itself against the bible and its dogmatic interpretation.[10] It is, therefore, particularly concerned with the hermeneutical problem. It desires to understand tradition correctly, ie reasonably and without prejudice. But there is a special difficulty about this, in that the sheer fact of something being written down confers on it an authority of particular weight. It is not altogether easy to realise that what is written down can be untrue. The written word has the tangible quality of something that can be demonstrated and is like a proof. It needs a special critical effort to free oneself from the prejudice in favour of what is written down and to distinguish here also, as with all oral assertions, between opinion and truth.[11]

It is the general tendency of the enlightenment not to accept any authority and to decide everything before the judgment seat of reason. Thus the written tradition of scripture, like any other historical document, cannot claim any absolute validity, but the possible truth of the tradition depends on the credibility that is assigned to it by reason. It is not tradition, but reason that constitutes the ultimate source of all authority. What is written down is not necessarily true. We may have superior knowledge: this is the maxim with which the modern enlightenment approaches tradition and which ultimately leads it to undertake historical research.[12] It makes the tradition as much an object of criticism as do the natural sciences the evidence of the senses. This does not necessarily mean that the 'prejudice against prejudices' was everywhere taken to the extreme consequences of free thinking and atheism, as in England and France. On the contrary, the German enlightenment recognised the 'true prejudices' of the christian religion. Since the human intellect is too weak to manage without prejudices it is at least fortunate to have been educated with true prejudices.

It would be of value to investigate to what extent this kind of modification and moderation of the enlightenment[13] prepared the way for the rise of the romantic movement in Germany, as undoubtedly did the critique of the enlightenment and the revolution by Edmund Burke.[14] But none of this alters the fundamental facts. True prejudices must still finally be justified by rational knowledge, even though the task may never be able to be fully completed.

Thus the criteria of the modern enlightenment still determine the self-understanding of historicism. This does not happen directly, but in a curious refraction caused by romanticism. This can be seen with particular clarity in the fundamental schema of the philosophy of history that romanticism shares with the enlightenment and that precisely the romantic reaction to the enlightenment made into an unshakeable premise: the schema of the conquest of mythos by logos. It is the presupposition of the progressive retreat of magic in the world that gives this schema its validity. It is supposed to represent the progressive law of the history of the mind, and precisely because romanticism has a negative attitude to this development, it takes over the schema itself as an obvious truth. It shares the presupposition of the enlightenment and only reverses the evaluation of it, seeking to establish the validity of what is old, simply because it is old: the 'gothic' middle ages, the christian European community of states, the feudal structure of society, but also the simplicity of peasant life and closeness to nature.

In contrast to the enlightenment's belief in perfection, which thinks in terms of the freedom from 'superstition' and the prejudices of the past, we now find that olden times, the world of myth, unreflective life, not yet analysed away by consciousness, in a 'society close to nature', the world of christian

[10] The enlightenment of the classical world, the fruit of which was Greek philosophy and its culmination in sophism, was quite different in nature and hence permitted a thinker like Plato to use philosophical myths to convey the religious tradition and the dialectical method of philosophising. Cf Erich Frank, *Philosophische Erkenntnis und religiöse Wahrheit*, p 31ff, and my review of it in the *Theologische Rundschau* 1950 (pp. 260–266). Cf also Gerhard Krüger, *Einsicht und Leidenschaft*, 2nd ed 1951. [Au.]

[11] A good example of this is the length of time it has taken for the authority of the historical writing of antiquity to be destroyed in historical studies and how slowly the study of archives and the research into sources have established themselves (cf R. G. Collingwood, *Autobiography*, Oxford, 1939, ch 11, where he more or less draws a parallel between the turning to the study of sources and the Baconian revolution in the study of nature). [Au.]

[12] Cf what we said about Spinoza's theological-political treatise. [Au.] See *Truth and Method*, p. 159ff. [Eds.]

[13] As we find, for example, in G. F. Meier's *Beiträge zu der Lehre von den Vorurteilen des menschlichen Geschlechts*, 1766. [Au.]

[14] Edmund Burke (1729–97), British writer and statesman (see *CTSP*, pp. 302–12). [Eds.]

chivalry, all these acquire a romantic magic, even a priority of truth.[15] The reversal of the enlightenment's presupposition results in the paradoxical tendency to restoration, ie the tendency to reconstruct the old because it is old, the conscious return to the unconscious, culminating in the recognition of the superior wisdom of the primaeval age of myth. But the romantic reversal of this criterion of the enlightenment actually perpetuates the abstract contrast between myth and reason. All criticism of the enlightenment now proceeds via this romantic mirror image of the enlightenment. Belief in the perfectibility of reason suddenly changes into the perfection of the 'mythical' consciousness and finds itself reflected in a paradisic primal state before the 'fall' of thought.

In fact the presupposition of a mysterious darkness in which there was a mythical collective consciousness that preceded all thought is just as dogmatic and abstract as that of a state of perfection achieved by a total enlightenment or that of absolute knowledge. Primaeval wisdom is only the counter image of 'primaeval stupidity'. All mythical consciousness is still knowledge, and if it knows about divine powers, then it has progressed beyond mere trembling before power (if this is to be regarded as the primaeval state), but also beyond a collective life contained in magic rituals (as we find in the early Orient). It knows about itself, and in this knowledge it is no longer simply 'outside itself'.[16]

There is the related point that even the contrast between genuine mythical thinking and pseudo-mythical poetic thinking is a romantic illusion which is based on a prejudice of the enlightenment: namely, that the poetic act, because it is a creation of the free imagination, is no longer in any way bound within the religious quality of the myth. It is the old quarrel between the poets and the philosophers in the modern garb appropriate to the age of belief in science. It is now said, not that poets tell lies, but that they are incapable of saying anything true, since they have an aesthetic effect only and merely seek to rouse through their imaginative creations the imagination and the emotions of their hearers or readers.

The concept of the 'society close to nature' is probably another case of a romantic mirror-image, whose origin ought to be investigated. In Karl Marx it appears as a kind of relic of natural law that limits the validity of his socio-economic theory of the class struggle.[17] Does the idea go back to Rousseau's description of society before the division of labour and the introduction of property?[18] At any rate, Plato has already demonstrated the illusory nature of this political theory in the ironical account he gives of a 'state of nature' in the third book of the *Republic*.[19]

These romantic revaluations give rise to the attitude of the historical science of the nineteenth century. It no longer measures the past by the yardsticks of the present, as if they represented an absolute, but it ascribes their own value to past ages and can even acknowledge their superiority in one or the other respect. The great achievements of romanticism—the revival of the past, the discovery of the voices of the peoples in their songs, the collecting of fairy-tales and legends, the cultivation of ancient customs, the discovery of the world views implicit in languages, the study of the 'religion and wisdom of India'—have all motivated the historical research that has slowly, step by step, transformed the intuitive revival into historical knowledge proper. The fact that it was romanticism that gave birth to the historical school confirms that the romantic retrieval of origins is itself based on the enlightenment. The historical science of the nineteenth century is its proudest fruit and sees itself precisely as the fulfilment of the enlightenment, as the last step in the liberation of the mind from the trammels of dogma, the step to the objective knowledge of the historical world, which stands as an equal besides the knowledge of nature achieved by modern science.

The fact that the restorative tendency of roman-

[15] I have analysed an example of this process in a little study on Immermann's 'Chiliastische Sonette' (*Die Neue Rundschau*, 1949). [Au.]

[16] Horkheimer and Adorno seem to me right in their analysis of the 'dialectic of the enlightenment' (although I must regard the application of sociological concepts such as 'bourgeois' to Odysseus as a failure of historical reflection, if not, indeed, a confusion of Homer with Johann Heinrich Voss [author of the standard German translation of Homer], who had already been criticised by Goethe). [Au.]

[17] Cf the reflections on this important question by G. von Lukács in his *History and Class Consciousness*, London 1969 (orig 1923). [Au.]

[18] Rousseau, *Discours sur l'origine et les fondements de l'inégalité parmi les hommes*. [Au.]

[19] Cf the present author's *Plato und die Dichter*, p. 12f. [Au.]

ticism was able to combine with the fundamental concern of the enlightenment to constitute the unity of the historical sciences simply indicates that it is the same break with the continuity of meaning in tradition that lies behind both. If it is an established fact for the enlightenment that all tradition that reason shows to be impossible, ie nonsense, can only be understood historically, ie by going back to the past's way of looking at things, then the historical consciousness that emerges in romanticism involves a radicalisation of the enlightenment. For the exceptional case of nonsensical tradition has become the general rule for historical consciousness. Meaning that is generally accessible through reason is so little believed that the whole of the past, even, ultimately, all the thinking of one's contemporaries, is seen only 'historically'. Thus the romantic critique of the enlightenment ends itself in enlightenment, in that it evolves as historical science and draws everything into the orbit of historicism. The basic discrediting of all prejudices, which unites the experiential emphasis of the new natural sciences with the enlightenment, becomes, in the historical enlightenment, universal and radical.

This is the point at which the attempt to arrive at an historical hermeneutics has to start its critique. The overcoming of all prejudices, this global demand of the enlightenment, will prove to be itself a prejudice, the removal of which opens the way to an appropriate understanding of our finitude, which dominates not only our humanity, but also our historical consciousness.

Does the fact that one is set within various traditions means really and primarily that one is subject to prejudices and limited in one's freedom? Is not, rather, all human existence, even the freest, limited and qualified in various ways? If this is true, then the idea of an absolute reason is impossible for historical humanity. Reason exists for us only in concrete, historical terms, ie it is not its own master, but remains constantly dependent on the given circumstances in which it operates. This is true not only in the sense in which Kant limited the claims of rationalism, under the influence of the sceptical critique of Hume,[20] to the a priori element in the knowledge of nature; it is still truer of historical consciousness and the possibility of historical knowledge. For that man is concerned here with himself and his own creations (Vico)[21] is only an apparent solution of the problem set by historical knowledge. Man is alien to himself and his historical fate in a quite different way from that in which nature, that knows nothing of him, is alien to him.

The epistemological question must be asked here in a fundamentally different way. We have shown above that Dilthey probably saw this, but he was not able to overcome the influence over him of traditional epistemology. His starting-point, the awareness of 'experience', was not able to build the bridge to the historical realities, because the great historical realities of society and state always have a predeterminant influence on any 'experience'. Self-reflection and autobiography—Dilthey's starting-points—are not primary and are not an adequate basis for the hermeneutical problem, because through them history is made private once more. In fact history does not belong to us, but we belong to it. Long before we understand ourselves through the process of self-examination, we understand ourselves in a self-evident way in the family, society and state in which we live. The focus of subjectivity is a distorting mirror. The self-awareness of the individual is only a flickering in the closed circuits of historical life. That is why the prejudices of the individual, far more than his judgments, constitute the historical reality of his being.

. . . .

Since the romantic period we can no longer hold the view that, should there be no direct understanding, interpretative ideas are drawn on, as needed, out of a linguistic store-room in which they are lying ready. Rather, language is the universal medium in which understanding itself is realised. The mode of realisation of understanding is interpretation. This statement does not mean that there is no special problem of expression. The difference between the language of a text and the language of the interpreter, or the gulf that separates the translator from the original, is not a merely secondary question. On the contrary, the fact is that the problems of linguistic expression are already problems of understanding. All understanding is interpretation, and all interpretation takes place in the medium of

[20] Immanuel Kant (1724–1804), German philosopher (see *CTSP*, pp. 377–99); David Hume (1711–76), English philosopher (see *CTSP*, pp. 313–23). [Eds.]

[21] Giovanni Battista Vico (1668–1744), Italian philosopher (see *CTSP*, pp. 293–301). [Eds.]

a language which would allow the object to come into words and yet is at the same time the interpreter's own language.

Thus the hermeneutical phenomenon proves to be a special case of the general relationship between thinking and speaking, the mysterious intimacy of which is bound up with the way in which speech is contained, in a hidden way, in thinking. Interpretation, like conversation, is a closed circle within the dialectic of question and answer. It is a genuine historical life-situation that takes place in the medium of language and that, also in the case of the interpretation of texts, we can call a conversation. The linguistic quality of understanding is the concretion of effective-historical consciousness.

The relation between language and understanding is seen primarily in the fact that it is the nature of tradition to exist in the medium of language, so that the preferred object of interpretation is a linguistic one.

(A) Language as Determination of the Hermeneutic Object

The fact that tradition is linguistic in character has hermeneutical consequences. The understanding of linguistic tradition retains special priority over all other tradition. Linguistic tradition may have less physical immediacy than monuments of plastic art. Its lack of immediacy, however, is not a defect, but this apparent lack, in the abstract alienness of all 'texts', expresses the fact that all language belongs in a unique way to the process of understanding. Linguistic tradition is tradition in the literal sense of the word, ie something handed down. It is not just something that has been left over, to be investigated and interpreted as a remnant of the past. What has come down to us by the way of linguistic tradition is not left over, but given to us, told us—whether in the form of direct repetition, of which myth, legend and custom are examples, or in the form of written tradition, the signs of which are immediately clear to every reader who is able to read them.

The full hermeneutical significance of the fact that tradition is linguistic in nature is clearly revealed when the tradition is a written one. In writing, language is detached from its full realisation. In the form of writing all tradition is simultaneous with any present time. Moreover, it involves a unique coexistence of past and present, insofar as present consciousness has the possibility of a free access to all that is handed down in writing. No longer dependent on repetition, which links past knowledge with the present, . . . in its direct acquaintance with literary tradition, understanding consciousness has a genuine opportunity to widen its horizon and thus enrich its world by a whole new and deeper dimension. The appropriation of literary tradition is even more valuable than the experience given by the adventure of travel and exposure to the world of a foreign language. The reader who studies a foreign language and literature has, at every moment, the possibility of free movement back to himself and thus is at once both here and there.

A written tradition is not a fragment of a past world, but has always raised itself beyond this into the sphere of the meaning that it expresses. It is the ideality of the word, which raises linguistic objects beyond the finiteness and transience of other remnants of past existence. It is not this document, as coming from the past, that is the bearer of tradition, but the continuity of memory. Through memory tradition becomes part of our own world, and so what it communicates can be directly expressed. Where we have a written tradition, we are not just told an individual thing, but a past humanity itself becomes present to us, in its general relation to the world. That is why our understanding remains curiously unsure and fragmentary when we have no written tradition of a culture, but only dumb monuments, and we do not call this information about the past 'history'. Texts, on the other hand, always express a whole. Meaningless strokes which seem strange and incomprehensible prove suddenly intelligible in every detail when they can be interpreted as writing—so much so that even the arbitrariness of a faulty tradition can be corrected if the context as a whole is understood.

Thus written texts present the real hermeneutical task. Writing involves self-alienation. Its overcoming, the reading of the text, is thus the highest task of understanding. Even the pure signs of an inscription can be seen properly and articulated correctly only if the text can be transformed back into language. This transformation, however, always establishes, as we have said, a relationship to what is meant, to the object that is being spoken about. Here the process of understanding moves entirely in the sphere of a meaning mediated by the linguistic tradition. Thus the hermeneutical task with an inscription starts only after it has been deciphered. Only in an extended sense do non-literary monuments present a hermeneutical task, for they cannot be understood of themselves. What they mean is a question of their interpretation, not of the deciphering and understanding of what they say.

In writing, language gains its true intellectual quality, for when confronted with a written tradition understanding consciousness acquires its full sovereignty. Its being does not depend on anything. Thus reading consciousness is in potential possession of its history. It is not for nothing that with the emergence of a literary culture the idea of 'philology', 'love of speech', was transferred entirely to the all-embracing art of reading, losing its original connection with the cultivation of speech and argument. A reading consciousness is necessarily historical and communicates justification if, with Hegel, one says that history begins with emergence of a will to hand things down, to make memory last.[22] Writing is not merely chance or extra addition that qualitatively changes nothing in the development of oral tradition. Certainly, there can be a will to make things continue, a will to permanency without writing. But only a written tradition can detach itself from the mere continuance of fragments left over from the life of the past, remnants from which it is possible to reconstruct life.

From the start, the tradition of inscriptions does not share in the free form of tradition that we call literature, inasmuch as it depends on the existence of the remains, whether of stone or whatever material. But it is true of everything that has come down to us that here a will to permanence has created the unique forms of continuance that we call literature. It presents us not only with a stock of memorials and signs. Literature, rather, has acquired its own simultaneity with every present. To understand it does not mean primarily to reason one's way back into the past, but to have a present involvement in what is said. It is not really about a relationship between persons, between the reader and the author (who is perhaps quite unknown), but about sharing in the communication that the text gives us. This meaning of what is said is, when we understand it, quite independent of whether we can gain from the tradition a picture of the author and of whether or not the historical interpretation of the tradition as a literary source is our concern.

Let us here recall that the task of hermeneutics was originally and chiefly the understanding of texts. Schleiermacher was the first to see that the hermeneutical problem was not raised by written words alone, but that oral utterance also presented—and perhaps in its fullest form—the problem of understanding. We have outlined above[23] how the psychological dimension that he gave to hermeneutics blocked its historical one. In actual fact, writing is central to the hermeneutical phenomenon, insofar as its detachment both from the writer or author and from a specifically addressed recipient or reader has given it a life of its own. What is fixed in writing has raised itself publicly into a sphere of meaning in which everyone who can read has an equal share.

Certainly, in relation to language, writing seems a secondary phenomenon. The sign language of writing refers back to the actual language of speech. But that language is capable of being written is by no means incidental to its nature. Rather, this capacity of being written down is based on the fact that speech itself shares in the pure ideality of the meaning that communicates itself in it. In writing, this meaning of what is spoken exists purely for itself, completely detached from all emotional elements of expression and communication. A text is not to be understood as an expression of life, but in what it says. Writing is the abstract ideality of language. Hence the meaning of something written is fundamentally identifiable and reproducible. What is identical in the reproduction is only that which was formulated. This indicates that 'reproduction' cannot be meant here in its strict sense. It does not mean referring back to some original source in which something is said or written. The understanding of something written is not a reproduction of something that is past, but the sharing of a present meaning.

Writing has the methodological advantage that it presents the hermeneutical problem in all its purity, detached from everything psychological. What is, however, in our eyes and for our purpose a methodological advantage is at the same time the expression of a specific weakness that is characteristic of writing even more than of language. The task of

[22] Hegel, *Die Vernunft in der Geschichte,* p. 145. [Au.]

[23] Pp. 163ff. and 264ff. in *Truth and Method.* [Au.]

understanding is seen with particular clarity when we recognise this weakness of all writing. We need only to think again of what Plato said, namely that the specific weakness of writing was that no one could come to the aid of the written word if it falls victim to misunderstanding, intentional or unintentional.[24]

Plato saw in the helplessness of the written word a more serious weakness than the weakness of speech (to astheneston ogon) and when he calls on dialectic to come to the aid of this weakness of speech, while declaring the condition of the written word to be beyond hope, this is obviously an ironic exaggeration with which to conceal his own writing and his own art. In fact, writing and speech are in the same plight. As in speech there is an art of appearances and an art of true thought—sophistry and dialectic—so in writing there is such a dual art: mere sophistry and true dialectic. There is, then, an art of writing that comes to the aid of thought and it is to this that the art of understanding—which affords the same help to what is written—is allied.

All writing is, as we have said, a kind of alienated speech, and its signs need to be transformed back into speech and meaning. Because the meaning has undergone a kind of self-alienation through being written down, this transformation back is the real hermeneutical task. The meaning of what has been said is to be stated anew, simply on the basis of the words passed on by means of the written signs. In contrast to the spoken word there is no other aid in the interpretation of the written word. Thus the important thing here is, in a special sense, the 'art' of writing.[25] The spoken word interprets itself to an astonishing degree, by the way of speaking, the tone of voice, the tempo etc, but also by the circumstances in which it is spoken.[26]

But there is also such a thing as writing that, as it were, reads itself. A remarkable debate on the spirit and the letter in philosophy between two great German philosophical writers, Schiller and Fichte,[27] has this fact as its starting-point. It is interesting that the dispute cannot be resolved with the aesthetic criteria used by the two men. Fundamentally they are not concerned with a question of the aesthetics of good style, but with a hermeneutical question. The 'art' of writing in such a way that the thoughts of the reader are stimulated and held in productive movement has little to do with the conventional rhetorical or aesthetic devices. Rather, it consists entirely in one's being led to think the material through. The 'art' of writing does not seek here to be understood and evaluated as such. The art of writing, like the art of speaking, is not an end in itself and therefore not the fundamental object of hermeneutical effort. The understanding is entirely taken up with what is being written about. Hence unclear thinking and 'bad' writing are not, for the task of understanding, exemplary cases for the art of hermeneutics to show itself in its full glory but, on the contrary, limiting cases which undermine the basic presupposition of all hermeneutical success, namely the clear unambiguity of the intended meaning.

All writing claims that it can be awakened into spoken language, and this claim to autonomy of meaning goes so far that even an authentic reading, eg the reading of a poem by the poet, becomes questionable if the direction of our listening takes us away from what our understanding should really be concerned with. Because the important thing is the communication of the true meaning of a text, its interpretation is already subject to an objective norm. This is the requirement that the Platonic dialectic makes when it seeks to bring out the logos as such and in doing so often leaves behind the actual partner in the conversation. In fact, the particular weakness of writing, its greater helplessness when compared with speech, has another side to it, in that it demonstrates with greater clarity the dialectical task of understanding. As in conversation, understanding must here seek to strengthen the meaning of what is said. What is stated in the text must be detached from all contingent factors and grasped in its full ideality, in which alone it has validity. Thus, precisely because it entirely detaches the sense of what is said from the person saying it, the written

[24] Plato, *Seventh Letter* 341c, 344c, and *Phaedrus*, 275. [Au.]

[25] This is the reason for the enormous difference that exists between what is spoken and what is written, between the style of spoken material and the far higher demands of style that a literary work has to satisfy. [Au.]

[26] Kippenberg relates that Rilke once read one of his *Duino Elegies* aloud in such a way that listeners were not at all aware of the difficulty of the poetry. [Au.]

[27] Cf. the correspondence that followed Fichte's essay 'Uber Geist und Buchstabe in der Philosophie" (Fichtes *Briefwechsel* 2, v). [Au.] Friedrich Schiller (1759–1805), German writer; Johann Gottlieb Fichte (1762–1814), German philosopher. [Eds.]

word makes the reader, in his understanding of it, the arbiter of its claim to truth. The reader experiences in all its validity what is addressed to him and what he understands. What he understands is always more than an alien meaning: it is always possible truth. This is what emerges from the detachment of what is spoken from the speaker and from the permanence that writing bestows. This is the deeper hermeneutical reason for the fact, mentioned above,[28] that it does not occur to people who are not used to reading that what is written down could be wrong, since anything written seems to them like a document that is self-authenticating.

Everything written is, in fact, in a special way the object of hermeneutics. What we found in the extreme case of a foreign language and the problems of translation is confirmed here by the autonomy of reading: understanding is not a psychic transposition. The horizon of understanding cannot be limited either by what the writer had originally in mind, or by the horizon of the person to whom the text was originally addressed.

It sounds at first like a sensible hermeneutical rule, generally recognised as such, that nothing should be put into a text that the writer or the reader could not have intended. But this rule can be applied only in extreme cases. For texts do not ask to be understood as a living expression of the subjectivity of their writers. This, then, cannot define the limits of a text's meaning. However, it is not only the limiting of the meaning of a text to the 'actual' thoughts of the author that is questionable. Even if we seek to determine the meaning of a text objectively by seeing it as a contemporary document and in relation to its original reader, as was Schleiermacher's basic procedure, such limitation is a very chancy affair. The idea of the contemporary addressee can claim only a restricted critical validity. For what is contemporaneity? Listeners of the day before yesterday as well as of the day after tomorrow are always among those to whom one speaks as a contemporary. Where are we to draw the line that excludes a reader from being addressed? What are contemporaries and what is a text's claim to truth in the face of this multifarious mixture of past and future? The idea of the original reader is full of unexamined idealisation.

[28] Cf. p. 844 above. [Au.]

Furthermore, our concept of the nature of literary tradition contains a fundamental objection to the hermeneutical legitimisation of the idea of the original reader. We saw that literature is defined by the will to hand on. But a person who copies and passes on is doing it for his own contemporaries. Thus the reference to the original reader, like that to the meaning of the author, seems to offer only a very crude historico-hermeneutical criterion which cannot really limit the horizon of a text's meaning. What is fixed in writing has detached itself from the contingency of its origin and its author and made itself free for new relationships. Normative concepts such as the author's meaning or the original reader's understanding represent in fact only an empty space that is filled from time to time in understanding.

(B) LANGUAGE AS DETERMINATION OF THE HERMENEUTIC ACT

This brings us to the second aspect of the relationship between language and understanding. Not only is the special object of understanding, namely literary tradition, of a linguistic nature, but understanding itself has a fundamental connection with language. We started from the proposition that understanding is already interpretation because it creates the hermeneutical horizon within which the meaning of a text is realised. But in order to be able to express the meaning of a text in its objective content we must translate it into our own language. This, however, involves relating it to the whole complex of possible meanings in which we linguistically move. We have already investigated the logical structure of this in relation to the special place of the question as a hermeneutical phenomenon. In considering now the linguistic nature of all understanding, we are again expressing from another angle what has been shown in the dialectic of question and answer.

Here we are moving into a dimension that is generally ignored by the dominant view that the historical sciences have of themselves. For the historian usually chooses the concepts by means of which he describes the historical nature of his objects, without expressly reflecting on their origin and justification. He is simply following here his interest in the material and takes no account of the fact that the descriptive aptness of his chosen concepts can be highly detrimental to his proper purpose, inasmuch as it assimilates what is historically different to what is familiar and thus, despite all objectivity, has already subordinated the alien being of the object to its own conceptual frame of reference. Thus, despite all his scientific method, he behaves just like everyone else, as a child of his time who is dominated unquestioningly by the concepts and prejudices of his own age.[29]

Insofar as the historian does not admit this naiveté to himself, he fails to reach the level of reflection that the subject demands. But his naiveté becomes truly abysmal when he starts to become aware of the problems it raises and so demands that in understanding history one must leave one's own concepts aside and think only in the concepts of the epoch one is trying to understand.[30] This demand, which sounds like a logical implementation of historical consciousness is, as will be clear to every thoughtful reader, a naive illusion. The naiveté of this claim does not consist in the fact that it remains unfulfilled because the interpreter does not attain the ideal of leaving himself aside. This would still mean that it was a legitimate ideal to which one must approximate as far as possible. But what the legitimate demand of the historical consciousness, to understand a period in terms of its own concepts, really means is something quite different. The call to leave aside the concepts of the present does not mean a naive transposition into the past. It is, rather, an essentially relative demand that has meaning only in relation to one's own concepts. Historical consciousness fails to understand its own nature if, in order to understand, it seeks to exclude that which alone makes understanding possible. To think historically means, in fact, to perform the transposition that the concepts of the past undergo when we try to think in them. To think historically always involves establishing a connection between those ideas and one's own thinking. To try to eliminate one's own concepts in interpretation is not only impossible, but manifestly absurd. To interpret means precisely to use one's own preconceptions so that the meaning of the text can really be made to speak for us.

In our analysis of the hermeneutical process we saw that to acquire a horizon of interpretation required a 'fusion of horizons'. This is now confirmed by the linguistic aspect of interpretation. The text is to be made to speak through interpretation. But no text and no book speaks if it does not speak the language that reaches the other person. Thus interpretation must find the right language if it really wants to make the text speak. There cannot, therefore, be any one interpretation that is correct 'in itself', precisely because every interpretation is concerned with the text itself. The historical life of a tradition depends on constantly new assimilation and interpretation. An interpretation that was correct 'in itself' would be a foolish ideal that failed to take account of the nature of tradition. Every interpretation has to adapt itself to the hermeneutical situation to which it belongs.

Being bound by a situation does not mean that the claim to correctness that every interpretation must make is dissolved into the subjective or the occasional. We must not here abandon the insights of the romantics, who purified the problem of hermeneutics from all its occasional elements. Interpretation is not something pedagogical for us either, but the act of understanding itself, which is realised not just for the one for whom one is interpreting, but also for the interpreter himself in the explicitness of linguistic interpretation. Thanks to the linguistic nature of all interpretation every interpretation includes the possibility of a relationship with others. There can be no speech that does not bind the speaker and the person spoken to. This is true of the hermeneutic process as well. But this relationship does not determine the interpretative process of understanding as if it were a conscious adaptation to a pedagogical situation, but rather this process is simply the concretion of the meaning itself. Let us recall our stress on the element of application, which had completely disappeared from hermeneutics. We saw that to understand a text always means to apply it to ourselves and to know that, even if it must always be understood in different ways, it is still the same text presenting itself to

[29] Cf. p. 325 in *Truth and Method;* in particular the quotation from Friedrich Schlegel. [Au.]

[30] Cf. my note on H. Rose's *Klassik als Denkform des Abendlandes,* in *Gnomen* 1940, p. 433f. I now see that the methodological introduction to *Platos dialektische Ethik* implicitly makes the same criticism. [Au.]

us in these different ways. That the claim to truth of every interpretation is not in the least relativised is seen from the fact that all interpretation is essentially linguistic. The linguistic explicitness that the process of understanding gains through interpretation does not create a second sense apart from that which is understood and interpreted. The interpretative concepts are not, as such, thematic in understanding. Rather, it is their nature to disappear behind what they bring, in interpretation, into speech. Paradoxically, an interpretation is right when it is capable of disappearing in this way. And yet is is true at the same time that it must be expressed as something that is intended to disappear. The possibility of understanding is dependent on the possibility of this kind of mediating interpretation.

This is also true in those cases when there is immediate understanding and no explicit interpretation is undertaken. For in these cases too interpretation must be possible. But this means that interpretation is contained potentially in the understanding process. It simply makes the understanding explicit. Thus interpretation is not a means through which understanding is achieved, but it has passed into the content of what is understood. Let us recall that this does not only mean that the significance of the text can be realised as a unity, but that the object of which the text speaks is also expressed. The interpretation places the object, as it were, on the scales of words.

There are a few characteristic variations to the universality of this statement which indirectly confirm it. When we are concerned with the understanding and interpretation of linguistic texts, interpretation in the medium of language itself shows what understanding always is: an assimilation of what is said to the point that it becomes one's own. Linguistic interpretation is the form of all interpretation, even when what is to be interpreted is not linguistic in nature, ie is not a text, but is a statue or a musical composition. We must not let ourselves be confused by these forms of interpretation which are not linguistic, but in fact presuppose language. It is possible to demonstrate something by means of contrast, eg by placing two pictures alongside each other or reading two poems one after the other, so that one is interpreted by the other. In these cases demonstration seems to obviate linguistic interpretation. But in fact this kind of demonstration is a modification of linguistic interpretation. In such demonstration we have the reflection of interpretation, which uses the demonstration as a visual short-cut. Demonstration is interpretation in much the same sense as is a translation which summarises the result of an interpretation, or the correct reading aloud of a text that must imply decision on the questions of interpretation, because one can only read aloud what one has understood. Understanding and interpretation are indissolubly bound up with each other.

It is obviously connected with the fact that interpretation and understanding are bound up with each other that the concept of interpretation can be applied not only to scientific interpretation, but to that of artistic reproduction, eg of musical or dramatic performance. We have shown above that this kind of reproduction is not a second reproduction behind the first, but makes the work of art appear as itself for the first time. It brings to life the signs of the musical or dramatic text. Reading aloud is a similar process, in that it is the awakening and conversion of a text into new immediacy.

From this it follows that the same thing must be true of all understanding in private reading. Reading fundamentally involves interpretation. This is not to say that understanding as one reads is a kind of inner production in which the work of art would acquire an independent existence—although remaining in the intimate sphere of one's own inner life—as in a production that is visible to all. Rather, we are stating the contrary, namely that a production that takes place in the external world of space and time does not in fact have any independent existence over against the work itself and can acquire such only through a secondary aesthetic distinction. The interpretation that music or a play undergoes when it is performed is not basically different from the understanding of a text when you read it: understanding always includes interpretation. The work of a literary critic also consists in making texts readable and intelligible, ie safeguarding the correct understanding of a text against misunderstandings. Thus there is no essential difference between the interpretation that a work undergoes in being reproduced and that which the critic performs. However secondary an interpretative artist may feel the justification of his interpretation in words may be, rejecting it as inartistic, he cannot want to deny that such an account can be given of his reproductive interpretation. He must also desire that his interpretation be correct and convincing, and it will not occur to him to deny its connection with the text he has before him. But this text is the same one that presents the academic interpreter with his task. Thus he will be unable to deny that this own understanding of a work, expressed in his reproductive interpretation, can itself be understood, ie interpreted and justified, and this interpretation will take place in a linguistic form. But even this is not a new creation of meaning. Rather, it also disappears again as an interpretation and preserves its truth in the immediacy of understanding.

This insight into the way in which interpretation and understanding are bound up with each other will destroy that false romanticism of immediacy that artists and connoisseurs have pursued, and still do pursue, under the banner of the aesthetics of genius. Interpretation does not seek to replace the interpreted work. It does not, for example, seek to draw attention to itself by the poetic power of its own utterance. Rather, it remains fundamentally accidental. This is true not only of the interpreting word, but also of reproductive interpretation. The interpreting word always has something accidental about it insofar as it is motivated by the hermeneutic question, not just for the pedagogical purposes to which, in the age of the enlightenment, interpretation had been limited, but because understanding is always a genuine event.[31] Similarly, interpretation that is a reproduction is accidental in a fundamental sense, ie not just when something is played, imitated, translated or read aloud for didactic purposes. These cases, where reproduction is interpretation in a special demonstrative sense, where it includes demonstrative exaggeration and highlighting, are in fact different only in degree, and not in kind, from other sorts of reproductive interpretation. However much it is the literary work or the musical composition itself that acquires its mimic presence through the performance, every performance still has its own emphasis. In this respect the difference from the demonstrative placing of accents for didactic reasons is not so great. All performance is interpretation. All interpretation is highlighting.

It is only because it has not any permanent being of its own and disappears in the work which it reproduces that this fact does not emerge clearly. But if we take a comparable example from the plastic arts, eg drawings after old masters made by a great artist, we find the same illuminative interpretation in them. The same effect is experienced when seeing revivals of old films or seeing again a film that one has just seen and remembers clearly: everything seems to be overplayed. Thus it is wholly legitimate for us to speak of the interpretation that lies behind every reproduction, and it must be possible to give a fundamental account of it. The total interpretation is made up of a thousand little decisions which all claim to be correct. Argumentative justification and interpretation do not need to be the artist's proper concern. Moreover, an explicit interpretation in language would only approximate the truth, and fall short of the rounded form achieved by an 'artistic' reproduction. Nevertheless, the inner relation of all understanding to interpretation, and the basic possibility of an interpretation in words, remains untouched by this.

We must understand properly the nature of the fundamental priority of language asserted here. Indeed, language often seems ill-suited to express what we feel. In the face of the overwhelming presence of works of art the task of expressing in words what they say to us seems like an infinite and hopeless undertaking. It seems like a critique of language that our desire and capacity to understand always go beyond any statement that we can make. But this does not affect the fundamental priority of language. The possibilities of our knowledge seem to be far more individual than the possibilities of expression offered by language. Faced with the socially motivated tendency towards uniformity with which language forces understanding into particular schematic forms which hem us in, our desire for knowledge seeks to release itself from these schematisations and predecisions. However, the critical superiority which we claim over language is not concerned with the conventions of linguistic expression, but with the conventions of meaning that have found their form in language. Thus it says nothing against the essential connection between understanding and language. In fact it confirms this connection. For all such criticism which rises above the schematism of our statements in order to understand again finds its expression in the form of language. Hence language always forestalls any objection to its jurisdiction. Its universality keeps pace with the universality of reason. Hermeneutical con-

[31] Cf. p. 274 in *Truth and Method*. [Au.]

sciousness is only participating in something that constitutes the general relation between language and reason. If all understanding stands in a necessary relation of equivalence to its possible interpretation and if there are basically no bounds set to understanding, then the linguistic form which the interpretation of this understanding finds must contain within it an infinite dimension that transcends all bounds. Language is the language of reason itself.

One says this, and then one hesitates. For this makes language so close to reason—which means to the objects that it names—that one may ask why there should be different languages at all, since all seem to have the same proximity to reason and to objects. When a person lives in a language, he is filled with the sense of the unsurpassable appropriateness of the words that he uses for the objects to which he is referring. It seems impossible that other words in other languages could name the objects equally well. The suitable word always seems to be one's own and unique, just as the object referred to is always unique. The agony of translation consists ultimately in the fact that the original words seem to be inseparable from the objects they refer to, so that in order to make a text intelligible one often has to give an interpretative paraphrase of it rather than translate it. The more sensitively our historical consciousness reacts, the more it seems to be aware of the untranslatability of what is written in a foreign language. But this makes the intimate unity of word and object a hermeneutical stumbling block. How can we possibly understand anything written in a foreign language if we are thus imprisoned in our own?

It is necessary to see the speciousness of this argument. In actual fact the sensitivity of our historical consciousness tells us the opposite. The work of understanding and interpretation always remains meaningful. This shows the superior universality with which reason rises above the limitations of any given language. The hermeneutical experience is the corrective by means of which the thinking reason escapes the prison of language, and it is itself constituted linguistically.

From this point of view the problem of language is not presented as the philosophy of language raises it. Certainly the variety of languages presents us with a problem. But this problem is simply how every language, despite its difference from other languages, is able to say everything it wants. We know that every language does this in its own way. But we then ask how, amid the variety of these forms of utterance, there is still the same unity of thought and speech, so that everything that has been transmitted in writing can be understood. Thus we are interested in the opposite of what philosophy of language seeks to investigate.

The intimate unity of language and thought is the premise from which philosophy of language also starts. It is this alone that has made it a science. For only because this unity exists is it worthwhile for the investigator to make the abstraction which causes language to be the object of his research. Only by breaking with the conventionalist prejudices of theology and rationalism could Herder and Humboldt[32] learn to see languages as views of the world. By acknowledging the unity of thought and language they were able to undertake the task of comparing the various forms of this unity. We are starting from the same insight, but we are going, as it were, in the opposite direction. Despite the multifariousness of ways of speech we seek to hold on to the indissoluble unity of thought and language as we encounter it in the hermeneutical phenomenon, namely as the unity of understanding and interpretation.

Thus the question that concerns us is that of the abstractness of all understanding. It only appears to be a secondary question. We have seen that interpretation is the realisation of the hermeneutical experience itself. That is why our problem is such a difficult one. The interpreter does not know that he is bringing himself and his own concepts into the interpretation. The linguistic formulation is so much part of the interpreter's mind that he never becomes aware of it as an object. Thus it is understandable that this side of the hermeneutic process has been wholly ignored. But there is the further point that the situation has been confused by incorrect theories of language. It is obvious that an instrumentalist theory of signs that sees words and concepts as handy tools has missed the point of the hermeneutical phenomenon. If we stick to what takes place in speech and, above all, in all intercourse with tradition carried on by the human sciences, we cannot fail to see that there is a constant process of concept-formation at work. This does not mean

[32] Johann Gottfried Herder (1744–1803), German philologist; Wilhelm von Humboldt (1767–1835), German philologist. [Eds.]

that the interpreter is using new or unusual words. But the use of familiar words does not proceed from an act of logical subsumption, through which an individual is placed under a universal concept. Let us remember, rather, that understanding always includes an element of application and thus produces a constant further development in the formation of concepts. We must consider this now if we want to liberate the linguistic nature of understanding from the presuppositions of philosophy of language. The interpreter does not use words and concepts like an artisan who takes his tools in his hands and then puts them away. Rather, we must recognise that all understanding is interwoven with concepts and reject any theory that does not accept the intimate unity of word and object.

Indeed, the situation is even more difficult. It is questionable whether the concept of language which modern science and philosophy of language take as their starting-point is adequate to the situation. It has recently been stated by some linguists—and rightly—that the modern concept of language presumes a linguistic consciousness that is itself a historical result and does not apply to the beginning of the historical process, especially to what the Greeks called language.[33] There is a development from the complete unconsciousness of language, that we find in classical Greece, to the instrumentalist devaluation of language that we find in modern times. This process of developing consciousness, which also involves a change in the attitude to language, makes it possible for 'language' as such, ie its form, separated from all content, to become an independent object of attention.

In this view we can doubt whether the relation between the attitude to language and the theory of language is correctly characterised, but there is no doubt that the science and philosophy of language operate on the premise that their only concern is the form of language. Is the idea of form still appropriate here? Is language a symbolic form, as Cassirer would have it? Does this take account of its unique quality, which is that language embraces everything—myth, art, law etc—that Cassirer also calls symbolic form?[34]

In analysing the hermeneutical phenomenon we have stumbled upon the universal function of language. In revealing its linguistic nature, the hermeneutical phenomenon itself is seen to have a universal significance. Understanding and interpretation are related to the linguistic tradition in a specific way. But at the same time they transcend this relationship not only because all the creations of human culture, including the nonlinguistic ones, seek to be understood in this way, but more fundamentally inasmuch as everything that is intelligible must be accessible to understanding and to interpretation. The same thing is as true of understanding as of language. Neither is to be grasped simply as a fact that can be empirically investigated. Neither is ever simply an object, but comprises everything that can ever be an object.[35]

If one recognises this basic connection between language and understanding, one will not be able to see the development from unconsciousness of language via consciousness of language to the devaluation of language[36] as an unambiguous historical process. This schema does not seem to me to be adequate even for the history of theories of language, as we shall see, let alone for the life of language. The language that lives in speech, which takes in all understanding, including that of the textual interpreter, is so much bound up with thinking and interpretation that we have too little left if we ignore the actual content of what languages hand down to us and seek to consider only language as form.

[33] J. Lohmann in *Lexis* III. [Au.]

[34] Cf. Ernst Cassirer, *Wesen und Wirkung des Symbolbegriffs*, 1956, which chiefly contains the essays published in the Warburg Library Series. R. Honigswald, *Philosophie und Sprache*, 1937, starts his critique here. [Au.]

[35] Honigswald puts it this way: 'Language is not only a fact, but a principle' (*loc. cit.*, p. 448). [Au.]

[36] This is how J. Lohmann (*op. cit.*) describes the development. [Au.]

Afterword: Criticism and the Claims of Reason

by Leroy Searle

I.

TWO EVENTS IN 1965 and 1966 provide useful points of perspective for literary criticism and theory in the ensuing two decades. In 1965, the English Institute offered an unprecedented program: a review and tribute to a living literary critic, Northrop Frye.[1] As Lionel Trilling had said of the decision at Columbia University not too many years earlier to offer a course in Modern Literature, it had long seemed imprudent to judge living authors, but once the decision was made, partly in response to student demands, it was pursued with what Trilling calls "a certain mean-spirited, last-ditch vindictiveness." As Trilling put it, "I recall that we said something like, 'Very well, if they want the modern, let them have it—let them have it, as Henry James says, full in the face.'"[2]

As I recall the beginning of my own graduate education in 1965, modernism in the curriculum was already taken for granted, as part of the order of things. The demand was for criticism not in the style of genteel appreciation but theory, in courses that took on the intellectual basis of literary study. Only a few graduate institutions offered such courses, and Frye's importance at that time was immense. Never had there been a critic of such imaginative scope, and *Anatomy of Criticism* had taken that archmodernist T. S. Eliot's idea in "Tradition and the Individual Talent" to the theoretical extreme, arguing not just for an "ideal order" among the monuments of the past but for a totalizing and comprehensive "order of words" that claimed to make sense of all literary artifacts.[3] Frye was the first Anglo-American critic to attempt a comprehensive theory of literature that was not obviously limited to the treatment of selected aspects of texts, and the way that theory was put together, while it now seems parochial, relied almost exclusively on work done in departments of literature. Frye remarks, apparently with pride, that he had developed his account of literary meaning inductively, working as independently of symbolic logic and semantics as he could (p. 72), just as he remarked of "the confused swirl of new intellectual activities today

[1] See Murray Krieger, ed., *Northrop Frye in Modern Criticism* (New York: Columbia University Press, 1966). See also Frank Lentricchia's discussion of Frye's importance in *After the New Criticism* (Chicago: University of Chicago Press, 1980), pp. 3–30.

[2] "On the Modern Element in Modern Literature," quoted from Irving Howe, ed., *The Idea of the Modern in Literature and the Arts* (New York: The Horizon Press, 1967), p. 64.

[3] See Eliot's "Tradition and the Individual Talent" in *CTSP*, pp. 784–87, and Frye, *Anatomy of Criticism: Four Essays* (Princeton: Princeton University Press, 1957), esp. pp. 3–29. Subsequent references to *Anatomy* will be included in the text.

[1957] associated with such words as communication, symbolism, semantics, linguistics, metalinguistics, pragmatics, cybernetics" that his "knowledge of most of the books dealing with this new material is largely confined, like Moses' knowledge of God in the mount, to gazing at their spines" (p. 350).

While this is in part a rhetorical device to minimize claims for virtually encyclopedic reading, it is also a recognition that the intellectual independence Frye sought for literary criticism should not be confused with insularity. He goes on to say that "it is clear to me that literary criticism has a central place in all this activity," though he had only the most tentative suggestions to offer on the theme of similarities between mathematics and literature as formal modes of thought.

In the papers presented at the 1965 English Institute (and later discussions at the Modern Language Convention), Frye was not handled gently; and while there was a hint of mean-spirited vindictiveness, the prevailing mood of the volume was uncertainty—not about Northrop Frye so much as about what his accomplishment represented. Instead of signaling the start of a new critical epoch, rationalized on the basis of literary archetypes, it seemed to signal the outer limit of formalism. Murray Krieger found Frye's archetypal vision too reminiscent of Sidney, too much occupied with a "golden world" and too little concerned with the sublunary world of ordinary human action,[4] but in fact Frye's vision is even more uncannily reminiscent of Plato's Forms, the archetypal archetypes. Frye's *Anatomy* turns Plato inside out, as the exiled poets return to the palace of Forms to claim their rightful domain. Yet it is not exactly a triumphant return, with justice done to the exiles. Rather, it is just one more occasion to renew the worry that the model of forms, based on the idea of mimesis, is the wrong model, the wrong idea, creating not a palace but a prison. But what other domicile, what other "conceptual universe," was there for poets and critics?

The second event, to which many allusions have been made in this volume, was the Johns Hopkins University conference on structuralism in 1966.[5] In some quarters, structuralism, following Lévi-Strauss, together with recently revived interest in the Russian Formalists, appeared to offer an invigorating alternative to generally moribund Anglo-American formalism, not least of all because it was not so restrictively focused on the literary. Frye's concern that literary criticism should have a "conceptual universe" of its own was that "the absence of systematic criticism has created a power vacuum, and all the neighboring disciplines have moved in" (p. 12). But continental critics, particularly the structuralists in France, rejected such territorial metaphors to argue for a more philosophical unification of the human sciences, under a comprehensive theory of structure and signification, joining the work of Lévi-Strauss with the linguistic theory of Ferdinand de Saussure.

If Northrop Frye's notices at Columbia turned out to be mixed, structuralism, as it were, closed in Baltimore on opening night. This is not to say at all that interest in problems of structure have not been profoundly consequential but

[4] See "Ariel and the Spirit of Gravity" in *Northrop Frye in Modern Criticism*.

[5] See Richard Macksay and Eugenio Donato, eds., *The Structuralist Controversy* (Baltimore: The Johns Hopkins University Press, 1972), originally published as *The Languages of Criticism and the Sciences of Man* (1970).

only to point out that the theoretical pretensions of structuralism as a metascience have fared less well than Frye's version of criticism as the study of archetypes. In American universities, "structuralism" of one sort was already old hat, as the designation of a largely abandoned linguistic theory, following not Saussure but Bloomfield, Trager, and Smith (with the generally unremarked irony that Bloomfield, Trager, and Smith offer an account of language in many respects more responsible than Saussure's). The continental version, combining anthropology and linguistics, presented an odd aspect, as if the Cambridge ethnologists (Frazer, Jane Ellen Harrison, Jesse Weston) had undergone a sea change, returning almost recognizable but now, as it were, under the sign of the Signifier. For this as well as other reasons, structuralism attracted more interest than adherents, as if it were not really worth the trouble to defend or attack so tame a creature. Structuralism appeared mainly as an extension of diverse formalisms, differing principally (though not trivially) in being international and more highly generalized. But structuralism, in its more highly generalized form, scarcely needed to be attacked by opponents: it attacked itself, in the sense that each effort to push the claims of formalist/structuralist thought to a more general form only revealed more starkly its problematic quality and its insufficiency.

In the past two decades, there has been no literary theorist like Frye, no single work with the scope of *Anatomy of Criticism,* in part, I would submit, because *Anatomy of Criticism* came quickly to resemble a structuralist project. Like the circus performer who brags that he can dive off the high tower into a five-foot box of sand, does so, and then slowly remarks, "I don't think I want to do that trick again," critics have become increasingly wary of grand synoptic models that build only a higher tower and then invite you to dive off into philosophical nothingness—or perhaps just into the parking lot.

In a gesture of collective journalism, reactions to structuralism were quickly dubbed "poststructuralism," suggesting that we were done with all that, as if time could heal all things. It would be more accurate to say that "poststructuralism" is just the sign of our inability to get *through* structuralism and that it represents, along with formalism, a way of thinking so ingrained in our collective history, our languages, and our critical procedures that we can scarcely see it—and can hardly see without it. The advent of deconstruction, following Jacques Derrida, is in this respect a significant negative exercise, making visible a collective theoretical frustration, and it is only bad habits (which deconstruction discloses as such) that lead us to think of deconstruction as something new, a way out, or even a way to go on.

In any case, since the late 1960s, we have had criticism, with its share of mean-spiritedness, "full in the face." The most obvious change has been the reversal of perspective about what must be included in the conceptual universe of "criticism." Frye's recommendation of "naive induction," to try to find in literature alone an account of literary meaning, now appears not only naive but precritical. One simply cannot proceed in ignorance of logic and philosophy, innocent of linguistics, isolated from intellectual history and anthropological learning and reflection, just as one cannot presume to be immune to practical and political considerations in reading and writing of any form. Unfortunately, "criticism" seen in this perspective becomes almost unmanageable, if not unthinkably difficult. It is not enough to read poems, novels, and plays avidly and intelligently: one must also know something about linguistics and language theory, historiography, anthropology, psychoanalysis, hermeneutics, and semiotics. It is not only an increase in the scope of critical training that is presumed (since few actually get such training) but an apparent loss of focus. Put otherwise, it is a situation in which the demands placed on the readers of critical theory have escalated, without any clear assurance that the increased effort is worthwhile.

If one had thought, for example, that the result of increased critical awareness would be some advance in *literary* theory, one would be disappointed for overlooking how much a problem "criticism" has become for itself—and not only in literary study. Again, literature is central, because it presents not incidental but fundamental philosophical difficulties for any attempt to explain what it is and what is important about it. Since Kant, the principle of the "critique" has been the cornerstone of rational inquiry, just as the limit of the critique is the problem of creativity. Accordingly, the apparent centrality of literary criticism among other disciplines is not necessarily a position to be envied, since the attempt of criticism to provide a rational explanation of imaginative creation always runs the risk of turning imagination into mechanism while turning explanation into a species of controlled raving.

Concerns that the cultural disciplines are in disarray, as expressed by Stanley Cavell for aesthetics and philosophy and Hayden White and Clifford Geertz for history and anthropology, arise from critical problems within those other disciplines, with the irony that each appeals in a different way to aesthetic and literary studies as a corrective model. The gesture is as telling as the arguments, all the more because the very models to which appeal is made—particularly Frye's archetypal approach and New Critical textual interpretation—have been under withering attack from within. Surely it would be no cause for celebration if anthropologists merely became New Critics, or historians became Archetypalists, all the more because so many literary critics are turning to the study of society and history, in dissatisfaction over the cultural and historical isolation that formalism and textual interpretation tend to impose, under the concept of the text as aesthetic "object."

It is partly for this reason that one can view deconstruction as a symptom as much as an intellectual position or a set of analytical and rhetorical strategies. It marks a limit, a point of difficult transition, when one cannot quite decide which side of a dividing line one would like to be on. It is worth recalling, for example, that Jacques Derrida, the most dramatic representative of deconstruction, is a "literary critic" only by association and that, as a philosopher, he has been drawn to problems of writing and textuality because they appear to him as repressed problems of philosophy—just as literary critics have been receptive to Derrida because philosophy and theory are the repressed problems of literature: at least Derrida is a philosopher who acknowledges literature as interesting and consequential. What is at stake is much simpler than the rhetoric of liminal negotiation in which the repressed returns: with Derrida, the problems of poetry and philosophy converge in the recognition that an entire tradition of thought has reached its limit, encountering not merely a rhetorical paradox that can be resolved by adjusting the domain of conceptual categories but a contradiction that affects categorial conceptualization itself.

Indeed, the "ancient quarrel" between philosophy and poetry of which Plato speaks in book X of *Republic* has revived in our time with as much energy and ambivalence as in Plato's dealings with the poets and the sophists (see *CTSP*, pp. 33–41). I do not mean to suggest that deconstruction in our time is merely the start of a new era of Sophistic, though it may be. Rather, it is a moment of disclosure: as structuralism follows formalism, deconstruction comes quickly, trailing tropes, because deconstruction, like the wisdom of the original Sophists, is the logical complement of a theory of Forms—or, put otherwise, a logical by-product of the idea of mimesis.

It seems especially significant, in this light, that in all of the materials collected in this anthology (as well as in other work of the last two decades), three major problems have dominated critical discussion: that of the aesthetic object, of the subject, and of oppression. I do not mean to suggest that critics set out to treat these familiar *topoi* of philosophical debate. Rather, it is that in setting out to go "beyond formalism," in Geoffrey Hartman's phrase, or, as the case may be, to posit "poststructuralism," these are the problems that refuse to go away because they are the fundamental problems of formalism, just as they are the daily bread of deconstruction. I take it that the extraordinary variety and vigor of critical debate for the last twenty years is no mere sound and fury, rather that it signifies a collective effort to formulate profound but elementary choices on these issues. The highly rhetoricized form of deconstruction that has turned the expression "the logocentric metaphysics of presence" into a commonplace has been an unremitting reminder that such choices are, finally, metaphysical, despite the fact that the practice of deconstruction appears primarily as a way to defer making any such choices at all, or to cloud the question of what makes a problem "metaphysical" in the first place. What I mean by this assertion will be my main task to explain in these concluding pages.

II.

In saying that the problem of the aesthetic object has been a dominant concern, I surely do not mean that the idea has been a locus of positive development. On the contrary, the "aesthetic object" has almost resembled a tin can tied to the tail of a high-spirited dog. Indeed, to go beyond formalism means primarily going beyond the idea of an aesthetic object. In any version of that idea, the "object" is set apart as a haven, a categorial space between philosophy and history, or between reason and the will, meant as a domain of freedom, uncoerced by external need and responsive to internal necessity. The critical dilemma is just that the arguments propounded to articulate the idea have the habit of unraveling before they can be finished, as one might argue Kant's *Critique of Judgment* unravels over the problem of the sublime and the faculty of Genius, threatening to take the *Critique of Pure Reason* with it. Alternatively, successful aesthetic arguments—that is, those that do find some way to determine what an aesthetic "object" is—become even more problematic by restricting the very freedom held to be essential.

In the case of Anglo-American formalism, since I. A. Richards the progressive definition of poems as objects has been based on the view that poems represent experiences of unique value. From his early view that the poem is an instrument by which conflicting "impulses" are balanced in the psyche of the poet, the argument evolves into the view one finds later in Cleanth Brooks, that the poem *is* an experience of unique value in which semantic conflict is balanced in the rhetorical deployment of tropes. The article of faith is just that the rhetoric of tropes can be mapped back onto the psyche, to make the poem not just a "piece of language," bound by paradox, but the locus of humane value. As Richards discovered in *Practical Criticism* and Brooks found in controversies with R. S. Crane, Bateson, and others, that faith can be justified only on the condition that the sense of the aesthetic "object" can be uniquely determined. What good is a map if you cannot read it, or if it never takes you to the same place twice?

This retrospective view is only to recall that the aestheticism of Anglo-American formalists did not start out as aestheticism but in a concern for poetry as an instrument of value in real and practical matters pertaining to the conduct of human life. The inability to agree on interpretations led primarily to intensified interest in the technology of interpreting, which, to the great frustration of interpreters, seemed only to put agreement about determinate or definitive meaning still farther out of reach. When Jonathan Culler, for example, argues against producing still more "interpretations" of poems, one might suggest that it is not so much going "beyond interpretation" as trying to go *before* it or get *behind* it, to reassert the connection between literature, historical culture, and personal experience that had led Richards to turn from moral philosophy to literature in the first place. In any case, the move is representative, for the presumption that one could find in the language of the poem a self-sufficient structure of meaning is inevitably self-limiting, tending to cut poetry off from its historical and cultural context, just as it cuts the poem off from the intention of its author. Not only that: the search for *the* meaning of poems quickly becomes obsessive when it turns out not to be available and becomes not a celebration of freedom but a form of coercion.

On this ground, one might view the last half of the decade of the 1960s as a time of flight, where the search for meaning, balked in texts, was sought in practical contexts or in radical undertakings that contained no small element of reaction against the failure of formalism to deliver. The most obvious reaction is the flight from the aesthetic object to the reading subject, whether in sociological studies of literary reception, diverse variants of "reader response" criticism, or renewed interest in psychoanalysis. David Bleich's proposal that ours is an age of revolution in the midst of a shift to a new "subjective paradigm" suggests why such reactions only replicate that to which they react. If anything can serve as a "paradigm" it must therefore be collective, in which case to say that it is "subjective" is to objectify subjectivity. The primary difference is that one now has to deal not just with the alienating pressure of an object that cannot be read but with the caprice of a will to possession that can fulfill itself only in narcissism or mere assertiveness. If so, why should poetry be any different than any other possible occasion of experience?

Since this verges on a clinical question, one might say that one needs poetry precisely as an antidote to alienation, whether self-regarding or assertive. In this sense, turning away from the aesthetic object involves at least the irony that one seeks confirmation of just the value postulated for it in treating it as both "aesthetic" and an "object." But where, then, does one turn? In reader response criticism, the self is likely to prove a disappointment, after one has recovered some sense of the integrity of one's own thoughts and emotions, partly because they are also unstable. Stanley Fish's concern for "interpretive communities," for example, is a way to relate the problem to the practical politics of human institutions, while theorists of reception may use a broad range of evidence, political, sociological, and psychological, to understand more precisely how books are read and why they may be used in particular ways.

Even without an immediate interest in readerly affect or response, critics have sought similar evidence, in similar contexts, in turning to Marx, to Freud, to Lévi-Strauss—save that in each case, Marx turns into Althusser, Freud into Lacan, Lévi-Strauss into Foucault. That is, in each domain, the spirit of deconstruction and revision has long been at work. If one appeals to political or psychoanalytic theory, or to anthropology *cum* archaeology, from the point of view of literature, one finds not a satisfactory explanation of why literature should matter but problems of ideology, dogma, and repression—in other words, the same symptoms that make the domain of the purely aesthetic object seem confining and oppressive. Realizing that literature as a social institution is part of an ideological apparatus may or may not be a discovery, which may or may not be pleasant; but it can easily lead to an increased suspicion that the domain of freedom reserved for but denied to the aesthetic object may be illusory.

The significance of theoretical revision in such areas as political economy, psychoanalysis, or cultural history and anthropology is primarily that primitive concepts, those concepts we think with or use in other definitions, but accept as given or obvious without definition, are being called in question consistently, across a broadening front. Marx's idea of production, as the cornerstone of his economic theory, is being rethought as not necessarily restricted to materiality, but, in the work of such thinkers as Pierre Macherey and Althusser, as covering the production of literature or any cultural institution. So conceived, the "means of production" start with the means of thought, and the condition of being alienated from the means of production provides a notional starting point for a critique of intellectual or psychological capitalism, in which literature and even language itself appear locked in internal contradictions. Deleuze and Guattari, for example, employ such an analytical strategy in *Anti-Oedipus* to subvert Freudian theory, to show that it is not just in *Civilization and Its Discontents* that Freud justifies repression, since the whole theory of Oedipal relations is based on an idea of the self or psyche that embodies the principle of repression. One does not need to go so far as Deleuze and Guattari's notion of "schizoanalysis" to see that the idea of the self since Descartes is the formalization of human powers, appearing to thought as an object with particular qualities; and just so, formalization is a restriction and limitation of those powers to act, to think, and to feel, and not at all, as theorists from Descartes to Freud have supposed, a necessary or universal structure. In the case of Foucault, the historization of the subject, as depending on powers, yields the notion of the *epistemé,* which, like Thomas Kuhn's metaphor of the paradigm, provides a term for order without an executive agent. As "power" then becomes a kind of field phenomenon, the epistemé appears to operate as a virtual subject, accountable to no one while seeming to account for everything.

It is in the work of Jacques Lacan, however, that this pattern is most revealing, specifically in Lacan's insight that the unconscious is like a language. While the point is not particularly surprising to seasoned readers of Coleridge or Blake, Proust or Valéry, it offers a fruitful complication that is, by a change of perspective, a simplification. It is this: Lacan's treatment of psychic process by way of signification and representation makes clear that "subject" and "object" are not primitive concepts but must be derived and formed from underlying processes—processes, moreover, that must be thought of as neither objects nor subjects but pure relations. While this approach makes Lacan rather frustrating to read, as if one had to do with discourse consisting mostly of prepositions, it suggests a rather satisfying formal symmetry. The flight from the confinement of the aesthetic object, in the direction of the subject, is a flight back into language, more particularly into the constitution of "objects" and "subjects" by processes that appear to be homologous with discourse. The unsettling difference, however, is that discourse, particularly literary discourse, no longer seems a haven for liberty but all too often as itself an instrument of repression.

Feminist theory and criticism over the past two decades have treated this complex issue in a variety of ways, ranging from speculations following Lacan on the importance of language, especially language in its full symbolic register, to the development of identity, to practical concerns about the literary canon and the profession of writing, that have systematically repressed or excluded women. As Sandra Gilbert and Susan Gubar have shown, the practical import of this repression or exclusion is incalculable, partly because it is transparently unjust or unreasonable that exclusion should have been so consistent merely on the grounds of gender. In this respect, the search for reasons becomes, in spite of itself, another variation on the theme of deconstruction: such exclusions have been rationalized on the basis of power, and when literature is seen in this light the irony is quite literally stunning. That is, the domain of the literary, or the idea of the aesthetic object, has been guarded as jealously as some set of trade secrets because it is a domain of power, particularly of productive power. Yet it is power, the use of which presupposes a benificent end or employment of that power, precisely as it seems to guarantee the domain of the imaginative protection against coercive powers.

If, that is, we had valued the aesthetic but had forgotten the reason, the flight from the aesthetic object *qua* object, the deconstruction of the subject as "self," and the return to language as power restore the reason: we need literature and art in a very practical way, as a space in which to think and reflect and feel, without immediate peril, not least of all to determine and to judge what we desire and what we need to live to the fullness of our powers and not merely to their limits. To be excluded from that space is to be rendered powerless and made subject to a disabling anxiety, precisely because one cannot *not* ask "why," cannot *not* resent the unfairness of unexplained denial. It is in the primitive clarity of our response to injustice that we may postulate what is perhaps the most important element of our common humanity: the desire not to be hurt, not to be subject to capricious force, to be valued or cared for and acknowledged, simply for living. From this, I would submit, all our ideas of "reason" and "rationality" derive. When that desire to be acknowledged is not met, or when we apprehend that the ground on which it is possible is threatened, then we look for reasons, and we do so always in the mode of the imaginative, the mode of speculation: "what if . . ." or "could it be that . . . ?"

When our speculations take us, as it were, full circle and we arrive at a point of mistrusting language, it is no ordinary problem we face. Instead, we see the form of rationality itself as depending on and not in opposition to the imaginative, just as reason and imagination both require the instrumentality of language. Correspondingly, it is no ordinary puzzle to determine how rationality can survive its own history, or live through the rigors of deconstruction that seem to indict language with duplicity, or presume its complicity in some necessary error that permits language to become articulation.

III.

Let us assume just this: that language is a power. By this, I mean only that the *shape* of language, as articulation, is the realization of a potential; and what is produced in the exercise of the power is a form. Linguistic insight is based on the ability to infer from manifest examples the function of the example from its form, as when one recognizes that the relation between a topic and a comment is invariant, no matter what the content of the topic or the comment. So too with subjects and predicates, noun phrases and verb phrases, parts of speech, inflectional patterns, and so on. It follows that items in a language have not "meaning" but only a distinctive shape and that understanding any articulate expression requires assigning an interpretation to that shape. Further, the assignment of interpretations is functional: "to," for example, can be assigned an interpretation as a preposition (going **to** the market) or as a marker of the infinitive (he wants **to go** shopping).

In this simple example, the notion that the two expressions have "meaning" arises only because speakers of English know how to assign interpretations to the expressions, and to argue in either case that meaning is determinate or indeterminate is rather beside the point. The "meaning" is determined by assigning the interpretation, and what is involved in that assignment may differ dramatically in different contexts without implying in any way that meaning is not determinate. The problem is just that we do infer function from form, without having to attend directly to what the function is, and only when the relational expectations in which the function consists are violated are we aware of our inferences. Thus, it seems that words have meanings, and we take the meaning to consist in the simple function of correspondence: nouns name things, verbs name actions, adjectives and adverbs name qualities of nouns and verbs, etc. Who ever says, "going to the to"? When Wallace Stevens says "the *the,*" however, he identifies the function of indication by a first order recursion, applying a word to a word.

It would be interesting to speculate on what might have occurred had Saussure reflected on this example, instead of "arbre / tree," "cheval / horse," and so on, as the paradigm case for language theory. As it is, Saussure's interest in historical philology, particularly the branching tree of the Indo-European family of languages, led him naturally to illustrate his lectures with examples in which historical contingency is ready at hand—how many different words are there, in various tongues (langue), for 'tree' or 'horse' and how is it that words preserve their identity in any given tongue? While much pertaining to Saussure must remain speculative, given the provenance of his (and Bally's) *General Course,* it seems quite clear that the distinction between the synchronic and diachronic is in fact the cornerstone of Saussure's conception of linguistics, from which this projective notion of a "semiology," or science of signs, is an extrapolation. Even clearer is that Saussure's model of signification, in which the sign is bifurcated into the signifying acoustical image and the signified concept, is a commonplace that is structurally identical to Plato's theory of forms, or any view of language that presumes the only function of words to be naming. Saussure is entirely unambiguous in his view that "the only essential thing" in language (langue) as a system of signs "is the union of meanings and sound images" (p. 15), just as he is certain the "both parts of the sign" (sound image or signifier, and meaning or signified) "are psychological."

What distinguishes Saussure's account of the sign is just his contention that linguistic signs, composed of sound and concept, or signifier and signified, "are realities that have their seat in the brain" (p. 15). Thus, when he argues that the relation between the signifier and the signified is arbitrary, it is so only with respect to the historical associations by which the union of sound images and meaning have been effected: he attributes reality to the sign, just as he deplores "starting from words in defining things" as a "bad procedure" (p. 14). Thus, when he later says that "in language there are only differences *without positive terms,*" the remark "is true only if the signified and the signifier are considered separately; when we consider the sign in its totality, we have something that is positive in its own class" (p. 120). Saussure goes farther still, to claim that the positive union of signifier and signified is "the sole type of facts that language has, for maintaining the parallelism between the two classes of differences [sound related to sound and idea related to idea]" and comprises "the distinctive function of the linguistic institution" (p. 121). It is for this reason that we find only six pages on grammar, justified on the assumption that the distinction between "paradigmatic" and "syntagmatic" associations was a "higher principle" sufficient to explain syntax—which is, evidently, why Saussure has no theory of syntax, since it cannot even be formulated under this "higher principle."

While this brief account suggests that Saussure has been rather freely rendered, if not positively misrepresented, in discussions of his views of language and the sign, the point is merely that Saussure includes only one relational principle in his account of the sign, the relation of correspondence. By making the reality of language psychological, Saussure succeeded mainly in complicating the problem of empirical reference, without providing any convincing way to solve the problem of semiological determination in any structure larger than the word. Again, his major contribution is his recognition that *langue,* considered synchronically, *is* a complex system, not just phonology, lexicography, and grammar, and that the diachronic question of language change is not an appropriate subject for predictions.

Where there is no significant advance is precisely in Saussure's account of signs, because he presumes that the relation between signifier and signified is one to one and generally unproblematic. In Plato's *Cratylus,* there is already a fuller discussion of the problem of arbitrariness in the union of signifier and signified, as well as the differential character of any signifying element, at the level of the phoneme, alphabetical letter, and the word, just as there is an ingenious speculative discussion of the possibility that one *could* implement a language in which the inherent character of the signifying elements would bear a systematic (and semantic) relation to the signified. So, too, St. Augustine's discussion of signs in both the *Confessions* (which Wittgenstein used as the epigraph to *Philosophical Investigations*) and *On Christian Doctrine* provides an account of different senses in which one item can be a sign for another that, in some respects, anticipates Peirce.

In all these cases, Plato, Augustine, and Saussure, the common treatment of the linguistic sign stems from a common relational principle, one to one correspondence, or, in Plato's terms, mimesis. Derrida's reiterative argument that this treatment of language, from Plato to Husserl, privileges speech over writing, in asserting the centrality of "logos," is true but only trivially: what is crucial is the insistence on a one-to-one link—under which condition it makes no difference at all which is privileged, speech or writing, since in either case the condition under which either could be identified is a condition of formal closure or distinction, singling out one item, be it signifier *or* signified, phoneme *or* grapheme, as different from another. Put otherwise, the decision to privilege speech over writing follows from the view that the "sign" is the union of signifier and signified, since the treatment of writing as speech transcribed is exactly the same as presuming that the idea (*eidos* or form) precedes the image—and that the relation of the image to the *eidos* is one of imitation or direct transcription.

What is remarkable is that anyone should have ever thought that this presumption was necessary, to say nothing of being sufficient. In Plato's *Republic,* where the paradigm for this view of cognition as mimetic is first articulated, deconstruction starts, as soon as it is posited that a Form is to a description of the form as an object is to an image of the object. Plato's account of the "double-divided line" separates the realm of the intelligible from the visible, and then divides each of these on the same principle (and according to the same proportion), to yield the faculties of *Nous, Dianoia, Psistis,* and *Eikasia* (or Reason, Understanding, Opinion, and 'Picture Thinking'). It is as if by doubling the cases it would escape notice that only one relation is employed, mimesis, and that the paradigm for its employment is visual representation, not cognition. That Plato elaborates his theory into a vision of the reality of transcendent Forms is just a consequence of proceeding according to commonsense empiricism: as objects can be represented, according to their aspect or appearance (the common meaning of "eidos," or form), so one presumes the prior existence of the object. By a reiterative application of the principle of mimesis, Plato merely sets the intelligible realm in relation to the visible, each of which has the same binary structure, on the model object:image, and then argues that the intelligible precedes the visible, making the visible the imitation. But it is obvious (even to Plato's Socrates) that there is no compelling reason to privilege the intelligible over the visible, especially since the notion of mimesis is *a posteriori* and must be exemplified in the visible before the concept of "an imitation" can be attained. The arguments to confer that privilege on the intelligible are driven by a practical need to represent reality as other than it appears—as *not* dominated by willful and capricious gods and powers that, as Shakespeare's Lear puts it, "kill us for their sport."

As it happens, Plato employs a linguistic example to form his concept of mimesis, the relation between "big" and "small" letters—the term he uses is *stoichia,* or "element"—where one uses the identification of the two (for example, small and capital alphas) as the paradigm case of a form.[6] The "deconstructive" moment is just when Socrates realizes that if the small letter is treated as an imitation of the big, then the "letter," either small *or* big, is an imitation of a discrete sound; but what is the sound an imitation of? Of course, it is not an imitation of anything, since it is just an instance of the primary fact of synthetic consciousness: any item to be cognized must be differentiable in some way from other items, which requires that it have a specific identity. As we will see, this is just one of many problems that arise in the *Republic* that are never solved there; but the trajectory of the problem in Plato's other, later dialogues is instructive, especially for literary criticism. The *Cratylus,* for example, treats the problem of the identity of sound images, as indicated above, while the *Parmenides, Theatetus,* and *Sophist* take on the extended problem of paradox and contradiction that follows directly from building a theory of forms using just the relation of mimesis.

In Plato's *Parmenides,* for example, Parmenides is brought in, anachronistically, to caution Socrates against taking too simple a view of Forms. What follows is one of Plato's most difficult arguments, in which one Aristoteles is led through the minefield of paradoxes that arise when Forms are generalized. In this dialogue, as in the *Sophist,* the status of difference is the overriding topic of the argument, but with special reference to the idea of the One. If the Forms are to be unitary, and also to exist apart from the particulars that participate in the forms, then it appears that the unitary form is no different from the particulars, at least as far as "form" is concerned. This is the classic "Third Man" paradox, one of a set of puzzles pertaining to self-prediction; but even as it demonstrates that archetypes, as "one" form, in which "many" participate, set in motion an

[6] See especially, *Republic,* 368c–d, 402a–c. So dominant is this little recognized figure that it can be found in almost all of Plato's dialogues, bearing no thematic weight but serving as a privileged example of the theory of forms. A fuller treatment of this issue is the subject of work in progress.

infinite regression, it does not remove the cognitive requirement that the "form" as type must be distinguished from its tokens as the very condition for recognizing the similarity among the tokens. *Parmenides* attempts an encyclopedic review of such paradoxes, but what frequently escapes notice is that the whole of the argument is a *reductio ad impossible* that, on the one hand, chastises Socrates for putting philosophy itself in peril by basing his account of the Forms on a model of direct mimesis and, on the other, demonstrates that *some* version of forms or ideas is essential if discourse itself is to be possible—even the discourse that seems to prove the impossibility of forms or ideas.

When put in these terms, the metaphysics of formalism does not offer a choice between speech or writing but between language or no language; and given such a choice, deconstruction is assured of its arena for the simple reason that it is a choice that can only be made or affirmed or even registered *in* language, even to call the sufficiency of language into question. So considered, "deconstruction" is not a tenable position, but a liminal state, the very identity of which is its instability. As in Plato's quarrels with the poets first, then the sophists, it is primarily this liminal instability that provoked his anxiety—compelling him to make a metaphysical choice. But in the light of the foregoing analysis, how might we characterize that choice? In the *Phaedo,* Plato has Socrates characterize it in the earliest description of hypothetical method, as the decision to lay down a theoretical principle, even though one has no proof for it, not merely heuristically but prospectively and projectively, to test it by consistency and by consensus. (See *Phaedo,* 99d, ff.) What makes such a choice "metaphysical" is just that it cannot be empirically justified, and thereby goes "beyond physics." What has made Plato's particular choice both fruitful and troublesome is that he assigned an ontological interpretation to the problem of knowledge, thereby effectively preempting the term "metaphysics," for 2,400 years; and he did so on the warrant of a view of the sign that has not changed substantially over the same period.

It should be obvious enough that Plato's objection to the poets was not that they were merely mimetic, at two removes from the truth of transcendent Forms, but that the poets were not mimetic at all: neither in nature nor in logical necessity could one find the "original" of which the poem is thought to be an "imitation." But if we take the metaphysical issue here to be the presumption that knowledge must be the establishment of a one-to-one correlation between being and its representation, it is equally obvious that in such matters "being" is *never* the problem: the problem is always with representation. What is at stake is not itself paradoxical: we know things as "true" when we have the means to establish invariant relations between terms, just as we use the same test of invariance as the operational criterion of "reality." The Greeks were wary of negative and "irrational" numbers and so did not develop algebra, while Arabic mathematicians were wary of "imaginary" roots and so did not develop analytical geometry or calculus; but we have no such problems, since in having the means to represent relations among integers relative to a null point, or to represent the roots of quadratic equations, complex and transfinite numbers, and so on, we quit worrying over whether a "negative number" can "exist" because we know how it is symbolically constituted and understand the functional relations into which it enters. Under just these conditions, negative numbers simply become a normal part of arithmetic, which we may use in a multitude of practical situations or for mental play. In this way, the metaphysical problem vanishes.

In fact, one could say that for more than three hundred years, a species of deconstruction has been afoot in the critique of metaphysics, from Bacon to Carnap, or from Bruno to Derrida, that has as its target not metaphysics per se but formalist metaphysics, derived from Plato. The most vigorous strain has been largely empiricist, notably in the development of positivism since Comte, where the assumption was that "metaphysics" could simply be done away with or exiled, just as Plato thought to get rid of the poets. The critique of metaphysics has been so successful as to discourage much interest in the history of such questions; but to use the general periodization suggested by Hazard Adams (in the introduction to this volume), the sequence from an age of ontology to an age of epistemology, to our own era of language, leads us to a point where it is mostly old habits that associate metaphysics with ontology. I would suggest that any significant linkage of this sort has long since dissolved, leaving us in some perplexity and no small irritation over the question of what makes anything "metaphysical."

If a consideration of language as a power permits us to go beyond the presumption that signification is a simple binary correspondence and that representation is by no means the same thing as a reference to some entity, whether empirical, psychological, or transcendental, then we should be able to proceed to consider how metaphysics is related to mediation, particularly linguistic mediation, and how both are implicated not in a concern with being but with our most fundamental ideas of reason or rationality. What I am suggesting, and will shortly argue, is that questions are metaphysical just as they require us to go beyond what already exists, to suggest speculatively a means for resolving conflicts and bringing order out of disorder. Metaphysical questions, in brief, are imaginative questions, and they matter because they are the means for insuring that we are not always subject to capricious force, living in terror either of what may be done to us or resorting to terrorism to avenge injustice. From this point of view, the claims of reason are real and they cannot be set aside.

Plato's deep and abiding anxiety about poets and sophists was metaphysical in just this sense. Ideas about the gods as, if you will, passionate and powerful children who first devour each other before turning to us, are problematic because their imaginative projection leaves humanity in endless subjugation to fear. The dream of reason is then the dream of justice; and as Plato's *Republic* starts in the house of Cephalus, at night, over a problem about interpreting a line from Simonides which calls justice "giving to each his due," it proceeds as an attempt to answer Thrasymachus, who erupts halfway through book I to proclaim that "justice" is merely the will of the stronger. This too is a claim that is never answered; but it is also a claim that refuses metaphysical discussion and insures that whatever a person may think is his or her "due" will never have the protection of common consent.

By the end of Book X, Plato at least has asserted the will of the philosopher as the stronger in his decision to exile poetry, with the palpable irony that the decision to do so has been rationalized on a far-from-probable analogy between poetry and painting, namely, that both are products of direct mimesis. While this marks the beginning of apologetic criticism, it also marks the beginning of formal philosophy in what Kenneth Burke has called the "bureaucratization of the imaginative."[7] Whether the "quarrel" between poetry and philosophy was already "ancient" matters little, once Plato institutionalized it; for he insured the recurrence of a characteristic piece of drama, in which philosophy chastises poetry for being capricious, and poetry retorts that philosophy is being oppressive. In practical terms, we might say that Plato's concern was eminently practical: could the *polis* survive if subject to mysterious and capricious powers? On the other side, one might say that the concern of the sophists and poets was equally practical: could the creative power that creates the *polis* in the first place survive subjugation to the powers of Platonic reason? In this view, the quarrel is not between reason and unreason, between mind and passion, but between functionally equivalent interpretations of rationality as rooted in practical and ethical concerns.

The sophists' appeals to paradox could thus be viewed as defensive maneuvers, not only to prevent a sort of hardening of the categories but to prevent outright suppression of mental liberty. The tactic resembles the ruse of Odysseus, calling himself No-man, to escape the Cyclops, Polyphemus, in several ways: it works, but at the cost of keeping Odysseus at sea for years. So with deconstruction: as a tactic of liberation, and a mode of discovery, it is bracing; but made permanent, it is akin to cerebral fibrillation. Odysseus presumed he had a home to go to, where he would not have to look the Cyclops in the eye every day; but when deconstruction is institutionalized, it resembles a decision to stay in the cave of Polyphemus and engage in an endless battle of wits with a very large and ill-tempered idiot. Part of the bureaucratization of the imaginative is the creation of imaginative bureaucrats who can no longer imagine any situation as not being affected by the local conditions of their institution.

It is surely not the case that there is no alternative; but articulating any alternative requires a reengagement with metaphysical questions, but not as "metaphysics" has already been institutionalized, in its linkage to an always mystified notion of Being. Perhaps the most interesting figure in this light is Charles Sanders Peirce, whose view of semiotics has the creation of institutions very much in mind, even as Peirce himself was evidently not suited to being institutionalized or even domesticated in the world of late-nineteenth-century academic philosophy. He may fare no better in the late twentieth century either, but on one point his example is crucial. The pragmaticist maxim that the meaning of a proposition is the sum of the consequences that follow from accepting it is a basis on which metaphysics can be reconceived in terms of mediation. The "semiology" that Saussure projected, or the "semiotics" that Peirce attempted to work out, has yet to be domesticated, but it may turn out that there will be no need to do so: if the bureaucracy of formalism is Byzantine, the bureaucracy of semiotics is,

[7] Kenneth Burke, *Perspectives by Incongruity,* ed. Stanley Edgar Hyman and Barbara Karmiller (Bloomington: Indiana University Press, 1964), pp. 76–80.

by comparison, Abyssinian. The central problem is still the notion of the "sign," viewed as a category of analysis. We might say that signs are all virtual but are habitually conceived as actual. As in the historical case of mathematics, the problem is not in "what" is represented, but in the means (and medium) of representation itself.

More specifically, the notion of the "sign" breaks down in two characteristic contexts, both of which are essential for thought. In the first case, the relation between perception and cognition, image and thought, is rendered static; in the second case, the relation between particular situations and the order or arrangement (i.e., the logical "syntax") in the situation is hypostatized by the notion of the sign. The consequence is that we are set off in search of "codes" without first having clarified the "instructions" that will permit the relation between encoding and decoding to be reversible, and we therefore mistake conventions for codes or functions for rules.

In other words, formalism gives way to structuralism, only to terminate in deconstruction, not because we need to be more ambitious in the treatment of signs, but because we do not have a convenient way to indicate the relational and mediating functions that generate structures, or produce "signs" as particular values of those functions. If we presume that ours is a time of transition between modes of thought, the old, mistrusted because it appears to have lost its generative power, is either held to or attacked mainly because it is not clear how to go on. If so, there should be no surprise in the fact that even the most destructive critique of a mode of thought is not sufficient to displace it, unless there is an alternative that is able to do the same work.

The mood of suspicion that has prevailed for most of the last two decades I take as a symptom of the will to go on, frustrated by the insufficiency of the alternatives that have been easy to identify, since all of those alternatives appear to suffer the same deficiencies. Going on, as Wittgenstein observed, is possible only as one understands the principles of relation that led one to the present moment. With respect to the problems of formalism, the risk is to misidentify the principles and, as the saying goes, throw the baby out with the bathwater. The desire to go on under such circumstances can become desperate, inducing one to go backwards, typically by leaving some insufficient opposition intact, trying to be "subjective" instead of "objective" or appealing to "emotion" or "affect" or "passion" as opposed to "logic" or "reason." To flee to the other pole of a binary opposition, when the problem is the inadequacy of the opposition itself, able to produce only a degenerative loop, takes away the advantage of critical reflection to show that being in such a loop is simply getting stuck.

From a more technical point of view, the main difference between a "sign" as conceived by formalists from Plato to Derrida and a "sign" as conceived by semioticians following Peirce is that in the former case the notion is binary, whereas in the latter it is at least trinary. The third term is necessary to designate the *function* of the form or sign, just as one might say that the practical failing of formalism and structuralism in criticism is just the inability to specify functions, once forms had been described. The following figure I offer with only brief comment, as one way to represent mediation according to functions, all of which must be fulfilled for predication to be possible.[8] The two contexts indicated (P and S) do the work of such notions as subject and object, with the difference that in each case the notion is represented as a relation between terms, both of which are necessary for us to form either images or ideas about any situation. The figure, that is to say, could be considered as a schematic representation of what Jurij Lotman calls a primary modeling system, with the distinguishing characteristic that each state of the system leads to the next, starting from any perception whatsoever. As a crude representation of a functional grammar, the figure takes into account the inherent dynamism of thought and language, without making either indeterminate. By the same means, it suggests how lines of thought—and texts—develop over time, engaged with a material world, in response to practical matters of choice and value.

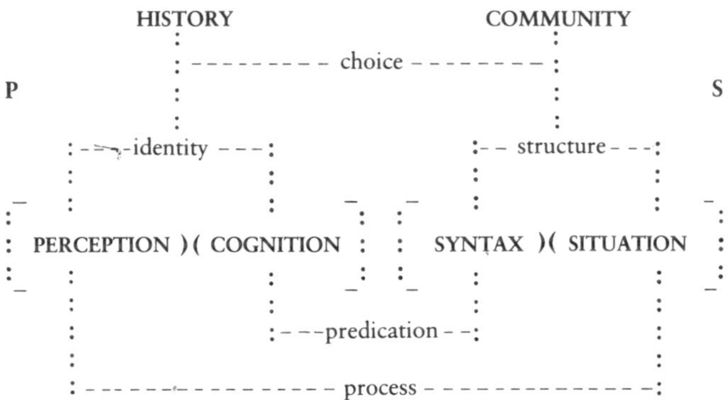

It is important to note that this diagram is merely a strategic instrument, for which no exclusive claims need to be made. The point is just this: having learned so meticulously from the formalists and structuralists to perceive patterns and relations, all based upon difference (or differ*a*nce), it remains to say what functional difference these differences make. Intertextuality and the proliferation of choices need not present added weight to wearied minds but an invitation to consider the claims of reason as coextensive with the pleasures of imagination, both of which seek the good.

[8] A fuller account of this model is available in my "Language Theory and Photographic Praxis," *Afterimage* 7 (Summer 1979): pp. 26–34. Here, I would note only that this model, originally developed in attempting to describe functions in mediation that could cover both pictorial and verbal artifacts, is intended as a very general model of mediation by which the "feedback" of conscious processes is traceable as a sequence of states. For example, any perception of a "situation" initiates a process by which the representation of the situation is differentiated as a gestalt image and a structural description. Predication, then, is the point of feedback, when the identity of the situation is related to a description of its structure. A second look at the same situation, then, produces a different result; and the inclusion of temporality provides a basis on which to relate one structure to two or more situations, etc. The function here labeled as "choice" provides the locus for describing the collective interests of historical communities, by which attention is ordered in conformity with sets of values. The same function is also the basis for treating themes as ordering elements.

Books Published on Critical Theory Since 1965: A Selection

Jonathan Arac, Wlad Godzick, and Wallace Martin, eds., *The Yale Critics: Deconstruction in America*

Roland Barthes, *The Pleasure of the Text*

———, *S/Z*

Georges Bataille, *Death and Sexuality: A Study of Eroticism and the Taboo*

Jean Baudrillard, *For a Critique of the Political Economy of the Sign*

Tony Bennett, *Formalism and Marxism*

Leo Bersani, *Baudelaire and Freud*

———, *A Future for Astyanax: Character and Desire in Literature*

David Bleich, *Subjective Criticism*

James H. Boone, *From Symbolism to Structuralism*

Wayne Booth, *Critical Understanding: The Powers and Limits of Pluralism*

———, *Modern Dogma and the Rhetoric of Assent*

———, *A Rhetoric of Irony*

Paul Bové, *Destructive Poetics: Heidegger and Modern American Poetry*

Gerald Bruns, *Inventions: Writing, Textuality, and Understanding in Literary History*

———, *Modern Poetry and the Idea of Language*

William E. Cain, *The Crisis in Criticism: Theory, Literature, and Reform in English Studies*

David Carroll, *The Subject in Question*

John Casey, *The Language of Criticism*

Seymour Chatman, *Story and Discourse*

Ralph Cohen, *The Unfolding of "The Seasons"*

———, ed., *New Directions in Literary History*

Stanley Corngold, *The Fate of the Self: German Writers and French Theory*

Walter Davis, *The Act of Interpretation: A Critique of Literary Reason*

George Dickie, *Aesthetics: An Introduction*

Serge Doubrovsky, *The New Criticism in France*

Jacques Dubois et al., *Rhetorique générale*

Terry Eagleton, *Literary Theory: An Introduction*

———, *Marxism and Literary Criticism*

Umberto Eco, *A Theory of Semiotics*

John Ellis, *The Theory of Literary Criticism: A Logical Analysis*

Shoshana Felman, ed., *Literature and Psychoanalysis*

Hollis Frampton, *Circles of Confusion*

William Gass, *The World within the Word*

Gerard Genette, *Narrative Discourse: An Essay in Method*

Erving Goffman, *Frame Analysis*

Lucien Goldmann, *Essays on Method in the Sociology of Literature*

———, *The Human Sciences and Philosophy*

Nelson Goodman, *Languages of Art*

———, *Ways of Worldmaking*

Gerald Graff, *Literature against Itself*

———, *Poetic Statement and Critical Dogma*

Gayle Greene and Coppelia Kahn, eds., *Making a Difference: Feminist Literary Criticism*

A. J. Griemas, *Sémantique structurale: Recherche de methode*

———, ed., *Sign, Language, Culture*

Susan Handelman, *The Slayers of Moses*

Josue Harari, ed., *Textual Strategies*

Ihab Hassan, *The Dismemberment of Orpheus*

———, *Paracriticisms*

Terence Hawkes, *Structuralism and Semiotics*

Paul Hernadi, *Beyond Genre*

———, ed., *What is Literature?*

Neil Hertz, *The End of the Line: Essays on Psychoanalysis and the Sublime*

Norman Holland, *5 Readers Reading*

———, *Poems in Persons*

———, *The I*

Robert C. Holub, *Reception Theory*

David Couzens Hoy, *The Critical Circle*
Luce Irigaray, *Speculum de l'autre femme*
Carol Jacobs, *The Dissimulating Harmony: The Image of Interpretation in Nietzsche, Rilke, Artaud, & Benjamin*
Fredric Jameson, *Marxism and Form*
———, *The Political Unconscious*
———, *The Prison-House of Language*
Gregory S. Jay and David Miller, eds., *After Strange Texts: The Role of Theory in the Study of Literature*
Barbara Johnson, *The Critical Difference*
Edith Kurzweil, *The Age of Structuralism*
Edmund Leach, *Genesis as Myth*
Vincent B. Leitch, *Deconstructive Criticism*
Frank Lentricchia, *After the New Criticism*
———, *Criticism and Social Change*
Lawrence Lipking, ed., *High Romantic Argument: Essays for M. H. Abrams*
Jean-François Lyotard, *Just Gaming*
———, *The Postmodern Condition*
Pierre Macherey, *A Theory of Literary Production*
Richard Macksey and Eugenio Donato, eds., *The Languages of Criticism and the Sciences of Man*
Robert R. Magliola, *Derrida on the Mend*
———, *Phenomenology and Literature*
Steven Mailloux, *Interpretive Conventions*
Joseph Margolis, *The Languages of Art and Art Criticism*
———, ed., *Philosophy Looks at the Arts*
Jeffrey Mehlman, *Revolution and Repetition: Marx/Hugo/Balzac*
———, *A Structural Study of Autobiography: Proust, Leiris, Sartre, Lévi-Strauss*
Christian Metz, *Film Language*
W. J. T. Mitchell, *The Politics of Interpretation*
———, ed., *Against Criticism: Literary Studies and the New Pragmatism*
———, *Iconology: Image, Text, Ideology*
Toril Moi, *Sexual/Textual Politics*
Arthur Moore, *Contestable Concepts in Literary Theory*
Wesley Morris, *Friday's Footprint*
———, *Toward a New Historicism*
Judith Newton and Deborah Rosenfelt, eds., *Feminist Criticism and Social Change*
Christopher Norris, *The Contest of Faculties: Deconstruction, Philosophy, and Theory*
———, *Deconstruction: Theory and Practice*
Daniel T. O'Hara, *The Romance of Interpretation: Visionary Criticism from Pater to de Man*
Stein Haugom Olsen, *The Structure of Literary Understanding*
Walter J. Ong., S. J., *Orality and Literacy: The Technologizing of the Word*
Richard Poirer, *The Performing Self*
Mary Louise Pratt, *Towards a Speech Act Theory of Literary Discourse*
Gerald Prince, *A Grammar of Stories*
Suresh Raval, *Metacriticism*
Michael Riffaterre, *Text Production*
Schlomith Rimmon-Kenan, *Narrative Fiction*
Richard Rorty, *Philosophy and the Mirror of Nature*
Adena Rosmarin, *The Power of Genre*
K. K. Ruthven, *Critical Assumptions*
———, *Feminist Literary Studies: An Introduction*
Michael Ryan, *Marxism and Deconstruction*
Jeffrey Sammons, *Literary Sociology and Practical Criticism*
Robert Scholes, *Semiotics and Interpretation*
———, *Structuralism in Literature*
———,. *Textual Power: Literary Theory and the Teaching of English*
Thomas Sebeok, *Semiotics: A Survey of the State of the Art*
———, *The Sign and Its Masters*
Karl D. Uitti, *Linguistics and Literary Theory*
Gregory Ulmer, *Applied Grammatology*
Evan Watkins, *The Critical Act: Criticism and Community*
René Wellek, *History of Modern Criticism 1750–1950*, vols. 5 and 6
Raymond Williams, *Marxism and Literature*
———, *Problems in Materialism and Culture*
W. K. Wimsatt, *Day of the Leopards: Essays in Defense of Poems*
Elizabeth Wright, *Psychoanalytic Criticism: Theory in Practice*

Index